D1531083

Dreamweaver® 3 Bible, Gold Edition

Dreamweaver® 3 Bible, Gold Edition

Joseph W. Lowery

IDG Books Worldwide, Inc.
An International Data Group Company

Foster City, CA ✦ Chicago, IL ✦ Indianapolis, IN ✦ New York, NY

Dreamweaver® 3 Bible, Gold Edition

Published by
IDG Books Worldwide, Inc.
An International Data Group Company
919 E. Hillsdale Blvd., Suite 400
Foster City, CA 94404
www.idgbooks.com (IDG Books Worldwide Web site)

Copyright © 2000 IDG Books Worldwide, Inc. All rights reserved. No part of this book, including interior design, cover design, and icons, may be reproduced or transmitted in any form, by any means (electronic, photocopying, recording, or otherwise) without the prior written permission of the publisher.

ISBN: 0-7645-3479-3

Printed in the United States of America

10 9 8 7 6 5 4 3 2

1B/SR/QY/QQ/FC

Distributed in the United States by IDG Books Worldwide, Inc.

Distributed by CDG Books Canada Inc. for Canada; by Transworld Publishers Limited in the United Kingdom; by IDG Norge Books for Norway; by IDG Sweden Books for Sweden; by IDG Books Australia Publishing Corporation Pty. Ltd. for Australia and New Zealand; by TransQuest Publishers Pte Ltd. for Singapore, Malaysia, Thailand, Indonesia, and Hong Kong; by Gotop Information Inc. for Taiwan; by ICG Muse, Inc. for Japan; by Intersoft for South Africa; by Eyrolles for France; by International Thomson Publishing for Germany, Austria, and Switzerland; by Distribuidora Cuspide for Argentina; by LR International for Brazil; by Galileo Libros for Chile; by Ediciones ZETA S.C.R. Ltda. for Peru; by WS Computer Publishing Corporation, Inc., for the Philippines; by Contemporanea de Ediciones for Venezuela; by Express Computer Distributors for the Caribbean and West Indies; by Micronesia Media Distributor, Inc. for Micronesia; by Chips Computadoras S.A. de C.V. for Mexico; by Editorial Norma de Panama S.A. for Panama; by American Bookshops for Finland.

For general information on IDG Books Worldwide's books in the U.S., please call our Consumer Customer Service department at 800-762-2974. For reseller information, including discounts and premium sales, please call our Reseller Customer Service department at 800-434-3422.

For information on where to purchase IDG Books Worldwide's books outside the U.S., please contact our International Sales department at 317-596-5530 or fax 317-572-4002.

For consumer information on foreign language translations, please contact our Customer Service department at 800-434-3422, fax 317-572-4002, or e-mail rights@idgbooks.com.

For information on licensing foreign or domestic rights, please phone +1-650-653-7098.

For sales inquiries and special prices for bulk quantities, please contact our Order Services department at 800-434-3422 or write to the address above.

For information on using IDG Books Worldwide's books in the classroom or for ordering examination copies, please contact our Educational Sales department at 800-434-2086 or fax 317-572-4005.

For press review copies, author interviews, or other publicity information, please contact our Public Relations department at 650-653-7000 or fax 650-653-7500.

For authorization to photocopy items for corporate, personal, or educational use, please contact Copyright Clearance Center, 222 Rosewood Drive, Danvers, MA 01923, or fax 978-750-4470.

Library of Congress Cataloging-in-Publication Data

Lowery, Joseph (Joseph W.)
Dreamweaver 3 bible / Joseph W. Lowery. --
Gold ed.
p. cm.
ISBN 0-7645-3479-3 (alk. paper)
1. Dreamweaver (Computer file) 2. Web sites --
Authoring programs. 3.Web publishing I. Title
TK5105.8885.D74 L685 2000b
005.7'2--dc21 00-039569

LIMIT OF LIABILITY/DISCLAIMER OF WARRANTY: THE PUBLISHER AND AUTHOR HAVE USED THEIR BEST EFFORTS IN PREPARING THIS BOOK. THE PUBLISHER AND AUTHOR MAKE NO REPRESENTATIONS OR WARRANTIES WITH RESPECT TO THE ACCURACY OR COMPLETENESS OF THE CONTENTS OF THIS BOOK AND SPECIFICALLY DISCLAIM ANY IMPLIED WARRANTIES OF MERCHANTABILITY OR FITNESS FOR A PARTICULAR PURPOSE. THERE ARE NO WARRANTIES WHICH EXTEND BEYOND THE DESCRIPTIONS CONTAINED IN THIS PARAGRAPH. NO WARRANTY MAY BE CREATED OR EXTENDED BY SALES REPRESENTATIVES OR WRITTEN SALES MATERIALS. THE ACCURACY AND COMPLETENESS OF THE INFORMATION PROVIDED HEREIN AND THE OPINIONS STATED HEREIN ARE NOT GUARANTEED OR WARRANTED TO PRODUCE ANY PARTICULAR RESULTS, AND THE ADVICE AND STRATEGIES CONTAINED HEREIN MAY NOT BE SUITABLE FOR EVERY INDIVIDUAL. NEITHER THE PUBLISHER NOR AUTHOR SHALL BE LIABLE FOR ANY LOSS OF PROFIT OR ANY OTHER COMMERCIAL DAMAGES, INCLUDING BUT NOT LIMITED TO SPECIAL, INCIDENTAL, CONSEQUENTIAL, OR OTHER DAMAGES. FULFILLMENT OF EACH COUPON OFFER IS THE RESPONSIBILITY OF THE OFFEROR.

Trademarks: All brand names and product names used in this book are trade names, service marks, trademarks, or registered trademarks of their respective owners. IDG Books Worldwide is not associated with any product or vendor mentioned in this book.

is a registered trademark or trademark under exclusive license to IDG Books Worldwide, Inc. from International Data Group, Inc. in the United States and/or other countries.

ABOUT IDG BOOKS WORLDWIDE

Welcome to the world of IDG Books Worldwide.

IDG Books Worldwide, Inc., is a subsidiary of International Data Group, the world's largest publisher of computer-related information and the leading global provider of information services on information technology. IDG was founded more than 30 years ago by Patrick J. McGovern and now employs more than 9,000 people worldwide. IDG publishes more than 290 computer publications in over 75 countries. More than 90 million people read one or more IDG publications each month.

Launched in 1990, IDG Books Worldwide is today the #1 publisher of best-selling computer books in the United States. We are proud to have received eight awards from the Computer Press Association in recognition of editorial excellence and three from Computer Currents' First Annual Readers' Choice Awards. Our best-selling *...For Dummies®* series has more than 50 million copies in print with translations in 31 languages. IDG Books Worldwide, through a joint venture with IDG's Hi-Tech Beijing, became the first U.S. publisher to publish a computer book in the People's Republic of China. In record time, IDG Books Worldwide has become the first choice for millions of readers around the world who want to learn how to better manage their businesses.

Our mission is simple: Every one of our books is designed to bring extra value and skill-building instructions to the reader. Our books are written by experts who understand and care about our readers. The knowledge base of our editorial staff comes from years of experience in publishing, education, and journalism — experience we use to produce books to carry us into the new millennium. In short, we care about books, so we attract the best people. We devote special attention to details such as audience, interior design, use of icons, and illustrations. And because we use an efficient process of authoring, editing, and desktop publishing our books electronically, we can spend more time ensuring superior content and less time on the technicalities of making books.

You can count on our commitment to deliver high-quality books at competitive prices on topics you want to read about. At IDG Books Worldwide, we continue in the IDG tradition of delivering quality for more than 30 years. You'll find no better book on a subject than one from IDG Books Worldwide.

John Kilcullen
Chairman and CEO
IDG Books Worldwide, Inc.

Eighth Annual Computer Press Awards 1992

Ninth Annual Computer Press Awards 1993

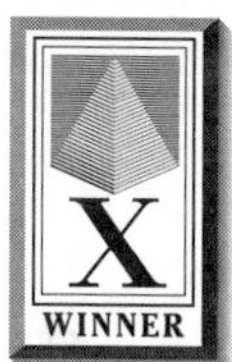

Tenth Annual Computer Press Awards 1994

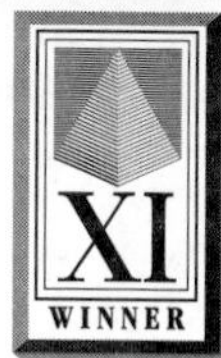

Eleventh Annual Computer Press Awards 1995

IDG is the world's leading IT media, research and exposition company. Founded in 1964, IDG had 1997 revenues of $2.05 billion and has more than 9,000 employees worldwide. IDG offers the widest range of media options that reach IT buyers in 75 countries representing 95% of worldwide IT spending. IDG's diverse product and services portfolio spans six key areas including print publishing, online publishing, expositions and conferences, market research, education and training, and global marketing services. More than 90 million people read one or more of IDG's 290 magazines and newspapers, including IDG's leading global brands — Computerworld, PC World, Network World, Macworld and the Channel World family of publications. IDG Books Worldwide is one of the fastest-growing computer book publishers in the world, with more than 700 titles in 36 languages. The "...For Dummies®" series alone has more than 50 million copies in print. IDG offers online users the largest network of technology-specific Web sites around the world through IDG.net (http://www.idg.net), which comprises more than 225 targeted Web sites in 55 countries worldwide. International Data Corporation (IDC) is the world's largest provider of information technology data, analysis and consulting, with research centers in over 41 countries and more than 400 research analysts worldwide. IDG World Expo is a leading producer of more than 168 globally branded conferences and expositions in 35 countries including E3 (Electronic Entertainment Expo), Macworld Expo, ComNet, Windows World Expo, ICE (Internet Commerce Expo), Agenda, DEMO, and Spotlight. IDG's training subsidiary, ExecuTrain, is the world's largest computer training company, with more than 230 locations worldwide and 785 training courses. IDG Marketing Services helps industry-leading IT companies build international brand recognition by developing global integrated marketing programs via IDG's print, online and exposition products worldwide. Further information about the company can be found at www.idg.com.

1/26/00

Credits

Acquisitions Editor
Kathy Yankton

Project Editors
Paul Winters
Julie M. Smith

Technical Editor
Simon White

Copy Editors
Michael Welch
Julie Campbell Moss

Proof Editor
Patsy Owens

Project Coordinators
Marcos Vergara
Danette Nurse

Media Development
Jeff Goens
Carmen Krikorian
Marisa Pearman
Jamie Smith

Graphics and Production Specialists
Robert Bihlmayer
Jude Levinson
Michael Lewis
Victor Pérez-Varela
Ramses Ramirez

Quality Control Technician
Dina F Quan

Book Designer
Drew R. Moore

Cover Illustration Design
Peter Kowaleszyn, Murder By Design, San Francisco

Illustrator
Mary Jo Weis

Proofreading and Indexing
York Production Services

About the Author

Joseph W. Lowery has been writing about computers and new technology since 1981. He is the author of the previous editions of *Dreamweaver Bible* and *Fireworks Bible* as well as *Buying Online For Dummies* (all from IDG Books Worldwide). He recently coauthored a book on Flash with designer Hillman Curtis and has also written books on HTML and using the Internet for business. Joseph is currently Webmaster for a variety of sites and is also a Web design trainer and consultant. Joseph and his wife, dancer/choreographer Debra Wanner, have a daughter, Margot.

For the Dreamweaver community — from the program creators to the program users — this book would not exist without your enthusiasm, support, and vision.

Foreword

We live in a time of great change and I feel privileged to have the opportunity to affect the expression of a new medium, the Internet. Everything about the Web is evolving quickly — the design, the tools, and even the medium itself. Dreamweaver is an evolutionary product for Macromedia as well as a revolutionary one. Not only is Dreamweaver the state-of-the-art Web authoring tool used by more professionals than any other, it has also evolved into an application platform central to Macromedia's ever-expanding Internet vision.

I think one of the reasons that Dreamweaver was so successful from the beginning is because it grew out of a community. Before Dreamweaver, there was a growing community of professional Web developers that no one was listening to. Developers cried, "Leave my code alone!" but all of the available visual editors altered their code. Developers pled, "Help me create tables," but no integrated tool could help. Developers demanded, "I need cutting-edge features," only to get last year's fading standards.

Macromedia decided to listen. The Dreamweaver project relied on an advisory board of designers and developers to identify the most desirable features. The development effort, however, was far more than a committee voting on a wish-list. An entire culture was evolving and the Dreamweaver team came out of that culture and remains a part of it still. Throughout the year we listen to our customers — both current and potential — to gather their reactions to the present release as well as better understand their requirements for the future.

One of the key underpinnings of Dreamweaver is its extensibility layer. By constantly expanding the core customizability of Dreamweaver, we enable our customers to streamline their workflow. We think it's better that the product adapt to the way you work rather than you adapt to product. The community of extension builders has taken Dreamweaver to unforeseen heights in creating a new set of power tools for its use. In fact, Macromedia itself has taken advantage of Dreamweaver's extensibility to craft a new product, Dreamweaver UltraDev.

What's in the future for Dreamweaver? Macromedia is committed to making tools for every aspect of what we call the Web Content Life Cycle. The most effective Web sites are continually developing and changing in response to their visitors' needs and reactions. We see Dreamweaver as a core element in Macromedia's mission to empower developers and their companies to create entertaining, educational, and effective Web content — and to successfully use that content to communicate and refine their message.

One person whose message needs no refining is Joseph Lowery. From the beginnings of Dreamweaver, Joe has provided the Dreamweaver community with remarkable works of clarity and substance. The *Dreamweaver 3 Bible* is the definitive resource for the Web authoring professional, not only because it covers the product in exhaustive detail, but also because the book provides a much-needed context for understanding new technologies. We're glad that Joe has shared his talents and energies with Macromedia and the Dreamweaver community and we look forward to growing together.

Kevin Lynch
President Products and Office of the President, Macromedia

Preface

Web designers are relentless explorers in the ever-expanding frontier that is the World Wide Web. Boundary-pushing is not only the norm, it's practically a job requirement — which is one of the reasons Dreamweaver is the leading Web design program today. Dreamweaver provides the tools you need to build any type of Web site you can imagine. Imagination, however, is not enough. A cutting-edge site requires cutting-edge resources — and that's the reason the *Dreamweaver 3 Bible, Gold Edition* was written.

Perhaps the most explosive technology today is database connectivity. More and more clients are demanding the accessibility and flexibility of a data-driven Web site — and more and more Web page designers are finding themselves on the edge of a potentially enormous learning curve. Numerous solutions are in use, all of which require a serious commitment and investment of time and energy. The four technologies covered in the Gold Edition of this book — ASP, ColdFusion, Lasso, and Tango — all share the requisite power to drive Web applications as well as strong connections to Dreamweaver. As a special bonus, you'll also find coverage of Macromedia's latest entry in the dynamic data realm, Dreamweaver UltraDev.

Dreamweaver is also at the forefront of another revolution: the wireless Web. The landscape of the Web is quickly moving beyond networked computers; Internet access is becoming totally portable. The Nokia WML Studio for Dreamweaver provides the toolset necessary to build wireless Web pages. This book not only explains how to create these pages step by step, but also explains the technology underlying the Wireless Markup Language.

Not only is Dreamweaver expanding across the globe, it's also moving up the enterprise. The Dreamweaver Objects for Aria from Macromedia grant access to a increasingly mission-critical facet of the Web world: Web site analysis and reporting. The Aria objects work with server-side components to provide real-time activity analysis for high-traffic sites. Information in this book can be used by any developer to design Web pages for any enterprise using the Aria system.

Extensibility has long been a Dreamweaver hallmark, although it was a little-known fact. That's all changed with Macromedia's introduction of the Extension Manager and the Dreamweaver Exchange. This book describes how to use the Extension Manager to add new features to Dreamweaver — at little or no cost — to greatly enhance your workflow, automate your production, and jazz up your Web pages. Moreover, you'll also find information here on how to package and submit your own extensions to the Dreamweaver Exchange for worldwide distribution.

This book is an expansion of *Dreamweaver 3 Bible*, and includes all material from that previous edition plus seven new chapters (in Parts IX and X) and a new appendix (E). The Gold Edition also gives me the opportunity to show off some of the reasons why I'm such a Dreamweaver supporter. A 32-page color insert illustrates key examples of what Dreamweaver is capable of. The color section is comprised of screen shots from the full spectrum of Web design — from brand-name enterprises to lesser-known design shops — all with a clarity of message, attention to detail, and an exciting vision. This book also features two CD-ROMs packed with trial programs and extensions from Dreamweaver authors to help you take your own vision further.

Weaving Your Dreams Into Reality

Among other accolades, Macromedia's Dreamweaver has one of the most appropriate product names in recent memory. Web page design is a blend of art and craft; whether you're a deadline-driven professional or a vision-filled amateur, Dreamweaver is the perfect tool for many Web designers. Dreamweaver is not only the first Web authoring tool to bring the ease of visual editing to an HTML code-oriented world, it also brings a point-and-click interface to complex JavaScript coding.

To use this book, you only need two items: the Dreamweaver software and a desire to make cutting-edge Web pages. (Actually, you don't even need Dreamweaver to begin; one of the two CD-ROMs that accompany this book contains a fully functional trial version.) From quick design prototyping to ongoing Web site management, Dreamweaver automates and simplifies much of a Webmaster's workload. Unfortunately, even Dynamic HTML, which Dreamweaver handles elegantly, cannot accomplish all the tasks of a modern Web page. As a result, this book contains step-by-step instructions on how to handle every Web design task — through Dreamweaver's visual interface or its integrated HTML code editors.

Underneath its simple, intuitive interface, Dreamweaver is a complex program that makes high-end Web concepts (Dynamic HTML, Cascading Style Sheets, and JavaScript behaviors) accessible for the first time. *Dreamweaver 3 Bible, Gold Edition* is designed to help you master every nuance of the program. Are you creating a straightforward layout with the visual editor? Do you need to extend Dreamweaver's capabilities by building your own custom objects? With Dreamweaver and this book, you can weave your dreams into reality for the entire world to experience.

What's New in Dreamweaver 3

If I had to sum up the differences between the earlier versions of Dreamweaver and Dreamweaver 3 in one word, that word would be *automation*. Major features, such as the History palette, Design Notes, and enhanced Fireworks communication, have been added and are aimed at increasing a Web designer's total productivity. With Dreamweaver 3, you can simply do more, faster.

Dreamweaver appeals to both the expert and the novice Web designer. Although the program is extraordinarily powerful, it's also fairly intuitive. Nonetheless, designers new to the Web often find the entire process overwhelming and understandably so. To give folks a birds-eye view of the overall use of Dreamweaver in Web site design and production, this edition includes a Quick Start in Chapter 2. In this chapter, you'll see how one designer — yours truly — works with Dreamweaver in every aspect of building Web pages and constructing a site.

The Macromedia family of products is working more closely together, with Dreamweaver 3 and Fireworks 3 leading the interprocess communication trend. The third versions of both software packages have been revamped to streamline their combined workflow; not only are there more parallel features, like the History palette, but Dreamweaver can also send commands to Fireworks which, in turn, can generate graphics to send back to Dreamweaver. You'll find all these new capabilities covered in Chapter 22.

Who Should Read This Book?

Dreamweaver attracts a wide range of Web developers. Because it's the first Web authoring tool that doesn't rewrite original code, veteran designers are drawn to using Dreamweaver as their first visual editor. Because it also automates complicated effects, beginning Web designers are interested in Dreamweaver's power and performance. *Dreamweaver 3 Bible, Gold Edition* addresses the full spectrum of Web professionals, providing basic information on HTML if you're just starting as well as advanced tips and tricks for seasoned pros. Moreover, this book is a complete reference for everyone working with Dreamweaver on a daily basis.

What Hardware and Software Do You Need?

Dreamweaver 3 Bible, Gold Edition includes coverage of Dreamweaver 3. If you don't own a copy of the program, this book's CD-ROM 1 contains a demo version for your trial use. Written to be platform-independent, this book covers both Macintosh and Windows 95/98/NT versions of Dreamweaver 3.

Macintosh

Macromedia recommends the following minimum requirements for running Dreamweaver on a Macintosh:

- ✦ Power Macintosh PowerPC (G3 or higher recommended)
- ✦ MacOS 8.1 or later
- ✦ 64MB of available RAM
- ✦ 20MB of available disk space
- ✦ 100MB of free hard-disk space
- ✦ Color monitor capable of 800×600 resolution
- ✦ CD-ROM drive

Windows

Macromedia recommends the following minimum requirements for running Dreamweaver on a Windows system:

- ✦ Intel Pentium processor, 90MHz or equivalent (Pentium II or higher recommended)
- ✦ Windows 95/98, NT 4.0 (with Service Pack 3) or later
- ✦ 64MB of available RAM
- ✦ 100MB of available disk space
- ✦ 256-color monitor capable of 800×600 resolution
- ✦ CD-ROM drive

Please note that these are the minimum requirements. As with all graphics-based design tools, more capability is definitely better for using Dreamweaver, especially in terms of memory and processor speed.

How This Book Is Organized

Dreamweaver 3 Bible, Gold Edition can take you from raw beginner to full-fledged professional if read cover-to-cover. However, you're more likely to read each section as needed, taking the necessary information and coming back later. To facilitate this approach, *Dreamweaver 3 Bible, Gold Edition* is divided into eight major task-oriented parts. Once you're familiar with Dreamweaver, feel free to skip around the book, using it as a reference guide as you build up your own knowledge base.

The early chapters present the basics, and all chapters contain clearly written steps for the tasks you need to perform. In later chapters, you encounter sections labeled "Dreamweaver Techniques." Dreamweaver Techniques are step-by-step instructions for accomplishing specific Web designer tasks; for example, building an image map that uses rollovers, or eliminating underlines from hyperlinks through Cascading Style Sheets. Naturally, you can also use the Dreamweaver Techniques as stepping-stones for your own explorations into Web page creation.

If you're running Dreamweaver while reading this book, don't forget to use the CD-ROMs. An integral element of the book, the two accompanying CD-ROMs offer a vast number of additional Dreamweaver behaviors, objects, commands, browser profiles, and other extensions in addition to relevant code from the book.

Part I: Getting Started with Dreamweaver

Part I begins with an overview of Dreamweaver's philosophy and design. To get the most out of the program, you need to understand the key advantages it offers and the deficiencies it addresses. Part I takes you all the way to setting up your first site. In Chapter 2, you'll get an overview of the Web development process as a quick start to Dreamweaver.

The other opening chapters give you a full reference to the Dreamweaver interface and all of its customizable features. You also learn how you can access Dreamweaver's full-bodied online Help and find additional resources on the Web. Chapter 6 takes you from the consideration of various Web site design models to publishing your finished site on the Internet while Chapter 7 shows you how to make the most of Dreamweaver's FTP Site window.

Part II: Using Basic HTML in Dreamweaver

Although Dreamweaver is partly a visual design tool, its roots derive from the language of the Web: HTML. Part II gives you a solid foundation in the basics of HTML, even if you've never seen code. Chapter 8 covers HTML theory, describing how a Web page is constructed and alerting you to some potential pitfalls to look out for.

The three fundamentals of Web pages are text, images, and links. You explore how to incorporate these elements to their fullest extent in Chapters 9, 10, and 11, respectively. Chapter 12 examines another fundamental HTML option: lists. You study the list in all of its forms: numbered lists, bulleted lists, definition lists, nested lists, and more.

Part III: Incorporating Advanced HTML

Part III begins to investigate some of the more advanced structural elements of HTML as implemented in Dreamweaver. Chapter 13 examines the various uses of tables — from a clear presentation of data to organizing entire Web pages. Here you learn how to use Dreamweaver 3's greatly enhanced visual table editing capabilities to resize and reshape your HTML tables quickly.

Chapter 14 is devoted to image maps and shows how to use Dreamweaver's built-in Image Map tools to create client-side image maps. The chapter also explains how you can build server-side image maps and demonstrates a revised technique for creating image map rollovers. Forms are the focus of Chapter 15, where you find all you need to know about gathering information from your Web page visitors. Chapter 16 investigates the somewhat complex world of frames — and shows how Dreamweaver has greatly simplified the task of building and managing these multifile creations, particularly with the new Frame objects. You also learn how to handle more advanced design tasks such as updating multiple frames with just one click.

Part IV: Extending HTML Through Dreamweaver

HTML is a language with extensive capabilities for expanding its own power. Part IV begins with Chapter 17, which introduces you to the world of CGI programs, external plug-ins, Java applets, ActiveX controls, and scripting with JavaScript and VBScript. You also find techniques for ensuring a secure middle ground of cross-browser compatibility in the ongoing browser wars.

With its own set of objects and behaviors, Dreamweaver complements HTML's extensibility. Chapter 18 shows you how you can use the built-in objects to accomplish most of your Web page-layout chores quickly and efficiently — and when you're ready for increased automation, the chapter explains how to build your own custom objects. Chapter 19 offers an in-depth look at the capabilities of Dreamweaver behaviors. Each standard behavior is covered in detail with step-by-step instructions. If you're JavaScript-savvy, then Chapter 20 gives you the material you need to construct your own behaviors and reduce your day-to-day workload. Finally, Chapter 21 explores the brave new world of Dreamweaver extensibility, with complete coverage of using and building commands as well as custom tags, translators, floaters, and C-level Extensions.

Part V: Adding Multimedia Elements

In recent years, the Web has moved from a relatively static display of text and simple images to a full-blown multimedia circus with streaming video, background music, and interactive animations. Part V contains the power tools for incorporating various media files into your Web site.

Graphics remains the key medium on the Web today and Macromedia's Fireworks is a top-notch graphics generator. Chapter 22 delves into methods for incorporating Fireworks graphics — with all the requisite rollover and other code intact. Special focus is given to the Dreamweaver-to-Fireworks communication link and how your Web production efforts can benefit from it.

Chapter 23 covers digital video in its many forms: downloadable AVI files, streaming RealVideo displays, and panoramic QuickTime movies. Chapter 24 focuses on digital audio, with coverage of standard WAV and MIDI sound files as well as the newer streaming audio formats, like MP3. A special section covers the exciting possibilities offered by Beatnik and the Rich Music Format, with full coverage of the Beatnik ActionSet.

In addition to Dreamweaver, Macromedia is perhaps best known for one other contribution to Web multimedia: Shockwave. Chapter 25 explores the possibilities offered by incorporating Shockwave and Flash movies into Dreamweaver-designed Web pages, and includes everything you need to know about configuring MIME types. You also find step-by-step instructions for building Shockwave inline controls and playing Shockwave movies in frame-based Web pages, as well as how to add Generator objects.

Part VI: Dynamic HTML and Dreamweaver

Dynamic HTML brought a new world of promises to Web designers — promises that went largely unfulfilled until Dreamweaver was released. Part VI of *Dreamweaver 3 Bible, Gold Edition* examines this brave new world of pixel-perfect positioning, layers that fly in and then disappear as if by magic, and Web sites that can change their look and feel at the click of a mouse.

Chapter 26 provides an overview of Dynamic HTML and explores the different implementations by the major browsers — with new information on how to embed cross-platform, cross-browser fonts in your Web pages. Chapter 27 takes a detailed look at the elegance of Cascading Style Sheets and offers techniques for accomplishing the most frequently requested tasks, such as creating an external style sheet. Much of the advantages of Dynamic HTML come from the use of layers, which enable absolute positioning of page elements, visibility control, and a sense of depth. You discover how to handle all these layer capabilities and more in Chapter 28. Chapter 29 focuses on timelines, which have the potential to take your Web page into the fourth dimension. The chapter concludes with a blow-by-blow description of how to create a multiscreen slide show, complete with layers that fly in and out on command.

Part VII: Creating Next-Generation Code with Dreamweaver

The Web is one fast-moving train, and if you're not running when you try to board, you're going to get left behind. Keeping up with the latest technological developments is essential for working Web designers. Sooner or later, your clients are going to demand the cutting-edge, and Part VII is here to help you create the sharpest sites online.

I can't think of any new technology on the Web that has so quickly gained the widespread acceptance that XML has. In a nutshell, XML (short for Extensible Markup Language) enables you to create your own custom tags that make the most sense for your business or profession. Although XML doesn't enjoy full browser support as of this writing, it's only a matter of time — and little time at that. Chapter 30 shows you how to apply this fast-approaching technology of tomorrow in Dreamweaver today.

Virtually every day another breakthrough in Web multimedia is announced — and through it's open-ended architecture, Dreamweaver 3 is ready to support them all. Macromedia has partnered with several leaders in this ever-growing field: Real Networks, IBM, and Live Pictures, to name a few. Chapter 31 delves into their contributions and demonstrates how you can use their technology to enhance your site's interactivity and razzmatazz.

The Web has become one vast information junkie: the more data you put online now, the more information required tomorrow. Part of this tremendous growth is due to the explosion of electronic commerce (e-commerce) — the Internet is almost at the point where if you can buy it, you can buy it online. To manage this overwhelming flood of info, Web designers are turning to database-driven pages and sites. Dreamweaver 3 now offers numerous connectivity and e-commerce solutions, surveyed in Chapter 32, to help Web designers create such active content.

Part VIII: Enhancing Web Site Management and Workflow in Dreamweaver

Although Web page design gets all the glory, Web site management pays the bills. In Part VIII, you see how Dreamweaver makes this essential part of any Webmaster's day easier to handle. Chapter 33 starts off the section with a look at the use of Dreamweaver Templates and how they can speed up production while ensuring a unified look and feel across your Web site. Chapter 34 covers the Library, which can significantly reduce any Webmaster's workload by providing reusable — and updateable — page elements. Finally, Chapter 35 describes Dreamweaver's built-in tools for maintaining cross- and backward-browser compatibility. A Dreamweaver Technique demonstrates a browser-checking Web page that automatically directs users to appropriate links.

Part IX: Connectivity with Dreamweaver

Most companies that have Web sites also have databases. Combining the two opens up all kinds of possibilities, from providing Web site visitors with custom-built pages on demand, to enabling e-commerce inventory control. In Part X, you look at a number of technologies for creating rich, database-driven Web sites in Dreamweaver. Chapter 36 introduces Active Server Pages (ASP), and looks at

Macromedia's Dreamweaver UltraDev. Chapter 37 explores ColdFusion, Allaire's popular active-content solution. Chapter 38 covers Lasso, and Lasso Studio for Dreamweaver, a great way to simplify rapid development of database-driven sites. Chapter 39 details the technology behind Tango, unique in that its final HTML output is quickly generated by a compiled program on the Tango Server at runtime.

Part X: Extending Dreamweaver

Extensibility has always been a hallmark of the Dreamweaver experience. Part X looks at new and exciting developments in Dreamweaver extensibility. Chapter 40 explores the new frontier of the wireless Web, using extensions to create WML (Wireless Markup Language) content. Chapter 41 examines Macromedia's Aria, an enterprise-level site analysis tool that combines server-side monitoring and directives embedded into Web pages themselves. Chapter 42 is devoted to another new Macromedia tool: the Extension Manager, which simplifies the process of installing or removing new features from Dreamweaver.

Appendixes

Appendix A describes the contents of the two CD-ROMs that accompany this book. Throughout this book, whenever you encounter a reference to files or programs on the CD-ROM, please check Appendix A for more information.

One special area of the Web — online learning — has experienced so much explosive growth that it has been granted its own special extension of Dreamweaver: CourseBuilder for Dreamweaver. Appendix B dives into this unique application and provides an overview of its most vital features.

Dreamweaver comes with a fully functional internal HTML editor, and the full version of the program is bundled with two industrial-strength external HTML editors: BBEdit for the Macintosh and HomeSite for Windows. Although both editors offer extensive online help, an abbreviated user's manual for both programs appears in Appendixes C and D. Each appendix also has detailed information on integrating the external editors with Dreamweaver.

Macromedia has made it clear that they want Dreamweaver users to consider Fireworks their best choice for image creation and optimization for the Web. Integration features in both products make the combination an efficient and complete Web content solution. Appendix E is a complete Fireworks Primer, covering the interface, import and export features, vector and bitmap drawing and editing, and automation features. If you're new to Fireworks, this primer will demystify Web graphics creation and have you creating GIFs and JPEGs quickly.

Conventions Used in This Book

I use the following conventions throughout this book.

Windows and Macintosh conventions

Because *Dreamweaver 3 Bible, Gold Edition* is a cross-platform book, it gives instructions for both Windows and Macintosh users when keystrokes for a particular task differ. Throughout this book, the Windows keystrokes are given first; the Macintosh keystrokes are given second in parentheses, as follows:

To undo an action, press Ctrl+Z (Command+Z).

The first action instructs Windows users to press the Ctrl and Z keys in combination, and the second action (in parentheses) instructs Macintosh users to press the Command and Z keys together.

Key combinations

When you are instructed to press two or more keys simultaneously, each key in the combination is separated by a plus sign. For example:

Ctrl+Alt+T (Command+Option+T)

The preceding tells you to press the three listed keys for your system at the same time. You can also hold down one or more keys and then press the final key. Release all the keys at the same time.

Mouse instructions

When instructed to *click* an item, move the mouse pointer to the specified item and click the mouse button once. Windows users use the left mouse button unless otherwise instructed. *Double-click* means clicking the mouse button twice in rapid succession.

When instructed to select an item, you may click it once as previously described. If you are selecting text or multiple objects, click the mouse button once, hold it down, and then move the mouse to a new location. The color of the selected item or items inverts to indicate the selection. To clear the selection, click once anywhere on the Web page.

Menu commands

When instructed to select a command from a menu, you see the menu and the command separated by an arrow symbol. For example, when instructed to execute the Open command from the File menu, you see the notation File ➪ Open. Some menus use submenus, in which case you see an arrow for each submenu, as follows: Insert ➪ Form Object ➪ Text Field.

Typographical conventions

I use *italic* type for new terms and for emphasis, and **boldface** type for text that you need to type directly from the computer keyboard.

Code

A special typeface indicates HTML or other code, as demonstrated in the following example:

```
<html>
<head>
<title>Untitled Document</title>
</head>
<body bgcolor="#FFFFFF">
</body>
</html>
```

This code font is also used within paragraphs to designate HTML tags, attributes, and values such as `<body>`, `bgcolor`, and `#FFFFFF`. All HTML tags are presented in lowercase, as written by Dreamweaver, although browsers are not generally case-sensitive in terms of HTML.

The ¬ character at the end of a code line means you should type the next line of code before pressing the Enter (Return) key.

Navigating Through This Book

Various signposts and icons are located throughout *Dreamweaver 3 Bible, Gold Edition* for your assistance. Each chapter begins with an overview of its information, and ends with a quick summary.

Icons appear in the text to indicate important or especially helpful items. Here's a list of the icons and their functions:

Tips provide you with extra knowledge that separates the novice from the pro.

Notes provide additional or critical information and technical data on the current topic.

Sections marked with a New Feature icon detail an innovation introduced in Dreamweaver 3.

Cross-Reference icons indicate places where you can find more information on a particular topic.

The Caution icon is your warning of a potential problem or pitfall.

The On the CD-ROM icon indicates that one of the accompanying CD-ROMs contains a related file in the given folder. See Appendix A for more information about where to locate specific items.

Further Information

You can find more help for specific problems and questions by investigating several Web sites. Macromedia's own Dreamweaver Web site is the best place to start:

```
www.dreamweaver.com
```

I heartily recommend that you visit and participate in the official Dreamweaver newsgroup:

```
news://forums.macromedia.com/macromedia.dreamweaver
```

You're also invited to visit my Web site for book updates and new developments:

```
www.idest.com/dreamweaver
```

You can also e-mail me:

```
jlowery@idest.com
```

I can't promise instantaneous turnaround, but I answer all my mail to the best of my abilities.

Acknowledgments

Whoever said "writing is a lonely business" never wrote a computer book. Sometimes I feel like the point man of a large swing band filled with seasoned pros. All the folks in this group can both play their parts exceedingly well, supporting the main theme, and are ready to solo at the drop of a hat. And now it's time to introduce, and applaud, the band. . . .

If this book feels richer, more dense in detail (not to mention a pound or two heavier) than the previous edition, a great deal of the credit goes to my technical editor, Simon White. Simon has been absolutely top-notch in providing insightful background comments, on-the-money tips, and real-world work experience. Simon is a Macromedia evangelist and routinely offers some of the best Web authoring advice around via the Dreamweaver newsgroup. A special thank-you goes out to his ace Web design shop in San Francisco, MediaFear, for letting me borrow him for a few days . . . oh, all right, months.

You can always tell someone who has only read about the Internet when they despair about how the Internet increases our isolation. Baloney. I've got more colleagues and friends around the world now than I ever did. The Dreamweaver community has been especially gracious and giving of their time and expertise to further the goals of this book. I'd like to express my gratitude to the growing pool of developers who have taken their valuable time to create Dreamweaver extensions and offer them freely to the public. While the group has literally become too numerous to mention, I would like to highlight a few luminaries: Andrew Wooldridge, Massimo Foti, Jaro von Flocken, Brendan Dawes, Taylor and Al Sparber. I'm particularly grateful because all of these authors (and many others) have kindly permitted their work to be included in this book's CD-ROMs. I now owe a good 40 percent of the user base a drink.

Macromedia has been wonderfully supportive of my efforts to bring out the most detailed *Bible* possible. I can only imagine the collective groan that goes up when yet another e-mailed question from me — with a deadline, no less — arrives. Warm thanks and heartfelt appreciation to Dave George, Sho Kuwamoto, Hava Edelstein, Heidi Bauer, Darrick Brown, and all the other Dreamweaver engineers and techs who opened up their brains for me to pick. A special "Gawd, what would I have done without you?" award goes to Lori Hylan for help above and beyond the call of duty. I'd also like to single out the Dreamweaver Technical Support staff whose answers to users' queries have been tremendous sources of information. And who's that in the back of the room? Macromedia management — in the form of David Mendels, Beth Davis, Eric Ott, Matt Brown, and others — has opened many, many doors to me and should stand up and take a bow. And finally, I and the rest of the Dreamweaver community are beholden to Kevin Lynch and Paul Madar for their vision and hard work in bringing this dream home.

To me, there's no higher compliment than to be told that I know my business. Well, the folks I work with at IDG Books Worldwide sure know their business: acquisitions editor Kathy Yankton; project editors Paul Winters and Julie Smith; copy editor Michael Welch, and all the additional support staff. And to someone whose business is to know my business, a double thank-you with a cherry on top for my agent, Laura Belt of Adler & Robin Books.

One last note of appreciation — for all the people who took a chance with some of their hard-earned money and bought the previous editions of this book. That small sound you hear in the background is me applauding you as thanks for your support. I hope my efforts continue to be worthy.

Contents at a Glance

Contents

Part IV: Extending HTML Through Dreamweaver 475

Part V: Adding Multimedia Elements 659

Getting Started with Dreamweaver

P A R T

I

✦ ✦ ✦ ✦

In This Part

✦ ✦ ✦ ✦

CHAPTER 1

What Is Dreamweaver?

✦ ✦ ✦ ✦

In This Chapter

Understanding the Dreamweaver philosophy

How Dreamweaver is designed

Using traditional HTML commands in Dreamweaver

Accessing next-generation features

Automating Web page production

Maintaining your Web site with Dreamweaver

✦ ✦ ✦ ✦

Dreamweaver, by Macromedia, is a professional Web site development program. Among its many distinctions, Dreamweaver was the first Web development program to take advantage of the capabilities of the latest generation of browsers, making it easy for developers to use advanced features such as Cascading Style Sheets and Dynamic HTML.

Dreamweaver is truly a tool designed by Web developers for Web developers. Designed from the ground up to work the way professional Web designers do, Dreamweaver speeds site construction and streamlines site maintenance. Throughout this chapter, you can see the philosophical underpinnings of the program and get a better sense of how Dreamweaver blends traditional HTML with cutting-edge techniques. You also learn some of the advanced features that Dreamweaver offers to help you manage a Web site.

The Real World of Dreamweaver

Dreamweaver is a program very much rooted in the real world. For example, Dreamweaver recognizes the problem of incompatible browser commands and addresses it by producing cross-browser compatible code. Dreamweaver even includes browser-specific HTML validation so you can see how your existing or new code works in a particular browser.

Dreamweaver 3 extends the real-world concept to the workplace. Features such as Dream templates streamline the production and maintenance process on large Web sites. Dreamweaver's advanced layers-to-tables feature make it possible to quickly position content during the design stage, while keeping your pages backwardly browser compatible when published. Dreamweaver's commands capability enables Web designers to automate their most difficult Web creations.

Integrated visual and text editors

In the early days of the World Wide Web, most developers "hand-coded" their Web pages using simple text editors such as Notepad and SimpleText. The second generation of Web authoring tools brought visual design or WYSIWYG ("what you see is what you get") editors to market. What these products furnished in ease of layout, they lacked in completeness of code. Professional Web developers found they still needed to hand-code their Web pages, even with the most sophisticated WYSIWYG editor.

Dreamweaver acknowledges this reality and has integrated a superb visual editor with a number of text editors. You can work with Dreamweaver's internal HTML Inspector or a dedicated external editor. Figure 1-1 shows Dreamweaver's visual editor and text editor working together. Any change made in the visual editor is instantly reflected in the text editor and vice versa. While Dreamweaver enables you to work with any text editor you like, it includes both HomeSite for Microsoft Windows developers and a trial version of BBEdit for Macintosh developers. Dreamweaver enables a natural, dynamic flow between the visual and text editors.

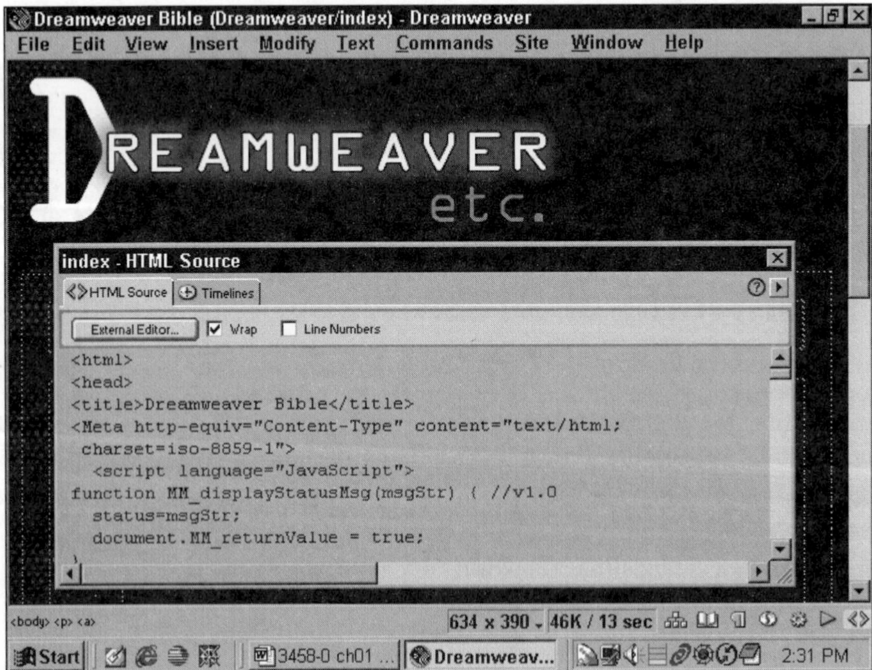

Figure 1-1: Dreamweaver enables you to work with a visual WYSIWYG editor and an HTML text editor simultaneously.

Dreamweaver 3 tightens the integration between the visual design and the underlying code with its introduction of the Quick Tag Editor. Web designers frequently need to adjust the HTML code minutely – changing an attribute here or adding a single tag there. The Quick Tag Editor, which appears as a small pop-up window in the Document window, makes these code tweaks quick and easy.

Roundtrip HTML

Most Web authoring programs modify any code that passes through their system—inserting returns, removing indents, adding `<meta>` tags, uppercasing commands, and so forth. Dreamweaver's programmers understand and respect that Web developers all have their own particular coding styles. An underlying concept, Roundtrip HTML, ensures that you can move back and forth between the visual editor and any HTML text editor without your code being rewritten.

Web site maintenance tools

The Dreamweaver creators also understand that creating a site is only a part of the Webmaster's job. Maintaining the Web site can be an ongoing, time-consuming chore. Dreamweaver simplifies the job with a group of site management tools, including a library of repeating elements and a file-locking capability for easy team updates.

In Dreamweaver, Web site maintenance is easier than ever—and very visual. Take note of the Site Map feature that enables you to view your Web site structure at a glance and to access any file for modification. Links are updated automatically, or are under user control, if a file moves from one directory to another. And, you can not only access a library of repeating elements to be inserted in the page, but also define templates to control the entire look and feel of a Web site—and modify a single template to update all the pages sitewide.

The Dreamweaver Interface

When creating a Web page, Webmasters do two things over and over: They insert an element—whether text, image, or layer—and then they modify it. Dreamweaver excels at such Web page creation. The Dreamweaver workspace combines a series of windows, palettes, and inspectors to make the process as fluid as possible, thereby speeding up the Webmaster's work.

Easy text entry

Although much of the World Wide Web's glitz comes from multimedia elements such as images and sound, Web pages are primarily a text-based medium. Dreamweaver recognizes this and makes the text cursor the default tool. To add text, just click in Dreamweaver's main workspace — the Document window — and start typing. As shown in Figure 1-2, the Text Property Inspector enables you to change characteristics of the text such as the size, font, position, or color.

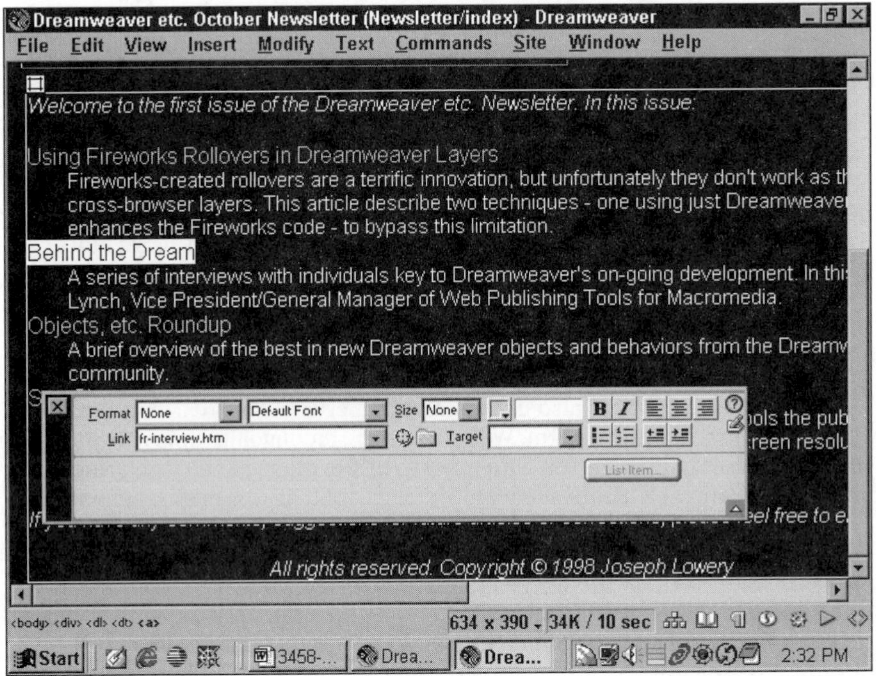

Figure 1-2: Use the Text Property Inspector to change the format of the selected text.

One-stop object modification

You can select Web page elements other than text from the Objects palette. Adding a picture to a Web page is as easy as clicking the Insert Image button from the Objects palette. Dreamweaver asks you to select the file for the image, and your image appears in your current cursor position. Once your graphic is onscreen, selecting it brings up the appropriate Property Inspector to enable you to make modifications. The same technique holds true for any other inserted element — from horizontal rules to Shockwave movies.

Complete custom environment

Dreamweaver enables you to customize your workspace to suit you best. A handy Launcher opens and closes various windows, palettes, and inspectors, all of which are movable. Just drag them wherever you want them onscreen. Want to see your page by itself? You can hide all windows at the touch of a function button; press it again, and your controls are revealed.

Dreamweaver's customization capabilities extend even further. If you find that you are inserting something over and over, such as a QuickTime video or .wav sound file, you can add that element to your Objects palette. Dreamweaver even enables you to add a specific element — a Home button, for example — to the Objects palette. In fact, you can add entire categories of objects if you like. Moreover, Dreamweaver 3 exposes the entire menu structure for customization — you can not only change keyboard shortcuts, but also add custom menus.

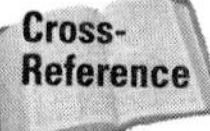

For more information on customizing your Objects palette, see Chapter 18. Information about changing the menu system is found in Chapter 21.

Simple selection process

As with most modern layout programs, in order to modify anything in Dreamweaver, you must select it first. The usual process for this is to click an object to highlight it or to click and drag over a block of text to select it. Dreamweaver adds another option for this process with the Tag Selector feature. Click anywhere on a Web page under construction and then look at Dreamweaver's status bar. The applicable HTML tags appear on the left side of the status bar.

In the example shown in Figure 1-3, the Tag Selector shows

```
<body> <table> <tr> <td> <div> <p>
```

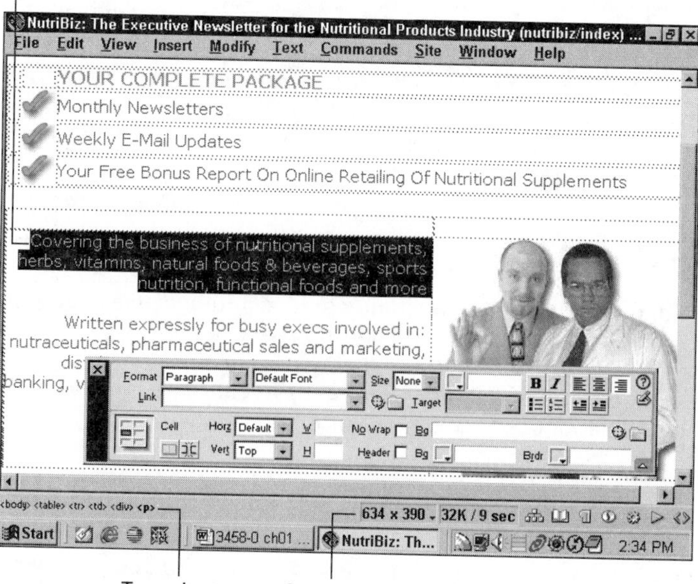

Figure 1-3: Choosing the <p> tag in Dreamweaver's Tag Selector is a quick and easy way to highlight the current paragraph on your Web page.

Click one of these tags, and the corresponding elements are selected on your page, ready for modification. The Tag Selector is a terrific time-saver; throughout this book, I point out how you can use it under various circumstances.

Enhanced layout options

Dreamweaver works much more like a desktop publishing program than do many other visual HTML editors. Today's browser capabilities permit images and text to be placed in specific locations on the Web page — a concept known as *absolute positioning*. To enable you to take full advantage of this power, Dreamweaver includes both rulers and grids. You can specify the type of measurement to be used (inches, pixels, or centimeters), as well as the spacing and appearance of the grid lines. You can even have objects snap to the grid for easy alignment.

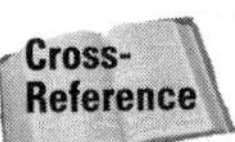

To find out more about absolute positioning, see Chapter 28.

Active content preview

In order for a browser to display anything beyond standard format graphics, a plug-in is generally required. Plug-ins extend the capability of most browsers to show animations, play music, or even explore 3D worlds. Dreamweaver is one of the first Web authoring tools to enable you to design your Web page with an active plug-in playing the extended file; with all other systems, you have to preview your page in a browser to see the active content.

The active content feature in Dreamweaver enables the playback of plug-ins such as Macromedia Flash, Shockwave, and others. However, this feature extends far beyond that. Many Web pages are coded with server-side includes, which traditionally required the page to be viewed through a Web server. Dreamweaver translates much of the server-side information so that the entire page — server-side includes and all — can be viewed in its entirety at design time.

Extended Find and Replace

The Web is a fluid medium. Pages are constantly in flux, and because changes are relatively easy to effect, corrections and additions are the norm. Quite often a Web designer needs to update or alter an existing page — or series of pages. Dreamweaver's enhanced Find and Replace feature is a real power tool when it comes to making modifications.

Find and Replace works in the Document window as well as the HTML Inspector to alter code and regular content. Moreover, changes are applicable to the current page, the working site, selected Web pages, or an entire folder of pages, regardless of the number. Complex Find and Replace queries can be stored and retrieved later to further automate your work.

Up-to-Date HTML Standards

Most Web pages are created in HyperText Markup Language (HTML). This programming language — really a series of tags that modify a text file — is standardized by an organization known as the World Wide Web Consortium (`www.w3.org`). Each new release of HTML incorporates an enhanced set of commands and features. The current version, HTML 4, is recognized by the majority of browsers in use today. Dreamweaver writes clear, easy-to-follow, real-world browser-compatible HTML 4 code whenever you insert or modify an element in the visual editor.

Straightforward text and graphics support

Text is a basic building block of any Web page, and Dreamweaver makes formatting your text a snap. Once you've inserted your text, either by typing it directly or pasting it from another program, you can change its appearance. You can use the generic HTML formats, such as the H1 through H6 headings and their relative sizes, or you can use font families and exact point sizes.

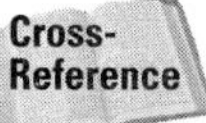

Chapter 9 shows you how to work with text in Dreamweaver.

Additional text support in Dreamweaver enables you to add both numbered and bulleted lists to your Web page. The Text Property Inspector gives you buttons for both kinds of lists as well as easy alignment control. Some elements, including lists, offer extended options. In Dreamweaver, clicking the Property Inspector's expander arrow opens a section from which you can access additional controls.

Graphics are handled in much the same easy-to-use manner. Select the image or its placeholder to enable the Image Property Inspector. From there, you can modify any available attributes, including the image's source, its width or height, and its alignment on the page. Need to touch up your image? Send it to your favorite graphics program with just a click of the Edit button.

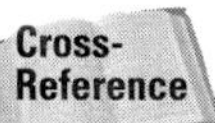

You learn all about adding and modifying Dreamweaver images in Chapter 10.

Enhanced table capabilities

Other features — standard, yet more advanced — are similarly straightforward in Dreamweaver. Tables are a key component in today's Web pages, and Dreamweaver gives you full control over all their functionality. Dreamweaver changes the work of resizing the column or row of a table, previously a tedious hand-coding task, into an easy click-and-drag motion. Likewise, you can delete all the width and height values from a table with the click of a button. Figure 1-4 shows the Table Property Inspector, which centralizes many of these options in Dreamweaver.

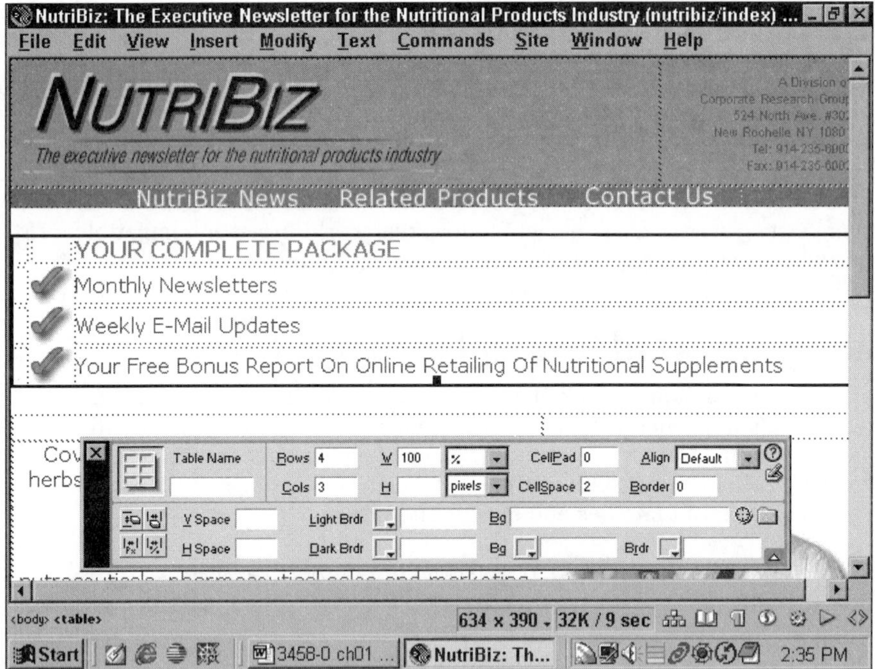

Figure 1-4: The Table Property Inspector is just one of Dreamweaver's paths to a full range of control over the appearance of your table.

Tables are flexible in Dreamweaver. Font changes can be applied to any number of selected cells, rows, or columns. Standard commands enable you to automatically format or sort a table as well.

Easy form entry

Forms, the basic vehicle for Web page data exchange, are just as easy to implement as tables in Dreamweaver. Switch to the Forms panel of the Objects palette and insert any of the available elements: text boxes, radio buttons, checkboxes, and even pop-up menus or scrolling lists. With the Validate Form behavior, you can easily specify any field as a required field and even check to ensure that the requested type of information has been entered.

Click-and-drag frame setup

Frames, which enable separate Web pages to be viewed on a single screen, are often considered one of the most difficult HTML techniques to master. Dreamweaver employs a click-and-drag method for establishing your frame outlines. After you've set up your frame structure, open the Frame Inspector (see Figure 1-5) to select any frame and modify it with the Property Inspector. Dreamweaver writes the necessary code for linking all the HTML files in a frameset, no matter how many Web pages are used. Dreamweaver 3 simplifies frame production even further with the new Frames panel of the Object palette.

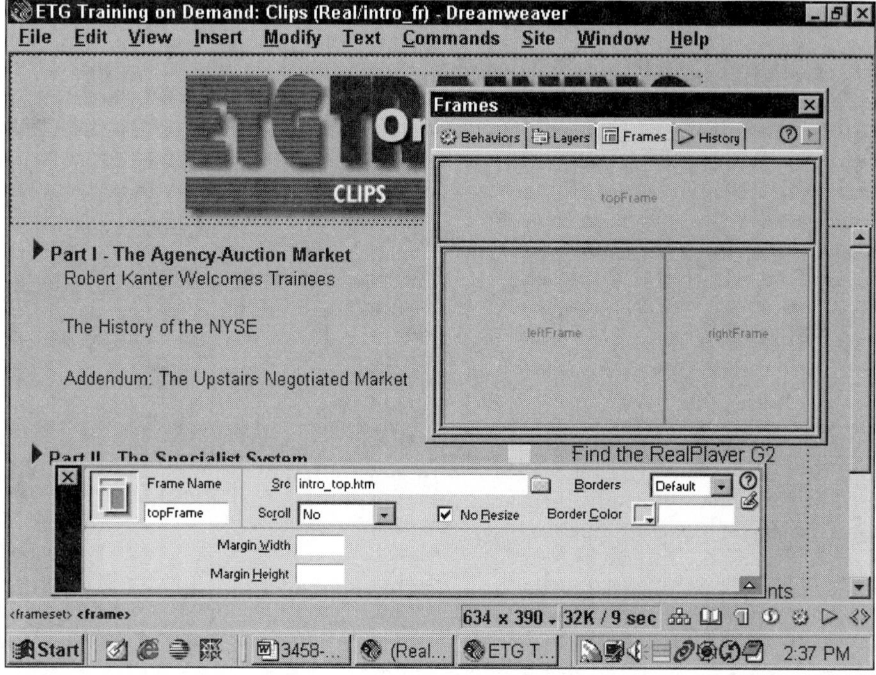

Figure 1-5: In Dreamweaver you use the Frame Inspector to choose which frame you want to modify through the Property Inspector.

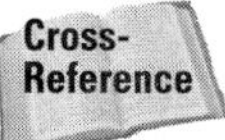

For more information on creating frame-based Web pages, see Chapter 16.

Multimedia enhancements

Dreamweaver enables you to drop in any number of multimedia extensions, plug-ins, applets, or controls. Just click the appropriate button on the Objects palette and modify with the Property Inspector. Two multimedia elements, Shockwave movies and Flash files — both from Macromedia — warrant special consideration in Macromedia's Dreamweaver. When you insert either of these objects, Dreamweaver automatically includes the necessary HTML code to ensure the widest browser acceptance, and you can edit all the respective properties.

Macromedia has formed partnerships with numerous cutting-edge multimedia companies such as RealNetworks, IBM, and Beatnik. Dreamweaver fully supports the fruits of those partnerships: custom objects that enable complex images, audio, and presentations to be easily inserted and displayed in Web pages.

Next-Generation Features

Dreamweaver was among the first Web authoring tools to work with the capabilities brought in by the 4.0 generation of browsers. Both Netscape Communicator 4+ and Microsoft Internet Explorer 4+ include variations of Dynamic HTML (DHTML). Moreover, both of these browsers adhere to the Cascading Style Sheet (CSS) standards to some degree, with support for absolute and relative positioning. Dreamweaver gives Web developers an interface that takes these advanced possibilities and makes them realities.

3D layers

One particular Dynamic HTML feature enables Dreamweaver to be called "the first 3D Web authoring tool." Until Dynamic HTML, Web pages existed on a two-dimensional plane—images and text could only be placed side by side. Dreamweaver supports control of Dynamic HTML layers, meaning that objects can be placed in front of or behind other objects. Layers can contain text, graphics, links, controls—you can even nest one layer inside another.

You create a layer in Dreamweaver by clicking the Layer button on the Objects palette. Once created, layers can be positioned anywhere on the page by clicking and dragging the selection handle. As with other Dreamweaver objects, you can modify a layer through the Property Inspector.

Detailed information on using Dynamic HTML in Dreamweaver starts in Chapter 26.

Animated objects

Objects in layers can be positioned anywhere on the Web page under construction, and they can also be moved when the page is viewed. Dreamweaver takes this capability and adds its Timeline Inspector, becoming a 4D Web authoring tool! The Timeline Inspector, shown in Figure 1-6, is designed along the lines of Macromedia's world-class multimedia creation program, Director. With timelines, you can control a layer's position, size, 3D placement, and even visibility on a frame-by-frame basis. With Dreamweaver, you no longer have to plot a layer's path on a timeline—now you can just draw it using the Record Path of Layer feature.

Figure 1-6: Use the Timeline Inspector to animate objects in layers using Dreamweaver's advanced Dynamic HTML features.

Dynamic style updates

Dreamweaver completely supports the Cascading Style Sheet (CSS) specification agreed upon by the World Wide Web Consortium. CSS gives Web designers more flexible control over almost every element on their Web pages. Dreamweaver applies CSS capabilities as if they were styles in a word processor. For example, you can make all the <h1> tags blue, italic, and in small caps. If your site's color scheme changes, you can make all the <h1> tags red — and you can do this throughout your Web site with one command. Dreamweaver gives you style control over type, background, blocks, boxes, borders, lists, and positioning.

Dreamweaver enables you to change styles online as well as offline. By linking a CSS change to a user-driven event such as moving the mouse, text can be highlighted or de-emphasized, screen areas can light up, and figures can even be animated. And it can all be done without repeated trips to the server or huge file downloads.

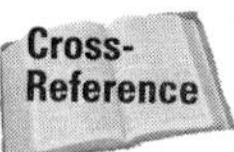

Details on using Cascading Style Sheets begin in Chapter 27.

JavaScript behaviors

Through the development of JavaScript behaviors, Dreamweaver combines the power of JavaScript with the ease of a drag-and-drop interface. A behavior is defined as a combination of an event and an action — whenever your Web page user does something and then something else happens, that's a behavior. What makes behaviors extremely useful is that they require no programming whatsoever.

Behaviors are JavaScript-based, and this is significant because JavaScript is supported to varying degrees by existing browsers. Dreamweaver has simplified the task of identifying which JavaScript command works with a particular browser. You simply select the Web page element that you want to use to control the action, and open the Behavior Inspector from the Launcher. As shown in Figure 1-7, Dreamweaver enables you to pick a JavaScript command that works with all browsers, a subset of browsers, or one browser in particular. Next, you choose from a full list of available actions, such as go to a URL, play a sound, pop up a message, or start an animation. You can assign multiple actions and even determine when they occur.

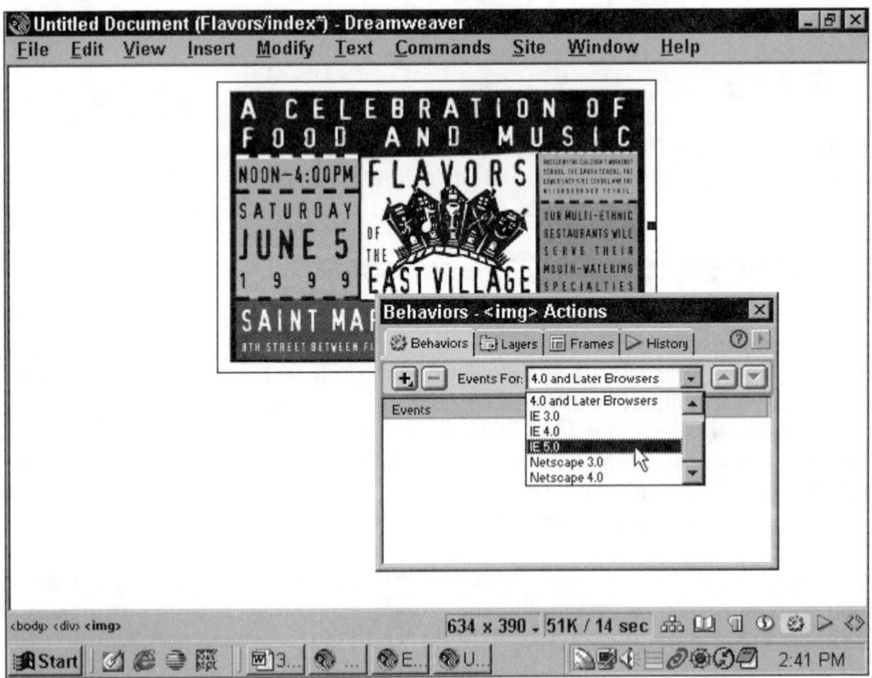

Figure 1-7: Dreamweaver offers only the JavaScript commands that work with the browser you specify.

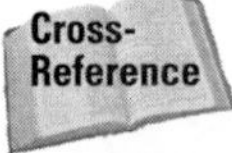

For complete details on working with JavaScript behaviors, see Chapter 19.

Roundtrip XML

A new type of markup language has excited a wide cross-section of Web designers, intranet developers, and corporate users. XML, which stands for Extensible Markup Language, has piqued the interest of many because of its underlying customizable nature. With XML, tags are created to describe the use of the information, rather than its appearance.

Dreamweaver is capable of exporting and importing XML tags, no matter what the tag definition. As XML grows in popularity, Dreamweaver is ready to handle the work.

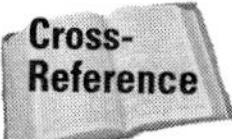

To learn more about XML and its use in Dreamweaver, see Chapter 30.

Program Extensibility

One of Dreamweaver's primary strengths is its extensibility. Virtually no two Web sites are alike, either in their design or execution. With such a tremendous variety of end results, the more flexible a Web authoring tool, the more useful it is to a wider group of designers. When it was introduced, Dreamweaver broke new ground with objects and behaviors that were easily customizable. Now, Dreamweaver lengthens its lead with custom floaters, commands, translators, and Property Inspectors. The basic underpinnings of Dreamweaver can even be extended with the C-Level Extensibility options.

Objects and behaviors

In Dreamweaver parlance, an object is a bit of HTML code that represents a specific image or HTML tag such as a `<table>` or a `<form>`. Dreamweaver's objects are completely open to user customization, or even out-and-out creation. If you'd rather import structured data into a table without a border instead of with the standard 1 pixel border, you can easily make that modification to the Insert Tabular Data object file—right from within Dreamweaver—and every subsequent table is inserted as you'd prefer.

Objects are a terrific timesaving device, essentially enabling you to drop in significant blocks of HTML code at the click of a mouse. Likewise, Dreamweaver behaviors enable even the most novice Web designer to insert complex JavaScript functions designed to propel the pages to the cutting edge. Dreamweaver ships with a full array of standard behaviors—but that's only the tip of the behavior iceberg. Because behaviors, too, are customizable and can be built by anyone with a working knowledge of JavaScript, many Dreamweaver designers have created custom behaviors and made them publicly available.

You can find a large assortment of custom objects, behaviors, and commands on the CD-ROMs that accompany this book.

Commands and floaters

Objects and behaviors are great ways to help build the final result of a Web page, but what about automating the work of producing that page? Dreamweaver employs commands to modify the existing page and streamline production. A great example is the Sort Table command, standard with Dreamweaver. If you've ever had to sort a large table by hand—meticulously moving data, one row at a time—you can appreciate the power of commands the first time you alphabetize or otherwise re-sort a table using this option.

Commands hold a great promise—they are, in effect, more powerful than either objects or behaviors combined. In fact, some of the more complex objects, such as the Rollover Image object, are actually commands. Commands can also extract information sitewide and offer a powerful programmable language within Dreamweaver.

Creating a Dreamweaver command is now easier than ever, thanks to the new History palette. Aside from displaying every action you undertake as you build your Web page, the History palette enables you to select any number of those actions and save them as a command. Your new command is instantly available to be called from the menu whenever you need it.

After only a few moments with Dreamweaver, you become accustomed to its use of floating palettes. In Dreamweaver 3, custom palettes, called *floaters*, can be created. These custom floaters can show existing resources or provide a whole new interface for modifying an HTML element.

Custom tags, translators, and Property Inspectors

In Dreamweaver, almost every part of the user interface can be customized—including the tags themselves. Once you've developed your custom third-party tags, you can display and modify their current properties with a custom Property Inspector. Moreover, if your custom tags include content not typically shown in Dreamweaver's Document window, a custom translator can be built, enabling the content to be displayed.

Programs such as Dreamweaver are generally built in the programming language called C or C++, which must be compiled before it is used. Generally, the basic functions of a C program are frozen solid; there's no way you can extend them. This is not the case with Dreamweaver, however. Dreamweaver offers a C-Level Extensibility that permits programmers to create libraries to install new functionality into the program. Translators, for example, generally rely on new C libraries to enable content to be displayed in Dreamweaver that could not be shown otherwise. Companies can use the C-Level Extensibility feature to integrate Dreamweaver into their existing workflow and maximize productivity.

Automation Enhancements

Web site design is the dream job; Web site production is the reality. Once a design has been finalized, its execution can become repetitive and burdensome. Dreamweaver offers a number of ways to automate the production work, keeping the look of the Web pages constant with the minimum work required.

Applying HTML Styles

Designers in every field depend on the consistency and flexibility of styles. Until recently, the only styles available to Web designers came through a Cascading Style Sheet (CSS). While CSS is, for many, an ideal solution, numerous clients are hesitant to authorize its use, for fear of alienating users with older browsers that don't support CSS. The Dreamweaver engineers have come up with a solution that maintains backward-compatibility while simplifying text formatting: HTML Styles.

The HTML Styles palette enables you to define, manage, and apply any combination of text formatting. You can apply your new style to either a selection or an entire paragraph—styles can be defined either to add formatting to the existing tags or to replace them. While redefining an existing HTML Style does not cause text to update, HTML Styles are sitewide and can be used to enforce a consistent look and feel without CSS limitations.

Importing office documents

Much of the Web's content originates from other sources—in-house documents produced by a word processor or spreadsheet program. Dreamweaver 3 bridges the gap between the offline and online world with two new import features: Import Word HTML and Import Tabular Data.

New Feature

Microsoft Word, perhaps the premier word processor, is great at creating and storing word processing documents but not so accomplished at outputting standard HTML. An HTML file derived from Word is, to put it mildly, bloated with extraneous and repetitive code. Dreamweaver 3's Import Word HTML feature strips out the unnecessary code and even permits you to format the code like your other Dreamweaver files. The Import Word HTML command offers a wide-range of options for cleaning up the code.

Of course, not all Web content derives from word processing documents — databases and spreadsheets are the other two legs of the modern office software triangle. Dreamweaver now includes the capability to incorporate data from any source that can export structured text files through the Import Tabular Data command. Just save your spreadsheet or database as a comma, tab, or otherwise delimited file and bring it directly into Dreamweaver in the table style of your choice.

History palette

The repetitiveness of building a Web site is often a matter of repeating the same series of commands over and over again. You might, for example, need to add a vertical margin of 10 pixels and a horizontal margin of 5, around most, but not all, of the images on a page. Rather than selecting each image and then entering these values time and again in the Property Inspector, you can now enter the values once and then save that action as a command.

The feature that brings this degree of automation to Dreamweaver is found in the History palette. The History palette, new to Dreamweaver 3, shows each step taken by a designer as the page is developed. While this visual display is great for complex, multilevel undo's, the capability to save any number of your steps as an instantly available command is truly timesaving.

Site Management Tools

Long after your killer Web site is launched, you'll find yourself continually updating and revising it. For this reason, site management tools are as important as site creation tools to a Web authoring program. Dreamweaver delivers on both counts.

Object libraries

In addition to site management functions that have become traditional, such as FTP publishing, Dreamweaver adds a whole new class of functionality called *libraries*. One of the truisms of Web page development is that if you repeat an element across your site, you're sure to have to change it — on every page. Dreamweaver libraries eliminate that drudgery.

You can define almost anything as a Library element: a paragraph of text, an image, a link, a table, a form, a Java applet, an ActiveX control, and so on. Just choose the item and open the Library palette (see Figure 1-8). Once you've created the Library entry, you can reuse it throughout your Web site. Each Web site can have its own library, and you can copy entries from one library to another.

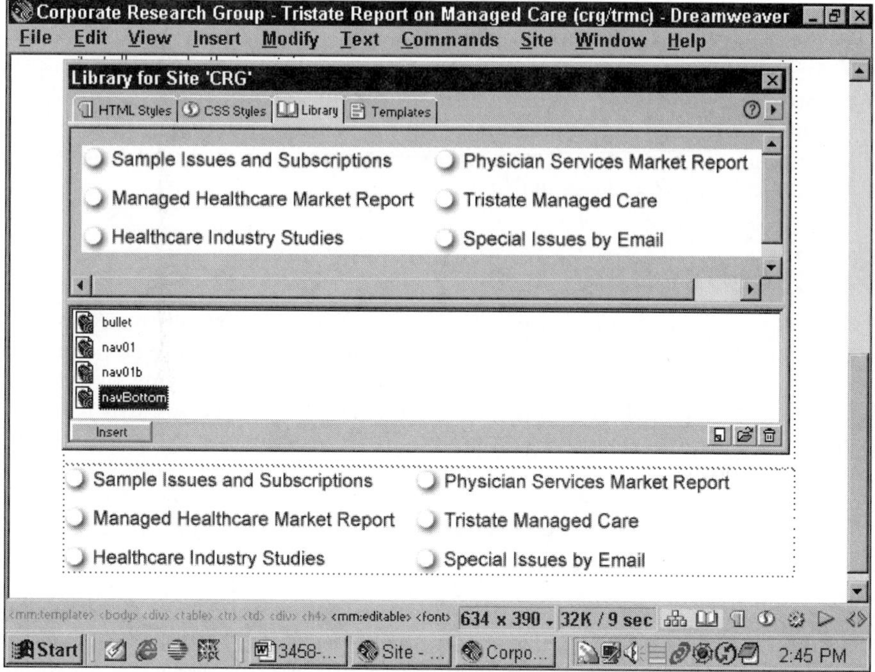

Figure 1-8: Use Dreamweaver's Library feature to simplify the task of updating elements repeated across many Web pages.

Being able to include "boilerplate" Web elements is one thing, being able to update them across the site simultaneously is quite another! You can easily change a Library entry through the Library palette. Once the change is complete, Dreamweaver detects the modification and asks if you want to update your site. Imagine updating copyright information across a 400+ page Web site in the wink of an eye, and you start to understand the power of Dreamweaver libraries.

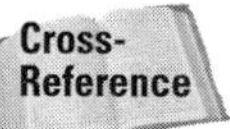

To find out more about making sitewide changes, see Chapter 34.

Templates

The more your Web site grows, the more you'll find yourself using the same basic format for different pages. Dreamweaver enables the use of Web page templates to standardize the look and feel of a Web site and to cut down on the repetitive work of creating new pages. A Dreamweaver template can hold the basic structure for the page — an image embedded in the background, a navigation bar along the left side, or a set-width table in the center for holding the main text, for example — with as many elements predefined as possible.

But Dreamweaver templates are far more than just molds for creating pages. Basically, templates work with a series of locked and editable regions. To update an entire site based on a template, all you have to do is alter one or more of the template's locked regions. Naturally, Dreamweaver enables you to save any template that you create in the same folder, so that your own templates, too, are accessible through the File ⇨ New from Template command. (You can find more about using and creating templates in Chapter 33.)

Browser targeting

Browser targeting is another site management innovation from Dreamweaver. One of the major steps in any site development project is to test the Web pages in various browsers to look for inconsistencies and invalid code. Dreamweaver's Browser Targeting function enables you to check your HTML against any existing browser's profile. Dreamweaver includes predefined profiles for several browsers, and you can create a profile for any browser you'd like to check.

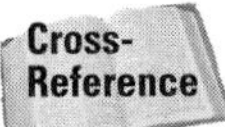

To learn how you can set up your own profile for Browser Targeting, see Chapter 35.

You can also preview your Web page in any number of browsers. Dreamweaver enables you to specify primary and secondary browsers that can display your page at the press of a function key. You can install up to 18 other browsers for previewing your Web page. The entire list of browsers is available through the Preview in Browser command under the File menu.

Converting Web pages

Although Web site designers may have access to the latest HTML tools and browsers, much of the public uses older, more limited versions of browsers. Dreamweaver gives you the power to build Web pages with the high-end capabilities of fourth-generation browsers — and then convert those pages so that older browsers can also read what you've created. Moreover, you can take previously designed Web pages that use tables and "upgrade" them to take advantage of the latest HTML features with the Tables to Layers command. Dreamweaver goes a long way toward helping you bridge the gap between browser versions.

Verifying links

Web sites are ever-evolving entities. Maintaining valid connections and links amid all that diversity is a constant challenge. Dreamweaver includes a built-in link checker so you can verify the links on a page, in a directory, or across your entire site. The Link Checker quickly shows you which files have broken links, which files have links to external sites, and which files may have been "orphaned" (so that no other file connects with them).

FTP publishing

The final step in Web page creation is publishing your page on the Internet. As any Webmaster knows, this "final step" is one that happens over and over again, as the site is continually updated and maintained. Dreamweaver includes an FTP publisher that simplifies the work of posting your site (FTP stands for file transfer protocol). More importantly, Dreamweaver enables you to synchronize your local and remote sites with one command.

You can work with sites originating from a local folder, such as one on your own hard drive. Or, in a collaborative team environment, you can work with sites being developed on a remote server. Dreamweaver enables you to set up an unlimited number of sites to include the source and destination directories, FTP user names and passwords, and more.

The Dreamweaver Site window, shown in Figure 1-9, is a visual interface in which you can click and drag files or select a number of files and transfer them with the Get and Put buttons. You can even set the preferences so the system automatically disconnects after remaining idle for a user-definable period of time.

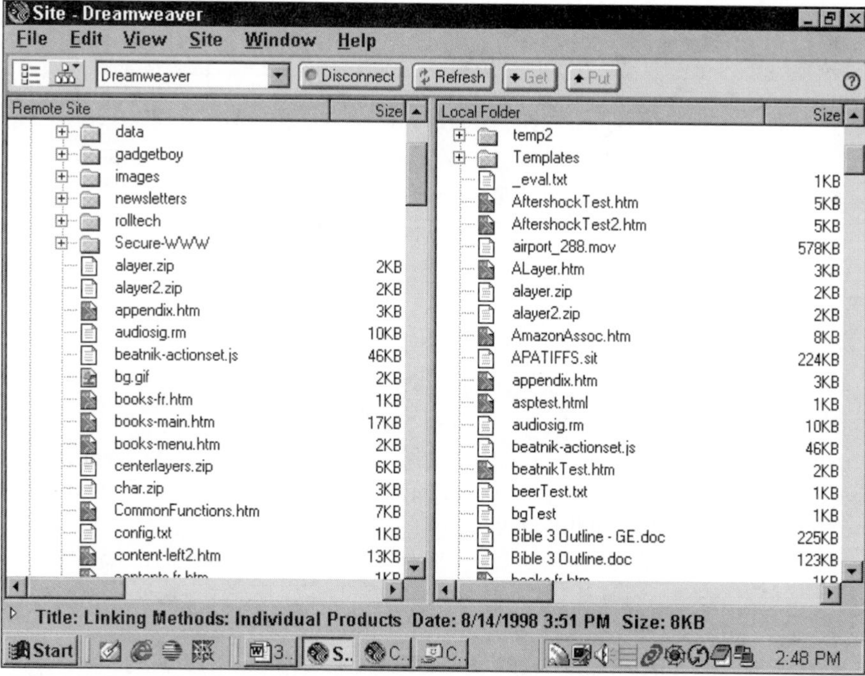

Figure 1-9: The FTP Site window enables you to publish your Web site directly from within Dreamweaver.

Site Map

Web sites can quickly outgrow the stage in which the designer can keep all the linked pages in mind. Dreamweaver includes a visual aid in the Web site management toolbox: the Site Map. With the Site Map, the Web designer can see how the entire Web site is structured. However, you can use the Site Map to do far more than just visualize the Web.

The Site Map, shown in Figure 1-10, can be used to establish the structure of the Web site in addition to viewing it. New pages can be created, and links can be added, modified, or deleted. In fact, the Site Map is so powerful, it becomes a site manager as well.

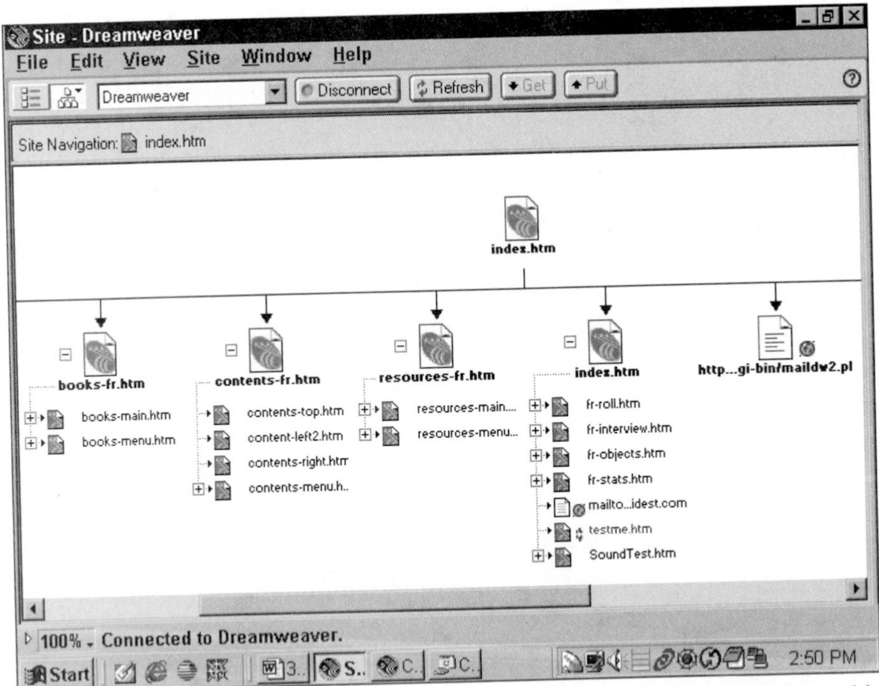

Figure 1-10: Use the Site Map to get an overall picture of your site — and then add new pages or links, right on the map.

File Check In/Check Out

On larger Web projects, more than one person is usually responsible for creation and daily upkeep of the site. An editor may need to include the latest company press release, or a graphic artist may have to upload a photo of the newest product — all on the same page. To avoid conflicts with overlapping updates,

Dreamweaver has devised a system under which Web pages can be marked as "checked out" and locked to prevent any other corrections until the file is once again "checked in."

Dreamweaver places a green checkmark over a file's icon in the Site Files window when it has been checked out by you, and a red mark if it has been checked out by another member of your team. And, so you won't have to guess who that team member is, Dreamweaver displays the name of the person next to the file name. You can also keep track of who last checked out a particular Web page (or image)—Dreamweaver keeps an ongoing log listing the file, person, and date and time of the check-out.

You can learn all about Dreamweaver's Web publishing capabilities in Chapter 7.

Summary

Building a Web site is half craft and half art, and Dreamweaver is the perfect tool for blending these often dueling disciplines. Dreamweaver's visual editor enables quick and artful page creation, and at the same time, its integrated text editors offer the detail-oriented focus required by programmers. Dreamweaver's key features include the following:

- ✦ Dreamweaver works the way professional Web developers do, with integrated visual and text editors. Dreamweaver won't convert your HTML code when it's used with preexisting Web pages.
- ✦ Dreamweaver supports HTML standard commands with easy entry and editing of text, graphics, tables, and multimedia elements.
- ✦ Dreamweaver makes cutting-edge features, such as Dynamic HTML and Cascading Style Sheets, easy to use.
- ✦ Dreamweaver offers you a variety of reusable JavaScript behaviors, object libraries, commands, and templates to streamline your Web page creation.
- ✦ Dreamweaver's wide range of site management tools include FTP publishing with a file-locking capability that encourages team creation and maintenance, as well as a built-in Link Checker and visual Site Map.

In the next chapter, you hit the ground running with a quick-start guide to Dreamweaver.

✦ ✦ ✦

QuickStart for Beginners

✦ ✦ ✦ ✦

In This Chapter

Establishing a local site

Mapping out the home page

Creating linked pages

Laying out the graphics

Adding content

Going live

✦ ✦ ✦ ✦

Designing a Web site is a big job, and Dreamweaver is a big program; both can be overwhelming when you first approach them. If you're new to Web design in general or Dreamweaver in particular, the best way to learn either is to build several sample sites. I've found that working on a project — especially a project that has meaning — helps most people to absorb all the little details needed to be productive.

The following chapter presents an overview of how one person — myself — goes about using Dreamweaver to begin to build a Web site. One of the hallmarks of any world-class software program, such as Dreamweaver, is its capability to be used in many ways by many different people. Don't get the idea that what follows is the only way to construct a site; it is, however, the basic methodology that I've used successfully over the years.

If you are totally new to Web site creation or Dreamweaver, I'd recommend reading through the chapter in one sitting. You get an overview of both the process and the program. Throughout this chapter, you can find many cross-references to other sections of the book where step-by-step instructions are detailed. As you begin to build your sites, use the chapter as a jumping-off place to delve deeper into each topic.

Setting Up a Site

The first phase of designing a Web site is pure input. You need to gather as much information from your client as possible. Some of the information relates to the overall message of the Web site: it's purpose, intended audience, and goals. Other information is more tangible: logos, textual content, and prior marketing materials. I've found it best to get up front as much info — in both categories — as possible.

Tip

Whenever possible, get your data in digital format; the images ideally should be in a format your graphics program can read and the content in a standard word processing file. Your workflow will be greatly enhanced if you don't have to spend time recreating logos or keying in faxed text.

As I am sketching out design ideas for the look of the site (on paper and in my head), I begin to set up the structure of the site on my computer system. Dreamweaver uses a folder on your hard drive as the local site root; when the site goes live on the Internet, the local site is mirrored on the Web server, also known as the *remote site*. So the very first physical step is to create a folder with the site or client name. All I need is a single folder to define a site in Dreamweaver and begin building my Web. Here's how I typically start:

1. Using the system file manager, create a folder on your local hard drive and give it a unique name, reflective of the client or site.
2. In Dreamweaver, open the Site window, as shown in Figure 2-1, by choosing the Show Site button from the Launcher.

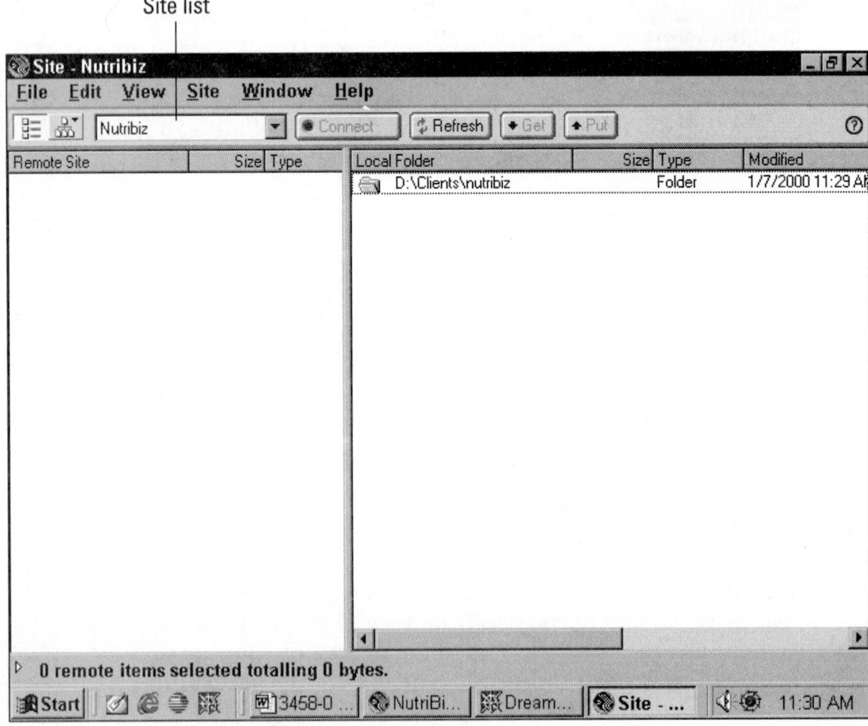

Figure 2-1: Use Dreamweaver's Site window to lay out the structure of your site.

Alternatively, you could select Window ➪ Site Files or use the keyboard shortcut F5.

3. From the site list, choose Define Sites.

   The Define Sites dialog box opens, displaying a list of your currently available sites.

4. Select the New button to set the parameters of your new site.

5. In the Site Definition dialog box, enter the name of the new site, its local root folder, the HTTP address, and the name of the home page.

A detailed breakdown of the process of defining a site can be found in Chapter 6.

After the site is initially defined, you have a folder and a single file set up as the home page, as shown in the Site Map view displayed in Figure 2-2. Dreamweaver's Site Map is not just a useful tool for maintaining a Web site; I recommend you use it to develop the entire structure of your Web site before you begin adding content.

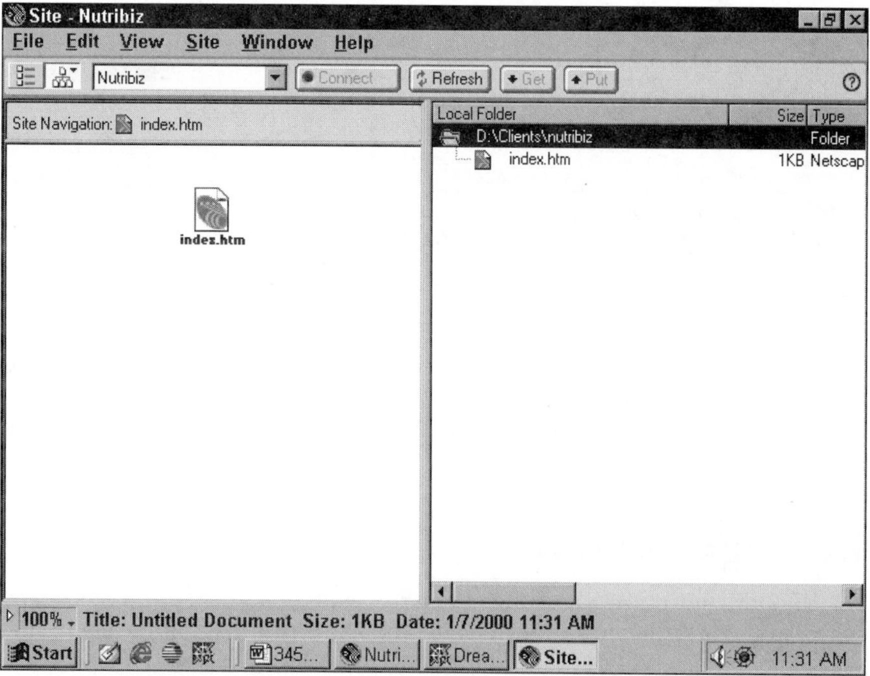

Figure 2-2: The Web site is defined and the home page created.

Using the techniques outlined in Chapter 6, I then create new blank files, already linked to my home page. These new pages act as placeholders for the content to come and help ease the building of the site by providing existing pages to link to and to preview the navigation of my site. To function properly, many of Dreamweaver's commands depend on a file being saved, so by prebuilding my site pages, I avoid unnecessary delays and warning dialog boxes. By the time I'm finished, my Web site is beginning to take form, as can be seen in Figure 2-3.

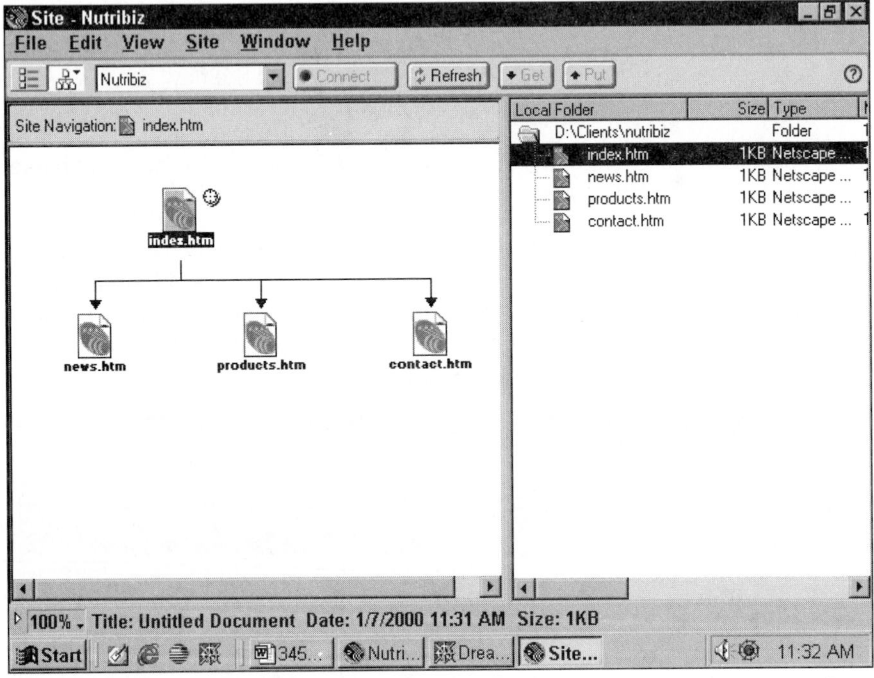

Figure 2-3: Dreamweaver's Site window is a valuable Web site prototyping tool.

While it's not necessary to create all the pages a site might use, I find it helpful to make the primary ones linked to the home page. Then, when I work on each section, such as Products, I use the Site window to create the pages in that division.

Home Page Layout

With the site's structure beginning to emerge, it's time to turn your attention to most visitors' first glance at the Web site: the home page. Although any page can act as a doorway to your site, the home page is by far the most commonly used entrance. I like to start my design on the home page for another reason also — I frequently reuse core elements from the home page, such as the logo and navigation system, throughout the site. By setting these designs early — and getting approval for them — I can save myself a fair amount of work down the road while maintaining a consistent look-and-feel to the site.

Starting with the <head>

One of the most important sections of a Web page is also one of those most frequently — and wrongly — ignored: the <head> section. Under normal circumstances, the <head> area (as opposed to the <body>) is not seen, but its effect is enormous. The <head> section contains vital information about the page and the site itself, including the page's title, its description, and the keywords used to describe the page for search engines. Much of this information is contained in a page's <meta> tags. I like to add this information at the beginning of my Web site development, partly to get the chore out of the way, but primarily so I don't forget to do it! Dreamweaver offers an easy way to input <head> information:

1. Choose View ➪ Head Content.

   The <head> section appears at the top of the Document window as shown in Figure 2-4.

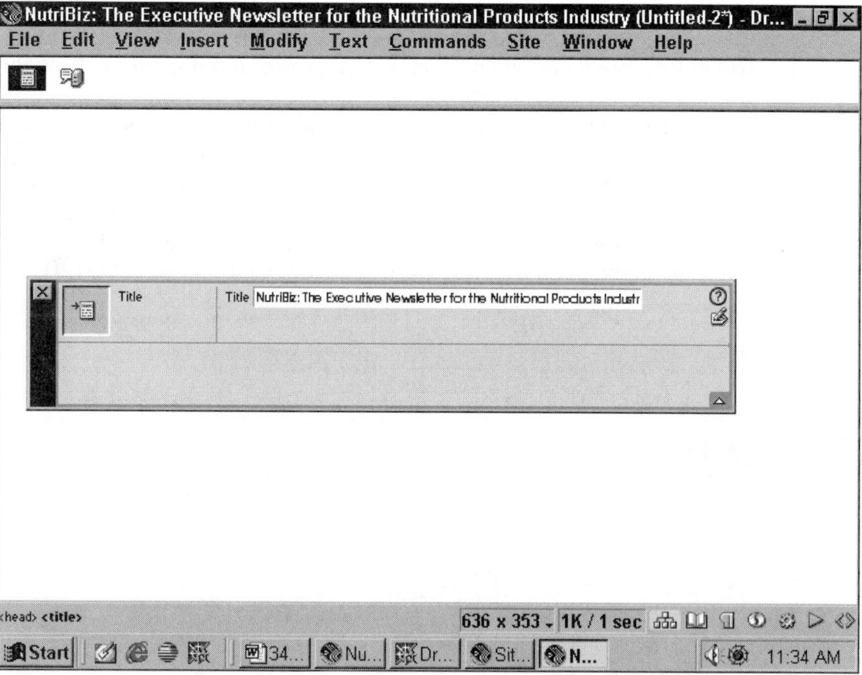

Figure 2-4: The <head> area holds important information for search engines.

2. Select the Title icon and enter the title of the Web page in the Property Inspector.

   The title is one of the primary elements search engines use to catalog pages.

3. From the Head pane of the Objects palette, insert both a Keywords and a Description object and fill them out appropriately.

   I prefer my clients to supply both the keywords and the description whenever possible. Naturally, they know their business best and how best to market it.

For a detailed description of the `<head>` section and its various tags, turn to Chapter 8.

Specifying page colors

After the first *Dreamweaver Bible* was published, I received an irate e-mail from a beginning Web designer who was infuriated by one of Macromedia's practices. By default, Dreamweaver pages all specify a white background color—and nothing else. The gentleman who was complaining set his browser colors to have a black background with white lettering—an austere look, but it was his preference. Whenever he previewed default Dreamweaver pages with his browser, his text seemed to disappear. His text was still there, of course, but because it was white text on a white background, it was invisible. The moral of this story is to always specify your background, text, and link colors if you want your Web pages to maintain your designed look.

After entering the `<head>` content, I next define the page's colors and margins through Dreamweaver's Page Properties dialog box, shown in Figure 2-5. Choose Modify ➪ Page Properties to set these parameters. This is also the location for setting up a background image, if you're using one. It's not unusual for me to alter these settings several times in the home page design stage as I try out different looks, so I've memorized the keyboard shortcut Ctrl+J (Command+J).

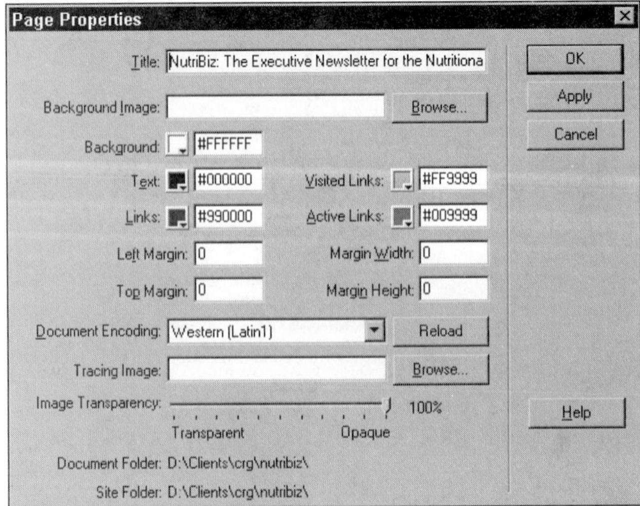

Figure 2-5: Be sure to set your page colors through the Page Properties dialog box.

Not sure about your color combinations? Dreamweaver has a useful command, Set Color Scheme, which contains background, text, and link color selections designed to work together.

Initial graphic layout

Like many small-shop Web designers, I create the majority of the graphics to use on my pages myself, and the Dreamweaver/Fireworks Studio has been a major boon to my productivity. Typically, I create or modify the logo for the home page in Fireworks while Dreamweaver is open, for instant placement and integration. Although the use of layers is always a possibility for placement, I prefer to lay out my pages with tables for most situations. Many designers new to the Web—especially those from a print background—prefer the exact positioning of layers and can use Dreamweaver's excellent layers-to-tables conversion features. The approach you prefer is up to you, but keep in mind that many clients still balk at using layers for fear of excluding visitors with older browsers.

Here's how a typical home page is developed:

1. Start by creating a logo for the Web in your favorite graphics editor.

   Remember that Web graphics are of a particular format, usually GIF or JPEG with a screen resolution of 72 dpi. Although most Web page visitors' monitors display thousands of colors, it's still good practice to use Web-safe colors wherever possible.

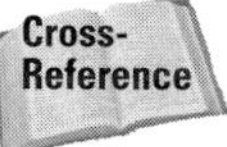

An explanation of Web graphic formats and Web-safe colors can be found in Chapter 10.

2. In Dreamweaver, create a 100 percent wide borderless table that roughly has enough rows and columns to hold your logo, navigational elements, and any other upfront information. In the example shown in Figure 2-6, I start with a two-row by two-column configuration and modify it as needed.

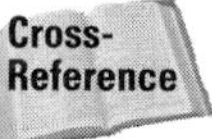

Tables are an important layout tool for Web designers. Chapter 13 shows you how to create and modify tables in Dreamweaver.

3. Add background color to the table or rows, if desired.

   Using a table's background color features is a good, no-overhead way to add color to your page. Dreamweaver enables me to sample colors directly from the logo to begin to tie the page together graphically.

4. If desired, adjust the positioning of the logo by using the Align option on the Property Inspector.

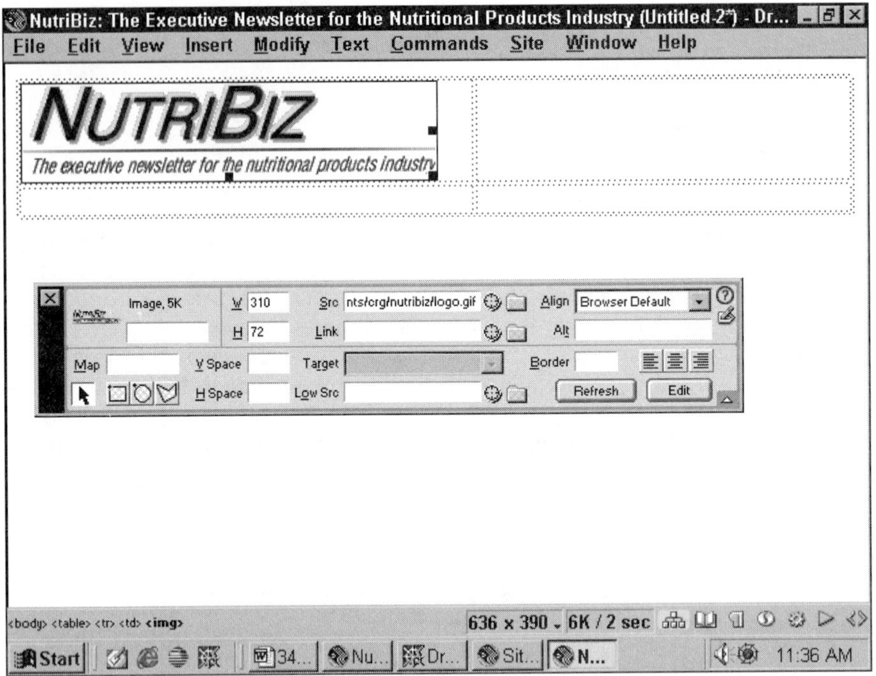

Figure 2-6: Placing the logo in a table to begin laying out the page.

I continue to add and modify elements to the logo area until I'm satisfied. In the case of the example site, I added right-justified contact information on one side of the table and then added navigation elements below the logo, as shown in Figure 2-7. I used a contrasting background color for the second smaller row to set off the navigation bar. Initially, the navigation bar is just text and not graphics; this enables me to prototype the page quickly, and I can always replace the text with images at a later date. The look of the text is controlled either by Cascading Style Sheets or Dreamweaver 3's new HTML Styles.

Note One advantage of using tables instead of layers is that tables can adjust in width more consistently across browsers than layers can. If, as in the example, I set the table to 100 percent width and the page to zero margins, I can be sure the background color will stretch across the page, regardless of the user's browser window size.

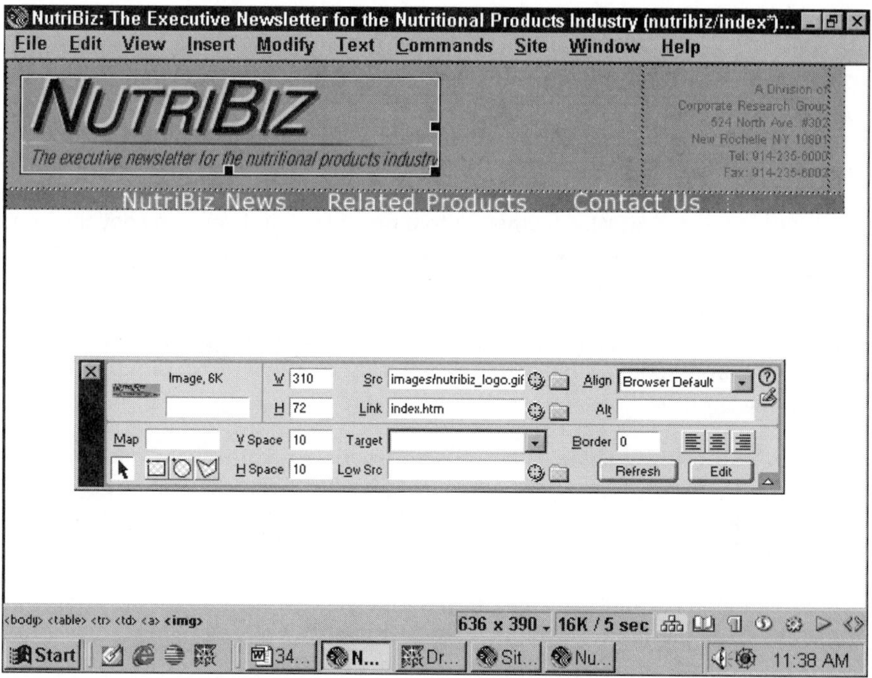

Figure 2-7: All the graphic elements are now in place in the logo area.

Including Client Text

Now that your home page is beginning to attract some eyeballs with its graphic look, it is time to throw in some content to get the message across. Text from a client comes in many forms: from the headings and paragraphs of a marketing brochure to bulleted copy points written especially for the Web, and everything in between. Your job as a Web designer is to make it all flow together in a logical, attractive, understandable fashion.

Many print designers coming to the Internet are appalled at the lack of typographic control on the Web. Particular fonts are, for the most part, suggested rather than specified, with alternatives always available. Sizes are often relative and line spacing — outside of Cascading Style Sheets — is nonexistent! A typical first response is to render blocks of text into graphics to achieve exactly the look desired. In a word, don't. Graphics, unlike text, aren't searchable, and displaying text as graphics defeats much of the purpose of the Web. Moreover, large blocks of graphics can take a long time to download. It's far better to learn the ins and outs of HTML text and take advantage of its universality. Besides, Cascading Style Sheets are increasingly a real option and give the Web designer almost as much control as the print designer.

To facilitate including client-generated text in my Web page designs, I often work with my word processing program and Dreamweaver open simultaneously. This arrangement enables me to quickly cut and paste text from one to the other.

Note

If you have a great deal of client text that's already formatted to include on your page—and a copy of Microsoft Word—take advantage of Dreamweaver's new Import Word HTML feature. When you run the command, Dreamweaver brings the Word-generated HTML document into a new page, and you can copy the needed sections (or all of it, if you like) and paste them directly into the home page. Dreamweaver preserves all the coding during the copy-and-paste operation.

I generally adopt a top-down approach when inserting text: I place the headings followed by the body copy. Then I can try different heading sizes, independently of the main paragraphs.

Tip

If you're copying multiple paragraphs from your word processing document, paste them in Dreamweaver using Edit ⇨ Paste as Text. This command preserves the paragraph breaks—although it converts them to line breaks in Dreamweaver—rather than running all the text together.

Although it depends on the design, I rarely let the text flow all the way across the page. If my page margins are set at zero—which they often are for the graphics I use—the text then bumps right up against the edge of the browser windows. I frequently use two techniques in combination. First, I place the text in a table, set at 95 percent width or less and centered on the page. This assures me that some "air" or gutter-space is on either side of my text, no matter how the browser window is sized. I'm also fond of the `<blockquote>` tag, which indents text by a browser-defined amount. You can access the `<blockquote>` tag by selecting your text and choosing the Indent button on the Property Inspector. The text blocks on the example page shown in Figure 2-8 use both techniques.

I feel that it's important you style your text in some fashion to maintain the desired look. Unless you specify the font, size, and color, you're at the mercy of your visitors' browser preferences—which can totally wreck your layout. You have two methods for defining text formatting: standard HTML tags and Cascading Style Sheets (CSS). Whenever possible, I try to use CSS because of its greater degree of control and flexibility. With CSS, if a client doesn't like the color of body text I've chosen or its size, I can modify it sitewide with one alteration. HTML tags, on the other hand, offer backwards compatibility with 3 browsers. However, for most clients, the relatively small percentage of visitors still using the earlier browser versions is a fair trade-off for the power of CSS.

Cross-Reference

To get the full scope of what CSS can do for you and your Web sites, see Chapter 27.

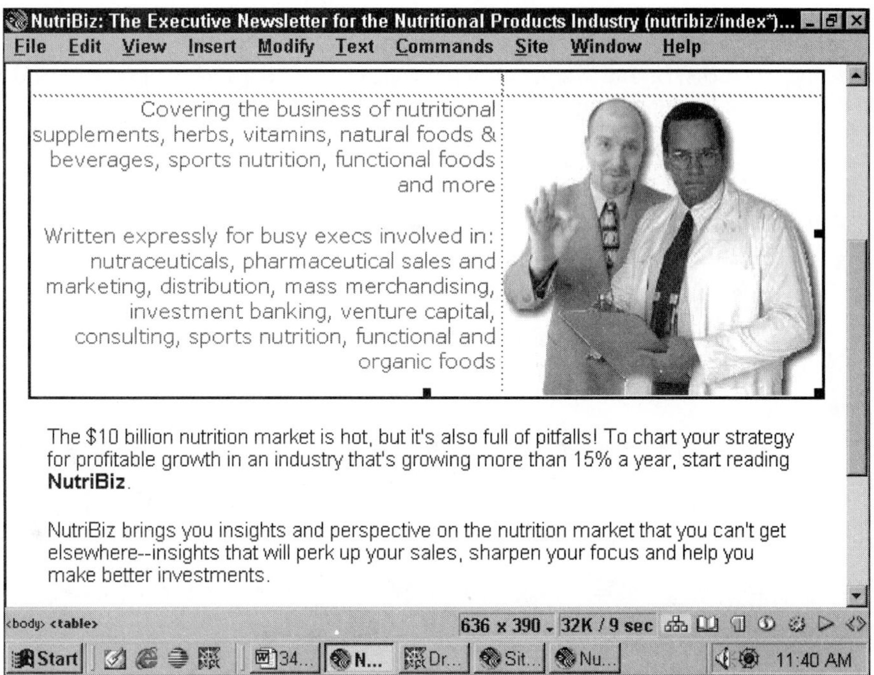

Figure 2-8: The text in the top paragraph (next to the image) is set within a centered table whereas the text below is indented with the `<blockquote>` tag.

Activating the Page

Study after study has proven that an engaged viewer remembers your message better than a passive viewer. One method of grabbing people's attention is to activate your Web page in some fashion, so that some element of the page reacts to the visitor's mouse movements. This reaction could be anything from a simple rollover to the complete rewriting of a frame. Activating a page requires a combination of HTML and JavaScript, frequently beyond the programming skill level — or interest — of the Web designer. Luckily, Dreamweaver makes such effects possible through behaviors.

Once I have the basic layout of a page accomplished, I go back and activate the page in a fitting manner. As with any flashy effect, too many behaviors can be more distracting than attractive, and it's best to use them only when called for. At the very least, I typically use some form of rollover for the navigation bar; this is especially feasible now with Dreamweaver's tighter integration with Fireworks. But even without Fireworks, Dreamweaver 3 enables you to construct a complete multistate navigation bar, or just use the Swap Image behavior to create your own.

Here's one method of activating your page:

1. In Fireworks, or another graphics program, create a series of rollover buttons with one image for each state.

   You need at least two states (Up and Over) and as many as four (Down and Over While Down).

2. In Dreamweaver, remove the temporary text links for the navigation bar.

3. If you've created your rollover buttons in Fireworks, you can just choose Insert Fireworks HTML from the Objects palette.

   Dreamweaver inserts a table of sliced images, such as those in Figure 2-9, complete with all the necessary code.

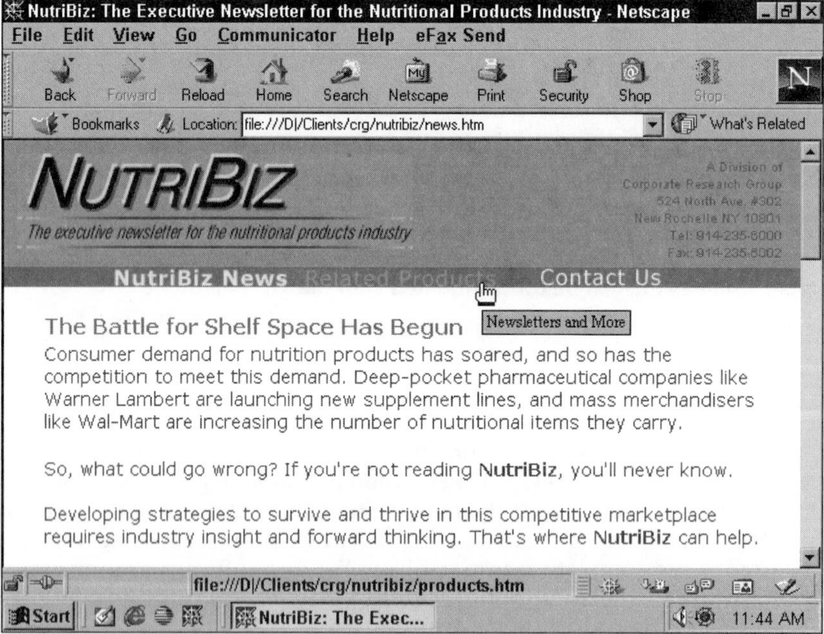

Figure 2-9: These rollover buttons were imported directly from Fireworks generated HTML.

4. If you're working with separate images for the various rollover states, either use the Swap Image behavior or insert a Navigation Bar object. Either method enables you to select the separate images for your rollover states.

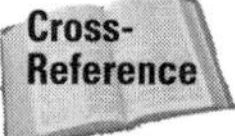

All of Dreamweaver's standard behaviors are covered in Chapter 19; information on the Navigation Bar object can be found in Chapter 10.

If I'm using tables for my layouts, I tend to nest the table containing the navigation bar inside the cell of another table. This technique gives me a fluid design that resizes and realigns well to match the user's browser window. For instance, in the example site, I merged all the columns in the row beneath the logo and then centered the table containing the navigation buttons.

Once I've completed the initial elements of my page, I take advantage of one of Dreamweaver's key features: Library items. By turning my navigation bar into a Library item, I can easily reuse it on the same page (as I do in the example page at the bottom), and on every other page of the site. Not only does this keep consistent elements on every page — an important consideration for design — but also, if I ever need to update the navigation system by changing a link or adding more buttons, I can do it in one step. Moreover, Dreamweaver's Library items, if activated with behaviors, retain all the necessary code.

Previewing and Posting the Page

No matter how beautiful or spectacular your home page design, it's not a Web page until it's viewed through a Web browser and posted on the Web. Now, "the Web" could just as easily be a company intranet as the Internet. But chances are, if the page is intended to be viewed by numerous people, it will be seen under a number of different circumstances. Different operating systems, browsers, screen sizes, and resolutions are just some of the variables you have to take as a given — which is why previewing and testing your Web page is vitally important.

Here are a few pointers for initially testing your pages in development:

✦ At the very least, you should look at your Web page through versions of both major browsers. Dreamweaver enables you to specify up to 13 browsers with its Preview in Browser feature; I currently have 5 available on my system.

✦ During the initial building phase, my routine is to preview my page with both my primary browser (as of this writing, Netscape 4.7) and secondary browser (Internet Explorer 5.0) whenever I add a major component to the page.

✦ I make it a point to resize the page several times to see how my layout is affected by different screen sizes. If the client has specified maximum browser compatibility as a site requirement, I also look at the page under various screen resolutions.

✦ When a page is largely completed, I run Dreamweaver's Check Target Browsers command to make sure I'm not committing some grievous error. If incompatibilities do appear — as they do especially when checking the earliest browsers as shown in Figure 2-10 — I have to decide whether to keep the offending tag or risk the page being visited by users with those browsers.

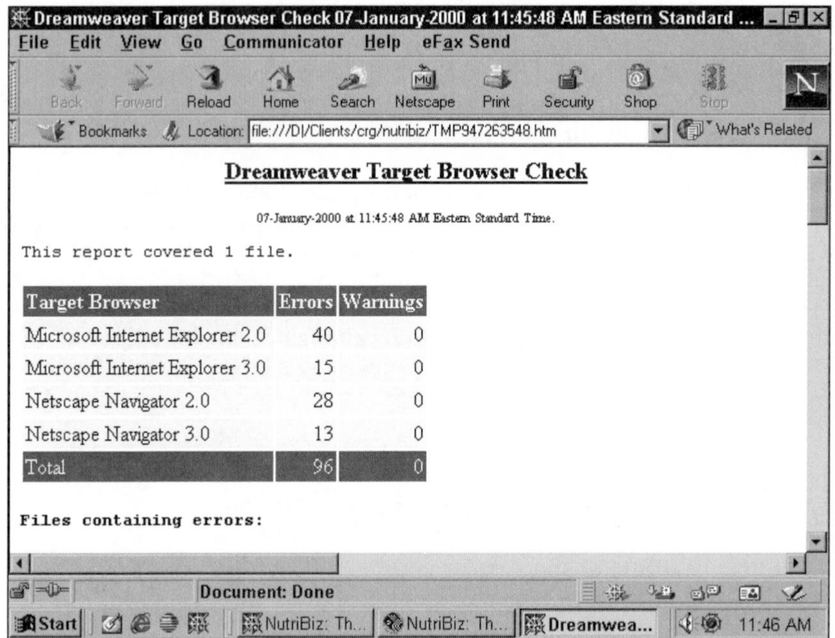

Figure 2-10: Errors from the Check Target Browser command are not uncommon when checking early browser versions.

I also make it a habit to routinely check the Download Stats found in Dreamweaver's status bar. The Download Stats show the "weight" of a page — its file size and the download time at a set speed. By default, the speed is set for a 28.8 modem, but you can alter that in the Status Bar panel of Preferences. Keep in mind that the Download Stats include all the dependent files (images and other media) as well as the size of the page itself.

To be sure that all my ducks are in a row — and all my links are valid, I run Dreamweaver's Check Links Sitewide command. Not only does this give me a report of broken links, but it also displays orphaned files and offers a list of external links that I can verify from its report.

My final testing phase is always conducted online. Here's the procedure I use for uploading my site and testing it:

1. Choose Window ⇨ Site Files to open the Site window.

   By this time I've already established a domain with an Internet host and edited my site definition to include the necessary FTP information.

2. Select the Connect button on the Site window.

   Dreamweaver logs into the remote system and displays the remote files in the pane opposite the local files.

3. Select the HTML files for the completed Web pages.
4. Choose the Put button.
5. By default, Dreamweaver asks if you'd like to include the dependent files; click Yes.

   Dreamweaver begins to transfer the HTML files as well as all dependent files. All necessary subfolders (images, media) are created to replicate the local site structure on the remote site.

Note

If the Include Dependent Files dialog box does not appear, open Preferences and, on the Site FTP category, select the Dependent Files: Prompt on Put/Check In option.

6. After the file transfer is complete, open a browser and connect to the URL for the site.
7. Navigate to every page and try all links and user actions, including rollovers. Note any "files not found" or other errors.
8. If errors occurred, return to Dreamweaver and verify the links for the problem files.
9. If necessary, repair the links and re-upload the HTML file. In most cases, you will not need to resend the dependent files.
10. Repeat Steps 6 through 9 with all available browsers and systems.

Tip

If the site is publicly viewable on the Internet, be sure to view the pages through an America Online (AOL) browser. Although AOL uses an Internet Explorer–derived browser, it also compresses graphics with its own algorithm and tends to open with smaller-than-normal windows. If you find problems, you might consult AOL's Webmaster Site at `http://webmaster.info.aol.com`.

Summary

When people ask me what I like about designing Web sites, I tell them that it appeals to me because it engages both my left and right brain. Web site design is, at turns, both creative and pragmatic, and Dreamweaver balances that equation with grace. Although everyone works differently, these are some of the points I try to keep in mind as I'm working:

✦ The more time spent in planning, the less time spent in revision. Get as much information as possible from the client before you begin designing.

✦ Use Dreamweaver's Site Map to prototype the site; the existing structure saves time as you begin to fill in the content.

- Work from the home page out. The home page is primarily used to succinctly express the client's message, and it often sets the tone for the entire site.
- Include some interactivity in your Web page. A static page may be beautiful to behold, but an active page enables the visitor to interact and leaves a more lasting impression.
- Preview your pages early and often during the development phase. It's far better to discover an incompatibility with the page half done than when you're demoing for the client.

In the next chapter, you get an in-depth tour of all of Dreamweaver's features.

✦ ✦ ✦

A Hands-On Tour of Dreamweaver

✦ ✦ ✦ ✦

In This Chapter

Understanding the screen layout

Inserting HTML elements with the Objects palette

Modifying tag properties with the Property Inspector

Switching views and windows with the Launcher

Working with dockable windows and palettes

Stepping through the menus

✦ ✦ ✦ ✦

Dreamweaver's user interface is clean, efficient, and powerful. By offering streamlined tools and controls, Dreamweaver helps you focus on the most important area of the screen: your Web page design. This chapter provides a detailed overview of the Dreamweaver workspace so you know where all the tools are when you need to use them.

Many other Web authoring programs surround your page-in-progress with numerous menu strips, icons, and other interface paraphernalia. Dreamweaver takes a more streamlined approach, however, which enables you to keep the focus on your workspace as your page develops. Dockable windows and palettes further reduce onscreen clutter; in Dreamweaver 3, every palette is dockable, including the HTML Source Inspector.

Viewing the Document Window

Dreamweaver's primary workspace is the Document window. When you first start Dreamweaver, you see what is essentially an empty canvas, as shown in Figure 3-1. This is where you create your Web pages by typing in headlines and paragraphs, inserting images and links, and creating tables, forms, and other HTML elements.

The Web design process consists of creating your page in Dreamweaver and then previewing the results in one or more browsers. As your Web page begins to take shape, Dreamweaver shows you a close representation of how the page looks when viewed through a browser such as Netscape Communicator or Internet Explorer. You can do this as often as you like — Dreamweaver displays the page in your favorite browser with the press of a button. You can even view active elements, such as QuickTime movies or Shockwave and Flash files, in your Web page as you're building it.

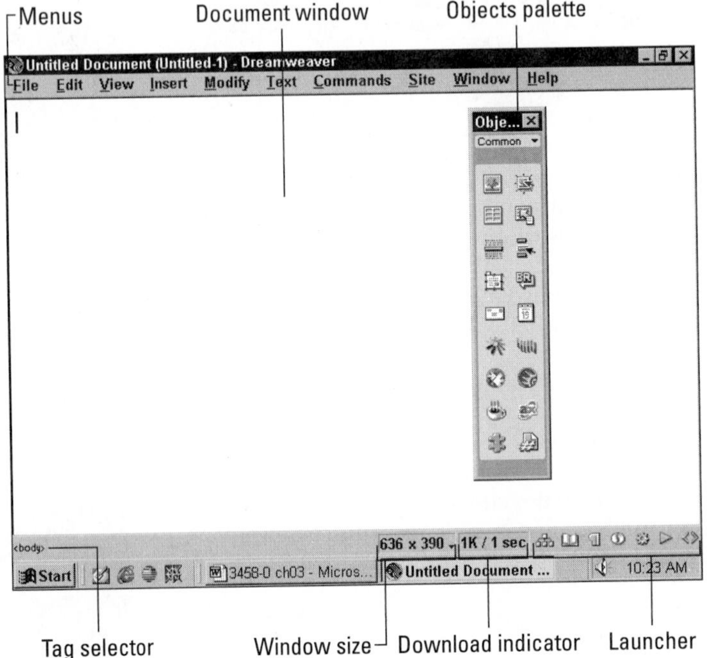

Figure 3-1: Dreamweaver's opening screen is designed to maximize your workspace with a minimum of distracting tools and windows.

Dreamweaver surrounds your "empty canvas" with the tools you need to create your Web masterpiece. We start our tour with the first of these: the status bar.

Working with the Status Bar

The status bar is found at the bottom of the Document window. Embedded here are four important tools: the Tag Selector, the Window Size pop-up menu, the Download Indicator, and the Launcher. Beyond displaying useful information such as which windows are open, these status bar tools are extremely helpful and provide the Web designer with several timesaving utilities.

Tip

If you don't see the status bar at the bottom of your screen, check the View menu. Make sure there's a checkmark next to the status bar item; if not, select it with your mouse to enable it.

Tag Selector

The Tag Selector is an excellent example of Dreamweaver's elegant design approach. On the left side of the status bar, you see a listing of the current HTML tags. When you first open a blank page in Dreamweaver, you see only the <body> tag. If you type a line of text and then press Enter (Return), the paragraph tag <p> appears. Your cursor's position in the document determines which tags are displayed in the Tag Selector. The Tag Selector constantly keeps track of where you are in the HTML document by displaying the tags surrounding your current cursor position. This becomes especially important when you are building complex Web pages that use such features as nested tables.

As its name implies, the Tag Selector does more than just indicate a position in a document. Using the Tag Selector, you can quickly choose any of the elements surrounding your current cursor. Once an element is selected, you can quickly modify or delete it. If you have the Property Inspector (described later in this chapter) onscreen, choosing a different code from the Tag Selector makes the corresponding options available in the Property Inspector.

Tip

If you want to quickly clear most of your HTML page, choose the <body> tag and press Delete. All graphics, text, and other elements you have inserted through the Document window are erased. Left intact is any HTML code in the <head> section, including your title, <meta> tags, and any preliminary JavaScript. The <body> tag is also left intact.

In a more complex Web page section such as the one shown in Figure 3-2, the Tag Selector shows a wider variety of HTML tags. As you move your pointer over individual codes in the Tag Selector, they are highlighted; click one, and the code becomes bold. Tags are displayed from left to right in the Tag Selector, starting on the far left with the most inclusive (in this case the <body> tag) and proceeding to the narrowest selection (here, the italic <i> tag) on the far right.

As a Web page developer, you're constantly selecting elements in order to modify them. Rather than relying on the click-and-drag method to highlight an area—which often grabs unwanted sections of your code, like <font> tags—use the Tag Selector to unerringly pick just the code you want. Dreamweaver's Tag Selector is a subtle but extremely useful tool that can speed up your work significantly.

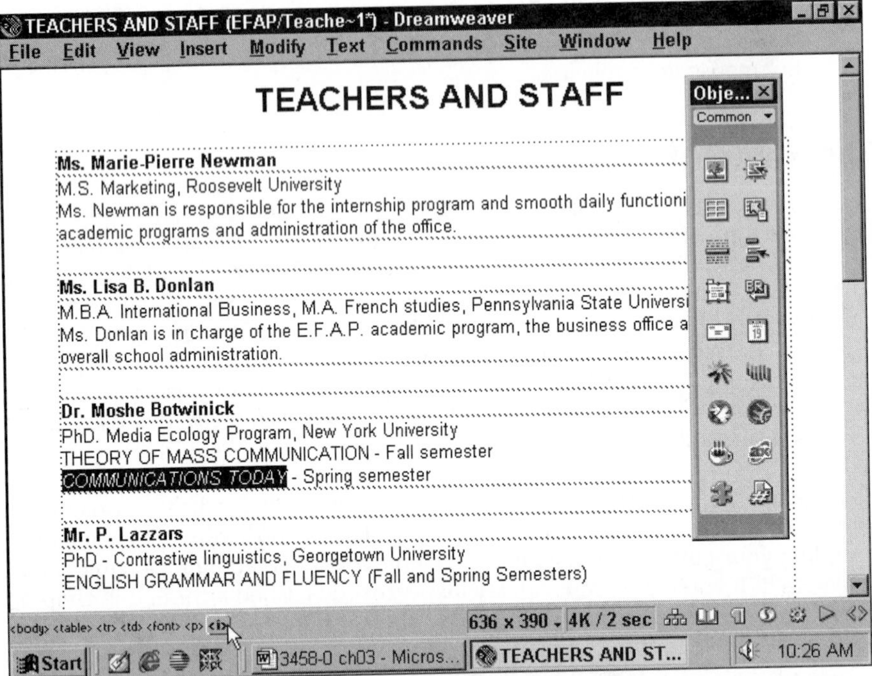

Figure 3-2: The Tag Selector enables you to highlight just the code you want. Here, selecting the <i> tag chooses only the italicized portion of the text.

Window Size pop-up menu

The universality of the Internet enables virtually any type of computer system from anywhere in the world to access publicly available Web pages. Although this accessibility is a boon to global communication, it forces Web designers to be aware of how their creations look under various circumstances — especially different screen sizes.

The Window Size pop-up menu gives designers a sense of how their pages look on different monitors. Located just right of center on the status bar, the Window Size pop-up menu indicates the screen size of the current Document window, in pixels, in *width* × *height* format. If you resize your Document window, the Window Size indicator updates instantly. This indicator gives you an immediate check on the dimensions of the current page.

But the Window Size pop-up menu goes beyond just telling you the size of your screen — it also enables you to quickly view your page through a wide variety of monitor sizes. Naturally, your monitor must be capable of displaying the larger screen dimensions before they can be selected. To select a different screen size, follow these steps:

1. Click once on the expander arrow to the right of the displayed dimensions.

   A menu listing the standard sizes, shown in Figure 3-3, pops up.

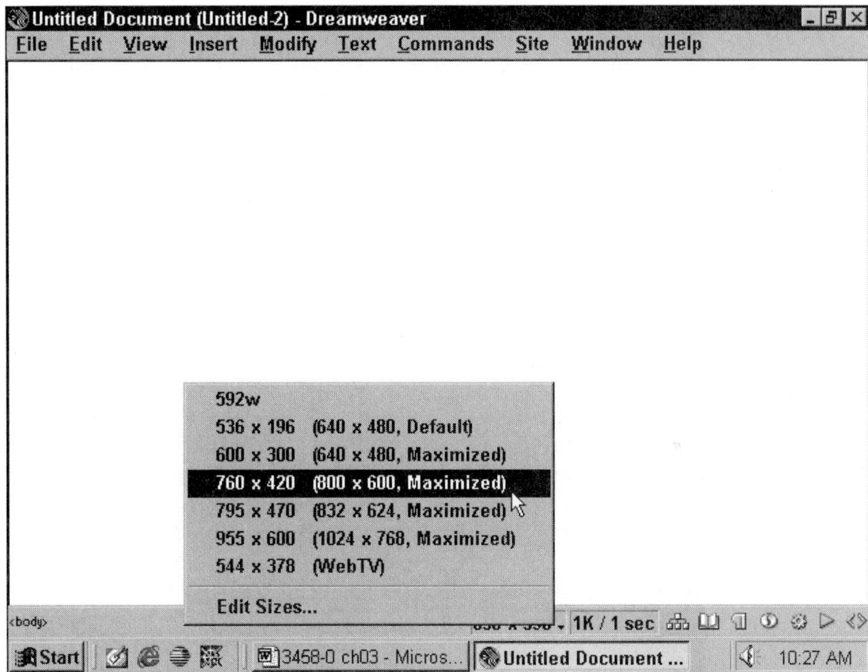

Figure 3-3: You can change your current screen size to any of seven standard sizes — or add your own custom sizes — with the new Window Size pop-up menu.

2. Holding down the mouse button, move your mouse over a desired screen size.
3. To select a size, release the mouse button.

The standard sizes, and the machines most commonly using them, are as follows:

- 592w
- 536×196 (640×480, Default)
- 600×300 (640×480, Maximized)
- 760×420 (800×600, Maximized)

✦ 795×470 (832×624, Maximized)

✦ 955×600 (1024×768, Maximized)

✦ 544×378 (WebTV)

The first option, 592w, is the only option that does not change the height as well as the width. Instead, this choice uses the current window height and just alters the width.

Tip You can set up your own custom screen settings by choosing Edit Sizes from the Window Size pop-up menu. This option opens the Status Bar panel of the Preferences dialog box. How you modify the pop-up list is described in Chapter 4.

The dimensions offered by the Window Size pop-up menu describe the entire editable area of a page. The Document window has been carefully designed to match specifications set by the primary browsers. Both the left and right margins are the same width as both the Netscape and Microsoft browsers, and the status bar matches the height of the browser's bottom row as well. The height of any given browser environment depends on which toolbars are being used; however, Dreamweaver's menu strip is the same height as the browsers' menu strips.

Tip If you want to compensate for the other browser user interface elements, such as the toolbar and the Address bar (collectively called "chrome"), you can increase the height of your Document window by approximately 72 pixels. Combined, Navigator's toolbar (44 pixels high) and Address bar (24 pixels) at 68 pixels are slightly narrower than Internet Explorer's total chrome. Microsoft includes an additional bottom separator that adds 6 pixels to its other elements (toolbar, 42 pixels; and Address bar, 24) for a total of 72 pixels. Of course, with so many browser variables, the best design course is to leave some flexibility in your design.

Download Indicator

So you've built your Web masterpiece, and you've just finished uploading the HTML, along with the 23 JPEGs, eight audio files, and three Flash movies that make up the page. You open the page over the Net and — surprise! — it takes five minutes to download. Okay, this example is a tad extreme, but every Web developer knows that opening a page from your hard drive and opening a page over the Internet are two vastly different experiences. Dreamweaver has taken the guesswork out of loading a page from the Web by providing the Download Indicator.

The Download Indicator is located to the right of the Window Size pop-up menu on the status bar. As illustrated in Figure 3-4, Dreamweaver gives you two values, separated by a slash character:

✦ The cumulative size of the page, including all the associated graphics, plug-ins, and multimedia files, measured in kilobytes (K).

✦ The time it takes to download at a particular modem connection speed, measured in seconds (sec).

You can check the download size of any individual graphic by selecting it and looking at the Property Inspector—you can find the file size in kilobytes next to the thumbnail image on the left.

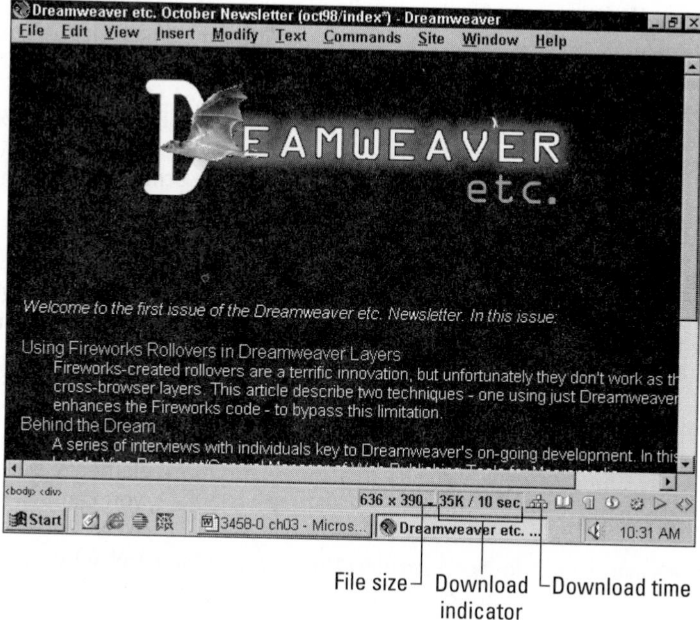

Figure 3-4: Take notice of the Download Indicator whenever you lay out a page with extensive graphics or other large multimedia files.

The Download Indicator is a handy real-world check. As you build your Web pages, it's a good practice to keep an eye on your file's download size—both in kilobytes and seconds. As a Web designer, you ultimately have to decide what your audience will deem is worth the wait and what will have them reaching for that Stop button. For example, the graphic shown in Figure 3-4 is attractive, but at 35K it's on the borderline of an acceptable size. Either the graphic should probably be resized or the colors reduced to lower the overall "weight" of the page.

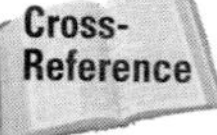

Not everybody has the same modem connection. If you are working with an intranet or on a broadband site, you can set your connection speed far higher. Likewise, if your site gets a lot of traffic, you can lower the connection speed. You change the anticipated download speed through Dreamweaver's Preferences dialog box, as explained in Chapter 4.

Launcher

On the far right of the status bar, you find the Launcher—or, rather, one of the Launchers. In addition to the one on the status bar (known as the Mini-Launcher), Dreamweaver offers an independent, draggable palette with larger, named buttons that is also known as the Launcher. Both Launchers open and close the same windows: Site, Library, HTML Styles, CSS Styles, Behavior, History, and HTML Source. A key new feature of the Launcher is that it's now completely customizable.

As with the Tag Selector, each one of the buttons in the Mini-Launcher lights up when the pointer passes over it and stays lit when selected. You can also use the Launcher to close the windows it has opened—just click the highlighted button. Dreamweaver enables you to keep open any or all of the different windows at the same time.

Clicking a Launcher or Mini-Launcher button when a window is already open has one of two effects. If the window for the button is on top, the window closes. If the window is hidden behind another floating window, the window corresponding to the button is brought forward.

If you don't want the Mini-Launcher to appear in the status bar, you can turn it off. Choose Edit ⇨ Preferences and then select the Status Bar category. Click Show Mini-Launcher in Status Bar to remove its checkmark and then click OK. Naturally, you can turn the Mini-Launcher back on by rechecking its box.

The features of the various windows controlled through the Mini-Launcher are discussed in the section "Using the Launcher," later in this chapter.

Selecting from the Objects Palette

The Objects palette holds the items most often used—the primary colors, as it were—when designing Web pages. Everything from images to ActiveX plug-ins to HTML comments can be selected from the Objects palette. Moreover, the Objects palette is completely customizable—you can add your own favorite items and even set up how the Objects palette is organized.

To see how you can build your own Dreamweaver objects and modify the Objects palette, turn to Chapter 18.

The Objects palette is divided into six separate panels of objects: Characters, Common, Forms, Frames, Head, and Invisibles. The initial view is of the Common panel. To switch from one panel to another, select the small expander arrow at the top of the Objects palette (see Figure 3-5) and then choose an option from the resulting pop-up menu. Each panel is described in detail in the following sections.

If the Objects palette is not available when you first start Dreamweaver, you can enable it by choosing Window ⇨ Objects or the keyboard shortcut, Ctrl+F2

(Command+F2). Likewise, choosing Window ➪ Objects (or the shortcut) again deselects it and closes the Objects palette. You can also remove the Objects palette from your screen by clicking its Close button.

Mac users have the added advantage of being able to windowshade the Objects palette by selecting the Collapse button.

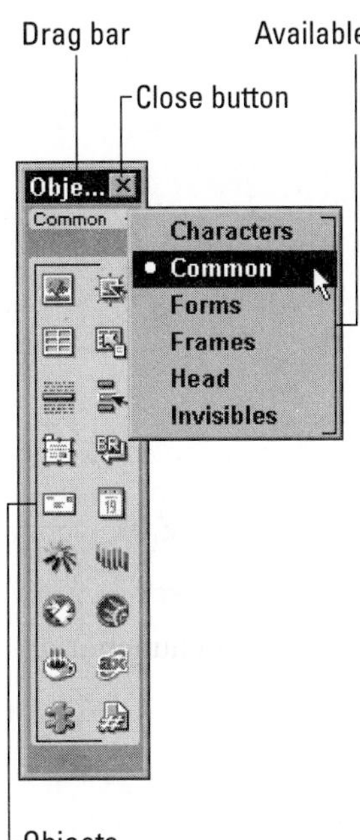

Figure 3-5: The Objects palette acts as a toolbox for holding your most commonly used Web page elements.

To reposition the Objects palette — or any of the Dreamweaver windows or floating toolbars — just place your cursor over the drag bar at the top of the window and drag it to a new location. The Objects palette can be placed anywhere on the screen, not just inside the Document window. Some Web designers like to size their Document window to a standard width that renders well across a variety of platforms and resolutions, and then place the Objects palette outside of that window so they have a clear canvas with which to work.

You can reshape the Objects palette by positioning your pointer over the palette's border so that a double-headed arrow appears. Click and drag the rectangle into a new size or shape, and the icons within the Objects palette rearrange themselves to fit. If your resized Objects palette is too small to contain all the objects, a small scroll arrow is displayed. Select the arrow, and the Objects palette scrolls to show additional objects; at the same time, another arrow appears at the opposite side of the window to indicate more hidden objects. Mac users can only resize the Objects palette by dragging the lower-right corner.

Common objects

The most often-used HTML elements, aside from text, are accessible through the Common Objects panel of the Objects palette. Table 3-1 explains what each of the Common Objects panel icons represents.

In Dreamweaver 3, the number of objects have increased to the point where, to show them all, the standard Object palette is widened to two columns. The following tables describe the icons in a left-to-right, top-to-bottom order.

Table 3-1
Common Objects Panel

Icon	*Name*	*Description*	*Detailed Information*
	Insert Image	Use for including any graphic (including animated GIFs) at the cursor position	See Chapter 10
	Insert Rollover Image	Inserts an image that changes into another image when the user's mousemoves over it	See the section "Inserting Rollover Images" in Chapter 10
	Insert Table	Opens a dialog box for creating a table at the cursor position	See Chapter 13
	Insert Tabular Data	Imports delimited data exported from a spreadsheet or database program	See the section "Importing Tabular Data" in Chapter 13
	Insert Horizontal Rule	Draws a line across the page at the cursor position	See the section "Dividing the Web Page with Horizontal Rules" in Chapter 10
	Insert Navigation Bar	Inserts a series of images with links used as buttons for navigation	See Chapter 10
	Draw Layer	Enables you to drag out a layer of specific size and shape at a specific location	See Chapter 28
	Insert Line Break	Puts in a ` ` tag that causes the line to wrap at the cursor position	See the section "Working with Paragraphs" in Chapter 9

Icon	Name	Description	Detailed Information
	Insert E-mail Link	Inserts a text link that opens an e-mail form when selected	See the section "Adding an E-mail Link" in Chapter 11
	Insert Date	Inserts the current date in a user-selected format	See the section "Incorporating Dates" in Chapter 9
	Insert Flash	Use to include a Flash movie	See Chapter 25
	Insert Shockwave	Use to include a Shockwave movie	See Chapter 25
	Insert Generator	Inserts a Generator template file with optional parameters	See the section "Adding Generator Templates" in Chapter 25
	Insert Fireworks HTML	Inserts images and code generated by Fireworks	See Chapter 22
	Insert Applet	Includes a Java applet at the cursor position	See the section "Adding Java Applets" in Chapter 17
	Insert ActiveX	Puts a placeholder for an ActiveX control at the cursor position, using the `<object>` tag	See the section "Working with ActiveX Components" in Chapter 17
	Insert Plug-in	Use for including a file that requires a plug-in	See the section "Incorporating Plug-ins" in Chapter 17
	Insert Server-Side Include	Opens the dialog box for inserting a server-side include	See the section "Applying Server-Side Includes" in Chapter 34

All of the common objects except for Insert Horizontal Rule, Insert Line Break, and Draw Layer open a dialog box that enables you to browse for a file or specify parameters.

Tip

If you'd prefer to enter all your information, including the necessary file names, through the Property Inspector, you can turn off the automatic appearance of the file requester when you insert any object through the Objects palette or the menus. Choose Edit ⇨ Preferences and, from the General Category, select Show Dialog When Inserting Objects to uncheck it.

Character objects

Certain special characters — such as © (the copyright symbol) — are represented in HTML by codes called *character entities*. In code, a character entity is either a name (such as `©` for the copyright symbol) or number (`©`). Each character entity has its own unique code.

Dreamweaver 3 adds a new facility to ease entering these complex, hard-to-remember codes, the Characters panel. Nine of the most commonly used characters are included as separate objects and a tenth object opens a dialog box with 99 special characters to choose from. Table 3-2 details the new Characters panel objects.

Table 3-2
Characters Panel

Icon	*Name*	*Description*	*Detailed Information*
©	Insert Copyright	Inserts the code for the copyright symbol	See the section "Inserting Symbols and Special Characters" in Chapter 8
®	Insert Registered Trademark	Inserts the code for the registered trademark symbol	See "Inserting Symbols and Special Characters" in Chapter 8
TM	Insert Trademark	Inserts the code for the trademark symbol	See "Inserting Symbols and Special Characters" in Chapter 8
£	Insert Pound	Inserts the code for the pound currency symbol	See "Inserting Symbols and Special Characters" in Chapter 8
¥	Insert Yen	Inserts the code for the yen currency symbol	See "Inserting Symbols and Special Characters" in Chapter 8
€	Insert Euro	Inserts the code for the Euro currency symbol	See "Inserting Symbols and Special Characters" in Chapter 8
—	Insert Em Dash	Inserts the code for the em dash symbol	See "Inserting Symbols and Special Characters" in Chapter 8
"	Insert Left Quote	Inserts the code for the opening curly quote symbol	See "Inserting Symbols and Special Characters" in Chapter 8
"	Insert Right Quote	Inserts the code for the closing curly quote symbol	See "Inserting Symbols and Special Characters" in Chapter 8
	Insert Other Character	Opens the dialog box for inserting special characters	See "Inserting Symbols and Special Characters" in Chapter 8

Form objects

The form is the primary method for implementing HTML interactivity. The Forms panel of the Objects palette gives you nine basic building blocks for creating your Web-based form. Table 3-3 describes each of the elements found in the Forms panel.

Table 3-3
Forms Panel

Icon	*Name*	*Description*	*Detailed Information*
	Insert Form	Creates the overall HTML form structure at the cursor position	See Chapter 15
	Insert Text Field	Places a text box or a text area at the cursor position	See the section "Using Text Boxes" in Chapter 15
	Insert Button Position	Inserts a Submit, Reset, or user-definable button at the cursor	See the section "Activating Your Form with Buttons" in Chapter 15
	Insert Check Box	Inserts a checkbox for selecting any number of options at the cursor position	See the section "Providing Checkboxes and Radio Buttons" in Chapter 15
	Insert Radio Button	Inserts a radio button for making a single selection from a set of options at the cursor position	See the section "Providing Checkboxes and Radio Buttons" in Chapter 15
	Insert List/Menu	Enables either a drop-down menu or a scrolling list at the cursor position	See the section "Creating Form Lists and Menus" in Chapter 15
	Insert File Field	Inserts a text box and Browse button for selecting a file to submit	See the section "Using the Hidden Field and the File Field" in Chapter 15
	Insert Image Field	Includes an image that can be used as a button	See the section "Activating Your Form with Buttons" in Chapter 15
	Insert Hidden Field	Inserts an invisible field used for passing variables to a CGI or JavaScript program	See the section "Using the Hidden Field and the File Field" in Chapter 15
	Insert Jump Menu	Opens a dialog box for building a pop-up menu that activates a link	See the section "Navigating with a Jump Menu" in Chapter 15

As demonstrated in Figure 3-6, you can use a table inside a form to get objects to line up properly. All forms return user input via a CGI or JavaScript program. See Chapter 15 for more detailed information.

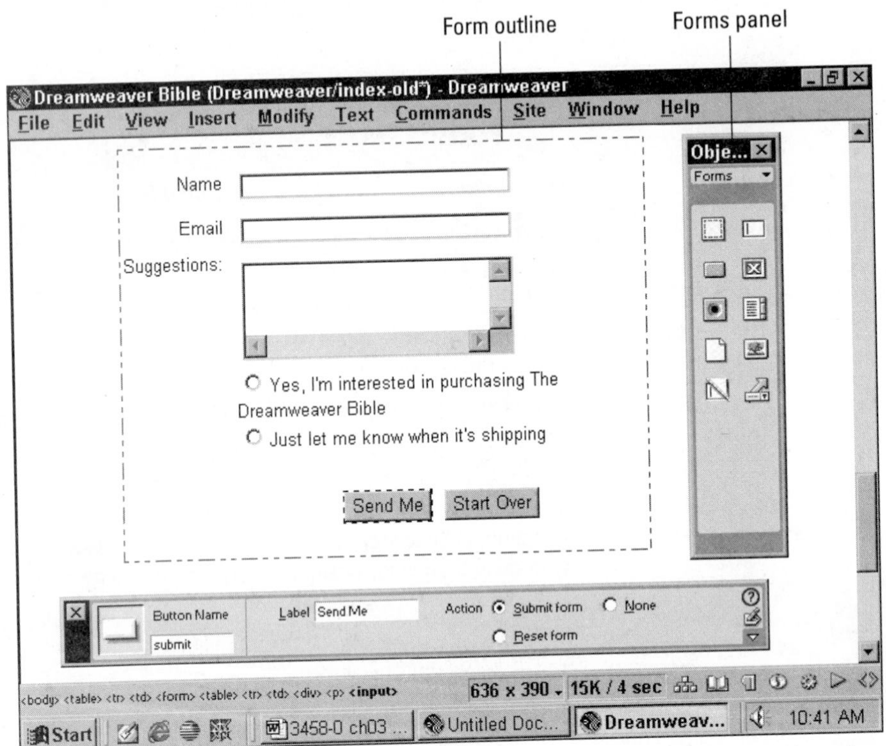

Figure 3-6: Dreamweaver puts a distinctive dashed line around any form if you have View ➪ Show Visibles checked.

Frame objects

In HTML terms, a frame is a collection of separate pages arranged on a single screen. Frames are contained within framesets, which until Dreamweaver 3 could be created only by dragging frame borders into position or selecting a menu option. Because it involves multiple pages, creating a frameset often proved difficult for the novice designer.

Dreamweaver 3 greatly simplifies the process for making standard framesets with the new Frames panel objects. Eight of the most commonly used designs are now immediately available. Select any frame object, and that frameset is made, incorporating the existing page.

The blue symbol in the frame object icons indicates which frame on the current page is placed when the frameset is created. For example, if you create a single page with the text "Table of Contents" and then choose the Insert Top Frame object, "Table of Contents" is moved below the newly inserted top frame. All of the Frames panel objects are explained in Table 3-4.

Table 3-4
Frames Panel

Icon	*Name*	*Description*	*Detailed Information*
	Insert Left Frame	Inserts a blank frame to the left of the current page	See Chapter 16
	Insert Right Frame	Inserts a blank frame to the right of the current page	See Chapter 16
	Insert Top Frame	Inserts a blank frame above the current page	See Chapter 16
	Insert Bottom Frame	Inserts a blank frame below the current page	See Chapter 16
	Insert Left, Top-Left Corner, and Top Frames	Makes a frameset with four frames where the current page is in the lower right	See Chapter 16
	Insert Left and Nested Top Frames	Makes a frameset where the top spans the lower two frames	See Chapter 16
	Insert Top and Nested Left Frames	Makes a frameset where the left spans the two rightmost frames	See Chapter 16
	Split Frame Center	Creates a frameset with four equal frames	See Chapter 16

Head objects

General document information—such as the title and any descriptive keywords about the page—are written into the `<head>` section of an HTML document. The objects of the Head panel enable Web designers to drop in these snippets of code in a handy object format. These objects insert `<meta>` tags with keywords for search engines, specify refresh times, and do many more tasks that impact a Web site's overall performance.

While Dreamweaver enables you to see the <head> objects onscreen via the View ➪ Head Content menu option, you don't have to have the <head> window open to drop in the objects. Simply click any of the nine objects detailed in Table 3-5, and a dialog box opens, prompting you for the needed information.

Table 3-5
Head Objects Panel

Icon	*Name*	*Description*	*Detailed Information*
	Insert Meta	Includes document information usable by servers and browsers	See the section "Understanding <meta> and other <head> tags" in Chapter 8
	Insert Keywords	Inserts keywords used by search engines to catalog the Web page	See the section "Understanding <meta> and other <head> tags" in Chapter 8
	Insert Description	Provides a description of the current page	See the section "Understanding <meta> and other <head> tags" in Chapter 8
	Insert Refresh	Sets a tag to refresh the current page or redirect the browser to another URL	See the section "Refreshing the page and redirecting users" in Chapter 8
	Insert Base	Specifies the base address of the current document	See the section "Understanding <meta> and other <head> tags" in Chapter 8
	Insert Link	Declares a relationship between the current document and another object or file	See the section "Linking to other files" in Chapter 8

Invisible objects

As any experienced Web designer knows, what you see onscreen is, increasingly, a small part of the code necessary for the page's generation. Often you need to include an element that Dreamweaver categorizes as an Invisible. The fourth panel of the Objects palette gives you quick access to the most commonly inserted behind-the-scenes tags, as described in Table 3-6.

Table 3-6
Invisible Objects

Icon	*Name*	*Description*	*Detailed Information*
	Insert Named Anchor	Puts a hyperlink at a particular place on a Web page	See the section "Navigating with Anchors" in Chapter 11
	Insert Comment	Places HTML comment tags inside your script; these comments are ignored by the browser	See the section "Commenting Your Code" in Chapter 9
	Insert Script	Inserts JavaScript or VBScript either directly or from a file	See the section "Adding JavaScript and VBScript" in Chapter 17
	Insert Non-Breaking Space	Inserts a hard space in the current cursor position	See the section "Inserting Symbols and Special Characters" in Chapter 8

Invisible elements can be turned on or off through the Preferences dialog box. Choose Edit ⇨ Preferences and then select the Invisible Elements category. A list of 12 options (including the objects listed in the Invisibles panel except for Insert Non-breaking Space) is displayed. To turn off an option, click once to remove the checkmark from the option's checkbox. For a complete description of all the Invisible elements and other preferences, see Chapter 4.

Getting the Most out of the Property Inspector

Dreamweaver's Property Inspector is your primary tool for specifying an object's particulars. What exactly those particulars are — in HTML, these are known as *attributes* — depends on the object itself. The contents of the Property Inspector change depending on which object is selected. For example, click anywhere on a blank Web page, and the Property Inspector shows text attributes for format, font name and size, and so on. If you click an image, the Property Inspector displays a small thumbnail of the picture, and the image's attributes for height and width, image source, link, and alternative text. Figure 3-7 shows a Property Inspector for a line of text with an attached hyperlink.

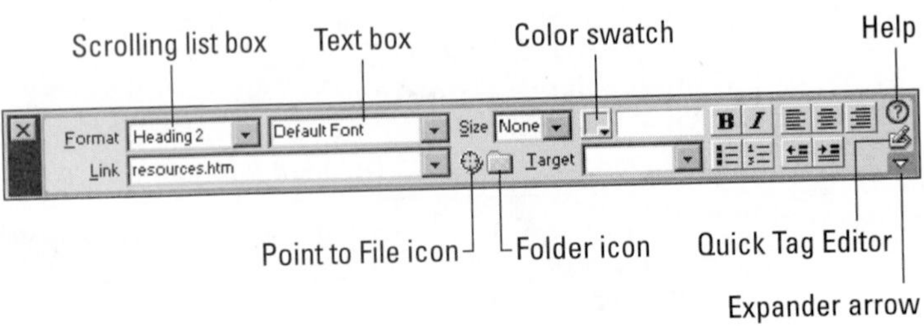

Figure 3-7: The Property Inspector takes many forms, depending on which HTML element you select.

Manipulating the Property Inspector

The Property Inspector is enabled by choosing Window ➪ Properties or selecting the keyboard shortcut, Ctrl+F3 (Command+F3). As with the Objects palette, the Property Inspector can be closed by selecting the Close button, unchecking Window ➪ Properties, or choosing the keyboard shortcut again. On the Mac, you can also windowshade the Property Inspector so that only the title bar is left showing by clicking the collapse button on its window.

You can reposition the Property Inspector in one of two ways. You can click and drag the title bar of the window and move it to a new location, or — unlike the Objects palette — you can click and drag any open gray area in the Inspector itself. This is handy for quickly moving the Inspector aside, out of your way. However, it only works for Windows.

The Property Inspector initially displays the most typical attributes for a given element. To see additional properties, click the expander arrow in the lower-right corner of the Property Inspector. Virtually all the inserted objects have additional parameters that can be modified. Unless you're tight on screen real estate, it's a good idea to keep the Property Inspector expanded so you can see all your options.

In addition to using the expander arrow, you can reveal (or hide) the expanded attributes by double-clicking any open gray area of the Property Inspector.

Property Inspector elements

Many of the attributes in the Property Inspector are text boxes; just click in any one and enter the desired value. If a value already appears in the text box, whether number or name, double-click it (or click and drag over it) to highlight the information and then enter your new data — the old value is immediately replaced. You can see the effect your modification has had by pressing the Tab key to move to the next attribute or by clicking outside of the Property Inspector.

New Feature

Dreamweaver 3 enables you to make small additions to the code without opening up the HTML Source Inspector through the Quick Tag Editor. Located on the right of the Property Inspector just below the Help button, the Quick Tag Editor pops open a small window to display the code for the currently selected tag. You can swiftly change attributes or add special parameters not found in the Property Inspector. The Quick Tag Editor is covered in depth in Chapter 8.

The Property Inspector also uses scrolling list boxes for several attributes that provide a limited number of responses for you to choose. To open the drop-down list of available options, click the arrow button to the right of the list box. Then choose an option by highlighting it.

Tip

Some options on the Property Inspector are a combination drop-down list and text box—you can select from available options or type in your own values. For example, when text is selected, the font name, size, and color options are all combination list/text boxes.

If you see a folder icon next to a text box (see the List item in the Inspector shown in Figure 3-7), you have the option of browsing for a file name on your local or networked drive, or manually inputting a name. Clicking the folder opens a standard Open File dialog box (called Select File in Dreamweaver); after you've chosen your file and clicked Open, Dreamweaver inputs the name and any necessary path information in the correct attribute.

Dreamweaver 3 enables you to quickly select an onscreen file in either a Document window or a Site window as a link, with its Point to File icon, found next to the Folder icon. Just click and drag the Point to File icon until it touches the file (or the file name from the Site window) you want to reference. The path is automatically written into the Link text box.

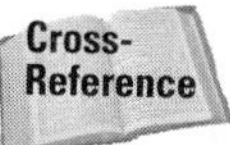

Dreamweaver can handle all forms of absolute and relative addressing. For more information on specifying HTML pages, be sure to see the section "Relative and Absolute Addresses" in Chapter 6.

Certain objects such as text, layers, and tables enable you to specify a color attribute. The Property Inspector alerts you to these options with a small color swatch next to the text box. You can type in a color's name (such as "blue") or its six-figure hexadecimal value ("#3366FF") or select the color swatch. Choosing the color swatch displays a color picker, shown in Figure 3-8, with the 212 colors common to both the Netscape and Microsoft browsers—the so-called browser-safe colors. (Some of the 212 Web-safe colors are duplicated to create a more user-friendly interface.) You can go outside of this range by clicking the small painter's palette in the lower-right corner of the color picker. This opens a full-range Color dialog box in which you can choose a color visually or enter its red, green, and blue values or its hue, saturation, and luminance values.

The color picker in Dreamweaver 3 (see Figure 3-8) is very flexible. Not only can you choose from a palette, but you can also select any color onscreen with Dreamweaver's Eyedropper tool. The Eyedropper button has two modes: When it's selected, the Eyedropper snaps the selected color to its nearest Web-safe neighbor; when it's disabled, colors are sampled exactly. If you'd like to access the system color picker, the Palette button opens it up for you. There's also an Eraser tool, located in the lower-right corner, that deletes any color choice previously inserted.

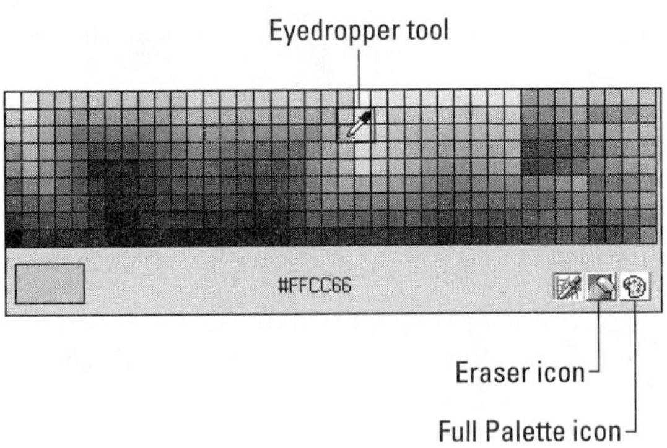

Figure 3-8: Dreamweaver 3's color picker enables you to choose from a wide selection of colors, right from the palette or right off the desktop, with the Eyedropper tool.

One final aspect of the Property Inspector is worth noting: The circled question mark in the upper-right corner of the Property Inspector is the Help button. Selecting this button invokes online help and displays specific information about the particular Property Inspector you're using. The Help button is also available throughout all of the windows opened by the Launcher, as described in the next section.

Using the Launcher

Dreamweaver's third main control panel, along with the Objects palette and the Property Inspector, is called the Launcher, shown in Figure 3-9.

Figure 3-9: The Launcher gives you access to seven different Dreamweaver functions, and up to thirteen if you customize it.

The Launcher opens and closes seven default windows, each of which handles a different aspect of the program:

✦ The Site window handles all elements of publishing to the Web, as well as basic file maintenance such as moving and deleting folders.

✦ The Library palette is used to manage the repeating elements feature, which enables Dreamweaver to simultaneously update any number of Web pages on a site.

✦ The HTML Styles palette manages Dreamweaver 3's new feature, which applies standard HTML formatting to text and paragraph selections.

✦ The CSS Styles palette coordinates the Cascading Style Sheet modifications on each Web page and, if used in conjunction with an external style sheet, throughout your entire Web site.

✦ The Behavior Inspector assigns one or more JavaScript actions to a JavaScript event selected from a browser-targeted list.

✦ The History palette shows a list of the user actions that can be replayed, undone, or saved as a command.

✦ The HTML Source Inspector is Dreamweaver's internal HTML editor, integrated with the Document window's visual editor.

Similar to the other control panels, the Launcher can be started by choosing Window ➪ Launcher, and closed by either selecting the Close button or choosing Window ➪ Launcher again. A standard title bar is available on the Launcher for dragging the palette into a new position. The Launcher also includes a small button in the lower-right corner (see Figure 3-9) that serves to change the panel's orientation from a horizontal shape to a vertical one, and vice versa.

The free-floating Launcher palette functions identically to the status bar Launcher. Each one of the Launcher buttons is highlighted when the pointer passes over it, and remains highlighted when chosen. As noted, the Launcher can be used to close the windows or bring them to the front as well as open them — just click the highlighted button. Any or all of the windows can be "launched" simultaneously.

In Dreamweaver 3, both the floating Launcher and status bar Launcher are customizable. You can display the icon for any or all of the 13 standard palettes. See the section "Floating Palettes" in Chapter 4.

Site window

The Site window is your gateway to the Web. Through it, you can transfer files from the development folder on your local drive to your online Web server. Any member of your development team can check out a file to work on with no fear that another member is making changes at the same time. The team leader can even check Dreamweaver's log to see who is working on what.

Web sites can become quite complex very quickly, and it's often difficult to remember how pages are linked together. Dreamweaver 3 offers a visual representation of your Web site through its Site Map window. The Site Map window not only enables you to quickly review the structure of a site, you can also use it to add, move, or modify links. You can learn all the details about the Site Map feature in Chapter 7.

Open the Site window by choosing the Site button, on either the Launcher palette or the status bar Launcher, by selecting Window ➪ Site Files or by pressing F5. As you can see in Figure 3-10, the Site window is two-paned: Local files are shown on the right side, and remote files are displayed on the left. The headings across the top of each pane and the panes themselves can be resized. Position your pointer over a border until a double-headed arrow appears and then click and drag the border to a new position.

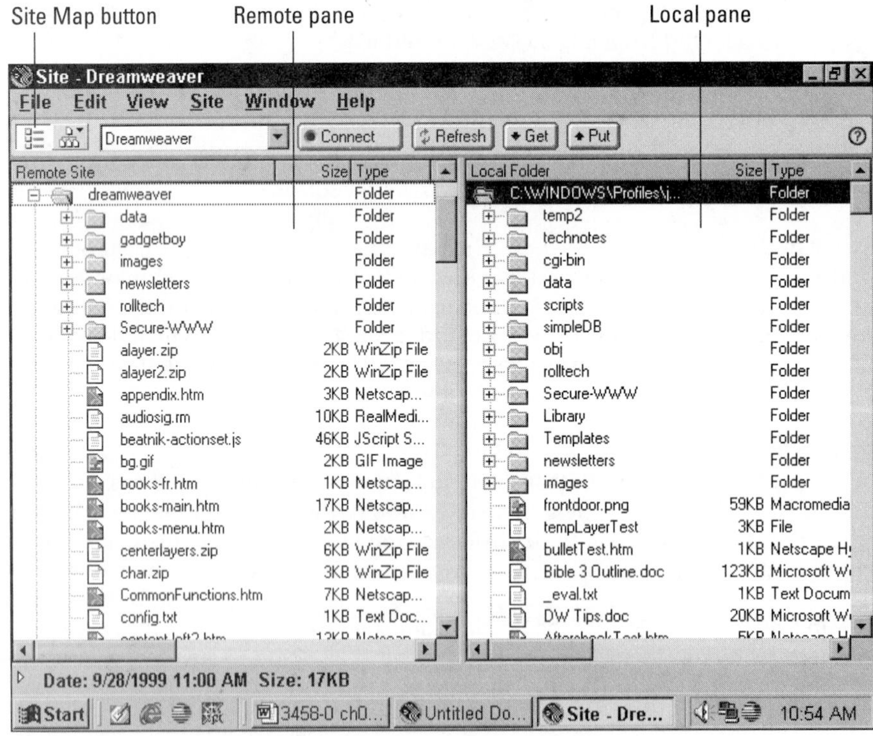

Figure 3-10: Dreamweaver's Site window handles the Webmaster's site management chores.

Tip

The files of both local and remote folders can be sorted by name, file size, file type, date modified, or checkout status – all the options corresponding to the headings across each pane. For example, to display your files in A-to-Z alphabetical order, click the Name button once. To show them in descending (Z-to-A) order, click the Name button again. If you're constantly updating your site, it's good practice to have your folders sorted in descending date order so that your most recently modified files appear at the top of each pane.

The major operations performed in the Site window include the following:

Site Window Function	***Site Window Action***
Connecting to the site	When your site is properly configured, the Connect button automatically calls your remote site and uses whatever login and password are necessary to get you online. After the connection is confirmed, the button changes into a Disconnect button.
Transferring files	To move files between your local drive and the remote server, use the Get and Put buttons. The Get button copies whatever files are highlighted in the Remote pane to the local folder, and the Put button copies files highlighted in the Local pane to the remote directory. To stop a transfer, select the Stop Current Task button – the stop sign in the lower-right corner of the window.
Locking files	When a team of Web designers is working on a site, you have to be able to prevent two people from working on the same file simultaneously. The Checked In/Checked Out indicator not only shows that a file is in use, but who has the file.
Site Map representation	As a site grows in complexity, it is often helpful to get an overview of a site's structure and its links. The Site Map feature gives a visual representation of the complete site and can be chosen by selecting the Site Map button.

Cross-Reference

Maintaining a Web site is a major portion of a Webmaster's responsibility. To learn more about Dreamweaver's site management features, see Part VIII.

Library palette

The Library palette manages Dreamweaver's repeating element feature. Through the Library palette you can turn any item — or series of items — on your Web page into a kind of "linked boilerplate." Not only can you drop your "boilerplate" text or images into any page of your site, but you can update them all by modifying just one item. The Library feature can save a Web development team many, many hours of work in both the creation and maintenance phases.

You can open the Library palette by selecting the Library button from the Launcher, by choosing Window ➪ Library, or by pressing F6. As you can see from Figure 3-11, the Library palette is a draggable, resizable window divided horizontally into two panes. The lower portion of the window displays the list of Library items for the current Web site. When one of these items is selected, the upper portion of the Library palette, the Preview pane, illustrates the item. You can resize the two panes by positioning your pointer over the separating border and then clicking and dragging the border to a new place.

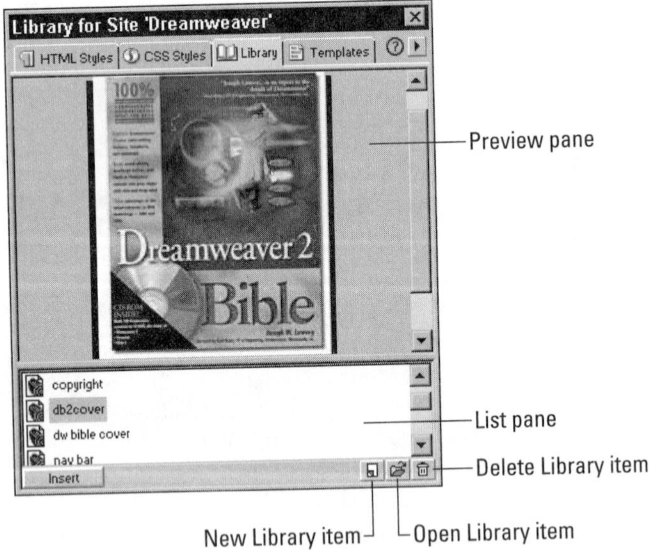

Figure 3-11: The Library palette manages the repeating elements throughout your Web site.

All of Dreamweaver 3's floating palettes, including the Library palette, now feature a context-sensitive menu accessible through the right-facing triangle button at the top of the palette. These menus are the same as those found when the palette is clicked with the right mouse button on Windows systems or Control+clicked on Macintosh systems.

The primary features of the Library palette are listed in the following table:

Library Palette Function	*Document Window Action*
Creating new entries	You define a Library item by first selecting it, either in the Document window or the HTML Source Inspector, and then clicking the Create button.
Deleting old entries	Remove an item from the Library by selecting the Delete button.
Editing entries	To alter a defined Library item, select it and press the Open button, or double-click the item. This opens another Dreamweaver window containing your Library item. After you've made your modifications, closing the window alerts Dreamweaver to your changes, and the item is updated.
Inserting entries	After you've built and defined your Library item, use the Insert button to insert it into your pages at the current cursor position.

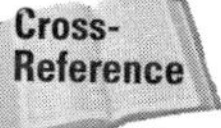

To find out more about the powerful Library feature, turn to Chapter 34.

HTML Styles palette

While Cascading Style Sheets are powerful, they have two major drawbacks: They're not compatible with 3.0 browsers, and they're difficult to master. To offset these disadvantages — and still make it easy to apply formatting to text and paragraphs — Dreamweaver 3 introduces HTML styles.

The HTML Styles palette lists all available styles and is used primarily to apply and remove formatting. Two basic types of HTML styles exist: paragraph and selection. A paragraph style is denoted by the ¶ symbol, while styles, which only affect a selection, are marked with an underlined, lowercase *a*, as shown in Figure 3-12. Styles with a plus sign next to them add their formatting to the existing tags; those styles without the plus sign replace the original formatting.

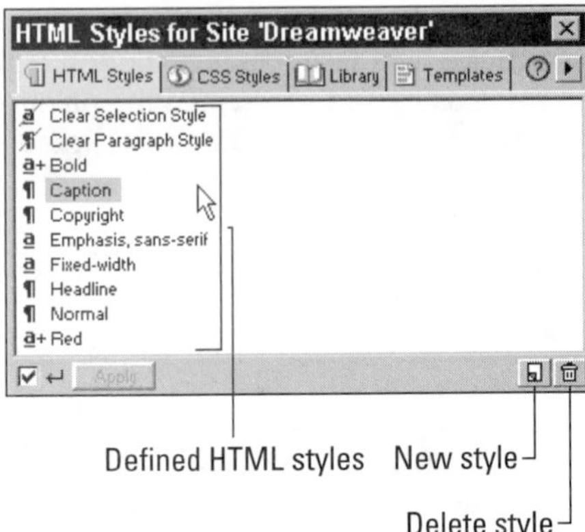

Figure 3-12: The new HTML Styles palette offers an easy way to apply consistent formatting to any text selection or paragraph.

Features of the HTML Styles palette are listed in the following table:

HTML Styles Palette Function	*Document Window Action*
Defining styles	New styles can be defined through the Define HTML Style dialog box, which is opened when the New Style button is selected.
Applying styles	All available styles are listed in the palette and applied by selecting one, if the Apply option is enabled. If the Apply option is not selected, you'll have to choose the style and then click the Apply button.
Removing styles	Existing HTML text formatting, whether applied through the HTML Styles palette or another means, can be removed by choosing either Clear Selection Style or Clear Paragraph Style.
Editing styles	Double-clicking an existing HTML style reopens the Define HTML Style dialog box. Styles that are already applied are not affected by any changes.

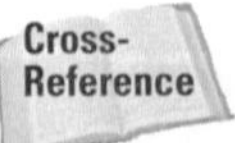

HTML styles are explained fully in the section "Using HTML Styles" in Chapter 9.

CSS Styles palette

Through the Styles palette, Dreamweaver makes creating and applying Cascading Style Sheets (CSSs) easy. CSSs give the Web designer a terrific degree of control over the appearance of text and other elements, throughout the creation stage and when the Web site is live. Styles can be used in conjunction with a single Web page or an entire site.

The Styles palette, shown in Figure 3-13, is accessed by clicking the Styles button from either the Launcher palette or the status bar Launcher. You can also open the Styles palette by choosing Window ➪ Styles or by pressing F7. You can drag or resize the Styles palette with the mouse.

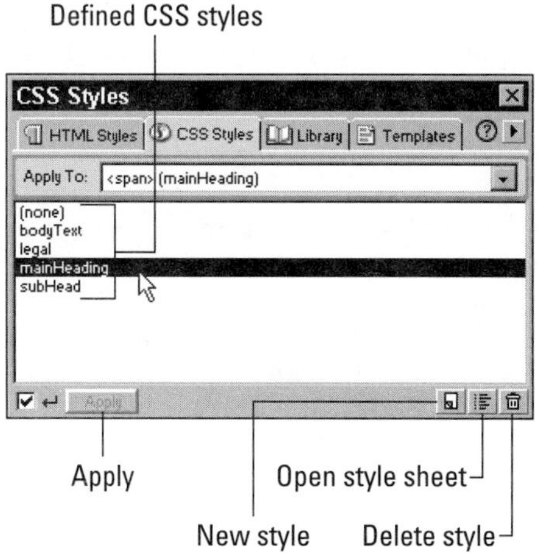

Figure 3-13: The CSS Styles palette displays custom styles and gives you access to Dreamweaver's point-and-click CSS editing capabilities.

The CSS Styles palette has the following three key uses:

CSS Styles Palette Function	*Document Window Action*
Defining styles	Through the Style Sheet button on the Styles palette, you can create, modify, and remove CSS formats. CSSs either redefine existing HTML tags or create new user-defined classes.
Applying styles	Once your styles are defined, you can easily apply them to any selected text throughout your Web page. Just click the desired style in the Styles palette list, if you have the Apply option selected; otherwise, you'll have to also click the Apply button.
Viewing styled tags	It can be difficult to tell which style has already been applied to which tag. With the Styles palette, pick any text or item on the screen, and the applied style (if any) is highlighted.

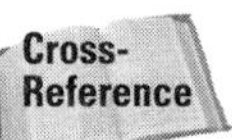

For more detailed information on how to use the CSS Styles palette, see Chapter 27.

Behavior Inspector

The Behavior Inspector enables nonprogrammers to build cutting-edge Web pages through prebuilt JavaScript actions. Briefly, behaviors are composed of two parts: an action and an event that triggers the action. Dreamweaver includes 25 standard behaviors, and because behaviors can be custom built, hundreds more are available on the Web — and, of course, on the CD-ROMs that accompany this book. Macromedia has recently launched the Dreamweaver Exchange, which is instantly accessible through the Get More Behaviors feature.

The Behavior Inspector is browser savvy and won't enable you to assign a JavaScript event that only works on 4.0 browsers when you need 3.0 compatibility. With the Behavior Inspector, not only can you link several actions to a single event, but you can also specify the order of the actions.

Use the Behavior button on either Launcher (palette or status bar) to open the Behavior Inspector. You can also press F8 or choose Window ➪ Behaviors. Like the other windows, you can resize or reposition the Behavior Inspector with the mouse using the click-and-drag technique. As shown in Figure 3-14, the Behavior Inspector displays the events on the left side and the actions on the right.

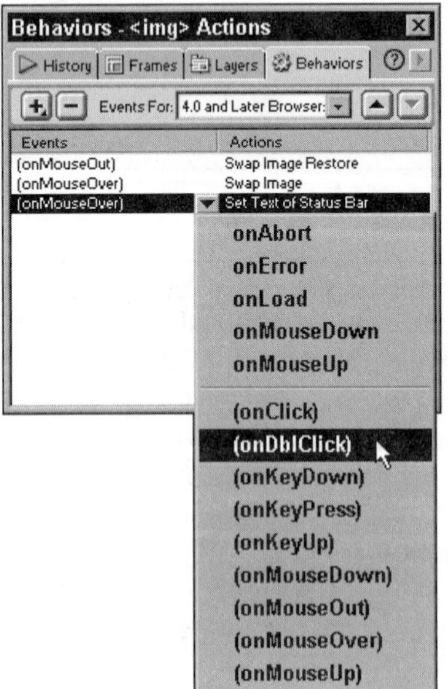

Figure 3-14: Linking an action to an event creates a JavaScript behavior in the Behavior Inspector.

Use the Behavior Inspector to perform the functions outlined in the following table:

Behavior Inspector Function	*Document Window Action*
Specifying a browser	The various browsers and browser versions understand specific JavaScript commands. You can target individual browsers by manufacturer or version number, or a combination of the two, by using the Browser pop-up menu.
Picking an action	Behaviors are linked to specific HTML tags; not all HTML tags have behaviors associated with them. Selecting the Behavior pop-up menu (by clicking the + button) displays a list of available actions. Remove an action by highlighting it and clicking the – button.
Changing an event	The events listed under the Events pop-up menu (the arrow button in between the action and the event) are determined by what's selected in the Browser pop-up menu.
Order the actions	Because you can assign more than one action to an event, Dreamweaver enables you to rearrange the order of the actions. Use the up/down-arrow keys to rearrange the order of your action list for each event.

Behaviors are user definable. In Chapter 19, you learn how to create your own actions.

Be sure to check out the Behaviors section of CD-ROM 1 that accompanies this book to add to your list of Dreamweaver action capabilities.

History palette

Web design is largely a process of experimentation and repetition. You try one approach, and if you're not satisfied, you undo what you've done and try something else. Then, when you find something you like, you do it over and over. In earlier versions of Dreamweaver, this process was performed rather blindly, if at all: You had little idea of what steps you were undoing, and automation was not an option.

The new History palette tracks every action taken by the user—from deleting text to inserting and resizing a layer. A slider, shown in Figure 3-15, points to the last action performed. Dragging the slider up undoes each step in turn; dragging the slider back down redoes the steps. Selected steps can be quickly repeated in the same document by selecting the Replay button. You can save any selection of steps as a Command for application at any other time, in any other document.

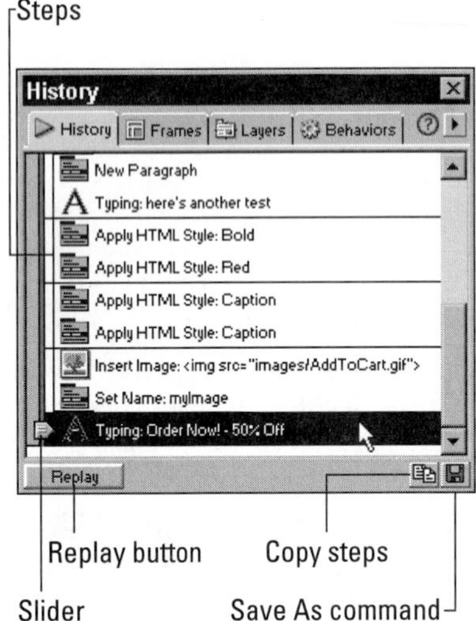

Figure 3-15: Undo or redo any series of actions by moving the slider in the new History palette.

The primary functions of the History palette are covered in the following table:

History Palette Function	*Document Window Action*
Undo actions	Reverses each action the slider passes over as it is dragged up the History palette.
Redo actions	Reapplies each action the slider passes over as it is dragged down the History palette.
Replay selected steps	Choosing the Replay button repeats selected steps, in sequence.
Save As selected steps as a command	Stores the selected actions under a user-selected name, which is dynamically added to the Command menu.

HTML Source Inspector

The last default window controlled by the Launcher is the HTML Source Inspector (shown in Figure 3-16) — the internal editor designed to complement Dreamweaver's visual layout facility. Although you can opt to use an external editor such as the bundled BBEdit or HomeSite for extensive coding, the HTML Source Inspector is great for making spot edits or quickly checking your code. The tight integration between Dreamweaver's text and visual editors enables simultaneous input and instant updating.

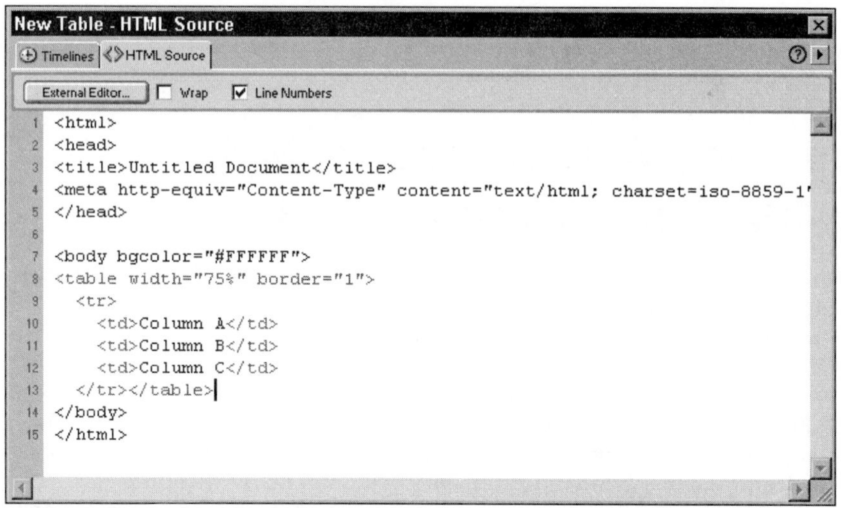
New Table - HTML Source
Timelines
<>HTML Source
External Editor...
Wrap
Line Numbers
<html>
<head>
<title>Untitled Document</title>
<meta http-equiv="Content-Type" content="text/html; charset=iso-8859-1'
</head>
<body bgcolor="#FFFFFF">
<table width="75%" border="1">
<tr>
<td>Column A</td>
<td>Column B</td>
<td>Column C</td>
</tr></table>
</body>
</html>

Figure 3-16: The HTML Source Inspector gives you instant access for tweaking your code – or adding entirely new elements by hand.

Tip

You can see the tight integration between the visual editor and the HTML Source Inspector when you have both windows open and you select an object in the Document window. The corresponding code is instantly displayed in the HTML Source Inspector. This feature is useful for quickly finding a specific HTML element for alteration.

Clicking the HTML button on either Launcher opens and closes the HTML Source Inspector, as does choosing Window ➪ HTML Source or pressing F10. Once the HTML Source Inspector is open, changes made in the Document window are incorporated in real time. However, in order to properly check the code, any changes made in the HTML Source Inspector are not updated in the Document window until the Document window is activated. You can alternate between the two windows by pressing Ctrl+Tab (Control+Tab).

By design, the HTML Source Inspector's layout is simple, to give maximum emphasis to your code. Only three primary controls really exist, aside from Help, Close, and the context menu, in the HTML Source Inspector. First, if you decide you need to do more extensive coding, you can select the External Editor button to open your full-featured editor. Second, you can turn on or off the line-wrap function by selecting the Wrap checkbox. This is useful if you encounter an error message that displays a line number; temporarily turn off the wrap feature to locate the line. The third option, Line Numbers, was added in Dreamweaver 3 and often proves helpful when attempting to debug a JavaScript-related problem.

Tip

You might notice that the code in the HTML Source Inspector is colored. The color coding (no pun intended) is set by the HTML Colors panel of the Preferences dialog box—you can even modify the background color of the Inspector.

Customizing Your Workspace with Dockable Windows and Palettes

Dreamweaver is known for its powerful set of tools: Objects, Behaviors, Layers, Timelines, and so much more. To be truly useful, each tool needs its own palette or window; but the more tools you use, the more cluttered your workspace can become.

To reduce the amount of screen real estate taken up by the individual windows, but still keep their power, Dreamweaver incorporates dockable windows and palettes. All of Dreamweaver's 12 floating palettes (including the HTML Source Inspector) can now be grouped into a single window (see Figure 3-17)—or several windows, if you like. The dockable window system is completely customizable to give you optimum control over your workflow.

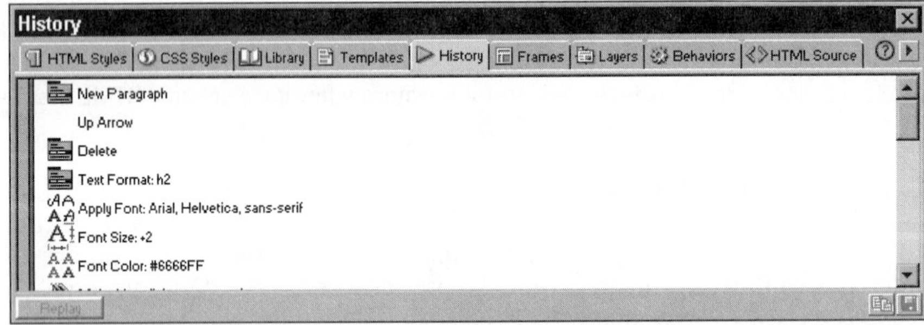

Figure 3-17: Dreamweaver 3 now enables you to group any or all of your floating windows and palettes into a docking window.

Whenever one window is docked with another, each becomes accessible by clicking the representative tab. Selecting the tab brings the window or palette to the front of the docked window. Grouping windows and palettes together is very straightforward. Simply drag one window by its tab on top of another window. When you see a border appear inside the stationary window, release your mouse button.

A new tab is created to the right of the existing tabs. To remove a palette from a docked window, click the tab and drag the window clear. When you release the mouse button, the palette returns to being an independent object but retains the size and shape of the previously docked window.

A couple of restrictions apply when docking palettes. First, while you can't dock the Object palette on another palette, you can combine any other palette in the Object palette's window. Second, neither the Property Inspector nor the Launcher can be docked.

As you group more palettes together, Dreamweaver displays a symbol for the window and its name on each tab. When too many palettes are combined to fit within the docking window, Dreamweaver shows just the symbol to make room for more. If you add an additional palette to a docking window that is too small, Dreamweaver automatically expands the docking window.

As noted earlier, when you move a palette from a docking window, the palette keeps the size and shape of the docking window. To resize any window, click and drag its borders. On the Mac, you only resize from the bottom-right corner of a window by dragging the resize handle.

Accessing the Menus

Like many programs, Dreamweaver's menus duplicate most of the features accessible through windows and palettes. Certain features, however, are available only through the menus or through a corresponding keyboard shortcut. This section offers a reference guide to the menus when you need a particular feature or command. (Note to Windows users: The menus referred to here are those for the Document window and not the Site window; those menu options particular to the Site window are covered in Chapter 7.)

Almost every element placed in the Document window has a shortcut menu associated with it. To access a shortcut menu, right-click (Control+click) any area or object. The new shortcut menus are context sensitive and change according to which object or area is selected. Using the shortcut menus can enhance your productivity tremendously.

The File menu

The File menu contains commands for file handling and overall site management. Table 3-7 describes the commands and their keyboard shortcuts.

Table 3-7
File Menu Commands

Command	*Description*	*Windows*	*Macintosh*
New	Adds a new Document window.	Ctrl+N	Command+N
New from Template	Creates a document based on an existing template.	N/A	N/A
Open	Displays the Open dialog box for opening an existing file.	Ctrl+O	Command+O
Open in Frame	Opens an existing file in the selected frame.	Ctrl+Shift+O	Command+Shift+O
Close	Closes the current window.	Ctrl+W or Ctrl+F4	Command+W
Save	Saves the current document, or displays the Save As dialog box for an unnamed document.	Ctrl+S	Command+S
Save As Template	Displays the Save As dialog box before saving the document.	N/A	N/A
Save As	Stores the current document as a template in the Templates folder of the current site.	N/A	N/A
Save Frameset	Saves a file describing the current frameset, or displays the Save As dialog box for an unnamed document.	N/A	N/A
Save Frameset As	Displays the Save As Frameset before saving the current frameset.	N/A	N/A
Save All	Saves all open documents (including framesets, if applicable).	Ctrl+Shift+S	Command+Shift+S
Revert	Loads the previously saved version of the current page.	N/A	N/A
Design Notes	Displays the Design Notes dialog box for the current document.	N/A	N/A

Command	*Description*	*Windows*	*Macintosh*
Import ➪ Import XML into Template	Creates a new document by inserting an XML file into the current template.	N/A	N/A
Import ➪ Import Word HTML	Opens an HTML file saved in Microsoft Word, and optionally, cleans up the code.	N/A	N/A
Import ➪ Import Table Data	Inserts a table derived from a file with delimited data.	N/A	N/A
Export ➪ Editable Regions as XML	Saves the current template's editable regions as an XML file.	N/A	N/A
Export ➪ CSS Styles	Creates an external style sheet based on CSS styles in the current document.	N/A	N/A
Export ➪ Table	Saves data in the current table as a delimited text file.	N/A	N/A
Convert ➪ 3.0 Browser Compatible	Creates a new Web page, converting all layers to tables.	N/A	N/A
Preview in Browser ➪ Your Browser List	Displays a list of browsers established in Preferences; choose one to preview the current page using that browser.	F12 (Primary) Shift+F12 (Secondary)	F12 (Primary) Shift+F12 (Secondary)
Preview in Browser ➪ Edit Browser List	Displays the Preview in Browser category of Preferences, where the user can add, edit, or delete additional preview browsers.	N/A	N/A
Check Links	Verifies hypertext links for the current document.	Shift+F8	Shift+F8
Check Target Browsers	Displays the Check Target Browsers dialog box, where the user can validate the current file against installed browser profiles.	N/A	N/A
Your Last Opened Files	Displays the last four opened files; select any name to reopen the file.	N/A	N/A
Exit (Quit)	Closes all open files and quits.	Ctrl+Q or Alt+F4	Command+Q

The Edit menu

The Edit menu gives you the commands necessary to quickly modify your page—or recover from a devastating accident. Many of the commands (Cut, Copy, and Paste) are standard in other programs; others, such as Paste As Text, are unique to Dreamweaver. Table 3-8 lists all of the features found under the Edit menu.

Table 3-8
Edit Menu Commands

Command	*Description*	*Windows*	*Macintosh*
Undo	Reverses the last action; the number of times you can Undo is determined by a Preferences setting.	Ctrl+Z	Command+Z
Repeat	Repeats the last action.	Ctrl+Y	Command+Y
Cut	Places a copy of the current selection on the clipboard, and removes the selection from the current document.	Ctrl+X	Command+X
Copy	Places a copy of the current selectionon the clipboard, and leaves the selection in the current document.	Ctrl+C	Command+C
Paste	Copies the clipboard to the current cursor position.	Ctrl+V	Command+V
Clear	Removes the current selection from the document.	Delete or Backspace	Delete
Copy Text Only	Copies the current selection onto the clipboard with the HTML codes.	Ctrl+Shift+C	Command+ Shift+C
Paste As Text	Pastes the current selection f rom the clipboard without any HTML codes rendered as text.	Ctrl+Shift+V	Command+ Shift+V
Select All	Highlights all the elements in the current document or frame.	Ctrl+A	Command+A
Select Parent Tag	Chooses the tag surrounding the current selection.	Ctrl+Shift+<	Command+ Shift+< and Command+ Shift+, (comma)

Command	Description	Windows	Macintosh
Select Child	Chooses the first tag contained within the current selection.	Ctrl+Shift+>	Command+ Shift+> and Command+ Shift+. (period)
Find	Displays the Find dialog box for searching the current document.	Ctrl+F	Command+F
Find Next (Find Again)	Repeats the previous Find operation.	F3	Command+G
Replace	Displays the Replace dialog box.	Ctrl+H	Command+H
Launch External Editor	Opens the External HTML Editor as defined in Preferences ⇨ External Editors.	Ctrl+E	Command+E
Preferences	Displays the Preferences dialog box.	Ctrl+U	Command+U or Command+K

The View menu

As you build your Web pages, you'll find that it's helpful to be able to turn certain features on and off. The View menu centralizes all these commands. Certain capabilities, such as rulers and grids, are useful only when combined with layers. Table 3-9 describes each command under the View menu.

Table 3-9
View Menu Commands

Command	Description	Windows	Macintosh
Head Contents	Displays symbols for elements inserted in the <head> section of the current document.	Ctrl+Shift+W	Command+ Shift+W
Invisible Elements	Controls whether the symbols for certain HTML tags are shown.	Ctrl+Shift+I	Command+ Shift+I
Layer Borders	Makes a border visible outlining an unselected layer.	N/A	N/A
Table Borders	Makes a border visible outlining an unselected table.	N/A	N/A

Continued

Table 3-9 *(continued)*

Command	***Description***	***Windows***	***Macintosh***
Frame Borders	Enables borders necessary for drag-and-drop frame creation.	N/A	N/A
Image Maps	Displays/hides the overlays for defined image maps.	N/A	N/A
Rulers ➪ Show	Displays the horizontal and vertical rulers.	Ctrl+Alt+Shift+R	Command+Option+Shift+R
Rulers ➪ Reset Origin	Resets the rulers' 0,0 coordinates to the upper-left corner of the window.	N/A	N/A
Rulers ➪ Pixels/Inches/Centimeters	Sets the rulers to a selected measurement system.	N/A	N/A
Grid ➪ Show	Displays a background grid using the current settings.	Ctrl+Alt+Shift+G	Command+Option+Shift+G
Grid ➪ Snap To	Forces inserted objects to align with the nearest snap setting.	Ctrl+Alt+G	Command+Option+G
Grid ➪ Settings	Displays the Grid Settings dialog box.	N/A	N/A
Prevent Layer Overlaps	Stops newly created layers from overlapping.	N/A	N/A
Tracing Image ➪ Show	Displays the image chosen as the Tracing Image according to the Page Properties settings.	N/A	N/A
Tracing Image ➪ Align with Selection	Aligns the top-left corner of the Tracing Image with the top-left corner of the selected object.	N/A	N/A
Tracing Image ➪ Adjust Position	Enables the Tracing Image to be moved using the cursor keys or numerically.	N/A	N/A
Tracing Image ➪ Reset Position	Resets the position of the Tracing Image to the upper-left corner of the document.	N/A	N/A
Tracing Image ➪ Load Image	Displays the Open File dialog box for inserting the tracing.	N/A	N/A
Plug-ins ➪ Play	Plays the selected plug-in.	Ctrl+Alt+P	Command+Option+P

Command	Description	Windows	Macintosh
Plug-ins ➪ Stop	Stops the selected plug-in from playing.	Ctrl+Alt+X	Command+ Option+X
Plug-ins ➪ Play All	Plays all plug-ins on the current page.	Ctrl+Alt+ Shift+P	Command+ Option+ Shift+P
Plug-ins ➪ Stop All	Stops all plug-ins on the current page from playing.	Ctrl+Alt+ Shift+X	Command+ Option+ Shift+X
Status Bar	Enables the status bar to be shown.	N/A	N/A

The Insert menu

The Insert menu contains the same items available through the Objects palette. In fact, if you add additional objects (as discussed in Chapter 18), you can see your objects listed on the Insert menu the next time you start Dreamweaver. All objects are inserted at the current cursor position.

Table 3-10 lists the items available to be inserted in the standard Dreamweaver.

Table 3-10
Insert Menu Commands

Command	Description	Windows	Macintosh
Image	Opens the Insert Image dialog box that enables you to input or browse for a graphics file.	Ctrl+Alt+I	Command+ Option+I
Rollover Image	Opens the Rollover dialog box for inserting a Rollover button.	N/A	N/A
Table	Opens the Insert Table dialog box for establishing a table layout.	Ctrl+Alt+T	Command+ Option+T
Tabular Data	Inserts a table derived from a file with delimited data.	N/A	N/A
Horizontal Rule	Inserts a horizontal line the width of the current window.	N/A	N/A

Continued

Table 3-10 *(continued)*

Command	***Description***	***Windows***	***Macintosh***
Navigation Bar	Opens the Navigation Bar dialog box for creating a series of Rollover buttons with links.	N/A	N/A
Layer	Inserts a layer of a preset size.	N/A	N/A
Form	Creates the form structure on your Web page.	N/A	N/A
Form Object ➪ Text Field/Button/ Check Box/Radio Button/List/Menu/ File Field/Image Field/Hidden Field	Inserts the selected form object at the current cursor position.	N/A	N/A
Form Object ➪ Jump Menu	Opens the Jump Menu dialog box for creating a list box with links.	N/A	N/A
Frames ➪ Left/ Right/Top/Bottom/ Left and Top/Left Top/Top Left/Split	Inserts the selected frameset.	N/A	N/A
Line Break	Inserts a line break tag.	Shift+Enter	Shift+Enter
E-mail Link	Opens the Insert E-mail Link dialog box to create a mailto: link.	N/A	N/A
Date	Opens the Insert Date dialog box for entering today's date.	N/A	N/A
Media ➪ Applet	Opens the Insert Applet dialog box that permits you to input or browse for a Java class source.	N/A	N/A
Media ➪ Flash	Opens the Insert Flash Movie dialog box so you can either type in or browse for a movie file.	Ctrl+Alt+F	Command+ Option+F
Media ➪ Shockwave	Opens the Insert Shockwave dialog box for you to input or browse for a Director file.	Ctrl+Alt+D	Command+ Option+D
Media ➪ Generator	Opens the Insert Generator dialog box to include a Generator template.	N/A	N/A
Media ➪ Fireworks HTML	Imports HTML and JavaScript generated by Fireworks.	N/A	N/A
Media ➪ ActiveX	Inserts an ActiveX placeholder.	N/A	N/A

Command	Description	Windows	Macintosh
Media ➪ Plug-in	Opens the Insert Plug-in dialog box so you can either input or browse for a plug-in.	N/A	N/A
Head ➪ Meta/ Keywords/ Description/ Refresh/Base/Link	Displays the appropriate dialog box for inserting the selected HTML tag in the `<head>` section.	N/A	N/A
Characters ➪ Copyright/ Registered/ Trademark/Pound/ Yen/Euro/ Em-Dash/Left Quote/Right Quote	Inserts the HTML code for the selected character entity.	N/A	N/A
Characters ➪ Other	Opens the Insert Other Character dialog box to choose a special character.	N/A	N/A
Server-Side Include	Opens the dialog box for inserting a server-side include.	N/A	N/A
Named Anchor	Displays the Insert Named Anchor dialog box.	Ctrl+Alt+A	Command+ Option+A
Comment	Displays the Insert Comment dialog box.	N/A	N/A
Script	Displays the Insert Script dialog box.	N/A	N/A
Non-breaking Space	Inserts a hard space.	Ctrl+Shift+ spacebar	Command+ Shift+ spacebar (or Option+ spacebar)
Get More Objects	Connects to the Dreamweaver Online Resource Center.	N/A	N/A

The Modify menu

Inserting objects is less than half the battle of creating a Web page. Most Web designers spend most of their time adjusting, experimenting with, and tweaking the various elements. The Modify menu lists all the commands for altering existing selections. Table 3-11 lists all the Modify options.

Table 3-11
Modify Menu Commands

Command	*Description*	*Windows*	*Macintosh*
Page Properties	Opens the Page Properties dialog box.	Ctrl+J	Command+J
Selection Properties	Displays and hides the Property Inspector.	Ctrl+Shift+J	Command+Shift+J
Quick Tag Editor	Displays the Quick Tag Editor for the current selection; repeating the keyboard shortcut toggles between the three Quick Tag Editor modes.	Ctrl+T	Command+T
Make Link	Presents the Select HTML File dialog box for picking a linking file.	Ctrl+L	Command+L
Remove Link	Deletes the current link.	Ctrl+Shift+L	Command+Shift+L
Open Linked Page	Opens the linked page in Dreamweaver.	N/A	N/A
Link Target ➪ Default/_blank/_parent/_self/_top	Selects the target for the current link.	N/A	N/A
Link Target ➪ Set	Enables you to name a target for the link.	N/A	N/A
Table ➪ Select Table	Highlights the entire table surrounding the current cursor position.	Ctrl+A	Command+A
Table ➪ Merge Cells	Merges selected cells using spans.	Ctrl+Alt+M	Command+Option+M
Table ➪ Split Cell	Splits cells into rows or columns.	Ctrl+Alt+S	Command+Option+S
Table ➪ Insert Row	Adds a new row above the current row.	Ctrl+M	Command+M
Table ➪ Insert Column	Adds a new column before the current column.	Ctrl+Shift+A	Command+Shift+A
Table ➪ Insert Rows or Columns	Opens the Insert Rows/Columns dialog box that enables multiple rows or columns to be inserted relative to the cursor position.	N/A	N/A

Command	*Description*	*Windows*	*Macintosh*
Table ➪ Delete Row	Removes the current row.	Ctrl+Shift+M	Command+ Shift+M
Table ➪ Delete Column	Removes the current column.	Ctrl+Shift+– (minus sign)	Command+ Shift+– (minus sign)
Table ➪ Increase Row Span/ Decrease Row Span	Increases or decreases by one row the span of the current cell.	N/A	N/A
Table ➪ Increase Column Span/ Decrease Column Span	Increases or decreases the column span of the current cell by one column.	Ctrl+Shift+] (Increase Col- umn Span) Ctrl+Shift+[(Decrease Column Span)	Command+ Shift+] (Increase Col- umn Span) Command+ Shift+[(Decrease Column Span)
Table ➪ Clear Cell Heights	Removes specified row height values for the entire selected table.	N/A	N/A
Table ➪ Clear Cell Widths	Removes specified column width values for the entire selected table.	N/A	N/A
Table ➪ Convert Widths to Pixels	Changes column widths from percents to pixels for the entire selected table.	N/A	N/A
Table ➪ Convert Widths to Percent	Changes column widths from pixels to percents for the entire selected table.	N/A	N/A
Layers and Hotspots ➪ Align Left	Aligns grouped layers or hotspots on the left edge.	Ctrl+left arrow	Command+ left arrow
Layers and Hotspots ➪ Align Right	Aligns grouped layers or hotspots on the right edge.	Ctrl+right arrow	Command+ right arrow
Layers and Hotspots ➪ Align Top	Aligns grouped layers or hotspots on the top edge.	Ctrl+up arrow	Command+ up arrow

Continued

Table 3-11 *(continued)*

Command	***Description***	***Windows***	***Macintosh***
Layers and Hotspots ➪ Align Bottom	Aligns grouped layers or hotspots on the bottom edge.	Ctrl+down arrow	Command+ down arrow
Layers and Hotspots ➪ Bring to Front	Places selected layers or hotspots in front of other all other layers or hotspots	N/A	N/A
Layers and Hotspots ➪ Send to Back	Places selected layers or hotspots behind all other layers or hotspots	N/A	N/A
Layers and Hotspots ➪ Make Same Width	Changes the width of grouped layers or hotspots to that of the last selected layer.	Ctrl+Shift+[	Command+ Shift+[
Layers and Hotspots ➪ Make Same Height	Changes the height of grouped layers or hotspots to that of the last selected layer.	Ctrl+Shift+]	Command+ Shift+]
Frameset ➪ Edit No Frames Content	Opens a new window for content to be seen by browsers that do not support frames.	N/A	N/A
Frameset ➪ Split Frame Left/Split Frame Right/Split Frame Up/Split Frame Down	Moves the current frame in the specified direction, and adds a new frame opposite.	N/A	N/A
Navigation Bar	Opens the Navigation Bar dialog box for editing the selected Navigation Bar.	N/A	N/A
Layout Mode ➪ Convert Tables to Layers	Places all content on the page in layers.	Ctrl+F6	Command+ F6
Layout Mode ➪ Convert Layers to Table	Places all content in layers in tables.	Ctrl+Shift+F6	Command+ Shift+F6
Library ➪ Add Object to Library	Opens the Library palette, and adds the selected object.	Ctrl+Shift+B	Command+ Shift+B
Library ➪ Update Current Page/ Update Pages	Replaces any modified Library items in the current page or current site.	N/A	N/A

Command	Description	Windows	Macintosh
Templates ➪ Apply Template to Page	Enables the selection of a template to be overlaid on the current page.	N/A	N/A
Templates ➪ Detach from Template	Breaks the link between the template and the current page.	N/A	N/A
Templates ➪ Open Attached Template	Opens the current template for editing.	N/A	N/A
Templates ➪ Update Current Page	Automatically updates the page with template changes.	N/A	N/A
Templates ➪ Update Pages	Enables the updating of an entire site or of all pages using a particular template.	N/A	N/A
Templates ➪ New Editable Region	Inserts the placeholder for a new editable region.	Ctrl+Alt+V	Command+Option+V
Templates ➪ Mark Selection as Editable	Converts the selected text or objects from locked to editable.	Ctrl+Alt+W	Command+Option+W
Templates ➪ Unmark Editable Region	Converts the selected region from editable to locked.	N/A	N/A
Templates ➪ No Editable Regions	Displayed in menu until editable regions are created	N/A	N/A
Timeline ➪ Add Object to Timeline	Opens the Timeline Inspector, and inserts the current image or layer.	Ctrl+Alt+Shift+T	Command+Option+Shift+T
Timeline ➪ Add Behavior to Timeline	Opens the Timeline Inspector, and inserts an `onFrame` event using the current frame.	N/A	N/A
Timeline ➪ Record Path of Layer	Plots the path of a dragged layer onto a timeline.	N/A	N/A
Timeline ➪ Add Keyframe	Inserts a keyframe at the current Playback Head position.	Shift+F9	Shift+F9
Timeline ➪ Remove Keyframe	Deletes the currently selected keyframe.	Delete	N/A
Timeline ➪ Change Object	Applies a timeline path to another object.	N/A	N/A
Timeline ➪ Remove Object/Remove Behavior	Deletes the currently selected object or behavior.	N/A	N/A

Continued

Table 3-11 (continued)

Command	Description	Windows	Macintosh
Timeline ⇨ Add Frame/Remove Frame	Inserts or deletes a frame at the current Playback Head position.	N/A	N/A
Timeline ⇨ Add Timeline/Remove Timeline/Rename Timeline	Inserts an additional timeline, deletes the current timeline, or renames the current timeline.	N/A	N/A
Translate ⇨ Date	Updates the date and time code inserted by the Date object.	N/A	N/A
Translate ⇨ Server-side Includes document.	Makes nonconditional server-side includes visible in the current	N/A	N/A

The Text menu

The Internet was initially an all-text medium, and despite all the multimedia development, the World Wide Web hasn't traveled far from these beginnings. The Text menu, as described in Table 3-12, covers overall formatting as well as text-oriented functions such as spell-checking.

Table 3-12
Text Menu Commands

Command	Description	Windows	Macintosh
Indent	Marks the selected text or the current paragraph with the `<blockquote>` tag to indent it.	Ctrl+]	Command+]
Outdent	Removes a `<dir>` or `<blockquote>` surrounding the selected text or current indented paragraph.	Ctrl+[	Command+[
Format ⇨ None	Removes all HTML formatting tags surrounding the current selection.	Ctrl+0 (zero)	Command+0 (zero)

Command	Description	Windows	Macintosh
Format ➪ Paragraph	Converts the selected text to paragraph format.	Ctrl+ Shift+P	Command+ Shift+P
Format ➪ Heading 1–6	Changes the selected text to the specified heading format.	Ctrl+1–6	Command+ 1–6
Format ➪ Preformatted Text	Formats the selected text with a monospaced font.	N/A	N/A
List ➪ None	Changes a list item into a paragraph.	N/A	N/A
List ➪ Unordered List	Makes the selected text into a bulleted list.	N/A	N/A
List ➪ Ordered List	Makes the selected text into a numbered list.	N/A	N/A
List ➪ Definition List	Converts the selected text into alternating definition terms and items.	N/A	N/A
List ➪ Properties	Opens the List Properties dialog box.	N/A	N/A
Alignment ➪ Left	Aligns the selected text to the left of the page, table, or layer.	Ctrl+Alt+L	Command+ Option+L
Alignment ➪ Center	Aligns the selected text to the center of the current page, table, or layer.	Ctrl+Alt+C	Command+ Option+C
Alignment ➪ Right	Aligns the selected text to the right of the page, table, or layer.	Ctrl+Alt+R	Command+ Option+R
Font ➪ Default	Changes the current selection to the default font.	N/A	N/A
Font ➪ Your Font List	Displays fonts in your current font list.	N/A	N/A
Font ➪ Edit Font List	Opens the Font List dialog box for adding or deleting fonts from the current list.	N/A	N/A
Style ➪ Bold	Makes the selected text bold.	Ctrl+B	Command+B
Style ➪ Italic	Makes the selected text italic.	Ctrl+I	Command+I
Style ➪ Underline	Underlines the selected text.	N/A	N/A
Style ➪ Strikethrough	Surrounds the selected text with the `<s>...</s>` tags for text with a line through it.	N/A	N/A

Continued

Table 3-12 *(continued)*

Command	***Description***	***Windows***	***Macintosh***
Style ➪ Teletype	Surrounds the selected text with the `<tt>...</tt>` tags for a monospaced font.	N/A	N/A
Style ➪ Emphasis	Surrounds the selected text with the `<emp>...</emp>` tags for slightly emphasized, usually italic, text.	N/A	N/A
Style ➪ Strong	Surrounds the selected text with the `<strong>...</strong>` tags for more emphasized, usually bold, text.	N/A	N/A
Style ➪ Code	Surrounds the selected text with HTML code for depicting programming code.	N/A	N/A
Style ➪ Variable	Surrounds the selected text with HTML code for depicting a variable in programming, typically in italic.	N/A	N/A
Style ➪ Sample/ Keyboard	Surrounds the selected text with HTML code for depicting monospaced fonts.	N/A	N/A
Style ➪ Citation	Surrounds the selected text with HTML code for depicting cited text, usually in italic.	N/A	N/A
Style ➪ Definition	Surrounds the selected text with HTML code for depicting a definition, usually in italic.	N/A	N/A
HTML Styles ➪ Clear Selection Style	Removes text formatting tags around the current selection.	N/A	N/A
HTML Styles ➪ Clear Paragraph Style	Removes text formatting tags for the paragraph containing the current selection.	N/A	N/A
HTML Styles ➪ Bold/Caption/ Copyright/Emphasis, sans-serif/Fixed-width/Headline/ Normal/Red	Applies the chosen style to the current selection or current paragraph.	N/A	N/A

Command	*Description*	*Windows*	*Macintosh*
HTML Styles ➪ New Style	Displays the HTML Styles dialog box to create a new text style.	N/A	N/A
HTML Styles ➪ New Style	Displays the HTML Styles dialog box to create a new text style.	N/A	N/A
CSS Styles ➪ None/ Your Style List	Applies a user-defined style to selected text. The None option removes previously applied styles.	N/A	N/A
CSS Styles ➪ Edit Style Sheet	Opens the Edit Style Sheet dialog box for adding, deleting, or modifying custom styles.	Ctrl+Shift+E	Command+ Shift+E
Size ➪ Default ➪ 1–7	Converts the selected text to the chosen font size.	N/A	N/A
Size Increase ➪ +1–+7	Increases the size of the selected text relative to the defined basefont size (default is 3).	N/A	N/A
Size Decrease ➪ –1 through –7	Decreases the size of the selected text relative to the defined basefont size (default is 3).	N/A	N/A
Color	Opens the operating system's Color dialog box to alter the color of selected or following text.	N/A	N/A
Check Spelling	Opens the Spell Check dialog box.	Shift+F7	Shift+F7

The Commands menu

Dreamweaver 3 offers a further enhancement to its already impressive extensibility palette: commands. Commands are user-definable code capable of affecting almost any tag, attribute, or item on the current page—or even the current site. Commands increase your productivity by automating many of the mundane, repetitive tasks in Web page creation.

Dreamweaver 3 comes with several handy commands, but they are truly just the tip of the iceberg. Commands, such as objects and behaviors, are written in HTML and JavaScript and can be created and modified by any capable JavaScript programmer.

Table 3-13 describes the standard Dreamweaver 3 commands.

Table 3-13
Commands Menu

Command	*Description*	*Windows*	*Macintosh*
Start/Stop Recording	Begins remembering the sequence of user commands; toggles with Stop Recording.	Ctrl+Shift+X	Command+ Shift+X
Play Recorded Command	Executes the last recorded command.	Ctrl+P	Command+P
Edit Command List	Opens the Edit Command List dialog box for arranging and deleting custom items from the Commands menu.	N/A	N/A
Get More Commands	Connects to the Dreamweaver Online Resource Center.	N/A	N/A
Clean Up HTML	Processes the current page according to various options to remove extraneous HTML.	N/A	N/A
Clean Up Word HTML	Processes the current page according to various options to remove extraneous HTML inserted by Microsoft Word.	N/A	N/A
Add/Remove Netscape Resize Fix	Inserts or deletes code to compensate for the bug affecting layers in Netscape 4+ browsers.	N/A	N/A
Optimize Image in Fireworks	Displays the Optimize Image dialog box for processing images. Requires Fireworks 3.	N/A	N/A
Apply Source Formatting	Structures the current page according to the Source Format Profile.	N/A	N/A
Format Table	Enables a predesigned format . to be set on the current table	N/A	N/A
Sort Table	Sorts the current table alphabetically or numerically.	N/A	N/A
Set Color Scheme	Selects a color scheme for the current page affecting background color, text color, and the link colors.	N/A	N/A
Your Commands	Automatically lists new commands added to the Commands folder	N/A	N/A

You can find a number of new commands on the CD-ROMs that accompany this book. Chapter 21 gives you information on how to build your own commands.

The Site menu

Web designers spend a good portion of their day directly interacting with a Web server: putting up new files, getting old ones, and generally maintaining the site. To ease the workflow, Dreamweaver 3 now includes the most commonly used commands in the Document window menu as well as the Site window menu.

The Site menus are very different on the Windows and Macintosh platforms. Because of these differences, the commands are listed in two different tables. All the commands found in the Windows Site menu are described in Table 3-14.

Table 3-14
Site Menu Commands (Windows)

Command	*Description*	*Shortcut*
Sites Files	Displays the Site window.	F5
Site Map	Displays the current site map.	Ctrl+F5
New Site	Presents the Site Definition dialog box for creating a new site.	N/A
Open Site ⇨ Your Site List	Displays a user-definable list of sites; when one is selected, the Site window opens pointing to the selected site.	N/A
Define Sites	Displays the Site Information dialog box for setting up a new site, or for modifying or deleting an existing site.	N/A
Get	Transfers the selected files from the remote site to the local folder.	Ctrl+Shift+D
Check Out	Marks selected files on the remote site as checked out.	Ctrl+Alt+Shift+D
Put	Transfers the selected files from the local folder to the remote site.	Ctrl+Shift+U
Check In	Marks selected files as checked in.	Ctrl+Alt+Shift+U
Undo Check Out	Removes the Check Out designation on selected files.	N/A
Check Links Sitewide ⇨ Selected	Verifies hypertext links for the current or selected documents.	Ctrl+F8

Continued

Table 3-14 *(continued)*

Command	*Description*	*Shortcut*
Locate in Local Site	Selects the current document in the Site Files list Local pane.	N/A
Locate in Remote Site	Selects the current document in the Site Files list Remote pane.	N/A

The Macintosh Site menu is set up somewhat differently from the Windows version, although the functionality is the same. Table 3-15 details the Site menu for Macintosh systems.

Table 3-15
Site Menu Commands (Macintosh)

Command	*Description*	*Macintosh*
New Site	Presents the Site Definition dialog box for creating a new site.	N/A
Open Site ➪ Your Site List	Displays a user-definable list of sites; when one is selected, the Site Window opens pointing to the selected site.	N/A
Define Sites	Displays the Site Information dialog box for setting up a new site, or for modifying or deleting an existing site.	N/A
Connect	Connects to the current site online.	N/A
Site Files View ➪ New Folder	Creates a new folder in the current site.	Command+Shift+ Option+N
Site Files View ➪ New File	Creates a new HTML file in the current site.	Command+ Shift+N
Site Files View ➪ Refresh Local	Rereads and displays the current local folder.	Command+F5
Site Files View ➪ Refresh Remote	Rereads and displays the current remote folder.	Option F5
Site Files View ➪ Select Newer Local	Highlights files that have been modified locally but not transferred to the remote site.	N/A
Site Map View ➪ View as Root	Makes the selected file the starting point for the map.	Command+ Shift+R

Command	Description	Macintosh
Site Map View ➪ Link to New File	Creates a new file and adds a link to the selected page.	Command+ Shift+N
Site Map View ➪ Link to Existing File	Adds a text link to an existing file to the selected page.	Command+ Shift+K
Site Map View ➪ Change Link	Selects a new page to use as a link instead of the selected file and updates the link.	Command+L
Site Map View ➪ Remove Link	Deletes the selected link.	Command+ Shift+L
Site Map View ➪ Show/Hide Link	Marks a file and all its dependent files as hidden or displayable.	Command+ Shift+Y
Site Map View ➪ Open Source of Link	Opens the HTML file containing the selected link	N/A
Site Map View ➪ New Home Page	Makes the selected file the starting point for the Site Map.	N/A
Site Map View ➪ Select Home Page	Presents a Select File dialog box to choose a file that becomes the new starting point for the Site Map.	N/A
Site Map View ➪ Save Site Map ➪ Save Site Map as PICT | JPEG	Stores the current site map as a graphic file in the chosen format.	N/A
Site Map View ➪ Show Files Marked as Hidden	Displays all hidden files with the file name in italics.	N/A
Site Map View ➪ Show Dependent Files	Shows all the graphic and other additional files	N/A
Site Map View ➪ Show Page Titles	Displays icons identified by page titles instead of by file names.	Command+ Shift+T
Site Map View ➪	Opens the Layout dialog box that determines the structure of the Site Map.	N/A
Site Map View ➪ Refresh Local	Redraws the Site Map.	Shift+F5
Get	Transfers the selected files from the remote site to the local folder.	Command+ Shift+D

Continued

Table 3-15 *(continued)*

Command	*Description*	*Macintosh*
Check Out	Marks selected files on the remote site as checked out.	Command+Shift+ Option+D
Put	Transfers the selected files from the local folder to the remote site.	Command+ Shift+U
Check In	Marks selected files as checked in.	Command+Shift+ Option+U
Undo Check Out	Removes the Check Out designation on selected files.	N/A
Open	Loads a selected file into Dreamweaver.	Command+Shift+ Option+O
Rename	Renames the selected file.	N/A
Unlock	Makes selected read-only files accessible.	N/A
Locate in Local Site	Selects the current document in the Site Files list Local pane.	N/A
Locate in Remote Site	Selects the current document in the Site Files list Remote pane.	N/A
Change Links Sitewide	Updates links from one pointing to one page to point to another.	Command+F8
Change Link Sitewide	Opens a dialog box to specify a link to change.	N/A
Synchronize	Transfers files between the local and remote sites so that the latest version of all selected files are on both sites.	N/A
Recreate Site Cache	Rebuilds the Site Cache to enable quicker updates.	N/A
FTP Log	Opens the FTP Log window.	N/A
Tool Tips	Enables long file names or page titles to be displayed when passed over by the pointer.	N/A

The Window menu

The Window menu manages both program and user-opened windows. Through this menu, described in Table 3-16, you can open, close, arrange, bring to the front, or hide all of the additional Dreamweaver screens.

Table 3-16
Window Menu Commands

Command	*Description*	*Windows*	*Macintosh*
Objects	Opens the Objects palette	Ctrl+F2	Command+F2
Properties	Shows the Property Inspector for the currently selected item	Ctrl+F3	Command+F3
Launcher	Opens the Launcher palette	Shift+F4	Shift+F4
Sites Files	Displays the Site window	F5	F5
Site Map	Displays the current site map	Ctrl -F5	Command -F5
Library	Opens the Library palette	F6	F6
CSS Styles	Opens the CSS Styles Inspector	F7	F7
HTML Styles	Opens the HTML Styles Inspector	Ctrl+F7	Command+F7
Behaviors	Shows the Behaviors Inspector	F8	F8
History	Displays the History palette	F9	F9
Timelines	Shows the Timelines Inspector	Ctrl+F9	Command+F9
HTML Source	Displays the HTML Source Inspector	F10	F10
Frames	Opens the Frames Inspector	Ctrl+F10	Command+F10
Layers	Opens the Layers Inspector	F11	F11
Templates	Opens the Template palette	Ctrl+F11	Command+F11
Arrange Floating Palettes	Moves all open windows to preset positions	N/A	N/A
Show/Hide Floating Palettes	Displays/hides all open windows	F4	F4
Your Open Windows	Displays a list of the currently open document windows	N/A	N/A

All the commands for Dreamweaver's various windows, palettes, and inspectors are toggles. Select a command once to open the window; select again to close it.

The Help menu

The final menu, the Help menu, offers access to Dreamweaver's excellent online help, as well as special examples and templates. Table 3-17 explains each of these useful options.

Table 3-17
Help Menu Commands

Command	*Description*	*Windows*	*Macintosh*
Using Dreamweaver	Opens the Dreamweaver online help system in your primary browser	F1	F1
What's New in Dreamweaver 3	Displays the What's New section of the help files	N/A	N/A
Guided Tour	Displays the Guided Tour section of the help files	N/A	N/A
Tutorial	Displays the Tutorial section of the help files	N/A	N/A
Extending Dreamweaver	Opens the Extending Dreamweaver online documentation in your primary browser	Shift+F1	Shift+F1
Dreamweaver Support Center	Connects to Macromedia's Dreamweaver Support Center	Ctrl+F1	Command+F1
Dreamweaver Exchange	Connects to the Dreamweaver Online Resource Center	N/A	N/A
Register Dreamweaver	Goes online to register your copy of Dreamweaver	N/A	N/A
About Dreamweaver	Displays the opening splash screen with credits and registration and version information	N/A	N/A

Summary

In this chapter, you've observed Dreamweaver's power and had a look at its well-designed layout. From the Objects palette to the various tools controlled through the Launcher, Dreamweaver offers you an elegant, flexible workspace for creating next-generation Web sites.

- ✦ The Document window is your main canvas for visually designing your Dreamweaver Web pages. This workspace includes simple, powerful tools such as the Tag Selector and the status bar Launcher.
- ✦ The Objects palette is Dreamweaver's toolbox. Completely customizable, the Objects palette holds the elements you need most often, in seven initial categories: Characters, Common, Forms, Frames, Head, Invisibles, and Other.

- Dreamweaver's mechanism for assigning details and attributes to an HTML object is the Property Inspector. The Property Inspector is context sensitive, and its options vary according to the object selected.
- The Launcher is the control center for Dreamweaver's specialized functions: the Site window, the Library palette, the HTML Styles palette, the CSS Styles palette, the Behavior Inspector, the History Inspector, and the HTML Source Inspector. You have two Launchers to choose from: one free-floating palette and the one accessible through the status bar, the Mini-Launcher.
- Dreamweaver 3 introduces two new palettes: History and HTML Styles.
- Dreamweaver's full-featured menus offer complete file manipulation, a wide range of insertable objects, the tools to modify them, and extensive online—and on-the-Web—help. Many menu items can be invoked through keyboard shortcuts.

In the next chapter, you learn how to customize Dreamweaver to work the way you work by establishing your own preferences for the program and its interface.

✦ ✦ ✦

Setting Your Preferences

✦ ✦ ✦ ✦

In This Chapter

Dreamweaver made to order

Customizing Dynamic HTML specs

Extending preferences outside Dreamweaver

Specifying your HTML formatting

✦ ✦ ✦ ✦

Everyone works differently. Whether you need to conform to a corporate style sheet handed down from the powers that be or you think "it just looks better that way," Dreamweaver offers you the flexibility to shape your Web page tools and your code output. This chapter describes the options available in Dreamweaver's Preferences and then details how you can tell Dreamweaver to format your source code your way.

Customizing Your Environment

The vast majority of Dreamweaver's settings are controlled through the Preferences dialog box. You can open Preferences by choosing Edit ➪ Preferences or by using the keyboard shortcut Ctrl+U (Command+U). Within Preferences, you find 16 different subjects listed on the left side of the screen. As you switch from one category to another by selecting its name from this Category list, the options available for that category appear in the main area of the dialog box. Although this chapter covers all the options available in each category, the categories are grouped by function, rather than examined in the same order as they appear in the Category list.

Most changes to Preferences take effect immediately after you close the window by clicking OK or the Close button. Only two preferences are not updated instantly:

✦ First, the Show Only Site Window on Startup option goes into effect on the next running of Dreamweaver.

✦ Second, if you elect to modify the Source Format, as described in the section "Understanding the Source Format," later in this chapter, you should complete this modification outside of Dreamweaver (in a text editor), save your work, and then start the program.

General Preferences

Dreamweaver's General Preferences, as seen in Figure 4-1, cover program appearance, user operation, and external editor integration. The appearance of the program's interface may seem to be a trivial matter, but Dreamweaver is a program for designers — to whom appearance is extremely important. These user-operation options are based purely on how you, the user, work best.

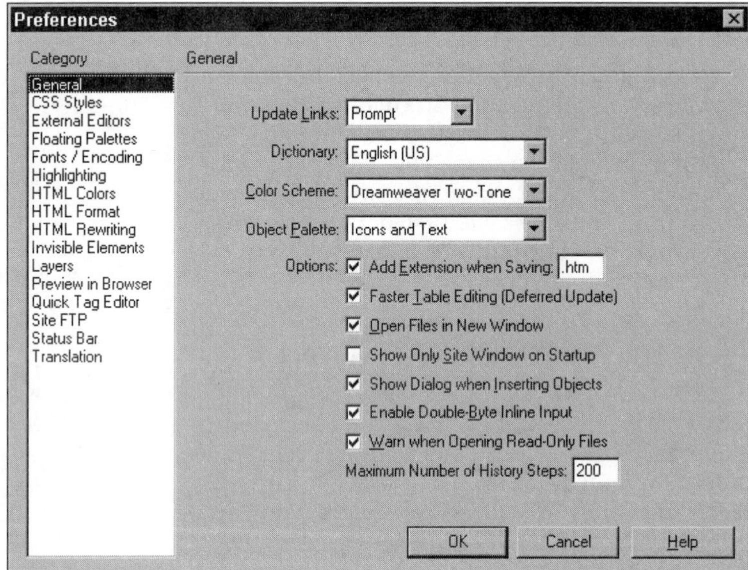

Figure 4-1: Dreamweaver's General Preferences enable you to change your program's appearance and certain overall operations.

In choosing all the preferences, including the General ones, you can work in two ways. If you are a seasoned Web designer, you probably want Dreamweaver to work in your established manner to minimize your learning curve. If you're just starting out as a Web page creator, work with the default options for a while and then go back and try other options. You should know right away which style works for you.

Update Links

As your site grows in complexity, you'll find that keeping track of the various links is an increasingly difficult task. Dreamweaver 3 has several enhanced features to help you manage links, and the Update Links option is one of them. Dreamweaver can check each link on a page when a file is moved — whether it is the Web page you're working on or one of the support files, such as an image, that goes on the page. The Update Links option determines how Dreamweaver reacts when it notes an altered link.

By default, the Update Links option is set to Prompt, which causes Dreamweaver 3 to alert you to any link changes and requires you to "OK" the code alterations by selecting the Update button. To leave the files as they are, you choose the Don't Update button. You can elect to have Dreamweaver automatically keep your pages up to date by selecting the Always option from the Update Links drop-down list. Finally, you can select the Never option, and Dreamweaver ignores the link changes necessary when you move, rename, or delete a file.

As a general rule, I keep my Update Links option set to Always. It is a very rare circumstance when I intentionally want to maintain a bad link on my Web page. Likewise, I recommend using the Never option with extreme caution.

The Update Links option replaces the Correct Relative Links on Save As option found in versions of Dreamweaver earlier than 2.

Dictionary

The Dictionary option enables you to select a spell-checking dictionary from any of those installed. In addition to the standard English-language version, which has three options — English (US), English (UK -ise), and English (UK -ize) — additional dictionaries exist online. As of this writing, dictionaries in these other languages are also available: German, Spanish, French, Italian, Brazilian-Portuguese, and Catalan. You can download these dictionaries from Macromedia's Dreamweaver Object Exchange at `www.macromedia.com/support/dreamweaver/dictionary.html`. Once downloaded, save the .dat file in the Configuration\Dictionaries folder and restart Dreamweaver.

To select a different dictionary for spell-checking, select the Dictionary option button and choose an item from the drop-down list. Dreamweaver also maintains a Personal dictionary (although it's not visible on the list) to hold those words you wish Dreamweaver to learn during the spell-checking process.

Color Scheme (Windows only)

The first option is purely a cosmetic one: the color scheme of the screens presented to you as you work with the program. Dreamweaver offers three different color combinations. This feature is Windows only as Macintosh users can affect Dreamweaver's look through the Appearances Control Panel. Windows users should click the arrow button next to Color Scheme to open the drop-down list and choose from the following options:

Color Scheme Option	*Description*
Dreamweaver Two-Tone	This default color scheme uses two shades of gray.
Desktop Two-Tone	Picks up your desktop primary color and one contrasting color to define window borders and other areas.
Desktop Standard	Uses the system default colors for a monochromatic approach.

Tip

On the Launcher palette, the icon text is anti-aliased to appear smooth against the default background, which is a light gray. If your desktop or system color is much darker in tone, you'll probably notice some distracting artifacts (miscolored pixels) around the letters. To fix this problem, switch to a lighter desktop color or choose the Dreamweaver Two-Tone color scheme.

Objects palette

Learning a new software program can be tough—just memorizing which icon means what can increase your learning curve. With Dreamweaver, you don't have to try to remember all the Object symbols right off the bat. If you like, you can opt to have the names of the Objects next to their icons—or even just the names themselves. You make this choice in the Objects palette option.

By default, the Objects palette is composed only of icons. When you pass your mouse over each one, a ToolTip appears that names the object. However, if you don't want to hunt for your object, you can select Icons and Text (or Text Only) from the Objects palette option. Whichever option you select, when you exit from Preferences, the Objects palette changes size and shape to accommodate the new format, as shown in Figure 4-2.

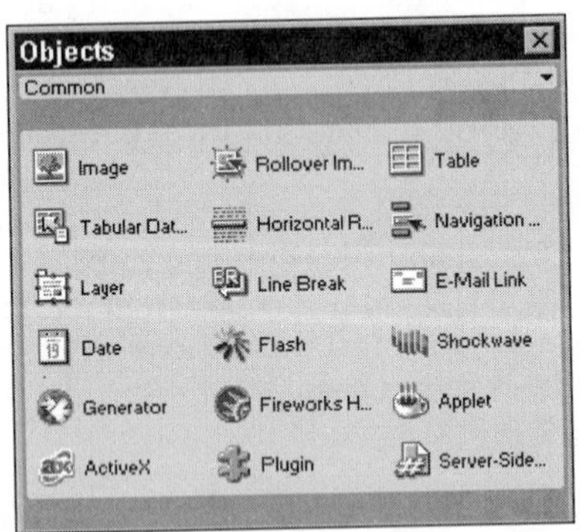

Figure 4-2: In Dreamweaver 3, the Objects palette can display each object's name along with its icon.

General options

The second main section of the General Preferences screen consists of numerous checkbox options you can turn on or off. Overall, these options fall into the user-interaction category or "What's good for you?" Take the Show Dialog when Inserting Objects option, for example. Some Web creators prefer to enter all their attributes at one time through the Property Inspector and would rather not have the dialog boxes appear for every inserted object. Others want to get their file sources in immediately and modify the rest later. Your selection depends on how you want to work.

The following paragraphs describe the listed options.

Add Extension when Saving

HTML files originally were identified — cleverly enough — by their .html file name extension. When Microsoft jumped on the Internet bandwagon, it reduced the extension to three letters, .htm, to fit its pre-Windows 95 format. But now many different Web file formats and extensions have exploded onto the Internet — .asp, .shtml, .stm, and .phtml, to name just a few. In early versions of Dreamweaver (before 2), the .htm extension was the default — and a difficult one to change at that. Dreamweaver 3 includes the capability to save your files using any file name extension you specify.

The Add Extension when Saving option is straightforward. Just enter the extension of your choosing in the text box and make sure the option is selected. For example, if you are building nothing but Active Server Pages for a particular Web site, you would change the Add Extension when Saving text box to .asp and select OK in the Preferences dialog box. Now, to save a file, you have to enter only the initial part of the file name, and the appropriate extension is automatically appended.

Faster Table Editing (Deferred Update)

When you enter text into a table, the current column width automatically expands while the other columns shrink correspondingly. If you're working with large tables, this updating process can slow your editing. Dreamweaver gives you the choice between faster input or instantaneous feedback.

When the Faster Table Editing preference is turned on, Dreamweaver updates the entire table only when you click outside the table, or if you press Ctrl+spacebar (Command+spacebar). If you prefer to see the table form as you type, turn this option off.

Two other ways to update tables: Select any tag in the Tag Selector (a useful approach when working with a very large table), or resize the Document window.

Open Files in New Window (Windows only)

Select the Open Files in New Window option when you need to have several Web pages open simultaneously. Alternatively, if you want to free up some of your system resources (such as memory) and you need only one Dreamweaver window, you can deselect this option.

If this option is not selected and changes are made to the current file, Dreamweaver asks if you'd like to save the current page when you attempt to load a new file.

Show Only Site Window on Startup

Some Web designers prefer to use the Site window as their "base of operations," rather than the Document window. For them, it's easier — particularly with many of Dreamweaver 3's new features — to construct and maintain their Web pages from the sitewide perspective offered through the Site window. Dreamweaver offers you the option to begin a Web authoring session with just the Site window.

Selecting the Show Only Site Window on Startup option displays just the Site window the next time you open Dreamweaver. The Site window is shown in the configuration used the last time you had it open — with or without the site map enabled and with the various columns positioned in the same manner. To bring up the Document window, choose File ⇨ New Window from the Site window menu.

Show Dialog when Inserting Objects

By default, almost all the objects that Dreamweaver inserts — via either the Objects palette or the Insert menu — open an initial dialog box to gather needed information. In most cases, the dialog box enables you to input a URL or browse for a source file. Turning off the Show Dialog option causes Dreamweaver to insert a default-sized object, or a placeholder, for the object. You must then enter all attributes through the Property Inspector.

Enable Double-Byte Inline Input

Some computer representations of languages, primarily Asian languages, require more raw descriptive power than others. The ideogram for "snow," for example, is far more complex than a four-letter word. These languages need twice the number of bytes per character and are known as *double-byte languages*. In versions of Dreamweaver before 2, all double-byte characters had to go through a separate text input window instead of directly into the Document window.

Dreamweaver 3 simplifies the page creation process for double-byte languages with the Enable Double-Byte Inline Input option. Once selected, this option enables double-byte characters to be entered directly into the Document window. To use the old method of inserting such characters, deselect this option.

Warn when Opening Read-Only Files

Read-only files have been locked to prevent accidental overwriting. Optionally, Dreamweaver 3 can warn you when such a file is opened. The warning is actually more than just an alert, however. Dreamweaver provides an option on the warning dialog box to make the file writable. Alternatively, you can just view the file.

Although Dreamweaver enables you to edit the file either way, if the document is still read-only when you save your changes, the Save As dialog box appears, and you are prompted to store the file under a new name.

Maximum Number of History Steps

Before Dreamweaver 3, the number of undo steps was limited by a system's memory — but there was no visual indication of what those steps were. The History palette, introduced in Dreamweaver 3, shows exactly what actions have been taken. A limit exists, however, to the number of steps that can be tracked. By default, the limit is set to 200.

Although 200 history steps are more than enough for most systems, you can alter this number by changing the Maximum Number of History Steps value. When the maximum number of history steps is exceeded, the oldest actions are wiped from memory and unrecoverable. The history steps are not discarded when a file is saved, unlike the previous undo steps.

Preferences for invisible elements

By their nature, all HTML markup tags remain unseen to one degree or another when presented for viewing through the browser. You may want to see certain elements while designing a page, however. For example, adjusting line spacing is a common task, and turning on the visibility of the line break tag <BR> can help you understand the layout.

Dreamweaver enables you to control the visibility of 12 different codes — or rather their symbols, as shown in Figure 4-3. When, for example, a named anchor is inserted, Dreamweaver shows you a small gold shield with an anchor emblem. Not only does this shield indicate the anchor's position, but you can also manipulate the code with cut-and-paste or drag-and-drop techniques. Moreover, double-clicking a symbol opens the pertinent Property Inspector and enables quick changes to the tag's attributes.

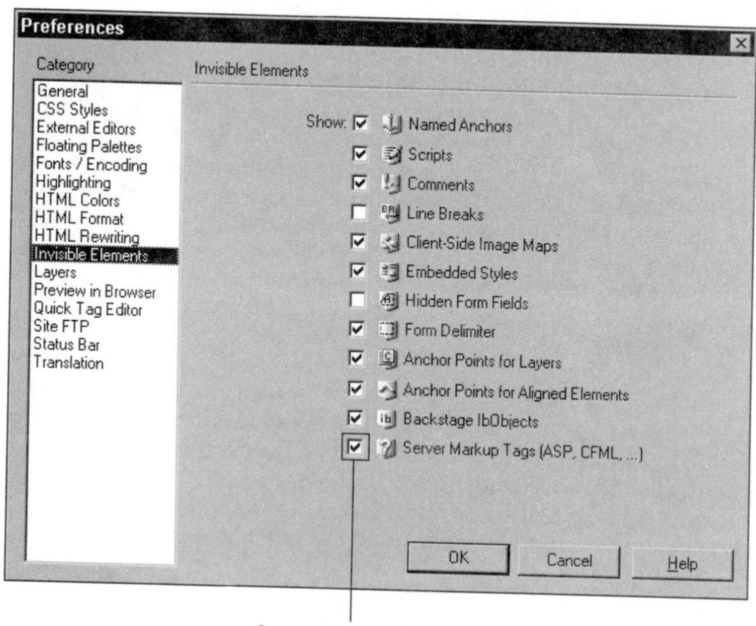

Figure 4-3: You can show or hide any or all of the 12 invisible elements listed in the Preferences dialog box.

You can temporarily hide all invisible elements by deselecting View ➪ Invisible Elements.

The 12 items controlled through the Invisible Elements panel are as follows:

- ✦ Named anchors
- ✦ Scripts
- ✦ Comments
- ✦ Line breaks
- ✦ Client-side image maps
- ✦ Embedded styles
- ✦ Hidden form fields
- ✦ Form delimiter
- ✦ Anchor points for layers
- ✦ Anchor points for aligned elements
- ✦ Backstage lbObjects
- ✦ Server markup tags (ASP, CFML, . . .)

Most of the Invisible Elements options display or hide small symbols in Dreamweaver's visual Document window. Several options, however, show an outline or another type of highlight. Turning off Form Delimiter, for example, removes the dashed line that surrounds a form in the Document window.

You may have noticed that the Cold Fusion tags and Active Server Page tags are now combined into one symbol, Server Markup tags. Dreamweaver 3's capability to handle dynamic pages generated by databases makes these new invisible elements essential.

Floating palettes

Although the various windows, palettes, and inspectors are convenient, sometimes you just want a clear view of your document. The Floating Palettes Preferences panel enables you to choose which of Dreamweaver's accessory screens stay on top of the Document window. As shown in Figure 4-4, you can adjust 14 different elements. By default, they are all set to float above the Document window. Dreamweaver 3 even provides a new option, All Other Floaters, to control the behavior of custom floaters.

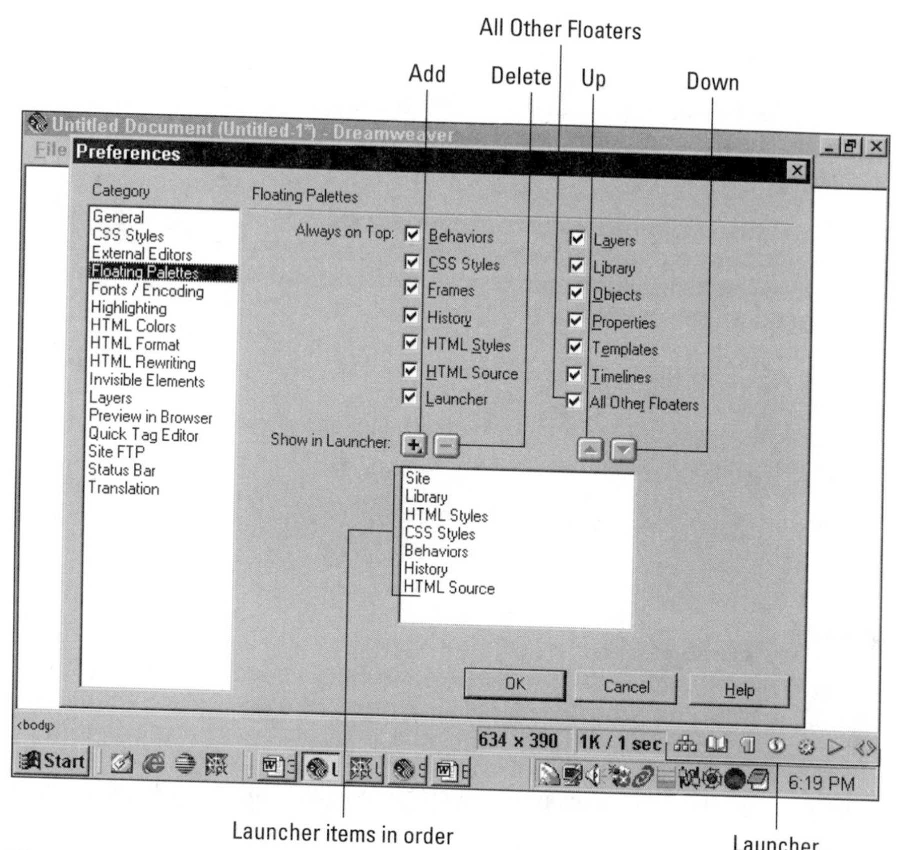

Figure 4-4: If you deselect any of the floating palettes screens, they move behind the Document window.

Tip

You can use the Show/Hide Floating Palettes key to bring back any screen element that has gone behind the Document window. Just press F4 twice.

If you often use the HTML Source Inspector, you might consider taking it off the "always on top" list. Then, after you've made your HTML code edits, click in the Document window. This sequence updates the visual document, incorporating any changes, and simultaneously pushes the HTML Source Inspector behind the Document window. You can switch between the two views of your Web page by using the Ctrl+Tab (Control+Tab) key combination.

Prior to Dreamweaver 3, the Launcher (both the floating palette and the status bar versions) displayed a preset series of icons; if you used a palette such as Templates often, you had to either open it through the Windows menu or memorize the keyboard shortcut. In Dreamweaver 3, the Launcher is completely customizable—you can add or remove icons for any of the available palettes. Moreover, the order of their appearance is up to you as well.

To add a new icon to the Launcher, follow these steps:

1. Click the Add (+) button and choose an available floating palette from the drop-down list.

   The chosen palette is added to the end of the list, and the icon appears on the right of the Launcher.

2. You can reposition the icon by using the up and down arrows with the palette's name selected.

To remove an icon from the Launcher, select the palette in the list and choose the Delete (–) button.

Highlighting preferences

Dreamweaver 3 is far more extensible than previous versions — custom functions are more prevalent, server-side markup is more acceptable, and more third-party tags are supported. Many of these features depend on "hidden" capabilities that are not noticeable in the final HTML page, but the Web designer must take them into account. Dreamweaver 3 uses user-selectable highlighting to mark areas on a Web page under construction.

The Highlighting panel of the Preferences dialog box, shown in Figure 4-5, enables you to choose the highlight color for four different types of extended objects: Editable and Locked Regions, both used in templates; Library items; and Third-Party Tags. In each case, to choose a highlight color, select the color swatch to open Dreamweaver's color picker. Then use the Eyedropper to pick a color from the Web-safe palette or from your desktop. After you've chosen an appropriate color, make sure to select the related Show checkbox so that the highlighting is displayed.

Quick Tag Editor preferences

The Quick Tag Editor is a new edition to Dreamweaver 3 designed to bridge the gap between the visual layout and the underlying code. With the Quick Tag Editor, you can quickly edit a tag or wrap the selection in a whole new tag, without opening the HTML Source Inspector. The Quick Tag Editor pops open a small draggable window when invoked, and its preferences, shown in Figure 4-6, control the appearance and behavior of that window.

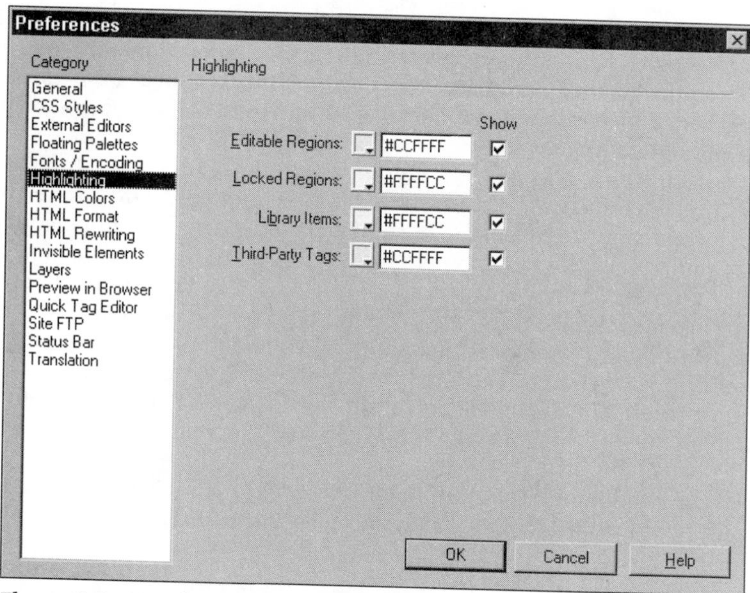

Figure 4-5: Use the Highlighting preferences to control how template regions, library items, and third-party tags appear in the Document window.

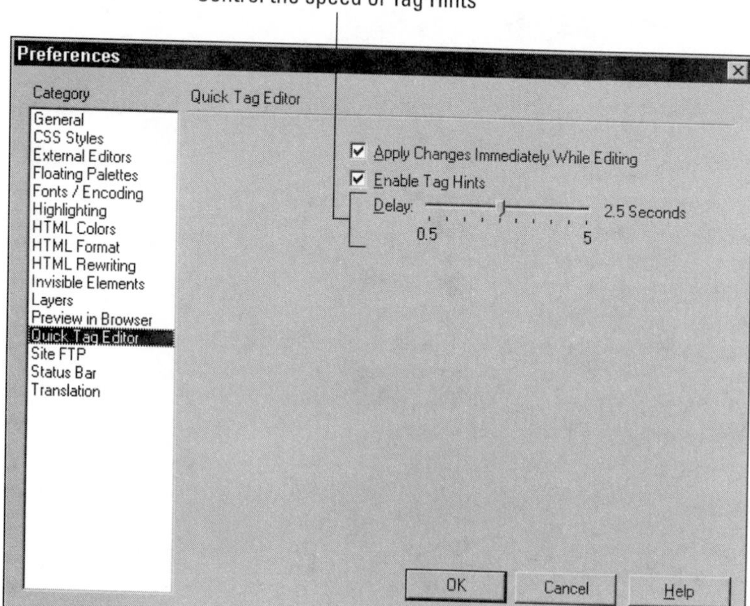

Figure 4-6: Adjust the Quick Tag Editor preferences to suit the way you like to add code to a page.

The Quick Tag Editor has three modes: Edit Tag, Insert HTML, and Wrap Tag. The first option, Apply Changes Immediately While Editing, affects only the Edit Tag mode. When this option is disabled, the Enter (Return) key must be pressed to confirm the edits. In the other two modes, you always must confirm your additions with the Enter (Return) key.

The second option, Enable Tag Hints, works in all three modes. A short time after the Quick Tag Editor is invoked, a list of possible tags appears. To reduce your typing, when the first letter of the tag is typed, the list scrolls to the tags starting with that letter. For example, if you want to wrap a `<blockquote>` tag around a paragraph, typing a *b* brings the list to the `<b>` (bold) tag; type the next letter, *l*, and the list scrolls to `<blockquote>`—at this point, all you have to do is press Enter (Return) to confirm your choice. The Tag Hint list does not appear at all if Enable Tag Hints is unchecked. You can also control the speed at which the Tag Hints list appears by moving the Delay slider; the range is from .5 seconds to 5 seconds.

If you like using the Tag Hints list, set the Delay slider to .5 second; with that setting, the list pops up almost immediately and speeds your work.

Status bar preferences

The status bar is a handy collection of four different tool sets: the Tag Selector, the Window Size pop-up menu, the Connection Speed Indicator, and the Mini-Launcher. The Status Bar panel of the Preferences dialog box, shown in Figure 4-7, controls options for three of the four tools.

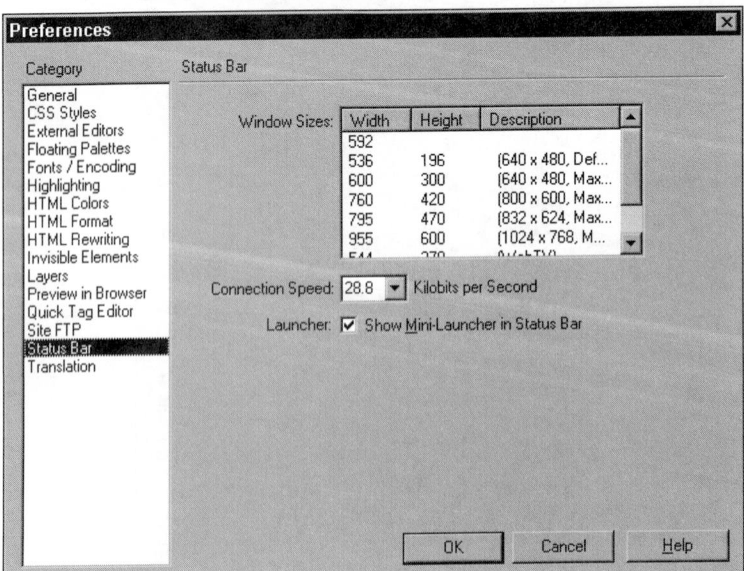

Figure 4-7: Use the Status Bar panel to evaluate your real-world download times.

Window Sizes

The Window Sizes list at the top of the Status Bar panel shows the current options for the Window Sizes pop-up menu. This list is completely user editable and enables you to add new window sizes, modify existing dimensions, add descriptions, or delete little-used measurements.

As discussed in Chapter 3, the Window Sizes pop-up is a feature in Dreamweaver 3 that enables you to instantly change your screen size so that you may view and build your page under different monitor conditions. To change any of the current dimensions, simply click the measurement you wish to alter and enter a new value. You can also change any description of the existing widths and heights by clicking in the Description column and entering your text. While you can enter as much text as you like, it's not practical to enter more than about 15 to 20 characters.

To enter a new set of dimensions in the Window Sizes list box, follow these steps:

1. From the Status Bar panel of the Preferences dialog box, locate the last entry in the current list.

   If the last entry is not immediately available, use the vertical scroll bar to move to the end.
2. Click once in the Width column on the line below the last entry.
3. Enter the desired width of the new window size in pixels.
4. Press Tab to move to the Height column.
5. Enter the desired height for the new window size. Press Tab again.
6. Optionally, you can enter short descriptive text in the Description column. Press Tab when you're finished.
7. To continue adding new sizes, repeat Steps 2 through 6. Select OK when you finish.

You don't have to enter the word *pixels* or the abbreviation *px* after your values in the Width and Height columns of the Window Sizes list box, but you can. If you enter any dimensions under 20, Dreamweaver converts the measurement to its smallest possible window size, 20 pixels.

Connection Speed

Dreamweaver understands that not all access speeds are created equal, so the Connection Speed option enables you to check the download time for your page (or the individual images) at a variety of rates. The Connection Speed setting evaluates the download statistics in the status bar. You can choose from seven preset connection speeds, all in kilobits per second: 14.4, 28.8, 33.6, 56, 64, 128, and 1,500. The lower speeds (14.4 through 33.6) represent older dial-up modem connection rates — if you are building a page for the mass market, you should consider selecting one of these slower rates. Although 56K modems are widespread on the market today, the true 56K connection is a rare occurrence. Use the 128 setting if your audience connects through an ISDN line. If everyone views your page through a direct LAN connection, change the connection speed to 1,500.

You are not limited to these preset settings. You can type any desired speed directly into the Connection Speed text box. You could, for example, specify a connection speed more often experienced in the real world, such as 23.3. If you find yourself, in the near future, designing for an audience using cable modems, you could change the Connection Speed to 150 or higher.

Show Mini-Launcher in Status Bar

The default setting enables the status bar Mini-Launcher. When this option is disabled, you always have to access the Launcher by choosing Window ⇨ Launcher from the menus.

External Editor preferences

Refinement is often the name of the game in Web design, and giving you quick access to your favorite modification tools — whether you're modifying code, graphics, or other media — is one of Dreamweaver's key features. In Dreamweaver 3, this access has been greatly expanded. The External Editors panel, shown in Figure 4-8, is where you specify the program you want Dreamweaver to call for any file type you define.

HTML Editor preferences

Dreamweaver recognizes the importance of your choice of a text editor. Although Dreamweaver ships with two extremely robust HTML editors, you can opt to use any other program. To select your editor, enter the path in the HTML Editor text box or select the Browse (Choose) button to choose the appropriate executable file.

The two included editors, BBEdit for Macintosh and HomeSite for Windows, are integrated with Dreamweaver to varying degrees. Both of the editors can be called from within Dreamweaver, and both have "Dreamweaver" buttons for returning to the main program — switching between the editor and Dreamweaver automatically updates the page. Like Dreamweaver's internal HTML editor, BBEdit highlights the corresponding code to a selection made in Dreamweaver; this property does not, however, extend to HomeSite.

You specify and control your external editor selection with the following options.

Enable BBEdit Integration (Macintosh only)

Dreamweaver for Macintosh ships with this option activated. If you prefer to use another editor or an older version of BBEdit that lacks the integration capabilities, deselect this option.

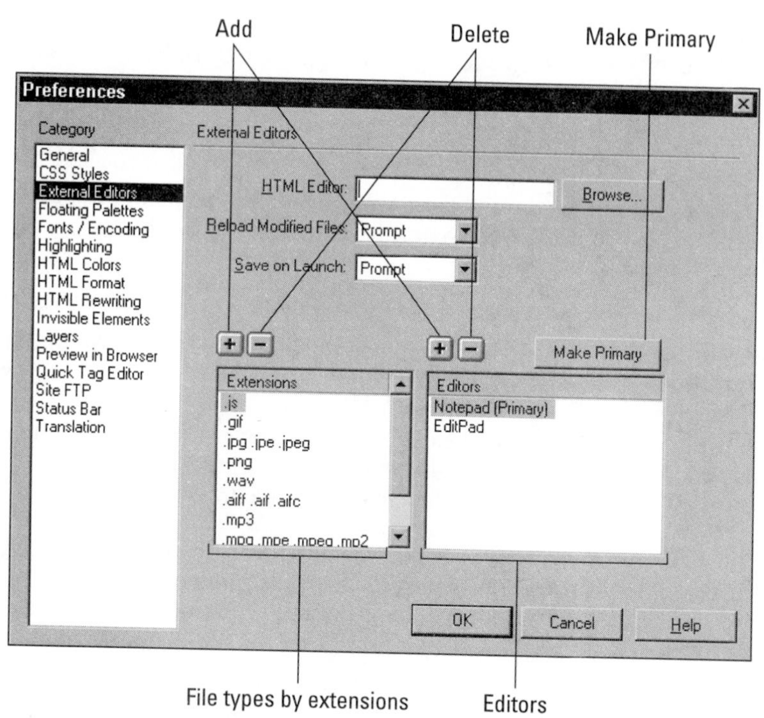

Figure 4-8: Assign your favorite HTML, graphics editors, and more through the newly extended External Editors panel of the Preferences dialog box.

Reload Modified Files

The drop-down list for this setting offers three options for working with an external editor:

✦ **Prompt:** Detects when files are updated by another program and enables you to decide whether to update them within Dreamweaver

✦ **Always:** Updates the file in Dreamweaver automatically when the file is changed in an outside program

✦ **Never:** Assumes that you want to make all updates from within Dreamweaver yourself.

Personally, I prefer to have Dreamweaver always update my files. I find it saves a couple of mouse clicks — not to mention time.

Save on Launch

Any external HTML editor—even the integrated HomeSite or BBEdit—opens and reads a previously saved file. Therefore, if you make any changes in Dreamweaver's visual editor and switch to your editor without saving, the editor shows only the most recently saved version. To control this function, you have three options:

- ✦ **Prompt:** Determines that unsaved changes have been made and asks you to save the file. If you do not, the external editor reverts to the last saved version.
- ✦ **Always:** Saves the file automatically before opening it in the external editor.
- ✦ **Never:** Disregards any changes made since the last save, and the external editor opens the previously saved file.

Here again, as with Reload Modified Files, I prefer to always save my files when switching back and forth. Keep in mind, however, that saving a file clears Dreamweaver's undo memory and the changes cannot be undone.

If you try to open a file that has never been saved in an external editor, Dreamweaver prompts you to save it regardless of your preference settings. If you opt not to save the file, the external editor is not opened because it has no saved file to display.

Media Editor preferences

Dreamweaver has the capability to call an editor for any specified type of file at the touch of a button. For example, when you import a graphic, you often need to modify its color, size, shape, transparency, or another feature to make it work correctly on the Web page. Rather than force you to start your graphics program independently, load the image, make the changes, and resave the image, Dreamweaver enables you to send any selected image directly to your editor. After you've made your modifications and saved the file, the altered image appears automatically in Dreamweaver.

In Dreamweaver 3, the capability to associate different file types with external editors has expanded to more than just images. Now you can link one or more editors to any type of media—images, audio, video, even specific kinds of code. The defined external editor is invoked when the file is double-clicked in the Site window. Because the editors are assigned according to file extension as opposed to media type, one editor could be assigned to GIF files and another to JPEGs. The selection is completely customizable.

When a file is double-clicked in the Site window, that file type's primary editor runs. Dreamweaver offers the capability to define multiple editors for any file extension. You might, for instance, prefer to open certain JPEGs in Fireworks and others in Photoshop. To choose an alternative editor, right-click (Control+click) the file name in the Site window and select the desired program from the Open With menu option. The Open With option also enables you to browse for a program.

To assign an editor to an existing file type, follow these steps:

1. Select the file type from the Extensions list.
2. Click the Add (+) button above the Editors list.

   The Add External Editor dialog box opens.
3. Locate the application file of the editor and click Open when you're ready.

   You can also select a shortcut or alias to the application.
4. If you want to select the editor as the primary editor, click Make Primary while the editor is highlighted.

To add a new file type, click the Add button above the Extensions list and enter the file extension — including the period — in the field displayed at the bottom of the list. For multiple file extensions, separate each extension with a space, such as this:

```
.doc .dot .rtf
```

Looking for a good almost-all-purpose editor? The QuickTime Pro Player makes a great addition to Dreamweaver as the editor for AIFF, AU, WAV, MP3, AVI, MOV and animated GIF files and others. The Pro Player is wonderful for quick edits and optimization especially with sound files. It's available from the Apple Web site (`www.apple.com/quicktime`) for both platforms for around $30.

Finally, to remove an editor or a file extension, select it and click the Delete (–) button above the corresponding list. Note that removing a file extension also removes the associated editor.

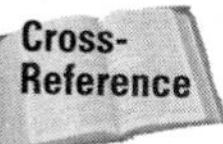

Be sure that your graphics program is adept at handling the three graphic formats used on the Web: GIFs, JPEGs, and PNG images. Macromedia makes Fireworks 3, a graphics editor designed for the Web that integrates nicely with Dreamweaver. In fact, it integrates so nicely, this book includes an entire chapter on it, Chapter 22.

Adjusting Advanced Features

Evolution of the Web and its language, HTML, never ends. New features emerge often from leading browser developers. A competing developer can introduce a similar feature that works in a slightly different way. The HTML standards organization — the World Wide Web Consortium, also known as the W3C — can then endorse one approach or introduce an entirely new method of reaching a similar goal. Eventually, one method usually wins the approval of the marketplace and becomes the accepted coding technique.

To permit the widest range of features, Dreamweaver enables you to designate how your code is written to accommodate the latest HTML features: layers and style sheets. The default preferences for these elements offer the highest degree of cross-browser and backward compatibility. If your Web pages are intended for a more specific audience, such as a Netscape Navigator–only intranet, Dreamweaver enables you to take advantage of a more specific feature set.

Layers preferences

Aside from helping you control the underlying coding method for producing layers, Dreamweaver enables you define the default layer. This capability is especially useful during a major production effort in which the Web development team must produce hundreds of layers spread over a Web site. Being able to specify in advance the initial size, color, background, and visibility saves numerous steps — each of which would have to be repeated for every layer. Figure 4-9 shows the layout of the Layers panel of the Preferences dialog box.

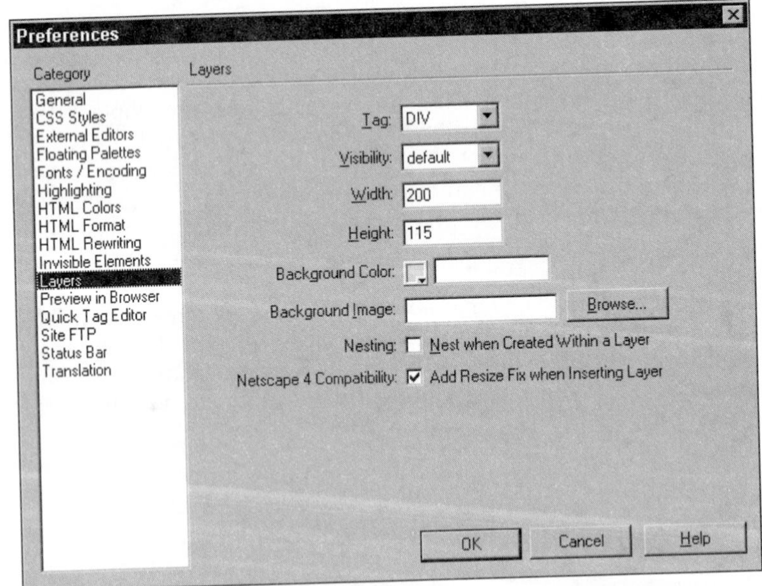

Figure 4-9: In Layers preferences, you can predetermine the structure of the default Dreamweaver layer.

The controls accessible through the Layers panel include the following.

Tag

Select the arrow button to see the tags for the four HTML code methods for implementing layers: `<div>`, `<span>`, `<layer>`, and `<ilayer>`. The first two, `<div>` and

<span>, were developed by the W3C as part of their Cascading Style Sheets recommendation and are supported by both the Netscape and Microsoft 4.0 browsers. Netscape developed the latter two HTML commands, <layer> and <ilayer>; currently only Communicator 4.0 supports these tags.

Dreamweaver uses the <div> tag for its default. Supported by both major 4.0 and above browsers, the <div> element offers the widest cross-browser compatibility. You should use only one of the other Tag options if you are building a Web site intended for a specific browser.

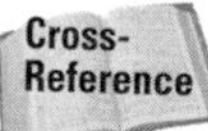

To learn more about the uses of the various positioning tags, see Chapter 28.

Visibility

Layers can be either visible or hidden when the Web page is first loaded. A layer created using the default visibility option is always displayed initially; however, no specific information is written into the code. Selecting Visible forces Dreamweaver to include a `visibility:visible` line in your layer code. Likewise, if you select Hidden from the Visibility options, the layer is initially hidden.

Use the Inherit option when creating nested layers. Creating one layer inside another makes the outer layer the parent, and the inner layer the child. If the parent layer is visible and the child layer is set to `visibility:inherit`, then the child is also visible. This option makes it possible to affect the visibility of many layers with one command—hide the parent layer, and all the inheriting child layers disappear as well.

Width and Height

When you choose Draw Layer from the Objects palette, you drag out the size and shape of your layer. Choosing Insert ➪ Layer puts a layer of a default size and shape at your current cursor position. The Width and Height options enable you to set these defaults. Select the text boxes and type your new values. Dreamweaver's default is a layer 200 pixels wide by 115 pixels high.

Background Color

Layers can have their own background color independent of the Web page's overall background color (which is set as a <body> attribute). You can define the default background color of any inserted layer through either the Insert menu or the Objects palette. For this preference setting, type a color, either by its standard name or as a hexadecimal triplet, directly into the text box. You can also click the color swatch to display the Dreamweaver browser-safe color picker.

Note that while you can specify a different background color for the layer, you can't alter the layer's default text and link colors (except on a layer-by-layer basis) as you can with a page. If your page and layer background colors are highly contrasting, be sure your text and links are readable in both environments. A similar caveat applies to the use of a layer's background image, as explained in the next section.

Background Image

Just as you can pick a specific background color for layers, you can select a different background image for layers. You can type a file source directly into the Background Image text box or select your file from a dialog box by choosing the Browse button. The layer's background image supersedes the layer background color, just as it does with the HTML page. Also, just as the page's background image tiles to fill the page, so does the layer's background image.

Nesting

The two best options about layers seem to be directly opposed: overlapping and nesting layers. You can design layers to appear one on top of another, and you can code layers so that they are within one another. Both techniques are valuable options, and Dreamweaver enables you to decide which one should be the overriding method.

If you are working primarily with nested layers and plan on using the inheritance facility, check the Nest when Created Within a Layer option. If your design entails a number of overlapping but independent layers, make sure this option is turned off. Regardless of your preference, you can reverse it on an individual basis by pressing the Ctrl (Command) key when drawing out your layers.

Netscape 4 Compatibility

Netscape 4 has a particularly annoying problem displaying Web pages with layers. When the user resizes the browser, all of the CSS positioning information is lost—in other words, all your layers lose their exact positioning and typically align themselves on the left. The only fix is to force Netscape to reload the page after the browser has been resized.

When the Netscape 4 Compatibility option is enabled, Dreamweaver 3 automatically includes a small JavaScript routine to handle the resizing problem. The code is inserted in the <head> section of the page when the first layer is added to the page. If additional layers are added, Dreamweaver is smart enough to realize that the workaround code has already been included and does not add more unnecessary code.

Many Web designers run into this problem as they begin to explore the possibilities of Dynamic HTML. I highly recommend that you enable the Netscape 4 Compatibility option to offset any problems.

CSS Styles preferences

The CSS Styles panel (see Figure 4-10) is entirely devoted to how your code is written. As specified by the W3C, Cascading Style Sheets (CSS) declarations—the specifications of a style — can be written in several ways. One method displays a series of items, separated by semicolons:

```
H1 { font-family: helvetica; font-size: 12pt; line-height: 14pt; ¬
font-weight: bold;}
```

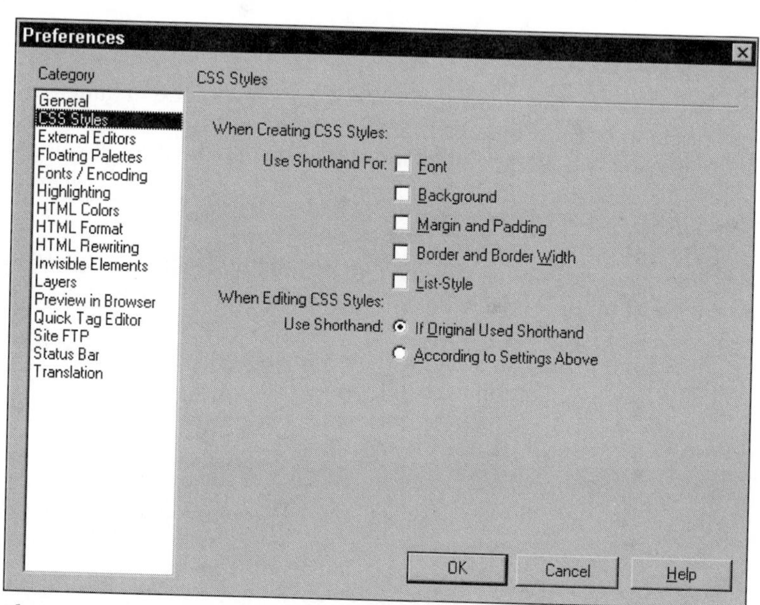

Figure 4-10: The CSS Styles panel enables you to code the style sheet sections of your Web pages in a graphics designer–friendly manner.

Certain properties (such as font) have their own grouping shorthand, developed to be more readable to designers coming from a traditional print background. A second, "shorthand" method of rendering the preceding declaration follows:

```
H1 { font: helvetica 12pt/14pt bold }
```

With the CSS Styles panel, you can enable the shorthand method for any or all of the five different properties that permit it. Select any of the checkboxes under Use Shorthand For to have Dreamweaver write your style code in this fashion.

The second option on the CSS Styles panel determines how Dreamweaver edits styles in previously coded pages. If you want to retain the format of the original page, click Use Shorthand If Original Used Shorthand. If you want Dreamweaver to write new code in the manner that you specify, select Use Shorthand According to Settings Above.

Although the leading varieties of the 4.0 and above browsers can read the style's shorthand with no difficulty, Internet Explorer 3.0 does not have this capability. IE3 is the only other mainstream browser that can claim support for Cascading Style Sheets, but it doesn't understand the shorthand form. If you want to maintain browser backward-compatibility, don't enable any of the shorthand options.

Translation preference

In order to properly view server-generated content for server-side includes or database-linked pages in Dreamweaver's Document window, the information has to be translated. Code in server-side includes looks something like the following:

```
<!--#include file="footer.inc" -->
```

With other Web authoring programs, you have to send all your files to the Web server and look at them online to view the complete content on the page. Dreamweaver 3 gives you the power to translate the server-side information so that you can design your page in context. The Translation panel, shown in Figure 4-11, specifies how translations are to be handled.

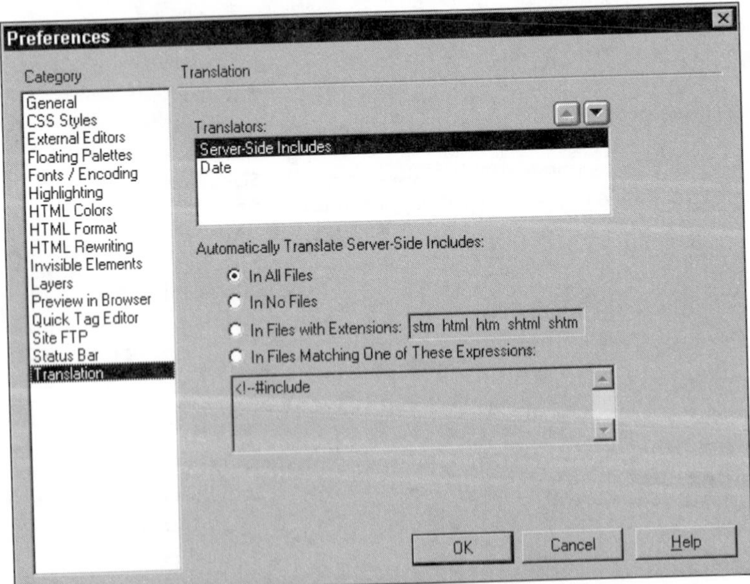

Figure 4-11: The Translation panel of the Preferences dialog box determines when your server-side content is capable of being viewed in the Document window.

Translators

The Translators list box displays the currently available translators. Dreamweaver 3 ships with two included translators: Server-Side Includes (SSI) and Date. Other translators can be custom written or purchased from third-party companies. When you add additional translators to the system — by copying their files to the Configuration\Translators folder — their names appear in the Translators list box, and the Up and Down buttons become active. The Up/Down buttons are used to specify the order in which the translations occur.

Translation options

The translation options in the lower portion of the Translation panel are specific to each translator. For server-side includes, the options are to automatically translate SSI under the following conditions:

- **In All Files:** Displays server-side includes unconditionally (default).
- **In No Files:** Never translates SSIs in the Document window.
- **In Files with Extensions:** Only files with the listed extensions are translated.
- **In Files Matching One of These Expressions:** If this option is selected, Dreamweaver scans the code of the entire page. If one or more of the listed expressions are found, all SSIs included on the page are translated.

To learn more about server-side includes, see Chapter 17. Translators are covered in Chapter 21.

Making Online Connections

Dreamweaver's visual layout editor offers an approximation of your Web page's appearance in the real world of browsers — offline or online. After you've created the initial draft of your Web page, you should preview it through one or more browsers. And when your project nears completion, you should transfer the files to a server for online, real-time viewing and further testing through a File Transfer Protocol program (FTP). Dreamweaver gives you control over all these stages of Web page development, through the Site FTP and Preview in Browser panels.

Site FTP preferences

As your Web site takes shape, you'll spend more time with the Site FTP portion of Dreamweaver. The Site FTP panel, seen in Figure 4-12, enables you to customize the look and feel of your site, as well as enter essential connection information.

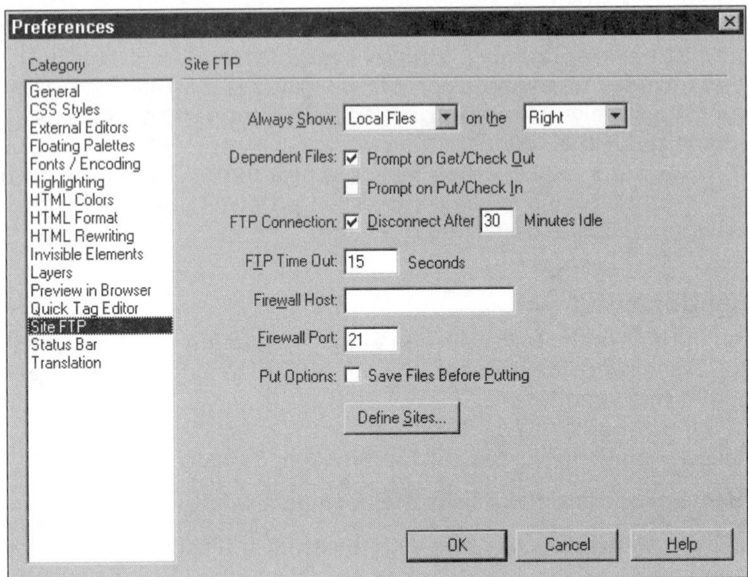

Figure 4-12: Options for Dreamweaver's Site window are handled through the Site FTP panel.

The available Site FTP preferences are described in the following sections.

Always Show Local/Remote Files on the Right/Left

The Site window is divided into two panes: one showing local files and one showing remote files on the server. By default, Dreamweaver puts the Local pane on the right and the Remote pane on the left. However, Dreamweaver enables you to customize that option. Like many designers, I'm used to using other FTP programs in which the Remote files are on the right and the Local files on the left; Dreamweaver 3 enables me to work the way I'm used to working.

To switch the layout of your Site window, select the file location you want to change to (Local Files or Remote Files) from the Always Show drop-down list or select the panel you want to change to (Right or Left) from the "on the" drop-down list. Be careful not to switch both options, or you end up where you started!

Dependent files

Web pages are seldom just single HTML files. Any graphic — whether it's in the background, part of your main logo, or used on a navigational button — is uploaded as a separate file. The same is true for any additional multimedia add-ons such as audio or video files. If you've enabled File Check In/Check Out when defining your site, Dreamweaver can also track these so-called dependent files.

Enabling the Prompt checkboxes causes Dreamweaver to ask you if you'd like to move the dependent files when you transfer an HTML file. You can opt to show the dialog box for Get/Check Out, Put/Check In, or both.

Tip

You're not stuck with your Dependent Files choice. If you turn off the Dependent Files prompt, you can make it appear by pressing the Alt (Option) key while clicking the Get or Put button.

FTP Connection: Disconnect After __ Minutes Idle

You can easily forget you're online when you are busy modifying a page. You can set Dreamweaver to automatically disconnect you from an FTP site after a specified interval. The default is 30 minutes; if you want to set a different interval, you can select the FTP Connection value in the Disconnect After text box. Dreamweaver then asks if you want to continue to wait or to disconnect when the time limit is reached, but you can maintain your FTP connection regardless by deselecting this option.

FTP Time Out

Client-server communication is prone to glitches. Rather than hanging up your machine while trying to reach a server that is down or slow, Dreamweaver alerts you to an apparent problem after a set period. You can determine the number of seconds you want Dreamweaver to wait by altering the FTP Time Out value. The default is 60 seconds.

Firewall information

Dreamweaver enables users to access remote FTP servers outside their network firewall. A firewall is a security component that protects the internal network from unauthorized outsiders, while enabling Internet access. To enable firewall access, enter the Firewall Host and External Port numbers in the appropriate text boxes; if you do not know these values, contact your network administrator.

If you're having trouble transferring files through the firewall via FTP, make sure the Use Firewall (in Preferences) option is enabled in the Site Definition dialog box. You can find the option on the Web Server Info panel.

Put options

In Dreamweaver 3, certain site operations, such as putting a file on the remote site, are now available in the Document window. It's not uncommon to make an edit to your page and then quickly choose the Site ⇨ Put command — without saving the file first. In this situation, Dreamweaver prompts you with a dialog box to save your changes. However, you can avoid the dialog box and automatically save the file by choosing the Save Files Before Putting option.

Preview in Browser preferences

Browser testing is an essential stage of Web page development. Previewing your Web page within the environment of a particular browser gives you a more exact representation of how it looks when viewed online. Because each browser renders the HTML slightly differently, you should preview your work in several browsers. Dreamweaver enables you to select both a primary and secondary browser, which can both be called by pressing a function key. You can name up to 18 additional browsers through the Preview in Browser panel shown in Figure 4-13. This list of preferences is also called when you choose File ➪ Preview in Browser ➪ Edit Browser List.

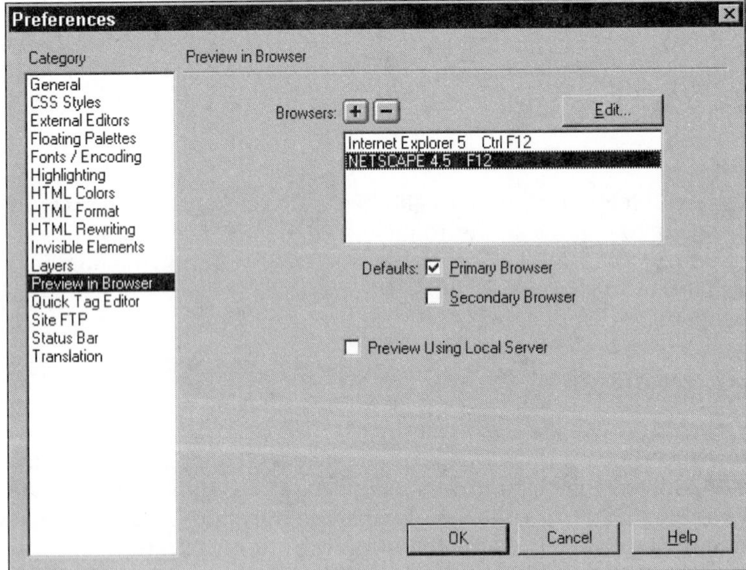

Figure 4-13: The Preview in Browser panel lists browsers currently available for preview and enables you modify the list.

If you are developing on Windows, your Web page is using site root relative paths for links, and you have a local server setup, enable the Preview Using Local Server option. This capability ensures that your previews link correctly. The other method to preview sites using site root relative paths places the files on a remote server.

Adding a browser to the preview list

To add a browser to your preview list, follow these steps:

1. Choose Edit ➪ Preferences or press the keyboard shortcut: Ctrl+U (Command+U).
2. Select the Preview in Browser category.

3. Select the Add (+) button.
4. In the Add Browser dialog box, type the browser name you want listed into the Name text box.
5. Enter the path to the browser file in the Path text box or click the Browse (Choose) button to pick the file from the Select Browser dialog box.
6. If you want to designate this browser as your Primary or Secondary browser, select one of those checkboxes in the Defaults section.
7. Click OK when you have finished.
8. You can continue to add browsers (up to a total of 20) by following Steps 3 through 7. Click OK when you have finished.

Once you've added a browser to your list, you can modify your selection by following these steps:

1. Open the Preview in Browser panel and highlight the browser you want to alter.
2. Select the Edit button to get the Edit Browser dialog box.
3. After you've made your modifications, click OK to close the dialog box.

You can quickly make a browser your Primary or Secondary previewing choice without going through the Edit screen. From the Preview in Browser panel, select the desired browser and check either Primary Browser or Secondary Browser. Note that if you already have a primary or secondary browser defined, this action overrides your previous choice.

You can also easily remove a browser from your preview list:

1. Open the Preview in Browser panel and choose the browser you want to delete from the list.
2. Select the Remove (–) button and click OK.

Customizing Your Code

For all its multimedia flash and visual interactivity, the Web is based on code. The more you code, the more particular about your code you are likely to become. Achieving a consistent look and feel to your code enhances its readability and, thus, your productivity. In Dreamweaver, you can even design the HTML code that underlies a Web page's structure.

Every time you open a new document, the default Web page already has several key elements in place, such as the language the page is to be rendered in. Dreamweaver also enables you to customize your work environment by selecting default fonts and even the colors of your HTML code.

Fonts/Encoding preferences

In the Fonts/Encoding panel, shown in Figure 4-14, you can control the basic language of the fonts as seen by a user's browser and the fonts that you see when programming. The Default Encoding section enables you to choose Western-style fonts for Web pages to be rendered in English, one of the Asian languages — Japanese, Traditional Chinese, Simplified Chinese, or Korean — or another language, such as Cyrillic, Greek, or Icelandic Mac.

Dreamweaver 3 has extended the number of encoding options to 10, as well as adding a generic Other category. Many of the encodings have platform-specific configurations, such as Icelandic Mac. Be sure to examine all the choices before you make a selection.

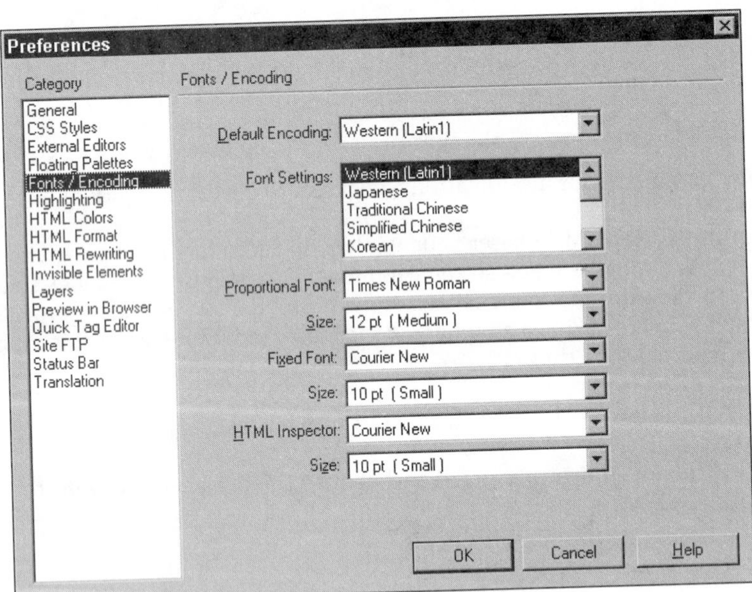

Figure 4-14: Use the Fonts/Encoding panel to set both the font encoding for each Web page and the fonts you use when programming.

In the bottom portion of the Fonts/Encoding panel, you can alter the default font and size for three different fonts:

- ✦ **Proportional Font:** This font option sets the default font used in Dreamweaver's Document window to depict paragraphs, headings, and lists.
- ✦ **Fixed Font:** In a fixed font, every character is allocated the same width. Dreamweaver uses your chosen fixed font to depict preformatted styled text.

✦ **HTML Inspector:** The HTML Inspector font is used by Dreamweaver's built-in text editor. You should probably use a monospaced font such as Courier or Monaco. A monospaced font makes it easy to count characters, which is often necessary when debugging your code.

For all three font options, select your font by clicking the list and highlighting your choice of font. Change the font size by selecting the value in the Size text box or by typing in a new number.

Don't be misled into thinking that by changing your Proportional Font preference to Arial or another font, all your Web pages are automatically viewed in that typeface. Changing these font preferences affects only the default fonts that you see when developing the Web page; the default font that the user sees is controlled by the user's browser. To ensure that a different font is used, you have to specify it for any selected text through the Text Properties Inspector.

HTML Rewriting preferences

The exception to Dreamweaver's policy of not altering imported code occurs when HTML is incorrectly structured. Dreamweaver automatically fixes tags that are nested in the wrong order or have additional, unnecessary closing tags — unless you tell Dreamweaver otherwise by setting up the HTML Rewriting preferences accordingly (see Figure 4-15).

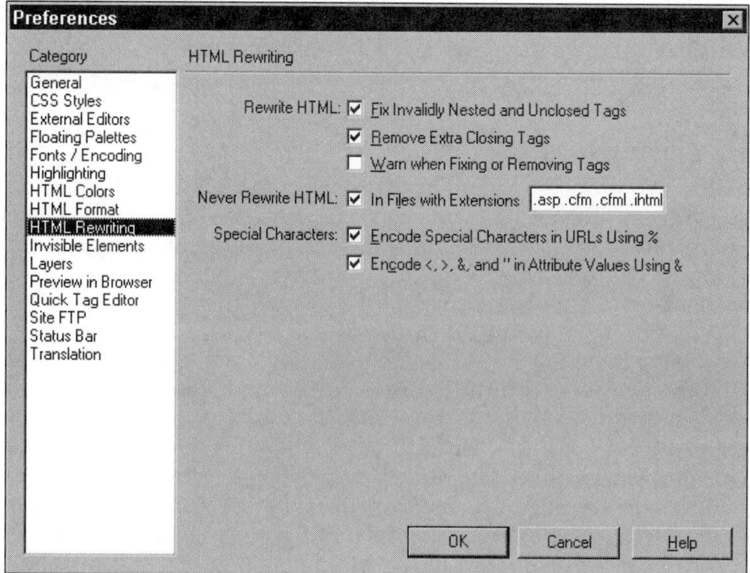

Figure 4-15: The HTML Rewriting panel can be used to protect nonstandard HTML from being automatically changed by Dreamweaver.

Dreamweaver 3 now accommodates many different types of markup languages, not just HTML, through the Never Rewrite HTML in Files with Extensions option. Moreover, you can prevent Dreamweaver from encoding special characters, such as spaces, tildes, and ampersands, in URLs or attribute values. Dreamweaver just got a whole lot more flexible.

Following are descriptions of the particular controls of the HTML Rewriting preferences.

Fix Invalidly Nested and Unclosed Tags

When enabled, this option repairs incorrectly placed HTML tags. For example, if a file contained the following line:

```
<h3><b>Welcome to the Monkey House!</h3></b>
```

Dreamweaver rewrites it as follows:

```
<h3><b>Welcome to the Monkey House!</b></h3>
```

Open that same file while the Fix option is turned off, and Dreamweaver highlights the misplaced code in the Document window. Double-clicking the code brings up a window with a brief explanation.

If a browser encounters nonstandard HTML, the code is probably ignored. Dreamweaver does not follow this protocol, however. Unless Dreamweaver is familiar with the type of code you are using, your code could be altered when the page is opened. If you are using specially formatted database tags or other non-standard HTML programming, be sure to open a test page first.

Remove Extra Closing Tags

When you're editing your code by hand, it's fairly easy to miss a closing tag. Dreamweaver cleans up such code if you enable the Remove Extra Closing Tags option. You may, for example, have the following line in a previously edited file:

```
<p>And now back to our show...</p></i>
```

Notice that the closing italic tag, `</i>`, has no matching opening partner. If you open this file in Dreamweaver with the Remove option enabled, Dreamweaver plucks out the offending `</i>`.

In some circumstances, you want to make sure your pages remain as originally formatted. If you edit pages in Dreamweaver that are preprocessed by a server unknown to Dreamweaver prior to the display of the pages, make sure to disable both the Fix Invalidly Nested and Unclosed Tags option where possible and the Remove Extra Closing Tags option.

Warn when Fixing or Removing Tags

If you're editing a lot of Web pages created on another system, you should enable the Warn when Fixing or Removing Tags option. If this setting is turned on, Dreamweaver displays a list of changes that have been made to your code in the HTML Corrections dialog box. As you can see from Figure 4-16, the changes can be quite extensive when Dreamweaver opens what it regards as a poorly formatted page.

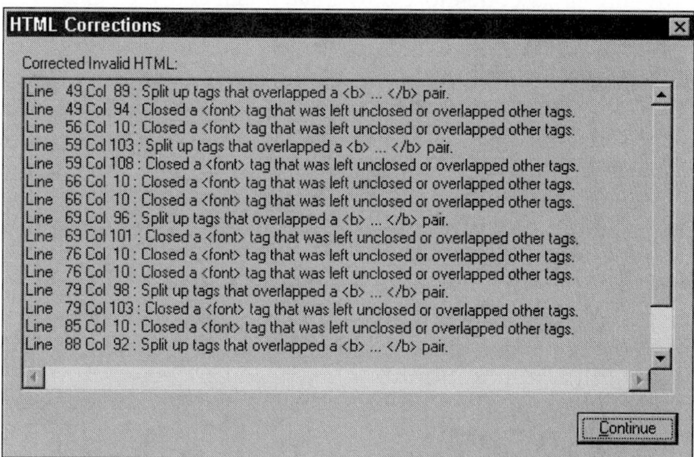

Figure 4-16: Dreamweaver can automatically catch and repair certain HTML errors. You can set Dreamweaver to send a report to the screen in the HTML Corrections dialog box.

Remember that once you've enabled these Rewrite HTML options, the fixes occur automatically. If this sequence happens to you by mistake, immediately close the file (without saving it!), disable the HTML Rewriting preferences options, and reopen the document.

Never Rewrite HTML preferences

Many of the database connectivity programs, such as Cold Fusion or Lasso, use proprietary tags embedded in a regular Web page to communicate with their servers. In previous versions, Dreamweaver often viewed these tags as invalid HTML and tried to correct them. Dreamweaver 3 enables you to explicitly protect file types, identified with a particular file extension.

To enter a new file type in the Never Rewrite HTML options, select the In Files with Extensions field. Enter the file extension of the file type, including the period, in the end of the list. Be sure to separate your extensions from the others in the list with a space on either side.

Special Character preferences

In addition to the rewriting of proprietary tags, many middleware vendors faced another problem when trying to integrate with Dreamweaver. By default, earlier versions of Dreamweaver encoded all URLs so that they could be understood by Unix servers. The encoding converted all special characters to their decimal equivalents, preceded by a percent sign. Spaces became `%20`, tildes (~) became `%7E`, and ampersands were converted to `&`. Although this is valid for Unix servers, and helps to make the Dreamweaver code more universal, it can cause problems for many other types of application servers.

Dreamweaver 3 gives you the option to disable the URL encoding, if necessary. Moreover, Dreamweaver 3 also enables you to turn off encoding that is applied to special characters in the attributes of tags. This latter problem was particularly vexing because, while you could rewrite the attributes in the HTML Source Inspector, if you selected the element in the Document window with the Property Inspector open, the attributes were encoded. Now, you can prevent that from happening with the selection of a single checkbox.

In general, however, it's best to leave both of the Special Characters encoding options enabled unless you find your third-party tags being rewritten destructively.

HTML Colors preferences

HTML code is a combination of the tags that structure the language and the text that provides the content. A Web page designer often has difficulty distinguishing swiftly between the two — and finding the right code to modify. Dreamweaver enables you to set color preferences for the code as it appears in the HTML Inspector. You can not only alter colors for the background, default tags, and text and general comments, but also specify certain tags to get certain colors.

To modify any of the basic elements (Background, Text, Comments, or Tag Default), select the color swatch next to the corresponding name, as illustrated in Figure 4-17. Select a color from any of the 216 displayed in the color picker or choose the small palette icon to select from the full range of colors available to your system. You can also use the Eyedropper tool to pick a color from the Document window.

To select a different color for a specific tag, first select the tag from the Tag Specific list box. Then choose either the Default option (which assigns the same color as specified for the Tag Default) or a custom color by clicking the color swatch and choosing the color. If you want to set all of the code and text enclosed by the selected tag to the same color, choose the Apply Color to Tag Contents option. This option is useful for setting off large blocks of code, such as the code included in the `<script>` section.

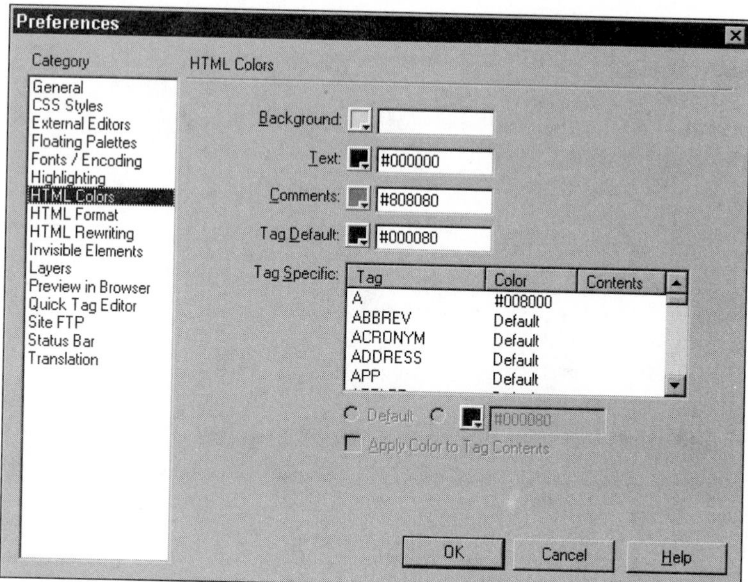

Figure 4-17: Use the HTML Colors panel to custom color–code the HTML Inspector.

HTML Format preferences

Dreamweaver includes two other tools for customizing your HTML. The first is an easy-to-use, point-and-click preferences panel called HTML Format. The second is a text file called the Source Format (SourceFormat.txt), which must be modified by hand and controls the output of every HTML tag. You can modify your HTML using either or both techniques. All of the options controlled by the HTML Format panel are written out to the text file.

Most of your HTML code parameters can be controlled through the HTML Format panel. The only reason to alter the SourceFormat.txt text file by hand is if you want to control the appearance of your HTML code at the tag level.

In the preferences panel, you can decide whether to use indentations — if so, whether to use spaces or tabs and how many of each — or to turn off indents for major elements such as tables and frames. You can also globally control the case of your HTML tags and their attributes. As you can see in Figure 4-18, the HTML Format panel is full featured.

To examine the available options in the HTML Format panel, let's separate them into four areas: indent control, line control, case control, and centering.

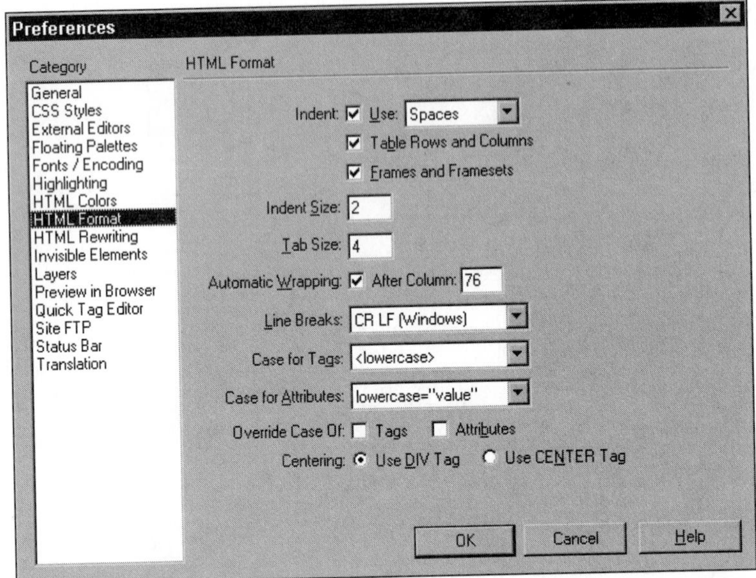

Figure 4-18: The HTML Format panel enables you to shape your HTML to your own specifications.

Indent control

Indenting your code generally makes it more readable. Dreamweaver defaults to indenting most HTML tags with two spaces, giving extra indentation grouping to tables and frames. All these parameters can be altered through the HTML Format panel of the Preferences dialog box.

The first indent option enables indenting, and you can switch from spaces to tabs. To permit indenting, make sure a checkmark is displayed in the Indent checkbox. Of the 52 separate HTML tags Dreamweaver identifies in its Source Format, 29 tags are designed to be indented. If you prefer your code to be displayed flush left, turn off the Indent option altogether.

To use tabs instead of the default spaces, click the Use arrow button and select tabs from the drop-down list. If you anticipate transferring your code to a word-processing program for formatting and printing, you should use tabs; otherwise, stay with the default spaces.

Dreamweaver formats both tables and frames as special indentation groups. Within each of these structural elements, the related tags are indented (or nested) more than the initial two spaces. As you can see in Listing 4-1, each table row (`<tr>`) is indented within the table tag, and the table data tags (`<td>`) are nested within the table row.

Listing 4-1: An indented code sample

```
<table border="1" width="75%">
 <tr>
 <td>Row 1, Column 1</td>
 <td>Row 1, Column 2</td>
 <td>Row 1, Column 3</td>
 </tr>
 <tr>
 <td>Row 2, Column 1</td>
 <td>Row 2, Column 2 </td>
 <td>Row 2, Column 3</td>
 </tr>
</table>
```

If you want to disable the special indentation grouping for tables, deselect Table Rows and Columns in the HTML Format panel. Turn off frame indenting by unchecking Frames and Framesets (this option is selected by default).

The other two items in the indent control section of HTML Format preferences are Indent Size and Tab Size. Change the value in Indent Size to establish the size of indents using spaces. To alter the size of tab indents, change the Tab Size value.

Line control

The browser is responsible for ultimately formatting an HTML page for viewing. This formatting includes wrapping text according to each user's screen size and the placement of the paragraph tags (`<p>...</p>`). Therefore, you control how your code wraps in your HTML editor. You can turn off the automatic wrapping feature or set it for a particular column through the line control options of the HTML Format panel.

To turn off the automatic word-wrapping capability, deselect AutoWrap. When you are trying to debug your code and looking for specific line numbers and character positions, enable this option. You can also set the specific column for the word wrap to take effect. Be sure AutoWrap is enabled and then type your new value in the After Column text box.

If you're using the HTML Inspector, selecting its Wrap option overrides the Automatic Wrapping setting in HTML Format.

The Line Breaks setting determines which line break character is appended to each line of the page. Each of the major operating systems employs a different ending character: Macintosh uses a carriage return (CR), Unix uses a line feed (LF), and Windows uses both (CR LF). If you know the operating system for your remote server, choosing the corresponding line break character helps the file to appear correctly when viewed online. Click the arrow button next to Line Breaks and select your system.

The operating system for your local development machine may be different from the operating system of your remote server. If so, using the Line Breaks option may cause your HTML to appear incorrectly when viewed through a simple text editor (such as Notepad or vi). The Dreamweaver HTML Inspector, however, does render the code correctly.

Case control

Whether an HTML tag or attribute is in uppercase or lowercase doesn't matter to most browsers—the command is rendered regardless of case. Case is only a personal preference among Web designers. That said, some Webmasters consider case a serious preference and insist on their codes being all uppercase, all lowercase, or a combination of uppercase and lowercase. Dreamweaver gives you control over the tags and attributes it creates, as well as over case conversion for files that Dreamweaver imports.

The Dreamweaver default for both tags and attributes is lowercase. Click the arrow button next to Case for Tags and/or Case for Attributes to alter the selection. After you have selected OK from the HTML Format panel, Dreamweaver changes all the tags in any currently open file. Choose File ➪ Save to write the changes to disk.

Lowercase tags and attributes are also less fattening, according to the W3C. Files with lowercase tag names and attributes compress better and thus transmit faster.

You can also use Dreamweaver to standardize the letter case in tags of previously saved files. To alter imported files, select the Override Case Of Tags and/or the Override Case Of Attributes options. When enabled, these options enforce your choices made in the Case for Tags and Case for Attributes option boxes in any file Dreamweaver loads. Again, be sure to save your file to keep the changes.

Centering

When an object—whether it's an image or text—is centered on a page, HTML tags are placed around the object (or objects) to indicate the alignment. Since the release of HTML 3.2, the `<center>` tag has been deprecated by the W3C in favor of using a `<div>` tag with an align="center" attribute. By default, Dreamweaver uses the officially preferred method of `<div align="center">`.

Many Web designers are partial to the older `<center>` tag and prefer to use it to align their objects. Dreamweaver 3 now offers a choice with the Centering option in the HTML Format panel. To use the new method, select the Use DIV Tag option (the default). To switch to the older `<center>` method, select the Use CENTER Tag option. Although use of `<center>` has been officially discouraged, it is so widespread that all browsers continue to support it.

Understanding the Source Format

As noted earlier, Dreamweaver pulls its code configuration guidelines from a text file named SourceFormat.txt. When Dreamweaver is installed, this file is put in the Dreamweaver\Configuration folder. When you make a modification to the HTML Format panel, the initial profile is renamed as SourceFormat.backup and then Dreamweaver writes a new SourceFormat.txt.

You can restore the default Source Profile settings at any time. When Dreamweaver is closed, delete SourceFormat.txt and then make a copy of the SourceFormat.original file. Finally, rename the copy as SourceFormat.txt.

Dreamweaver uses a specialized HTML format to create a SourceFormat.txt that can be viewed and edited in any text editor. Three main sections exist, each denoted with a `<?keyword>` format: `<?options>`, `<?elements>`, and `<?attributes>`. Prior to each section, Dreamweaver uses the HTML comment tags to describe them. The file closes with the `<?end>` keyword.

The Source Format (see Listing 4-2) starts with two HTML comments. The first describes the overall document (`Dreamweaver source formatting profile`), followed by the Options section.

Listing 4-2: The Source Format

```
<!-- Dreamweaver source formatting profile -->

<!-- options

    INDENTION     : indention options
        ENABLE     - allows indention
        INDENT     - columns per indention
        TABS       - columns per tab character
        USE        - TABS or SPACES for indention
        ACTIVE     - active indention groups (IGROUP)

    LINES         : end-of-line options
        AUTOWRAP    - enable automatic line wrapping
        BREAK       - CRLF, CR, LF
        COLUMN      - auto wrap lines after column

    OMIT         : element omission options
        OPTIONS     - options

    ELEMENT        : element options
        CASE       - "UPPER" or "lower" case
        ALWAYS     - always use preferred element case (instead of original case)
```

Continued

Listing 4-2 *(continued)*

```
   ATTRIBUTE    : attribute options
       CASE      - "UPPER" or "lower" case
       ALWAYS    - always use preferred attribute case (instead of original
case)

-->
<?options>
<indention enable indent="2" tabs="4" use="spaces" active="1,2">
<lines autowrap column="76" break="CRLF">
<omit options="0">
<element case="lower">
<attribute case="lower">
<colors text="0x00000000" tag="0x00000000" unknowntag="0x00000000" ¬
comment="0x00000000" invalid="0x00000000" object="0x00000000">

<!-- element information
    line breaks              : BREAK = "before, inside start, ¬
inside end, after"
    indent contents          : INDENT
    indent group             : IGROUP = "indention group number" (1 through 8)
    specific name case       : NAMECASE = "CustomName"
    prevent formatting       : NOFORMAT
-->
<?elements>
<address break="1,0,0,1">
<applet break="0,1,1,0" indent>
<base break="1,0,0,1">
<blockquote break="1,0,0,1" indent>
<body break="1,1,1,1">
<br break="0,0,0,1">
<caption break="1,0,0,1">
<center break="1,1,1,1" indent>
<cfabort break="1,0,0,1">
<cfapplication break="1,0,0,1">
<cfbreak break="1,0,0,1">
<cfcol break="1,0,0,1">
<cfcontent break="1,0,0,1">
<cfcookie break="1,0,0,1">
<cferror break="1,0,0,1">
<cffile break="1,0,0,1">
<cfform break="1,1,1,1" indent>
<cfgrid break="0,1,1,1" indent>
<cfgridcolumn break="1,0,0,1">
<cfgridrow break="1,0,0,1">
<cfheader break="1,0,0,1">
<cfhtmlhead break="1,0,0,1">
<cfhttp break="1,1,1,1" indent>
<cfhttpparam break="1,0,0,1">
<cfif break="1,1,1,1" indent>
<cfelse break="1,0,0,1" indent>
<cfelseif break="1,1,1,1">
```

```
<cfinclude break="1,0,0,1">
<cfindex break="1,0,0,1">
<cfinput break="1,0,0,1">
<cfinsert break="1,0,0,1">
<cfldap break="1,0,0,1">
<cflocation break="1,0,0,1">
<cfloop break="1,1,1,1" indent noformat>
<cfmail break="1,1,1,1" indent>
<cfmodule break="1,0,0,1">
<cfobject break="1,0,0,1">
<cfoutput noformat>
<cfparam break="1,0,0,1">
<cfpop break="1,0,0,1">
<cfquery break="1,1,1,1" indent noformat>
<cfreport break="1,1,1,1" indent>
<cfsearch break="1,0,0,1">
<cfselect break="1,1,1,1" indent>
<cfset break="1,0,0,1">
<cfslider break="1,0,0,1">
<cftable break="1,1,1,1" indent>
<cftextinput break="1,0,0,1">
<cftransaction break="1,1,1,1" indent>
<cftree break="1,1,1,1" indent>
<cftreeitem break="1,0,0,1">
<cfupdate break="1,0,0,1">
<dd break="1,0,0,1" indent>
<dir break="1,0,0,1" indent>
<div break="1,0,0,1" indent>
<dl break="1,0,0,1" indent>
<dt break="1,0,0,1" indent>
<embed break="0,1,1,0" indent>
<form break="1,1,1,1" indent>
<frame break="1,0,0,1">
<frameset break="1,0,0,1" indent igroup="2">
<h1 break="1,0,0,1" indent>
<h2 break="1,0,0,1" indent>
<h3 break="1,0,0,1" indent>
<h4 break="1,0,0,1" indent>
<h5 break="1,0,0,1" indent>
<h6 break="1,0,0,1" indent>
<head break="1,1,1,1">
<hr break="1,0,0,1">
<html break="1,1,1,1">
<ilayer break="1,0,0,1">
<input break="1,0,0,1">
<isindex break="1,0,0,1">
<layer break="1,0,0,1">
<li break="1,0,0,1" indent>
<link break="1,0,0,1">
<map indent>
<menu break="1,0,0,1" indent>
<meta break="1,0,0,1">
```

Continued

Listing 4-2 *(continued)*

```
<object break="0,1,1,0" indent>
<ol break="1,1,1,1" indent>
<option break="1,0,0,1">
<p break="1,0,0,1" indent>
<param break="1,0,0,1">
<pre break="1,0,0,1" noformat>
<script break="1,0,0,1" noformat>
<select break="1,1,1,1" indent>
<server break="1,0,0,1" noformat>
<style break="1,0,0,1" noformat>
<table break="1,1,1,1" indent igroup="1">
<td break="1,0,0,1" indent igroup="1">
<textarea break="1,0,0,1" noformat>
<th break="1,0,0,1" indent igroup="1">
<title break="1,0,0,1">
<tr break="1,0,0,1" indent igroup="1">
<ul break="1,1,1,1" indent>

<!-- attribute information
    specific name case        : NAMECASE = "CustomName"
    values follow attr case   : SAMECASE
-->
<?attributes>
<onAbort namecase="onAbort">
<onBlur namecase="onBlur">
<onChange namecase="onChange">
<onClick namecase="onClick">
<onDragDrop namecase="onDragDrop">
<onError namecase="onError">
<onFocus namecase="onFocus">
<onKeyDown namecase="onKeyDown">
<onKeyPress namecase="onKeyPress">
<onKeyUp namecase="onKeyUp">
<onLoad namecase="onLoad">
<onMouseDown namecase="onMouseDown">
<onMouseMove namecase="onMouseMove">
<onMouseOut namecase="onMouseOut">
<onMouseOver namecase="onMouseOver">
<onMouseUp namecase="onMouseUp">
<onMove namecase="onMove">
<onReset namecase="onReset">
<onResize namecase="onResize">
<onSelect namecase="onSelect">
<onSubmit namecase="onSubmit">
<onUnload namecase="onUnload">
<onDblClick namecase="onDblClick">
<onAfterUpdate namecase="onAfterUpdate">
<onBeforeUpdate namecase="onBeforeUpdate">
```

```
<onHelp namecase="onHelp">
<onReadyStateChange namecase="onReadyStateChange">
<onScroll namecase="onScroll">
<onRowEnter namecase="onRowEnter">
<onRowExit namecase="onRowExit">
<align samecase>
<checked samecase>
<codetype samecase>
<compact samecase>
<ismap samecase>
<frame samecase>
<method samecase>
<multiple samecase>
<noresize samecase>
<noshade samecase>
<nowrap samecase>
<selected samecase>
<shape samecase>
<type samecase>
<valign samecase>
<visibility samecase>
<?end>
```

Options

The Options section parallels the options set in the HTML Format panel. Either you can use Dreamweaver's point-and-click interface by choosing Edit ➪ Preferences and then selecting the HTML Format category; or you can edit the <?options> section of the SourceFormat.txt file. In the Options description, five parameters are outlined: indention, lines, omit, element, and attribute.

The indention item denotes the indent options:

```
ENABLE - allows indention
INDENT - columns per indention
TABS - columns per tab character
USE - TABS or SPACES for indention
ACTIVE - active indention groups (IGROUP)
```

The final indention option, ACTIVE, relates to the special grouping function that Dreamweaver calls IGROUPS. By default, Dreamweaver assigns `IGROUP #1` to Table Rows and Columns and `IGROUP #2` to Frames and Framesets.

The line options are detailed as follows:

```
AUTOWRAP - enable automatic line wrapping
BREAK - CRLF, CR, LF
COLUMN - auto wrap lines after column
```

As mentioned earlier, the BREAK options are used to insert the type of line break character recognized by your Web server's operating system. Use CRLF for Windows, CR for Macintosh, and LF for Unix.

The next Options section, OMIT, is reserved by Dreamweaver for further expansion and is not currently used.

The Element and Attribute sections control the case of HTML elements (or tags) and attributes:

```
CASE - "UPPER" or "lower" case
ALWAYS - always use preferred element case (instead of original case)
```

If the ALWAYS keyword is used, Dreamweaver alters the case of tags and/or attributes when you import a previously saved file.

The following section of the Source Format that starts with <?options> contains the actual options read by Dreamweaver at startup. This listing shows the default options from the default SourceFormat.txt file for Dreamweaver 3:

```
<?options>
<indention enable indent="2" tabs="8" use="spaces" active="1,2">
<lines autowrap column="76">
<omit options="0">
<element case="lower">
<attribute case="lower">
```

Elements

The Element information in the next section of the Source Format describes the syntax and options for individually controlling each HTML tag.

```
line breaks : BREAK = "before, inside start, inside end, after"
indent contents : INDENT
indent group : IGROUP = "indention group number" (1 through 8)
specific name case : NAMECASE = "CustomName"
prevent formatting : NOFORMAT
```

break

The syntax for break refers to the number of line breaks surrounding the opening and closing HTML tags. For example, the default syntax for the <h1> tag follows:

```
<h1 break="1,0,0,1" indent>
```

The preceding produces code that looks like the following:

```
<h1>Welcome!</h1>
```

If you want to display the opening and closing tags on their own lines, you could change the `break` value as follows:

```
<h1 break="1,1,1,1" indent>
```

The preceding gives you the following result:

```
<h1>
 Welcome!
</h1>
```

Use zero in the "before" and "after" positions when you want a tag to appear in line with the other code, as in this map tag:

```
<map break="0,1,1,0" indent>
```

The Elements list only contains tags that have opening and closing elements, which are also known as *container tags*. Any single-element tags, such as the image tag, `<img>`, are presented in line with other elements.

Note

For all of the Source Format's comprehensiveness, one type of tag is unavailable: comment tags. While you can't adjust their spacing, you can alter the color of comments through Preferences, in the HTML Colors category.

You're not restricted to using 1 and 0 values for `break`. If you want to isolate a tag so that it really stands out, use 2 in the "before" and "after" positions. For example:

```
<p break="2,1,1,2" indent>
```

The preceding produces completely separated paragraphs such as the following:

```
<p>
Synapse Advertising is your first choice for the best in subliminal advertising.
</p>

<p>
Call Synapse when you want your clients to come a-knockin' at your door -- ¬
and have no idea why!
</p>
```

indent

The indent keyword ensures that the text contained between the opening and closing tags wraps to the same text column as the tag, rather than appearing flush left. The difference is apparent when you compare almost any text format tag, from paragraph `<p>`, to any heading `<h1>` through `<h6>` tag, to the preformatted tag `<pre>`.

```
<p>Four score and seven years ago our fathers brought forth ¬
on this continent, a new nation, conceived in liberty, and ¬
dedicated to the proposition that all men are created ¬
equal.</p>
```

```
<pre>The above speech was offered by President Abraham Lincoln and is known as ¬
the Gettysburg Address. Now recognized by many as the leading speech of the ¬
Lincoln presidency, the Gettysburg Address was initially received to mixed ¬
reviews...</pre>
```

igroup

The igroup keyword is used only when applied to special indentation groups such as tables and frames. For example, all the elements contained in a table have `igroup="1"` as part of their source profile, as shown in the following:

```
<table break="1,1,1,1" indent igroup="1">
<td break="1,0,0,1" indent igroup="1">
<th break="1,0,0,1" indent igroup="1">
<tr break="1,0,0,1" indent igroup="1">
```

The igroup attribute in the indention option activates the indentation set for all the tags in that group. For example, if the `indention` option read as follows:

```
<indention enable indent="2" tabs="8" use="spaces" active="2">
```

then indenting would be turned off for igroup number 1, tables.

The active igroup causes each element to use the indentation level of the outermost group member as its left margin—and indent from there. Thus, with the indented `<table>...</table>` pair as the outer igroup member, the `<tr>...</tr>` pair is indented two more spaces and the `<td>...</td>` pair is indented another two spaces, so it looks like the following:

```
<table border="2" width="50%">
 <tr>
 <td>Symbol</td>
 <td>Element</td>
 </tr>
 <tr>
 <td>H</td>
 <td>Hydrogen</td>
 </tr>
</table>
```

You can currently define up to six igroups, in addition to the preset tables and frames.

namecase

You can override the general case conventions for any element with the namecase keyword. If you want to use a title case or mixed case for certain tags, you define them in the following way:

```
<applet break="0,1,1,0" indent namecase="Applet">
<blockquote break="1,0,0,1" indent namecase="BlockQuote">
```

You may also use the namecase keyword when defining a custom tag for use in conjunction with a new object. Let's say you've created a series of objects for use with Cold Fusion and you want them to stand out in the code. To accentuate your new tag pair, <cfif>...</cfif>, you could add the following line to your Source Format:

```
<cfif break="1,1,1,1" indent namecase="CFIf">
```

This line ensures that a Cold Fusion "if" tag is always inserted in the specified mixed case.

noformat

As the name implies, the noformat keyword presents the tag-surrounded text without any additional formatting. This keyword is primarily used when the tag is used to reproduce verbatim information, such as when using the preformatted tag <pre>. The noformat keyword is also used when the element requires attributes and values in a specific format, such as with <style> or <script>.

Attributes

The Attributes section has only two options: namecase, which works as previously described in the "Elements" section, and samecase. The namecase option is used to maintain a consistent mixed case approach to JavaScript events, such as onKeyDown. The samecase option ensures that an attribute and its value use the same case as its tag. If the <input> tag is uppercase, then the named attribute and the value are uppercase.

Never use the samecase option with any attribute that requires a case-sensitive value. The most common instance of this situation is an attribute such as src that takes a file name as its value—which, in most cases, is case sensitive.

Case is generally determined for all attributes by the following line found in the Objects section:

```
<attribute case="lower">
```

As with elements, you can alter the case of attributes individually by specifying them in this section. For example, if you always want the source attribute of the image tag to be uppercase, you can include the following line in the Attributes section:

```
<src namecase="SRC">
```

The preceding produces code such as the following:

```
<img SRC="logo.gif>
```

This capability is handy when you are scanning your code and quickly want to find all the source files.

Modifying the Source Format

Because you have to restart Dreamweaver in order for any Source Format modifications to take effect, you should edit the file with Dreamweaver closed. You can use any editor capable of saving an ASCII or regular text file. If you want to preserve the previous profile, you can use the Save As feature of your editor to save the file under a different name, such as SourceFormat.backup, prior to making any changes. Then, after you complete your alterations, use Save As again and name it SourceFormat.txt.

Make your changes only to those sections marked with the `<?keyword>`, such as `<?options>` or `<?elements>`. Remember that Dreamweaver is not case sensitive when it comes to changing commands — other than with the namecase keyword — so you can write lines such as the following:

```
<element case="LOWER">
```

In the preceding, all your tags are still created, as specified, in lowercase.

Dreamweaver is fairly protective of its Source Format. If you accidentally misspell a keyword (for example, "ident" instead of "indent"), Dreamweaver ignores and then deletes the misspelled keyword. Likewise, misplaced keywords — for instance, using the enable keyword when defining an element instead of an option — are removed from the file when Dreamweaver loads.

One of the Dreamweaver 3 commands enables you to apply the Source Format to an existing page — typically one created outside of Dreamweaver. To use this capability, you first make changes to the Source Format and save it. Then restart Dreamweaver and open the page you want to affect. Finally, choose Command ⇨ Apply Source Formatting. Whatever modifications you made to the Source Format are written to the existing code.

The Source Format is an HTML tinker's paradise. You can shape your code as precisely as necessary, and Dreamweaver outputs it for you. Feel free to experiment and try different code arrangements. Just be sure to have a copy of the original Source Format available as a reference.

Summary

Creating Web pages, like any design job, is easier when the tools fit your hands. Through Preferences and the Source Format, you can make Dreamweaver work the way you work.

- ✦ Dreamweaver enables you to customize your Web page design and HTML coding environment through a series of easy-to-use, point-and-click panels.
- ✦ You can decide how best to use cutting-edge features, such as layers and style sheets, depending on the degree of cross-browser and backward compatibility you need.
- ✦ Dreamweaver gives you plenty of elbow room for previewing and testing by providing for 20 selections on your browser list.
- ✦ The Source Format can be modified. You can make alterations, from across-the-board case changes to tag-by-tag presentation, to define the way Dreamweaver writes your HTML code.

In the next chapter, you learn how to get online and offline help from Dreamweaver.

✦ ✦ ✦

Using the Help System

♦ ♦ ♦ ♦

In This Chapter

Browsing for help

Step-by-step techniques

Learning with the Tutorial

Online assistance

♦ ♦ ♦ ♦

Dreamweaver includes a multifaceted Help system that you can rely on in any number of situations:

- To provide quick context-sensitive answers to questions about how to use specific Dreamweaver features
- To learn the program using step-by-step instructions presented in a tutorial format
- To explain various concepts and capabilities through the hyperlinked Help pages and their embedded Show Me movies
- To seek specific programming assistance from the peer-to-peer network of the online newsgroups or the Dreamweaver technical support team at Macromedia

Navigating the Help Screen

To assist your understanding of Dreamweaver — in both the short term and the long term — Macromedia includes a full electronic manual with the program.

- Choose Help ⇨ Using Dreamweaver or press the keyboard shortcut F1 to open the Dreamweaver HTML Help pages.

If you have defined a primary browser in Dreamweaver through the Preferences, or with File ⇨ Preview in Browser ⇨ Edit Browser List, that browser opens and the Help pages are loaded. Otherwise, Dreamweaver uses your system's default browser to display the Help pages.

The Dreamweaver Help pages are presented within an HTML frameset as shown in Figure 5-1. At the top of the frame, you find the main control buttons for switching between the Help Contents, Index, and Search modes as well as two navigational buttons that are used to move from topic to topic. The frame on the far left changes according to the current mode (Contents, Index, or Search). The main portion of the frame is reserved for showing the Help pages themselves.

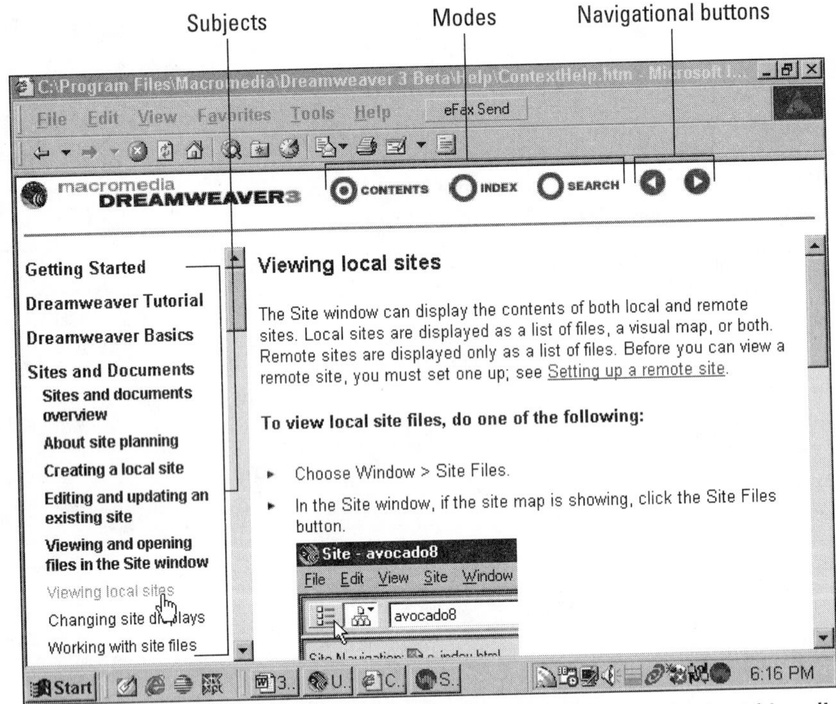

Figure 5-1: The Dreamweaver Help pages comprise a hyperlinked, multimedia manual that is displayed in your primary or default browser.

Dreamweaver 3 adds a whole new level of online help documentation for the advanced user: Extending Dreamweaver. The Extending Dreamweaver Help pages are the online edition of the new manual that comes with Dreamweaver 3, and they explain how to customize the various aspects of the program. The Extending Dreamweaver Help pages are available from the Help menu or by selecting Shift+F1.

Browsing the Help Contents

To get the most benefit from the Help pages, maximize your browser window. You can alternate between the Contents and Index by selecting one or the other control button. When you choose Contents, the frame on the left side provides a list of main Dreamweaver subjects and a handy scroll bar for moving through the list.

Selecting any main topic — displayed in bold — in the Help Contents reveals another list of subtopics. You can collapse the main topic by selecting it again or by choosing another main topic. Note that you must click a subtopic to load the information into the main viewing frame. If there is too much information to be displayed on a single screen, another scroll bar appears on the far-right side of the frame. To see the additional text, you can drag the scroll bar or select the frame and use your PgUp and PgDn keys.

Dreamweaver takes advantage of your browser's HTML capabilities, and many Help pages contain hyperlinks to other Help screens. If you follow a hyperlink to a new section from the main screen, the Contents updates to reflect your new position.

Using the navigational controls

As you browse through the Help pages, you find you can use your browser's Back and Forward buttons to revisit pages you have already viewed. You can also use the Help pages' own navigational system to move back and forth or from topic to topic.

The Next and Previous buttons, shown in Figure 5-2, are tied to the Help pages' content structure and only display current subtopics within each major subject. As you would expect, selecting the Next button displays the next topic or subtopic, and Previous displays the prior ones.

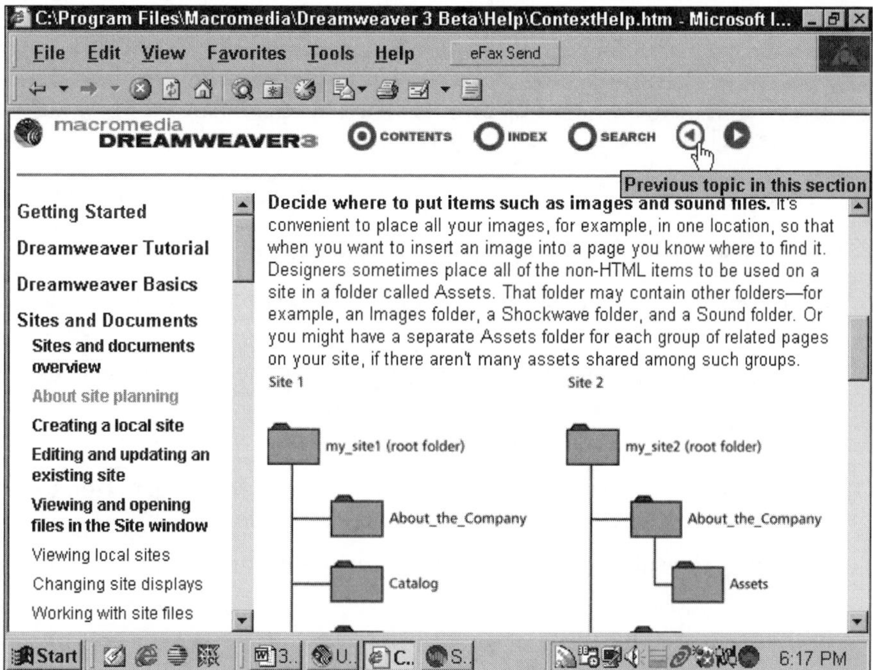

Figure 5-2: Move from topic to topic with the Next and Previous buttons.

If you reach the last subtopic and attempt to use the Next button, you get a JavaScript alert saying you are at the end of a section. A similar event occurs when you are looking at the first subtopic and try to view the Previous one. To go to another major subject, you have to select it from the Contents listing and then select one of the subtopics.

Playing the Show Me movies

Dreamweaver incorporates a number of multimedia feature demonstrations called Show Me movies. Each Show Me movie is a separate Shockwave animation that graphically illustrates the workings of the interface or one of the more advanced Dreamweaver capabilities.

To run the Show Me movies, you must have the Shockwave (for Director) plug-in for your browser installed. If you installed Dreamweaver through its CD-ROM, the appropriate plug-in was included in the installation. If you downloaded Dreamweaver from Macromedia or another Web site (or if you are using the trial version that comes with this book), you can get the plug-in by visiting `www.macromedia.com/shockwave/download`.

The Guided Tour of Dreamweaver, accessible by choosing Help ⇨ Guided Tour or by selecting the Guided Tour topic in the Help pages, contains a Show Me movie that lists all the available animations. You start the tour by clicking the first topic, Workspace Overview. This loads the first movie, an introduction to the Dreamweaver workspace. After you've viewed the movie, select continue to view the next topic or the Home button to return to the Guided Tour screen and choose your next topic.

Be sure the sound is turned up on your system when running the Show Me movies. All the movies punctuate their actions with sound.

A few simple controls are available for viewing any of the Show Me movies:

1. When you are ready to view the movie, select the title from the menu.
2. At the end of each screen's presentation, the Next button begins to flash. Click the Next button to proceed.

   You can also skip to the next screen by selecting the Next button at any time, as shown in Figure 5-3.
3. To review a previous step, select the Back button.
4. When you have finished viewing the movie, select the Home button to return to the Guided Tour or choose any other topic.
5. To replay the entire movie, select the Rewind button that appears on the final screen.

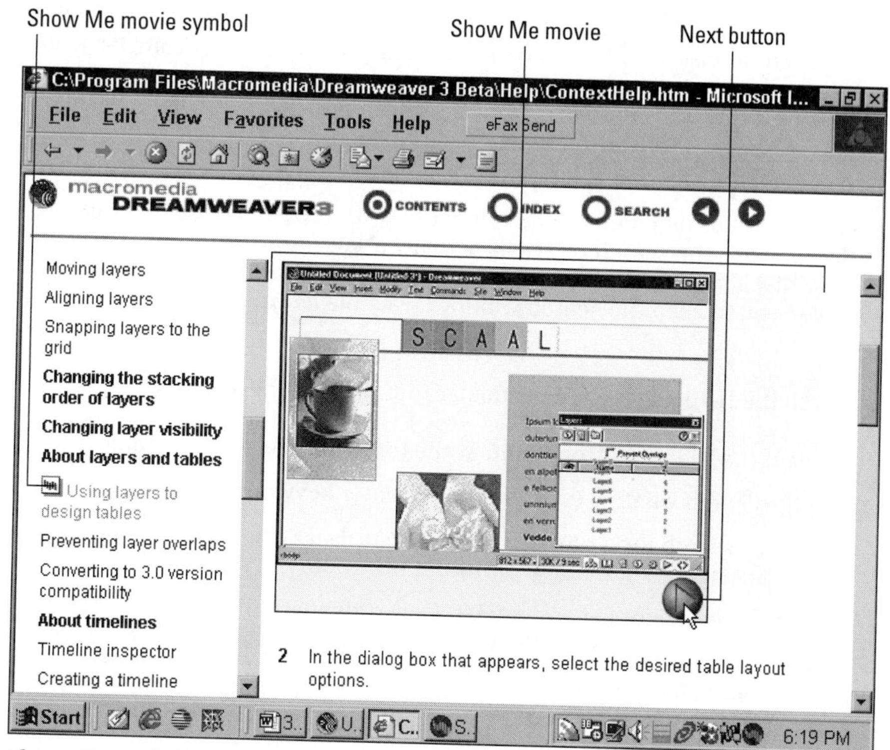

Figure 5-3: All the Show Me movies, such as this one about working with layers, provide excellent introductions to the subjects.

The Show Me movies offer limited controls: forward, back, and rewind. However, with the Shockwave Remote, you can also pause, fast forward, and control the volume of any movie. The Shockwave Remote is available from Macromedia's spin-off company, Shockwave.com, or by going to `www.macromedia.com/shockwave/download`.

Using the Help Index

Selecting the Index control button loads an alphabetical listing of topics covered in the Dreamweaver Help pages. To find the subject you need, scroll down the list by dragging the scroll bar at the near right. You can also click anywhere in the frame and use your system's PgUp and PgDn keys to navigate through the Index.

When you find your subject, select it from the list. The corresponding Help page appears in the main frame. Note that when an index listing is divided into a topic and related subtopics, you must choose one of the subtopics to get the related Help page. In this case, the topics themselves are not linked to any specific Help page.

The A–Z index is quite extensive and can take several moments to completely load. Be sure to wait until the browser indicates that the frame is completely loaded before scrolling all the way down.

Searching the help files

Dreamweaver has included a search function with the Help pages. As designed by Macromedia, the search engine is actually a Java applet that runs within your browser displaying the Help pages. One major advantage to this approach is that it enables you to keep the search window available as you look for the material you need.

To search the Help pages for a particular topic, follow these steps:

1. Select the Search button found at the top of the Help Pages frame.
2. In the Search window (see Figure 5-4), enter keywords in the upper text box.
   - To search for a phrase, enter the words as you would normally, for example, "shockwave" (without the quotes).
   - To search for several related keywords that do not have to appear next to each other, enter the words with a plus sign between them, like this:

     templates + regions
   - By default the search is not case sensitive. To turn on this feature, select the Case sensitive checkbox.
3. After you've entered your search criteria, select the List Topics button.

   As each page is searched, pages matching your search criteria are displayed in the results window.
4. To see an individual page, double-click its title in the results window. You can also select the title of the page and click the Display button.

   The page linked to the title is displayed in the main frame of the Help pages.
5. Repeat Steps 2 through 4 to continue searching.
6. Click the Cancel button to close the Search window.

To return to either the Contents or the Index listing, select the Contents or Index command buttons, respectively.

Stepping through the Tutorial

The Dreamweaver Help pages include a step-by-step tutorial that demonstrates how to use the latest Dynamic HTML features to create a Web page. To access the tutorial, choose Help ➪ Tutorial or, from the Help pages, select the Dreamweaver Tutorial topic.

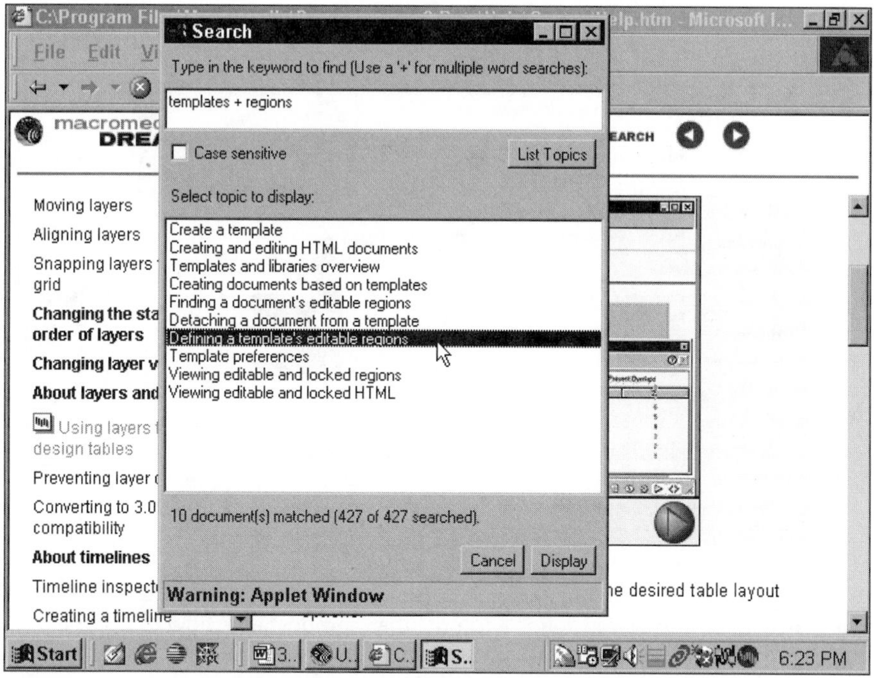

Figure 5-4: Quickly find the topics you're looking for with the Help pages search engine.

The Dreamweaver 3 Tutorial takes the form of a complete sample Web site for a fictitious company, Scaal Coffee. In the process of building its Web pages, you get to try your hand at defining a local site, editing existing pages, working with templates, formatting complex page layouts, attaching behaviors, and even creating a jump menu. (A jump menu is a drop-down list that "jumps" to a new page when you make a choice from the list.)

To see the sample Web site, choose File ➪ Open and browse to the Dreamweaver 3\Tutorial\Scaal_site. Then select the scaal_home.html file to open it. The example home page, shown in Figure 5-5, should be previewed in a 4 or above browser to understand how the various pages link together.

Note The tutorial folder holds both completed and semicompleted pages. The completed pages are included to give you an idea of how the site should ultimately look. The semicompleted files enable you to work on specific techniques during the tutorial without having to build every page from the ground up each time. For easy identification, the file names for the pages-in-progress begin with the prefix "DW3," for example, DW3_scaal_home.html.

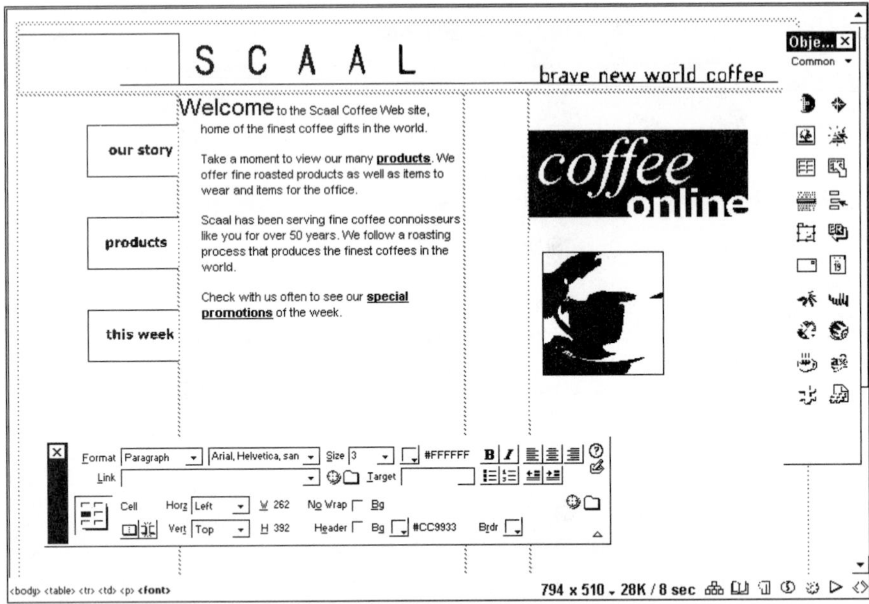

Figure 5-5: Dreamweaver includes a tutorial that demonstrates how to use the program to build an advanced Web page, step by step.

Getting Help Online

Without a doubt, one of the factors that has helped the Web to grow so rapidly is the fact that it is largely self-documenting. Want to learn more about developing Web pages? Find out on the Web! The same holds true for Dreamweaver. An extensive array of information about Dreamweaver is available online — and more coming every day.

Macromedia has done — and continues to do — an excellent job of supporting Dreamweaver on the Web. To that end, Macromedia has developed and continues to sponsor three Web sites: the Dreamweaver Support Center, the Online Resource Center, and the Dynamic HTML Zone. The Dreamweaver Support Center is a part of the general Macromedia site and focuses exclusively on providing support for Dreamweaver. Let's take a look at this one first.

Note As with many popular Web sites, the Macromedia sites are constantly in a state of revision. The following information was current when written, but some of the content or structure may have changed by the time you read it. If all else fails, you should always be able to find assistance by starting at `www.macromedia.com` and looking for the Dreamweaver support area.

Dreamweaver support site

Macromedia's primary help center on the Web for Dreamweaver is a terrific resource. Visit the Dreamweaver Support Center at `www.macromedia.com/support/dreamweaver/contents.html` to find the latest technical data, free downloads, and peer-to-peer connections — and it's all specific to Dreamweaver, naturally. One of the most impressive aspects of the site is its multilevel approach; there's material here for everyone, from rank beginner to the savviest code jockey.

When you visit the Dreamweaver Support Center, you find various areas of help as well as a search facility. Macromedia generally updates the site, shown in Figure 5-6, on a monthly or better basis. It's definitely worth bookmarking in your browser and visiting often.

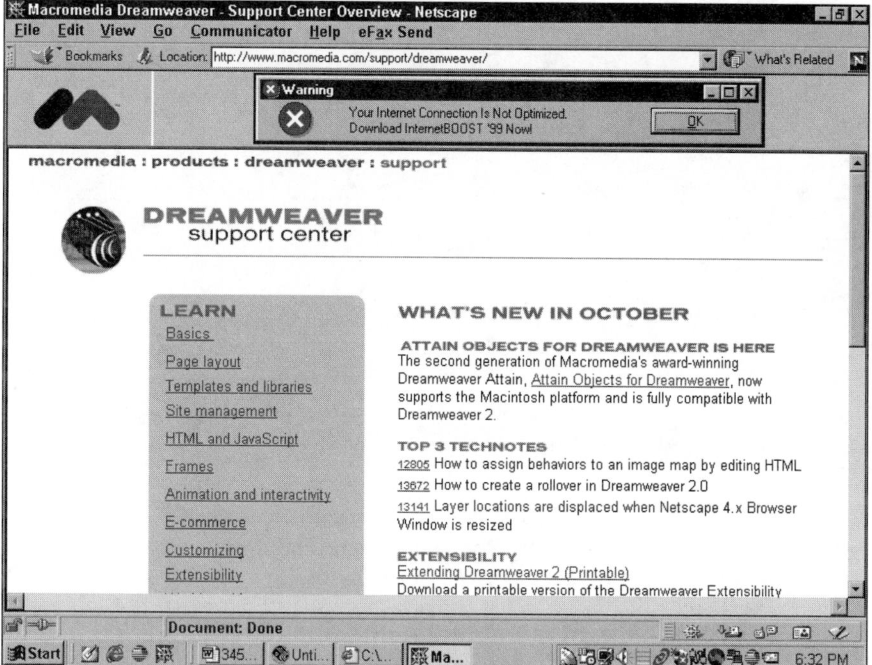

Figure 5-6: The Dreamweaver Support Center Web site is a central resource for gathering the newest information and software related to Dreamweaver.

Dynamic HTML Zone

The Dynamic HTML Zone, at `www.dhtmlzone.com`, is another extremely valuable online resource center. This site is also hosted by Macromedia, but here the focus is less on Dreamweaver than on implementing Dynamic HTML features in your Web pages. The Dynamic HTML Zone, shown in Figure 5-7, is a great jumping-off place for learning about DHTML through a variety of methods. The following is just some of what you can find at "the DZone."

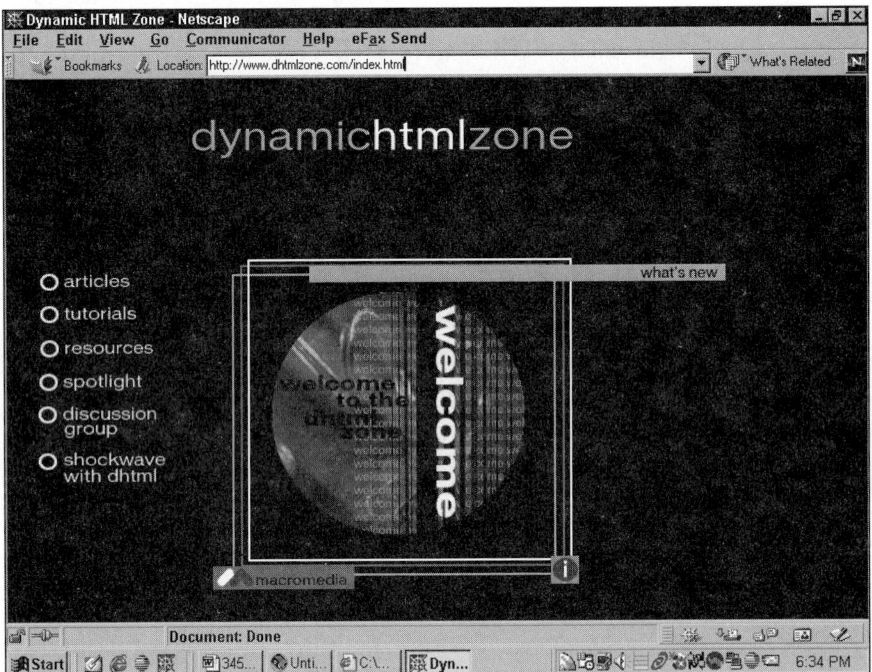

Figure 5-7: Visit the Dynamic HTML Zone for the latest information on building your Web pages with cutting-edge DHTML capabilities.

Articles

The Dynamic HTML Zone contains a collection of some of the finest technical papers about creating DHTML pages on the Web. Both browser-specific and cross-browser features are explained by experts in the field. Sample articles include "Creating Multimedia with Dynamic HTML: An Overview," "Cross-Browser Dynamic HTML," and "Techniques for Building Backward Compatible DHTML."

Tutorials

Learning from tutorials can be dry and tedious — but not at the DZone! Visit SuperFly Fashions and learn helpful general techniques, such as working with CSS layers and initializations. You also find more advanced methods, such as pull-down menus and scrolling text. The tutorials come with an overview as well as a line-by-line analysis of the JavaScript subroutines and other needed HTML code.

Resources

The Resources area is a collection of links to articles, reference guides, demos, various tutorials, and browser data — all related to DHTML. Pulling equally from the Microsoft and Netscape camps, as well as independent organizations such as C|Net and the W3C, these links are a great jumping-off place for all things DHTML.

Spotlight

Want to see what else is being accomplished with Dynamic HTML? Check out the Spotlight area. In addition to the site that's currently "in the spotlight," this page maintains an archive of past sites so honored.

Shockwave in DHTML

Combining the interactivity of Shockwave with the flexibility of Dynamic HTML is an exciting concept, and this area of the DZone gives you all the tools you need to make this marriage happen. You can find both technical white papers and full-featured demos to learn from.

Summary

Dreamweaver is a full-featured program incorporating many new technologies. This chapter describes the substantial alternatives available to you for shortening your learning curve. Key methods include the following:

- ✦ The expansive electronic manual, Dreamweaver Help pages, which explains how to accomplish specific Web page building tasks through hyperlinked text and embedded multimedia.
- ✦ Built-in tutorials for learning how to get started with Dreamweaver, by making a Web page with some of the latest effects.
- ✦ Examples of the most popular HTML features as created in Dreamweaver. You can also use the examples as templates, by substituting your own objects and text for Macromedia's.

✦ A wealth of information, online. Constantly updated, always available, Dreamweaver's online resources are a tremendous benefit to any Web designer or developer, no matter what your level of skills.

In the next chapter, you see how to set up your first Dreamweaver site, step by step.

✦ ✦ ✦

Setting Up Your First Site

✦ ✦ ✦ ✦

In This Chapter

Web site design and structure

Making a local site

All about paths and addresses

Previewing your Web site

Publishing online

✦ ✦ ✦ ✦

Web sites are far more than collections of HTML documents. Every image — from the smallest navigational button to the largest image map — is a separate file that must be uploaded with your HTML page. And if you add any additional elements, such as a background sound, digital video, or Java applet, their files must be transferred as well. To preview the Web site locally and view it properly on the Internet, you have to organize your material in a specific manner.

Each time you begin developing a new site, you can follow the straightforward procedure described in this chapter. These steps lay the groundwork for Dreamweaver to properly link your local development site with your remote online site. For those who are just starting to create Web sites, this chapter begins with a brief discussion of approaches to online design. The remainder of the chapter is devoted to the mechanics of setting up your site — which type of Internet addressing to use, file management in Dreamweaver, and publishing to the Web with Dreamweaver's Site FTP facility.

Planning Your Site

Planning in Web design, just as in any other design process, is essential. Careful planning not only cuts your development time considerably, but also makes it far easier to achieve a uniform look and feel for your Web site — which thus makes your site friendlier and easier to use. This first section briefly covers some of the basics of Web site design: what to focus on, what options to consider, and what pitfalls to avoid. If you are an established Web site developer who has covered this ground before, feel free to skip this section.

Primary considerations

Even before you choose from various models to design your site, you need to address the all-important issues of message, audience, and budget.

What do you want to say?

If I had to pick one overriding concern for Web site design, it would be to answer the following question: "What are you trying to say?" The clearer your idea of your message, the more focused your Web site will be. To this end, I find it useful to try to state the purpose of a Web site in one sentence. "Creating the coolest Web site on the planet" doesn't count. Though it could be regarded as a goal, it's so open-ended that it's almost no concept at all.

Here are some examples of clearly stated Web site concepts:

- "To provide the best small-business resource center focused on Microsoft's Office software."
- "To chronicle the world's first voyage around the world by hot air balloon."
- "To advertise music lessons offered by a collective of keyboard teachers in New York City."

Who is your audience?

Right behind a site's concept—some would say neck-and-neck with it—is the site's audience. Who are you trying to reach? Quite often a site's style is heavily influenced by a clear vision of the site's intended audience. Take, for example, Macromedia's Dynamic HTML Zone (`www.dhtmlzone.com`), discussed in Chapter 5. This is an excellent example of a site that is perfectly pitched toward its target; in this case, the intended audience is composed of professional developers and designers. Hence, you'll find the site snazzy but informative and filled with exciting examples of cutting-edge programming techniques.

In contrast, a site that is devoted to mass market e-commerce must work with a very different group in mind: shoppers. Everyone at one time or another falls into this category, so we're really talking about a state of mind, rather than a profession. Many shopping sites use a straightforward page design—one that is easily maneuverable and comforting in its repetition. At such a site, visitors can quickly find what they are looking for and—with as few impediments as possible—buy it.

What are your resources?

Unfortunately, Web sites aren't created in a vacuum. Virtually all development work happens under real-world constraints of some kind. A professional Web designer is accustomed to working within a budget. In fact, the term *budget* can apply to several concepts.

First, you have a monetary budget — how much is the client willing to spend? This translates into a combination of development time (for designers and programmers), materials (custom graphics, stock photos, and the like), and ongoing maintenance. You can build a large site with many pages that pulls dynamically from an internal database and requires little hands-on upkeep. Or you can construct a small, graphics-intensive site that must be updated weekly by hand. Yet it's entirely possible that both sites will end up costing the same.

Second, budget also applies to the amount of time you can afford to spend on any given project. The professional Web designer is quick to realize that time is an essential commodity. The resources needed when undertaking a showcase for yourself with no deadline are very different from contracting on June 30 for a job that must be ready to launch on July 4.

The third real-world budgetary item to consider is bandwidth. The Web, with faster modems and an improved infrastructure, is slowly shedding its image as the "World Wide Wait." That means today's Webmaster must keep a steady eye on a page's weight — how long it takes to download under the most typical modem rates. Of course, you can always decide to include that animated video masterpiece that takes 33 minutes to download on a 28.8 modem — you just can't expect anyone to wait to see it.

In conclusion, when you are trying to define your Web page, filter it through these three ideas: message, audience, and the various faces of the budget. The time spent visualizing your Web page in these terms is time decidedly well spent.

Design options

Many Web professionals borrow a technique used extensively in developing other mass-marketing forms: storyboarding. Storyboarding for the Web entails first diagramming the various pages in your site — much like the more traditional storyboarding in videos or filmmaking — and then detailing connections for the separate pages to form the overall site. How you connect the disparate pages determines how your visitors will navigate the completed Web site.

Several basic navigational models exist; the modern Web designer should be familiar with them all because each one serves a different purpose and they can be mixed and matched as needed.

The linear approach

Prior to the World Wide Web, most media formats were linear — that is, one image or page followed another in an unalterable sequence. In contrast, the Web and its interactive personality enable the user to jump from topic to topic. Nevertheless, you can still use a linear approach to a Web site and have one page appear after another, as in a multimedia book.

The linear navigational model, shown in Figure 6-1, works well for computer-based training applications and other expository scenarios in which you want to tightly control the viewer's experience. Some Web designers use a linear-style entrance or exit from their main site, connected to a multilevel navigational model. One advantage that Dynamic HTML brings is that you can achieve the effects of moving through several pages in a single page through layering.

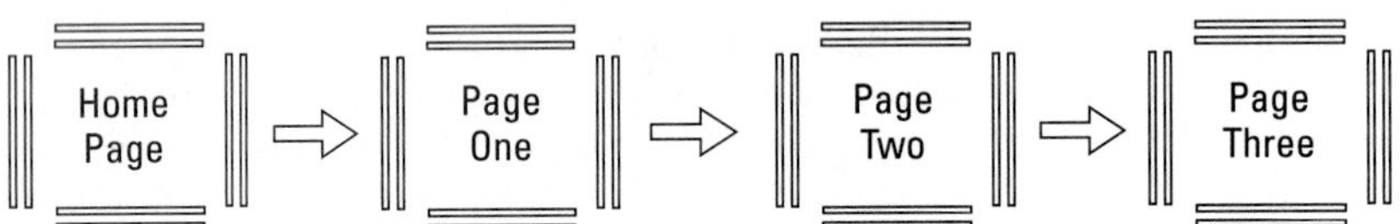

Figure 6-1: The linear navigational model takes the visitor through a series of Web pages.

Keep in mind that Web search engines can index the content of every page of your site separately. Each page of your site—not just your home page—then becomes a potential independent entrance point. So be sure to include, on every page, navigational buttons back to your home page, especially if you use a linear navigational model.

The hierarchical model

Hierarchical navigational models emerge from top-down designs. These start with one key concept that becomes your home page. From the home page, users branch off to several main pages; if needed, these main pages can, in turn, branch off into many separate pages. Everything flows from the home page; it's much like a company's organization chart, with the CEO on top followed by the various company divisions.

The hierarchical Web site, shown in Figure 6-2, is best known for maintaining a visitor's sense of place in the site. Some Web designers even depict the treelike structure as a navigational device and include each branch traveled as a link. This enables visitors to quickly retrace their steps, branch by branch, to investigate different routes.

The spoke-and-hub model

Given the Web's flexible hyperlink structure, the spoke-and-hub navigational model works extremely well. The hub is, naturally, the site's home page. The spokes projecting out from the center connect to all the major pages in the site. This layout permits fairly immediate access to any key page in just two jumps—one jump always leading back to the hub/home page and one jump leading off to a new direction. Figure 6-3 shows a typical spoke-and-hub structure for a Web site.

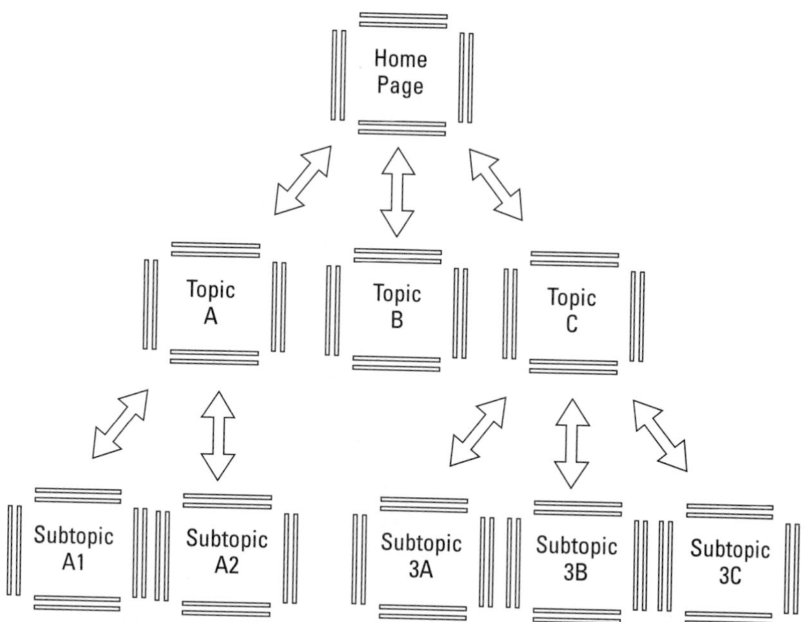

Figure 6-2: A hierarchical Web layout enables the main topics to branch into their own subtopics.

The main drawback to the spoke-and-hub structure is the constant return to the home page. Many Web designers get around this limitation by making the first jump off the hub into a Web page using frames, in which the navigational bars are always available. This design also enables visitors using nonframes-capable browsers to take a different path.

The full Web design

The seemingly least structured approach for a Web site—full Web—takes the most advantage of the Web's hyperlink capabilities. This design enables virtually every page to connect to every other page. The full Web design, shown in Figure 6-4, works well for sites that are explorations of a particular topic because the approach encourages visitors to experience the site according to their own needs, not based on the notions of any one designer. The danger in using full Web for your site design is that the visitor can literally get lost. As an escape hatch, many Web designers include a link to a clickable site map, especially for large-scale sites of this design.

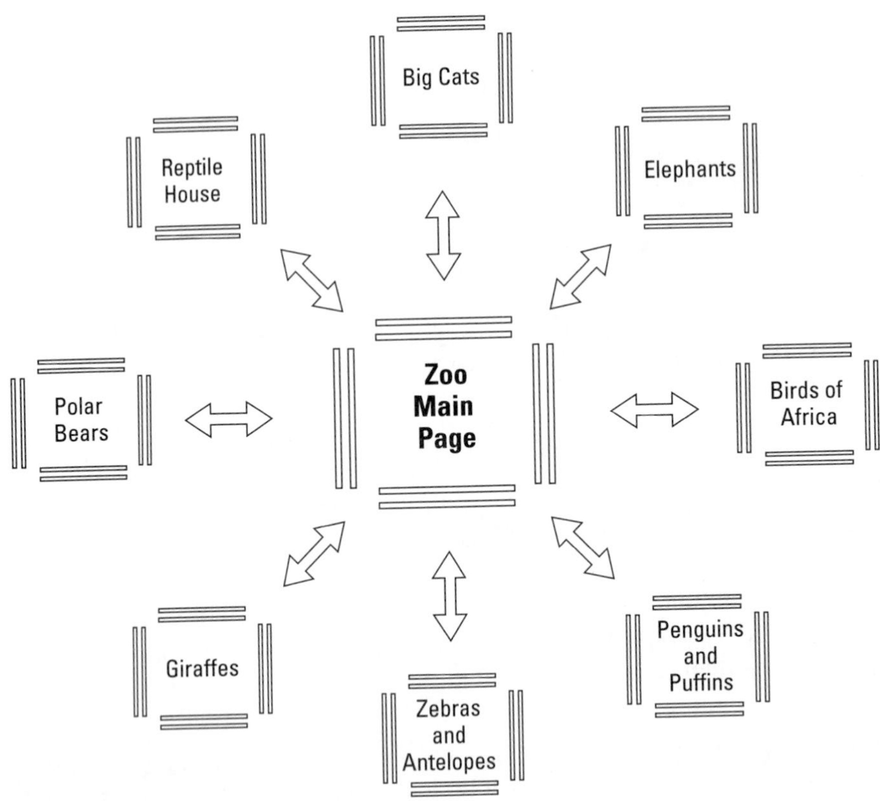

Figure 6-3: This storyboard diagram for a zoo's Web site shows how a spoke-and-hub model might work.

Defining a Local Site

Now that you've decided on a design and mapped your site, you're ready to set it up in Dreamweaver. Once your site is on your Web server and fully operational, it consists of many files — HTML, graphics, and others — that make up the individual Web pages. All of these associated files are kept on the server in one main folder, which may use one or more subfolders. This main folder is called the *remote site root*. In order for Dreamweaver to properly display your linked pages and embedded images — just as they are displayed online — the program creates a mirror of your remote site on your local development system. This primary mirror folder on your system is known as the *local site root*.

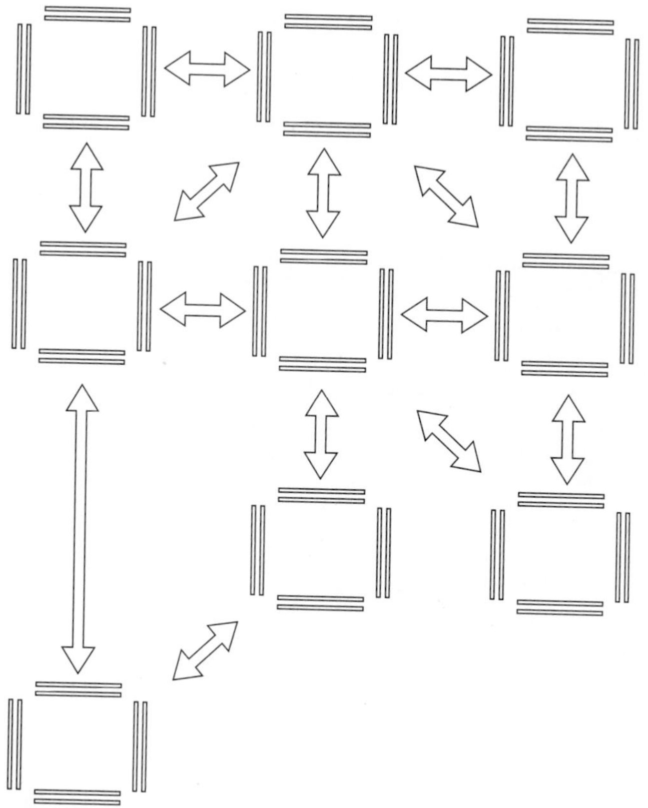

Figure 6-4: In a full Web design, each page can have multiple links to other pages.

It's necessary for you to establish the local site root at the beginning of a project. This ensures that Dreamweaver duplicates the complete structure of the Web development site when it comes time to publish your pages to the Web. One of Dreamweaver's key site management features enables you to select just the HTML pages for publication; Dreamweaver then automatically transfers all the associated files, creating any needed folders in the process. The mirror images of your local and remote site roots are critical to Dreamweaver's capability to expedite your workload in this way.

Tip

If you do decide to transfer an existing Web site to a new Dreamweaver local site root, run Dreamweaver's Link Checker after you've consolidated all your files. Choose File ⇨ Check Links Sitewide or press the keyboard shortcut Ctrl+F8 (Command+F8). The Link Checker tells you of broken links and orphan files as well. For more information on the Link Checker, see Chapter 7.

To set up a local site root folder in Dreamweaver, follow these steps:

1. Select Site ➪ New Site from the main Dreamweaver menu.

   The Site Definition dialog box opens, as shown in Figure 6-5. The Site Definition dialog box has five categories: Local Info, Web Server Info, Check In/Out, Site Map Layout, and Design Notes.

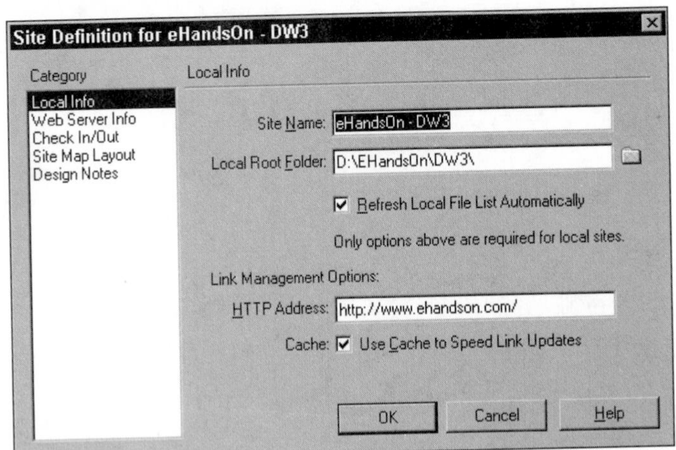

Figure 6-5: Set up your local site root through the Site Definition dialog box.

2. From the Local Info category, type a name for your site in the Site Name text box.

   This name appears in the user-defined site list displayed when you select Site ➪ Open Site.

3. Specify the folder to serve as the local site root, by either typing the path name directly into the Local Root Folder text box or clicking the folder icon. The folder icon opens the Choose Local Directory dialog box. When you've made your choice there, click the Select button.

4. Leave the Refresh Local File List Automatically option selected. This option ensures that new files are automatically included in the list and relieves you from having to select the Refresh command.

   If you're just working on the site locally with no intention of uploading it to a server, you don't have to enter any additional information.

5. Enter the full URL for your site in the HTTP Address text box.

   When checking links for your Web site, Dreamweaver uses the HTTP address to determine whether absolute links, such as `http://www.idest/dreamweaver/index.htm`, reference external files or files on your site.

6. For fastest performance, select the Cache option.

   Typically, the use of the cache speeds up link updates.

7. Select the Web Server Info category from the Site Definition dialog box.

8. From the Server Access options in the Web Server Info category, choose the Web server description that applies to your site:

   - **None:** Choose this option if your site is being developed locally and will not be uploaded to a Web server.

     If you selected None for Server Access, click OK to close the dialog box.

   - **Local/Network:** Select this option if you are running a local Web server or if your Web server is mounted as a network drive.

     If you selected Local/Network for Server Access, enter the name of the remote folder in the Remote Folder text box or click the folder icon to locate the folder. Then click OK to close the dialog box.

   - **FTP:** Select this option if you connect to your Web server via File Transfer Protocol (FTP).

     If FTP is selected, the following options appear:

FTP Host	The host name of the FTP connection for your Web server, usually in the form `www.domain.com`. Do not include the full URL, such as `ftp://www.sitename.com/index.html`.
Host Directory	The directory in which publicly accessible documents are stored on the server. Typical Host Directory names are `www/public/docs/` and `public_html/htdoc/`. Your remote site root folder will be a subfolder of the Host Directory. If you are unsure of the exact name of the Host Directory, check with your Web server administrator for the proper directory path.
Login	The login name you have been assigned for access to the Web server.
Password	The password necessary for you to gain access to the Web server. Many servers are case sensitive when it comes to logins and passwords.
Save	Dreamweaver automatically selects this option after you enter a password. Deselect this box only if you and others access the server from the current system.

Use Passive FTP	Passive FTP establishes the FTP connection through the local software rather than the server. Certain firewall configurations use passive FTP; check with your network administrator to see if you need it.
Use Firewall	This option is selected for you if you've set the Preferences with the correct host and port information.

9. Click OK when you finish entering your FTP information.

Turning on the Check In/Out system

When the Web site is being developed or maintained by a team of designers and programmers, Dreamweaver's file Check In/Out is especially useful. In a typical session, a graphic designer may get the current version of a page off the Web site in order to revise a logo. If Check In/Out is enabled, Dreamweaver places a checkmark next to the file in the remote directory pane of the Site window for all team members to see. Moreover, Dreamweaver displays the name of the person checking out the file and records the file transfer in a log.

To enable this file-control feature, select the Check In/Out category, shown in Figure 6-6, in the Site Definition dialog box. Click the Enable File Check In and Check Out option. Once the overall capability is selected, the Check Out Files when Opening option is available. When this option is turned on, Dreamweaver marks your files as checked out automatically when you open them. This feature works when opening files from either the remote or the local directories of the Site window.

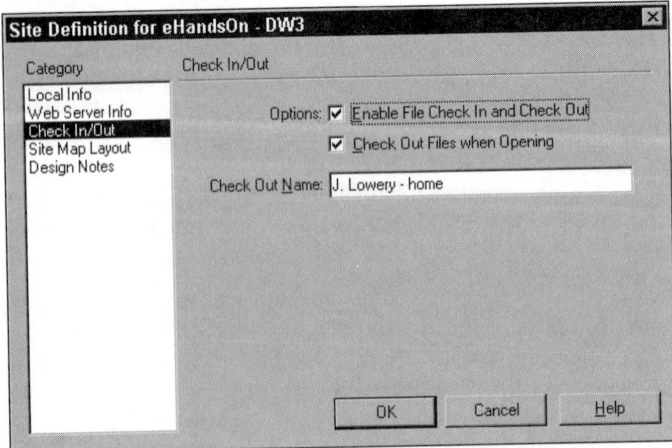

Figure 6-6: You can keep track of who's got what file with Dreamweaver's Check In/Out capability.

The final option on the Check In/Out panel of the Site Definition dialog box is to enter a check-out name. When a file is checked out, this name is posted next to the file in the Site window in the Checked Out By column. The naming facility is helpful in several ways. First, you can identify yourself and your department, as in "Margot L. - Graphic Design." Or, if you are working on the same site from multiple machines, you can keep track of where the latest version of a particular file is stored by using labels such as "Home - Mac" and "Office - Win98-03."

Managing site info

You can change any of the information associated with your local site roots by selecting Site ⇨ Define Sites from either the main Dreamweaver menu or from the Site window menu. You'll also find the Define Sites option wherever a site listing is seen. Choose the site you want to modify from the Site list box at the top of the Site Information dialog box; you'll see the corresponding information for you to edit.

After your participation in a project has ended, you can remove the site from your list. Select Site ⇨ Define Sites to open the Site Information dialog box, choose the site you want to remove in the Site list box, and click the Delete Site button. Note that this action removes the site only from Dreamweaver's internal list; it does not delete any files or folders from your hard drive.

With the local site root folder established, Dreamweaver can properly manage links no matter which address format is used. The various address formats are explained in the following section.

Relative and Absolute Addresses

In Dreamweaver, you can specify the type of link as well as the link itself. HTML links or URLs come in three formats: absolute addresses, document-relative addresses, and site root–relative addresses.

Before you begin coding your Web pages with one form of addressing or another, it's best to understand the differences between them so that you can pick the best format for your Web site. Otherwise, you might find that you have to recode most, if not all, of the links on your site — a time-consuming, tedious task.

Absolute addresses

An absolute address is the full Uniform Resource Locator (URL), specifying the type of protocol, the domain name or ID, the path, and the file name. Most often, the absolute address takes a form similar to the following:

```
http://www.idest.com/dreamweaver/index.htm
```

Absolute addresses are generally used when you are linking to a Web page on another server. Although you could code all the links on your Dreamweaver pages with absolute addresses, this approach has two drawbacks. First, it takes a lot more typing than using relative addresses; second — and much more significantly — you have to redo every single link if your linked files get moved.

As an example of a worst-case scenario, let's assume the Dreamweaver site listed just previously (currently in a subfolder on my own domain) becomes so popular that I decide to move it to its own domain. With absolute addressing in effect, I will have to change every link that points to my home page, to something like this:

```
http://www.dreamweaver-etc.com/index.html
```

The best policy is to avoid using an absolute address except when you have no other choice — specifically, when the file is on another server out of your control.

Should you ever need to rename every link in your Web site, Dreamweaver 3 offers extensive automated help through the enhanced Find and Replace features, where you can establish substitutes for multiple files in one operation. For more information on these features, see Chapter 9.

Document-relative addresses

Whereas an absolute address includes every part of the URL, a relative address omits one or more elements. As its name implies, a document-relative address assumes that the current HTML page is the point of departure, and all elements leading up to the document name are left out of the address. For example, if I were using absolute addresses to establish a link between a button on my home page (index.html) and another page (say, objects.html) stored in the same folder, I would set the link to

```
http://www.idest.com/dreamweaver/objects.html
```

However, because they are in the same folder, I could use document-relative addressing and shorten the link to

```
objects.html
```

This is possible because the linked page is in the same location, relative to the current document (index.html). More importantly, if the site changes servers or domains, all the links will still be valid.

To use document-relative addresses in Dreamweaver, you must first save your file in an established local site root. If you attempt to link anything on the current page without first saving it, Dreamweaver suggests that you save it first. If you don't save the file, the link is inserted with a `file://path` prefix, where `path` is the location of the object on your local drive. For example:

```
file://C|/Dreamweaver/Dev/images/button04.gif
(file:///Macintosh HD/Dreamweaver/Dev/¬
images/button04.gif)
```

The file:// references will not work properly if posted to a remote server.

You can specify a link to a subfolder using document-relative addressing. It's a relatively common practice for Web designers to store their graphics in a separate folder from their HTML pages. To insert a logo kept in a subfolder called images, for instance, you would use the following syntax in the link:

```
images/logo.gif
```

The slash character indicates a subfolder contained in the same directory as the current document. You can also nest folders, like this:

```
images/flags/states/ny/cities/nyc.gif
```

which links to a graphic located five subfolders deep, relative to the current page.

It is also possible to use relative document addressing to link to an object located in a folder above the current one in the directory structure. The symbol indicating a higher folder is two dots and a slash (../) and looks like this:

```
../../resume.html
```

Such a link moves up the directory tree two folders from the current document and then calls a document found there.

Document-relative addressing is a good all-around solution for small-to-medium Web sites. If you are working on a large-scale Web site that employs multiple servers, site root–relative addresses (explained next) are a better choice.

Site root–relative addresses

Just as a document-relative address omits the protocol, server, and path portion of a URL, a site root–relative address leaves off the protocol and server segments but retains the path. Why is this difference important? The answer lies in the capability of Web servers to host more than one site at a time—or to enable one site to be spread across multiple servers.

All Web site folders are stored on a Web server in a special directory that has been designated as being publicly accessible — unlike other, administrator-only areas of the system. This special directory is known as the *Host Directory*; recall that it is noted in one of the fields of Dreamweaver's Site Information dialog box when the local root folder is established. A site root–relative address uses the Host Directory as its base, much as a document-relative address uses the current HTML page.

The format for a site root–relative address calls for the link to start with a slash, followed by the folder name. Let's again use my Dreamweaver site as an example. Suppose I'm keeping it in the root directory of my domain. I could use the following form of site root–relative addressing:

```
/dreamweaver-etc/objects.html
```

Note the beginning forward-slash character in the preceding line of code. Site root–relative addressing is used on larger sites that require multiple servers to handle the substantial number of hits received. The same material can be mirrored onto several Web servers that the system administrator has set up as aliases of one another. Site root–relative addressing also enables a site to be easily moved from one server to another.

Prior to Dreamweaver 3, the primary drawback to using site root–relative addressing is that browsers cannot recognize a site root when it is used locally. In other words, if you attempted to call a graphic with a link such as this:

```
/dreamweaver-etc/images/logo.gif
```

when previewed on your system with your primary or alternate browser, the image would not display, although you could still see it within the Dreamweaver Document window. Dreamweaver 3 now translates server-side links to client-side when the Preview in Browser feature is used.

To view saved content that is site root–relative addressed outside of Dreamweaver, however, you must move the file to a remote server to view the page in your browser.

Creating and Saving New Pages

You've considered message, audience, and budget issues. You've chosen a design. You've set up your site and its address. All the preliminary planning is completed, and now you're ready to really rev up Dreamweaver and begin creating pages. This section covers the basic mechanics of opening and saving Web pages in development.

Building Placeholder Pages

One technique that I've found helpful over the years—and especially so with the use of document-relative addressing in Dreamweaver Web projects—is what I call *placeholder pages*. These placeholder pages can fill the need to include links, in as effortless a manner as possible, as you create each Web page.

Let's say, for example, you've just finished laying out most of the text and graphics for your home page and you want to put in some navigational buttons. You drop in your button images and align them just so. All that's missing is the link. If you're using document-relative addressing, the best way to handle assigning the link is to click the Browse folder icon in the Property Inspector and select your file. But what do you do if you haven't created any other pages yet and there aren't any files to select? That's when you can put placeholder pages to work.

After you've designed the basics of your site and created your local site root, as described elsewhere in this chapter, start with a blank Dreamweaver page. Type a single identifying word on the page and save it in the local site root. Do this for all the Web pages in your plan. When it comes time to make your links, all you have to do is point and click to the appropriate placeholder page. This arrangement also gives you an immediate framework for link testing. When it comes time to work on the next page, just open up the correct placeholder page and start to work.

Another style of working involves using the Site window, rather than the Document window, as your base of operations. It's easy in Dreamweaver 3 to choose File ⇨ New File (Site ⇨ Site Files View ⇨ New File) from the Site window menu several times and create the basic files of your site. You can even create a file and immediately link to it by choosing File ⇨ Link to New File (Site ⇨ Site Map View ⇨ Link to New File); a dialog box opens that enables you to specify the file name, title of the new document, and text for the link. Moreover, any needed subfolders, such as ones for images or other media, can be created by selecting File ⇨ New Folder (Site ⇨ Site Files View ⇨ New Folder).

Starting Dreamweaver

Start Dreamweaver as you would any other program. Double-click the Dreamweaver program icon, or single-click if you are using Internet Explorer's Desktop Integration feature in Windows.

After the splash screen, Dreamweaver opens with a new blank page. This page is created from the Default.html file found in the Dreamweaver\Configuration\Templates folder. Of course, it's likely that you'll want to replace the original Default.html file with one of your own—perhaps with your copyright information. All of your blank pages will then be created from a template that you've built.

If you do decide to create your own Default template, it's probably a good idea to rename the Dreamweaver Default template – as Original-Default.html or something similar – prior to creating your new, personalized Default template.

Opening an existing file

If you're looking to work on a Web page in Dreamweaver that was created in another application, choose File ➪ Open, or the keyboard shortcut Ctrl+O (Command+O). From the standard Open File dialog box, you can browse to your file's location and select it.

If you have just started Dreamweaver or if your current document is blank, your selected file loads into the current window. If on Windows systems, however, you have another Web page open or have begun creating a new one, Dreamweaver opens your file in a new window. On Macs, files always open in their own window and the initial untitled document remains.

When you first open an existing Web page, Dreamweaver checks the HTML syntax. If it finds any errors, Dreamweaver corrects them and then informs you of the corrections through the HTML Parser Results dialog box. As discussed in Chapter 4, you can turn off this HTML syntax-checking feature. Select Edit ➪ Preferences and then, from the HTML pane of the Preferences dialog box, deselect one or more of the checkbox options for HTML syntax checking.

Opening a new window

You can work on as many Dreamweaver documents as your system memory can sustain. When you choose File ➪ New or one of the keyboard shortcuts (Ctrl+N or Command+N), Dreamweaver opens a new blank page in a separate window. Once the window is open, you can switch among the various windows. To do this in Windows, you select the appropriate icon in the taskbar or use the Alt+Tab method. To switch between Dreamweaver windows on a Macintosh, click the individual window or use the Window menu.

Opening a new page

After working for a while on a design, you sometimes need to start over or switch entirely to a new project. In either case, choose File ➪ New or one of the keyboard shortcuts Ctrl+N (Command+N). This closes the current document and opens a new blank page in the same window.

You can also drag and drop an HTML file onto the Dreamweaver Document window or onto the Dreamweaver icon on your desktop.

Opening Other Types of Files

Dreamweaver defaults to displaying all types of files used to create Web pages, with these extensions: .htm, .html, .asp, .cfm, .cfml, .txt, .shtm, .shtml, .stm, .lasso, .xml. To look for specific types of files, select the Files of Type (Show) arrow button. Dreamweaver enables you to search for several individual file types, including server-side includes (.shtml, .shtm, or .stm), Active Server Pages (.asp), Cold Fusion (.cfm or .cfml), PHP (.php), and Lasso (.lasso). You can also search for text documents, Cascading Style Sheets, and Dreamweaver Library or Template pages. If you need to load a different file type, select the All Files option.

If you are working consistently with a different file format, you can add your own extensions and file types to the Dreamweaver Open File dialog box. In the Configuration folder is an editable text file called Extensions.txt. Open this file in your favorite text editor to make any additions. If you use Dreamweaver, be sure to edit the file in the HTML Inspector to see the correct format.

The syntax must follow the format of the standard Extensions.txt file:

```
HTM,HTML,ASP,CFM,CFML,TXT,SHTM,SHTML,STM,LASSO:All Documents
HTM,HTML:HTML Documents
SHTM,SHTML,STM:Server-Side Includes
XML:XML Files
LBI:Library Files
DWT:Template Files
CSS:Style Sheets
ASP:Active Server Pages
CFM,CFML:Cold Fusion Templates
TXT:Text Files
PHP:PHP Files
LASSO:Lasso Files
```

To add an entry, place your cursor at the end of the line above where you want your new file format to be placed and press Enter (Return). Type your file extension(s) in capital letters, followed by a colon, and then the text description. Save the Extensions.txt file and restart Dreamweaver to see your modifications.

If you've made any modifications to your page, Dreamweaver asks if you would like to save the page. Click the Yes (Save) button to save the file or the No (Don't Save) button to continue without saving it. To abort the new page opening, click Cancel.

Each time you open a new page, whether in the existing window or in a new window, Dreamweaver temporarily names the file "Untitled-*n*," where *n* is the next number in sequence. This prevents you from accidentally overwriting a new file opened in the same session.

Saving your page

Saving your work is very important in any computer-related task, and Dreamweaver is no exception. To initially save the current page, choose File ➪ Save or the keyboard shortcut Ctrl+S (Command+S). The Save dialog box opens; you can enter a file name and, if desired, a different path.

By default, all files are saved with an .htm file name extension for Windows and .html for Macintosh. The file extensions are always visible on Macintosh, but not on Windows. To save your file with another extension, such as .shtml, change the Save as Type option to the specific file type and then enter your full file name, without the extension.

It seems kind of backward in this day and age of long file names, but it's still a good idea to choose names for your files without spaces or punctuation other than an underscore or hyphen. Otherwise, not all servers will read the file name correctly, and you'll have problems linking your pages.

Closing the page

When you're finished with a page — or if your system is running low on resources — you can close a file without quitting Dreamweaver. To close a page, select File ➪ Close or the keyboard shortcuts Ctrl+W (Command+W). If you made any changes to the page since you saved it last, Dreamweaver prompts you to save it.

On Window systems, if you have only one Dreamweaver window open and you close the current page, Dreamweaver asks if you'd like to quit the program. As with other Macintosh applications, all windows can be closed and the application still accessible through the menu bar.

Quitting the program

Once you're done for the day — or, more often, the late, late night — you can close Dreamweaver by choosing File ➪ Exit (File ➪ Quit) or one of the standard keyboard shortcuts Ctrl+Q (Command+Q).

In Windows systems, to make sure you're really ready to shut down the program, Dreamweaver 3 asks you to confirm your desire to quit. If you're confident that you won't quit the program accidentally, select the Don't Warn Me Again option to stop this dialog box from reappearing.

You won't receive an opportunity to confirm your choice if you quit from the Site window in Windows or on Macintosh systems. That's because, on Windows, Dreamweaver's Site window and Document window are really separate applications.

Previewing Your Web Pages

When using Dreamweaver or any other Web authoring tool, it's important to constantly check your progress in one or more browsers. Dreamweaver's Document window offers a near-browser view of your Web page, but because of the variations among the different browsers, it's imperative that you preview your page early and often. Dreamweaver offers you easy access to a maximum of 20 browsers — and they're just a function key away.

You add a browser to your preview list by selecting File ➪ Preview in Browser ➪ Edit Browser List or by choosing the Preview in Browser category from the Preferences dialog box. Both actions open the Preview in Browser Preferences panel. The steps for editing your browser list are described in detail in Chapter 4. Here's a brief recap:

1. Select File ➪ Preview in Browser ➪ Edit Browser List.
2. To add a browser (up to 20), click the Add (+) button and fill out the following fields:

Name	How you want the browser listed.
Application	Type in the path to the browser program or click the Browse (Choose) button to locate the browser application file.
Primary Browser/Secondary Browser	If desired, select one of these checkboxes to designate the current browser as such.

3. After you've added a browser to your list, you can easily edit or delete it. Choose File ➪ Preview in Browser ➪ Edit Browser List as before and highlight the browser you want to modify or delete.
4. To alter your selection, click the Edit button. To delete your selection, click the Remove (-) button.
5. After you've completed your modifications, click OK to close the dialog box.

Once you've added one or more browsers to your list, you can preview the current page in these browsers. Select File ➪ Preview in Browser ➪ BrowserName, where BrowserName indicates the particular program. Dreamweaver saves the page to a temporary file, starts the browser, and loads the page.

Note that in order to view any changes you've made to your Web page under construction, you must select the Preview in Browser menu option again (or press one of the function keys for primary/secondary browser previewing, described in the following paragraph). Clicking the Refresh/Reload button in your browser does not load in any modifications. The temporary preview files are deleted when you quit Dreamweaver.

You can also use keyboard shortcuts to preview two different browsers, by pressing a function key: Press F12 to preview the current Dreamweaver page in your primary browser and Shift+F12 to preview the same page in your secondary browser. These are the Primary and Secondary Browser settings you establish in the Preferences Preview in the Browser dialog box, explained in Chapter 4.

In fact, with Dreamweaver's Preview in Browser Preferences, you can so easily switch the designations of primary and secondary browser that you can use that setup for "debugging" a Web page in any browser, simply by changing the preferences. Go to the Preview in Browser Preferences pane, select the browser you want to use for debugging, and check the appropriate checkbox to designate the browser as primary or secondary. In the list of browsers in this Preferences pane, the indicator of F12 or Shift+F12 appears next to the browser's name.

Tip

In addition to checking your Web page output on a variety of browsers on your system, it's also a good idea to preview the page on other platforms. If you're designing on a Macintosh, try to view your pages on a Windows system, and vice versa. Watch out for some not-so-subtle differences between the two environments, in terms of color rendering (colors in Macs tend to be brighter than in PCs) and text size.

Putting Your Pages Online

The final phase of setting up your Dreamweaver site is publishing your pages to the Web. When you begin this publishing process is up to you. Some Web designers wait until everything is absolutely perfect on the local development site and then upload everything at once. Others like to establish an early connection to the remote site and extend the transfer of files over a longer period of time.

I fall into the latter camp. When I start transferring files at the beginning of the process, I find that I catch my mistakes earlier and avoid having to effect massive changes to the site after everything is up. For example, in developing one large site, I started out using file names with mixed case, as in `ELFhome.html`. After publishing some early drafts of a few Web pages, however, I discovered that the host had switched servers; on the new server, file names had to be all lowercase. Had I waited until the last moment to upload everything, I would have been faced with an unexpected and gigantic search-and-replace job.

Tip: In general, Unix servers are case sensitive, whereas Windows servers are not. Check with your hosting administrator if you're not sure of the server type.

Once you've established your local site root — and you've included your remote site's FTP information in the setup — the actual publishing of your files to the Web is a straightforward process. To transfer your local Web pages to an online site, follow these steps:

1. Choose Site ➪ Open Site ➪ Site Name, where Site Name is the current site.

   The Site window opens, displaying the current site.

2. From the Site window, click the Connect button. (You may need to complete your connection to the Internet prior to choosing the Connect button.)

   Dreamweaver displays a message box showing the progress of the connection.

3. If you didn't enter a password in the Site Information dialog box, or if you entered a password but didn't opt to save it, Dreamweaver asks you to type in your password.

   Once the connection is complete, the directory listing of the remote site appears in the Remote (left-hand by default) pane of the Site window.

4. In the Local (right-hand by default) pane, highlight the HTML files you would like to transfer.

5. Click the Put button at the top of the Site window.

6. Dreamweaver asks if you would like to move the dependent files as well. Select Yes to transfer all embedded graphics and other objects, or No if you'd prefer to move these yourself. You can also select the Don't Ask Me Again box to make transfers of dependent files automatic in the future.

   Dreamweaver displays the progress of the file transfer in the Site window's status bar.

7. When each file transfer is finished, Dreamweaver places a green checkmark next to each file (if File Check In/Out has been enabled in the Site FTP Preferences pane).

8. When you've finished transferring your files, click the Disconnect button.

Remember, the only files you have to highlight for transfer to the remote site are the HTML files. As noted previously, Dreamweaver automatically transfers any dependent file (if you enable it), which means that you'll never forget to move a GIF again! (Nor will you ever move an unnecessary file, such as an earlier version of an image, by mistake.) Moreover, Dreamweaver automatically creates any subfolders necessary to maintain the site's integrity. These two features combined can save you substantial time and worry.

Some files, especially CGI programs, require that you set the file permissions before they can be used. For information about setting file permissions from within Dreamweaver, see Chapter 17.

So now your site has been prepped from the planning stages, through the local site root and onto the Web. Congratulations — all that's left is to fill those pages with insightful content, amazing graphics, and wondrous code. Let's get to it!

Summary

In this chapter, you studied some options for planning your Web site and what you need to do in Dreamweaver to initialize the site. This planning and initialization process is not a detailed one, but taking particular steps can greatly smooth your development path down the road.

- ✦ Put as much time into planning your site as possible. The more clearly conceived the site, the cleaner the execution.
- ✦ Set up your local site root in Dreamweaver right away. The local site root is essential for Dreamweaver to properly publish your files to the remote site later.
- ✦ If you're working in a team environment, enable the Check In/Out features to prevent two or more team members from editing the same file at the same time.
- ✦ Decide on the type of addressing to use in your links. Document-relative addressing is good for most small-to-medium Web sites, and site root–relative addressing is best for most large sites. Use absolute addressing only when linking to an outside server.
- ✦ Preview early, often, and with various browsers. Dreamweaver gives you quick function key access to a primary and secondary browser. Check your pages frequently in these browsers and then spend some time checking your pages against other available browsers and browser versions.
- ✦ Establish an early connection to the Web and use it frequently. You can begin publishing your local site through Dreamweaver's Site window almost immediately.

In the next chapter, you learn how to use Dreamweaver to begin coding your Web pages.

✦ ✦ ✦

Publishing with the Site Window

✦ ✦ ✦ ✦

In This Chapter

Site management principles

Working with the Site window

Managing Web site files

Using the Site window's file Check In/Check Out

Running the Link Checker

Exploring the Site Map

✦ ✦ ✦ ✦

Site management is an essential part of a Webmaster's job description. Far from static designs, the Web site is not like a magazine advertisement that you're finished with as soon as you send the file to the printer. Publishing your Web site pages on the Internet is really just the first step in an ongoing — often day-to-day — management task.

Dreamweaver includes an integrated but separate process known as the Site window to handle all your Web management needs. With the Site window, you can

✦ Transfer files to your remote site from your local development site and back again

✦ Issue system commands to enable CGI programs on the server

✦ Monitor your Web site for broken links and orphaned files

✦ Check a file in or out during team Web development

This chapter covers these site management functions and more. However, before you begin exploring the Site window features, it's helpful to know a little more about site management in Dreamweaver.

Site Management with Dreamweaver

At the simplest level, *site management* means transferring your files from the local drive to a publishing server. This is standard File Transfer Protocol (FTP), and many designers are accustomed to working with tools such as WS_FTP and Fetch. These utilities, however, only help you to move files back and forth. In a medium-to-large Web site, other issues must be addressed. For instance:

- What happens when a large group is working on a single Web site? What prevents the graphics designer from altering the same file the JavaScript programmer is modifying?
- How can you tell which version of your logo is the final one among the 15 working versions in your local site root folder?
- Do you have to update all your files every time some change is made to a few? Or can you only update those that have changed? How can you tell which ones have changed?

To help the Dreamweaver developer cope with these issues and avoid the type of frustration they can produce, a useful site management tool is included within Dreamweaver: the Site window. Its key features include the following:

- A quick, visual view of the elements of your site, on your local and remote directories
- Fast drag-and-drop functionality for transferring files with dependent file support
- Site management check-in and check-out tools for groups working on files within the same Web site
- A Link Checker that helps you identify broken or unused objects being posted to your site
- A Site Map that enables you to both visualize your Web site structure and alter it

On Windows systems, the Site window runs as a connected but independent process, so that you can close your document window when you're finished designing and then publish your files to the Web through the Site window.

Note

The Dreamweaver commands related to the Site window features are in different places on the Windows and Macintosh systems. In Windows, the Site window has its own menu bar; all the Windows-oriented references in this chapter refer to this menu. In addition, Dreamweaver 3 includes a new Site menu in the Document window that repeats many commands for easy access. Because Macintosh systems don't have a separate menu for a program's individual windows, Dreamweaver organizes the Site functions in a Site category of the main menu strip.

Setting Up a New Site

The first step in developing an effective site — one that links to other Web pages, uses images and library files, and offers other site root–relative links — is, of course, to establish a site. Dreamweaver has made this very easy to do.

For complete, detailed information on establishing your initial site, see Chapter 6.

You need to create a folder on your development system that contains all the HTML, as well as graphics, media, and other files, needed by the site. To create a new site, choose Site ➪ New Site. The Site Definition dialog box opens with the Local Info panel selected, as shown in Figure 7-1. Here you find the information and settings for the current site you are developing. Once you've entered this information, you seldom need to modify it.

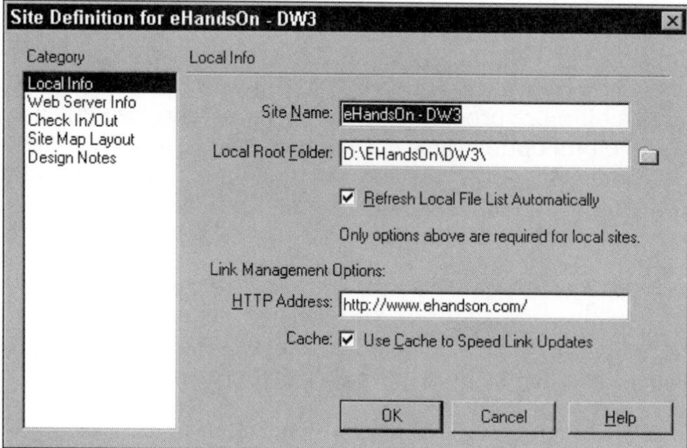

Figure 7-1: The Site Definition dialog box contains settings for the current site you are developing.

The data in the Site Definition dialog box is divided into five categories: Local Info, Web Server Info, Check In/Out, Site Map Layout, and Design Notes.

Local directory information

The local directory is in a folder on your development system, either on your own hard drive or on a network server.

Site Name

This is the name that appears in the Site ➪ Open Site list. The site name is a reference only you need to know, and it can be as fancy as you want. No hard-and-fast rules exist for creating a site name, except you should keep the name simple so you can easily reference it later. In a large Web design firm, you may need to develop more structured methods for naming various clients' Web sites.

Local Root Folder

The Local Root Folder is the location on your hard drive, or in a network folder, where you place your HTML pages, images, plug-in files, and Library items. Remember, the root folder is essential to an effective Dreamweaver site. As you add links to other Web pages and images, Dreamweaver needs to maintain the relative links between files. The benefit of this becomes apparent when you upload your files to a Web server. By maintaining a root-relative relationship, you ensure that all of the files and associated images can transfer seamlessly together onto any Web site. You won't have to go back and replace the code for any broken images.

Refresh Local File List Automatically

When the Refresh Local File List Automatically option is selected, Dreamweaver updates the list every time a new file is added by Dreamweaver or any other program. Although it takes a bit more processing power to constantly watch and update the folder, it's a helpful option (new in Dreamweaver 3), and I recommend always selecting it. Without the option checked, you need to choose View ➪ Refresh Local (Site ➪ Site Files View ➪ Refresh Local) or use the keyboard shortcut, Shift+F5, to see the latest files.

HTTP Address

The information entered in the HTTP Address field is used when you access the Link Checker. In this field, you enter the remote URL that corresponds to the local root folder, as if it were a regular Web address.

For example, say you are developing a Web site for My Frozen Custard, Inc. In the HTTP Address field, you would enter the URL for the Web site, like this:

```
http://www.myfrozencustard.com/
```

With this information, the Link Checker can compare absolute addresses embedded in your Web page to see whether those addresses refer to internal or external files.

Cache

Put a checkmark in the Cache checkbox to speed up Dreamweaver's links and site management tasks.

Web Server Info

The Web Server Info category contains all of the information required for you to post your files to a remote server. The setup allows for any type of host directory. Typically, though, you upload your files to either a Unix or an NT Web server.

From the Web Server Info panel (see Figure 7-2), choose Local/Network from the Server Access drop-down menu to enter or select a folder on your hard drive or on the network from which your files will be served. Select FTP from the Server Access drop-down menu to be presented with a dialog box requesting information needed to access your remote site.

If you don't know the name of your FTP host server or any of the other required host site information (directory, login ID, password, and firewall preferences), contact your ISP or system administrator. If a hosting server is not yet established, keep Server Access set to None.

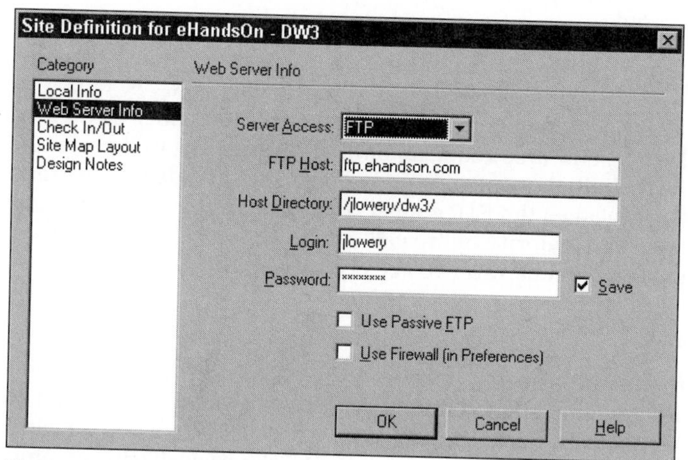

Figure 7-2: Information entered in the Web Server Info panel is essential for Dreamweaver to connect with your remote site.

FTP Host

The FTP Host is the name of the server on which you will be placing your files. The names for the host will be something like these:

```
www.yourdomain.com
ftp.yourdomain.com
```

Do not include the protocol information, such as `http://` or `ftp://`, in the FTP host name.

Host Directory

The host directory is the one in which publicly accessible documents are stored on the server. Your remote site root folder will be a subfolder of the host directory. Here's an example of the host directory information:

```
/usr/www/htdocs/jlowery
```

Check with your Web server administrator for the proper directory path.

Login ID and Password

A login ID and password are required to transfer your files from your local root folder to the host. Your login ID is a unique name that tells the host who you are. Your password should be known only by you and the host. Every time you upload or download a file from the host server, you are asked for your password. If you don't want to have to retype your password each time you log on, just select the Save checkbox next to your password, and Dreamweaver remembers it.

For security reasons, it is highly recommended that you do not allow anyone to know your password.

Use Passive FTP

During a normal FTP process, one computer (the client) establishes a connection with another (the server) and then requests data to be sent. Firewall-protected servers do not allow the initial connection to be made, so no data can be transferred. Passive FTP establishes the FTP connection through the local software rather than the server. The majority of firewall configurations use passive FTP; check with your network administrator to see if you need it.

Use Firewall

Firewalls are security features used by many companies to prevent unwanted access to internal documents. Many different types of firewalls exist, and all have a multitude of security settings. For instance, some firewalls enable people within a company to move documents back and forth through the firewall without any problems. Other companies will not allow Java or ActiveX controls to be moved through the firewall.

If you have a firewall that requires additional security to upload and download files, you should enable the Use Firewall checkbox in the Site Definition window. Selecting this checkbox requires that you go to Dreamweaver Preferences and fill out additional information on proxy servers. A proxy server enables you to navigate files through a firewall.

To make the appropriate proxy server changes, go to Edit ➪ Preferences and choose the Site Window category from the Preferences dialog box. This panel of settings contains selections for firewall information. Enter the firewall host name and port number, which can be provided to you by your ISP or system administrator. By default, most firewalls use port 21.

Check In/Out

In this panel (see Figure 7-3), you can enable or disable Dreamweaver's Check In and Check Out. When you select Enable File Check In and Check Out, the two other fields become available. You then can select the Check Out Files While Opening option, which automates the check-out process to some degree.

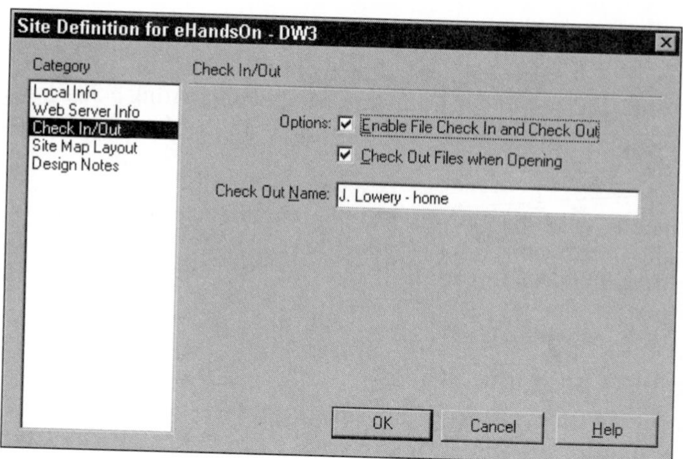

Figure 7-3: Turn on the file-locking feature of Dreamweaver in the Check In/Out panel of the Site Definition dialog box.

The name you enter in the Check Out Name field is used to inform others in your group when you have downloaded a file from the host server. Because the Check Out Name is one of several columns of information in the Local and Remote panes of the Site window, it's a good idea to keep the name relatively short. (Your initials are an ideal choice for Check Out Name, if that is appropriate.)

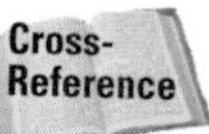

For detailed information on the Site Window preferences, see Chapter 4.

Modifying the Site Map

You can control the way that Dreamweaver displays a Site Map in the Site Map Layout panel (see Figure 7-4). In the Site Definition dialog box, select Site Map Layout from the Category list to access the Site Map options.

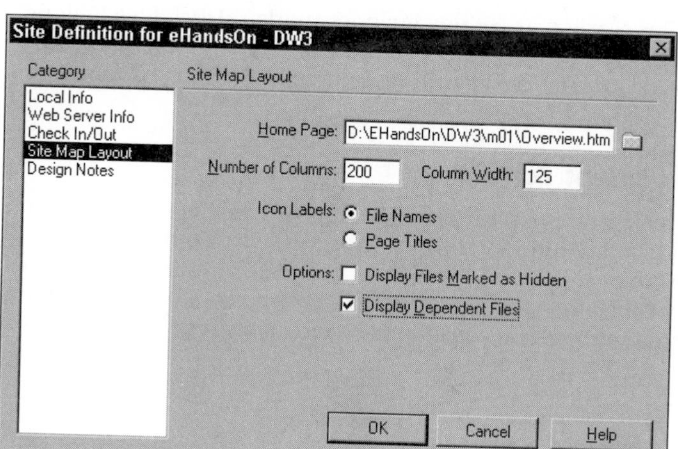

Figure 7-4: You can control what the Site Map shows as well as its overall appearance through the Site Map Layout panel.

Home Page

By default, Dreamweaver looks for a file called index.html, index.htm, or default.htm (in that order) in your Local root folder from which to begin creating a Site Map. You can choose another page to appear at the top level of your Site Map by selecting a different file to serve as your home page.

It's best to include a home page if you plan on using the Site Map feature at all when defining the site. If one is not available, you can just enter the name for the file, like index.htm, in the Home Page field and press Tab; Dreamweaver will create the file for you.

Number of Columns/Column Width

These options control the way your Site Map is displayed on your screen. You can modify these values in order to make the Site Map fit more easily onto a single page for printing.

By default, the Site Map displays horizontally. You can switch the layout to vertical by changing the Number of Columns field to 1.

Icon Labels

The Icon Labels option enables you to select whether the icons in your Site Map should be displayed using their file names or their page titles. Page titles are derived from the `<title>` tag in the `<head>` section of an HTML document. While this method can be more descriptive, you have to remember to insert the title, either through the Page Properties dialog box or by revealing the Head Content, selecting the Title icon, and entering the desired text in the Title Property Inspector. If you don't assign each page a title, Dreamweaver uses "Untitled Document" as the title.

Options

Checking Display Files Marked as Hidden includes hidden HTML files in your Site Map Layout; checking Display Dependent Files includes non-HTML files, such as graphics image files or external JavaScript files, in your Site Map Layout.

Integrating Design Notes

Web sites can be quite complex creations, particularly when worked on by a team of designers, coders, and content providers. Dreamweaver 3 introduces a new feature aimed at enhancing the communication between various team members: Design Notes. A Design Note can be attached to any Dreamweaver-created page or any media inserted into a Dreamweaver page and easily read from within Dreamweaver.

To be truly useful, the entire team needs to gain access to the Design Notes. Dreamweaver 3 enables you to maintain the Design Notes on the remote server, just like another dependent file. The preferences in the Define Sites dialog box set up this option as well as giving you a simple way to remove all unused Design Notes.

Options

Design Notes have only two options. The first, Maintain Design Notes, enables Design Notes functionality for the site. It must be enabled to add or modify a Design Note for any page within the site. This option also causes a Design Note to follow its associated file if that file is moved. The second option, Upload Design Notes for Sharing, automatically gets or puts the Design Note whenever its associated file is transferred.

Clean Up

If the Maintain Design Notes option is enabled and a Dreamweaver file is deleted from within Dreamweaver, the associated Design Note is removed also. However, if you delete, move, or rename your HTML files in any other way—with a file manager or other program—the Design Note is left. Select the Clean Up button to remove any Design Notes that no longer have associated HTML files.

Using the Site Window

In Dreamweaver 3, some site commands, such as Put File, can be called without using the Site window, but the Site window is "home base" for almost all of Dreamweaver's sitewide functions. You can open the Site window by any of the following methods:

- Choose Site ➪ Open Site ➪ Your Site.
- Select the Site button from the Launcher or Site window from the Mini Launcher.
- Choose Window ➪ Site File.
- Press the keyboard shortcut F5.

The Site window is your vehicle for moving files back and forth between your local and remote folders. Figure 7-5 illustrates the various parts of the Site window.

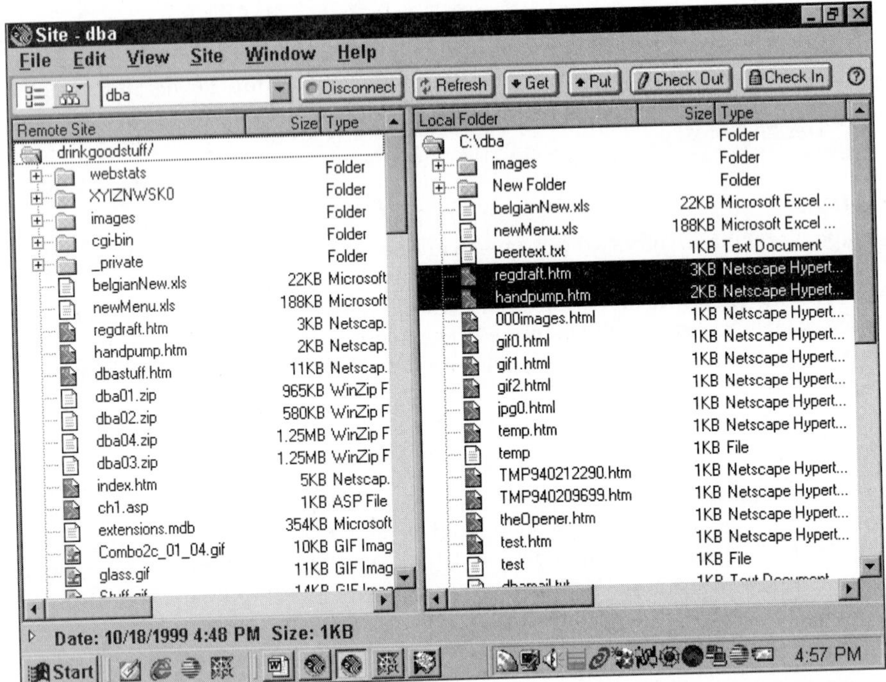

Figure 7-5: The Site window is used for transferring files to and from your remote Web server.

Remote Site and Local Root Directory windows

The Site window is arranged in two main windows: The remote site is on the left and the local root directory is on the right. These two windows enable you to view all the files contained within the two directories.

Another helpful view enables you to see which files have been most recently added or modified since the last FTP transfer. Choose either Select Newer Local or Select Newer Remote in the Edit menu (or on a Macintosh, Site ⇨ Site Files View ⇨ Select Newer Local or Site Files View ⇨ Select Newer Remote). Dreamweaver compares the files within the two folders to see which ones have been saved since the last FTP session. The newer files are highlighted and can be easily transferred by selecting the Get or Put button (described in a later section).

Tip

In large sites, the Select Newer Remote operation can take a fairly long time to complete. If possible, selecting individual folders to be checked, while leaving the others unscanned, can speed up the process.

Connect/Disconnect button

The Connect/Disconnect button enables you to begin or end a live session with a remote host server. By clicking the Connect button, you start a new FTP session. You must have a way to connect to the Internet when you select Connect. You won't see any information in the Remote Site pane until you connect to it.

After Dreamweaver has made the connection to your remote site—as identified in the Site Information dialog box—the Connect button becomes the Disconnect button. To end your FTP session with the host server, click the Disconnect button.

You can monitor all of your site management transactions by looking at the FTP Log. Select Window ➪ Site FTP Log (Windows) or Site ➪ FTP Log (Macintosh) from within the Site window. A new window pops up and shows you all your transactions as you perform them.

Get and Put buttons

Two of the most useful controls on the Site window are the Get and Put buttons. The Get button retrieves selected files and folders from the host server. The Put button transfers selected files from your local root directory to the host server. Dreamweaver offers several ways to transfer files in the Site window during an active FTP session.

To transfer one or more files from the local directory to the host server, use one of the following methods:

✦ Select the files from the Local Folder pane and drag them over to the Remote Folder pane.

✦ Use the keyboard shortcut—select the files and press Ctrl+Shift+U (Command+Shift+U).

✦ Highlight the files and choose Site ➪ Put.

✦ Select the files in the Local Folder pane and click the Put button.

If the file you are transferring has any dependent files, such as inserted images or Java applets, the Dependent Files dialog box (see Figure 7-6) asks if you want to include dependent files. If you select Yes, all such files are transferred. Select No to move only the file you selected.

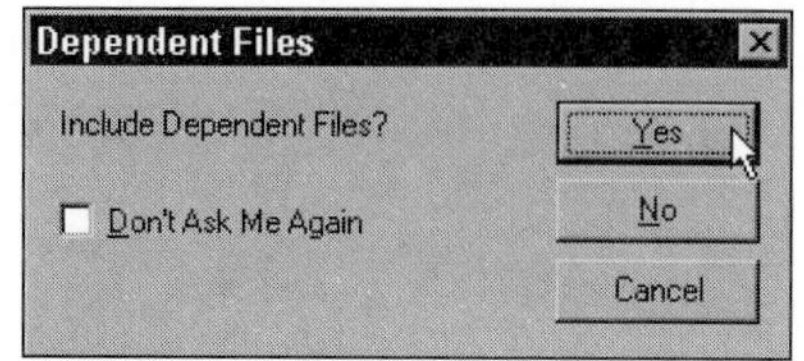

Figure 7-6: After selecting the HTML files, say Yes to the Dependent Files dialog box to transfer all the needed files.

Tip

The Dependent Files dialog box includes a checkbox that asks if you want to be reminded of this feature again. If you choose this option, but later want the reminder to reappear, you can select either of the Dependent Files options from the Site Window panel of Preferences. To bring up the Dependent Files dialog box on a case-by-case basis, press Alt (Option) when selecting the Get, Put, Check In, or Check Out buttons.

To transfer one or more files from the host server to the local folder, use one of these techniques:

✦ Select the files you want from the Remote Site pane and drag them over to the Local Folder pane.

✦ Use the keyboard shortcut — select the files and press Ctrl+Shift+D (Command+Shift+D).

✦ Highlight the files and select Site ➪ Get.

✦ Select the files in the remote directory and click the Get button.

Caution

If you select either Site ➪ Get or the Get button without having selected any files in the Remote Site pane, all the files from your host server are moved. Dreamweaver does warn you, however.

Refresh button

As the name implies, the Refresh button re-reads the currently selected directory, whether locally or remotely. This can be useful when other people are working on the same site at the same time — refreshing your screen enables you to see if any additional files have been added or removed during your FTP session. You also need to refresh the Site window if you have modified a file during the FTP session. If you have enabled the Refresh Local Files Automatically option in the Define Site preferences, you only have to use this button to refresh the remote files.

The View (Windows) or Site ➪ Site Files View (Macintosh) menu options also enable you to refresh the two windows. You can choose from two refresh commands: Refresh Local and Refresh Remote.

Stop Current Task button

Use the Stop Current Task button to halt the current transfer of files in an active FTP session. The Stop Current Task button is the octagonal red X button located in the lower-right corner of the Site window; it appears only while you are actually moving files.

Check Out/Check In buttons

The Check In/Check Out buttons, which are visible only if you've selected the Check In/Out category in the Site Definition window (as previously shown in Figure 7-3), enable a user to officially check out an item from either the local or host server. The Check Out button provides a visual cue to everyone with access to the server that a file is currently in use. Details on how to use this feature are covered in the next section.

Checking a File In and Out

Your control over the files used for your Web site is very important if you are developing a site with a team. On larger sites, the various Webmaster chores — design, programming, management — are distributed among several people. Without proper check-in and check-out procedures, it's easy for the same HTML page to get updated by more than one person, and you can wind up with incompatible versions.

Dreamweaver's Check In/Check Out facility solves this file-control problem by permitting only one person at a time to modify a Web page or graphic. Once a file has been checked out — accessed by someone — the file must be checked in again before another person using the Site window can download it and work on it.

Dreamweaver handles the functionality of Check In/Check Out very efficiently. Whenever you establish an active FTP session between your local root folder and the remote server, any files you get or put are displayed with a green checkmark. If other people in your group are also moving files back and forth, their transferred files are marked with a red checkmark. This method provides a quickly recognized, visual representation of the status of files you and your teammates are handling. Files that do not have either a red or green checkmark are not currently checked out by anyone and are available to work on.

If you want to see who is working on what, you can view user names in the Remote Site window. (You may have to scroll the window horizontally to see the column.) The name shown is the Check Out name that they use for logging on to the remote server. The Check Out name is entered through the Site Information dialog box.

Knowing who is working on what, and when, is a good control mechanism, but to really prevent duplication, site file control has to go one step further. Under Dreamweaver's Check In/Check Out system, when you transfer a file from your local root folder to the host server, the file on your local folder becomes read-only. Making the file read-only enables others to see the Web page but prevents anyone else from overwriting the file. The file must be checked in again before others can modify it.

Dreamweaver accomplishes Check In/Check Out by using a set of special files. When a file is checked out, a text file of the same file name but with the extension .lck is placed on the server. The .lck file contains the name of the user who checked out the file, as well as the date and the time that the file was checked out. The .lck files cannot be viewed in the Site window display but can be seen when a third-party FTP program is used.

Unfortunately, Dreamweaver is not able to make checked-out files in the host server read-only. This means someone in your group using an FTP program other than the Site window could easily overwrite the checked-out file on the server.

To check out one or more files, use any of the following methods:

- ✦ Select the files you want to transfer and then click the Check Out button at the top of the Site window. All the files are downloaded into your local folder and checked out in your name (denoted by a green checkmark).
- ✦ Select the files and choose Site ➪ Check Out.
- ✦ Select the files and use the keyboard shortcut Ctrl+Alt+Shift+D (Command+Option+Shift+D).

To check one or more files back in, do either of the following:

- ✦ Select the files you want to transfer and then click the Check In button at the top of the Site window. All of the selected files will be uploaded from your local folder to the remote site, and the green checkmark will be removed from their names.
- ✦ Select the checked-out files and choose Site ➪ Check In.
- ✦ Select the files and use the keyboard shortcut Ctrl+Alt+Shift+U (Command+Option+Shift+U).

To change the checked-out status of a file, use one of these methods:

- ✦ Select the file that's checked out and then click the Check In button at the top of the Site window.
- ✦ Select the file and choose Site ➪ Undo Check Out, or use the keyboard shortcut Ctrl+Shift+L (Command+Shift+L).

Synchronizing local and remote sites

The necessity of having sets of files stored both locally and remotely often leads to confusion over which file is the most current. The problem is far more likely to occur if you're working in a team situation where numerous people are maintaining the same site. Until now, you had to either examine the date and time stamps of the files carefully to determine which was newer, or use a combination of Dreamweaver commands Select Newer Local and Select Newer Remote to achieve synchronicity between the sites.

Dreamweaver 3 introduces a one-step command to solve this local-remote dilemma: Synchronize. Found under the Site menu in Windows and on the menu bar in Macintosh systems, the Synchronize command ensures that the most current version of the same files are on both systems. Synchronize can also delete files on one site that do not appear on another. You can apply the Synchronize command sitewide or to selected files or folders.

To synchronize your files, follow these steps:

1. If you want to synchronize only selected files or folders, select those in the local pane of the Site window.
2. Choose Site ➪ Synchronize.

   The Synchronize Files dialog box opens, as shown in Figure 7-7.

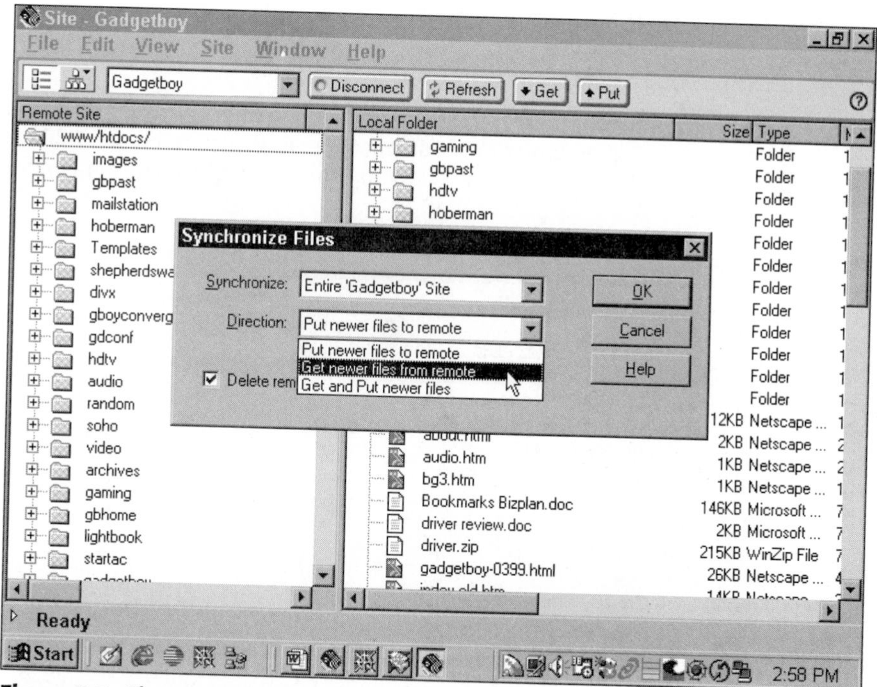

Figure 7-7: The new Synchronize command makes sure that both the local and remote sites contain the same files.

3. To synchronize the full site, select Entire *Site Name* Site from the Synchronize list, where *Site Name* is the current site. Otherwise, choose Selected Local Files Only.

4. Set the direction of the synchronization:

   - **Put Newer Files to Remote:** Examines local files and transfers those with more recent modification dates to the remote server.
   - **Get Newer Files from Remote:** Examines remote files and transfers those with more recent modification dates to the local server.
   - **Get and Put Newer Files:** Transfers the most current versions of all files to and from both sites.

5. By selecting the Delete Remote Files Not on Local Drive option, you can remove any local files without a corresponding file on the server side when using the Get Newer Files from Remote direction. If the Put Newer Files to Remote direction is chosen with the Delete option, files on the remote site without a local equivalent are removed.

As with all file deletions, these operations cannot be undone. Use this feature with extreme care.

6. When you're ready, click OK to begin the process.

   Dreamweaver compares the local and remote sites and begins displaying files in a new Site dialog box for confirmation, as shown in Figure 7-8. If no files are mismatched, Dreamweaver tells you that no synchronization is necessary.

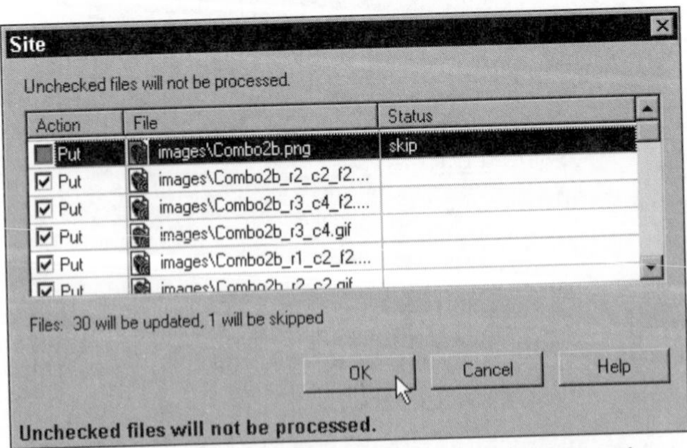

Figure 7-8: Confirm files to get or put or to be deleted during the Synchronization process in the Site dialog box.

7. Deselect any file for action by removing its checkmark from the Action column.

8. Click OK when you're ready.

   Dreamweaver displays the process of the synchronization in the dialog box and the status bar of the Site window.

9. When the synchronization is complete, you can keep a record of the changes by selecting the Save Log button; if you do, Dreamweaver asks for a file location. When you're done, select the Close button.

On Windows, if you have Dreamweaver windows open other than just the Site window, the Site dialog box may be not appear on top of the Site window. Select the other Dreamweaver windows to find the Site dialog box.

Synchronization is a powerful new addition to Dreamweaver's arsenal of site management tools. However, care needs to be taken when first using the feature to make sure that team members system clocks are in sync.

Checking Links

During a Web site's development, hundreds of different files and links are often referenced from within the HTML code. Unfortunately, it's not uncommon for a user to enthusiastically follow a link only to encounter the dreaded Web server error 404: File Not Found. Broken links are one of a Webmaster's most persistent headaches, because a Web page may have not only internal links pointing to other pages on the Web site, but external links as well — over which the Webmaster has no control.

Orphaned files constitute a parallel nightmare for the working Web developer. An orphaned file is one that is included in the local or remote site but is no longer actively referenced by any Web page. Orphaned files take up valuable disk space and can erroneously be transferred from an old site to a new one.

Dreamweaver includes for the Web designer a useful feature to ease the labor in solving both of these problems: the Link Checker. The Link Checker command can be used to check a single page, selected pages, a subfolder, or an entire site. Once the Link Checker has completed its survey, you can view broken links, external files (links outside the site, such as absolute references and mailto: links), and orphaned files. You can also repair broken links immediately or save the Link Checker results in a file for later viewing.

To check for links, follow these steps:

1. Make sure that the most current versions of the files have been saved.
2. To check a single document from within Dreamweaver, open the file and then choose File ➪ Check Links, or use the keyboard shortcut Shift+F8.
3. To check for links on an entire site from within Dreamweaver, choose Site ➪ Check Links Sitewide or use the keyboard shortcut Ctrl+F8 (Command+F8).

When Dreamweaver has finished checking for all the links on your page or site, it opens the Link Checker dialog box. The Link Checker dialog box, shown in Figure 7-9, provides a summary report of the broken links, external links, and when an entire site is reviewed, orphaned files. You can also use the Save button to store for future reference, in a tab-delimited text file, a report of the problems that the Link Checker has found.

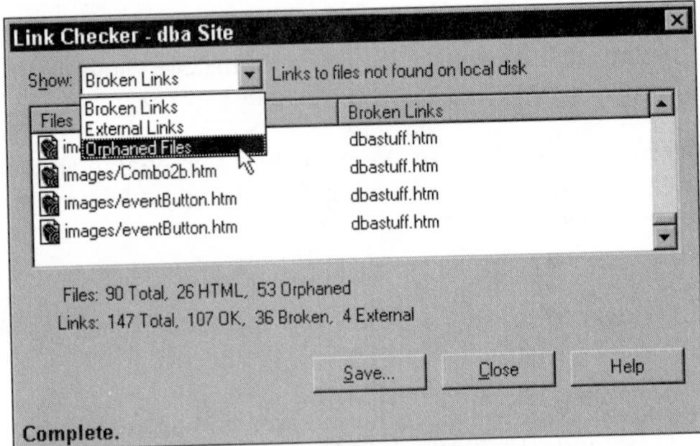

Figure 7-9: The Link Checker dialog box helps you determine which files have broken links and then fix the links directly.

When you list broken links, you can observe any file that is included as a link, inserted as an image, or embedded in the page, but which cannot be located. If you want to fix the broken link, you can do so by double-clicking the highlighted broken-link file. This brings up the file in Dreamweaver, where you can fix any problems using the Property Inspector. You can use the Property Inspector to locate the `Src` attribute. To open the page from the Link Checker, double-click the Dreamweaver icon next to the broken link.

You can also fix the link directly in the Link Checker window by following these steps:

1. Run the Link Checker command, either for the entire site or a single Web page.
2. In the Link Checker window, select the path and file name of the broken link you want to repair.
3. Enter the correct path for the missing file.

You can also access the Link Checker for both your local and remote folders. After you've selected your files or folders, choose File ➪ Check Links, from the main Dreamweaver menu, to check either the selected files or the entire Web site. Or, you can right-click (Control+click) any of the selected files to display the shortcut menu and choose the Check Link options from there.

Launching External Editors

As Web pages grow in complexity, many different types of media are involved in the creation of a page. Graphic editors, audio editors, word processors, spreadsheet programs, and database systems are all used in the creation and modification of files that can be included on a Web page—and the list grows daily. While multi-tasking computers enable you to run any of these programs simultaneously with Dreamweaver, until now you had to seek out the file or its corresponding editor in a separate file manager. With Dreamweaver 3's capability to invoke editors for any file type, the workflow has been greatly simplified.

New Feature

Earlier versions of Dreamweaver enabled you to automatically summon an external HTML editor as well as a graphic editor. In Dreamweaver 3, you can assign an editor to any file type—actually you can assign multiple editors to the same file type for maximum flexibility. Because the editors are assigned according to file extension rather than kind of file, you can associate different editors for every different graphic format, if you so choose.

To launch a file's primary editor from the Site window, just double-click the file name. If you have multiple editors assigned to a file type, you can open the file with an alternate editor by right-clicking (Control+clicking) the file name and choosing the editor from the Open With menu option. There's even a Browse option under the Open With menu to enable you to select an unassigned editor.

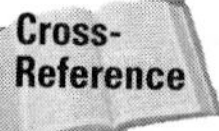

To learn how to set up editors for any media type, see the "External Editor Preferences" section in Chapter 4.

You may note that certain editors are preassigned on Windows systems. For example, on my system, if I double-click any .zip file, WinZip loads the archive. Dreamweaver recognizes file extension associations registered on your system. If a file extension has a particular association, it's listed under the Type category in the Site window. My file chap07.zip, for instance, is shown to be a WinZip file.

Tip

Macintosh users should check to see if the desired editor opens when the file is double-clicked before assigning new editors in Dreamweaver. On Macintosh, Dreamweaver uses system assignments if available.

Working with the Site Map

A Web site consists primarily of pages linked to other pages, which in turn can be linked to more pages. The more complex the site, the more difficult it becomes to comprehend—or remember—the entire structure when looking at just a directory listing.

With Dreamweaver 3, you can easily view your entire Web site and all its links as a hierarchical tree using the Site Map feature. Not only do problems such as broken links jump out at you—after all, they're depicted in red—but also the Site Map can give you a much needed overview of the entire site. Poor site design can lead to visitors getting "lost" or frustrated with the number of links it takes to get to an important page. Dreamweaver 3's Site Map gives you a visual reference and enables you to create the structure for entire sites in a point-and-click environment.

The Site Map is a graphical representation of your site, with all its Web pages symbolized by icons, as shown in Figure 7-10. The Site Map resembles both an organizational chart and a flow chart. The Web site's home page is shown at the top of the chart. A link from one page to another is represented by a connecting line with an arrowhead. Any document, other than the home page, that is linked to additional pages indicates these pages with a plus or minus symbol in Windows systems and a right or down arrow in Macintosh systems. By default, Dreamweaver displays your Site Map only two levels deep. Selecting the plus/minus (arrow) symbols shows and hides the view of the linked pages on deeper levels.

To open the Site Map from the Document window, choose Window ➪ Site Map or use the keyboard shortcut Ctrl+F5 (Command+F5). If the Site window is open, you can select the Site Map button to bring up the Site Map. The Site Map button has two settings, which you can activate by clicking and holding down the corresponding button. The Map Only setting displays just the Site Map. The Map and Files setting shows the Site Map in one pane of the Site window and the Local Files pane in the other.

The Site Map represents internal HTML pages with Dreamweaver page icons. If the link is good, the name is in blue type; if the link is broken, it's red. External files—files on another site—and special links, such as a `mailto:` or `javascript:` link, are indicated with globes. Initially, the Site Map displays only the HTML files, and not any hidden or dependent files, in a site. (Hidden and dependent files are covered later in this section.)

If your site has enabled Dreamweaver's Check In/Check Out features, you see additional symbols on the Site Map. A file checked out by you is indicated by a green checkmark. If the file has been checked out by someone else, the checkmark is red. It's not uncommon for teams to prevent an important Web page from being altered by making it read-only (Windows) or locking it (Macintosh). Such files are noted with a lock symbol.

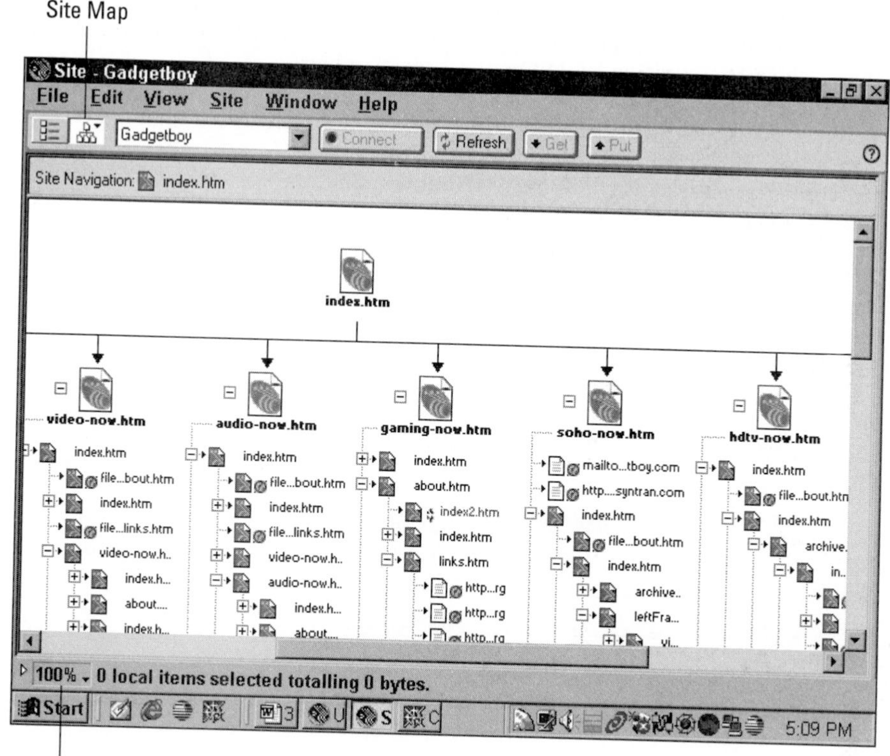

Figure 7-10: Clicking the Site Map icon in the Site window brings up a graphical representation of your site.

To view a Site Map of your site, it must be in a local folder. To view a Site Map of a remote site, you must first download it to a local folder.

Storyboarding with the Site Map

Increasingly, Web designers lay out the structure of their sites before filling in the details with text, image, and media content. This approach is all but essential on larger sites where development is divided among many people. In many ways, laying out the site's structure ahead of the content makes the content phase go much faster. You can, for example, pick an existing page (even if it is empty of content) from the Select File dialog box when building your links, rather than entering a nonexistent page's file name in the Link text box — and then trying to remember to create it later.

All you need to begin building your site with the Site Map is a single file, typically the site's home page. This home page is then defined as such in the Site Map Layout panel of the Site Definition dialog box.

To create a Web site structure from the Site Map, follow these steps:

1. Open the Site Map by choosing Window ➪ Site Map or one of the other methods previously described.
2. Select the icon of the site's home page.
3. Choose Site ➪ Link to a New File (Site ➪ Site Map View ➪ Link to a New File). You can also right-click (Ctrl+click) the page's icon and choose Link to New File from the shortcut menu. Or use the key shortcut: Ctrl+Shift+N (Command+Shift+N).

   The Link to New File dialog box appears, as shown in Figure 7-11.

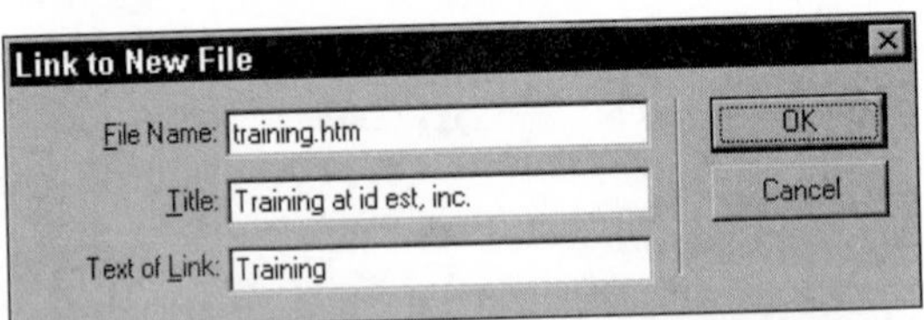

Figure 7-11: Use the Site Map to build the Web site's structure by creating new linked pages in one operation.

4. In the Link to New File dialog box, enter the correct file name, with an extension such as .htm or .html, in the File Name text box. Press Tab to move to the next text box.
5. Enter a title for the new page in the Title text box. Press Tab.
6. Enter the descriptive word or phrase to appear as a link on the original page in the Text of Link text box. Select OK or press Enter (Return) when you're done.

   The HTML page is created, and an icon for the new page appears, with a line connecting it to the original page.
7. To add another link to the home page, select the home page icon again and repeat Steps 3 through 6.
8. To add a new link to the newly created page, select its icon and repeat Steps 3 through 6.

When text links are added to a page, they are placed at the bottom of an existing page, one after another in the same line, like a text-only navigation bar. If the page is new, the text links are naturally the only items on the page.

Connecting to existing pages

Adding existing files to the Site Map is even easier than adding a new file, especially if the file to which you're linking is already in the same site. Part of building a Web-like structure is connecting from one page to another. With the Site Map, this is literally a drag-and-drop affair.

When an HTML icon is selected in the Site Map, a Point to File icon appears. The Point to File feature on the Site Map is basically used the same way it is on the Property Inspectors — just click the symbol and drag your pointer to another file. You can point and link to files in the current site whether or not they're already in the Site Map.

To link to a file that's in the current site but not on the Site Map (in other words, a file that's not linked to the home page or any connected pages), it's best to have both the Site Map and the Local Files panels displayed. To show both panels, select and hold down the Site Map button and then choose Map and Files from the drop-down list. Next, in the Site Map panel, select the file you want to link from — and a Point to File icon appears. Click and drag the Point to File icon from the Site Map to the Local Files panel to select the linking page. A line is drawn from the Point to File icon to the selected file, as shown in Figure 7-12. When your pointer is over the desired file, release the mouse button. The link is added, with a new icon appearing on the Site Map, and a text link is added to the originating page.

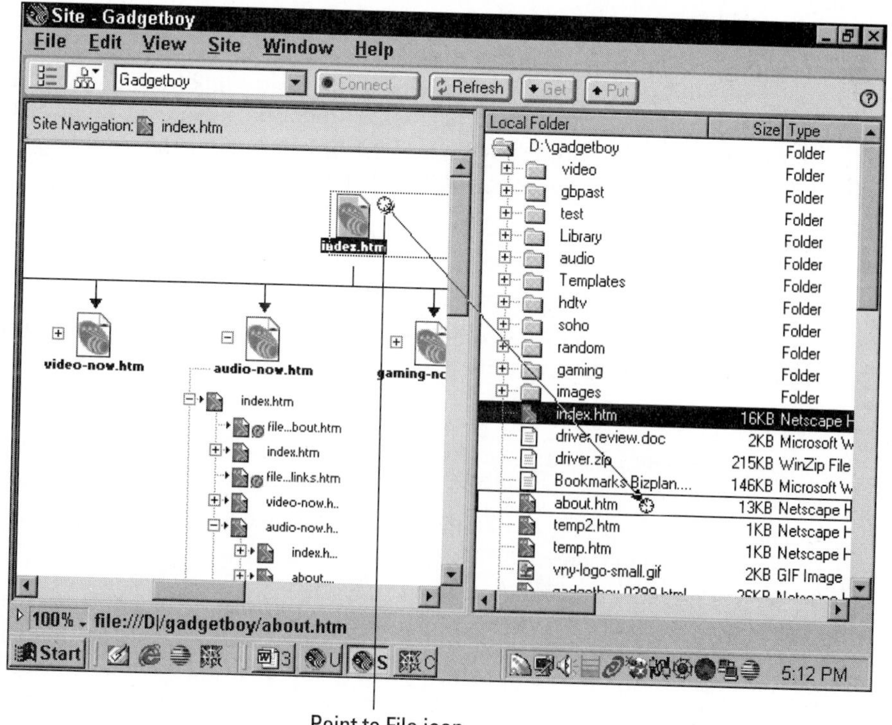

Figure 7-12: Quickly link to an existing file with Dreamweaver's Point to File feature.

If you're linking from one Site Map page to another, the Point to File icon is handy. Just select the originating page's icon and drag its Point to File symbol to the page you want to link to. Rather than draw another line across the screen—which would quickly render the Site Map screen indecipherable with crisscrossing lines—links to existing Site Map files are shown in italics.

Several other methods exist for linking to an existing file. First, you can open a Select File dialog box by selecting the originating file and then choosing Site ➪ Link to Existing File (Site ➪ Site Map View ➪ Link to an Existing File). The keyboard shortcut for this command is Ctrl+Shift+K (Command+Shift+K). You can also invoke the command by choosing Link to an Existing File from the shortcut menu, brought up by right-clicking (Control+clicking) the originating file's Site Map icon. Any of these techniques opens the Select File dialog box to enable you to browse for your file, which is useful for selecting files not in the current site.

If you want to drag and drop external files to create a link, you can use the Site Map in combination with the Windows Explorer or Finder, depending on your operating system. Instead of pointing from the originating file to the linked file, you drag the name or icon representing the external file from Windows Explorer (Finder) and drop it on the Site Map icon of the originating page. To accomplish this, it's best to either have the Site Map and Windows Explorer (Finder) windows side by side or, if they are overlapping, have the Windows Explorer (Finder) window in front.

Modifying links

If you have spent any time in Web site design and management, you know nothing is written in stone. Luckily, Dreamweaver 3 makes changing a link from one page to another a breeze and handles the tedious task of updating changes in all linked pages. Moreover, if you have multiple pages linking to a single page, you can make all the pages in the Web site link to a different page.

To change a link from one page to another, follow these steps:

1. Select the icon of the linked page you want to alter in the Site Map.
2. Choose Site ➪ Change Link (Site ➪ Site Map View ➪ Change Link) or use the keyboard shortcut Ctrl+L (Command+L).

   The Select File dialog box opens.
3. Enter the path and file name in the File Name text box or select the Browse (Choose) button to locate the file. Click OK when you've selected your file.

   Dreamweaver displays the Update Files dialog box with all the connecting pages, as shown in Figure 7-13.
4. To change the link in all the files, choose the Update button.
5. To change the link in some of the files, select the files first, using either the Shift+click or Ctrl+click (Command+click) method, and then choose the Update button.
6. To cancel the link change, choose the Don't Update button.

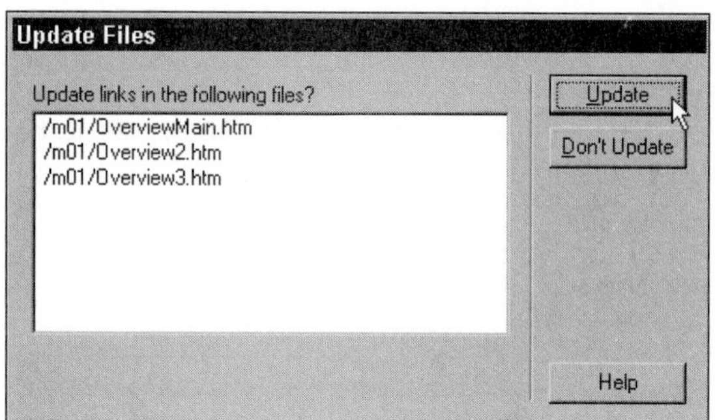

Figure 7-13: Changing a link in the Site Map brings up the Update Files dialog box.

If you have multiple pages linking to a single page that you want to alter, you can change a link sitewide. Simply select the icon for the linked page you want to modify and choose Site ➪ Change Link Sitewide. As with the Change Link command, the Update Files dialog box opens; the balance of the procedure remains the same.

I recommend that you enable the Refresh Local File List Automatically option found in the Define Sites dialog box. Dreamweaver picks up changes made inside of its own program and outside of it—even the Site Map view is updated when a change is made on a page.

Deleting links

You can delete a link from one page in several ways. First, select the icon and then do any of the following:

- ✦ Press the Delete key (Windows only).
- ✦ Choose Site ➪ Remove Link (Site ➪ Site Map View ➪ Remove Link).
- ✦ Press Ctrl+Shift+L (Command+Shift+L).
- ✦ Right-click (Control -click) the icon and, from the shortcut menu, choose Remove Link.

In all cases, the link is deleted without confirmation, and the deletion cannot be undone.

Deleting a link does not delete the file itself, just the link. For the text link, the href attribute is eliminated, but the actual text remains.

Changing titles

Dreamweaver 3 gives you an easy way to change a Web page's title right in the Site Map. Before you can use this feature, however, you must be sure the titles are used to identify the icons, rather than the file names. Choose View ➪ Show Page Titles (Site ➪ Site Map View ➪ Show Page Titles) or use the keyboard shortcut, Ctrl+Shift+T (Command+Shift+T), to switch to a title view.

To retitle a Web page, click the title twice, slowly — make sure you don't double-click the title, which will open the file. Alternatively, you can select the icon and then click the title. You can also select the icon and then choose File ⇨ Rename (Site ⇨ Rename) from the menus. In Windows, F2 is the key shortcut. All of these methods make the title an editable field that you can then modify.

Modifying pages through the Site Map

Once you've created and refined your site structure, you're ready to begin adding the content. The Site Map enables you to open a single page or a collection of pages. You can even quickly locate the text or graphic that serves as the source for the link in the connecting page.

Open a page in Dreamweaver's Document window for editing by double-clicking the page's icon in the Site Map. To open more than one page, you must first select all icons. Multiple files can be selected by selecting one file and then Shift+clicking the additional files. Another method of multiple selection is to click into an empty area in the Site Map and then drag a rectangle around the desired files. After all the needed files are selected, choose File ⇨ Open Selection (Site ⇨ Open), and the key shortcut is Ctrl+Alt+Shift+O (Command+Option+Shift+O). Every file opens in a separate Dreamweaver Document window.

Occasionally, you need to go right to the source of a link. Dreamweaver 3 enables you to open the connecting page and instantly select the actual link used to make the connection. To view the actual text or graphic used to make a link, first select the file's icon in the Site Map. Then, choose Site ⇨ Open Source of Link (Site ⇨ Site Map View ⇨ Open Source of Link). Dreamweaver loads the page containing the link, opens the Property Inspector, and selects the link.

Altering the home page

As noted earlier, the Site Map assigns a home page to use as the base for its organization. As with most items in Dreamweaver, this assignation can be changed. But why would you want to change a Web site's home page? One of the primary purposes for the Site Map is to provide a visual representation of a site's structure — one that can easily be presented to a client for discussion. You can set up multiple views of a site, each with its own structure, by just switching the home page.

You can replace the home page with an existing page or a new one. To create a new page and make it the home page, select Site ⇨ New Home Page (Site ⇨ Site Map View ⇨ New Home Page). The New Home Page dialog box opens with two fields to fill out: File Name and Title. After you enter the needed information, the file is created, and the icon appears by itself in the Site Map. Now you can use the Link to Existing File and Link to New features to build your new site organization.

To change the home page to an existing file, choose Site ⇨ Set as Home Page (Site ⇨ Site Map View ⇨ Set as Home Page). The Select File dialog box opens and enables you to choose a new file. Once you've selected a file, the Site Map is recreated using the new file as a base and displaying any existing links.

Viewing the Site Map

The more complex the site, the more important it is to be able to view the Site Map in different ways. To cut down on the number of pages showing, Dreamweaver 3 enables you to hide any pages you choose. For maximum detail, you can also display all the dependent files (such as a page's graphics) in the Site Map. You even have the option of temporarily limiting the view to a particular "branch" of the Site Map. Dreamweaver also enables you to zoom out to get the big picture of a particularly large site or save the Site Map as a graphic.

If the Site Map columns are too narrow to see the full title or file name, use the ToolTips feature. Enabling View ➪ Tool Tips (Site ➪ Tool Tips) causes Dreamweaver to display the full text of the title or file name in a ToolTip box when your pointer passes over the name.

Working with hidden and dependent files

Web sites are capable of containing several hundred, if not several thousand, pages. In these situations, the Site Map can become overcrowded. Dreamweaver can mark any file (and its associated linked files) as hidden with a single command, View ➪ Show/Hide Link (Site ➪ Site Map View ➪ Show/Hide Link). The key shortcut is Ctrl+Shift+Y (Command+Shift+Y). The Show/Hide Link command is a toggle—applying it a second time to a file removes the "hidden" designation.

To see previously hidden files, choose View ➪ Show Files Marked as Hidden (Site ➪ Site Map View ➪ Show Files Marked as Hidden). Hidden files made visible are displayed in italics.

Dependent files include any image, external style sheet, or media file (such as a Flash movie). By default, dependent files are not displayed in the Site Map; however, you can opt to view them by choosing View ➪ Show Dependent Files (Site ➪ Site Map View ➪ Show Dependent Files). Once visible on the Site Map, you can send any image to its designated image editor by double-clicking its icon. You can also open the Styles palette by double-clicking any external CSS file.

Focusing on part of a Site Map

Most of the time, the overall view, centered on the Web site's home page, is most useful. Sometimes, though, you want to examine a section of the site in greater detail. Dreamweaver enables you to set any page to be treated like a temporary home page or root, ignoring all linking pages above it.

To view just a portion of your Web site, first select the page you wish to choose as the new root. Next, choose View ➪ View As Root (Site ➪ Site Map View ➪ View As Root) or use the keyboard shortcut Ctrl+Shift+R (Command+Shift+R). The Site Map now depicts your selected file as if it were the home page. Notice also that the Site Navigation bar has changed, as shown in Figure 7-14. The Site Navigation bar shows the actual home page and any pages that have been chosen as roots, separated by right-pointing arrows. You can switch from one root to another, or to the actual home page, by clicking its icon in the Site Navigation bar.

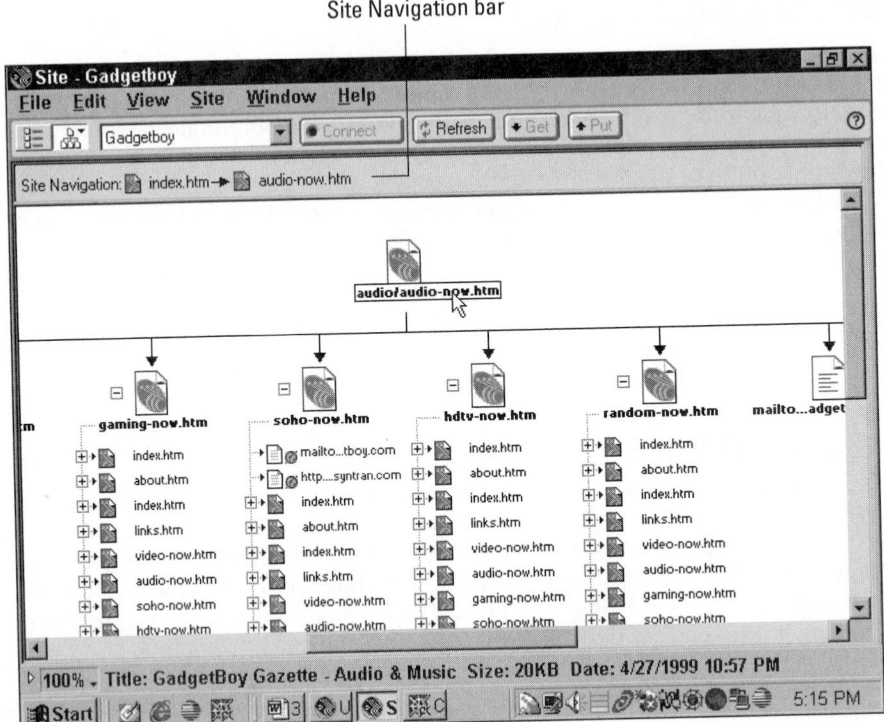

Figure 7-14: To view a section of your Site Map in detail, use the View As Root command.

Zooming out of your Site Map

What do you do when your site is so big that you can't see it all in one screen? Dreamweaver 3 provides a Zoom feature that enables you to pull back for a more encompassing view. The Site Map Zoom button is located on the far left of the Site Window's status bar. Selecting the Zoom button reveals the magnification options to choose from: 100%, 75%, 50%, 25%, and 12%.

If you find that Dreamweaver is displaying page icons only, with no file names or titles, you can expand the column width in the layout. Choose View ➪ Layout (Site ➪ Site Map View ➪ Layout) and change the value in the Column Width text box to a higher number. The default column width is 125 pixels.

Converting the Site Map into a graphic

Web designers like to believe that the whole world is wired and on the Web, but in truth, we're not there yet. Sometimes it's necessary to present a client or other interested party with a printout of a site design. Dreamweaver makes it possible to take a snapshot of the current Site Map and save it as a graphic file that can then be inserted into another program for printing—or attached to an e-mail for easy transmission.

To convert the Site Map into a graphic in Windows, choose File ➪ Save Site Map and then choose either BMP or PNG from the drop-down box in the Save box. On the Macintosh, choose Site ➪ Site Map View ➪ Save Site Map, and then the menu flies out to give you two file type options: Save Site Map as PICT or Save Site Map as JPEG.

When you save a Site Map as a graphic, the image is saved at the size necessary to contain all the displayed icons. Figure 7-15 shows a 448 × 722 pixel-sized graphic, saved from a Site Map, in Fireworks.

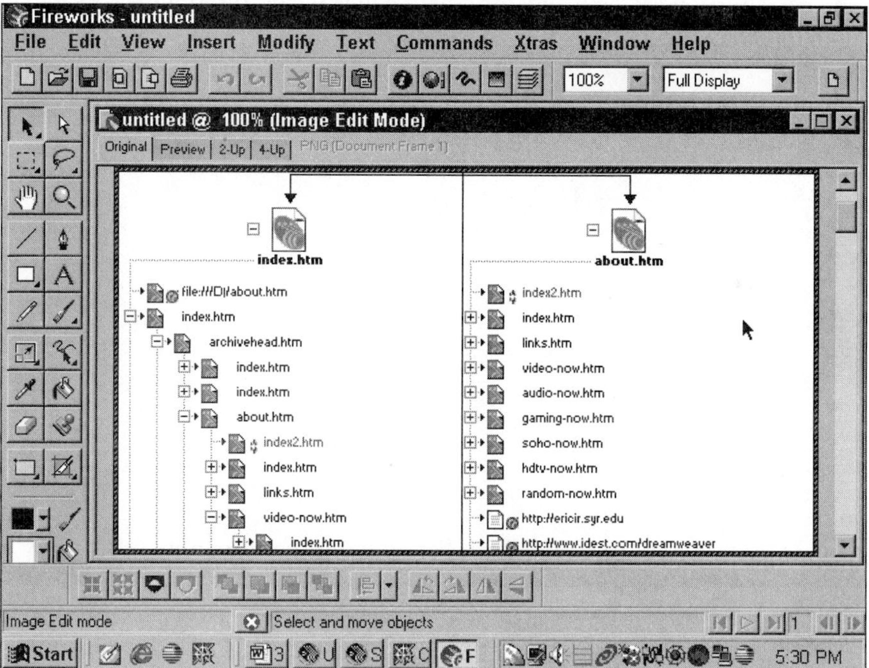

Figure 7-15: This Site Map image, ready for editing in Fireworks 3, was created in Dreamweaver.

Summary

With the Site window and Dreamweaver's site management tools, a group or an individual Web designer can manage even large and diverse sites.

✦ Setting up a new site is an essential element in managing a Dreamweaver Web site. Without the root directory for the local files, Dreamweaver cannot properly manage the Web pages and associated links.

- ✦ The Site window enables you to drag and drop files from the host server to the local root folder.
- ✦ All file check-in and check-out functions for teams can be handled through the Site window.
- ✦ Broken links can be quickly found and fixed with the Link Checker. You can also find orphaned files and identify external links.
- ✦ With Dreamweaver 3's new Synchronize command, keeping your local and remote sites in sync is easier than ever.
- ✦ Dreamweaver's Site Map enables you to quickly visualize your overall site structure.
- ✦ The Site Map is also useful for creating new pages and their associated links. You can storyboard the entire site structure — links and all — before adding any content.

In the next chapter, you learn how to speed up your Web site production through the use of Dreamweaver templates.

✦ ✦ ✦

PART

Using Basic HTML in Dreamweaver

✦ ✦ ✦ ✦

In This Part

✦ ✦ ✦ ✦

Understanding How HTML Works

✦ ✦ ✦ ✦

In This Chapter

Laying the HTML foundation

Working with the <head> section

Developing the <body> section

Adding special characters

✦ ✦ ✦ ✦

In a perfect world, you could lay out the most complex Web site with a visual authoring tool and never have to see the HTML, much less code in it. Dreamweaver takes you a long way toward this goal — in fact, you can create many types of Web pages using only Dreamweaver's Document window. As your pages become more complex, however, you will probably need to tweak your HTML just a tad.

This chapter gives you a basic understanding of how HTML works and gives you the specific building blocks you need to begin creating Web pages. Also, in this chapter you get your first look at a Dreamweaver 3 innovation: the Quick Tag Editor for swiftly altering the code, right in the visual environment. The other Dreamweaver-specific material in this chapter — primarily describing how Dreamweaver sets and modifies a page's properties — is suitable for even the most accomplished Web designers. Armed with these fundamentals, you are ready to begin your exploration of Web page creation.

The Structure of an HTML Page

The simplest explanation of how HTML works derives from the full expansion of its acronym: HyperText Markup Language. *HyperText* refers to one of the World Wide Web's main properties — the capability to jump from one page to another, no matter where the pages are located on the Web. *Markup Language* means that a Web page is really just a heavily annotated text file. The basic building blocks of HTML, such as <strong> and <p>, are known as markup elements, or tags. The terms *element* and *tag* are used interchangeably.

An HTML page, then, is a set of instructions (the tags) suggesting to your browser how to display the enclosed text and images. The browser knows what kind of page it is handling based on the tag that opens the page, `<html>`, and the tag that closes the page, `</html>`. The great majority of HTML tags come in such pairs, in which the closing tag always has a forward slash before the keyword. Two examples of tag pairs are: `<p>...</p>` and `<title>...</title>`. A few important tags are represented by a single element: the image tag `<img>`, for example.

The HTML page is divided into two primary sections: the `<head>` and the `<body>`. Information relating to the entire document goes in the `<head>` section: the title, description, keywords, and any language subroutines that may be called from within the `<body>`. The content of the Web page is found in the `<body>` section. All the text, graphics, embedded animations, Java applets, and other elements of the page are found between the opening `<body>` and the closing `</body>` tags.

When you start a new document in Dreamweaver, the basic format is already laid out for you. Listing 8-1 shows the code from a Dreamweaver blank Web page.

Listing 8-1: **The HTML for a New Dreamweaver Page**

```
<html>
<head>
<title>Untitled Document</title>
<meta http-equiv="Content-Type" content="text/html; charset=iso-8859-1">
</head>

<body bgcolor="#FFFFFF">

</body>
</html>
```

Notice how the `<head>...</head>` pair is separate from the `<body>...</body>` pair, and that both are contained within the `<html>...</html>` tags.

Also notice that the `<body>` tag has an additional element:

```
bgcolor="#FFFFFF"
```

This type of element is known as an *attribute*. Attributes modify the basic tag and either can be equal to a value or can stand alone; in this example, the attribute, `bgcolor`, is set to a hexadecimal number that represents the color white. Thus, this attribute sets the background color of the body—the page—to white. Not every tag has attributes, but when they do, the attributes are specific.

Tip

If you're using the PC version of Dreamweaver, you have access to an excellent HTML guide through the HomeSite editor. From the HomeSite window, select Help ➪ Help Topics and then open the HTML Reference from the Help pane.

One last note about an HTML page: You are free to use carriage returns, spaces, and tabs as needed to make your code more readable. The interpreting browser ignores all but the included tags and text to create your page. Some minor, browser-specific differences in interpretation of these elements are pointed out throughout the book, but by and large, you can indent or space your code as you desire.

Defining <head> Elements

Information pertaining to the Web page overall is contained in the `<head>` section of an HTML page. Browsers read the `<head>` to find out how to render the page—for example, is the page to be displayed using the Western, the Chinese, or some other character set? Search engine spiders also read this section to quickly glean a summary of the page.

When you begin inserting JavaScript (or code from another scripting language such as VBScript) into your Web page, all the subroutines and document-wide declarations go into the `<head>` area. Dreamweaver uses this format by default when you insert a JavaScript behavior.

Dreamweaver enables you to insert, view, and modify `<head>` content without opening an HTML editor. Dreamweaver 3's View Head Content capability enables you to work with `<meta>` tags and other `<head>` HTML code as you do with the regular content in the visual editor.

Establishing page properties

When you first start Dreamweaver, your default Web page is untitled, with no background image but a plain white background. You can change all these properties and more through Dreamweaver's Page Properties dialog box.

As usual, Dreamweaver gives you more than one method for accessing the Page Properties dialog box. You can select Modify ➪ Page Properties, or you can use the keyboard shortcut Ctrl+J (Command+J).

Tip

Here's the other way to open the Page Properties dialog box. Right-click (Control+click) any open area in the Document window—that is, any part of the screen not occupied by an image, table, or other object (text outside of tables is okay to click, however). From the bottom of the Shortcut menu, select Page Properties.

The Page Properties dialog box, shown in Figure 8-1, gives you easy control of your HTML page's overall look and feel.

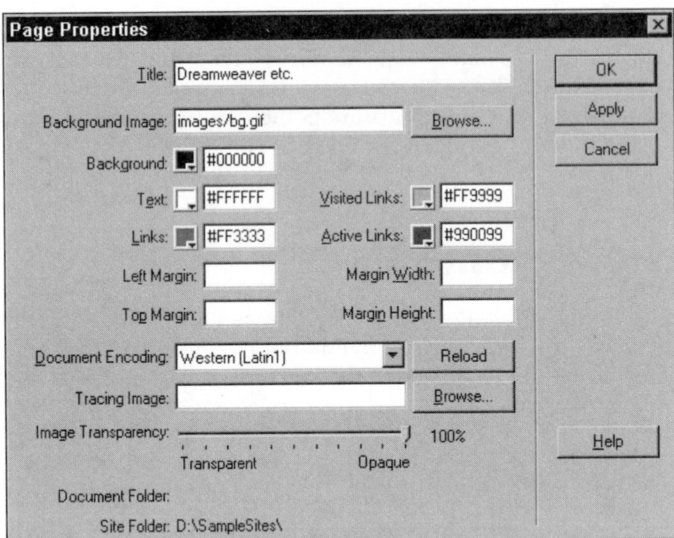

Figure 8-1: Change your Web page's overall appearance through the Page Properties dialog box.

Technically, some of the values you assign through the Page Properties dialog box are applied to the <body> tag; because they affect the overall appearance of a page, however, they are covered in this <head> section.

The key areas of the Page Properties dialog box are as follows:

Page Property	***Description***
Title	The title of your Web page. The name you enter here appears in the browser's title bar when your page is viewed. Search engine spiders also read the title as one of the important indexing clues.
Background Image	The file name of the graphic you want in the page background. Either type in the path directly or pick a file by clicking the Browse (Choose) button. You can embed the graphic of your choice in the background of your page; if the image is smaller than your content requires, the browser tiles the image to fill out the page. Specifying a background image overrides any selection in the Background color field.

Page Property	*Description*
Background	Click this color swatch to change the background color of the Web page. Select one of the browser-safe colors from the pop-up menu, or enter its name or hexadecimal representation (for example, "#FFFFFF") directly into the text box.
Text	Click this color swatch to control the color of default text.
Links	Click this color swatch to modify the color of any text designated as a link, or the border around an image link.
Visited Links	Click this color swatch to select the color that linked text changes to after a visitor to your Web page has selected that link and then returned to your page.
Active Links	Click this color swatch to choose the color to which linked text changes briefly when a user selects the link.
Left Margin, Top Margin, Margin Width, Margin Height	Enter values here to change the default margin settings used by browsers. The Left and Top Margin settings are used by Microsoft, whereas Margin Width and Margin Height are used by Netscape.
Document Encoding	The character set in which you want your Web page to be displayed. Choose one from the drop-down list. The default is Western (Latin 1).
Tracing Image	Selects an image to use as a layout guide.
Image Transparency	Sets the degree of transparency for the tracing image.

The Page Properties dialog box also displays the document folder if the page has been saved, and the current site root folder if one has been selected.

The Tracing Image option is a powerful feature for quickly building a Web page based on design comps. For details about this feature and how to use it, see the section "Tracing Your Design with Layers" in Chapter 28.

Choosing Colors from an Onscreen Image

One of the features found throughout Dreamweaver 3, the Eyedropper tool, is especially useful in the Page Properties options. The Eyedropper tool appears whenever you open any of Dreamweaver's color swatches, such as those attached to the Background, Text, and Links colors. You can not only pick a color from the Web-safe palette that appears, but also use the Eyedropper to select any color on any page — including system colors such as those found in dialog boxes and menu strips.

Continued

Continued

To use the Eyedropper tool to choose a color for the background (or any of the other options) from an onscreen image, follow these steps:

1. Insert your image on the page and, using the vertical scroll bar, position the Document window so that the image and the Page Properties dialog box can be viewed simultaneously.

   If your image is too big to fit both it and the Page Properties dialog box on the same screen, temporarily resize your image by dragging its sizing handles. You can restore the original image size when you're done by selecting the Refresh button on the Image Property Inspector.

2. Open the Page Properties dialog box by choosing Modify ⇨ Page Properties or using the keyboard shortcut Ctrl+J (Command+J).

3. Drag the Page Properties dialog box to a place where the image can be seen.

4. Select the Background color swatch (or whichever one you wish to change).

   The Dreamweaver color picker opens and the pointer becomes an eyedropper.

5. Move the Eyedropper tool over the image until you find the correct color. (On Windows, you must hold the mouse button down as you drag the Eyedropper off the Dreamweaver dialog box to the image.) As you move the Eyedropper over an image, its colors are reflected in the color well and its hex value is shown on the color picker. Click once when you've found the appropriate color.

   The color picker closes.

6. Repeat Steps 4 and 5 to grab other colors from the screen for other color swatches. Click OK when you've finished modifying the page properties.

You don't have to keep the image on your page to get its color. Just insert it temporarily and then delete it after you've used the Eyedropper to grab the shade you want.

Choosing a Page palette

Getting the right text and link colors to match your background color has been largely a trial-and-error process. Generally, you'd set the background color, add a contrasting text color, and then add some variations of different colors for the three different link colors — all the while clicking the Apply button and checking your results until you found a satisfactory combination. This is a time-intensive chore, to say the least.

However, Dreamweaver 3 ships with a command that enables you to quickly pick an entire palette for your page in one fell swoop. The Set Color Scheme command, shown in Figure 8-2, features palette combinations from noted Web designers Lynda Weinman and Bruce Heavin. The colors available in the command are all Web safe — which means that they will appear the same in the major browsers on all Macintosh and Windows systems without dithering.

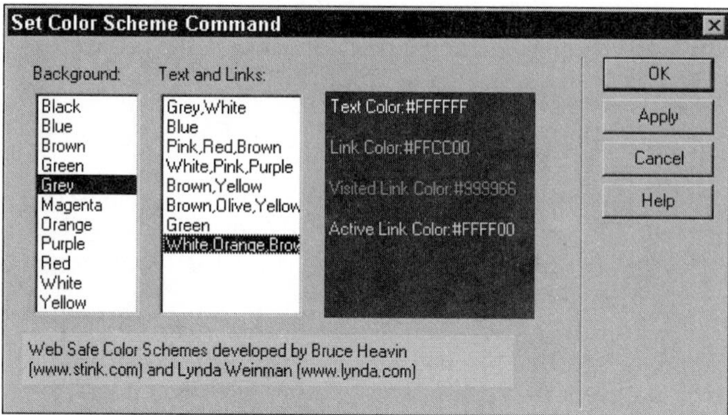

Figure 8-2: Get a Web-safe page palette with one click by using the Set Color Scheme command.

To use the Set Color Scheme command, follow these steps:

1. Choose Command ➪ Set Color Scheme.

   The Set Color Scheme dialog box opens.

2. Select the background color from the Background column on the left.

   The Text and Links column is updated to show available combinations for the selected background color.

3. Select a color set from the Text and Links column to see various combinations in the Preview pane.

   The color names — such as White, Pink, Brown — refer to the Text, Link, and Visited Link colors, generally. If only one color name is offered, the entire color scheme uses shades of that color. Note that the background color changes slightly for various color combinations to work better with the foreground color choices.

4. Click Apply to see the effect on your current page. Click OK when you finish.

To learn more about commands in general – including how to build your own – check out Chapter 21.

Understanding <meta> and other <head> tags

Summary information about the content of a page — and a lot more — is conveyed through `<meta>` tags used within the `<head>` section. The `<meta>` tag can be read by the server to create a header file, which makes it easier for indexing software used by search engines to catalog sites. Numerous different types of `<meta>` tags exist, and you can insert them in your document just like other objects.

One <meta> tag is included by default in every Dreamweaver page. The Document Encoding option of the Page Properties dialog box determines the character set used by the current Web page and is displayed in the <head> section as follows:

```
<meta http-equiv="Content-Type" content="text/html; charset=iso-8859-1">
```

The preceding <meta> tag tells the browser that this page is, in fact, an HTML page and that the page should be rendered using the specified character set (the `charset` attribute). The key attribute here is `http-equiv`, which is responsible for generating a server response header.

Tip

Once you've determined your <meta> tags for a Web site, the same basic <meta> information can go on every Web page. Dreamweaver gives you a way to avoid having to insert the same lines again and again: templates. Once you've set up the <head> elements the way you'd like them, choose File ➪ Save As Template. If you want to add <meta> or any other <head> tags to an existing template, you can edit the template and then update the affected pages. For more on templates, turn to Chapter 33.

In Dreamweaver 3, you can insert a <meta> tag or any other tag using the <head> tag objects, which you access via the Head panel in the Objects palette or the Insert ➪ Head menu option. The new <head> tag objects are described in Table 8-1 and subsequent subsections.

Table 8-1
Head Tag Objects

Head Tag Object	Description
Meta	Inserts information that describes or affects the entire document.
Keywords	Includes a series of words used by the search engine to index the current Web page and/or site.
Description	Includes a text description of the current Web page and/or site.
Refresh	Reloads the current document or loads a new URL within a specified number of seconds.
Base	Establishes a reference for all other URLs in the current Web page.
Link	Inserts a link to an external document, such as a style sheet.

Inserting tags with the Meta object

The Meta object is used to insert tags that provide information for the Web server, through the HTTP-equiv attribute, and other overall data that you want to include in your Web page but not make visible to the casual browser. Some Web pages, for example, have built-in expiration dates after which the content is to be considered outmoded. In Dreamweaver, you can use the Meta object to insert a wide range of descriptive data.

You can access the Meta object on the Head panel of the Objects palette or via the Insert menu by choosing Insert ➪ Head ➪ Meta. Like all the Head objects, you don't have to have the Head Content visible to insert the Meta object; although you do have to choose View ➪ Head Content if you wish to edit the object. To insert a Meta object, follow these steps:

1. Select Insert ➪ Head ➪ Meta or the Meta object from the Head panel of the Objects palette. Your current cursor position is irrelevant.

   The Insert Meta dialog box opens, as shown in Figure 8-3.

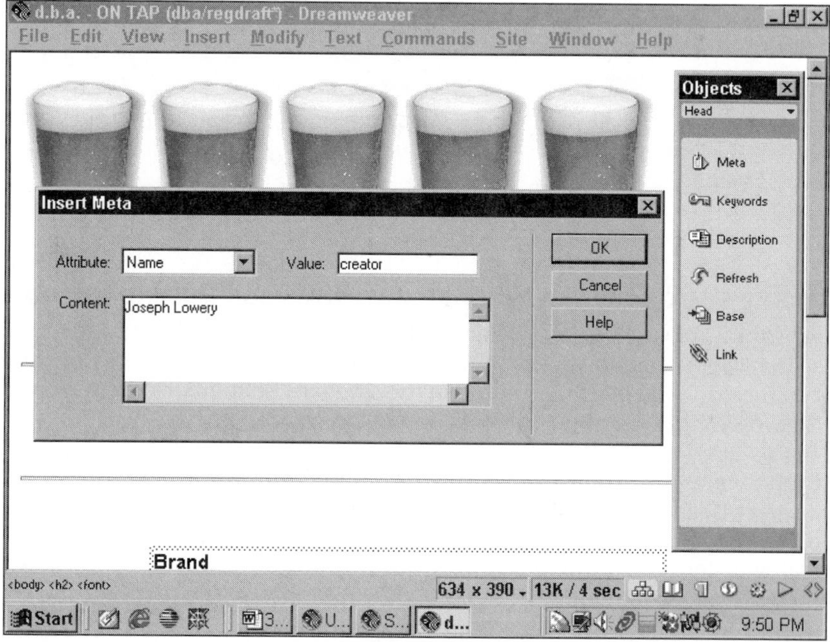

Figure 8-3: The Meta object enables you to enter a full range of `<meta>` tags in the `<head>` section of your Web page.

2. Choose the desired attribute: Name or an HTTP-equivalent from the Attribute list box. Press Tab.
3. Enter the value for the selected attribute in the Value text box. Press Tab.
4. Enter the value for the content attribute in the Content text box.
5. Click OK when you're done.

You can add as many Meta objects as you need to by repeating Steps 1 through 4. To edit an existing Meta object, you must first choose View ➪ Head Content to reveal the `<head>` code, indicated by the various icons. Select the Meta tag icon and make your changes in the Property Inspector.

Built-in Meta Commands

Although Dreamweaver presents six different Head objects, `<meta>` tags form the basis of four of them: Meta, Keywords, Description, and Refresh. By specifying different `name` attributes, the purpose of the `<meta>` tags changes. For example, a Keywords object uses this format:

```
<meta name="keywords" content="dreamweaver, web, authoring, ¬
HTML, DHTML, CSS, Macromedia">
```

whereas a Description object inserts this type of code:

```
<meta name="description" content="This site is devoted to ¬
extensions made possible by Macromedia's Dreamweaver, the ¬
premier Web authoring tool.">
```

It is possible to create all your `<meta>` tags with the Meta object by specifying the name attribute and giving it the pertinent value, but it's easier to just use the standard Dreamweaver 3 Head objects.

Aiding search engines with the Keywords and Description objects

Let's take a closer look at the tags that convey indexing and descriptive information to search engine spiders. In Dreamweaver 3, these chores are handled by the Keywords and Description objects. As noted in the sidebar, "Built-in Meta Commands," the Keywords and Description objects output specialized `<meta>` tags.

Both objects are straightforward to use. Choose Insert ➪ Head ➪ Keywords or Insert ➪ Head ➪ Description. You can also choose the corresponding objects from the Head panel of the Objects palette. Once selected, these objects open similar dialog boxes with a single entry area, a large text box, as shown in Figure 8-4. Enter the values — whether keywords or a description — in the text box and click OK when you're done. You can edit the Keywords and Description objects, like the Meta object, by selecting their icons in the Head area of the Document window, revealed by choosing View ➪ Head Contents.

Although you can enter paragraph returns in your Keywords and Description objects, there's no reason to. Browsers ignore all such formatting when processing your code.

What you place in the Keywords and Description objects can have a big impact on your Web page's accessibility. If, for example, you want to categorize your Web page as an homage to the music of the early seventies, you could enter the following in the Content area of the Keywords object:

```
music, 70s, 70's, eagles, ronstadt, bee gees, pop, rock
```

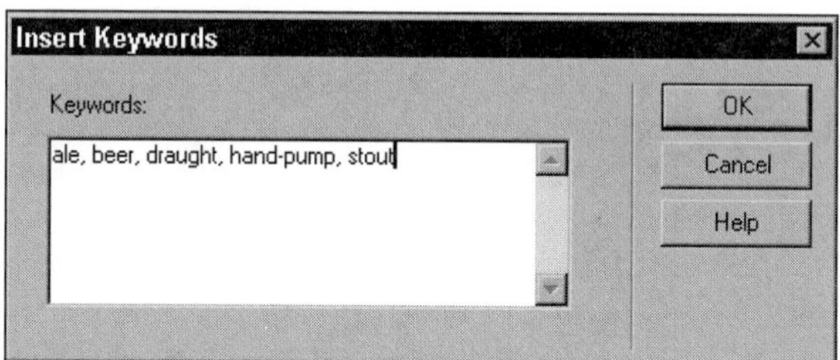

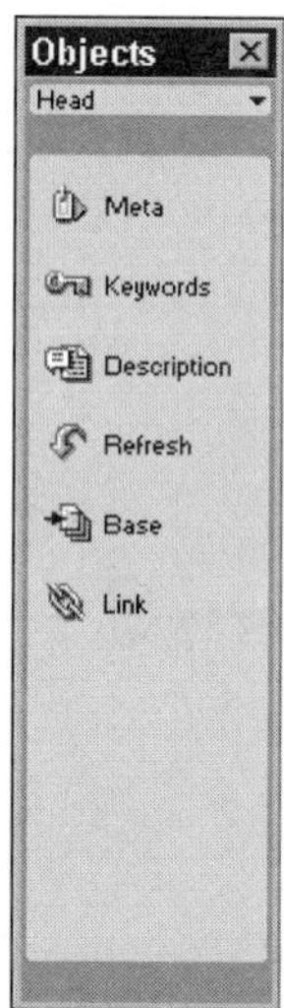

Figure 8-4: Entering information through the Keywords object helps search engines correctly index your Web page.

In the preceding case, the content list is composed of words or phrases, separated by commas. Use sentences in the Description object, like this:

```
The definitive look back to the power pop rock stylings of early 1970s music, ¬
with special sections devoted to the Eagles, Linda Ronstadt, and the Bee Gees.
```

Keep in mind that the content in the Description should complement and extend both the Keywords and the Web page title. You have more room in both the Description and Keywords objects — really, an unlimited amount — than in the page title, which should be on the short side in order to fit into the browser's title bar.

When using `<meta>` tags with the Keywords or Description objects, don't stuff the `<meta>` tags with the same word repeated over and over again. The search engines are engineered to reject multiple words, and your description will not get the attention it deserves.

Refreshing the page and redirecting users

The Refresh object forces a browser to reload the current page or to load a new page after a user-set interval. The Web page visitor usually controls refreshing a page; if, for some reason, the display has become garbled, the user can choose Reload from the menu to redraw the screen. Impatient Web surfer that I am, I often stop a page from loading to see what text links are available and then — if I don't see what I need — hit Reload to bring in the full page. The code inserted by the Refresh object tells the server, not the browser, to reload the page. This can be a powerful tool but leads to trouble if used improperly.

To insert a Refresh object, follow these steps:

1. Choose Insert ➪ Head ➪ Refresh or select the Insert Refresh object from the Head panel of the Objects palette.

   The Insert Refresh dialog box, shown in Figure 8-5, opens.

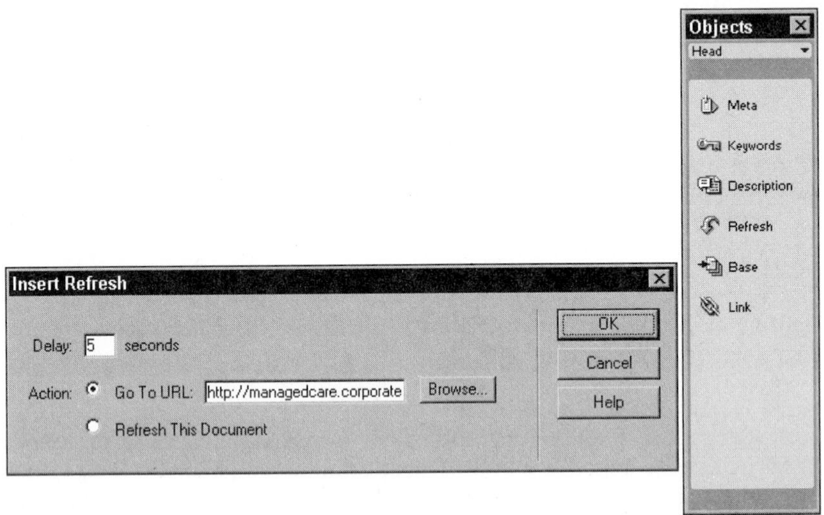

Figure 8-5: Use the Refresh object to redirect visitors from an outdated page.

2. Enter the number of seconds you want to wait before the Refresh command takes effect in the Delay text box.

   The Delay value is calculated from the time the page finishes loading.

3. Select the desired Action:
   - Go to URL
   - Refresh This Document

4. If you selected Go to URL, enter a path to another page in the text box or select the Browse button to select a file.

5. Click OK when you're done.

The Refresh object is most often used to redirect a visitor to another Web page. The Web is a fluid place, and sites often move from one address to another. Typically, a page at the old address contains the Refresh code that automatically takes the user to the new address. It's good practice to include a link to your new URL on the "change-of-address" page because not all browsers support the Refresh option. One other tip: Keep the number of seconds to a minimum—there's no point in waiting for something to happen automatically when you could click a link.

If you elect to choose the Refresh This Document option, use extreme caution. You can easily set up an endless loop for your visitors in which the same page is constantly being refreshed. If you are working with a page that updates often, enter a longer Refresh value such as 300 or 500. Also, you should be sure to include a link to another page to enable them to exit from the continually refreshed page.

Changing bases

Through the Base object, the `<head>` section enables you to exert fundamental control over the basic HTML element: the link. The code inserted by this object specifies the base URL for the current page. If you use relative addressing (covered in Chapter 6), you can switch all your links to another directory—even another Web site—with one command. The Base object takes two attributes: `Href`, which redirects all the other relative links on your page; and `target`, which specifies where the links will be rendered.

To insert a Base object in your page, follow these steps:

1. Choose Insert ⇨ Head ⇨ Refresh or select the Insert Base object from the Head panel of the Objects palette.

   The Insert Base dialog box opens.
2. Input the path that you want all other relative links to be based on in the Href text box or choose the Browse button to pick the path.
3. If desired, enter a default target for all links without a specific target to be rendered in the Target text box.
4. Click OK when you're done.

How does a `<base>` tag affect your page? Let's say you define one link as follows:

```
images/backgnd.gif
```

Normally, the browser looks in the same folder as the current page for a subfolder named images. A different sequence occurs, however, if you set the `<base>` tag to another URL in the following way:

```
<base href="http://www.testsite.com/client-demo01/">
```

With this `<base>` tag, when the same `images/backgnd.gif` link is activated, the browser looks for its file in the following location:

```
http://www.testsite.com/client-demo01/images/backgnd.gif
```

Because of the all-or-nothing capability of <base> tags, many Webmasters use them cautiously, if at all.

Linking to other files

The Link object is used to indicate a relationship between the current page and another page or file. Although many other intended uses exist, the <link> tag is most commonly used to apply an external Cascading Style Sheet (CSS) to the current page. This code is entered automatically in Dreamweaver when you create a new linked style sheet (as described in Chapter 27), but to apply an existing style sheet, you need to use the Link object. The Link tag is also used to include TrueDoc dynamic fonts.

To insert a Link object, first choose Insert ➪ Head ➪ Link or select the Insert Link object from the Head panel of the Objects palette. This opens the Insert Link dialog box, shown in Figure 8-6.

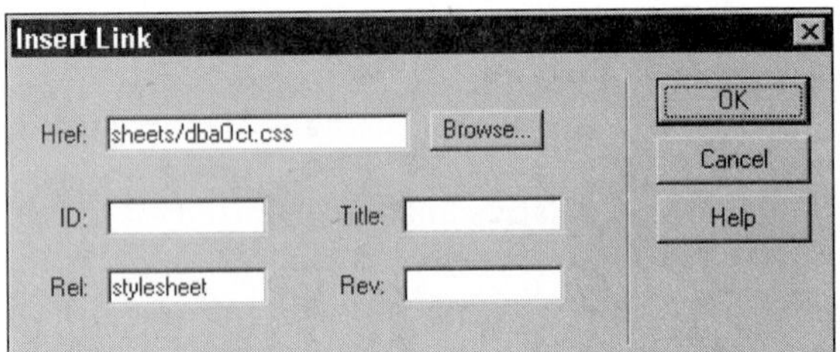

Figure 8-6: The Link object is primarily used to include external style sheets.

Next, enter the necessary attributes:

Attribute	***Description***
Href	The path to the file being linked. Use the Browse button to open the Select File dialog box.
ID	The ID attribute can be used by scripts to identify this particular object and affect it if need be.
Title	The Title attribute is displayed as a ToolTip by Internet Explorer browsers.
Rel	A keyword that describes the relationship of the linked document to the current page. For example, an external style sheet uses the keyword `stylesheet`.
Rev	Rev, like Rel, also describes a relationship but in the reverse. For example, if home.html contained a link tag with a Rel attribute set to intro.html, intro.html could contain a link tag with a Rev attribute set to home.html.

Aside from the style sheet use, there's little browser support for the other link functions. However, the W3C supports an initiative to use the <link> tag to address other media, such as speech synthesis and Braille devices, and it's entirely possible that the Link object will be used for this purpose in the future.

Adding to the <body>

The content of a Web page — the text, images, links, and plug-ins — is all contained in the <body> section of an HTML document. The great majority of <body> tags can be inserted through Dreamweaver's visual layout interface.

To use the <body> tags efficiently, you need to understand the distinction between logical styles and physical styles used in HTML. An underlying philosophy of HTML is to keep the Web as universally accessible as possible. Web content is intended to be platform- and resolution-independent, but the content itself can be styled by its intent as well. This philosophy is supported by the existence of logical <body> tags (such as <code> and <cite>), with which a block of text can be rendered according to its meaning, and physical style tags for directly italicizing or underlining text. HTML enables you to choose between logical styles, which are relative to the text, or physical styles, which can be regarded as absolute.

Logical styles

Logical styles are contextual rather than explicit. Choose a logical style when you want to ensure that the meaning, rather than a specific look, is conveyed. Table 8-2 shows a listing of logical style tags and their most common usage. Tags not supported through Dreamweaver's visual interface are noted.

Table 8-2
HTML Logical Style Tags

Tag	*Usage*
<big>	Increases the size of the selected text relative to the surrounding text. Not currently supported by Dreamweaver.
<cite>	Citations, titles, and references; usually shown in italic.
<code>	Code; for showing programming code, usually displayed in a monospaced font.
<dfn>	Defining instance; used to mark the introduction of a new term.
<em>	Emphasis; usually depicted as underlined or italicized text.

Continued

Table 8-2 (continued)

Tag	*Usage*
`<kbd>`	Keyboard; used to render text to be entered exactly.
`<s>`	Strikethrough text; used for showing text that has been deleted.
`<samp>`	Sample; a sequence of literal characters.
`<small>`	Decreases the size of the selected text relative to the surrounding text. Not currently supported by Dreamweaver.
`<strong>`	Strong emphasis; usually rendered as bold text.
`<sub>`	Subscript; the text is shown slightly lowered below the baseline. Not currently supported by Dreamweaver.
`<sup>`	Superscript; the text is shown slightly raised above the baseline. Not currently supported by Dreamweaver.
`<tt>`	Teletype; displayed with a monospaced font such as Courier.
`<var>`	Variable; used to distinguish variables from other programming code.

Logical styles are going to become increasingly important as more browsers accept Cascading Style Sheets. Style sheets make it possible to combine the best elements of both logical and physical styles. With style sheets, you can easily make the text within your `<code>` tags blue, and the variables, denoted with the `<var>` tag, green.

If a tag is not currently supported by Dreamweaver, you must enter the tag by hand – either through the HTML Source Inspector, the Quick Tag Editor, or another text editor – and preview the result in a browser. For example, you can use the `<sub>` tag to create a formula for water (H_2O), but you don't see the subscripted 2 in the formula until you view the page through a browser.

Physical styles

HTML picked up the use of physical styles from modern typography and word processing programs. Use a physical style when you want something to be absolutely bold, italic, or underlined (or, as we say in HTML, `<b>`, `<i>`, and `<u>`, respectively). You can apply the bold and the italic tags to selected text through the Property Inspector or by selecting Text ➪ Style; the underline style is available only through the Text menu.

With HTML version 3.2, a fourth physical style tag was added: `<font>`. Most browsers recognize the size attribute, which enables you to make the selected text larger or smaller, relatively or directly. To change a font size absolutely, select your text and then select Text ➪ Size; Dreamweaver inserts the following tag, where n is a number from 1 to 7:

```
<font size=n>
```

To make text larger than the default text, select Text ➪ Size Increase and then choose the value you want. Dreamweaver inserts the following tag:

```
<font size=+n>
```

The plus sign indicates the relative nature of the font. Make text smaller than the default text by selecting Text ➪ Size Decrease; Dreamweaver inserts this tag:

```
<font size=-n>
```

You can also expressly change the type of font used and its color through the face and color attributes. Because you can't be sure what fonts will be on a user's system, common practice and good form dictate that you should list alternatives for a selected font. For instance, rather than just specifying Palatino—a sans serif font common on PCs but relatively unknown on the Mac—you could insert a tag such as the following:

```
<font face=" Palatino, Times New Roman, Times, sans-serif">
```

In the preceding case, if the browser doesn't find the first font, it looks for the second one (and so forth, as specified). Dreamweaver handles the font face attribute through its Font List dialog box, which is explained fully in Chapter 9.

Working with the HTML Source Inspector

The HTML Source Inspector is used for viewing, inputting, and modifying code for your Web page. Although Dreamweaver offers many options for using the visual interface of the Document window, sometimes you just have to tweak the code by hand. Dreamweaver's acceptance by professional coders is due in large part to the easy access of the underlying code. For large-scale additions and changes, you might consider using an external HTML editor such as BBEdit or Homesite, but for many situations, the built-in HTML Source Inspector is perfectly suited and much faster to work with.

You have several ways to open the HTML Source Inspector:

✦ Choose Window ➪ HTML Source.

✦ Select the HTML Source button in either Launcher.

✦ Use the primary keyboard shortcut F10.

✦ Press another keyboard shortcut Ctrl+Tab (Control+Tab); this shortcut also alternates between the Document window and the HTML Source Inspector.

Once opened, the HTML Source Inspector (Figure 8-7) behaves like any other floating palette in Dreamweaver: the window can be resized, moved, or hidden, and the inspector can be grouped with any other palette or dragged out onto its own. When the HTML Source Inspector is opened initially, it is automatically selected. If you click in the Document window with the HTML Source Inspector open, the inspector dims but still reflects changes made in the document.

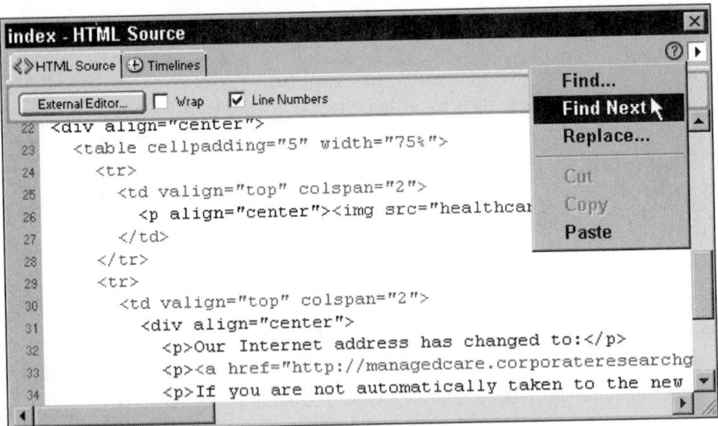

Figure 8-7: New features, such as the Line Numbers option, make it easier to follow the code in the HTML Source Inspector.

By and large, the HTML Source Inspector acts like a regular text editor. Simply click anywhere in the inspector to add or modify code. Double-click a word to select it. Select an entire line by moving your pointer to the left edge of the code—where the pointer becomes a right-pointing arrow—and clicking once. Multiple lines can be selected in this same fashion by dragging the right-pointing arrow. Once a section of code is selected, you can drag and drop it into a new location; pressing the Ctrl (Option) key while dragging makes a copy of the selection. Moving from word to word is accomplished by pressing Ctrl (Command) in combination with any of the arrow keys.

Dreamweaver 3 brings a couple of new enhancements to the HTML Source Inspector. You can now number the code lines by selecting the Line Numbers option, in addition to a Wrap option that causes lines to wrap at the width of the palette. This becomes useful when you're debugging a page and the browser references a problem at a specific line number.

The second enhancement is the inclusion of a context-sensitive menu. Clicking the right-facing triangle button at the top of the inspector reveals a menu of six choices: Find, Find Next, Replace, Cut, Copy, and Paste. These are all duplicates of the standard Edit menu commands, which are also accessible via their keyboard shortcuts.

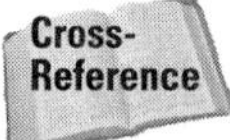

The HTML Source Inspector is customizable in numerous ways. You can change the color coding so that various tags are highlighted or more subdued; you can even change the way the lines wrap, with indents for certain tag pairs. All the options are outlined for you in Chapter 4.

Rapid Tag Modification with the Quick Tag Editor

I tend to build Web pages in two phases: First, I generally lay out my text and images to create the overall design, and then I go back, adding details and alterations to get the page just right. The second phase of Web page design often requires that I make a small adjustment to the HTML code, typically through the Property Inspector; but occasionally I need to go right to the source — code, that is.

Until now, the only direct access Dreamweaver made available to the underlying code was through the window known as the HTML Source Inspector. Dreamweaver 3 introduces a new feature for making minor but essential alterations to the code: the Quick Tag Editor. The Quick Tag Editor is a small pop-up window that appears in the Document window and enables you to edit an existing tag, add a new tag, or wrap the current selection in a tag. One other feature makes the Quick Tag Editor even quicker to use: A handy list of tags or attributes appears to cut down on your typing.

To call up the Quick Tag Editor, use any of the following methods:

✦ Choose Modify ➪ Quick Tag Editor.

✦ Press the keyboard shortcut Ctrl+T (Command+T).

✦ Select the Quick Tag Editor icon on the Property Inspector.

The Quick Tag Editor has three modes: Insert HTML, Wrap Tag, and Edit HTML. Although you can get to all three modes from any situation, which mode appears initially depends on the current selection. The Quick Tag Editor's window appears above the current selection when using either the menu or keyboard method of opening it (Figure 8-8) or next to the Property Inspector when you select the icon. In either case, you can move the Quick Tag Editor window to a new location onscreen by dragging its title bar.

Regardless of which mode the Quick Tag Editor opens in, you can toggle to the other modes by pressing the keyboard shortcut Ctrl+T (Command+T).

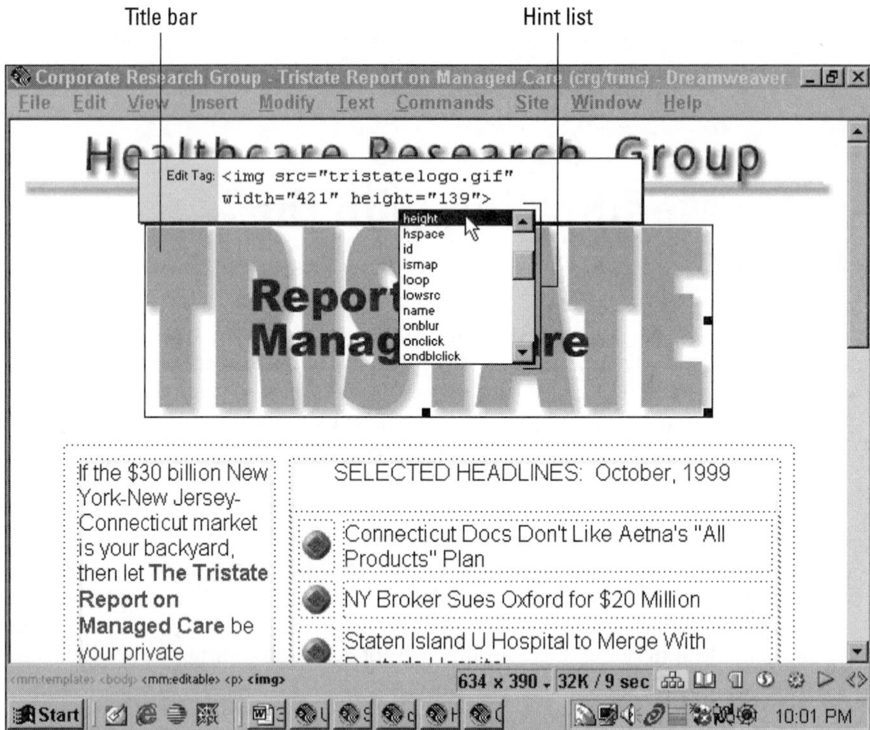

Figure 8-8: The new Quick Tag Editor is great for quickly tweaking your code.

Insert HTML mode

The Insert HTML mode of the Quick Tag Editor is used for adding new tags and code at the current cursor position; it is the initial mode when nothing is selected. The Insert HTML mode starts with a pair of angle brackets enclosing a blinking cursor. You can enter any desired tag — whether standard HTML or custom XML — and any attribute or content within the new tag. When you're done, just press Enter (Return) to confirm your addition.

To add new tags to your page using the Quick Tag Editor Insert HTML mode, follow these steps:

1. Position your cursor where you would like the new code to be inserted.
2. Choose Modify ➪ Quick Tag Editor or use the keyboard shortcut, Ctrl+T (Command+T), to open the Quick Tag Editor.

   The Quick Tag Editor opens in Insert HTML mode as shown in Figure 8-9.

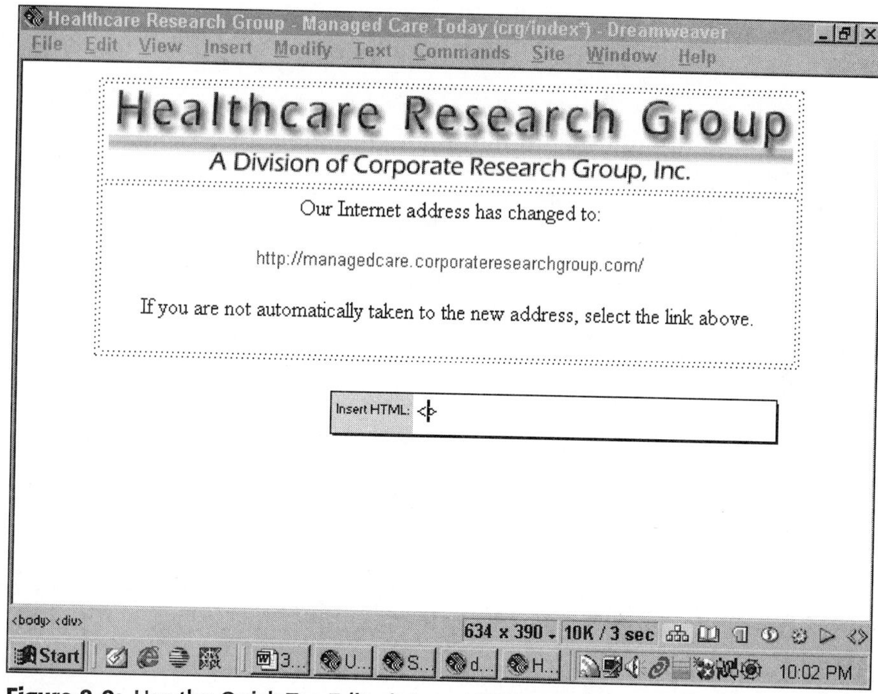

Figure 8-9: Use the Quick Tag Editor's Insert HTML mode to add tags not available through Dreamweaver's visual interface.

3. Enter your HTML or XML code.

Use the right-arrow key to move quickly past the closing angle bracket and add text after your tag.

4. If you pause while typing, the hint list appears, selecting the first tag that matches what you've typed so far. Use the arrow keys to select another tag in the list and press Enter (Return) to select a tag.
5. Press Enter (Return) when you're done.

The Quick Tag Editor is fairly intelligent and tries to help you write valid HTML. If, for example, you leave off a closing tag, such as </b>, the Quick Tag Editor automatically adds it for you.

Working with the Hint List

The Quick Tag Editor has a rather nifty feature referred to as the *hint list*. To make it even quicker to use the Quick Tag Editor, a list of tags pops up when you pause in your typing. When you're entering attributes within a tag, a list of appropriate parameters pops up instead of tags. These lists are tied to what, if anything, you've already typed. Say, for instance, you've begun to enter **blockquote** and have only gotten as far typing **b** and **l**. When the hint list appears, it scrolls to "blink"—the first tag in the list starting with those two letters. If you continue typing "o," "blockquote" is selected. All you have to do to insert it into your code is to press Enter (Return).

Here's a few other hint list hints:

- ✦ Scroll to a tag by using the up- or down-arrow keys.
- ✦ Double-clicking the selected hint list item also inserts it into the code.
- ✦ Once the hint list is open, press Esc if you decide not to enter the selected tag or attribute.
- ✦ If an attribute has a set series of values that can be applied (for example, the `<div>` tag align attribute can only be set to left, right, or center), those values are accessible via the hint list.
- ✦ Control how quickly the hint list appears—or even if it appears at all—by altering the Quick Tag Editor preferences.

The tags and attributes that appear in the hint list are contained in the TagAttributeList.text file found in the Dreamweaver Configuration folder. The list is in a format known as Data Type Declaration or DTD where each tag is listed as a separate element, and under each of those elements any corresponding attributes are displayed. Here, for example, is the DTD listing for the background sound tag, `<bgsound>`:

```
<!ELEMENT BGSOUND Name="Background sound" >
<!ATTLIST BGSOUND
     Balance
     Loop
     Src
     Volume
>
```

As with almost all other Dreamweaver aspects, the TagAttribute.txt list can be modified to include any special tags and their attributes you might need to include on a regular basis. Just relaunch Dreamweaver after making your changes in a standard text editor, and your modifications are included the next time you use the Quick Tag Editor.

Wrap Tag mode

Part of the power and flexibility of HTML is the capability to wrap one tag around one or more other tags and content. To make a phrase appear bold and italic, the code is written this way:

```
<b><i>On Sale Now!</i></b>
```

Note how the inner <i>...</i> tag pair is enclosed by the <b>...</b> pair. The Wrap Tag mode of the Quick Tag Editor surrounds any selection with your entered tag in one easy operation.

The Wrap Tag mode appears initially when you have selected just text (with no surrounding tags) or an incomplete tag (the opening tag and contents but no closing tag). The Wrap Tag mode is visually similar to the Insert HTML mode, as can be seen in Figure 8-10. However, rather than just include exactly what you've entered into the Quick Tag Editor, Wrap Tag mode also inserts a closing tag that corresponds to your entry. For example, let's say I want to apply a tag not available in Dreamweaver's Document window, the subscript or <sub> tag. After highlighting the text I want to mark up as subscript (a "2" in the formula, H_20, for example), I open the Quick Tag Editor and enter **sub**. The resulting code looks like this:

```
H<sub>2</sub>0
```

Caution You can only enter one tag in Wrap Tag mode; if more than one tag is entered, Dreamweaver displays an alert informing you that the tag you've entered appears to be invalid HTML. The Quick Tag Editor is then closed, and the selection is cleared.

To wrap a tag with the Quick Tag Editor, follow these steps:

1. Select the text or tags you want to enclose in another tag.
2. Choose Modify ➪ Quick Tag Editor or use the keyboard shortcut, Ctrl+T (Command+T), to open the Quick Tag Editor.

   The Quick Tag Editor opens in Wrap Tag mode.
3. If you select a complete tag, the Quick Tag Editor opens in Edit HTML mode; press the keyboard shortcut, Ctrl+T (Command+T), to toggle to Wrap Tag mode.
4. Enter the desired tag.

Figure 8-10: Enclose any selection with a tag by using the Quick Tag Editor's Wrap Tag mode.

5. If you pause while typing, the hint list appears, selecting the first tag that matches what you've typed so far. Use the arrow keys to select another tag in the list and press Enter (Return) to select a tag from the hint list.
6. Press Enter (Return) to confirm your tag.

   The Quick Tag Editor closes, and Dreamweaver adds your tag before your selection and a corresponding closing tag after it.

Edit HTML mode

If a complete tag — either a single tag, such as `<img>`, or a tag pair, such as `<h1>...</h1>` — is selected, the Quick Tag Editor opens in Edit HTML mode. Unlike the other two modes where you are presented with just open and closing angle brackets and a flashing cursor, the Edit HTML mode displays the entire selected tag with all the attributes, if any. The Edit HTML mode is always invoked when you start the Quick Tag Editor by clicking its icon in the Property Inspector.

The Edit HTML mode has many uses. I've found it to be terrific for adding a parameter not found on Dreamweaver's Property Inspector. For example, when building a form that returns the information formatted, you need to declare the enctype attribute to be equal to "text/plain." However, the enctype attribute cannot be assigned from the Property Inspector for the `<form>` tag. So, I just select the tag from the Tag Selector and then click the Quick Tag Editor icon to open the Quick Tag Editor. The `<form>` tag appears with my current parameters, as shown in Figure 8-11.

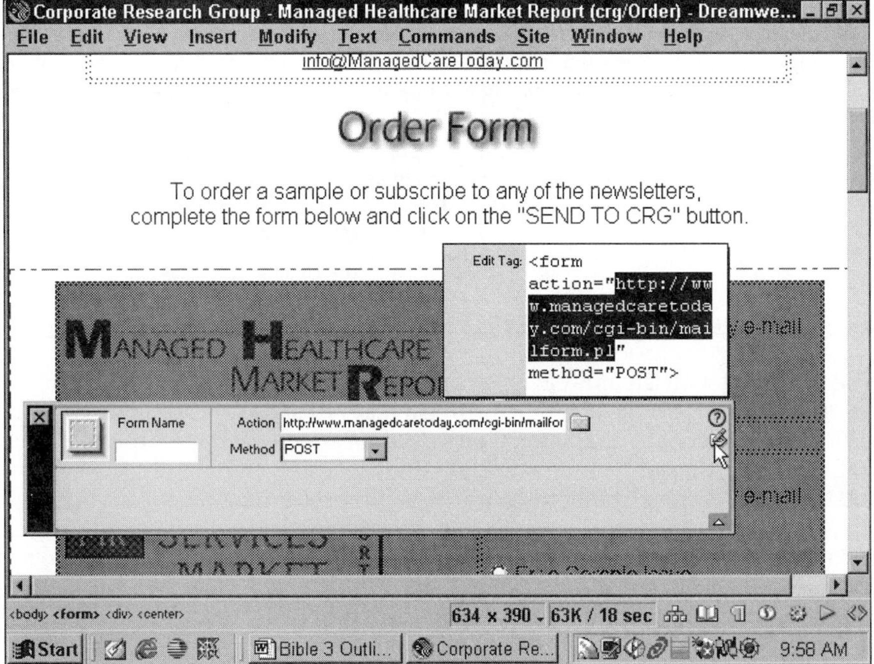

Figure 8-11: In Edit HTML mode, the Quick Tag Editor shows the entire tag with attributes and their values.

To use the Quick Tag Editor in Insert HTML mode, follow these steps:

1. Select an entire tag by clicking its name in the Tag Selector.
2. Choose Modify ➪ Quick Tag Editor.
3. To change an existing attribute, tab to the current value and enter a new one.
4. To add a new attribute, tab and/or use the arrow keys to position the cursor after an existing attribute or after the tag and enter the new parameter and value.

If you don't close the quotation marks for a parameter's value, Dreamweaver does it for you.

5. If you pause briefly while entering a new attribute, the hint list appears with attributes appropriate for the current tag. If you select an attribute from the hint list, press Enter (Return) to accept the parameter.
6. When you're done editing the tag, press Enter (Return).

New Feature

In addition to this new capability to edit complete tags, Dreamweaver has a couple of navigational commands to help select just the right tag. The Select Parent Tag command – keyboard shortcut Ctrl+Shift+< (Command+Shift+<) – highlights the tag immediately surrounding the present tag. Going the other direction, Select Child Tag – keyboard shortcut Ctrl+Shift+> (Command+Shift+>) – chooses the next tag, if any, contained within the current tag. Both commands are available under the Edit menu. Exercising these commands is equivalent to selecting the next tag in the Tag Selector to the left (parent) or right (child).

Inserting Symbols and Special Characters

When working with Dreamweaver, you're usually entering text directly from your keyboard, one keystroke at a time, with each keystroke representing a letter, number, or other keyboard character. Some situations, however, require special letters that have diacritics or common symbols such as the copyright mark, which are outside of the regular, standard character set represented on your keyboard. HTML enables you to insert a full range of such character entities through two systems. The more familiar special characters have been assigned a mnemonic code name to make them easy to remember; these are called *named characters*. Less typical characters must be inserted by entering a numeric code; these are known as *decimal characters*. For the sake of completeness, named characters also have a corresponding decimal character code.

Both named and decimal character codes begin with an ampersand (&) symbol and end with a semicolon (;). For example, the HTML code for an ampersand symbol follows:

```
&amp;
```

Its decimal character equivalent follows:

```
&#38;
```

If, during the browser-testing phase of creating your Web page, you suddenly see an HTML code onscreen rather than a symbol, double-check your HTML. The code could be just a typo; you may have left off the closing semicolon, for instance. If the code is correct and you're using a named character, however, switch to its decimal equivalent. Some of the earlier browser versions are not perfect in rendering named characters.

Named characters

HTML coding conventions require that certain characters, including the angle brackets that surround tags, be entered as character entities. Table 8-3 lists the most common named characters.

Table 8-3
Common Named Characters

Named Entity	*Symbol*	*Description*
`<`	<	A left angle bracket or the less-than symbol
`>`	>	A right angle bracket or the greater-than symbol
`&`	&	An ampersand
`"`	"	A double quotation mark
` `	°	A nonbreaking space
`©`	©	A copyright symbol
`®`	®	A registered mark
`™`	™	A trademark symbol, which cannot be previewed in Dreamweaver but is supported in Internet Explorer

Those characters that you can type directly into Dreamweaver's Document window, including the brackets and the ampersand, are automatically translated into the correct named characters in HTML. Try this with the HTML Source Inspector open. Also, you can enter a nonbreaking space in Dreamweaver by typing Ctrl+Shift+spacebar (Command+Shift+spacebar) or by choosing the Non-breaking Space object.

Decimal characters

To enter almost any character that has a diacritic — such as á, ñ, or â — in Dreamweaver, you must explicitly enter the corresponding decimal character into your HTML page. As mentioned in the preceding section, decimal characters take the form of &#number;, where the number can range from 00 to 255. Not all numbers have matching symbols; the sequence from 14 through 31 is currently unused, while the upper range 127 through 159 is only partially supported by Internet Explorer and Netscape Navigator. Also, not all fonts have characters for every entity.

Using the Character objects

Not only is it difficult to remember the various name or number codes for the specific character entity you need, it's also a bit of a process to enter the code by hand. The Dreamweaver engineers recognized this need and, in Dreamweaver 3, introduced a series of Character objects on their own panel of the Object palette.

Ease-of-use is the guiding principal for the new Character objects. Nine of the most commonly used symbols, such as © and ™, are instantly available as separate objects. And a single object exists offering access to 99 different character entities. Inserting the single Character objects is a straightforward point-and-click affair. Either drag the desired symbol to a place in the Document window or position your cursor and select the object.

The nine individual Character objects are detailed in Table 8-4.

Table 8-4
Character Objects

Icon	*Name*	*HTML Code Inserted*
©	Insert Copyright	`©`
®	Insert Registered Trademark	`®`
TM	Insert Trademark	`™`
£	Insert Pound	`£`
¥	Insert Yen	`¥`
€	Insert Euro	`€`
—	Insert Em-Dash	`—`
“	Insert Left Quote	`“`
”	Insert Right Quote	`”`

You may notice that the Character objects insert a mix of named and number character entities. Not all browsers recognize the easier-to-identify named entities, so for the widest compatibility, Dreamweaver uses the number codes for a few objects.

The final object on the Characters panel is used for inserting these or any other character entity. The Other Characters object displays a large table with symbols for 99 different characters, as shown in Figure 8-12. Simply select the desired symbol, and

Dreamweaver inserts the appropriate HTML code into the current cursor position. By the way, the very first character—which appears to be blank—actually inserts the code for a nonbreaking space, also accessible via a keyboard shortcut, Ctrl+Shift+ spacebar (Command+Shift+spacebar). The nonbreaking space is also available on the Invisibles panel of the Objects palette.

Keep in mind that the user's browser must support the character entity for it to be visible to the user. In the case of the Euro symbol, that support is still very haphazard.

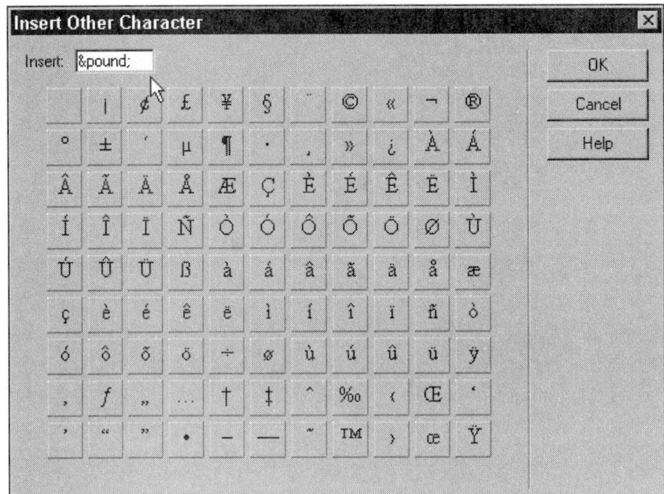

Figure 8-12: Use the Other Character objects to insert the character entity code for any of 99 different symbols.

Summary

Creating Web pages with Dreamweaver is a special blend of using visual layout tools and HTML coding. Regardless, you need to understand the basics of HTML so that you have the knowledge and the tools to modify your code when necessary. This chapter covered these key areas:

✦ An HTML page is divided into two main sections: the `<head>` and the `<body>`. Information pertaining to the entire page is kept in the `<head>` section; all the actual content of the Web page goes in the `<body>` section.

✦ You can change the color and background of your entire page, as well as set its title, through the Page Properties dialog box.

✦ Use `<meta>` tags to summarize your Web page so that search engines can properly catalog it. In Dreamweaver 3, you can use the View Head Contents feature to easily alter these and other `<head>` tags.

✦ When possible, use logical style tags, such as `<strong>` and `<cite>`, rather than hard-coding your page with physical style tags. Style sheets bring a great deal of control and flexibility to logical style tags.

✦ Special extended characters such as symbols and accented letters require the use of HTML character entities, which can either be named (as in `"`) or in decimal format (as in `"`).

In the next chapter, you learn how to insert and format text in Dreamweaver.

✦ ✦ ✦

Adding Text to Your Web Page

✦ ✦ ✦ ✦

In This Chapter

Creating headlines in Dreamweaver

Styling paragraphs

Using special text formats

Changing fonts, font size, and font color

Running the Spell Checker

Automating your work with Find and Replace

Handling whitespace

Inserting HTML comments

✦ ✦ ✦ ✦

If content is king on the Web, then certainly style is queen—together they rule hand in hand. Entering, editing, and formatting text on a Web page is a major part of a Webmaster's job. Dreamweaver gives you the tools to make the task as clear-cut as possible. From headlines to comments, this chapter covers the essentials of working with basic text.

At first, Web designers didn't have many options for manipulating text. However, now the majority of browsers understand a number of text-related commands, and the designer can specify the font as well as its color and size. Dreamweaver 3 includes a range of text manipulation tools. These topics are covered in this chapter, along with an important discussion of manipulating whitespace on the Web page.

Starting with Headings

Text in HTML is primarily composed of headings and paragraphs. Headings separate and introduce major sections of the document, just as a newspaper uses headlines to announce a story and subheads to provide essential details. HTML has six levels of headings; the syntax for the heading tags is `<hn>`, where *n* is a number from 1 to 6. The largest heading is `<h1>` and the smallest is `<h6>`.

Remember that HTML headings are not linked to any specific point size, unlike type produced in a page layout or word processing program. Headings in an HTML document are sized relative to one another, and their final, exact size depends on the browser used. The sample headlines in Figure 9-1 depict the basic headings as rendered through Internet Explorer 5.0 and as compared to the default paragraph font size. As you can see, some headings are rendered in type smaller than that used for the default paragraph. Headings are usually displayed with a boldface attribute.

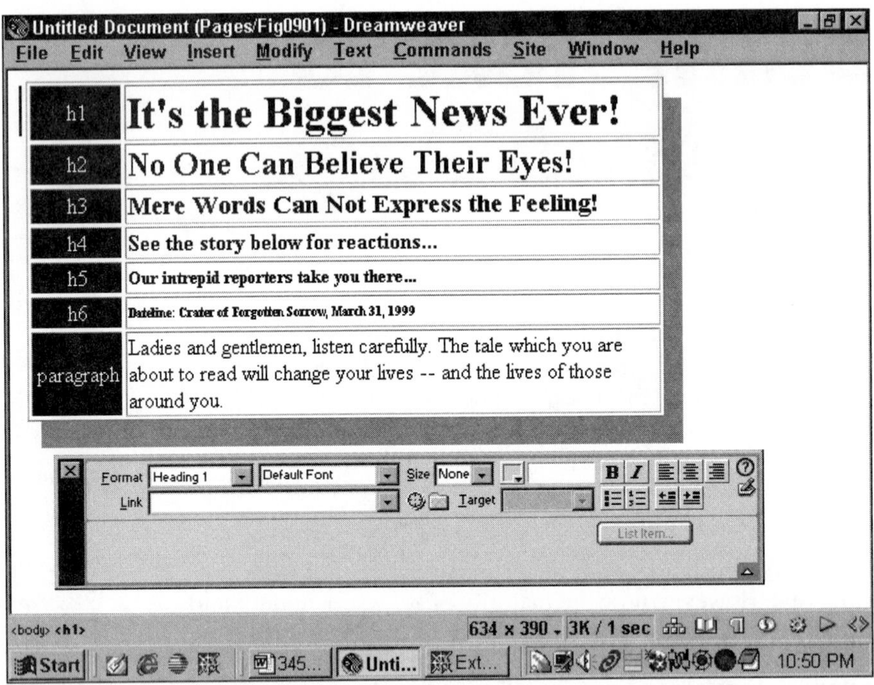

Figure 9-1: You can use up to six different sizes of headings in your HTML page.

Two methods set text as a particular heading size in Dreamweaver. In both cases, you first need to select the text you want to affect. If you are styling a single line or paragraph as a heading, just position the cursor anywhere in the paragraph to select it. If you want to convert more than one paragraph, click and drag out your selection.

Tip

You can't mix heading levels in a single paragraph. That is, you can't have in the same line a word with an `<h1>` heading next to a word styled with an `<h4>` heading. Furthermore, headings belong to a group of HTML text tags called *block elements*. All block elements are rendered with a paragraph return both above and below, which isolates ("blocks") the text. To work around both of these restrictions, you can use `<font size=n>` tags to achieve the effect of varying sizes for words within the same line or for lines of different sizes close to one another. The `<font size=n>` tag is covered later in this chapter in the section "Styling Your Text."

Once the text for the heading is selected, you can choose your heading level by selecting Text ➪ Format and then one of the Headings 1 through 6 from the submenu. Alternately, you can make your selection from the Text Property Inspector. (If it's not already open, display the Property Inspector by selecting Window ➪ Properties.) In the Text Property Inspector, open the Format drop-down list (see Figure 9-2) and choose one of the six headings.

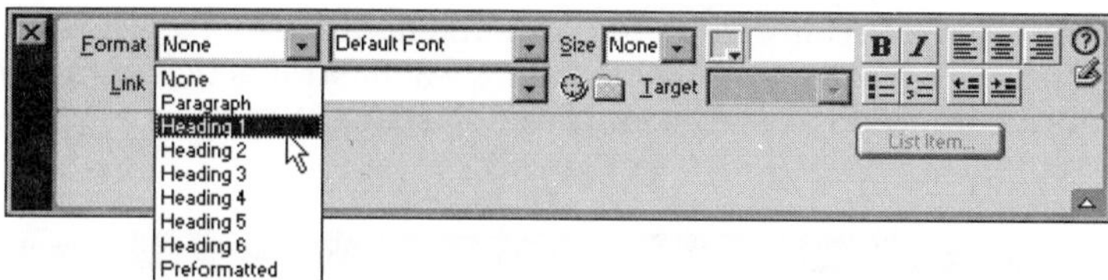

Figure 9-2: You can convert any paragraph or line into a heading through the Format options in the Text Property Inspector.

Headings are often used in a hierarchical fashion, largest to smallest — but you don't have to do it that way. You can have an <h4> line followed by an <h1> paragraph, if that's what your design needs. Be careful using the smallest heading, <h6>; it's likely to be difficult to read on any resolution higher than 800×600.

Working with Paragraphs

Usually the bulk of text on any Web page is composed of paragraphs. Paragraphs in HTML are denoted by the <p> and </p> pair of tags. When your Web page is processed, the browser formats everything between those two tags as one paragraph and renders it to fit the user's screen, word wrapping as needed at the margins. Any additional line breaks and unnecessary whitespace (beyond one space between words and between sentences) in the HTML code are ignored.

In the early version of HTML, paragraphs used just the opening <p> tag, and browsers rendered everything between <p> tags as one paragraph; the closing tag was optional. As of HTML 3.2, however, an optional closing </p> tag was added. Because so many Web pages have been created with just the opening paragraph tag, most browsers still recognize the single-tag format. To be on the safe side in terms of future compatibility, you should enclose your paragraphs within both opening and closing tags when you do any hand-coding.

Dreamweaver starts a new paragraph every time you press Enter (Return) when composing text in the Document window. If you have the HTML Inspector open when you work, you can see that Dreamweaver inserts the following code with each new paragraph:

```
<p> </p>
```

The code between the tags creates a nonbreaking space that enables the new line to be visible. You won't see the new line if you have just the paragraph tags with nothing (neither a character nor a character entity, such as) in between:

```
<p></p>
```

When you continue typing, Dreamweaver replaces the nonbreaking space with your input, unless you press Enter (Return) again. Figure 9-3 illustrates two paragraphs with text and a third paragraph with the nonbreaking space still in place.

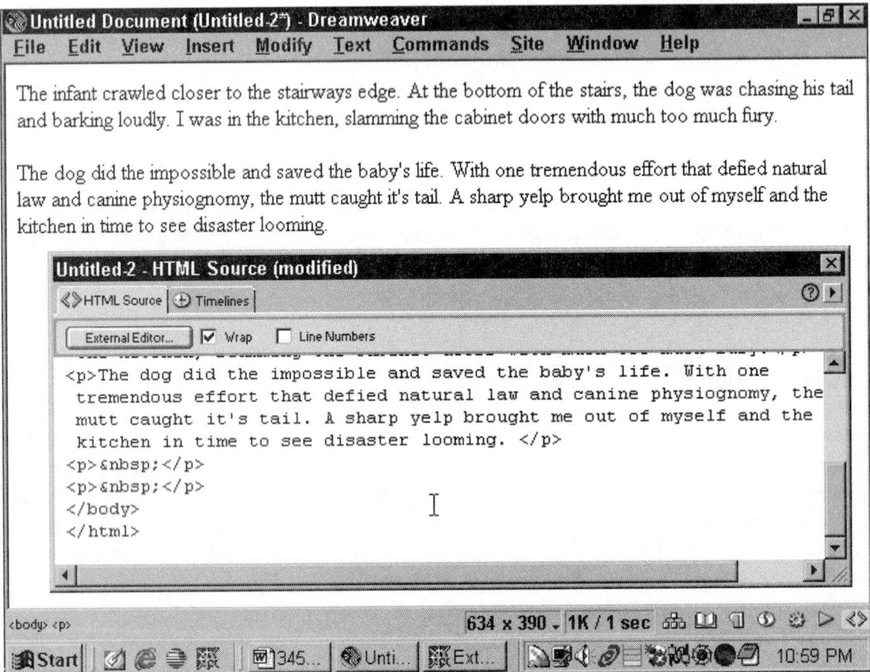

Figure 9-3: Dreamweaver automatically wraps any text inserted into the Document window. If you press Enter (Return) without entering text, Dreamweaver enters paragraph tags surrounding a nonbreaking space.

You can easily change text from most other formats, such as a heading, to paragraph format. First, select the text you want to alter. Then, in the Property Inspector, open the Format options drop-down list and choose Paragraph. You can also choose Text ➪ Format ➪ Paragraph from the menu or use the keyboard shortcut Ctrl+T (Command+T). Hint: Think T for text.

All paragraphs are initially rendered on the page in the default font at the default size. The user can designate these defaults through the browser preferences, although most people don't bother to alter them. If you want to change the font name or the font size for selected paragraphs explicitly, use the techniques described in the upcoming section, "Styling Your Text."

Tip

Remember, you can always use the Tag Selector on the status bar to select and highlight any tag surrounding your current cursor position. This method makes it easy to see exactly what a particular tag is affecting.

Editing paragraphs

By and large, the editing features of Dreamweaver are similar to other modern word processing programs — with one or two Web-oriented twists. Dreamweaver has Cut, Copy, and Paste options, as well as Undo and Redo commands. You can search for and replace any text on your Web page under construction and even check its spelling.

The "twists" come from the relationship between the Document window and the HTML Inspector. Dreamweaver has some special functionality for copying and pasting text. Let's see how that works.

Inserting text

You've already seen how you can position the cursor on the page and directly enter text. In this sense, Dreamweaver acts like a word processing program, rather than a page layout program. On a blank page, the cursor starts at the top-left corner of the page. Words automatically wrap to the next line when the text exceeds the right margin. Press Enter (Return) to end the current paragraph and start the next one.

Indenting text

In Dreamweaver, you cannot indent text as in a word processor. Tabs normally have no effect in HTML. To indent a paragraph's first line, one method uses nonbreaking spaces, which can be inserted with the keyboard shortcut Ctrl+Shift+spacebar (Command+Shift+spacebar). Nonbreaking spaces are an essential part of any Web designer's palette because they provide single-character spacing — often necessary to nudge an image or other object into alignment. You've already seen the code for a nonbreaking space — ` ` — that Dreamweaver inserts between the `<p>...</p>` tag pair to make the line visible.

Aside from the keyboard shortcut, two other methods insert a nonbreaking space. You can enter its character code — ` ` — directly into the HTML code. You can also style your text as preformatted; this technique is discussed later in this chapter.

Tip

Another method exists for indenting the first line of a paragraph: Cascading Style Sheets. You can set an existing HTML tag, such as `<p>`, to any indent amount using the Text Indent option found on the Block panel of the Style Sheet dialog box. Be aware, however, that style sheets are only partially implemented in browsers. A full discussion of text indent and other style sheet controls is in Chapter 27.

Cutting, copying, and pasting

Text can be moved from one place to another—or from one Web document to another—using the standard cut-and-paste techniques. No surprises here: before you can cut or copy anything, you must select it. Select by clicking the mouse at the beginning of the text you want to cut or copy, drag the highlight to the end of your selection, and then release the mouse button.

Here are some other selection methods:

- Double-click a word to select it.
- Move the pointer to the left margin of the text until the pointer changes to a right-facing arrow. Click once to highlight a single line. Click and drag down the margin to select a group of lines.
- Position the cursor at the beginning of your selection. Hold down the Shift key and then click once at the end of the selection.
- You can select everything in the body of your document by using Edit ➪ Select All or the keyboard shortcut Ctrl+A (Command+A).
- Use the Tag Selector to select text or other objects contained within specific tags.
- You can also select text by holding down Shift and using the right- or left-arrow key to select one character at a time. If you hold down Ctrl+Shift (Command+Shift), you can click the right- or left-arrow key to select a word at a time.

When you want to move a block of text, first select it and then use Edit ➪ Cut or the keyboard shortcut Ctrl+X (Command+X). This sequence places the text on your system's clipboard. To paste the text, move the pointer to the new location and click once to place the cursor. Then select Edit ➪ Paste or the keyboard shortcut Ctrl+V (Command+V). The text is copied from the clipboard to its new location. You can continue pasting this same text from the clipboard until another block of text is copied or cut.

To copy text, the procedure is much the same. Select the text using one of the preceding methods and then use Edit ➪ Copy or Ctrl+C (Command+C). The selected text is copied to the clipboard, and the original text is left in place. Then position the cursor in a new location and select Edit ➪ Paste (or use the keyboard shortcut).

Using drag-and-drop

The other, quicker method for moving or copying text is the drag-and-drop technique. Once you've selected your text, release the mouse button and move the cursor over the highlighted area. The cursor changes from an I-beam to an arrow. To move the text, click the selected area with the arrow cursor and drag your mouse to a new location. The arrow cursor now has a box attached to it, indicating that it is carrying something. As you move your cursor, a bar (the insertion point) moves with you, indicating where the text will be positioned. Release the mouse button to drop the text. You can copy text in the same manner by holding down the Ctrl (Option) key as you drag and drop your selected text. When copying this way, the box attached to the cursor is marked with a plus sign (on Macintosh computers the box is the same size as the text selection and no plus sign appears).

To completely remove text, select it and then choose Edit ⇨ Clear or press Delete. The only way to recover deleted text is to use the Undo feature described in the following section.

Undo and Redo

The Undo command has to be one of the greatest inventions of the twentieth century. Make a mistake? Undo! Want to experiment with two different options? Undo! Change your mind again? Redo! The Undo command reverses your last action, whether you changed a link, added a graphic, or deleted the entire page. The Redo command enables you to reverse your Undo actions.

Dreamweaver 3 now displays all of your previous actions on the History palette, so you can easily see what steps you took. To use the Undo command, you can either choose Edit ⇨ Undo or press the keyboard shortcut Ctrl+Z (Command+Z); this undoes a single action at a time. To undo multiple actions, drag the slider in the History palette to the last action you want to keep or just click in the slider track at that action.

The complement to Undo is the Redo command. To reverse an Undo command, choose Edit ⇨ Redo or Ctrl+Y (Command+Y). To reverse several Undo commands, drag the slider in the History palette back over the grayed-out steps; alternately, you can click in the slider track once at the step up to which you'd like to redo.

Inserting Text from Other Applications

The Paste command can also insert text from another program into Dreamweaver. If you cut or copy text from a file in any other program—whether it is a word processor, spreadsheet, or database program—Dreamweaver inserts it at the cursor position. The results of this Paste operation vary, however.

Dreamweaver can paste only plain, unformatted text. In addition, if you use the regular Paste command, all the text on the clipboard is inserted as a single paragraph, no matter how many returns are in the original text. To retain text in separate paragraphs coming from a file in another program, you must copy and then paste them into Dreamweaver using the Paste As Text command, covered in detail later in this chapter.

If you need to import a great deal of text and want to retain as much formatting as possible, you can use another application, such as the latest version of Microsoft Word, to save your text as an HTML file. Then open that file in Dreamweaver with the Import Word HTML command.

The best use I've found for the Redo command is in concert with Undo. When I'm trying to decide between two alternatives, such as two different images, I'll replace one choice with another and then use the Undo/Redo combination to go back and forth between them. Because Dreamweaver replaces any selected object with the current object from the clipboard – even if one is a block of text and the other is a layer – you can easily view two separate options with this trick. The History palette enables you to apply this procedure over any number of steps.

Dreamweaver's implementation of the Undo command enables you to back up as many steps as set in the Maximum Number of History Steps found in Preferences. The History steps can even undo actions that had taken place before a document was saved. Note that the History palette has additional features besides multiple undo's.

Copy Text Only and Paste As Text

A preceding section mentioned that Dreamweaver includes a couple of "twists" to the standard Cut, Copy, and Paste options. You've seen how regular text entered into the Document window is converted to text marked up by HTML tags, visible in the HTML Inspector. Dreamweaver includes two functions that enable you to translate text and corresponding codes back and forth from one form to the other.

To understand these two features, Copy Text Only and Paste As Text (both on the Edit menu), let's examine how they are used. Table 9-1 explains each command.

Table 9-1
Results of Copy/Paste Compared to Copy/Paste As Text Commands

Selected Text	*Copy From*	*Command Used*	*Paste To*	*Result*
Example Text	Document window	Copy	Other program	<b>Example Text</b>
Example Text	Document window	Copy Text Only	Other program	Example Text
<b>Example Text</b>	HTML Inspector or other program	Paste window	Document	**Example Text**
<b>Example Text</b>	HTML Inspector or other program	Paste As Text	Document window	<b>Example Text</b>
Example Text	Document window	Paste As Text	HTML Inspector	<b>Example Text</b>

Notice that in the final row of Table 9-1, if you copy formatted text such as the boldface “Example Text” sample and use the Paste As Text command to insert it in the HTML Inspector, you get the following:

```
&lt;b&gt;Example Text&lt;/b&gt;
```

If you remember the section on named character entities in Chapter 8, you may recognize < as the code for the less-than symbol (<) and > as the code for the greater-than symbol (>). These symbols are used to represent tags such as <b> and </b> to prevent a browser from interpreting them as tag delimiters.

So what possible real-life uses could there be for the Copy/Paste As Text command and Dreamweaver’s implementation of the regular Copy/Paste commands? First, these commands are a major benefit for programmers, teachers, and writers who constantly have to communicate in both HTML code and regular text. If an instructor is attempting to demonstrate a coding technique on a Web page, for example, she can just copy the code in the HTML Inspector (or the Document window) and use Paste As Text to put it into the Document window—instantly transforming the code into something readable online. Previously, this task required a tedious hand-coding process to convert the angle brackets to character entities.

Another use of this approach transfers code from another text editor directly into the Dreamweaver Document window. You copy the code in the other window normally, position the cursor in Dreamweaver, and then paste in the Document window. No need to open the HTML Inspector and hunt for the right place in the code—another troublesome task eliminated.

I find these commands to be a major boost to my productivity and an excellent example of how Dreamweaver is firmly rooted in the real world of the Webmaster.

Checking your spelling

A typo can make a significant impression. Not many things are more embarrassing than showing a new Web site to a client and having that client point out a spelling error. Dreamweaver includes an easy-to-use Spell Checker to avoid such awkward moments. I make it a practice to spell-check every Web page before it’s posted online.

You start the process by choosing Text ⇨ Check Spelling or you can press the keyboard shortcut Shift+F7. This sequence opens the Check Spelling dialog box, as seen in Figure 9-4.

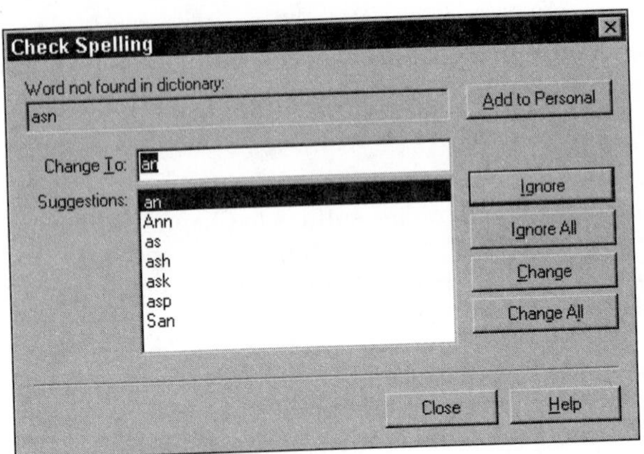

Figure 9-4: Dreamweaver's Spell Checker double-checks your spelling and can find the typos on any Web page.

Once you've opened the Check Spelling dialog box, Dreamweaver begins searching your text for errors. Unless you have selected a portion of your document, Dreamweaver checks the full document regardless of where your cursor is placed. When text is selected, Dreamweaver checks the selection first and then asks if you'd like to do the entire document.

Dreamweaver checks your Web page text against two dictionaries: a standard English (or your chosen language) dictionary and a personal dictionary, to which you can add words. If the Spell Checker finds any text not in either of the program's dictionaries, the text is highlighted in the Document window and appears in the Word not found in dictionary field of the dialog box. A list of suggested corrections appears in the Suggestions list box, with the topmost one highlighted and also displayed in the Change To box. If Dreamweaver cannot find any suggestions, the Change To box is left blank. At this point, you have the following options:

✦ **Add to Personal:** Select this button to include the highlighted word in your personal dictionary and prevent Dreamweaver from tagging it as an error in the future.

✦ **Ignore:** Select this button when you want Dreamweaver to leave the currently highlighted word alone and continue searching the text.

✦ **Ignore All:** Select this button when you want Dreamweaver to disregard all occurrences of this word in the current document.

✦ **Change:** If you see the correct replacement among the list of suggestions, highlight it and select the Change button. If no suggestion is appropriate, you can type the correct word into the Change To text box and then select this button.

✦ **Change All:** Choosing this button causes all instances of the current word to be replaced with the word in the Change To text box.

Spell-Checking in Non-English Languages

Macromedia has made additional language dictionaries available. As of this writing, dictionaries in these other languages are also available: German, Spanish, French, Italian, Brazilian-Portuguese, and Catalan. You can download these dictionaries from Macromedia's Dreamweaver Object Exchange at `www.macromedia.com/support/dreamweaver/dictionary.html`.

To use the dictionaries, download the compressed file to your system. After uncompressing them, store the file with the .dat extension in the Configuration\Dictionaries folder and restart Dreamweaver. Finally, open Preferences (Edit ➪ Preferences) and, from the General panel, select the Dictionary option button. Choose the new language from the drop-down list, and you're ready to spell correctly in another tongue.

Have you ever accidentally added a misspelled word to your personal dictionary and then been stuck with the error for all eternity? Dreamweaver enables you to recover from your mistake by giving you access to the dictionary itself. The personal dictionary, stored in the Dreamweaver\Configuration\Dictionaries\personal.dat file, can be opened and modified in any text editor.

Using Find and Replace

Dreamweaver's Find and Replace features are both timesaving and lifesaving (well, almost). You can use Find and Replace to cut your input time substantially by searching for abbreviations and expanding them to their full state. You can also find a client's incorrectly spelled name and replace it with the correctly spelled version—that's a lifesaver! However, that's just the tip of the iceberg when it comes to what Find and Replace can really do. The Find and Replace engine should be considered a key power tool for any Web developer. You can not only search multiple files but also easily check the code separately from the content.

Here's a short list of what the Find and Replace feature makes possible:

- ✦ Search the Document window to find any type of text.
- ✦ Search the underlying HTML to find tags, attributes, or text within tags.
- ✦ Look for text within specific tags with specific attributes—or look for text that's outside of a specific tag with specific attributes.
- ✦ Find and replace patterns of text, using wildcard characters called *regular expressions*.
- ✦ Apply any of the preceding Find and Replace operations to the current document, the current site, any folder, or any group of selected files.

As in earlier Dreamweaver versions, three basic commands make up the Find and Replace set: Find, Find Next (Find Again, on the Macintosh), and Replace. You can use all three commands in Dreamweaver's Document window, the HTML Inspector, and, in Windows systems, the Site window. In every situation, you can use Find independently or in conjunction with Replace.

Where your Find and Replace operations can be applied depends on whether you launch the Find/Replace command from the Document window or the Site window. Table 9-2 details the differences.

Table 9-2
Find/Replace Selection Options

To Find/Replace In	*Launch From*
Current document	Document window
Current site	Document window or Site window
All files in a specific folder	Document window or Site window
Selected file or files	Site window

Finding on the visual page

The most basic method of using Find and Replace takes place in the Document window. Whenever you need to search for any text that can be seen by the public on your Web page—whether it's to correct a spelling or change a name—Dreamweaver makes it fast and simple.

The Find and Replace dialog box, unlike most of Dreamweaver's dialog boxes, is actually a *nonmodal window*. This technical term just means that you can easily move back and forth between your Document window and the Find and Replace dialog box without having to close the dialog box first, as you do with the other Dreamweaver windows.

To find some text on your Web page, follow these steps:

1. From the Document window, choose Edit ➪ Find or use the keyboard shortcut Ctrl+F (Command+F).
2. In the Find dialog box, shown in Figure 9-5, make sure that Text is the selected Find What option.
3. In the text box next to the Find What option, type the word or phrase you're looking for.

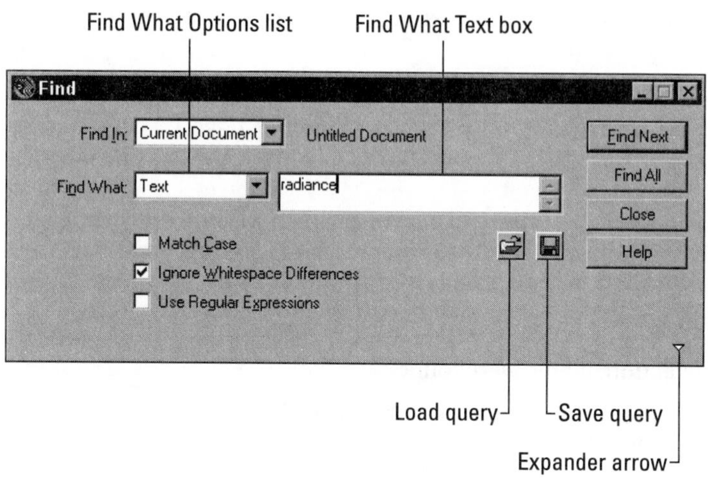

Figure 9-5: The Find dialog box.

If you select your text *before* launching the Find dialog box, it automatically appears in the Find What text box. If the text is even moderately lengthy, you might notice the lines wrapping differently than they do on the screen. This is because Dreamweaver is actually using the text as it appears in the HTML Inspector. For this reason, it's best to keep the Ignore Whitespace Differences option (described in the next step) selected.

4. Select the appropriate search options, if any:

   - If you want to find an exact replica of the word as you entered it, select the Match Case checkbox; otherwise, Dreamweaver searches for all variations of your text, regardless of case.
   - To force Dreamweaver to disregard any whitespace variations, such as additional spaces, hard spaces or tabs, select the Ignore Whitespace Differences option.
   - Selecting Use Regular Expressions enables you to work with Dreamweaver's wildcard characters (discussed later in this section). Use Regular Expressions and Ignore Whitespace Differences are mutually exclusive options.

5. Select the Find Next button to begin the search from the cursor's current position.

   - If Dreamweaver finds the desired text, it highlights the text in the Document window.
   - If Dreamweaver doesn't find the text in the remaining portion of the document, it asks if you want to continue searching from the beginning. Select Yes to continue or No to exit.

6. If you want to look for the next occurrence of your selected text, click the Find Next button again.
7. To look for all occurrences of your text, choose Find All.

   The Find dialog box expands to display the List window. Dreamweaver lists each found occurrence on a separate line in the List window.

You can quickly move from one found selection to another by double-clicking the line in the List window. Dreamweaver highlights the selection, scrolling the Document window, if necessary.

   After searching the page, Dreamweaver tells you how many occurrences of your selection, if any, were found.

8. You can enter other text to search or exit the Find dialog box by clicking the Close button.

The text you enter in the Find dialog box is kept in memory until it's replaced by your next use of the Find feature. After you have executed the Find command once, you can continue to search for your text without redisplaying the Find dialog box, by selecting Edit ⇨ Find Next (Find Again) or the keyboard shortcut F3 (Command+G). If Dreamweaver finds your text, it is highlighted — in fact, Dreamweaver acts exactly the same as when the Find dialog box is open. The Find Next (Find Again) command gives you a quick way to search through a long document — especially when you put the F3 (Command+G) key to work.

The preceding tip about redoing a search is unfortunately not uniform across all of Dreamweaver's search capabilities. Using F3 (Command+G) to avoid redisplaying the dialog box works only if you redo a text tag or text (advanced) search from the Document window – not for an HTML Source search. For example, if you search for HTML Source - `<font face="Arial">` and it is found, the HTML Inspector opens with the tag highlighted. Now if you close the HTML Inspector and the Find dialog box and press F3 (Command+G), Dreamweaver searches for Text - `<font face="Arial">` instead because Dreamweaver remembers only if it last did a tag or text (advanced). Similarly, if opened when the Site window has focus, it defaults to HTML Source. The Site window has no Find Next command, though, so if you're working there exclusively, you have no way to repeat an HTML Source find except to execute Find command from the menus and choose the Find Next button.

When you add the Replace command to a Find operation, you can search your text for a word or phrase and, if it's found, replace it with another word or phrase of your choice. As mentioned earlier, the Replace feature is a handy way to correct mistakes and expand abbreviations. Figure 9-6 shows an example of the latter operation. This example intentionally uses the abbreviation DW throughout the input text of a Web page article. Then the example uses the Replace All function to expand all the DWs to Dreamweaver — in one fell swoop. This technique is much faster than typing "Dreamweaver" nine times.

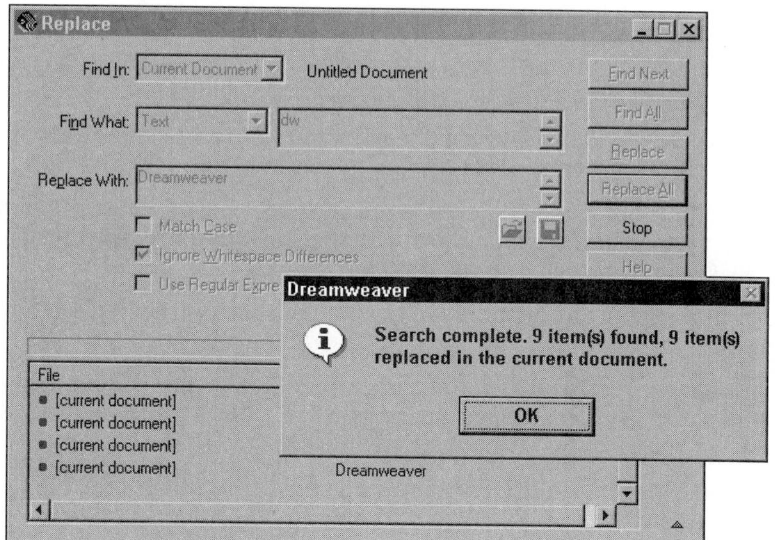

Figure 9-6: Use the Edit ➪ Replace command to correct your text, one item at a time or all at once.

When you replace text in the Document window, it is replaced regardless of its formatting. For example, suppose you had the following paragraph:

Mary's accusation reminded Jon of studying synchrones in high school. Synchrones, he recalled, were graphs in which the lines constantly approached zero, but never made it. "Yeah," he thought, "That's me, all right. I'm one big synchrone."

Upon discovering that "synchrone" should actually be "asymptote," you could use the Find and Replace feature to replace all the plain, italic, and bold versions of the "synchrone" text simultaneously.

It's possible to alter formatting as well – to change all the formatting to just underlining for example – but for that, you need to perform your Find and Replace operations in the HTML Inspector, as discussed in the following section.

Follow these steps to use Dreamweaver's Replace feature in the Document window:

1. Choose Edit ➪ Replace, or the keyboard shortcut Ctrl+H (Command+H), to open the Replace dialog box.
2. In the Replace dialog box, make sure that Text is the selected Find What option and then, in the text box next to the Find What option, type the word or phrase you're looking for.

3. In the Replace With text box, type the substitute word.

4. Click the Find Next button. Dreamweaver begins searching from the current cursor position. If Dreamweaver finds the text, it is highlighted.

   If the text is not found, Dreamweaver asks if you want to continue searching from the top of the document. Select Yes to continue or No to exit.

5. To replace the highlighted occurrence of your text, select the Replace button. Dreamweaver replaces the found text with the substitute text and then automatically searches for the next occurrence.

6. If you want to replace all instances of the Find text, select the Replace All button.

   When Dreamweaver has found all the occurrences of your Find text, it displays the number of replacement operations and a line for each in the List window.

   Double-clicking a line in the List window highlights the changed text in the Document window.

7. When you've finished using the Replace dialog box, click the Close button to exit.

Storing and Retrieving Queries

Dreamweaver enables you to develop extremely complex queries. Rather than forcing you to reenter queries over and over again, Dreamweaver enables you to save and load them when needed. You can store and retrieve both Find and Find/Replace queries; Dreamweaver saves them with .dwq and .dwr file extensions, respectively.

To save a query, select the diskette icon on the Find or Replace dialog box. The standard Save Query (Save Query to file) dialog box appears for you to enter a file name; the appropriate file extension is appended automatically. To load a previously saved query, select the folder icon on the Find or Replace dialog box to open the Load Query dialog box. From the Find dialog box, you can only open .dwq files, but you can load both .dwq and .dwr files from the Replace dialog box.

While saving and opening queries is an obvious advantage when working with complex wildcard operations, you can also make it work for you in an every day situation. If, for example, you have a set series of acronyms or abbreviations that you must convert repeatedly, you can save your simple text queries and use them as needed without having to remember all the details.

A note for advanced users: Dreamweaver queries are actually XML files. For sufficiently complex operations, you could open the query file in a text editor (or Dreamweaver) and modify the code by hand. To learn more about XML, see Chapter 30.

Searching the code

The power curve ramps up significantly when you start to explore Dreamweaver's HTML Find and Replace capabilities. Should your client decide that he wants the company's name to appear in blue, bold, 18-point type throughout the 300-page site, you can accommodate him with a few keystrokes — instead of hours of mind-numbing grunt work.

You can perform three different types of searches that use the HTML in your Web page:

- You can search for text anywhere in the HTML code. With this capability, you can look for text within alt or any other attribute — and change it.
- You can search for text relative to specific tags. Sometimes you need to change just the text contained within the `<b>` tag and leave all other matching text alone.
- You can search for specific HTML tags and/or their attributes. Dreamweaver's Find and Replace feature gives you the capability to insert, delete, or modify tags and attributes.

Looking for text in the HTML Inspector

Text that appears onscreen is often replicated in various sections of your offscreen HTML code. It's not uncommon, for example, to use the alt attribute in an `<img>` tag that repeats the caption under the picture. What do you think would happen under those circumstances if you replaced the wording with the standard Find and Replace features in the Document window? You're still left with the task of tracking down the alt attribute and making that change as well. Dreamweaver enables you to act on both content and programming text in one operation — a major savings in time and effort, not to mention aggravation.

To find and replace text in both the content and the code, follow these steps:

1. Choose Edit ➪ Find or Edit ➪ Replace to open the Find and Replace dialog box.
2. Select the parameters of your search from the Find In option: Current Document, Current Site, or Folder.

   Remember, you can also search specific files if you launch the Find and Replace dialog box from the Site window.
3. Choose the Find What option button and select the HTML Source option from the drop-down list.
4. Enter the text you're searching for in the text box next to the Find What option.
5. If you are replacing, enter the new text in the Replace With text box.

6. Select any options desired: Match Case, Ignore Whitespace Differences, or Use Regular Expressions.
7. Choose your Find/Replace option: Find Next, Find All, Replace, or Replace All

   If you don't have the HTML Inspector open, it appears with the text selected when you use the Find Next option.
8. Select Close when finished.

As with all Find and Replace operations – especially those in which you decide to Replace All – you need to exercise extreme caution when replacing text throughout your code. If you're unsure about what's going to be affected, choose Find All first and, with your HTML Inspector open, step through all the selections to be positive no unwanted surprises exist. Should you replace some code in error, you can always undo the operation.

Using advanced text options in Find and Replace

In Find and Replace operations, the global Replace All isn't appropriate for every situation; sometimes you need a more precise approach. Dreamweaver enables you to fine-tune your searches to pinpoint accuracy. You can look for text within particular tags — and even within particular tags with specific attributes. Moreover, you can find (and replace) text that is outside of particular tags with specific attributes.

Dreamweaver assists you by providing a drop-down list of every standard HTML tag, as well as numerous special function tags such as those used for Cold Fusion applications. You can also search for your own custom tags. You don't have to try to remember which attributes go with which tag either. Dreamweaver also supplies you with a context-sensitive list of attributes that changes according to the tag selected.

In addition to using the tag's attributes as a search filter, Dreamweaver 3 can also search within the tag for text or another tag. Most HTML tags are so-called container tags that consist of an opening tag and a closing tag, such as `<b>` and `</b>`. You can set up a filter to look for text within a tag that contains (or explicitly doesn't contain) specific text or another tag. For example, if you were searching the following code:

```
The <b>big, red</b> boat was a <b>big</b> waste of money.
```

you could build a Find and Replace operation that changed the one phrase (`<b>big, red</b>`) but not the other (`<b>big</b>`) — or vice versa.

To look for text in or out of specific tags and attributes, follow these steps:

1. Choose Edit ➪ Find or Edit ➪ Replace to open the Find and Replace dialog box.
2. Select the parameters of your search from the Find In option: Current Document, Current Site, or Folder.

3. Choose the Find What option button and select the Text (Advanced) option from the drop-down list.

   The add and delete (+ and –) tag options are made available, as shown in Figure 9-7.

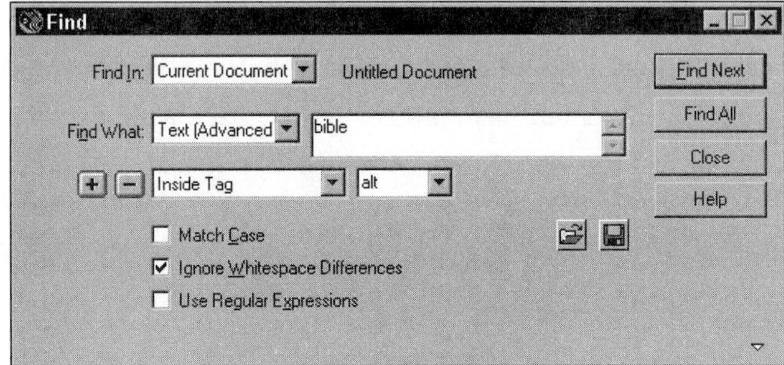

Figure 9-7: The advanced text features of Find and Replace enable you to manipulate text and code simultaneously.

4. Enter the text you're searching for in the text box next to the Find What option.
5. Select either Inside Tag or Not Inside Tag from the option list.
6. Select the tag to include or exclude from the adjacent option list.
7. To add a further restriction on the search, click the add button (the plus sign).

   Another line of search options is added to the dialog box.
8. Select the additional search filter. The available options include the following:

Filter	Description
With Attribute	Enables you to select any attribute from the adjacent option list. You can set this attribute to be equal to, less than, greater than, or not equal to any given value by choosing from the available drop-down lists.
Without Attribute	Finds text within a particular tag that does not include a specific attribute. Choose the attribute to be equal to, less than, greater than, or not equal to any given value by choosing from the available drop-down lists.
Containing	Searches the tag for either specified text or another user-selectable tag found within the initial tag pair.
Not Containing	Searches the tag for either text or a tag not found within the initial tag pair.

Inside Tag	Enables you to look for text that is within two (or more) sets of specific tags.
Not Inside Tag	Enables you to look for text that is in one tag, but not in another tag, or vice versa.

9. To continue adding filter conditions, select the add button (the plus sign) and repeat Steps 7 and 8.
10. To remove a filter condition, select the delete button (the minus sign).
11. If you are replacing, enter the new text in the Replace With text box.
12. Select any options desired: Match Case, Ignore Whitespace Differences, or Use Regular Expressions.
13. Choose your Find/Replace option: Find Next, Find All, Replace, or Replace All.
14. Select Close when finished.

You can continue to add conditions by clicking the add (+) button. In fact, I was able to add so many conditions, the Find/Replace dialog box began to disappear off the screen! To erase all conditions, change the Find What option to Text or HTML Source and then change it back to Text (Advanced).

Replacing HTML tags and attributes

Let's say a new edict has come down from the HTML gurus of your company: No longer is the `<strong>` tag to be used to indicate emphasis; from now on; use only the `<b>` tag. Oh, and by the way, change all the existing pages — all 3,000+ Web and intranet pages — so that they're compliant. Dreamweaver makes short work out of nightmare situations such as these by giving you the power to search and replace HTML tags and their attributes.

But Dreamweaver doesn't stop there. Not only can you replace one tag with another, you can also perform the following:

- ✦ Change or delete the tag (with or without its contents)
- ✦ Set an attribute in the tag to another value
- ✦ Remove any or all attributes
- ✦ Add text and/or code before or after the starting or the ending tag

To alter your code using Dreamweaver's Find and Replace feature, follow these steps:

1. As with other Find and Replace operations, choose Edit ⇨ Find or Edit ⇨ Replace to open the Find and Replace dialog box.
2. Select the parameters of your search from the Find In option: Current Page, Current Site, or Folder.

3. Choose the Find What option button and select the tag option from the drop-down list.

   The dialog box changes to include the tag functions.

4. Select the desired tag from the option list next to the Find What option.

You can either scroll down the list box to find the tag or you can type the first letter of the tag in the box. Dreamweaver scrolls to the group of tags that begin with that letter when the list is visible (Windows only).

5. If desired, you can limit the search by specifying an attribute and value or with other conditions, as discussed in detail in the previous section.

If you want to search for just a tag, select the delete button (the minus key) to eliminate the additional condition.

6. Make a selection from the Action list, shown in Figure 9-8. The options are as follows:

Action	Description
Replace Tag & Contents	Substitutes the selected tag and all included content with a text string. The text string can include HTML code.
Replace Contents Only	Changes the content between the specified tag to a given text string, which can also include HTML code.
Remove Tag & Contents	Deletes the tag and all contents.
Strip Tag	Removes the tag but leaves the previously enclosed content.
Change Tag	Substitutes one tag for another.
Set Attribute	Sets an existing attribute to a new value or inserts a new attribute set to a specific value.
Remove Attribute	Deletes a specified attribute.
Add Before Start Tag	Inserts a text string (with or without HTML) before the opening tag.
Add After End Tag	Inserts a text string (with or without HTML) after the end tag.
Add After Start Tag	Inserts a text string (with or without HTML) after the opening tag.
Add Before End Tag	Inserts a text string (with or without HTML) before the end tag.

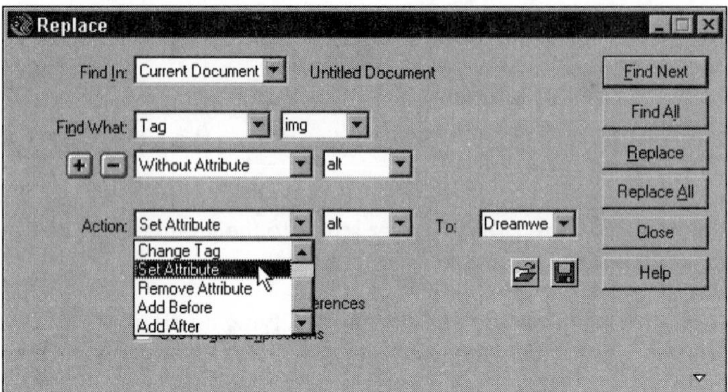

Figure 9-8: The Action list enables you to replace tags or modify them by setting the existing attributes or adding new ones.

Not all the options listed in the preceding table are available for all tags. Some so-called empty tags, such as `<img>`, consist of a single tag and not tag pairs. Empty tags have only Add Before and Add After options instead of Add Before Start Tag, Add After Start Tag, Add Before End Tag, and Add After End Tag.

7. Select any options desired: Match Case, Ignore Whitespace Differences, or Use Regular Expressions.

8. Choose your Find/Replace option: Find Next, Find All, Replace, or Replace All.

9. Select Close when finished.

You don't have to apply a single action to all the instances Dreamweaver locates if you choose Find All. In the list of found expressions, select a single item and then choose Replace. Dreamweaver makes the revision and places a green dot next to the item so you can tell it has been altered. If you want, you can then select another item from the list, choose a different action, and then select Replace.

Concentrating your search with regular expressions

As powerful as all the other Find and Replace features are, they are boosted to a new level of flexibility with the addition of regular expressions. I've referred to regular expressions as being similar to wildcards in other programs, but their capabilities are really far more extensive.

Regular expressions are best described as a text pattern matching system. If you can identify any pattern in your text, you can manipulate it with regular expressions. What kind of pattern? Let's say you have a spreadsheet-like table with lots of numbers, showing both dollars and cents, mixed with explanatory text. With regular expressions, you can match the pattern formed by the dollar sign and the decimal point and reformat the entire table, turning all the figures deep blue with a new font — all in one Find and Replace operation.

If you're into Unix, you recognize regular expressions as being very close to the grep utility—*grep*, by the way, stands for Get Regular Expressions and Print. The Find and Replace feature in BBEdit also features a grep-like syntax.

You can apply regular expressions to any of the types of Find and Replace operations previously discussed, with just a click of the Using Regular Expressions checkbox. Note that when you select Using Regular Expressions, the Ignore Unnecessary Whitespace option is deselected. This is because the two options are mutually exclusive and cannot be used together.

The most basic regular expression is the text itself. If you enable the feature and then enter **th** in the Find What text box, Dreamweaver locates every example of "th" in the text and/or source. Although this capability by itself has little use, it's important to remember this functionality as you begin to build your patterns.

Wildcard characters

Initially, it's helpful to be able to use what traditionally are know as *wildcards*—characters that match different types of characters. The wildcards in regular expressions represent single characters and are described in Table 9-3. In other words, no single regular expression represents all the characters, as the asterisk does when used in PC file searches (such as *.*). However such a condition can be represented with a slightly more complex regular expression (described later in this section).

Table 9-3
Regular Expression Wildcard Characters

Character	*Matches*	*Example*
.	Any single character	**w.d** matches **wid**e but not world.
\w	Any alphanumeric character, including the underscore	**w\wd** matches **wid**e and **world**.
\W	Any nonalphanumeric character	**jboy\Widest.com** matches **jboy@idest.com**.
\d	Any numeric character 0–9	**y\dk** matches **Y2K**.
\D	Any nonnumeric character	**\D2\D** matches **Y2K** and **H20**.
\s	Any whitespace character, including space, tab, form feed, or line feed	**\smedia** matches **media** but not Macromedia.
\S	Any nonwhitespace character	**\Smedia** matches Macro**media** but not media.

Continued

Table 9-3 *(continued)*

Character	*Matches*	*Example*
\t	A tab	Matches any single tab character in the HTML source.
\f	Form feed	Matches any single form-feed character in the HTML source.
\n	Line feed	Matches any single line-feed character in the HTML source.
\r	Carriage return	Matches any single carriage-return character in the HTML source.

The backslash character (\) is used to escape special characters so that they can be included in a search. For example, if you want to look for an asterisk, you need to specify it like this: *. Likewise, when trying to find the backslash character, precede it with another backslash character: \\.

Matching character positions and repeating characters

With regular expressions, not only can you match the type of character, but you can also match its position in the text. This feature enables you to perform operations on characters at the beginning, end, or middle of the word or line. Regular expressions also enable you to find instances in which a character is repeated an unspecified number of times or a specific number of times. Combined, these features broaden the scope of the patterns that can be found.

Table 9-4 details the options available for matching by text placement and character repetition.

Table 9-4
Regular Expression Character Positions and Repeating Characters

Character	*Matches*	*Example*
^	Beginning of a line	**^c** matches the first c in "**C**all me Ishmael."
$	End of a line	**d$** matches the final "d" in "Be afraid. Be very afrai**d**."
\b	A word boundary, such as a space or carriage return	**\btext** matches **text**book but not SimpleText.

Character	*Matches*	*Example*
\B	A nonword boundary inside a word	**\Btext** matches Simple**Text** but not textbook.
*	The preceding character zero or more times	**b*c** matches **BBC** and **c**old.
+	The preceding character one or more times	**b+c** matches **BBC** but not cold.
?	The preceding character zero or one time	**st?un** matches **stun** and **sun** but not strung.
{n}	Exactly *n* instances of the preceding character	**e{2}** matches reed and each pair of two e's in "Ai**ee**eeeee!" but nothing in Dreamweaver.
{n,m}	At least *n* and *m* instances of the preceding character	**C{2,4}** matches #**CC**00FF and #**CCCC**00 but not the full string #CCCCCC.

Matching character ranges

Beyond single characters, or repetitions of single characters, regular expressions incorporate the capability of finding or excluding ranges of characters. This feature is particularly useful when you're working with groups of names or titles. Ranges are specified in set brackets. A match is made when any one of the characters, not necessarily all of the characters, within the set brackets is found.

Descriptions of how to match character ranges with regular expressions can be found in Table 9-5.

Table 9-5
Regular Expression Character Ranges

Character	*Matches*	*Example*
[abc]	Any one of the characters a, b, or c	**[lmrt]** matches the l and m's in **lemm**ings and the r and t in **r**oad**t**rip.
[^abc]	Any character except a, b, or c	**[^etc]** matches **GIFs** but not etc in the phrase "GIFs etc."
[a-z]	Any character in the range from a to z	**[l-p]** matches l and o in **lo**wery and m, n, o an p in **pointman**.
x|y	Either x or y	**boy|girl** matches both **boy** and **girl**.

Using grouping with regular expressions

Grouping is perhaps the single most powerful concept in regular expressions. With it, any matched text pattern is easily manipulated — for example, the following list of names:

- John Jacob Jingleheimer Schmidt
- James T. Kirk
- Cara Fishman

could be rearranged so that the last name is first, separated by a comma, like this:

- Schmidt, John Jacob Jingleheimer
- Kirk, James T.
- Fishman, Cara

Grouping is handled primarily with parentheses. To indicate a group, enclose it in parentheses in the Find text field. Regular expressions can manage up to nine grouped patterns. Each grouped patterned is designated by a dollar sign ($) in front of a number, (1–9) in the Replace text field, like this: **$3**.

Remember that the dollar sign is also used after a character or pattern to indicate the last character in a line.

Table 9-6 shows how regular expressions use grouping.

Table 9-6
Regular Expressions Grouping

Character	*Matches*	*Example*
(p)	Any pattern p	**(\b\w*)\.(\w*\b)** matches two patterns, the first before a period and the second, after; such as in a file name with an extension. The backslash before the period escapes it so that it is not interpreted as a regular expression.
$1, $2 . . . $9	The *n*th pattern noted with parentheses	The replacement pattern **$1's extension is ".$2"** would manipulate the pattern **(\b\w*)\.(\w*\b)** so that Chapter09.txt and Image12.gif would become **Chapter09's extension is ".txt"** and **Image12's extension is ".gif."**

The <br> tag

Just like headings, the paragraph tag falls among the class of HTML objects called *block elements*. As such, any text marked with the <p>...</p> tag pair is always rendered with an extra line above and below the text. To have a series of blank lines appear one after the other, use the break tag <br>.

Break tags are used within block elements, such as headings and paragraphs, to provide a line break where the <br> is inserted. Dreamweaver provides two ways to insert a <br> tag: You can choose the Enter Line Break button from the Invisibles panel of the Objects palette, or you can use the keyboard shortcut Shift+Enter (Shift+Return).

Figure 9-9 clearly demonstrates the effect of the <br> tag. The menu items in Column A on the left are the result of using the <br> tag within a paragraph. In Column B on the right, paragraph tags alone are used. The <h1> heading is also split at the top (modified through style sheet selections) with a break tag to avoid the insertion of an unwanted line.

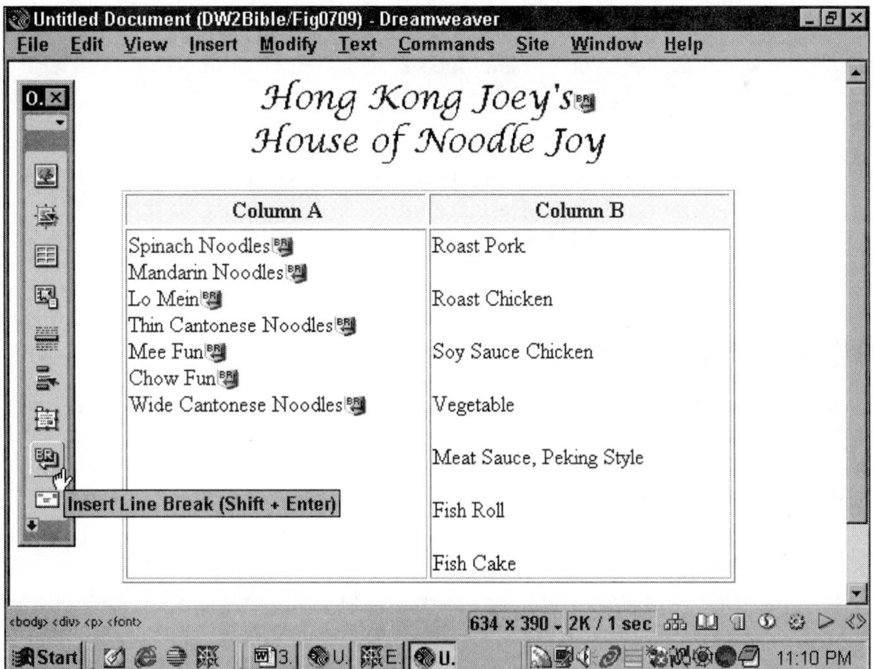

Figure 9-9: Use break tags to wrap your lines without the additional line spacing brought about by <p> tags.

Overcoming Line-Spacing Difficulties

Line spacing is a major issue and a common problem for Web designers. A design often calls for lines to be tightly spaced, but also of various sizes. If you use the break tag to separate your lines, you get the tight spacing required, but you won't be able to make each line a different heading size. As far as HTML and your browser are concerned, the text is still one block element, no matter how many line breaks are inserted. If, on the other hand, you make each line a separate paragraph or heading, the line spacing will be unattractively "open."

You can use one of several workarounds for this problem. First, if you're using line breaks, you can alter the size of each line by selecting it and choosing a different font size, either from the Property Inspector or the Text ⇨ Size menu. The only drawback to this approach is that the attribute you insert with this action — `<font size=n>` — is not recognized by older browsers.

A second option renders all the text as a graphics object and inserts it as an image. This gives you total control over the font's appearance and line spacing, as well as across-the-board browser compliance at the cost of added download time.

For a third possible solution, take a look at the section on preformatted text later in this chapter. Because you can apply styles to a preformatted text block (which can include line breaks and extra whitespace), you can alter the size, color, and font of each line, if necessary.

By default, Dreamweaver marks `<br>` tags with a symbol: a gold shield with the letters BR and the standard Enter/Return symbol. You can turn off this display feature by choosing Preferences ⇨ Invisible Elements and deselecting the Line Breaks checkbox.

Other whitespace tags

If you can't get the alignment effect you want through the regular text options available in Dreamweaver, two other HTML tags can affect whitespace: `<nobr>` and `<wbr>`. Although a tad on the obscure side, these tags can be just the ticket in certain circumstances. Let's see how they work.

The <nobr> tag

Most of the time, you want the user's browser to handle word-wrapping chores automatically. Occasionally, however, you may need to make sure that a particular string of text is rendered in one piece. For these situations, you can use the no break tag `<nobr>`. Any text that comes in between the opening and closing tag pair — `<nobr>...</nobr>` — is displayed in one continuous line. If the line of text is wider than the current browser window, a horizontal scroll bar automatically appears along the bottom of the browser.

The <nobr> tag is supported only through the Netscape and Microsoft browsers and must be entered by hand into your HTML code. Use the <nobr> tag under very special circumstances.

The <wbr> tag

The companion to the <nobr> tag is the word break tag <wbr>. Similar to a soft hyphen in a word processing program, the <wbr> tag tells the browser where to break a word, if necessary. When used within <nobr> tags, <wbr> is the equivalent of telling a browser, "Keep all this text in one line, but if you have to break it, break it here."

Like the <nobr> tag, <wbr> is supported only by Netscape and Microsoft browsers and must be entered by hand in either the HTML Inspector or your external editor.

Importing Word HTML

Microsoft Word has offered an option to save its documents as HTML since the release of Word 97. Unfortunately, Microsoft's version of HTML output is, at best, highly idiosyncratic. While you could always open a Word HTML file in Dreamweaver, if you ever had to modify the page—which you almost always do—it took so long to find your way through the convoluted code that you were almost better off building the page from scratch. Fortunately, that's no longer the case with Dreamweaver 3.

The capability to Import Word HTML is a key new feature of Dreamweaver 3. Dreamweaver can successfully import and automatically clean up files from Microsoft Word 97, Word 98, or Word 2000. The cleanup takes place automatically upon import, but you can also finely tune the modifications that Dreamweaver makes to the file. Moreover, you can even apply the current Source Format profile so that the HTML is styled to look like native Dreamweaver code.

Naturally, before you can import a Word HTML file, you have to have created one. To export a document in HTML format in Word 97/98, you choose File ⇨ Save as HTML; in Word 2000, the command has changed to File ⇨ Save as Web Page. Although the wording change may seem to be a move toward less jargon, it's significant what Word actually exports. With Word 2000 (and all the Office 2000 products), Microsoft heartily embraced the XML standard and uses a combination of standard HTML and custom XML code throughout their exported Web pages. For example, here's the opening tag from a Word 2000 document, saved as a Web page:

```
<html xmlns:o="urn:schemas-microsoft-com:office:office"
xmlns:w="urn:schemas-microsoft-com:office:word"
xmlns:dt="uuid:C2F41010-65B3-11d1-A29F-00AA00C14882"
xmlns="http://www.w3.org/TR/REC-html40">
```

which Dreamweaver alters to:

```
<html>
```

If you accept the defaults, importing a Word HTML file is a two-step affair:

1. Choose File ➪ Import ➪ Import Word HTML.

   The Import Word HTML dialog box opens (Figure 9-10), and Dreamweaver detects whether the HTML file was exported from Word 97/98 or 2000. The interface options change accordingly.

If Dreamweaver can't determine what version of Word generated the file, an alert appears. Although Dreamweaver will still try to clean up the code, it may not function correctly. The same alert appears if you inadvertently select a standard non-HTML Word document.

2. Click OK to confirm the import operation.

   Dreamweaver creates a new HTML document, imports the file, and cleans up the code. If the Show Log on Completion option is selected, Dreamweaver informs you of the modifications made.

For most purposes, accepting the defaults is the best way to quickly bring in your Word HTML files. However, because Web designers have a wide range of code requirements, Dreamweaver provides a full set of options so you can tailor the Word-to-Dreamweaver transformation to your liking. Two different sets of options exist — one for documents saved from Word 97/98 and one for those saved from Word 2000. The different sets of options can be seen on the Detailed tab of the Import Word HTML dialog box; the Basic tab is the same for both file types. Table 9-7 details the Basic tab options, the Word 97/98 options, and the Word 2000 options.

Table 9-7
Import Word HTML Options

Option	*Description*
Basic	
Remove all Word-specific markup	Deletes all Word-specific tags, including Word XML, conditional tags, empty paragraphs, and margins in `<style>` tags.
Clean up CSS	Deletes all Word-specific CSS code, including inline CSS styles where styles are nested, "mso" designated styles, non-CSS style declarations, CSS style attributes from tables and orphaned (unused) style definitions.

Option	*Description*
Clean up <font> tags	Deletes <font> tags that set the default body text to an absolute font size 2.
Fix invalidly nested tags	Deletes tags surrounding paragraph and block-level tags.
Set background color	Adds a background color to the page. Word does not supply one. The default added color is white (#ffffff). Colors can be entered as hexadecimal triplets with a leading hash mark or as a valid color name – that is, red.
Apply source formatting	Formats the imported code according to the guidelines of the current Source Format profile used by Dreamweaver.
Show log on completion	Displays a dialog box that lists all alterations when the process is complete.
Detailed Options for Word 97/98	
Remove Word specific markup	Enables the general clean up of Word-inserted tags.
Word meta and link tags from <head>	Specifically enables Dreamweaver to remove Word-specific <meta> and <link> tags from the <head> section of a document.
Clean up <font> tags	Enables the general clean up of <font> tags.
Convert size [7-1] to	Specifies which tag, if any, is substituted for a <font size=*n*> tag. Options are: • <h1> through <h6> • <font size=1> through <font size=7> • Default size • Don't change
Detailed Options for Word 2000	
Remove Word specific markup	Enables the general clean up of Word-inserted tags.
XML from <html> tag	Deletes the Word-generated XML from the <html> tag.
Word meta and link tags from <head>	Specifically enables Dreamweaver to remove Word-specific <meta> and <link> tags from the <head> section of a document.
Word XML markup	Enables the general clean up of Word-inserted XML tags.

Continued

Table 9-7 (continued)

Option	*Description*
Detailed Options for Word 2000	
`<![if...]><![endif]>` conditional tags and their contents	Removes all conditional statements.
Remove empty paragraphs and margins from styles	Deletes `<p>` tags without a closing `</p>` and styles tags including margin attributes — for example, `style='margin-top:0in'`.
Clean up CSS	Enables the general clean up of Word inserted CSS tags.
Remove inline CSS styles when possible	Deletes redundant information in nested styles.
Remove any style attribute that starts with "mso"	Eliminates all Microsoft Office (mso) specific attributes.
Remove any non-CSS style declaration	Deletes nonstandard style declarations.
Remove all CSS styles from table rows and cells	Eliminates style information from `<table>`, `<tr>`, and `<td>` tags.
Remove all unused style definitions	Deletes any declared styles that are not referenced in the page.

You don't have to remember to run the Import Word HTML command to take advantage of Dreamweaver's cleanup features. If you've already opened a document saved as Word HTML, you can choose Commands ⇨ Clean Up Word HTML and gain access to the exact same dialog box for the existing page.

Styling Your Text

When the Internet was founded, its intended focus was to make scientific data widely accessible. Soon it became apparent that even raw data could benefit from being styled contextually, without detracting from the Internet's openness and universality. Over the short history of HTML, text styles have become increasingly important, and the W3C has sought to keep a balance between substance and style.

Dreamweaver enables the Web designer to apply the most popular HTML styles directly through the program's menus and Property Inspector. Less prevalent styles can be inserted through the integrated text editors or by hand.

Working with preformatted text

Browsers ignore formatting niceties considered irrelevant to page content: tabs, extra line feeds, indents, and added whitespace. You can force browsers to read all the text, including whitespace, exactly as you have entered it. By applying the preformatted tag, `<pre>`, you tell the browser that it should keep any additional whitespace encountered within the text. By default, the `<pre>` tag also renders its content with a monospace font such as Courier. For these reasons, the `<pre>` tag was used to lay out text in columns in the early days of HTML, before tables were widely available.

You can apply the preformatted tag either through the Property Inspector or the menus. Before you use either technique, however, be sure to select the text or position the cursor where you want the preformatted text to begin. To use the Property Inspector, open the Format list box and choose Preformatted. To use the menus, choose Text ⇨ Format ⇨ Preformatted.

The `<pre>` tag is a block element format, like the paragraph or the headings tags, rather than a style. This designation as a block element format has two important implications. First, you can't apply the `<pre>` tag to part of a line; when you use this tag, the entire paragraph is altered. Second, you can apply styles to preformatted text — this enables you to increase the size or alter the font, but at the same time maintain the whitespace feature made possible with the `<pre>` tag. All text in Figure 9-10 uses the `<pre>` tag; the column on the left is the standard output with monospaced font; the column on the right uses a different font in a larger size.

Depicting various styles

As explained in Chapter 8 HTML's logical styles are used to mark text relatively or within a particular context, rather than with a specific look. The eventual displayed appearance of logical styles is completely up to the viewer's browser. This is useful when you are working with documents from different sources — reports from different research laboratories around the country, for instance — and you want certain conformity of style. Logical styles are utilitarian; physical styles such as boldface and italic are decorative. Both types of styles have their uses in material published on today's Web.

All of Dreamweaver's styles are accessed by choosing Text ⇨ Style and selecting from the 13 available style name options. A checkmark appears next to the selected tags. Style tags can be nested (put inside one another), and you can mix logical and physical tags within a word, line, or document. You can have a bold, strikethrough, variable style; or you can have an underlined cited style. (Both variable and cite are particular logical styles covered later in this section.) If, however, you are trying to achieve a particular look using logical styles, you should probably use the Cascading Style Sheets feature.

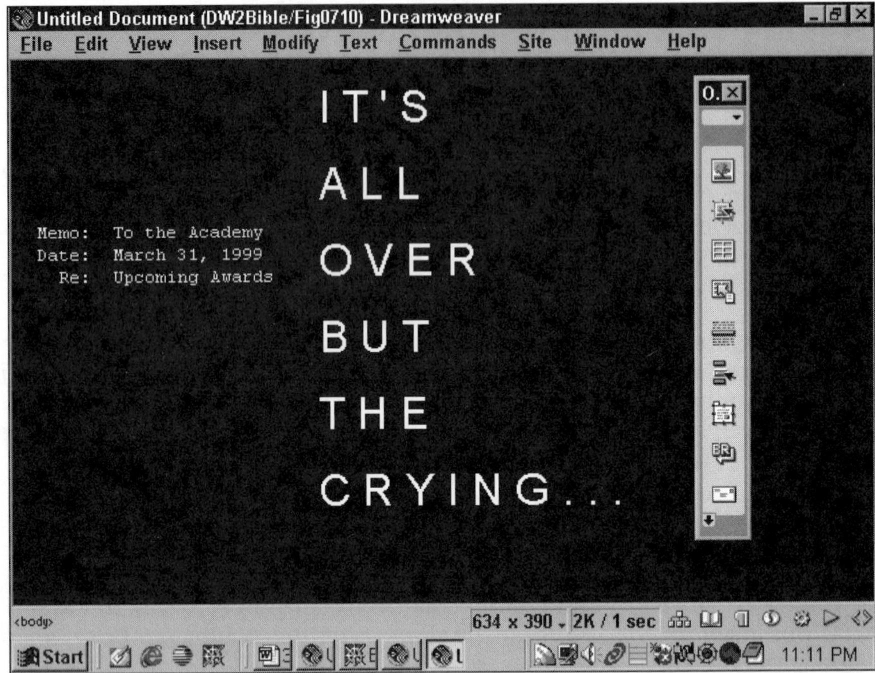

Figure 9-10: Preformatted text gives you full control over the line breaks, tabs, and other whitespace in your Web page.

The styles that can be applied through regular HTML are just the tip of the iceberg compared to the possibilities with Cascading Style Sheets. For details on using this feature, see Chapter 27.

Take a look at Figure 9-11 for a comparison of how the styles are rendered in Dreamweaver, Internet Explorer 5.0, and Netscape Communicator 4.7. While the various renderings are mostly the same, notice the browser differences in the Definition styles and the difference in how the Keyboard style is rendered in Dreamweaver and either browser.

Two of the three physical style tags — bold and italic — are both available from the Text Property Inspector and through keyboard shortcuts (Ctrl+B or Command+B, and Ctrl+I or Command+I, respectively). The Underline tag, <u>, is available only through the Text ⇨ Style menu. Underlining text on a Web page is generally discouraged, to avoid confusion with links, which are typically displayed underlined.

Both physical and logical style tags are described, with example uses, in Table 9-8.

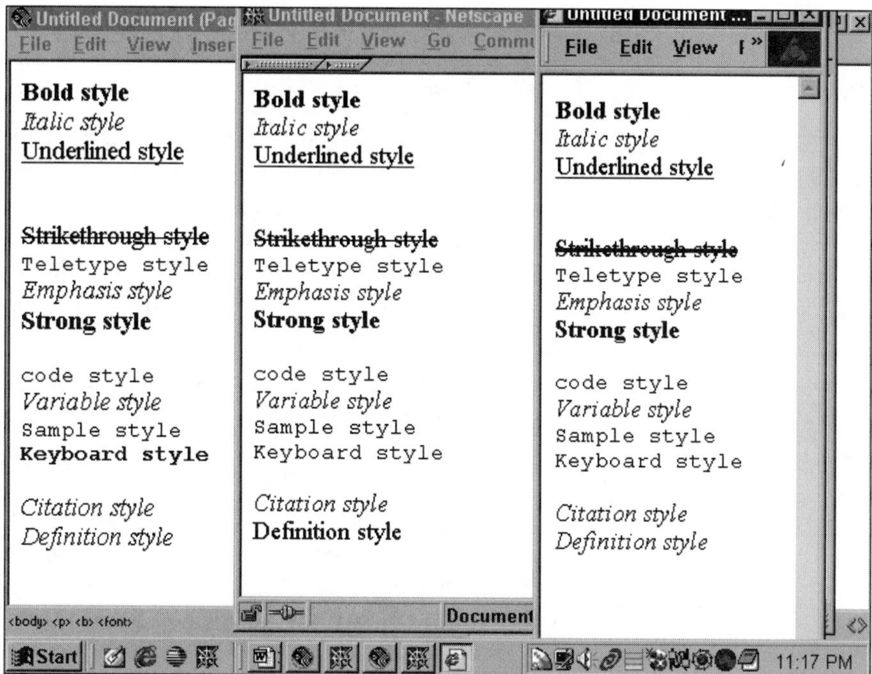

Figure 9-11: In this comparison chart, the various renderings of Dreamweaver style tags are from Dreamweaver, Netscape Communicator 4.7, and Internet Explorer 5.0 (from left to right).

Table 9-8
Dreamweaver Style Tags

Style	*Tag*	*Description*
Bold	<b>	Text is rendered with a bold style.
Italic	<i>	Text is rendered with an italic style.
Underline	<u>	Text is rendered underlined.
Strikethrough	<s>	Used primarily in edited documents to depict edited text. Usually rendered with a line through the text.
Teletype	<tt>	Used to represent an old-style typewriter. Rendered in a monospace font such as Courier.

Continued

Table 9-8 (continued)		
Style	***Tag***	***Description***
Emphasis	<em>	Used to accentuate certain words relative to the surrounding text. Most often rendered in italic.
Strong Emphasis	<strong>	Used to strongly accentuate certain words relative to the surrounding text. Most often rendered in boldface.
Code	<code>	Used to depict programming code, usually in a monospaced font.
Sample	<samp>	Used to display characters in a literal sequence, usually in a monospaced font.
Variable	<var>	Used to mark variables in programming code. Most often displayed in italics.
Keyboard	<kbd>	Used to indicate what should be user input. Often shown in a monospaced font, sometimes in boldface.
Citation	<cite>	Used to mark citations, references, and titles. Most often displayed in italic.
Definition	<dfn>	Used to denote the first, defining instance of a term. Usually displayed in italic.

Using the <address> tag

Currently, Dreamweaver does not support one useful style tag: the <address> tag. Rendered as italic text by browsers, the <address>...</address> tag pair often marks the signature and e-mail address of a Web page's creator. The <address> tags should go around a paragraph tag pair; otherwise, Dreamweaver flags the closing </p> as invalid.

The easiest way to do this in Dreamweaver 3 is to use the new Quick Tag Editor. Select your text and press Ctrl+T (Command T) to automatically enter Wrap Tag mode. If Tag Hints is enabled, all you'll have to type is **ad** and press Enter (Return) twice to accept the hint and confirm the tag.

If you're applying the <address> tag to multiple lines, use <br> tags to form line breaks. The following example shows the proper use of the <address> tags:

```
<address><p>The President<br>
 1600 Pennsylvania Avenue<br>
 Washington, DC 20001</p></address>
```

This preceding code is shown on a Web browser as follows:

The President

1600 Pennsylvania Avenue

Washington, DC 20001

To remove a standard style, highlight the styled text, choose Text ⇨ Style, and select the name of the style you want to remove. The checkmark disappears from the style name. To remove a nonstandard tag such as `<address>`, choose the tag in the Tag Selector and right-click (Control+click) to open the shortcut menu and select Remove Tag.

Using HTML Styles

In the world of Web design, consistency is a good thing. A site where headings, subheads, and body text are consistent from page to page is far easier for the visitor to quickly grasp than one where each page has its own style. While the best approach for a consistently designed site may be the use of Cascading Style Sheets (CSS), that approach requires 4.0 and above browsers, and many clients are not willing to write off those potential Web visitors using older software.

To bridge the gap between old and new—and to make it easier to apply the same set of tags over and over again—Dreamweaver 3 introduces HTML Styles. HTML Styles are similar to CSS in that you define a custom style for text and give it any attributes you want: font name, size, color, format, and so on. Then you apply that style to either a selection or an entire block of text. The primary difference is that, with HTML Styles, Dreamweaver adds the necessary standard HTML tags, instead of CSS style declarations, to recreate your style. In other words, if you always set your legal disclaimers in Verdana at a –1 size in a deep red color, you can define your "legal" style once and apply it over and over again with one step, anywhere on the site.

HTML Styles, however, are not a replacement for CSS styles, and you should keep in mind some important differences:

✦ Modifying a HTML Style definition affects only subsequent applications of the style. When a CSS style is altered, the change is immediately seen wherever the style has been applied on the current page as well as in all future applications.

✦ HTML Styles use standard text tags and cannot, therefore, create some of the special effects possible in CSS. For example, you could not create a HTML Style that eliminates the underline from a link or changes the leading of a paragraph.

✦ Although defined HTML Styles are accessible from anywhere within a site, they are applied on a document-to-document basis, whereas with CSS, an external style sheet could be defined and linked to pages anywhere on your site.

Even with these differences, however, HTML Styles are an enhancement to a designer's workflow and extremely easy to use.

In the remainder of this section, when I refer to a style or styles, I'm referring to HTML Styles. CSS Style references are designated as such.

Applying HTML Styles

Dreamweaver 3 ships with eight predefined styles that are available for immediate use from the HTML Styles palette. The HTML Styles palette, shown in Figure 9-12, displays all currently available styles as well as options for removing style formatting, editing existing styles, adding new styles, or removing styles from the palette.

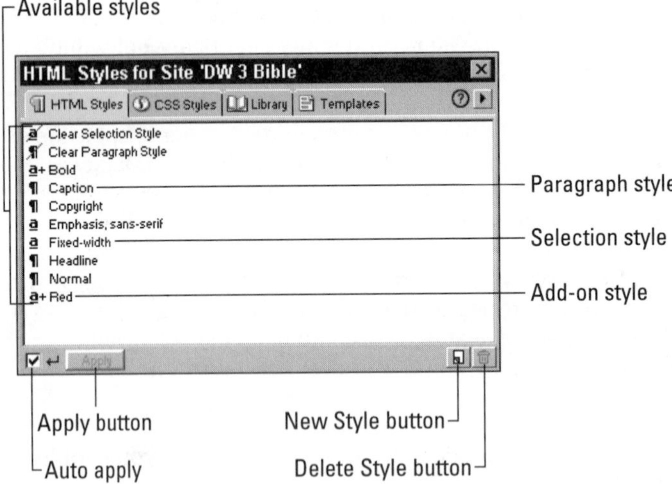

Figure 9-12: Manage your standard formatting through the HTML Styles palette.

HTML Styles are divided into two distinct types: paragraph and selection styles. A paragraph style affects an entire block element, whether it is a single heading, a paragraph, or another block element such as a block quote. Paragraph styles are designated with a ¶ symbol in the HTML Styles palette. A paragraph style is applied to the entire current block element, whether the cursor has selected the text or is just within the block. A selection style, on the other hand, applies formatting only to selected text. Selection styles are marked in the HTML Styles palette with an underlined lowercased *a*, like this a.

It's possible for both paragraph and selection styles to either clear the existing style before adding the new formatting or add the new formatting to the existing style. The default behavior is for existing formatting to be removed; if the style is to be added, a small plus sign (+) is shown in front of the style name.

To apply an HTML Style, follow these steps:

1. Open the HTML Styles palette in one of the following ways:
   - Select Window ➪ HTML Styles.
   - Choose the HTML Styles button from either Launcher.
   - Press the keyboard shortcut, Ctrl+F7 (Command+F7).
2. To apply a style to the currently selected text, choose any designated (a) HTML Style.

Tip: It's easiest to always have the Auto Apply option selected, so that your choices immediately are applied; if this option is not selected, click the Apply button.

3. To apply a style to the current block element, choose any so-designated (¶) HTML Style.

Removing HTML Styles

As useful as applying new HTML Styles is, I find that the capability to remove all such formatting even more beneficial. It's not unusual for me to style a paragraph and then want to try a completely different approach—with the HTML Styles palette, I can wipe out all the formatting in one click and start fresh.

As with applying styles, you can remove either a paragraph or a selection style. Both are available as the first items in the HTML Styles palette. Clear Selection Style removes all <font> and other text formatting tags surrounding the current selection while Clear Paragraph Style eliminates all such tags from the current block element.

Caution: Removing a paragraph style removes all styles to the paragraph, not just ones you may have added via the HTML Styles palette. For example, if a line is styled like this:

```
<h1><font color="#FFFF00">Welcome</font></h2>
```

Selecting Clear Paragraph Style converts the line to this:

```
<p>Welcome</p>
```

The Clear Selection Style command does not require that the formatting tags be adjacent to the selection. If you select some text in the middle of a paragraph styled in a particular color and font, choosing Clear Selection Style inserts appropriate tags before and after the selection so that the selection has no style whatsoever, but the surrounding text remains styled. A before and after view of the process is shown in Figure 9-13.

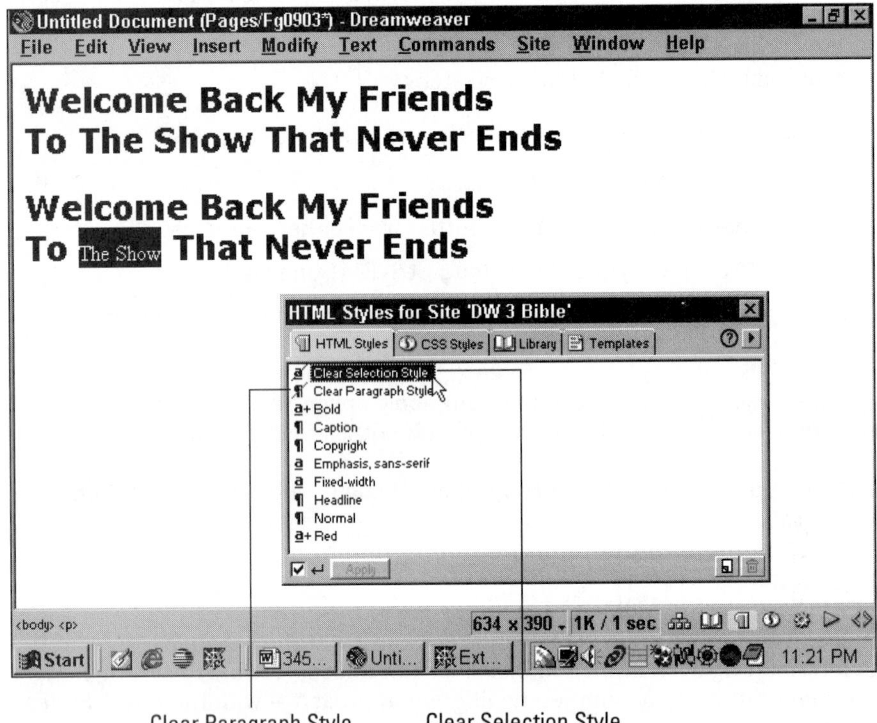

Figure 9-13: You can remove all styling from a bit of text and keep the surrounding styling with the Clear Selection Style command.

If you no longer wish to have a defined style displayed in the HTML Styles palette, select that style and choose the Delete Style button. Alternatively, you could select the style and choose Delete Style from the context-sensitive menu on the palette.

Defining HTML Styles

Naturally, the standard list of styles is just a jumping-off place for the HTML Styles palette. To get the most out the feature, you should design your own custom styles. Dreamweaver gives you a number of methods to define a style:

✦ **Style by Example** — Create a new style from formatted text onscreen.

✦ **Modify an Existing Style**—Edit a standard or custom style to your liking. You can even duplicate the style first, so both old and new versions are available.

✦ **Build a New Style**—Select all the desired attributes for your selection or paragraph style and try it out right away on selected text.

All style definitions are managed in the Define HTML Style dialog box, shown in Figure 9-14. How the dialog box is opened depends on which method you're using to create or modify your style.

✦ To create a style from example, select tags you want to include in the style from the Document window or the Tag Selector and then choose the New Style button from the HTML Styles palette.

✦ To modify an existing style, double-click its name in the HTML Styles palette list.

✦ To create a new style built on an existing one, select the style and then, from the context-sensitive menu of the HTML Styles palette, select Duplicate.

✦ To create a style from the ground up, choose the New Style button on the HTML Styles palette.

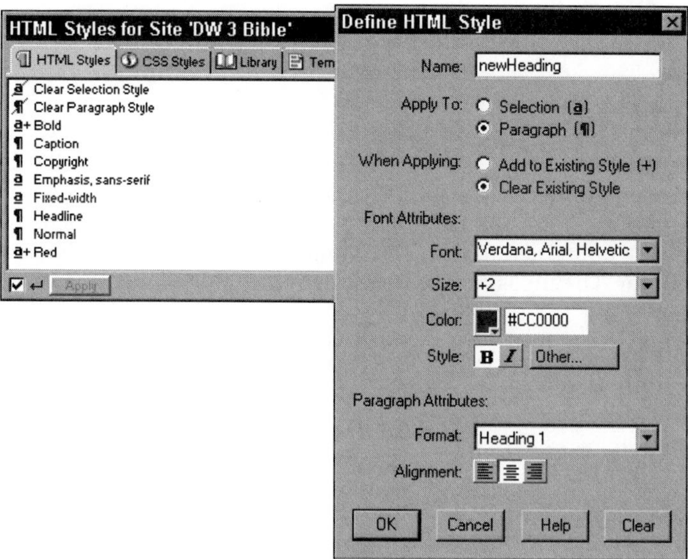

Figure 9-14: Build or modify styles in the Define HTML Style dialog box.

To define an HTML Style, follow these steps:

1. Open the Define HTML Style dialog box using one of the previously described methods.

2. Enter a unique name for your style, if creating a new one.
3. Choose whether your style is to apply to a selection or a paragraph.
4. Select whether your style will add to the existing style or clear existing style.
5. Choose the desired font attributes:
   - Font
   - Size
   - Color
   - Style: Bold, Italic, or Bold-Italic
   - Other . . . (Additional Optional Styles): Underline, Strikethrough, Teletype, Emphasis, Strong, Code, Variable, Sample, Keyboard, Citation, Definition
6. If defining a paragraph style, select from the following attribute options:
   - Format: None, Heading 1 through Heading 6, or Preformatted
   - Alignment: Right, Center, Left.
7. Click OK when you're done.

Tip To start over at any time, select the Clear button.

Changing default styles

If you find yourself using the same HTML Styles in all or most of your work—and don't want to keep copying the styles.xml file from site to site as described in the previous sidebar—you can alter the default styles that Dreamweaver opens with. The standard styles are contained in the aptly named defaultStyles.xml file, found in the Configuration folder. The file is a series of XML tags that look like this:

```
<mm:style name="Bold" type="char" apply="add" bold />
<mm:style name="Caption" format="p" align="center" apply="replace" ¬
font="Arial, Helvetica, sans-serif" size="2" color="#808080" bold italic />
```

Although you could write in the style by hand, following the given format, there's an easier way:

1. Create a style within a site that you want to add to the Dreamweaver default HTML Styles.
2. In your favorite text editor, open styles.xml found in the Library folder of your site.

3. Locate and copy the tag that describes the desired style or styles. The name of the style is the first attribute of the XML tag.

   Be sure to get all of the tag, including the closing />.

4. Open the defaultStyles.xml file found under the Dreamweaver Configuration folder in the text editor.

5. Paste the style(s) in the defaultStyles.xml file and save it.

6. Relaunch Dreamweaver.

Your new styles will be available with every new site.

Modifying Text Format

As a Web designer, you easily spend at least as much time adjusting your text as you do getting it into your Web pages. Luckily, Dreamweaver puts most of the tools you need for this task right at your fingertips. All the text-formatting options are available through the Text Property Inspector. Instead of hand-coding `<font>`, `<blockquote>`, and alignment tags, just select your text and click a button.

Note In HTML text formatting today, programmers are moving toward using Cascading Style Sheets and away from hard-coding text with `<font>` and other tags. Both 4.0+ versions of the major Web browsers support Cascading Style Sheets to some extent, and Internet Explorer has had some support since the 3.0 version. The current realities of browser competition, however, dictate that to take advantage of the widest support range, Web designers must continue to use the character-specific tags. Even after Cascading Style Sheets gain widespread acceptance, you'll probably still need to apply tags on the "local level" occasionally.

Moving HTML Styles from Site to Site

Custom HTML styles are available from any page in your site. But what happens if you start a new site? Do you have to recreate your custom styles again? Every new site starts with the same set of default styles standard in Dreamweaver. (The next section describes how to alter even those defaults.) But you can easily transfer styles you've created for one site to another, just by copying the right file.

The information describing the custom HTML styles are stored in each site's Library folder in a file named styles.xml. To transfer the HTML styles, just copy the styles.xml file from one site's Library folder to the Library folder for another site. Library folders are created within a site when they are first needed, so if you've just defined your site, the Library folder may not exist yet. You can, however, safely create it within the local site root and move your styles.xml file into the folder.

Adjusting font size

The six HTML heading types enable you to assign relative sizes to a line or to an entire paragraph. In addition, HTML gives you a finer degree of control through the size attribute of the font tag. In contrast to publishing environments, both traditional and desktop, font size is not specified in HTML with points. Rather, the `<font>` tag enables you to choose one of seven different explicit sizes that the browser can render (absolute sizing), or you can select one relative to the page's basic font. Figure 9-15 shows the default absolute and relative sizes, compared to a more page designer–friendly point chart (accomplished with Dreamweaver's Cascading Style Sheets features).

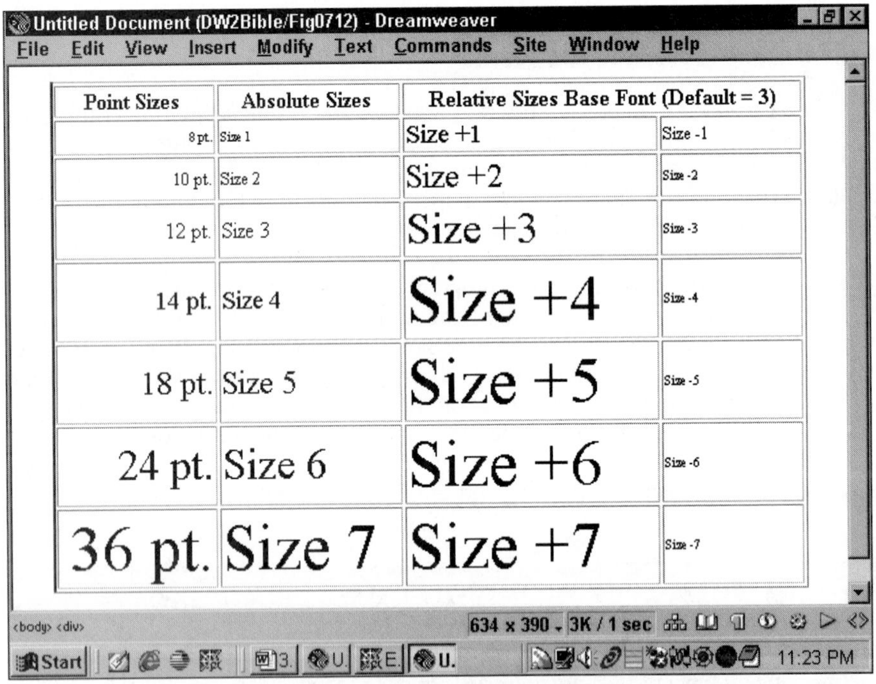

Point Sizes	Absolute Sizes	Relative Sizes Base Font (Default = 3)	
8 pt.	Size 1	Size +1	Size -1
10 pt.	Size 2	Size +2	Size -2
12 pt.	Size 3	Size +3	Size -3
14 pt.	Size 4	Size +4	Size -4
18 pt.	Size 5	Size +5	Size -5
24 pt.	Size 6	Size +6	Size -6
36 pt.	Size 7	Size +7	Size -7

Figure 9-15: In this chart, you can see the relationships between the various font sizes in an HTML browser and as compared to "real-world" point sizes.

Which way should you go — absolute or relative? Some designers think that relative sizing gives them more options. As you can see by the chart in Figure 9-15, browsers are limited to displaying seven different sizes no matter what — unless you're using Cascading Style Sheets. Relative sizing does give you additional flexibility, though, because you can resize all the fonts in an entire Web page with one command. Absolute sizes, however, are more straightforward to use and can be coded in Dreamweaver without any additional HTML programming. Once again, it's the designer's choice.

Absolute size

You can assign an absolute font size through either the Property Inspector or the menus. In both cases, you choose a value, 1 (smallest) through 7 (largest), to which you want to resize your text; you might note that this order is the reverse of the heading sizes, which range from H1 to H6, largest to smallest.

To use the Property Inspector to pick an absolute font size, follow these steps:

1. Select your text.
2. In the Property Inspector, open the Font Size drop-down list of options.
3. Choose a value from 1 to 7.

To pick an absolute font size from the menu, follow these steps:

1. Select your text.
2. Choose Text ➪ Size and pick a value from 1 to 7, or Default (which is 3).

You can also use the keyboard shortcuts for changing absolute font sizes. Headings 1 through 6 correspond to Ctrl+1 through Ctrl+6 (Command+1 through Command+6). The Paragraph option is rendered with a Ctrl+Shift+P (Command+Shift+P); you can remove all formatting with Ctrl+0 (Command+0).

Relative size

To what exactly are relative font sizes relative? The default font size, of course. The advantage of relative font sizes is that you can alter a Web page's default font size with one command, the `<basefont>` tag. The tag takes the following form:

```
<basefont size=value>
```

where value is a number from 1 to 7. The `<basefont>` tag is usually placed immediately following the opening `<body>` tag. Dreamweaver does not support previewing the results of altering the `<basefont>` tag, and the tag has to be entered by hand or through the external editor.

You can distinguish a relative font size from an absolute font size by the plus or minus sign that precedes the value. The relative sizes are plus or minus the current `<basefont>` size. Thus a `<font size=+1>` is normally rendered with a size 4 font because the default `<basefont>` is 3. If you include the following line in your Web page:

```
<basefont size=5>
```

text marked with a `<font size=+1>` is displayed with a size 6 font. Because browsers display only seven different size fonts with a `<basefont size=5>` setting — unless you're using Cascading Style Sheets — any relative size over `<font size=+2>` won't display differently when previewed in a browser.

Relative font sizes can also be selected from either the Property Inspector or the menus. To use the Property Inspector to pick a relative font size, follow these steps:

1. Select your text or position the cursor where you want the new text size to begin.
2. In the Property Inspector, open the Font Size drop-down list of options.
3. To increase the size of your text, choose a value from +1 through +7.

   To decrease the size of your text, choose a value from –1 to –7.

To pick a relative font size from the menus, follow these steps:

1. Select your text or position the cursor where you want the new text size to begin.
2. To increase the size of your text, choose Text ➪ Size Increase and pick a value from +1 to +7.

   To reduce the size of your text, choose Text ➪ Size Decrease and pick a value from –1 to –7.

Dreamweaver's Color Pickers

Dreamweaver includes a color picker containing the 212 colors common to the Macintosh and Windows palettes – you already know these as the browser-safe colors. While it's generally believed that 216 common colors exist, the Macromedia engineers found that Internet Explorer on Windows systems renders four incorrectly: colors #0033FF (0,51,255), #3300FF (51,0,255), #00FF33 (0,255,51), and #33FF00 (51,255,0).

If you choose a color outside of the "safe" range, you have no assurances of how the color is rendered on a viewer's browser. Some systems select the closest color in RGB values; some use dithering (positioning two or more colors next to each other to simulate another color) to try to overcome the limitations of the current screen color depth. So be forewarned: If at all possible, stick with the browser-safe colors, especially when coloring text.

Mac Users: The color picker for Macintosh systems is far more elaborate than the one available for Windows users. The Mac version has several color schemes to use: CMYK (for print-related colors), RGB (for screen-based colors), HTML (for Web-based colors) and Crayon (for kid-like colors). The CMYK, HTML, and RGB systems offer you color swatches and three or four sliders with text entry boxes and accept percentage values for RGB and CMYK and hex values for HTML. Both RGB and HTML also have a snap-to-Web color option for matching your chosen color to the closest browser-safe color. The Hue, Saturation, and Value (or Lightness) sliders also have color wheels.

Adding font color

Unless you assign a color to text on your Web page, the browser uses its own default, typically black. As noted in "Establishing Page Properties" in Chapter 8, you can change the font color for the entire page by choosing Modify ➪ Page Properties and selecting a new color from the Text Color swatch. You can also color any specific headings, words, or paragraphs that you have selected in Dreamweaver.

Tip: When adding a new font color, size, or name to text that already has one `<font>` tag applied to it, it's best to use the Tag Selector to highlight the text by selecting that `<font>` tag. If you select your text by clicking and dragging, you're likely to not select the entire contents of the tag, which results in multiple `<font>` tags being applied.

The `<font>` tag goes to work again when you add color to selected elements of the page—this time, with the color attribute set to a particular value. HTML color is expressed in either a hexadecimal color number or a color name. The hexadecimal color number is based on the color's red-green-blue value and is written as follows:

```
#FFFFFF
```

The preceding represents the color white. You can also use standard color names instead of the hexadecimal color numbers. A sample color code line follows:

```
I'm <font color="green">GREEN</font> with envy.
```

Dreamweaver understands both color names and hexadecimal color numbers, but its HTML code output is in hexadecimal color numbers only.

Again, you have two ways to add color to your text in Dreamweaver. The Property Inspector displays a drop-down list of the browser-safe colors and also gives you an option to choose from a full-spectrum Color dialog box. If you approach your coloring task via the menus, the Text ➪ Color command takes you immediately to the Color dialog box.

To use the Property Inspector to color a range of text in Dreamweaver, follow these steps:

1. Select the text you want to color or position the cursor where you want the new text color to begin.
2. From the Property Inspector, you can
   - Type a hexadecimal color number directly into the Font Color text box
   - Type a color name directly into the Font Color text box
   - Select the Font Color swatch to open the browser-safe color picker
3. If you chose to type a color name or number directly into the Font Color text box, press Tab or click the Document window to see the color applied.

4. If you clicked the Font Color swatch, select your color from the browser-safe colors available. As you move your pointer over the color swatches, Dreamweaver displays the color in the corner and the color's hexadecimal number below.

5. For a wider color selection from the Color dialog box, select the Palette icon in the lower-right corner of the color swatch.

To access the full-spectrum color picker in Windows, follow these steps:

1. Select your text or position your cursor where you want the new text color to begin.

2. Choose Text ➪ Color to open the Color dialog box, as shown in Figure 9-16.

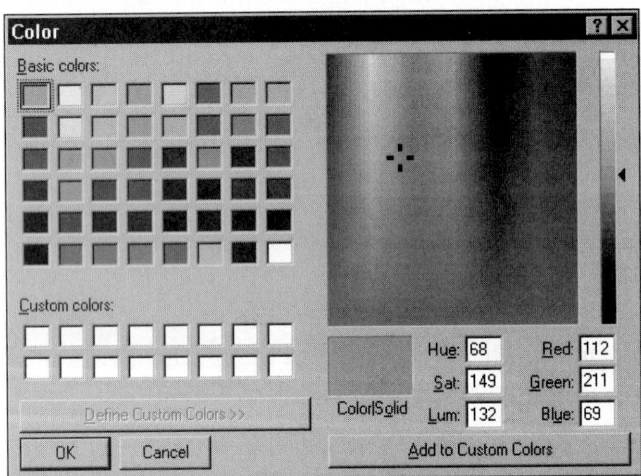

Figure 9-16: Use the Color dialog box in Windows to choose a color for your font outside of the browser-safe palette.

3. Select one of the 48 preset standard colors from the color swatches on the left of the Color dialog box, or use either of the following methods:

   • Select a color by moving the Hue/Saturation pointer and the Luminance pointer.

   • Enter decimal values directly into either the Red, Green, and Blue boxes or the Hue, Saturation, and Luminance boxes.

4. If you create a custom color, you can add it to your palette by selecting Add to Custom Colors. You can add up to 16 custom colors.

5. Click OK when you are finished.

When you add a custom color to your palette in Windows, the new color swatch goes into the currently selected swatch or, if no swatch is selected, the next available swatch. Make sure you have selected an empty or replaceable swatch before selecting the Add to Custom Color button. To clear the custom colors, first set the palette to white by bringing the Luminance slider all the way to the top. Then, select the Add to Custom Color button until all the color swatch text boxes are empty.

To access the full-spectrum color picker in Macintosh systems, follow these steps:

1. Select the text or position your cursor where you want the new text color to begin.
2. Choose Text ➪ Color to open the Color dialog box.
3. From the Color dialog box, select the Color Palette icon.

   The Macintosh color picker opens.
4. In the Macintosh color picker, the list of available pickers is displayed in the left pane, and each particular interface is shown in the right. Choose the specific color picker icon from the left pane and create the color desired in the right.

   The number and type of color pickers vary from system to system, depending on the version of the operating system and whether you've added any third-party color pickers.
5. When you've found the desired color, click OK.

Assigning a specific font

Along with size and color, you can also specify the typeface in which you want particular text to be rendered. Dreamweaver uses a special method for choosing font names for a range of selected text, due to HTML's unique way of handling fonts. Before you learn how to change a typeface in Dreamweaver, let's further examine how fonts in HTML work.

About HTML fonts

Page layout designers can incorporate as many different fonts as available to their own systems. Web layout designers, on the other hand, can use only those fonts on their viewers' systems. If you designate a paragraph to be in Bodoni Bold Condensed, for instance, and put it on the Web, the paragraph is displayed with that font only if that exact font name is on the user's system. Otherwise, the browser uses the default system font, which is often Times or Times New Roman.

Fonts are specified with the `<font>` tag, aided by the `name` attribute. Because a designer can never be certain of which fonts are on visitors' computers, HTML enables you to offer a number of options to the browser, as follows:

```
<font name="Arial, Helvetica, sans-serif">Swiss Maid Foundry</font>
```

The browser encountering the preceding tag first looks for the Arial font to render the enclosed text. If Arial isn't there, the browser looks for the next font in the list, which in this case is Helvetica. Failing to find any of the specified fonts listed, the browser uses whichever font has been assigned to the category for the font — sans-serif in this case.

The W3C and some Web browsers recognize five main categories of fonts: serif, sans-serif, monospace, cursive, and fantasy. Internet Explorer has a higher compliance rating on this issue than Netscape Communicator.

Selecting a font

The process for assigning a font name to a range of text is similar to that of assigning a font size or color. Instead of selecting one font name, however, you're usually selecting one font series. That series could contain three or more fonts, as previously explained. Font series are chosen from the Property Inspector or through a menu item. Dreamweaver enables you to assign any font on your system — or even any font you can name — to a font series, as covered in the section "Editing the Font List," later in this chapter.

To assign a specific font series to your text, follow these steps:

1. Select the text or position your cursor where you want the new text font to begin.
2. From the Property Inspector, open the drop-down list of font names. You can also choose Text ⇨ Font from the menu bar. Your font list is displayed.
3. Select a font from the Font List. To return to the system font, choose Default Font from the list.

It's also possible to enter the font name or font series directly in the Property Inspector's Font drop-down list box.

Font peculiarities are one of the key reasons to always test your Web pages on several platforms. Macintosh and Windows have different names for the same basic fonts (Arial in Windows is almost identical to Helvetica in Macintosh, for instance), and even the standard font sizes vary between the platforms. On the plus side, standard Microsoft fonts (Arial, Verdana for example) are more common on the Macintosh since Mac OS 8.1, but differences still exist. Overall, PC fonts are larger than fonts on a Macintosh. Be sure to check out your page on as many systems as possible before finalizing your design.

Editing the Font List

With the Edit Font List dialog box, Dreamweaver gives you a point-and-click interface for building your font lists. Once the Edit Font List dialog box is open, you can delete an existing font series, add a new one, or change the order of the list so your favorite ones are on top. Take a look at Figure 9-17 to see the sections of the Edit Font List dialog box: the current Font List, the Available Fonts on your system, and the Chosen Fonts. The Chosen Fonts are the individual fonts that you've selected to be incorporated into a font series.

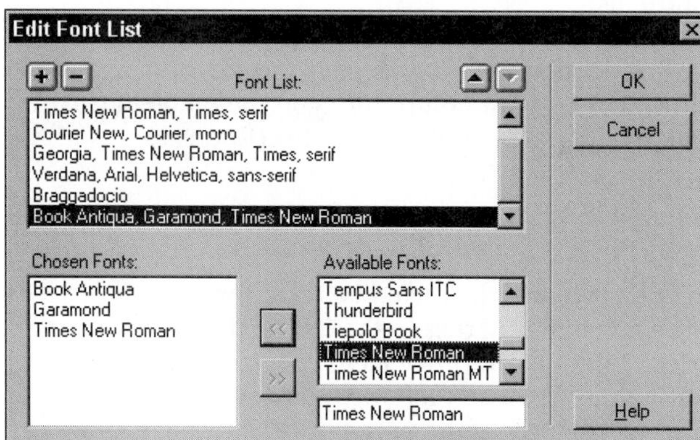

Figure 9-17: Dreamweaver's Edit Font List dialog box gives you considerable control over the fonts that you can add to your Web page.

Let's step through the process of constructing a new font series and adding it to the font list:

1. To open the Edit Font List dialog box, either choose Edit Font List through the Font Name option arrow in the Property Inspector, or select Text ➪ Font ➪ Edit Font List.
2. If the Chosen Fonts box is not empty, clear the Chosen Fonts box by selecting the plus (+) button at the top of the dialog box. You can also scroll down to the bottom of the current Font List and select "(Add fonts in list below)."
3. Select a font from the Available Fonts list.
4. Click the << button to transfer the selected font to the Chosen Fonts list.
5. To remove a font you no longer want or have chosen in error, highlight it in the Chosen Fonts list and select the >> button.
6. Repeat Steps 3 through 5 until the Chosen Fonts list contains the alternative fonts desired.
7. If you want to add another, separate font series, repeat Steps 2 through 5.
8. Click OK when you are finished adding fonts.

To change the order in which font series are listed in the Font List, follow these steps:

1. In the Font List dialog box, select the font series that you want to move.
2. If you want to move the series higher up the list, select the up-arrow button at the top-right of the Font List. If you want to move the series lower down the list, select the down-arrow button.

To remove a font series from the current Font List, highlight it and select the minus (–) button at the top-left of the list.

Remember, you need to have the fonts on your system to make them a part of your font list. To add a font unavailable on your computer, type the name of the font into the text box below the Available Fonts list and press Enter (Return).

Aligning text

You can easily align text in Dreamweaver, just like in a traditional word processing program. HTML supports the alignment of text to the left or right margin, or in the center of the browser window. Like a word processing program, Dreamweaver aligns text one paragraph at a time. You can't left-align one word, center the next, and then right-align the third word in the same paragraph.

To align text, you can use one of three methods: a menu command, the Property Inspector, or a keyboard shortcut. To use the menus, choose Text ➪ Alignment and then pick the alignment you prefer (Left, Right, or Center). Table 9-9 explains the Text Property Inspector's Alignment buttons and the associated keyboard shortcuts.

Table 9-9
Text Alignment Options in the Property Inspector

Button	*Alignment*	*Keyboard Shortcut*
	Left	Ctrl+Alt+L (Command+Option+L)
	Center	Ctrl+Alt+C (Command+Option+C)
	Right	Ctrl+Alt+R (Command+Option+R)

A fourth way to align text is through the Cascading Style Sheets. Any style can be set to align your text. Moreover, not only Left, Right, and Center are supported; so is Justify, which causes text to be flush against both left and right margins, creating a block-like appearance. The Justify value is supported in browsers 4.0 and above.

Traditional HTML alignment options are limited. For a finer degree of control, be sure to investigate precise positioning with layers in Chapter 28.

Indenting entire paragraphs

HTML offers a tag that enables you to indent whole paragraphs, such as inset quotations or name-and-address blocks. Not too surprisingly, the tag used is called the `<blockquote>` tag. Dreamweaver gives you instant access to the `<blockquote>` tag through the Indent and Outdent buttons located on the Text Property Inspector, as shown in Figure 9-18.

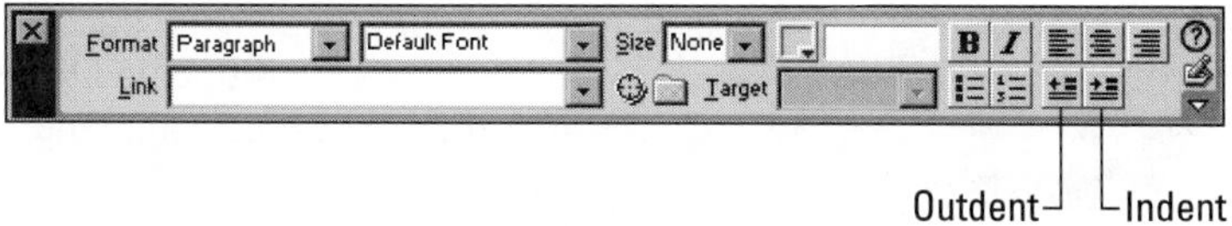

Figure 9-18: Indent paragraphs and blocks of text with the Indent and the Outdent buttons.

To indent one or more paragraphs, select them and click the Indent button in the Property Inspector. Paragraphs can be indented multiple times; each time you click the Indent button, another `<blockquote>...</blockquote>` tag pair is added.

Note that you can't control how much space a single `<blockquote>` indents a paragraph — that characteristic is determined by the browser.

If you find that you have over-indented, you can use the Outdent button, which is also located on the Property Inspector. The Outdent button has no effect if your text is already at the left edge.

You also have the option of indenting your paragraphs through the menus; choose Text ➪ Indent or Text ➪ Outdent.

You can tell how many `<blockquote>` tags are being used to create a particular look by placing your cursor in the text and looking at the Tag Selector.

Incorporating Dates

With the Web constantly changing, keeping track of when information is updated is important. Dreamweaver includes a new command that enables you to insert today's date in your page, in almost any format imaginable. Moreover, you can set the inserted date to be automatically updated every time the page is saved. This means every time you make a modification to a page and save it, the current date is added.

The Insert Date command uses your system clock to get the current date. In addition, you can elect to add a day name (for example, Thursday) and time to the basic date information. Once the date text is inserted, it can be formatted like any other text—adding color or a specific font type or changing the date's size.

To insert the current date, follow these steps:

1. Choose Insert ⇨ Date or select the Insert Date object from the Common panel of the Objects palette.

   The Insert Date dialog box, shown in Figure 9-19, is displayed.

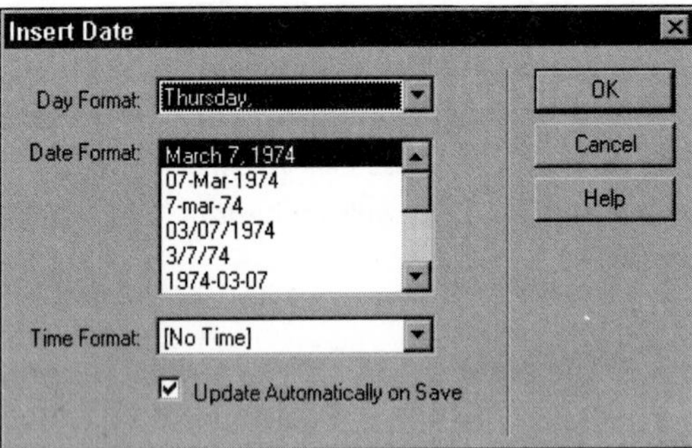

Figure 9-19: Keep track of when a file is updated by using the Insert Date command.

2. If desired, select a Day Format to include in the date from the drop-down list. The options are:

[No Day]	Thu
Thursday	thu,
Thursday,	thu
Thu,	

3. Select the desired date format from the drop-down list. The example formats are:

March 7, 1974	7./03/7.4
07.-Mar-1974	07.03.1974
7.-mar-7.4	07.03.74
03./07/1994	7.-03-197.4
3./7/74	7. March, 197.4
1974.-03-07	74.-03-07
7./3/7.4	

Tip

If you are creating Web pages for the global market, consider using the format designated by the 1974-03-07 example. This year-month-day format is an ISO (International Organization for Standardization) standard and is computer sortable.

4. Select the desired time format, if any, from the drop-down list. The two example formats are:

   [No Time]

   12.:18 PM

   22.:18

5. If you want the date modified to include the current date every time the file is saved, select the Update Automatically on Save option.

6. Click OK when you're done.

Tip

It's no problem at all to format an inserted date when the Update Automatically on Save option is *not* selected—then it's just plain text, and the formatting can be added easily through the Text Property Inspector. However if the date is to be automatically updated, it's inserted as a special Macromedia datatype with its own Property Inspector. You can style it, however, by selecting options from the Text menu or applying an HTML or CSS style.

If your date object includes the Automatic Update option, you can modify the format. Select the date and, in the Property Inspector, choose the Edit Date Format button. The Edit Date Format dialog box opens and is identical to the Insert Date dialog box, except the Update Automatically on Save option is not available.

Commenting Your Code

When will you know to start inserting comments into your HTML code? The first time you go back to an earlier Web page, look at the code and say, "What on earth was I thinking?" You should plan ahead and develop the habit of commenting your code now.

Browsers run fine without your comments, but for any continued development—of the Web page or of yourself as a Webmaster—commenting your code is extremely beneficial. Sometimes, as in a corporate setting, Web pages are codeveloped by teams of designers and programmers. In this situation, commenting your code may not just be a good idea; it may be required.

An HTML comment looks like the following:

```
<!-- Created by Hummer Associates, Inc. -->
```

You're not restricted to any particular line length or number of lines for comments. The text included between the opening of the comment, `<!--`, and the closing, `-->`, can span regular paragraphs or HTML code. In fact, one of the most common uses for comments during the testing and debugging phase of page design is to "comment out" sections of code as a means of tracking down an elusive bug.

To insert a comment in Dreamweaver, first place your cursor in either the Document window or the HTML Inspector where you want the comment to appear. Then select the Insert Comment button from the Invisibles panel of the Objects palette. This sequence opens the Insert Comment dialog box, where you can insert the desired text; click OK when you've finished. Figure 9-20 shows the Insert Comment dialog box, with the corresponding completed comment in the HTML Inspector.

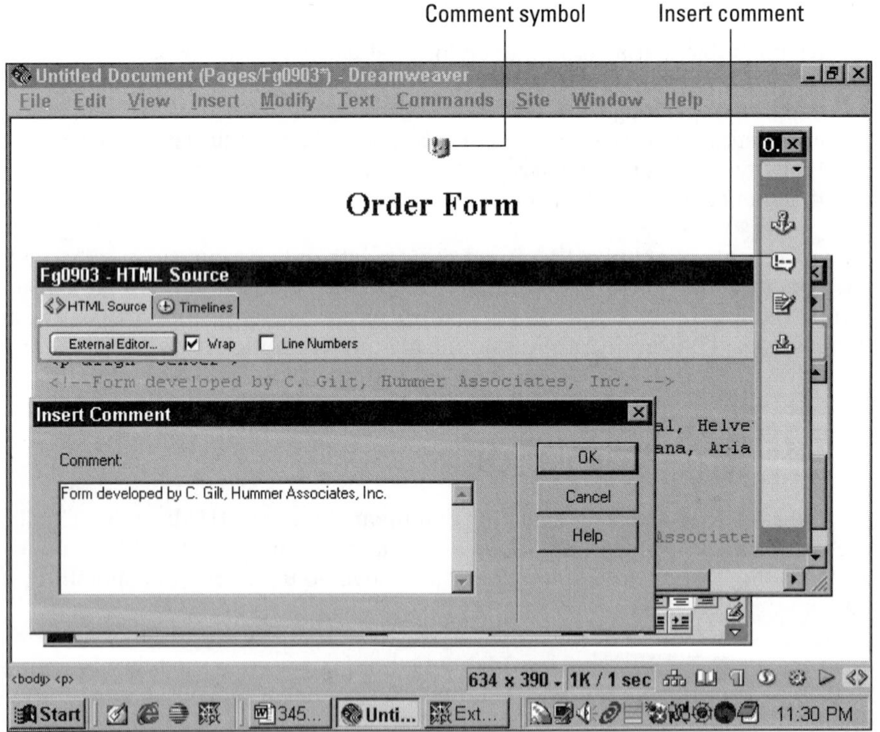

Figure 9-20: Comments are extremely useful for inserting into the code information not visible on the rendered Web page.

By default, Dreamweaver inserts a Comment symbol in the Document window. As with the other Invisibles, you can hide the Comment symbol by choosing Edit ➪ Preferences and then deselecting the Comments checkbox in the Invisible Elements panel. You can also hide any displayed Invisibles by selecting View ➪ Invisible Elements or using the keyboard shortcut, Ctrl+Shift+I (Command+Shift+I).

When you need to edit a comment, double-click the Comment symbol to display the current comment in an editable window. After you've finished making your changes to the comment, select the Close button of the Comment window. A comment can be moved or duplicated by selecting its symbol and using the Cut, Copy, and Paste commands under the Edit menu. You can also right-click (Command+click) the Comment symbol to bring up the shortcut menu. Finally, you can click and drag Comment symbols to move the corresponding comment to a new location.

Summary

Learning to manipulate text is an essential design skill for creating Web pages. Dreamweaver gives you all the tools you need to insert and modify the full range of HTML text quickly and easily.

- ✦ HTML headings are available in six different sizes: `<h1>` through `<h6>`. Headings are used primarily as headlines and subheads to separate divisions of the Web page.
- ✦ Blocks of text are formatted with the paragraph tag `<p>`. Each paragraph is separated from the other paragraphs by a line of whitespace above and below. Use the line break tag, `<br>`, to make lines appear directly above or below one another.
- ✦ Dreamweaver offers a full complement of text-editing tools — everything from Cut and Paste to Find and Replace. Two commands, Copy Text Only and Paste As Text, are unique to Dreamweaver and make short work of switching between text and code.
- ✦ Dreamweaver's Find and Replace feature goes a long way toward automating your work on the current page as well as throughout the Web site. Both content and code can be searched in a basic or very advanced fashion.
- ✦ Where possible, text in HTML is formatted according to its meaning. Dreamweaver applies the styles selected through the Text ➪ Style menu. For most styles, the browser determines what the user views.
- ✦ You can format Web page text much as you can text in a word processing program. Within certain limitations, you can select a font's size and color, as well as the font itself.
- ✦ Dreamweaver's HTML Styles feature enables you to consistently and quickly format your text.

✦ HTML comments are a useful (and often requisite) vehicle for embedding information into a Web page that remains unseen by the casual viewer. Comments can annotate program code or insert copyright information.

In the next chapter, you learn how to insert and work with graphics.

✦ ✦ ✦

CHAPTER 10

Inserting Images

✦ ✦ ✦ ✦

In This Chapter

Image file formats

Working with foreground and background images

Modifying image height, width, and margins

Using the lowsrc attribute

Aligning and wrapping

Dividing your page with HTML lines

Graphics in motion

Adding rollovers

Inserting navigational buttons

The Internet started as a text-based medium primarily used for sharing data among research scientists and among U.S. military commanders. Today, the Web is as visually appealing as any mass medium. Dreamweaver's power becomes even more apparent as you use its visual layout tools to incorporate background and foreground images into your Web page designs.

Completely baffled by all the various image formats out there? This chapter opens with an overview of the key Web-oriented graphics formats, including PNG. Also, this chapter covers techniques for incorporating both background and foreground images — and modifying them using new methods available in Dreamweaver 3. Animation graphics and how you can use them in your Web pages are also covered here, as are techniques for creating rollover buttons. Finally, this chapter delves into integration with Fireworks, Macromedia's award-winning Web graphics tool; Dreamweaver and Fireworks make a potent team for creating and publishing Web graphics.

Web Graphic Formats

If you've worked in the computer graphics field, you know that virtually every platform — as well as every paint and graphics program — has its own proprietary file format for images. One of the critical factors in the Web's rapid, expansive growth is the use of cross-platform graphics. Regardless of the system you use to create your images, these versatile files ensure that the graphics can be viewed by all platforms.

The trade off for universal acceptance of image files is a restricted field: just two file formats, with a possible third just coming into view. Currently, only GIF and JPEG formats are fully supported by browsers. A third alternative, the PNG graphics format, is experiencing a limited but growing acceptance.

You need to understand the uses and limitations of each of the formats so you can apply them successfully in Dreamweaver. Let's look at the fundamentals.

GIF

GIF, the Graphics Interchange Format, was developed by CompuServe in the late 1980s to address the problem of cross-platform compatibility. With GIF viewers available for every system from PC and Macintosh to Amiga and NeXT, the format became a natural choice for an inline (adjacent to text) image graphic. GIFs are bitmapped images, which means that each pixel is given or mapped to a specific color. You can have up to 256 colors for a GIF graphic. These images are generally used for illustrations, logos, or cartoons—anything that doesn't require thousands of colors for a smooth color blend, such as a photograph. With a proper graphics tool, you can reduce the number of colors in a GIF image to a minimum, thereby compressing the file and reducing download time.

The GIF format has two varieties: "regular" (technically, GIF87a) and an enhanced version known as GIF89a. This improved GIF file brings three important attributes to the format. First, GIF89a supports transparency, where one or more of the colors can become invisible. This property is necessary for creating nonrectangular-appearing images. Whenever you see a round or irregularly shaped logo or illustration on the Web, a rectangular frame is displayed as the image is loading—this is the actual size and shape of the graphic. The colors surrounding the irregularly shaped central image are set to transparent in a graphics-editing program (such as Fireworks or Adobe Photoshop) before the image is saved in GIF89a format.

Note

Most of the latest versions of the popular graphic tools default to using GIF89a, so unless you're working with older, legacy images, you're not too likely to encounter the less flexible GIF87a format.

Although the outer area of a graphic seems to disappear with GIF89a, you won't be able to overlap your Web images using this format without using layers. Figure 10-1 demonstrates this situation. In this figure, the same image is presented twice—one lacks transparency, and one has transparency applied. The image on the left is saved as a standard GIF without transparency, and you can plainly see the shape of the full image. The image on the right was saved with the white background color made transparent, so the central figure seems to float on the background.

The second valuable attribute contributed by GIF89a format is interlacing. One of the most common complaints about graphics on the Web is lengthy download times. Interlacing won't speed up your GIF downloads, but it gives your Web page visitors something to view other than a blank screen. A graphic saved with the interlace feature turned on gives the appearance of "developing," like an instant picture, as the file is downloading. Use of this design option is up to you and your clients. Some folks swear by it; others can't abide it.

Figure 10-1: The same image, saved without GIF transparency (left) and with GIF transparency (right)

Animation is the final advantage offered by the GIF89a format. Certain software programs enable you to group your GIF files together into one large page-flipping file. With this capability, you can bring simple animation to your page without additional plug-ins or helper applications. Unfortunately, the trade off is that the files get very big, very fast. For more on animated GIFs in Dreamweaver, see the section "Applying Simple Web Animation," later in this chapter.

JPEG

The JPEG format was developed by the Joint Photographic Experts Group specifically to handle photographic images. JPEGs offer millions of colors at 24 bits of color information available per pixel, as opposed to the GIF format's 8-bit and 256 colors. To make JPEGs usable, the large amount of color information must be compressed, which is accomplished by removing what the algorithm considers redundant information.

The more compressed your JPEG file, the more degraded the image. When you first save a JPEG image, your graphics program asks you for the desired level of compression. As an example, take a look at the three pictures in Figure 10-2. Here you can compare the effects of JPEG compression ratios and resulting file sizes to the original image itself. As you can probably tell, JPEG does an excellent job of compression, with even the highest degree of compression having only a little visible impact. Keep in mind that each picture has its own reaction to compression.

Figure 10-2: JPEG compression can save your Web visitors substantial download time, with little loss of image quality.

With the JPEG image-compression algorithm, the initial elements of an image "compressed away" are least noticeable. Subtle variations in brightness and hue are the first to disappear. When possible, preview your image in your graphics program while adjusting the compression level to observe the changes. With additional compression, the image grows darker and less varied in its color range.

With JPEGs, what is compressed for storage must be uncompressed for viewing. When a JPEG picture on your Web page is accessed by a visitor's browser, the image must first be downloaded to the browser and then uncompressed before it can be viewed. This dual process adds additional time to the Web-browsing process, but it is time well spent for photographic images.

JPEGs, unlike GIFs, have neither transparency nor animation features. A newer strand of JPEG called Progressive JPEG gives you the interlace option of the GIF format, however. Although not all browsers support the interlace feature of Progressive JPEG, they render the image regardless.

PNG

The latest entry into the Web graphics arena is the Portable Network Graphics format, or PNG. Combining the best of both worlds, PNG has lossless compression, like GIF, and is capable of millions of colors, like JPEG. Moreover, PNG offers an interlace scheme that appears much more quickly than either GIF or JPEG, as well as transparency support that is far superior to both the other formats.

One valuable aspect of the PNG format enables the display of PNG pictures to appear more uniform across various computer platforms. Generally, graphics made on a PC look brighter on a Macintosh, and Mac-made images seem darker on a PC. PNG includes gamma correction capabilities that alter the image depending on the computer used by the viewer.

Before the 4.0 versions, the various browsers supported PNG only through plug-ins. After PNG was endorsed as a new Web graphic format by the W3C, both 4.0 versions of Netscape and Microsoft browsers added native, inline support of the new format. Perhaps most important, however, Dreamweaver was among the first Web authoring tools to offer native PNG support. Inserted PNG images preview in the Document window just like GIFs and JPEGs. Browser support is currently not widespread enough to warrant a total switch to the PNG format (it's still lacking in Internet Explorer for Macintosh, for example), but its growing acceptance certainly bears watching.

If you're really excited about the potential of PNG, check out Macromedia's Fireworks, the first Web graphics tool to use PNG as its native format. Fireworks takes full advantage of PNG's alpha transparency features and enhanced palette.

Two excellent resources for more on the PNG format is the PNG home page at `www.cdrom.com/pub/png` and the W3C's PNG page at `www.w3.org/Graphics/PNG`.

Using Inline Images

An inline image can appear directly next to text — literally in the same line. The capability to render inline images is one of the major innovations of the World Wide Web's transition from the Internet. This section covers all the basics of inserting inline images into Dreamweaver and modifying their attributes.

Inserting images

Dreamweaver can open and preview any graphic in a GIF, JPEG, or PNG format. With Dreamweaver, you have five methods for placing a graphic on your Web page.

- ✦ From the Objects palette, select the Insert Image button.
- ✦ From the menu bar, choose Insert ➪ Image.
- ✦ From the keyboard, press Ctrl+Alt+I (Command+Option+I).
- ✦ Point to an image file in the Site window using Dreamweaver 3's Point to File feature.
- ✦ Drag either the Insert Image button or an icon from your file manager (Explorer or Finder) to your page.

The first four methods require that you first position the cursor at the point where you want the image to appear on the page; only the drag-and-drop method enables you to place the image inline with any existing element.

After you've used one of the preceding methods, Dreamweaver opens the Select Image Source dialog box (shown in Figure 10-3) and asks you for the path or address to your image file. Remember that in HTML, all graphics are stored in separate files linked from your Web page. The image's address can be just a file name, a directory path and file name on your system, a directory path and file name on your remote system, or a full URL to a graphic on a completely separate Web server. You don't have to have the file immediately available to insert the code into your HTML.

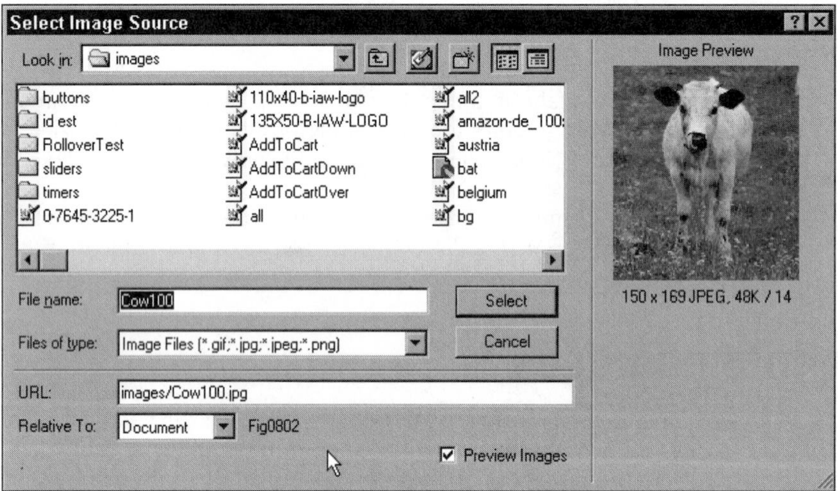

Figure 10-3: In this Select Image Source dialog box, you can keep track of your image's location relative to your current Web page.

From the Select Image Source dialog box, you can browse to your image folder, and preview images before you load them. To enable this feature, make sure the Preview Images option is selected. Dreamweaver can preview GIF, JPEG, or PNG files.

In the lower portion of the dialog box, the URL text box displays the format of the address Dreamweaver inserts into your code. Below the URL text box is the Relative To list box. Here you can choose to declare an image to be relative to the document you're working on (the default) or relative to the site root. (After you've saved your document, you see its name displayed beside the Relative To box.)

To take full advantage of Dreamweaver's site management features, you must open a site, establish a local site root, and save the current Web page before beginning to insert images. For more on how to begin a Dreamweaver project, and about document-relative and site root–relative addressing, see Chapter 6.

Relative to Document

Once you've saved your Web page and chosen Relative to Document, Dreamweaver displays the address in the URL text box. If the image is located in a folder on the same level as, or within, your current site root folder, the address is formatted with just a path and file name. For instance, if you're inserting a graphic from the subfolder named images, Dreamweaver inserts an address like the following:

```
images/men10.jpg
```

If you try to insert an image currently stored outside of the local site root folder, Dreamweaver temporarily appends a prefix that tells the browser to look on your local system for the file. For instance, the file listing would look like the following in Windows:

```
file:///C|/Dreamweaver/Figs/men10.jpg
```

while on the Macintosh, the same file is listed as follows:

```
file:///Macintosh HD/Dreamweaver/Figs/men10.jpg
```

Dreamweaver also appends the `file:///C|` prefix (or just `file:///Macintosh HD` in Macintosh) if you haven't yet saved your document. It is strongly recommended that you save your file before you begin developing the Web page. You can easily upload Web pages with this `file:///C|` (`file:///Macintosh HD`) prefix in place—and miss the error completely. Because your local browser can find the referenced image on your system, even when you are browsing the remote site, the Web page appears perfect. However, anyone else browsing your Web site only sees placeholders for broken links. Saving your page before you begin enables Dreamweaver to help you avoid these errors. To this end, do not check the Don't show me this message again checkbox that appears when you're reminded to save your file the first time. This message can save you an enormous amount of grief!

After you select your image file, you see the prompt window shown in Figure 10-4. Dreamweaver asks if you want to copy this image to your local site root folder. Whenever possible, keep all of your images within the local site root folder so that Dreamweaver can handle site management efficiently. Click Yes, and you next see a Save Copy As dialog box, which points to the local site root folder. If you select No, the file is inserted with the `src` attribute pointing to the path of the file.

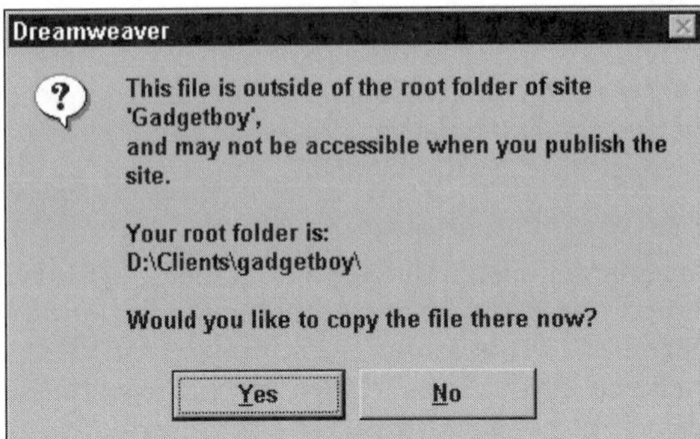

Figure 10-4: Dreamweaver reminds you to keep all your graphics in the local site root folder for easy site management.

Relative to Site Root

Should you select Site Root in the Relative To field of the Select Image Source dialog box, and you are within your site root folder, Dreamweaver appends a leading forward slash to the directory in the path so the browser can correctly read the address. Thus, the same men10.jpg file appears in both the URL box and the HTML code as follows:

```
/images/men10.jpg
```

When you use site root–relative addressing and you select a file outside of the site root, you get the same reminder from Dreamweaver about copying the file into your local site root folder — just as with document-relative addressing.

Modifying images

When you insert an image in Dreamweaver, the image tag, `<img>`, is inserted into your HTML code. The `<img>` tag takes several attributes, all of which can be entered through the Property Inspector. Code for a basic image looks like the following:

```
<img src="images/Collection01.gif" width="172" height="180">
```

Dreamweaver centralizes all of its image functions in the Property Inspector. The Image Property Inspector, shown in Figure 10-5, displays a small thumbnail of the image as well as its file size. Dreamweaver automatically inserts the image file name in the Src text box (as the `src` attribute). To replace a currently selected image with another, click the folder icon next to the Src text box, or double-click the image itself. This sequence opens the Select Image Source dialog box. When you've selected the desired file, Dreamweaver automatically refreshes the page and corrects the code.

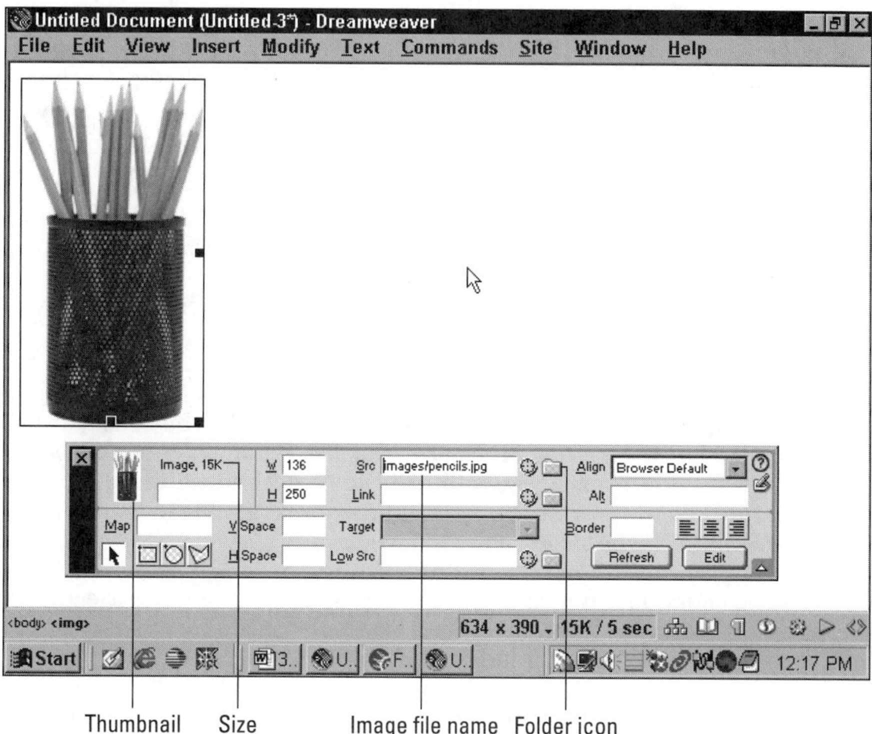

Figure 10-5: The Image Property Inspector gives you total control over the HTML code for every image.

With the Property Inspector open when you insert your image, you can begin to modify it immediately.

Editing the image

Dreamweaver is a terrific Web authoring tool, but it's not a graphics editor. Quite often, after you've inserted an image into your Web page, you find that the picture needs to be altered in some way. Perhaps you need to crop part of the image or make the background transparent. Dreamweaver enables you to specify your primary graphics editor for each type of graphic in the External Editors panel of Preferences.

Once you've picked an image editor, clicking the Edit button in the Property Inspector opens the application with the current image. After you've made the modifications, just save the file in your image editor and switch back to Dreamweaver. The new, modified graphic has already been included in the Web page.

Dreamweaver seamlessly refreshed the images being edited in all the image editors I tested. However, there have been reports of images not reappearing in their modified form. If this happens, click the Refresh button in the Property Inspector after you select your image.

Adjusting height and width

The `width` and `height` attributes are important: Browsers build Web pages faster when they know the size and shape of the included images. Dreamweaver reads these attributes when the image is first loaded. The width and height values are initially expressed in pixels and are automatically inserted as attributes in the HTML code.

Browsers can dynamically resize an image if its height and width on the page are different from the original image's dimensions. For example, you can load your primary logo on the home page and then use a smaller version of it on subsequent pages by inserting the same image with reduced height and width values. Because you're only loading the image once and the browser is resizing it, download time for your Web page can be significantly reduced.

Resizing an image just means you're changing its appearance onscreen; the file size stays exactly the same. To reduce a file size for an image, you need to scale it down in a graphics program such as Fireworks.

You don't have to use pixels to enter your resizing measurements into Dreamweaver's Property Inspector. You can also use inches (in), picas (pc), points (pt), millimeters (mm), or centimeters (cm). The values must be entered without spaces between the number and the measurement abbreviation, as follows:

```
72pt
```

You can also combine measurement systems. Suppose, for example, you want to resize a picture's height to 2 inches and 5 centimeters. In the Property Inspector, you enter the following value in the H text box:

```
2in+5cm
```

Dreamweaver translates both inches and centimeters to their equivalent in pixels and then adds them together. The measurements are system-dependent; on the Macintosh, an inch equals 72 pixels and on Windows, an inch is 96 pixels.

When you use values with a combined measurement system, you can only add values—you can't subtract them. When you press the Tab key or click outside of the height and width boxes, Dreamweaver converts your value to pixels.

With Dreamweaver, you can visually resize your graphics by using the click-and-drag method. A selected image has three sizing handles located on the right, bottom, and lower-right corners of its bounding box. Click any of these handles and drag it out to a new location – when you release the mouse, Dreamweaver resizes the image. You can hold down the Shift key while dragging the corner sizing handle, and Dreamweaver maintains the current height/width aspect ratio.

If you alter either the height or the width of an image in the Property Inspector, Dreamweaver displays the values in bold in their respective fields. You can restore an image's default measurements by selecting the H or the W independently — or you can choose the Refresh button to restore both values.

If you elect to enable your viewer's browser to resize your image on the fly using the height/width values you specify, keep in mind that the browser is not a graphics-editing program and that its resizing algorithms are not sophisticated. View your resized images through several browsers to make sure that the results are acceptable.

Using margins

You can offset images with surrounding whitespace by using the margin attributes. The amount of whitespace around your image can be designated both vertically and horizontally through the `vspace` and `hspace` attributes, respectively. These margin values are entered, in pixels, into the V Space and H Space text boxes in the Image Property Inspector.

The V Space value adds the same amount of whitespace along the top and bottom of your image; the H Space value increases the whitespace along the left and right sides of the image. These values must be positive; HTML doesn't allow images to overlap text or other images (outside of layers). Unlike in page layout, "negative whitespace" does not exist.

Titling your image

When you first insert a graphic into the page, the Image Property Inspector displays a blank text box next to the thumbnail and file size. Fill in this box with a unique name for the image, to be used in JavaScript and other applications.

As a page is loading over the Web, the image is first displayed as an empty rectangle if the `<img>` tag contains the width and height information. Sometimes these rectangles include a brief title to describe the coming image. You can enter this alternative text in the Alt text box of the Image Property Inspector.

Good coding practice associates an Alt title with all of your graphics. Aside from giving the user some clue as to what's coming, these mini-titles are also used to display the screen tips that pop up in some browsers when the user's pointer passes over the graphic. The real benefit of mini-titles, however, is providing input for browsers not displaying graphics. Text-only browsers are still in use, and some users, interested only in content, turn off the graphics to speed up the text display. Moreover, the W3C is working toward standards for browsers for the visually impaired, and the Alt text can be used to describe the page.

Bordering a graphic

When you're working with thumbnails (a series of small versions of images) on your Web page, you may need a quick way to distinguish one from another. The `border` attribute enables you to place a one-color rectangular border around any graphic. The width of the border is measured in pixels, and the color is the same as the default for the page's text color as specified in the Page Properties dialog box. To turn on the border, enter a value in the Border text box located on the lower half of the Image Property Inspector. Entering a value of zero explicitly turns off the border.

One of the most frequent cries for help among beginning Web designers (using Dreamweaver or another program) results from the sudden appearance of a bright blue border around their image. Whenever you assign a link to an image, HTML automatically places a border around that image; the color is determined by the Page Properties' Link color, where the default is bright blue. Dreamweaver intelligently assigns a zero to the `border` attribute whenever you enter a URL in the Link text box. If you've already declared a border value and enter a link, Dreamweaver won't zero-out the border. You can, of course, override the no-border option by entering a value in the Border text box.

Specifying a lowsrc

Another option for loading Web page images, the `lowsrc` attribute, displays a smaller version of a large graphic file while the larger file is loading. The `lowsrc` file can be a grayscale version of the original, or a version that is physically smaller or reduced in color or resolution. This option is designed to reduce the file size significantly for quick loading.

Select your `lowsrc` file by choosing the File icon next to the Low text box in the Image Property Inspector. The same criteria that applies to inserting your original image also applies to the `lowsrc` picture.

One handy `lowsrc` technique first proportionately scales down a large file in a graphics-processing program. This file becomes your `lowsrc` file. Because browsers use the final image's height and width information for both the `lowsrc` and the final image, your visitors immediately see a "blocky" version of your graphic, which is replaced by the final version when the picture is fully loaded.

Working with alignment options

Just like text, images can be aligned to the left, right, or center. In fact, images have much more flexibility than text in terms of alignment. In addition to the same hori-zontal alignment options, you can align your images vertically in nine different ways. You can even turn a picture into a floating image type, enabling text to wrap around it.

Horizontal alignment

When you change the horizontal alignment of a line — from left to center or from center to right — the entire paragraph moves. Any inline images that are part of that paragraph also move. Likewise, selecting one of a series of inline images in a row and realigning it horizontally causes all the images in the row to shift.

In Dreamweaver, the horizontal alignment of an inline image is changed in exactly the same way you realign text, with alignment buttons found on the Property Inspector. As with text, buttons exist for Left, Center, and Right. Although these are very conveniently placed on the lower portion of the Graphics Property Inspector, the alignment attribute is actually written to the `<p>` or other block element enclosing the image.

Vertical alignment

Because you can place text next to an image — and images vary so greatly in size — HTML includes a variety of options for specifying just how image and text line up. As you can see from the chart in Figure 10-6, a wide range of possibilities is available.

To change the vertical alignment of any graphic in Dreamweaver, open the Align drop-down list in the Image Property Inspector and choose one of the options. Dreamweaver writes your choice into the `align` attribute of the `<img>` tag.

The various vertical alignment options are listed in the following table, and you can see examples of each type of alignment in Figure 10-6.

Vertical Alignment Option	*Result*
Browser Default	No alignment attribute is included in the `<img>` tag. Most browsers use the baseline as the alignment default.
Baseline	The bottom of the image is aligned with the baseline of the surrounding text.
Top	The top of the image is aligned with the top of the tallest object in the current line.

Continued

Vertical Alignment Option	*Result*
Middle	The middle of the image is aligned with the baseline of the current line.
Bottom	The bottom of the image is aligned with the baseline of the surrounding text.
Text Top	The top of the image is aligned with the tallest letter in the current line.
Absolute Middle	The middle of the image is aligned with the middle of the text or object in the current line.
Absolute Bottom	The bottom of the image is aligned with the descenders (as in y, g, p, and so forth) that fall below the current line.
Left	The image is aligned to the left edge of the browser or table cell, and all text in the current line flows around the right side of the image.
Right	The image is aligned to the right edge of the browser or table cell, and all text in the current line flows around the left side of the image.

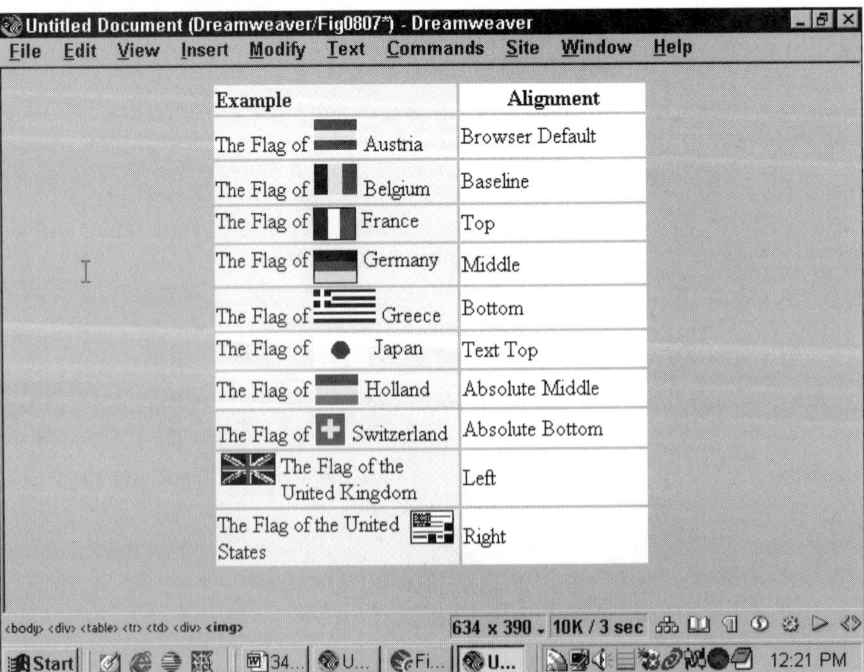

Figure 10-6: You can align text and images in one of nine different ways using the Align option box on the Image Property Inspector.

The final two alignment options, Left and Right, are special cases; details about how to use their features are covered in the following section.

Wrapping text

Long a popular design option in conventional publishing, wrapping text around an image on a Web page is also supported by most, but not all, browsers. As noted in the preceding section, the Left and Right alignment options turn a picture into a floating image type, so called because the image can move depending on the amount of text and the size of the browser window.

> **Tip:** Using both floating image types (Left and Right) in combination, you can actually position images flush-left and flush-right, with text in the middle. Insert both images side by side and then set the leftmost image to align left and the rightmost one to align right. Insert your text immediately following the second image. Unless you place a `<p>` or `<br>` at the top, this arrangement does not render correctly in Dreamweaver (the first line overlaps the left image), but it does display as expected in most browsers.

Your text wraps around the image depending on where the floating image is placed (or anchored). If you have the feature enabled in the Invisibles pane of Preferences, Dreamweaver inserts a Floating Image Anchor symbol to mark the floating image's place. Figure 10-7 shows two examples of text wrapping. In the top case, the Floating Image Anchor symbol is placed at the front of the first paragraph, which causes the three paragraphs to flow around the right-aligned image. In the bottom case, you can't see the Floating Image Anchor because the left-aligned image overlaps the anchor, which is placed at the front of the first paragraph.

The Floating Image Anchor is not just a static symbol. You can click and drag the anchor to a new location and cause the paragraph to wrap in a different fashion. Be careful though—if you delete the anchor, you also delete the image it represents.

You can also wrap a portion of the text around your left- or right-aligned picture and then force the remaining text to appear below the floating image. However, the HTML necessary to do this task cannot currently be inserted by Dreamweaver and must be coded by hand. You have to force an opening to appear by inserting a break tag, with a special `clear` attribute, where you want the text to break. This special `<br>` tag has three forms:

`<br clear=left>`	Causes the line to break, and the following text moves down vertically until no floating images are on the left.
`<br clear=right>`	Causes the line to break, and the following text moves down vertically until no floating images are on the right.
`<br clear=all>`	Moves the text following the image down until no floating images are on either the left or the right.

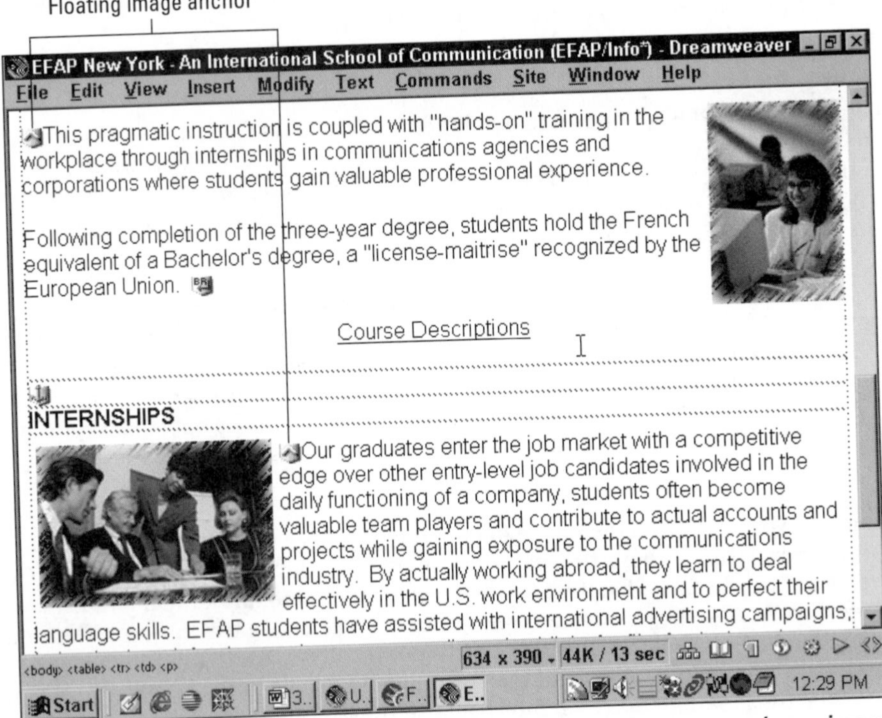

Figure 10-7: Aligning an image left or right enables text to wrap around your images.

One of the Dreamweaver objects included on CD-ROM 1 that accompanies this book is an enhanced break tag that enables you to include any version of the `clear` attribute. To access these objects, copy the new_break.htm and new_break.gif files from the Dreamweaver\Configuration\Objects\Invisibles folder into the same folder on your system, and then restart Dreamweaver.

Putting Pictures in the Background

In this chapter, you've learned about working with the surface graphics on a Web page. As seen in Chapter 8, you can also have an image in the background of an HTML page. This section covers some of the basic techniques for incorporating a background image in your Dreamweaver page.

Remember, you add an image to your background in Dreamweaver by modifying the Page Properties. Either choose Modify ➪ Page Properties or select Page Properties from the shortcut menu that pops up when you right-click (Command+click) any open area on the Web page. In the Page Properties dialog box, select a graphic by choosing the Browse (Choose) button next to the Background Image text box. You can use any file format supported by Dreamweaver – GIF, JPEG, or PNG.

Two key differences exist between background images and the foreground inline images discussed in the preceding sections of this chapter. First and most obvious, all other text and graphics on the Web page are superimposed over your chosen background image. This capability can bring extra depth and texture to your work; unfortunately, you have to make sure the foreground text and images work well with the background.

You can quickly try out a number of professionally designed background and foreground color combinations with the Set Color Scheme command. For more information on how to use this Dreamweaver command, see Chapter 8.

Basically, you want to ascertain that enough contrast exists between foreground and background. You can set the default text and the various link colors through the Page Properties dialog box. When trying out a new background pattern, you should set up some dummy text and links. Then use the Apply button on the Page Properties dialog box to test different color combinations. See Figure 10-8 for an example of this test at work.

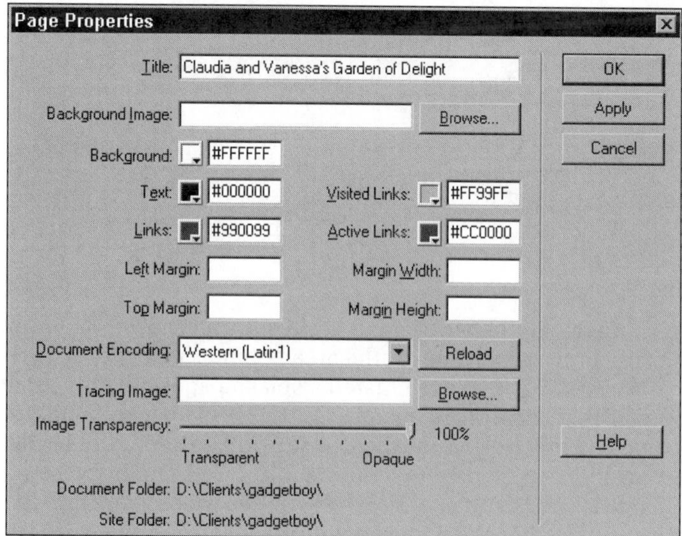

Figure 10-8: If you're using a background image, be sure to check the default colors for text and links to make sure enough contrast exists between background and foreground.

Tiling Images

Web designers use the tiling property of background images to create a variety of effects with very low file-size overhead. The columns typically found on one side of Web pages are a good example of tiling. Columns are popular because they enable the designer to place navigational buttons in a visual context. An easy way to create a column that runs the full length of your Web page uses a long, narrow background image.

Take a look at the following figure. The background image is 45 pixels high, 800 pixels wide, and only 6K in size. When the browser window is set at 640×480 or 800×600, the image is tiled down the page to create the vertical column effect. You could just as easily create an image 1,000 pixels high by 40 pixels wide to create a horizontal column.

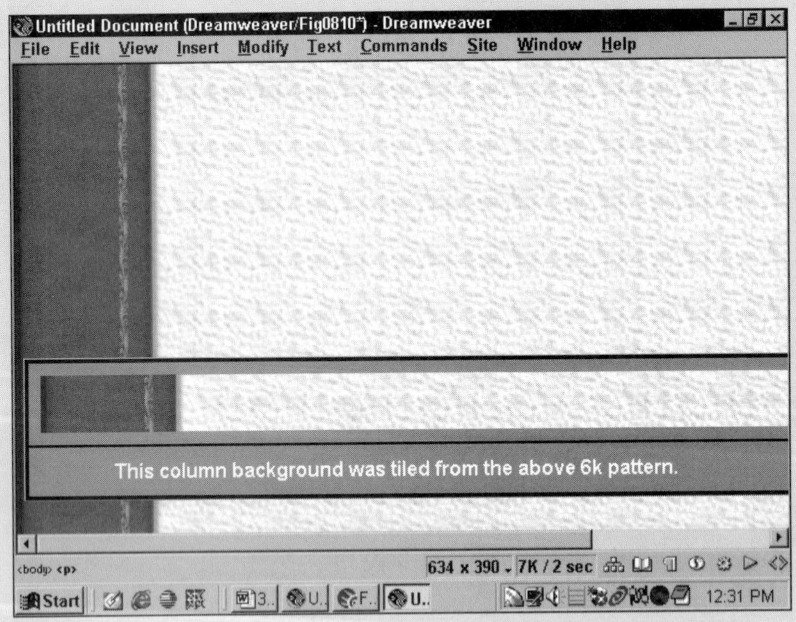

The second distinguishing feature of background images is that the viewing browser completely fills either the browser window or the area behind the content of your Web page, whichever is larger. So, if you've created a splash page with only a 200×200 foreground logo, and you've incorporated an amazing 1,024×768 background that took you weeks to compose, no one can see the fruits of your labor in the background—unless they resize their browser window to 1,024×768. On the other hand, if your background image is smaller than either the browser window or what the Web page content needs to display, the browser and Dreamweaver repeat (or tile) your image to make up the difference.

Dividing the Web Page with Horizontal Rules

HTML includes a standard horizontal line that can divide your Web page into specific sections. The horizontal rule tag, <hr>, is a good tool for adding a little diversion to your page without adding download time. You can control the width (either absolutely or relative to the browser window), the height, the alignment, and the shading property of the rule. These horizontal rules appear on a line by themselves; you cannot place text or images on the same line as a horizontal rule.

To insert a horizontal rule in your Web page in Dreamweaver, follow these steps:

1. Place your cursor where you want the horizontal rule to appear.
2. From the Common pane of the Objects palette, select the Insert Horizontal Rule button or choose the Insert ➪ Horizontal Rule command.

   Dreamweaver inserts the horizontal rule and opens the Horizontal Rule Property Inspector, as shown in Figure 10-9.

Figure 10-9: The Horizontal Rule Property Inspector controls the width, height, and alignment for these HTML lines.

3. To change the width of the line, enter a value in the width (W) text box. You can insert either an absolute width in pixels or a relative value as a percentage of the screen.

   • To set a horizontal rule to an exact width, enter the measurement in pixels in the width (W) text box and press the Tab key. Then select pixels in the drop-down list.

   • To set a horizontal rule to a width relative to the browser window, enter the percentage amount in the width (W) text box and press Tab. Then select the percent sign (%) in the drop-down list.

4. To change the height of the horizontal rule, type a pixel measurement in the height (H) text box.

   For both the width and height values, you can also enter a value in inches (in), picas (pc), points (pt), millimeters (mm), or centimeters (cm), just as with images. When you press Tab to leave the text box, Dreamweaver converts your entry to pixels.

5. To change the alignment from the default (centered), open the Align drop-down list and choose another alignment.

6. To disable the default "embossed" look for the rule, deselect the Shading checkbox.

7. If you intend to address (call) your horizontal rule in a JavaScript or another application, you can give it a unique name. Type it into the unlabeled name text box located directly to the left of the H text box.

To modify any inserted horizontal rule, simply click it. (If the Property Inspector is not already open, you have to double-click the rule.) As a general practice, size your horizontal rules using the percentage option if you are using them to separate items on a full screen. If the horizontal rules are being used to divide items in a specifically sized table column or cell, use the pixel method.

Tip

To use the Shading property of the horizontal rule properly, your background should be a shade of gray. The default shading is black along the top and left, and white along the bottom and right. The center line is generally transparent (although Internet Explorer enables you to assign a color attribute). If you use a different background color or image, be sure to check the appearance of your horizontal rules in that context.

Many designers prefer to create more elaborate horizontal rules; in fact, these rules are an active area of clip art design. These types of horizontal rules are regular graphics and are inserted and modified as such.

Applying Simple Web Animation

Why include a section on animation in a chapter on inline images? On the Web, animations are, for the most part, inline images that move. Outside of the possibilities offered by Dynamic HTML (covered in Part VI), Web animations typically either are animated GIF files or are created with a program such as Flash that requires a plug-in. This section takes a brief look at the capabilities and uses of GIF animations.

A GIF animation is a series of still GIF images flipped rapidly to create the illusion of motion. Because animation-creation programs compress all the frames of your animation into one file, a GIF animation is placed on a Web page in the same manner as a still graphic.

In Dreamweaver, click the Insert Image button in the Objects palette or choose Insert ⇨ Image and then select the file. Dreamweaver shows the first frame of your animation in the Document window. To play the animation, preview your Web page in any graphics-capable browser.

As you can imagine, GIF animations can quickly grow to be very large. The key to controlling file size is to think small: Keep your images as small as possible with a low bit-depth (number of colors) and use as few frames as possible.

To create your animation, use any graphics program to produce the separate frames. One excellent technique uses an image-processing program such as Adobe Photoshop and progressively applies a filter to the same image over a series of frames. Figure 10-10 shows the individual frames created with Photoshop's Lighting Effects filter. When animated, a spotlight appears to move across the word.

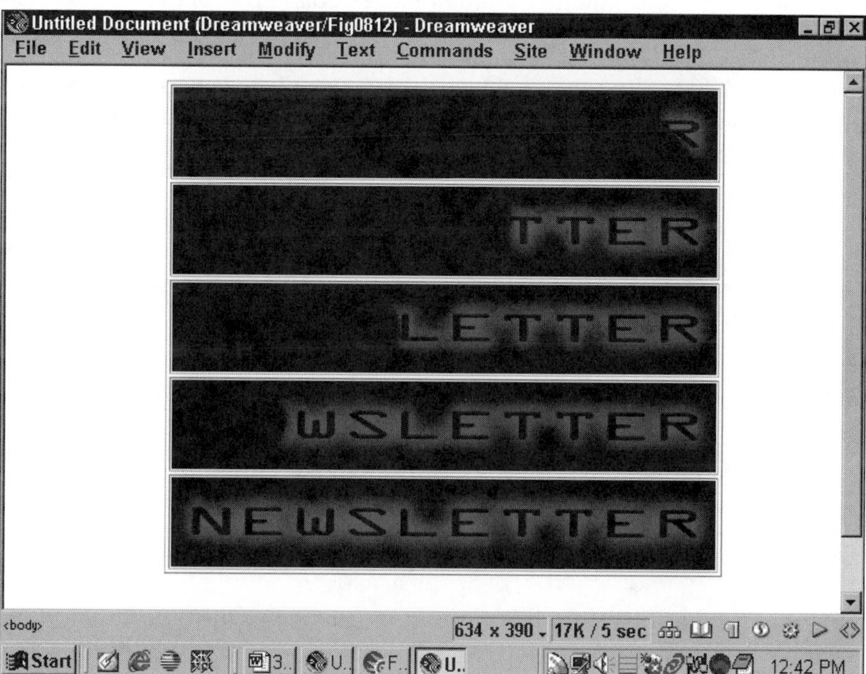

Figure 10-10: Five of twelve frames are compressed into one animated file.

You need an animation program to compress the separate frames and build your animated GIF file. Many commercial programs, including Macromedia's Fireworks, can handle GIF animation. QuickTime Pro can turn individual files or any other kind of movie into an animated GIF, too. Most animation programs enable you to control the number of times an animation loops, the delay between frames, and how transparency is handled within each frame.

If you want to use an advanced animation tool but still have full backward compatibility, check out Flash, from Macromedia. Flash is best known for outputting small vector-based animations that require a plug-in to view, but it can also save animations as GIFs or AVIs. The program is discussed in Chapter 25.

Dreamweaver Technique: Including Banner Ads

Banner ads have become an essential aspect of the World Wide Web; for the Web to remain, for the most part, freely accessible, advertising is needed to support the costs. Banner ads have evolved into the de facto standard. Although numerous variations exist, a banner ad is typically an animated GIF of a particular width and height and under a specified file size.

Two organizations, the Standards and Practices Committee of the Internet Advertising Bureau (IAB) and the Coalition for Advertising Supported Information and Entertainment (CASIE), established a series of standard sizes for banner ads. Although no law dictates that their guidelines have to be followed, the vast majority of commercial sites adhere to the suggested dimensions. The most common banner sizes (in pixels) and their official names are listed in Table 10-1.

Table 10-1
IAB/CASIE Advertising Banner Sizes

Dimensions	*Name*
468×60	Full Banner
392×72	Full Banner with Vertical Navigation Bar
234×60	Half Banner
125×125	Square Button
88×31	Micro Button

Dimensions	Name
120×90	Button 1
120×60	Button 2
120×240	Vertical Banner

File size for a banner ad is not as clearly determined, but it's just as important. The last thing a hosting site wants is for a large, too heavy banner to slow down the loading of its page. Usually a commercial site has an established maximum file size for a particular banner ad size. Generally banner ads are around 10K and no more than 12K. The lighter your banner ad, the faster it loads and — as a direct result — the more likely Web page visitors stick around to see it.

Inserting a banner ad on a Web page is very straightforward. As with any other GIF file, animated or not, all you have to do is insert the image and assign the link. As any advertiser can tell you, the link is as important as the image itself, and you should take special care to ensure that it is correct when inserted. Advertising links are often quite complex as they not only link to a specific page, but may also carry information about the referring site. Several companies monitor how many times an ad is selected — the *clickthru rate* — and often a CGI program is used to communicate with these companies and handle the link. Here's a sample URL from CNet's `News.com` site:

```
http://home.cnet.com/cgi-acc/clickthru.acc?¬
clickid=00001e145ea7d80f00000000&adt=003:10:100&edt=cnet&cat=1:1002:&site=CN
```

Obviously, copying and pasting such URLs is highly preferable to entering them by hand.

It's not unusual for an advertisement to come from an outside source, so a Web page designer often has to allow space for the ad without incorporating the actual ad. Some Web designers use special placeholder images. In Dreamweaver, placeholder ads can easily be maintained as a Library item and placed as needed, as shown in Figure 10-11. If you'd prefer not to use placeholder graphics such as these, you could also just insert a plain `<img>` tag — with no `src` parameter — using the Quick Tag Editor. When an `<img>` tag without a `src` is in the code, Dreamweaver displays a broken image icon that could then be resized to the proper banner ad dimensions in the Property Inspector. (The broken image icon used to be inserted whenever an Insert Image operation was canceled, but that functionality was removed in Dreamweaver 3.)

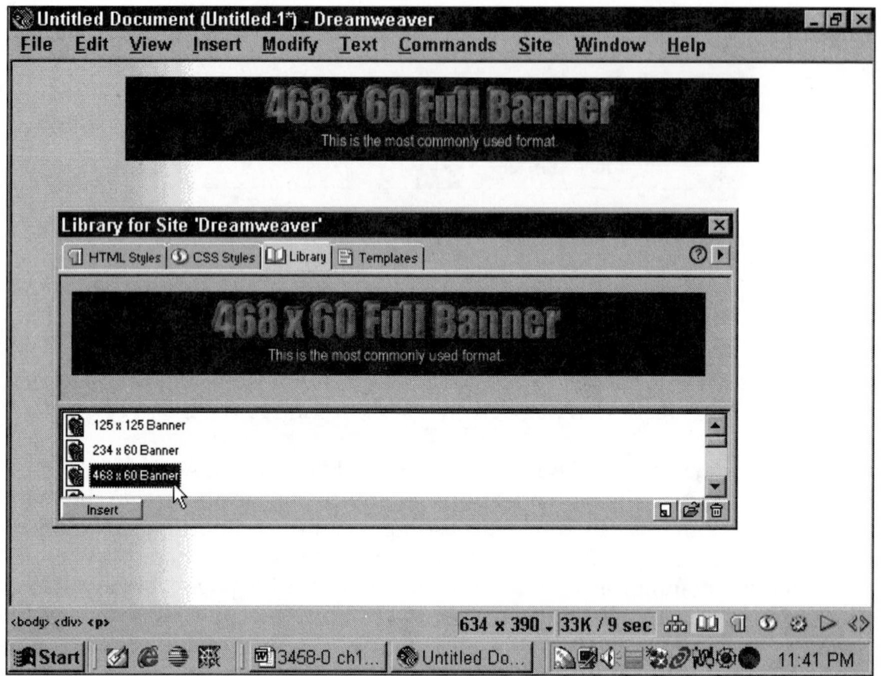

Figure 10-11: Use the Library to store standard banner ad images for use as placeholders.

Inserting Rollover Images

Rollovers are among the most popular of all Web page effects. A rollover (also known as a *mouseover*) occurs when the user's pointer passes over an image and the image changes in some way. It may appear to glow or change color and/or shape; when the pointer moves away from the graphic, the image returns to its original form. The rollover indicates interactivity and attempts to engage the user with a little bit of flare.

Rollovers are usually accomplished with a combination of HTML and JavaScript. Dreamweaver was among the first Web authoring tools to automate the production of rollovers through its Swap Image and Swap Image Restore behaviors. Later versions of Dreamweaver make rollovers even easier with the Rollover Image object. With the Rollover Image object, if you can pick two images, you can make a rollover.

Technically speaking, a rollover is accomplished by manipulating an `<img>` tag's `src` attribute. You'll recall that the `src` attribute is responsible for providing the actual file name of the graphic to be displayed; it is, quite literally, the source of the image. A rollover changes the value of `src` from one image file to another. Swapping the `src` value is analogous to having a picture within a frame and changing the picture while keeping the frame.

The picture frame analogy is appropriate on one other level: It serves as a reminder of the size barrier inherent in rollovers. A rollover changes only one property of an <img> tag, the source — it cannot change any other property such as the height or width. For this reason, both your original image and the image that is displayed during the rollover should be the same size. If they are not, the alternate image is resized to match the dimensions of the original image.

Dreamweaver's Rollover Image object automatically changes the image back to its original source when the user moves the pointer off the image. Optionally, you can elect to preload the images with the selection of a checkbox. Preloading is a Web page technique that reads the intended file or files into the browser's memory before they are displayed. With preloading, the images appear on demand, without any download delay.

Rollovers are typically used for buttons that, when clicked, open another Web page. In fact, JavaScript requires that an image include a link before it can detect when a user's pointer moves over it. Dreamweaver automatically includes the minimum link necessary: the #target link. Although JavaScript recognizes this symbol as indicating a link, no action is taken if the image is clicked by the user; the #, by itself, is an empty link. You can, naturally, supply whatever link you want in the Rollover Image object.

To include a Rollover Image object in your Web page, follow these steps:

1. Place your cursor where you want the rollover image to appear and choose Insert ➪ Rollover Image or select Insert Rollover Image from the Common panel of the Objects palette. You can also drag the Insert Rollover Image button to any existing location on the Web page.

   Dreamweaver opens the Insert Rollover Image dialog box shown in Figure 10-12.

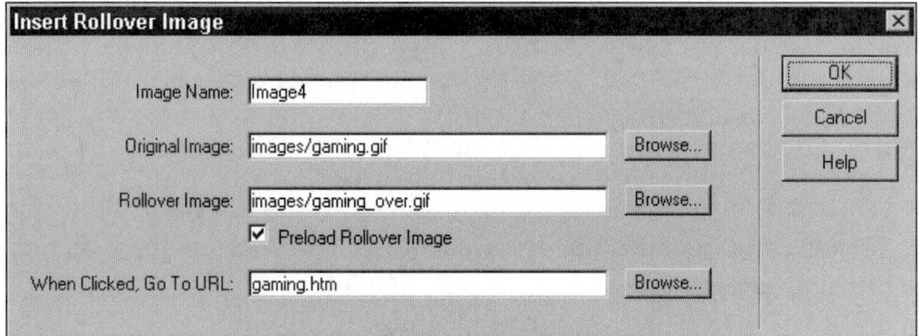

Figure 10-12: The Rollover Image object makes rollover graphics quick and easy.

2. If desired, you can enter a unique name for the image in the Image Name text box, or you can leave the name automatically generated by Dreamweaver.
3. In the Original Image text box, enter the path and name of the graphic you want displayed when the user's mouse is not over the graphic. You can also choose the Browse (Choose) button to select the file. Press Tab when you're done.
4. In the Rollover Image text box, enter the path and name of the graphic you want displayed when the user's pointer is over the graphic. You can also choose the Browse (Choose) button to select the file.
5. If desired, specify a link for the image by entering it in the When Clicked, Go To URL text box. If you are entering a path and file by hand, be sure to delete the initial target link, #. If you use the Browse (Choose) button to select your file, the target link is deleted for you.
6. To enable images to load only when they are required, deselect the Preload Images option. Generally, it is best to leave this option selected (the default) so that no delay occurs in the rollover appearing.
7. Click OK when you're finished.

Keep in mind that the Rollover Image object inserts both the original image and its alternate, whereas the Swap Image technique is applied to an existing image in the Web page. If you prefer to use the Rollover Image object rather than the Swap Image behavior, nothing prevents you from deleting an existing image from the Web page and inserting it again through the Rollover Image object. Just make sure that you note the path and name of the image before you delete it, so you can find it again.

Adding a Navigation Bar

Rollovers are nice effects, but a single button does not make a navigation system for a Web site. Typically, several buttons with a similar look and feel are placed next to each other to form a *navigation bar*. To make touring a site as intuitive as possible, the same navigation bar is usually repeated on each page or used once, as a frame element. Consistency of design and repetitive use of the navigation bar simplifies getting around a site—even for a first-time user.

New Feature

Some designers build their navigation bars in a separate graphics program and then import them into Dreamweaver. Fireworks, with its capability to export both images and code, makes this a strong option. Other Web designers, however, prefer to build separate rollover images in a graphics program and then assemble all the pieces at the HTML layout stage. Dreamweaver now automates such a process with its new Navigation Bar object.

The Navigation Bar object incorporates rollovers — and more. A Navigation Bar element can use up to four different images, each reflecting a different user action:

- Up — The user's pointer is away from the image.
- Over — The pointer is over the image.
- Down — The user has clicked the image.
- Over While Down — The user pointer is over the image after it has been clicked.

You don't have to use all four states — it's up to you whether you use just the first two, like a standard rollover, or add the third and possibly the fourth. You can even skip the Over state and just use Up and Down. While it's possible to display an Over While Down state without a Down state, it doesn't make much sense to do so.

One key difference separates a fully functioning navigation bar from a group of unrelated rollovers. When the Down state is available, if the user clicks one of the buttons, any other Down button is changed to the Up state. The effect is like a series of mutually exclusive radio buttons: You can show only one selected in a group. The Down state is often used to indicate the current selection.

Tip While you can use the Navigation Bar object on any type of Web design, it works best in a frameset situation with a frame for navigation and one for content. If you insert a navigation bar with Up, Over, Down, and Over While Down states for each button in the navigation frame, you can target the content frame and gain the full effect of the mutually exclusive Down states.

Before you can use Dreamweaver 3's Navigation Bar object, you have to create a series of images for each button — one for each state you plan to use. It's completely up to the designer how the buttons appear, but it's important that a consistent look and feel be applied for all the buttons. For example, if rolling over Button A reveals a green glow, rolling over Buttons B, C, and D should also cause the same green glow, as demonstrated in Figure 10-13.

To insert a navigation bar, follow these steps:

1. From the Objects palette, select the Insert Navigation Bar object.

   The Insert Navigation Bar dialog box appears, as shown in Figure 10-14.

2. Enter a unique name for the first button in the Element Name field and press Tab.

Caution Be sure to use Tab rather than Enter (Return) when moving from field to field. When Enter (Return) is pressed, Dreamweaver attempts to build the navigation bar. If you have not completed the initial two steps (providing an Element Name and a source for the Up Image), an alert is displayed; otherwise, the navigation bar is built.

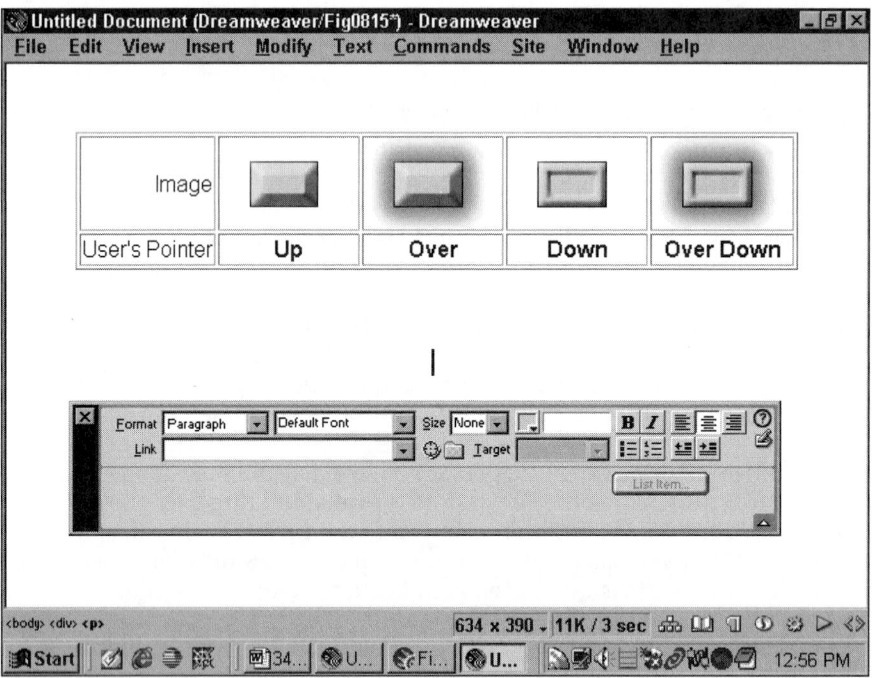

Figure 10-13: Before you invoke the Navigation Bar object, create a series of buttons with a separate image for each state to be used.

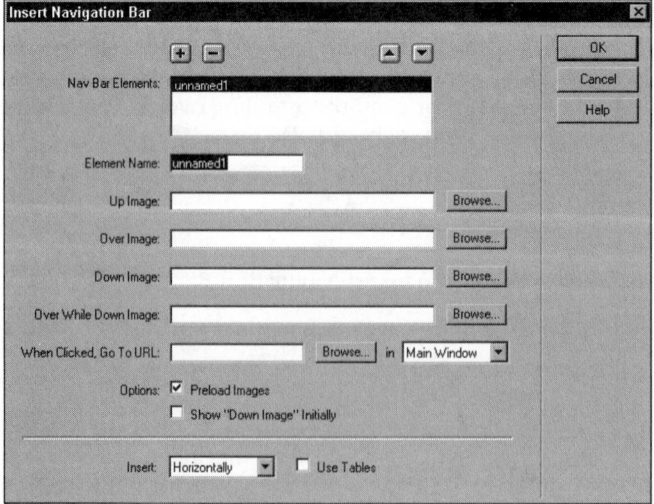

Figure 10-14: Add elements one at a time in the Insert Navigation Bar dialog box.

3. In the Up Image field, enter a path and file name or browse to a graphic file to use.
4. Select files for each of the remaining states you wish to use: Over, Down, and Over While Down.
5. Enter a URL or browse to a file in the When Clicked, Go To URL field.
6. If you're using a frameset, select a target for the URL from the drop-down list.
7. Enable or disable the Preload Images option as desired.

   For a multistate button to be effective, the reaction has to be immediate, and the images must be preloaded. It is highly recommended that the Preload Images option be enabled.
8. If you want the current button to display the Down state first, select the Show "Down Image" Initially option.

   When this option is chosen, an asterisk appears next to the current button in the Nav Bar Element list. Generally, you don't want more than one Down state showing at a time.
9. To set the orientation of the navigation bar, select either Horizontally or Vertically from the Insert drop-down list.
10. If you want to contain your images in a table, keep the Use Table option selected.

    If you decide not to use tables in a horizontal configuration, images are presented side by side; when a vertical navigation bar is built without tables, Dreamweaver inserts a line break (`<br>` tag) between each element.
11. Select the add (plus) button and repeat Steps 2 through 8 to add the next element.
12. To reorder the elements in the navigation bar, select an element in the Nav Bar Elements list and use the up and down buttons to reposition it in the Element list.
13. To remove an element, select it and click the delete (minus) button.

Each page can have only one Dreamweaver-built navigation bar. If you try to insert a second, Dreamweaver asks if you'd like to modify the existing series. Clicking OK opens the Modify Navigation Bar dialog box, shown in Figure 10-15, which is identical to the Insert Navigation Bar dialog box, except you can no longer change the orientation or table settings. You can also alter the inserted navigation bar by choosing Modify ⇨ Navigation Bar.

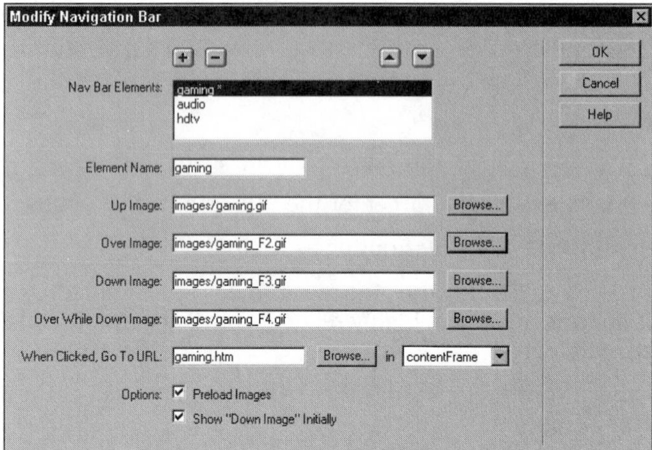

Figure 10-15: Once you've inserted your nav bar, you can adjust it through the Modify Navigation Bar dialog box.

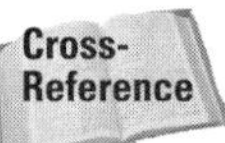

If you're looking for even more control over your navigation bar, Dreamweaver also includes a new behavior, Set Navigation Bar, which is fully covered in Chapter 19.

Summary

In this chapter, you learned how to include both foreground and background images in Dreamweaver. Understanding how images are handled in HTML is an absolute necessity for the Web designer. Some of the key points follow:

✦ Web pages are restricted to using specific graphic formats. Virtually all browsers support GIF and JPEG files. PNG is also gaining acceptance. Dreamweaver can preview all three image types.

✦ Images are inserted in the foreground in Dreamweaver through the Insert Image command of the Objects palette. Once the graphic is inserted, almost all modifications can be handled through the Property Inspector.

✦ You can use HTML's background image function to lay a full-frame image or a tiled series of the same image underneath your text and graphics. Tiled images can be employed to create columns and other designs with small files.

✦ The simplest HTML graphic is the built-in horizontal rule. Useful for dividing your Web page into separate sections, the horizontal rule can be sized either absolutely or relatively.

✦ With the Rollover Image object, you can easily insert simple rollovers that use two different images. To build a rollover that uses more than two images, you have to use the Swap Image behavior.

✦ Animated images can be inserted alongside, and in the same manner as, still graphics. The individual frames of a GIF animation must be created in a graphics program and then combined in an animation program.

✦ Since the release of Fireworks 2, images can now be optimized from within Dreamweaver. Moreover, it's easier to integrate code generated from Fireworks — and you can even specify Dreamweaver-style HTML.

✦ You can add a series of interrelated buttons — complete with four-state rollovers — by using the new Navigation Bar object.

In the next chapter, you learn how to use hyperlinks in Dreamweaver.

✦ ✦ ✦

Establishing Web Links

In This Chapter

All about Internet addresses

Linking Web pages

Pointing to a file

Creating anchors within Web pages

URL targeting

To me, links are the Web. Everything else about the medium can be replicated in another form, but without links, there would be no World Wide Web. As your Web design work becomes more sophisticated, you'll find more enhanced uses for links: sending mail, connecting to an FTP site — even downloading software. In this chapter, you learn how Dreamweaver helps you manage the various types of links, set anchors within documents to get smooth and accurate navigation, and establish targets for your URLs. But first, let's begin with an overview on Internet addresses to give you the full picture of the possibilities.

Understanding URLs

URL stands for Uniform Resource Locator. An awkward phrase, it nonetheless describes itself well — the URL's function is to provide a standard method for finding anything on the Internet. From Web pages to newsgroups to the smallest graphic on the most esoteric of pages, everything can be referenced through the URL system.

The URL can use up to six different parts, although all parts are not necessary for the URL to be read. Each part is separated by some combination of a slash, colon, and hash mark delimiter. When entered as an attribute's value, the entire URL is generally enclosed within quotes to ensure that the address is read as one unit. A generic URL using all the parts looks like the following:

```
method://server:port/path/file#anchor
```

Here's a real-world example that also uses every section:

```
http://www.idest.com:80/dreamweaver/index.htm#bible
```

In order of appearance in the body of an Internet address, left to right, the parts denote the following:

✦ The method used to access the resource. The method to address Web servers is the HyperText Transport Protocol (HTTP). Other methods are discussed later in this section.

✦ The name of the server providing the resource. The server can either be a domain name (with or without the "www" prefix) or an Internet Protocol (IP) address, such as 199.227.52.143.

✦ The port number to be used on the server. Most URLs do not include a port number, which is analogous to a telephone extension number on the server, because most servers use the defaults.

✦ The directory path to the resource. Depending on where the resource (for example, the Web page) is located on the server, the following paths can be specified: no path (indicating that the resource is in the public root of the server), a single folder name, or a number of folders and subfolders.

✦ The file name of the resource. If the file name is omitted, the Web browser looks for a default page, often named index.html or index.htm. The browser reacts differently depending on the type of file. For example, GIFs and JPEGs are displayed by themselves; executable files and archives (Zip, StuffIt, and so on) are downloaded.

✦ The named anchor in the HTML document. This part is another optional section. The named anchor enables the Web designer to send the viewer to a particular section of an HTML page.

Because it is used to communicate with servers, the HTTP access method is far and away the most prevalent method on today's World Wide Web. In addition to the HTTP access method, other methods connect with other types of servers. Table 11-1 discusses some of these options.

Table 11-1
Various Internet Access Methods and Protocols

Name	*Syntax*	*Usage*
File Transfer Protocol	ftp://	Links to an FTP server that is generally used for uploading and downloading files. The server can be accessed anonymously, or it may require a user name and password.
Gopher	gopher://	Connects to a directory tree structure primarily used for disseminating all-text documents.
HyperText Transfer Protocol	http://	Used for connecting to a document available on a World Wide Web server.

Name	*Syntax*	*Usage*
JavaScript	javascript://	Executes a JavaScript function.
Mailto	mailto:	Opens an e-mail form with the recipient's address already filled in. These links are useful when embedded in your Web pages to provide visitors with an easy feedback method.
News	news://	Connects to the specified Usenet newsgroup. Newsgroups are public, theme-oriented message boards where anyone can post or reply to a message.
Telnet	telnet://	Enables users to log directly onto remote host computers and interact directly with the operating system software.

Part of the richness of today's Web browsers stems from their capability to connect with all the preceding (and additional) services.

The mailto: access method enables you not only to open up a preaddressed e-mail form but also to specify the topic, with a little extra work. For example, if Joe Lowery wants to include a link to his e-mail address with the subject heading "Dreamweaver Bible," he can insert a link such as the following:

```
mailto:jlowery@idest.com?subject=BibleFeedback
```

The question mark acts as a delimiter that enables a variable and a value to be passed to the browser. When you're trying to encourage feedback from your Web page visitors, every little bit helps. A note of caution: This method is not standardized HTML, and while it works with most browsers and mail programs, you could get unexpected results with some systems.

Surfing the Web with Hypertext

Most often, you assign a link to a word or phrase on your page, an image such as a navigational button, or a section of graphic for an image map (a large graphic in which various parts are links). Once you have created the link, you have to preview it in a browser; links are not active in Dreamweaver's Document window.

Designate links in HTML through the anchor tag pair: <a> and </a>. The anchor tag generally takes one main attribute — the hypertext reference, which is written as follows:

```
href="link name"
```

When you create a link in Dreamweaver, the anchor pair surrounds the text or object that is being linked. For example, if you link the phrase "Back to Home Page," it may look like the following:

```
<a href="index.html">Back to Home Page</a>
```

When you attach a link to an image, logo.gif, your code looks as follows:

```
<a href="home.html"><img src="images/logo.gif"></a>
```

Creating a basic link in Dreamweaver is easy. Simply follow these steps:

1. Select the text, image, or object you want to establish as a link.
2. In the Property Inspector, enter the URL in the Link text box as shown in Figure 11-1. You can use one of the following methods to do so:
   - Type the URL directly into the Link text box.
   - Select the folder icon to the right of the Link text box to open the Select File dialog box, where you can browse for the file.
   - Select the Point to File icon and drag your mouse to an existing page or link. This feature is explained later in this section.

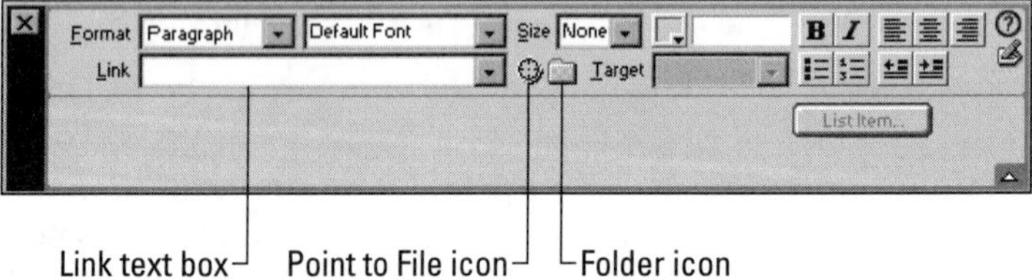

Figure 11-1: You can enter your link directly into the Link text box, select the folder icon to browse for a file, or point to it directly with the Point to File icon.

Only a few restrictions exist for specifying linked URLs. Dreamweaver does not support any letters from the extended character set (also known as High ASCII), such as ¡, à, or ñ. Complete URLs must have fewer than a total of 255 characters. You should be cautious about using spaces in path names and, thus, URLs. Although most browsers can interpret the address, spaces are changed to a %20 symbol for proper Unix usage, which can make your URLs difficult to read.

Links without Underscores

To remove the underlined aspect of a link, you can use one of two methods. The classic method—which works for all graphics-capable browsers—uses an image rather than text as the link. You must make sure the `border` attribute of your image is set to 0 because a linked image usually displays a blue border if a `border` attribute exists. Dreamweaver adds border="0" to all image links now, as a default.

The second, newer method uses Cascading Style Sheets. While this is an excellent one-stop solution, bear in mind that these can be read only by the more recent browser versions (generally 4.0 and above). Refer to the Dreamweaver Technique for eliminating the underlines in links in Chapter 27.

Whitespace in your HTML usually doesn't have an adverse effect. However, Netscape browsers are sensitive to whitespace when assigning a link to an image. If you isolate your image tag from the anchor tags as in the following example:

```
<a href="index.htm">
<img src="images/Austria.gif" width="34" ¬
height="24">
</a>
```

Netscape browsers attach a small blue underscore—a tail, really—to your image. Because Dreamweaver codes the anchor tag properly, without any additional whitespace, this odd case applies only to hand-coded or previously coded HTML.

Text links are most often rendered with a blue color and underlined. You can alter the document link color by choosing Modify ➪ Page Properties and selecting the Link Color swatch. In Page Properties, you can also alter the color to which the links change after being selected (the Visited Link Color) and the color flashed when the link is clicked (the Active Link Color).

Want to add a little variety to your text links? You can actually change the color of the link on an individual basis. To do this, you have to enter the link in the Property Inspector before you apply the color. Be sure to exercise a little discretion though—you don't want to use so many different colors that your Web page visitors can't figure out the navigation.

Pointing to a file

Dreamweaver has an alternative method of identifying a link—pointing to it.

By using the Point to File icon on the Property Inspector, you can quickly fill in the Link text box by dragging your mouse to any existing named anchor or file visible in the Dreamweaver environment. The Point to File feature saves you from having to browse through folder after folder as you search for a file you can clearly see onscreen.

You can point to a file in another open Dreamweaver window or one in another frame in the same window. If your desired link is a named anchor located further down the page, Dreamweaver automatically scrolls to find it. You can even point to a named anchor in another page, and Dreamweaver enters the full syntax correctly. Named anchors are covered in detail later in this chapter.

Perhaps one of the slickest applications of the Point to File icon is when it is used in tandem with the Site window. The Site window lists all the existing files in any given Web site, and when both it and the Document window are onscreen, you can quickly point to any file.

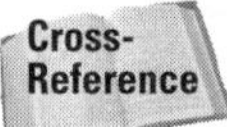

For more details about using the Site window in this fashion, see Chapter 7.

Pointing to a file uses what could be called a "drag-and-release" mouse technique, as opposed to the more ordinary point-and-click or drag-and-drop method. To select a new link using the Point to File icon, follow these steps:

1. Select the text or the graphic that you'd like to make into a link.
2. In the Property Inspector, click and hold the Point to File icon located to the right of the Link text box.
3. Holding down the mouse button, drag the mouse until it is over an existing link or named anchor in the Document window or a file in the Site window.

   As you drag the mouse, a line extends from the Point to File icon, and the reminder "Point to a file to make a link" appears in the Link text box.
4. When you locate the file you want to link to, release the mouse button. The file name with the accompanying path information is written into the Link text box as shown in Figure 11-2.

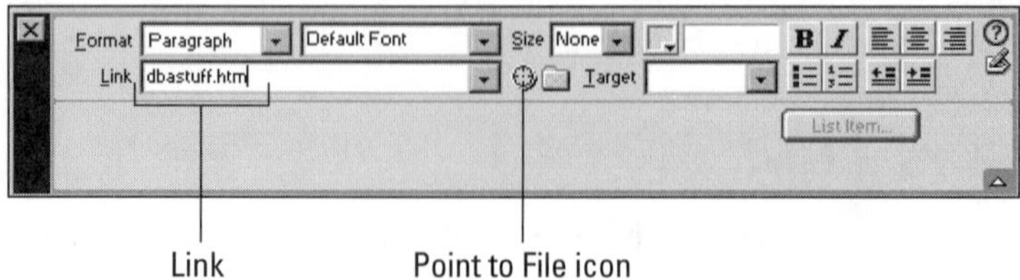

Figure 11-2: The Point to File capability enables you to quickly insert a link to any onscreen page.

Addressing types

As you learned in Chapter 6, three types of URLs are used as links: absolute addresses, document-relative addresses, and site root–relative addresses. Let's briefly recap these address types.

- Absolute addresses require the full URL, as follows:

  ```
  http://www.macromedia.com/software/dreamweaver/
  ```

  This type is most often used for referencing links on another Web server.

- Document-relative addresses know the method, server, and path aspects of the URL. You need to include only additional path information if the link is outside of the current Web page's folder. Links in the current document's folder can be addressed with their file name only. To reference an item in a subfolder, just name the folder, enter a forward slash, and then enter the item's file name, as follows:

  ```
  images/background.gif
  ```

- Site root–relative addresses are indicated with a leading forward slash. For example:

  ```
  /upndown.html
  ```

  The preceding address links to a file named upndown.html stored in the primary directory of the current site. Dreamweaver now translates site-relative to document-relative links when the Preview in Browser feature is used.

A Webmaster must often perform the tedious but necessary task of verifying the links on all the Web pages in a site. Because of the Web's fluid nature, links can work one day and then be broken the next. Dreamweaver has enhanced its powerful link-checking capabilities with link-updating features. To find out how to keep your site up to date with a minimum of effort, see Chapter 7.

Adding an E-mail Link

E-mail links are very common on the Web. Rather than opening a new Web page like a regular link, when an e-mail link is clicked, a window for sending a new e-mail message is displayed. The message window is already preaddressed to the recipient, making it convenient to use. All the user has to do is add a subject, enter a message, and select Send.

Until now, e-mail links had to be added by hand. Dreamweaver 3 includes an object that streamlines the process. Just enter the text of the line, and the e-mail address and the link is ready. E-mail links, like other links, do not work in Dreamweaver when clicked and must be previewed in the browser.

To enter an e-mail link with the new object, follow these steps:

1. Position your cursor where you want the e-mail link to appear.
2. From the Common panel of the Object palette, select the Insert E-Mail Link button.

   The Insert E-Mail Link dialog box, shown in Figure 11-3, appears.

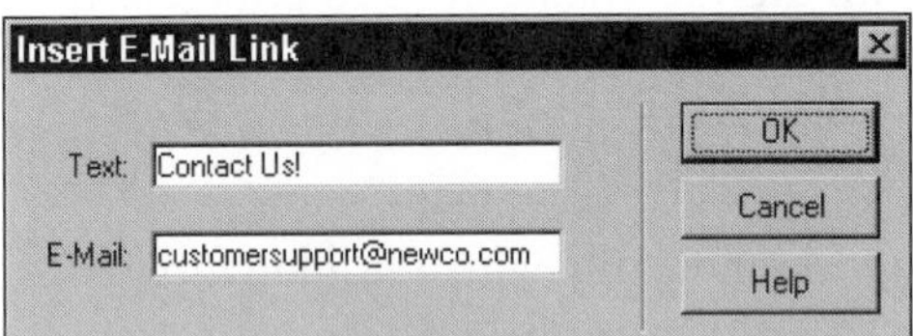

Figure 11-3: The new Insert E-Mail Link object creates links that make it simple for your Web page visitors to send an e-mail.

3. In the Insert E-Mail Link dialog box, enter the visible text for the link in the Text field.
4. Enter the e-mail address in the E-Mail field.

The e-mail address must be in the format name@company.com. Dreamweaver does not check to make sure you've entered the proper format.

5. Click OK when you're done.

If you already have the text for the e-mail link in the document, you can also use the Property Inspector to insert an e-mail link. Just highlight the text and in the Link field of the Property Inspector, enter the URL in this format:

```
mailto:name@company.com
```

Make sure that the URL is a valid e-mail address with the @ sign properly placed.

Here's a bit of the frustration that Web designers sometimes face: On some browsers, notably Internet Explorer, the user may see a dialog box when the e-mail link is first selected. The dialog box informs them that they are about to send an e-mail over the Internet. The user has an option to not see these warnings, but there's no way for the Web designer to prevent them from appearing.

Navigating with Anchors

Whenever you normally link to an HTML page, through absolute or relative addressing, the browser displays the page from the top. Your Web visitors must scroll to any information rendered below the current screen. One HTML technique, however, links to a specific point anywhere on your page regardless of the display window's contents. This technique uses named anchors.

Using named anchors is a two-step process. First you place a named anchor somewhere on your Web page. This placement is coded in HTML as an anchor tag using the `name` attribute, with nothing in between the opening and closing tags. In HTML, named anchors look like the following:

```
<a name="bible"></a>
```

The second step includes a link to that named anchor from somewhere else on your Web page. If used, a named anchor is referenced in the final possible portion of an Internet address, designated by the hash mark (#), as follows:

```
<a href="http://www.idest.com/dreamweaver/index.htm#bible>
```

You can include any number of named anchors on the current page or another page. Named anchors are commonly used with a table of contents or index.

To insert a named anchor in Dreamweaver, follow these steps:

1. Place the cursor where you want the named anchor to appear.
2. Choose Insert ⇨ Named Anchor. You can also select the Insert Named Anchor button from the Invisibles panel of the Objects palette. Or use the key shortcut Ctrl+Alt+A (Command+Option+A).
3. The Named Anchor dialog box opens. Type the anchor name into the text box.

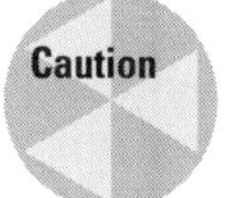

Named anchors are case sensitive and must be unique within the page.

When you press Enter (Return), Dreamweaver places a named anchor symbol in the current cursor location and opens the Named Anchor Property Inspector (shown in Figure 11-4).

4. To change an anchor's name, click the named anchor symbol within the page and alter the text in the Property Inspector.

As with other invisible symbols, the named anchor symbol can be cut and pasted or moved using the drag-and-drop method.

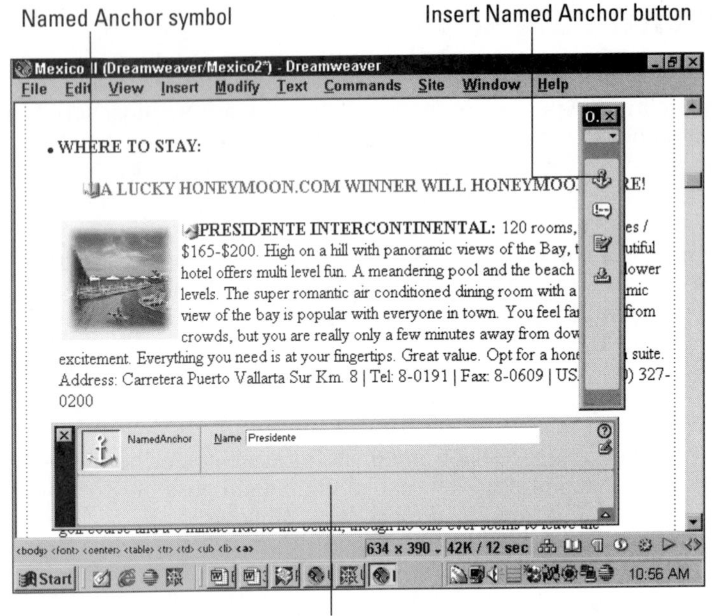

Figure 11-4: The Named Anchor tag enables you to link to specific areas of a Web page.

Moving within the same document

One of the major advantages of using named anchors is the almost instantaneous response the viewer receives when they click them. The browser only needs to scroll to the particular place in the document because the entire page is loaded. For long text documents, this capability is an invaluable time-saver.

Once you have placed a named anchor—or all of them at once—in your document, you can link to these anchors. Follow these steps to create a link to a named anchor in the same document:

1. Select the text or image that you want to designate as a link.
2. In the Link text box of the Property Inspector, type a hash mark, #, followed by the exact anchor name. For example:

   ```
   #top
   ```

   Remember, anchor names are case sensitive and must be unique in each document.

Tip

You should place the named anchor one line above the heading or image to which you want to link the viewer. Browsers tend to be quite literal. If you place the named anchor on the same line, the browser renders it up against the top of the window. Placing your named anchor up one line gives your topic a bit of breathing room in the display.

In Dreamweaver, you can also use the Point to File icon to choose a named anchor link. If your named anchor is in the same document, just drag the Point to File icon to the named anchor symbol. When you release the mouse, the proper named anchor is inserted into the Link text box. If the named anchor is on the same page but offscreen, Dreamweaver automatically scrolls the Document window as you approach the edge. In Windows, the closer you move to the edge, the faster Dreamweaver scrolls. Dreamweaver even returns the screen to your original location, with the new link at the top of the screen, after you release the mouse button.

In long documents with a table of contents or index linking to a number of named anchors, it's common practice—and a good idea—to place a link back to the top of the page after every screen or every topic. This technique enables your users to return to the menu quickly and pick another topic without having to manually scroll all the way back.

Using named anchors in a different page

If your table of contents is on a separate page from the topics of your site, you can use named anchors to send the viewer anywhere on a new page. The technique is exactly the same as already explained for placing named anchors, but one minor difference exists when it comes to linking. Instead of placing a hash mark and name to denote the named anchor, you must first include the URL of the linked page.

Let's say you want to call the disclaimer section of a legal page from your table of contents. You could insert something like the following in the Link text box of the Property Inspector:

```
legal.htm#disclaimer
```

This link, when activated, first loads the referenced Web page (legal.htm) and then goes directly to the named anchor place (#disclaimer). Figure 11-5 shows how you would enter this in the Property Inspector. Keep in mind, you can use any form of addressing prior to the hash mark and named anchor.

Tip

One of the more obscure uses for named anchors comes into play when you are trying to use Dreamweaver's JavaScript Behavior feature. Because JavaScript needs to work with a particular type of tag to perform `onMouseOver` and other events, one trick marks some text or image with a link to #nowhere. You can use any name for the nonexistent named anchor. In fact, you don't even have to use a name—you can just use a hash mark by itself (#). One problem area: Netscape browsers have a tendency to send the page to the top if a link of this type is used. Many programmers have begun to substitute a JavaScript function instead, such as `javascript://void()`.

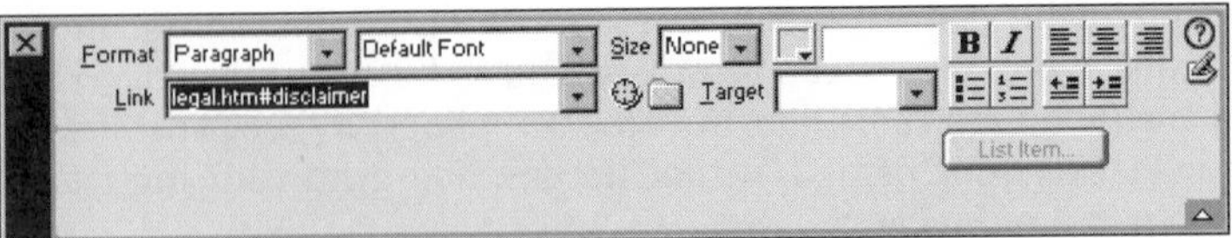

Figure 11-5: You can also link to any part of a separate Web page using named anchors.

Targeting Your Links

Thus far, all of this chapter's links have had a similar effect: They open another Web page or section in your browser's window. What if you want to force the browser to open another window and load that new URL in the new window? HTML enables you to specify the target for your links.

Targets are most often used in conjunction with frames — that is, you can make a link in one frame open a file in another. (Chapter 16 covers the subject of frames in depth.) Here, though, let's take a look at one of the HTML predefined targets useful in a situation where you want to load another URL into a new window.

To specify a new browser window as the target for a link in Dreamweaver, follow these steps:

1. Select the text or image you want to designate as your new link.
2. In the Property Inspector, enter the URL into the Link text box.

   After you've entered a link, the target option becomes active.
3. Choose the option button next to the Target list box and select _blank from the drop-down list. You can also type it in the list box.

   Dreamweaver inserts a _blank option in the Target list box, as shown in Figure 11-6. Now, when your link is activated, the browser spawns a new window and loads the referenced link into it. The user has both windows available.

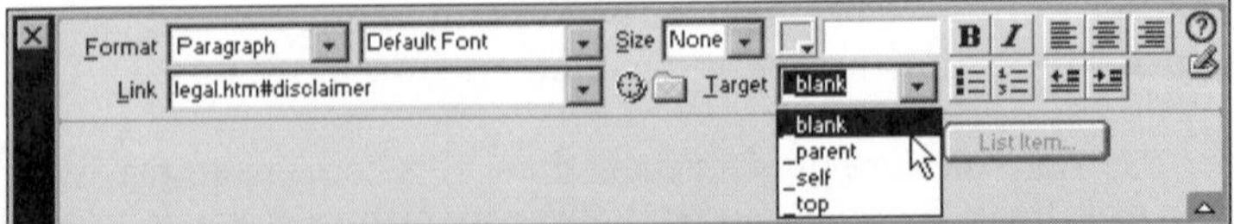

Figure 11-6: You can force a user's browser to open a separate window to display a specific link with the Target command.

The _blank target is most often used when the originating Web page is acting as a jump station and has numerous links available. By keeping the original Web page open, the user can check out one site without losing the origin point.

Three other system-wide targets exist: _top, _parent, and _self. Both _top and _parent are primarily used with framesets: _top target replaces the outermost frameset and _parent replaces the frameset containing the current page. These two have the same effect, except in the case of nested framesets. The _self target is the default behavior and only the current page is replaced.

You can even use the _blank target technique on named anchors in the same document, thereby emulating frames to some degree.

Some key online services, such as America Online and WebTV, don't enable their built-in browsers to open new windows. Every link that is accessed is displayed in the same browser window.

Summary

Whether they are links for Web site navigation or jumps to other related sites, hypertext links are an essential part of any Web page. Dreamweaver gives you full control over your inserted anchors.

- ✦ Through a unique URL, you can access virtually any Web page, graphic, or other item available on the Internet.
- ✦ The HyperText Transfer Protocol (HTTP) is the most common method of Web connection, but Web pages can link to other formats, including FTP, e-mail, and newsgroups.
- ✦ Any of the three basic address formats — absolute, document relative, or site root relative — can be inserted in the Link text box of Dreamweaver's Property Inspector to create a link.
- ✦ Dreamweaver has a quick linking capability through its Point to File feature.
- ✦ Named anchors give you the power to jump to specific parts of any Web page, whether the page is the current one or located on another server.
- ✦ With the `_blank target` attribute, you can force a link to open in a new browser window, leaving your original window available to the user.

In the next chapter, you learn how to use various types of lists in Dreamweaver.

✦ ✦ ✦

CHAPTER 12

Creating Lists

✦ ✦ ✦ ✦

In This Chapter

Bulleting your points

Using a numbered list

Building a glossary

Inserting menu and directory lists

Dreamweaver Technique: Making graphic bullets

✦ ✦ ✦ ✦

Lists serve several different functions in all publications, including Web pages. A list can itemize a topic's points or catalog the properties of an object. A numbered list is helpful for giving step-by-step instructions. From a page designer's point of view, a list can break up the page and simultaneously draw the viewer's eye to key details.

Lists are an important alternative to the basic textual tools of paragraphs and headings. In this chapter, you study Dreamweaver's tools for designing and working with each of the three basic types of lists available under HTML:

- ✦ Unordered lists
- ✦ Ordered lists
- ✦ Definition lists

The various list types can also be combined to create outlines. Dreamweaver supplies a straightforward method for building these nested lists.

Creating Bulleted (Unordered) Lists

What word processing programs and layout artists refer to as *bulleted lists* are known in HTML as *unordered lists*. An unordered list is used when the sequence of the listed items is unimportant, as in a recipe's list of ingredients. Each unordered list item is set off by a leading character, and the remainder of the line is indented. By default, the leading character is the bullet; in HTML, you also can specify two other symbols by conventional means and a custom bullet through Cascading Style Sheets.

You can either create the unordered list from scratch or convert existing text into the bulleted format.

To begin an unordered list from scratch, position the cursor where you want to start the list. Then click the Unordered List button supplied conveniently on the Text Property Inspector (see Figure 12-1) or use the Text ➪ List ➪ Unordered List command.

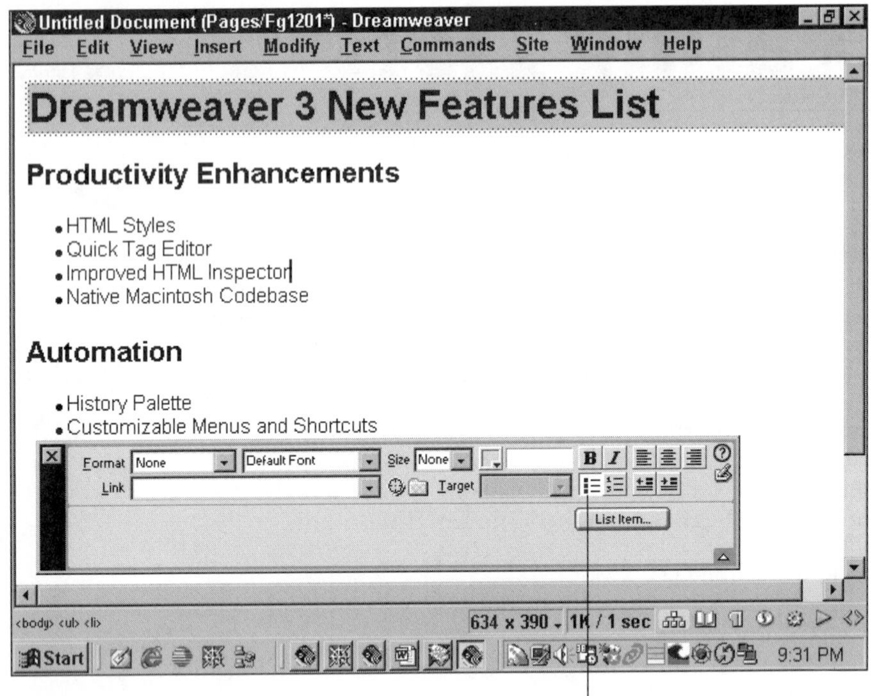

Figure 12-1: An itemized list that doesn't need to be in any specific order is perfect for formatting as an unordered list.

If you are changing existing text into a list, select the paragraphs first and then execute the Unordered List button or menu command.

Dreamweaver creates one list item for every paragraph. As you can see from Figure 12-1, list items are generally rendered closer together than regular paragraphs. Unlike block elements such as paragraphs or headings, HTML doesn't insert additional lines above and space below each line of a list.

In terms of lists in Dreamweaver, the word *paragraph* is used literally to mean any text designated with a paragraph tag. Certainly you can apply a heading format to an HTML list, but you probably won't like the results: The heading format reinserts those additional lines below and above each list item—the ones generally not used by the list format. If you want your list items to appear larger in size, you should change the font size through the Property Inspector or with Text ➪ Size Increase.

Editing unordered lists

Once a series of paragraphs is formatted as an unordered list, you can easily add additional bulleted items. The basic editing techniques are the same for all types of lists:

- ✦ To continue adding items at the end of a list, simply press Enter (Return) to create each new paragraph. Another bullet is inserted.
- ✦ To insert an item within an unordered list, place your cursor at the end of the item above the desired position for the added item and press Enter (Return).
- ✦ List items can be copied or cut and pasted in a different place on the list. Place your cursor in front of the list item below where you want the repositioned item to appear and choose Edit ➪ Paste.
- ✦ To end a bulleted list, you can press Enter (Return) twice or deselect the Unordered List button on the Text Property Inspector.

List tags

You may occasionally need to tweak your list code by hand. Two HTML tags are used in creating an unordered list. The first is the outer tag, which defines the type of list; the second is the item delimiter. Unordered lists are designated with the `<ul>...</ul>` tag pair, and the delimiter is the `<li>...</li>` pair. The unordered list code in the HTML Inspector looks like the following:

```
<ul>
  <li>Cascading Style Sheet Support</li>
  <li>Roundtrip HTML</li>
  <li>JavaScript Behaviors</li>
  <li>Repeatable Library Elements</li>
</ul>
```

If a list item is too long to fit in a single line, the browser indents the line when it wraps. By inserting a line break code, you can emulate this behavior even when you're working with lines that aren't long enough to need wrapping. To insert a line break, choose the Insert Line Break button from the Invisibles panel of the Objects palette, or select Insert ➪ Line Break. Or use the key combination Shift+Enter (Shift+Return), or just type `<br>` in your code. Figure 12-2 shows examples of both appro-aches: the long paragraph that wraps naturally and the inserted line breaks to force the wrapping.

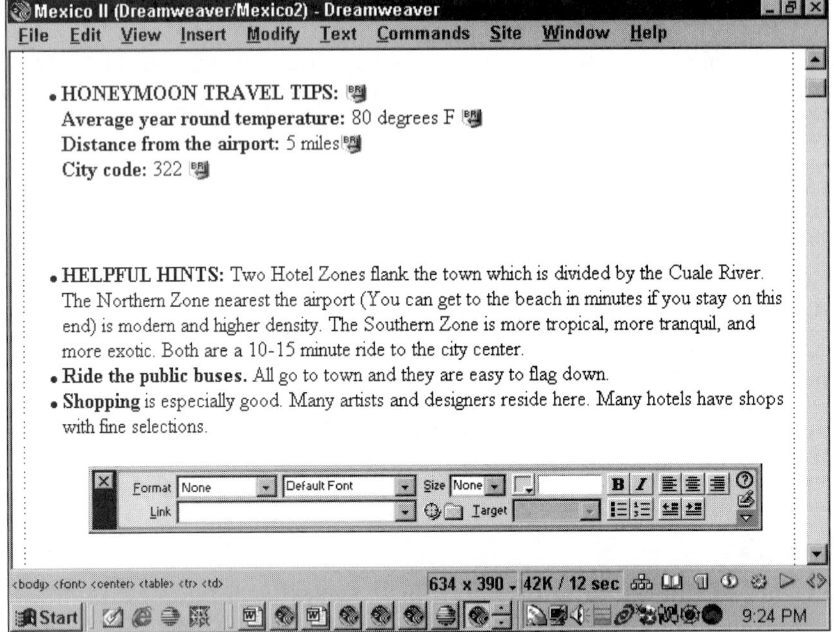

Figure 12-2: A list is indented if the text wraps around the screen or if you insert a line break.

Using other bullet symbols

Although HTML doesn't include a wide range of different symbols to use in an unordered list, you have a few options. Most browsers recognize three different bullet styles: bullet (the default), circle, and square. You can apply the style to the entire unordered list or to one list item at a time.

To change the bullet style of the overall unordered list, follow these steps:

1. Position your cursor anywhere in an existing list.
2. If necessary, click the expander arrow on the Text Property Inspector to display the additional options. Click the List Item button.
3. In the List Properties dialog box that appears (see Figure 12-3), open the Style options list.
4. Select one of the four options:
   - **[Default]:** No style is listed, and the browser applies its default, usually rendered as a bullet.
   - **Bullet:** A solid circle.
   - **Circle:** An open circle.
   - **Square:** A solid square.

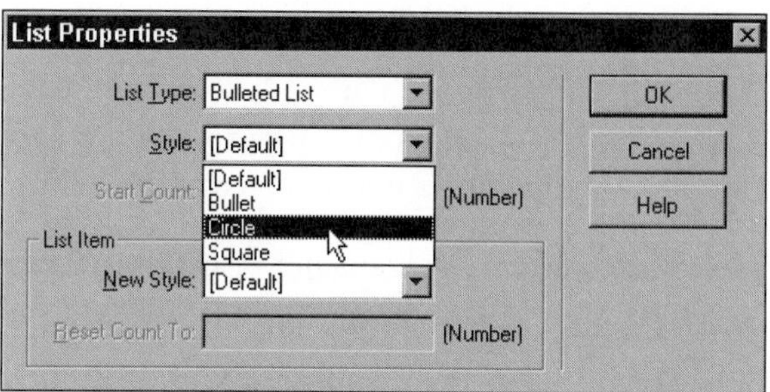

Figure 12-3: You can change the style of the entire list or just one list item through the List Properties dialog box.

5. Click OK.

If you find the List Item button inactive in your Text Property Inspector, make sure that you have – at most – one list item selected. Selecting more than one list item deactivates the List Item button.

When you try to change the style of just one list item, Dreamweaver alters all the successive list items as well. By default, list items don't specify a bullet style. Therefore, when a new style is inserted, all the following items adopt that style.

When you need to change the bullet style of just one item in a list, follow these steps:

1. Select the list item you wish to change.
2. Make sure the Text Property Inspector is expanded and select the List Item button.
3. From the List Properties dialog box, in the List Item section, open the New Style drop-down list.
4. Select one of the four bullet options (described in the preceding steps).

You can alter the type of bullet used in two other ways. The time-tested solution substitutes a graphic for the bullet. Just as with graphical horizontal rules, the Web offers a substantial clip art collection of bullets. You have to insert a graphic for each bullet, however. The quickest method is the drag-and-drop copy technique: Hold down the Ctrl (Command) key and then click and drag the bullet graphic — this sequence places a copy of the bullet wherever you release the mouse.

The newer technique for installing bullet styles uses style sheets. Style sheets can switch a list or list item's bullet style the same as the List Properties dialog box, but with a style sheet you can perform one additional task. You can assign the bullet style type to a specific file — in other words, you can customize your bullet image. The drawback to using this technique is that the list aspect of style sheets is currently supported only by Internet Explorer versions 4.0 and higher. Netscape 4.0 browsers display the regular bullet symbol; however, testing of an unreleased version of Netscape 6.0 show it working properly.

Cascading Style Sheets are covered in depth in Chapter 27. Here is a brief version of the steps for using a style sheet to assign a new bullet symbol:

1. Select the Style Palette button from the Launcher or choose Window ➪ Styles.
2. In the Style Inspector, select the New Style button.
3. In the New Style dialog box, choose the Redefine HTML Tag radio button.
4. From the option list, choose the `li` tag and click OK.
5. In the Style Definition dialog box that appears (see Figure 12-4), choose List in the Category list.

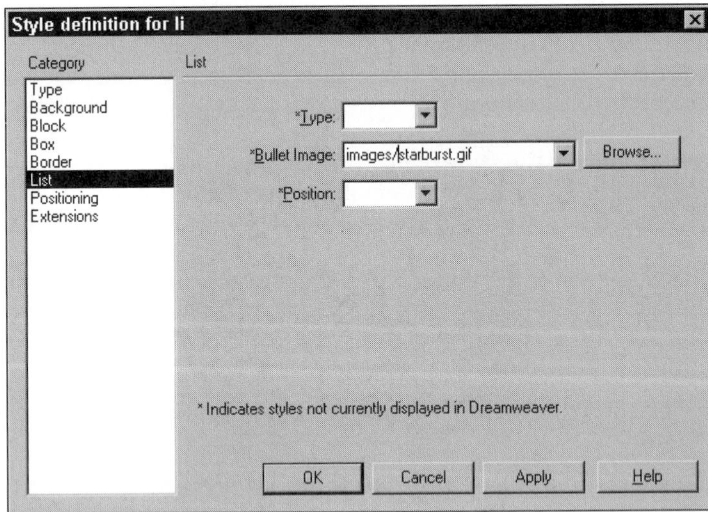

Figure 12-4: You can use Cascading Style Sheets to specify a bullet image for your Web page.

6. Find your graphics file by clicking the Browse (Choose) button next to the Button Image text box. Click OK when you're done.

Your newly defined bullet image doesn't preview in Dreamweaver, but you can view it in Internet Explorer 4.0 or higher.

Mastering Numbered (Ordered) Lists

Unlike a bulleted list, in which sequence is not vital, order is important in the numbered list. This relationship translates in HTML as: "The opposite of an unordered list is an ordered list." The major advantage of an ordered list is the automatic generation of list item numbers and automatic renumbering when you're editing. If you've ever had to renumber a legal document because paragraph 14.b became paragraph 2a, then you recognize the time-saving benefits of this feature.

Ordered lists offer a slightly wider variety of built-in styles than unordered lists, but you cannot customize the leading character further. For instance, you cannot surround a character with parentheses or offset it with a dash. Once again, the browser is the final arbiter of how your list is viewed.

Many of the same techniques used with unordered lists work with ordered lists. To start a new numbered list in Dreamweaver, place your cursor where you want the new list to begin. Then, in the Text Property Inspector, select the Ordered List button or choose Text ➪ List ➪ Ordered List.

As with unordered lists, you can also convert existing paragraphs into a numbered list. First select your text and then select either the Ordered List button or the Text ➪ List ➪ Ordered List command.

As shown in Figure 12-5, the default numbering system is Arabic numerals: 1, 2, 3, and so forth. In the following section, you learn how to alter this default.

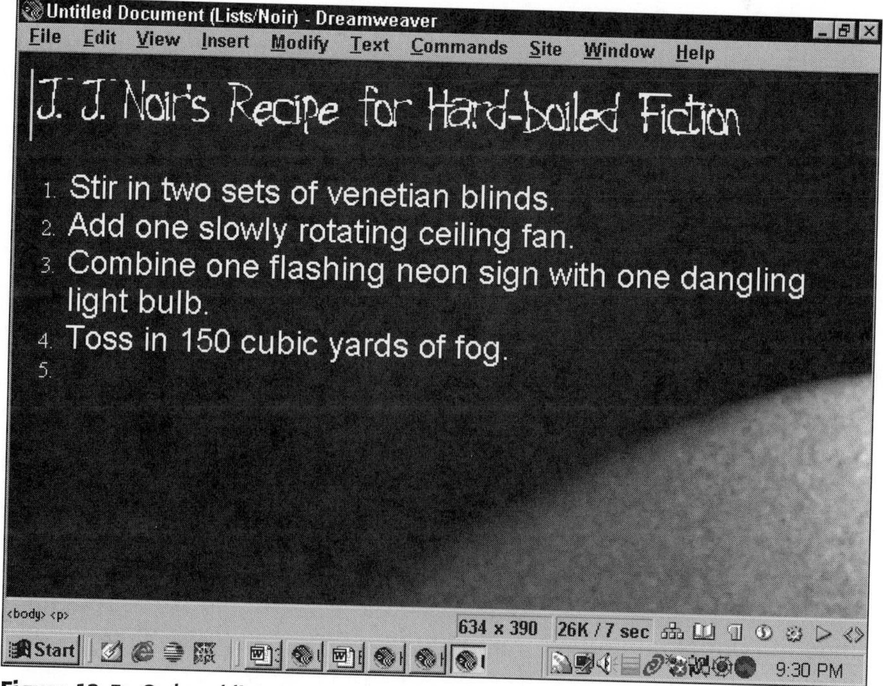

Figure 12-5: Ordered lists are used on this page to create a numbered sequence.

Editing ordered lists

The HTML code for an ordered list is <ol>. Both <ol> and <ul> use the list item tag, <li>, to mark individual entries, and Dreamweaver handles the formatting identically:

```
<ol>
  <li>Stir in two sets of venetian blinds.</li>
  <li>Add one slowly rotating ceiling fan.</li>
  <li>Combine one flashing neon sign with one dangling light bulb.</li>
  <li>Toss in 150 cubic yards of fog.</li>
  <li></li>
</ol>
```

The empty list item pair, <li>...</li>, is displayed on the page as the next number in sequence.

Modifications to an ordered list are handled in the same manner as for an unordered list. The results are far more dramatic, however.

- ✦ To continue adding to the sequence of numbers, position your cursor at the end of the last item and press Enter (Return). The next number in sequence is generated, and any styles in use (such as font size or name) are carried over.
- ✦ To insert a new item in the list, put your cursor at the end of the item above where the new item will be positioned, and press Enter (Return). Dreamweaver inserts a new number in sequence and automatically renumbers the following numbers.
- ✦ To rearrange a numbered list, highlight the entire list item you want to move. Using the drag-and-drop method, release the mouse when your cursor is at the front of the item below the new location for the moved item.
- ✦ To end an item in a numbered list, press Enter (Return) twice or press Enter (Return) and deselect the Ordered List button.

Using other numbering styles

In all, you can apply five different numbering styles to your numbered lists:

- ✦ **Arabic numerals:** 1, 2, 3, and so forth (this is the default style)
- ✦ **Roman Small:** i, ii, iii, and so forth
- ✦ **Roman Large:** I, II, III, and so forth
- ✦ **Alphabet Small:** a, b, c, and so forth
- ✦ **Alphabet Large:** A, B, C, and so forth

You can restyle your entire list all at once, or you can just change a single list item. To change the style of the entire ordered list, follow these steps:

1. Position your cursor anywhere in an existing list.
2. If necessary, click the expander arrow on the Text Property Inspector to display the additional options. Select the List Item button.

   The List Properties dialog box opens, with Numbered List showing as the List Type.
3. Open the drop-down list of Style options and choose any of the five preceding numbering types.
4. Click OK.

As with unordered lists, when you modify the style of one ordered list item, all the subsequent items adopt that style. To alter the style of a single and all subsequent items, follow these steps:

1. Select the item you wish to change.
2. In the expanded portion of the Text Property Inspector, select the List Item button.
3. In the List Properties dialog box from the List Item section, open the New Style list of options.
4. Select one of the five numbering options.

Although you can't automatically generate an outline with a different numbering system for each level, you can simulate this kind of outline with nested lists. See "Using Nested Lists" later in this chapter.

Making Definition Lists

A definition list is another list in HTML that doesn't use leading characters, such as bullets or numbers, in the list items. Definition lists are commonly used in glossaries or other types of documents in which you have a list of terms followed by their description or explanation.

Browsers generally render a definition list with the definition term flush left and the definition data indented, as shown in Figure 12-6. As you can see, no additional styling is added. You can, however, format either the item or the definition with the Text ➪ Style options.

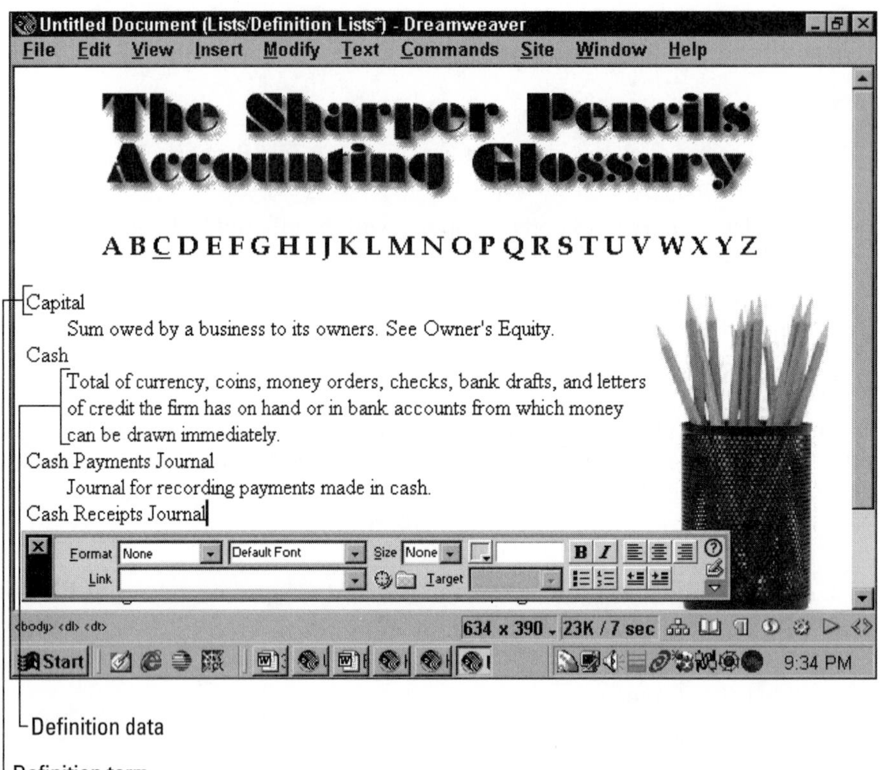

Figure 12-6: Definition lists are ideal for glossaries or other situations in which you have a list of terms followed by their definition.

To begin your definition list in Dreamweaver, follow these steps:

1. Choose Text ➪ List ➪ Definition List.
2. Type in the definition term and press Enter (Return) when you are finished. Dreamweaver indents the line.
3. Type in the definition data and press Enter (Return) when you are finished.
4. Repeat Steps 2 and 3 until you have finished your definition list.
5. Press Enter (Return) twice to stop entering definition list items.

If you have an extended definition, you may want to format it in more than one paragraph. Because definition lists are formatted with the terms and their definition data in alternating sequence, you have to use the line break tag, `<br>`, to create blank space under the definition if you want to separate it into paragraphs. Select the Insert Line Break button from the Objects palette to enter one or two `<br>` tags to separate paragraphs with one or two additional lines.

When you insert a definition list, Dreamweaver denotes it in code using the <dl>...</dl> tag pair. Definition terms are marked with a <dt> tag, and definition data uses the <dd> tag. A complete definition list looks like the following in HTML:

```
<dl>
  <dt>Capital</dt>
  <dd>Sum owed by a business to its owners. See Owner's Equity.</dd>
  <dt>Cash</dt>
  <dd>Total of currency, coins, money orders, checks, bank drafts, and letters
    of credit the firm has on hand or in bank accounts from which money can be
    drawn immediately.</dd>
  <dt>Cash Payments Journal</dt>
  <dd>Journal for recording payments made in cash.</dd>
</dl>
```

When originally proposed by the World Wide Web Consortium, the <dt> column was intended to take up only one-third of the browser window, but the latest, most common browsers don't follow this design specification.

You can vary the structure of a definition list from the standard definition term followed by the definition data format, but you have to code this variation by hand. For instance, if you want a series of consecutive terms with no definition in between, you need to insert the <dt>...</dt> pairs directly in the HTML Inspector.

Using Nested Lists

You can combine—nest—lists in almost any fashion. For instance, you can mix an ordered and unordered list to create a numbered list with bulleted points. You can have one numbered list inside of another numbered list. You can also start with one numbering style such as Roman Large, switch to another style such as Alphabet Small, and return to Roman Large to continue the sequence (like an outline).

Dreamweaver offers an easy route for making nested lists. The Indent button in the Text Property Inspector—when used within a list—automatically creates a nested list. As an example, the ordered list in Figure 12-7 has a couple of bulleted points (or unordered list items) inserted within it. Notice how the new items are indented one level.

Follow these steps to create a nested list in Dreamweaver:

1. Select the text in an existing list that you want to reformat with a different style.
2. In the Text Property Inspector, choose the Indent button. You can also select the Text ➪ Indent command. Dreamweaver indents the selected text and creates a separate list in the HTML code with the original list's properties.
3. Go to the List Properties dialog box and select another list type or style, as described in preceding sections.

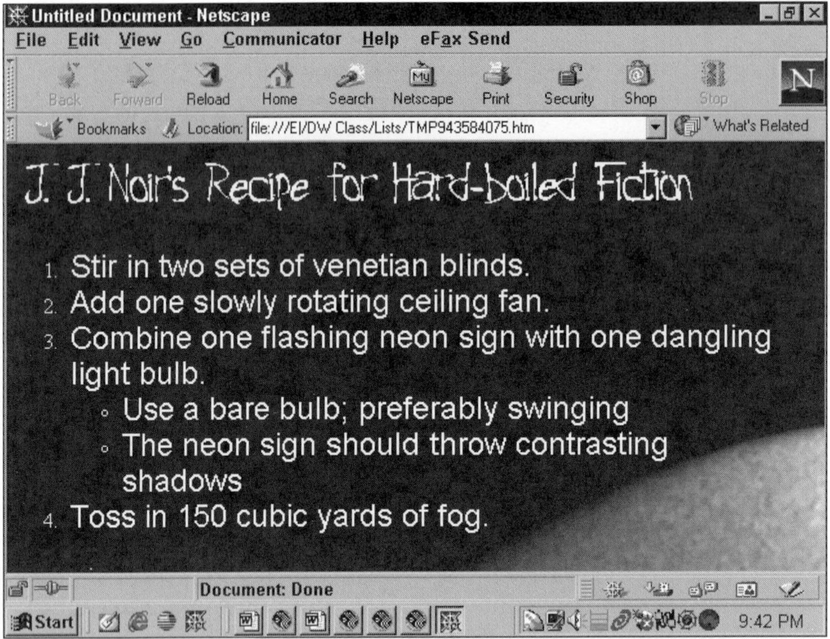

Figure 12-7: Dreamweaver automatically generates the code necessary to build nested lists when you use the Indent button on the Property Inspector.

You can unnest your list and reverse the effects of the Indent button by selecting the Outdent button in the Text Property Inspector or choosing Text ➪ Outdent. Be careful, however, when selecting your text for this operation. When you use the mouse to perform a click-and-drag selection, Dreamweaver tends to grab the closing list item tag above your intended selection. A better way to highlight the text in this case uses the Tag Selector on the status bar. Place the cursor in the indented list you want to outdent and choose the innermost <ol> or <ul> tag from the Tag Selector.

To examine the origins of the term *nested list*, take a look at the code created for this list type by Dreamweaver:

```
<ol>
  <li>Stir in two sets of venetian blinds.</li>
  <li>Add one slowly rotating ceiling fan.</li>
  <li>Combine one flashing neon sign with one dangling light bulb.</li>
    <ul>
      <li>Use a bare bulb, preferably swinging.</li>
      <li>The neon sign should throw contrasting shadows.</li>
    </ul>
  <li>Toss in 150 cubic yards of fog.</li>
</ol>
```

Notice how the unordered tag pair, <ul>...</ul>, is completely contained between the ordered list items.

If you don't indent your list items before you change the list format, Dreamweaver breaks the current list into three separate lists: one for the original list above the selected text, another for the selected text itself, and a third list for the items following the selected text. If you don't want this arrangement, choose the Indent button in the Text Property Inspector, and Dreamweaver nests the list as described previously.

Accessing Special List Types

Dreamweaver gives you access to a couple of special-use list types: menu lists and directory lists. When the tags for these lists — `<menu>` and `<dir>`, respectively — were included in the HTML 2.0 specification, they were intended to offer several ways to present lists of short items. Unfortunately, browsers tend to render both tags in the same manner: as an unordered list. You can use Cascading Style Sheets to restyle these built-in tags for use in 4.0 and higher browsers.

Menu lists

A menu list generally comprises single items, with each item on its own individual line.

Because menu lists are rendered as unordered lists with leading bullets, you probably want to display the menu list in a more compact manner. Add the attribute compact as follows:

```
<menu compact>
```

To apply a menu list style, follow these steps:

1. In an existing list, select one item that you want to convert to a menu list.
2. In the expanded Text Property Inspector, select the List Item button.
3. In the List Properties dialog box, open the List Type drop-down list and choose Menu List, as shown in Figure 12-8.
4. Click OK.

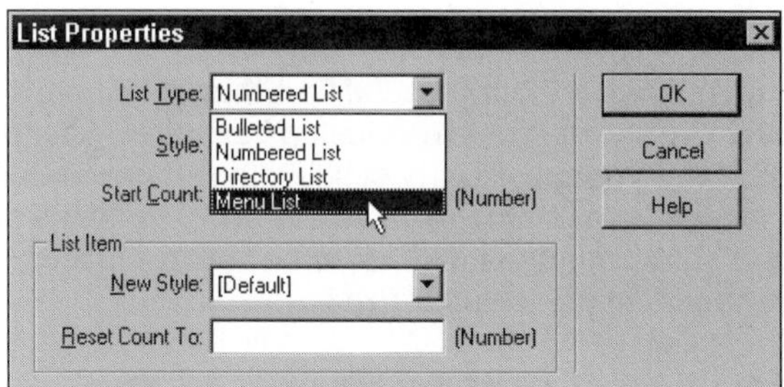

Figure 12-8: Making a menu list.

To apply CSS techniques to either the `<menu>` or the `<dir>` tags in Dreamweaver, you must either hand-code all of the entry or use a little trick. Here's the trick: Because Dreamweaver doesn't list the menu or directory list tags in its list of HTML tags to redefine in the New Style dialog box, type **menu** or **dir** in the list box, instead of picking it from a list. But be certain you're entering the missing tag names in the text box when Redefine HTML Tag is selected; otherwise, Dreamweaver puts a period in front of your tag name, and it won't be recognized.

Directory lists

The directory list was originally intended to provide Web designers with an easy way to create multiple-column lists of short items. Unfortunately, the most current browsers present the directory list's items in one long list, rather than in columns.

The directory list format is applied in the same way as the menu list, and here as well, most browsers render the format as an unordered list with bullets.

To apply a directory list style, follow these steps:

1. In the current list, select one item you want to convert to a directory list.
2. In the expanded Text Property Inspector, select the List Item button.
3. In the List Properties dialog box, open the List Type list (previously shown in Figure 12-8) and choose Directory List.
4. Click OK.

Nested directory lists exhibit a cool feature in most browsers—they automatically change the list style for each level. In many browsers, the outermost level is displayed with a bullet, the second level with a circle, and the third level with a square. Automatic outlining from an unexpected source! One drawback to note: Dreamweaver doesn't preview the changing styles—it only shows the bullets.

Dreamweaver Technique: Building Graphical Bullets

HTML unordered lists are functional and often useful, but they're not particularly decorative. A Web designer might very well want to spice up his bulleted list of items with graphics. Although CSS offers the possibility of selecting an image to use as the bullet, this solution is not available to Netscape browsers or 3.0 versions of Internet Explorer. Moreover, you don't have much control over the vertical placement of the bullet, so the image often appears higher than desired.

Substituting a graphical bullet for the HTML versions is practical and often desirable. Because a small, single image is used repeatedly, the impact on a Web page's size is negligible, and the image downloads quickly. You can include graphical bullets in two basic ways: inline and tables. Inline graphical bullets put the bullet image right next to the text, whereas the table technique keeps all the bullets in one column and the bullet items in another. Which technique you use depends on the length of the bulleted item. If your bulleted items are short enough so that they won't wrap, use the inline technique; on the other hand, if the text is likely or definitely wrapping from one line to the next, use the table technique.

To use graphic images as bullets in an inline technique, follow these steps:

1. Create your image in a graphics editor such as Fireworks and save the file so that it is accessible to your local site.
2. If necessary, convert your unordered list to standard paragraph format by selecting the entire list and deselecting the Bullet button on the Property Inspector.
3. Choose Insert Image from the Objects palette and place the graphic button before the first line item.
4. Select the correct vertical alignment for the image from the Align list on the image Property Inspector.

   Although your alignment choice may vary according to the height of your text and your image, Absolute Middle works in many situations.
5. If necessary, add a nonbreaking space or two between the image and the list item by pressing Ctrl+Shift+spacebar (Control+Shift+spacebar).
6. Select the image and any added nonbreaking spaces.
7. Ctrl+drag (Control+drag) the selection to copy it to the beginning of the next line item as shown on Figure 12-9.
8. Repeat Step 7 for each line item.

The following technique requires a basic understanding of tables in HTML in general and Dreamweaver in particular. If you're not familiar with inserting and formatting tables, you may want to look at Chapter 13 before proceeding.

If your text lines are too long, they wrap at the browser window and — here's the unsightly part — under the graphical bullet. To avoid this wrapping problem, use the table technique, detailed in the following steps:

1. Create your bullet in your favorite graphics program.
2. If necessary, convert your unordered list to standard paragraph format by selecting the entire list and deselecting the Bullet button on the Property Inspector.

Figure 12-9: Copying your graphic bullets after you've set the alignment saves you many steps later.

3. Position your cursor above the first line item and choose the Insert Table object from the Objects palette.

4. In the Insert Table dialog box, set the Columns value to 2 and the Rows to the number of line items you have. If desired, turn off the borders by setting Border value to 0. Click OK when you're done.

   The table is inserted in the Document window.

5. Select the first column of the table by dragging down its length.

6. In the Property Inspector, set the Horiz (horizontal alignment) value to Right and the Vert (vertical alignment) to Top.

7. Select the second column by dragging down its length.

8. In the Property Inspector, set the Horiz (horizontal alignment) value to Left and the Vert (vertical alignment) to Top.

9. Select the Insert Image object and place your bullet image in the first column, first row.

10. Select the first line item and drag it into the second column, first row.
11. Copy the bullet image from the first cell and paste it into the first column for every remaining row.
12. Repeat Step 10 for each of the remaining line items, putting each on its own row.

When you're done, the bullet images line up evenly as do the line items, as shown in Figure 12-10. You may find it necessary to adjust the vertical alignment on either the bullet or line item column to get the look you want.

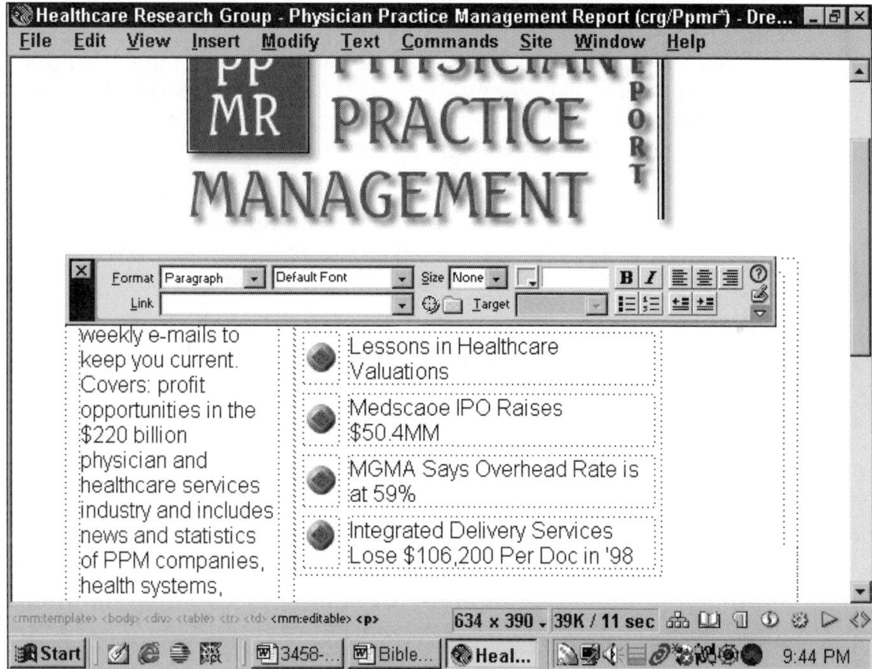

Figure 12-10: Placing bullet items in a table enables you to keep an equal spacing with longer, wrapping lines.

I've built a Dreamweaver extension that automates the process of replacing an unordered list with graphical bullets. If you have Fireworks 3, you can use the BulletBuilder command, which converts list items to paragraph lines and places a custom bullet — available in ten different shapes and any Fireworks style — before the line. You'll find this extension on CD-ROM 2 that accompanies this book.

Summary

Lists are extremely useful to the Web site designer from the perspectives of both content and layout. Dreamweaver offers point-and-click control over the full range of list capabilities.

- ✦ The three primary list types in HTML are unordered, ordered, and definition lists.
- ✦ Use unordered lists when you want to itemize your text in no particular order. Dreamweaver can apply any of the three built-in styles to unordered lists, or you can customize your own list style through style sheets.
- ✦ An ordered list is a numbered list. Items are automatically numbered when added, and the entire list is renumbered when items are rearranged or deleted. Dreamweaver gives you access to five different styles of numbering — everything from regular Arabic to Roman numerals.
- ✦ Definition lists are designed to display glossaries and other documents in which terms are followed by definitions. A definition list is generally rendered without leading characters such as bullets or numbers; instead, the list terms are displayed flush left, and the definitions are indented.
- ✦ Dreamweaver gives you the power to nest your lists at the touch of a button — the Indent button on the Text Property Inspector. Nested lists enable you to show different outline levels and to mix ordered and unordered lists.
- ✦ Menu and directory lists are also supported by Dreamweaver. Both of these special lists render in a similar fashion, but they can be adapted through style sheets for extensive use.
- ✦ It's easy to substitute graphic images for standard bullets in Dreamweaver. Two different techniques are used — inline and table — depending on the length of the line item.

In the next chapter, you learn how to create and use tables in Dreamweaver.

✦ ✦ ✦

P A R T

Incorporating Advanced HTML

✦ ✦ ✦ ✦

In This Part

✦ ✦ ✦ ✦

Setting Up Tables

✦ ✦ ✦ ✦

In This Chapter

All about tables in HTML

Setting up a Dreamweaver table

Customizing tables

Importing tabular data

Formatting tables

Using tables as a design tool

✦ ✦ ✦ ✦

Tables bring structure to a Web page. Whether used to align numbers in a spreadsheet or to arrange columns of text on a page, an HTML table brings a bit of order to other wise free-flowing content. Initially, tables were implemented to present raw data in a more readable format. More recently, Web designers have taken up tables as the most capable tool to control page layout.

Dreamweaver's implementation of tables reflects this current trend in Web page design. Drag-and-drop table sizing, easy organization of rows and columns, and instant table refor-matting all help get the job done in the shortest time possible. Table editing features enable you to select and modify anything in a table from a single cell to multiple columns. Moreover, using Dreamweaver commands, you can sort your table in a variety of ways or completely reformat it.

Although the absolute positioning capabilities offered by Dynamic HTML give Web designers more exact layout control, many Web designers use a combination of tools to get desired effects and maintain wide browser compatibility. In other words, HTML tables are going to be around for a long time.

HTML Table Fundamentals

A table is basically a grid that expands as you add text or images. Tables consist of three main components: rows, columns, and cells. *Rows* go across a table from left to right, and *columns* go up and down. A *cell* is the intersection of a row and a column; it's where you enter your information. Cells expand to fit whatever they hold. If you have enabled the table border, your browser shows the outline of the table and all its cells.

In HTML, all the structure and all the data of a table are contained between the table tag pair, `<table>` and `</table>`. The `<table>` tag can take numerous attributes, determining a table's width and height (which can be given in absolute measurement or as a percentage of the screen) as well as the border, alignment on the page, and background color. You can also control the size of the spacing between cells and the amount of padding within cells.

HTML uses a strict hierarchy when describing a table. You can see this clearly in Listing 13-1, which shows the HTML generated from a default table in Dreamweaver.

Listing 13-1: Code for an HTML Table

```
<table border="1" width="75%">
  <tr>
    <td> </td>
    <td> </td>
    <td> </td>
  </tr>
  <tr>
    <td> </td>
    <td> </td>
    <td> </td>
  </tr>
  <tr>
    <td> </td>
    <td> </td>
    <td> </td>
  </tr>
</table>
```

The ` ` seen in the table code is HTML for a nonbreaking space. Dreamweaver inserts the code in each empty table cell because some browsers collapse the cell without it. Enter any text or image in the cell, and Dreamweaver automatically removes the ` ` code.

Rows

After the opening `<table>` tag comes the first row tag `<tr>`. Within the current row, you can specify attributes for horizontal alignment or vertical alignment. In addition, recent browsers recognize row color as an added option.

Cells

Cells are marked in HTML with the `<td>...</td>` tag pair. No specific code exists for a column; rather, columns are seen as the number of cells within a row. For example, in Listing 1-1, notice the three sets of `<td>` tags between each `<tr>` pair. This means the table has three columns. A cell can span more than one row or column — in these cases, you see a `rowspan=value` or `colspan=value` attribute in the `<td>` tag.

Cells can also be given horizontal or vertical alignment attributes; these attributes override any similar attributes specified by the table row. When you give a cell a particular width, all the cells in that column are affected. Width can be specified in either an absolute pixel measurement or as a percentage of the overall table.

After the initial `<table>` tag, you can place an optional caption for the table. In Dreamweaver, you have to enter the `<caption>` tag by hand or through your HTML editor.

Column/row headings

A special type of cell called a *table header* is used for column and row headings. Information in these cells is marked with a `<th>` tag and is generally rendered in boldface, centered within the cell.

Inserting Tables in Dreamweaver

You can control almost all of a table's HTML features through Dreamweaver's point-and-click interface. To insert a Dreamweaver table in the current cursor position, use one of the following three methods:

✦ Select the Insert Table button on the Objects palette.

✦ Choose Insert ➪ Table from the menus.

✦ Use the keyboard shortcut: Ctrl+Alt+T (Command+Option+T).

The Insert Table dialog box, shown in Figure 13-1, contains the following default values when it is first displayed:

Attribute	*Default*	*Description*
Rows	3	The number of horizontal rows.
Columns	3	The number of vertical columns.
Width	75%	Sets the preset width of the table. Available in a percentage of the containing element (screen, layer, or another table) or an absolute pixel size.

Continued

Attribute	*Default*	*Description*
Border	1 pixel	The width of the border around each cell and the entire table.
Cell Padding	(Empty)	The space between a cell's border and its contents. Although not shown, Dreamweaver displays 1 pixel of cell padding unless a different value is entered.
Cell Spacing	(Empty)	The number of pixels between each cell. Although not shown, Dreamweaver displays 2 pixels of cell spacing unless a different value is entered.

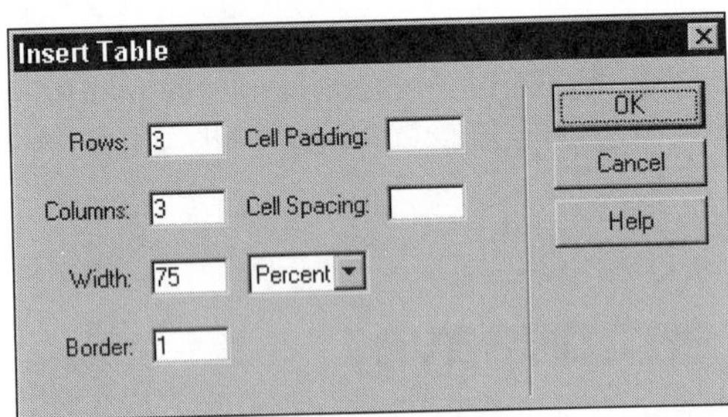

Figure 13-1: The Insert Table dialog box starts out with a default of three columns and three rows; you can adjust as needed.

If you aren't sure of the number of rows and/or columns you need, put in your best guess—you can add or delete rows or columns as necessary.

The default table is sized to take up 75 percent of the browser window. You can alter this percentage by changing the value in the Width text box. The table maintains this proportion as you add text or images, except in two situations:

✦ When an image is larger than the specified percentage

✦ When the `nowrap` attribute is used for the cell or table row and there is too much text to fit

In either case, the percentage set for the table is ignored, and the cell and table expand to accommodate the text or image. (For further information on the `nowrap` attribute, see the section "Cell Wrap," later in this chapter.)

If you prefer to enter the table width as an absolute pixel value, as opposed to the relative percentage, type the number of pixels in the Width text box and select pixels in the drop-down list of width options.

Figure 13-2 shows three tables: At the top is the default table with the width set to 75 percent. The middle table, set to 100 percent, will take up the full width of the browser window. The third table is fixed at 300 pixels — approximately half of a 640×480 window.

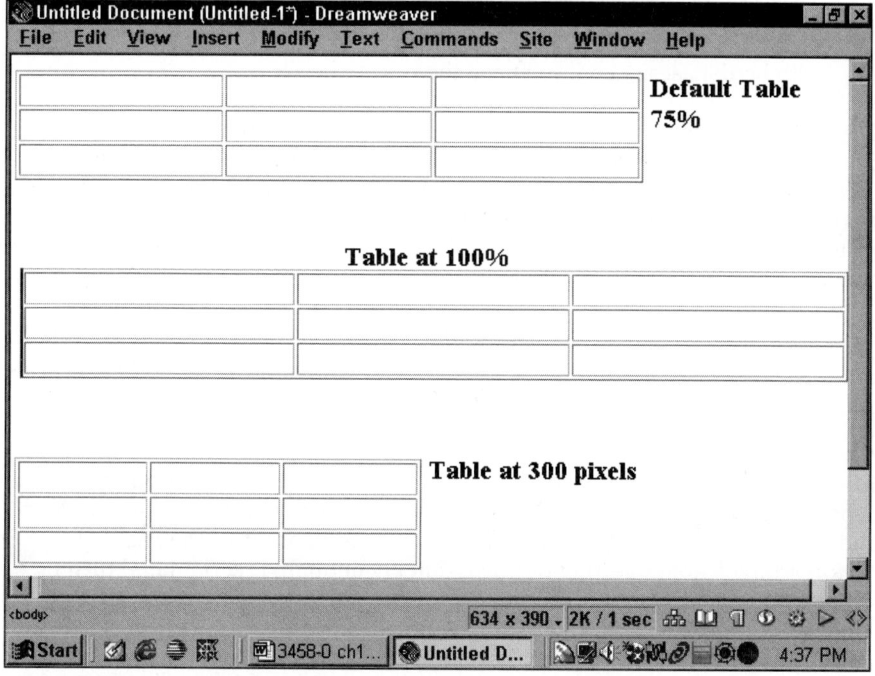

Figure 13-2: The width of a table can be relative to the browser window or set to an absolute width in pixels.

You don't have to declare a width for your table at all. If you delete the value in the Width text box of the Insert Table dialog box, your table starts out as small as possible and only expands to accommodate inserted text or images. However, this can make it difficult to position your cursor inside a cell to enter content. You can always delete any set size – pixel or percentage – later.

Setting Table Preferences

Two preferences directly affect tables. Both can be set by choosing Edit ➪ Preferences and looking in the General category.

The first pertinent option is the Show Dialog when Inserting Objects checkbox. If this option is turned off, Dreamweaver always inserts a default table (3 rows by 3 columns at 75 percent width of the screen with a 1-pixel border), without displaying a dialog box and asking for your input. Should you wish to change these values, you can adjust them from the Table Property Inspector once the table has been inserted.

New Feature

In Dreamweaver 3, the Insert Table object remembers your last settings, so you're no longer forced to keep changing the default settings to something you prefer. For example, if you primarily use tables without a border, choose the Insert Table object, and in the Border field of the dialog box, enter a 0. You won't have to deal with borders again, until you need them.

The second notable preference is labeled Faster Table Editing (Deferred Update). Because tables expand and contract dynamically depending on their contents, Dreamweaver gives you the option of turning off the continual updating. (Depending on the speed of your system, the updating can slow down your table input.) If the Faster Table Editing option is enabled, the table is updated whenever you click outside of it or when you press the keyboard shortcut, Ctrl+Space (Command+Space).

Note

If you have enabled Faster Table Editing and begin typing in one cell of your table, notice that the text wraps within the cell, and the table expands vertically. However, when you click outside of the table or press Ctrl+Space (Command+Space), the table cells adjust horizontally as well, completing the redrawing of the table.

You should decide whether to leave the Faster Table Editing option on or turn it off, depending on your system and the complexity of your tables. Nested tables tend to update more slowly, and you may need to take advantage of the Faster Table Editing option if tables aren't getting redrawn quickly enough. I recommend turning off Faster Table Editing until it seems that you need it.

Modifying Tables

Most modifications to tables start in the Property Inspector. Dreamweaver helps you manage the basic table parameters — width, border, and alignment — and provides attributes for the other useful but more arcane features of a table, such as converting table width from pixels to percentage of the screen, and vice versa.

Selecting table elements

As with text or images, the first step in altering a table (or any of its elements) is selection. Dreamweaver simplifies the selection process, making it easy to change both the properties and the contents of entire tables, selected rows or columns, and even nonadjacent cells. You can change the font size and color of a row with a click or two of the mouse — instead of highlighting and modifying each individual cell.

In Dreamweaver, you can select the following elements of a table:

✦ The entire table

✦ A single row

✦ Multiple rows, either adjacent or separate

✦ A single column

✦ Multiple columns, either adjacent or separate

✦ A single cell

✦ Multiple cells, either adjacent or separate

Once a table element is selected, you can modify its contents.

Selecting an entire table

Several methods are available for selecting the entire table, whether you're a menu- or mouse-oriented designer. To select the table via a menu, do one of the following:

✦ Choose Modify ➪ Table ➪ Select Table.

✦ With the cursor positioned in the table, choose Edit ➪ Select All or use the keyboard shortcut, Ctrl+A (Command+A).

✦ Right-click (Control+click) inside a table to display the shortcut menu and choose Table ➪ Select Table.

To select an entire table with the mouse, use one of these techniques:

✦ Click the bottom or right border of the table. You can also click anywhere along the table border when the pointer becomes a four-sided arrow.

✦ Select the `<table>` tag in the Tag Selector.

✦ Click immediately to one side of the table and drag the mouse over the table.

However you select the table, the selected table is surrounded by a black border with sizing handles on the right, bottom, and bottom-right corner (as shown in Figure 13-3), just like a selected graphic.

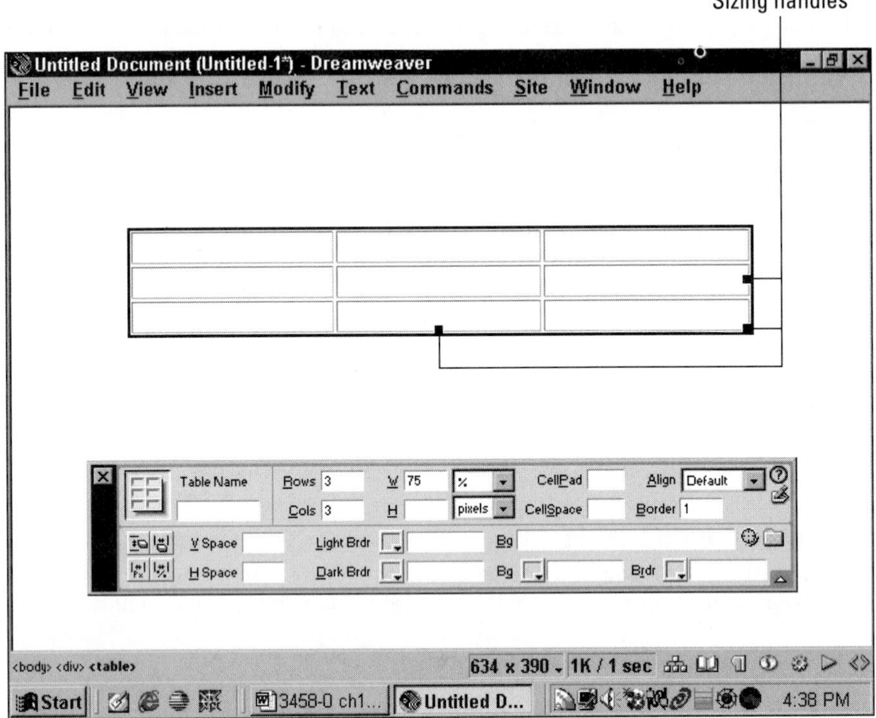

Figure 13-3: A selected table can be identified by the black border outlining the table and the three sizing handles.

Selecting a row or column

Altering rows or columns of table text without Dreamweaver is a major time-consuming chore. Each cell has to be individually selected, and the changes applied. Dreamweaver 3 has an intuitive method for selecting single or multiple columns and rows, comparable — and in some ways, superior — to major word processing programs.

As with entire tables, you have several methods for selecting columns or rows. None of the techniques, however, use the menus; row and column selection is handled primarily with the mouse. In fact, you can select an entire row or column with one click.

The one-click method for selecting a single column or row requires that you position your pointer directly over the column or to the left of the row you want to choose. Move the pointer slowly toward the table — when the pointer becomes a single arrow, with the arrowhead pointing down for columns and to the right for rows, click the mouse. All the cells in the selected column or row are bounded with a black border. Any changes now made in the Property Inspector, such as a change in font size or color, affect the selected column or row.

You can select multiple, contiguous columns or rows by dragging the single arrow pointer across several columns or rows. To select a number of columns or rows that are not next to one another, use the Ctrl (Command) key. Press the Ctrl (Command) key while selecting each individual column, using the one-click method. (Not even Word 2000 can handle this degree of complex table selection.)

If you have trouble positioning the mouse so that the single arrow pointer appears, you can use two other methods for selecting columns or rows. With the first method, you can click and drag across all the cells in a column or row. The second method uses another keyboard modifier, the Shift key. With this technique, click once in the first cell of the column or row. Then, hold down the Shift key while you click in the final cell of the column or row. You can also use this technique to select multiple adjacent columns or rows; just click in another column's or row's last cell.

Selecting cells

Sometimes you need to change the background color of just a few cells in a table, but not the entire row—or you might need to merge several cells to form one wide column span. In these situations, and many others, you can use Dreamweaver 3's cell selection capabilities. Like columns and rows, you can select multiple cells, whether they are adjacent to one another or separate.

Individual cells are generally selected by dragging the mouse across one or more cell boundaries. To select a single cell, click anywhere in the cell and drag the mouse into another cell. As you pass the border between the two cells, the initial cell is highlighted. If you continue dragging the mouse across another cell boundary, the second cell is selected, and so on. Note that you have to drag the mouse into another cell and not cross the table border onto the page; for example, to highlight the lower-right cell of a table, you need to drag the mouse up or to the left.

You can also select a single cell by pressing the Ctrl (Command) key and clicking once in the cell, or you can select the rightmost `<td>` tag in the Tag Selector.

Extended cell selection in Dreamweaver is handled identically to extended text selection in most word processing programs. To select adjacent cells, click in the first desired cell, press and hold the Shift key, and click in the final desired cell. Dreamweaver selects all in a rectangular area, using the first cell as the upper-left corner of the rectangle and the last cell as the lower-right. You could, for instance, select an entire table by clicking in the upper-left cell and then Shift+clicking the lower-right cell.

Just as the Shift key is used to make adjacent cell selections, the Ctrl (Command) key is used for all nonadjacent cell selections. You can highlight any number of individual cells — whether or not they are next to one another — by pressing the Ctrl (Command) key while you click in the cell.

If you Ctrl+click (Command+click) a cell that is already selected, that cell is deselected – regardless of the method you used to select the cell initially.

Editing a table's contents

Before you learn how to change a table's attributes, let's look at basic editing techniques. Editing text in Dreamweaver tables is slightly different from editing text outside of tables. When you begin to enter text into a table cell, the table borders expand to accommodate your new data. The other cells appear to shrink, but they, too, expand once you start typing in text or inserting an image. Unless a cell's width is specified, the cell currently being edited expands or contracts, and the other cells are forced to adjust their width. Figure 13-4 shows the same table (with one row and three columns) in three different states. In the top table, only the first cell contains text; notice how the other cells have contracted. In the middle table, text has been entered into the second cell as well, and you can see how the first cell is now smaller. Finally, in the bottom table, all three cells contain text, and the other two cells have adjusted their width to compensate for the expanding third cell.

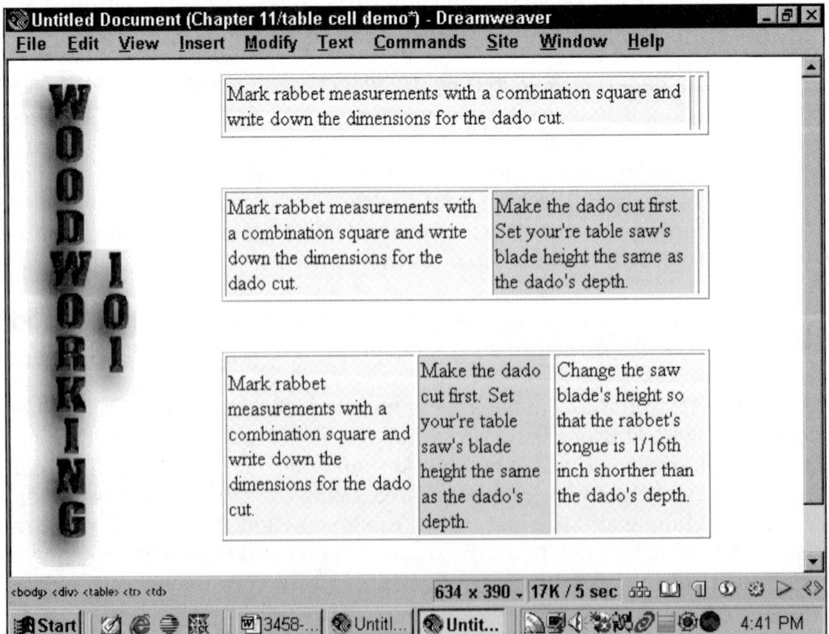

Figure 13-4: As text is entered into a cell, the cell expands; other cells contract, even if they already contain text.

If you look closely at the bottom table in Figure 13-4, you can also see that the text doesn't line up vertically. That's because the default vertical alignment in Dreamweaver, as in most browsers, provides for entries to be positioned in the middle of the cell. (Later in this section, you learn how to adjust the vertical alignment.)

Moving through a table

When you've finished entering your text in the first cell, you can move to the next cell in the row by pressing the Tab key. When you reach the end of a row, pressing Tab takes your cursor to the first cell of the next row. To go backward, cell to cell, press Shift+Tab.

Pressing Tab has a special function when you're in the last cell of a row—it adds a new row, with the same column configuration as the current one.

The Home and End keys take you to the beginning and end, respectively, of the cursor's current line. If a cell's contents are large enough for the text to wrap in the cell, move to the top of the current cell by pressing Ctrl+Home (Command+up arrow or Command+Home). To get the bottom of the current cell in such a circumstance, press Ctrl+End (Command+down arrow).

When you're at the beginning or end of the contents in a cell, the arrow keys can also be used to navigate from cell to cell. Use the left and right arrows to move from cell to cell in a row, and the up and down arrows to move down a column. When you come to the end of a row or column, the arrow keys move to the first cell in the next row or column. If you're moving left to right horizontally, the cursor goes from the end of one row to the beginning of the next row—and vice-versa, if you move from right to left. When moving from top to bottom vertically, the cursor goes from the end of one column to the start of the next, and vice-versa when moving bottom to top.

Cutting, copying, and pasting in tables

In the early days of Web design (about three years ago), woe if you should accidentally leave out a cell of information. It was often almost faster to redo the entire table than to make room by meticulously cutting and pasting everything, one cell at a time. Dreamweaver ends that painstaking work forever with its advanced cutting and pasting features. You can copy a range of cells from one table to another and main-tain all the attributes, such as color and alignment as well as the content—text or images—or you can copy just the contents and ignore the attributes.

Dreamweaver has one basic restriction to table cut-and-paste operations: Your selected cells must form a rectangle. In other words, although you can select non-adjacent cells, columns, or rows and modify their properties, you can't cut or copy them. Should you try, you get a message from Dreamweaver like the one shown in Figure 13-5; the table above the notification in the figure illustrates an incorrect cell selection.

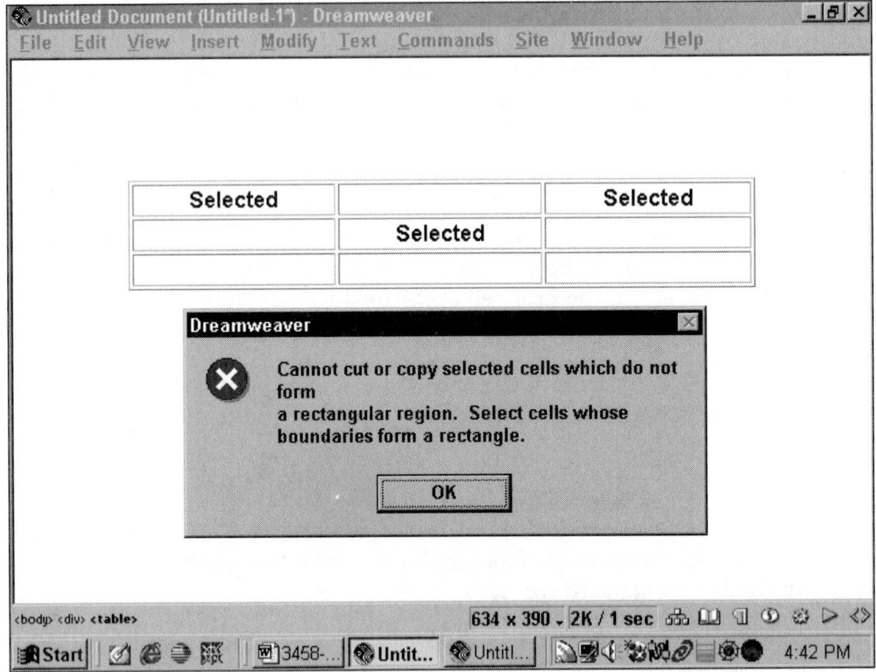

Figure 13-5: Dreamweaver enables you to cut or copy selected cells only when they form a rectangle, unlike the cells in the table depicted here.

Copying attributes and contents

When you copy or cut a cell using the regular commands, Dreamweaver automatically copies everything—content, formatting, and cell format—in the selected cell. Then, pasting the cell reproduces it all—however, you can get different results depending on where the cell (or column or row) is pasted.

To cut or copy both the contents and the attributes of any cell, row, or column, follow these steps:

1. Select the cells you wish to cut or copy.

   Remember that to cut or copy a range of cells in Dreamweaver, they must form a solid rectangular region.

2. To copy cells, choose Edit ➪ Copy or use the keyboard shortcut, Ctrl+C (Command+C).

3. To cut cells, choose Edit ➪ Cut or use the keyboard shortcut, Ctrl+X (Command+X).

   If you cut an individual cell, the contents are removed, but the cell remains. If, however, you cut an entire row or column, the cells are removed.

4. Position your cursor to paste the cells in the desired location:

   - To replace a cell with a cell on the clipboard, click anywhere in the cell to be replaced. If you cut or copied multiple cells that do not make up a full column or row, click in the upper-left corner of the cells you wish to replace. For example, a range of six cells in a 2×3 configuration replaces the same configuration when pasted.

     Dreamweaver alerts you to the differences if you try to paste one configuration of cells into a different cell configuration.

   - To insert a new row with the row on the clipboard, click anywhere in the row below where you'd like the new row to appear.
   - To insert a new column with the column on the clipboard, click anywhere in the column to the right of where you'd like the new column to appear.
   - To replace an existing row or column in a table, select the row or column. If you've cut or copied multiple rows or columns, you must select an equivalent size and shape of cells to replace.
   - To insert a new table based on the copied or cut cells, click anywhere outside of the table.

5. Paste the copied or cut cells by choosing Edit ➪ Paste or pressing Ctrl+V (Command+V).

To move a row or column that you've cut from the interior of a table to the exterior (the right or bottom), you have to first expand the number of cells in the table. To do this, first select the table by choosing Modify ➪ Table ➪ Select Table or using one of the other techniques previously described. Next, in the Table Property Inspector, increase the number of rows or columns by altering the values in the Rows or Cols text boxes. Finally, select the newly added rows or columns and choose Edit ➪ Paste.

Copying contents only

It's not uncommon to need to move data from one cell to another, while keeping the destination cell's attributes, such as its background color or border, intact. For this, you need to use Dreamweaver's facility for copying just the contents of a cell.

To copy only the contents, you select a cell as previously described and then, instead of choosing Edit ➪ Copy, choose Edit ➪ Copy Text Only or use the keyboard shortcut, Ctrl+Shift+C (Command+Shift+C). Instead of selecting the entire cell, you can select a portion of the text and use the Copy Text Only command to avoid pasting in the format of the copied text.

Unlike the copying of both contents and attributes described in the previous section, content-only copying has a couple of limitations:

- ✦ First, you can copy the contents only one cell at a time. You can't copy contents only across multiple cells.
- ✦ Second, you can't replace the entire contents of one cell with another and maintain all the text attributes (font, color, and size) of the destination cell. If you select all the text to be replaced, Dreamweaver also selects the `<font>` tag that holds the attributes and replaces those as well. The workaround is to select all but one letter or word, paste the contents, and then delete the unwanted text.

Working with table properties

The `<table>` tag has a large number of attributes, and most of them can be modified through Dreamweaver's Property Inspector. As with all objects, the table must be selected before it can be altered. Choose Modify ➪ Table ➪ Select Table or use one of the other selection techniques previously described.

Once you've selected the table, if the Property Inspector is open, it presents the table properties as shown in Figure 13-6. Otherwise, you can open the Table Property Inspector by choosing Window ➪ Properties Inspector.

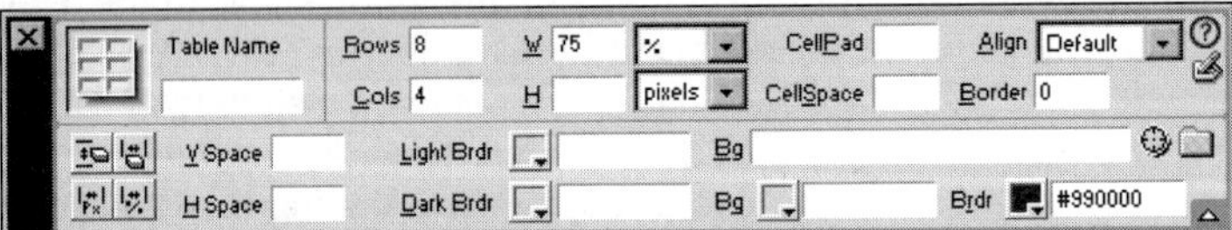

Figure 13-6: The expanded Table Property Inspector gives you control over all the tablewide attributes.

Setting alignment

Aligning a table in Dreamweaver goes beyond the expected left, right, and center options—you can also make a table into a free-floating object around which text can wrap to the left or right.

With HTML, you can align a table using two different methods, and each gives you a different effect. Using the text alignment method (Text ➪ Alignment) results in the conventional positioning (left, right, and center), and using the Table Property Inspector method enables you to wrap text around your realigned table. Figure 13-7 compares some of the different results you get from aligning your table with the two methods.

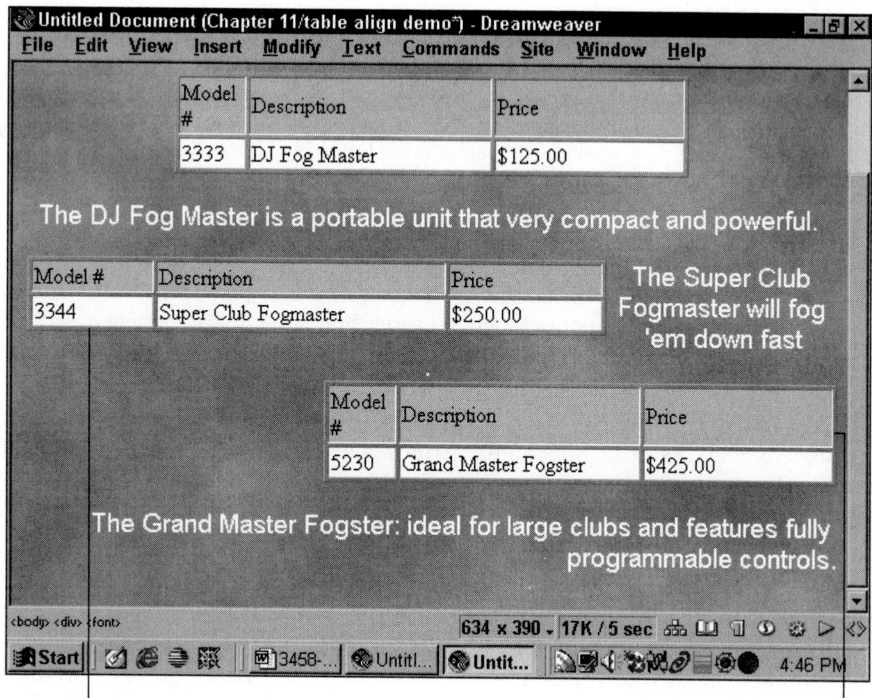

Figure 13-7: Tables can be centered, as well as aligned left or right—with or without text wrapping.

To align your table without text wrapping, follow these steps:

1. Select your table using one of the methods described earlier.
2. In the Property Inspector, make sure the Align option is set to Default.
3. Select the Text ⇨ Alignment command and then choose one of the three options: Left, Center, or Right.

   Dreamweaver surrounds your table code with a division tag pair, `<div>...</div>`, with an `align` attribute set to your chosen value.

To align your table with text wrapping, making your table into a floating object, follow these steps:

1. Select the table.
2. In the Table Property Inspector, open the Align drop-down list and choose one of the four options:

Alignment Option	*Result*
Default	No alignment is written. Table aligns to the browser's default, usually left, with no text wrapping.
Left	Aligns the table to the left side of the browser window and wraps text around the right side.
Right	Aligns the table to the right side of the browser window and wraps text around the left side.
Center	The table aligns to the center of the browser window. Text does not wrap around either side. Note: This alignment option works only with 4.0 browsers.

Dreamweaver codes these alignment attributes in the `<table>` tag. As with floating images, Dreamweaver places an anchor point for floating elements on the Web page. However, you cannot drag-and-drop or cut-and-paste the anchor point, unlike most other Invisible symbols, for a floating table.

Resizing a table

The primary sizing control on the Table Property Inspector is the Width text box. You can enter a new width value for the entire table in either a screen percentage or pixels. Just enter your value in the Width text box and then select % or pixels in the drop-down list of options.

Dreamweaver also provides a quick and intuitive way to resize the overall table width, column widths, or row height. Pass your pointer over any of the table's borders, and the pointer becomes a two-headed arrow; this is the resizing pointer. When you see the resizing pointer, you can click and drag any border to new dimensions.

As noted earlier, tables are initially sized according to their contents. Once you move a table border in Dreamweaver, however, the new sizes are written directly into the HTML code, and the column width or row height is fixed — unless the contents cannot fit. If, for example, an inserted image is 115 pixels wide and the cell has a width of only 90 pixels, the cell expands to fit the image. The same is true if you try to fit an extremely long, unbroken text string, such as a complex URL, in a cell that's too narrow to hold it.

Dreamweaver enables you to set the height of a table using the Height text box in much the same way as the Width box. However, the height of a table — whether in pixels or a percentage — is maintained only as long as the contents do not require a larger size. A table's width, though, takes precedence over its height, and a table expands vertically before it expands horizontally.

Changes to a cell or column's width are shown in the `<td>` tags, as are changes to a row's height and width, using the `width` and `height` attribute, respectively. You can see these changes by selecting the table, cell, column, or row affected and looking at the W (Width) and H (Height) text box values.

For an overall view of what happens when you resize a cell, row, or column, it's best to look at the HTML. Here's the HTML for an empty table, resized:

```
<table border="1" width="70%">
  <tr>
    <td width="21%"> </td>
    <td width="34%"> </td>
    <td width="45%"> </td>
  </tr>
  <tr>
    <td width="21%" height="42"> </td>
    <td width="34%" height="42"> </td>
    <td width="45%" height="42"> </td>
  </tr>
  <tr>
    <td width="21%" height="42"> </td>
    <td width="34%" height="42"> </td>
    <td width="45%" height="42"> </td>
  </tr>
</table>
```

Notice how all the widths for the cells and the entire table are expressed as percentages. If the table width were initially set at a pixel value, the cell widths would have been, too. The row height values, on the other hand, are shown as an absolute measurement in pixels.

You can switch from percentages to pixels in all the table measurements, and even clear all the values at once—with the click of the right button. Four measurement controls appear in the lower-left portion of the expanded Table Property Inspector, as shown in Figure 13-8.

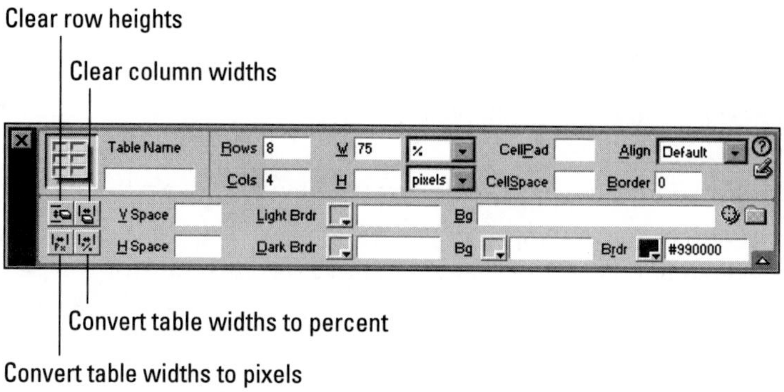

Clear row heights

Clear column widths

Convert table widths to percent

Convert table widths to pixels

Figure 13-8: You can make tablewide changes with the four control buttons in the Table Property Inspector.

From left to right, the measurement controls are as follows:

Measurement Control Button	*Description*
Clear Row Heights	Erases all the `height` attributes in the current table
Clear Column Widths	Deletes all the `width` attributes found in the `<td>` tags
Convert Table Widths to Pixels	Translates the current widths of all cells and for the entire table from percentages to pixels
Convert Table Widths to Percent	Translates the current widths of all cells and for the entire table from pixels to percentages

Selecting Clear Row Heights doesn't affect the table height value.

If you clear both row heights and column widths, the table goes back to its "grow as needed" format and, if empty, shrinks to its smallest possible size.

When converting width percentages to pixels, and vice versa, keep in mind that the percentages are relative to the size of the browser window—and in the development phase that browser window is Dreamweaver. You should expand Dreamweaver's Document window to the same sizes as what you expect to be seen in various browser settings.

Inserting rows and columns

The default Dreamweaver table configuration of three columns and three rows can be changed at any time. You can add rows or columns almost anywhere in a table, using various methods.

You have three methods for adding a single row:

✦ Position the cursor in the last cell of the last row and press Tab to add a new row below the present one.

✦ Choose Modify ➪ Table ➪ Insert Row to insert a new row above the current row.

✦ Right-click (Control+click) to open the shortcut menu and select Table ➪ Insert Row. Rows added in this way are inserted above the current row.

You have two ways to add a new column to your table:

✦ Choose Modify ⇨ Table ⇨ Insert Column to insert a new column to the left of the current column.

✦ Right-click (Control+click) to open the shortcut menu and select Table ⇨ Insert Column from the shortcut menu. The column is inserted to the left of the current column.

You can add multiple rows and columns in one of two different ways:

✦ Increase the number of rows indicated in the Rows text box of the Table Property Inspector. All new rows added in this manner appear below the last table row. Similarly, you can increase the number of columns indicated in the Cols text box of the Table Property Inspector. Columns added in this way appear to the right of the last column.

✦ Use the Insert Rows or Columns dialog box.

The Insert Rows or Columns feature enables you to include any number of rows or columns anywhere relative to your current cursor position.

To add multiple columns using the Insert Rows or Columns dialog box, follow these steps:

1. Open the Insert Rows or Columns dialog box (shown in Figure 13-9) by selecting Modify ⇨ Table ⇨ Insert Rows or Columns or by choosing Table ⇨ Insert Rows or Columns from the shortcut menu.

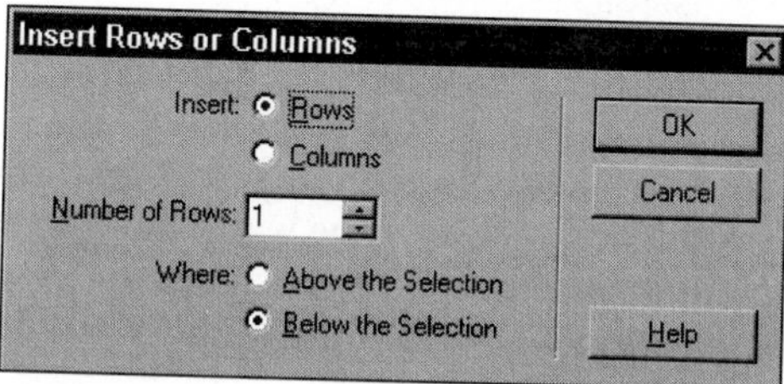

Figure 13-9: Use the Insert Rows or Columns feature to add several columns or rows simultaneously.

2. Select either Rows or Columns.

3. Enter the number of rows or columns you wish to insert—you can either type in a value or use the arrows to increase or decrease the number.

4. Select where you want the rows or columns to be inserted.
   - If you have selected the Rows option, you can insert the rows either Above or Below the Selection (the current row).
   - If you have selected the Columns options, you can insert the columns either Before or After the Current Column.
5. Click OK when you're finished.

Deleting rows and columns

When you want to delete a column or row, you can use either the shortcut menu or the Table Property Inspector. On the shortcut menu, you can remove the current column or row by choosing Delete Column or Delete Row, respectively. Using the Table Property Inspector, you can delete multiple columns and rows by reducing the numbers in the Cols or Rows text boxes. Columns are deleted from the right side of the table, and rows are removed from the bottom.

Watch out—exercise extreme caution when deleting columns or rows. Dreamweaver does not ask for confirmation and removes these columns and/or rows whether or not data exists in them.

Setting table borders and backgrounds

Borders are the solid outlines of the table itself. A border's width is measured in pixels; the default width is 1 pixel. This width can be altered in the Border field of the Table Property Inspector.

You can make the border invisible by specifying a border of 0 width. You can still resize your table by clicking and dragging the borders, even when the border is set to 0. When the View ⇨ Table Borders option is selected, Dreamweaver displays a thin dashed line to represent the border.

When the border is visible, you can also see each cell outlined. The width of the outline around the cells stays constant, regardless of the width of the border. However, you can control the amount of space between each cell with the Cell Space value in the Table Property Inspector, covered later in this chapter.

To change the width of a border in Dreamweaver, select your table and enter a new value in the Border text box. With a wider border, you can see the default shading: The top and left side are a lighter shade, and the bottom and right sides are darker. This gives the table border a pseudo-3D appearance. Figure 13-10 shows single-cell tables with borders of various widths.

In Dreamweaver, you can assign colors to the border, and to both the light and dark sides of the border. Each of these colors is chosen through the Table Property Inspector, as follows:

✦ To choose a color for the border, select the Border color swatch or enter a color name in the adjacent text box.

✦ To choose a color for the light (top and left) border, select the Light Brdr color swatch or enter a color name in the adjacent text box.

✦ To choose a color for the dark (bottom and right) border, select the Dark Brdr color swatch or enter a color name in the adjacent text box.

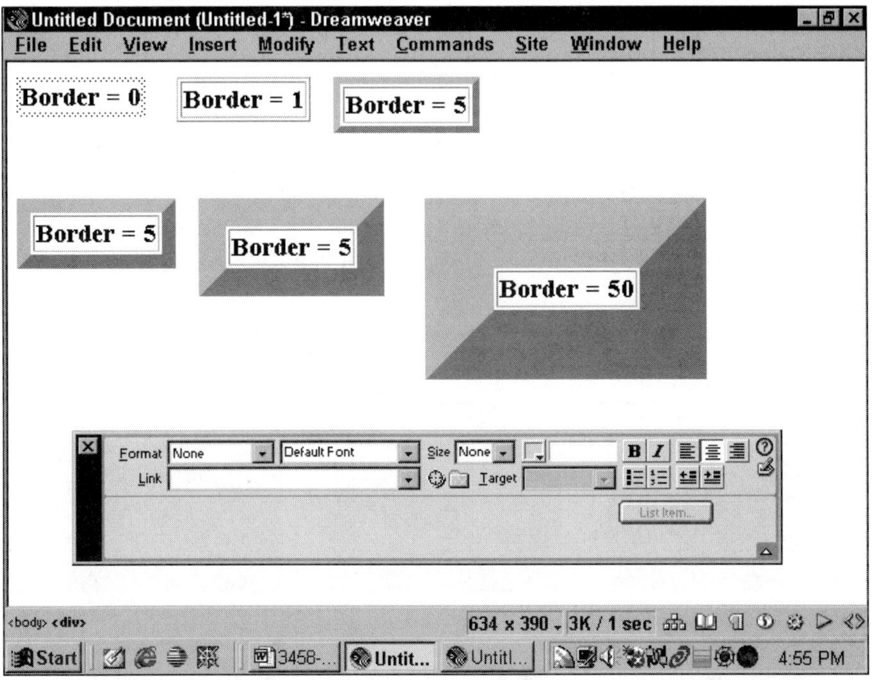

Figure 13-10: Changing the width of the border can give your table a 3D look.

If you assign a border color, any Light Brdr and/or Dark Brdr choices override it.

Tip

You can change the "light source" of the shadow for your table. To make the light appear to come from the bottom right instead of the upper left, choose a dark shade for the Light Brdr color and a light shade for the Dark Brdr color.

In addition to colored borders, a table can also have a colored background. (By default, the table is initially transparent.) Choose the background color in the Table Property Inspector by selecting a color in the Bg Color swatch or entering a color name in the adjacent text box. As you see later in the chapter, you can also assign background colors to rows, columns, and individual cells — if used, these specific colors all override the background color of the overall entire table.

Working with cell spacing and cell padding

HTML gives you two methods to add white space in tables. Cell spacing controls the width between each cell, and cell padding controls the margins within each cell. These values can be set independently through the Table Property Inspector.

Although not indicated in the Table Property Inspector, the default value is 2 pixels for cell spacing and 1 pixel for cell padding. Some Web page designs call for a close arrangement of cells and are better served by changing either (or both) the CellSpace or CellPad values to 1 or 0.

To change the amount of white space between each cell in a table, enter a new value in the CellSpace text box of the Table Property Inspector. If you want to adjust the amount of white space between the borders of the cell and the actual cell data, alter the value in the CellPad text box of the Table Property Inspector. Figure 13-11 shows an example of a table with wide (10 pixels) cell spacing and cell padding values.

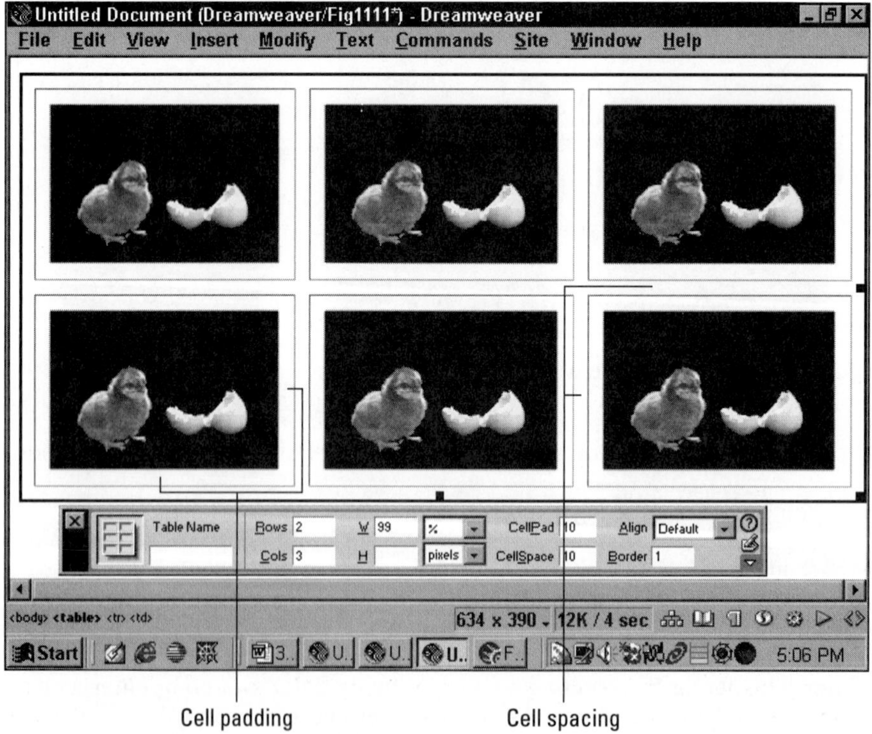

Figure 13-11: You can add additional white space between each cell (cell spacing) or within each cell (cell padding).

Merging and splitting cells

You have seen how cells in HTML tables can extend across (span) multiple columns or rows. By default, a cell spans one column or one row. Increasing a cell's span enables you to group any number of topics under one heading. You are effectively merging one cell with another to create a larger cell. Likewise, a cell can be split into multiple rows or columns.

Dreamweaver enables you to combine and divide cells in two different ways. If you're more comfortable with the concept of merging and splitting cells, you can use two handy buttons on the Property Inspector. If, on the other hand, you prefer the older method of increasing and decreasing row or column span, you can still access these commands through the main and shortcut menus.

To combine two or more cells, first select the cells you want to merge. Then, from the Property Inspector, select the Merge Cells button or press the keyboard shortcut M. If the Merge button is not available, multiple cells have not been selected.

To divide a cell, follow these steps:

1. Position your cursor in the cell to split.
2. From the Property Inspector, select the Split Cell button or press the keyboard shortcut, Ctrl+Alt+S (Command+Option+S).

   The Split Cell dialog box (shown in Figure 13-12) appears.

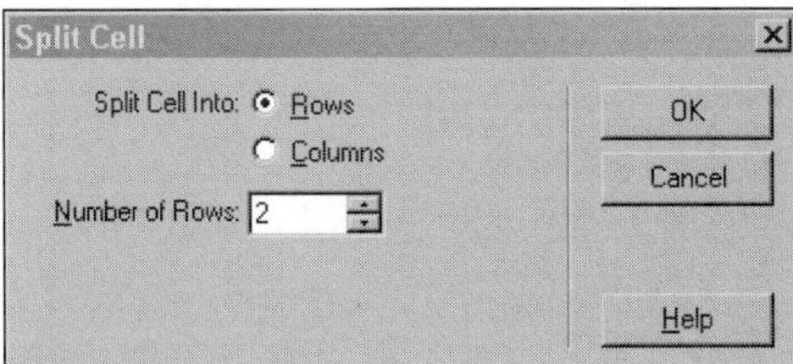

Figure 13-12: Use the Split Cell dialog box to divide cells horizontally or vertically.

3. Select either the Rows or Columns option to decide whether the cell will be split horizontally or vertically.
4. Enter the Number of Rows or Columns in the text box or use the arrows to change the value.
5. Select OK when you're done.

The same effect can be achieved by using the menus. To do so, first position the cursor in the cell to be affected and then choose one of the following commands:

Command	***Description***
Increase Row Span	Joins the current cell with the cell below it
Decrease Row Span	Separates two or more previously spanned cells from the bottom cell
Increase Column Span	Joins the current cell with the cell immediately to its right
Decrease Column Span	Separates two or more previously spanned cells from the right edge

Existing text or images are put in the same cell if the cells containing them are joined to span rows or columns. Figure 13-13 shows a table containing both row and column spanning.

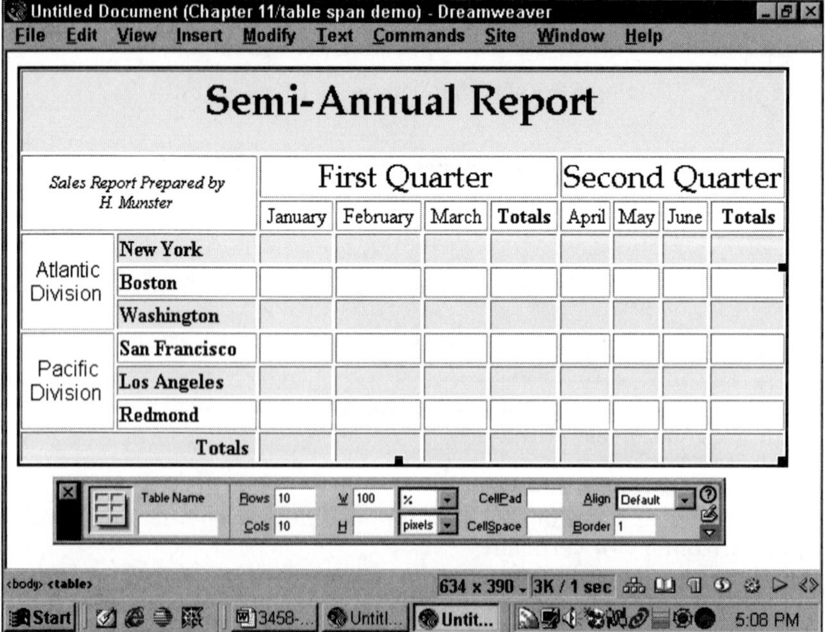

Figure 13-13: This spreadsheet-like report was built using Dreamweaver's row- and column-spanning features.

When you need to build a complex table such as this one, it's best to map out your table before you begin constructing it, and complete it prior to entering your data.

Setting cell, column, and row properties

In addition to the overall table controls, Dreamweaver helps you set numerous properties for individual cells one at a time, by the column or by the row. When attributes overlap or conflict, such as different background colors for a cell in the same row and column, the more specific target wins out. The hierarchy, from most general to most specific, is as follows: tables, rows, columns, and cells.

You can call up the specific Property Inspector by selecting the cell, row, or column you want to modify. The Cell, Row, and Column Property Inspectors each affect similar attributes. The following sections explain how the attributes work in general and—if any differences exist—specifically in regard to the cell, column, or row.

Horizontal alignment

You can set the Horizontal Alignment attribute, `align`, to specify the default alignment, or Left, Right, or Center alignment, for the element in the cell, column, or row. This attribute can be overridden by setting the alignment for the individual line or image. Generally, Left is the default horizontal alignment for cells.

Vertical alignment

The HTML `valign` attribute determines whether the cell's contents are vertically aligned to the cell's top, middle, bottom, or along the baseline. Typically, browsers align cells vertically in the middle by default. Select the Vertical Alignment option arrow in the Cell, Column, or Row Properties dialog box to specify a different alignment.

Top, Middle, and Bottom vertical alignments work pretty much as you would expect. A Baseline vertical alignment displays text near the top of the cell and positions the text—regardless of font size—so that the baselines of all the text in the affected row, column, or cell are the same. You can see how images and text of various sizes are displayed under the various vertical alignment options in Figure 13-14.

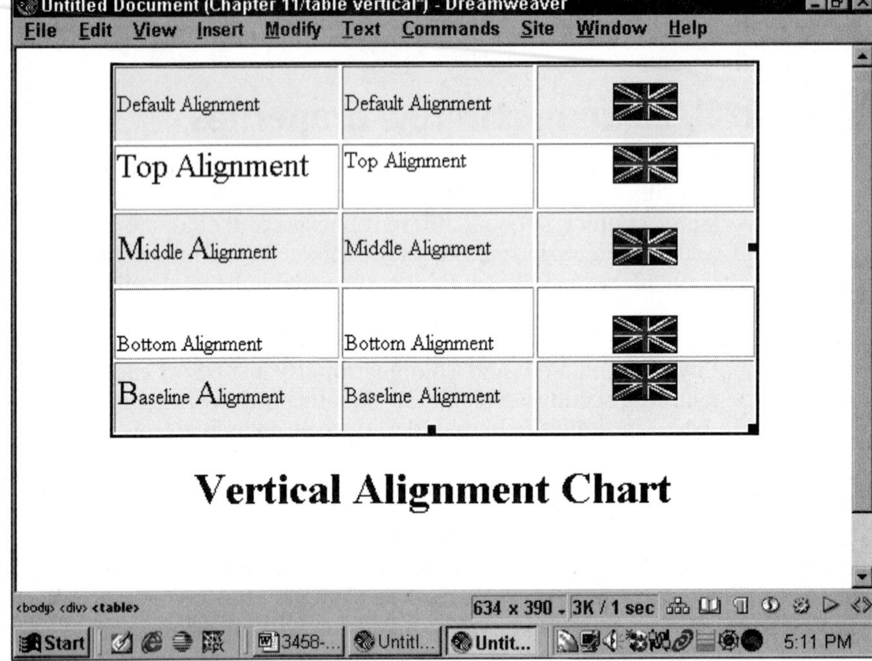

Figure 13-14: You can vertically align text and images in several arrangements in a table cell, row, or column.

Cell wrap

Normal behavior for any cell is to automatically wrap text or a series of images within the cell's borders. You can turn off this automatic feature by selecting the No Wrap option in the Property Inspector for cell, column, or row.

I've had occasion to use this option when I absolutely needed three images to appear side by side in one cell. In analyzing the results, I found that on some lower-resolution browsers, the last image wrapped to the next line.

Table header cells

Quite often in tables, a column or row functions as the heading for that section of the table, labeling all the information in that particular section. Dreamweaver has an option for designating these cells: the Header option. Table header cells are usually rendered in boldface and centered in each cell. Figure 13-15 shows an example of a table in which both the first row and first column are marked as table header cells.

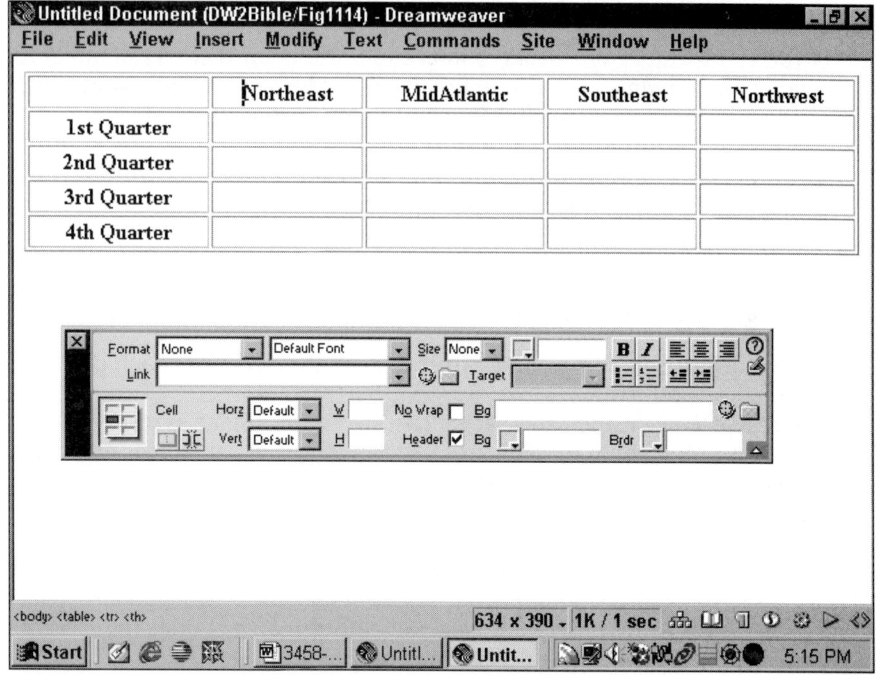

Figure 13-15: Table header cells are a good way to note a category's label — either for a row or a column, or both.

Width and height

The gridlike structure of a table makes it impossible to resize only one cell in a multicolumn table. Therefore, the only way you can enter exact values for a cell's width is through the Width section available only in the Column Properties dialog box. In this section of the dialog box, you can enter values in pixels or as a percen-tage of the table. The default enables cells to automatically resize with no restrictions outside of the overall dimensions of the table.

Similarly, whenever you change a cell's height, the entire row is altered. If you drag the row to a new height, the value is written into the H (Height) text box for all cells in the row. On the other hand, if you specify a single cell's height, the row resizes, but you can see the value only in the cell you've changed.

Color elements

Just as you can specify color backgrounds and borders for the overall table, you can do the same for columns, rows, or individual cells. Corresponding color swatches and text boxes are available in all dialog boxes for the following categories:

✦ **Background Color:** Specifies the color for the selected cell, row, or column. Selecting the color swatch opens the standard 212 Web-safe color picker.

✦ **Border Color:** Controls the color of the single-pixel border surrounding each cell.

✦ **Light Border:** Sets the color for the bottom and right borders of each cell.

✦ **Dark Border:** Sets the color for the top and left borders of each cell.

Note

Notice that the light and dark shading concept for cell borders is reversed from the light and dark shading for table borders. However, the cell border attributes are just like the table attributes in that, if specified, the light and dark cell borders override any border color that might be chosen.

As with all Dreamweaver color pickers, you can use the Eyedropper tool to select a color from the Web-safe palette or from any item on a page. You can also select the Eraser tool to delete any previously selected color. Finally, choose the Palette tool to open the Color dialog box and select any available color.

Working with Table Formats

Tables keep data organized and generally make it easier to find information quickly. Large tables with many rows, however, tend to become difficult to read unless they are formatted with alternating rows of color or some other device. Formatting a large table is often an afterthought as well as a time-consuming affair. Unless, of course, you're using Dreamweaver's Format Table command.

The Format Table command permits you to choose from 17 preset formats or customize your own. This versatile command can style the top row, alternating rows in the body of the table, the left column, and the border. It's best to completely build the structure of your table — although you don't have to fill it with data — before formatting it; otherwise, you might have to reformat it when new rows or columns are added.

To apply one of the preset table formats, follow these steps:

1. Select your table by choosing Modify ➪ Table ➪ Select Table or by using one of the other techniques.
2. Choose Commands ➪ Format Table.

The Format Table dialog box (shown in Figure 13-16) opens.

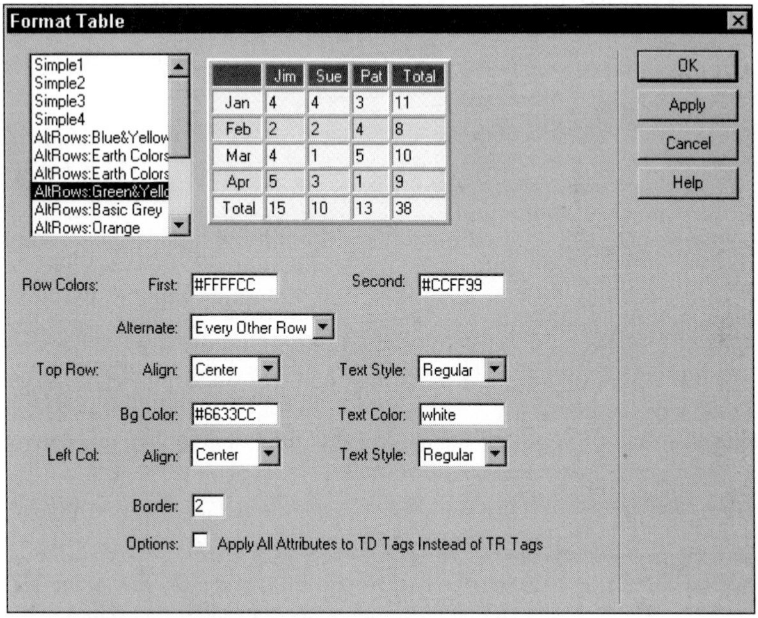

Figure 13-16: Select any one of 17 different preset formats from the Format Table dialog box or customize your own.

3. Select any of the options from the scrolling list box on the left side of the Format Table dialog box.

   As you select an option, a representation of the table appears to the right, and the attribute values used are displayed below.

4. When you've found a table format that's appropriate, select OK to close the dialog box, and the format is applied.

The preset formats are divided into three groups: Simple, AltRows, and DblRows. The Simple formats maintain the same background color for all rows in the body of the table but change the top row and the left column. The AltRows formats alternate the background color of each row in the body of the table; you have eight different color combinations from which to choose. The final category, DblRows, alternates the background color of every two rows in the body of the table.

Although 17 different formats may seem like a lot of choices, it's really just the jumping-off place for what's possible with the Format Table command. Each variable applied to create the preset formats can be customized. Moreover, you don't have to apply the changes to your selected table to see the effect — you can preview the results directly in the Table Format dialog box. Following are the variable attributes in the Table Format dialog box:

Attribute	*Description*
Row Colors: First	Enter a color (in color name or hexadecimal format) for the background colors of the first row in the body of a table. The Row Colors do not affect the top row of a table.
Row Colors: Second	Enter a color (in color name or hexadecimal format) for the background colors of the second row in the body of a table. The Row Colors do not affect the top row of a table.
Row Colors: Alternate	Establishes the pattern for using the specified Row Colors. Options are `<do not alternate>`, Every Other Row, Every Two Rows, Every Three Rows, and Every Four Rows.
Top Row: Align	Sets the alignment of the text in the top row of the table to left, right, or center.
Top Row: Text Style	Sets the style of the text in the top row of the table to Regular, Bold, Italic, or Bold Italic.
Top Row: Bg Color	Sets the background color of the top row of the selected table. Use either color names or hexadecimal values.
Top Row: Text Color	Sets the color of the text in the top row of the selected table. Use either color names or hexadecimal values.
Left Col: Align	Sets the alignment of the text in the left column of the table to Left, Right, or Center.
Left Col: Text Style	Sets the style of the text in the left column of the table to Regular, Bold, Italic, or Bold Italic.
Border	Determines the width of the table's border in pixels.
Options: Apply All Attributes to TD Tags Instead of TR Tags	Writes attribute changes at the cell level, `<td>`, rather than the default, the row level, `<tr>`.

The final option in the Format Table dialog box, Apply All Attributes to TD Tags Instead of TR Tags, should be used in only one of two situations: One, the selected table is nested inside of another table and you want to override the outer table's `<tr>` format; or two, you anticipate moving cells from one table to another and want to maintain the formatting. Generally, the code produced by selecting this option is bulkier and could impact a page's overall download size, if the table is sufficiently large.

Currently, there's no way to save your custom format without editing the tableFormats.js JavaScript file in the Commands folder. Otherwise, you need to reenter the selections each time you apply them.

Sorting Tables

Have you ever painstakingly built a table, alphabetizing every last entry by last name and first name, only to have the client call up with a list of 13 additional names that just have to go in? "Oh, and could you sort them by zip code instead of last name?" Dreamweaver contains a Table Sort command designed to make short work of such requests. All you need to do is select your table, and you're ready to do a two-level-deep sort, either alphabetically or numerically.

The Table Sort command can rearrange any size table; more important, it's HTML savvy and gives you the option of keeping the formatting of your table rows. This capability enables you to maintain a table with alternating row colors and still sort the data — something not even the most powerful word processors can handle. The Table Sort command is useful for generating different views of the same data, without having to use a database.

The Table Sort command is straightforward to use; just follow these steps:

1. Select your table by choosing Modify ➪ Table ➪ Select Table or by using one of the other techniques.
2. Choose Commands ➪ Sort Table.

   The Sort Table dialog box (shown in Figure 13-17) opens.

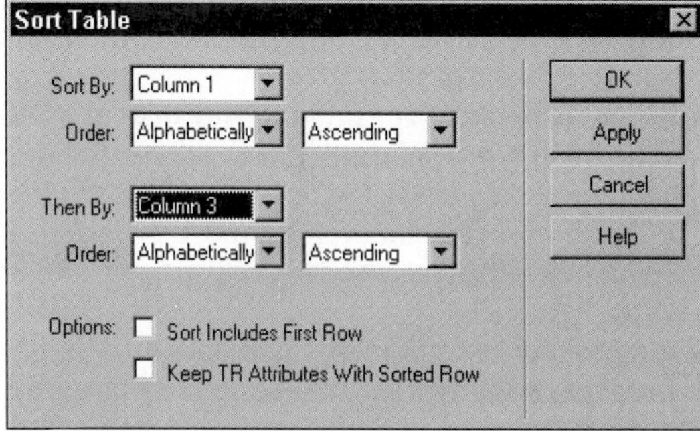

Figure 13-17: Sort your tables numerically or alphabetically with the Sort Table command.

3. Choose the primary sort column from the Sort By option list.

   Dreamweaver automatically lists the number of columns in the selected table in the option list.

4. Set the type of the primary sort by choosing either Alphabetically or Numerically from the first Order option list.

5. Choose the direction of the sort by selecting either Ascending or Descending from the second Order option list.

6. If you wish to add a second level of sorting, repeat Steps 3 through 5 in the Then By section.

7. If your selected table does not include a header row, select the Sort Includes First Row option.

8. If you have formatted your table with alternating row colors, choose the Keep TR Attributes with Sorted Row option.

9. Click OK when you're finished.

As with any sorting program, if you leave blank cells in the column you're basing the sort on, those rows appear as a group on top of the table for an ascending sort and at the end for a descending sort. Be sure that all the cells in your sort criteria column are filled correctly.

Importing Tabular Data

In the computer age, there's nothing much more frustrating than having information in a digital format and still having to enter it manually—either typing it in or cutting and pasting—to get on the Web. This frustration is multiplied when it comes to table data, whether created in a spreadsheet or database program. You have to transfer lots of small pieces of data, and it all has to be properly related and positioned.

Dreamweaver 3's new Import Table Data goes a long way toward alleviating the tedium – not to mention the frustration – of dealing with tabular information. The Import Table Data command reads any delimited text file and inserts the information in a series of rows and columns. You can even set most characteristics for the table to be created, including the width, cell padding, cell spacing, and border.

Quite often, the first step in the process of importing table data into Dreamweaver is to export it from your other program. Most spreadsheet and database programs have some capability of outputting information in a text file; each bit of data (whether it's from a cell of a spreadsheet or field of a database) is separated—or *delimited*—from every other data by a special character, typically a tab or comma. In Dreamweaver, you can choose which delimiter is used in the Import Table Data dialog box to ensure a clean transfer with no loss of data.

Although you have many types of delimiters to choose from, I generally default to exporting tab-delimited files. With a tab-delimited file, you usually don't have to worry if any of your data contains the delimiter—which would throw off the import. However, testing shows that Dreamweaver 3 correctly handles comma-delimited files with and without quotes, so you could also use that format safely.

To import a tabular data file, follow these steps:

1. Be sure the data you wish to import has been saved or exported in the proper format: a delimited text file.
2. Choose File ➪ Import ➪ Import Table Data.

   The Import Table Data dialog box, shown in Figure 13-18, is displayed.

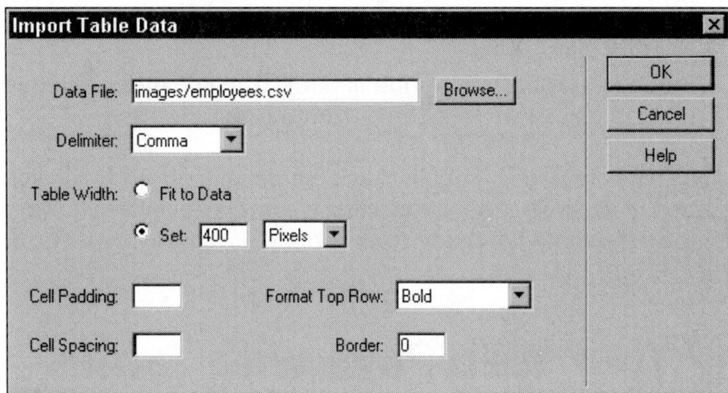

Figure 13-18: Any external data, saved in a delimited text file, can be brought into Dreamweaver through the Import Table Data command.

3. Select the Data File Browse (Choose) button to find the desired file.
4. Choose the delimiter used to separate the fields or cells of data from the Delimiter option list. The choices are Tab, Comma, Semicolon, Colon, and Other.

If you select a file with a .csv extension, the Comma delimiter is automatically chosen. CSV is short for Comma Separated Values.

5. If you choose Other from the Delimiter list, a blank field appears to the right of the list. Enter the special character, such as a pipe (|), used as the delimiter in the exported file.

   Now that the imported file characteristics are set, you can predefine the table the information will be imported into, if desired.

6. If you want to set a particular table width, enter a value in the Set field and choose either Pixels or % from the option list. If you want the imported file to determine the size of the table, keep the Fit to Data option selected.
7. Enter any Cell Padding or Cell Spacing values desired, in their respective fields.

   As with standard tables, by default Cell Padding is set to 2 pixels and Cell Spacing to 1 if no specific values are entered.
8. If you'd like to style the first row, choose Bold, Italic, or BoldItalic from the Format Top Row option list.

   This option is typically used when the imported file contains a header row.
9. Set the Border field to the desired width, if any. If you don't want a border displayed at all, set the Border field to 0.
10. Click OK when you're done.

Even though the Import Table Data option is under the File menu, it doesn't open a new file — the new table is created at the current cursor position.

If your data comes in wrong, double-check the delimiter used by opening the file in a text editor. If Dreamweaver is expecting a comma delimiter and your file uses tabs, data is not separated properly.

Structuring Your Web Page with Tables

At the beginning of this chapter, it was pointed out that experienced Web designers regard tables as one of their primary layout tools. This is because, outside of Dynamic HTML's layers, tables are the only way you can even get close to positioning your page elements the way you want them to appear. Granted, it's a lot of work to do this with tables, but designers are a persistent group — and when you have a vision to impart to the world, you do what's necessary.

To get the look you want, it often becomes necessary to design your entire Web page with tables — or, at least, the majority of it. And to achieve complete control of the page, you frequently put nested tables — tables within tables — to work.

Dreamweaver enables what is, for some Web designers, a much more intuitive method of using tables to design your entire page: converting layers to tables. Because this new feature requires an understanding of how layers work, you can find details about how to use it in Chapter 28.

Nesting Tables

Dreamweaver has no practical restrictions on nesting tables. You can put as many tables within other tables as you can handle. All you have to do is position your cursor in the cell where you want the new table to appear and select the Insert Table button on the Objects palette. Although it's not absolutely faultless, nested tables give you an increasingly fine degree of control over your Web page layout. One example of a full-page table layout is shown in Figure 13-19.

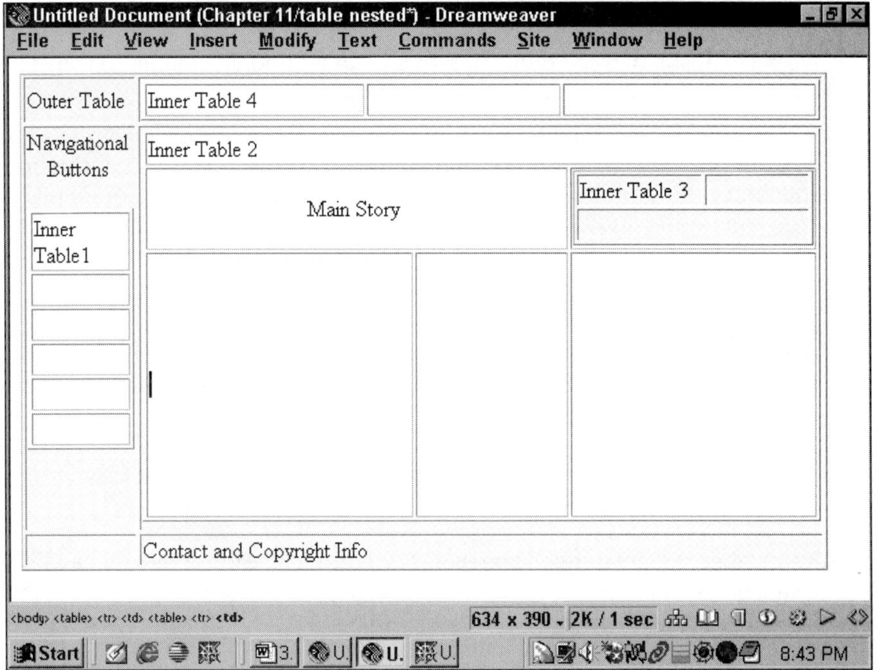

Figure 13-19: Nested tables can give the Web designer tighter command of the Web page elements.

Following are some pointers to consider when working with nested tables:

- ✦ Sketch your work before you begin. Even just a simple diagram can save you hours of experimentation and rework.
- ✦ Work from the outside in. Create your largest table first and then create the smaller tables within it.

✦ Don't be afraid to move a table. No matter how much you plan, you almost never get it right the first time. As long as you select your entire table, all the elements in it remain intact. Unfortunately, you can't drag and drop a table. So after you've selected the table, choose Edit ➪ Cut, reposition the cursor, and then choose Edit ➪ Paste — or use those fabulous keyboard shortcuts.

✦ Let the Tag Selector be your guide. Because the Tag Selector displays tags in the nesting order (outside-to-inside is shown left-to-right), you can quickly select the table on which you need to work. Then you can switch to either the HTML Inspector or BBEdit, and the table will be highlighted in your code.

✦ You can't split a cell, so nest a table. If you've already begun embedding objects in your table and you find you need to split a cell into two or more parts, it's far easier to nest a two-cell table than to add an additional column to the entire table and readjust your column and row spans.

✦ When resizing row heights, work from the top down. Dragging a row's border to a new size sets an absolute value in the <td> tag. If you adjust the bottom row first — let's say you set it to about one-fifth of the screen, or 80 pixels high — and then modify a row height above, the table gets larger. That's because Dreamweaver maintains the 80 pixels, not the 20 percent.

✦ Use absolute measurements on the outside and relative measurements on the inside. Though it's not a hard-and-fast rule, it is generally better to lock the outer table into a specific absolute pixel width and then set the inner table to 100 percent widths. Why? It saves the calculation time of trying to figure out the width, and the inner tables blend better this way.

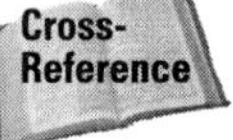

For more information about how to modify an existing object, see Chapter 18.

✦ Remember the default cell spacing. Trying to figure out why you can't close that gap? It could be because, even though the CellSpace text box is blank, Dreamweaver still displays a default 2 pixels for cell spacing. Enter a zero as the CellSpace value to clear out the excess air.

Summary

Tables are an extremely powerful Web page design tool. Dreamweaver enables you to modify both the appearance and the structure of your HTML tables through a combination of Property Inspectors, dialog boxes, and click-and-drag mouse movements. Mastering tables is an essential task for any modern Web designer and worth the somewhat challenging learning curve. The key elements to keep in mind are as follows:

✦ An HTML table consists of a series of rows and columns presented in a gridlike arrangement. Tables can be sized absolutely, in pixels, or relative to the width of the browser's window, in a percentage.

- Dreamweaver inserts a table whose dimensions can be altered through the Objects palette or the Insert ➪ Table menu. Once in the page, the table needs to be selected before any of its properties can be modified through the Table Property Inspector.
- Table editing is greatly simplified in Dreamweaver. You can select multiple cells, columns, or rows — and modify all their contents in one fell swoop.
- You can assign certain properties — such as background color, border color, and alignment — for a table's columns, rows, or cells through their respective dialog boxes. A cell's properties override those set for its column or row.
- Dreamweaver 3 brings power to table building with the Format Table and Sort Table commands and now a greater connection to the outside world with its Import Tabular Data option.
- Putting a table within another table — also known as *nesting tables* — is a powerful (and legal) design option in HTML. Nested tables offer a positioning alternative to Dynamic HTML's layers, while retaining backward browser compatibility.

In the next chapter, you learn how to create and use client-side image maps.

✦ ✦ ✦

Making Client-Side Image Maps

✦ ✦ ✦ ✦

In This Chapter

Image map overview

Using the Image Map Editor

Making a server-side image map

Dreamweaver Technique: Creating image map rollovers

✦ ✦ ✦ ✦

By their very nature, HTML images are rectangular. Though you can make portions of a rectangular graphic transparent, giving the impression of an irregularly shaped picture, the image itself — and thus its clickable region — is still a rectangle. For more complex images, in which shapes overlap and you want several separate areas of a picture to be hyperlinked, not just the overall graphic, you need an image map.

For version 3, Dreamweaver has moved the image map tools front and center so now you can draw and manage your hotspots right on your graphics in the Document window. The onscreen image map tools do make it much easier to manipulate your hotspots, but there's another major advantage: You can now attach behaviors to hotspots.

This chapter introduces you to Dreamweaver's hotspot tools and also covers more advanced techniques for creating server-side and rollover image maps.

Client-Side Image Maps

As an almost literal example of an image map, imagine a map of the United States being used on a Web page. Suppose you want to be able to click each state and link to a different page in your site. How would you proceed? With the exception of Colorado and Wyoming, all the states have highly irregular shapes, so you can't use the typical side-by-side arrangement of rectangular images. You need to be able to specify a region on the graphic, to which you could then assign a link. This is exactly what an image map represents.

Two different kinds of image maps exist: client-side and server-side. With a server-side image map, all the map data is kept in a file on the server. When the user clicks a particular spot on the image, often referred to as a *hotspot*, the server compares the coordinates of the clicked spot with its image map data. If the coordinates match, the server loads the corresponding link. The key advantage to a server-side image map is that it works with any image-capable browser. The disadvantages are that it consumes more of the server's processing resources and tends to be slower than the client-side version.

With client-side image maps, on the other hand, all the data that is downloaded to the browser is kept in the Web page. The comparison process is the same, but it requires a browser that is image map savvy. Originally, only server-side image maps were possible. It wasn't until Netscape Navigator 2.0 was released that the client-side version was even an option. Microsoft began supporting client-side image maps in Internet Explorer 3.0. The vast majority of image maps used on the Web today are client-side, and server-side image maps should only be considered for special purposes.

In HTML, a client-side image map has two parts. In the `<img>` tag, Dreamweaver includes a `usemap=mapname` attribute. The mapname value refers to the second part of the image map's HTML, the `<map>` tag. One of the first steps in creating an image map is to give it a unique name. Dreamweaver stores all your mapping data under this map name. Here's an example of the code for an image map with three hotspots:

```
<img src="images/imagemap.jpg" width="640" height="480" ¬
usemap="#navbar"></p>
<map name="navbar">
  <area shape="poly"
coords="166,131,165,131,160,143,164,179,127,180,143,200,156,203,118,229,119,¬
236,158,229,177,217,199,238,212,247,220,242,196,203,232,190,241,189,241,182,¬
223,177,185,182,175,134,166,132" href="/starpro.html" alt="High Risk Funds">
  <area shape="circle" coords="312,202,56" href="/nestegg.html" ¬
alt="Mutual Funds">
  <area shape="rect" coords="389,138,497,244" href="/prodfunds.html" ¬
alt="Money Markets">
</map>
```

Dreamweaver directly supports client-side image maps. Once you've inserted an image into your Web page, it can be an image map. Select any image and open the expanded version of the Property Inspector. The image map tools are in the lower-left corner, as shown in Figure 14-1.

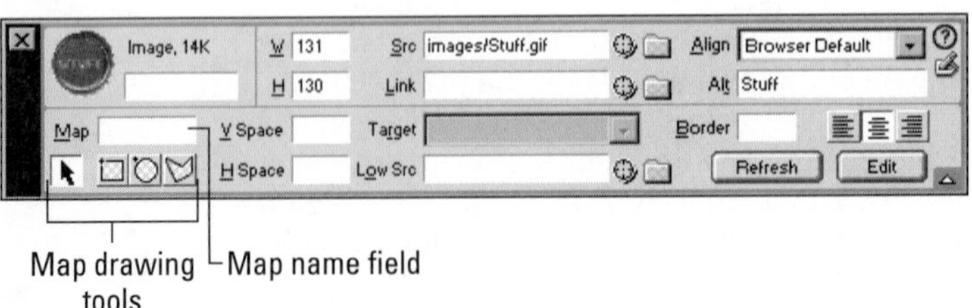

Figure 14-1: From the Image Property Inspector, select the image map tools to draw hotspots directly on graphics within Dreamweaver.

Creating Image Hotspots

Image maps are created with tools similar to those you find in any drawing program. (They're described in detail in the section "Using the Drawing Tools," later in this chapter.) After you've selected your graphic, you can click a tool to describe a rectangle, oval, or polygon shape.

You can make an image map from any graphic format supported by Dreamweaver: GIF, JPEG, or PNG.

Follow these steps to create hotspots on an image in Dreamweaver:

1. Select your image and, if necessary, open the Image Property Inspector to full height by clicking the expander arrow.
2. Enter a unique name for your image map in the Map Name text box.

   Dreamweaver initially displays a placeholder name, Map, which you can use or replace. It's generally a good practice to use a name that is more meaningful, such as navMap.
3. Choose the appropriate drawing tool to outline your hotspot: Rectangle, Circle, or Polygon. Outline one hotspot.

   When you complete the hotspot, Dreamweaver displays the Hotspot Property Inspector, shown in Figure 14-2.

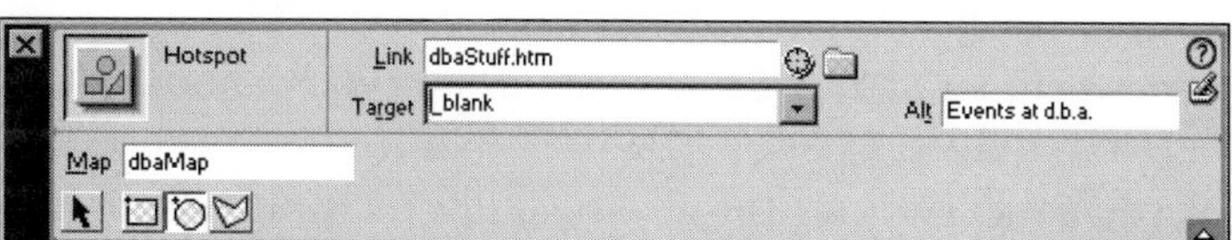

Figure 14-2: Enter image map attributes through the Hotspot Property Inspector.

4. Enter the URL for this image map in the Link text box or click the folder icon and browse for the file.
5. If desired, enter a frame name or other target in the Target text box.

A target can refer to a specific section of a frameset or to a new browser window. For more information on using targets in frames, see Chapter 16. To learn more about targeting a new browser window, see the section "Targeting Your Links" in Chapter 11.

6. In the Alt text box, you can enter text you want to appear as a ToolTip that appears when the user's mouse moves over the area.

In Windows, the information taken from the Alt text box appears as a ToolTip only in Netscape browsers. Another attribute, `title`, is used in Microsoft browsers. Dreamweaver 3 automatically adds both the `alt` and the `title` attributes for cross-browser compatibility.

7. Repeat Steps 3 through 6 to add additional hotspots to the graphic.
8. Click OK when you're finished.

Using the drawing tools

You'll find the hotspot drawing tools to be straightforward and easy to use. Each one produces a series of coordinates that are incorporated into the HTML code.

In the following steps, you use the hotspot drawing tools to outline a hotspot:

1. Select the Rectangle tool from the toolbar.
2. Click one corner of the area you want to map and drag toward the opposite corner to draw a rectangle.
3. Release the mouse button. Dreamweaver inverts the defined area.
4. Fill in the Link, Target, and Alt text boxes.

Follow these steps to use the Circle drawing tool in the Image Map Editor:

1. Select the Circle tool from the toolbar.
2. Click at one corner of the perimeter of the area you want to define and drag out the circle until it reaches the correct size.
3. Release the mouse button. Dreamweaver inverts the defined area.
4. As before, complete the Link, Target, and Alt text boxes.

To define an irregularly shaped hotspot, use the Polygon drawing tool. Follow these steps:

1. Select the Polygon tool from the toolbar.
2. Click the first point for your hotspot object.
3. Release the mouse button and move the mouse to the next point.
4. Continue outlining the object by clicking and moving the mouse.
5. When the hotspot is completely outlined, double-click the mouse to close the area.
6. Fill in the Link, Target, and Alt text boxes.

The Polygon tool does not work properly if the image is in a layer. To work around this issue, temporarily move the image out of the layer, apply the polygon hotspot, and then drag the image back into the layer.

You can use the drawing tools in any combination. In Figure 14-3, all three drawing tools have been used to create three different hotspots. The star-shaped image is currently selected, as indicated by the control points visible on that hotspot. The other two defined areas (the circular and rectangular objects) are shown with light blue overlays around them.

Figure 14-3: The image map drawing tools enable you to define both regular and irregularly shaped areas.

After you've created your hotspots, you may want to view your page without the highlighted areas. To turn off the overlays, choose View ➪ Hotspots to disable the option.

Setting the Default URL

What happens when Web site visitors pass their pointers over parts of your image that are not the primary hotspots? Prior to the fourth generation of browsers, a default URL property was supported to handle this issue. Now, however, the necessary code, `<area shape="default" href="url">`, is ignored by Internet Explorer 4 and above, although it remains supported by Netscape.

One workaround to this drawback is to completely cover the graphic with an area, using the Rectangle drawing tool, and then assign the desired default URL. If you add the overall rectangle hotspot after other hotspots have been created, be sure to send the full-graphic rectangle behind the other hotspots using the Modify ⇨ Layers and Hotspots ⇨ Send to Back command. Where hotspots overlap, browsers detect only the uppermost hotspot.

Modifying an image map

Dreamweaver gives you several options for modifying the image maps you create. First, you can move any previously defined area by selecting it and then clicking and dragging to a new location. For precise pixel-by-pixel movement, select the area and use your keyboard arrow keys to move it in any direction.

Each of the hotspots has a number of control points that can be used to resize or reshape it. To move any of the control points, first select the hotspot Pointer tool.

- ✦ The rectangle has four control points, one at each corner. Drag any corner to resize or reshape the rectangle. Press Shift while dragging to constrain the rectangle's width-to-height ratio.
- ✦ Circle hotspots also have four control points. Dragging any of these points increases or decreases the diameter of the circle, leaving the opposing side stationary. For example, if you drag the top control point of a hotspot circle up, the hotspot expands from the bottom.
- ✦ Each point in a polygon hotspot is a control point that can be dragged into a new position to reshape the hotspot.

Hotspots can also be aligned with other hotspots or resized to match. The alignment commands are found under the Modify ⇨ Layers and Hotspots menu and are the following:

Align Left	Aligns selected hotspots to the leftmost edge of the selection.
Align Right	Aligns selected hotspots to the rightmost edge of the selection.
Align Top	Aligns selected hotspots to the topmost edge of the selection.

Align Bottom	Aligns selected hotspots to the bottommost edge of the selection.
Make Same Width	Converts all selected hotspots to the width of the last selected hotspot.
Make Same Height	Converts all selected hotspots to the height of the last selected hotspot.
Bring to Front	Brings the selected hotspot in front of all other overlapping hotspots.
Send to Back	Sends the selected hotspot behind all other overlapping hotspots.

Although Dreamweaver lists keyboard shortcuts for all the alignment options under Modify ⇨ Layers and Hotspots, these apply only to layers. You must use the menus (either the main or shortcut) to align hotspots.

Of course, Dreamweaver also enables you to delete any existing area. Simply select the area and press the Delete or Backspace key.

Converting Client-Side Maps to Server-Side Maps

Although most Web browsers support client-side image maps, some sites still rely on server-side image maps. You can take a client-side image map generated by Dreamweaver and convert it to a server-side image map—you can even include pointers for both maps in the same Web page, to accommodate older browsers as well as the newer ones. Such a conversion does require, however, that you use a text editor to modify and save the file. You also need to add one more attribute, `ismap`, to the `<img>` tag; this attribute tells the server that the image referenced in the `src` attribute is a map.

Adapting the server script

First, let's examine the differences between a client-side image map and a server-side image map from the same graphic. The HTML for a client-side image map looks like this:

```
<map name="navbar">
  <area shape="rect" coords="1,1,30,33" href="home.html" alt="Home Page">
  <area shape="circle" coords="65,64,62" href="contacts.html" ¬
alt="Information">
  <area shape="default" href="index.html">
</map>
```

The same definitions for a server-side image map are laid out like this:

```
rect home.html 1,1 30,33
circle contacts.html 65,64 62
default index.html
```

As you can see, the server-side image map file is much more compact. Notice first that all of the `alt="string"` code is thrown out because ToolTips can be shown only through client-side image maps.

A server expects the information in this form:

```
shape URL coordinates
```

So, you need to remove the `<area>` tag and its delimiters, as well as the phrases `shape=`, `coords=`, and `href=`. Then you reverse the order of the URL and the coordinates.

The last step in this phase of adapting the server-side script is to format the coordinates correctly. The format depends on the shape being defined.

- ✦ For rectangles, group the x, y points into comma-separated pairs with a single space in between each pair.
- ✦ For circles, separate the center point coordinates from the diameter with a space.
- ✦ For polygons, group the x, y points into comma-separated pairs with a single space in between each pair—just like rectangles.

Your new map file should be stored on your server, probably in a subfolder of the cgi-bin directory.

Not all servers expect server-side image maps in the same format. The format offered here conforms to the NCSA HPPD standard. If you're unsure of the required format, or of where to put your maps on your server, check with your server administrator before creating a server-side image map.

Including the map link

The second phase of converting a client-side map to a server-side one involves making the connection between the Web page and the map file. A client-side image map link directly calls the URL associated with it. In contrast, all references from a server-side link call the map file—which in turn calls the specified URL.

Attaching Behaviors to Image Maps

A hotspot is basically an interactive trigger. Although hotspots are used most frequently to open new Web pages, they can also be used to trigger other events. In Dreamweaver, behaviors, assigned to linked text or images, can perform a range of actions: Swap an image on the page, show or hide a layer, or even open another smaller browser window. Dreamweaver 3, with its upfront image maps, makes it straightforward to assign behaviors to hotspots as well.

To attach a behavior to a hotspot, first select the hotspot and then choose the Add Action button from the Behavior Inspector. Select your behavior from the list and enter its parameters. After you've confirmed your options, you may find it necessary to change the event from its default, which is often `onMouseDown` or `onMouseOver`. To do so, select the down triangle in-between the event and the action in the Behavior Inspector and choose a new event from the list.

Here's a cool and useful feature: If you copy an image with defined hotspots and behaviors, all the associated behaviors are copied as well as the image map.

The connection to a server-side map is handled in the normal manner of adding a link to a graphic. You can, of course, do this directly in Dreamweaver. Simply select your graphic and, in the Image Property Inspector, insert the map file URL in the Link text box. Be sure the image's Border property is set to zero to avoid the link outline.

The final addition to your script is the `ismap` attribute. Place the `ismap` attribute in the `<img>` tag of the graphic being used for the image map, like this:

```
<img href="images/biglogo.gif" width="200" height="350" ismap>
```

As noted earlier, it is entirely possible to use client-side and server-side image maps together. The easiest way to do it is to keep the image map data as written by Dreamweaver and add the `ismap` attribute. The HTML example seen in the previous section, "Client-Side Image Maps," would then read as follows:

```
<a href="http://www.idest.com/cgi-bin/maps/imap.txt">
<img src="images/imagemap.jpg" width="640" height="480" usemap="#navbar" ¬
ismap><a/>
```

Dreamweaver Technique: Building an Image Map Rollover

One of the most popular Web page techniques today is known as a *rollover*. A rollover occurs when a user's mouse moves over a button or graphic in the page, and the button or graphic changes in some way. You saw how to create these graphic rollovers in Chapter 10. Here in this section, let's try out one method for applying the same technique to an image map.

The following method uses advanced techniques involving JavaScript behaviors and layers. If you're unfamiliar with these concepts, you might want to examine Chapters 19 and 28 before proceeding.

Before we get underway, keep in mind that this technique — because it uses layers — works only with 4.0 browsers and above.

Step 1: Create two images

As with behavior-based button rollovers, you use two images to represent the "off" and "over" states of the graphic. However, because we are using image maps here, rather than separate graphics, you only need a total of two images (versus two for every button). In our example, three buttons are "carved" from one graphic; but there could very easily have been eight or a dozen separate buttons, which would have required 16 or 24 separate images. All we need is our two image maps.

After building your first image, bring it into your favorite image processing program and make the alterations necessary to create the second image. Figure 14-4 shows examples of the two images you need (above and below), inserted into Dreamweaver. As you can see, all that was necessary to make the "over" image was to add a glow effect to each of the three hotspots.

One of the methods used in this technique involves clipping a region of an image. Presently, layers support only rectangular clipping. Keep this in mind as you build your primary image and avoid placing hotspots too close together.

Step 2: Set up the layers

This technique takes advantage of three different layer properties: absolute positioning, visibility, and clipping. The idea is to display just a portion of a hidden layer during a `onMouseOver` event. To perform this function without rewriting the code, a layer for each of the hotspots is necessary. Each layer will later be clipped to show just that hotspot. The beauty of this technique is that while it uses multiple layers, only two images are required, as the "over" image is used for each rollover.

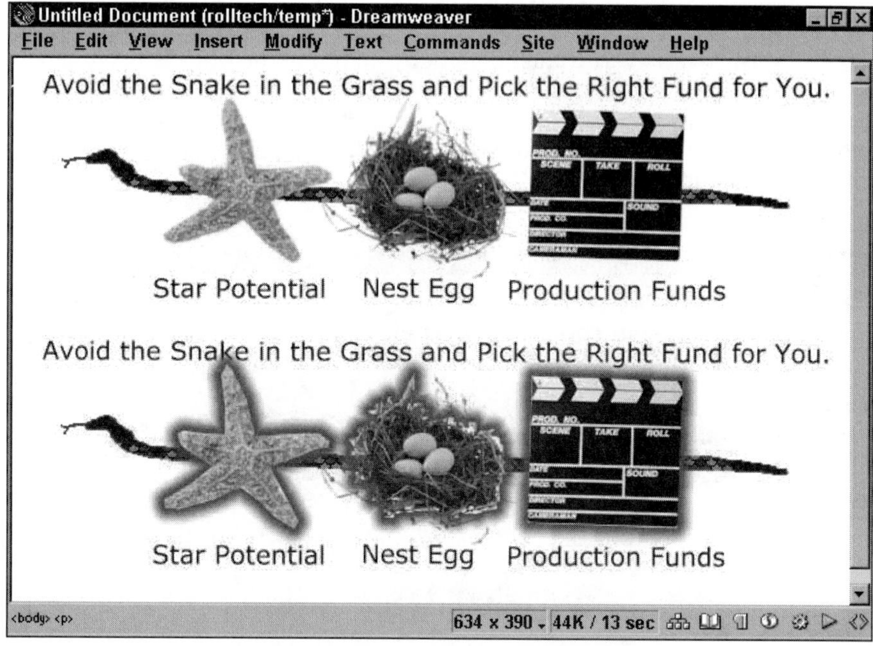

Figure 14-4: You need two separate images, representing "over" and "off," for a rollover image map.

To get started, we just need two layers — one for each of our images.

Follow these steps to establish the initial layers:

1. Choose Insert ⇨ Layer or select the Draw Layer button on the Objects palette to create the overLayer01. If you use the menu option instead of drawing out the layer, it is created at a standard size, and you won't have to spend as much time adjusting the layer sizes later.
2. Making sure the cursor is in the layer, choose Insert ⇨ Image or select the Insert Image button on the Objects palette. Load your "over" graphic. If the layer is smaller than the image, the layer automatically expands.
3. Repeat Step 1 to create the offLayer. Be sure to give it a unique name.
4. Repeat Step 2 and insert the "off" graphic.
5. If necessary, open the Layers Inspector by choosing Window ⇨ Layers or pressing F11, and make sure of the following:
   - Both layers must have unique names. In this example, we use offLayer and overLayer01.
   - The offLayer must be visible.

- The overLayer01 must be hidden.
- The overLayer01 must be exactly on top of the offLayer, so that when you make a portion of the overLayer01 visible, it obscures the offLayer.

Figure 14-5 shows how the screen looks with both layers in place and the visibility properties set correctly.

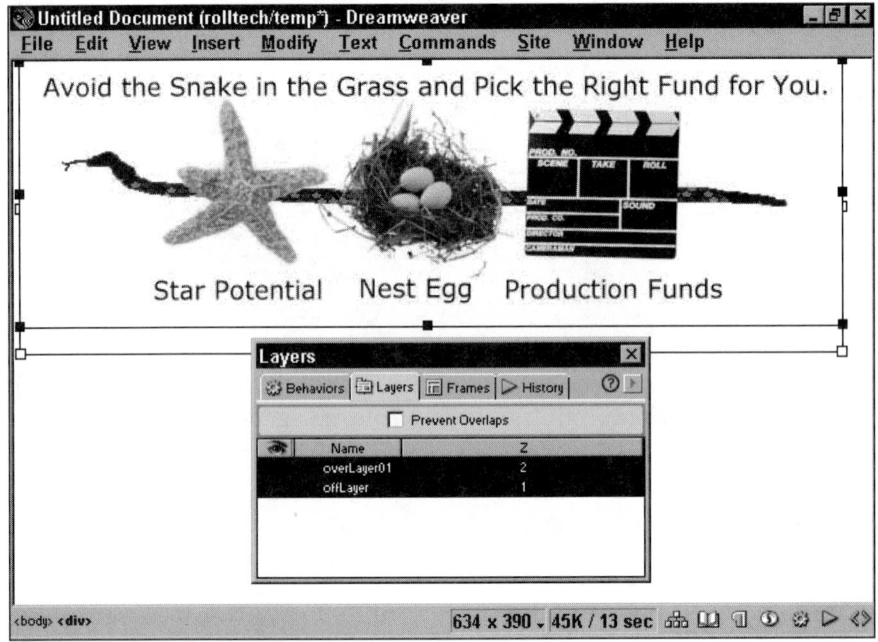

Figure 14-5: Two image maps are placed on top of each other in layers, and the top layer is hidden.

After you've created your initial layers, you need to create a layer for each remaining hotspot. I name these layers sequentially, such as overLayer02 and overLayer03. Then insert the "over" graphic in each of these layers. Finally, all the overLayers should be in the same position as, but on top of, the offLayer and hidden. Basically you have a stack of identical overLayers on top of the offLayer.

Tip

If you have many hotspots, you may want to name the overLayers something more recognizable. For example, with my three shapes, I could name the layers overLayer_star, overLayer_nest, and overLayer_clapboard. You need to be able to match the layers to the hotspot as part of the technique. And a proper naming scheme can smooth your workflow.

Aligning Layers

Now in Dreamweaver 3, you can use the new layer alignment commands to easily line up the two layers. The commands are covered in detail in Chapter 25, but here are the steps briefly. Group the two windows by selecting both layers in the Layers Inspector while pressing the Shift key. Choose two of the Modify ⇨ Layers options – Align Left and Align Top, for example – so that they are in the same position. The layer alignment commands all work the same; all layers are aligned to the edge of the last layer selected. If the layers are different shapes, you can make them the same size by choosing Modify ⇨ Layers ⇨ Make Same Width and/or Modify ⇨ Layers ⇨ Make Same Height.

Step 3: Make the image map

The first part of this step is to make the actual image map that will eventually be used to activate the `onMouseOver` and `onMouseOut` events. Follow these steps to complete this task:

1. Select the image in one of the layers. You can use either image (the "over" or the "off") to draw the image map. I preferred the overLayer, with the slightly fuzzier edges.
2. In the Map Name field of the Property Inspector, give your map a unique name.
3. Draw out the image maps using the drawing tools.

As noted earlier, a known problem in Dreamweaver 3 prevents you from drawing a polygon hotspot while an image is in a layer. To circumvent this issue, temporarily move your graphic out of the layer and draw the polygon hotspot. When you're finished, move the graphic back in the layer.

4. In the Hotspot Inspector, give each area a URL in the Link box.
5. Complete the Target and Alt text boxes, if desired.

   Normally, when building an image map, this is where you would stop. However, because we're using multiple layers, we need to apply the same image map to each of the remaining layers in our technique.
6. Using the Layers Inspector, select the next layer and then choose the image.
7. In the Map Name field, enter the same name as previously assigned.

   This ensures that all the layers use the same image map; if you do not perform this step, the off and over images will appear to flicker.
8. Repeat Steps 6 and 7 for each of the remaining layers.

Step 4: Attach the behaviors

Dreamweaver includes a JavaScript behavior called Show/Hide Layers that does exactly what we need for this technique.

Follow these steps to assign the Show/Hide Layers behavior to the layers:

1. Be sure the offLayer (the layer holding the basic, unchanged image) is visible and all the overLayers are hidden. You can select the visibility options in the Layers Inspector to open and close the "eyes" of the respective layers.
2. Select the first hotspot of the image in the offLayer.
3. Open the Behavior Inspector by clicking the Behavior button in the Launcher or selecting Window ➪ Behaviors.
4. Choose 4.0 and Later Browsers from the Browser option list, if it's not already selected.
5. Still in the Behavior Inspector, select the + (Add Behavior) button and choose Show-Hide Layers from the pop-up list.
6. When the Show-Hide Layers dialog box opens, Dreamweaver searches for all the layers in your document. After they are displayed, select overLayer01 and click the Show button (see Figure 14-6). Click OK when you've finished.

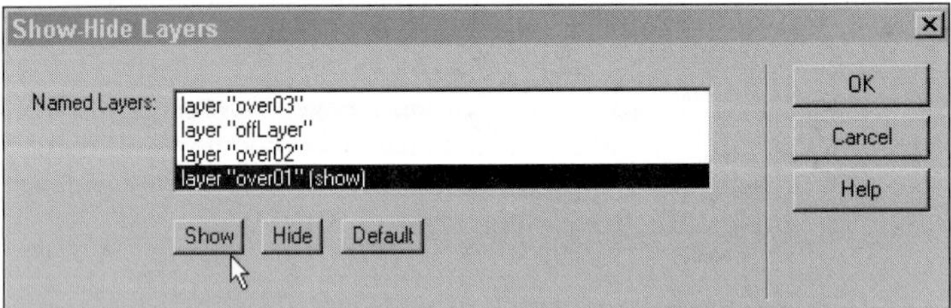

Figure 14-6: Highlight overLayer01 and then choose the Show option to ensure that the Show-Hide Layer action makes the appropriate layer visible.

7. Now we need to change the event that triggers the behavior from `onMouseDown` to `onMouseOver`. To do this, click the Add Event button in the Behavior Inspector. The Add Event button is the down arrow between the Event and Action lists. Choose `onMouseOver` from the Add Event drop-down list.
8. So far, we've assigned one behavior to make overLayer01 visible when the pointer is over the image. Now we have to assign another behavior to hide overLayer01 when the pointer moves away from the image.

9. Click the Add Behavior button and again select Show-Hide Layers from the option list.
10. Now select overLayer01 again and click the Hide button. Click OK when you're finished.
11. Finally, change the Event to `onMouseOut` for this new behavior, following the same procedure as in Step 7.

So what we now have is two behaviors assigned to one image. Now, you need to repeat the attachment of the behaviors to each of the additional hotspots in your graphic. However, instead of showing and hiding overLayer01, each hotspot has its own overLayer to show and hide. For example, after I've selected my second hotspot, I show and hide overLayer02, and so on.

Step 5: Add the clipping

Let's review what we have done so far:

✦ Before we began working in Dreamweaver, we built two different images — one to depict the regular ("off") state, and another for the "over" state.

✦ We used Dreamweaver to create a series of identically sized and positioned layers. We then inserted our two images into the hidden layers, with the "over" graphic placed on top layers.

✦ Next, we created hot spots on our graphics and assigned the same image map name to each of the graphics in all the layers.

✦ Then, we used Dreamweaver to assign JavaScript behaviors that reveal the hidden layer when the user's pointer passes over the hotspot and hide it again when the pointer moves away from the hotspot.

If you test the image map rollover at this stage, you'll see the entire "over" graphic for every hotspot. To achieve the rollover effect, each of the overLayers must be clipped. All that is left to do now is assign the clipping values.

The clipping property of a layer essentially crops the visible portion of that layer. Four values are used to define the clipped section: Left, Top, Right, and Bottom. These values are pixel measurements relative to the upper-left corner of the layer. Although you could bring your image into an image editor to find the measurements, you can, with a slight bit of trickiness, also get the measurements right from Dreamweaver.

To get the relative pixel values within a layer, I use another temporary layer drawn over my clipped area. I can shape this temporary layer to the exact size of the clip and then note the layer's coordinates and dimensions. Because one layer can nest inside another, you can find the relative positioning—the Left and Top values—very easily. Finding the Right and Bottom values then requires only a minor calculation.

To add the clipping values to your overLayers, follow these steps:

1. From the Layers palette, select the first of the overLayers.

   Although it's not necessary, it's a good idea to select the Prevent Overlaps option from the Layers palette to stop your clipped sections from overlapping.
2. Click the graphic in the overLayer.
3. Press the left-arrow key once to move your cursor in front of the image but within the layer.
4. Choose Insert ➪ Layer.

   This new layer is a temporary one that will be used for measurement purposes only and then deleted.
5. Drag the temporary layer into position for the first area to be clipped.
6. Use the resizing handles to reshape the temporary layer until it frames the area you want to clip as shown in Figure 14-7.

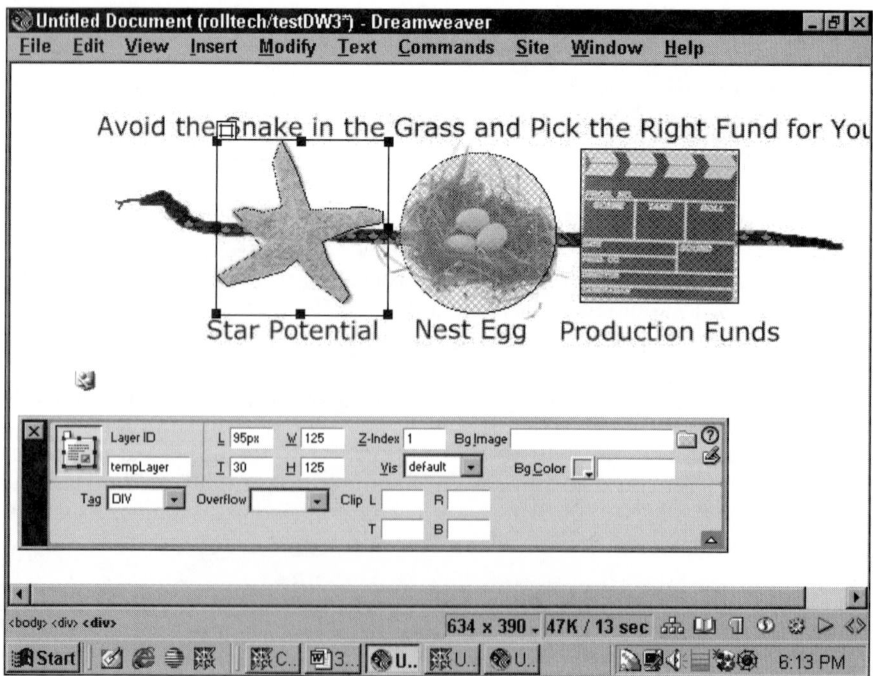

Figure 14-7: You can use a temporary layer to get the exact clipping measurements.

7. In the Property Inspector, note the values for Left, Top, Width, and Height (L, T, W, and H, respectively) of the temporary layer.
8. From the Layers palette, select the overLayer.
9. In the Clip section of the Property Inspector, enter the Left and Top values as noted from the temporary layers.
10. For the Clip Right (R) value, enter the sum of the temporary layer's Left and Width values.
11. For the Clip Bottom (B) value, enter the sum of the temporary layer's Top plus its Height values.

    For example, the example temporary layer's initial values were: Left - 95, Top - 30, Width - 125, and Height - 125. This translates into the following clip values: Left - 95, Top - 30, Right - 220 (Left + Width), and Bottom - 155 (Top + Height).

    After you've entered the last clipping value (and pressed Tab or Enter/Return to confirm), Dreamweaver displays just the clipped area.
12. Repeat this procedure (Steps 1 through 11) for each of the remaining overLayers, until all have clip values.

Once you've implemented these changes, test your object. You should see the type of reaction demonstrated in Figure 14-8.

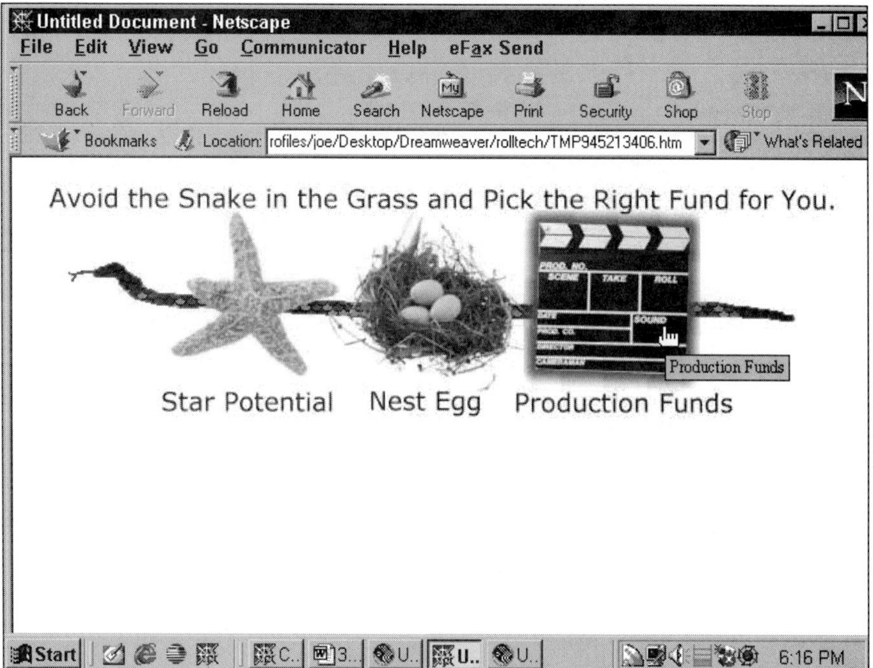

Figure 14-8: The completed image map rollover technique in action.

When you preview your work in a browser, make sure that visibility is set correctly for each layer.

Summary

Image maps provide a necessary capability in Web page design. Without them, you wouldn't be able to link irregularly shaped graphics or to group links all in one image. Dreamweaver's built-in Image Map Editor gives you all the tools you need to create simple, effective client-side image maps.

- Image maps enable you to define separate areas of one graphic and link them to different URLs. Image maps come in two varieties: client-side and server-side. Dreamweaver creates client-side image maps through its Image Map Editor.
- Dreamweaver offers three basic drawing tools for creating rectangular, circular, and irregularly shaped image maps, selectable from the Image Property Inspector.
- If your Web site uses server-side image maps, you can make them by modifying and converting Dreamweaver-generated client-side image maps.
- It's possible to create the effect of a graphic rollover, common on Web pages, using client-side image maps. This chapter's Dreamweaver Technique shows you how.

In the next chapter, you learn about forms in Dreamweaver.

✦ ✦ ✦

Working with Interactive Forms

✦ ✦ ✦ ✦

In This Chapter

Forms overview

Including forms in your Web page

Using text fields and text areas

Enabling options with radio buttons, checkboxes, and drop-down lists

Building a Jump menu

Incorporating buttons in your form

Adding hidden fields and password fields

✦ ✦ ✦ ✦

A form, in the everyday world as well as on the Web, is a type of structured communication. When you apply for a driver's license, you're not told to just write down all your personal information, you're asked to fill out a form that asks for specific parts of that information, one at a time, in a specific manner. Web-based forms are just as precise, if not more so.

Dreamweaver has a robust and superior implementation of HTML forms — from the dedicated Forms panel in the Objects palette to various form-specific Property Inspectors. In addition to their importance as a tool for communication between the browsing public and Web site administrators, forms are integral to building some of Dreamweaver's own objects.

In this chapter, you learn how forms are structured and then created within Dreamweaver. Each form object is explored in detail — text fields, radio buttons, checkboxes, menus, list boxes, command buttons, hidden fields, and password fields.

How HTML Forms Work

Forms have a special function in HTML: They support interaction. Virtually all HTML elements apart from forms are concerned with design and presentation — delivering the content to the user, if you will. Forms, on the other hand, give the user the ability to pass information back to Web site creators and administrators. Without forms, the Web would be a one-way street.

Forms have many, many uses on the Web, such as for surveys, electronic commerce, guest books, polls, and even real-time custom graphics creation. For such feedback to be possible, forms require an additional component to what's seen onscreen so that each form can complete its function. Every form needs some type of connection to a Web server, and usually this connection uses a common gateway interface (CGI) script, although JavaScript and Java can also be used. This means that, in addition to designing your forms onscreen, you or someone who works with you must implement a program that collects and manages the information from the form.

Forms, like HTML tables, can be thought of as self-contained units within a Web page. All the elements of a form are contained within the form tag pair `<form>` and `</form>`. Unlike tables, you cannot nest forms, although there's nothing to stop you from having multiple forms on a page.

The `<form>` tag has three attributes, only two of which are commonly used:

✦ The `method` attribute tells the server how the contents of the form should be presented to the CGI program. The two possible `method` values are `get` and `post`. `Get` passes the attached information to a URL; it is rarely used these days because it places limitations on the amount of data that can be passed to the gateway program. `Post` causes the server to present the information as standard input and imposes no limits on the amount of passed data.

✦ The second `<form>` attribute is action. The `action` attribute determines what should be done with the form content. Most commonly, `action` is set to a URL for running a specific CGI program or for sending e-mail.

✦ The third attribute for `<form>` is `enctype`, which specifies the MIME media type. It is infrequently used.

Typical HTML for a `<form>` tag looks something like this:

```
<form method="post" action="http://www.idest.com/_cgi-bin/mailcall.pl">
```

The .pl extension in the preceding example form tag stands for *Perl*—a scripting language often used to create CGI programs. Perl can be edited in any regular text editor.

Within each form is a series of input devices — text boxes, radio buttons, check-boxes, and so on. Each type handles a particular sort of input; in fact, the main tag for these elements is the `<input>` tag. With one exception, the `<textarea>` tag, all form input types are called by specifying the `type` attribute. The text box tag, for example, is written as follows:

```
<input type=text value="lastname">
```

All form-input tags have value attributes. Information input by the user is assigned to the given value. Thus, if I were to fill out a form with a text box asking for my last name, such as the one produced by the foregoing tag, part of the message sent would include the following string:

```
lastname=Lowery
```

Web servers send all the information from a form in one long text string to whatever program or address is specified in the `action` attribute. It's up to the program or the recipient of the form message to parse the string. For instance, if I were to fill out a small form with my name, e-mail address, and a quick comment such as "Good work!", the server would send a text string similar to the following:

```
name=Joseph+Lowery&address=jlowery@idest.com&comment=Good+work%21
```

As you can see, the various fields are separated by ampersands, and the individual words within the responses are separated by plus signs. Characters outside of the lower end of the ASCII set are represented by their hexadecimal values. Decoding this text string is called parsing the response.

If you're not using the mailto method for getting your Web feedback, don't despair. Most CGI programs parse the text string as part of their basic functionality before sending it on its way.

Inserting a Form in Dreamweaver

A form is inserted just like any other object in Dreamweaver. Place the cursor where you want your form to start and then either select the Insert Form button from the Forms panel of the Objects palette or choose Insert ➪ Form from the menus. Dreamweaver inserts a red dashed outline stretching across the Document window to indicate the form.

If you have the Property Inspector open, the Form Property Inspector appears when you insert a form. As you can see from Figure 15-1, you can specify only three values regarding forms: the Form Name, the Action, and the Method.

Specifying a form name enables the form to be directly referenced by JavaScript or other languages. Because of the interactive nature of forms, Web programmers often use this feature to gather information from the user.

In the Action text box, you can directly enter a URL or mailto address, or you can select the folder icon and browse for a file.

Sending your form data via a mailto address is not without its problems. Some browsers, most notably Internet Explorer, are set to warn the user whenever a form button using mailto is selected. While many users let the mail go through, they do have the option to stop it from being sent.

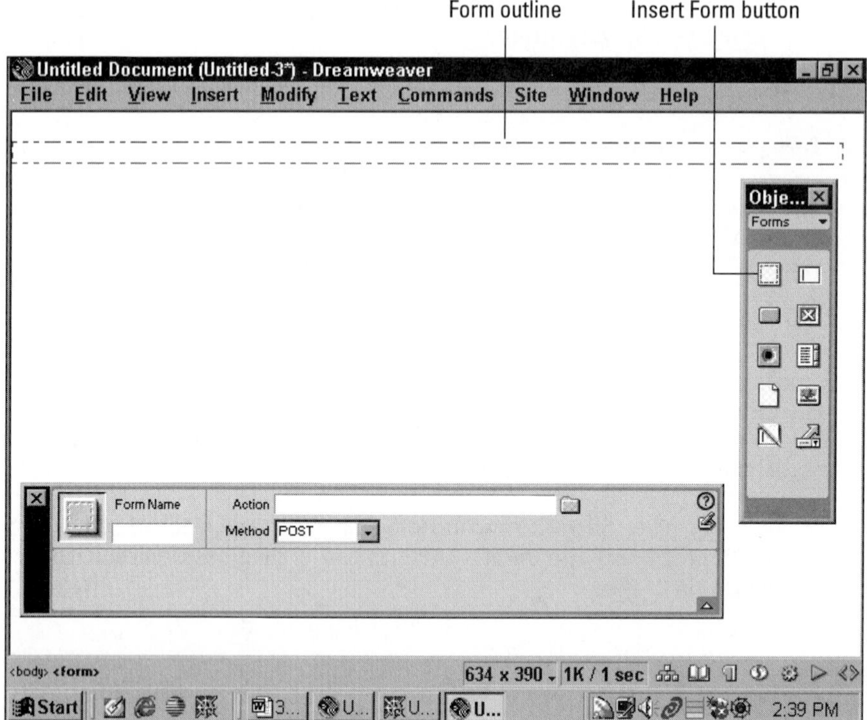

Figure 15-1: Inserting a form creates a dashed red outline of the form and displays the Form Property Inspector, if available.

The Method defaults to POST, the most commonly used option. You can also choose GET or DEFAULT, which leaves the method up to the browser. In most cases, you should leave the method set to POST.

Forms cannot be placed inline with any other element such as text or graphics.

Keep in mind a few considerations when it comes to mixing forms and other Web page elements:

- ✦ Forms expand as objects are inserted into them; you can't resize a form by dragging its boundaries.
- ✦ The outline of a form is invisible; there is no border to turn on or off.
- ✦ Forms and tables can be used together only if the form either completely encloses or is completely enclosed inside the table. In other words, you can't have a form spanning part of a table.

✦ Forms can be inserted within layers, and multiple forms can be in multiple layers. However, the layer must completely enclose the form. As with forms spanning tables, you can't have a form spanning two or more layers. (A workaround for this limitation is discussed in Chapter 28.)

Tip

You can turn off the red dashed form outline in Dreamweaver's preview, if you like. Choose Edit ➪ Preferences and, in the Invisible Elements panel, deselect the Form Delimiter option.

Using Text Boxes

Anytime you use a form to gather text information typed in by a user, you use a form object called a *text field*. Text fields can hold any number of alphanumeric characters. The Web designer can decide whether the text field is displayed in one line or several. When the HTML is written, a multiple-line text field uses a `<textarea>` tag, and a single-line text field is coded with `<input type=text>`.

Declaring the Enctype

The `<form>` attribute `enctype` is helpful in formatting material returned via a form. `Enctype` can have three possible values. By default `enctype` is set to `application/x-www-form-urlencoded`, which is responsible for encoding the form response with ampersands between entries, equal signs linking form element names to their values, spaces as plus signs, and all nonalphanumeric characters in hexadecimal, such as `%3F` (a question mark).

The second `enctype` value, `text/plain` is useful for e-mail replies. Instead of one long string, your form data is transmitted in a more readable format with each form element and its value on a separate line as in this example:

```
fname=Joseph
lname=Lowery
email=jlowery@idest.com
comment=Please send me the information on your new products!
```

The final `enctype` value, `multipart/form-data`, is used only when a file is being uploaded as part of the form. There's a further restriction: The Method should be set to POST, instead of GET.

Dreamweaver doesn't include a space on the Form Property Inspector for the `enctype` attribute, so you have to add it manually either through the HTML Source Inspector or the Quick Tag Editor. To use the Quick Tag Editor, select the `<form>` tag in the Tag Selector and press Ctrl+T (Command+T). Tab to the end of the tag and enter `enctype="value"`, substituting one of the three possible values.

Text fields

To insert a single-line text field in Dreamweaver, you can use any of the following methods:

✦ From the Forms panel of the Objects palette, select the Insert Text Field button to place a text field at your current cursor position.

✦ Choose Insert ➪ Form Object ➪ Text Field from the menu, which inserts a text field at the current cursor position.

✦ Drag the Insert Text Field button from the Objects palette to any existing location in the Document window and release the mouse button to position the text field.

When you insert a text field, the Property Inspector, when displayed, shows you the attributes that can be changed (see Figure 15-2). The size of a text field is measured by the number of characters it can display at one time. You can change the length of a text field by inserting a value in the Char Width text box. By default, Dreamweaver inserts a text field approximately 20 characters wide. The *approximately* is important here because the *final* size of the text field is ultimately controlled by the browser used to view the page. Unless you limit the number of possible characters by entering a value in the Max Chars text box, the user can enter as many characters as desired, and the text box scrolls to display them.

Note that the value in Char Width determines the visible width of the field, whereas the value in Max Chars actually determines the number of characters that can be entered.

The Init Value text box on the Text Field Property Inspector is used to insert a default text string. The user can overwrite this value, if desired.

Password fields

Normally, all text entered into text fields displays as you expect — programmers refer to this process as *echoing*. You can turn off the echoing by selecting the Password option in the Text Field Property Inspector. When a text field is designated as a password field, all text entered by the user shows up as asterisks in Windows systems or as dots on Macintoshes.

Use the password field when you want to protect the user's input from prying eyes (as your PIN number is hidden when you enter it at an ATM, for instance). The information entered in a password field is not encrypted or scrambled in any way, and when sent to the Web administrator, it displays as regular text.

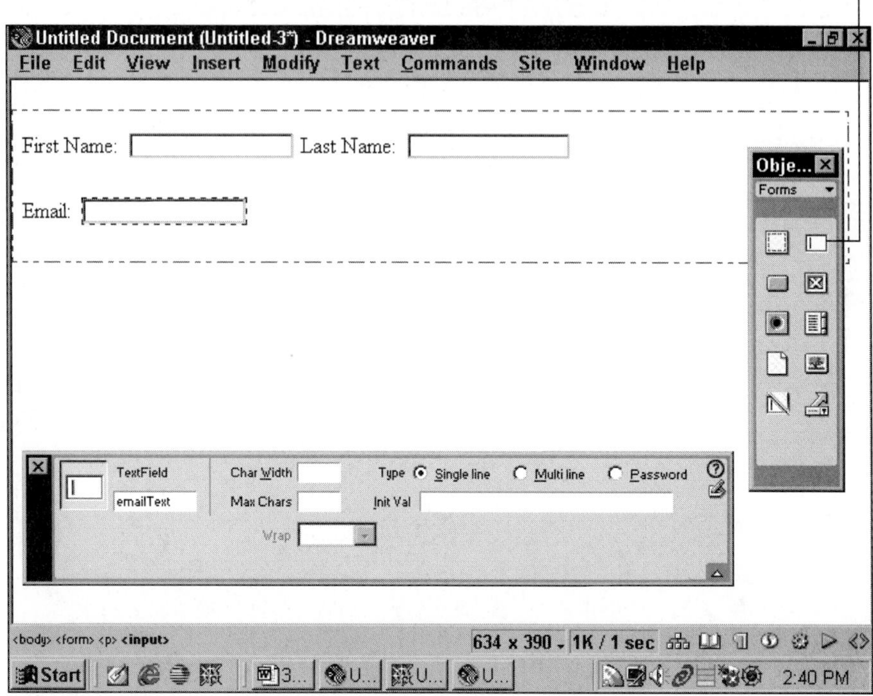

Figure 15-2: The text field of a form is used to enable the user to type in any required information.

Only single-line text fields can be set as password fields. You cannot make a multi-line `<textarea>` tag act as a password field without employing JavaScript or some other programming language.

Multiline text areas

When you want to give your users a generous amount of room to write, set the text field to the Multiline option on the Text Field Property Inspector. This converts the default 20-character width for single-line text fields to a text area approximately 18 characters wide and 3 lines high, with a horizontal and vertical scroll bar. Figure 15-3 shows a typical multiline text field embedded in a form.

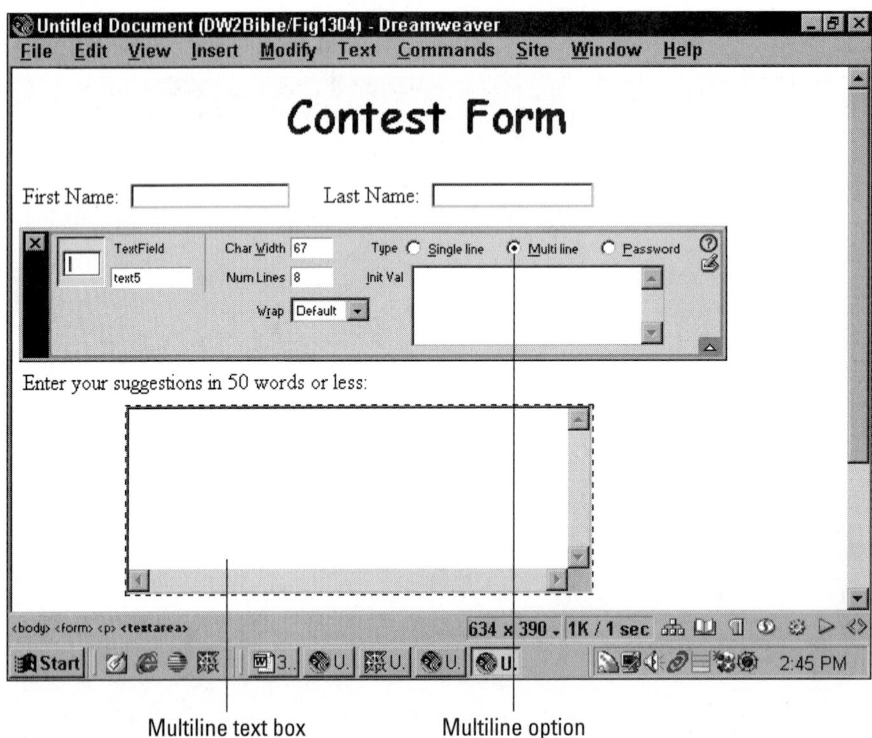

Figure 15-3: The Multiline option of the Text Field Property Inspector opens up a text box for more user information.

You control the width of a multiline text area by entering a value in the Char Width text box of the Text Field Property Inspector, just as you do for single-line text fields. The height of the text area is set equal to the value in the Num Lines text box. As with the default single-line text field, the user can enter any amount of text desired. Unlike the single-line text field, which can restrict the number of characters that can be input through the Max Chars text box, you cannot restrict the number of characters the user enters into a multiline text area.

By default, text entered into a multiline text field does not wrap when it reaches the right edge of the text area; rather, it keeps scrolling until the user presses Enter (Return). Dreamweaver 3 enables you to force the text to wrap by selecting Virtual or Physical from the Wrap drop-down list. The Virtual option wraps text on the screen but not when the response is submitted. To wrap text in both situations, use the Physical wrap option.

One other option is to preload the text area with any default text you like. Enter this text in the Init Val text box of the Text Field Property Inspector. When Dreamweaver writes the HTML code, this text is not entered as a value, as for the single-line text field, but rather goes in between the `<textarea>...</textarea>` tag pair.

Neat Forms

Text field width is measured in a monospaced character width. Because regular fonts are not monospaced, however, lining up text fields and other form objects can be problematic at best. The two general workarounds are preformatted text and tables.

Switching the labels on the form to preformatted text enables you to insert any amount of white space to properly space (or *kern*) your text and other input fields. Previously, Web designers were stuck with the default preformatted text format—the rather plain-looking Courier monospaced font. Now, however, newer browsers (3.0 and later) can read the `face=fontname` attribute. So you can combine a regular font with the preformatted text option and get the best of both worlds.

Going the preformatted text route requires you to insert a lot of spaces. So when you are working on a larger, complex form, using tables is probably a better way to go. Besides the speed of layout, the other advantage that tables offer is the capability to right-align text labels next to your text fields. The top form in the following figure gives an example of using preformatted text to get different-sized form fields to line up properly, while the bottom form in the figure uses a table.

Combining differently sized text fields on a single row—for example, when you're asking for a city, state, and zip code combination—can make the task of lining up your form even more difficult. Most often, you'll spend a fair amount of time in a trial-and-error effort to make the text fields match. Be sure to check your results in the various browsers as you build your form.

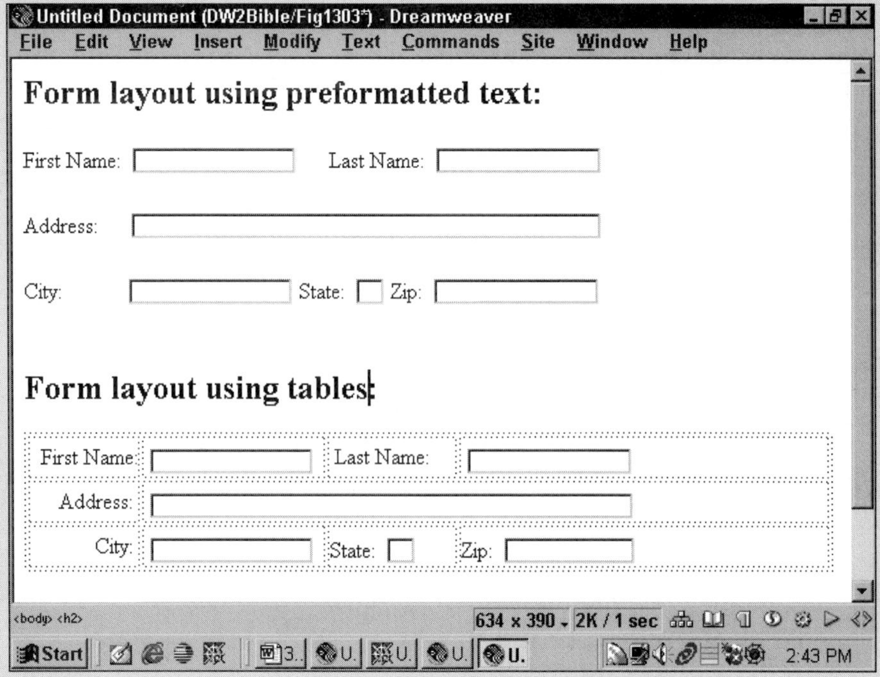

Providing Checkboxes and Radio Buttons

When you want your Web page reader to choose between a specific set of options in your form, you can use either checkboxes or radio buttons. Checkboxes enable you to offer a series of options from which the user can pick as many as desired. Radio buttons, on the other hand, enable your user to choose only one selection from a number of options.

Tip

You can achieve the same functionality as checkboxes and radio buttons with a different look by using the drop-down list and menu boxes. These options for presenting choices to the user are described shortly.

Checkboxes

Checkboxes are often used in a "Select All That Apply" type of section, when you want to enable the user to choose as many of the listed options as desired. You insert a checkbox in much the same way you do a text box: Select or drag the Insert Check Box object from the Objects palette or choose Insert ➪ Form Object ➪ Check Box.

Like other form objects, checkboxes can be given a unique name in the text box provided in the Check Box Property Inspector (Figure 15-4). If you don't provide one, Dreamweaver inserts a generic one, such as checkbox4.

In the Checked Value text box, fill in the information you want passed to a program when the user selects the checkbox. By default, a checkbox starts out unchecked, but you can change that by changing the Initial State option to Checked.

Radio buttons

Radio buttons on a form provide a set of options from which the user can choose only one. If users change their minds after choosing one radio button, selecting another one automatically deselects the first choice. You insert radio buttons in the same manner as checkboxes. Choose or drag Insert Radio Button from the Forms panel of the Objects palette, or choose Insert ➪ Form Object ➪ Radio Button.

Unlike checkboxes and text fields, each radio button in the set does not have a unique name — instead, each group of radio buttons does. Giving the entire set of radio buttons the same name enables browsers to assign one value to the radio button set. That value is determined by the contents of the Checked Value text box. Figure 15-5 shows two different sets of radio buttons. One is named computersRadio and the other, osRadio.

Figure 15-4: Checkboxes are one way of offering the Web page visitor any number of options to choose.

To designate the default selection for each radio button group, you select the particular radio button and make the Initial State option Checked instead of Unchecked. In the form shown in Figure 15-5, the default selection for the osRadio group is Macintosh.

Tip

Because you must give radio buttons in the same set the same name, you can speed up your work a bit by creating one button, copying it, and then pasting the others. Don't forget to change the Checked Value for each button, though.

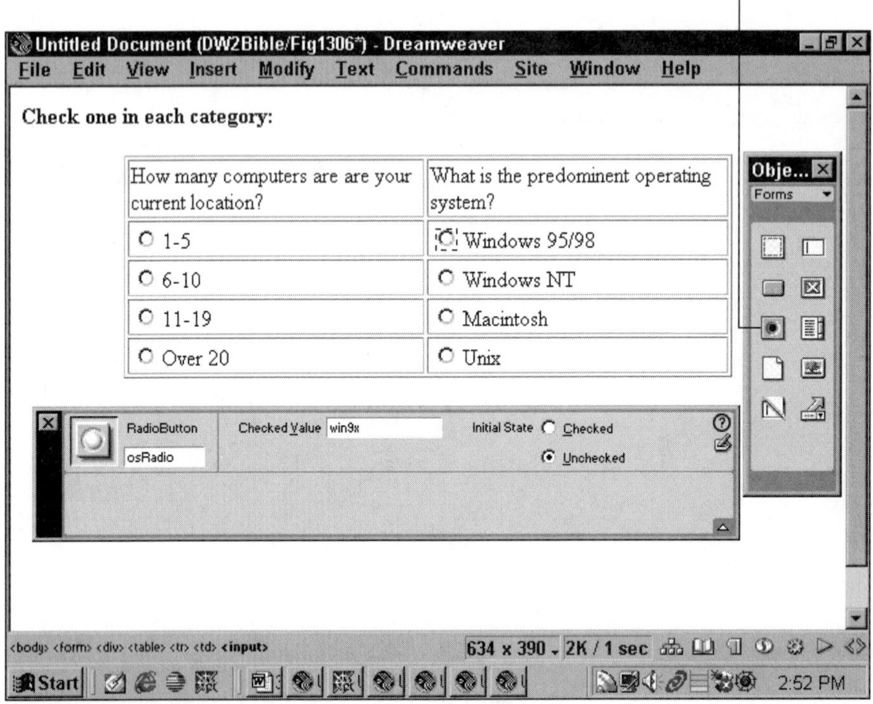

Figure 15-5: Radio buttons enable a user to make just one selection from a group of options.

Creating Form Lists and Menus

Another way to offer your user options, in a more compact form than radio buttons and checkboxes, is with form lists and menus. Both objects can create single-line entries in your form that expand or scroll to reveal all the available options. You can also determine how deep you want the scrolling list to be; that is, how many options you want displayed at a time.

Drop-down menus

A drop-down menu should be familiar to everyday users of computers: The menu is initially displayed as a single-line text box with an option arrow button at the right end; when the button is clicked, the other options are revealed in a list or menu. (Whether the list "pops up" or "drops down" depends on its position in the browser window at the time it is selected. Normally, the list drops down, unless it is close to the bottom of the screen.) The user selects one of the listed options, and when the mouse is released, the list closes up and the selected value remains displayed in the text box.

Insert a drop-down menu in Dreamweaver as you would any other form object, with one of these actions:

✦ From the Forms panel of the Objects palette, select the Insert List/Menu button to place a drop-down menu at the current cursor position.

✦ Choose Insert ➪ Form Object ➪ List/Menu from the menu to insert a drop-down menu at the current cursor position.

✦ Drag the Insert List/Menu button from the Property Inspector to any location in the Document window and release the mouse button to position the drop-down menu.

With the List/Menu object inserted, make sure the Menu option (not the List option) is selected in the Property Inspector, as shown in Figure 15-6. You can also name the drop-down menu by typing a name in the Name text box; if you don't, Dreamweaver supplies a generic "select" name.

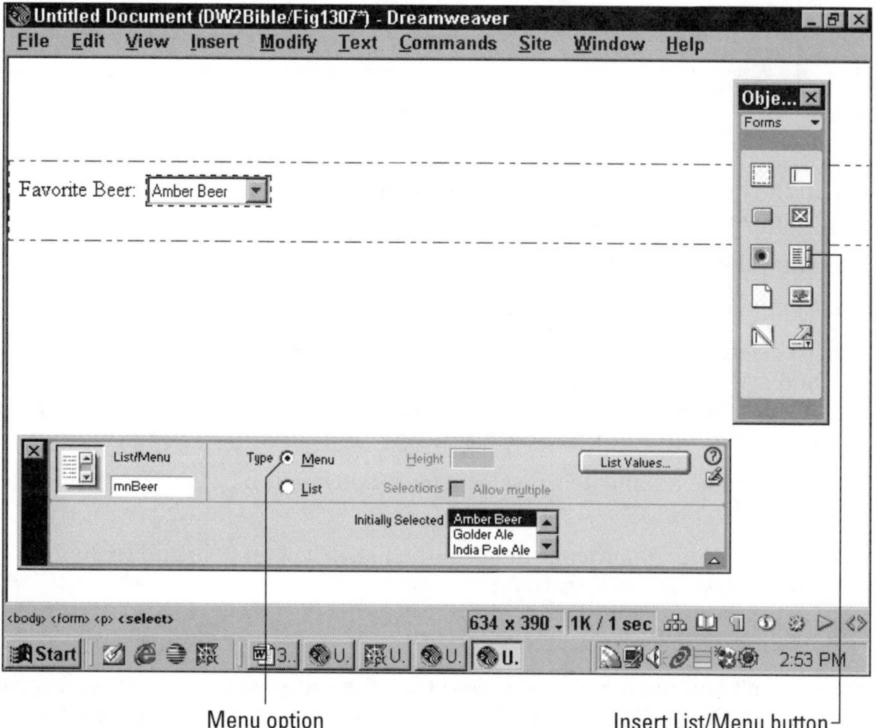

Figure 15-6: Drop-down menus are created by inserting a List/Menu object and then selecting the Menu option in the List/Menu Property Inspector.

Menu values

The HTML code for a drop-down menu uses the `<select>...</select>` tag pair surrounding a number of `<option>...</option>` tag pairs. Dreamweaver gives you a straightforward user interface for entering labels and values for the options on your menu. The menu item's label is what is displayed on the drop-down list; its value is what is sent to the server-side processor when this particular option is selected.

To enter the labels and values for a drop-down menu — or for a scrolling list — follow these steps:

1. Select the menu for which you want to enter values.
2. From the List/Menu Property Inspector, select the List Values button. The List Values dialog box appears (see Figure 15-7).

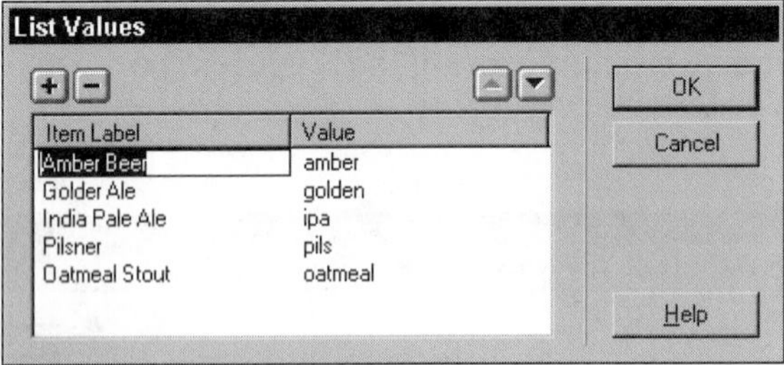

Figure 15-7: Use the List Values dialog box to enter and modify the items in a drop-down menu or scrolling list.

3. In the Item Label column, enter the label for the first item. Press the Tab key to move to the Value column.
4. Enter the value to be associated with this item. Press the Tab key.
5. Continue entering items and values by repeating Steps 3 and 4.
6. To delete an item's label and value in the List Values dialog box, highlight it and select the – (delete) button at the top of the list. To delete either the item's label or value, but not both, highlight either the label or the value and press the Delete or Backspace key.
7. To continue adding items, select the + (add) button or continue using the Tab key.
8. To rearrange the order of items in the list, select an item and then press the up- or down-arrow keys to reposition it.
9. Click OK when you've finished.

If you haven't entered a value for every item, the server-side application receives the label instead. Generally, however, it is a good idea to specify a value for all items.

You can preselect any item in a drop-down menu so that it appears in the list box initially and is highlighted when the full list is displayed. Dreamweaver enables you to pick your selection from the Initially Selected menu in the Property Inspector. The Initially Selected menu is empty until you enter items through the List Values dialog box. You can preselect only one item for a drop-down menu.

Scrolling lists

A scrolling list differs from a drop-down menu in three respects. First, and most obviously, the scrolling list field has up- and down-arrow buttons, rather than an option arrow button, and the user can scroll the list, showing as little as one item at a time, instead of the entire list. Second, you can control the height of the scrolling list, enabling it to display more than one item — or all available items — simultaneously. Third, you can enable the user to select more than one item at a time, as with checkboxes.

A scrolling list is inserted in the same manner as a drop-down menu — through the Objects palette or the Insert ➪ Form Object menu. Once the object is inserted, select the List option in the List/Menu Property Inspector.

You enter items for your scrolling list just as you do with a drop-down menu, by starting with the List Values button and filling in the List Values dialog box.

As it does for drop-down menus, Dreamweaver automatically shows the first list item in the scrolling list's single-line text box. However, all the list items are displayed in the Document window, as shown in Figure 15-8.

By default, the Selections checkbox for Allow multiple is enabled in the List/Menu Property Inspector, and the Height box (which controls the number of items visible at one time) is empty.

When multiple selections are enabled (by selecting the Allow multiple checkbox), the user can then make multiple selections by using two keyboard modifiers, the Shift and Control keys:

- ✦ To select several adjacent items in the list, the user must click the first item in the list, press the Shift key, and select the last item in the list.
- ✦ To select several nonadjacent items, the user must hold down the Control key while selecting the items.

Other than the highlighted text, no other acknowledgment (such as a checkmark) appears in the list. As with drop-down menus, the Web designer can preselect options by highlighting them in the Initially Selected menu. Use the same techniques with the Shift and Control keys as a user would.

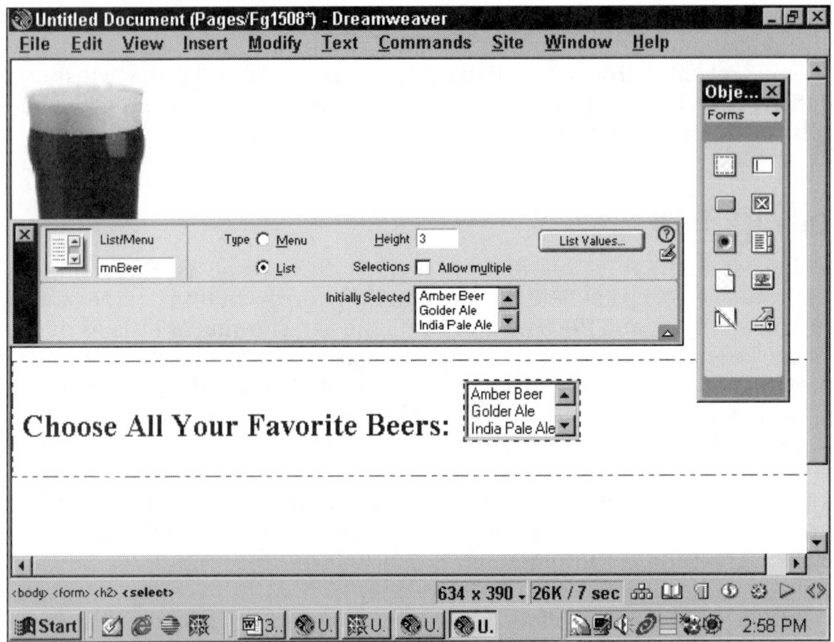

Figure 15-8: Scrolling lists enable multiple selections.

Keep in mind several factors as you are working with scrolling lists:

✦ If you disable the Allow Multiple Selections box and do not set a Height value greater than 1, the list appears as a drop-down menu.

✦ If you do not set a Height value at all, the number of items that appear onscreen is left up to the browser. Internet Explorer, by default, shows four items at a time, and Navigator displays all the items in your list. To exercise control over your scrolling list, it is best to insert a Height value.

✦ The widths of both the scrolling list and the drop-down menu are determined by the number of characters in the longest label. To widen the List/Menu object, you must directly enter additional spaces (` `) in the HTML code; Dreamweaver does not recognize additional spaces entered through the List Values dialog box. For example, to expand the Favorite Beer List/Menu object in our example, you'd need to use the HTML Inspector or another editor to change the following code:

```
<option value="oatmeal">Oatmeal Stout</option>
```

to this:

```
<option value="oatmeal">Oatmeal Stout ¬
   </option>
```

Navigating with a Jump Menu

It's not always practical to use a series of buttons as the primary navigation tool on a Web site. For sites that want to offer access to a great number of pages, a *jump menu* can be a better way to go. A jump menu uses the menu form element to list the various options; when one of the options is chosen, the browser loads — or jumps to — a new page. In addition to providing a single mechanism for navigation, a jump menu is easy to update because it doesn't require relaying out the page. Because they are JavaScript-driven, jump menus can even be updated dynamically.

Dreamweaver 3 includes a jump menu object that handles all the JavaScript coding for you — all you have to provide is a list of item names and associated URLs. Dreamweaver even drops in a Go button for you, if you choose. The Jump Menu object is easily used in a frame-based layout for targeting specific frames. Once inserted, the Jump Menu object is modified like any other list object, through the List/Menu Property Inspector.

To insert a jump menu, follow these steps:

1. Position your cursor in the current form, if one exists, where you'd like the jump menu to appear.

   If you haven't already inserted a form, don't worry. Dreamweaver automatically inserts one for you.

2. From the Forms panel of the Objects palette, choose the Insert Jump Menu button.

   The Insert Jump Menu dialog box, shown in Figure 15-9, is displayed.

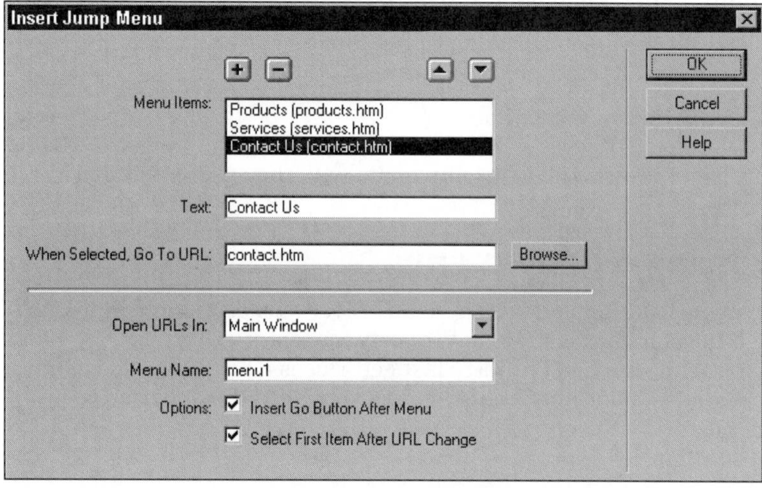

Figure 15-9: Consolidate your Web site navigation through a jump menu.

3. In the Insert Jump Menu dialog box, enter the label for the first item in the Text field.

   When you confirm your entry by tabbing out of the field, Dreamweaver updates the Menu Items list.

4. Enter the path and file name of the page you want opened for the current item in the When Selected, Go To URL field; alternatively, you can select the Browse (Choose) button to select your file.

5. To add additional jump menu items, select the add (+) button and repeat Steps 3 and 4.

6. You can adjust the positioning of the items in the jump menu by selecting an item in the Menu List and using the up and down arrows to move it higher or lower.

7. Pick the destination target for the page from the Open URLs In list.

   Unless you're working in a frameset, you have only one option — Main Window. When a Jump Menu object is added in a frameset, Dreamweaver displays all frame names as well as Main Window as options.

Tip

The Main Window option always replaces your current page with the new page. If you want to have your new page open in a separate window, and keep your current page active, you'll have to edit the HTML. Select the jump menu object on the page and open the Quick Tag Editor. In the code, locate the onChange event and change "parent" to "_blank." If you're working with a Go button, you need to follow the same procedure with the `onClick` event of the tag.

8. If desired, enter a unique name for the jump menu in the Menu Name field.

9. To add a button that activates the jump menu choice, select the Insert Go Button After Menu option.

10. To reset the menu selection to the top item after every jump, choose the Select First Item After URL Change.

11. Click OK when you're done.

Dreamweaver inserts the new jump menu with the appropriate linking code.

Modifying a jump menu

Once you've inserted your Jump Menu object, you can modify it in one of two ways: through the standard List/Menu Property Inspector or through the Jump Menu behavior. While the List Property Inspector uses a List Value dialog box, editing the Jump Menu behavior opens a dialog box similar to the one used to insert the jump menu object.

To alter the items in an existing jump menu via the List/Menu Property Inspector, select the jump menu and click the List Values button. In the List Values dialog box, you see the jump menu labels on the left and the URLs on the right. You can add, move, or delete items as you would with any other list.

Note one caveat for adding new URLs to the jump menu through the Property Inspector: Any file names with spaces or special characters should be URL-encoded. In other words, if one of your file names is `about us.htm`, it should be entered using the hexadecimal equivalent for a space (%20): `about%20us.htm`.

If you'd prefer to work in the same environment as you did when creating the Jump Menu object, go the Behavior Inspector route. Select the jump menu and from the Behavior Inspector double-click the Jump Menu event. The Jump Menu dialog box opens—it is identical to the Insert Jump Menu dialog box except the Go button option is not available.

Activating Go buttons

The Dreamweaver jump menu is activated immediately whenever a user makes a choice from the list. So why would you want a Go button? The Go button, as implemented in Dreamweaver, is useful for selecting the first item in a jump menu list. To ensure that the Go button is the sole means for activating a jump selection, you need to remove an attached behavior. Select the jump menu item and then open the Behavior Inspector. From the Behavior Inspector, delete the Jump Menu event.

Some Web designers prefer to use a non-URL choice for the first item, such as "Please Select A Department." When entering such a non-URL option, set the Go to URL (or the Value in the List Value Properties) to #.

The generic Go button is a nice convenience, but it's a little, well, generic. To switch from a standard Go button to a graphical Go button of your choosing, follow these steps:

1. Insert the image that you want to use as your new Go button next to the jump menu.
2. With the new graphic selected, open the Behavior Inspector.
3. Select Jump Menu Go from the Add Event drop-down list.

   Dreamweaver displays a dialog box showing all available jump menus.
4. Choose the name of the current jump menu from the Jump Menu Go dialog box list; click OK when you're done.
5. If necessary, delete the Dreamweaver-inserted Go button.

Activating Your Form with Buttons

Buttons are essential to HTML forms. You can place all the form objects you want on a page, but until your user presses that Submit button, there's no interaction between the client and the server. HTML provides three basic types of buttons: Submit, Reset, and Command buttons.

Submit, Reset, and Command buttons

A Submit button sends the form to the specified Action (generally the URL of a server-side program or a mailto address) using the noted Method (generally `post`). A Reset button clears all the fields in the form. Submit and Reset are both reserved HTML terms used to invoke specific actions.

Wrapping Graphics around a Jump Menu

Jump menus are useful in many circumstances, but as a raw form element, they often stick out of a Web page design like a sore thumb. Some designers solve this dilemma by including their jump menu within a specially constructed graphic. The easiest way to create such a graphic is to use a program like Fireworks, which enables a single image to be sliced up into separate parts. The slices are then exported to an HTML file and reassembled in a table.

When you create your graphic, you need to leave room for the jump menu to be inserted in Dreamweaver. This usually entails designating one slice as a nongraphic or text-only slice in your graphics program. Fireworks uses a transparent GIF—called a *shim*—as a placeholder. Once you bring the HTML into Dreamweaver, delete the shim image and insert the Jump Menu object in its place.

Here are a few pointers for wrapping a graphic around a jump menu:

- ✦ Use a flat color—not a gradient—as the background for the menu.
- ✦ Select the background color of the graphic to be the background color of the cell of the table holding your jump menu.
- ✦ Make sure you leave enough height in your graphic to accommodate the jump menu in all browsers. Netscape displays a standard list/menu form element approximately 24 pixels high on a PC; I typically leave about 30 pixels in my graphic.
- ✦ Form elements are drawn by the user's operating system and are vastly different on each platform. Test your designs extensively.

✦ Integrate your Go button, if you're using one, right in the graphic. Be sure to set it as its own slice, so it comes in as a separate image and can be activated with a Jump Menu Go behavior.

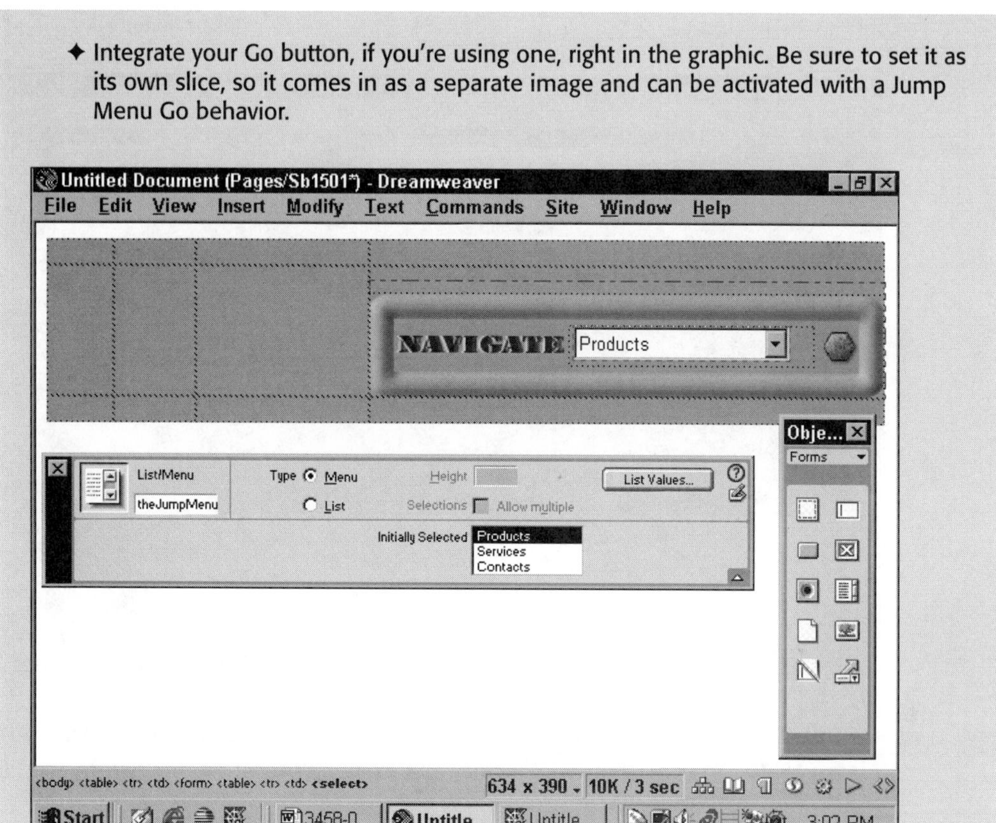

A Command button permits the execution of functions defined by the Web designer, as programmed in JavaScript or other languages.

To insert a button in Dreamweaver, follow these steps:

1. Position the cursor where you want the button to appear. Then either select the Insert Button icon from the Form pane of the Objects palette, or choose Insert ⇨ Form Object ⇨ Button from the menus. Or you can simply drag the Insert Button button from the Objects palette and drop it into place on an existing form.

2. Choose the button Action type. As shown in Figure 15-10, the Button Property Inspector indicates that the Submit form button action is selected. (This is the default.) To make a Reset button, select the Reset form option. To make a Command button, select the None option.

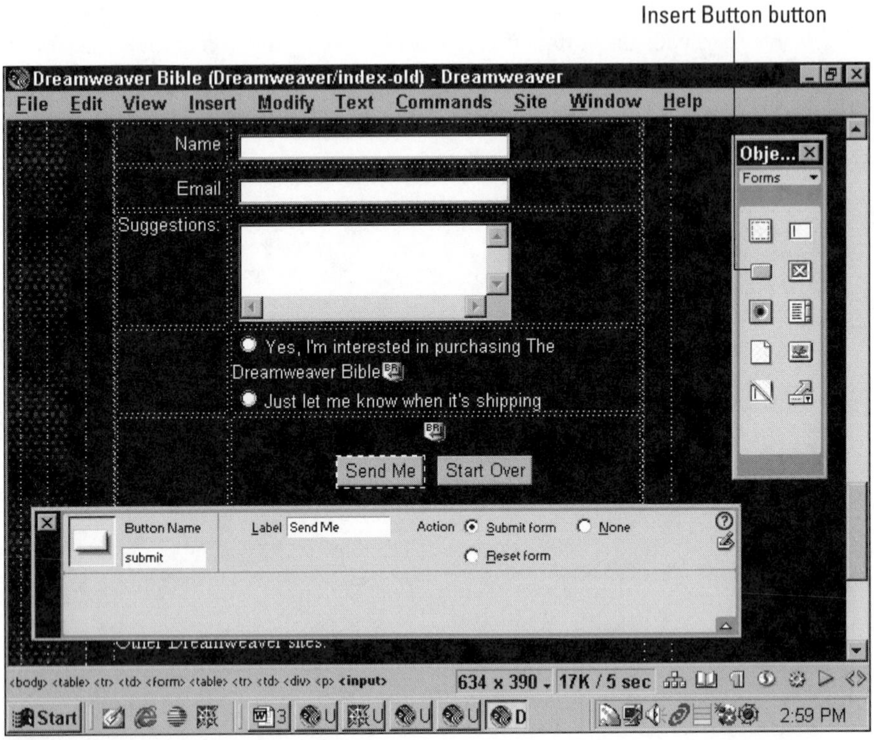

Figure 15-10: You can choose a function and a label for a button through the Button Property Inspector.

3. To change the name of any button as you want it to appear on the Web page, enter the new name in the Label text box.

When working with Command buttons, it's not enough to just insert the button and give it a name. You have to link the button to a specific function. A common technique is to use JavaScript's `onClick` event to call a function detailed in the `<script>` section of the document:

```
<input type="BUTTON" name="submit2" value="yes" ¬
onClick="doFunction()">
```

Graphical buttons

HTML doesn't limit you to the browser-style default buttons. You can also use an image as a Submit, Reset, or Command button. Dreamweaver has the capability to add an image field just like other form elements: Place the cursor in the desired position and choose Insert ➪ Form Object ➪ Image Field, or select the Image Field button from the Forms panel of the Objects palette. You can use multiple image fields in a form to give the user a graphical choice, as shown in Figure 15-11.

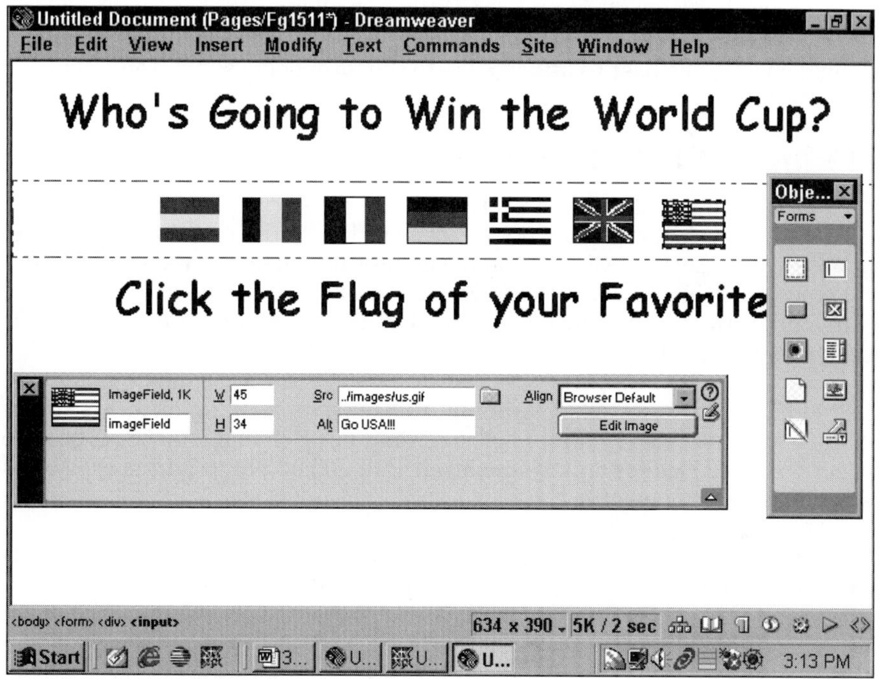

Figure 15-11: Each flag in this page is not just an image; it's an image field that also acts as a Submit button.

When the user clicks the picture that you've designated as an image field for a Submit button, the form is submitted. Any other functionality, such as resetting the fields, must be coded in JavaScript or another language and triggered by attaching an `onClick` event to the button. This can be handled through the Dreamweaver behaviors, covered in Chapter 17 or by hand-coding the script and inserting the `onClick` code.

In fact, when the user clicks a graphical button, not only does it submit your form, but also it passes along the *x, y* coordinates of the image. The *x* coordinate is submitted using the name of the field and an `.x` attached; likewise, the *y* coordinate is submitted with the name of the field and a `.y` attached. Although this latter feature isn't often used, it's always good to know all the capabilities of your HTML tools.

For detailed information about how to use a graphic as a form button, see the section, "Posting Form Data with a Submit Button," in Chapter 18.

Using the Hidden Field and the File Field

You should also be aware of a couple of other special-purpose form fields. The *hidden field* and the *file field* are supported through all major browsers. The hidden field is extremely useful for passing variables to your gateway programs, and the file field enables the user to attach a file to the form being submitted.

The hidden input type

When passing information from a form to a CGI program, the programmer often needs to send data that should not be made visible to the user. The data could be a variable needed by the CGI program to set information on the recipient of the form, or it could be a URL to which the CGI program will redirect the user after the form is submitted. To send this sort of information unseen by the form user, you must use a hidden form object.

The hidden field is inserted in a form much like the other form elements. To insert a hidden field, place your cursor in the desired position and choose Insert ➪ Form Object ➪ Hidden Field or choose the Insert Hidden Field button from the Forms panel of the Objects palette.

The hidden object is another input type, just like the text, radio button, and checkbox types. A hidden variable looks like this in HTML:

```
<input type="hidden" name="recipient" value="jlowery@idest.com">
```

As you would expect, this tag has no representation when it's viewed though a browser. However, Dreamweaver does display a Hidden Form Element Invisible symbol in the Document window. You can turn off the display of this symbol by deselecting the Hidden Form Element option from the Invisible Elements panel of Preferences.

The file input type

Much more rarely used is the file input type, which enables any stored computer file to be attached to the form and sent with the other data. Used primarily to enable the easy sharing of data, the file input type has been largely supplanted by modern e-mail methods, which also enable files to be attached to messages.

The file field is inserted in a form much like the other form elements. To insert a file field, place your cursor in the desired position and choose Insert ➪ Form Object ➪ File Field or choose the Insert File Field button from the Forms panel of the Objects palette. Dreamweaver automatically inserts a text box for the file name to be input, with a Browse (Choose) button on the right. In a browser, the user's selection of the Browse (Choose) button displays a standard Open File dialog box from which a file can be selected to go with the form.

Summary

HTML forms provide a basic line of communication from Web page visitor to Web page administrator. With Dreamweaver, you can enter and modify most varieties of form inputs, including text fields and checkboxes.

- ✦ For the most part, a complete form requires two working parts: the form object inserted in your Web page and a CGI program stored on your Web server.
- ✦ To avoid using a server-side script, you can use a mailto address rather than a URL pointing to a program in a form's `action` attribute. However, you still have to parse the form reply to convert it to a usable format.
- ✦ The basic types of form input are text fields, text areas, radio buttons, checkboxes, drop-down menus, and scrolling lists.
- ✦ Dreamweaver includes a Jump Menu object, which uses a drop-down list as a navigational system.
- ✦ Once a form is completed, it must be sent to the server-side application. This is usually done through a Submit button on the form. Dreamweaver also supports Reset and user-definable Command buttons.

In the next chapter, you learn how to use Dreamweaver to develop frames and framesets.

✦ ✦ ✦

CHAPTER 16

Using Frames and Framesets

✦ ✦ ✦ ✦

In This Chapter

Fundamentals of HTML frames and framesets

Creating frames visually

Fast framesets with Frame objects

Altering frames and framesets

Opening links in specific frames

Working with borders, scroll bars, and margins

Inserting frameless content

✦ ✦ ✦ ✦

The first time I fully appreciated the power of frames, I was visiting a site that displayed examples of what the Webmaster considered "bad" Web pages. The site was essentially a jump-station with a series of links. The author used a frameset with three frames: one that ran all the way across the top of the page, displaying a logo and other basic information; one narrow panel on the left with a scrolling set of links to the sites themselves; and the main viewing area, which took up two-thirds of the center screen. Selecting any of the links caused the site to appear in the main viewing frame.

I was astounded when I finally realized that each frame was truly an independent Web page and that you didn't have to use only Web pages on your own site—you could link to any page on the Internet. That was when I also realized the amount of work involved in establishing a frame Web site: Every page displayed on that site used multiple HTML pages.

Dreamweaver takes the head-pounding complexity out of coding and managing frames with a point-and-click interface. You get easy access to the commands for modifying the properties of the overall frame structure as well as each individual frame. This chapter gives you an overview of frames, as well as all the specifics you need for inserting and modifying frames and framesets. Special attention is given to defining the unique look of frames through borders, scroll bars, and margins.

Frames constitute one of the Webmaster's major design tools. A frame is a Web page that is subdivided into both static and changing HTML pages. Not too long ago, the evolution of frames was right where Dynamic HTML is today, in terms of general acceptance. The use of frames and framesets has become even more widespread over the last year or so, and the technology is now supported through every major browser version. It's safe to say that every Web designer today needs a working knowledge of frames to stay competitive.

Frames and Framesets: The Basics

It's best to think of frames in two major parts: the frameset and the frames. The frameset is the HTML document that defines the framing structure — the number of individual frames that make up a page, their initial size, and the shared attributes among all the frames. A frameset by itself is never displayed. Frames, on the other hand, are complete HTML documents that can be viewed and edited separately or together in the organization described by the frameset.

A frameset takes the place of the <body> tags in an HTML document, where the content of a Web page is found. Here's what the HTML for a basic frameset looks like:

```
<frameset rows="50%,50%">
  <frame src="top.html">
  <frame src="bottom.html">
</frameset>
```

Notice that the content of a <frameset> tag consists entirely of <frame> tags, each one referring to a different Web page. The only other element that can be used inside of a <frameset> tag is another <frameset> tag.

Columns and rows

Framesets, much like tables, are made up of columns and rows. The columns and rows attributes (cols and rows) are lists of comma-separated values. The number of values indicates the number of either columns or rows, and the values themselves establish the size of the columns or rows. Thus, a <frameset> tag that looks like this:

```
<frameset cols="67,355,68">
```

denotes three columns of widths 67, 355, and 68, respectively. And this frameset tag:

```
<frameset cols="270,232" rows="384,400">
```

declares that two columns exist with the specified widths (270 and 232) and two rows with the specified heights (384 and 400).

Sizing frames

Column widths and row heights can be set as absolute measurements in pixels, or expressed as a percentage of the entire screen. HTML frames also support an attribute that assigns the size relative to the other columns or rows. In other words, the relative attribute (designated with an asterisk) assigns the balance of the remaining available screen space to a column or row. For example, the following frameset:

```
<frameset cols="80,*">
```

sets up two frames, one 80 pixels wide and the other as large as the browser window allows. This ensures that the first column will always be a constant size—making it perfect for a set of navigational buttons—while the second is as wide as possible.

The relative attribute can also be used proportionally. When preceded by an integer, as in `n*`, this attribute specifies that the frame is allocated *n* times the space it would have received otherwise. So frameset code like this:

```
<frameset rows="4*,*">
```

ensures that one row is proportionately four times the size of the other.

Creating a Frameset and Frames

Dreamweaver offers two ways to divide your Web page into frames and make your frameset. The first method uses the menus. Choose Modify ➪ Frameset and, from the submenu, select the direction in which you would like to split the frame: left, right, up, or down. Left or right splits the frame in half vertically; up or down splits it horizontally in half.

To create a frameset visually, using the mouse, follow these steps:

1. Turn on the frame borders in your Dreamweaver Document window by selecting View ➪ Frame Borders.

   A 3-pixel-wide inner border appears along the edges of your Document window.

2. Position the cursor over any of the frame borders.

3. Press Alt (Option).

   If your pointer is over a frame border, the pointer changes into a two-headed arrow when over an edge and a four-headed arrow (or a drag-hand on the Mac) when over a corner.

4. Drag the frame border into the Document window. Figure 16-1 shows a four-frame frameset being created.

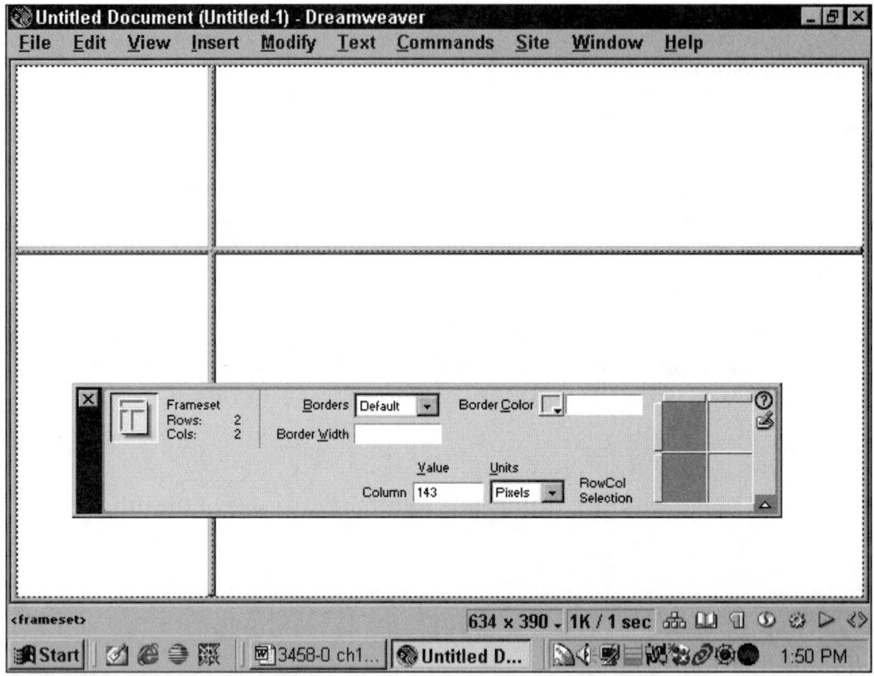

Figure 16-1: After you've enabled the frame borders, you can drag out your frameset structure with the mouse.

Dreamweaver initially assigns a temporary file name and an absolute pixel value to your HTML frameset code. Both can be modified later, if you wish.

With the menu method of frameset creation, you can initially create only a two-way frame split. To further split the frame using the menu commands, you must first select each frame. However, by Alt+dragging (Option+dragging) the corner of the frame border, you can quickly create a four-frame frameset.

When the frameset is selected, Dreamweaver displays a black, dotted line along all the frame borders and within every frame. You can easily reposition any frameset border by clicking and dragging it. If you just want to move the border, make sure you don't press the Alt or Option key while dragging the border; this action creates additional frames.

If you create a four-frame frameset in two stages, by first splitting the Web page in one direction and then dragging a frame border to split it in another, you'll find a small aberration in the HTML code. Dreamweaver adds the relative indicator (*) to the second set of frames, as shown in this code:

```
<frameset rows="265,237" cols="323*,455">
```

Although, in most cases, this coding does not create any problems for the user, it could lead to undesired results when the window is resized. To avoid this possible problem, when you know you are building a four-frame frameset, drag the frame border from the corner to create the frameset all at once. If you must create the frameset in two steps, change the relative value to a pixel or percentage value.

Adding more frames

You're not at all limited to your initial frame choices. In addition to being able to move them visually, you can also set the size through the Frameset Property Inspector, as described in the next section. Furthermore, you can continue to split either the entire frame or each column or row as needed. When you divide a column or row into one or more frames, you are actually nesting one frameset inside another.

Tip

Once you've created the basic frame structure, you can select View ➪ Frame Borders again (it's a toggle) to turn the borders off and create a more accurate preview of your page.

Using the menus

To split an existing frame using the menus, position the cursor in the frame you want to alter and choose Modify ➪ Frameset ➪ Split Frame Left, Right, Up, or Down. Figure 16-2 shows a two-row frameset in which the bottom row was split into two columns and then repositioned. The Frameset Property Inspector indicates that the inner frameset (2 columns, 1 row) is selected. The direction in the command (Left, Right, Up, and Down) indicates the frame the existing page will be placed in. For example, I selected Split Frame Right for Figure 16-2, and the current page is placed in the right frame.

You can clearly see the "nested" nature of the code in this HTML fragment describing the frameset in Figure 16-2:

```
<frameset rows="163,333" cols="784">
  <frame src="file://Dev/UntitledFrame-34">
  <frameset cols="115,663" rows="*">
    <frame src="file://Dev/UntitledFrame-57">
    <frame src="file://Dev/UntitledFrame-35">
  </frameset>
</frameset>
```

Tip

You can also split an existing frame by Alt+dragging (Option+dragging) the current frame's border, but you have to choose an inner border that does not extend across the page.

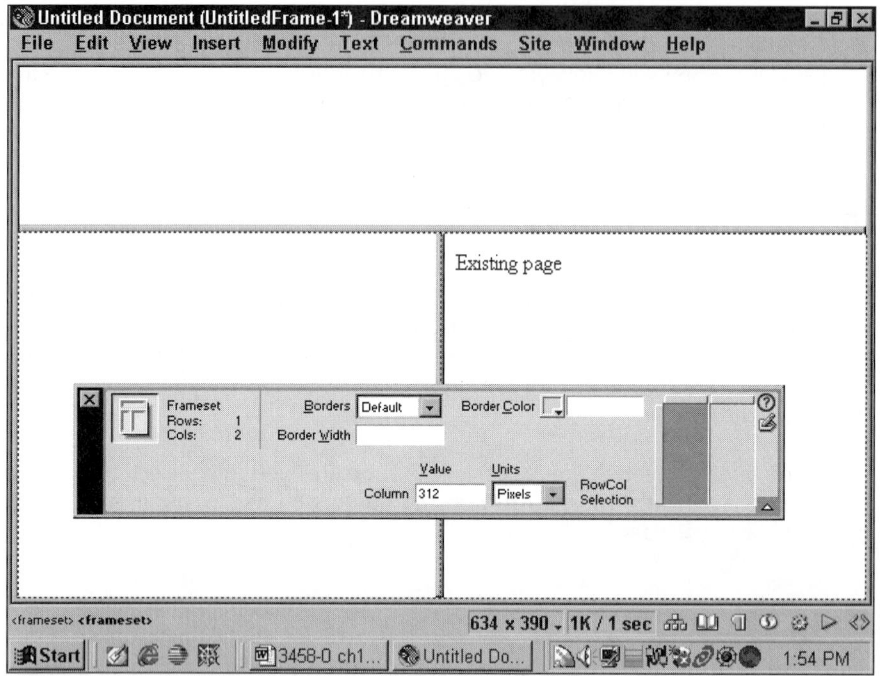

Figure 16-2: Use the Modify ⇨ Frameset menu option to split an existing frame into additional columns or rows and create a nested frameset.

Using the mouse

When you need to create additional columns or rows that span the entire Web page, use the mouse method instead of the menus. Option+drag or Alt+drag any of the current frame's borders that go across the entire page, such as one of the outer borders. Figure 16-3 shows a new row added along the bottom of our previous frame structure.

Tip

You can also split a smaller frame by first selecting it and then Alt+dragging or Option+dragging one of its borders. As you can see in this chapter, you select a frame by Alt+clicking (Windows) or Option+Shift+clicking (Macintosh) inside the frame.

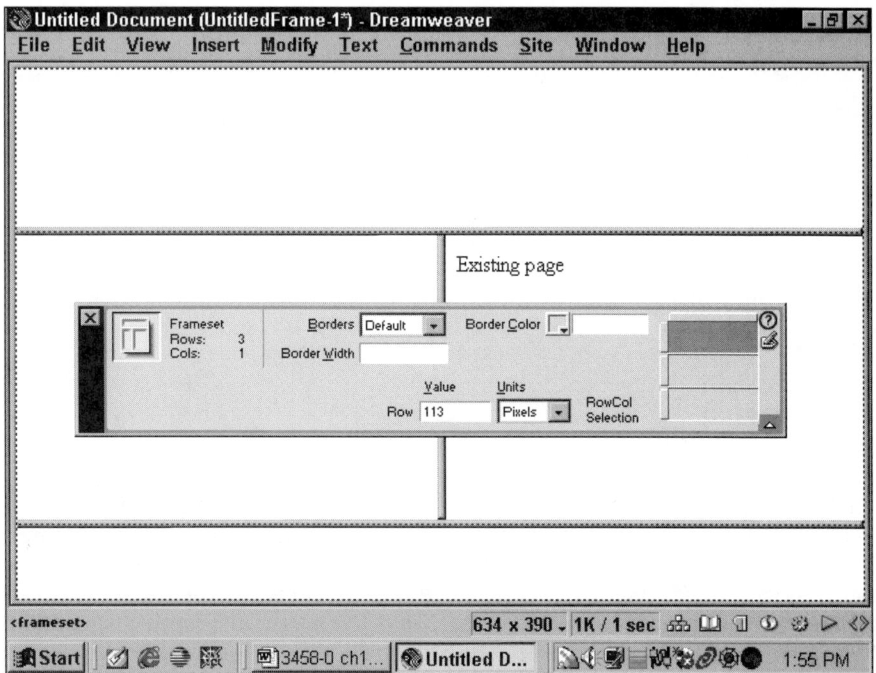

Figure 16-3: An additional frame row was added using the Alt+drag (Option+drag) method.

Quick Framesets with the Frame Objects

Dragging out your frameset in Dreamweaver is a clear-cut method of setting up the various frames. However, now matter how easy it is, it can still be a bit of a chore to create even simple framesets by clicking and dragging. To hasten the development workflow, Dreamweaver 3 introduces Frame objects, which can build a frameset with a single click.

Although a frame-based Web design could potentially be quite complex with numerous nested framesets, most of the sites using frames follow a more simple, general pattern. Dreamweaver 3 offers eight of the most common frameset configurations in the new Frames panel of the Objects palette, shown in Figure 16-4. Choose one of the basic designs, and you're ready to tweak the frame sizes and begin filling in the content. It's a great combination of ease-of-use mixed with design flexibility.

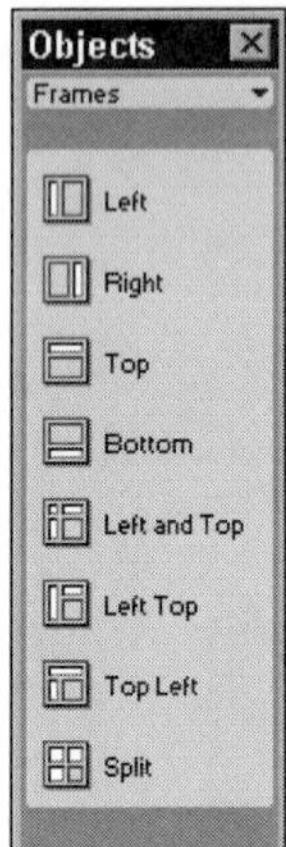

Figure 16-4: The new Frames panel holds eight of the most commonly used frameset configurations.

The Frames panel is roughly organized from simplest framesets to most complex. You might notice that each of the icons on the panel shows an example frameset with one blue section. The placement of the color is quite significant. The blue indicates in which frame the current page will appear when the frameset is constructed. For example, if I had begun to construct my main content page, and then decided to turn it into a frameset with a separate navigation strip frame beneath it, I would choose the Bottom Frames object. Figure 16-5 provides a before-and-after example with the preframe content on the left and the same content after a Bottom Frame object has been applied.

The eight different framesets available from the Frames panel are

- ✦ **Left:** Inserts a blank frame to the left of the current page.
- ✦ **Right:** Inserts a blank frame to the right of the current page.
- ✦ **Top:** Inserts a blank frame above the current page.
- ✦ **Bottom:** Inserts a blank frame below the current page.
- ✦ **Left and Top:** Makes a frameset with four frames where the current page is in the lower right.
- ✦ **Left Top:** Makes a frameset where the left spans the two rightmost frames; a nested frameset is used to create the right frames. The existing page is placed in the lower-right frame.
- ✦ **Top Left:** Makes a frameset where the top spans the lower two frames; the lower frames are created using a nested frameset. The existing page is placed in the lower-right frame.
- ✦ **Split:** Creates a frameset with four equal frames and moves the existing page to the lower right.

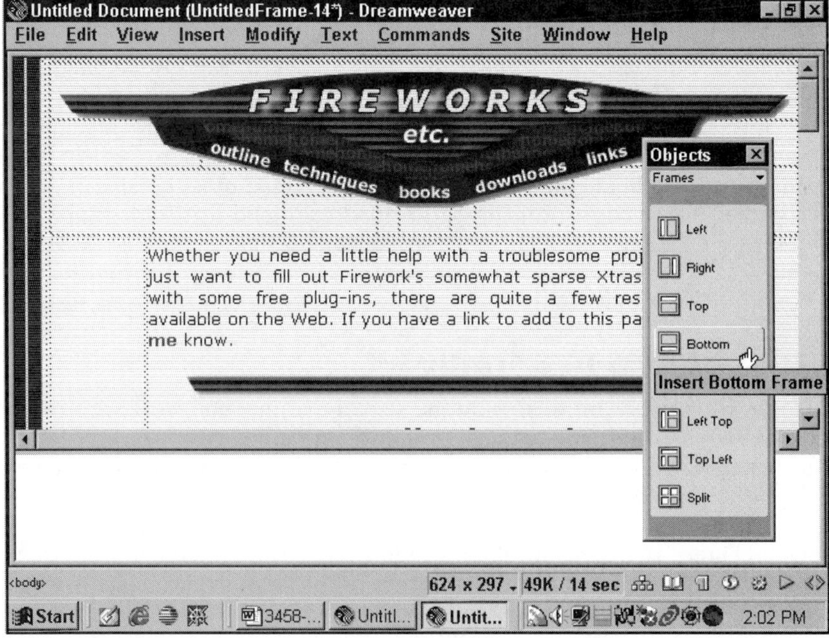

Figure 16-5: Existing content is incorporated in a new frameset when a Frames object is chosen.

Using the Frame objects is quite literally a one-click operation. Just select the desired frameset, and Dreamweaver automatically turns on Frame Borders, if necessary, and creates and names the required frames. For all Frame objects, the existing page is moved to a frame where the scrolling option is set at Default, and the size is relative to the rest of the frameset. In other words, the existing page can be scrolled and expands to fill the content. For this reason, it's best to apply a Frame object to an existing page only if it is intended to be the primary content frame. Otherwise, it's better to select the Frame object while a blank page is open and then use the File ➪ Open in Frame command to load any existing pages into the individual frames.

For almost all of the Frame objects, Dreamweaver creates one or more frames with a set size. Although by default, the set width or height is 80 pixels, you can easily resize the frame by dragging the frame border. The only frameset that does not have at least one set frame is the Split object where the four frames are divided equally. Dreamweaver also sets the Scroll option to No for frames with absolute sizes.

Working with the Frameset Property Inspector

The Frameset Property Inspector manages those elements, such as the borders, that are common to all the frames within a frameset; it also offers more precise sizing control over individual rows and columns than you can do visually. To access the Frameset Property Inspector, choose Window ➪ Properties, if the Property Inspector is not already open, and then select any of the frame borders.

When a browser visits a Web page that uses frames, it displays the title found in the frameset HTML document for the entire frame. You can set that title in Dreamweaver by selecting the frameset and then choosing Modify ➪ Page Properties. In the Page Properties dialog box, enter your choice of title in the Title text box, as you would for any other Web page. All the other options in the Page Properties dialog box—including background color and text color—apply to the `<noframes>` content, covered in the section "Handling Frameless Browsers," later in this chapter.

Resizing frames in a frameset

With HTML, when you want to specify the size of a frame, you work with the row or column in which the frame resides. Dreamweaver gives you two ways to alter a frame's size: by dragging the border or, to be more precise, by specifying a value in the Property Inspector.

As shown in Figure 16-6, Dreamweaver's Frameset Property Inspector contains a Row/Column selector to display the structure of the selected frameset. For each frameset, you select the tab along the top or left side of the Row/Column selector to choose the column or row you want to modify.

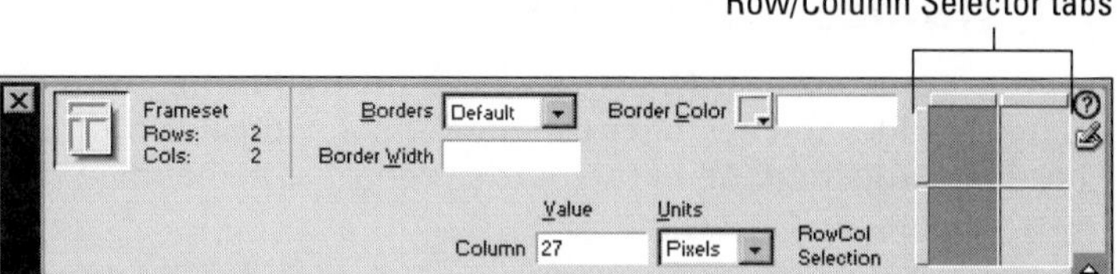

Figure 16-6: In the Frameset Property Inspector, you use the Row/Column Selector tabs to choose which frame you are going to resize.

Tip

The Row/Column Selector shows only one frameset at a time. So if your design uses nested framesets, you won't see an exact duplicate of your entire Web page in the Row/Column Selector.

Whether you need to modify just a row, a column, or both a row and a column depends on the location of the frame.

✦ If your frame spans the width of an entire page, like the top or bottom row in Figure 16-3, select the corresponding tab on the left side of the Row/Column Selector.

✦ If your frame spans the height of an entire page, select the equivalent tab along the top of the Row/Column Selector.

✦ If your frame does not span either height or width, like the middle row in Figure 16-3, you need to select both its column and its row and modify the size of each in turn.

Once you have selected the row or column, follow these steps to specify its size:

1. To specify the size in pixels, enter a number in the Property Inspector's Value text box and select Pixels as the Units option.
2. To specify the size as a percentage of the screen, enter a number from 1 to 100 in the Value text box and select Percent as the Units option.
3. To specify a size relative to the other columns or rows, first select Relative as the Units option. Now you have two options:
   - To set the size to occupy the remainder of the screen, delete any number that may be entered in the Value text box; optionally, you can enter 1.
   - To scale the frame relative to the other rows or columns, type the scale factor in the Value text box. For example, if you want the frame to be twice the size of another relative frame, put a 2 in the Value text box.

Tip

The Relative size operator is generally used to indicate you want the current frame to take up the balance of the frameset column or row. This makes it easy to specify a size without having to calculate pixel widths and ensures that the frame has the largest possible size.

Manipulating frameset borders

By default, Dreamweaver sets up your framesets so all the frames have gray borders that are 6 pixels wide. You can alter the border color, change the width, or eliminate the borders altogether. All of the border controls are handled through the Frameset Property Inspector.

Tip

Border controls for individual frames also exist. Just as table cell settings can override options set for the entire table, the individual frame options override those determined for the entire frameset, as described in the section "Working with the Frame Property Inspector," later in this chapter. Use the frameset border controls when you want to make a global change to the borders, such as turning them all off.

If you are working with nested framesets, it's important that you select the outermost frameset before you begin making any modifications to the borders. You can tell that you've selected the outermost frameset by looking at the Dreamweaver Tag Selector; it shows only one `<frameset>` in bold. If you select an inner nested frameset, you see more than one `<frameset>` in the Tag Selector.

Eliminating borders

When a frameset is first created, Dreamweaver leaves the borders display up to the browser's discretion. You can expressly turn the frameset borders on or off through the Property Inspector.

To eliminate borders completely, enter a zero in the Border Width text box. Even if no width value is displayed, the default is a border 6 pixels wide. If you turn off the borders for your frameset, you can still work in Dreamweaver with View ➪ Frame Borders enabled, which gives you quick access to modifying the frameset. The borders are not displayed, however, when your Web page is previewed in a browser.

Border appearance options

You can control the appearance of your borders to a limited degree. In the Borders drop-down list of options, choosing Yes causes browsers to draw the borders with a 3D appearance. Select No, and the frameset borders are drawn as a single color. Browsers generally interpret the three-dimensional look as the default option.

Border color options

To change the frameset border color, select the Border Color text box and then enter either a color name or a hexadecimal color value. You can also select the color swatch and choose a new border color from the browser-safe color picker. Clicking the Palette icon on the color picker opens the extended color selector, just as for other color swatches in Dreamweaver.

If you have nested framesets on your Web page, make sure you've selected the correct frameset before you make any modifications through the Property Inspector. You can move from a nested frameset to its "parent" by using the keyboard shortcut Alt+up arrow (Command+up arrow). Likewise, you can move from a parent frameset to its "child" by pressing Alt+down arrow (Command+down arrow).

Saving a frameset and frames

As mentioned earlier, when you're working with frames, you're working with multiple HTML files. You must be careful to save not only all the individual frames that make up your Web page but also the frameset itself.

Dreamweaver makes it easy to save framesets and included frames by providing several special commands. To save a frameset, choose File ➪ Save Frameset to open the standard Save File dialog box. You can also save a copy of the current frameset by choosing File ➪ Save Frameset As. You don't have to select the frameset border or position your cursor in any special place to activate these functions.

Saving each frame in the frameset can be a chore unless you choose File ➪ Save All. The first time this command is invoked, Dreamweaver cycles through each of the open frames and displays the Save File dialog box. Each subsequent time you choose File ➪ Save All, Dreamweaver automatically saves every updated file in the frameset.

To copy an individual frame, you must use the regular File ➪ Save As command.

Closing a frameset

There's no real trick to closing a Dreamweaver frameset: just choose File ➪ Close. If the frameset is your last open file, Dreamweaver asks if you'd like to quit the program (unless you've previously selected the Don't Ask Me Again option).

Modifying a Frame

What makes the whole concept of a Web page frameset work so well is the flexibility of each frame.

- ✦ You can design your page so that some frames are fixed in size while others are expandable.
- ✦ You can attach scroll bars to some frames and not others.
- ✦ Any frame can have its own background image, and yet all frames can appear as one seamless picture.

✦ Borders can be enabled — and colored — for one set of frames but left off for another set.

Dreamweaver uses a Frame Property Inspector to specify most of a frame's attributes. Others are handled through devices already familiar to you, such as the Page Properties dialog box.

Page properties

Each frame is its own HTML document, and as such, each frame can have independent page properties. To alter the page properties of a frame, position the cursor in the frame and then choose Modify ➪ Page Properties. You can also use the keyboard shortcuts, Ctrl+J or Command+J. Or you can select Page Properties from the shortcut menu by right-clicking (Control+clicking) any open space on the frame's page.

From the Page Properties dialog box, you can assign a title, although it is not visible to the user unless the frame is viewed as a separate page. If you plan on using the individual frames as separate pages in your `<noframes>` content (see "Handling Frameless Browsers," at the end of this chapter), it's good practice to title every page. You can also assign a background and the various link colors by selecting the appropriate color swatch or entering a color name into the correct text box.

Working with the Frame Property Inspector

To access the Frame Property Inspector, you must first select a frame. Selecting a frame is different from just positioning the cursor in the frame. You have two ways to properly select a frame: using the Frames Inspector or using the mouse.

The Frames Inspector shows an accurate representation of all the frames in your Web page. Open the Frames Inspector by choosing Window ➪ Frames. As you can see in Figure 16-7, the Frames Inspector displays names, if assigned, in the individual frames, and (no name) if not. Nested framesets are shown with a heavier border.

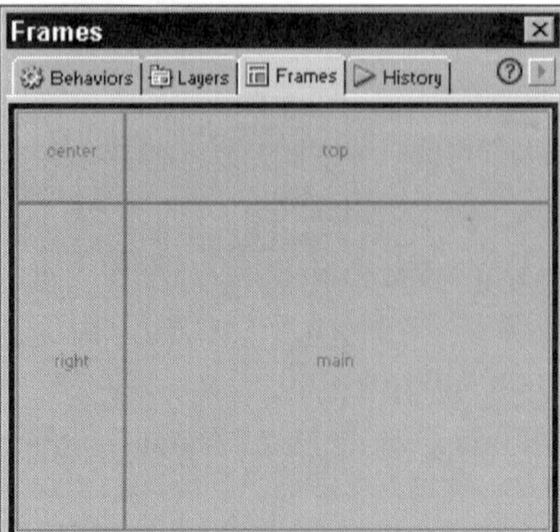

Figure 16-7: Use the Frames Inspector to visually select a frame to modify.

Joining Background Images in Frames

One popular technique is to insert background images into separate frames so they blend into a seamless single image. This takes careful planning and coordination between the author of the graphic and the designer of the Web page.

To accomplish this image consolidation operation, you must first "slice" the image in an image-processing program, such as Fireworks or Adobe Photoshop. Then save each part as a separate graphic, making sure that no border is around these image sections—each cut-up piece becomes the background image for a particular frame. Next, set the background image of each frame to the matching graphic. Be sure to turn off the borders for the frameset and set the Border Width to zero.

You can find a command on CD-ROM 1 that accompanies this book to help you eliminate your borders. Look for the Zero Page Borders Command in Andrew Wooldridge's folder.

Correct sizing of each piece is important to ensure that no gaps appear in your joined background. A good technique is to use absolute pixel measurements for images that fill the frame and, where the background images tile, set the frame to Relative spacing. In the following figure, the corner frame has the same measurement as the background image (107×126 pixels), and all the other frames are set to Relative.

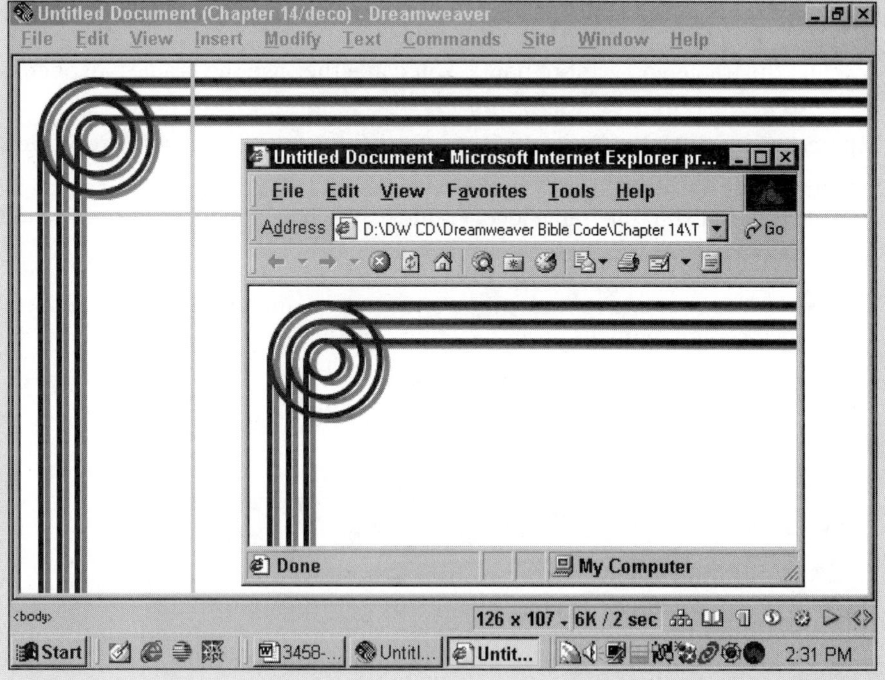

To select a frame, click directly on its represented image in the Frames Inspector. If the Frame Property Inspector is open, it reflects the selected frame's options. For more complex Web pages, you can resize the Frames Inspector to get a better sense of the page layout. To close the Frames Inspector, select the Close button or choose Window ➪ Frames again.

When you are working with multiple framesets, use the Tag Selector together with the Frames Inspector to identify the correct nested frameset. Selecting a frameset in the Tag Selector causes it to be identified in the Frame Inspector with a heavy black border.

To select a frame with the mouse, press Alt (Option+Shift) and click in the desired frame. Once the frame is selected, you can move from one frame to another by pressing Alt (Command) and then using the arrow keys.

Naming your frames

Naming each frame is essential to getting the most power from a frame-structured Web page. The frame's name is used to make the content inserted from a hyperlink appear in that particular frame. For more information about targeting a link, see the section "Targeting Frame Content," later in this chapter.

Frame names must follow specific guidelines, as explained in the following steps:

1. Select the frame you want to name. You can either use the Frames Inspector or Alt+click (Option+Shift+click) inside the frame.
2. If necessary, open the Property Inspector by choosing Window ➪ Properties.
3. In the Frame Property Inspector, shown in Figure 16-8, add the frame's name in the text box next to the frame logo. Frame names have the following restrictions:
   - You must use one word, with no spaces.
   - You may not use special characters such as quotation marks, question marks, and hyphens.
   - You may use the underscore character.
   - You may not use certain frame names: `_blank`, `_parent`, `_self`, and `_top`.

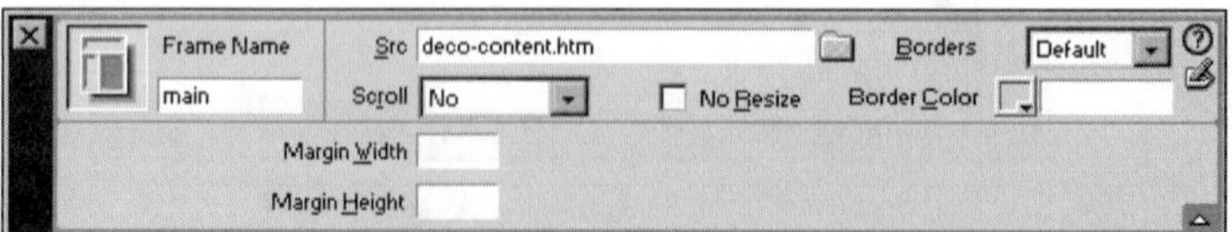

Figure 16-8: The Frame Property Inspector enables you to name your frame and control all of a frame's attributes.

Opening a Web page into a frame

You don't have to build all Web pages in frames from scratch. You can load an existing Web page into any frame. If you've selected a frame and the Frame Property Inspector is open, just type the link directly into the Src text box or choose the folder icon to browse for your file. Or you can position your cursor in a frame (without selecting the frame) and choose File ⇨ Open in Frame.

Setting borders

You can generally set most border options adequately in the Frameset Property Inspector; you can also override some of those options, such as color, for each frame. These possibilities have practical limitations, however.

To set borders from the Frame Property Inspector for a selected frame, you can make the borders three-dimensional by choosing Yes in the Borders drop-down option list, or use the monochrome setting by choosing No. Leaving the Borders option at Default gives control to the frameset settings. You can also change a frame's border color by choosing the Border Color swatch in a selected frame's Property Inspector.

Now, about those limitations: They come into play when you try to implement one of your border modifications. Because frames share common borders, it is difficult to isolate an individual frame and have the change affect just the selected frame. As an example, Figure 16-9 shows a frameset in which the borders are set to No for all frames except the one on the lower right. Notice how the left border of the lower-right frame extends to the top, all the way over the upper frame. You have two possible workarounds for this problem. First, you can design your frames so that their borders do not touch, as in a multirow frameset. Second, you can create a background image for a frame that includes a border design.

Adding scroll bars

One of the features that has given frames the wide use they enjoy of late is the capability to enable or disable scroll bars for each frame. Scroll bars are used when the browser window is too small to display all the information in the Web page frame. The browser window size is completely user controlled, so the Web designer must apply the various scroll bar options on a frame-by-frame basis, depending on the look desired and the frame's content.

Four options are selectable from the Scroll drop-down list on the Frame Property Inspector:

- **Default:** Leaves the use of scroll bars up to the browser.
- **Yes:** Forces scroll bars to appear regardless of the amount of content.
- **No:** Disables scroll bars.
- **Auto:** Turns scroll bars on if the content of the frame extends horizontally or vertically beyond what the browser window can display.

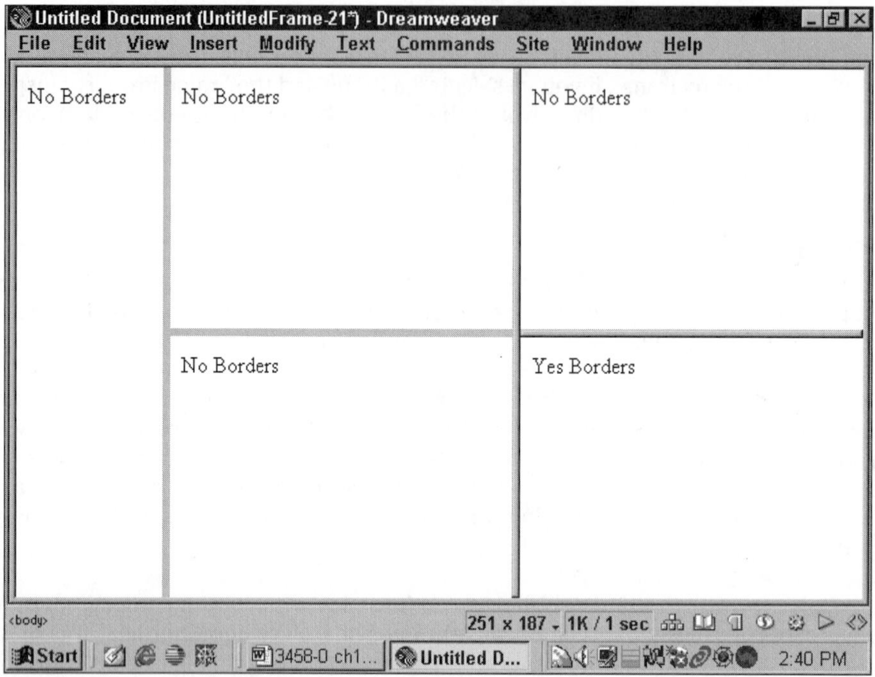

Figure 16-9: If you want to use isolated frame borders, you have to carefully plan your Web page frameset to avoid overlapping borders.

Figure 16-10 uses an automatic vertical scroll bar in the lower frame; you can see it on the far right.

Resizing

By default, all frames are resizable by the user; that is, a visitor to your Web site can widen, narrow, lengthen, or shorten a frame by dragging the border to a new position. You can disable this resizing capability, however, on a frame-by-frame basis. In the Frame Property Inspector, select the No Resize option to turn off the resizing feature.

Although it might be tempting to select No Resize for every frame, it's best to enable resizing, except in frames that require a set size to maintain their functionality (for instance, a frame containing navigational controls).

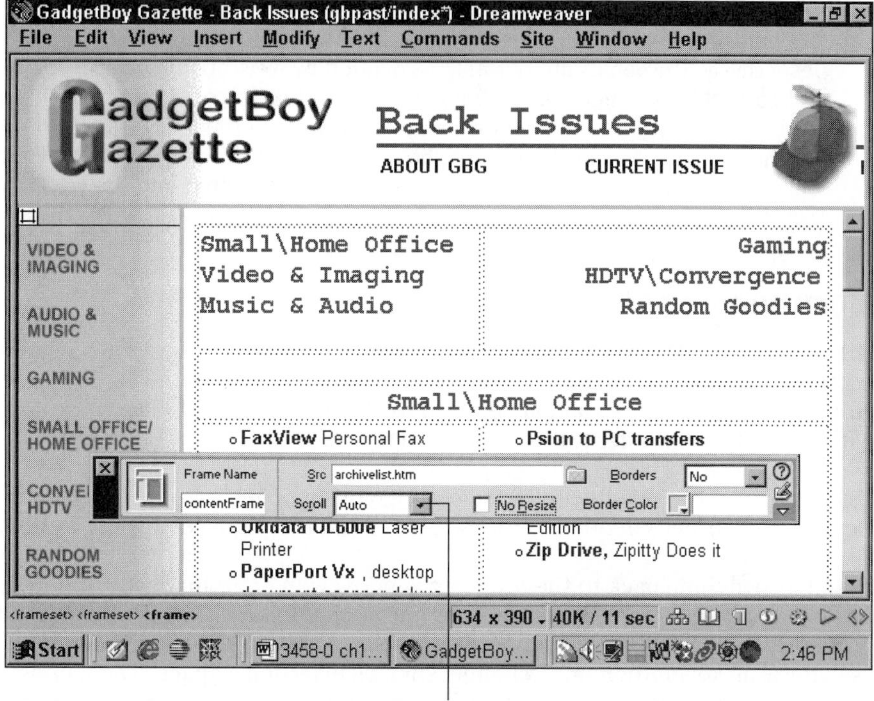

Figure 16-10: The top frame of the Web page has the scroll bars turned off, and the bottom right frame has scroll bars enabled.

Setting margins

Just as you can pad table cells with additional space to separate text and graphics, you can offset content in frames. Dreamweaver enables you to control the left/right margins and the top/bottom margins independently. By default, about 6 pixels of space are between the content and the left or right frame borders, and about 15 pixels of space are between the content and the top or bottom frame borders. You can increase or decrease these margins, but even if you set the values to zero, some room still exists between the borders and the content.

To alter the left and right margins, change the value in the Frame Property Inspector's Margin Width text box; to change the top and bottom margins, enter a new value in the Margin Height text box. If you don't see the Margin Width and Height text boxes, select the Property Inspector expander arrow.

Dreamweaver currently inserts only the `marginwidth` and `marginheight` attributes when you enter values in the Margin Width and Margin Height text boxes, respectively. The values are not fully recognized by Netscape browsers. To ensure full compatibility, enter the following attributes as well: `topmargin=value` and `leftmargin=value`. Although Dreamweaver 3 now includes fields to input the Left Margin, Top Margin, Margin Height, and Margin Width in the Page Properties dialog box, if applied to a frameset, these values are written into the No Frames Content page.

Modifying content

You can update a frame's content in any way you see fit. Sometimes, it's necessary to keep an eye on how altering a single frame's content affects the entire frameset. Other times, it is easier — and faster — to work on each frame individually and later load them into the frameset to see the final result.

With Dreamweaver's multiwindow structure, you can have it both ways. Work on the individual frames in one or more windows and the frameset in yet another.

Although switching back to the frameset window won't automatically update it to show your changed frames, you can use one shortcut. After saving changes in the full frame windows, go to the frameset window. In any window you've altered elsewhere, make another small change, such as inserting a space. Then, choose File ⇨ Revert. This command is normally used to revert to the previously saved version, but in this case, you're using it to update your frames.

To preview changes made to a Web page using frames, you must first save the changed files. Currently, Dreamweaver creates a temporary file of the frameset, but not any of the included frames.

Deleting frames

As you're building your Web page frameset, you inevitably try a frame design that does not work. How do you delete a frame once you've created it? Click the frame border and drag it into the border of the enclosing, or parent, frame. When no parent frame is present, drag the frame border to the edge of the page. If the frame being deleted contains any unsaved content, Dreamweaver asks if you'd like to save the file before closing it.

Tip

Because the enclosing frameset and each individual frame are all discrete HTML pages, each keeps track of its own edits and other changes — and therefore each has its own undo memory. If you are in a particular frame and try to undo a frameset alteration, such as adding a new frame to the set, it won't work. To reverse an edit to the frameset, you have to select the frameset and then choose File ⇨ Undo, or use one of the keyboard shortcuts (Ctrl+Z or Command+Z). To reverse the creation of a frameset, you must select Undo twice.

Targeting Frame Content

One of the major uses of frames is for navigational control. One frame acts as the navigation center, offering links to various Web pages in a site. When the user selects one of the links, the Web page appears in another frame on the page; and that frame, if necessary, can scroll independently of the navigation frame. This technique keeps the navigation links always visible and accessible.

When you assign a link to appear in a particular frame of your Web page, you are said to be assigning a target for the link. You can target specific frames in your Web page, and you can target structural parts of a frameset. In Dreamweaver, targets are assigned through the Text and Image Property Inspectors.

Targeting sections of your frameset

In the earlier section on naming frames, you learned that certain names are reserved. These are the four special names HTML reserves for the parts of a frameset that are used in targeting: `_blank`, `_parent`, `_self`, and `_top`. With them, you can cause content from a link to overwrite the current frame or to appear in an entirely new browser window.

To target a link to a section of your frameset, follow these steps:

1. Select the text or image you want to use as your link.
2. In the Text (or Image) Property Inspector, enter the URL and/or named anchor in the Link text box. Alternately, you can select the folder icon to browse for the file.
3. Select the Target text box. You may need to expand the Image Property Inspector to see the Target text box.
4. Select one of the following reserved target names from the drop-down list of Target options (see Figure 16-11) or type an entry into the text box:
    - **_blank:** Opens the link into a new browser window and keeps the current window available.
    - **_parent:** Opens the link into the parent frameset of the current frame, if any.
    - **_self:** Opens the link into the current frame, replacing its contents (the default).
    - **_top:** Opens the link into the outermost frameset of the current Web page, replacing all frames.

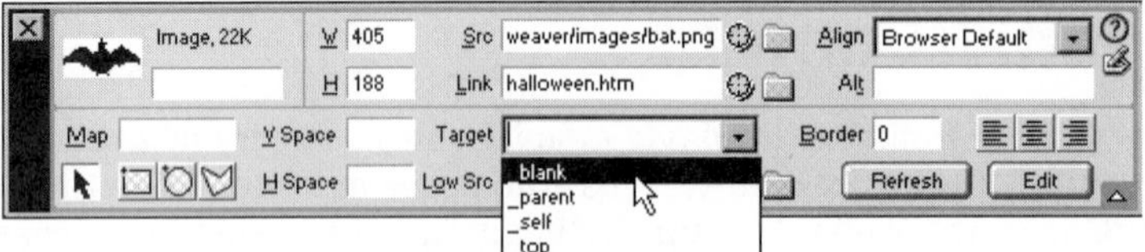

Figure 16-11: Choose your frame target from the Property Inspector's Target drop-down list.

The generic nature of these reserved target names enables them to be used repeatedly on different Web pages, without your having to code a particular reference each time.

For an example of structural targeting, look at the code for the Dreamweaver Help system. The Index frame, for example, uses the implied `_self` target whenever a major Help topic is selected, to open an HTML document that shows all the subtopics.

A phenomenon known as *recursive frames* can be dangerous to your site setup. Let's say you have a frameset named index_frame.html. If you include in any frame on your current page a link to index_frame.html and set the target as _self, when the user selects that link, the entire frameset loads into the current frame—including another link to index_frame.html. Browsers can handle about three or four iterations of this recursion before they crash. To avoid the problem, set your frameset target to _top.

Targeting specific frames in your frameset

Earlier I stressed the importance of naming each frame in your frameset. Once you have entered a name in the Name text box of the Frame Property Inspector, Dreamweaver dynamically updates the Target list to include that name. This feature enables you to target specific frames in your frameset in the same manner that you target the reserved names noted previously.

Although you can always type the frame name directly in the Name text box, the drop-down option list comes in handy for this task. You avoid not only having to keep track of the various frame names in your Web page, but typing errors as well. Targets are case sensitive, and names must match exactly or the browser won't be able to find the target.

Updating two frames or more at once

Sooner or later, most Web designers using frames have the need to update more than one frame with a single click. The problem is, you can't group two or more URLs together in an anchor tag. Here is an easy-to-implement solution, thanks to Dreamweaver's behaviors.

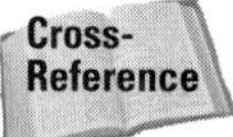

If you're not familiar with Dreamweaver's JavaScript behaviors, you might want to look over Chapter 19 before continuing.

To update more than one frame target from a single link, follow these steps:

1. Select your link in the frame.
2. Open the Behavior Inspector from the Launcher or by choosing Window ➪ Behaviors.
3. Make sure that 4.0 Browsers is selected in the Show Events For pop-up menu of the Behavior Inspector.
4. Select the + (add behavior) button to display the list of available behaviors.
5. Choose Go To URL from the drop-down option list.
6. Dreamweaver displays the Go To URL dialog box (see Figure 16-12) and scans your document for all named frames. Select a target frame from the list of windows or frames.

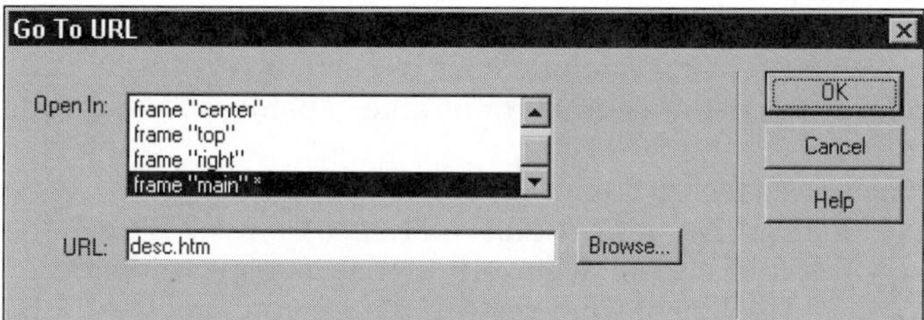

Figure 16-12: You can cause two or more frames to update from a single link by using Dreamweaver's Go To URL behavior.

You won't be able to use this behavior until you name your frames as detailed in the section "Naming Your Frames," earlier in this chapter.

7. Enter a URL or choose the Browse (Choose) button to select one.

   Dreamweaver places an asterisk after the targeted frame to indicate that a URL has been selected for it. You can see this in Figure 16-12.
8. Repeat Steps 6 and 7 for any additional frames you want to target.
9. Click OK when you're finished.

   Dreamweaver automatically selects the `onClick` event for the Go To URL behavior.

Now, whenever you click your one link, the browser opens the URLs in the targeted frames in the order specified.

Handling Frameless Browsers

Not all of today's browsers support frames. Netscape began supporting frames in Navigator version 2.0; Microsoft didn't start until IE version 3.0 — and a few of the earlier versions for both browsers are still in use, particularly among AOL users. Some less prevalent browsers also don't support frames. HTML has a built-in mechanism for working with browsers that are not frame-enabled: the <noframes>...</noframes> tag pair.

When you begin to construct any frameset, Dreamweaver automatically inserts a <noframes> area just below the closing </frameset> tag. If a browser is not frames-capable, it ignores the frameset and frame information and renders what is found in the <noframes> section.

What should you put into the <noframes> section? To ensure the widest possible audience, Webmasters typically insert links to a nonframe version of the site. The links can be as obvious or as discreet as you care to make them. Perhaps a more vital reason is that most of the search engine indexing systems (called *spiders*) don't work with frames. If your frameset is index.html and you want the spider to find the rest of your site, you need to have a link to each page in the noframes content. Many Webmasters also include links to current versions of Communicator or Internet Explorer, to encourage their nonframe-capable visitors to upgrade.

Dreamweaver includes a facility for easily adding and modifying the <noframes> content. Choose Modify ➪ Frameset ➪ Edit NoFrames Content to open the NoFrames Content window. As you can see in Figure 16-13, this window is identical to the regular Dreamweaver Document window, with the exception of the "NoFrames Content" in the title bar. In this window, you have access to all the same objects and palettes that you normally do. When you have finished editing your <noframe> content, Choose Modify ➪ Frameset ➪ Edit NoFrames Content again to deselect the option and return to the frameset.

Here are some pointers to keep in mind when working in the NoFrames Content window:

✦ The page properties of the <noframes> content are the same as the page properties of the frameset. You can select the frameset and then choose Modify ➪ Page Properties to open the Page Properties dialog box. While in the NoFrames Content window, you can also right-click (Control+click) in any open space to access the Page Properties command.

✦ Dreamweaver disables the File ➪ Open commands when the NoFrames Content window is onscreen. To move existing content into the <noframes> section, use Dreamweaver's Copy and Paste features.

✦ The <noframes> section is located in the frameset page, which is the primary page examined by search engine "spiders." It's a good idea to enter <meta> tag information detailing the site, as described in Chapter 8, in the frameset page. While you're in the NoFrames Content window, you can open the HTML Inspector and add the <meta> tags.

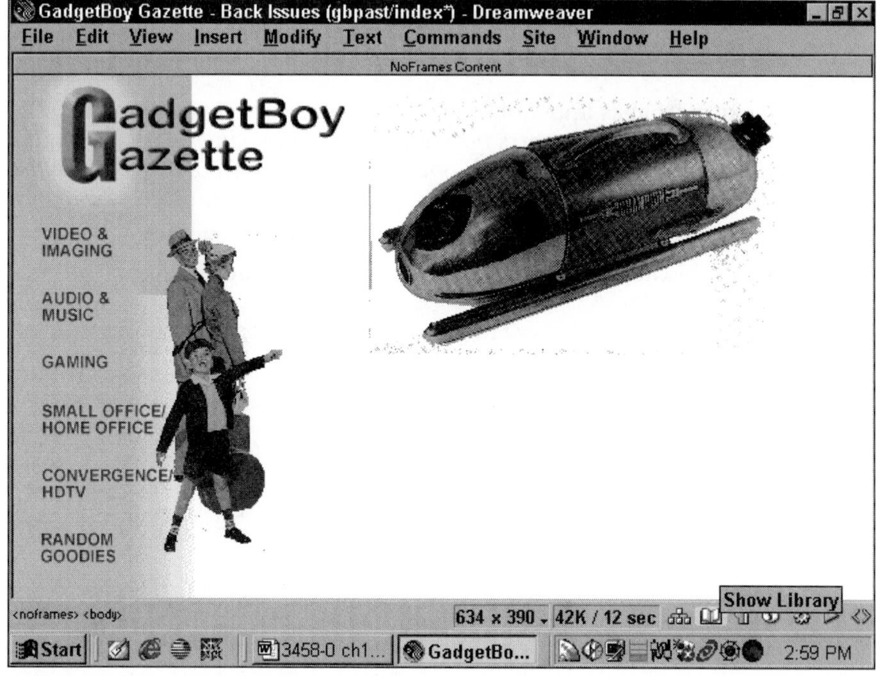

Figure 16-13: Through the Edit NoFrames Content command, Dreamweaver enables you to specify what's seen by visitors whose browsers are not frame-capable.

Summary

Frames are a significant Webmaster design tool. With frames and framesets, you can divide a single Web page into multiple, independent areas. Dreamweaver gives Web designers quick and easy access to frame design through the program's drag-and-drop interface.

✦ A framed Web page consists of a separate HTML document for each frame and one additional file that describes the frame structure, called the *frameset.*

✦ A frameset comprises columns and rows, which can be sized absolutely in pixels, as a percentage of the browser window, or relative to the other columns or rows.

✦ Dreamweaver enables you to reposition the frame borders by dragging them to a new location. You can also add new frames by Alt+clicking (Option+clicking) any existing frame border.

✦ Framesets can be nested to create more complex column and row arrangements. Selecting the frame border displays the Frameset Property Inspector.

- Select any individual frame through the Frame Inspector or by Alt+clicking (Option+Shift+clicking) within any frame. Once the frame is selected, the Frame Property Inspector can be displayed.
- You make your links appear in a specific frame by assigning targets to the links. Dreamweaver supports both structured and named targets. You can update two or more frames with one link by using a Dreamweaver JavaScript behavior.
- You should include information and/or links for browsers that are not frame-capable, through Dreamweaver's Edit NoFrames Content feature.

In the next chapter, you learn how to access external programs through your Web pages in Dreamweaver.

✦ ✦ ✦

Extending HTML Through Dreamweaver

P A R T

IV

✦ ✦ ✦ ✦

In This Part

✦ ✦ ✦ ✦

CHAPTER 17

Accessing External Programs

✦ ✦ ✦ ✦

In This Chapter

Working with CGI programs

Embedding plug-ins

Using ActiveX controls

Applying Java applets

Including JavaScript or VBScript in Dreamweaver

✦ ✦ ✦ ✦

Until recently, you could create relatively static Web pages made of text and images with "basic" HTML, but you needed additional code for more action. Without using some of the advanced capabilities of Dynamic HTML — viewable only with a fourth-generation browser — animated GIFs have been your sole option for any sort of motion on a self-contained Web page. HTML need not stand alone, however; the capabilities of the language can be extended using several methods.

You can do all of the following using external programs with HTML:

✦ Collect data from the user

✦ Add multimedia elements such as audio, video, animation, and virtual reality

✦ Enable a Web browser to present almost any kind of information in its native format

✦ Dynamically create Web pages based on a user's request

Dreamweaver gives you various methods — some specific to the file type and others more generic — for accessing a full range of external programs invaluable to the Web author. In this chapter, you learn how to send information to and from the server through CGI programs, install feature-extending plug-ins and ActiveX controls, incorporate custom-built Java applets, and work with scripting languages such as JavaScript and VBScript.

Generally, the techniques for melding any of the external capabilities with your Web page are quite straightforward. Often, however, learning to use the outside program takes a fair amount of time — whether that program is writing your CGI script or encoding your digital video. You may want to approach each specific technique on a project-by-project basis, rather than try to master all the disciplines at once. No matter how you choose to work, you can always count on Dreamweaver's own extensibility to incorporate every new technology.

Using CGI Programs

When someone clicks a link to a Web page, a message is sent to a particular Web server, which then sends the components of that Web page — the HTML file and any associated graphic files — back to the user. Most information is usually sent over the Web from the server to the client. But how do you send information in the opposite direction, from the client to the server?

The standard method is to use a Common Gateway Interface (CGI) program. CGI programs, or scripts (the terms are used interchangeably), perform many different kinds of Internet functions, but they all entail collecting data from the user and passing it to the server. Whether the server stores the information in a database, manipulates it and passes it on to another system, or generates a new Web page to be sent to the user depends on the design of the CGI program.

Creating and calling scripts

CGI programs can be written in any number of computer languages, including C/C++, Fortran, Perl, TCL, Unix shell, Visual Basic, and AppleScript. The only requirement is that the program must be executable by the type of server processing the information. Perl (Program Extraction and Report Language) is one of the most popular languages used to write CGI programs. Perl is an interpreted language — that is, the source code is an ordinary text file compiled at runtime, unlike Java or C++ code, which are previously compiled. Because it is text-based, Perl is easy to modify and particularly strong in parsing and manipulating text — an important capability for interpreting data from forms and other Web-based tasks.

Perl, however, is difficult to debug — you don't get much in the way of error reporting from the Perl interpreter.

Note

Keep in mind that with CGI programs, you're essentially running a program on a different, remote computer and what's true for your computer setup may not be true for the server. Your best ally is the system administrator of your Web server. Chances are good that questions about running CGI programs have been asked many times before, and a FAQ or equivalent file is probably available.

Every CGI script must be customized to some extent in order to communicate with a particular server. You can develop your custom CGI program in two ways: Build it from scratch yourself, or modify an existing script. Modifying an existing script is much easier and a customary practice on the Web. Someone else has probably already developed a CGI script for your situation, and it is probably available for download on the Internet.

Tip

Three great sources for CGI scripts are Matt's Script Archives (`www.worldwidemart.com/scripts`); Extropia, formerly Selena Sol's Public Domain Archives (`www.extropia.com`); and—for all your scripting needs—The CGI-Resource Index (`www.cgi-resources.com`).

Once your CGI program is completed, three steps remain before it can be used:

✦ The CGI script must be uploaded to your Web server and stored in a special directory—often named cgi-bin.

✦ The file permissions need to be set depending on the program's function. File permissions determine whether a file can be read, written to, and/or executed and by whom. File permissions are explained in the following section.

✦ The CGI program must be referenced or called from the Web page.

Web designers most often use the HTML `<form>` structure to call a CGI script and simultaneously pass the data from the user to the server. Dreamweaver enables you to specify the necessary information through various form objects.

Setting file permissions in Dreamweaver

An important aspect of installing CGI programs is properly setting the file permissions for the CGI file. Because of security concerns, most Web servers restrict access on certain files to particular users. A file can be read, overwritten, or executed. With Unix servers, you can set these three operations for each of three different groups of people: the creator or owner of the file, the group administering the Web server, and outside visitors. These settings are called *file permissions.*

Typically, a CGI file is set to the following parameters:

✦ It can be read, overwritten, or executed by its owner.

✦ It can be read and executed by the administrative group but not overwritten.

✦ It can be read and executed by outside visitors but not overwritten.

File permissions are set on a Unix machine through the `site chmod` command issued directly to the server. The permissions previously listed are accomplished when the `site chmod` command is set to 755 and the file name is referenced; an example follows:

```
site chmod 755 mailer.pl
```

To set the file permissions in Dreamweaver, follow these steps:

1. Open the Site window. Choose File ➪ Open Site (Site ➪ Open Site) and then select the site you want to work with from the submenu.
2. Go online and select the Connect button from the Site window.
3. From the Site window menus, choose Window ➪ Site Log (Site ➪ FTP Log).
4. In the Site Log window's FTP command line, use the `site chmod` command with the appropriate code number and file name reference (see the example in Figure 17-1) and press Enter (Return).

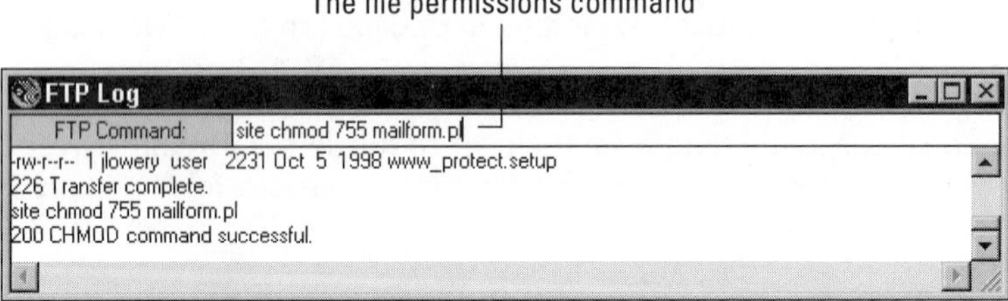

Figure 17-1: Before a CGI program can be used, the file permissions must be set through Dreamweaver's Site Log window.

Sending data to CGI programs

Two primary methods send data to the Web server for processing by a CGI script. The first technique attaches the information directly to a selected URL; another method uses a form to post the data when the user selects the Submit button.

The URL method is useful when you need to send known data. The form method is useful for sending variable or user-supplied information. Both techniques can be used within the Dreamweaver interface.

Passing data through a URL

Although the URL route is not as commonly employed as the forms method, certain information lends itself well to being passed to the server directly through a URL. Anytime you need to send a specific value to your CGI program, you can use the URL method.

Following is the general syntax of the statement that sends data to the URL. You use a question mark to separate the CGI program address from the data itself. The data takes the following form:

```
1st_field=value+2nd_field=value
```

In practice, information passed to a program via a link looks like the following:

```
<a href= "http://www.testcenter.com/cgi-bin/¬
response.pl?choice=left+entry=nada_ad">
```

In Dreamweaver, enter the data as part of the Link information, as shown in Figure 17-2. Most often, you should enter the URL to a CGI program as an absolute address, with the full "http://domain/path" attached, to properly reference the cgi-bin directory.

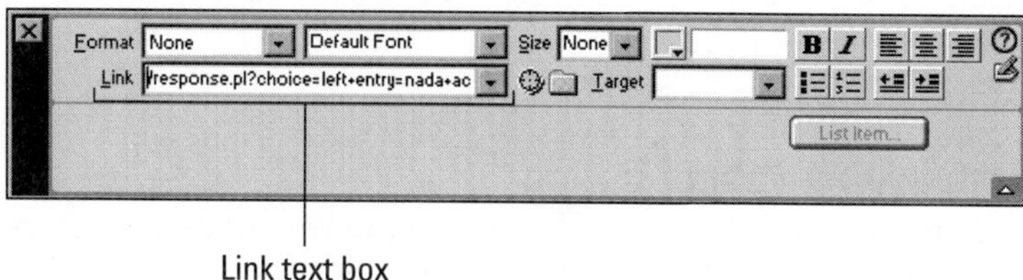

Figure 17-2: In the Link text box, enter the specific information to be passed directly to a CGI program.

Using forms to send information

Forms are the most common method to transmit data from the user to a CGI program on a server. With the push of a single Submit button, all of the information the user has filled in or selected on the form—text, menu options, radio button options, and so forth—is sent. The data arrives in the program's standard input. The CGI script manipulates the data before sending it on to a database or in an e-mail message.

To find out more about building forms in Dreamweaver and the various form fields, see Chapter 15.

Most CGI scripts require that the form use the `post` method (as opposed to `get`) to send data to the server. When you first insert a form in Dreamweaver, you notice that the default method listed in the form's Property Inspector is POST, as shown in Figure 17-3.

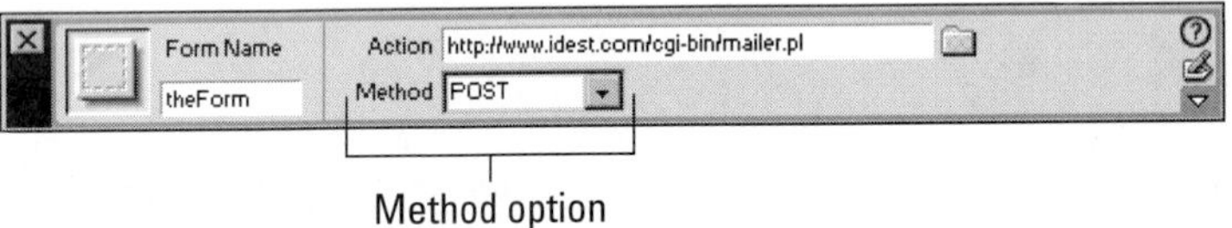

Figure 17-3: Use the POST method to send information via a form to most CGI programs.

Aside from choosing a method, the only other task to ready a form for submission is to assign an action — which, oddly enough, is really the URL of the CGI program (see the Action box in Figure 17-3).

Again, this URL is most often supplied in absolute address form, like the following:

```
http://www.idest.com/cgi-bin/mailer.pl
```

Posting form data with a Submit button

Once you have set up the form properly and installed the Web page and corresponding CGI program, data is sent to the server when the user selects the Submit button. You don't need to assign an `onClick` or other event to the button.

As noted in Chapter 15, "Submit" and "Reset" are the default labels for these two buttons. You can easily modify the label of a button by entering new text in the Label text box, as shown in Figure 17-4.

With Dreamweaver, you can also use an image to create a graphical button for handling the submitting chores. However, it's necessary to use a little JavaScript — very little — to accomplish the task. Moreover, you currently have to hand-code the addition. Basically, you have to add a link tag (`<a>...</a>`) around the Image Field button that calls the JavaScript equivalent to Submit or Reset. The code refers to the form in which the button is located (here, "theForm") and uses the following format:

```
<a href="javascript:document.theForm.submit()"><img src=mySubmit></a>
```

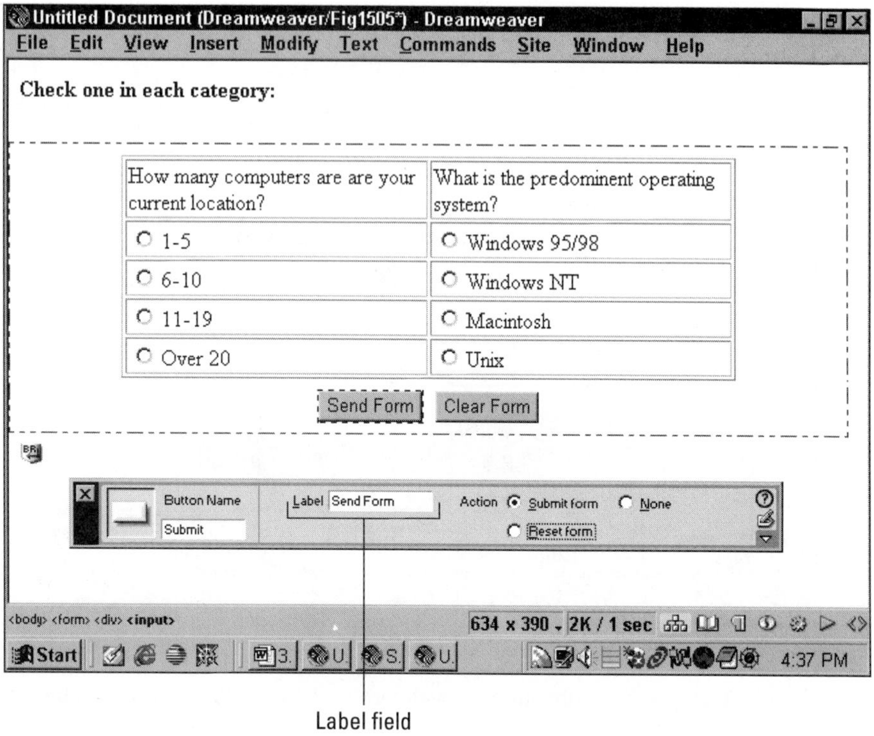

Label field

Figure 17-4: Change the text of the Submit and Reset buttons by entering a name in the Label field of the Property Inspector.

I've bolded the additional code to make it easy to see. To make a Reset button, just substitute `reset()` for `submit()` in the preceding code.

I've found it best to always name my form — doing so makes coding much simpler. Typically, only one form is used on a page, so I've adopted a general technique of naming the form `theForm`, although you can choose your own naming convention.

To use an image for a Submit button, follow these steps:

1. Choose Insert ⇨ Image or select the Insert Image button from the Common panel of the Objects palette.
2. In the Insert Image dialog box, enter the path to your image or select the folder icon to locate the file. The image can be in GIF, JPEG, or PNG format.
3. Give the image a name and, if desired, alternative text using the appropriate text boxes in the Property Inspector (see Figure 17-5).

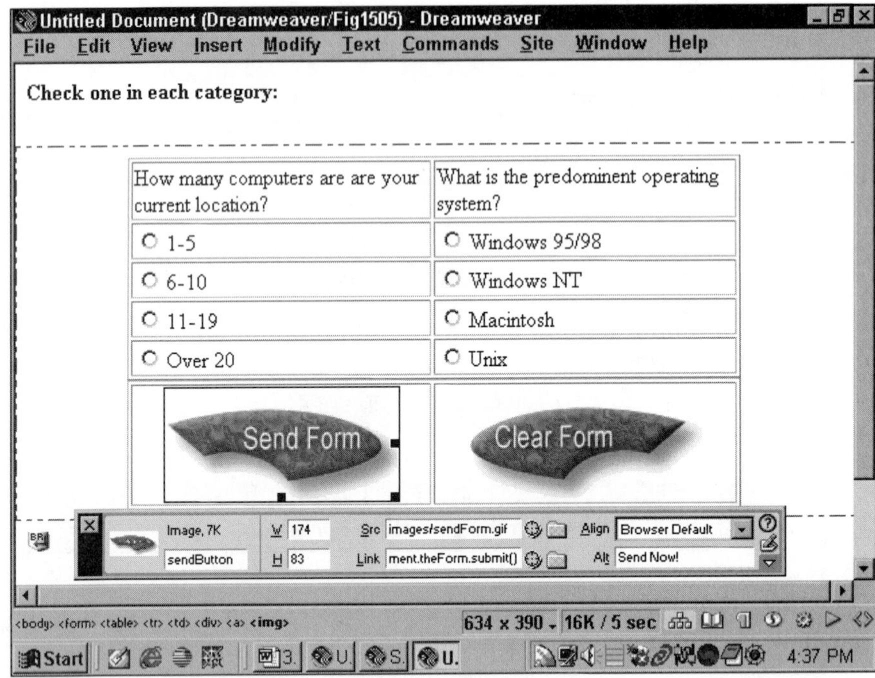

Figure 17-5: You can substitute any valid graphic for the Submit button by using an image and JavaScript.

4. In the Link field of the Property Inspector, enter the following code for a graphical Submit button:

```
javascript:document.theForm.submit()
```

or this code for a Reset button:

```
javascript:document.theForm.reset()
```

Be sure to change the code to reflect your specifics: the name of your form as well as the name of your images.

Using the Hidden Field

Many CGI scripts require that certain information not input by the user be submitted in order to process the form properly. A good example is a text string that tells the CGI program which fields of the form are required. This type of data is hidden from the user and passed to the program through the unseen form object, the appropriately named *Hidden Field.*

Although generally placed at the top of the form, Hidden Fields can be included anywhere between the `<form>` tag pair. You can include a Hidden Field by choosing the

Insert Hidden Field button in the Forms panel of the Objects palette or by selecting Insert ⇨ Form Object ⇨ Hidden Field. Enter the information you want to pass to the CGI program in the Value text box of the Property Inspector, as shown in Figure 17-6.

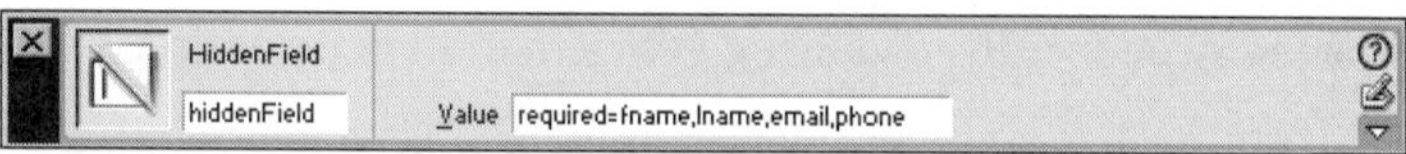

Figure 17-6: Pass variables that you want to remain unseen by your Web page visitor by using the Hidden Field in your form.

When a Hidden Field is included in your form, Dreamweaver designates it with a Hidden Field icon. Like all invisible elements, the Hidden Field icon can be hidden by deselecting its option in the Invisible Elements panel of Preferences.

Incorporating Plug-ins

Plug-ins are small software programs introduced by Netscape to enable its browser to display many types of files, not only HTML. Although some of the most well-known plug-ins are employed in the multimedia world—Macromedia's Shockwave, for example—hundreds of different kinds of plug-ins are available for all kinds of files. Plug-ins are generally designed so that the document blends seamlessly with the other portions of the HTML page.

Keep in mind that you're not really inserting a plug-in; you're inserting a file that requires a plug-in. Although the Dreamweaver menus and dialog boxes refer to "inserting a plug-in," a reference to a specific file is actually inserted. That file is of a particular MIME (Multipurpose Internet Mail Extension), which tells the browser what kind of file is being called. Once the browser knows the file's MIME type, it can invoke the correct plug-in.

Just like plug-ins, the code used to insert the plug-in was also originally developed by Netscape. Plug-ins are incorporated into HTML through the <embed> tag. Although plug-in features and their associated attributes vary widely, the minimum requirements for a plug-in are the source file and the dimensions (height and width) of the object. Typical HTML for a plug-in looks like the following:

```
<embed src="movies/oscars.avi" height="200" width="300">
```

Although Netscape developed the plug-in concept, Microsoft has embraced it to some degree. Internet Explorer recognizes the <embed> tag and works with some plug-ins—even if an equivalent ActiveX control is unavailable.

Beyond the excitement and novelty that plug-ins can add to your page, one inescapable fact remains: If a user doesn't have the plug-in installed, the plug-in file can't be experienced. Users generally have to download and install the plug-in — and then restart their browsers — before they can perceive any new material. Although this sequence is not a particularly difficult task, it nevertheless stops many people from viewing your creation in its entirety.

Tip

Plug-in Plaza (`www.browserwatch.internet.com/plug-in.html`) is an excellent resource for links to the entire spectrum of plug-ins. You can access plug-ins by category or by searching the entire list.

Dreamweaver has an open-ended approach to plug-ins. After you've inserted the Plug-in object, Dreamweaver displays a placeholder for it and enables you to enter the basic attributes through the Property Inspector (see Figure 17-7). Custom attributes are inserted through the Parameters dialog box. You can enter as many attributes as necessary.

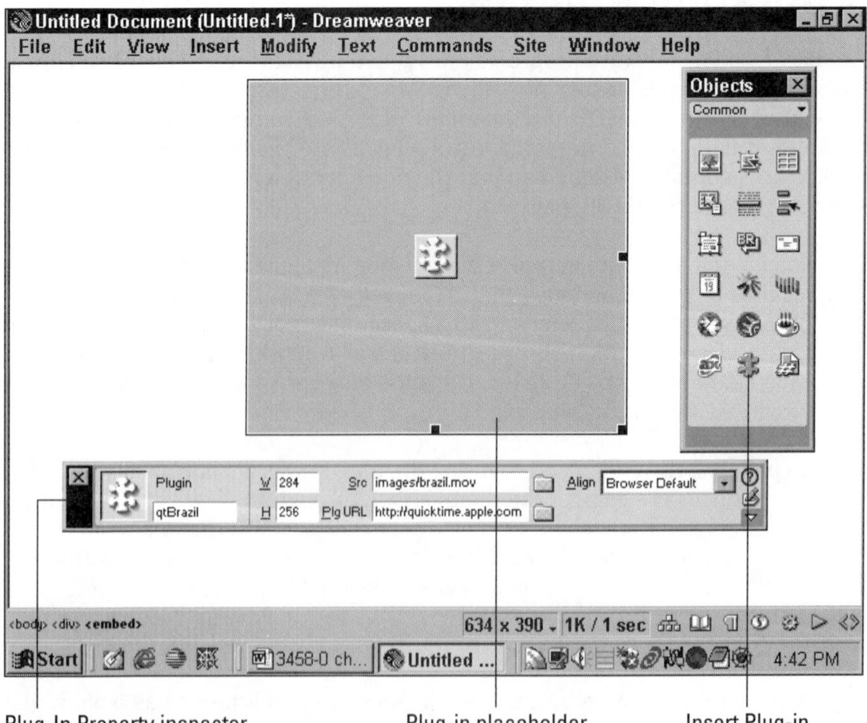

Figure 17-7: Use the Plug-in object from the Objects palette to begin the process of embedding your plug-in.

Embedding a plug-in

Dreamweaver provides a generic Plug-in object available through the menus or through the Objects palette. Like any other HTML object, a plug-in can be aligned with text or an image, or even included in a table. Some plug-ins work automatically with no user interaction; others come with their own control panel.

To embed a plug-in into your Web page, follow these steps:

1. Insert the Plug-in object by choosing Insert ➪ Plug-in or by selecting the Plug-in object from the Objects palette. You can also drag the Insert Plug-in object from the Objects palette to any place in the Document window with any existing text or object.
2. In the Select File dialog box, enter the path and file name for your plug-in file in the File Name text box, or select the Browse (Choose) button to locate your file.

   A placeholder icon for the plug-in appears in the Document window.
3. Size the plug-in placeholder with either of these methods:
   a. Enter the appropriate values in the W (Width) and the H (Height) text boxes of the Property Inspector.
   b. Click the resizing handles on the plug-in placeholder and drag out the placeholder to a new size.
4. In the Plg URL text box, enter the Internet address that visitors to your Web page can visit if they do not have the necessary plug-in installed. For example, in the case of QuickTime movies, you would use `http://quicktime.apple.com`.
5. To name the plug-in, enter a unique name in the unlabeled text box on the left side of the Property Inspector. Such names are useful when the plug-in is addressed from a JavaScript function.
6. To change the alignment relative to other inline objects, click the Align arrow button and choose one of the options in the drop-down list.
7. To add additional whitespace around the plug-in, enter pixel values in the V Space text box for the top and bottom of the object, and in the H Space text box for the left and right sides.
8. To surround the plug-in with a border, enter a pixel value in the Border text box.
9. To add additional attributes, select the Parameters button. These options are discussed in the following section.

Once you've entered the basic values for your plug-in, Dreamweaver enables you to preview it right in the Document window as well as through an appropriate browser. See the section "Playing Plug-ins," later in this chapter, for more details.

Setting plug-in parameters

Because individual attributes for plug-ins can take any form, Dreamweaver offers a completely generic method of entering parameters and associated values. Parameters generally fall into one of two categories: those that take a value and those that stand alone. You can enter both types through the Parameters dialog box.

To set additional parameters to a plug-in, follow these steps:

1. From the extended Property Inspector, select the Parameters button.

   The Parameters dialog box is displayed with its two columns: Parameters and Values.

2. Click the + (add) button and enter the first attribute in the Parameter column. Press Tab to move to the Value column and enter the desired value. If the attribute is a standalone and doesn't take a value, simply press Tab again to return to the Parameter column.
3. Repeat Step 2 until all parameters are entered. Press Shift+Tab to move backwards through the list.
4. To delete a parameter, highlight it and select the – (delete) button.
5. To move a parameter from one position in the list to another, highlight it and select the up- or down-arrow buttons in the Parameters dialog box, as shown in Figure 17-8.

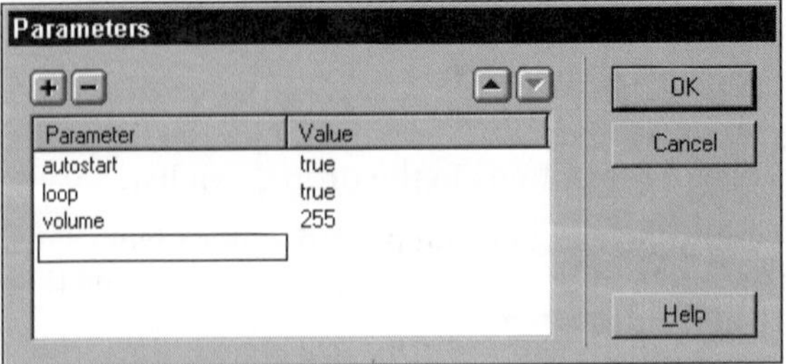

Figure 17-8: Enter specific attributes for each plug-in through the Parameters dialog box.

6. When you are finished inserting your parameters, select the OK button.

Many plug-ins require that the Web server recognize the affiliated MIME types. MIME types are a standard method of specifying various file formats. If your plug-in works locally but not remotely, the server probably needs to be configured for the particular MIME type. Contact your server administrator for further details.

Playing plug-ins

Plug-ins were invented for browsers, by browsers. But you can play any file for which you have a plug-in right in Dreamweaver's Document window—and you can keep right on designing. Of course, you could use this capability to play an MP3 music file in the background as you work, but it really has far more practical uses.

One use for the Dreamweaver play plug-in feature is to align Web page elements with portions of your digitized video or Flash movie. Previously, this process involved flipping back and forth between the Dreamweaver Document window and the browser preview as you moved elements ever so slightly. Now, Dreamweaver's playback capabilities enable you to line up your static elements with the dynamic ones.

Dreamweaver can play any file that uses plug-ins with the `<embed>` tag. Naturally, you have to have the plug-in installed on your local system. You can play any one selected plug-in file or all the plug-ins on the page.

Dreamweaver looks in its own Configuration\Plugins folder as well as the Plugins folder of the installed Netscape browser to determine which plug-ins are available. If you have it installed for Netscape, you don't have to reinstall it for Dreamweaver.

To play a selected plug-in, simply click the Play button (the green triangle) in the expanded Property Inspector. You can also choose View ➪ Plugins ➪ Play or use the keyboard shortcut Ctrl+P (Command+P). To stop the plug-in from playing, click the red Stop button in the Property Inspector (shown in Figure 17-9) or choose View ➪ Plugins ➪ Stop. The keyboard shortcut for stopping a plug-in from playing is Ctrl+. (period) (Command+.).

For the full effect on a media-rich page, play all the embedded plug-ins at once. To do this, choose View ➪ Plugins ➪ Play All or use the keyboard shortcut Ctrl+Shift+P (Command+Shift+P). You can stop any or all plug-ins from playing by choosing View ➪ Plugins ➪ Stop All or by using the keyboard shortcut Ctrl+Shift+. (period) (Command+Shift+.).

Caution

Unfortunately, not all plug-ins are created equal, and Dreamweaver can't play every one available. Dreamweaver maintains a list of those it can't play in the file UnsupportedPlugins.txt found in the Configuration folder. As of this writing, only one plug-in is noted as being "bad"—Video for Windows. Should you encounter any other plug-in that Dreamweaver cannot play, you can add its name to the UnsupportedPlugins.txt file, and Dreamweaver alerts you whenever you try to embed a file of this type.

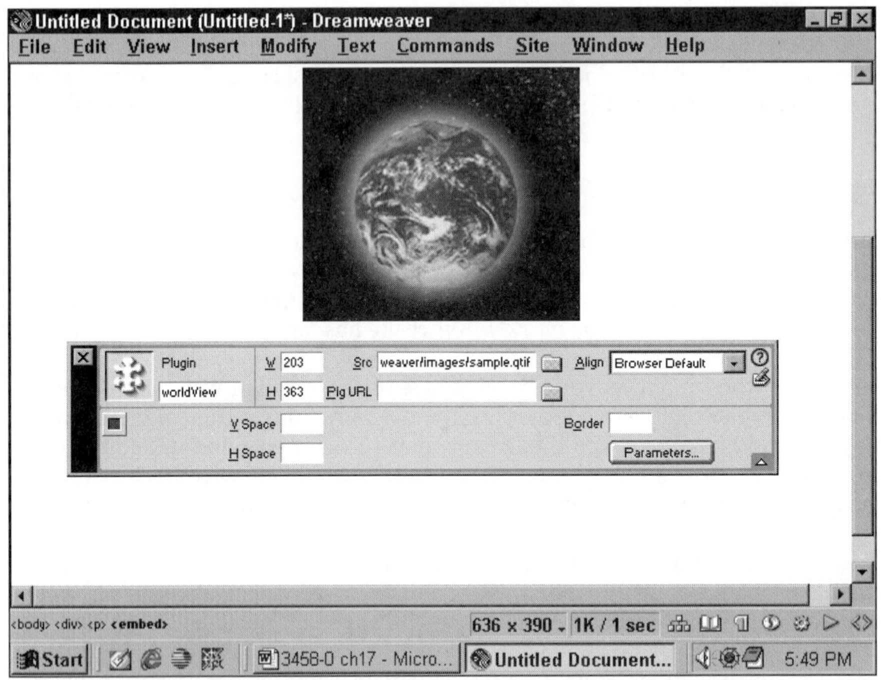

Figure 17-9: Files embedded in your Web page, such as this QuickTime movie, can be played back in the Document window as you design.

Detecting particular plug-ins

When a user visits your Web site via Netscape Navigator 3.0 or later, you can find out what plug-ins are installed and act accordingly. You may, for example, want to redirect a user who can't accommodate Shockwave files to a separate, less media-intensive page. You can achieve this redirection by creating a mechanism within your page to recognize the Shockwave plug-in.

To detect the presence of a specific plug-in, you need to use a little JavaScript in the `<head>` section of your document. You also need to know either the official name of the plug-in or its MIME type. As an example, the following code checks for a Shockwave plug-in by name; if that name isn't found, the user is redirected to another page:

```
<script language="javascript">
if (!navigator.plugins['Shockwave for Director']){
location="http://www.nadaville.com/simple.html"
}
</script>
```

You can also have your document discover whether a particular MIME type is supported, regardless of which plug-in is used. This next example checks for anything that can play a .wav audio file and, if the means is found, plays some background music:

```
<script language="javascript">
if (navigator.mimetypes['audio/wav']){
document.write('<embed name="audioBG" src="moody.wav" loop=true
autostart=true hidden=true volume=100 height=2 width=2>');
}
</script>
```

Both of these `if` statements can be used to detect any plug-in and MIME type by simply substituting the appropriate plug-in name and the MIME type you are attempting to detect.

To see which plug-ins are installed in your own system — and their proper names and MIME types — choose Help ⇨ About Plug-ins from within Navigator or Communicator.

Working with ActiveX Components

Microsoft developed ActiveX components largely in response to Netscape's plug-ins, and although the two technologies are similar, some significant differences exist. Standing on the shoulders of Microsoft's Object Linking and Embedding (OLE) technology, ActiveX controls work only with Internet Explorer 3 and later. A plug-in that enables Navigator to run ActiveX components is available but not widely used. ActiveX technology is only available on the Windows platform.

ActiveX controls, though difficult to develop, are fairly easy to implement in any Web page. Aside from the usual attributes such as a source file and the object dimensions, ActiveX uses two special parameters: a Class ID and the `codebase` property.

The Class ID is a unique code used to identify the specific ActiveX control. Every ActiveX control has a Class ID that must be used when calling the control. The Class ID is a lengthy combination of numbers and letters; here's the RealPlayer ActiveX Class ID code:

```
CLSID:CFCDAA03-8BE4-11CF-B84B-0020AFBBCCFA
```

To escape the considerable risk of typing errors when entering a Class ID code, you should cut and paste the code.

The codebase property is an Internet location where the ActiveX control can be automatically downloaded and installed if the browser does not find the control on the user's system. The primary difference between ActiveX's codebase parameter and a plug-in's pluginspage attribute is that the ActiveX control can be transferred and installed without requiring the browser to close and restart. A typical codebase value follows — the Director 7 ActiveX control value:

```
http://download.macromedia.com/pub/shockwave/cabs/director/sw.cab#version=7,0,2,0
```

Microsoft uses the <object>...</object> tag pair to include ActiveX controls in the HTML code. Unlike Netscape's <embed> tag, the <object> tag is recognized by the W3C as a valid specification for HTML 3.2 and later.

Optimally, everyone would adhere to the same standard; however, because neither browser recognizes the other's tag 100 percent of the time, you can actually combine an <object> and an <embed> tag to cover both browsers. This procedure is explained in the following section.

Dreamweaver provides a separate object for adding ActiveX controls to your Web pages. In addition, Dreamweaver makes it easy to add those complex Class ID codes by maintaining a user-definable list — accessible right from the ActiveX Property Inspector.

Incorporating an ActiveX control

As with plug-ins, Dreamweaver includes an ActiveX object to simplify inserting ActiveX controls. The primary difference between an ActiveX object and a Plug-in object — aside from the two special ActiveX parameters previously noted — is the location for the ActiveX source file. For example, if you want to embed an ActiveX control to show a digital video in AVI format, you first insert the control object by selecting the Insert ActiveX button from the Objects palette. Then you see the ActiveX Property Inspector (rather than an Insert ActiveX file dialog box). The source file is actually one of the parameters of the <object> tag, FileName, and must be entered through the Parameters dialog box (Embed Src text box).

Although you see a Play button on the ActiveX Property Inspector, like the one on the Plugin Property Inspector, you can't actually play ActiveX files in the Document window. If you have checked the Embed option, the Play button uses the comparable plug-in to play the file if it's installed on your system.

Follow these steps to insert an ActiveX control into your Web page:

1. Position the cursor where you want the ActiveX file to appear. Choose Insert ➪ ActiveX or select the Insert ActiveX button from the Objects palette.

   An ActiveX placeholder appears in the Document window, and the ActiveX Property Inspector displays (see Figure 17-10).

2. In the ClassID text box, enter the Microsoft ID for the ActiveX control.

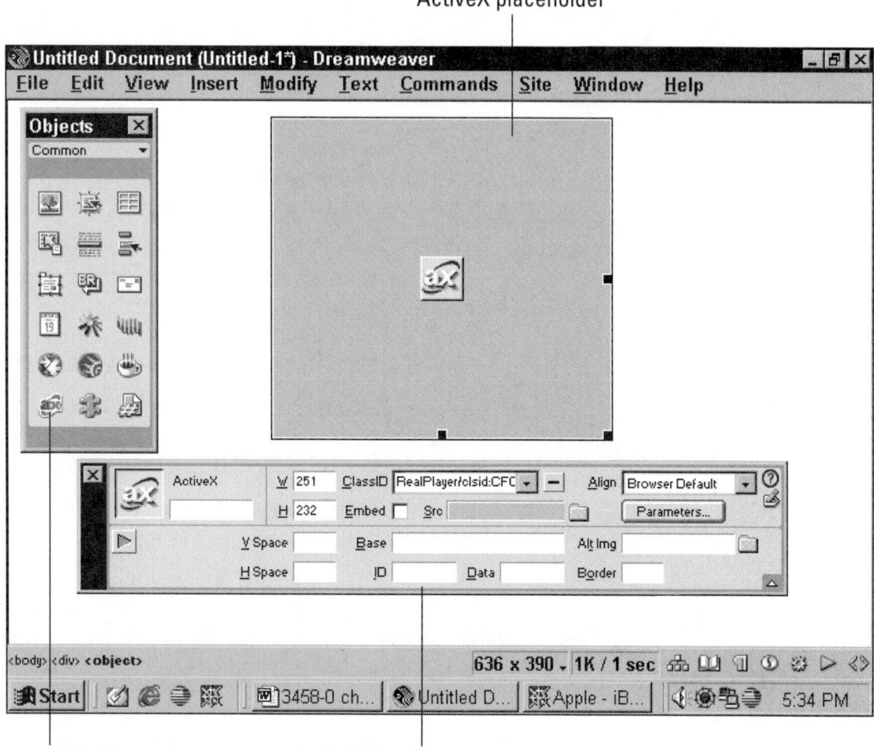

Figure 17-10: ActiveX controls are inserted with the help of Dreamweaver's ActiveX object and its Property Inspector.

If you've previously entered this particular Class ID, select the arrow button and choose the ID from the drop-down list, as shown in Figure 17-10.

3. Change the Width and Height values in the W and H text boxes to match the desired control display.
4. If you know the `codebase` URL, enter it in the Base text box.
5. Enter other relative parameters for the object as needed (see Table 17-1).
6. Click the Parameters button to display the Parameters dialog box.
7. Click the + (add) button and enter the first parameter: `FileName`. Press Tab to move to the Value column and enter the path and file name for your file.
8. Press Tab and continue entering the desired parameters in the left column, with their values in the right column. Click OK when you're finished.
9. Preview your ActiveX control in action through Internet Explorer 3 or 4.

Table 17-1
ActiveX Object Properties

ActiveX Object Property	*Description*
Align	To alter the alignment of the ActiveX control, choose an option from the Align drop-down list. In addition to the Browser Default, your options include Baseline, Top, Middle, Bottom, Texttop, Absolute Middle, Absolute Bottom, Left, and Right.
Alt Image	Enter a path to an alternative image for display to browsers, such as Netscape, that don't understand the `<object>` tag. The Alt Image is available only if you are not using the Embed option. This image does not display in Dreamweaver.
Border	To place a border around your control, enter a number in the Border text box. The number determines the width of the border in pixels. The default is zero or no border.
Data	Specify a data file for the ActiveX control in this text box. Not all ActiveX controls use this attribute.
Embed	This property designates whether the matching code for the plug-in is to be included (see the following section "Combining ActiveX Controls and Plug-in Objects," in this chapter).
H Space	You can increase the space to the left and right of the object by entering a value in the H (Horizontal) Space text box. The default is zero.
ID	The ID field is used to define the optional ActiveX ID parameter, most often used to pass data between ActiveX controls.
Name	If desired, you can enter a unique name in the unlabeled field at the left of the Property Inspector. JavaScript and VBScript use this name to identify the ActiveX control.
Src	This sets the source for the plug-in if the Embed checkbox is selected (as described in the following section).
V Space	To increase the amount of space between the top and bottom of the ActiveX object and the other elements on the page, enter a pixel value in the V (Vertical) Space text box. The default is zero.

Combining ActiveX controls and plug-in objects

Dreamweaver takes advantage of the fact that Netscape browsers do not recognize the <object> tag, and that Microsoft browsers ignore the <embed> tag placed inside the <object> tag. How could this be an advantage, you ask? Because of their mutual exclusivity, you can include both types of tags in the same Web page and still avoid conflicts.

The following example code shows you how the approach works in HTML. The <embed> section is bold to show how one tag fits within another.

```
<object width="137" height="136" classid="clsid:CFCDAA03-8BE4-11cf¬
-B84B-0020AFBBCCFA">
      <param name="FileName" value="images/braz.wav">
      <embed width="137" height="136" filename="images/braz.wav"
      src="images/braz.wav"></embed>
    </object>
```

Notice the values common to both tags, including the dimensions and the source file. (The source file is the `src` attribute in <embed> and the `FileName` parameter in the <object> tag.) Dreamweaver automatically inserts these values when you enable the Embed option on the ActiveX Property Inspector.

If you're going to use the Embed option with your ActiveX object, you should wait until you've entered the necessary `FileName` parameter (through the Edit Parameters button) before you select the Embed checkbox. When the `FileName` parameter is already specified, Dreamweaver automatically writes the same value in the Embed Scr text box. If you forget and turn on the Embed option before entering the `FileName` parameter, just turn off Embed, reselect it, and the proper value appears as the Embed source file.

Adding Java Applets

Java is a platform-independent programming language developed by Sun Microsystems. Although Java can also be used to write entire applications, its most frequent role is on the Web in the form of an applet. An *applet* is a self-contained program that can be run within a Web page.

Java is a compiled programming language similar to C++. Once a Java applet is compiled, it is saved as a class file. Web browsers call Java applets through, aptly enough, the <applet> tag. When you insert an applet, you refer to the primary class file much as you call a graphic file for an image tag.

Each Java applet has its own unique set of parameters — and Dreamweaver enables you to enter as many as necessary, in the same manner as plug-ins and ActiveX controls. In fact, the Applet object works almost identically to the Plug-in and ActiveX objects.

Keep two caveats in mind if you're planning to include Java applets in your Web site. First, most (but not all) browsers support some version of Java – the newest release has the most features but the least support. Second, all the browsers that support Java enable the user to disable it because of security issues. Make sure to use the Alt property to designate an alternative image or some text for display by browsers that do not support Java.

A Java applet can be inserted in a Web page with a bare minimum of parameters: the code source and the dimensions of the object. Java applets derive much of their power from their configurability, and most of these little programs have numerous custom parameters. As with plug-ins and ActiveX controls, Dreamweaver enables you to specify the basic attributes through the Property Inspector, and the custom ones via the Parameters dialog box.

To include a Java applet in your Web page, follow these steps:

1. Position the cursor where you want the applet to originate and choose Insert ⇨ Applet. You can also select the Insert Applet button from the Objects palette.

   The Insert Applet dialog box opens.

2. From the Select File dialog box, enter the path to your class file in the File Name text box or select the Browse (Choose) button to locate the file.

   An Applet object placeholder appears in the Document window. In the Applet Property Inspector (Figure 17-11), the selected source file appears in the Code text box, and the folder appears in the Base text box.

The path to your Java class files cannot be expressed absolutely; it must be given as an address relative to the Web page that is calling it.

3. Enter the height and width of the Applet object in the H and W text boxes, respectively. You can also resize the Applet object by clicking and dragging any of its three sizing handles.

4. You can enter any of the usual basic attributes, such as a name for the object, as well as values for `Align`, `V` and/or `H Space`, and `Alt` in the appropriate text boxes in the Property Inspector.

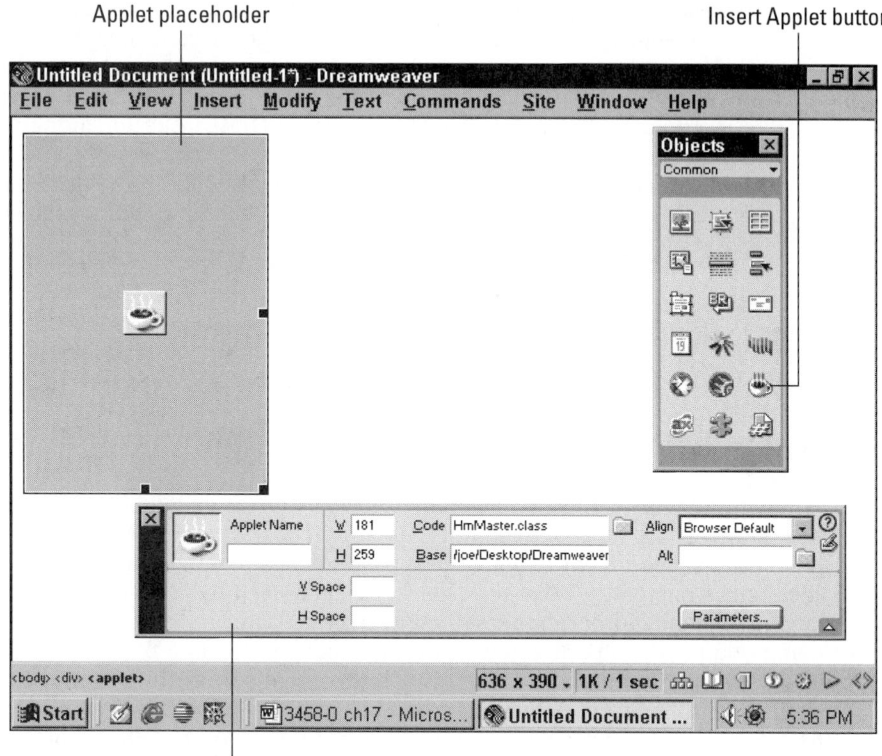

Figure 17-11: Use the Insert Applet button to insert a Java Applet object and display the Applet Property Inspector.

5. If desired, enter the online directory where the applet code can be found in the Base text box. If none is specified, the document's URL is assumed to be this attribute, known as the *codebase*.
6. To enter any custom attributes, select the Parameters button to open the Parameters dialog box.
7. Select the + (add) button and enter the first parameter. Press Tab to move to the Value column.
8. Enter the value for the parameter, if any. Press Tab.
9. Continue entering desired parameters in the left column, with their values in the right. Click OK when you're finished.

Tip

Because of the importance of displaying alternative content for users not running Java, Dreamweaver provides a method for displaying something for everyone. To display an image, enter the URL to a graphics file in the Alt text box. To display text as well as an image, you have to do a little hand-coding. First, select a graphics file to insert in the Alt text box and then open the HTML Inspector. In the `<img>` tag found between the `<applet>` tags, add an `alt="your_message"` attribute by hand (where the text you want to display is the value for the `alt` attribute). Now your Java applet displays an image for browsers that are graphics-enabled but not Java-enabled, and text for text-only browsers such as Lynx.

Some Java class files have additional graphics files. In most cases, you need to store both the class files and the graphics files in the same folder.

Adding JavaScript and VBScript

When initially developed by Netscape, JavaScript was called LiveScript. This browser-oriented language did not gain importance until Sun Microsystems joined the development team and the product was renamed JavaScript. Although the rechristening was a stroke of marketing genius, it has caused endless confusion among beginning programmers — JavaScript and Java have almost nothing in common outside of their capability to be incorporated in a Web page. JavaScript is used primarily to add functionality on the client side of the browser (for tasks such as verifying form data and adding interactivity to interface elements) or to script Netscape's servers on the server side. Java, on the other hand, is an application development language that can be used for a wide variety of tasks.

Conversely, VBScript is a full-featured Microsoft product. Both VBScript and JavaScript are scripting languages — which means you can write the code in any text editor and compile it at runtime. JavaScript enjoys more support than VBScript — JavaScript can be rendered by both Netscape and Microsoft browsers (as well as other browsers like WebTV, Opera, and Sun's HotJava), whereas VBScript is read only by Internet Explorer on Windows systems — but both languages have their fans. In Dreamweaver, both types of code are inserted in the Web page in the same manner.

Inserting JavaScript or VBScript

If only mastering JavaScript or VBScript itself were as easy as inserting the code in Dreamweaver! Simply go to the Objects palette's Invisibles pane and select the Insert Script button, or choose Insert ➪ Script from the menus and enter your code in the small Insert Script window. After you click OK, a Script icon appears in place of your script.

Of course, JavaScript or VBScript instruction is beyond the scope of this book, but every working Web designer must have an understanding of what these languages can do. Both languages refer to and, to varying degrees, manipulate the information on a Web page. Over time, you can expect significant growth in the capabilities of the JavaScript and VBScript disciplines.

Dreamweaver, through the application of its behaviors, goes a long way toward making JavaScript useful for nonprogrammers. To learn more about Behaviors, see Chapter 19.

Use the Script Property Inspector (Figure 17-12) to select an external file for your JavaScript or VBScript code. You can also set the language type by opening the Language drop-down list and choosing either JavaScript or VBScript. Because different features are available in the various releases of JavaScript, you can also specify JavaScript 1.1 or JavaScript 1.2. If you need to choose a specific version of JavaScript, you must do it when you initially insert the script—you cannot change the setting from the Script Property Inspector. Naturally, you could also make the adjustment in the HTML Inspector.

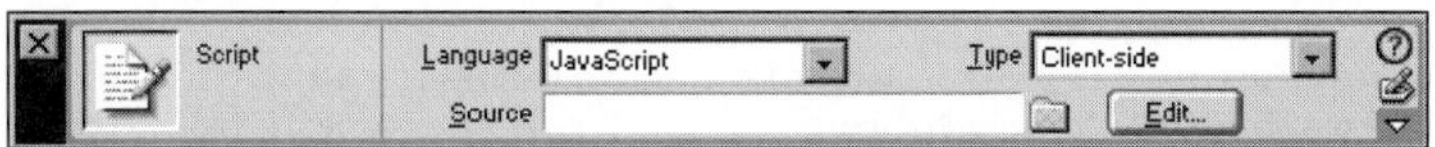

Figure 17-12: Insert either JavaScript or VBScript through the Objects palette's Script object available on the Invisibles panel.

When you choose JavaScript or VBScript as your Language type, Dreamweaver writes the code accordingly. Both languages use the `<script>` tag pair, and each is specified in the `language` attribute, as follows:

```
<script language="JavaScript">alert("Look Out!")</script>
```

With Dreamweaver, you are not restricted to inserting code in just the `<body>` section of your Web page. Many JavaScript and VBScript functions must be located in the `<head>` section. To insert this type of script, first select View ➪ Head Content. Next, select the now-visible `<head>` window and choose Insert ➪ Script or click the Insert Script object. Enter your script as described earlier in this section and then select the main Document window, or choose View ➪ Head Content again to deselect it.

You can also indicate whether your script is based on the client side or server side by choosing the Type option from the Property Inspector. If you choose Server-side, your script is enclosed in `<server>...</server>` tags and is interpreted by the Web server hosting the page.

Editing JavaScript or VBScript

Dreamweaver provides a large editing window for modifying your script code. To open this Script Properties window, select the placeholder icon for the script you want to modify and then choose the Edit button on the Script Property Inspector. You have the same functionality in the Script Properties window as in the Script Property Inspector; namely, you can choose your language or link to an external script file (see Figure 17-13).

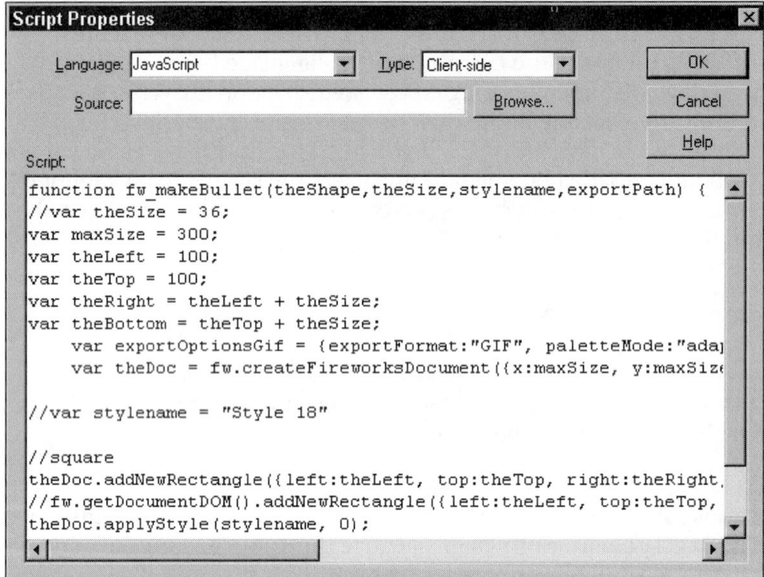

Figure 17-13: The generous Script Properties window provides plenty of room for modifying your JavaScript or VBScript.

Tip

Some older browsers "break" when loading a JavaScript Web page and display the code written between the <script>...</script> tag pair. Although Dreamweaver doesn't do it by default, you can use a trick to prevent this anomaly. In the HTML Inspector or your external editor, insert the opening comment tag (<--) right after the opening <script> tag. Then insert the closing comment tag (-->), preceded by two forward slashes, right before the closing </script>. An example follows:

```
<script language="Javascript">
<!--
[JavaScript code goes here]
//-->
</script>
```

The comment tags effectively tell the older browser to ignore the enclosed content. The two forward slashes in front of the closing comment tag are JavaScript's comment indicator, which tells it to ignore the rest of the line.

Summary

To paraphrase a popular commercial, "Web pages aren't just for HTML anymore." The possibilities expand tremendously when you start to explore any of the technologies discussed in this chapter: CGI, plug-ins, ActiveX, Java, and JavaScript or VBScript. Dreamweaver maintains an open-ended design for external programs.

✦ CGI scripts are primarily used to send information back and forth between the user and the Web server. The Web server can then, under the direction of the CGI program, store the information in a database or forward it to another URL or e-mail address.

✦ Plug-ins enable browsers to display formats other than HTML. A plug-in can display multimedia content inline with other HTML objects such as images and tables. Dreamweaver supports a Plug-in object that enables the `<embed>` code to be customized through the Parameters dialog box.

✦ Dreamweaver enables you to play any or all of the plug-ins — right in the Document window as you're creating your Web page.

✦ Microsoft browsers employ ActiveX controls in a manner similar to Netscape's plug-ins. Each ActiveX control has its own unique Class ID, as well as a codebase attribute that enables users to get the control without interrupting their workflow. The Dreamweaver ActiveX object enables you to easily combine both ActiveX controls and their corresponding plug-in with the Embed option.

✦ Java applets can be inserted as Applet objects in a Dreamweaver Web page. Java source files, called *classes*, can be linked to the Applet object through the Property Inspector.

✦ Dreamweaver offers a simple method for including both JavaScript and VBScript code in the `<body>` section of your HTML page. Script functions that need to be inserted in the `<head>` section can now be added by selecting View ⇨ Head Content.

In the next chapter, you learn how you can use and create your own Dreamweaver objects.

✦ ✦ ✦

CHAPTER 18

Creating and Using Objects

✦ ✦ ✦ ✦

In This Chapter

The basics of using objects

Modifying the Object menu and Objects palette

Inserting downloaded and other new objects

Creating a custom object

Enhancing custom objects with JavaScript functions

✦ ✦ ✦ ✦

Sometimes the simplest ideas are the most powerful. The Dreamweaver development team had a simple idea: Why not code the insertable objects in HTML? After all, when you choose to insert anything into a Web page — from a horizontal rule to a Shockwave movie — you are just putting HTML in the page. If the objects are just HTML files, what are the possible benefits? For one, the objects can be easily modified. Also, HTML requires no special program to code, and coding the language itself is not extraordinarily difficult. In addition, the core users of Dreamweaver are experts in HTML. Now, a simple idea is turned into a powerful tool.

All the objects included with Dreamweaver can be modified and customized to fit any Web designer's working preferences. Furthermore, custom objects can easily be created. This capability not only enables you to include regular HTML tags that repeatedly occur in your designs, but also opens the door to an impressive new level of expandability. Dreamweaver's capability to accommodate any number of custom objects means you can take advantage of new technologies immediately.

Building a site that needs the latest tags just released by the W3C? Go right ahead — make an object that inserts any or all of the tags. You may not be able to see the result in Dreamweaver, but if your browser can handle the tags, you can preview them there.

Find yourself including the same ActiveX control over and over again, with only one change in the parameters? Create a custom object that inserts that control, with all the constant attributes — and add a parameter form to enter the variable attributes.

This chapter shows you the tremendous potential of Dreamweaver objects. After studying the use of the standard objects, you learn how you can customize your object working environment. Then, you find out how to create your own objects and take advantage of the new extensibility features in Dreamweaver 3.

Inserting Dreamweaver Objects

If you've been using Dreamweaver, you've been using objects. Even if your first exposure to Dreamweaver has been working through the first half of this book, you've already used several types of objects. Aside from text, everything inserted in a Web page can be considered an object: images, comments, plug-ins, named anchors — they're all objects, and are all extremely easy to use.

Dreamweaver offers several ways to include any object. For a few objects, you even have as many as four different techniques from which to choose:

- ✦ From the menu, choose Insert and then any of the listed objects.
- ✦ From the Objects palette (see Figure 18-1), click any button on the six standard panes — Characters, Common, Forms, Frames, Head, and Invisibles — to insert an object at the current cursor position.
- ✦ Drag any button off the Objects palette and drop it next to any existing content on your Web page.
- ✦ Many objects have a keyboard shortcut, such as Ctrl+Alt+I (Command+Alt+I) for Image or Ctrl+Alt+F (Command+Alt+F) for a Flash movie. Keyboard shortcuts insert the chosen object at the current cursor location.

Figure 18-1: You'll find yourself returning to the Objects palette as an easy way to include HTML elements.

When you insert one of the objects from the Invisibles pane—such as the Non-Breaking Space, Comment, or Named Anchor—Dreamweaver by default inserts an icon to show the object's placement. If you find these icons distracting, you can turn them all off by choosing the toggle command, View ➪ Invisible Elements. If you have an invisible element "turned off" in Preferences, you never see the icon, regardless of the status of the View menu command.

Modifying the Objects Palette

The Objects palette is one of the most customizable of all of Dreamweaver's features. In addition to the flexibility of having it "float" anywhere on the screen, you can also resize and reshape the palette to your liking—you can even dock it with other floating windows. Most important, you can rearrange its contents, add new panes, and, as noted earlier, include custom objects.

Moving and reshaping the Objects palette

If you work with your Document window fully expanded, you often find yourself repositioning the Objects palette. Just click and drag the title bar on top of the palette to quickly move it out of the way. You can also press F4 to send the Objects palette (and any other open palette or inspector) behind the Document window or Site window. Pressing F4 again brings them back to the front.

If you don't like the long, vertical shape that Dreamweaver uses by default for the Objects palette, you can change its appearance. Place your pointer over any border of the palette until the usual pointing arrow changes into a two-headed arrow—now you can click and drag the Objects palette into a new shape. You can drag any corner to form a rectangular shape in Windows, as shown in Figure 18-2 (with Macintosh, use the lower-right corner), or you can extend the palette horizontally instead of vertically.

Figure 18-2: Reshape the Objects palette to your liking.

When screen real estate is at a premium, you can reduce the overall size of the Objects palette—even down to just a one-button size. If you shrink it down small enough so that all the buttons don't show at once, one or two scroll arrows appear. Click an arrow to see the next button in the palette.

The Objects palette is the only one of the "big three" floating windows — Objects, Properties, and Launcher — that can be included in Dreamweaver's docking system, but it's a one-way connection. You can dock the Objects palette to any other, but you can't dock the others to the solo Objects palette. If you're working with a variety of Dreamweaver's other features, such as layers, templates, behaviors, and so on, you might want to group the Objects palette with these other windows to reduce your workspace clutter.

Reorganizing the objects and adding panes

The six panes of the Objects palette — Characters, Common, Forms, Frames, Head, and Invisibles — correspond to the six folders found in the Dreamweaver Configuration\Objects directory. Each folder has two items for each object: an HTML file and a GIF file. The HTML file is the source code for the object, and the GIF file is the button image. If you want to move an item from one Objects palette pane to another, just transfer the two files related to that object from one folder to the other.

For example, let's say you're doing a lot of JavaScript work and you want to move the Insert Script object from the Invisibles pane to the Common pane. To accomplish this task, you need to move script.htm and script.gif from the Invisibles folder to the Common folder. You can click and drag the files or cut and paste them (Windows only). You must restart Dreamweaver to see the changes.

You're not limited to the six panes on the Objects palette. The standard panes — Characters, Common, Forms, Frames, Head, and Invisibles — correspond to identically named subfolders in the Objects directory. If you want to add another pane, simply add a new subfolder. For example, I've developed a number of custom objects for inserting sound and digital video files, which I wanted to group on a new pane of the Objects palette. In my file management program, I created a folder called Media within the Dreamweaver\Configuration\Objects folder and moved all my special object files into the new folder. After restarting Dreamweaver, Media appears as my seventh pane in the Objects palette.

Dreamweaver recognizes only one level of subfolders within the Objects folder as new Objects palette panes. You cannot, for instance, create a subfolder called Videos within the Media subfolder that will be recognized by Dreamweaver as a submenu.

Dreamweaver alphabetizes the Object panes by folder name. If you want your new custom pane to appear first on the Objects palette, you must name its folder so that it appears further down alphabetically (that is, closer to A) than the Common folder.

Use one of two tricks: You can start the custom folder name with a space or a tilde (~), such as ~Media, for instance; or you can rename the Common folder so that its name appears later in the alphabet.

You can customize not only the Objects palette but also the menus. All menus are now controlled via the menus.xml file found in the Configuration\Menus folder. For an in-depth look at how you can change your Insert—or any other—menu, as well as keyboard shortcuts, see Chapter 21.

Adding Other Objects

Before you begin building your own custom objects, you may want to look around and see if someone else has already created something similar. In addition to having the standard objects that ship with Dreamweaver, numerous Web sites have objects (and behaviors) that are available for download. You can even search an ongoing database of Dreamweaver objects (as well as behaviors, commands, and so on) at the Dreamweaver Extension Database, located on my site, Dreamweaver etc. (`www.idest.com/dreamweaver`). Of course, a variety of objects are available on the CD-ROM media accompanying this book.

No matter where you get your objects, the procedure for installing them is the same. To incorporate new objects into your Dreamweaver system, follow these steps:

1. Uncompress the files if necessary. Object files come with an HTML file and a GIF file, and the two files are usually compressed for easy download or transfer.
2. If necessary, make a new folder for your objects. All objects must be stored in a subfolder of the Dreamweaver\Configuration\Objects folder. You can either store the object files in a standard subfolder (Characters, Common, Forms, Frames, Head, or Invisibles, for instance) or in a new folder that you create.
3. Transfer the object files to the desired folder. Be careful: Make sure you transfer both the HTML and the GIF file together.

The new object is automatically added as the last item on the Insert menu. If you want to customize the Insert menu to list the new object in a different location, you need to change the menus.xml file, found in the Configuration\Menus folder.

4. Restart Dreamweaver.

The extension community has grown by leaps and bounds in recent times, and far too many sites exist to mention here. However, CD-ROM 1 that accompanies this book includes a Web resource directory with links to all the extension authors that I am aware of as this writing.

Online Sources for Dreamweaver Extensions

You can find new objects and behaviors at numerous online sources. However, like traditional Web development, creating Dreamweaver extensions is an ever-growing affair—if you can't find what you're looking for at any one site, visit the Dreamweaver Extension Database hosted by Dreamweaver etc.

Macromedia

`www.macromedia.com/support/dreamweaver/upndown/objects`

The official Object and Behavior Exchange site accepts objects submitted from all over. After evaluations by the Dreamweaver engineers, objects are posted for downloading. Before you can access this area of the Macromedia site, you must accept the terms of a licensing agreement.

Dreamweaver Depot

`http://weblogs.userland.com/dreamweaver`

Run by Andrew Wooldridge, the Dreamweaver Depot initially specialized in Netscape-only objects and behaviors, but the site now offers cross-browser and Internet Explorer-specific extensions as well. The Depot also has a forum and a chat room for Dreamweaver aficionados.

Massimo's Corner of the Web

`www.massimocorner.com`

Massimo Foti produces high-quality extensions that fulfill many specific functions faced by a Web developer. For example, his site features extensions devoted to redirecting browsers as well as controlling remote windows and scrolling layers.

Webmonkey Editor Extensions Collection

`www.hotwired.com/webmonkey/javascript/code_library/ed_ext`

Although this area on the Hot Wired site could potentially hold other Web authoring tools' extensions, Dreamweaver is currently the only one on the market with the capability. You can find several professional-quality objects and behaviors, both cross-browser and browser-specific ones.

Yaromat

`www.yaromat.com`

Featuring objects, commands, and behaviors by Jaro von Flocken, Yaromat houses some of the most creative Dreamweaver extensions on the Web. His Layer f(x) behavior brings mathematical precision to layer movements, and his other creations are equally dramatic.

Dreamweaver etc.

`www.idest.com/dreamweaver`

Maintained by Joseph Lowery, author of this book, the Dreamweaver etc. site includes all the objects found on this book's CD-ROMs, plus new ones posted after this book's publication.

Creating Custom Objects

Each custom object, like standard objects, is made from two files: an HTML file describing the object, and a GIF file depicting the button. The complexity of the HTML depends on the complexity of the object. You can build just about anything—from a simple object that replicates a repeatedly used item, to a high-end object that uses advanced JavaScript techniques for creating special function layers and windows. You can even make objects that create other objects.

To support the "higher end" of the custom object scale, Dreamweaver includes proprietary extensions to JavaScript and a Document Object Model (DOM), which combines a subset of Netscape Navigator 4.0's DOM, a subset of the DOM Level 1 established by the W3C, and a host of custom Dreamweaver extensions. You study these techniques further into the chapter. As the following section shows, however, many objects don't require any JavaScript and are easy to construct.

Making simple objects

To make a simple object that inserts any HTML-created item, put only the code necessary to create the object into a file and then save the file in one of the object folders. The key phrase in the preceding sentence is *only the code necessary*. Unlike a regular Web page, you don't include the framing `<html>...<body>...</body>...</html>` sections for a simple custom object—all you need is the essential code necessary to make the object.

For example, let's say you are asked to enhance 100 Web pages and make each page capable of showing a different QuickTime movie. Each of the .mov files is different, so you can't use Dreamweaver's Library feature. The easiest way to handle this situation is to create a dummy version of what you need and then turn that dummy into an object.

Step 1: Creating the item

First, create your item as you normally would in Dreamweaver. For this example, let's insert a plug-in and add all the standard attributes: `name`, `height` and `width`, `pluginspage`, `border`, `v space`, and `h space`—and even a few special parameters such as autostart and stretch. The only attribute that the example omits is the attribute that changes: the file source. You also want the movie to be centered, wherever it's located, and you center the plug-in. When finished, the complete code for the page and plug-in, as generated by Dreamweaver, looks like the following:

```
<html>
<head>
<title>Untitled Document</title>
<meta http-equiv="Content-Type" content="text/html; charset=iso-8859-1">
</head>
<body bgcolor="#FFFFFF">
```

```
<div align="center">
  <embed src="" width="135" height="135" name="qtMovie" ¬
pluginspage="http://www.apple.com/quicktime/" vspace="5" hspace="5" ¬
border="5" stretch="true" autostart="false"></embed>
</div>
</body>
</html>
```

Step 2: Creating the object

To create a simple object from the preceding, just cut everything in the code but the item (or items) you want repeated. In the HTML Inspector, select all the code from the opening <html> tag up to and including the <body> tag and then delete. Then delete the closing tags, </body> and </html>. The only remaining code is the following:

```
<div align="center">
  <embed src="" width="135" height="135" name="qtMovie" ¬
pluginspage="http://www.apple.com/quicktime/" vspace="5" hspace="5" ¬
border="5" stretch="true" autostart="false"></embed>
</div>
```

After you eliminate all the code except for your object's code and return to the visual editor, the Document window changes from a white background to a dark-gray background. This change occurs because Dreamweaver makes the bgcolor attribute of the <body> tag white by default — to create a simple object, you need to delete the entire <body> tag, including the color information.

Step 3: Saving the object

Now your object is ready to be saved. For Dreamweaver to recognize this or any other snippet of code as an object, the file must be saved in the Configuration\Objects folder. You can choose to save your object in any of the existing subfolders — Characters, Common, Forms, Frames, Head, or Invisibles — or you can create a new subfolder within the Objects folder. For this example, create a new folder called Media for this and other similar objects.

Caution

You must save your new object in a subfolder within the Objects folder. Dreamweaver doesn't recognize objects saved individually in the Objects folder.

After the file is saved, you can restart Dreamweaver to test your object — or you can use the Reload Extensions feature.

To force Dreamweaver to reload objects, behaviors, inspectors, and commands, click the expander arrow on the Objects palette while holding down the Ctrl (Command) key. In addition to the different Objects palette panes, Dreamweaver displays the Reload Extensions menu item, as shown in Figure 18-3. Select this option, and soon your new objects will be available — although there's one final step to consider.

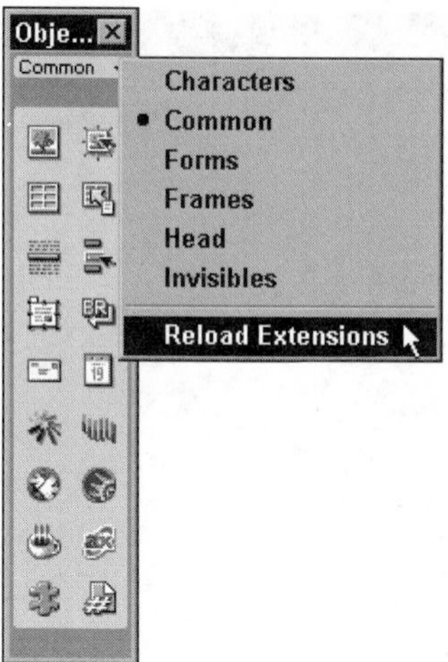

Figure 18-3: Press the Ctrl (Command) key and click the Objects palette expander arrow to access the Reload Extensions command.

Macintosh users should approach the Reload Extensions feature with care, if at all. On Macs, when you invoke the Reload Extensions command, the Apple menu is disabled until Dreamweaver exits.

Step 4: Creating a button for the object

As shown in Figure 18-4, Dreamweaver displays an "unknown object" placeholder in the Objects palette because you haven't yet made a button image for the qtMovie object. In addition, unless you specifically include the new object in the menu configuration file, menus.xml, the object is listed in the bottom portion of the Insert menu. This arrangement is fine for debugging, but if you want to continue using your object, it's more efficient to create a button image for it and revise the menus.xml file to include it. The following section shows you how to complete this task.

Building an object button

Object buttons are GIF files, ideally sized at 18 pixels square. To make the object button, you can use any graphics-creation program that can save GIF files. If your button image file is not 18 pixels by 18 pixels, Dreamweaver resizes it to those dimensions. Your button can be as colorful as you want — as long as it can still fit in an 18-pixel square.

To create an object button, you can open and modify any of the existing GIF files for the standard buttons. Just be sure to use the Save As command of your paint program – and not the Save command – to save your modified version.

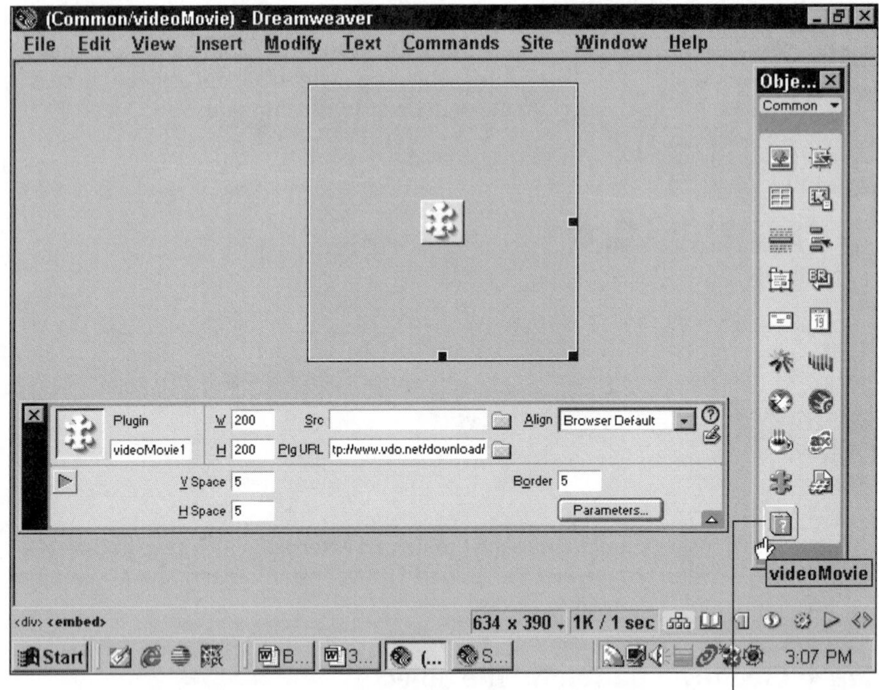

Figure 18-4: You can create custom objects such as the qtMovie object shown here.

After you've created your button image, save the GIF file in the same folder as the HTML file for the new object.

At this time, you may also want to modify the menus.xml file as described in Chapter 21.

Putting JavaScript to Work in Custom Objects

The remaining sections of this chapter deal with using JavaScript to create more complex objects.

If you're totally unfamiliar with JavaScript, you might want to review this section with a good supporting resource at hand. An excellent choice is Danny Goodman's *JavaScript Bible,* published by IDG Books Worldwide.

Using the objectTag() function

When Macromedia built a JavaScript interpreter into Dreamweaver, a number of extensions were included to facilitate object and behavior creation. One of these functions, `objectTag()`, is the key to building advanced objects. All of the standard Dreamweaver-built objects use the `objectTag()` function. This function has a single purpose: It writes any specified value into the HTML document.

The `objectTag()` is multifunctional; it can insert code in the `<head>` as well as the `<body>`. Moreover, the function handles the placement intelligently; `objectTag()` knows which tags should be placed where. Consequently, you don't have to make any special declarations to place code in the `<head>` section.

You can see a simple use of the `objectTag()` function by looking at the source code for Dreamweaver's Insert Line-Break object. In the Objects\Common folder, open line_break.htm and look at the code for this object in the HTML Inspector. Just like most JavaScript functions that can affect any portion of the page, the `objectTag()` function is written in the `<head>` section. Here's the function in its entirety:

```
function objectTag() {
  // Return the html tag that should be inserted
  return "<BR>";
}
```

You can designate a ToolTip to appear when your mouse passes over your new object's button. Enter the desired name in the `<title>` section of the HTML object file. The designated `<title>` also appears on any dialog boxes used by the object.

Aside from the comment line, `objectTag()` returns a only value. In the preceding example, the value happens to be `"<BR>"`. You can insert any HTML code as the return value. However, because JavaScript formats any value as a string, you need to apply JavaScript string-formatting syntax, as follows:

✦ To use the `objectTag()` function to return an HTML tag and a variable, use quotes around each string literal, but not around the variable, and join the two with a plus sign. For example, the following `objectTag()` function code inserts `<img src=images/whatzit.gif>` in the current cursor position:

```
nada = "images/whatzit.gif"
return "<img src=" + nada + ">";
```

✦ To make an object that returns separate lines of code, put each tag on its own line, with the symbol for a newline, `\n`, at the end of the string, surrounded by quotes; then add a plus sign at the end of the line. For example, the following `objectTag()` function inserts a Flash movie of a particular size and shape:

```
function objectTag() {
  // Return the html tag that should be inserted
  return '\n' +
'<object classid="clsid:D27CDB6E-AE6D-11cf-96B8-444553540000" \n' +
'codebase="http://active.macromedia.com/flash2/cabs/swflash.¬
cab#version=4,0,0,0". "width="145" height="135"> \n' +
' <param name="movie" value="newMovie.swf"> \n' +
' <param name="PLAY" value="false"> \n' +
' <embed src="newMovie.swf" \n' +
'pluginspage="http://www.macromedia.com/shockwave/download/index.cgi?¬
P1_Prod_Version=ShockwaveFlash" width="145" height="135"
play="false"></embed> \n' +
'</object>'
}
```

Some developers prefer to set the entire collection of strings to a variable and return that variable. In this case, you'd be better served by using JavaScript's add-by-value operator (+=), as in this example:

```
var retval = ''
retval += '<table width="' + newWidth + '" height="' +
newHeight + '" border="0" cellspacing="0" cellpadding="0">\n'
retval += '  <tr>\n'
retval += '    <td>' + newCode + '</td>\n'
retval += '  </tr>\n'
retval += '</table>\n'
return retval
```

✦ Use single quotes to surround the return values that include double quotes. For every opening quote of one kind, make sure a matching closing quote exists of the same kind. For example:

```
return '<img src="images/eiffel.jpg">'
```

✦ Use the backslash character, \, to display special inline characters such as double and single quotes or newline.

```
return "<strong>You\'re Right!</strong>"
```

Unless you're mixing variables with the HTML you're using for your object, you should use the "object-only" method described in the previous section, "Making Simple Objects." Reserve the `objectTag()` function for your intermediate-to-advanced object-creation projects.

Offering help

As objects grow in their features, they often grow in their complexity. An object with multiple parameters — especially if it is intended for public release — could potentially benefit from a Help button. Dreamweaver offers just such a button to aid custom object builders and their users.

Including the `displayHelp()` function causes Dreamweaver to display a Help button, directly beneath the OK and Cancel buttons found to the right of a user-created parameter form. When selected, this button calls whatever is defined in the function.

For example, if you wanted to define a Help button that would put up an informative message within Dreamweaver, you might code the `displayHelp()` function this way:

```
displayHelp() {
  alert("Be sure to name all your layers first")
}
```

You're not restricted to in-program alerts. If you have a much larger help file, you can display it in your primary browser by using Dreamweaver's built-in `browseDocument()` function. With the following definition, when the Help button is selected, Dreamweaver first opens the primary browser (if it's not already running) and shows the object-specific help file:

```
displayHelp() { dreamweaver.browseDocument¬
("http://www.idest.com/dreamweaver/help/entitiesHelp.htm")
}
```

Note that the preceding code includes an absolute URL that pulls a page off the Web. You can also reference a file locally. The best way to do this is to use another Dreamweaver JavaScript function, `getConfigurationPath()`. Just as it sounds, this function returns the current path to the Configuration folder. Using this as a base, you can reference other files installed on the system. In this example, the help file is stored in a folder called HelpDocs, which in turn is stored within the Configuration folder:

```
function displayHelp() {
  var helpPath = dreamweaver.getConfigurationPath() + ¬
"/HelpDocs/replicatorHelp.htm"
  dreamweaver.browseDocument(helpPath)
}
```

Attaching a parameter form

To be truly useful, many objects require additional attributes. Several of the standard objects in Dreamweaver use parameter forms to simplify entry of these attributes. A *parameter form* is the portion of the object code that creates a dialog box. Dreamweaver uses the HTML form commands for handling the parameter form duties.

To see how a parameter form is structured, look at the parameter forms used in the standard objects. Select the Insert Script button in the Invisibles pane of the Objects palette. The Insert Script dialog box that appears on the screen is a basic parameter form.

Next, open the Script object source file (Objects\Invisibles\script.htm) in Dreamweaver to see how the parameter form is built. As shown in Figure 18-5, the `<body>` of the file consists of a single `<form>` element with two items inside, a text field and a menu list.

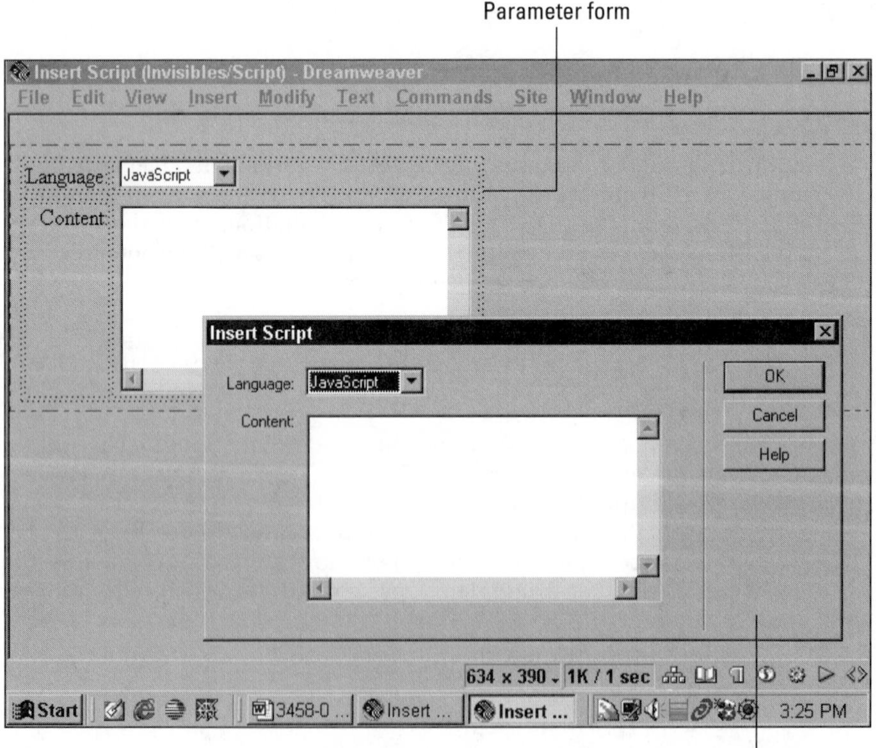

Figure 18-5: To see how the parameter form is used, compare the Script source file to its completed object.

Sizing the Parameter Form Dialog Box

Although you cannot control all aspects of your parameter form — Dreamweaver automatically inserts the OK and Cancel buttons on the upper right — you can designate the dimensions of the parameter's dialog box. Normally, Dreamweaver automatically sizes the dialog box, but for a complex object, you can speed up the display by using the `windowDimensions()` function. Moreover, if your object is intended for general distribution, you can set different window dimensions for the Macintosh and Windows platforms.

The `windowDimensions()` function takes one argument, `platform`, and returns a string in the following form:

```
"width_in_Pixels,height_in_Pixels"
```

The size specified should not include the area for the OK and Cancel buttons. If the dimensions offered are too small to display all the options in the parameter form, scroll bars automatically appear.

The following example of the `windowDimensions()` function creates a parameter form dialog box 650 pixels by 530 pixels if viewed on a Macintosh, and 670 pixels by 550 pixels if viewed on a Windows system:

```
function windowDimensions(platform){
     if (platform.charAt(0) == 'm'){ // Macintosh
       return "650,530";
     }
     else { // Windows
       return "670,550";
     }
}
```

Macromedia recommends that you not use the `windowDimensions()` function unless you want your dialog box to be larger than 640 × 480 pixels. Like all Dreamweaver extensions to the Application Programming Interface (API), the `windowDimensions()` function can be used to build both objects and actions.

The `<body>` section of the HTML source code for the Script object contains only the `<form>` with two fields: a `<select>` field (the menu list used to select the language) and a `<textarea>` field for the actual script:

```
<FORM NAME="theform">
  <table>
    <tr>
      <td align="right" nowrap>Language:</td>
      <td>
        <select name="Language">
          <option value="JS" selected>JavaScript</option>
```

```
          <option value="JS11">JavaScript 1.1</option>
          <option value="JS12">JavaScript 1.2</option>
          <option value="VB">VBScript</option>
        </select>
      </td>
    </tr>
    <tr>
      <td align="right" height="5"></td>
      <td rowspan="2">
        <textarea name="script" cols="50" rows="8"></textarea>
      </td>
    </tr>
    <tr>
      <td align="right" valign="top" nowrap>Content:</td>
    </tr>
  </table>
</FORM>
```

When the parameter form is displayed as an object, Dreamweaver automatically adds the OK and Cancel buttons; a Help button is added if the `displayHelp()` function is defined. When you select the OK button, the `objectTag()` function combines the values in the `<select>` and `<textarea>` tags with the necessary HTML tags to write the `<script>` code.

Using the form controls

Dreamweaver uses the HTML `<form>` tag and all of its various input types to gather attribute information for objects. To use the form elements in a parameter form, their input data must be passed to the JavaScript functions. Because Dreamweaver uses a subset of the Navigator 4.0 Document Object Model (DOM), as shown in Table 18-1, you are restricted to using specific methods for the various input types to gather this information. Properties marked with an asterisk are read-only.

Table 18-1
Form Elements in the Dreamweaver Document Object Model

Object	*Properties*	*Methods*	*Events*
`form`	`elements*` (an array of `button`, `checkbox`, `password`, `radio`, `reset`, `select`, `submit`, `text`, and `text area` objects); child objects by name	None	None

Object	Properties	Methods	Events
button reset submit	form*	blur() focus()	onClick
checkbox radio	checked form*	blur() focus()	onClick
password text textarea	value form*	blur() focus() select()	onBlur onFocus
select	form* options[n]. defaultSelected* options[n].index* options[n].selected* options[n].text* options[n].value* selectedIndex	blur() (Windows only) focus() (Windows only)	onBlur (Windows only) onChange onFocus() (Windows only)

JavaScript uses a hierarchical method of addressing the various elements on any given Web page. Moving from most general to most specific, each element is separated by a period. For example, the background color property of a page would be `document.bgColor`. The status of a checkbox named "sendPromo" on a form called "orderForm" would be `document.orderForm.sendPromo.checked`. The more complex your objects, the more important it is for you to master this syntax.

Input fields: Text, textarea, password, file, image, and hidden

When information is entered in one of the input type fields, the data is stored in the value property of the specific object. For example, look again at the code for the Plug-in object and notice the text field where the selected file's name is displayed:

```
<INPUT TYPE="text" name="pluginfilename" size="30">
```

When the `objectTag()` function is run, the contents of that text box are assigned to a variable, and that variable is included in the output written to the Web page:

```
function objectTag() {
  // Return the html tag that should be inserted
  var retval = '<EMBED SRC="' +
escape(document.forms[0].pluginfilename.value) + '"></EMBED>';
```

```
    // clear the field for next insertion
    clearForm();
    return retval;
}
```

In the preceding case, the input file name is located in:

```
document.forms[0].pluginfilename.value
```

Because the form was also named ("theForm"), this same value could also be written as follows:

```
document.theForm.pluginfilename.value
```

The "escape" function is an internal JavaScript function that converts a text string so that it can be read by a Web server. Any special characters are encoded into their hexadecimal ASCII equivalents. A single space between words, for instance, is converted to `%20`.

The text input types recognize two events in the Dreamweaver DOM: `onBlur` and `onFocus`. When a user selects a text field, either by tabbing to or clicking it, that text field is said to have focus — and the `onFocus` event is fired. When the user leaves that field, the field loses focus or blurs — and the `onBlur` event is triggered. Because the DOM does not recognize the `onChange` event handler with text fields, you can use a combination of `onFocus` and `onBlur` to check for changes and act accordingly.

Submit, Reset, and Command buttons

The button input types are used in parameter forms to trigger custom JavaScript functions. Instead of sending data to an external server, the data is sent to a specified internal function. The buttons respond only to `onClick` events and cannot pass any particular properties of their own, such as value or name.

Command buttons are used extensively in the Character Entities object shown in Figure 18-6. (The object is available on this book's CD-ROM 1 and was developed before Dreamweaver 3's new Other Characters object was created.) Each character entity is a separate Command button, written in the following form:

```
<input type="BUTTON" value="&#161;"
onClick="getChar('&amp;#161;','&#161;')">
```

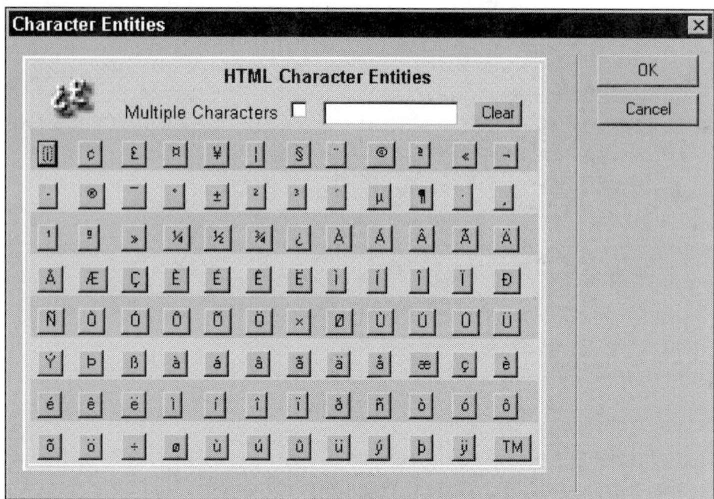

Figure 18-6: This custom Character Entities object uses 97 separate Command buttons.

Each character entity symbol in each line has a specific purpose. The value is the character displayed on the button; the first argument in the `getChar()` function is written to a hidden field and eventually sent to the Web page; and the second argument is used to display the selected character in a text box.

```
function getChar(val,val2) {
  document.theForm.charValue.value=val
  document.theForm.txChar.value=val2
}
```

When this object is at work, the user makes a selection and clicks OK, and the `objectTag()` function reads the value from the hidden field and writes it into the Web page:

```
function objectTag() {
  return document.theForm.charValue.value;
}
```

Command buttons can be used to fire any custom JavaScripts and pass any necessary information to be eventually processed by the `objectTag()` function.

Checkboxes

Checkboxes enable an option to be selected or deselected, so the only information that a function needs from a checkbox is whether it has been selected. Dreamweaver's DOM enables you to read the checked property of the Checkbox object and act accordingly. The Character Entities object discussed in the preceding section, for instance, uses a checkbox to turn on and off the Multiple Characters option. If the checkbox (named cbMultiple) is selected, then `document.theForm.cbMultiple.checked` is true, and one set of statements is executed; otherwise, the second set of statements is run. The code for checkboxes follows:

```
function getChar(val,val2) {
if(document.theForm.cbMultiple.checked) {
  document.theForm.charValue.value=
  document.theForm.charValue.value+val
  document.theForm.txChar.value=
  document.theForm.txChar.value+val2
  } else {
  document.theForm.charValue.value=val
  document.theForm.txChar.value=val2
  }
}
```

Checkboxes are excellent for setting up either/or situations. You can also use checkboxes to set (turn on) particular attributes. You may, for instance, use a checkbox to make it possible for the user to enable an automatic startup for an QuickTime movie, or to turn the control panel on or off.

Radio buttons

Radio buttons offer a group of options, from which the user can only select one. The group is composed of `<input type=radio>` tags with the same name attribute; there can be as few as two in the group or as many as necessary.

The input type `radio`, like `checkbox`, makes use of the checked property to see which option was selected. The method used to figure out which of the radio buttons was chosen depends on the number of buttons used on the form:

- ✦ With just two or three buttons, you may want to use a simple if-else construct to determine which radio button was selected.
- ✦ If you are offering many options, you can use a loop structure to look at the `checked` property of each radio button.

With only a couple of radio buttons in a group, you can examine the one radio-type item in the array (starting with 0) and see if it was checked. In the following code, if one radio button is selected, the variable (`theChoice`) is set to one value — otherwise, it is set to the other value:

```
if (document.forms[0].comm[0].checked == "1")
      theChoice = "left";
   else
      theChoice = "right";
```

When you have many radio buttons, or you don't know how many radio buttons you will have, use a counter loop such as this next example from the Enhanced LineBreak object (available on CD-ROM 1 that accompanies this book):

```
for (var i = 0; i < document.theForm.lbreak.length; i++) {
     if (document.theForm.lbreak[i].checked) {
          break
     }
}
```

In this example, `lbreak` is the name of the group of radio buttons on the parameter form, and the `length` property tells you how many radio buttons are in the group. When the loop finds the selected radio button in the array, the loop is broken, and the program proceeds to the next group of statements.

Unfortunately, once you know which radio button is checked, there's no easy way to get its value. The Dreamweaver DOM doesn't support the value property for the radio input type. As a result, you have to assign the value to a variable based on which radio button was selected. You can complete this task in a simple series of if-else statements:

```
if (i == 0){
val = ""
     } else {
     if (i == 1) {
     val = "left"
          } else {
          if (i == 2) {
          val = "right"
               } else {
               val = "all"
               }
          }
     }
```

Alternatively, you can put all the values in an array and assign them in a statement like the following:

```
return "<br clear=" + newValue[i].name + ">"
```

List boxes and drop-down menus

List boxes and drop-down menus are perfect for offering a variety of options in a compact format. Drop-down menus enable the user to choose an option from a scrolling list; list boxes offer multiple choices from a similar list. Both use the `<select>` tag to set up their available options. When you include a list box or drop-down menu from Dreamweaver, you enter the options by selecting the List Value button and entering the item labels and their associated values in the dialog box.

The code for the Direction list box — taken from Matthew David's Marquee object, which is shown in Figure 18-7 and is available on CD-ROM 1 that accompanies this book — is written as follows:

```
<select name="direction">
     <option value="LEFT" selected>LEFT</option>
     <option value="RIGHT">RIGHT</option>
     <option value="UP">UP</option>
     <option value="DOWN">DOWN</option>
</select>
```

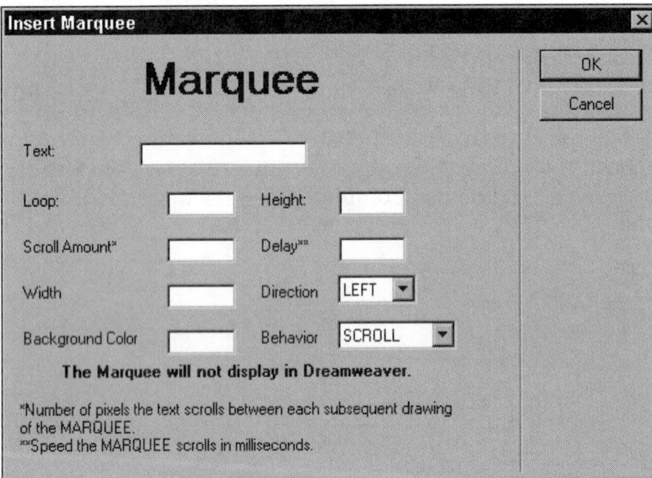

Figure 18-7: The Marquee custom object is designed to take advantage of an Internet Explorer special function: the capability to make a scrolling text display.

Each list box or drop-down menu must have a unique name — in the preceding code, that name is "direction," given in the `<select>` tag. To discover which option the user selected when working with a drop-down menu, you need to examine the selected Index property of the named `<select>` object. Each `<option>` in a `<select>` tag is placed in an array in the order listed in the displayed menu. Remember, arrays always start with a 0 in JavaScript.

The following code looks at each member of the array; if that option is the one in which the `selectedIndex` property is `true`, then the proper value is assigned to a variable:

```
if(document.forms[0].direction.selectedIndex == 0) {
  direct_choice = 'LEFT'
   } else {
   if(document.forms[0].direction.selectedIndex == 1) {
  direct_choice = 'RIGHT'
  } else {
       if(document.forms[0].direction.selectedIndex == 2) {
       direct_choice = 'UP'
  } else {
```

```
        if(document.forms[0].direction.selectedIndex == 3) {
        direct_choice = 'DOWN'
    }
   }
  }
  }
```

The process is slightly different when you have multiple options in a list box. In this situation, you should set up a loop to examine the `options[n].selected` property. All the options in a `<select>` tag set have additional properties that can be read by Dreamweaver's DOM, as follows:

Select Option	***Description***
`options[n].defaultSelected`	Returns `true` for the option (or options, when multiple selections are enabled) for every `<option>` tag with a selected attribute.
`options[n].index`	Returns the option's position in the array.
`options[n].selected`	Returns `true` if the option is chosen by the user.
`options[n].text`	Returns the text of the item as it appears in the list.
`options[n].value`	Returns the value of the item assigned in the `<option>` statement.

The following method cycles through all of the `<options>` to find which one(s) were selected:

```
for (var i = 0; i < document.theForm.optList.length; i++) {
  if (document.theForm.optList.options[i].selected) {
      result += "n\ " + document.theForm.optList.options[i].
      value
      }
  }
return result
}
```

Adding images to your objects

Custom objects don't have to be just text, of course. You can include images in your object, just as you would in a regular Web page — with one catch: Dreamweaver has to be able to find your image files. If you are not distributing your custom object, you can use images from any folder on your system. On the other hand, if your objects are going out to other users, you have to either include the image files with the object or use existing graphics stored in known locations.

What existing graphics are on every Dreamweaver system in specific locations? The GIF files for each object, of course. The button for the custom Character Entities object (previously shown in Figure 18-6) is used in the dialog box for the object itself. Because the two files always have to be in the same folder, you can include the image file on the same level. The size of the GIF files is fairly small (18 pixels by 18 pixels), so you can simply double the size of the image and have Dreamweaver rescale it.

The opposite approach for using one image for both the Objects palette and your dialog box is to make a larger image, say 32×32. Often this results in a better looking graphic in both places.

Of course, you can create your own custom graphics for your objects and include those files with the associated HTML and GIF button files. You can even spice up your Dreamweaver standard objects, as shown in Figure 18-8.

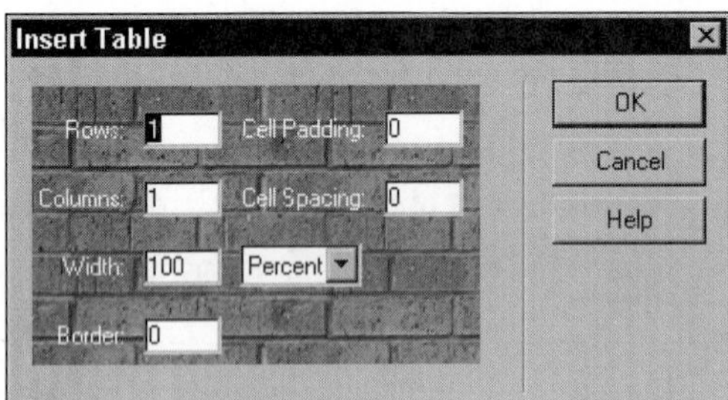

Figure 18-8: You can include graphics in custom objects; in this Insert Table dialog box, the standard Dreamweaver object is altered to add a brick background.

You can count on several other useful graphical objects, all found in the Configuration\Shared\MM\Images folder. In addition to the plus and minus buttons used in the Dreamweaver dialog boxes for behaviors and parameters, there are GIF files for standard up and down arrows, a transparent 1-pixel image to use for spacing, and more.

Using layers and Flash movies in objects

Standard HTML layout options are fairly limiting. You can however, use layers in your custom Object dialog boxes. With the expansive possibilities of layers, you can build a Wizard-type object that leads users through a series of complex steps, with instructions on every screen. You can also use layers to describe the effect of the user's choices.

For an excellent example of the use of layers to create a Dreamweaver extension, take a look at the Drag Layer behavior, discussed in Chapter 19. This behavior uses five different layers to reveal new options as the user makes certain choices; there's even an error layer to inform the user of a precondition to using the object.

Layers enable you to pack in a lot of information—and amass a great deal of input—in a single parameter form. One of the best examples of a multilayered object is Dreamweaver CourseBuilder Knowledge Object. CourseBuilder is a version of the program customized for Web learning, and the Knowledge object is the primary interface. Amazingly enough, all the key functionality of the program is contained in the one object.

Another available option in Dreamweaver objects is the capability to use Flash movies — or any plug-in on the system — within the parameter form. All that's required is that the user have the same plug-in available on their system.

With Flash's scalable vector graphics, animation capabilities, and interactivity, user interfaces have the potential to take a tremendous leap forward. Instead of a Help message, you could build in a training video that demonstrates particularly difficult concepts.

Incorporating a Flash file in your object's parameter form is no different from using it in your Web page. Just choose Insert ➪ Flash or select the Insert Flash button from the Objects palette. Dreamweaver automatically reads the correct size from the Flash file. Make sure any other parameters you desire are set, and you've just created an advanced user interface! To get an idea of what's possible, take a look at Figure 18-9, which shows an Insert Flash 3 object that uses Flash as the interface, playing in Dreamweaver.

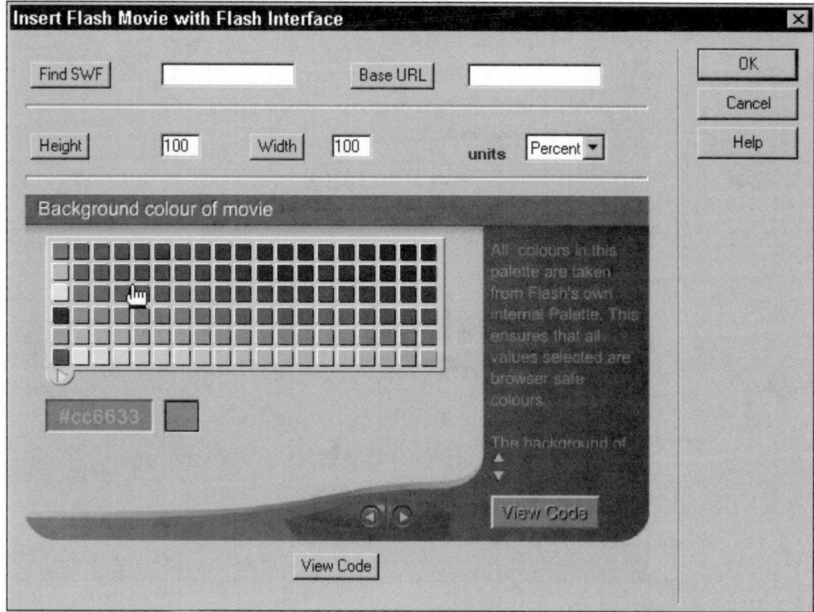

Figure 18-9: Spice up your object's user interface like this Insert Flash 3 object from the Web designer team of Spooky and the Bandit at `www.spookyandthebandit.com`.

Summary

In one sense, objects are analogous to the macros in a word processing program that enable repetitive work to be greatly simplified. Objects can be so much more than just duplication tools, however — they can extend the reach of Dreamweaver's power and instantly incorporate new standards and technology. The standard Dreamweaver objects can be used effortlessly. Just like all objects, they are simply HTML files, and thus provide excellent examples for creating custom objects.

✦ Objects can be inserted from either the Objects palette or the Insert menu.

✦ Both the Objects palette and the Insert menu can be easily modified by adjusting the menus.xml file.

✦ Simple objects can be created by inserting the HTML code necessary to make the object into a file and then saving the file in one of the object's subfolders.

✦ More complex objects can take advantage of Dreamweaver's built-in JavaScript interpreter, its Document Object Model (DOM), special JavaScript functions, and enhanced Application Programming Interface (API). In Dreamweaver, you can even use layers to construct custom objects.

In the next chapter, you learn how to use Dreamweaver behaviors.

✦ ✦ ✦

CHAPTER 19

Using Behaviors

✦ ✦ ✦ ✦

In This Chapter

Behavior basics

Adding a behavior's event and action

Looking at the standard behaviors

Managing behaviors

✦ ✦ ✦ ✦

Behaviors are truly the power tools of Dreamweaver. With Dreamweaver behaviors, any Web designer can make layers appear and disappear, execute any number of rollovers, or control a Shockwave movie — all without knowing even a snippet of JavaScript. In the hands of an accomplished JavaScript programmer, Dreamweaver behaviors can be customized or created from scratch to automate the most difficult Web effect.

Creating behaviors is one of the more challenging Dreamweaver features to master. Implementing these gems, however, is a piece of cake. This chapter examines the concepts behind and the reality of using behaviors — detailing the use of all the behaviors included with Dreamweaver and some from other notable third-party sources. This chapter also contains tips on managing your ever-increasing library of behaviors.

Here's a guarantee for you: Once you get the hang of using Dreamweaver behaviors, your Web pages will never be the same.

Understanding Behaviors, Events, and Actions

A *behavior*, in Macromedia parlance, is the combination of an event and an action. In the electronic age, one pushes a button (the event), and something (the action) occurs — such as changing the channel on the TV. In Dreamweaver, events can be anything as interactive as a user's click of a link or something as automatic as the loading of a Web page. Behaviors are said to be *attached* to a specific element on your page, whether it's a text link, an image, or even the `<body>` tag.

Dreamweaver has simplified the process of working with behaviors by including default events in every possible object on the Web page. Instead of having to think about both *how* you want to do something and *what* you want to do, you only have to focus on the *what*—the action.

To help you understand conceptually how behaviors are structured, let's examine the four essential steps for adding a behavior to your Web page:

✦ **Step 1: Pick a tag.** All behaviors are connected to a specific HTML element. You can attach a behavior to everything from the `<body>` to the `<textarea>` of a form. If a certain behavior is unavailable, it's because the necessary element isn't present on the page.

✦ **Step 2: Choose your target browser.** Different browsers—and the various browser versions—support different events. Dreamweaver enables you to choose either a specific browser, such as Internet Explorer 4, or a browser range, such as version 3 and 4 browsers.

✦ **Step 3: Select an action.** Dreamweaver makes active only those actions available to your specific page. You can't, for instance, choose the Show-Hide Layer action until you insert one or more layers. Behaviors guide you to the workable options.

✦ **Step 4: Enter the parameters.** Behaviors get their power from their flexibility. Each action comes with a specific parameter form (which represents the dialog box that the user sees) designed to customize the JavaScript code output. Depending on the action, you can choose source files, set attributes, and enable features. The parameter form can even dynamically update to reflect your current Web page.

Dreamweaver 3 comes with 25 cross browser–compatible actions, and third-party developers have made many additional actions available, with even more in the works. Behaviors greatly extend the range of possibilities for the modern Web designer—without learning to program JavaScript. All you need to know about attaching behaviors is presented in the following section.

Attaching a Behavior

When you see the code generated by Dreamweaver, you understand why setting up a behavior is also referred to as *attaching* a behavior. As previously noted, Dreamweaver needs a specific HTML tag in order to assign the behavior (Step 1). The link tag `<a>` is often used because, in JavaScript, links can respond to several different events, including `onClick`. Here's an example:

```
<a href="#" onClick="MM_popupMsg('Thanks for coming!')">Exit Here</a>
```

You're not restricted to one event per tag or even one action per event. Multiple events can be attached to a tag to handle various user actions. For example, you may have an image that does all of the following things:

- Highlights when the user's pointer moves over the image
- Reveals a hidden layer in another area of the page when the user clicks the mouse button over on the image
- Makes a sound when the user releases the mouse button over the image
- Starts a Flash movie when the user's pointer moves away from the image

Likewise, a single event can trigger several actions. Updating multiple frames through a single link used to be difficult — but no more. Dreamweaver makes it easy by enabling you to attach several Go to URL actions to the same event, `onMouseClick`. In addition, you are not restricted to attaching multiple instances of the same action to a single event. For example, in a site that uses a lot of multimedia, you could tie all of the following actions to a single `onClick` event:

- Begin playing an audio file (with the Play Sound action).
- Move a layer across the screen (with the Play Timeline action).
- Display a second graphic in place of the first (with the Swap Image action).
- Show the copyright information for the audio piece in the status bar (with the Set Text of Status Bar action).

You can even determine the order in which the actions connected to a single event are executed.

With Dreamweaver behaviors, hours of complex JavaScript coding is reduced to a handful of mouse clicks and a minimum of data entry. All behavior assigning and modification are handled through the Behavior Inspector.

Using the Behavior Inspector

The Behavior Inspector is a two-paned window (see Figure 19-1) that neatly sums up the behaviors concept in general. A list of assigned events is located on the left side of the window. The selected tag is displayed at the top of the Events pane, with a drop-down list of browsers, which includes the following:

- 3.0 and Later Browsers
- 4.0 and Later Browsers
- IE 3.0
- IE 4.0
- IE 5.0
- Netscape 3.0
- Netscape 4.0

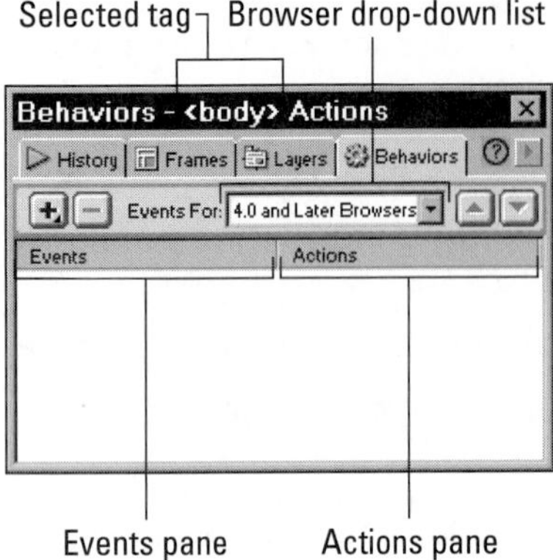

Figure 19-1: You can handle everything about a behavior through the Behavior Inspector.

When you select one of these options, the default event for the selected tag is noted by Dreamweaver. After you've selected an action and completed the dialog box, the default event appears in the Events pane alongside the action in the Actions pane. You can choose a different event by selecting the down arrow next to the default event. Select any event in the drop-down list. Double-click the action to open the associated Parameter window, where you can modify the action's attributes.

As usual in Dreamweaver, you have your choice of methods for opening the Behavior Inspector:

✦ Choose Window ⇨ Behaviors.

✦ Select the Show Behaviors button from either Launcher.

✦ Use the keyboard shortcut F8 (an on/off toggle).

Tip The Behavior Inspector can be closed by toggling it off with F8 or hidden with the other floating windows by pressing F4.

After you have attached a behavior to a tag and closed the associated action's parameter form, Dreamweaver writes the necessary HTML and JavaScript code into your document. Because it involves functions that can be called from anywhere in the document, the JavaScript code is placed in the `<head>` section of the page, and the code that links the selected tag to the functions is written in the `<body>` section. A few actions, including Play Sound, place additional HTML code at the bottom of the `<body>`, but most of the code—there can be a lot of code to handle all the cross-browser contingencies—is placed in the `<head>` HTML section.

Adding a behavior

Now let's look more closely at the procedure for adding (or attaching) a behavior. As noted earlier, you can assign only certain events to particular tags, and those options are further defined by the type of selected browser.

Even in the latest browsers, key events such as `onMouseDown`, `onMouseOver`, and `onMouseOut` work only with anchor tags. To circumvent this limitation, Dreamweaver can enclose an element, such as `<img>`, with an anchor tag that links to nowhere—`src="#"`. Events that use the anchor tag in this fashion are seen in parentheses in the pop-up menu of events.

To add a behavior to your Web page, follow these steps:

1. Select an object in the Document window.

If you want to assign a behavior to the entire page, select the `<body>` tag from the Tag Selector.

2. Open the Behavior Inspector by choosing Window ➪ Behaviors or selecting the Show Behaviors button from either Launcher. You can see the selected tag at the top of the Events pane.
3. If necessary, select a different browser target from the drop-down list in the Events pane.
4. Select the + (add action) button to reveal the available options, as shown in Figure 19-2. Choose one from the pop-up menu.

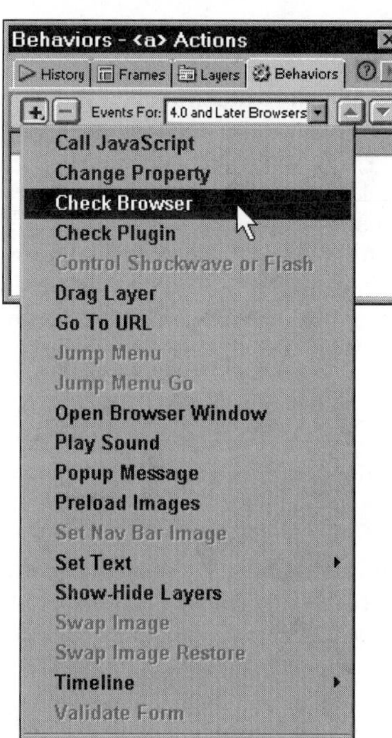

Figure 19-2: The Add Action pop-up menu dynamically changes according to what's on the current page and which tag is selected.

5. Enter the necessary parameters in the Action's dialog box.
6. Click OK when you're finished.

Dreamweaver 3 includes a new menu item at the bottom of the Add Action list: Get More Behaviors. To use this feature, go online and then choose the option. You will be connected with the Dreamweaver Exchange, a new service from Macromedia with a huge selection of extensions of all flavors, including behaviors.

The standard events

Every time Dreamweaver attaches a behavior to a tag, it also inserts an event for you. The default event that is chosen is based on two selections: the browser type and the tag selected. The different browsers in use have widely different capabilities, notably when it comes to understanding the various event handlers and associated tags.

For every browser and browser combination shown in the Browser drop-down list, Dreamweaver has a corresponding file in the Configuration\Behaviors\Events folder. Each of the tags listed in each file, such as I.E. 4.0.htm, has at least one event associated with it. The entries look like this:

```
<INPUT TYPE="Text" onBlur="*" onChange="" onFocus="" onSelect="">
```

The default event for each tag is marked with an asterisk; in the example, `onBlur` is the default event. After you've selected an action and completed the dialog box, the default event appears in the Events pane alongside the action in the Actions pane.

If you find yourself changing a particular default event over and over again to some other event, you might want to modify the Event file to pick your alternative as the default. To do this, open the relevant browser file found in the Configuration\Behaviors\Events folder in a regular text editor (not Dreamweaver) and move the asterisk to a different event for that particular tag. Resave the file and restart Dreamweaver to try out your new default behavior.

Should the default event not be the one you prefer to use, you can easily choose another. Choose a different event by selecting the down arrow next to the displayed default event in the Behavior Inspector and select any event in the drop-down list (see Figure 19-3).

Dreamweaver ships with a set list of events recognized by particular browsers. The Dreamweaver\Configuration\Behaviors\Events folder contains HTML files corresponding to the six browsers offered in the Events pane's drop-down list.

You can open these files in Dreamweaver, but Macromedia asks that you not edit them — with one exception. Each file contains the list of tags that have supported *event handlers* (the JavaScript term for events) in that browser.

Figure 19-3: You can change the event by selecting the Events arrow button.

The older the browser, the fewer event handlers are included — unfortunately, this also means that if you want to reach the broadest Internet audience, your event options are limited. In the broadest category, 3.0 and Later Browsers, only 13 different tags can receive any sort of event handler. This is one of the reasons why, for example, Internet Explorer 3 can't handle rollovers: the browser doesn't understand what an `onMouseOut` event is, and so the image can't revert to its original state.

If you do open and examine an event file in Dreamweaver, notice a group of yellow tags and a few form objects (see Figure 19-4). The yellow tags identify what Dreamweaver sees as invalid HTML. Those form objects — the buttons, checkbox, radio button, and text — render normally but aren't active.

It's far better to use a standard text editor such as HomeSite or BBEdit to open and modify an event file than to use Dreamweaver. By default, Dreamweaver attempts to correct the invalid HTML it finds in the file, and if you save the file with these unwanted corrections in place, your file will be corrupted, and you'll lose access to certain events.

In this case, viewing the HTML is far more instructive than the Document window, as you can see by looking at Listing 19-1. This example gives the event handler definitions for the 3.0 and Later Browsers category.

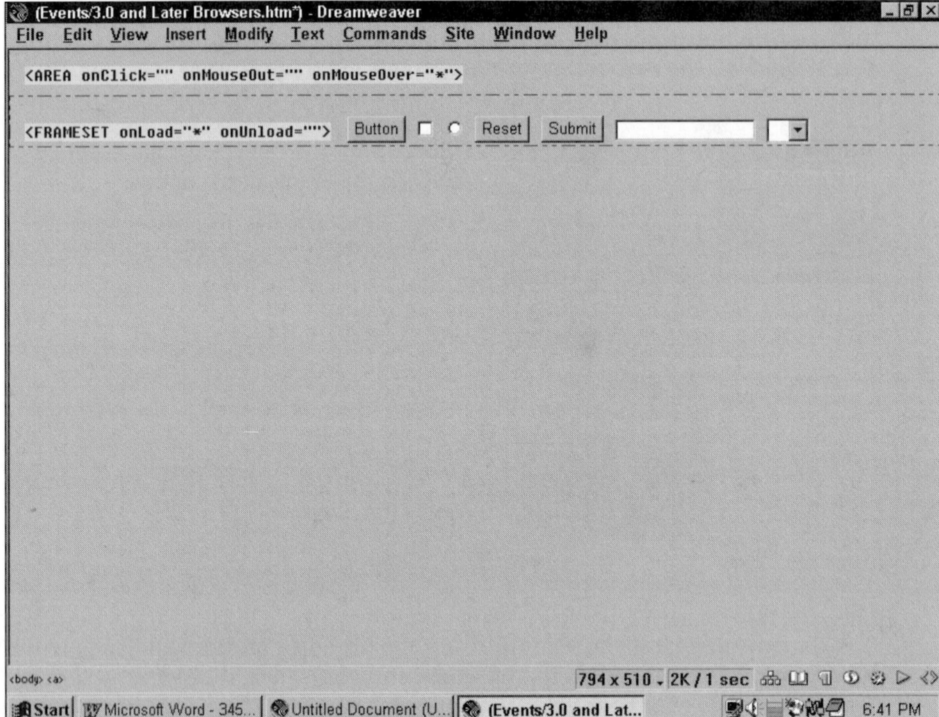

Figure 19-4: The event files define the tags that support particular event handlers in a selected browser.

Listing 19-1: **The Events File for 3.0 and Later Browsers**

```
<A onMouseOver="*">
<AREA onClick="" onMouseOut="" onMouseOver="*">
<BODY onLoad="*" onUnload="">
<FORM onReset="" onSubmit="*">
<FRAMESET onLoad="*" onUnload="">
<INPUT TYPE="Button" onClick="*">
<INPUT TYPE="Checkbox" onClick="*">
<INPUT TYPE="Radio" onClick="*">
<INPUT TYPE="Reset" onClick="*">
<INPUT TYPE="Submit" onClick="*">
<INPUT TYPE="Text" onBlur="*" onChange="" onFocus="" onSelect="">
<SELECT onBlur="" onChange="*" onFocus="">
<TEXTAREA onBlur="" onChange="*" onFocus="" onSelect="">
```

By contrast, the events file for Internet Explorer 5.0 shows support for every tag under the HTML sun — 92 in all — with almost every tag able to handle any type of event.

Although any HTML tag could potentially be used to attach a behavior, the most commonly used by far are the `<body>` tag (for entire-page events such as `onLoad`), the `<img>` tag when used as a button, and the link tag, `<a>`.

To locate the default events for any tag as used by a particular browser, consult Table 19-1. The table also shows, at a glance, which browsers support which tags to receive events.

Standard actions

As of this writing, 25 standard actions ship with Dreamweaver 3. Each action operates independently and differently from the others, although many share common functions. Each action is associated with a different dialog box or parameter form to enable easy attribute entry.

The following sections describe each of the standard actions: what the action does, what requirements must be met for it to be activated, what options are available, and most important of all, how to use it. Each action is written to work with all browser versions 4 and above; however, some actions do not work as designed in the older browsers. The charts included with every action show the action's compatibility with older browsers. (The information in these charts was adapted from the Dreamweaver Help pages and is used with permission.)

The following descriptions assume that you understand the basics of assigning behaviors and that you know how to open the Behavior Inspector.

Call JavaScript

With Call JavaScript, you can execute any JavaScript function — standard or custom — with a single mouse click or other event. As your JavaScript savvy grows, you'll find yourself using this behavior again and again.

Call JavaScript is straightforward to use; simply type in the JavaScript code or the name of the function you want to trigger into the dialog box. If, for example, you wanted to get some input from a visitor, you could use JavaScript's built-in `prompt()` method, like this:

```
result=prompt("Whom shall I say is calling?","")
```

When this code is triggered, a small dialog box appears with your query (here, "Whom shall I say is calling?") and a space for an input string. The second argument in the `prompt()` method enables you to include a default answer — to leave it blank, just use two quotes.

Table 19-1
Default Events by Browser

Tag	*3.0 and Later Browsers*	*4.0 and Later Browsers*	*IE 3.0*	*IE 4.0*	*IE 5.0*	*Netscape 3.0*	*Netscape 4.0*
<a>	onMouseOver	onClick	onMouseOver	onClick	onClick	onClick	onClick
<acronym>					onClick		
<address>				onClick	onClick		
<applet>				onLoad	onLoad		
<area>	onMouseOver	onMouseOver		onClick	onClick	onMouseOver	onMouseOver
<b>				onMouseOver	onMouseOver		
<bdo>					onClick		
<big>				onMouseOver	onMouseOver		
<blink>				onMouseOver	onMouseOver		
<body>	onLoad	onLoad	onLoad	onLoad	onLoad	onLoad	onLoad
<button>				onClick	onClick		
<caption>				onMouseOver	onMouseOver		
<center>				onMouseOver	onMouseOver		
<cite>				onMouseOver	onMouseOver		
<code>				onMouseOver	onMouseOver		
<col>				onMouseOver	onLoseCapture		
<colgroup>					onLoseCapture		
<dd>				onMouseOver	onMouseOver		
<del>					onMouseOver		
<dfn>				onMouseOver	onMouseOver		
<dir>				onMouseOver	onMouseOver		
<div>				onClick	onClick		

Tag	3.0 and Later Browsers	4.0 and Later Browsers	IE 3.0	IE 4.0	IE 5.0	Netscape 3.0	Netscape 4.0
<dl>				onMouseOver	onMouseOver		
<dt>				onMouseOver	onMouseOver		
<em>				onMouseOver	onMouseOver		
<embed>				onLoad	onLoad		
<fieldset>				onClick	onClick		
<font>				onMouseOver	onMouseOver		
<form>	onSubmit	onSubmit	onSubmit	onSubmit	onSubmit	onSubmit	onSubmit
<frame>				onLoad	onLoad		
<frameset>	onLoad	onLoad	onLoad	onLoad	onLoad	onLoad	onLoad
<h1>...<h6>				onMouseOver	onMouseOver		
<hr>				onMouseOver	onMouseOver		
<i>				onMouseOver	onMouseOver		
<iframe>				onFocus	onFocus		
<ilayer>							onLoad
<img>		onMouseDown		onClick	onClick	(None selected)	onMouseDown
<input type= button | checkbox | image | radio | reset | submit>	onClick	onClick	onClick	onClick	onClick	onClick	onClick

Continued

Table 19-1 (continued)

Tag	3.0 and Later Browsers	4.0 and Later Browsers	IE 3.0	IE 4.0	IE 5.0	Netscape 3.0	Netscape 4.0
<input type= file | password>		onChange		onChange	onChange	onChange	onChange
<input type= text>	onBlur	onBlur	onBlur	onBlur	onBlur	onBlur	onBlur
<ins>				onMouseOver	onMouseOver		
<kbd>				onClick	onClick		
<label>				onClick	onClick		
<layer>							onMouseOver
<legend>					onClick		
<li>				onMouseOver	onMouseOver		
<listing>				onMouseOver	onMouseOver		
<map>				onClick	onClick		
<marquee>				onMouseOver	onMouseOver		
<menu>				onMouseOver	onMouseOver		
<nobr>				onMouseOver	onMouseOver		
<object>				onLoad	onLoad		
<ol>				onMouseOver	onMouseOver		
<p>				onMouseOver	onMouseOver		
<plaintext>				onMouseOver	onMouseOver		
<pre>				onMouseOver	onMouseOver		
<q>				onMouseOver	onMouseOver		

Tag	3.0 and Later Browsers	4.0 and Later Browsers	IE 3.0	IE 4.0	IE 5.0	Netscape 3.0	Netscape 4.0
<rt>					onClick		
<s>				onMouseOver	onMouseOver		
<samp>				onMouseOver	onMouseOver		
<select>	onChange	onChange	onChange	onChange	onChange	onChange	onChange
<small>				onMouseOver	onMouseOver		
<span>				onMouseOver	onMouseOver		
<strike>				onMouseOver	onMouseOver		
<strong>				onMouseOver	onMouseOver		
<sub>				onMouseOver	onMouseOver		
<sup>				onMouseOver	onMouseOver		
<table>				onMouseOver	onMouseOver		
<tbody>				onMouseOver	onMouseOver		
<td>				onMouseOver	onMouseOver		
<textarea>	onChange	onChange	onChange	onChange	onChange	onChange	onChange
<tfoot>				onMouseOver	onMouseOver		
<th>				onMouseOver	onMouseOver		
<thead>				onMouseOver	onMouseOver		
<tr>				onMouseOver	onMouseOver		
<tt>				onMouseOver	onMouseOver		
<u>				onMouseOver	onMouseOver		
<ul>				onMouseOver	onMouseOver		
<var>				onMouseOver	onMouseOver		
<xmp>				onMouseOver	onMouseOver		

You can use either single or double quotes in your Call JavaScript behavior; Dreamweaver automatically adjusts for whichever you choose. However, I find it easier to use single quotes because Dreamweaver translates double quotes into character entities; that is, " becomes `"`.

Naturally, you could use Call JavaScript to handle much more complex chores as well. To call a specific custom function that is already in the `<head>` section of your page, just enter its name — along with any necessary arguments — in the Call JavaScript dialog box, shown in Figure 19-5.

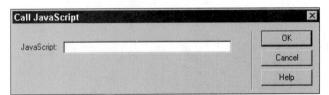

Figure 19-5: Trigger any JavaScript function by attaching a Call JavaScript behavior to an image or text.

To use the Call JavaScript behavior, follow these steps:

1. Select the object to trigger the action.
2. From the Behavior Inspector, select the add action button and choose Call JavaScript.
3. In the Call JavaScript dialog box, enter your code in the text box.
4. Click OK when you're done.

In the following charts that detail action behaviors for both newer and older browsers, the phrase "Fails without error" means that the action won't work in the older browser, but neither does it generate an error message for the user to see. Where the table indicates "error," it means the user receives a JavaScript alert message.

Here's the browser compatibility chart for the Call JavaScript behavior:

Call JavaScript	***Netscape 3.x***	***Internet Explorer 3.0***	***Internet Explorer 3.01***
Macintosh	Okay	Fails without error	
Windows	Okay		Okay

Change Property

The Change Property action enables you to dynamically alter a property of one of the following tags:

```
<layer>     <div>      <form>     <textarea>
<span>      <img>      <select>
```

You can also alter the following `<input>` types:

```
radio       checkbox   text       password
```

Exactly which properties can be altered depends on the tag as well as on the browser being targeted. For example, the `<div>` tag and Internet Explorer 4.0 combination enables you to change virtually every style sheet option on the fly. The Change Property dialog box (see Figure 19-6) offers a list of the selected tags in the current page.

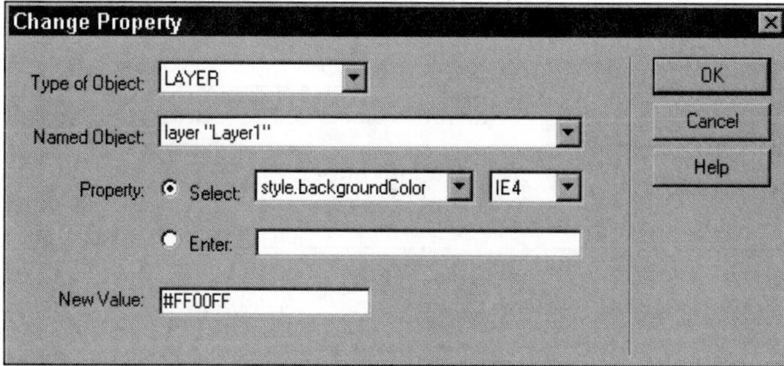

Figure 19-6: The Change Property action enables you to alter attributes of certain tags dynamically.

It's important that you name the objects you want to alter so that Dreamweaver can properly identify them. Remember to use unique names that begin with a letter and contain no spaces or special characters.

This behavior is especially useful for changing the properties of forms and form elements. Be sure to name the form if you wish to use Change Property in this manner.

To use the Change Property action, follow these steps:

1. Select the object to trigger the action.
2. From the Behavior Inspector, select the add action button and choose Change Property.

3. In the Change Property dialog box, choose an object type, such as FORM or SELECT, from the Type of Object drop-down list.
4. In the dynamic Named Object drop-down list, choose the object on your page you wish to affect.
5. Click the Select radio button. Select the target browser in the small list box on the far right and then choose the property to change. If you don't find the property in the drop-down list box, you can type it yourself into the Enter text box.

Many properties in the various browsers are read-only and cannot be dynamically altered. Those properties listed in the option list are always dynamic.

6. In the New Value text box, type the property's new value to be inserted when the event is fired.
7. Click OK when you're done.

Here's the browser compatibility chart for the Change Property behavior:

Change Property	***Netscape 3.x***	***Internet Explorer 3.0***	***Internet Explorer 3.01***
Macintosh	Okay	Fails without error	
Windows	Okay		Okay

Check Browser

Some Web sites are increasingly split into multilevel versions of themselves to gracefully handle the variety of browsers in operation. The Check Browser action acts as a type of browser "router" capable of sending browsers to appropriate URLs, or just letting them stay on the current page. The Check Browser action is generally assigned to the `<body>` tag and uses the `onLoad` event. If used in this fashion, it's a good idea to keep the basic page accessible to all browsers, even those with JavaScript disabled.

The Check Browser parameter form (see Figure 19-7) is quite flexible and enables you to specify decimal version numbers for the two main browsers. For instance, you may want to let all users of Navigator 4.04 or later stay on the current page and send everyone else to an alternative URL. The URLs can be either relative, such as `alt/index.html`, or absolute, such as `www.idest.com/alt/index.html`.

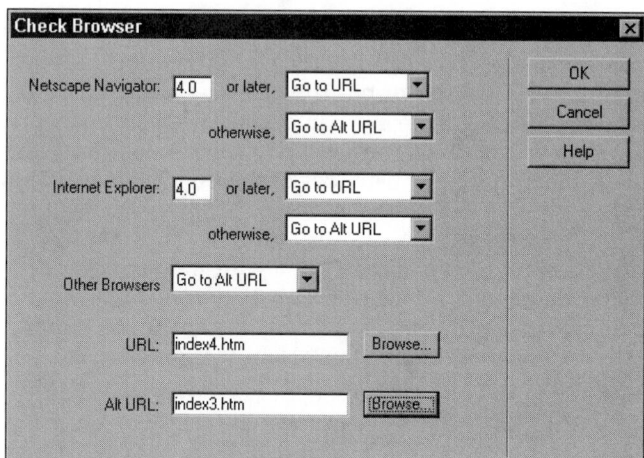

Figure 19-7: The Check Browser action is a great tool for segregating old and new browsers.

To use the Check Browser action, follow these steps:

1. Select the object to trigger the action.
2. From the Behavior Inspector, select the add action button and choose Check Browser.
3. Specify the Netscape Navigator and Internet Explorer versions and whether you want the browser to stay on the current page, go to another URL, or proceed to a third alternative URL.

With both major browsers, you can specify the URL that the lower version numbers should visit.

4. Set the same options for all other browsers, such as Opera.
5. Enter the URL and alternate URL options in their respective text boxes or select the Browse (Choose) button to locate the files.

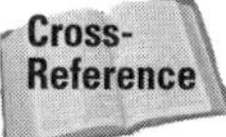

The Check Browser action works well with another Dreamweaver feature: Convert to 3.0 Compatible. Learn all about this new capability in Chapter 7.

Here's the browser compatibility chart for the Check Browser behavior:

Check Browser	*Netscape 3.x*	*Internet Explorer 3.0*	*Internet Explorer 3.01*
Macintosh	Okay	Fails without error	
Windows	Okay		Okay

Check Plugin

If certain pages on your Web site require the use of one or more plug-ins, you can use the Check Plugin action to see if a visitor has the necessary plug-in installed. Once this has been examined, Check Plugin can route users with the appropriate plug-in to one URL, and users without it to another URL. You can look for only one plug-in at a time, but you can use multiple instances of the Check Plugin action, if needed.

By default, the parameter form for Check Plugin (see Figure 19-8) offers five plug-ins: Flash, Shockwave, LiveAudio, Netscape Media Player, and QuickTime Plug-in. You can check for any other plug-in by entering its name in the Enter text box; use the name that appears when choosing Help ➪ About Plugins in the Navigator menus.

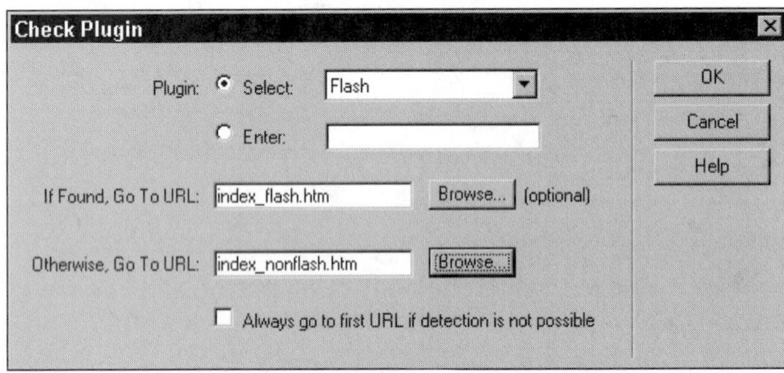

Figure 19-8: Running a media-intensive site? Use the Check Plugin action to divert visitors without plug-ins to alternative pages.

If you use a particular plug-in regularly, you may want to also modify the Check Plugin.js file found in your Actions folder. Add your new plug-in name to the PLUGIN_NAMES array and the corresponding PLUGIN_VALUES array in the initGlobal function.

Although Check Plugin cannot check for specific ActiveX controls, this action can route the Internet Explorer user to the same page as users who have plug-ins. The best way to handle both browsers is to use both ActiveX controls and plug-ins, through the `<object>` and `<embed>` methods explained in Chapter 17.

Another method for determining whether a plug-in or other player is available is to use the Check MIME action included on CD-ROM 1 that accompanies this book. This action works in the same way as the Check Plugin action, except you enter the MIME type.

To use the Check Plugin action, follow these steps:

1. Select the object to trigger the action.
2. From the Behavior Inspector, select the add action button and choose Check Browser.
3. Select a plug-in from the drop-down list. You can also type another plug-in name in the Enter text box.

Note

The names presented in the drop-down list are abbreviated, more recognizable names and not the formal names inserted into the code. For example, when the option `Shockwave` is selected, the phrase `Shockwave for Director` is actually input into the code. On the other hand, any plug-in name you enter manually into the Enter field is inserted verbatim.

4. If you want to send users who are confirmed to have the plug-in to a different page, enter that URL (absolute or relative) in the If Found, Go To URL text box or use the Browse (Choose) button to locate the file. If you want them to stay on the current page, leave the text box empty.
5. In the Otherwise, Go To URL text box, enter the URL for users who do not have the required plug-in.
6. Should the browser detection method fail — as with certain browsers, such as some versions of Internet Explorer on the Macintosh — you can keep the user on the initial page by enabling the Always go to first URL if detection is not possible option. Otherwise, if the detection fails, for any reason, the users are sent to the URL listed in the Otherwise field.

Here's the browser compatibility chart for the Check Plugin behavior:

Check Browser	*Netscape 3.x*	*Internet Explorer 3.0*	*Internet Explorer 3.01*
Macintosh	Okay	Fails without error	
Windows	Okay		Okay

Control Shockwave or Flash

The Control Shockwave or Flash action enables you to command your Shockwave and Flash movies through external controls. With Control Shockwave or Flash, you can build your own interface for your Shockwave or Flash material. This action can be used in conjunction with the `autostart=true` attribute (entered through the Property Inspector's Parameter dialog box for the Shockwave or Flash file) to enable a replaying of the movie.

You must have a Shockwave or Flash movie inserted in your Web page in order for the Control Shockwave or Flash action to be available. The parameter form for this action (see Figure 19-9) lists all the Shockwave or Flash movies by name that are found in either an `<embed>` or `<object>` tag. You can set the action to control the movie in one of four ways: Play, Stop, Rewind, or Go to Frame. You can choose only one option each time you attach an action to an event. If you choose the last option, you need to specify the frame number in the text box. Note that specifying a Go to Frame number does not start the movie there; you need to attach a second Control Shockwave or Flash action to the same event to play the file.

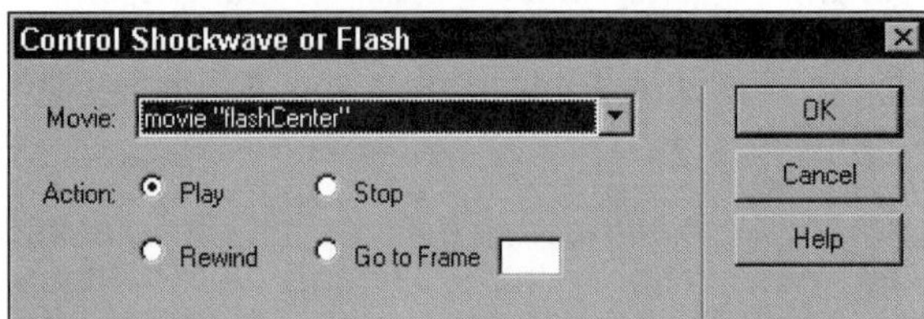

Figure 19-9: Build your own interface and then control a Shockwave and Flash movie externally with the Control Shockwave or Flash action.

Be sure to name your Shockwave or Flash movie. Otherwise, the Control Shockwave or Flash action lists both `unnamed <embed>` and `unnamed <object>` for each file, and you cannot write to both tags as you can with a named movie.

To use the Control Shockwave or Flash action, follow these steps:

1. Select the object to trigger the action.
2. From the Behavior Inspector, select the add action button and choose Control Shockwave or Flash.
3. In the Control Shockwave or Flash dialog box, select a movie from the Named Shockwave Object drop-down list.
4. Select a control by choosing its radio button:
   - **Play:** Begins playing the movie at the current frame location.
   - **Stop:** Stops playing the movie.
   - **Rewind:** Returns the movie to its first frame.
   - **Go to Frame:** Displays a specific frame in the movie. Note: For this option, you must enter a frame number in the text box.
5. Select OK when you're done.

Here's the browser compatibility chart for the Control Shockwave or Flash behavior:

Control Shockwave or Flash	*Netscape 3.x*	*Internet Explorer 3.0*	*Internet Explorer 3.01*
Macintosh	Okay	Fails without error	
Windows	Okay		Fails without error

Drag Layer

The Drag Layer action provides some spectacular — and interactive — effects with little effort on the part of the designer. Drag Layer enables your Web page visitors to move layers — and all that they contain — around the screen with the drag-and-drop technique. With the Drag Layer action, you can easily set up the following capabilities for the user:

- ✦ Enable layers to be dragged anywhere on the screen.
- ✦ Restrict the dragging to a particular direction or combination of directions — a horizontal sliding layer can be restricted to left and right movement, for instance.
- ✦ Limit the drag handle to a portion of the layer such as the upper bar or enable the whole layer to be used.
- ✦ Provide an alternative clipping method by enabling only a portion of the layer to be dragged.
- ✦ Enable changing of the layers' stacking order while dragging or on mouse release.
- ✦ Set a snap-to target area on your Web page for layers that the user releases within a defined radius.
- ✦ Program a JavaScript command to be executed when the snap-to target is hit or every time the layer is released.

Layers are one of the more powerful features of Dreamweaver. To get the most out of the layer-oriented behaviors, familiarize yourself with layers by examining Chapter 28.

Layers must be inserted in your Web page before the Drag Layer action becomes available for selection from the Add Action pop-up menu. You must attach the action to the `<body>` — you can, however, attach separate versions of Drag Layer to different layers for different effects.

Drag Layer's parameter form (see Figure 19-10) includes a Get Current Position button that puts the left and top coordinates of a selected layer into the appropriate boxes for the Drop Target parameters. If you plan on using targeting, place your layer at the target location before attaching the behavior.

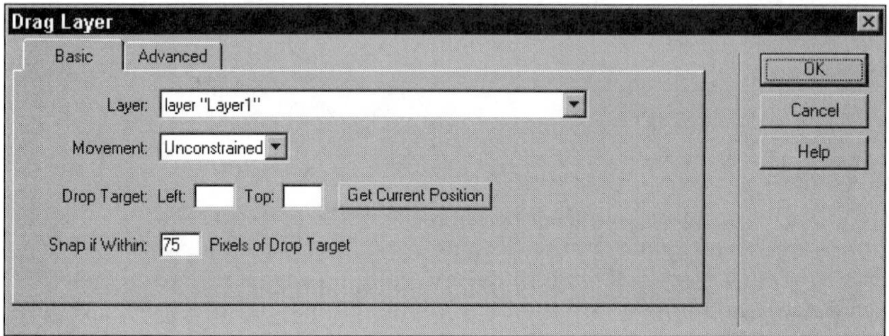

Figure 19-10: With the Drag Layer action, you can set up your layers to be repositioned by the user.

To use the Drag Layer action, follow these steps:

1. Select the `<body>` tag.
2. From the Behavior Inspector, select the add action button and choose Drag Layer.
3. In the Layer drop-down list of the parameter form in the Basic tab panel, select the layer you want to make draggable.
4. To limit the movement of the layer, change the Movement option from Unconstrained to Constrained. Text boxes for Up, Down, Left, and Right appear. Enter pixel values in the text boxes to control the range of motion:
   - To constrain movement vertically, enter positive numbers in the Up and Down text boxes and zeros in the Left and Right text boxes.
   - To constrain movement horizontally, enter positive numbers in the Left and Right text boxes and zeros in the Up and Down text boxes.
   - To enable movement in a rectangular region, enter positive values in all four text boxes.
5. To establish a location for a target for the dragged layer, enter coordinates in the Drop Target: Left and Top text boxes. Select the Get Current Position button to fill these text boxes with the layer's present location.
6. To set a snap-to area around the target coordinates where the layer falls, if released in the target location, enter a pixel value in the Snap if Within text box.

7. For additional options, select the Advanced tab.
8. If you want to limit the area to be used as a drag handle, select the radio button for Drag Handle: Area Within Layer. Left, Top, Width, and Height text boxes appear. In the appropriate text boxes, enter the Left and Top coordinates of the drag handle in pixels, as well as the Width and Height dimensions.

Note

If you want to enable the whole layer to act as a drag handle, make sure the Drag Handle: Entire Layer radio button is selected.

9. To control the positioning of the dragged layer, set the following While Dragging options:
   - To keep the layer in its current depth and not bring it to the front when it is dragged, deselect the checkbox for While Dragging: Bring Layer to the Front.
   - To change the stacking order of the layer when it is released, select either Leave on Top or Restore z-order from the drop-down list.
10. To execute a JavaScript command while the layer is being dragged, enter the command or function in the Call JavaScript text box.
11. To execute a JavaScript command when the layer is dropped on the target, enter the code in the When Dropped: Call JavaScript text box. If you want the JavaScript to execute only when the layer is snapped to its target, select the Only if snapped option — this option requires that a value be entered in the Snap if Within text box.
12. Click OK when you're done.

Note

If you — or someone on your team — have got the JavaScript programming skills, you can gather information output from the Drag Layer behavior to enhance your pages. Dreamweaver declares three variables for each draggable layer: MM_UPDOWN (the *y* coordinate), MM_LEFTRIGHT (the *x* coordinate), and MM_SNAPPED (true, if the layer has reached the specified target). Before you can get any of these properties, you must get an object reference for the proper layer. Another function, MM_findObj(layername), handles this chore.

Here's the browser compatibility chart for the Drag Layer behavior:

Drag Layer	*Netscape 3.x*	*Internet Explorer 3.0*	*Internet Explorer 3.01*
Macintosh	Fails without error	Fails without error	
Windows	Fails without error		Fails without error

Go to URL

Dreamweaver brings the same power of links — with a lot more flexibility — to any event with the Go to URL action. One of the trickier tasks in using frames on a Web page is updating two or more frames simultaneously with a single button click. The Go to URL action handily streamlines this process for the Web designer. Go to URL can also be used as a preload router that sends the user to another Web page once the `onLoad` event has finished.

The dialog box for Go to URL (see Figure 19-11) displays any existing anchors or frames in the current page or frameset. To load multiple URLs at the same time, open the drop-down list and select the first frame that you want to alter; then enter the desired page or location in the URL text box. Select the second frame from the list and enter the next URL (or Browse/Choose to find it). If you select a frame to which you have previously assigned a URL, that address appears in the URL text box.

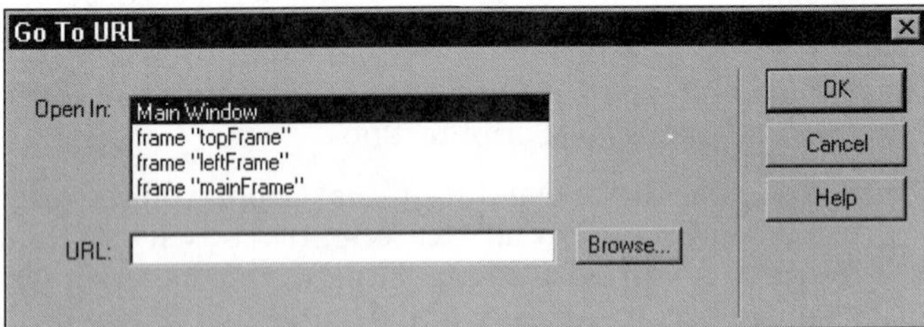

Figure 19-11: Update two or more frames at the same time with the Go to URL action.

To use the Go to URL action, follow these steps:

1. Select the object to trigger the action.
2. From the Behavior Inspector, select the add action button and choose Go to URL.
3. From the Go to URL dialog box, select the target for your link from the list in the Open In window.
4. Enter the path of the file to open in the URL text box or click the Browse (Choose) button to locate a file.

   An asterisk appears next to the frame name to indicate that a URL has been chosen.
5. To select another target to load a different URL, repeat Steps 3 and 4.
6. Click OK when you're done.

Here's the browser compatibility chart for the Go to URL behavior:

Go to URL	***Netscape 3.x***	***Internet Explorer 3.0***	***Internet Explorer 3.01***
Macintosh	Okay	Fails without error	
Windows	Okay		Okay

Jump Menu and Jump Menu Go

Although most behaviors insert original code to activate an element of the Web page, several behaviors are included to edit code inserted by a Dreamweaver object. The Jump Menu and Jump Menu Go behaviors both require a previously inserted Jump Menu object before they become active. The Jump Menu behavior is used to edit an exiting Jump Menu object, while the Jump Menu Go behavior adds a graphic image as a "Go" button.

To use the Jump Menu behavior to edit an existing Jump Menu object, follow these steps:

1. Select the Jump Menu object previously inserted into the page.
2. In the Behavior Inspector, double-click the listed Jump Menu behavior.
3. Make your modifications in the Jump Menu dialog box, as shown in Figure 19-12.

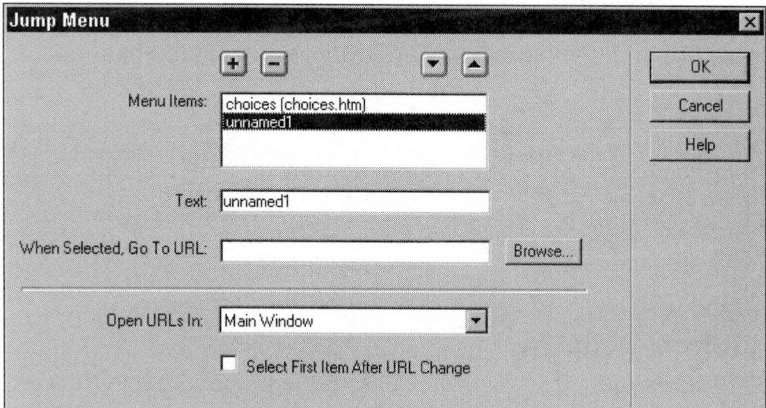

Figure 19-12: The Jump Menu behavior is used to modify a previously inserted Jump Menu object.

You can alter the existing menu item names or their associated URLs, add new menu items, or reorder the list through the Jump Menu dialog box.

4. Select OK when you're done.

To add a button to activate the Jump Menu object, follow these steps:

1. Select the image or form button you'd like to make into a Go button.

   A Jump Menu object must be on the current page for the Jump Menu Go behavior to be available.

2. From the Behavior Inspector, select Jump Menu Go from the Add behavior list.

   The Jump Menu Go dialog box, shown in Figure 19-13, is displayed.

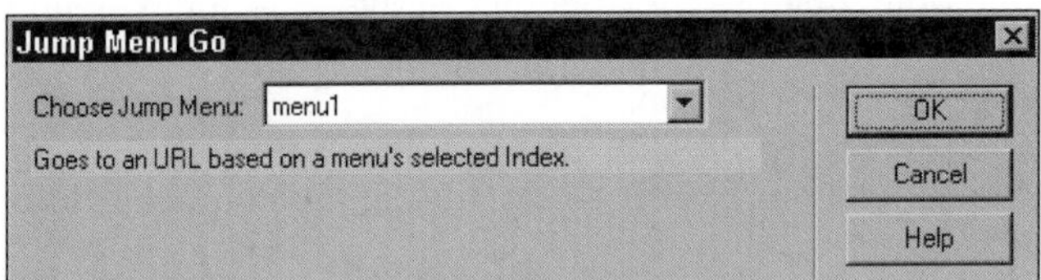

Figure 19-13: Add a graphic or standard button as a Go button with the Jump Menu Go behavior.

3. Select the name of the Jump Menu object you want to activate from the option list.

4. Click OK when you're done.

Here's the browser compatibility chart for both Jump Menu behaviors:

Jump Menu	*Netscape 3.x*	*Internet Explorer 3.0*	*Internet Explorer 3.01*
Macintosh	Okay	Fails without error	
Windows	Okay		Fails without error

Open Browser Window

Want to display your latest design in a borderless, nonresizable browser window that's exactly the size of your image? With the Open Browser Window action, you can open a new browser window and specify its exact size and attributes. You can even set it up to receive JavaScript events.

You can also open a new browser window with a regular link by specifying `target="_blank"`, but you can't control any of the window's attributes with that method. You do get this control with the parameter form of the Open Browser Window action (see Figure 19-14); here you can set the window width and height, and whether or not to display the Navigation Toolbar, Location Toolbar, Status Bar, Menu Bar, Scrollbars, and Resize Handles. You can also name your new window, a necessary step for advanced JavaScript control.

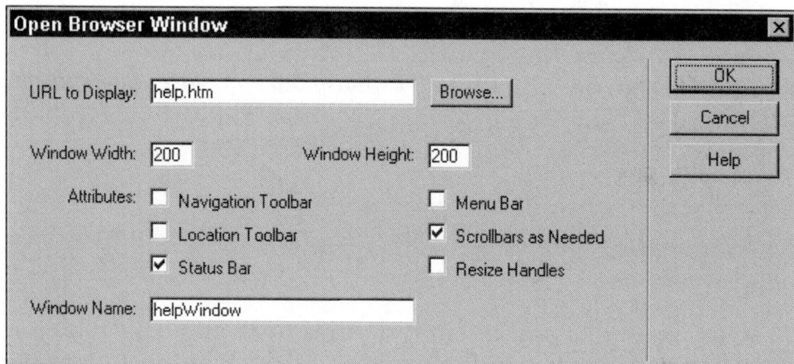

Figure 19-14: Use the Open Browser Window action to program in a pop-up advertisement or remote control.

You have to explicitly select any of the attributes you want to appear in your new window. Your new browser window contains only the attributes you've checked, plus basic window elements such as a title bar and a Close button.

To use the Open Browser Window action, follow these steps:

1. Select the object to trigger the action.
2. From the Behavior Inspector, select the add action button and choose Open Browser Window.
3. In the URL to Display text box, enter the address of the Web page you want to display in the new window. You can also select the Browse (Choose) button to locate the file.
4. To specify the window's size and shape, enter the width and height values in the appropriate text boxes.

   You must enter both a width and height measurement, or the new browser window opens to its default size.
5. Check the appropriate Attributes checkboxes to enable the parameters you want.

6. If you plan on using JavaScript to address or control the window, type a unique name in the Window Name text box. This name cannot contain spaces or special characters. Dreamweaver alerts you if the name you've entered is unacceptable.

7. Click OK when you're done.

Here's the browser compatibility chart for the Open Browser Window behavior:

Open Browser Window	*Netscape 3.x*	*Internet Explorer 3.0*	*Internet Explorer 3.01*
Macintosh	Okay	Fails without error	
Windows	Okay		Okay

Play Sound

The Play Sound action is used to add external controls to an audio file that normally uses the Netscape LiveAudio plug-in or the Windows Media Player. Supported audio file types include .wav, .mid, .au, and .aiff files — generally to add background music with a hidden sound file. The Play Sound action inserts an `<embed>` tag with the following attributes set:

✦ loop=false

✦ autostart=false

✦ mastersound

✦ hidden=true

✦ width=0

✦ height=0

Instead of automatically detecting which sound files have been inserted in the current Web page, Play Sound looks for the sound file to be inserted though the action's dialog box (see Figure 19-15).

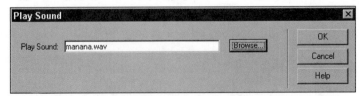

Figure 19-15: Give your Web page background music and control it with the Play Sound action.

Dreamweaver can detect if a visitor's browser has the Windows Media Player installed and, if so, issue the appropriate commands.

To use the Play Sound action, follow these steps:

1. Select the object to trigger the action.
2. From the Behavior Inspector, select the add action button and choose Play Sound.
3. To play a sound, enter the path to the audio file in the Play Sound text box or select the Browse (Choose) button to locate the file.
4. Select OK when you're done.

Here's the browser compatibility chart for the Play Sound behavior:

Play Sound	*Netscape 3.x*	*Internet Explorer 3.0*	*Internet Explorer 3.01*
Macintosh	Okay	Fails without error	
Windows	Okay		Fails without error

Popup Message

You can send a quick message to your users with the Popup Message action. When triggered, this action opens a JavaScript Application Alert with your message. You enter your message in the Message text box on the action's parameter form (see Figure 19-16).

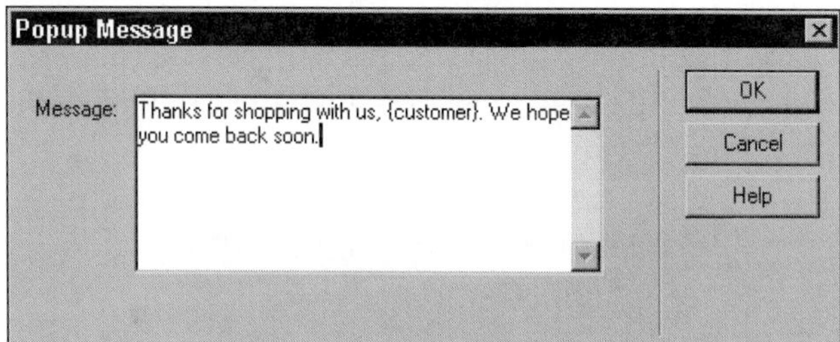

Figure 19-16: Send a message to your users with the Popup Message action.

To use the Popup Message action, follow these steps:

1. Select the object to trigger the action.
2. From the Behavior Inspector, select the add action button and choose Popup Message.

3. Enter your text in the Message text box.
4. Click OK when you're done.

You can include JavaScript functions or references in your text messages by surrounding the JavaScript with curly braces. For example, today's date could be incorporated in a message like this:

```
Welcome to our site on {new Date()}!
```

You could also pull data entered into a form to incorporate into a message, as in this example:

```
Thanks for filling out our form, ¬
{document.theForm.firstname.value}.
```

If you need to display a curly brace in a message, you must precede it with a backslash character, \.

Here's the browser compatibility chart for the Popup Message behavior:

Popup Message	*Netscape 3.x*	*Internet Explorer 3.0*	*Internet Explorer 3.01*
Macintosh	Okay	Fails without error	
Windows	Okay		Okay

Preload Images

Designs commonly require a particular image or images to be displayed immediately when called by an action or a timeline. Because of the nature of HTML, all graphics are separate files that normally are downloaded when needed. To get the snappy response required for certain designs, graphics need to be preloaded or cached so that they will be available. The Preload Images action performs this important service. You designate the images you want to cache for later use through the Preload Images parameter form (see Figure 19-17).

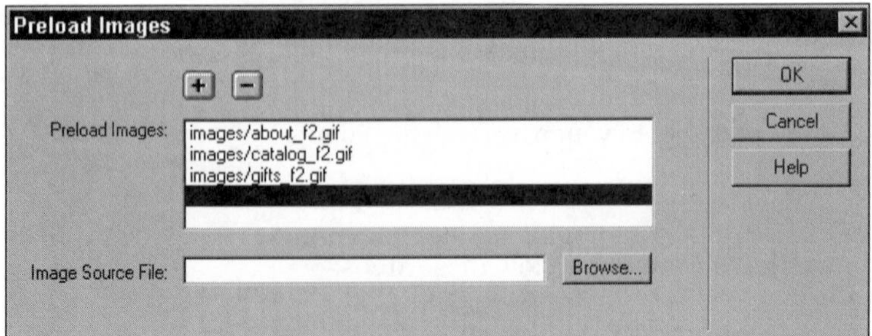

Figure 19-17: Media-rich Web sites respond much faster when images have been cached with the Preload Images action.

You don't need to use the Preload Images action if you're creating rollovers. Both the Rollover object and the Swap Image action enable you to preload images from their dialog boxes.

To use the Preload Images action, follow these steps:

1. Select the object to trigger the action.
2. From the Behavior Inspector, select the add action button and Preload Images.
3. In the action's parameter form, enter the path to the image file in the Image Source File text box or select the Browse (Choose) button to locate the file.
4. To add another file, click the + (add) button and repeat Step 2.

After you've specified your first file to be preloaded, be sure to press the + (add) button for each successive file you want to add to the list. Otherwise, the highlighted file is replaced by the next entry.

5. To remove a file from the Preload Images list, select it and click the – (delete) button.
6. Click OK when you're done.

Here's the browser compatibility chart for the Preload Images behavior:

Preload Image	*Netscape 3.x*	*Internet Explorer 3.0*	*Internet Explorer 3.01*
Macintosh	Okay	Fails without error	
Windows	Okay		Fails without error

Set Nav Bar Image

The Set Nav Bar Image action, like the Jump Menu actions, enables you to edit an existing Dreamweaver object. The Nav Bar object, inserted from the Common panel of the Objects palette, consists of a series of user-specified images acting as a group of navigational buttons. The Set Nav Bar Image action enables you to modify the current Nav Bar object, adding, reordering, or deleting images as buttons as well as setting up advanced rollover techniques. In fact, the Set Nav Bar Image action could be thought of as a superduper Swap Image behavior.

To refresh your memory about the capabilities of the Nav Bar Image, see Chapter 10.

The main aspect that sets a nav bar apart from any other similar series of rollover images is that the nav bar elements relate to one another. When you select one element of a nav bar, by default, all the other elements are swapped to their up state. The Set Nav Bar Image action enables you to modify that default behavior to a rollover in another area or any other image swap desired. You can also use the Set Nav Bar Image to include another image button in the nav bar.

To modify an existing Nav Bar object, follow these steps:

1. Choose any image in a Nav Bar object.
2. From the Behavior Inspector, double-click any of the Set Nav Bar Image actions displayed for the image.

   The same Set Nav Bar Image dialog box (Figure 19-18) opens regardless of whether you select an action associated with the `onClick`, `onMouseOver`, or `onMouseOut` event.

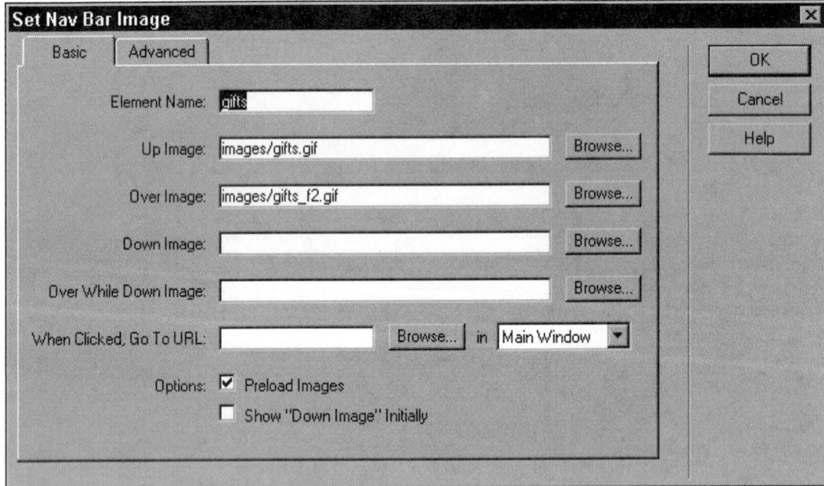

Figure 19-18: Modify an existing Nav Bar element through the Set Nav Bar Image action.

3. Make any desired edits — changing the Up, Over, Down, or Over While Down state images or their respective URLs or targets — from the Basic tab of the dialog box.
4. To change any other images when the current image is interacted with, select the Advanced tab.

5. On the Advanced tab of the dialog box, choose which state you want to trigger any changes from the drop-down list:
   - Over Image or Over While Down
   - Down State
6. Select the image you wish to change from the Also Set Image list.

   Dreamweaver lists all the named images on the current page, not just those in the nav bar.
7. Select the path of the new image to be displayed in the To Image Field text field.

   An asterisk appears after the current image in the list box, signifying that a swap image has been chosen.
8. If you chose Over Image or Over While Down as the triggering event, an optional field, If Down, enables you to specify another graphic to swap the image of the down state image as well.
9. To alter other images with the same triggering event, repeat Steps 6 through 8.

Here's the browser compatibility chart for the Set Nav Bar Image behavior:

Set Nav Bar Image	*Netscape 3.x*	*Internet Explorer 3.0*	*Internet Explorer 3.01*
Macintosh	Okay	Fails without error	
Windows	Okay		Fails without error

Set Text of Frame

Dreamweaver has grouped together four similar behaviors under the Set Text heading. The first of these, Set Text of Frame, enables you to do much more than change a word or two — you can dynamically rewrite the entire code for any frame. You can even incorporate JavaScript functions or interactive information into the new frame content.

The Set Text of Frame action replaces all the contents of the `<body>` tag of a frame. Dreamweaver supplies a handy "Get Current HTML" button that enables you to easily keep everything you want to retain and change only a heading or other element. Naturally, you must be within a frameset to use this behavior, and the frames must be named correctly — that is, uniquely without special characters or spaces.

To change the content of a frame dynamically, follow these steps:

1. Select the triggering object.
2. In the Behavior Inspector, choose Set Text ➪ Set Text of Frame from the Add Behavior list.

   The Set Text of Frame dialog box opens as shown in Figure 19-19.

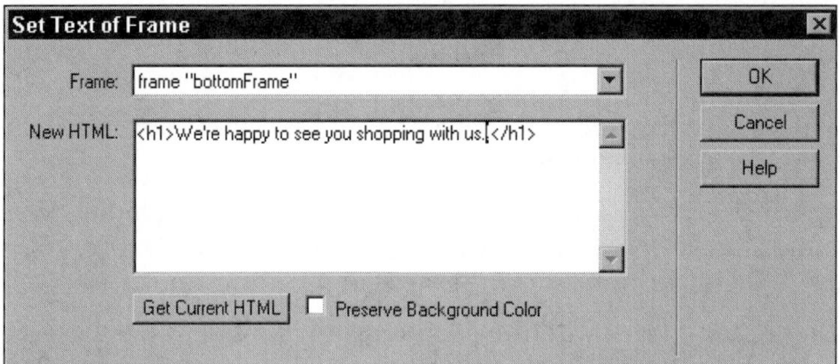

Figure 19-19: The Set Text of Frame behavior enables you to interactively update the contents of any frame in the current frameset.

3. Choose the frame you wish to alter from the Frame option list.
4. Enter the code for the changing frame in the New HTML text area.

   Keep in mind that you're changing not just a word or phrase, but all the HTML contained in the `<body>` section of the frame.
5. If you want to keep the majority of the code, select the Get Current HTML button and change only those portions necessary.

The same JavaScript capabilities outlined in the Popup Message section are available in the Set Text of Frame behavior.

6. To maintain the frames `<body>` attributes, such as the background and text colors, select the Preserve Background Color option.

   If this option is not selected, the frames background and text colors are replaced by the default values (a white background and black text).
7. Click OK when you're done.

Here's the browser compatibility chart for the Set Text of Frame behavior:

Set Text of Frame	*Netscape 3.x*	*Internet Explorer 3.0*	*Internet Explorer 3.01*
Macintosh	Okay	Fails without error	
Windows	Okay		Okay

Set Text of Layer

The Set Text of Layer behavior is similar to the previously described Set Text of Frame behavior in that it replaces the entire HTML contents of the target. The major difference, of course, is that with one you're replacing the code of a layer and with the other, the `<body>` tag of a frame. You're also able to include any valid JavaScript functions within a pair of curly braces, `{}`, in the HTML code as with other Set Text behaviors. You should also note that, unlike Set Text of Frame, no button exists for getting the current HTML in Set Text of Layer.

To set the text of a layer dynamically, follow these steps:

1. Make sure that the layer you want to change has been created and named properly.
2. Select the tag, link, or image you want to trigger the behavior.
3. From the Behavior Inspector, select the add action button and choose Set Text ➪ Set Text of Layer from the option list.

   The Set Text of Layer dialog box opens, as shown in Figure 19-20.

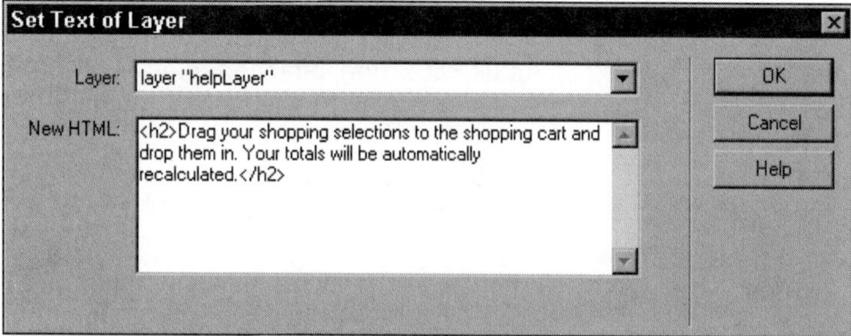

Figure 19-20: Replace all the HTML in a layer with the Set Text of Layer behavior.

4. Select the layer to modify from the Layer option list.
5. Enter the replacement code in the New HTML text area.

Although no "Get Current HTML" button exists here as with the Set Text of Frame behavior, a workaround does exist. Before invoking the behavior, select and copy all the elements inside the layer. Because Dreamweaver copies tags as well as text in the Document window, you can then just paste the clipboard into the New HTML text area. Be careful not to select the layer tag, `<div>`, or the layer's contents—if you do, you are pasting a layer in a layer.

6. Click OK when you're done.

Here's the browser compatibility chart for the Set Text of Layer behavior:

Set Text of Layer	*Netscape 3.x*	*Internet Explorer 3.0*	*Internet Explorer 3.01*
Macintosh	Fails without error	Fails without error	
Windows	Fails without error		Fails without error

Set Text of Status Bar

Use the Set Text of Status Bar action to show your choice of text in a browser's status bar, based on a user's action such as moving the pointer over an image. The message stays displayed in the status bar until another message replaces it. System messages, such as URLs, tend to be temporary and visible only when the user's mouse is over a link.

The only limit to the length of the message is the size of the browser's status bar; you should test your message in various browsers to make sure that it is completely visible.

To display a message only when a user's pointer is over an image, use one Set Text of Status Bar action, attached to an `onMouseOver` event, with your associated text. Use another Set Text of Status Bar action, attached to an `onMouseOut` event, that has a null string (a couple of spaces) as the text.

All text is entered in the Set Text of Status Bar parameter form (see Figure 19-21) in the Message text box.

Set Text of Status Bar

Message: Today is {new Date()}.

OK

Cancel

Help

Figure 19-21: Use the Set Text of Status Bar action to guide your users with instructions in the browser window's status bar.

To use the Set Text of Status Bar action, follow these steps:

1. Select the object to trigger the action.
2. From the Behavior Inspector, select the add action button and choose Set Text of Status Bar.

As with the other Set Text behaviors, you can include valid JavaScript functions and variables in the Set Text of Status Bar behavior by offsetting them with curly braces.

3. Enter your text in the Message text box.
4. Click OK when you're done.

Here's the browser compatibility chart for the Set Text of Status Bar behavior:

Set Text of Status Bar	***Netscape 3.x***	***Internet Explorer 3.0***	***Internet Explorer 3.01***
Macintosh	Okay	Fails without error	
Windows	Okay		Okay

Set Text of Text Field

The final Set Text behavior enables you to update any text or textarea field, dynamically. The Set Text of Text Field behavior accepts any text or JavaScript input (JavaScript functions and variables must be enclosed in a set of curly braces). A text field must be present on the page for the behavior to be available.

To change the displayed text of a text field, follow these steps:

1. From the Behavior Inspector, choose Set Text ➪ Set Text of Text Field from the Add Action list.

   The Set Text of Text Field dialog box is displayed, as shown in Figure 19-22.

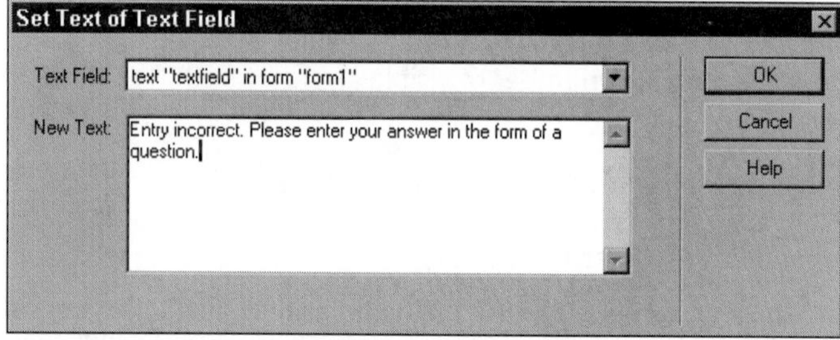

Figure 19-22: Dynamically update text form elements with the Set Text of Text Field behavior.

2. Choose the desired text field from the drop-down list.
3. Enter the new text and/or JavaScript in the New Text text area.
4. Click OK when you're done.

Here's the browser compatibility chart for the Set Text of Text Field behavior:

Set Text of Text Field	*Netscape 3.x*	*Internet Explorer 3.0*	*Internet Explorer 3.01*
Macintosh	Okay	Fails without error	
Windows	Okay		Okay

Show-Hide Layer

One of the key features of Dynamic HTML layers is their capability to appear and disappear on command. The Show-Hide Layer action gives you easy control over the visibility attribute for all layers in the current Web page. In addition to explicitly showing or hiding layers, this action can also restore layers to the default visibility setting.

The Show-Hide Layer action typically reveals one layer while concealing another; however, you are not restricted to hiding or showing just one layer at a time. The action's parameter form (see Figure 19-23) shows you a list of all the layers in the current Web page, from which you can choose as many as you want to show or hide.

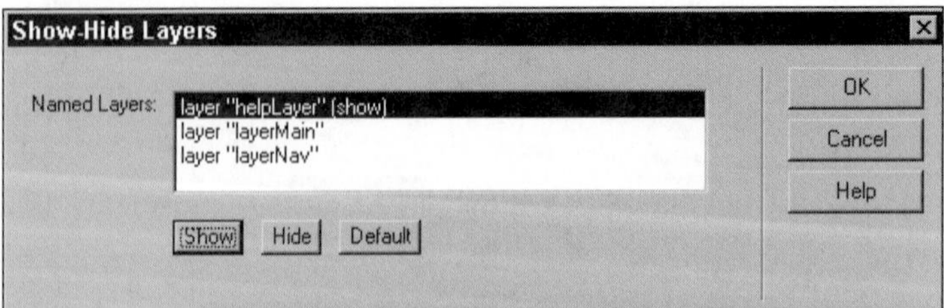

Figure 19-23: The Show-Hide Layers action can make any number of hidden layers visible, hide any number of visible layers, or both.

To use the Show-Hide Layer action, follow these steps:

1. Select the object to trigger the action.
2. From the Behavior Inspector, select the add action button and choose Show-Hide Layer.

When the dialog box opens, the parameter form shows a list of the available layers in the open Web page.

3. To reveal a hidden layer, from the Show-Hide Layer dialog box, select the layer from the Named Layers list and click the Show button.
4. To hide a visible layer, select its name from the list and click the Hide button.
5. To restore a layer's default visibility value, select the layer in the list and click the Default button.

Here's the browser compatibility chart for the Show-Hide Layer behavior:

Show-Hide Layer	*Netscape 3.x*	*Internet Explorer 3.0*	*Internet Explorer 3.01*
Macintosh	Fails without error	Fails without error	
Windows	Fails without error		Fails without error

Swap Image and Swap Image Restore

Button rollovers are one of the most commonly used techniques in Web design today. In a typical button rollover, a user's pointer moves over one image, and the graphic appears to change in some way, seeming to glow or change color. Actually, the `onMouseOver` event triggers the almost instantaneous swapping of one image for another. Dreamweaver automates this difficult coding task with the Swap Image action and its companion, the Swap Image Restore action.

In recognition of how rollovers most commonly work in the real world, Dreamweaver makes it possible to combine Swap Image and Swap Image Restore in one easy operation — as well as to preload all the images. Moreover, you can use a link in one frame to trigger a rollover in another frame without having to tweak the code as you did in early versions.

When the parameters form for the Swap Image action opens, it automatically loads all the images it finds in the current Web page (see Figure 19-24). You select the image you want to change — which could be the same image to which you are attaching the behavior — and enter the address for the file you want to replace the rolled-over image. You can swap more than one image with each Swap Image action. For example, if you want an entire submenu to change when a user rolls over a particular option, you can use a single Swap Image action to switch all of the submenu button images.

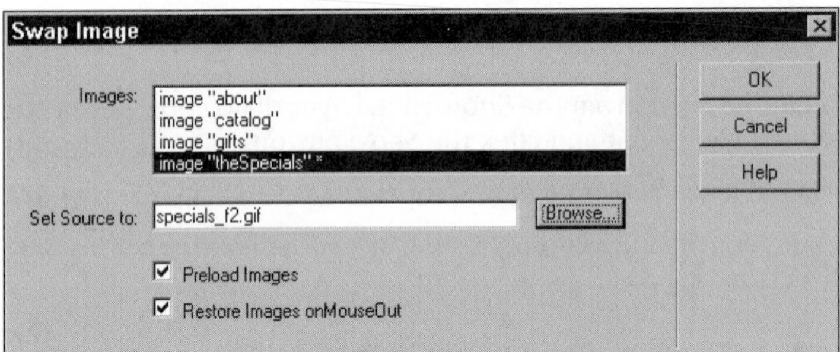

Figure 19-24: The Swap Image action is used primarily for handling button rollovers.

If you choose not to enable the Restore Images `onMouseOut` option, which changes the image back to the original, you need to attach the Swap Image Restore action to another event. The Swap Image Restore action can be used only after a Swap Image action. No parameter form exists for the Swap Image Restore action — just a dialog box confirming your selection.

If the swapped-in image has different dimensions than the image it replaces, the swapped-in image is resized to the height and width of the first image.

To use the Swap Image action, follow these steps:

1. Select the object to trigger the action.
2. From the Behavior Inspector, select the add action button and choose Swap Image.
3. In the parameter form, choose an available image from the Named Images list of graphics on the current page.
4. In the Set Source To text box, enter the path to the image that you want to swap in. You can also select the Browse (Choose) button to locate the file.

   An asterisk appears at the end of the selected image name to indicate an alternate image has been selected.
5. To swap additional images using the same event, repeat Steps 3 and 4.
6. To preload all images involved in the Swap Image action when the page loads, make sure the Preload Images option is checked.
7. To cause the selected images to revert to their original source, make sure that the Restore Images `onMouseOut` option is selected.
8. Click OK when you're done.

Here's the browser compatibility chart for the Swap Image and Swap Image Restore behaviors:

Swap Image and Swap Image Restore	*Netscape 3.x*	*Internet Explorer 3.0*	*Internet Explorer 3.01*
Macintosh	Okay	Fails without error	
Windows	Okay		Fails without error

Timelines: Play Timeline, Stop Timeline, and Go to Timeline Frame

Any Dynamic HTML animation in Dreamweaver happens with timelines, but a timeline can't do anything without the actions written to control it. The three actions in the timeline set — Play Timeline, Stop Timeline, and Go to Timeline Frame — are all you need to set your Web page in motion.

Before the Timeline actions become available, at least one timeline must be on the current page. All three of these related actions are located in the Timeline pop-up menu. Generally, when you are establishing controls for playing a timeline, you first attach the Go to Timeline Frame action to an event and then attach the Play Timeline action to the same event. By setting a specific frame before you enable the timeline to start, you ensure that the timeline always begins at the same point.

For more detailed information on using timelines, see Chapter 29.

The Play Timeline and Stop Timeline actions have only one element on their parameter form: a drop-down list box offering all timelines in the current page.

The Go to Timeline Frame action's parameter form (see Figure 19-25), aside from enabling you to pick a timeline and enter a specific go-to frame, also gives you the option to loop the timeline a set number of times.

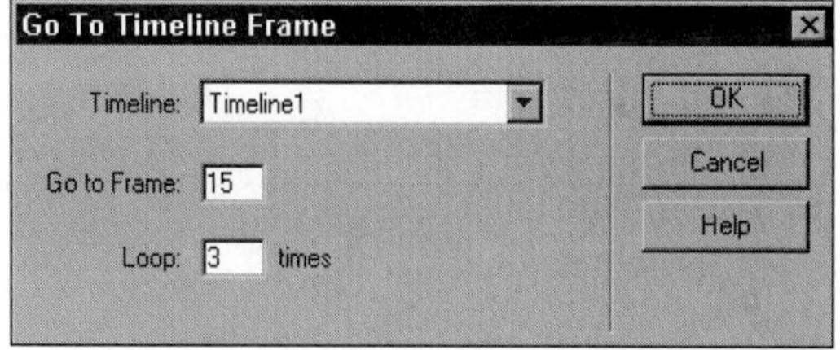

Figure 19-25: Control your timelines through the three Timeline actions. The Go to Timeline Frame parameter form enables you to choose a go-to frame and designate the number of loops for the timeline.

If you want the timeline to loop an infinite number of times, leave the Loop text box empty and turn on the Loop option in the Timeline Inspector.

To use the Go to Timeline Frame action, follow these steps:

1. Select the object to trigger the action.
2. From the Behavior Inspector, select the add action button and choose Go to Frame.
3. In the dialog box Timeline list, choose the timeline for which you want to set the start frame.
4. Enter the frame number in the Go to Frame text box.
5. If you want the timeline to loop a set number of times, enter a value in the Loop text box.
6. Click OK when you're done.

To use the Play Timeline action, follow these steps:

1. Select an object to trigger the action and then choose Timeline ➪ Play Timeline from the Add Action pop-up menu in the Behavior Inspector.
2. In the parameter form's Timeline list, choose the timeline that you want to play.

To use the Stop Timeline action, follow these steps:

1. Select an object to trigger the action and then choose Timeline ➪ Stop Timeline from the Add Action pop-up menu in the Behavior Inspector.
2. In the parameter form's Timeline list, choose the timeline that you want to stop.

You can also choose All Timelines to stop every timeline on the current Web page from playing.

Here's the browser compatibility chart for the Timeline behaviors:

Timelines: Play Timeline, Stop Timeline, and Go to Timeline Frame	***Netscape 3.x***	***Internet Explorer 3.0***	***Internet Explorer 3.01***
Macintosh	Image source animation and invoking behaviors work, but layer animation fails without error.	Fails without error	
Windows	Image source animation and invoking behaviors work, but layer animation fails without error.	Fails without error	

Validate Form

When you set up a form for user input, each field is established with a purpose. The name field, the e-mail address field, the zip code field — each has its own requirements for input. Unless the CGI program is specifically written to check the user's input, forms usually take input of any type. Even if the CGI program can handle it, this server-side method ties up server time and is relatively slow. The Validate Form action checks any text field's input and returns the form to the user if any of the entries are unacceptable. You can also use this action to designate any text field as a required field.

Validate Form can be used to check either individual fields or multiple fields for the entire form. Attaching a Validate Form action to an individual text box alerts the user to any errors as the form is being filled out. To check the entire form, the Validate Form action must be linked to the form's Submit button.

The Validate Form dialog box (see Figure 19-26) enables you to designate any text field as required, and you can evaluate its contents. You can require the input of a text field to be a number, an e-mail address (for instance, `jdoe@anywhere.com`), or a number within a range. The number range you specify can include positive whole numbers, negative numbers, or decimals.

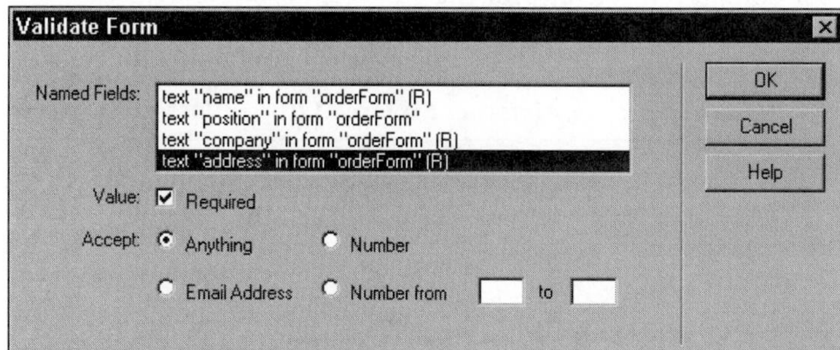

Figure 19-26: The Validate Form action can check your form's entries without CGI programming.

To use the Validate Form action, follow these steps:

1. Select the form object, such as a Submit button or text field, to trigger the action.

Tip

You can also attach the Validate Form to a checkbox or radio button, but it's really useful only if you want to require the field.

2. From the Behavior Inspector, select the add action button and choose Validate Form.
3. If validating an entire form, select a text field from the Named Fields list.

If you are validating a single field, the selected form object is chosen for you and appears in the Named Fields list.

4. To make the field required, select the Value: Required checkbox.
5. To set the kind of input expected, choose from one of the following Accept options:
   - **Anything:** Accepts any input.
   - **Number:** Enables any sort of numeric input. You cannot mix text and numbers, however, as in a telephone number such as (212) 555-1212.
   - **Email Address:** Looks for an e-mail address with the @ sign.
   - **Number from:** Enables you to enter two numbers, one in each text box, to define the number range.
6. Click OK when you're done.

Date validation is currently problematic when attempted with Dreamweaver's Validate Form action—you can't enter a date such as "011200" and have it recognize the entry as a number, because of the leading zero. For easy date validation, use the Validate Form Plus action included on this book's CD-ROM 1.

Here's the browser compatibility chart for the Validate Form behavior:

Validate Form	*Netscape 3.x*	*Internet Explorer 3.0*	*Internet Explorer 3.01*
Macintosh	Okay	Fails without error	
Windows	Okay		Okay

Managing and Modifying Your Behaviors

The standard behaviors that come with Dreamweaver are indeed impressive, but they're really just the beginning. Because existing behaviors can be modified and new ones created from scratch, you can continue to add behaviors as you need them.

The process of adding a behavior is simplicity itself. Just copy the HTML file to the Configuration\Behaviors\Actions folder and restart Dreamweaver.

If you find that your Add Action pop-up list is starting to get a little unwieldy, you can create subfolders to organize the actions better. When you create a folder within the Actions folder, that subfolder appears on the Add Action pop-up menu as a submenu, as you saw when you worked with the Timelines actions in the preceding section. Figure 19-27 shows a sample arrangement. This example has a subfolder called Beatnik - Advanced and another called Tracks to organize these diverse behaviors from Beatnik. You can even create sub-subfolders to maintain several levels of nested menus.

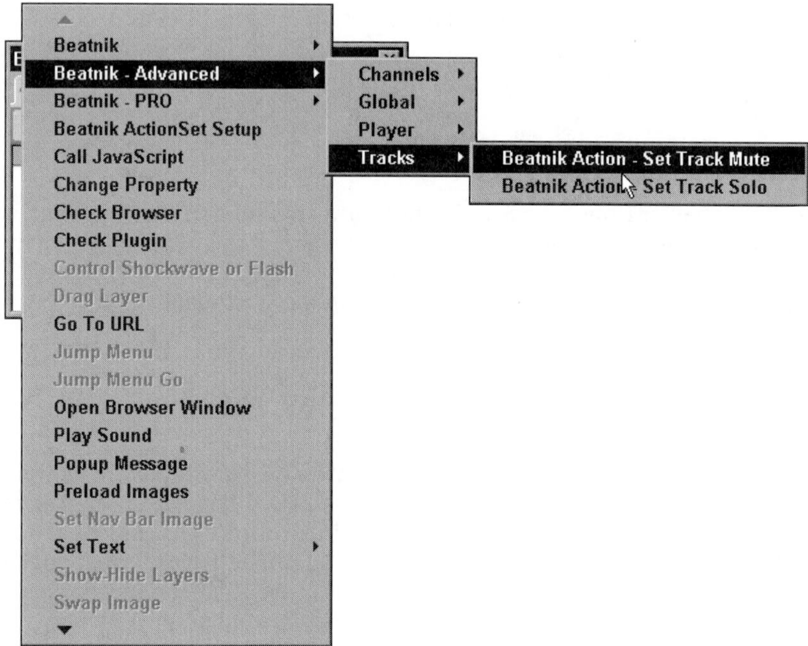

Figure 19-27: To create a new submenu in the Actions pop-up menu, just create a folder in the Actions directory.

Altering the parameters of a behavior

You can alter any of the attributes for your inserted behaviors at any time. To modify a behavior you have already attached, follow these steps:

1. Open the Behavior Inspector (go to Window ➪ Behaviors or click the Show Behaviors button in either Launcher, or press F8).
2. Select the object in the Document window or the tag in the Tag Selector to which your behavior is attached.
3. Double-click the action that you want to alter. The appropriate dialog box opens, with the previously selected parameters.
4. Make any modifications to the existing settings for the action.
5. Click OK when you are finished.

Sequencing your behaviors

When you have more than one action attached to a particular event, the order of the actions is often important. For example, you should generally implement the Go to Timeline Frame action ahead of the Play Timeline action. To specify the sequence in which Dreamweaver triggers the actions, reposition as necessary in the Actions page by highlighting one and using the up and down arrow buttons to reposition it in the list.

Deleting behaviors

To remove a behavior from your list of actions attached to a particular event, simply highlight the behavior and select the – (delete) button. If the removed behavior is the last action added, the event is also removed from the list; this process occurs after you select any other tag or click anywhere in the Document window.

Summary

Dreamweaver behaviors can greatly extend the Web designer's palette of possibilities — even a Web designer who is an accomplished JavaScript programmer. Behaviors simplify and automate the process of incorporating common, and not so common, JavaScript functions. The versatility of the behavior format enables anyone proficient in JavaScript to create custom actions that can be attached to any event. When considering behaviors, keep the following points in mind:

✦ Behaviors are a combination of events and actions.

✦ Behaviors are written in HTML and are completely customizable from within Dreamweaver.

✦ Different browsers support different events. Dreamweaver enables you to select a specific browser or a browser range, such as all 4.0 browsers, on which to base your event choice.

✦ Dreamweaver includes 25 standard actions. Some actions are not available unless a particular object is included on the current page.

In the next chapter, you learn how to create your own behaviors using Dreamweaver's custom JavaScript extensions.

✦ ✦ ✦

CHAPTER 20

Creating a Behavior

✦ ✦ ✦ ✦

In This Chapter

The basics of building a behavior

Working with the Document Object Model

Exploring the Dreamweaver API

Streamlining your code with common functions

Accessing useful behavior techniques

✦ ✦ ✦ ✦

The technology of a Dreamweaver behavior is open, and anybody with the requisite JavaScript and HTML skills can write one. To talk about "writing" a behavior, though, is a bit of a misnomer. You never actually touch the event portion of the behavior—you work only on the action file. To help the creation process, Macromedia has a complete Extending Dreamweaver document covering all the custom functions, JavaScript extensions, and the Document Object Model (DOM) that Dreamweaver recognizes.

Behaviors in Dreamweaver 3 have been greatly expanded in their functionality and implementation. By incorporating a much broader DOM, Dreamweaver 3 can read and affect virtually any element on the current HTML page. You can even use behaviors to open other existing documents or create new Web pages from scratch. Perhaps more importantly, the JavaScript API (built-in JavaScript extensions) has, in the words of Dreamweaver engineers, "exploded" to over 400 functions affecting every area of extensibility. Although this chapter covers the new features pertaining directly to behaviors, the majority of the JavaScript API is beyond the scope of this book. But before we delve into the nuts-and-bolts of behavior building, let's first get an overview of the process of creating a behavior.

Creating a Behavior from Scratch

Writing a behavior is not so complex when you take it one step at a time. In all, you need to follow just six basic steps to create a behavior from scratch:

✦ **Step 1: Define your behavior.** A behavior is an automatic method of incorporating a particular JavaScript function. The best way to begin building your behavior is to write that function. The function that you write is actually incorporated into the Dreamweaver action.

- **Step 2: Create the action file.** One of the key functions in Dreamweaver behaviors is, aptly enough, `behaviorFunction()`, which inserts your function into the `<head>` section of the Web page. Dreamweaver enables you to include multiple functions as well as single ones.
- **Step 3: Build the user interface.** As you look through the standard Dreamweaver behaviors, you see a dialog box that acts as the user interface in all but a few instances. The user interface that you create is based on HTML forms and is alternately referred to as a *parameter form.*
- **Step 4: Apply the behavior.** Both an event and an action are required to make up a behavior. The `applyBehavior()` function ties your new function to a specific tag and event. The `applyBehavior()` function also passes the necessary arguments to the function in the `<head>` section.
- **Step 5: Inspect the behavior.** From a user's point of view, building a Web page is often a trial-and-error process. You try one setting and if it doesn't work, you try another. To modify settings for a particular behavior, the user double-clicks the behavior name to reopen the dialog box and change the settings. The `inspectBehavior()` function handles the restoration of the previous values to the parameters form for easy editing.
- **Step 6: Test your behavior.** The final step, as in any software development, is testing. You need to try out your new behavior in a variety of Web browsers and debug it, if necessary (and it's always necessary).

To demonstrate the process of creating a behavior, the next few sections take you through a real-world example: the construction of a Set Layer Z Index action by Massimo Foti. Although it's easy to change the depth of a layer—its Z index—in the design phase, having a layer pop to the front is also a desirable dynamic effect. Mr. Foti has designed a cross-browser behavior that enables Web designers to control layer depth interactively. Set Layer Z Index is a relatively simple, but elegant behavior and as such, perfect for understanding how behaviors in general are constructed.

Dreamweaver includes a standard behavior—Change Property—that can also change the Z index of a layer, but it isn't cross-browser. To get the same effectiveness as Mr. Foti's behavior, you'd have to apply Change Property twice: once for Netscape browsers and again for Internet Explorer.

Step 1: Define your behavior

Behaviors are born of need, desire, or a combination of both. After repeating a single operation a thousand times, you probably find yourself thinking, "there's got to be a better way." The better way usually automates the process in any possible way. In the case of inserting JavaScript functions into Web pages, the better way is to create a behavior.

Starting from this vantage point already accomplishes the first phase of behavior creation: defining the behavior. If one were to add the necessary code to a single page to change the Z index of a layer dynamically, it would look like this:

```
<html>
<head>
<title>Untitled Document</title>
<meta http-equiv="Content-Type" content="text/html; charset=iso-8859-1">
<script language="JavaScript">
<!--
function tmt_LayerIndex(theTarget, theValue) {
    if (document.layers) {
        target = eval(theTarget);
        target.zIndex = theValue;
    }
    if (document.all) {
        eval("theTarget=theTarget.replace(/.layers/gi, '.all')");
        eval(theTarget + ".style.zIndex = theValue");
    }
}
//-->
</script>
</head>
<body bgcolor="#FFFFFF">
<a href="#" onClick="tmt_LayerIndex('document.layers[\'backLayer\']','4')" ¬
>Click to Bring Layer to Front</a>
<div id="backLayer" style="position:absolute; left:125px; top:95px; ¬
width:327px; height:142px; z-index:1; background-color: #CCCCFF; ¬
layer-background-color: #CCCCFF; border: 1px none #000000">
  <p>Back layer</p>
</div>
<div id="frontLayer" style="position:absolute; left:238px; top:45px; ¬
width:162px; height:258px; z-index:2; background-color: #FFCCCC; ¬
layer-background-color: #FFCCCC; border: 1px none #000000">
  <p>Front Layer</p>
</div>
</body>
</html>
```

Notice the lines in boldface. These are the key parts in the file: the function in the `<script>` section (the action) and the runtime function call attached to the text (the event). After being tested in several browsers, the function is judged to be sound and can be made into a behavior.

When you define your behavior in this manner, it tells you the arguments you need to generalize. In this example, two exist: `theTarget` and `theValue`. Ideally, your action should be flexible enough to enable any argument to be user defined. Here there are at most two attributes to take in through my parameter form and pass to my function.

Once you've created and tested your function in Dreamweaver, save it. I've found it helpful to go back to the original file as I build my action and verify that I have everything in working order.

Step 2: Create the action file

In the next phase of behavior creation, you build the skeleton of the action file and begin filling in the necessary JavaScript functions. Each action file must have, at a minimum, the following four functions:

- `canAcceptBehavior()`: Determines if the behavior should be available. If it is not to be available, the entry in the Add Action pop-up menu is not selectable.
- `behaviorFunction()`: Inserts the general function in the `<head>` section of the Web page.
- `applyBehavior()`: Attaches the runtime function to the selected tag and inserts the chosen event.
- `inspectBehavior()`: Enables the user to reopen the parameter form and make modifications to the original settings.

Note: One of the easiest ways to start an action file is to adapt one that is already built. You can open and modify any of the existing Dreamweaver standard actions, as long as you remember to use the File ➪ Save As feature command and give your file a new name.

Behaviors and other extensions can include external JavaScript files through the `<script language="javascript" src="script.js"></script>` construct. All of the Dreamweaver behaviors have been rewritten to take advantage of this facility. The key benefit of this approach is to enable easy sharing of JavaScript code between functions. Although you can still combine the user interface and JavaScript aspects of a behavior in one file, the standard practice now is to store your parameter form instructions in the HTML file, such as Control Sound.htm, and the JavaScript in a .js file with an identical name, such as Control Sound.js.

Note: The current example is fairly straightforward and does not incorporate the external JavaScript file technique.

Here are the steps to follow in the initial behavior creation phase:

1. Choose File ➪ New to open a new file.
2. Select Modify ➪ Page Properties to change the title of your behavior.
3. Choose File ➪ Save to save the HTML file under a new name in the Configuration\Behaviors\Action folder.
4. Open the HTML Inspector or your favorite text editor to work on the code for your new action.

Tip

It's best to work on the parameter form — the user interface — in Dreamweaver and, if your function code is extensive, work on your JavaScript file in an external editor, such as HomeSite or BBEdit.

5. Enter a new `<script language='javascript'>...</script>` tag pair in the `<head>` section of the document.
6. Open your original function test file.
7. Copy the function from the original file to the new behavior file.

   In our example, the function `tmt_LayerIndex()` is copied.

Caution

Make sure your behavior name is unique. Whenever you first open the Behavior Inspector, Dreamweaver checks to see if multiple function names exist. In the case of repetitive function names, Dreamweaver recognizes the earlier file but not the later one.

8. Add the following functions to the `<script>` tag:

```
function canAcceptBehavior(){
    return true;
}

function behaviorFunction(){
    return tmt_LayerIndex;
}

function applyBehavior(){
    return "";
}

function inspectBehavior(msgStr){
}
```

   Only one function, `behaviorFunction()`, is completed at this time; the rest are placeholders for necessary functions.

Tip

The `behaviorFunction()` is not limited to returning just one function; it can also return multiple functions. For more on this capability, see the section "Dreamweaver Behavior Techniques," later in this chapter.

After you've laid out the basic behavior structure, the next step is to define when the behavior can be used. This is handled by the `canAcceptBehavior()` function. If the behavior has no special requirements — such as needed images on the page — you can leave the function as is. Our example behavior uses layers so the behavior should be available only if layers exist on the current page. To check for layers, use this code:

```
function canAcceptBehavior(){
  var nameArray = getObjectRefs("NS 4.0","document","LAYER");
  return (nameArray.length > 0);
}
```

Here, if the Dreamweaver function `getObjectRefs()` finds any layer objects, the `nameArray` length is greater than zero, and the `canAcceptBehavior` function returns true; otherwise, false is returned, and the behavior name in the Add Action list of the Behavior Inspector is dimmed and inactive.

Step 3: Build the user interface

The user interface of a behavior is a parameter form, constructed with HTML form elements. The key indicator of what you need to include in your action's parameter form is the number and type of arguments required by your completed function.

In the Set Layer Z Index example, the function requires two primary arguments: `theTarget` and `theValue`. The interface needs to enable the user to choose the target parameter — the layer being affected — and the value of the Z index. To be useful, the action should list all available layers by name.

All user interface constructions are contained in the `<body>` section of your HTML action file. You can use Dreamweaver's visual editor to create and modify your form quickly. Many Web designers use tables to line up the various form elements; if you use this approach, be sure to place the table inside the form and not the other way around. Although you could insert a form in the cell of a table, you are limited to just entering form elements in that cell — and you return to no structure at all.

Follow these steps to create your user interface:

1. Open your HTML action file in Dreamweaver.
2. In the Document window, choose Insert ➪ Form or select the Insert Form button from the Forms panel of the Objects palette. Name the form in the Property Inspector for easy JavaScript identification.
3. For better alignment, place a table in your form by choosing Insert ➪ Table or by selecting the Insert Table button from the Common panel of the Objects palette.
4. Enter your form elements as needed. Be sure to name each one individually (with the exception of a radio button grouping) for JavaScript purposes.

As with Dreamweaver objects, you don't see the OK, Cancel, and Help buttons that appear when the parameter form is actually used. Dreamweaver automatically applies these buttons to the upper-right part of your interface.

The interface for the Set Layer Z Index action, as shown in Figure 20-1, uses a drop-down menu form element to list all available layers and a text box to get the desired Z index from the user.

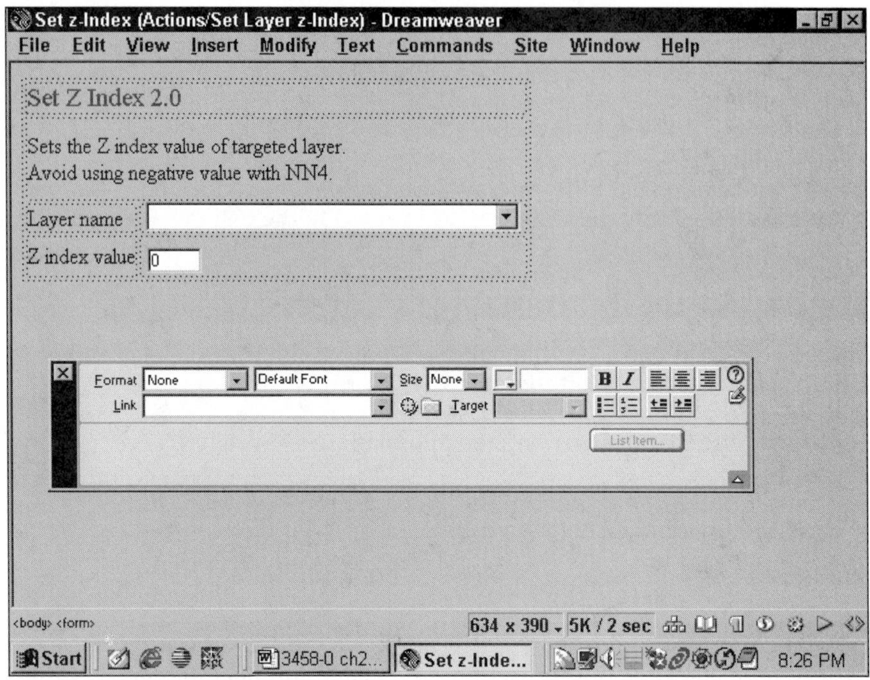

Figure 20-1: The parameter form uses text boxes to gather the user input and transmit it to the proper functions.

Initializing the user interface

The last part of setting up the user interface writes a function that initializes the interface and sets the cursor in the right field, or whatever is applicable. To complete this task, use the `initializeUI()` function, generally located in the Local Functions section of the JavaScript code. For the Set Layer Z Index action, all the layers in the current page must be displayed in the drop-down list. To do this, the `initializeUI()` function calls another specialized function:

```
function initializeUI() {
  yyGetlayers(theForm.le.options);
}
```

The `yyGetlayers()` function actually comes from another developer, Jaro von Flocken, who developed some groundbreaking layer behaviors. The function accepts the name of the list form array, `theForm.le.options`, as an argument and populates the list accordingly.

Finally, you need to attach the `initializeUI()` to `<body>` with an `onLoad` event in the HTML file. Again, you can proceed in one of two ways. First, you can locate the `<body>` tag and amend it so that it reads as follows:

```
<body onLoad="initializeUI()">
```

The second method uses the Call JavaScript behavior (as detailed in Chapter 19). In this case, enter only the code `intializeUI()` in the Call JavaScript dialog box.

Step 4: Apply the behavior

Now you can write the code that links your function to a specific tag and event. You can think of this process in three steps:

1. Make sure that the user entered information in the right places.
2. Put the user's input on the parameter form into a more usable format.
3. Return the runtime function call.

All of these steps are contained in the `applyBehavior()` function maintained in the JavaScript file.

You gather information from an action's parameter form in the same way that you gather data from a custom object. Using the same techniques discussed in Chapter 18, you receive the input information and usually convert it to local variables that are easier to handle. The number of variables is equal to the number of arguments expected.

If any of the input from the parameter form potentially may be sent out to a Web server—say, a URL or a file—you need to encode the text string so that it can be read by Unix servers. Use the built-in JavaScript function `escape` to convert space and special characters in the URL to Unix-friendly strings. The companion function, `unescape()`, reverses the process and is used in the `inspectBehavior()` function.

Follow these steps to build your `applyBehavior()` function:

1. Make the necessary variables:

   ```
   var theTarget
   var theValue
   ```

2. Get the information from the form. This process depends on the type of input field used. For the drop-down list, you need to find the value from an array of all layers, like this:

   ```
   divArray = getObjectRefs("NS 4.0", "document", "LAYER");
   theTarget="'" + escQ(divArray[theForm.le.selectedIndex]) + "'";
   ```

   The `escQ()` is another custom function for putting the layer name in the proper format.

3. Return the function runtime call, incorporating the variables. The `applyBehavior()` function must return a complete string. Enclose the argument variables with single quotes. If you use any internal quotes, they should be preceded by or escaped with a backslash.

4. Run an error check to see if values are entered where necessary; if not, inform the user.

```
myErr = (myErr=="")? "":"The following fields must be ¬
filled: "+myErr;
if (!myErr)
return "tmt_LayerIndex("+ theTarget+ ", " + theValue ¬
+ ")";
else return myErr;
```

Only one more step remains before you're ready to begin testing your action.

Step 5: Inspect the behavior

Now it's time to add the `inspectBehavior()` function to the JavaScript file. Basically, this function is called when the user double-clicks the action in the Behavior Inspector. It restores the information already entered through the parameter form and enables the user to change the parameters. In many ways, `inspectBehavior()` can be considered the reverse of the `applyBehavior()` function: rather than reading the form and writing the information to the Web page, `inspectBehavior()` reads the information and writes it back to the form.

Interpreting the string of information from a form is referred to as *parsing the string*. The Set Layer Z Index action passes a message string similar to the following:

```
onClick="tmt_LayerIndex('document.layers[\'backLayer\']','4')"
```

Dreamweaver uses several built-in functions to aid the parsing process, but the key function is `getTokens()`. The `getTokens()` function accepts a string to parse and the separators for which to look. It returns an array of strings. You can call `getTokens()`, passing the function call string as the first argument. The second argument should contain parentheses, a quote, and a comma as separators, as follows:

```
var argArray = getTokens(msgStr,"()',");
```

Once the string arguments are in an array, they can be extracted and placed back in the parameter form. Follow these steps to write the `inspectBehavior()` function:

1. Declare a variable and set it equal to the `getTokens()` function.

2. Assign the array elements to the same variables you used in the `applyBehavior()` function:

```
var theValue=unescQ(argArray[1]);
```

3. Now put the variables back in the form:

```
theForm.le.selectedIndex=j;
theForm.theZvalue.value=argArray[2]
```

4. The complete inspectBehavior() function looks like the following:

```
function inspectBehavior(msgStr){
    aargArray = extractArgs(msgStr);
    var argArray = getTokens(msgStr,"()',");
    var ii=0; var j=0;
    divArray = getObjectRefs("NS 4.0", "document", "LAYER");
    for (j=0;j<divArray.length;j++){
        myImg=unescQ(argArray[1]);
        if (myImg==divArray[j]){
            theForm.le.selectedIndex=j;
        }
    }
    theForm.theZvalue.value=argArray[2]
}
```

Tip

This example is a fairly simple inspectBehavior() function. Keep in mind that the more input you allow from your user, the more complicated it is to restore the information through this function. As with many aspects of building behaviors, one of the best ways to construct your inspectBehavior() function is by examining the code of working examples provided in the Macromedia-built behaviors, as well as examples contributed by other developers.

Step 6: Test your behavior

Testing and debugging is the final, necessary phase of building an action. To test your behavior, follow these steps:

1. Restart Dreamweaver.
2. Insert an image or a link in a blank Web page.
3. Select the element to use as your trigger.
4. Open the Behavior Inspector.
5. Select onClick from the Add Event pop-up menu.
6. Select the + (add action) button and choose your behavior.
7. Fill out the parameters form as required.

   Your action's name appears in the Actions pane, as shown with the Set Layer Z Index example in Figure 20-2.
8. Double-click the action to verify that your prior choices have been restored.
9. Test the behavior in various Web browsers.

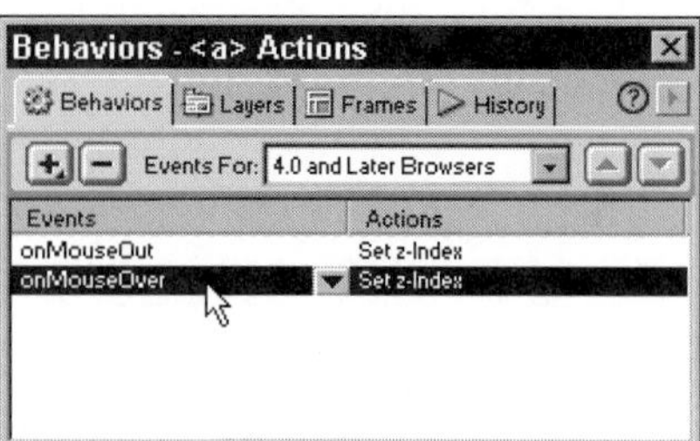

Figure 20-2: Even custom behaviors appear in the Behavior Inspector when created properly.

When you first select an event to add, Dreamweaver examines all of the actions in the Actions folder. If a problem is found, such as two files having the same function name, you are alerted to the conflict, and the list displays only the older file. You have to correct the problem with the other action and restart Dreamweaver before the file appears in the list again.

If your action is intended for distribution and not your own personal use, you should expand your testing considerably, especially on the user-interface side. As the action programmer, you know what values are expected and know—often subconsciously—how to avoid the pitfalls into which a new user may easily stumble. Be especially mindful of accepting input through a text box. Unless you're just passing a message to be displayed onscreen or in the browser status bar, you often have to validate the incoming text string. Telling the user to enter a number in a particular range doesn't guarantee correct results.

Debugging the behavior

Finding a bug is every programmer's least favorite moment—but getting rid of that bug can be the best. Basic JavaScript debugging techniques, including using the `alert()` function to keep track of variables, are without a doubt your first course of action. With its built-in JavaScript interpreter, Dreamweaver can give you error messages in the same manner as a browser. Dreamweaver's error handling is very good, with many error messages pointing directly to the problem code.

If the errors are severe enough to stop Dreamweaver from recognizing your action file as such, the file is not listed in the Action pop-up menu until the problem is resolved. Generally this situation means that you must restart Dreamweaver after each modification until the problem is resolved. Once you are debugging and modifying the minor errors, the following technique enables you to make changes without restarting Dreamweaver:

1. First, open your Action file and make the necessary changes. Save the file.
2. Assign your action to a tag and open the behavior's dialog box. Without entering any parameters, click Cancel to close the parameter form.
3. Remove the action from the Actions pane by selecting the Delete button.
4. Reassign your action, and Dreamweaver loads the new version.

Remember that JavaScript is case sensitive. If you get a message that a function cannot be found, make sure the names match exactly.

Extending Dreamweaver Documentation

To help developers create behaviors, Macromedia has released the Extending Dreamweaver documentation. Extending Dreamweaver is the background documentation of the various functions available for building behaviors. As such, it provides a useful framework for discussing the underpinnings of Dreamweaver behaviors and how you can use the extensions and built-in functions. The Extending Dreamweaver documentation can be found under the Help menu or use the keyboard shortcut Shift+F1.

Although Extending Dreamweaver covers all types of Dreamweaver extensions, behavior developers are interested in three main sections: the Document Object Model, the Dreamweaver JavaScript API, and the behaviors chapters. The more you understand about each of the various components and their included functions, the more flexibility you have in building your behaviors.

The material in this section is intended for programmers familiar with JavaScript and, as such, is fairly advanced.

Document Object Model

JavaScript is an interpreted programming language that addresses elements in the browser and on the Web page in a hierarchical fashion. To access the properties of any object on the page, JavaScript employs a Document Object Model (DOM). The DOM breaks down the page into successively smaller parts, until each element and its specific properties are identified.

As noted in the introduction, Dreamweaver 3 has significantly expanded the DOM by integrating a subset of the Netscape 3 DOM from the earlier version of Dreamweaver with a subset of the W3C's new implementation of the DOM. They've also tossed in a couple of features not implemented in either specification, but incredibly useful nonetheless. But perhaps the largest expansion in the DOM comes from the integration of the History palette. In order to make any user action repeatable, every user action needed a JavaScript equivalent.

Understanding nodes

Dreamweaver's DOM makes available, or *exposes*, virtually every element on a Web page. The DOM is often described using a tree metaphor, with the HTML document as the trunk. Instead of regarding the `<head>` and the `<body>` as the major branches, however, Dreamweaver's DOM, like the W3C DOM, uses four separate branches, or *nodes*, to divide the document:

✦ **DOCUMENT_NODE:** Enables access to objects directly relating to the overall document.

- **ELEMENT_NODE:** Contains references to all tags in the HTML document.
- **TEXT_NODE:** Describes the contiguous block of text within tags.
- **COMMENT_NODE:** Represents the comments within an HTML document and the text strings they contain.

Just as one tree branch can lead to another, nodes can contain other nodes. For example, a layer can contain a table that holds table rows that, in turn, hold table data. One node containing another is said to be in a *parent-child* relationship, and a node that cannot contain any other nodes is referred to as a *leaf node*, as it is incapable of supporting any more "branches." Figure 20-3 illustrates the node concept.

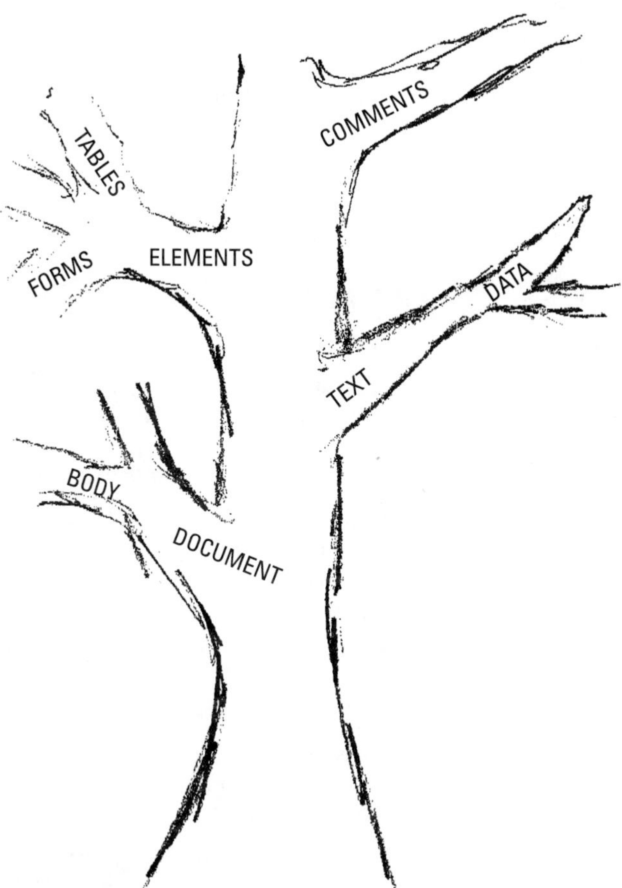

Figure 20-3: Nodes are used to express the structure of the HTML document and its relationship to the browser.

DOM properties

When referencing a specific tag, the DOM syntax goes from the most general to the most specific. For example, let's say you want to find out what a user entered into a specific text box, a property called *value*. You need to start from the document itself and work your way down, as follows:

```
var theText = document.theForm.textboxName.value
```

The DOM dictates what properties are accessible and in what form. Not all properties and methods are supported. You can't, for instance, directly reference the value of a button on a form. Instead, you have to assign that value to a hidden or other text field and access that value.

The portion of the DOM relating directly to forms and form elements is discussed in Chapter 18. The same rules of use and the same restrictions for implementing forms in objects apply likewise to implementing forms in behaviors. Additionally, the Dreamweaver DOM addresses other major objects as outlined in Table 20-1. Read-only properties are marked with an asterisk; otherwise, properties can be both read and set.

Table 20-1
Dreamweaver Document Object Model Properties

Property	*Nodes*	*Description*	*Return Values*
`nodeType*`	All	Returns the node of the current selection	`DOCUMENT_NODE` `ELEMENT_NODE` `TEXT_NODE` `COMMENT_NODE`
`parentNode*`	All	Returns the parent tag or, if the HTML tag is selected, the document object	Any node
`parentWindow*`	`DOCUMENT_NODE`	Returns the JavaScript object of the document's parent window	A string
`childNodes*`	All	Returns the nodelist of immediate children to the current selection	An array
`documentElement*`	`DOCUMENT_NODE`	Corresponds to the `<html>` tag of the current document	`"<html> <head>...</body> </html>"` (when used with outerHTML)

Property	Nodes	Description	Return Values
body*	DOCUMENT_NODE	Corresponds to <body> tag of the current document	"<body>...</body>" (when used with outerHTML)
URL*	DOCUMENT_NODE	Returns the current document's path	"FILE://C|/DOCS/NEW.HTML" for example
tagName*	ELEMENT_NODE	Returns the HTML name for a tag	"IMG" or "TABLE", for example
attrName	ELEMENT_NODE	Returns the value of the named attribute	"grey" or "#33CC66", for example
innerHTML	ELEMENT_NODE	Returns the HTML source within the specified tag	"<b>First Name</b>"
outerHTML	ELEMENT_NODE	Returns the HTML source, including the specified tag	"<p><b>First Name</b></p>"
data	TEXT_NODE COMMENT_NODE	Returns the text string contained within a specified tag or comment	"J. Lowery" where the tag reads <p>J. Lowery</p>

* Read-only.

DOM methods

Methods, in programming, are functions attached to a particular object, such as the document object. Dreamweaver includes several methods in the DOM to help manipulate the HTML page. With the node structure, you can apply these methods to the current document, frameset, frame, or a selected object.

Using these methods, your behaviors can inspect the current page and, if desired, change or even delete any attributes found. Table 20-2 outlines the methods contained in the Dreamweaver 3 DOM.

Table 20-2
Dreamweaver DOM Methods

Method	Returns	Description
`getElementsByTagName (tagName)`	A nodelist	Builds an array of the specified tag on the current page
`getTranslatedAttribute (attrName)`	The value	Gets the translated value of the named attribute; used in conjunction with Dreamweaver translators
`hasChildNodes()*`	Boolean value	Determines if current selection has children
`hasTranslatedAttributes()`	Boolean value	Determines if the tag has translated attributes; used in conjunction with Dreamweaver translators
`getAttribute(attrName)`	The value	Gets the value of a named attribute
`setAttribute(attrName, attrValue)`	Nothing	Sets a particular attribute to the specified value
`removeAttribute (attrName)`	Nothing	Deletes the specified attribute

Dreamweaver JavaScript API extensions

With Dreamweaver 3, the JavaScript API has expanded tremendously with functions for virtually everything Dreamweaver does. More than 400 custom Dreamweaver functions now exist, many of which were created to facilitate the new History palette. Although in-depth discussion of the full API is beyond the scope of this book, behavior programmers should be familiar with what is available in the API. The JavaScript API section of Extending Dreamweaver is categorized within the following areas:

Behaviors	General Editing	Quick Tag Editor
Clipboard	Global Applications	Selection
Command	Global Document	Site
Conversion	History	String Manipulation
CSS Style	HTML Style	Table Editing
External Application	Keyboard	Toggle
File Manipulation	Layer and Image Map	Translation
Find/Replace	Menu	Visual Layout
Frame and Frameset	Path	Window

Behavior writers will find the API functions under Behaviors, File Manipulation, Global Document, Path, Selection, and String Manipulation to be of particular interest.

The Macromedia engineers didn't stop with just Dreamweaver document APIs; there are also specific APIs for file I/O, design notes, Fireworks integration, and HTTP connectivity. Extending Dreamweaver has basic documentation about them all.

To make the behavior programmer's life a little easier, I've included coverage of some of the most often used API extensions. Although the following sections are in no way exhaustive, they do give a good example of how API functions work in Dreamweaver in general and behaviors in particular.

Notice that the API extensions have "dreamweaver." or "dom" as a prefix. The dreamweaver prefix can also be abbreviated as "dw" as in "dw.getDocumentDOM()." The "dom" functions refer to the DOM of a document returned by the `getDocumentDOM()` function as explained in the following section.

The dreamweaver.getDocumentDOM() function

The `getDocumentDOM()` function is the starting point for many Dreamweaver JavaScript manipulations. Setting this function equal to a variable returns the entire Document Object Model of the specified document, enabling the DOM (and thus the document) to be read and edited. Generally, `getDocumentDOM()` is used in this fashion:

```
var theDom = dreamweaver.getDocumentDOM("document")
```

Here, `theDom` now represents the root of the current document and everything connected to it. Once you have accessed the DOM in this manner, you need to request more specific information. If, for example, you wanted to examine the `<body>` of the current document, you could code it this way:

```
var theDom = dreamweaver.getDocumentDOM("document")
var theBody = theDom.body
```

You could also use JavaScript dot notation to shorten the code:

```
var theBody = dreamweaver.getDocumentDOM("document").body
```

Many behaviors require repeated access to the DOM; it's good practice to set it to one variable early on in your script.

The `getDocumentDOM()` function requires one argument, *sourceDoc*, which, as expected, refers to the source document. The argument must be one of the following:

- **`"document"`:** Sets the reference to the current document. Although the `"document"` argument can be used from anywhere to read the DOM, any edits applied using it must be ultimately called from within the `applyBehavior()`, `deleteBehavior()`, or `objectTag()` functions — or any function in a Command or Property Inspector file.

✦ `"parent"`: Sets the source document to the parent of the current document. This argument is generally used to determine if a document is within a frameset, like this:

```
var frameset = dreamweaver.getDocumentDOM("parent");
if (frameset) { ... do code ... }
```

✦ `"parent.frames[number]"` **or** `"parent.frames['framename']"`: To access another document in the frameset of which the current document is a member, use one of these two argument forms. The first, `"parent.frames [number]"`, is usually used when the names of the current frames are unknown or to cycle through any number of frames. The second, `"parent.frames ['framename']"`, is applied in specific cases where the names of the other frames are known and modifications need to be made only to them.

✦ **A URL:** Occasionally, the behavior builder needs to reference existing documents, either locally or on the Web. Using a URL—either absolute or relative—as an argument enables you to retrieve information on almost any document you can specify. When using a relative URL, such as this one from Dreamweaver's displayHelp.js file,

```
var idRoot = dreamweaver.getDocumentDOM¬
('../../../Help/contextID.html')
```

the URL is relative to the location of the behavior or other extensibility file.

Where API functions require the DOM object, such as the `dom.getSelection()` function and others that are discussed in the following sections, you must first get the DOM of the applicable document. In all examples that follow, the variable the DOM is understood to have been established, like this:

```
var theDOM = dreamweaver.getDocumentDOM("document")
var theSel = theDOM.getSelection()
```

The dom.getSelection() function

How a behavior performs is quite often dictated by what tag the user selects prior to attaching the behavior. The `getSelection()` function is the *first step* toward getting all the information necessary to control your behavior based on a user selection. I emphasize "first step" because this function returns the selection in the form of *byte offsets in memory*. A *byte offset* is a number that points to a memory address. In the case of the `getSelection()` function, the two byte offsets that are returned mark the beginning and end of the selection in memory. For example, say you open a new page in Dreamweaver, type in a phrase such as "The Key Points", and then select the first word. If you used the `getSelection` function like this:

```
var selArray = theDOM.getSelection()
alert(selArray)
```

the message box would return

```
161,164
```

which denotes the beginning byte (161) and the ending byte (164) offset of the selected word, "The." If your beginning and ending byte offsets are the same (as in "164,164"), then nothing is selected. This fact comes in handy when you want to make sure that the user has selected something before proceeding.

To examine what is contained within the byte offsets returned by the getSelection() function, you have to use the offsetsToNode() function, explained later in this section.

The dom.setSelection() function

Just as getSelection() retrieves the memory offsets of the current selection, the setSelection() function sets a new pair of memory offsets and thus a new selection. The setSelection() function takes two arguments: *offsetBegin* and *offsetEnd*.

setSelection() is most often used to restore a user's selection after various document manipulations have taken place. In this example, the selection is first stored in a variable via getSelection() and then, after much document modification, restored by setSelection:

```
var currSelection = theDOM.getSelection()
// document altering code goes here
theDom.setSelection(currSelection[0],currSelection[1])
```

Should the new setting not conform to a valid HTML selection, such as the attributes within a tag, the selection expands to include the entire tag.

You can also use setSelection to deselect anything on the page after completing a behavior. All that's required is that the two arguments be equal. Using the preceding example, the following code:

```
theDOM.setSelection(currSelection[1],currSelection[1])
```

would place the cursor after the previous selection, while

```
theDOM.setSelection(currSelection[0],currSelection[0])
```

would place it before.

The dom.offsetsToNode() function

The offsetsToNode() function serves as a translator, converting the byte memory offsets retrieved by getSelection() into readable data. For this reason, you often see the following code combination:

```
selArr = theDOM.getSelection();
selObj = theDOM.offsetsToNode(selArr[0],selArr[1]);
```

where getSelection() returns the array of the selection and the object referenced by that array. As indicated, offsetsToNode() takes two arguments: *offsetBegin* and *offsetEnd*, usually expressed as the initial (0) and next (1) array elements.

Once you've used offsetsToNode to get the selected object, you can examine or manipulate it. For example, in the custom Replicator command (included on CD-ROM 1 that accompanies this book), I used offsetsToNode to see if the selection made was appropriate (text only) and, if not, call a help function:

```
var offsets = theDOM.getSelection()
var selObj = theDOM.offsetsToNode(offsets[0],offsets[1])
if (selObj.nodeType == Node.TEXT_NODE) {
  helpMe2()
}
```

The dom.nodeToOffsets() function

As the name indicates, nodeToOffsets() is the inverse of offsetsToNode(). Instead of converting memory offsets to an object, nodeToOffsets takes an object reference and returns its memory offsets. This is useful when you need to manipulate a substring of the selection, usually text.

For example, in the custom command Change Case (included on CD-ROM 1 that comes with this book), after the selected object is retrieved via getSelection and offsetsToNode, nodeToOffsets expresses it in an array that can be uppercased or lowercased at the click of a button. Here's a fragment of the code from the custom upperCase() function:

```
var theDom = dreamweaver.getDocumentDOM("document");
var offsets = theDom.getSelection()
var theNode = theDom.offsetsToNode(offsets[0],offsets[1])
if (theNode.nodeType == Node.TEXT_NODE) {var nodeOffsets = ¬
theDom.nodeToOffsets(theNode)
offsets[0] = offsets[0]-nodeOffsets[0]
offsets[1] = offsets[1]-nodeOffsets[0]
var nodeText = theNode.data
theNode.data = nodeText.substring(0,offsets[0]) +
 nodeText.substring(offsets[0], offsets[1]).toUpperCase() +
 nodeText.substring(offsets[1], nodeText.length);
```

Because nodeToOffsets returns two memory offsets, you can use these as the arguments in setSelection to choose an object on the page. If, for instance, you wanted to select the first link on the page, you could use the code as follows:

```
var theDom = dreamweaver.getDocumentDOM("document")
var theLink = theDom.links[0]
var offsets = theDom.nodeToOffsets(theLink)
theDom.setSelection(offsets[0],offsets[1])
```

The dreamweaver.getTokens() function

The getTokens() function is often used in the inspectBehavior() function because it does such a good job of parsing a string. A *token* is a group of text characters that do not contain any of the specified separators. Generally, the *separators* in a function are the parentheses that surround the arguments and the commas that separate them.

The getTokens() function takes two arguments — the string to be parsed and the separators — and puts the results in an array. For example, note the following string:

```
doGroovoid('false','Fanfare-Arrival')
```

To extract the two arguments from this statement, use the getTokens() function as follows:

```
getTokens("doGroovoid('false','Fanfare-Arrival')","'(),")
```

If you set this function equal to an array called argArray, you get the following results:

```
argArray[0] = 'doGroovoid'
argArray[1] = 'false'
argArray[2] = 'Fanfare-Arrival'
```

Usually the first element of the array, the function name, is ignored.

The dreamweaver.getElementRef() function

The getElementRef() function is used to gather browser-specific references to a particular object and placing them into an array.

The getElementRef() function takes two arguments: the first argument is either *NS 4.0* or *IE 4.0,* which reference the Netscape and Internet Explorer formats, respectively, and the second argument is the tag being examined. The string returned puts the specified tag in the format of the named browser. If, for example, getElementRef() is used to get the object reference to a specific layer in Netscape terms, like this:

```
var theObjNS = dreamweaver.getElementRef("NS 4.0", tagArr[i])
```

the variable, theObjNS, would be set to something like:

```
document.layers['newLayer']
```

On the other hand, the same layer, in Internet Explorer terms, like this:

```
var theObjNS = dreamweaver.getElementRef("IE 4.0", tagArr[i])
```

would return a string like document.all.newLayer1.

Both getElementRef() and getObjectRefs() return browser-correct references for both browsers for the following tags: <a>, <area>, <applet>, <embed>, <select>, <option>, <textarea>, <object>, and <img>. Additionally, references for the tags <div>, <span>, and <input> are returned correctly for Internet Explorer, as <layer> and <ilayer> are for Netscape. Absolutely positioned <div> and <span> tags are also returned correctly for Netscape, but others return the message "cannot reference <tag>".

Naming objects and layers is often critical in JavaScript, as it certainly is with getElementRef() and getObjectRef(). Dreamweaver can't return references for unnamed objects; you get back an "unnamed <tag>" message for those. Furthermore, Dreamweaver can't handle references to a named object if it is in an unnamed layer or form. Although Dreamweaver automatically names layers as they are created, forms require that names be entered by the designer, in the Property Inspector.

The dreamweaver.getBehaviorTag() function

The getBehaviorTag() function returns the tag selected to implement the current behavior. The getBehaviorTag() function can also be incorporated into the behavior setup code to steer the user in the appropriate direction.

The getBehaviorTag() function returns the entire tag — attributes, values, and any text selected. For this reason, you need to seek out only the relevant portion of tag. One technique for doing this is to use JavaScript's indexOf property to determine if the tag is within the returned string. To make this even easier, it's best to uppercase or lowercase the tag. For example, the following code looks to see if the tag selected for the behavior is an <img> tag and, if it's not, alerts the users to what's required:

```
function initializeUI(){
var theTag = dreamweaver.getBehaviorTag().toUpperCase();
if (theTag.indexOf('IMG') != -1)){
// Behavior UI initilaization goes here
} else{
alert("This behavior requires you select an IMAGE to proceed.")
}
}
```

This is different from using the canAcceptBehavior function to block access to a behavior. With the getBehaviorTag() technique, the user is informed of what the problem is, rather than simply being denied access.

The dreamweaver.getBehaviorElement() function

Another method to discover which tag was selected for the invoked behavior is the getBehaviorElement() function. The major difference between this function and the getBehaviorTag() function is that the former returns the DOM reference to the tag, whereas the latter returns the tag itself. Once you have the DOM reference of the behavior tag, you can uncover a terrific amount of information about the tag and its attributes.

Like getBehaviorTag(), getBehaviorElement() is most often used to determine if the user has selected an appropriate tag for the chosen behavior. If the tag is inappropriate, a helpful message can be displayed to guide the user to a better option. The getBehaviorElement() function returns either a DOM reference or null. Circumstances under which null is returned by getBehaviorElement() are as follows:

- ✦ The function was not invoked from a script called by the Behavior Inspector.
- ✦ The behavior called is part of a timeline.
- ✦ The function was invoked from a script called by dreamweaver.popupAction().
- ✦ The function was invoked as part of a Behavior Inspector that is attaching an event to a link wrapper (<a href="#">...</a>), and the link wrapper has not yet been created.
- ✦ The function is called outside of a behavior.

The following example assumes that the required tag must be an embedded plug-in that is visible on the page:

```
function initializeUI(){
var theTag = dreamweaver.getBehaviorElement();
var tagGood = (theTag.tagName == "EMBED" && theTag.getAttribute("HIDDEN") ¬
== null);
if (tagGood) {
// Behavior User Interface code goes here
} else{
alert("This behavior can not be applied to hidden plug-ins")
}
}
```

The dreamweaver.browseForFileURL() function

The `browseForFileURL()` function enables the user to locate a file via a dialog box, rather than enter the entire path by hand. You can specify whether you want an Open, Save, or Select style dialog box, as well as the label in the title bar. You can even enable the Preview panel for images. No matter which options you choose, the `browseForFileURL()` function returns the path and file name in the form of a relative URL.

The `browseForFileURL()` function follows this syntax:

```
browseForFileURL('Open'|'Save'|'Select', 'Title Bar Label', true|false)
```

The first argument, either `Open`, `Save`, or `Select`, specifies the type of dialog box. The Select File dialog box displays additional local root information in its lower portion. The second argument is displayed in the title bar of the dialog box; if you don't want to insert your own title, you must use two quotes, as in this example:

```
browseForFileURL('open','',false)
```

The final argument is a Boolean and indicates whether or not the Preview panel for selecting images is to be displayed. If no title bar label is given and the Preview panel argument is true, the title displayed is "Select Image Source."

The `browseForFileURL()` function is generally contained within another function that is called by an `onClick` event attached to a Browse (Choose) button, which in turn is next to a text field that enables the user to enter the path by hand. Standard now, in the _common.js file, is the `browseFile()` function, which takes one argument, `fieldToStoreURL`. For instance, the code for a Browse (Choose) button may read as follows:

```
<input type="text" name="textFile">
<input value="Browse..." type="button" ¬
onClick="browseFile(document.theForm.textFile.value)" name="button">
```

The `browseFile()` function then calls the built-in `browseForFileURL()` function, which opens the Select File dialog box and, if the dialog box is returned with a file name, assigns that file name to a variable. In the standard `browseFile()` function, shown here, the returned file name is then assigned to a text box value for the given field, which makes the name appear in the text box:

```
function browseFile(fieldToStoreURL){
  var fileName = "";
  fileName = browseForFileURL();  //returns a local filename
  if (fileName) fieldToStoreURL.value = fileName;
}
```

The `browseForFileURL()` function does not return absolute URLs.

The dreamweaver.getDocumentPath() function

Dreamweaver includes several local document functions that aid in the reading, editing, and storing of current and external documents. The `getDocumentPath()` function is one of these; as the name states, this function returns the path of the specified document. The path returned is in the file://URL format, so that a file located at c:\sites\index.html would return file://c|/sites/ as its path.

The `getDocumentPath()` function takes one argument: the source document. This argument can be `"document"`, `"parent"`, `"parent.frames[number]"`, or `"parent.frames[framename]"` as described earlier in the `getDocumentDOM()` function. If the document specified has not been saved, `getDocumentPath()` returns an empty string.

The dreamweaver.getConfigurationPath() function

The Configuration folder can be considered the hub of Dreamweaver extensibility. It contains not only all the standard HTML files, such as the behaviors and objects, that are read into the system when Dreamweaver starts, but also various other files that control the look and feel of the menus in other areas. As such, it's often useful to be able to find the path to the Configuration folder so that other files can be created, read, edited, and stored. And that's exactly what `getConfigurationPath()` does.

One sample use of this function included with Dreamweaver is part of the secret behind the Rollover object. To a trained eye, the Rollover object is unlike any other — in fact, it's not really an object at all; it's a command masquerading as an object. The `getConfigurationPath()` function plays a key role in the JavaScript file, rollover.js, with this code:

```
var rolloverCmdURL = dreamweaver.getConfigurationPath() + ¬
"/Commands/Rollover.htm";
   var rolloverDoc    = dreamweaver.getDocumentDOM( rolloverCmdURL );
```

In the first line, `getConfigurationPath`, is used to locate the Rollover.htm file in the Command subfolder and assign it to a variable. This then enables the object to retrieve the DOM for manipulation with the `getDocumentDOM()` function.

Like `getDocumentPath()`, `getConfigurationPath()` formats the path as a file://URL.

The dreamweaver.getSiteRoot() function

Dreamweaver depends on the establishment of a local site root for much of its Web site management facility: all site root–relative links and references are based upon the location of the site root folder. The capability to uncover its file location is important for any behaviors or other extensibility files that work on the site root level. Dreamweaver supplies such a capability with the `getSiteRoot()` function.

Very straightforward to use, `getSiteRoot()` does not take an argument and returns a file://URL format reference to the local site root of the currently selected document. If an empty string is returned, it means that the file has not been saved.

The dreamweaver.releaseDocument() function

If you're working with a complex document with a lot of images, layers, tables, and text, you're going to have a lot of HTML to deal with. Accessing the DOM for that page can take up a significant chunk of your memory. If you're working with multiple pages, you could begin to run low on memory before the behavior closes and the memory is automatically freed. With the `releaseDocument()` function, you can get back the memory as soon as possible, whenever you request it.

The `releaseDocument` function's one argument is the DOM of the document in question. This is acquired by using the `getDocumentDOM()` function. You can see this function demonstrated in Dreamweaver's displayHelp.js file, which is used to direct all the help requested, contextually.

The dreamweaver.browseDocument() function

Should a help file get too big for an alert dialog box, you might need to provide access to a larger file. Dreamweaver enables you to open any specified file—including an expanded help file—within the primary browser. The `browseDocument()` function takes one argument, the path to the required file:

```
dreamweaver.browseDocument("http://www.idest.com/help/etable.htm")
```

As noted in Chapter 18, you can use `browseDocument` to access an absolute URL from the Web or a file from a local drive. To display a local file, you need to combine `browseDocument` with another function such as `getConfigurationPath()`. The example offered here shows how to use the two functions together to programmatically display Dreamweaver's InsertMenu.htm file:

```
function displayMenu() {
  var menuPath = dreamweaver.getConfigurationPath() + ¬
"/Objects/InsertMenu.htm"
  dreamweaver.browseDocument(menuPath)
}
```

The dreamweaver.openDocument() and dreamweaver.createDocument() functions

The `openDocument()` and `createDocument()` functions provide similar capabilities while possessing similar restrictions. The `openDocument()` function is equivalent to selecting File ➪ Open and selecting a file from the dialog box. The `createDocument()` function, as the name implies, creates a new, blank document, based on the standard Default.htm file. In either case, the document loads into a Dreamweaver window and is brought forward.

The `createDocument()` function does not need an argument to work and automatically returns the DOM of the new document. For example, the following code:

```
var theNewDoc = dreamweaver.createDocument()
```

is the same as using `getDocumentDOM()` for a new page.

The `openDocument()` function requires an argument in the form of a file://URL. If the URL is given in relative terms, the file is relative to the extensibility file calling the function. For instance, to open a file located one directory up from the Commands folder, you need to refer to it as follows in a custom command:

```
dreamweaver.openDocument("../Extensions.txt")
```

You can also use the same technique referred to earlier in the `browseDocument()` function to access files with the Configuration folder as a base.

Although this function and its companion, `createDocument()`, cannot be used within a behavior, they can be called from a custom command or Property Inspector. Therefore, it's possible to use the `popupCommand()` function to access a command that employs `openDocument()` or `createDocument()`.

The dreamweaver.saveDocument() function

Once all your edits and modifications have been finished, you need a way to store that file. The aptly named `saveDocument()` function performs just that chore for you. This function takes two arguments, *documentObject* and *fileURL*; the first corresponds to the DOM of the file desired to be saved, and the second is the address for it to be saved to. Again *fileURL* is relative to the extensibility file.

The `saveDocument` function returns true if successful and false if the file-storing attempt fails. If the file specified is noted as read-only, Dreamweaver attempts to check it out; if it is unsuccessful, an error message appears.

The dreamweaver.editLockedRegions() function

Dreamweaver templates are based on a combination of locked and editable regions. Normally, these regions are designated in the Document window, but you can use the `editLockedRegions()` function to lock and unlock a template's regions programatically. The `editLockedRegions()` function works by entering true as the function's argument if you want to unlock all of the current document's locked regions, and false to lock them again. After the routine calling `editLockedRegions()` ends, all regions revert to their default status.

Due to the potentially undesirable results using this function, Macromedia recommends that only custom data translators use the `editLockedRegions()` function.

The dreamweaver.popupAction() and dreamweaver.runCommand() functions

Although the popupAction() and popup.Command() functions are not directly useful to behavior creators because they cannot be called from within a behavior, they do enable considerable cross-pollination of Dreamweaver extensible objects. Invoking these functions calls an existing behavior or command and presents its dialog box to the user — except you use these functions to call the behaviors or commands from within a custom object, command, or Property Inspector.

The popupAction() function takes two arguments: the name of the action file and the general function call of the action. The action chosen must be in the Action subfolder. For example, code to call the Control Sound behavior could look like this:

```
var goCS = dreamweaver.popupAction("Control Sound.htm","MM_controlSound(,,)")
```

Tip

To call an action in a subfolder of the Action subfolder, you need to specify the path. For example, if you want to call one of the standard Timeline actions, it's necessary to state the action name as "Timeline/Go to Frame.htm."

The general function call can be found near the end of the applyBehavior() function, where the return value is specified, or as the behaviorFunction() return value. The popupAction() function returns the completed function call, including whatever parameters are selected by the user. In the previous example, if the user had chosen "Play" and selected "brazil.mid" as the file, the result (goCS) would be similar to the following:

```
"MM_controlSound('play',document.CS911946210190.'brazil.mid')"
```

Note

The second argument is a unique name generated by Dreamweaver as part of the function.

Everything is written into the user's page, except the event handler and its corresponding function call. This is left to the calling object, command, or Property Inspector to handle.

The runCommand() function is a bit simpler; this function requires only one argument: the name of the command file. Any file named must be located in the Commands folder. The runCommand() function does not return a value but simply executes the specified command.

The dreamweaver.latin1ToNative() and dreamweaver.nativeToLatin1() functions

Dreamweaver provides two functions to help with the localization of your behaviors around the globe. Many countries use font encodings other than Latin 1, which is standard in the United States and several Western European countries. To convert a string of text for a user interface from Latin 1 encoding to that of the user's machine, use the `latin1ToNative()` function. The argument, a text string, should be already translated into the other language. To convert a text string from the user's encoding system to Latin 1, use the inverse function, `nativeToLatin1()`.

Neither of these functions has an effect in Windows systems, which are already based on Latin 1.

The dreamweaver.relativeToAbsoluteURL() function

As more programs such as Fireworks and Director 7 are capable of outputting HTML, behaviors and other extensions are being employed to access their documents. It's often necessary to find the absolute URL of a selected file in order to get the document's DOM or open it. The `relativeToAbsoluteURL()` function returns this needed information, given three arguments:

✦ **docBaseURL:** The portion of the current document's relative path name excluding the file name. For example, if the file in question were to be found at images\austria.gif, the docBaseURL would be images/.

✦ **siteRootURL:** The file URL of the current site root, as returned from the `getSiteRoot()` function.

✦ **relativeURL:** The full relative path name of the selected file (for example, images/austria.gif).

The syntax for the function is as follows:

```
var absoluteURL = dreamweaver.relativeToAbsoluteURL( docBaseURL, ¬
siteRootURL, relativeURL )
```

Of the three arguments, only *docBaseURL* is a little tricky to get. Once you have the *relativeURL*, which can be returned from the `browseForFileURL()` function, you need to examine the path name and extract the first part of the path leading up to the actual file name. To do so, use the JavaScript function `lastIndexOf` to find the final "/" character and extract the previous substring. For example:

```
function docBase() {
var docURL = dreamweaver.getDocumentPath("document");
var index = docURL.lastIndexOf('/');
if ( -1 == index ){ // If there is no additional path
  return "";     // return nothing.
  }
  else {
  return docURL.substring(0, index);
  }
}
```

Behavior API

You've seen most of the behavior API functions applied in a previous section, "Create the Action File." The API is used to create a behavior. The primary functions are as follows:

Function	Role
`canAcceptBehavior()`	Determines whether an action is available
`windowDimensions()`	Sets the width and height of the parameter form
`applyBehavior()`	Attaches the behavior function to the selected tag
`inspectBehavior()`	Restores user-selected values to the parameter form for reediting
`behaviorFunction()`	Writes a function into the `<head>` of the HTML file
`deleteBehavior()`	Removes a behavior from the HTML file
`identifyBehaviorArguments()`	Notes the behavior arguments that need to be altered if the file is moved
`displayHelp()`	Attaches a Help button to the behavior's dialog box

For discussions of the uses of the `canAcceptBehavior()`, `applyBehavior()`, `inspectBehavior()`, and `behaviorFunction()` functions, see the preceding sections. Following are discussions of the other behavior API functions.

The windowDimensions() function

To speed display, the `windowDimensions()` function sets specific dimensions for the parameters form that the user sees as the dialog box. If this function is not defined, the window dimensions are computed automatically. This function takes one argument, *platform*, which is used to specify whether the user's system is Macintosh or Windows. The function returns a string with the width and height in pixels. For example:

```
function windowDimensions(platform){
if (platform.charAt(0) == 'm'){ // Macintosh
        return "650,500";
        }
        else { // Windows 95 or NT
        return "675,525";
}
}
```

You can see this function in some of the standard behaviors. However, Macromedia recommends that it be used only when you need the behavior's dialog box to be larger than 640×480.

The deleteBehavior() function

Normally, Dreamweaver automatically handles removal of a behavior's event handler and associated JavaScript when the user chooses the Remove Behavior button in the Behavior Inspector. However, as behaviors grow in complexity and become capable of adding additional support code to the HTML document, it becomes necessary to use the `deleteBehavior()` function on a case-by-case basis. To better understand how `deleteBehavior()` is used, it's best to look at a couple of examples.

Two standard behaviors, Control Sound and Swap Image, use the `deleteBehavior()` function. Control Sound inserts an `<embed>` tag that contains a unique ID. To remove the code, `deleteBehavior()` first reads a function call string, just like the one returned by `applyBehavior()`. If the function finds an `<embed>` tag with the matching ID that is not referenced elsewhere on the page, the code is deleted. Here's the implementation of `deleteBehavior()` for Control Sound:

```
function deleteBehavior(fnCallStr) {
  var argArray,sndName,doc,tagArray,i,embedName;

  argArray = extractArgs(fnCallStr);
  if (argArray.length > 2) {
    sndName = dreamweaver.getTokens(argArray[2],".")[1]; //remove ¬
"document.", use unique name
    //Find all EMBED calls that we created (name starts with "CS"), add ¬
to menu
    doc = dreamweaver.getDocumentDOM("document"); //get all
    tagArray = doc.getElementsByTagName("EMBED");
    for (i=0; i<tagArray.length; i++) {  //with each EMBED tag
      embedName = tagArray[i].name;
      if (embedName == sndName) { //if same embed
        if ( -1 == doc.body.outerHTML.indexOf( argArray[2] ) ) // and embed ¬
ref'd no where else
          tagArray[i].outerHTML = "";
        break;
  } } }
}
```

Swap Image doesn't insert additional `<embed>` or other tags; it inserts additional event handlers to make implementing rollovers a one-step process. When a Swap Image behavior is deleted from the page, all the additional event handlers must be stripped out as well. To do so, the `deleteBehavior()` function first reads in the behavior function call string and then searches for the *Preload ID*. This is a unique name inserted by Dreamweaver if the user checked the Preload option when running the behavior. If the preload ID is found, the preload handler, such as `onLoad = MM_preloadImages()`, is removed. Next, the Swap Image `deleteBehavior()` searches to see if the Swap Image Restore code was added—and if so, deletes that event handler as well.

The identifyBehaviorArguments() function

If you've ever had to relocate a Web site from one directory to another, you know the laborious job of making sure all your references are intact. Dreamweaver takes some of the tedium out of this chore. When you use Save As from Dreamweaver, all of the file paths within HTML attributes, such as the image source files and links, are automatically updated. Dreamweaver extends the same functionality to URLs contained within behaviors.

For example, suppose you have constructed a Web page that uses the Check Browser action to route users to various URLs, depending on the browser they are using. Should you elect to save your Web page in a different folder, for whatever reason, Dreamweaver automatically updates the referenced URLs.

For this property to work correctly, a new function must be included in the behavior. The function, `identifyBehaviorArguments()`, passes the argument structure to Dreamweaver so it can update the URLs, if necessary. The function also identifies the layer objects in the behavior that Dreamweaver must correct if the Convert Layers to Tables command is used.

The `identifyBehaviorArguments()` function accepts a string that contains the behavior function call, with arguments. The function then extracts the arguments into an array and identifies which arguments in the array are URLs, which ones are layer objects, and which ones are neither. Four identifying values are returned:

- **URL:** When the argument is a file or file path
- **NS4.0ref:** When the argument identifies a layer in Netscape syntax, such as `document.layers[\'Layer1\']`
- **IE4.0ref:** When the argument identifies a layer in Internet Explorer syntax, such as `document.all[\'Layer1\']`
- **Other:** When the argument is none of the preceding

You can see an example of the `identifyBehaviorArguments()` function in the Check Plugin action:

```
function identifyBehaviorArguments(fnCallStr) {
  var argArray;

  argArray = extractArgs(fnCallStr);
  if (argArray.length == 5) {
    return "other,URL,URL,other";
  }
}
```

As with the `inspectBehavior()` function, the array for the function call string is one element longer than the number of arguments—the initial array element is the function name itself.

The displayHelp() function

The `displayHelp()` function inserts a Help button on your custom behavior dialog boxes, below the standard OK and Cancel buttons. This function takes no arguments and is usually defined to display a help message or file. The two typical techniques are to use either the `alert()` method or the Dreamweaver JavaScript extension, `browseDocument()`.

To display a brief message, use the `alert()` method, as in the following code:

```
function displayHelp() {
  alert("This behavior works only with .rmf files.")
}
```

When you need to bring up a much longer file, use the `browseDocument()` function:

```
function displayHelp() {
  dreamweaver.browseDocument("http://www.idest.com/help/rep.htm")
}
```

You can also reference local files using `browseDocument()`. See the `browseDocument()` description in the section "Dreamweaver JavaScript API Extensions," earlier in this chapter.

Do not include the JavaScript file displayHelp.js in your behaviors. This is the Dreamweaver file used for calling its own Help pages.

Useful Common Functions

As with most other object-oriented programming languages, it's good programming practice to build a function once and recall it when needed. Dreamweaver 3 includes a large library of such useful functions, which are maintained in the Shared\Macromedia\Scripts\CMN folder. The functions are grouped by category into JavaScript files; currently 13 such files exist, including docInfo.js, DOM,js, file.js, and string.js. Although they are used extensively throughout the standard behaviors, nothing prevents you from using them in your own routines. To access them, you need to insert only a line in your behavior JavaScript file like this:

```
<SCRIPT SRC="../../Shared/MM/Scripts/CMN/string.js"></SCRIPT>
```

Table 20-3 shows a breakdown of some of the most commonly used functions available in the Shared folder and the file in which they can be found.

Table 20-3
Useful Common Functions

Function	*File*	*Description*
`extractArgs()`	string.js	Takes a function call and extracts the arguments into an array without quotes.
`escQuotes()`	string.js	Reviews a string and adds the escape character, `/`, in front of any single quote, double quote, or backslash found.
`unescQuotes()`	string.js	Removes any escape characters found in a string.
`browseFile()`	file.js	Opens the Select File dialog box and inserts the results into a specified text box.
`stripStar()`	menuItem.js	Removes asterisks from the end of a string.
`stripValue()`	menuItem.js	Removes any specified value from the end of a string.
`addStarToMenuItem()`	menuItem.js	Adds an asterisk to a selected menu item on the end, as in Swap Image.
`addValueToMenuItem()`	menuItem.js	Adds any specified value to a selected menu item, as `(show)`, `(hide)`, and `(default)` are added in Show/Hide Layers.
`niceNames()`	niceName.js	Changes JavaScript object references such as `document.layers['onLayer'].document.theForm` to a more readable format such as `form "theForm" in layer "onLayer"`.
`nameReduce()`	niceName.js	Extracts object names and array numbers and quotes them, if necessary.
`errMsg()`	errmsg.js	Concatenates strings given in an argument. For example, `errMsg("Now is the %s for %s to fight", var1, var2)` returns `"Now is the time for all men to fight"` if var1 is set to `"time"` and var2 is set to `"all men"`. However, if var1 is set to `"not the time"` and var2 is set to `"anyone"`, then `errMsg` returns `"Now is not the time for anyone to fight."`
`findObject()`	UI.js	Returns the JavaScript object reference for any named object. For example, if you have an image named `imgOne` in a form in a layer, `onLayer`, `findObject("imgOne")` returns `document.layers['onLayer'].imgOne`.

<table>
<tr><th>Function</th><th>File</th><th>Description</th></tr>
<tr><td>getParam()</td><td>string.js</td><td>Returns an array of named objects within a given tag found on the current page.</td></tr>
<tr><td>badChars()</td><td>string.js</td><td>Removes inappropriate characters such as ~!@#$%^&*()_+|`-=\\{}[]:\";'<> , . / and space.</td></tr>
<tr><td>getAllObjectRefs()</td><td>docInfo.js</td><td>Returns an array of object references for any specified tag in the current document or, if the document is in a frameset, in all frames.</td></tr>
<tr><td>getAllObjectTags()</td><td>docInfo.js</td><td>Returns an array of tags for any specified tag in the current document or, if the document is in a frameset, in all frames.</td></tr>
</table>

Dreamweaver Behavior Techniques

Creating a behavior is often far more than just stringing together a number of predefined functions. Specific techniques exist for many special needs, and if you don't know them, you can spend many hours redeveloping the wheel. In this section, you learn several methods that can help you streamline your work.

Specifying an event

In Dreamweaver, every tag capable of being used to launch a behavior has a default event. Although you can alter the default events for various tags by editing the HTML files in the Events folder, as described in Chapter 19, these changes affect only your own system, not those of other users. You can, however, specify the desired event on a behavior-by-behavior basis — in fact, you can specify a series of desired events.

The event specification takes place in the `canApplyBehavior()` function. Usually, this function returns either true or false, depending on whether the proper conditions for implementing the behavior have been met. If, however, the conditions have been met *and* you want to specify an event to use, `canApplyBehavior()` can be set to return a string of acceptable events.

In the following example, the page is inspected, and if a layer is found, the default event is overridden in favor of `onKeyDown`:

```
function canAcceptBehavior(){
  var nameArray = dreamweaver.getObjectRefs("NS 4.0","document","LAYER");
  if (nameArray.length > 0){
    return "onKeyDown";
  }else{
  return FALSE;
}
```

It's also possible to specify a series of preferred events, in reverse order of preference, like this:

```
return "onKeyDown, onKeyPress, onKeyUp"
```

If one event handler is not available — perhaps because the user specified an older browser — the next is selected.

Returning a value

Most event handlers don't require a return value to be implemented, but some, such as `onMouseOver` and `onMouseOut`, do. Generally, Dreamweaver behaviors don't take this into account, but you can by declaring a special variable, `document.MM_returnValue`. You can see the return value variable in operation in the standard Display Status Message behavior.

The `document.MM_returnValue` variable is declared as the last line in the function definition. Thus, Display Status Message reads as follows:

```
function MM_displayStatusMsg(msgStr) { //v2.0
  status=msgStr;
  document.MM_returnValue = true;
}
```

Naturally, the return value can also be `false`.

Including multiple functions

Although little known, the capability to return multiple functions began in Dreamweaver 1.2. Previously, all behavior functions had to be self-contained, and one could not call on any helper functions. Now, however, multiple functions can easily be defined and returned via `behaviorFunction()`. Once written into the user's page, all the returned functions are stored in a single `<script>...</script>` tag pair.

The technique for inserting multiple functions is fairly straightforward. First, list your defined functions in a comma-delimited string in `behaviorFunction()`. The one trick is to make sure that your primary function — the one called by the event handler — is listed last. This technique is illustrated in the following code for my custom Resize Layer Patch behavior:

```
function behaviorFunction(){
  return 'reDo,resizePatch';
}
```

Here, my primary function is `resizePatch()` and is used as such in `applyBehavior()`:

```
function applyBehavior() {
  return 'resizePatch()';  //return fn call with args
}
```

Summary

Although creating a custom behavior is not a simple task, it is a vastly rewarding one — both from the programmer's and the user's perspective. Dreamweaver gives you tremendous power to automate advanced Web page techniques, and Dreamweaver 3 has greatly enhanced that power with an expanded Document Object Model. As you ponder building your own behaviors, remember the following:

- If you can achieve a result in JavaScript, chances are good you can make a behavior to automate that task.
- Dreamweaver 3 includes an expanded Document Object Model (DOM) that enables the programmer to examine and modify virtually every aspect of an HTML page.
- You can use Dreamweaver's built-in JavaScript extensions and API functions to build your own actions.
- Dreamweaver's JavaScript extensions enable you to open existing documents, as well as create and save new ones.
- Many useful functions can be found in the standard _common.js file.

In the next chapter, you learn how to customize Dreamweaver further through commands, Property Inspectors, and more.

✦ ✦ ✦

CHAPTER 21

Customizing Dreamweaver

✦ ✦ ✦ ✦

In This Chapter

Automating Web development with commands

Including custom XML tags

Examining new Property Inspectors

Expanding Dreamweaver's core functionality

Translating server-side content

✦ ✦ ✦ ✦

The Web is a dynamic environment, with new technologies continually emerging. Until recently, HTML standards were changing every year or so, and even now, products are routinely introduced that use the Web as a jumping-off place for new methods and tools. Keeping pace with the constantly shifting work environment of the Web was beyond the capabilities of any suite of Web authoring tools, much less a single one — until Dreamweaver debuted, of course.

The initial version of Dreamweaver had a high degree of extensibility built right in, with its customizable HTML objects and JavaScript behaviors. Macromedia takes this core of flexibility to new heights with Dreamweaver 3. With the implementation of the W3C Document Object Model and a tremendous number of API functions, objects and behaviors have been beefed up so that they are much more powerful than ever. In addition, Dreamweaver presents a host of ways to extend its power:

- ✦ **Menus:** The entire menu system has been rewritten for Dreamweaver 3 and is now completely customizable. You can add context menu items, rearrange the main menu, change keyboard shortcuts, and even add completely new menus, all by modifying an XML file.
- ✦ **Commands:** Commands are JavaScript and HTML code that manipulate the Web page during the design phase, much as behaviors are triggered at runtime. Commands have been expanded in Dreamweaver 3 to include new menu commands to read and react to dynamically constructed menus.
- ✦ **Custom tags:** With the rapid rise of XML, custom tag support becomes essential in a professional Web authoring tool. Dreamweaver gives you the power to create any custom tag and control how it displays in the Document window.

✦ **Property Inspectors:** Custom Property Inspectors go hand-in-hand with custom tags, permitting the straightforward entry of attributes and values in a manner consistent with the Dreamweaver user interface.

✦ **Floaters:** Property Inspectors are limited to a specific size and shape, but the new custom floating palettes or floaters are not. Floaters also have the advantage of being onscreen with other elements, unlike Command dialog boxes.

✦ **Translators:** Translators enable server-side content to be viewed in the Document window at design time, as well as in the browser at runtime.

✦ **C-level extensions:** Some special uses require a root-level addition to Dreamweaver's capabilities. Macromedia's engineers have "popped the hood" on Dreamweaver and made it possible for a C or C++ language library to interface with it through C-level extensions.

While a few of these extension features require programming skills outside of those common to the typical Web designer, most are well within the reach of an HTML- and JavaScript-savvy coder. As with behaviors and objects, the source code for all but the C-level extensions is readily available and serves as an excellent training ground. This chapter, combined with these standard scripts, provides all the tools you need to begin carving out your own personalized version of Dreamweaver.

Adding New Commands

By their very nature, objects and behaviors are single-purpose engines. A custom object inserts a single block of HTML into the `<body>` of a Web page, while custom behaviors add JavaScript functions to the `<head>` and attributes of one tag. Commands, on the other hand, are multifaceted, multipurpose, go-anywhere and do-anything mechanisms. Commands can do everything objects and behaviors can do, combined—and more. In fact, commands can even masquerade as objects.

For all their power, however, commands are one of the most accessible of the Dreamweaver extensions. This section describes the basic structure of commands as well as the use of the standard commands that ship with Dreamweaver. You can also find information about how to create your own commands and control their integration into Dreamweaver.

Understanding Dreamweaver commands

When I first encountered commands, I thought, "Great! Dreamweaver now has a macro language," and I envisioned instantly automating simple Web design tasks. Before long, I realized that commands were even more powerful—and a bit trickier than a macro recorder. Dreamweaver's adoption of the W3C Document Object Model (DOM) is one of the factors that makes commands feasible. The DOM in

Dreamweaver makes available, or *exposes*, every part of the HTML page — every tag, every attribute, every bit of content — which can then be read, modified, deleted, or added to. Moreover, Dreamweaver commands can open, read, and modify other files on local systems.

The command can have a parameter form or not, depending on how the command was written. Generally, commands are listed in the Commands menu, but by altering the CommandMenu.htm file (as described later in the chapter), you can cause your command to appear as part of any other menu — or to not appear at all. Because one command can call another, such hidden commands are more easily modified.

My vision of a macro recorder has come true in Dreamweaver 3 with the addition of the Start Recording and Play Recording commands. Now, any onscreen action can be instantly logged and replayed – and through the History palette, even converted into a permanent, repeatable command.

But how specifically are commands being used? Here's a short list of the commands that have been built by Web designers outside of Macromedia:

✦ **iCat Commands:** Opens up a browser window and connects you to the iCat Web site for online e-commerce registration. Additional commands build the database of online store items and synchronize the information on both local and remote servers. By Eric Greene for iCat.

✦ **Site Log:** Keeps track of the changes made to a Web site for team development use. By Andrew Wooldridge.

✦ **Tag Killer:** Removes all instances of any tag from a Web page. By Massimo Foti.

✦ **Scratch Pad:** Keeps snippets of code available for easy cutting and pasting on a single page or across Web sites. By Andrew Wooldridge.

✦ **Borderless Frames:** Sets all frames in a frameset to no borders. By Massimo Foti.

✦ **Quick Site:** Prototypes a simple Web site by creating files and generating a navigation bar to all pages. By Andrew Wooldridge.

✦ **Replicator:** Duplicates any selected element any number of times. By this book's author, Joseph Lowery.

As should be obvious from this list, commands come close to being limited only by the author's imagination. The next section takes a brief look at the commands that ship with Dreamweaver 3 and their uses.

Dreamweaver 3 comes with nine standard commands that, in addition to adding some extra functionality, give you a taste of just how powerful commands can be:

✦ **Clean Up HTML:** Removes unnecessary or redundant HTML for a smaller file size and more readable code.

✦ **Clean Up Word HTML:** Deletes unnecessary XML or redundant HTML from a Microsoft Word file saved as a Web page.

✦ **Add/Remove Netscape Resize Fix:** Initially inserts code necessary to work around a problem with layers in Netscape browsers. When a Netscape 4.*x* browser is resized, all layers created with `<div>` tags lose their precise positioning; the inserted code causes browsers to reload whenever necessary. Reapplying the command deletes the code.

✦ **Optimize Image in Fireworks:** Opens the Fireworks Export Preview dialog box, which enables images to be rescaled, cropped, color-corrected, or exported in a different format. Requires Fireworks 3.

✦ **Create Web Photo Album:** Turns a folder of images into a Web page of thumbnail images, each linked to the original image. Requires Fireworks 3.

✦ **Apply Source Formatting:** Styles HTML in Web pages created outside of Dreamweaver to resemble Dreamweaver-created code.

✦ **Set Color Scheme:** Selects the colors for the current page's background, text, and link states.

✦ **Sort Table:** Performs a one- or two-level sort on any table, using any column in an ascending or descending manner.

✦ **Format Table:** Applies one of 17 different predesigned formats or any designated custom format to the selected table.

All but two of the standard commands are described in detail elsewhere in the book. You can find a description of Set Color Scheme in Chapter 8, and Chapter 13 covers the two Table commands. Chapter 4 explains the use of the Netscape Layer Fix, and you can find information on the two Fireworks commands in Chapter 22.

The Clean Up HTML command

Even if you never open the HTML Inspector or touch the code in an external editor, your HTML can still become unwieldy. One of the most common problems is redundant `<font>` tags that result from doing something like selecting some text and then first changing the font itself, and next the font size, and finally the font color. This is likely to give you code that resembles the following:

```
<font face="Arial"><font size="4">¬
<font color="green">Bonanza!</font></font></font>
```

The Clean Up HTML command is, quite literally, custom made to consolidate code such as this and remove some of the code clutter that can accumulate during a page's design. In all, you have six different cleansing operations from which to choose. The Clean Up HTML command is applicable only to the current page and cannot be applied sitewide.

To use the Clean Up HTML command, follow these steps:

1. Choose Commands ➪ Clean Up HTML.

   The Clean Up HTML dialog box appears, as shown in Figure 21-1.

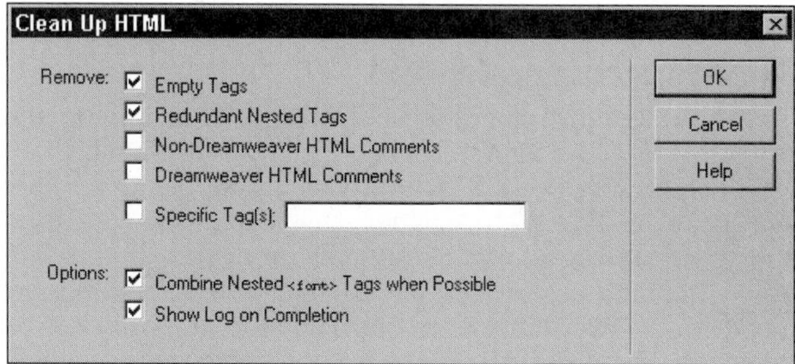

Figure 21-1: Reduce your page's file size and make your HTML more readable with the Clean Up HTML command.

2. To delete tag pairs with no code between them (such as `<i></i>`), make sure the Remove: Empty Tags option is selected.

3. To eliminate superfluous tags that repeat the same code as the tags surrounding them, as in this example:

```
<font color="white">And the <font color="white">¬
truth</font> is plain to see.</font>
```

   choose the Remove: Redundant Tags option.

4. To delete any HTML comments not created by Dreamweaver to mark a Library or Template item, choose Remove: Non-Dreamweaver HTML Comments.

5. To clear all Dreamweaver-specific comments, such as:

```
<! #BeginEditable "openingPara" -->
```

   select the Remove: Dreamweaver HTML Comments option.

6. To erase any specific tag and its attributes, select the Remove: Specific Tag(s) option and enter the tag name(s) in the text box.

Tag names are entered without angle brackets; separate multiple tags with a comma.

7. To consolidate `<font>` tags, select the Combine Nested `<font>` Tags When Possible option.

8. To view a report of the changes applied to your document, select the Show Log on Completion option.

9. Click OK when you're done.

Dreamweaver performs the actions requested on the current document. If the Show Log option has been selected, an alert displays the changes made, if any.

The Apply Source Formatting command

All the code created by Dreamweaver is structured according to a document called the "Source Format Profile." The Source Format Profile controls which codes are indented and which are on their own line, as well as numerous other specifications of HTML writing. Occasionally, a Web designer must work with Web pages created earlier or by other designers using other programs, or even by hand. The Apply Source Formatting command can rewrite the original code so that it is structured according to the current Source Format Profile. The more accustomed your eye is to following Dreamweaver-style HTML, the more you value this command.

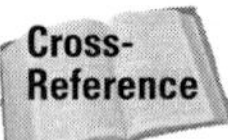

To learn more about the Source Format Profile, see Chapter 4.

The Apply Source Formatting command is an example of a Dreamweaver command that doesn't display a dialog box to gather the user's selected parameters — because you have no parameters to set. To invoke the command, choose Commands ➪ Apply Source Formatting. The command is applied immediately, with no confirmation or feedback offered indicating that it is complete.

Recording and replaying commands

I'm a big fan of any kind of work-related automation and consider myself a power user of word processing macros, so you can imagine my delight when a similar capability was added to Dreamweaver. The capability to record your onscreen actions and then replay them instantly — with the option of saving them as a command or simply pasting them into another document — is a tremendous work-saver. Most every onscreen action can be replicated.

How could you use such a macro-like capability in Dreamweaver? Let's say you have a series of ten images on a page, and you want to surround each of them with a 2-pixel border and center them on the page. Now, you could do this one at a time entering in the same border value and selecting the center alignment button, but it would get pretty tedious after the third or fourth image. With Dreamweaver, here's the basic automation procedure:

1. Select the first image.

2. Choose Commands ➪ Start Recording or use the keyboard shortcut, Ctrl+Shift+X (Command+Shift+X).

The cursor changes to a recording tape symbol, indicating you're in recording mode.

3. Enter the new values in the Property Inspector.
4. Choose Commands ➪ Stop or the same keyboard command again: Ctrl+Shift+X (Command+Shift+X).
5. Select another image.
6. Choose Commands ➪ Play Recorded Command or use the keyboard shortcut Ctrl+P (Command+P).
7. Repeat Steps 5 and 6 for every image you want to affect as shown in Figure 21-2.

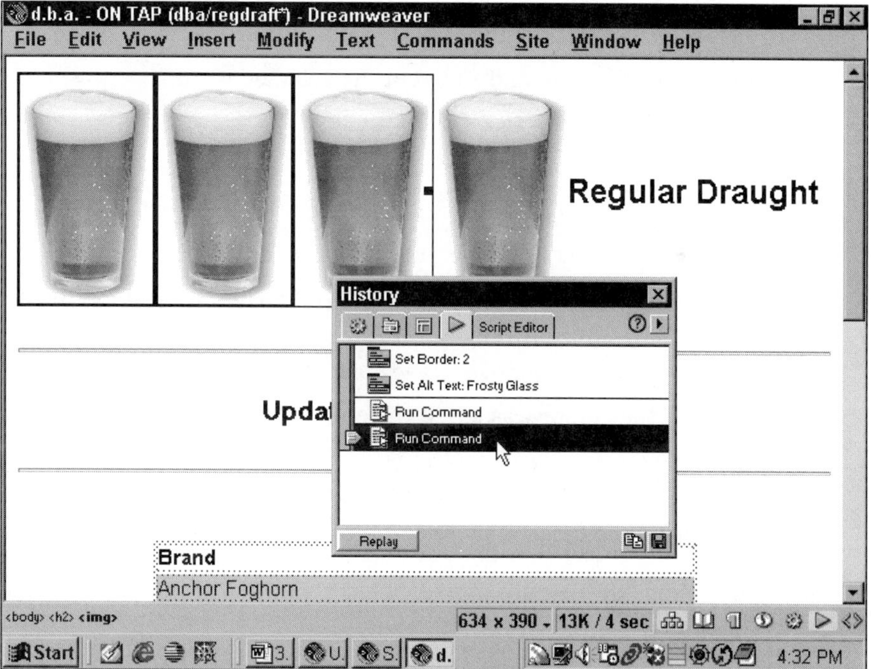

Figure 21-2: After the steps for formatting the first image were recorded, formatting the other images is a one-step process with Dreamweaver's command recorder.

Most of the commands and onscreen moves can be replicated in this manner, but not always. The major exception is the use of the mouse. Dreamweaver can not repeat mouse moves and selections. You could not, for example, begin to create a drop-cap by recording the drag selection of the first letter in each paragraph. You can however use the arrow keys and any keyboard-related combination.

For example, let's say you had a standard list of names in your document, like this:

```
Joseph Lowery
Andrew Wooldridge
Al Sparber
Simon White
```

that you wanted to change to *Lastname, Firstname* format. To do this with command recording, you'd follow this procedure.

1. Position your cursor at the beginning of the first name.
2. Choose Commands ➪ Start Recording.
3. Press Shift+right arrow to select the first word.

   Dreamweaver highlights the first word and the following space.
4. Press Ctrl+X (Command X) to cut the selected word.
5. Press End to move to the end of the line.
6. Type a comma and a space.
7. Press Ctrl+V (Command+V) to paste the previously cut word.
8. Press Backspace to remove the trailing space.

   Now that the first line is complete, it's important to position the cursor to perform the recorded command again.
9. Press right arrow to move to the start of the next line.

   Because the cursor was left at the end of the last line, the right-arrow key moves it to the front of the following line.
10. Choose Commands ➪ Stop Recording.
11. Choose Commands ➪ Play Recorded Command for each name in the list.

If you try to include a mouse move or selection when recording a command or playing back a recorded command, Dreamweaver issues a warning and asks if you'd like to stop recording. If you choose to continue, Dreamweaver ignores the attempted mouse move and resets the pointer in its previous position.

Tip

If you try to record your navigations around a table, Dreamweaver does not record the Tab or Shift+Tab keys. However, you can still record your table moves by using Home and End in combination with the arrow keys. To move from cell to cell, from left to right, press End and then right arrow. To move right to left, press Home and then left arrow. You can also move up and down columns by pressing Home or End and then either up or down arrow.

Recorded actions are maintained in memory and when you issue the Start Recording command again, the previously recorded steps are replaced. You can, however, convert recorded steps to a command to use over and over in any document or site you'd like by using the History palette.

1. Record a series of actions as described previously.
2. Play the recorded actions at least once by choosing Commands ⇨ Play Recorded Command.

   On the History palette, the collective recorded actions are displayed as a single step, Run Command
3. In the History palette, select Run Command.
4. Select the Save As Command button from the bottom of the History palette.

Scripting commands

Commands, like most behaviors, are a combination of JavaScript functions and HTML forms; the HTML provides the user interface for any parameters that need to be set, and JavaScript carries out the particular command. Although you can combine both languages in a single HTML file, many programmers, including those from Macromedia, keep the JavaScript in a separate .js file that is incorporated in the HTML file with a `<script>` tag, like this one:

```
<SCRIPT LANGUAGE="javascript" SRC="Clean Up HTML.js">
```

This separation enables easy modification of the user interface and the underlying code, and the sharing of the JavaScript functions.

Commands are very open-ended. In fact, only two Dreamweaver functions are specific to commands — `canAcceptCommand()` and `commandButtons()` — and neither function is required. Two other command-oriented functions, `receiveArguments()` and `windowDimensions()`, are also used elsewhere, but again, neither are required.

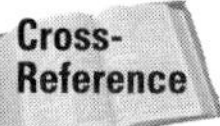

The DOM in Dreamweaver is covered in great detail in Chapter 20.

The `canAcceptCommand()` function controls when the command is active in the menus and when it is ghosted. If `canAcceptCommand()` is not defined, the command is always available. This function returns true or false; if false is returned, the command is ghosted in the menus.

You can see `canAcceptCommand()` in action in both the Sort Table and Format Table commands. For either of these commands to be effective, a table must be indicated. Rather than require that a table be selected, the `canAcceptCommand()`

function calls a subroutine, `findTable()`, which returns true if the user's cursor is positioned inside a table:

```
function canAcceptCommand(){
  if (findTable())
    return true;
  else
    return false;
}

function findTable(){
  var tableObj="";
  var selArr = dreamweaver.getSelection();
  var selObj = dreamweaver.offsetsToNode(selArr[0],selArr[1]);

  while (tableObj=="" && selObj.parentNode){
    if (selObj.nodeType == Node.ELEMENT_NODE && selObj.tagName=="TABLE")
    tableObj=selObj;
  else
    selObj = selObj.parentNode;
  }
  return tableObj;
}
```

Macromedia recommends that the `canAcceptCommand()` function not be defined unless at least one case exists in which the command should not be available. Otherwise, the function is asked to run for no purpose, which degrades performance.

The `commandButtons()` function defines the buttons that appear on the parameter form to the right. This expanded functionality is extremely useful when developing commands. Some commands require that an operation be enabled to run repeatedly and not just the one time an OK button is selected. As noted earlier, you don't have to declare the function at all, in which case the form expands to fill the dialog box entirely.

Each button that is declared has a function associated with it, which is executed when the user selects that particular button. All the buttons for a command are listed in an array, returned by `commandButtons()`. The following example declares three buttons: OK, Cancel, and Help:

```
function commandButtons() {
    return new Array("OK","goCommand()","Cancel","window.close()","Help",¬
"displayHelp()")
}
```

Notice that two of the buttons, OK and Help, call custom functions, but the Cancel button simply calls a built-in JavaScript function to close the window. No real limitations exist to the number of buttons a command can hold other than user interface design sense.

The `receiveArguments()` function is used in conjunction with `runCommand()`. Whenever `runCommand()` calls a specific command — from a behavior, object, or other command — it can pass arguments. If `receiveArguments()` is set up, that function is executed, and the arguments read into `receiveArguments()`. This function enables the same command to be called from different sources and have different effects, depending on the arguments passed. The `receiveArguments()` function is used extensively in menu commands and is explained more fully in that section later in this chapter.

As with behaviors and objects, the `windowDimensions()` function can be used with commands to set a specific size for the associated dialog box. If windowDimensions is not defined, the dialog box's size is set automatically. Macromedia recommends that `windowDimensions()` not be used unless your parameter form exceeds 650 × 480.

The remainder of the user interface for a command — the parameter form — is constructed in the same manner, using the same tools as objects and behaviors. A command parameter form or dialog box uses an HTML `<form>` in the `<body>` of the file. If no `<form>` is declared, the command executes without displaying a dialog box. All of the form elements used in objects — text boxes, radio buttons, checkboxes, and lists — are available in commands.

For detailed information about how to retrieve information in a parameter form, see Chapter 18.

Dreamweaver Techniques: Useful command routines

When programming a command, I often get stuck on one small point. "If only I knew how to _________, I'd be home free," is my usual refrain. The following routines and explanations are presented in the interest of helping you "fill in the blank" as you begin to construct your own custom commands.

Getting a user's selection

Although many commands work with the entire HTML document, some require just a portion of text or an object that has been selected by the user. While it seems like a simple task, some quirks in the API make getting a selection a little tricky.

Selecting text

The usual method for finding out — and acting on — what the user has selected requires the `getSelection()` function. As discussed in Chapter 20, `getSelection()` returns two-byte offsets that mark the beginning and end of the user's selection. The difficulty appears when you try to extract the character data that corresponds to those byte offsets. The `offsetsToNode()` function, which is used to make this translation, expands the offsets to the nearest tag—the innerHTML, in other words. For example, the following function attempts to get the user's selection and report it in an alert:

```
function testCase() {
 var theDom = dreamweaver.getDocumentDOM("document");
 var offsets = dreamweaver.getSelection()
 var theNode = dreamweaver.offsetsToNode(offsets[0],offsets[1])
 var nodeText = theNode.data
 alert(nodeText)
}
```

If a user selects the word "grey" in the paragraph "The old grey mare just ain't what she used to be," the function returns the entire line. In order get just what is selected, you need to use the nodeToOffsets() function in combination with offsetsToNode() and the JavaScript substring() function.

The example code in Listing 21-1 demonstrates the proper substring technique; it is taken from the Change Case command, included on CD-ROM 1 that accompanies this book:

Listing 21-1: Getting Selected Text

```
function lowerCase(){
 var theDom=dreamweaver.getDocumentDOM("document");
 var offsets = dreamweaver.getSelection()
 var theNode = dreamweaver.offsetsToNode(offsets[0],offsets[1])
 if (theNode.nodeType == Node.TEXT_NODE) {
 var nodeOffsets = dreamweaver.nodeToOffsets(theNode)
 offsets[0] = offsets[0]-nodeOffsets[0]
 offsets[1] = offsets[1]-nodeOffsets[0]
 var nodeText = theNode.data
 theNode.data = nodeText.substring(0,offsets[0]) +
  nodeText.substring(offsets[0], offsets[1]).toLowerCase() +
  nodeText.substring(offsets[1], nodeText.length);
 window.close()
 } else { //it's not a TEXT_NODE
 var nodeOffsets = dreamweaver.nodeToOffsets(theNode)
 offsets[0] = offsets[0]-nodeOffsets[0]
 offsets[1] = offsets[1]-nodeOffsets[0]
 var nodeText = theNode.innerHTML
 theNode.innerHTML = nodeText.toLowerCase()
 window.close()
 }
}
```

Notice two conditions in the example function — either the selected string is text (a TEXT_NODE), or it's not. If the node is something other than a TEXT_NODE, the `data` property is not available, and `innerHTML` must be used instead. This situation occurs when a user selects an entire paragraph. In fact, all the user has to select is the last character before the closing tag — such as a period at the end of a paragraph — and the node type switches to ELEMENT_NODE.

Selecting objects

By comparison, you have far fewer hoops to jump through to reference a selected object. To find a selected object, you need to get only its `outerHTML` property, as shown in Listing 21-2.

Listing 21-2: Getting a Selected Object

```
function replicate(){
  var theDom = dreamweaver.getDocumentDOM("document");
  var offsets = dreamweaver.getSelection()
  var selObj = dreamweaver.offsetsToNode(offsets[0],offsets[1])
  if (selObj.nodeType == Node.TEXT_NODE) {
    helpMe2()
    window.close()
    return;
  }
  var theCode = selObj.outerHTML
```

Listing 21-2 also includes a small error routine that looks to see if the user's selection is text (`selObj.nodeType == Node.TEXT_NODE`) and, if so, puts up an advisory and then closes the window to enable the user to reselect.

Using a command as an object

Commands offer a tremendous range of power and can perform actions not available to behaviors or objects. To take advantage of this power with a point-and-click interface, it's best to "disguise" your command as an object. As an object, your command appears in both the Objects palette and the Insert menu.

A Dreamweaver object usually consists of two files: an HTML file for the code and a GIF image for the button, all in the Object folder. When using a command as an object, however, you can have as many as five files split between the Object and Command folders. The standard Rollover object is a good example: three associated Rollover files are in the Object folder and two in the Command folder. Here is how they are used:

- **Object/Rollover.gif:** The image for the Rollover button that appears in the Objects palette
- **Object/Rollover.htm:** A shell file (called by the Rollover button) that reads Object/Rollover.js
- **Object/Rollover.js:** Contains the `objectTag()` function, which references the Command/Rollover.htm file
- **Command/Rollover.htm:** Builds the user interface for the "object" and reads all external JavaScript files, including Command/Rollover.js
- **Command/Rollover.js:** Contains the actual code for the function that performs the required operations, which returns its value to the Object/Rollover.htm file by way of the Object/Rollover.js file

The key to understanding how to use a command as an object is the code linking the two. In the Object/Rollover.js file is the `objectTag()`, which is used to write an object into an existing Web page with its return value. In this case, the function first gets the Document Object Model of the relevant Command file (Command/Rollover.htm); this procedure enables the current function to reference any variable set in the other file. Then the `popupCommand` is executed, which runs Command/Rollover.htm—which, in turn, launches the dialog box and gets the user parameters. Finally, a result from that command is set to the return value of `objectTag()` and written into the HTML page. Here's the `objectTag()` function in its entirety from Object/Rollover.js:

```
function objectTag() {
   var rolloverCmdURL = dreamweaver.getConfigurationPath() + ¬
"/Commands/Rollover.htm";
   var rolloverDoc    = dreamweaver.getDocumentDOM( rolloverCmdURL );
   dreamweaver.popupCommand( "Rollover.htm" );
   return( rolloverDoc.parentWindow.getRolloverTag() );
}
```

Some custom commands disguised as objects make the DOM connection in the command file, rather than the object file. The iCat objects, for example, all establish the link in the primary functions of their command JavaScript files, in this manner:

```
var dom = dreamweaver.getDocumentDOM("../Objects/iCat/Add To Cart.htm");
dom.parentWindow.icatTagStr = icatTagStr;
```

Then, the corresponding `objectTag()` function simply returns the `icatTagStr` variable.

Placing code in the <head> section

It's fairly straightforward to insert text wherever the cursor has been set in the document — you just set a text string equal to the [innerHTML | data] property of the DOM at that point. But how do you insert code in the <head> section of a Web page where the cursor is generally not found? Certain code, such as <script> tags that hold extensive JavaScript functions, must be inserted in the <head>. By design, behaviors return code specifically intended for the <script> tag — except you can't easily use a behavior to include a line like

```
<script language="Javascript" src="extend.js"></script>
```

You can insert such a line with commands, however, and this technique, developed by Dreamweaver extensions author Massimo Foti, shows the way.

Unfortunately, no equivalent to the .body property exists in the Dreamweaver DOM for the <head> section. The way around this minor limitation is to first locate the sole <head> tag in a document. This task can be accomplished in two lines of JavaScript code:

```
theDom = dreamweaver.getDocumentDOM("document")
theHeadNode = theDom.getElementsByTagName("HEAD")
```

Now the script variable needs to be set. Whenever Dreamweaver encounters a closing <script> tag (such as </script>) in a JavaScript function, the tag is flagged because it seems to be missing a mate. To avoid this problem, split the tag up into two concatenated strings, like this:

```
theScript = '<script language="Javascript" src="extend.js"><' + '/script>'
```

Finally, find the first item in the <head> section and append the script to its innerHTML property:

```
theHeadNode.item(0).innerHTML = theHeadNode.item(0).innerHTML + theScript
```

The full function looks like this:

```
function insertScript() {
  var theDom, theHeadNode, theScript
  theDom = dreamweaver.getDocumentDOM("document")
  theHeadNode = theDom.getElementsByTagName("HEAD")
  theScript = '<script language="Javascript" src="extend.js"><' + 'script>'
}
```

You can find numerous examples of Massimo Foti's commands and other extensions on CD-ROM 1 that accompanies this book. Just look in the Additional Extensions folder under his name.

Using commands to call other commands

In the earlier section "Using a Command as an Object," the `runCommand()` function plays a key role. It's worth emphasizing that this same function is used when you want one command to invoke another command. The proper syntax is

```
var doNew = dw.runCommand("commandFileName")
```

where *commandFileName* is the name of an HTML file in the Command folder. No value is returned with `runCommand()`; the function executes whatever command is called, passing any optional arguments. The function takes the format

```
dreamweaver.runCommand("myCommand.htm","argument01", "argument02")
```

The called command's dialog box is presented and must be completed or canceled before the originating command is able to continue.

Many commands – especially those disguised as objects – are not intended to be directly accessed by the user. However, Dreamweaver lists any valid command found in the Command folder on the menu – unless you add a comment as the first line of your HTML file in this format:

```
<!-- MENU-LOCATION=NONE -->
```

This code line inhibits the command name from being automatically displayed in the Commands menu list.

Creating a blank document

Commands aren't limited to working on the current document—you can use a command to read, modify, and even create new files. Any new file created using the `createDocument()` function is an HTML page based on the Default.htm file found in the Configuration\Templates folder—this is the same file used as the base for any files created when File ➪ New is chosen.

Occasionally, however, a command needs to make a new non-HTML document, such as an XML or SMIL file or other file type that doesn't use the `<html>...</html>` structure. To accomplish this task, you first create an HTML file and then replace its entire contents with your own data—or nothing at all. The following custom function, developed by Andrew Wooldridge, makes and saves a new, blank text file:

```
function doNew() {
var newDOM = dreamweaver.createDocument();
var theDoc = newDOM.documentElement;
theDoc.outerHTML = ".";
theDoc.innerHTML = " ";
dreamweaver.saveDocument(newDOM, '../../empty.txt');
}
```

Remember, all the Dreamweaver document functions — such as `saveDocument()` — use addresses relative to the file calling them. For example, if the `doNew()` function just described is included in a command, and therefore stored in the Commands folder, the empty.txt document is saved two folders above the Commands folder or in the Dreamweaver root directory, as the full path to the Commands folder is Dreamweaver\Configuration\Commands.

You can find a command incorporating this technique on CD-ROM 1 that accompanies this book along with many other commands by Andrew Wooldridge. Andrew has a deep understanding of commands and continually stretches the boundaries of what they can accomplish.

You'll find all of Hava's commands to be heavily commented and very worthwhile for programmers of any level.

Commands from a Developer's Developer

Hava Edelstein, a JavaScript engineer with Macromedia, has contributed five commands especially valuable for developers. You can find them on her Web site (`www.hava.com`). Here is an overview of these very useful commands:

✦ **Eval:** This command enables you to quickly spot-check JavaScript statements and perform one-time alterations to your document. A must-have for the serious command developer.

✦ **Show Browser References:** Navigator and Internet Explorer handle objects' references — especially those objects in layers — quite differently. This command enables you to select any object on the page and then find its proper JavaScript reference, which can be easily cut and pasted into your code.

✦ **Show Document Tree:** Want to see how the current document is structured from a DOM point of view? Run this command to create a new document with all the details, most notably the Node_Type of each node. Included in this command is a useful subroutine, `traverseNodes()`, which travels recursively through a document's nodes.

✦ **Set All Checkboxes:** If you've ever had to work with a large form with many checkboxes, you can appreciate this command. Each checkbox on the page is presented and can be set as checked or unchecked. Of special note to programmers is the included function, `setSingleWordAttribute()`, which enables an attribute such as hidden or checked to be set; this functionality is not present in the standard Dreamweaver function `setAttribute()`.

✦ **Show Table Properties:** While the capability to display the properties of a selected table may not seem all that compelling, it's what's under the hood here that counts. This command encompasses three useful utility functions: `getTagAttributes()`, `stripQuotesIfTheyExist()`, and `deleteExtraWhiteSpace()`.

Managing Menus and Keyboard Shortcuts

Dreamweaver offers numerous ways to perform most every task: through the Property Inspector, pop-up context menus, keyboard shortcuts, and even entering code directly. However, in the search for ever-faster, more efficient ways of working, it's often desirable to take control of the menus and other command methods and make them work the way you or your team prefer to work. If, for example, you insert a great number of layers and always define your links via the Property Inspector, you'd probably be better off redefining Ctrl+L (Command+L) to Insert Layer rather than its default, Insert Link. In previous versions of Dreamweaver, a limited amount of menu customization was enabled by adjusting the CommandMenu.htm and InsertMenu.htm files; however, there was no way to adjust most existing shortcuts or to add new menus. Dreamweaver 3 now makes any type of menu customization possible.

New Feature

Dreamweaver 3 completely restructures how all menus and keyboard shortcuts are handled. The CommandMenu.htm and InsertMenu.htm files have been replaced by a single file, menus.xml, found in the Configuration\Menus folder. With menus.xml, the entire menu structure is under your control. You can not only add new items but also rename menu items, change their keyboard shortcuts, determine when a menu item is active or dimmed—and even add entirely new menu strips. Moreover, all of this functionality is available with the context pop-up menus as well.

This new menu customization brings a whole new level of functionality to Dreamweaver. It's entirely possible for a company to create custom subsets of the program for certain departments. For example, let's assume each of several departments in a large firm is responsible for its own section of the Web site. A customized version of Dreamweaver could include a predefined site and disable the Define Site commands in the Site menu, as well as offer a specialized menu for calling up help screens, tied to the standard F1 keyboard shortcut for Help.

In addition to the fully open architecture of the menus.xml file, new command menu items, created by the History palette, can be managed right in the Document window. Before we delve into the relatively more complex menus.xml structure, let's take a look at the Edit Command List function.

Handling History palette commands

Whenever you save a series of History palette steps as a command, it is instantly added to the bottom of the Commands menu list. Dreamweaver enables you to manage these custom added items—renaming them or deleting them—through the Edit Command List feature.

To manage History palette recorded commands, follow these steps:

1. Choose Commands ➪ Edit Command List.

   The Edit Command List dialog box appears as shown in Figure 21-3.

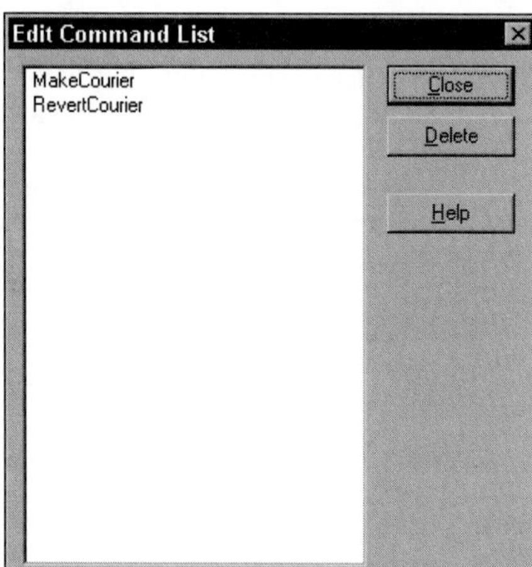

Figure 21-3: Manage your recorded commands through the Edit Command List dialog box.

2. To remove a command, select it and choose Delete.
3. To rename a command, select it and enter the new name or alter the existing one.

The Edit Command List affects only those commands saved from the History palette. To manage other commands—whether included in Dreamweaver or added later—you have to alter the menus.xml file, as discussed in the following section. This procedure is also required to reorder the Commands menu list.

Adjusting the Menu XML file

When Dreamweaver is launched, the menus.xml file is read by the program and the menu system is built. You can even customize menus.xml and then reload the file from within Dreamweaver—and instantly update your menu and shortcuts. The key, of course, is in editing the XML file.

Before you begin editing the menus.xml file, it's important that you create a backup of the file. The syntax for menus.xml is fairly sophisticated, and Dreamweaver ignores any incorrect entries, which could result in numerous menu items being made inoperative. Also, it's best to use a robust text editor, rather than Dreamweaver itself, to make changes to the menus.xml file.

The typical procedure for changing an existing menu item or shortcut is to open the file in a text editor (after having made a backup of the original) and make the necessary changes. When adding menus or menu items, you need to follow the file's syntax, as described in the following sections.

Generic shortcuts

The menus.xml file is divided into two main sections: `<shortcutlist>` and `<menubar>`. The `<shortcutlist>` divisions are, as you might suspect, a list of keyboard shortcuts, while the `<menubar>` areas are concerned with the various menu bars, in the main Document window, in the Site window (Windows only), and the numerous context menus. `<shortcutlist>` and `<menubar>` share several characteristics. They both follow the same basic structure:

```
<shortcutlist id=shortcutListID>
   <shortcut attributeName = value/>
   <shortcut attributeName = value/>
   <shortcut attributeName = value/>
</shortcutlist>

<menubar name=name id=menubarID platform=win|mac>
   <menu attributeName = value>
        <menuitem attributeName = value/>
        <menuitem attributeName = value/>
        <menuitem attributeName = value/>
   </menu>
</menubar>
```

Shortcuts for menu items are primarily defined within the `<menubar>` code; the `<shortcutlist>` is primarily concerned with those shortcuts that do not have a menu item associated with them, such as moving from one word to another. By default, Dreamweaver defines four `<shortcutlist>` sections: one for the Document window, the Site window (Windows only), the HTML Source Inspector, and the Timeline Inspector.

The key difference between the `<shortcutlist>` and the `<menubar>` sections is that while you can define new menu items or change existing ones in the `<menubar>` portion of the code, you can only alter existing shortcuts—you cannot add new shortcuts.

Each `<shortcutlist>` tag has one required attribute, the ID. The ID refers to a specific window or floating palette and must be unique within the `<shortcutlist>` section. The same ID is repeated in the `<menubar>` section to refer to the same window or palette. For example, the Document window ID is `DWMainWindow`, while the one for the context menu of the Timeline Inspector is `DWTimelineContext`. The `<shortcutlist>` tag can also have another attribute, platform, which must be set to either win or mac, for Windows and Macintosh systems, respectively. If no platform attribute is listed, the <shortcutlist> described applies to both platforms. Here, for example, is the beginning of the shortcutlist definition for the Site window, which only appears in the Windows version of the software:

```
<shortcutlist id="DWMainSite" platform="win">
```

A separate <shortcut> tag exists for every keystroke defined in the <shortcutlist>. The <shortcut> tag defines the key used, the tag's ID, the command or file to be executed when the keyboard shortcut is pressed, and the applicable platform, if any. Shortcuts can be defined for single special keys or key combinations using modifiers. The special keys are:

✦ F1 through F12

✦ PgDn, PgUp, Home, End

✦ Ins, Del, BkSp, Space

✦ Esc and Tab

Modifiers can be used in combination with standard keys, special keys, or themselves. A combination keyboard shortcut is indicated with a plus sign between keys. Available modifiers include those described in Table 21-1.

Table 21-1
Dreamweaver Shortcut Modifier Keys

Key	*Example*	*Use*
Cmd	Command+S	Indicates the Ctrl (Windows) and the Command (Macintosh) key modifier
Alt or Opt	Alt+V; Option+V	Indicates the Alt (Windows) or Option (Macintosh) key modifier
Shift	Shift+F1	Indicates the Shift key on both platforms
Ctrl	Ctrl+U	Indicates the Ctrl (Windows) or Control (Macintosh)

You can also combine multiple modifiers, as in this example:

```
Cmd+Shift+Z
```

The balance of the <shortcut> tag is identical in format to that used in the <menuitem> tag and is described in the section that follows.

Menubar definitions

Each <menubar> section of the menus.xml file describes a different menu strip, either on a window or the context menu associated with a floating palette. Nested within the <menubar> tag are a series of <menu> tags, each detailing a drop-down menu. The individual menu items are defined in the <menuitem> tags contained within each <menu> tags. Here, for example, is the context menu for the HTML Styles palette (I've abbreviated the complete <menuitem> tag for clarity):

```
<menubar name="" id="DWHtmlStyleContext">
    <menu name="HTML Style Popup" id="DWContext_HTMLStyle">
        <menuitem name="Edit..." />
        <menuitem name="Duplicate..." />
        <menuitem name="Delete" />
        <menuitem name="Apply" />
        <separator />
        <menuitem name="New..." />
    </menu>
</menubar>
```

<menubar> and <menu> tags are alike in that they both require a name—which is what appears in the menu system—and an ID. The ID must be unique within the <menubar> structure to avoid conflicts. If a conflict is found (that is, if one item has the same ID as another), the first item in the XML file is recognized, and the second item is ignored.

Note You can put a dividing line between your menu items by including a <separator/> tag between any two <menuitem> tags.

Numerous other attributes exist for the <menuitem> tag. The required attributes are name, ID, and either file or command as marked with an asterisk in Table 21-2.

Table 21-2
Menuitem Tag Attributes

Attribute	*Possible Value*	*Description*
name*	Any menu name	The name of the menu item as it appears on the menu. An underscore character causes the following letter to be underlined for Windows' shortcuts – for example, "_Frames" becomes "Frames."
id*	Any unique name	The identifying term for the menu item.
key	Any special key or keyboard key plus modifier(s)	The keyboard shortcut used to execute the command.

Attribute	Possible Value	Description
platform	win or mac	The operating system valid for the current menuitem. If the platform parameter is omitted, the menuitem is applicable for both systems.
enabled	JavaScript function	If present, governs whether a menu item is active (the function returns true) or dimmed (the function returns false). Including enabled=true assures that the function is always available.
command* (required if file is not used) for simple functions.	JavaScript function	Executed when the menu item is selected. This inline JavaScript function capability is used
file* (required if command is not used)	Path to a JavaScript file	The JavaScript file is executed when the menu item is selected; the path is relative to the Configuration folder.
checked	JavaScript function	Displays a checkmark next to the menu item if the function returns true.
dynamic	N/A	Specifies that the menu item is set dynamically by the function(s) found in the file.

The menus.xml file is quite extensive. The main menu for Dreamweaver—the one you most likely want to modify—can be found by searching for the second instance of its ID, DWMainWindow. The first instance is used by the corresponding <shortcutlist> tag.

You can create submenus by nesting one set of <menu> tags within another. For example, here's a simplified look at the File ➪ Import commands, as structured in menus.xml:

```
<menu name="_File" id="DWMenu_File">
[other menu items...]
   <menu name="_Import" id="DWMenu_File_Import">
      <menuitem name="Import _XML into Template..."/>
      <menuitem name="Import _Word HTML..."/>
      <menuitem name="Import _Table Data..."    />
   </menu>
[other menu items...]
</menu>
```

Note how within the <menu> tag that defines the File menu, another <menu> tag defining the Import submenu is nested.

Although it wasn't available at the time of this writing, Macromedia is reported to be working on a menu manager extension to automate the modification of the menus. Check the Dreamweaver Exchange Web site for its availability.

Building menu commands

When examining the menu.xml file, you'll notice that many of the menu items have JavaScript functions written right into the `<menuitem>` tag, such as this one for File ➪ Open:

```
<menuitem name="_New" key="Cmd+N" enabled="true" command="dw.createDocument()" ¬
id="DWMenu_File_New" />
```

Here, when the user selects File ➪ New, Dreamweaver executes the API function, `dw.createDocument()` in what is referred to as a *menu command.* Menu commands are used to specify the action of every menu item; what makes them unique is that they can be used to create and activate dynamic menus. Dynamic menus update according to user selections; the Preview in Browser browser list and HTML Styles menu items are both dynamic menus.

A menu command, like most of the other Dreamweaver extensions, is a combination of HTML and JavaScript. If the menu command is extensive and cannot be referenced as one or two functions directly in the menus.xml file, it is contained in an HTML file, stored in the Configuration\Menus folder. Menu commands can even use a dialog box like standard commands for accepting user input.

Many examples of menu commands written by the Dreamweaver engineers are to be found in the MM subfolder of the Menus folder.

Menu commands have access to all of the Dreamweaver API functions and a few of their own. None of the seven menu command API functions, listed in Table 21-3, are required, and three are automatically called when the menu command is executed.

Table 21-3
Command Menu API Functions

Function	*Returns*	*Description*
`canAcceptCommand()`	Boolean	Determines whether the menu item is active or dimmed.

Function	Returns	Description
commandButtons()	An array of labels and unctions, separated by commas	Sets the name and effect of buttons on the dialog box.
getDynamicContent()	An array of menu item names and unique IDs, separated by a semicolon	Sets the current listing for a menu.
isCommandChecked()	Boolean	Adds a checkmark next to item if true is returned.
receiveArguments()	N/A	Handles any arguments passed by <menuitem> tag.
setMenuText()	A text string	Sets the name of the menu item according to the given function. Not to be used in conjunction with getDynamicContent().
windowDimensions()	"Width,Height" (in pixels)	Determines the dimensions of the dialog box.

Working with Custom Tags

With the advent of XML—in which no standard tags exist—the capability to handle custom tags is essential in a Web authoring tool. Dreamweaver incorporates this capability through its third-party tag feature. After you've defined a third-party tag, Dreamweaver displays it in the Document window by highlighting its content, inserting a user-defined icon, or neither. Third-party tags are easily selected through the Tag Selector on the status bar and, thus, easy to cut, copy, and paste or otherwise manipulate. Perhaps most important, once a third-party tag is defined, you can apply a custom Property Inspector that permits tag attributes to be entered in a standardized user interface.

Third-party tags can be defined directly within Dreamweaver. Just as Object files use HTML to structure HTML code for easy insertion, Dreamweaver uses XML to make an XML definition for the custom tag. A custom tag declaration consists solely of one tag, <tagspec>, with up to seven attributes. The attributes for <tagspec> are as follows:

✦ **tag_name:** Defines the name of the tag as used in the markup. Any valid name—no spaces or special characters allowed—is possible. A tag with the attribute tag_name="invoice" is entered in the document as <invoice>.

✦ **tag_type:** Determines whether the tag has a closing tag (nonempty) and is thus capable of enclosing content or if the tag describes the content itself (empty). For example, the <invoice> tag could have a tag_type="nonempty" because all the content is between <invoice> and </invoice>.

✦ **render_contents:** Sets whether the contents of a nonempty type tag are displayed or not. The render_contents attribute value is either true or false; if false, the tag's icon is displayed instead of the contents.

✦ **content_model:** Establishes valid placement and content for the tag in the document. The three possible options are as follows:

- **block_model:** Tags defined with content_model="block_model" only appear in the <body> section of a document and contain block-level HTML tags, such as <p>, <div>, <blockquote>, and <pre>.
- **head_model:** To define a tag that appears in the <head> section and can contain text, set content_model="head_model".
- **marker_model:** Tags with the attribute content_model=marker_model are capable of being placed anywhere in the document with no restrictions on content. The marker_model value is most often used for inline tags that are placed within a paragraph or division.
- **script_model:** Like the marker_model, script_model tags can be placed in either the <head> or <body> section. All content within a script_model tag is ignored by Dreamweaver, which permits server-specific scripts to be included without alteration.

✦ **start_string:** The initial delimiter for a custom string-delimited tag; start_string and end_string must both be defined if one is declared. Lasso tags, for example use a start_string of an left bracket, [.

✦ **end_string:** The closing delimiter for a custom string-delimited tag. The end_string for a Lasso tag is the right bracket,].

✦ **detect_in_attribute:** A Boolean value that sets whether or not Dreamweaver should ignore string-delimited tags used as attributes in other tags. While the default is false, for most string-delimited functions, the detect_in_attribute value should be set to true.

✦ **parse_attribute:** A Boolean value that determines if Dreamweaver should inspect and parse the attributes within string-delimited tags. By default, Dreamweaver parses all attributes; set parse_attribute to false to force Dreamweaver to ignore the attributes.

✦ **icon:** Empty tags or nonempty custom tags with render_content disabled require a GIF file to act as an icon in the Document window. The icon attribute should be set to any valid URL, relative or absolute (as in icon="images/invoice.gif").

✦ **icon_width:** Sets the width in pixels of the icon used to represent the tag. The value can be any positive integer.

✦ **icon_height:** Sets the height in pixels of the icon used to represent the tag. The value can be any positive integer.

The icons used by Dreamweaver to represent the Invisible Elements such as the `<br>` tag are 16 pixels wide by 14 pixels high.

Here's the complete code for a sample custom tag, the Cold Fusion Directory tag:

```
<tagspec tag_name="CFDIRECTORY" tag_type="empty" render_contents="false" ¬
content_model="marker_model" icon="ColdFusion.gif" icon_width="16" ¬
icon_height="16"></tagspec>
```

You can see an example of the Cold Fusion custom tags in Figure 21-4.

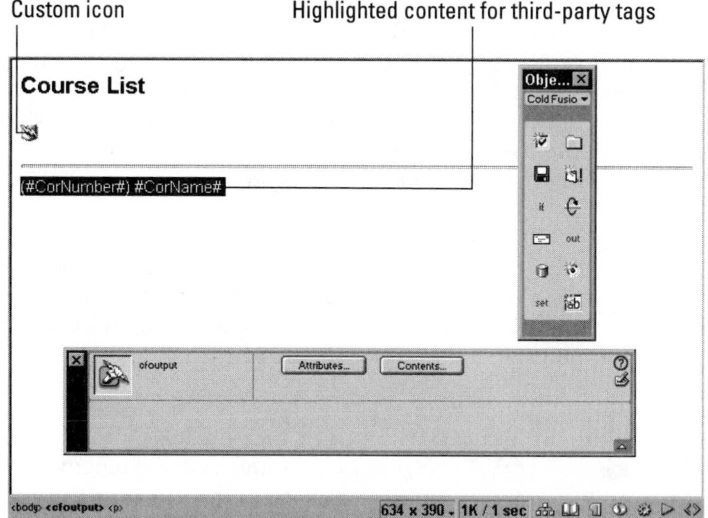

Figure 21-4: Third-party tags such as these from Cold Fusion can be displayed – and manipulated – in the Document window.

If the content is to be rendered for a custom tag, you can easily view it in the Document window by enabling the Third-Party Tags Highlighting option in Preferences. Make sure that View ➪ Invisible Elements is enabled.

Once a custom tag is defined, the definition is saved in an XML file in the ThirdPartyTags folder, found in the Configuration directory. If you are establishing a number of custom tags, you can place all the definitions in the same file. Macromedia refers to this as the Tag DB or Database.

Andrew Wooldridge has created an extremely useful command called `Build_Custom_Tag` for defining XML third-party tags. You can find it CD-ROM 1 that accompanies this book.

Customizing Property Inspectors

The Property Inspector is used throughout Dreamweaver to display the current attributes of many different types of tags: text, images, layers, plug-ins, and so on. Not only do Property Inspectors make it easy to see the particulars for an object, they make it a snap to modify the same parameters. With the inclusion of custom tags in Dreamweaver, the capability to add custom Property Inspectors is a natural parallel. Moreover, you can create custom Property Inspectors for existing tags, which display in place of the built-in Property Inspectors.

Like objects, commands, and behaviors, custom Property Inspectors are composed of HTML and JavaScript; the Property Inspector HTML file itself is stored in the Configuration\Inspectors folder. However, the layout of the Property Inspector is far more restrictive than it is with the other Dreamweaver extensions. The dialog box for an object, command, or behavior can be any size or shape desired — any custom Property Inspector must fit the standard Property Inspector dimensions and design. Because of the precise positioning necessary to insert parameter form items such as text boxes and drop-down menu lists, layers are used extensively to create the layout.

Quite elaborate Property Inspectors are possible. The XSSI IF Property Inspector built by Webmonkey, shown in Figure 21-5, has three separate tabs (based on layers) for accessing different possible parameters of the object. Property Inspectors, like other extension types, can also incorporate CSS styles, Flash movies, and Shockwave files.

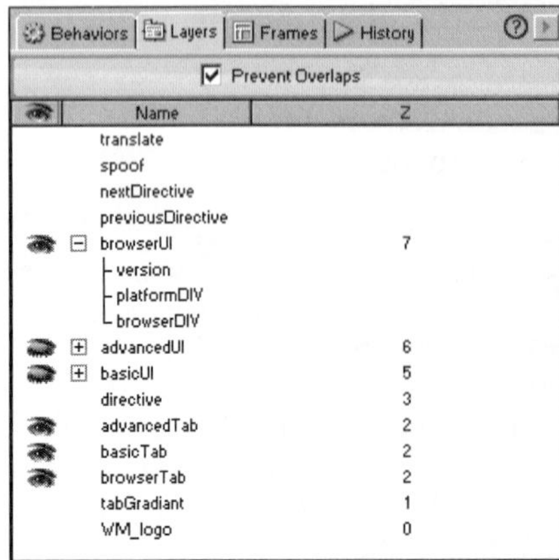

Figure 21-5: Some custom Property Inspectors, such as this one from Webmonkey, take advantage of Dreamweaver's layer and CSS styles support.

Coding a Property Inspector

Like many of the other standard extension files, most of the Property Inspector files that ship with Dreamweaver are composed of an HTML file that calls a separate JavaScript file. It is entirely possible, however, to combine HTML and JavaScript into a single file. No matter how it's structured, a custom Property Inspector HTML file needs three key elements to be properly defined:

- ✦ An initial HTML comment line that identifies which tag the Property Inspector is for.
- ✦ The function `canInspectSelection()`, which determines if the Property Inspector should be displayed according to the current selection.
- ✦ A second function, `inspectSelection()`, that updates the tag's HTML when new values are entered in the Property Inspector.

If any of these elements are missing or incorrectly declared, Dreamweaver ignores the file and does not display the Property Inspector.

In addition to the mandatory functions and definition, custom Property Inspectors are capable of using any of the other Dreamweaver JavaScript functions described in Chapter 20, with the exception of the `getBehaviorTag()` and `getBehaviorElement` functions. If you include the `displayHelp()` function, a small question mark in a circle appears in the upper-right corner of your custom Property Inspector, which, when selected by the user, executes whatever routines your Help function has declared.

The Property Inspector definition

The initial HTML comment — placed above the `<html>` tag — defines the Property Inspector. More than one Property Inspector can be defined for a particular tag, making it possible for separate inspectors to be used if different attributes are specified. Therefore, each Property Inspector is assigned a priority that determines the one to be displayed. Property Inspectors are further defined by whether the current selection is within the tag indicated or contains the entire tag; this feature enables two different Property Inspectors to be defined, as with the `<table>` tag. Finally, optional graphic elements are definable: a horizontal line to delineate the upper and lower portions of a Property Inspector, and a vertical line to separate the object's name from the other parts of the Property Inspector.

The Property Inspector definition follows this syntax:

```
<!-- tag:ID,priority:Number,selection:Type,hline,vline -->
```

For example, the Property Inspector for the `<link>` tag (a `<head>` element) is defined like this:

```
<!-- tag:LINK,priority:5,selection:within,vline,hline -->
```

The individual sections of the definition are as follows:

✦ **tag:** The name of the tag for which the Property Inspector is intended. Although it's not mandatory, the tag name is customarily uppercased. The tag ID can also be one of three keywords: *COMMENT*, when a comment class tag is indicated; *LOCKED*, when a locked region is to be inspected; or *ASP*, for all ASP elements.

The asterisks on either side of the tag keywords are mandatory.

✦ **priority:** The priority of a Property Inspector is given as a number from 1 to 10. The highest priority, 10, means that this Property Inspector takes precedence over any other possible Property Inspectors. The lowest priority, 1, marks the Property Inspector as the one to use when no other Property Inspector is available.

An example of how `priority` is used can be found in the `<meta>` tag and the Description and Keyword objects. The Property Inspectors for Description and Keyword have a higher priority than the one for the basic `<meta>` tag, which permits those inspectors to be shown initially if the proper criteria is met; if the criteria is *not* met, the Property Inspector for the `<meta>` tag is displayed.

✦ **selection:** Depending on the current selection, the cursor is either within a particular tag or exactly enclosing it. The selection attribute is set to within or exact, according to the condition under which the Property Inspector should be displayed.

✦ **hline:** Inserts a one-pixel horizontal gray line (see Figure 21-6) dividing the upper and lower halves of the expanded Property Inspector.

✦ **vline:** Places a one-pixel vertical gray line (see Figure 21-6) between the tag's name field and the other properties on the upper half of the Property Inspector.

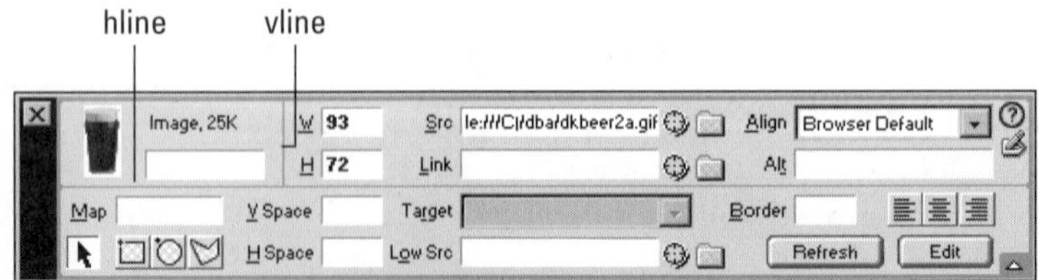

Figure 21-6: The Property Inspector for the `<img>` tag uses both the `hline` and `vline` attributes.

The canInspectSelection() function

To control the circumstances under which your custom Property Inspector is displayed, use the `canInspectSelection()` function. Like `canAcceptBehavior()` and `canAcceptCommand()` for behaviors and commands, respectively, if `canInspectSelection()` returns true, the Property Inspector is shown; if it returns false, the custom Property Inspector is not shown.

As noted earlier, the `canInspectSelection()` function is mandatory. If no conditions exist under which the Property Inspector should not be displayed, use the following code:

```
function canInspectSelection(){
  return true;
}
```

Several of the standard Dreamweaver `<head>` elements have Property Inspector files that use the `canInspectSelection()` function to limit access to specific tags. In this example, drawn from the `<meta>` Description object, the current selection is examined to see if a `<meta>` tag is selected, and the `name` attribute is set to description:

```
function canInspectSelection(){
  var selArr=dreamweaver.getSelection();
  var metaObj = dreamweaver.offsetsToNode(selArr[0],selArr[1]);
  return (metaObj.tagName && metaObj.tagName == "META" &&
        metaObj.getAttribute("name") &&
    metaObj.getAttribute("name").toLowerCase()=="description");
}
```

The inspectSelection() function

The `inspectSelection()` function is the workhorse of the custom Property Inspector code and is responsible for pulling the information from the selected tag for display in the various Property Inspector fields. Depending on the code design, the `inspectSelection()` function can also be used to update the HTML code when the attribute values are modified in the Property Inspector.

Here's a simple example of how the `inspectSelection()` function is used, drawn from the Link Property Inspector file:

```
function inspectSelection(){
  var Href = findObject("Href");

  if (linkObj.getAttribute("href"))
    Href.value=linkObj.getAttribute("href");
  else
    Href.value = "";
}
```

In this example, if an attribute (`href`) exists, its value is assigned to the Property Inspector's appropriate text box value (`Href.value`). The remainder of the `inspectSelection()` function for the `<link>` tag consists of a series of statements like those in the example code.

You can design a Property Inspector that displays a different interface depending on whether or not it is expanded, as the Keywords Property Inspector does. If an inspector is not expanded, the `argument(0)` property is set to the value `min`; when it is expanded, `argument(0)` is equal to the value `max`.

Many Property Inspectors update their HTML tags when a change occurs in one of the input boxes. No real standard method exists to accomplish this, due to the many possible variations with Property Inspectors. However, one of the most commonly used events is `onBlur()`, as in this example, again taken from the Link Property Inspector file:

```
<input type="text" name="Rel" onBlur="setLinkTag()" style="width:120">
```

The `setLinkTag()` function that is called is a local one that reads the new value in the current text box and sets it equal to the corresponding attribute.

Designing a Property Inspector

All the attributes for a Property Inspector must fit into a tightly designed space. While it's helpful to look at examples found in the Inspectors folder, many of the standard Property Inspectors are built-in to the core functionality of the program and are not immediately accessible on the design level. The following specifications and tips are offered to make it easier to design your own custom Property Inspectors:

- ✦ The full dimensions of available layout space in a Property Inspector are 482 pixels wide by 87 pixels high.
- ✦ The top (unexpanded) portion of the Property Inspector is 42 pixels high, while the bottom portion is 44 pixels high.
- ✦ If the `hline` attribute is specified in the Property Inspector definition, a single-pixel line is drawn the entire width of the Inspector, 43 pixels from the top.
- ✦ If the `vline` attribute is specified, a single-pixel line is drawn across the top half of the Property Inspector, 118 pixels from the left.
- ✦ The background color for the Property Inspector is a light gray, which translates into #D0D0D0FF in hexadecimal, or an RGB value of 208, 208, 208.
- ✦ The default text displayed within a Property Inspector is from the Arial, Helvetica, sans-serif font families, sized at 9 points. If you enter text with the standard default text selected, it is rendered in this style.

✦ The image placed on the upper left of the Property Inspector is generally sized at 36 pixels square and placed 3 pixels from the top and 2 pixels from the left. Although you are under no requirement to keep this size image — or its placement — following these guidelines helps make your custom Property Inspectors resemble the standard Dreamweaver ones.

✦ It's a good idea to lay out your Property Inspector with the View ➪ Invisible Elements command disabled. The small icons that indicate layers can alter the perceived spacing.

✦ Keep the Layers palette visible. Many custom Property Inspectors use multiple layers to position the elements exactly — several of the Webmonkey-designed XSSI Property Inspectors employ upwards of 20 layers, as shown in Figure 21-7 — and the Layers palette makes selecting individual layers for adjustment a snap.

✦ Use nested layers to position and group associated items in the Property Inspector. Almost all form objects used in Property Inspectors for user input, such as text boxes and drop-down lists, are identified by labels. Placing both label and text boxes in their own layers, while grouping them under one parent layer, provides maximum flexibility and ease of placement.

✦ Apply CSS styles within the Property Inspector to easily manage font sizes and design your Property Inspector in a WYSIWYG environment.

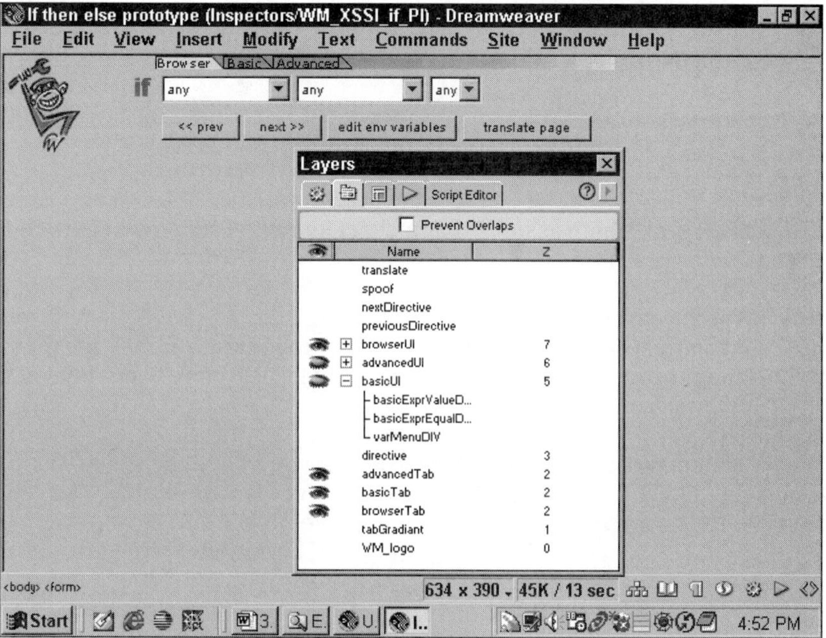

Figure 21-7: Property Inspectors, such as Webmonkey's custom XSSI IF inspector, use absolute and relative layers to position layout components and toggle different options.

Making Custom Floaters

Property Inspectors are an excellent way to manage the attributes of most elements in a single consistent user interface. The Property Inspector user interface, however, is not the best solution for all situations. Recognizing this, the Macromedia engineers have introduced a new extension for Dreamweaver 3: floaters.

A floater—short for *floating palette*—is a cross between a Property Inspector and a command. Like Property Inspectors, floaters can stay on the screen while you work on the Web page; like commands, floaters are not restricted to a set size and shape. Custom floaters have the same basic interface as standard Dreamweaver floating palettes. Any floating palette can be resized or grouped with other floating palettes, standard or custom. Once grouped, a custom floater also has a tab which, when selected, brings the floater interface to the front. The only minor difference between a built-in and a custom floating palette is that only the standard floaters can have icons in the tabs; custom floaters display only their names.

Floaters, like most other extensions, are a combination of HTML and JavaScript: HTML is the main file that is called and provides the user interface via an HTML form, while JavaScript provides the functionality from the `<head>` of the HTML page. Floaters are stored in the Configuration\Floaters folder. However, unlike commands or objects, it's not enough just to save your custom floater in a particular folder to make it accessible. A function that displays the floater, either `dw.setFloaterVisibility(floaterName,true)` or `dw.toggleFloater(floaterName)` must be called. Most often these functions are called from a `<menuitem>` tag in the menus.xml file, as with this custom floater:

```
<menuitem name="HelpBuilder" enabled="true" ¬
command="dw.toggleFloater('helpBuilder')" ¬
checked="dw.getFloaterVisibility('helpBuilder')" />
```

The checked attribute assures that a checkmark is displayed next to the menu item if the floater is visible.

When naming your custom floater, be sure to avoid names reserved for Dreamweaver's built-in floaters: objects, properties, launcher, site files, site map, library, css styles, html styles, behaviors, timelines, html, layers, frames, templates, or history.

As indicated in the preceding paragraphs, floaters have their own API functions, and several methods of the Dreamweaver object are applicable. The API functions, none of which are required, are listed in Table 21-4:

Table 21-4
Floater API Functions

Function	*Returns*	*Use*
`documentEdited()`	N/A	Executes after the current document has been edited.
`selectionChanged()`	N/A	Executes after the current selection has been altered.
`initialPosition(platform)`	A string in the format "left,top"	Sets the position of the floater onscreen when it is first called. If left onscreen when Dreamweaver quits, it reopens in the last location.
`initialTabs()`	A string in the format "floater1,floater2"	Indicates what other floaters are grouped with the current floater when it first appears.

Macromedia strongly cautions programmers from using `documentEdited()` and `selectionChanged()` unless absolutely needed. Both functions—because they constantly watch the document—can have an adverse affect on performance if implemented. Macromedia suggests programmers incorporate the `setTimeout()` method to temporarily pause these functions so that the user can continue to interact with the program.

Within the Dreamweaver API are two pairs of methods and a single function, which relate to floaters:

✦ `getHideAllFloaters()`: Reads the Show/Hide Floating palette menu option state to determine if all floaters should be hidden (true) or shown (false).

✦ `setHideAllFloaters()`: Sets the Show/Hide Floating palette to a particular state to Hide (true) or Show (false).

✦ `getFloaterVisibility(floaterName)`: Reads whether the given floater is currently displayed and frontmost (true) or hidden (false).

✦ `setFloaterVisibility(floaterName,isVisible)`: Brings the named floater forward if the `isVisible` argument is true.

✦ `toggleFloater(floaterName)`: Toggles the visibility state of the given floater between hiding and bringing to the front.

Floaters have a great deal of potential with their flexible interface and constant onscreen presence. The example shown in Figure 21-8, built by Brendan Dawes, scans an entire Web site, looking for an item with an attached Design Note and then lists the object, with its keys and values.

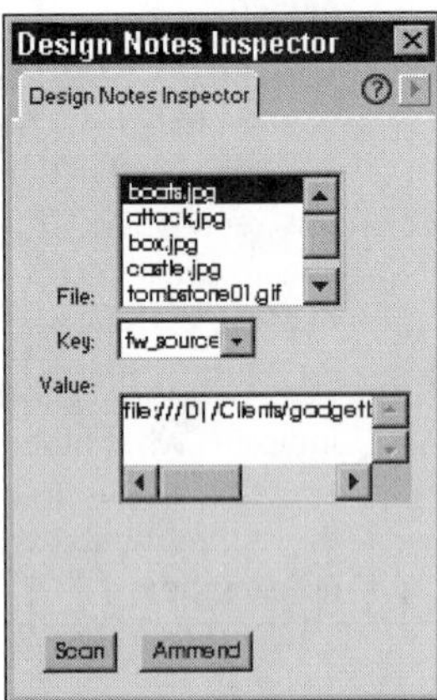

Figure 21-8: Brendan Dawes' custom floater shows all available design notes within a site.

Developing Translators

In order for any markup tag to be depicted in the Document window — whether it's `<b>` for bold or a custom third-party tag such as Tango's `<@cols>` — it must be translated. Dreamweaver's built-in rendering system translates all the standard HTML code, along with a few special custom tags such as those for ASP and Cold Fusion. However, in order to display any other custom tags, or those that perform special functions such as server-side includes, a special translator must be built.

As part of its expansion efforts, Dreamweaver permits the inclusion of custom translators. This enhancement enables programs that output nonstandard HTML to be displayed onscreen integrated with the regular code. One of Dreamweaver's main claims to fame is its capability to accept code without rewriting it. With Dreamweaver translators, custom code can not only be inserted but also shown — and edited — visually.

Here's a brief overview of how translators work:

1. When Dreamweaver starts, all the properly coded translators in the Configuration\Translators folder are initialized.
2. If a document is loaded with nonstandard HTML, the code is checked against the installed translators.
3. The Translator Preferences are examined. Should the translator in question be set for automatic translation, the next step is carried through. Otherwise, the translation does not take place until the user chooses Modify ➪ Translate ➪ *TranslatorName*.
4. The code is processed with the translator and temporarily converted to a format acceptable to Dreamweaver.
5. Dreamweaver renders the code onscreen.
6. If a change is made to the page, Dreamweaver retranslates the document and refreshes the screen. (Numerous other conditions can occur under which Dreamweaver translates a page, all of which are detailed in the following section, "Enabling Translators.")
7. When the page is saved, the temporary translation is discarded, and the original code, with any modifications, is stored.

Developers continue to break new ground with the use of translators. Some of the translators that have been developed so far include those for the following:

✦ **Server-Side Includes:** Standard with Dreamweaver, the SSI translator effortlessly inserts at design time files that you normally don't see until delivered by the Web server. (To learn more about SSI, see Chapter 34.)

✦ **XSSI:** The Extended Server-Side Include (XSSI) extension, developed by Webmonkey authors Alx, Nadav, and Taylor for Macromedia, includes a translator that brings the Apache-served code right in the Document window. (See the XSSI sidebar in Chapter 34.)

✦ **Live Picture:** The code for a Live Picture graphic, which enables panning and zooming, is structured inside a `<meta>` tag. The translator for this code incorporates a temporary JPEG representation of the more detailed image in the page for a smoother design session. (You can find details on the Live Picture enhancement in Chapter 31.)

✦ **Tango:** Developed by Pervasive Software, the Tango translator compensates for differences between their database-oriented code and standard HTML. Additionally, Tango includes a manually controlled Sample Data translator that enables the Web designer to view the page complete with example database output. (Tango is covered in Chapter 32.)

Enabling translators

As noted earlier, you can determine when you want a particular translator to do its job. Translation can be fully automatic or completely manual — or one of several states in between. You can even determine the order in which the translators look at a page. All of these features are controlled by the Translation panel in the Dreamweaver Preferences dialog box.

Some extensions handle the translator setup automatically; others require that you specify certain translation options before the custom translator is fully enabled. To access the Translator controls, choose Edit ➪ Preferences and select the Translation category. The Translation panel, as shown in Figure 21-9, appears.

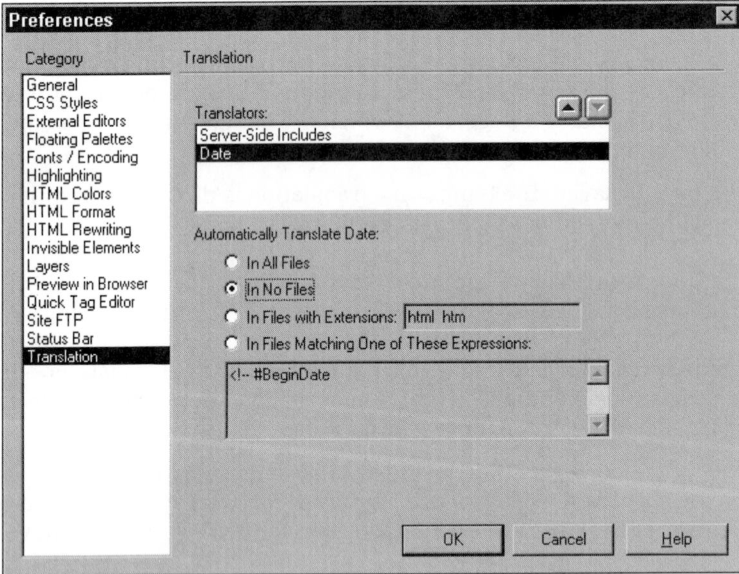

Figure 21-9: Setting your Translation preferences gives you control over results appearing in the Document window.

Four basic possibilities exist for automatic translation to occur:

✦ **In All Files:** Translation takes place whenever a modification or other qualifying condition (as noted in the following section) takes place.

✦ **In No Files:** The user must select the proper Translate command from the menu.

✦ **In Files with Extensions:** Translation is limited to specific file types, as identified by their file extension.

✦ **In Files Matching One of These Expressions:** Translation takes place only if the code includes one of the Regular Expressions listed. (Regular Expressions are a Find and Replace technology discussed in Chapter 9.)

Sometimes it's necessary for one translator to set the stage for another. In these cases, you can select a particular translator from the list and use the up and down arrows to move it higher or lower on the list. The higher translators are invoked before the lower ones.

For all but the manual option (In No Files), the translation is triggered by any of the following events in Dreamweaver:

✦ A file is opened

✦ A change is made in the HTML Inspector and then refreshed in the Document window.

✦ An object is inserted through the Objects palette or the Insert menu.

✦ The Document window is updated after a change to the current file has occurred in another application such as HomeSite or BBEdit.

✦ A dependent file, such as an image, is edited, and the modifications are stored.

✦ The `innerHTML` or `outerHTML` property of any tag object, or the data property of any comment object, is set in a DOM-related JavaScript function.

✦ The properties of an object are altered.

✦ Any of the conversion or layout commands are chosen: Convert ➪ 3.0 Browser Compatible, Convert ➪ Tables to Layers, Layout ➪ Reposition Content Using Layers, or Layout ➪ Convert Tables to Layers.

To manually trigger a translation, choose Modify ➪ Translate ➪ *TranslatorName*, where *TranslatorName* is any of the installed custom translators.

Translator functions

Like other Dreamweaver extensions such as behaviors and commands, translators are HTML files with JavaScript. Translators have no user interface. Other than deciding when to invoke it, you have no parameters to set or options to choose from; all the pertinent code is in the `<head>` section of a translator. In the translator's `<head>`, along with any necessary support routines, you can find two essential JavaScript functions: `getTranslatorInfo()` and `translateMarkup()`. Any other Dreamweaver JavaScript API functions not specific to behaviors can be used in a translator as well.

Due to the limitations of JavaScript, much of the heart of custom translation is handled by specially written C-level extensions. These compiled code libraries enhance Dreamweaver's capabilities so that new data types can be integrated. C-level extensions are covered later in this chapter.

The getTranslatorInfo() function

The settings that appear for each selected translator in the Translation panel of Preferences are determined by the `getTranslatorInfo()` function. The function itself simply sets up and returns an array of text strings that are read by Dreamweaver during initialization.

The structure of the array is fairly rigid. The number of array elements is specified when the `Array` variable is declared, and a particular text string must correspond to the proper array element. The array order is as follows:

✦ ***translatorClass:*** The translator's unique name used in JavaScript functions. The name has to begin with a letter and can contain alphanumeric characters as well as hyphens or underscores.

✦ ***title:*** The title listed in the menu and the Translation panel. This text string can be no longer than 40 characters.

✦ ***nExtensions:*** The number of file extensions, such as .cfml, to follow. This declaration tells Dreamweaver how to read the next portion of the array. If this value is set to zero, then all files are acceptable.

✦ ***extension:*** The actual file extension without the leading period.

✦ ***nRegularExpressions:*** The number of regular expressions to be declared. Should this value be equal to zero, the array is closed.

✦ ***RegularExpression:*** The regular expression to be searched for by Dreamweaver.

The number of array elements — and thus, the detail of the function — depends entirely on the translator. Here, for example, is the code for `getTranslatorInfo()` from Live Picture's translator, where a file must have a particular `<meta>` tag to be translated:

```
function getTranslatorInfo(){
  returnArray = new Array( 5 )
  returnArray[0] = "FPX";      // translatorClass
  returnArray[1] = "Flashpix Image Translator";     // title
  returnArray[2] = "0"         // number of extensions
  returnArray[3] = "1";        // number of expressions
  returnArray[4] = "<meta http-equiv=\"refresh\" content=\"0;url=http://";
  return returnArray
}
```

By comparison, the standard SSI translator's `getTranslatorInfo()` function has 10 array elements, and Webmonkey's XSSI has 17.

The translateMarkup() function

While the `getTranslatorInfo()` function initializes the translator, the `translateMarkup()` function actually does the work. As noted earlier, most of the translators rely on a custom C-level extension to handle the inner workings of the function, but `translateMarkup()` provides the JavaScript shell.

The `translateMarkup()` function takes three arguments, which must be declared but whose actual values are provided by Dreamweaver:

- ✦ ***docName:*** The file URL for the file to be translated.
- ✦ ***siteRoot:*** The site root of the file to be translated. Should the file be outside the current site, the value would be empty.
- ✦ ***docContent:*** A text string with the code for the page to be translated.

Typically, the *docContent* text string is parsed using either JavaScript or a C-level extension within the `translateMarkup()` function that returns the translated document. This translated document is then displayed by Dreamweaver.

Here's the `translateMarkup()` function from the standard SSI translator:

```
function translateMarkup( docNameStr, siteRootStr, inStr ) {
  var outStr = ""
  if ( inStr.length > 0 )
  {
  outStr = SSITranslator.translateMarkup( docNameStr, siteRootStr, inStr )
  }
  return outStr
}
```

In this example, notice that the translated document in the form of `outStr` is created by the custom function `SSITranslator.translateMarkup()`. The `SSITranslator` portion of this function calls the C-level extension, built by Macromedia for this purpose.

Locking code

Translations are generally intended for onscreen presentation only. Although there's no rule saying that translated content can't be written out to disk, most applications need the original content to run. To protect the original content, Dreamweaver includes a special locking tag. This XML tag pair, `<MM:BeginLock>...<MM:EndLock>`, stops the enclosed content (the translation) from being edited, while simultaneously storing a copy of the original content in a special format.

The <MM:BeginLock> tag has several attributes:

✦ **translatorClass:** The identifying name of the translator as specified in getTranslatorInfo(). Required.

✦ **type:** The type or tag name for the markup to be translated.

✦ **depFiles:** A comma-separated list of any files on which the locked content depends. If any of the listed dependent files are altered, the page is retranslated.

✦ **orig:** A text string with the original markup before translation. The text string is encoded to include three standard HTML characters. The < becomes %3C;, the > becomes %3E;, and the quote character is converted to %22;.

To see how the special locking tag works, look at an example taken from the Tango Sample Data translator. Tango uses what are called "meta tags" that begin with an @ sign, such as the <@TOTALROWS> tag. The Tango Sample Data translator replaces what will be a result drawn from a database with a specified sample value. The original code is

```
<@TOTALROWS samptotalrows=23>
```

Once the code is translated, Dreamweaver refreshes the screen with this code:

```
<MM:BeginLock translatorClass="TANGO_SAMPLEDATA"  type ="@TOTALROWS" ¬
orig="%3C@TOTALROWS samptotalrows=23%3E">23<MM:EndLock>
```

The "23" in bold is the actual translated content that appears in Dreamweaver's Document window.

You don't actually see the locking code—even if you open the HTML Inspector when a page is translated. To view the code, select the translated item, copy it, and then paste it in another text application, or use the Paste As Text feature to see the results in Dreamweaver.

Extending C-Level Libraries

All programs have their limits. Most limitations are intentional and serve to focus the tool for a particular use. Some limitations are accepted because of programming budgets—for both money and time—with the hope that the boundaries can be exceeded in the next version. With Dreamweaver, one small section of those high, sharply defined walls has been replaced with a doorway: C-level extensions. With the proper programming acumen, you can customize Dreamweaver to add the capabilities you need.

Like most modern computer programs, the core of Dreamweaver is developed using C and C++, both low-level languages that execute much faster than any non-compiled language, such as JavaScript. Because C is a compiled language, you can't just drop in a function with a few lines of code and expect it to work—it has to be integrated into the program. The only possible way to add significant functionality is through another compiled component called a *library*. With the C-level extensions capability, Dreamweaver permits the incorporation of these libraries, known as DLLs (Dynamic Link Libraries) on Windows systems and CFMs (Code Fragment Managers) on Macintosh systems.

One excellent example of the extended library is `DWFile`. This C-level extension is used by several Dreamweaver partners, including RealNetworks and iCat, to perform tasks outside the capabilities of JavaScript; namely, reading and writing external text files. By adding this one library, Dreamweaver can now work with the support files necessary to power a wide range of associated programs. `DWFile` is described in detail later in this section.

C-level extensions are also used in combination with Dreamweaver's translator feature. As discussed earlier in this chapter, translators handle the chore of temporarily converting nonstandard code to HTML that Dreamweaver can present onscreen—while maintaining the original code in the file. Although much of this functionality isn't impossible for JavaScript, the conversion would be too slow to be effective. C-level extensions are definitely the way to go when looking for a powerful solution.

Programming in C or C++, as required by C-level extensions, is beyond the scope of this book. Developers are encouraged to examine Macromedia's Extending Dreamweaver PDF file found on the Dreamweaver Web site.

Calling a C-level extension

C-level extensions, properly stored in the Configuration\JSExtensions folder, are read into Dreamweaver during initialization when the program first starts. The routines contained within the custom libraries are accessed through JavaScript functions in commands, behaviors, objects, translators, and other Dreamweaver extensions.

Let's take a look at how Macromedia's C-level extensions `DWFile` is used. `DWFile` has seven main functions:

✦ **exists():** Checks to see if a specified file name exists. This function takes one argument, the file name.

✦ **read():** Reads a text file into a string for examination. This function also takes one argument, the file name.

- **write():** Outputs a string to a text file. This function has three arguments; the first two — the name of the file to be created and the string to be written — are required. The third, the mode, must be the word "append." This argument, if used, causes the string to be added to the end of the existing text file; otherwise, the file is overwritten.
- **getAttributes():** Returns the attributes of a specified file or folder. Possible attributes are R (read-only), D (directory), H (hidden), and S (system file or folder).
- **getModificationDate():** Returns the date a specified file or folder was last modified.
- **createFolder():** Creates a folder, given a file URL.
- **listFolder():** Lists the contents of a specified folder in an array. This function takes two arguments: the file URL of the desired folder (required) and a Keyword, either "files" (which returns just file names) or "directories" (which returns just directory names). If the Keyword argument is not used, you get both files and directories.

The following JavaScript function, which could be included in any Dreamweaver extension, uses `DWFile` to see if a file, named in a passed argument, exists. If it does, the contents are read and presented in an alert; if the file doesn't exist, the function creates it and writes out a brief message.

```
function fileWork(theFile) {
  var isFile = DWFile.exists(theFile)
  if (isFile) {
        alert(DWFile.read(theFile))
  } else {
    DWFile.write(theFile,"File Created by DWFile")
  }
}
```

Note how the C-level extension name, `DWFile`, is used to call the library and its internal functions. Once the library has been initialized, it can be addressed like any other internal function, and its routines are simply called as methods of the function using JavaScript dot notation, such as `DWFile.exists(theFile)`.

Building C-level extensions

A C-level extension must follow strict guidelines in order to be properly recognized by Dreamweaver. Specifically, two files must be included in the library when created in C, and each function must be declared for correct interpretation by Dreamweaver's JavaScript interpreter.

Macromedia engineers have developed a C-Level Extension API in the form of a C header, `mm_jsapi.h`. This header contains definitions for over 20 data types and functions. To insert `mm_jsapi.h` in your custom library, add the following statement:

```
#include "mm_jsapi.h"
```

You can find the latest version of `mm_jsapi.h` on the Dreamweaver Web site.

After you've included the JavaScript API header, you need to declare a specific macro, `MM_STATE`. This macro, contained within the `mm_jsapi.h` header, holds definitions necessary for the integration of the C-level extension into Dreamweaver's JavaScript API. The `MM_STATE` must be defined only once.

Each library can be composed of numerous functions available to be called from within Dreamweaver. For Dreamweaver's JavaScript interpreter to recognize the functions, each one must be declared in a special function, `JS_DefineFunction()`, defined in the library. All of the `JS_DefineFunction()` functions are contained in the `MM_Init()` function. The syntax for `JS_DefineFunction()` is as follows:

```
JS_DefineFunction(jsName, call, nArgs)
```

where *jsName* is the JavaScript name for the function, *call* is a pointer to a C-level function, and *nArgs* is the number of arguments that the function can expect. For example, the `MM_Init()` function for `DWFile` might look like this:

```
void
MM_Init()
{
  JS_DefineFunction("exist", exist, 1);
  JS_DefineFunction("read", exist, 1);
  JS_DefineFunction("write", exist, 2);
}
```

Because `MM_Init()` depends on definitions included in the C header, `mm_jsapi.h`, it must be called after the header is included.

Tip

If you're building cross-platform C-level extensions, consider using Metrowerks CodeWarrior integrated development environment. CodeWarrior can edit, compile, and debug C, C++, and even Java or Pascal for both Windows and Macintosh operating systems. Perhaps most important, Macromedia engineers used CodeWarrior to test C-level extensions.

Summary

Dreamweaver's commitment to professional Web site authoring is at its most profound when examining the program's customization capabilities. Virtually every Web site production house can benefit from some degree of personalization — and some clients absolutely require it. As you consider making your productive life easier by extending Dreamweaver, keep the following points in mind:

- Dreamweaver includes a full range of customizable features: objects, behaviors, commands, third-party tags, Property Inspectors, and translators. You can even extend the program's core feature set with the C-Level Extensibility option.
- You can use commands to affect any part of your HTML page and automate repetitive tasks.
- In addition to accessing custom commands through the Command menu, you can configure them as objects for inclusion in the Objects palette. You can also make a command appear in any other standard Dreamweaver menu by altering the CommandMenu.htm file.
- To make it easy to work with XML and other non-HTML tags, Dreamweaver enables you to create custom tags complete with individual icons or highlighted content.
- Attributes for third-party tags are viewable — and modifiable — by creating a custom Property Inspector.
- Dreamweaver's C-Level Extensibility feature enables C and C++ programmers to add new core functionality to a program.
- Tags from server-side applications can be viewed in the Document window, just as they would be when browsed online, when a custom translator is used. A custom translator often requires a C-level extension.

In the next chapter, you see how Dreamweaver and Fireworks work closely together to smooth your workflow.

✦ ✦ ✦

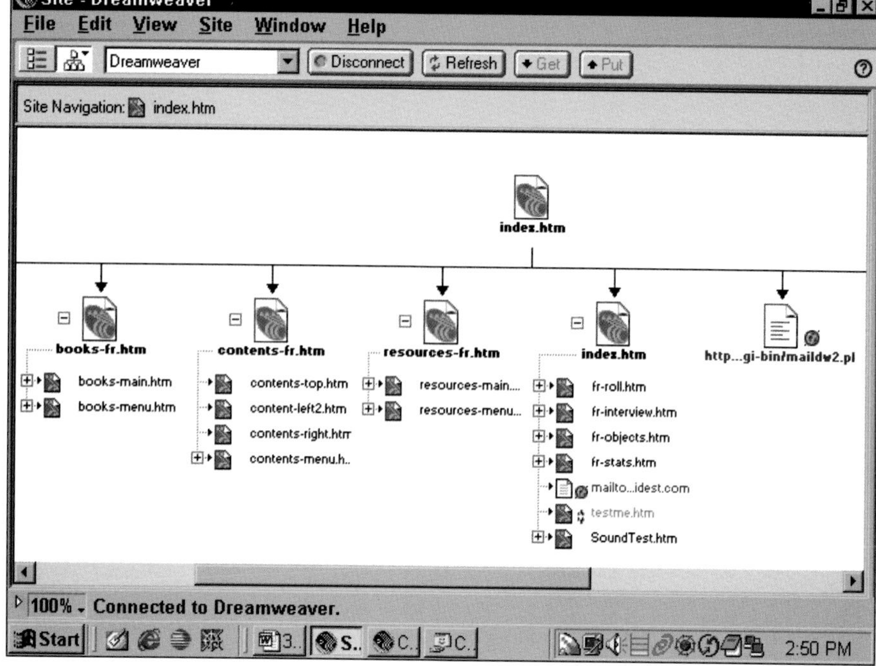

Figure 1 Use the Site Map to get an overall picture of your site — and then add new pages or links, right on the map.

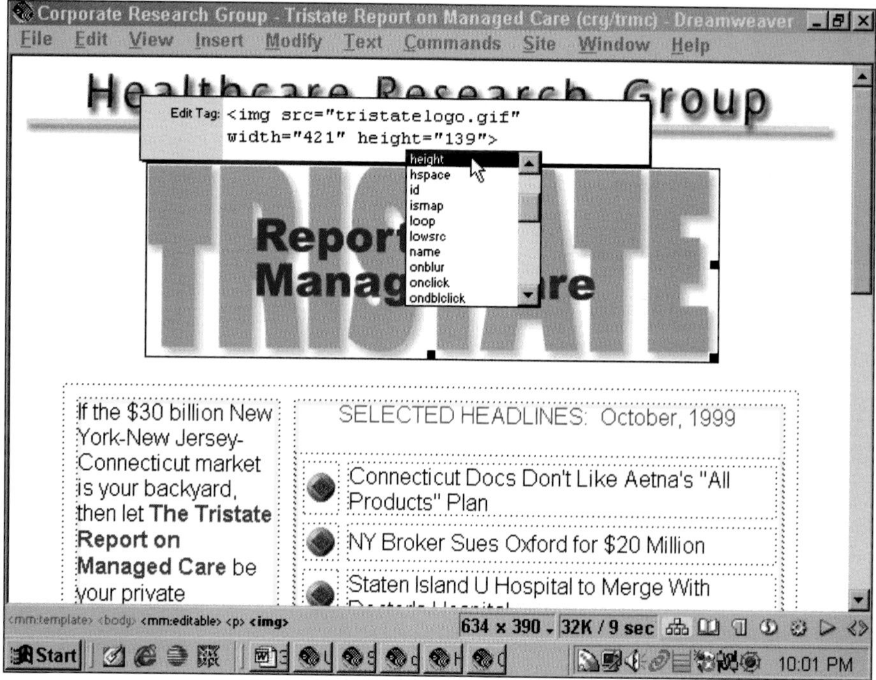

Figure 2 The new Quick Tag Editor is great for quickly tweaking your code.

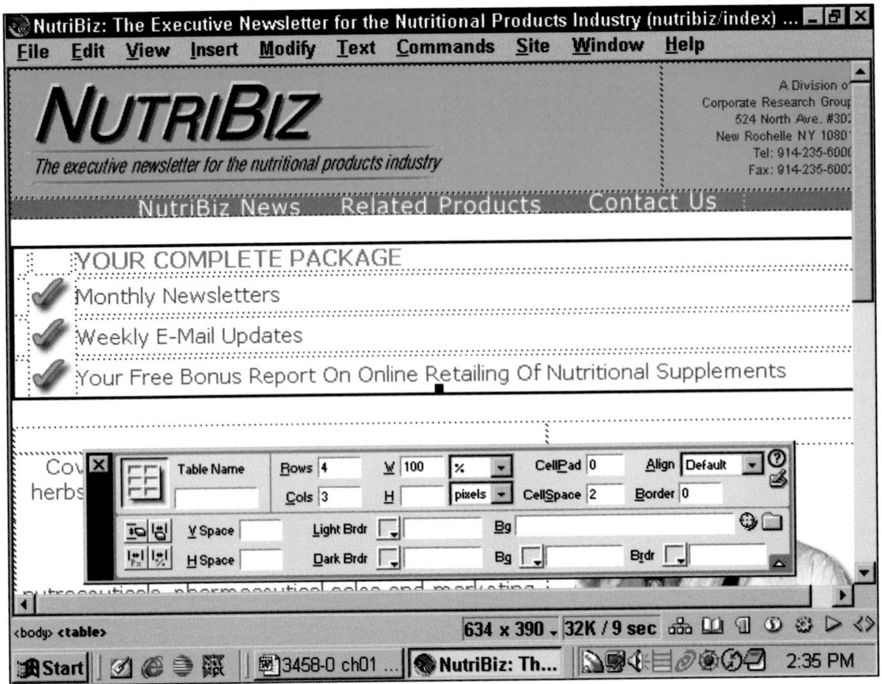

Figure 3 The Table Property Inspector is just one of Dreamweaver's paths to a full range of control over the appearance of your table.

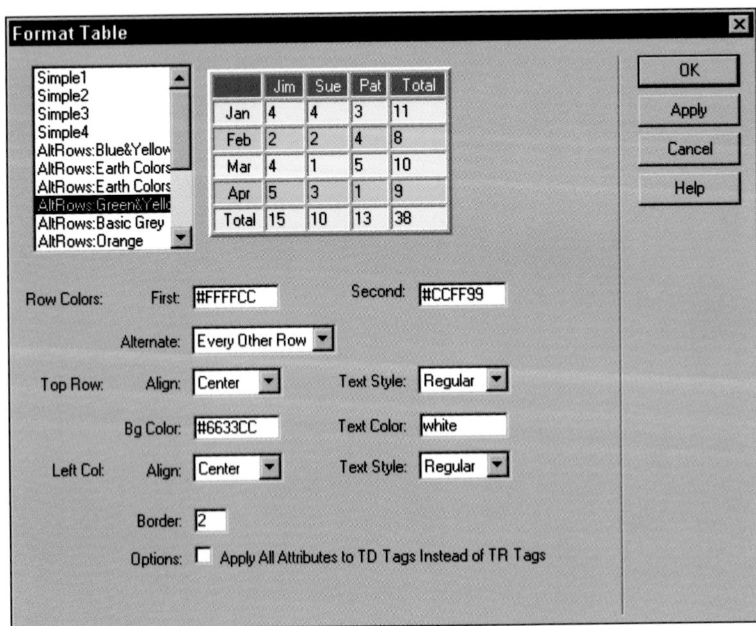

Figure 4 Select any one of 17 different preset formats from the Format Table dialog box or customize your own.

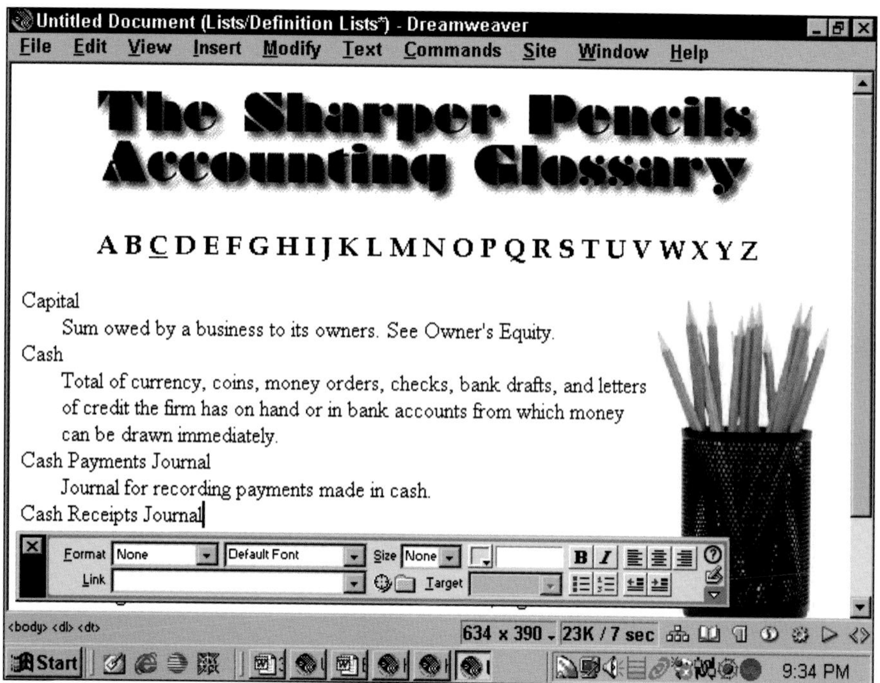

Figure 5 Definition lists are ideal for glossaries or other situations in which you have a list of terms followed by their definitions.

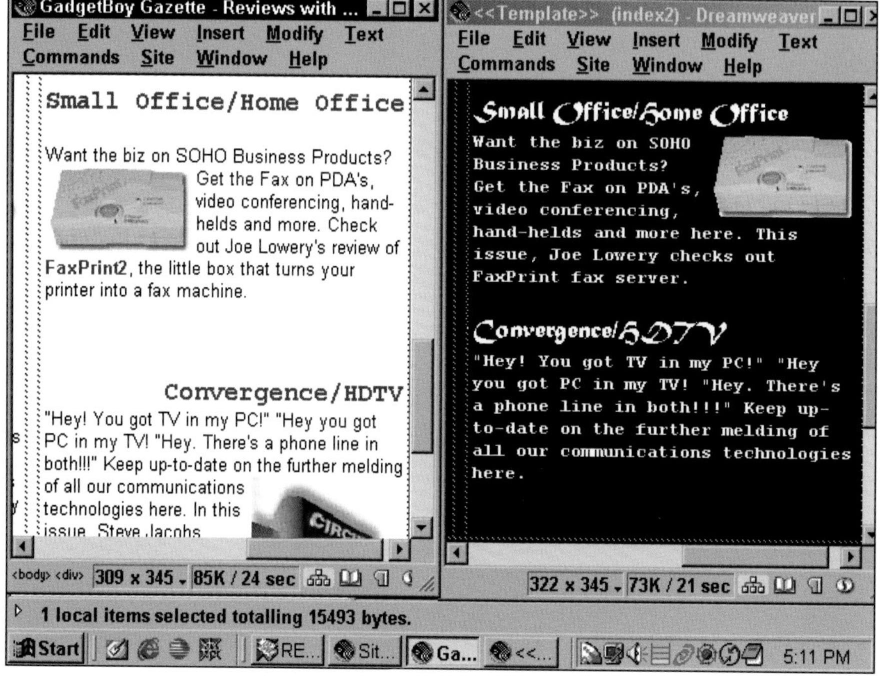

Figure 6 You can apply a template to a document created from another template to achieve different designs with identical content.

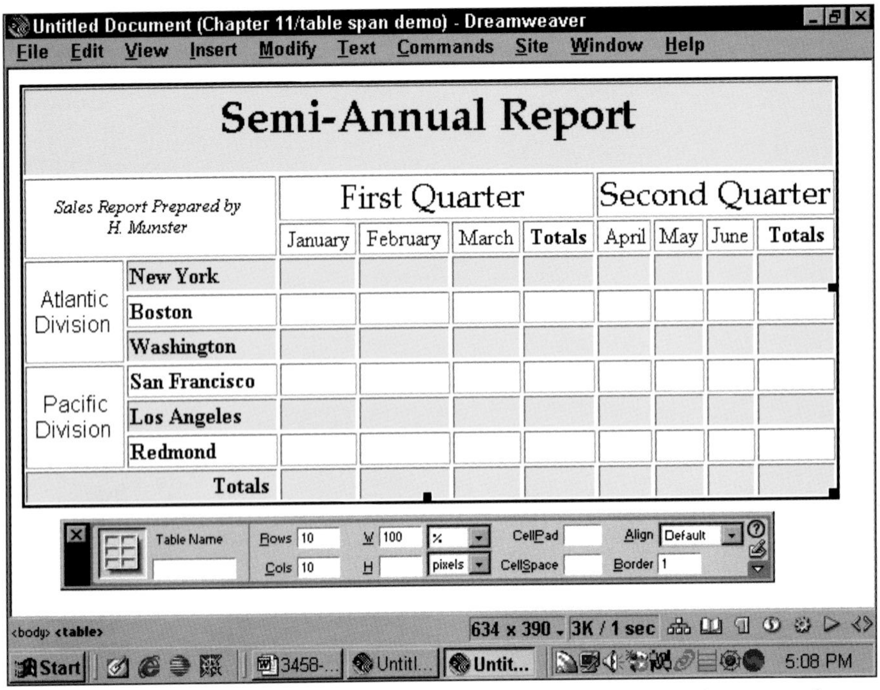

Untitled Document (Chapter 11/table span demo) - Dreamweaver

File Edit View Insert Modify Text Commands Site Window Help

Semi-Annual Report

Sales Report Prepared by H. Munster		First Quarter				Second Quarter			
		January	February	March	**Totals**	April	May	June	**Totals**
Atlantic Division	**New York**								
	Boston								
	Washington								
Pacific Division	**San Francisco**								
	Los Angeles								
	Redmond								
	Totals								

Table Name | Rows 10 | Cols 10 | W 100 % | H pixels | CellPad | CellSpace | Align Default | Border 1

<body> <table> 634 x 390 3K / 1 sec

Start | 3458-... | Untitl... | Untit... 5:08 PM

Figure 7 This spreadsheet-like report was built using Dreamweaver's row- and column-spanning features.

Figure 8 Existing content is incorporated in a new frameset when a Frames object is chosen.

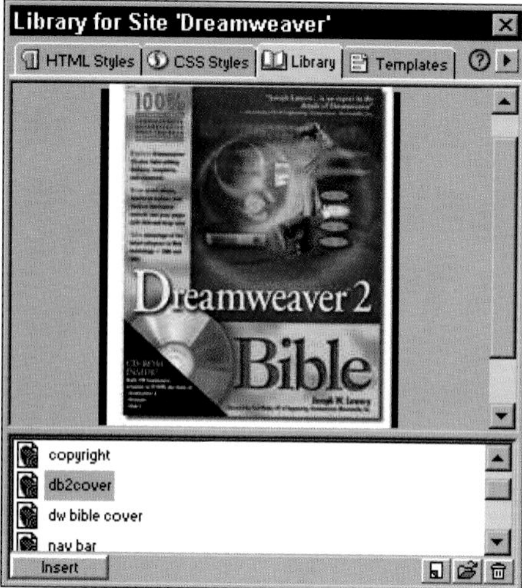

Figure 9 The Library palette manages the repeating elements throughout your Web site.

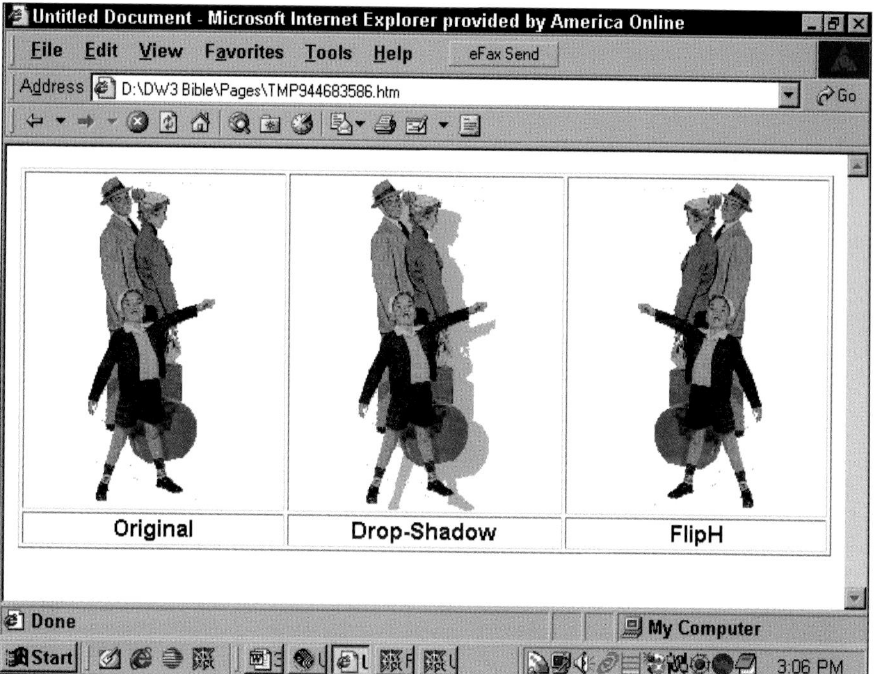

Figure 10 Internet Explorer's filters and transitions offer a full spectrum of graphic effects.

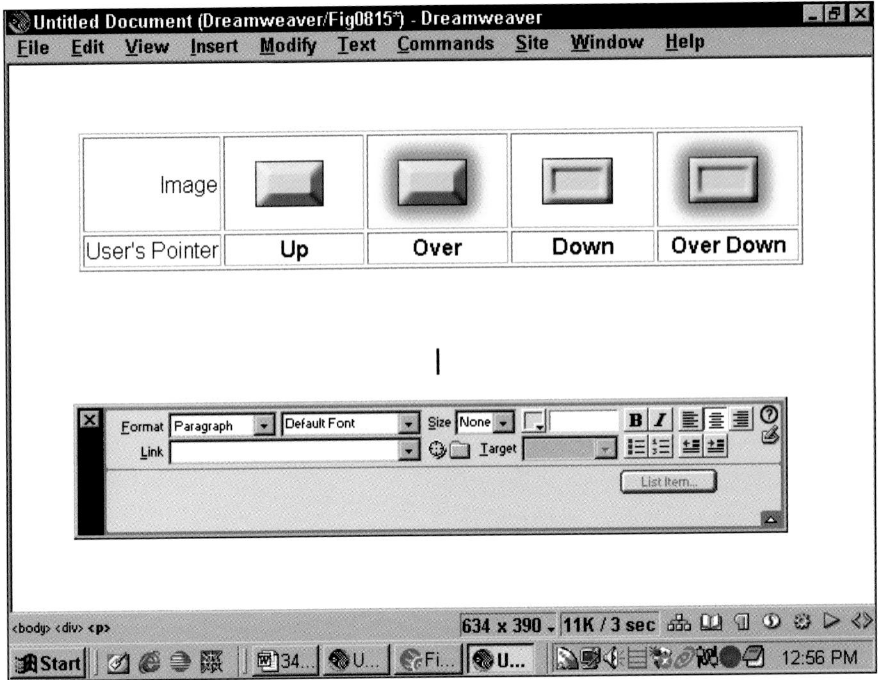

Figure 11 Before you invoke the Navigation Bar object, create a series of buttons with a separate image for each state to be used.

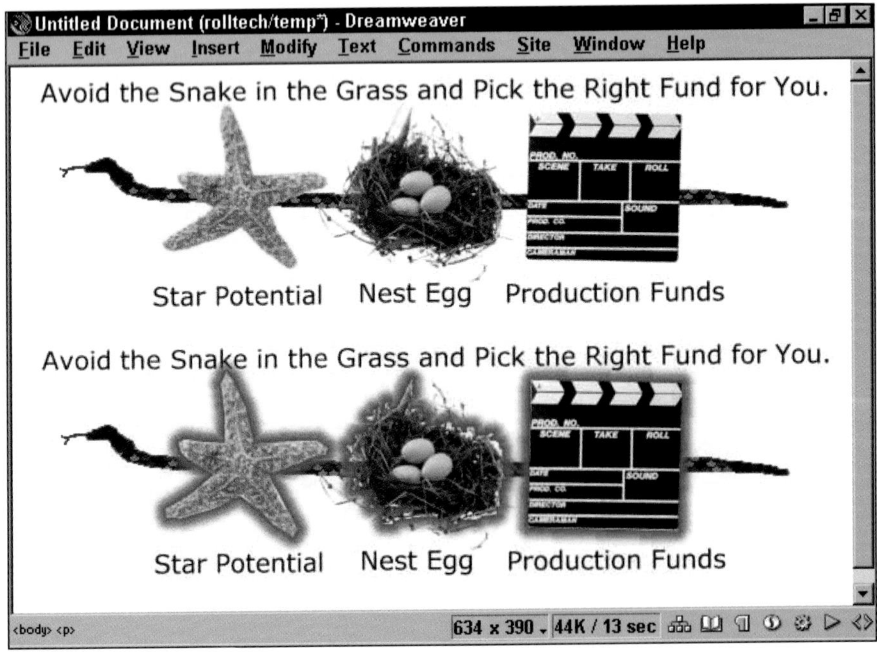

Figure 12 You need two separate images, representing "over" and "off," for a rollover image map.

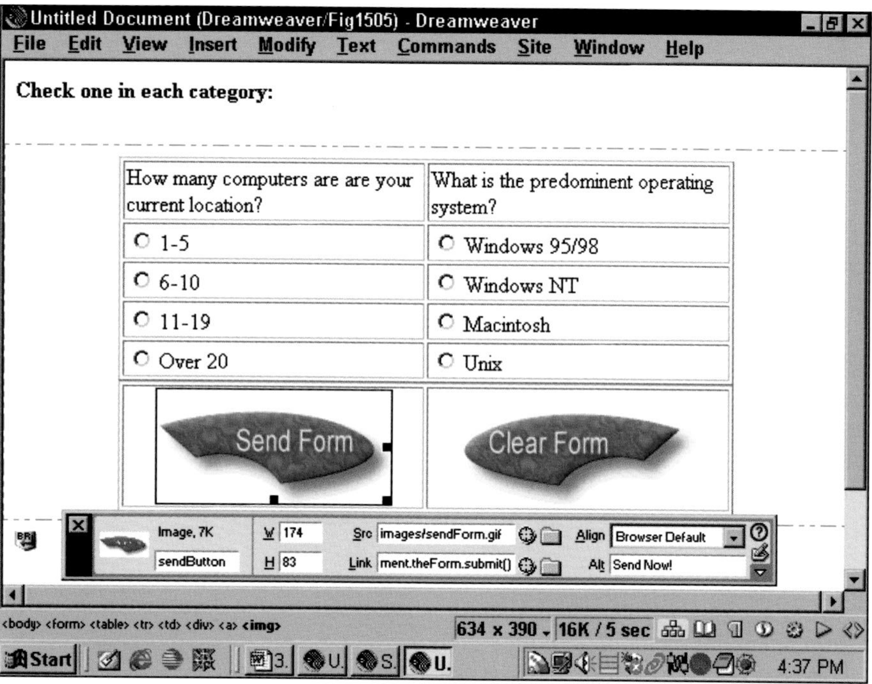

Figure 13 You can substitute any valid graphic for the Submit button by using an image and JavaScript.

Figure 14 A trick using a second temporary layer can make it easier to position your clipping.

Figure 15 With Fireworks 3 installed, you can optimize your images from within Dreamweaver.

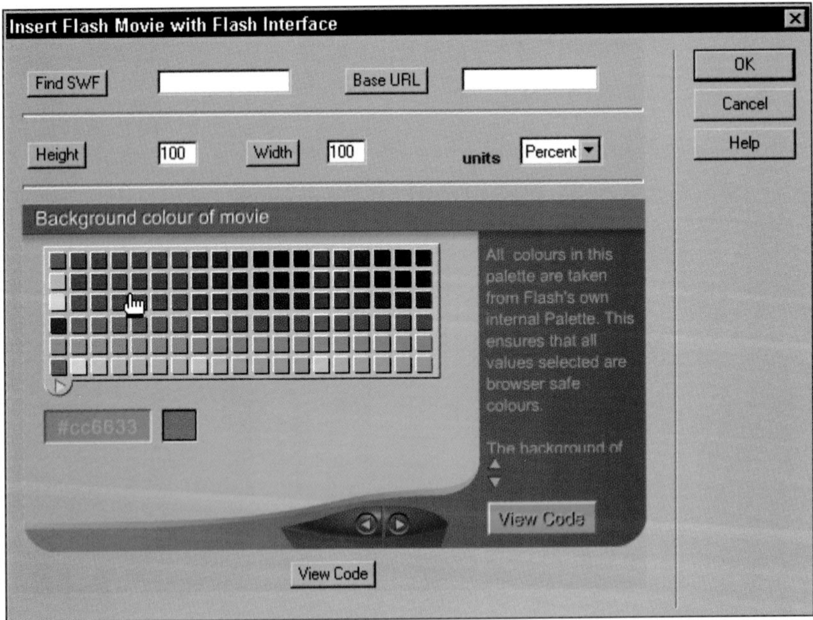

Figure 16 Spice up your object's user interface like the Web designer team of Spooky and the Bandit — at `www.spookyandthebandit.com` — did with this Insert Flash 3 object.

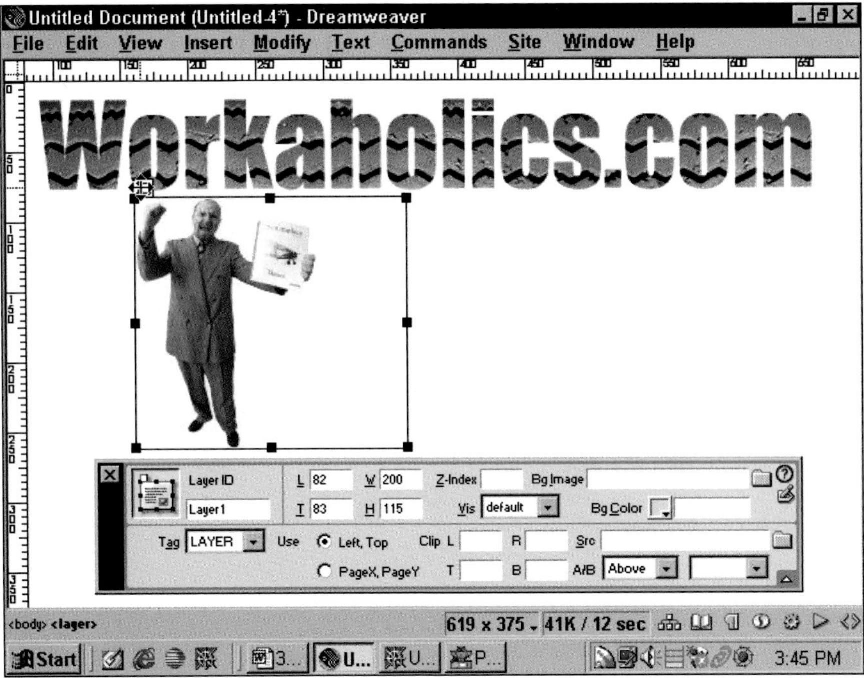

Figure 17 Use the horizontal and vertical rulers to assist your layer placement and overall Web page layout.

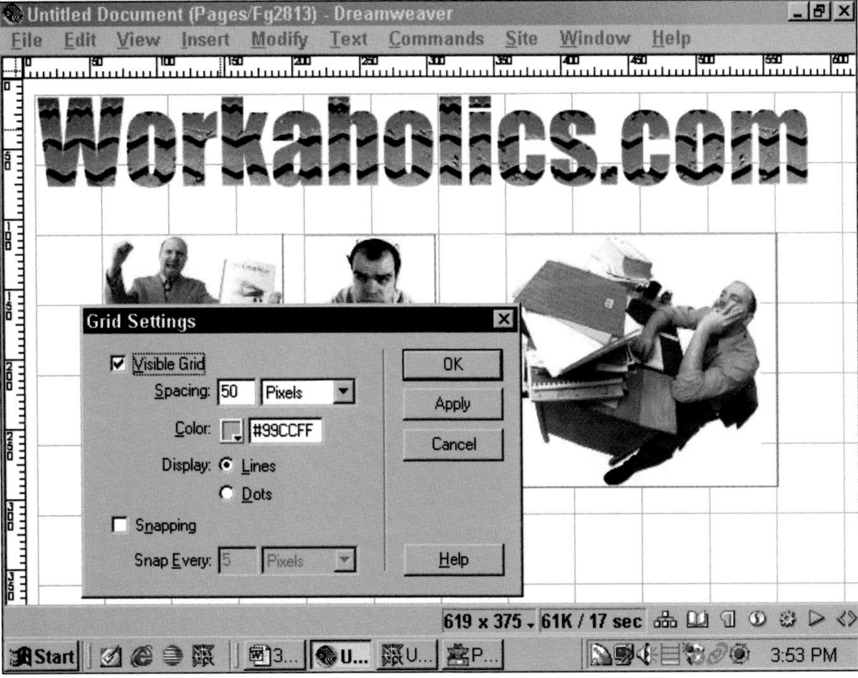

Figure 18 Dreamweaver's grid feature is extremely handy for aligning a series of objects.

Figure 19 Files embedded in your Web page, such as this QuickTime movie, can be played back in the Document window as you design.

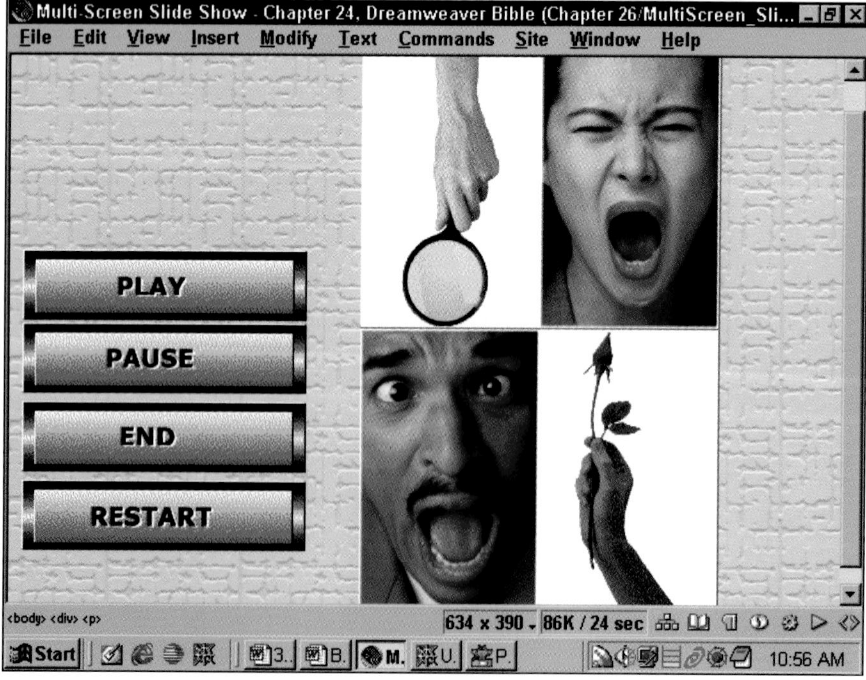

Figure 20 Before activating any layers or setting up the slideshow, design the layout.

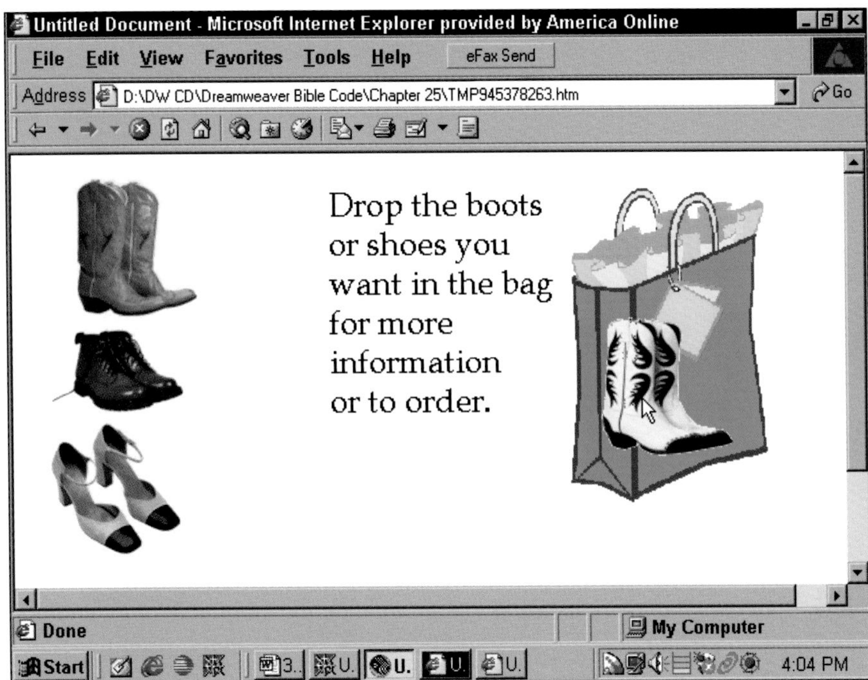

Figure 21 On this interactive page, visitors can drop merchandise into the shopping bag; this feature is made possible with the Drag Layer action.

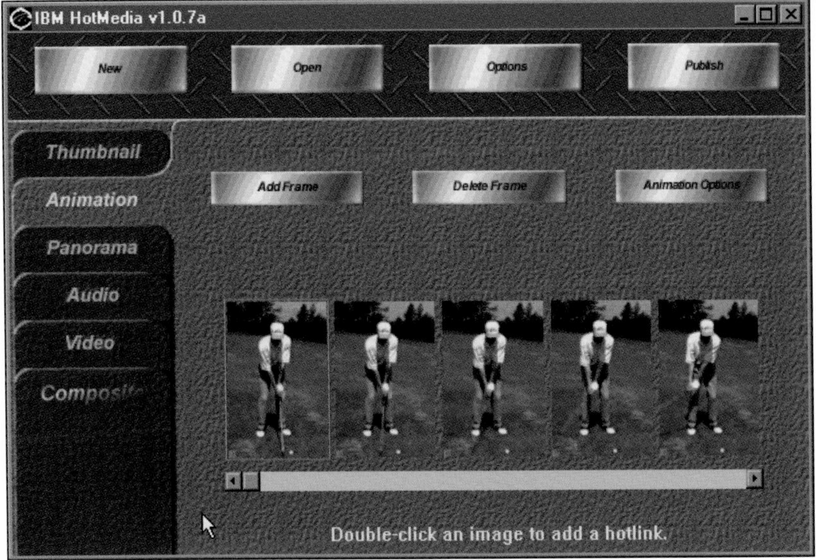

Figure 22 The IBM HotMedia Assembly utility combines numerous media types to create compelling interactive advertising.

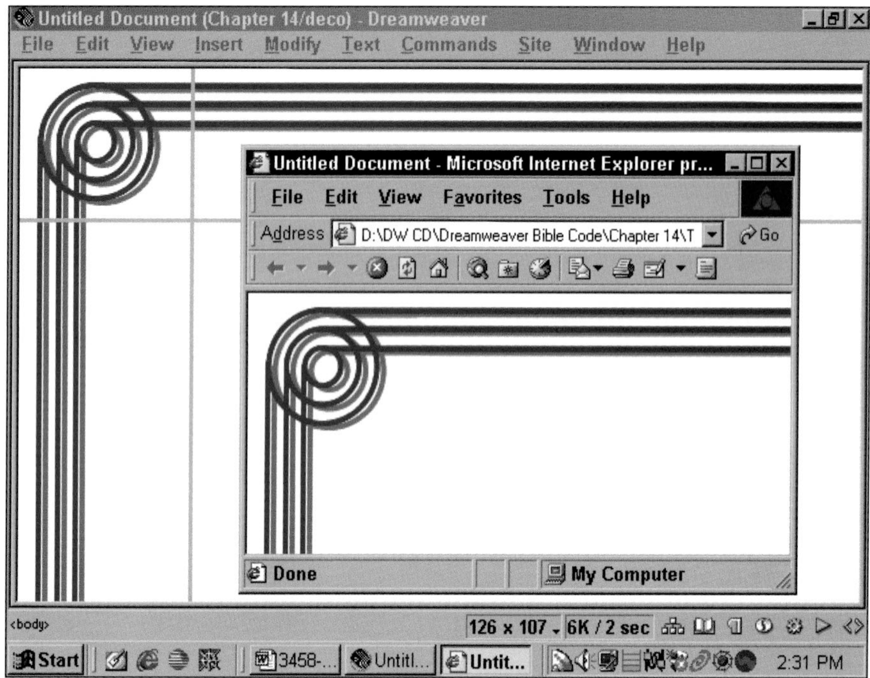

Figure 23 One popular design technique is to insert background images into separate frames so they blend into a seamless single image.

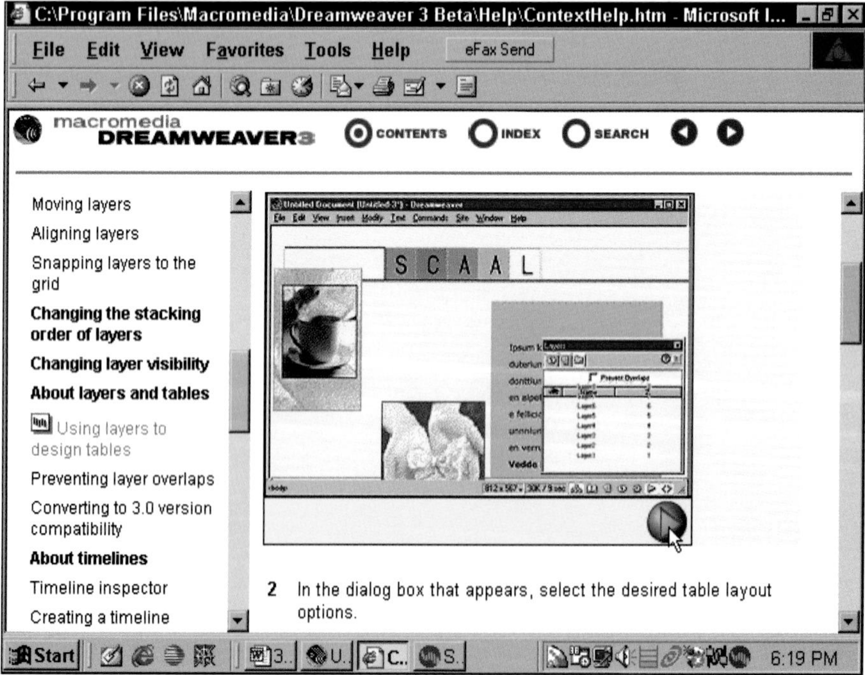

Figure 24 All the Show Me movies, such as this one about working with layers, provide excellent introductions to the subjects.

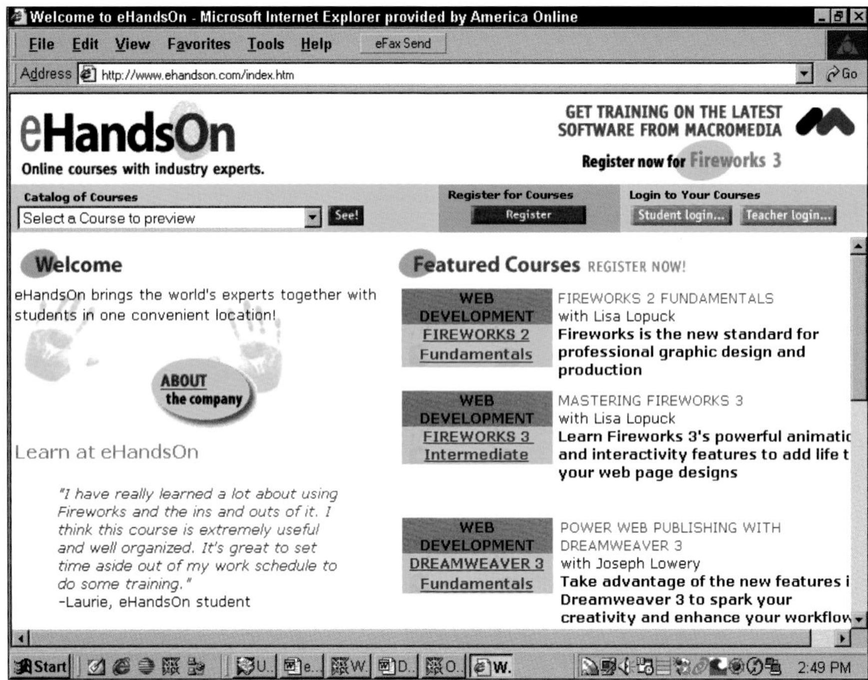

Figure 25 Designer Lisa Lopuck seamlessly weaves form elements into her design for this online learning center.

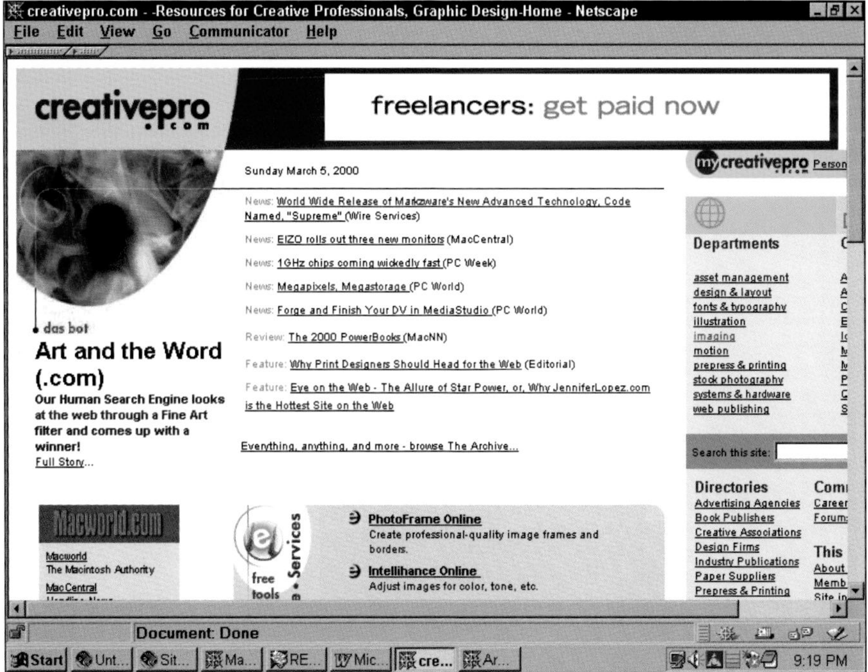

Figure 26 Creativepro keeps its site fresh by frequently updating the central image and lead story under the company logo.

Figure 27 The Glass Bottom site uses tables at 100 percent to maintain design integrity regardless of the browser window width.

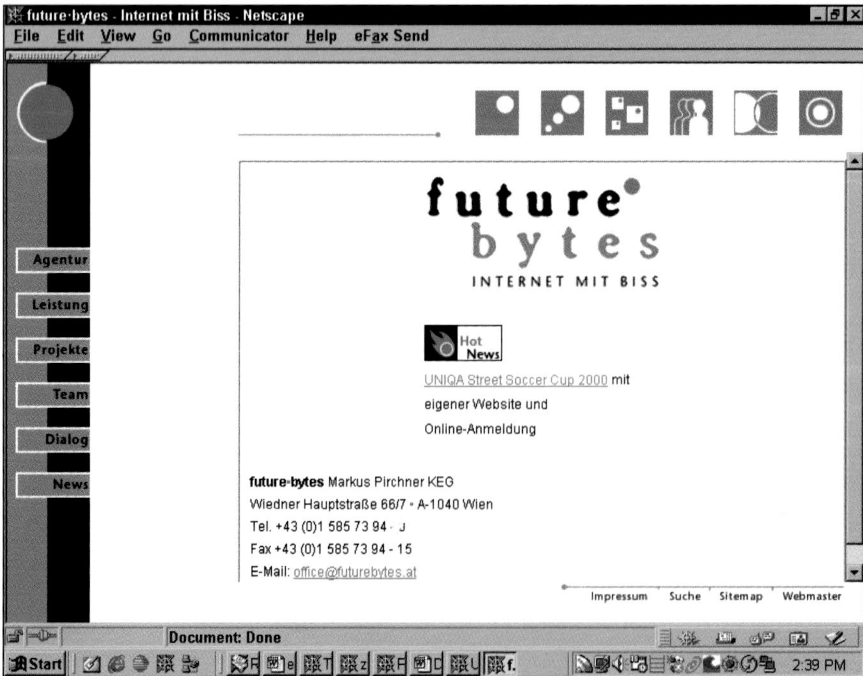

Figure 28 Austrian design firm Future-Bytes links the iconic navigation system along the top to the side menu with a series of swap image behaviors targeted to a separate frame.

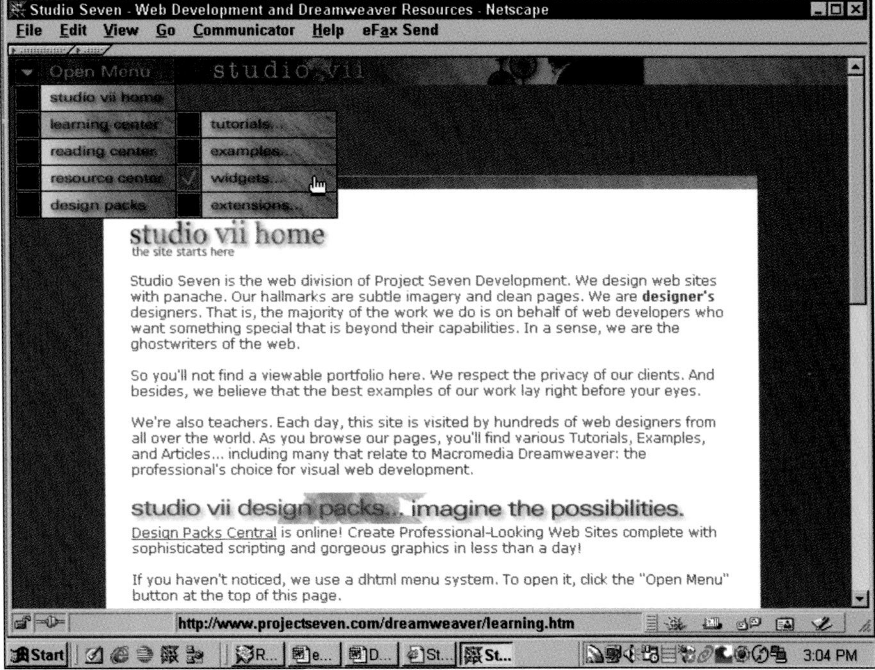

Figure 29 In this page from the Studio Seven site a combination of timeline and other behaviors is used to smoothly drop down the main menu, followed by a roll out of submenus.

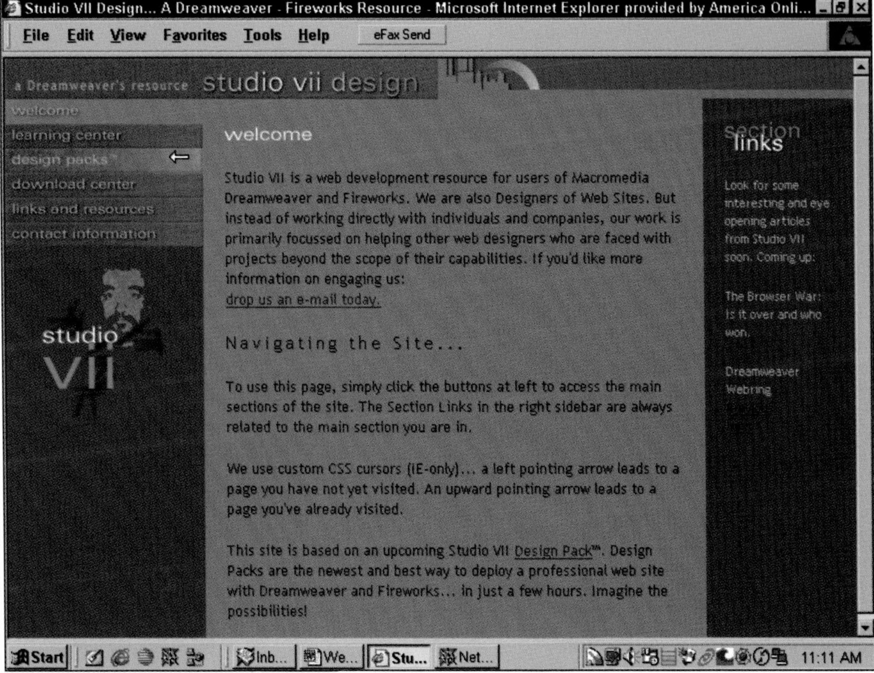

Figure 30 This entire site displays designer Al Sparber's mastery of muted color and Cascading Style Sheets.

Figure 31

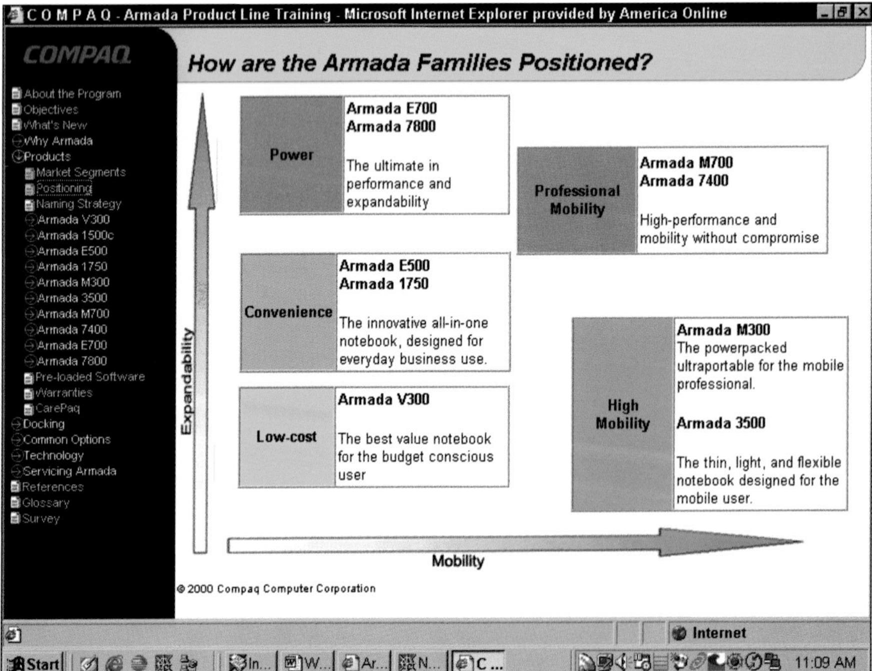

Figure 32 Expandable/collapsible menus guide the visitor through the online training course at the Compaq site.

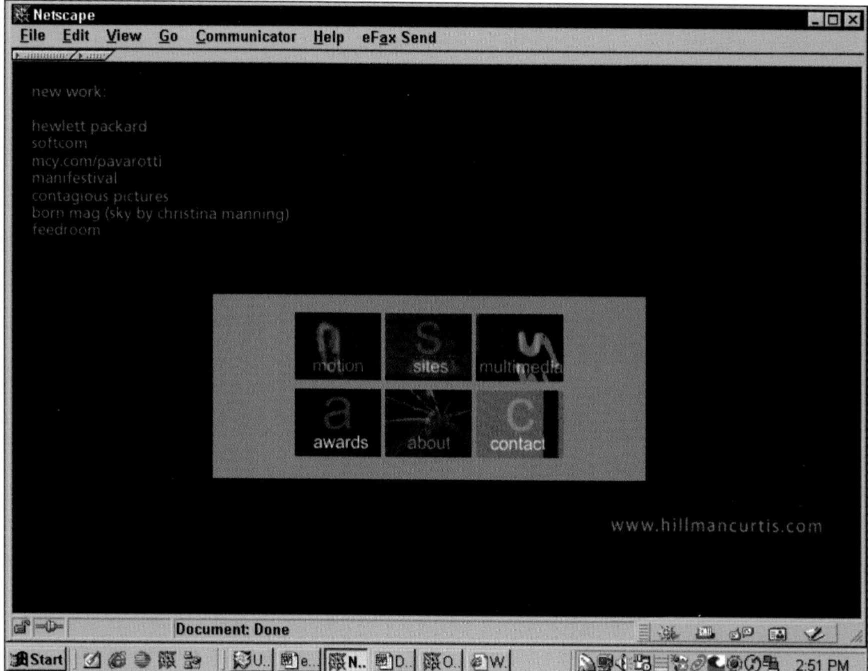

Figure 33 Hillman Curtis, master of motion graphics, incorporates Flash navigation buttons into a table that stays centered on the screen through use of tables, 100 percent wide and 100 percent high.

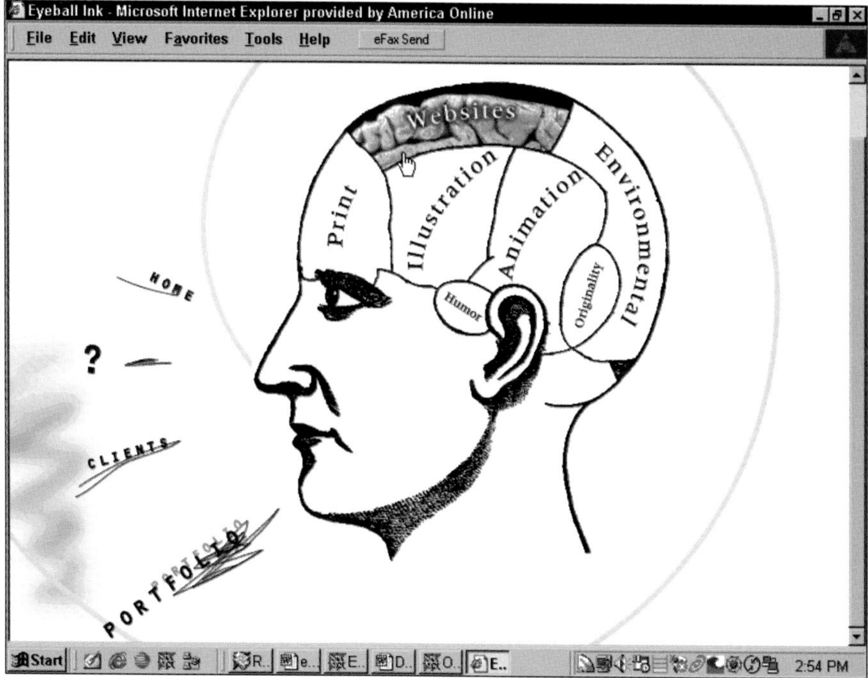

Figure 34 A complex series of swap image behaviors, generated in Fireworks, makes this unique navigation system by designer Ruth Peyser come to life.

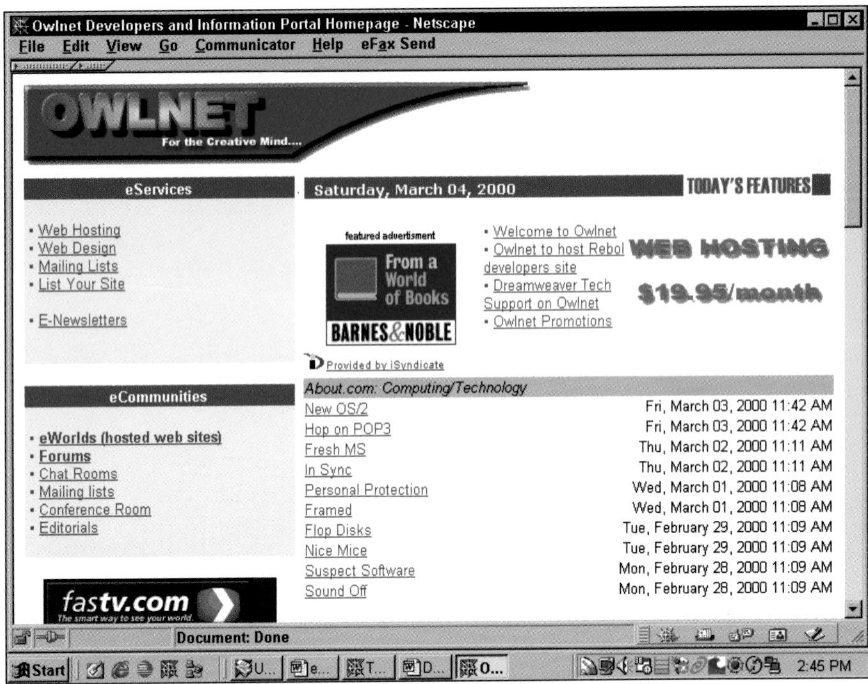

Figure 35 A series of well-divided tables makes it easy to sift through Web host OwlNet's many offerings.

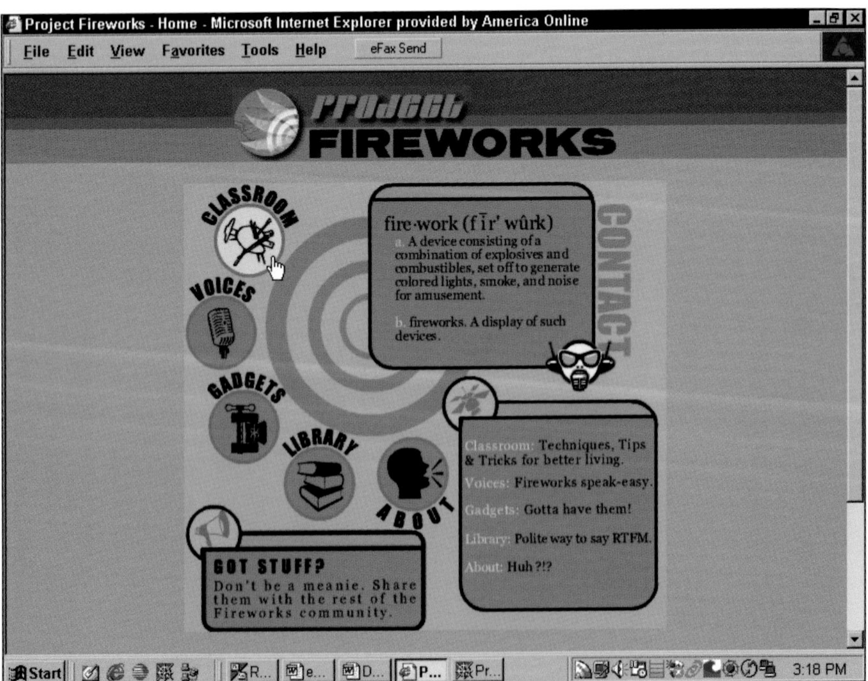

Figure 36 Designer Kleanthis Economou exhibits a true sense of retro with his Project Fireworks site.

Figure 37 Universal display is key to eTranslate's main page, which restricts the format to 600 pixels wide through a table layout.

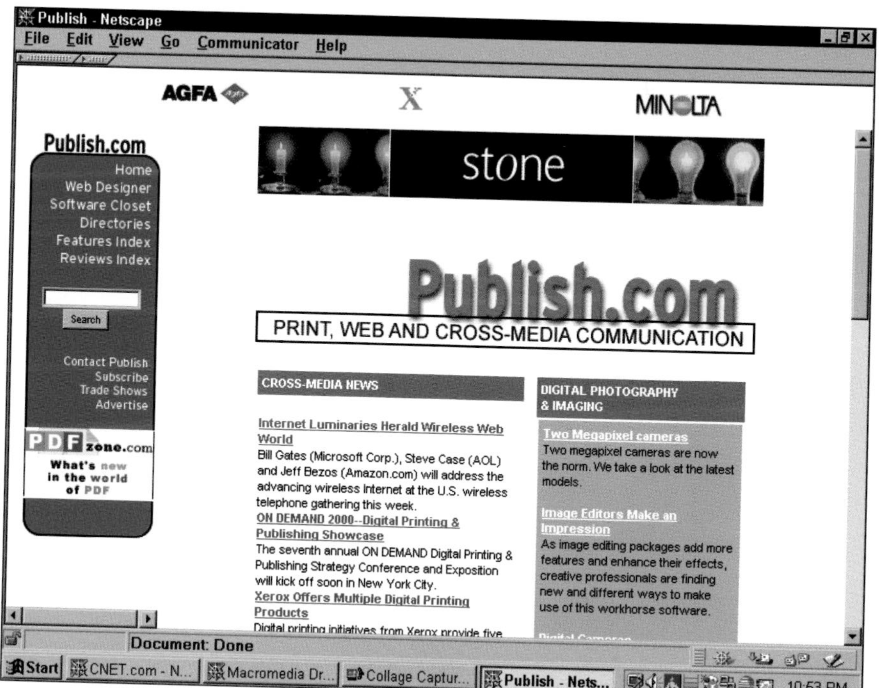

Figure 38 A clear-cut navigation bar in the left-hand frame persists as you navigate the Publish.com site.

Figure 39 Although the Lizardbyte site makes strong use of Flash, its static pages are equally striking.

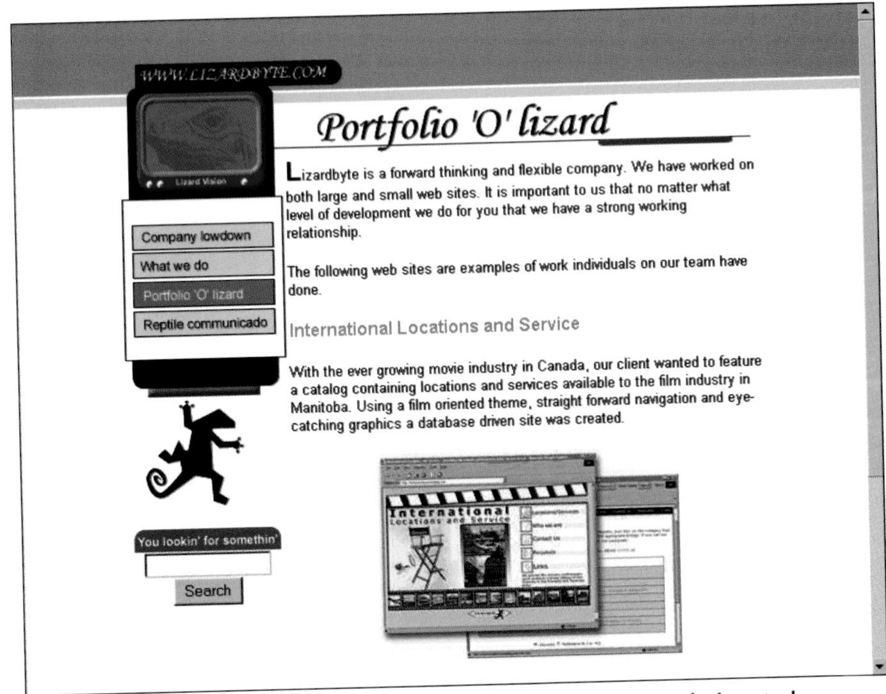

Figure 40 An excellent use of disjointed rollovers causes menu choices to be revealed in the Lizard Vision monitor.

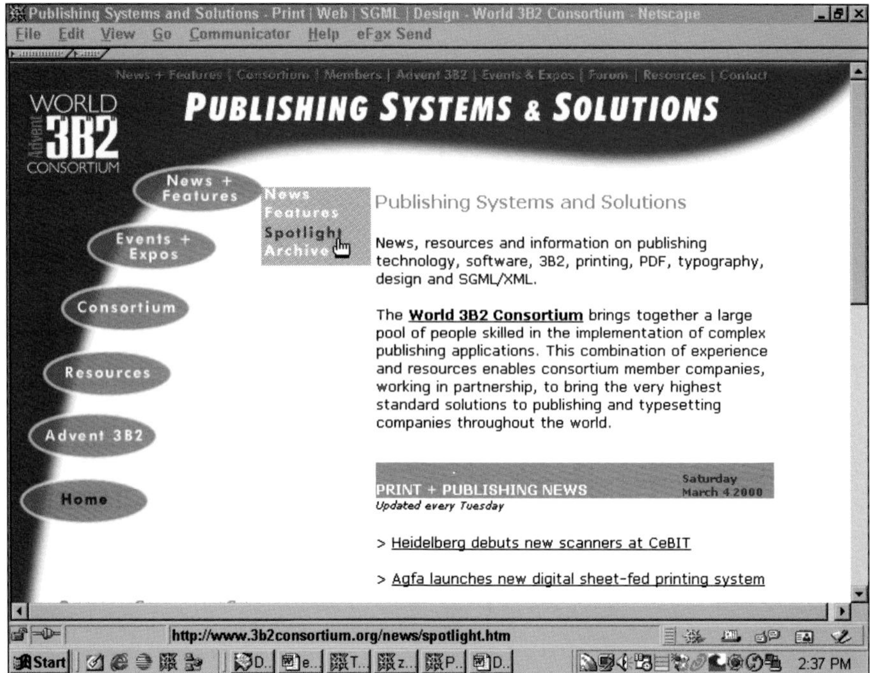

Figure 41 Dreamweaver's Show-Hide Layers behavior is used through this site to aid in navigation.

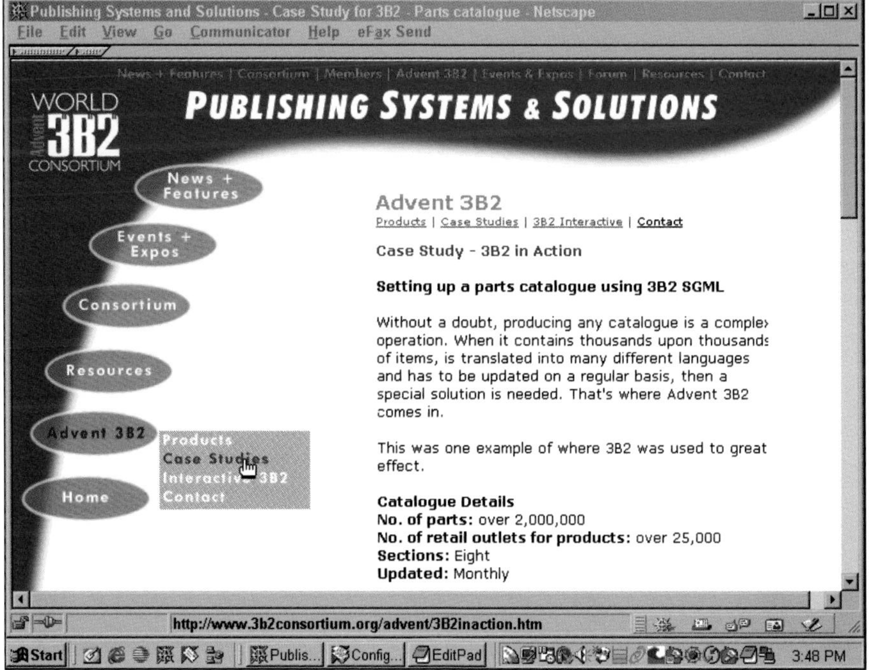

Figure 42 The swooping frame was developed in Fireworks.

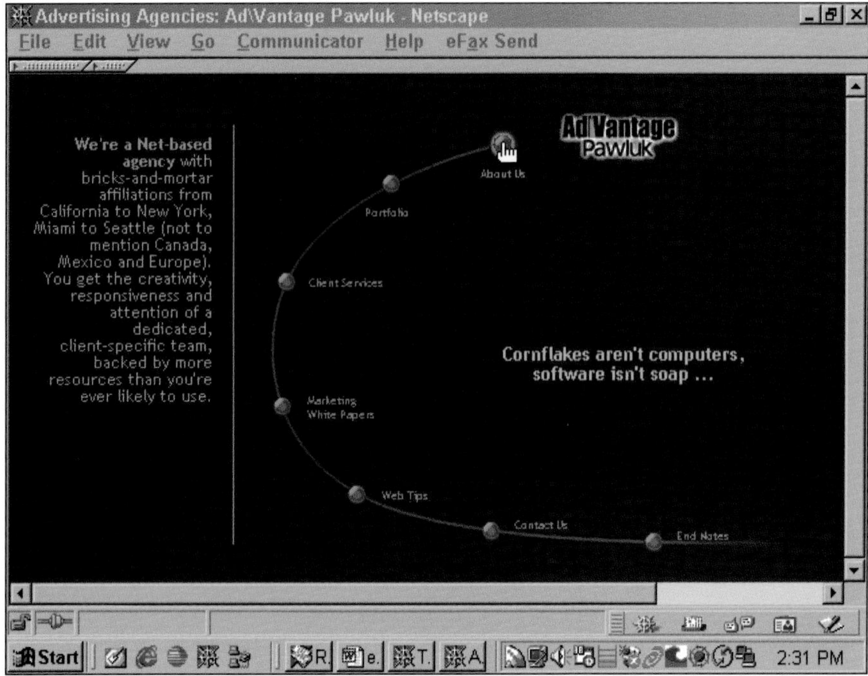

Figure 43 The arcing navigation system is balanced by a series of layers revealed as each key graphic is rolled over by the user's mouse in the Ad/Vantage Pawluk site.

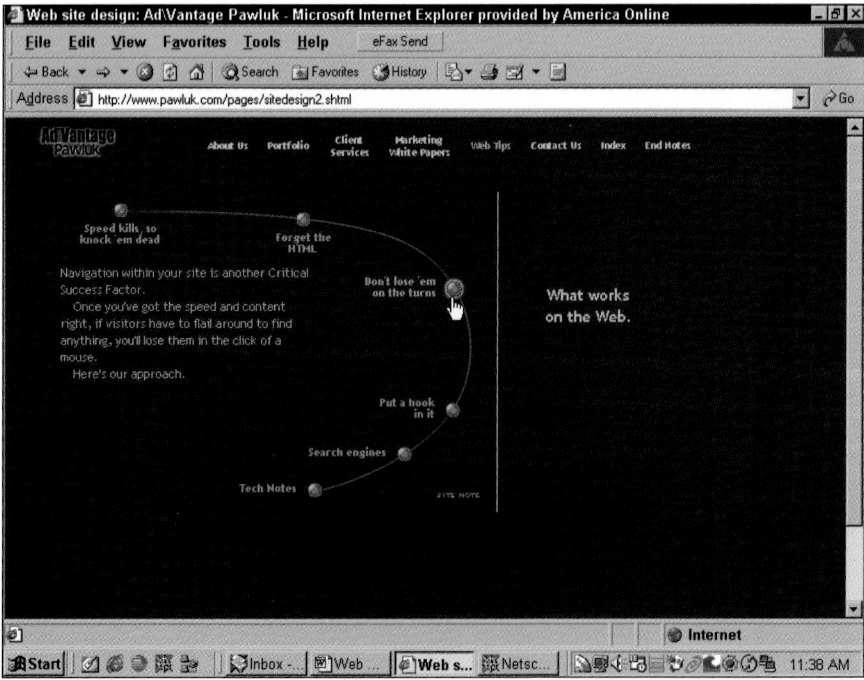

Figure 44 On another page within the site, this theme is repeated with a variation.

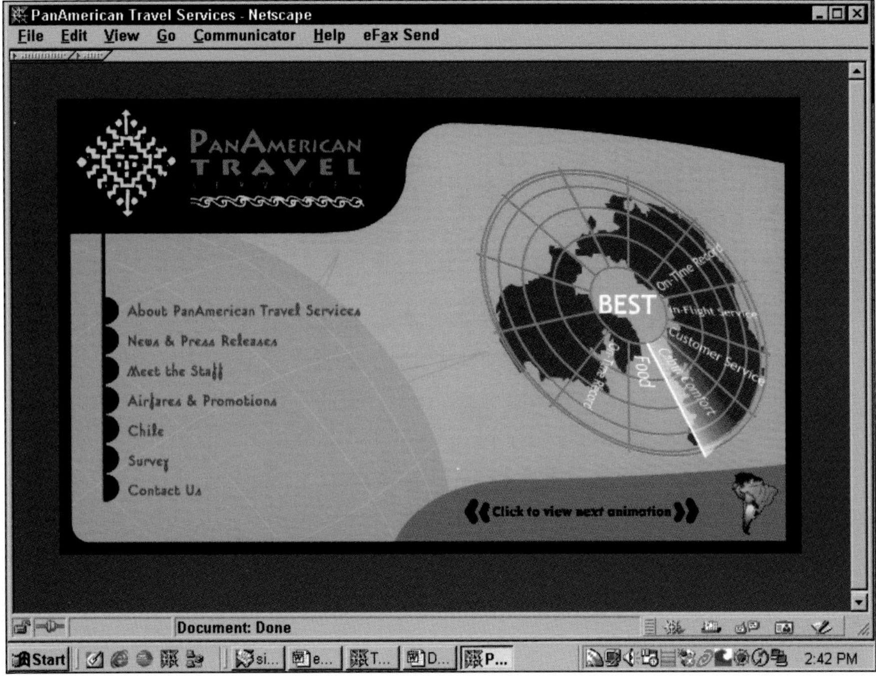

Figure 45 A series of gateway screens detects your browser and determines whether or not Flash is available on your system before the opening screen of PanAm Tours is displayed.

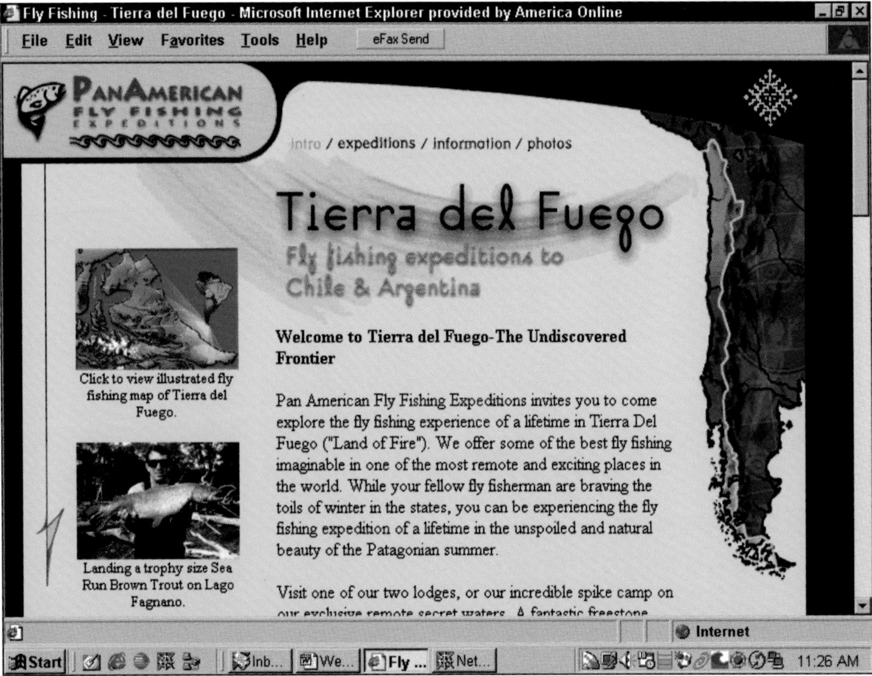

Figure 46 Inner pages of PanAm Tours use remote browser windows to reveal close-ups of embedded thumbnails.

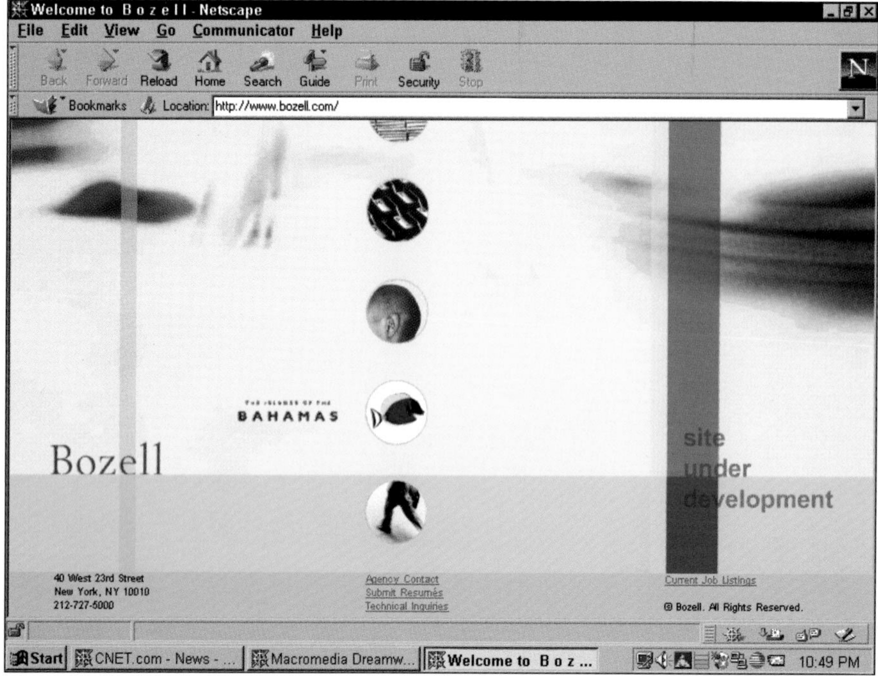

Figure 47 A smoothly flowing series of icons, courtesy of a full-frame Generator movie, makes the Bozell site move while maintaining important links on the lower frame.

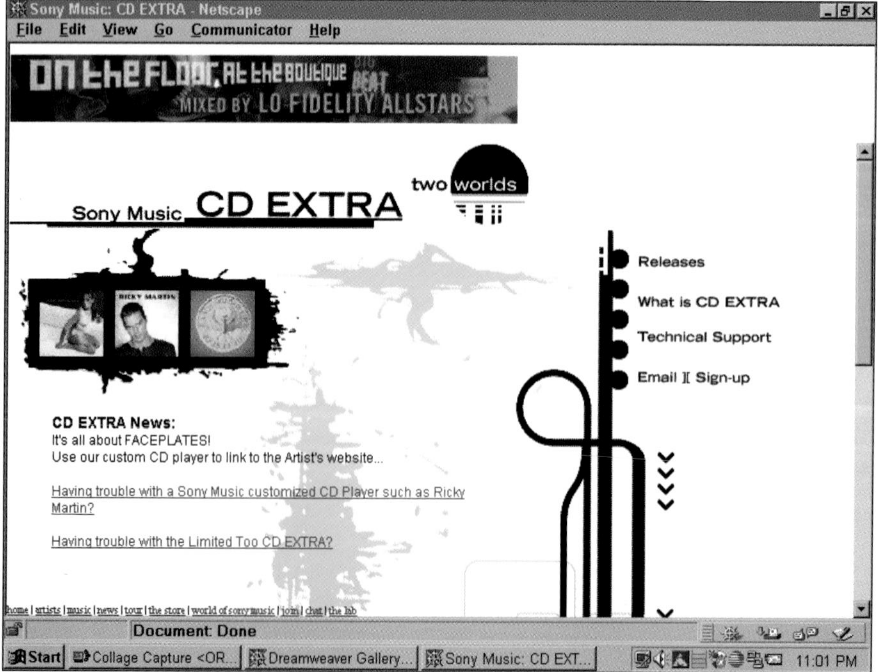

Figure 48 A lightweight, yet full-screen, background image and the buttons that rollover to animated GIFs gives the Sony CD Extra site a cutting-edge feel.

Figure 49 Sonicopia is a fully "sonified" site – in addition to background music, which smoothly fades up, virtually every link and graphic triggers a different sound effect or chord.

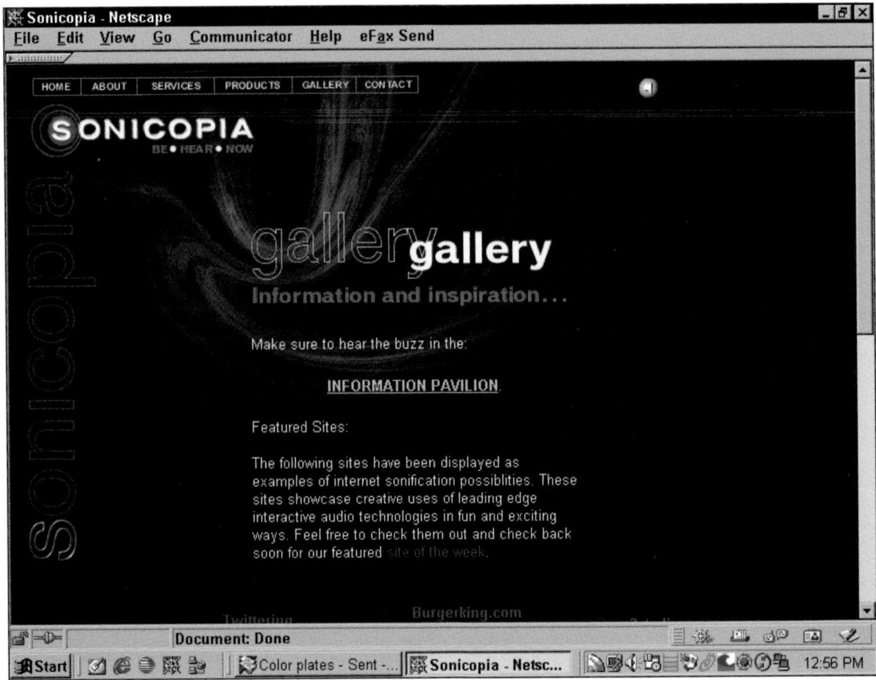

Figure 50 The background music is carried from page to page via a frameset device.

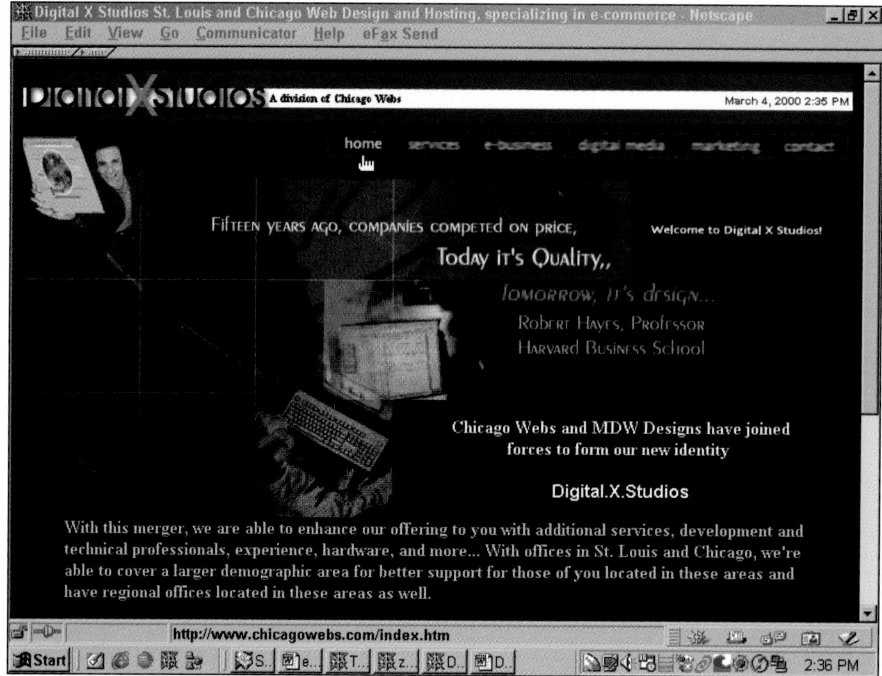

Figure 51 The Digital X Studios navigation bar uses reverse-image psychology: they initially appear blurred but become sharp when rolled over.

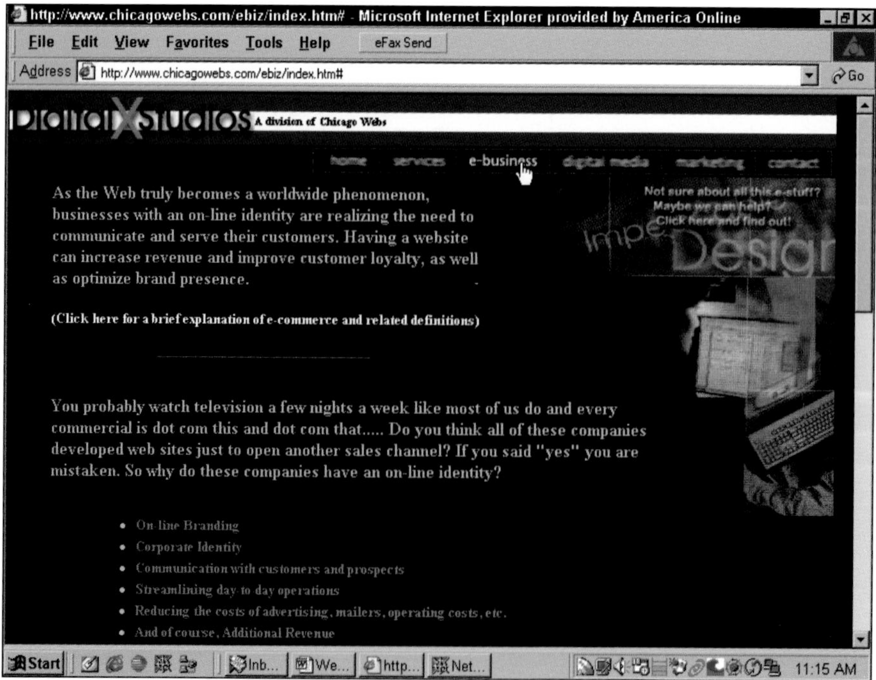

Figure 52 A series of nested tables separates the text from the images.

Figure 53 Beringer Winery embraces a very clean, crisp look for the Web site by combining rollovers with image maps.

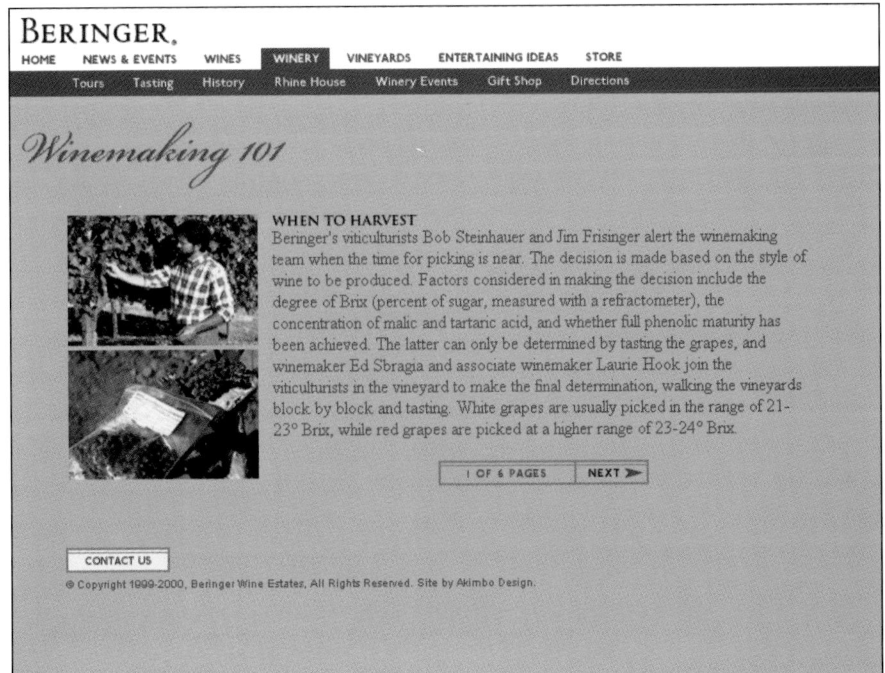

Figure 54 Each main topic of the Beringer navigation bar becomes highlighted and displays a submenu in an image map.

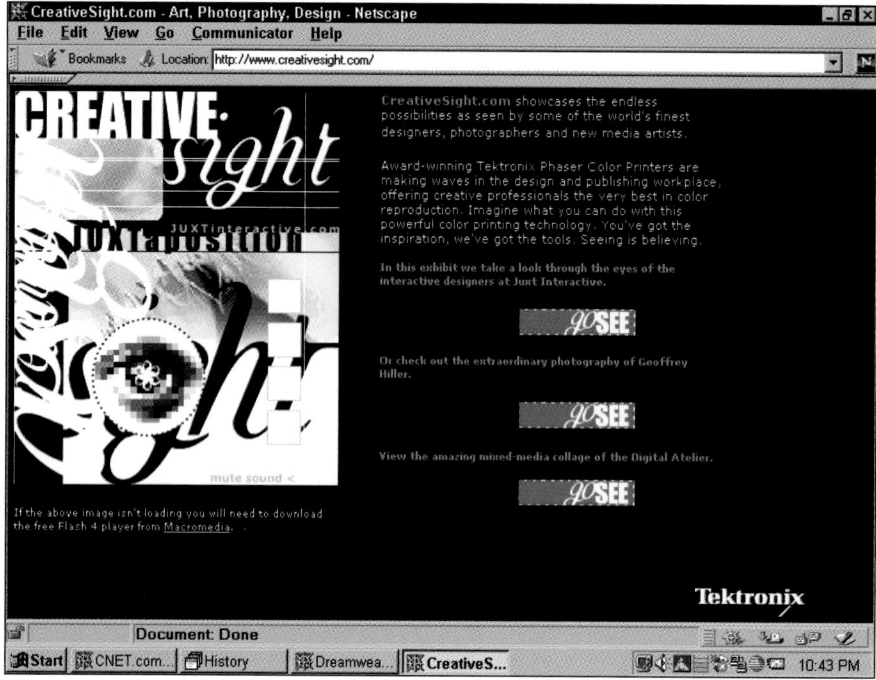

Figure 55 As a showcase for a variety of artists' media, CreativeSight.com must maintain a great deal of flexibility.

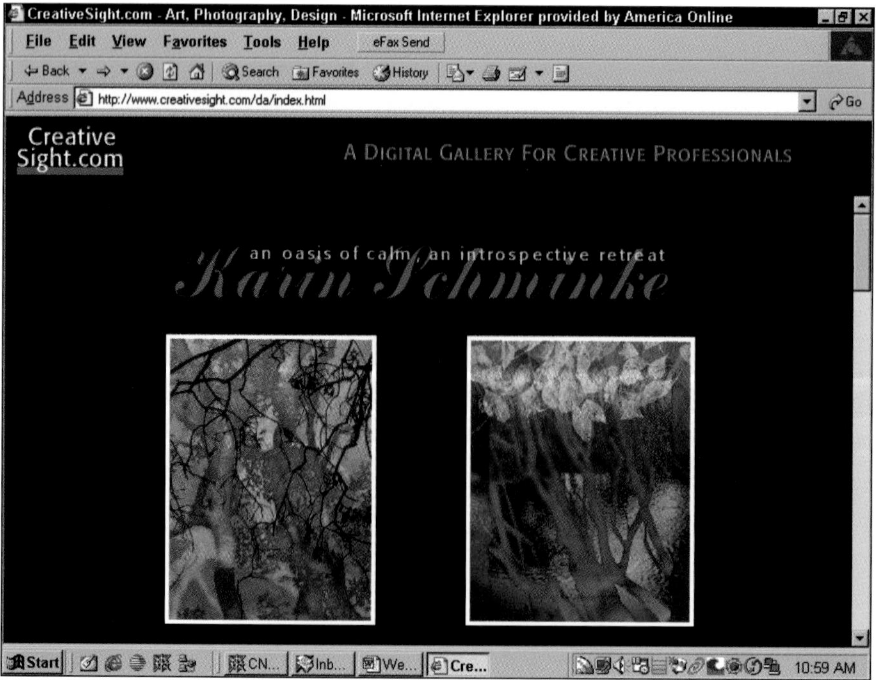

Figure 56 Although presented in a fairly large format, each of the artists' thumbnails, when selected, opens a dedicated, remote window for the graphic.

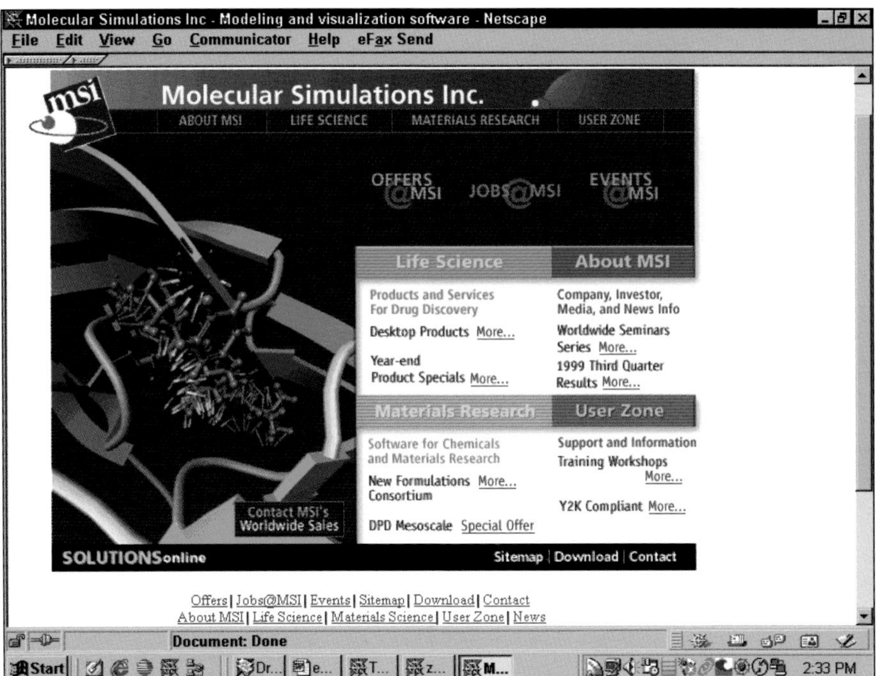

Figure 57

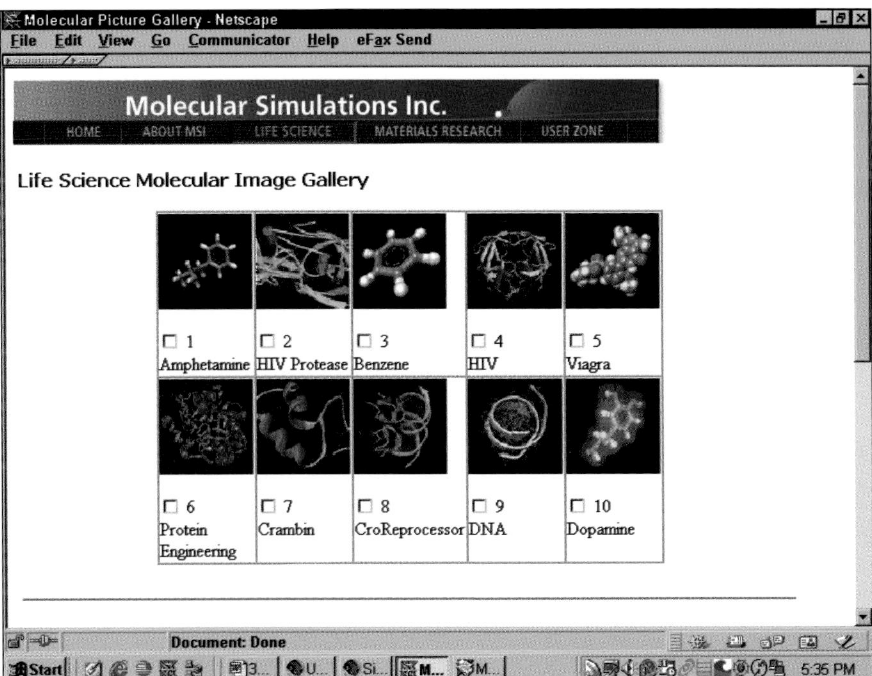

Figure 58 The easily altered homepage graphics keep the Molecular Simulations Inc. site lively while the graphic order form displays a precise product.

Figure 59 Although you must have a Shockwave player to view the Fox Kids UK site in its entirety, the site uses a simple, colorful, animated GIF to entice visitors.

Figure 60 Underneath the hood a series of cookie behaviors checks to see if the visitor has been to the site before.

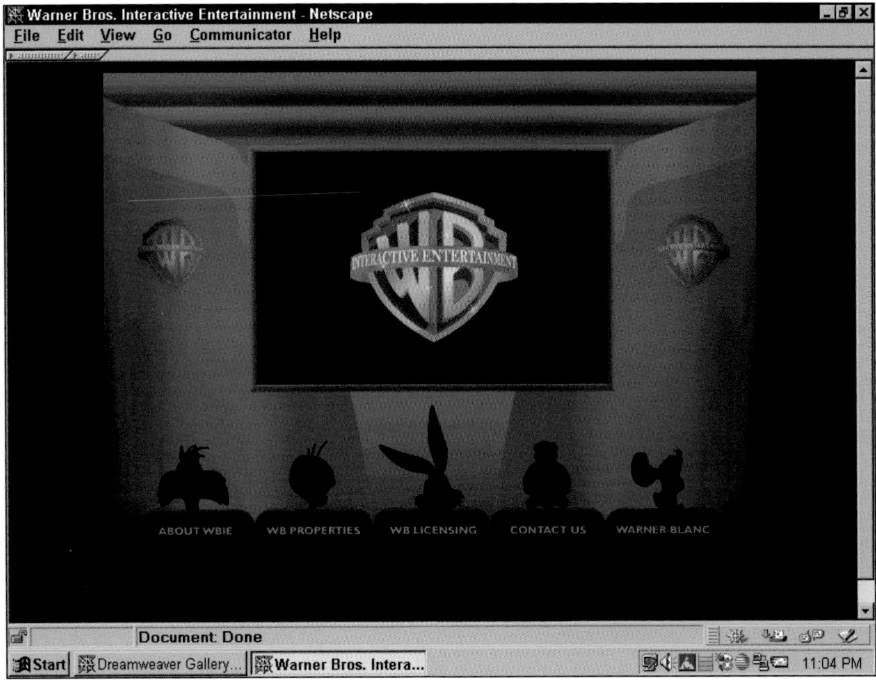

Figure 61 A darkened screening room — complete with very recognizable silhouettes — provides the entryway to the Warner Bros. site.

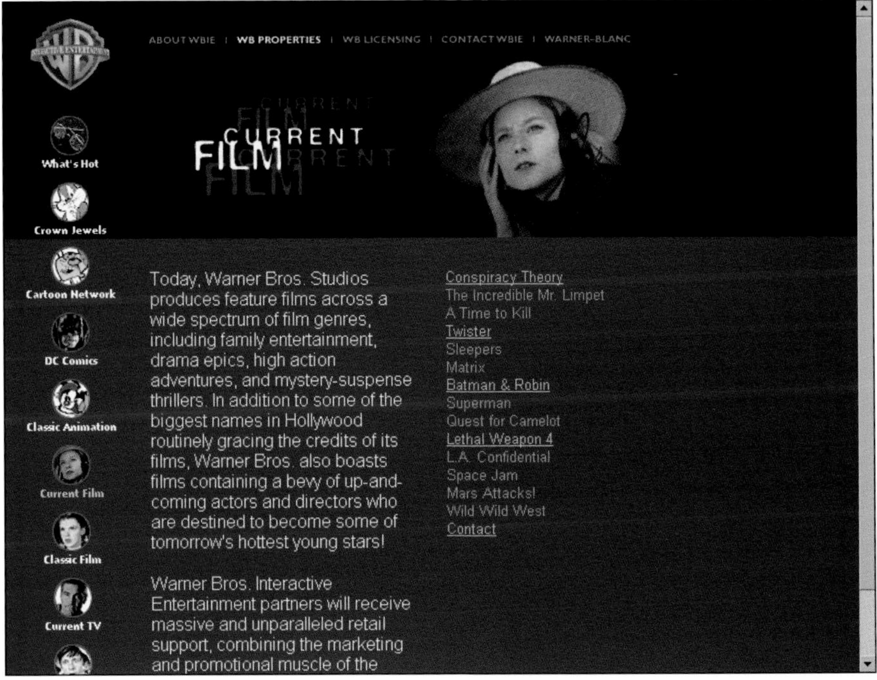

Figure 62 Once inside, navigation is split into two areas: primary categories appear across the top with submenus along the side.

Figure 63 Eddie Traversa is well known in the Dreamweaver community for creating Dynamic HTML. His Nirvana site features floating angels, harmonic music, and scrolling layers.

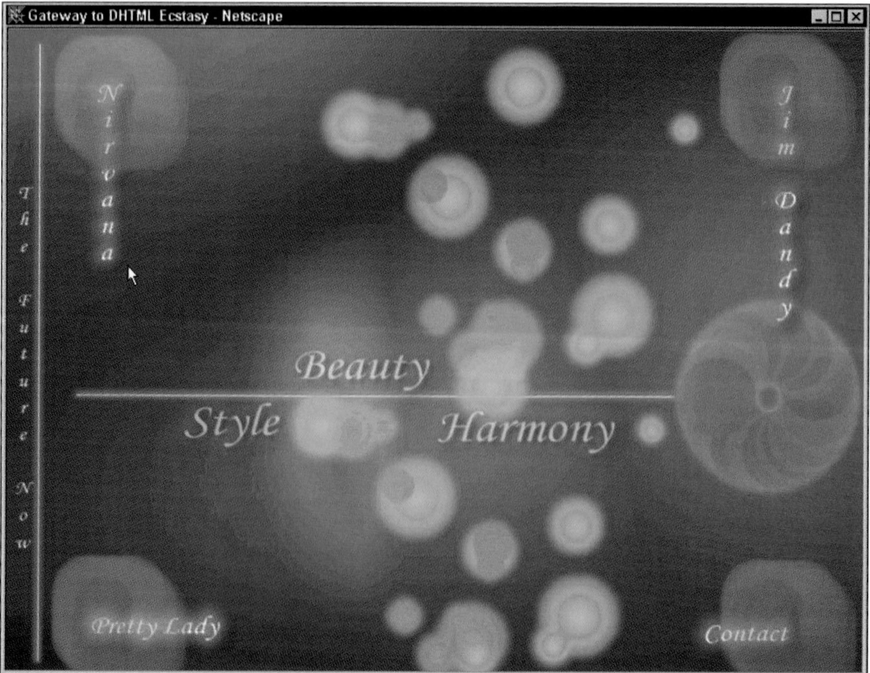

Figure 64 While Traversa's sites tend to be bandwidth-intensive, their visionary experience is certainly worthwhile.

Adding Multimedia Elements

PART

V

✦ ✦ ✦ ✦

In This Part

✦ ✦ ✦ ✦

CHAPTER 22

Integrating Fireworks

Imagine demonstrating a newly completed Web site to a client who *didn't* ask for an image to be a little bigger, or the text on a button to be reworded, or the colors for the background to be revised. In the real world, Web sites — particularly the images — are constantly being tweaked and modified. This fact of Web life explains why Fireworks, Macromedia's premier Web graphics tool, is so popular. One of Fireworks' main claims to fame is that everything is editable all the time. If that were all that Fireworks did, the program would have already earned a place on every Web designer's shelf just for its sheer expediency. But Fireworks is far more capable a tool — and now, that power can be tapped directly in Dreamweaver.

With the combination of Dreamweaver 3 and Fireworks 3, an even greater level of integration between the two Macromedia products has been achieved. You can optimize your images – reduce the file size, crop the graphic, make colors transparent – within Dreamweaver using the Fireworks interface. Moreover, you can edit your image in any fashion in Fireworks and, with one click of the Update command, automatically export the graphic with its original export settings. Perhaps most importantly of all, now Dreamweaver can control Fireworks – creating graphics on the fly – and then integrate the results in Dreamweaver.

A key Fireworks feature is the capability to output HTML and JavaScript for easy creation of rollovers, sliced images, and image maps with behaviors. With Fireworks, you can specify Dreamweaver-style code, so that all your Web pages are consistent. Once HTML is generated within Fireworks, Dreamweaver's new Insert Fireworks HTML object makes code insertion effortless.

Web pages and Web graphics are closely tied to one another. With the tight integration between Dreamweaver and Fireworks, the Web designer's world is moving toward a single design environment.

✦ ✦ ✦ ✦

In This Chapter

Exploring the Fireworks/ Dreamweaver Connection

Using Fireworks from within Dreamweaver

Sending a graphic to Fireworks

Embedding Fireworks code

Driving the Fireworks graphics engine

✦ ✦ ✦ ✦

Easy Graphics Modification

It's not uncommon for graphics to need some alteration before they fully integrate into a Web design. In fact, I'd say it's far more the rule than the exception. The traditional workflow generally goes like this:

1. Create the image in one or more graphics-editing programs.
2. Place the new graphic on a Web page via your Web authoring tool.
3. Note where the problems lie — perhaps the image is too big or too small, maybe the drop shadow doesn't blend into the background properly, or maybe the whole image needs to be flipped.
4. Reopen the graphics program, make the modifications, and save the file again.
5. Return to the Web page layout to view the results.
6. Repeat Steps 3 through 5 ad infinitum until you get it right.

Although you're still using two different programs even with Dreamweaver and Fireworks integration, one of the techniques available enables you to open a Fireworks window on the Dreamweaver screen. Now you can make your alterations with the Web page noticeable in the background. I've found that this small advantage cuts my trial-and-error to a bare minimum and streamlines my workflow.

If you're not familiar with Fireworks, you're missing an extremely powerful graphics program made for the Web. Fireworks combines the best of both vector and bitmap technologies and was one of the first graphics programs to use PNG as its native format. Exceptional export capabilities are available in Fireworks with which images can be optimized for file size, color, and scale. Moreover, Fireworks is terrific at generating GIF animations, rollovers, image maps, and sliced images.

With the latest versions of Dreamweaver and Fireworks, you have two ways to alter your inserted graphics: the Optimize Image in Fireworks command and the Edit button in the Image Property Inspector.

The full integration described in this chapter requires that Fireworks 3 be installed after Dreamweaver 3. Certain features, such as the Optimize Image in Fireworks command, work with Dreamweaver 3 and Fireworks 2, but any others requiring direct communication between the two programs work only with Fireworks 3.

Optimizing an image in Fireworks

Although you can design the most beautiful, compelling image possible in your graphics program, if it's intended for the Internet, you need to view it in a Web page. Not only must the graphic work in the context of the entire page, you have to take the file size of the Web graphic into account. All these factors mean that most, if not all, images need to undergo some degree of modification once they're included in a Web page. Fireworks 3 makes these alterations as straightforward as possible by including a command for Dreamweaver during its installation.

The Optimize Image in Fireworks command opens the Export module of Fireworks, as shown in Figure 22-1, right in Dreamweaver's Document window.

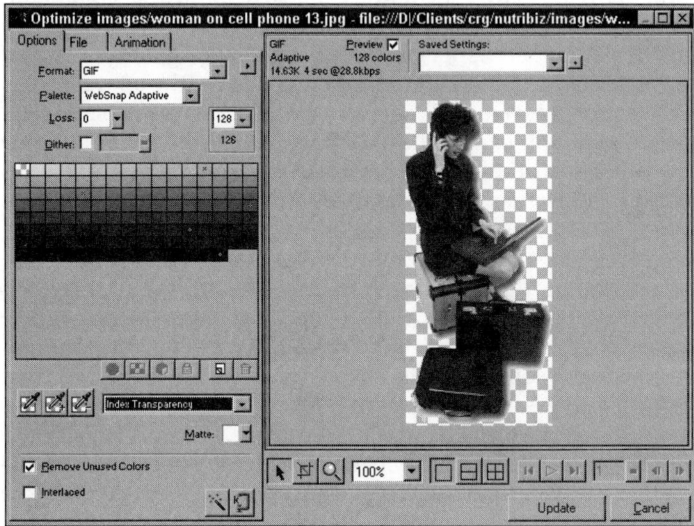

Figure 22-1: With Fireworks 3 installed, you can optimize your images from within Dreamweaver.

The Export module consists of three tabbed panels: Options, File, and Animation. Although a complete description of all of its features is beyond the scope of this book, here's a breakdown of the major uses of each area:

- ✦ **Options:** The Options panel is primarily used to try different export options and preview them. You can switch file formats from GIF to JPEG (or Animated GIF or PNG) as well as alter the palette, color depth, and dithering. Transparency for GIF and PNG images is set in the Options panel. Fireworks also has an Export to Size wizard that enables you to target a particular file size for your graphic.
- ✦ **File:** An image's dimensions are defined in the File panel. Images can be rescaled by a selected percentage or pixel size. Moreover, you can crop your image either numerically — by defining the export area — or visually with the Cropping tool.
- ✦ **Animation:** Frame-by-frame control for animated GIFs is available on the Animation panel. Each frame's delay (how long it is onscreen) is capable of being defined independently, and the entire animation can be set to either play once or loop a user-determined number of times.

If you crop or rescale an inserted image in Fireworks, you need to update the height and width in Dreamweaver. The easiest way to accomplish this is to select the Refresh button in the image's Property Inspector.

Fireworks saves its source files in an expanded PNG format to maintain full editability of the images. Graphics for the Web must be exported from Fireworks in GIF, JPEG, or standard PNG format. Dreamweaver's Optimize Image in Fireworks command can modify either the source or exported file. In most situations, better results are achieved from using the source file, especially when optimizing includes rescaling or resampling. However, some situations require that you leave the source file as is and modify only the exported files. Let's say, for example, that one source file is used to generate several different export files, each with different backgrounds (or *canvases*, as they are called in Fireworks). In that case, you'd be better off modifying the specific exported file rather than the general source image.

Dreamweaver enables you to choose which type of image you'd like to modify. When you first execute the Optimize Image in Fireworks or the Edit Image command, a Find Source dialog box (Figure 22-2) appears. If you want to locate and use the source file, choose Yes; to use the exported image that is inserted in Dreamweaver, select No. If you opt for the source file — and the image was created in Fireworks 3 — Dreamweaver reads the Design Note associated with the image to find the location of the source file and open it. If the image was created with an earlier version of Fireworks or the image has been moved, Dreamweaver asks you to locate the file with a standard Open File dialog box. By setting the Fireworks Source Files option, you can always open the same type of file: source or exported. Should you change your mind about how you'd like to work, open Fireworks and select File ➪ Preferences, and then choose the desired option from the Editing panel.

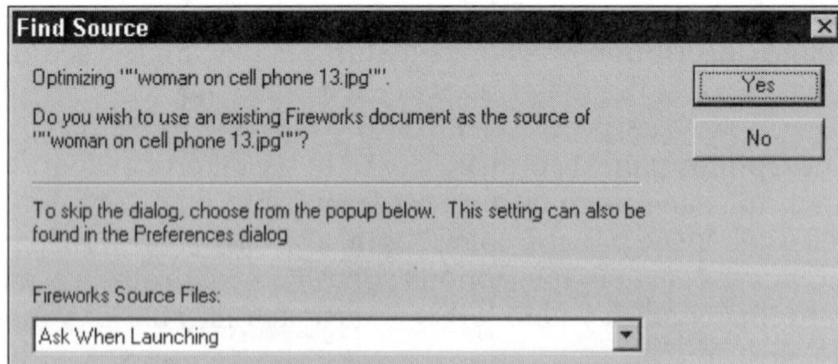

Figure 22-2: Set the Find Source dialog box to always use the source graphics image or the exported image, or to choose for each optimization.

Exploring Fireworks Source and Export Files

The separate source file is an important concept in Fireworks, and its use is strongly advised. Generally, when working in Fireworks, you have a minimum of two files for every image output to the Web: your source file and your exported Web image. Whenever major alterations are made, it's best to make them to the source file and then update the export files. Not only is this an easier method of working, but also you get a better image this way.

Source files are always Fireworks-style PNG files. Fireworks-style PNG files differ slightly from regular PNG format because they include additional information, such as paths and effects used that can be read only by Fireworks. The exported file is usually in GIF or JPEG format, although it could be in standard PNG format. Many Web designers keep their source files in a separate folder from their exported Web images so the two don't get confused. This source-and-export file combination also prevents you from inadvertently re-editing a lossy compressed file such as a JPEG image and reapplying the compression.

Note

Make sure that your source file and exported file are the same dimensions if you choose File ➪ Update. If your exported file is a cropped version of the source file, the complete source file is used as the basis for the export file, and any cropping information is discarded. To maintain the cropping, choose File ➪ Export instead of File ➪ Update.

To use the Optimize Image in Fireworks command, follow these steps:

1. Select the image you'd like to modify in Dreamweaver.

Note

You must save the current page at least once before running the Optimize Image in Fireworks command. The current state of the page doesn't have to have been saved, but a valid file must exist for the command to work properly. If you haven't saved the file, Dreamweaver alerts you to this fact when you call the command.

2. Choose Commands ➪ Optimize Image in Fireworks.
3. The Find Source dialog box opens, asking if you'd prefer to work with the Fireworks source file or the selected exported file. Choose Yes to use the PNG format source file and No to work with the exported file.

   The Optimize Images dialog box appears.
4. Make whatever modifications are desired from the Options, File, or Animation tabs of the Optimize Images dialog box.
5. When you're finished, select the Update button.

If you're working with a Fireworks source file, the changes are saved to both your source file and exported file; otherwise, only the exported file is altered.

Editing an image in Fireworks

Optimizing an image is great when all you need to do is tweak the file size or rescale the image. Other images require more detailed modification—as when a client requests that the wording or order of a series of navigational buttons be changed. Dreamweaver enables you to specify Fireworks as your graphics editor; and if you've done so, you can take advantage of Fireworks' capability to keep every element of your graphic always editable. And believe me, this is a major advantage.

In Dreamweaver 3, external editors can be set for any file format; you can even assign more than one editor to a file type. When installing the Dreamweaver 3/Fireworks 3 Studio, Fireworks is preset as the primary external editor for GIF, JPEG, and PNG files. The external editor assignment is handled through Dreamweaver Preferences.

To assign Fireworks to an existing file type, follow these steps:

1. Choose Edit ➪ Preferences.
2. Select the External Editors category.
3. Select the file type (GIF, JPEG, or PNG) from the Extensions list as shown in Figure 22-3.

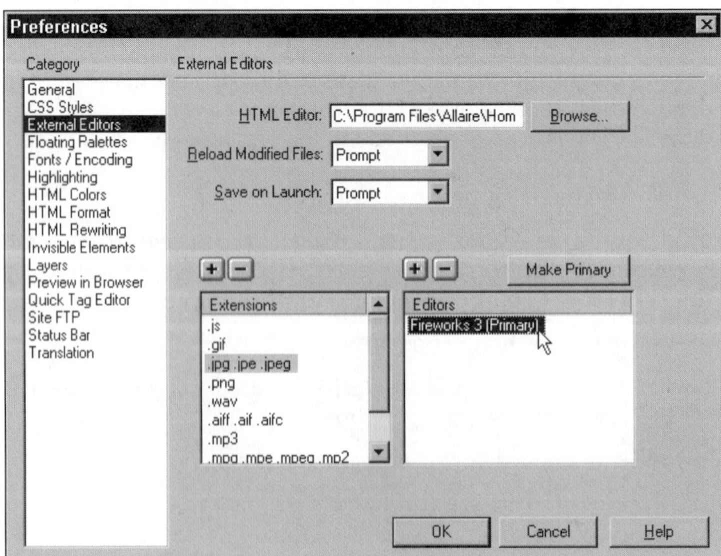

Figure 22-3: Define Fireworks as your External Editor for GIF, JPEG, and PNG files to enable the back-and-forth interaction between Dreamweaver and Fireworks.

4. Choose the Add button above the Editors list.

   The Add External Editor dialog box opens.

5. Locate the editor application and click Open when you're ready.

The default location in Windows systems is in C:\Program Files\Macromedia\Fireworks 3\Fireworks 3.exe; in Macintosh it's Macintosh HD:Applications:Fireworks 3:Fireworks 3. (The .exe extension may or may not be visible in your Windows system.)

6. Click Make Primary while the editor is highlighted.

Now, whenever you want to edit a graphic, select the image and click the Edit button in the Property Inspector. (You can also right-click [Control+click] the image and select Edit Image to start editing it.) Fireworks starts up, if it's not already open. As with the Optimize Image in Fireworks command, if the inserted image is a GIF or a JPEG and not a PNG format, Fireworks asks if you'd like to work with a separate source file. If so, you're given an opportunity to locate the file.

After you've made your alterations to your file in Fireworks, choose File ➪ Update or use the keyboard shortcut Ctrl+S (Command+S). If you're working with a Fireworks source file, both the source file and the exported file are updated and saved.

Recognizing Design Notes from Fireworks

Design Notes are one of the innovative methods for sharing information between graphic designers who use Fireworks and Web designers using Dreamweaver. Both programs are capable of saving Design Notes with their creations. A Design Note is basically an external file that contains editable information about any graphic or element inserted in Dreamweaver — or any page created by Dreamweaver. Fireworks also has the capability of adding Design Notes to a file; in fact, whenever an exported image is saved into a Dreamweaver site, a Design Note that stores the location of the source file for the graphic is automatically added. This enables Dreamweaver to optimize or edit the source file of an included image without asking the user to locate the file.

From within Dreamweaver, you can read Fireworks Design Notes — or add your own information. However, you have to make sure that Design Notes are enabled for the current site. To enable Design Notes, follow these steps:

1. Choose Site ➪ Define Sites.
2. From the Define Sites dialog box, select your current site and then Edit.
3. In the Edit Site dialog box, select the Design Notes category.
4. In the Design Notes panel, enable the Maintain Design Notes option.
5. If you want other team members to be able to view the Design Notes, select Upload Design Notes for Sharing.

6. Click OK to close the Edit Sites dialog box and then Done to close the Define Sites dialog box.

To view or add Design Notes to a Fireworks (or any other) image, select the file and right-click (Control+click) to open the context menu; then choose Design Notes. The Design Notes dialog box is displayed; select the All Info tab to see the path to the source file. The source file information is contained in a Design Note key called `fw_source` and looks like this:

```
fw_source=file:///D|/DW3 Bible/images/house.png
```

You can add additional information to the Design Note for the graphic by selecting the Add button and filling in the Name and Value fields. Tab out of the Value field to confirm your entry, rather than pressing Enter (Return).

Inserting Rollovers

The rollover is a fairly common, but effective, Web technique to indicate interactivity. Named after the user action of "rolling the mouse pointer over" the graphic, this technique uses from two to four different images per button. With Fireworks, you can both create the graphics and output the necessary HTML and JavaScript code from the same program. Moreover, Fireworks has some sophisticated twists to the standard "on/off" rollovers to further easily enhance your Web page.

Rollovers created in Fireworks can be inserted into Dreamweaver through several methods. First, you can use Fireworks to just build the images and then export them and attach the behaviors in Dreamweaver. This technique works well for graphics going into layers or images with other attached behaviors. The second method of integrating Fireworks-created rollovers involves transferring the actual code generated by Fireworks into Dreamweaver. This technique previously involved opening the HTML Inspector and copying and pasting the code — now, with Dreamweaver 3, you can handle the procedure completely with one object: Insert Fireworks HTML.

Using Dreamweaver's behaviors

With its full-spectrum editability, Fireworks excels at building consistent rollover graphics simply. The different possible states of an image in a rollover — Up, Over, Down, and Over Down — are handled in Fireworks as separate frames. As with an animated GIF, each frame has the same dimensions as the document, but the content is slightly altered to indicate the separate user actions. For example, Figure 22-4 shows the different frame states of a rollover button, side-by-side.

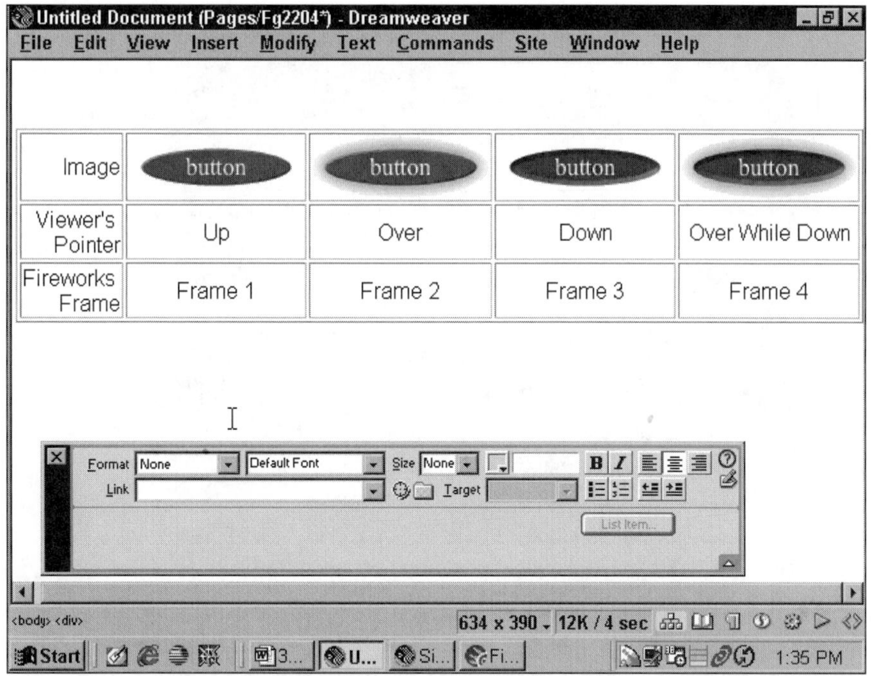

Figure 22-4: A Fireworks-created rollover can be made of four separate frames.

Many Web designers use just the initial two states — Up and Over — in their rollover buttons. The third state, Down, takes place when the user clicks the button, and it is useful if you want to indicate that moment to the user. The Down state also indicates which button has been selected (which is "down") when a new page appears, but the same navigation bar is used, notably with frames. The fourth state, Over While Down, is called when the previously selected button is rolled over by the user's pointer.

To insert Fireworks-created graphics using Dreamweaver behaviors, follow these steps:

1. Create your graphics in Fireworks, using a different frame for each rollover state.
2. In Fireworks 3, choose File ➪ Export Special ➪ Export as Files.

   The Export Special dialog box opens (see Figure 22-5).

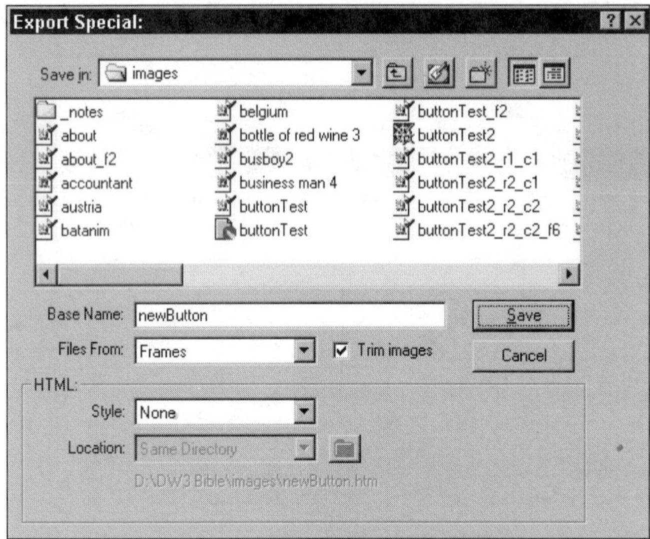

Figure 22-5: From Fireworks, you can export each frame as a separate file to be used in Dreamweaver rollovers.

3. Enter a new Base Name in the text box, if desired.

   The Base Name is used in Fireworks to name multiple images exported from a single file. When exporting frames, the default settings append "_f*n*", where *n* is the number of the frame. Frame numbers 1–9 are listed with a leading zero (for example, MainButton_f01).

4. In the Files From list box, select Frames.
5. If necessary, change the HTML Style list box option to None.
6. Select the Save button to store your frames as separate files.

Note You can attach the rollover behaviors to your images in several ways in Dreamweaver. The following technique uses Dreamweaver's Rollover object.

7. From the Common panel of the Objects palette, choose the Insert Rollover Image object.
8. In the Insert Rollover Image dialog box, choose the Original Image Browse (Choose) button to locate the image stored with the first frame designation, _f01.
9. If desired, give your image a different unique name than the one automatically assigned in the Image Name text box.

10. Choose the Rollover Image Browse button to locate the image stored with the second frame designation, _f02.
11. Click OK when you're done.
12. If you'd like to use the Down (_F03) and Over Down (_F04) images, attach additional swap image behaviors by opening the Swap Image behavior and following the steps outlined in Chapter 19.

Many Web designers build their entire navigation bar—complete with rollovers—in Fireworks. Rather than create and export one button at a time, all the navigation buttons are created as one graphic, and slices or hotspots are used to make the different objects or areas interact differently. You learn more about slices and hotspots later in this chapter.

Using Fireworks' code

In some ways, Fireworks is a hybrid program, capable of simultaneously outputting terrific graphics and sophisticated code. You can even select the type of code you want generated in Fireworks 3: Dreamweaver 2, 3.0, or 3.0 Library compatible; or code compatible with other programs such as GoLive and FrontPage. You also find a more general Generic code option. All these options are chosen during the Export procedure.

For rollovers, Fireworks generally outputs to two different sections of the HTML document, the `<head>` and the `<body>`; only the FrontPage style keeps all the code together. The `<head>` section contains the JavaScript code for activating the rollovers and preloading the images; `<body>` contains the HTML references to the images themselves, their links, and the event triggers (`onClick` or `onMouseOver`) used.

The general procedure is to first create your graphics in Fireworks and then export them, simultaneously generating a page of code. Now, the just-generated Fireworks HTML page can be incorporated in Dreamweaver. Dreamweaver 3 adds two slick methods for including your Fireworks-output code and images. The Insert Fireworks HTML object places the code—and the linked images—right at your current cursor position. You also have the option of exporting your Fireworks HTML directly to the clipboard and pasting it, verbatim, into Dreamweaver.

Just as an image requires a link to create a rollover in Dreamweaver, Fireworks images need to be designated as either a *slice* or a *hotspot*. The Fireworks program describes slices and hotspots as being part of the graphic's Web layer. The Web layer can be hidden or locked, but not deleted. Figure 22-6 shows the same button with both a slice and a hotspot attached.

Figure 22-6: The Fireworks image on the left uses a slice object, whereas the image on the right uses a polygon hotspot.

Slices are rectangular areas that permit different areas of the same graphic to be saved as separate formats — the entire graphic is formatted as an HTML table. Each slice can also be given its own URL; Fireworks requires either slices or hotspots to attach behaviors.

A Fireworks *hotspot* is a region defined for an image map. Hotspots can be rectangular, elliptical, or polygonal — just like those created by Dreamweaver with the Image Map tools. Because Fireworks is an object-oriented graphics program, any selected image (or part of an image) can be automatically converted to a hotspot. Like slices, hotspots can have both URLs and behaviors assigned to them.

Note In addition to the technique outlined in the text that follows, you could also use Fireworks 3's new Button Editor to create your rollover images and behaviors.

To include Fireworks-generated code in your Dreamweaver document, first follow these steps in Fireworks:

1. Create your graphics in Fireworks 3, placing the image for each interactive state on its own frame.
2. When the object is selected, choose Insert ➪ Hotspot or Insert ➪ Slice to add the item to your Web layer for attaching behaviors.

Alternatively, you can use any of the Hotspot or Slice tools found in the Fireworks toolbox.

3. Select the hotspot or slice and use Fireworks' Object Inspector to assign an Internet address to the selected graphic.

4. Open Fireworks' Behavior Inspector and choose the add behavior button (the + sign).

5. Select Simple Rollover.

The Simple Rollover behavior is used to create single-button or multiple-button rollovers in which one image is replaced by another image in the same location. Use Swap Image to create more complex rollovers such as those in which the rollover triggers an image change in another location.

6. Export the object by choosing File ➪ Export.

7. From the Export dialog box, enter a name in the Base Name text box and choose Use Slice Objects or Slice Along Guides from the Slices drop-down list.

8. Select the type of HTML code from the Style drop-down list.

   The Dreamweaver-related choices are Dreamweaver 2, Dreamweaver 3, and Dreamweaver 3 Library. Choose the Dreamweaver 3 HTML Style for graphics you intend to use once and Dreamweaver 3 Library for graphics that you plan to use throughout the site.

9. Choose the location to store your HTML code.

   The Location options are Same Directory, One Level Up, Custom and Copy to Clipboard. Many designers use the One Level Up convention to separate their images from the code. Select Copy to Clipboard to paste directly into Dreamweaver without creating an HTML file. Note that Dreamweaver 3 Library code must be saved in a site's Library folder.

10. Click Export when you're done.

When Fireworks completes the exporting, you have one HTML file (unless you've chosen the Copy to Clipboard HTML location) and one object file for each slice and frame. Now you're ready to integrate these images and the code into your Dreamweaver page. Which method you use depends on the HTML style selected when the graphics were exported from Fireworks:

✦ If you chose Dreamweaver 3, use the Insert Fireworks HTML object.

✦ If you chose Dreamweaver 3 Library, open the Library palette in Dreamweaver and insert the corresponding Library item.

✦ If you chose Copy to Clipboard, position your cursor where you'd like the graphics to appear and select Edit ➪ Paste or Ctrl+V (Command+V).

As you can see, the process for inserting Fireworks graphics and code has been greatly simplified in Dreamweaver 3. All three options are straightforward. Both the Library and Clipboard methods are one-step, self-explanatory techniques — and the Insert Fireworks HTML is hardly more complex. To insert the Fireworks code and images into your Dreamweaver page using the Insert Fireworks HTML object, follow these steps:

1. Make sure that you've exported your graphics and HTML from Fireworks with Dreamweaver 3 HTML Style selected.
2. Select the Insert Fireworks HTML object from the Common panel of the Objects palette.

   The Insert Fireworks HTML dialog box, shown in Figure 22-7, appears.

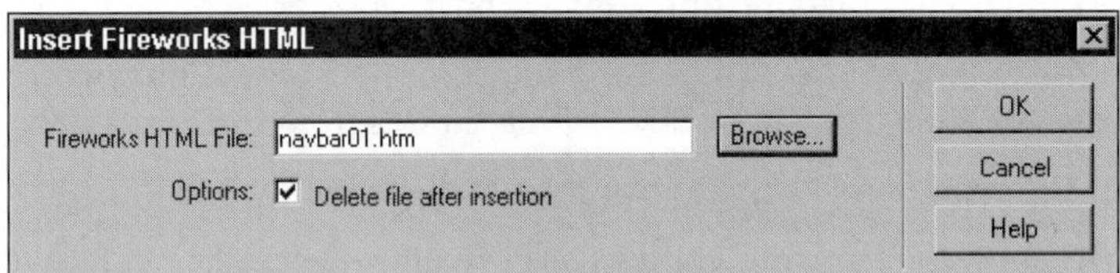

Figure 22-7: Import Fireworks code directly into Dreamweaver with the Insert Fireworks HTML object.

3. If you want to remove the Fireworks-generated HTML file after the code is inserted, select the Delete File After Insertion option.
4. Enter the path to the Fireworks HTML file or select the Browse button to locate the file.
5. Click OK when you're done.

   Dreamweaver inserts the Fireworks HTML and graphics at the current cursor location.

If you're a hands-on kind of Web designer, you can also use the HTML Inspector to copy and paste the JavaScript and HTML code. If you do, you can find helpful comments in the Fireworks file such as "Begin copying here" and "Stop copying here."

All the methods for inserting Fireworks HTML work with images with either hotspots or sliced objects (or both), with or without behaviors attached.

Controlling Fireworks with Dreamweaver

Dreamweaver and Fireworks integration extends deeper than just the simplified insertion of code and graphics. Dreamweaver can communicate directly with Fireworks, driving it to execute commands and return custom-generated graphics. This facility enables Web designers to build their Web page images based on the existing content. This interprogram communication promises to streamline the work of the Webmaster like never before — and that promise is already beginning to come through with existing Dreamweaver commands.

Web Photo Album

Online catalogs and other sites often depend on imagery to sell their products. Full-scale product shots can be large and time consuming to download, so it's not uncommon for Web designers to display a thumbnail of the images instead. If the viewer wants to see more detail, clicking the thumbnail loads the full-size image. Although it's not difficult to save a scaled-down version of an image in a graphics program and link the two in a Web layout program, creating page after page of such images is an overwhelming chore. The Dreamweaver/Fireworks interoperability offers a way to automate this tedious task.

A new Dreamweaver command, Create Web Photo Album, examines any user-specified folder of images and then uses Fireworks to scale the graphics to a set size. When the scaling is completed, the thumbnail graphics are brought into a Dreamweaver table, complete with links to a series of pages with the full-size image. Create Web Photo Album is an excellent example of the potential that Dreamweaver and Fireworks intercommunication offers.

The Create Web Photo Album command works with a folder of images in any format that Fireworks reads: GIF, JPEG, TIFF, Photoshop, PICT, BMP, and more. The images can be scaled to fit in a range of sizes, from 36 × 36 to 200 × 200. These thumbnails are exported in one of four formats:

✦ **GIF WebSnap 128:** Uses the WebSnap Adaptive palette, limited to 128 colors or fewer

✦ **GIF WebSnap 256:** Same as preceding format, with as many as 256 colors available

✦ **JPEG Better Quality:** Sets the JPEG quality setting at 80 percent, with no smoothing

✦ **JPEG Smaller File:** Sets the JPEG quality setting at 60 percent with a smoothing value of 2

The images are also exported in one of the same four settings, at a user-selected scale; the default scale is 100 percent.

To create a thumbnail gallery using Create Web Photo Album, follow these steps:

1. Choose Commands ➪ Create Web Photo Album.

   The Create Web Photo Album dialog box appears, as shown in Figure 22-8.

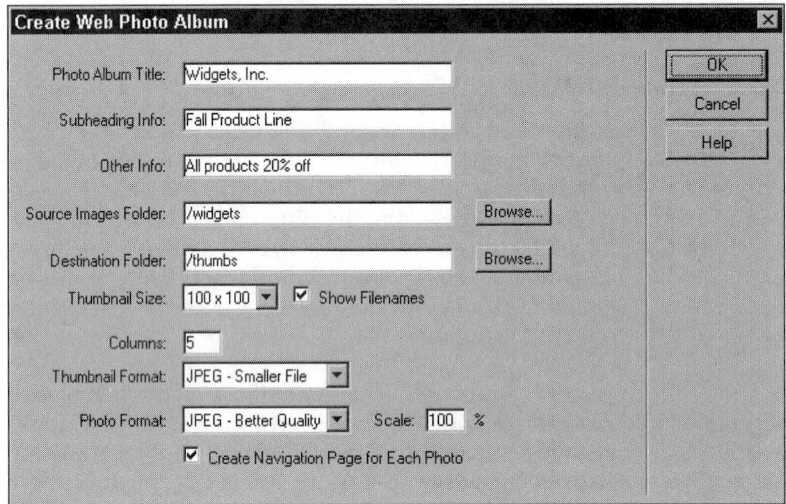

Figure 22-8: Build a thumbnail gallery page, linked to full-size originals.

2. Enter the Photo Album Title, Subheading Info, and Other Info into their respective text fields, if desired.

3. Enter the path to the folder of source images or select the Browse (Choose) button to locate the folder in the Source Images Folder field.

4. Enter the path to the Destination Folder or select the Browse (Choose) button to locate the folder in its field.

   Dreamweaver creates up to three subfolders in the Destination Folder: one for the original, rescaled images, another for the thumbnail images, and a third for the HTML pages created.

5. Select the desired thumbnail size from the drop-down list with the following options: 36 × 36, 72 × 72, 100 × 100, 144 × 144, and 200 × 200.

6. Select the Show Filenames option if you want the file name to appear below the image.
7. Choose the number of Columns for the table.
8. Select the export settings for the thumbnail images from the Thumbnail Format option list.
9. Select the export settings for the linked large-sized images from the Photo Format option list.
10. Choose the size of the linked large-sized images in the Scale field.
11. Select the Create Navigation Page for Each Photo option, if desired.

    Each photo's navigation page includes links to the Next and Previous images as well as the Home (main thumbnail) page, as shown in Figure 22-9.

Figure 22-9: You can add simple, clear navigation options to your Web Photo Album.

12. Click OK when you're done.

If not open, Fireworks starts and begins processing the images. When all the images are created and exported, Fireworks returns control to Dreamweaver. Dreamweaver then creates a single HTML page with the title, subheading, and other information up top, followed by a borderless table. As shown in Figure 22-10, each image is rescaled proportionately to fit within the limits set in the dialog box.

Figure 22-10: Build a thumbnail gallery with Fireworks right from Dreamweaver with the Create Web Photo Album command.

Custom Graphic Makers: StyleBuilder and BulletBuilder

Excited by the potential of Dreamweaver and Fireworks communication, I built two custom extensions: StyleBuilder and BulletBuilder. StyleBuilder enables you to convert any standard text in your Dreamweaver Web page to a graphic. StyleBuilder converts all text in a standard HTML tag, such as <h1> or <b>, any custom XML tag, or any selection. The graphics are based on Fireworks styles, displayed in a small swatch in the dialog box, along with basic information such as the font name and size used. Fireworks styles can be updated at any time, and the swatch set recreated on the fly in Fireworks.

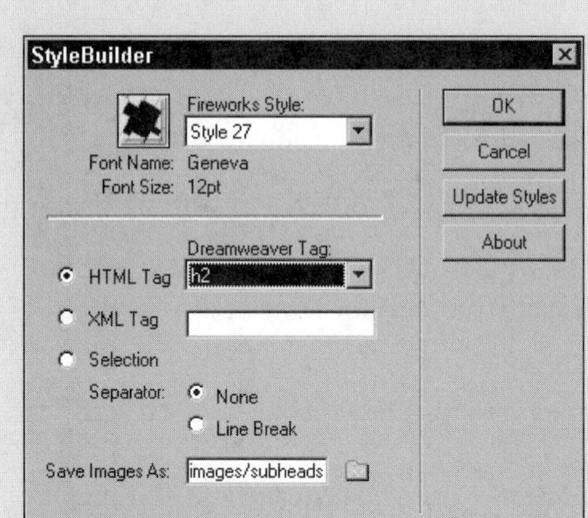

BulletBuilder is similar, but instead of changing text to graphics, this command converts the bullets of an unordered list to different graphic shapes. You can choose from ten different shapes, including diamonds, stars, starbursts, and four different triangles. The chosen shape is rendered in any available Fireworks style at a user-selected size.

Both commands can be found in the Commands folder on CD-ROM 1 that accompanies this book.

Building Dreamweaver/Fireworks extensions

To make communication between Dreamweaver and Fireworks viable, two conditions had to be met. First, Fireworks had to be scriptable; although Fireworks 2 had some batch processing capability, it was fairly limited. Second, a link between the two programs needed to be forged. The Dreamweaver 3/Fireworks 3 combination meets both criteria — and then some.

As with Dreamweaver 3, almost every operation is under command control in Fireworks 3. This is most apparent when using either program's History palette. If your action appears as a repeatable item in the History palette, a corresponding JavaScript function controls it. Fireworks' wealth of JavaScript functions also serves to expose its control to Dreamweaver – and the first condition for interoperability is handled. To create a strong link between programs, Dreamweaver engineers expanded on the Fireworks API used in the Optimize Image in Fireworks command, where Dreamweaver actually launches a streamlined version of Fireworks. This operation is controlled by a C-level extension called FWLaunch.

Here's a step-by-step description of how Dreamweaver typically is used to communicate with Fireworks:

1. The user selects a command in Dreamweaver.
2. Dreamweaver opens a dialog box, as with other extensions.
3. After the user has filled in the dialog box and clicked OK, the command begins to execute.
4. All user-supplied parameters are read and used to create a JavaScript scriptlet or function, which serve as instructions for Fireworks.
5. If used, the scriptlet is stored on the disk.
6. Fireworks is launched with a command to run the Dreamweaver-created scriptlet or function.
7. Fireworks processes the scriptlet or function, while Dreamweaver tracks its progress via a cookie on the user's machine.
8. Once Fireworks is finished, a positive result is returned.

   The Fireworks API includes several error codes if problems such as a full disk are encountered.
9. While tracking the Fireworks progress, Dreamweaver sees the positive result and integrates the graphics by rewriting the DOM of the current page.
10. The dialog box is closed, and the current page is refreshed to correctly present the finished product.

To successfully control Fireworks, you need a complete understanding of the Fireworks DOM and its extension capabilities. Macromedia provides documentation for extending Fireworks from its support site:
`www.macromedia.com/support/fireworks`.

Tip

I've also found the History palette in Fireworks to be useful—especially the Copy Command to Clipboard function. To see the underlying JavaScript used to create an object in Fireworks, first make the object. Then highlight the History palette steps and select the Copy to Clipboard button. Paste the clipboard contents in a text editor to see the exact steps Fireworks used; you can then begin to generalize the statements with variables and other functions.

On the Dreamweaver side, seven useful methods are in the FWLaunch C Library, detailed in Table 22-1.

Table 22-1
FWLaunch Methods

Method	*Returns*	*Use*
`bringDWToFront()`	N/A	Brings the Dreamweaver window in front of any other application running.
`bringFWToFront()`	N/A	Brings the Fireworks window in front of any other application running.
`execJsInFireworks (javascriptOrFileURL)`	Result from running the scriptlet in Fireworks. If the operation fails, returns an error code: 1: The argument proves invalid 2: File I/O error 3: Improper version of Dreamweaver 4: Improper version of Fireworks 5: User canceled operation	Executes the supplied JavaScript function or scriptlet.
`mayLaunchFireworks()`	Boolean	Determines if Fireworks may be launched.
`optimizeInFireworks (fileURL, docURL, {targetWidth}, {targetHeight})`	Result from running the scriptlet in Fireworks. If the operation fails,returns an error code: 1: The argument proves invalid 2: File I/O error	Performs an Optimize in Fireworks operation, opening the Fireworks Export Preview dialog box.

Continued

Table 22-1 *(continued)*

Method	***Returns***	***Use***
`optimizeInFireworks (fileURL, docURL, {targetWidth}, {targetHeight})` *(continued)*	3: Improper version of Dreamweaver 4: Improper version of Fireworks 5: User canceled operation	
`validateFireworks (versionNumber)`	Boolean	Determines if the user has a specific version of Fireworks.

Summary

Creating Web pages is almost never done with a single application: In addition to a Web layout program, you need a program capable of outputting Web graphics — and Fireworks is a world-class Web graphics generator and optimizer. Macromedia has integrated several functions with Dreamweaver and Fireworks to streamline production and ease modification. Here are some of the key features:

✦ You can update images placed in Dreamweaver with Fireworks in two ways: Optimize or Edit. With the Optimize Image in Fireworks command, just the Export Preview portion of Fireworks opens; with the Edit Image command, the full version of Fireworks is run.

✦ Graphics and HTML exported from Fireworks can be incorporated into a Dreamweaver page in numerous ways: as a Library item, an HTML file (complete with behavior code), or just pasted from the clipboard.

✦ New interapplication communication between Dreamweaver and Fireworks makes commands such as Create Web Photo Album possible.

✦ Dreamweaver includes a special C-level extension called FWLaunch, which provides the primary link to Fireworks.

In the next chapter, you see how you can add downloaded or streaming video to your Dreamweaver-created Web pages.

✦ ✦ ✦

Adding Video to Your Web Page

✦ ✦ ✦ ✦

In This Chapter

Creating video for the Web

Including video clips in your Web pages

Inserting QuickTime Player movies

Using streaming video

✦ ✦ ✦ ✦

In a world accustomed to being entertained by moving images 50 feet high, it's hard to understand why people are thrilled to see a grainy, jerky, quarter-screen sized video on a Web page. And in truth, it's the promise of video on the Web, not the current state of it, that has folks excited. Many of the industry's major players, including Microsoft and Apple, are spending big bucks to bring that promise a little closer to reality.

QuickTime and RealVideo are the most popular formats on the Web, and both are cross-platform. Video can be downloaded to the user and then automatically played with a helper application, or it can be streamed to the user so that it plays while it's downloading.

This chapter looks at the many different methods for incorporating video — whether you're downloading an MPEG file or streaming a RealVideo movie — into your Web pages through Dreamweaver.

Video on the Web

It may be hard for folks not involved in the technology of computers and the Internet to understand why the high-tech Web doesn't always include something as "low-tech" as video. After all, television has been around forever, right? The difficulties arise from the fundamental difference between the two media: television and radio signals are analog, and computers are pure digital. Sure, you can convert an analog signal to a digital one — but that's just the beginning of the solution.

The amount of information stored on a regular (analog) VHS cassette is truly remarkable. Moving that amount of information about in the ones and zeros of the digital world is a formidable task. For example, storing the digital video stream from any Digital Video camcorder uses up storage space at the rate of about one gigabyte every five minutes, and that video is already compressed. Large file sizes also translate into enormous bandwidth problems when you are transmitting video over the Web.

To resolve this issue of megasized files, industry professionals and manufacturers have developed various strategies, or *architectures*, for the creation, storage, and playback of digital media. Each architecture has a different file format, and thus each requires the user to have a playback system — whether a plug-in, ActiveX control, or Java applet — capable of handling that particular format.

In an effort to keep file sizes as small as possible, Web videos are often presented in very small dimensions. It's not uncommon to display a video at a puny 180 by 120 pixels. Furthermore, you'll notice a major difference between conventional and Web-based video in terms of quality. Television video displays at roughly 30 frames per second, film, 24 frames per second; but the best Web video rarely gets above 15 frames per second — virtually guaranteeing choppy motion in scenes with any action in them. Lossy compression also leads to artifacting — visible flaws introduced by the compression itself.

Given all the restrictions that video suffers on the Web, why use it at all? Simply because nothing else like it exists, and when you need video, you have to use video. Take heart, though. Advances are occurring at a rapid rate, both in the development of new video architectures and codecs and in new, higher-speed Internet delivery systems, such as cable modems and DSL phone lines. What you learn in this chapter enables you to include video in your Dreamweaver-built Web pages today and gives you a good foundation for accommodating future enhancements.

The Streaming Media Big Three

Technologies — and the companies that create them — come and go on the Internet. Over the past few years, quite a few different streaming media solutions have presented themselves and then faded away, leaving us with the current "Big Three": RealMedia, QuickTime, and Windows Media. These three technologies together represent almost the entire streaming media market, and the vast majority of Internet users have at least one of the corresponding players; many have two or even all three.

RealMedia

RealNetworks released the first streaming media system — RealAudio — in 1995. Over the years, RealAudio has evolved into RealMedia and now supports video, images, text, Flash movies, and standard audio types such as AIFF and MP3. All of these media types can be combined into a single presentation using SMIL (Synchronized Multimedia Integration Language).

The three primary software components of RealMedia are as follows:

✦ **RealPlayer:** The client software for viewing RealMedia. RealPlayer Basic is free, and RealPlayer Pro offers the user more features for $30. Either one can view all RealMedia content. A user who enjoys streaming media could quite easily browse the Web with RealPlayer 7 (see Figure 23-1) because its many Web links and ads, as well as the Flash navigation elements that often surround presentations, offer the user a lot of choices. RealPlayer 7 is available at `www.real.com/player`.

Figure 23-1: RealPlayer 7's busy interface enables the user to forego a Web browser completely when browsing for streaming media.

✦ **RealProducer:** Encoding software that turns standard MPEG and QuickTime Video into RealMedia files, which have the file name extension .rm. Again, you can pay for a free RealProducer Basic and an enhanced Pro version, available at `www.realnetworks.com/products/producer`.

✦ **RealServer:** Server software for serving RealMedia over RTSP (Real-Time Streaming Protocol). You can still offer RealMedia to your users over the Web's regular HTTP without any special server software. RealServer Basic is limited to ten users; to upgrade from that, you pay by the number of users. It's available at `www.realnetworks.com/products/basicserverplus`.

RealNetworks has led the way in cross-platform authoring and playback. Versions of RealPlayer are available for Windows, Macintosh, Unix, Linux, and OS/2, and versions of RealProducer for almost as many platforms. WebTV even plays RealAudio 3.0. By contrast, QuickTime is limited to Windows and Macintosh, and Microsoft's streaming video solution is basically Windows-only.

RealNetworks has also led the way in sheer numbers of eyeballs; for years they were the only option for large-scale streaming media sites. Even now, when they face the stiffest competition they've ever had, their market share is still about 55 percent. RealPlayer is included with major browsers, as well as with Windows, Mac OS and Red Hat Linux.

See `www.real.com` for examples of RealMedia content.

QuickTime

What "QuickTime" refers to is widely misunderstood. Some people confuse the video format QuickTime Video with QuickTime itself, but QuickTime Video is just one of the things a QuickTime movie might contain. Sometimes the high-profile QuickTime Player 4 is confused with QuickTime, but it is just one dependent application.

The best way to explain QuickTime is to say that it's a multimedia operating system, enabling applications such as CD-ROM titles to run on top of it and use the features it provides. These features include support for audio, video, images, 3D objects, MIDI music (including a software wavetable synthesizer) and — with QuickTime 4 — streaming video, Flash movies, and MP3 audio. Once you have QuickTime 4 installed on your computer, suddenly Director can access digital video. Flash 4 can export complete QuickTime presentations, and otherwise pedestrian applications can suddenly play synthesized music.

With the inclusion of streaming video in QuickTime, Apple dressed up QuickTime 3's MoviePlayer with an eye-catching brushed aluminum look and changed its name to QuickTime Player 4. Apple positioned themselves as a competitor to RealNetworks in the Web broadcasting field and now have almost 35 percent of the streaming market. QuickTime movies have a .mov file name extension.

Like RealMedia, QuickTime streaming has three main software components:

✦ **QuickTime and QuickTime Player:** All the viewing goodness of QuickTime and QuickTime Player (Figure 23-2) is free and is available for Macintosh and Windows at `www.apple.com/quicktime`. QuickTime is also included with all Macintosh computers and installed on Windows by CD-ROM titles. Just as they can with RealPlayer, users can spend more time in QuickTime Player and less in a browser because of the favorites storage and Flash navigation elements in many streaming presentations.

Figure 23-2: QuickTime Player has an uncluttered appearance that focuses the eye on the content.

✦ **QuickTime Pro and QuickTime Player Pro:** For about $30, Apple sells you a key code that unlocks the content creation features of QuickTime and turns it into QuickTime Pro, enabling QuickTime-dependent applications to create a vast range of QuickTime content. QuickTime Player becomes QuickTime Player Pro: a great piece of software that provides easy content conversion and cut-and-paste video compositing, although the interface is spartan and sometimes hides functionality. Apple has a directory of third-party QuickTime authoring tools at `www.apple.com/quicktime/authoring`.

✦ **QuickTime Streaming Server:** QuickTime Streaming Server delivers video over the Web using the standard RTSP, just like RealPlayer. Apple released QuickTime Streaming Server as open source software, and it is available completely free — no per stream charge, either — for Mac OS X, Darwin, and Linux. See `www.apple.com/quicktime/servers`.

Examples of QuickTime streaming content can be found on the QuickTime home page at `www.apple.com/quicktime`.

Windows Media

Microsoft has released a succession of media technologies over the years in an effort to gain some sort of foothold in content creation and delivery. The history of Microsoft multimedia is an incredible story of acquisitions, rebranding, orphaned technologies, and outright copying everybody else.

With Windows Media, though, Microsoft has gone all out, providing a solid — if unexciting — solution with lots of partners. Still, Windows Media's greatest asset is its automatic inclusion with every Windows PC, virtually guaranteeing it a huge installed base as time goes on. For now, though, Windows Media owns a little more than 10 percent of the market. Windows Media files have file name extensions of .asf or .asx.

The software involved in Windows Media includes:

✦ **Windows Media Player:** The supercharged Windows Media Player (see Figure 23-3) doesn't do as much all by itself as the other streaming players. Strangely, the Windows Media Player doesn't contain any buttons or menu items that actually start playing audio or video, in spite of the Favorites menu — which opens Web sites with embedded video in your browser — and a promising-looking button bar that says "Music" and "Radio." Although beta versions of the Windows Media Player exist for Macintosh and Unix, they seem to be unsupported. I was not able to get the Macintosh version to work at all, in spite of trying with multiple Web sites. For the time being, consider Windows Media to mean Windows-only. The Windows Media Player home page is at `www.microsoft.com/windows/mediaplayer`.

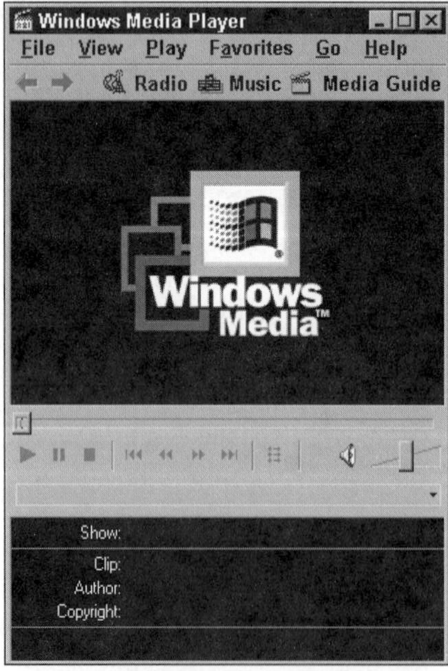

Figure 23-3: The Windows Media Player is heavily integrated with Internet Explorer but doesn't do much on its own.

✦ **Content creation and server software:** A directory of tools for working with Windows Media can be found at `www.microsoft.com/windows/windowsmedia`. Most are from Microsoft themselves, and all are Windows-only.

The Windows Media home page is located at `www.windowsmedia.com` and includes example content.

Working with Video Clips

If you have short video clips you'd like to put on the Web, you may not need the industrial strength — or the hassle and expense — of a streaming media solution. Short video clips can be included in a Web page just by linking to them or embedding them.

Depending on the viewer's software setup, video clips either download completely and then start playing, start playing right away and stutter as they wait for data, or start playing as soon as enough of the video has arrived that uninterrupted playback is possible, as shown in Figure 23-4.

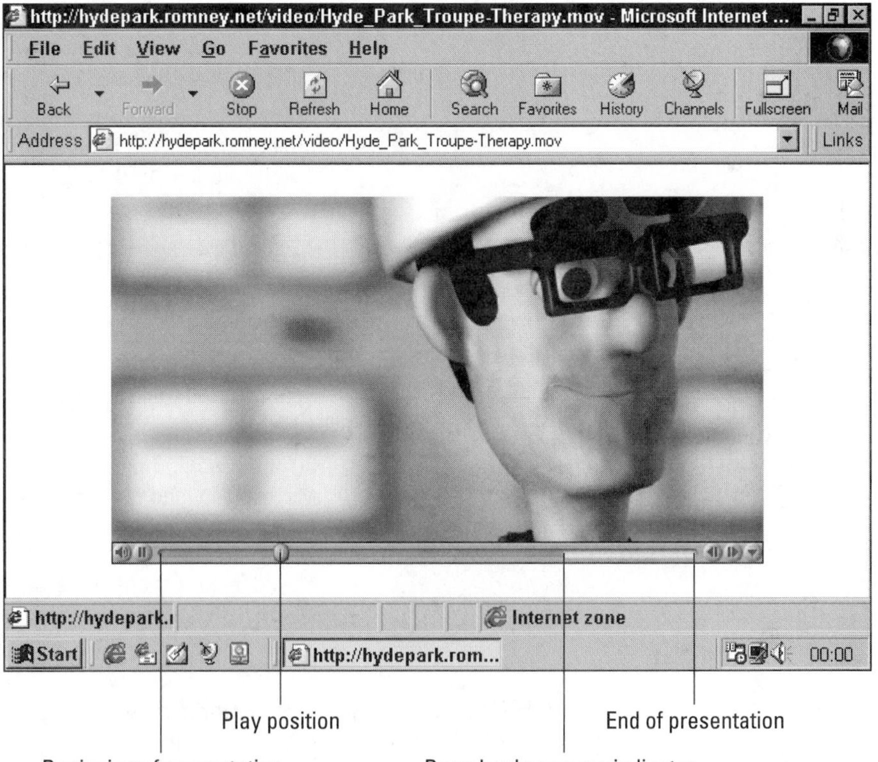

Figure 23-4: QuickTime Player starts playing video clips when it has downloaded enough that playback will be uninterrupted.

Video clips come in a few common formats, detailed in Table 23-1. In addition to the video format itself, what *codec* (en**co**der/**dec**oder) a particular video clip uses is also important. A codec provides video compression and is required for the decompression at playback time. Many codecs are included with Windows and with QuickTime, so codecs are not usually a problem, unless you're authoring for platforms other than Windows and Macintosh.

Table 23-1
Video Clip File Formats

Video Format	*Typical File Name Extension*	*Description*
MPEG	.mpg, .mpeg, .mpe	The MPEG video format is the work of the Motion Picture Experts Group. Windows computers play MPEG video clips with Windows Media Player or another, older Microsoft player. Macintosh systems play MPEG clips with QuickTime.
QuickTime	.mov	QuickTime movies can contain a multitude of media types and usually require QuickTime for playback.
QuickTime Video	.mov	A QuickTime movie that contains plain video only, and can be played by almost any video player on a machine that doesn't have QuickTime installed, as long as the right codec is available.
Video for Windows (AVI)	.avi	The popular but now officially unsupported format used by Microsoft's Video for Windows (aka ActiveMovie, aka NetShow). As with QuickTime Video, clips can be played in almost any player, as long as the right codec is installed.

One codec to watch out for if you're making cross-platform movies is the Intel Indeo Video codec, sometimes used for Video for Windows (AVI) files. The Indeo codec for Macintosh is not included with QuickTime and must be installed manually by Macintosh users.

MPEG, QuickTime Video, or AVI clips are good candidates for linking or embedding due to the wide variety of players on multiple platforms that can play them. QuickTime movies are best aimed squarely at the QuickTime Player because of the multiple media types that they contain.

Linking to video

To include a video clip in your Dreamweaver Web page, follow these steps:

1. Select the text or image that you want to serve as the link to the video file.

If you use an image as a link, you might want to use a frame from the video clip in order to provide a preview.

2. In the Property Inspector, enter the name of the video file in the Link text box or select the folder icon to browse for the file.
3. Because video files can be quite large, it's also good practice to note the file size next to the link name or enter it in the Alt text box, as shown in Figure 23-5.

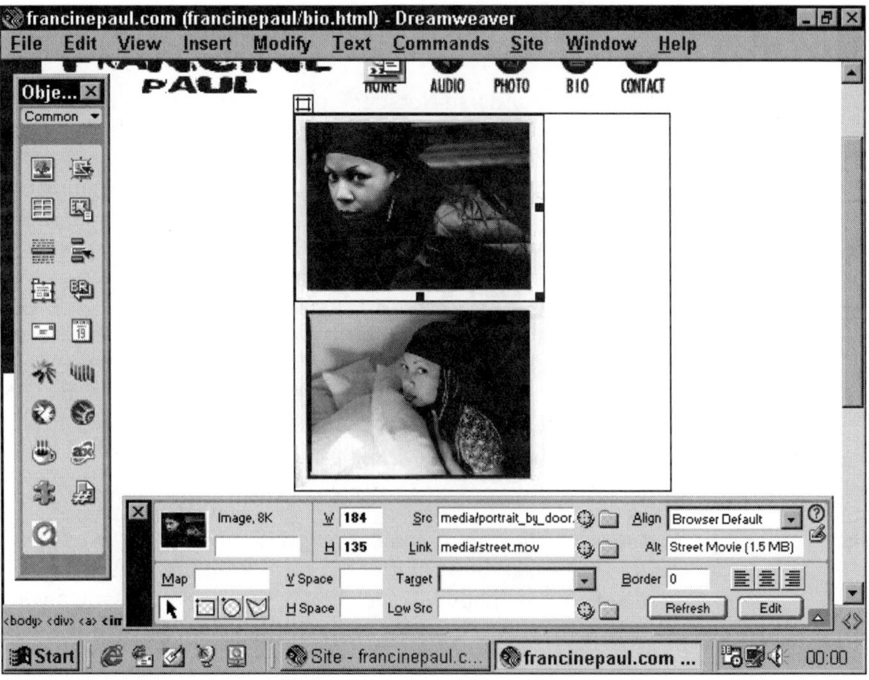

Figure 23-5: You can insert any video file for user download by creating a link to it, as if it were a simple Web page.

Embedding video

You can gain more control over the way your video clip plays by embedding it in the Web page with the `<embed>` tag. Modifying the attributes of the `<embed>` tag enables you to modify how the video is presented. Video clips inserted this way play back in whatever players are available, just as linked video clips do.

Note: The Windows Media Player in Internet Explorer plays video inserted using the `<embed>` tag, despite the fact that you can also address it as an ActiveX Control.

To embed a simple video clip in a Web page, follow these steps:

1. Choose Insert ➪ Plug-in or select the Plug-in object from the Common pane of the Objects palette, or drag the Plug-in object to a location on your Web page.
2. In the Insert Plug-in dialog box, enter the path to the video clip in the Plug-in Src text box, or select the folder icon to browse for the file.
3. In the Plug-in Property Inspector, enter the dimensions of your video clip in the width and height boxes, marked W and H, respectively.

Playing Videos within Dreamweaver

Dreamweaver can access and use Netscape plug-ins to display video right in the Document window at design-time. These plug-ins can be installed in Netscape's Plugins folder, in Internet Explorer's Plugins folder, or in Dreamweaver's own Plugins folder. Dreamweaver checks all three every time it starts up. Installing the correct plug-ins into Netscape and enabling Dreamweaver to use them from there can make maintaining your plug-ins easier, because many come with browser-specific installation programs that are hard to adapt to Dreamweaver.

Whenever a file is embedded for playback via a plug-in, a green Play button appears in the Property Inspector. To play a particular video in Dreamweaver's Document window, all you have to do is select the plug-in placeholder and click the Play button. The video begins playing, and the green Play button becomes a red Stop button, as shown in Figure 23-6. To stop playback — surprise — just click the Stop button.

Tip: How can playing a video during the design phase be useful? I've used this capability to sample the background color of the page from the background of a video's title or ending frame so that the video clip fits seamlessly into the page.

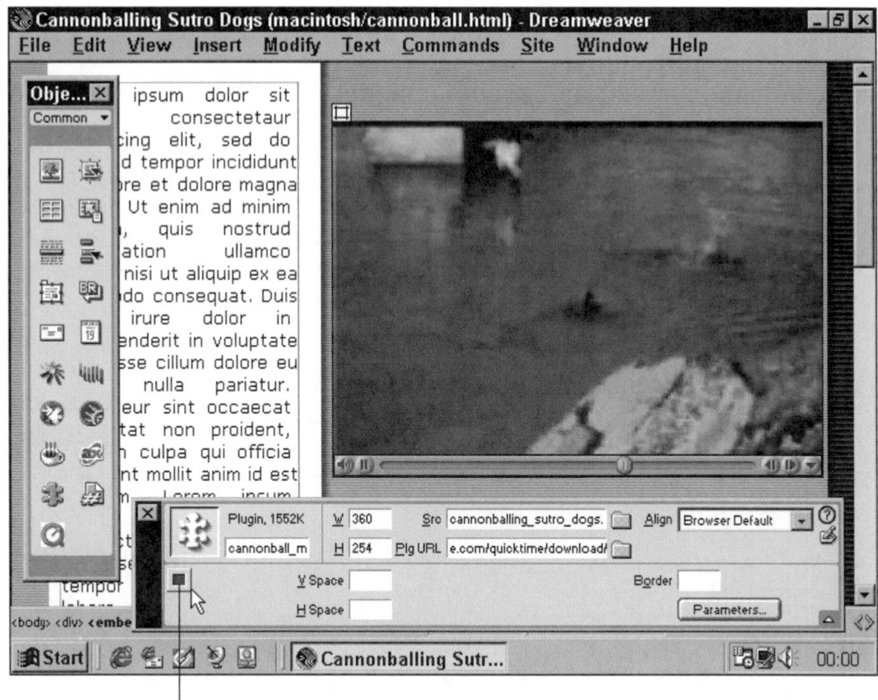

Play/Stop button

Figure 23-6: Playing video within Dreamweaver is as simple as having the right plug-in installed and clicking Play.

You can also use the menus and the corresponding keyboard shortcuts to control the digital video in the Document window: View ➪ Plugins ➪ Play or Ctrl+P (Command+P), and View ➪ Plugins ➪ Stop or Ctrl+. (period) (Command+. (period)). If you have multiple videos inserted on the page, you can play them all by choosing View ➪ Plugins ➪ Play All or by using the keyboard shortcut Ctrl+Shift+P (Command+Shift+P), and stop them with View ➪ Plugins ➪ Stop All or Ctrl+Shift+. (period) (Command+Shift+. (period)).

Caution

Unsupported plug-ins are listed in the UnsupportedPlugins.txt file in Dreamweaver's Configuration folder. The one plug-in identified by Macromedia as not working with Dreamweaver is the Video for Windows plug-in on Windows. If you're relying on this plug-in for video playback, you still have to preview your video files through a browser.

Inserting QuickTime Movies

The HTML command for incorporating a QuickTime movie (or any other media that requires a plug-in) is the `<embed>` tag. Because so many different types of plug-ins exist, Dreamweaver uses a generic Plugin Inspector that enables an unlimited number of parameters to be specified. If you regularly work with QuickTime movies, a custom QuickTime Dreamweaver object such as the one from Brendan Dawes (available on CD-ROM 1 that comes with this book) in Figure 23-7 can streamline the process. Although you still need to add some parameters by hand, having easy access to the most common ones can be a real time-saver.

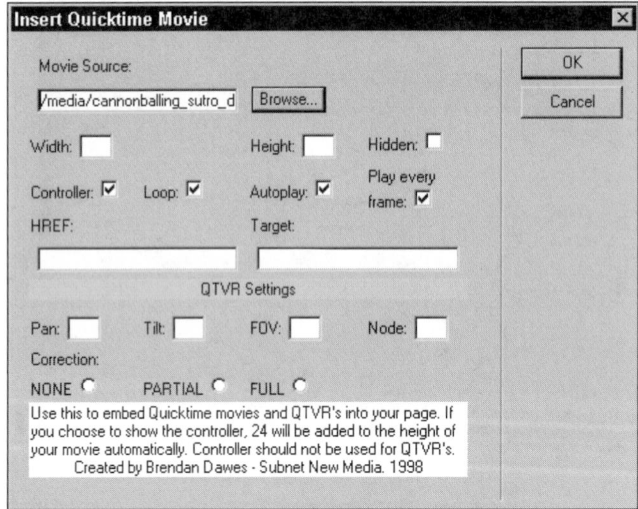

Figure 23-7: Add a third-party QuickTime object to Dreamweaver to simplify embedding QuickTime movies.

You can find Brendan Dawes' QuickTime 4 object in a folder on CD-ROM 1 that accompanies this book. Copy the folder to your own Objects folder and restart Dreamweaver.

Only three `<embed>` tag parameters are absolutely required for a QuickTime movie: the source of the file, the movie's width, and the movie's height, but the QuickTime plug-in also offers an amazing array of additional `<embed>` tag attributes to enable you to fine-tune the way content is presented.

The QuickTime Plugin is used by both Netscape and Internet Explorer on both Windows and Macintosh to enable the browser to interface with QuickTime.

To insert a QuickTime movie in your Web page, follow these steps:

1. First, insert the Plug-in object. Choose Insert ⇨ Plug-in or select the Plug-in object from the Common pane of the Objects palette, or drag the Plug-in object to a location on your Web page.
2. In the Insert Plug-in dialog box, enter the QuickTime movie's path and file name in the Plug-in Source text box, or select the folder to browse for the file.

If you're working on a Macintosh and your QuickTime movie doesn't have a file name extension, add **.mov** to the end of its name before embedding it or placing it on the Web.

3. In the Plug-in Property Inspector (see Figure 23-8), enter the width and height values in the W and H text boxes, respectively. Alternately, you can drag any of the sizing handles on the Plug-in placeholder in the Document window to a new size.

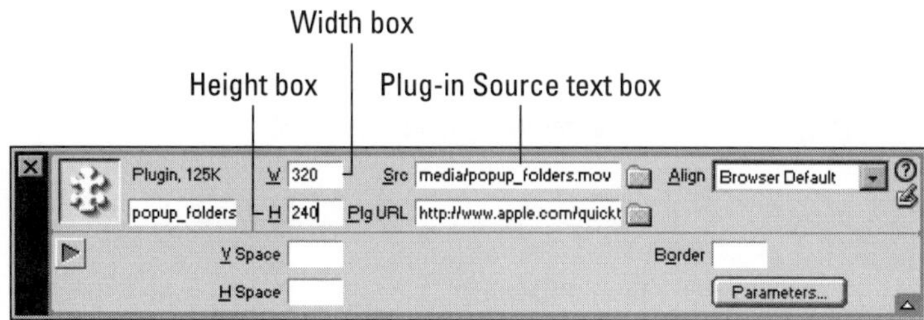

Figure 23-8: When inserting a QuickTime movie, specify the properties and values in the Plug-in Property Inspector.

If you don't know the dimensions of your QuickTime movie, open it in the QuickTime Player and choose Movie ⇨ Get Info and select Size from the options list on the right of the dialog box that appears.

4. In the Plg URL text box, enter `www.apple.com/quicktime`. This is the Web address that users who don't have QuickTime are directed to by their browser.
5. Select the Parameters button to open the Parameters dialog box, where you can enter additional `<embed>` tag attributes. Enter the attribute name in the left column and the value in the right column. Press Tab to move from one column to another. Table 23-2 describes the available parameters for a QuickTime movie. Add any additional parameters that you may require and click OK when you're done.

Table 23-2
QuickTime 4 Plugin Parameters

QuickTime Plugin Parameter	*Possible Values*	*Description*
`autoplay`	true (the default) or false	When set to false, a movie won't play until the user presses play in the controller. Otherwise, it starts playing as soon as enough data is downloaded to ensure uninterrupted playback.
`bgcolor`	RGB colors in hexadecimal such as "#FFFFFF", or valid HTML color names, such as "red"	Sets the color of the space set aside by the width and height attributes but not taken up by the QuickTime movie. Add a border to a QuickTime movie by setting the appropriate bgcolor and increasing the width and height attributes by a few pixels.
`cache`	true (the default) or false	Specifies whether the browser should store the movie in its cache for later retrieval. Doesn't work in IE.
`controller`	true (default for most movies) or false (the default for Flash only or QuickTime VR movies)	Displays the controller panel attached to the bottom of the movie.
`dontflatten whensaving`	Does not take a value. Include the parameter only.	When included, saving the movie using the Save As QuickTime option on the QuickTime Plugin's controller menu saves the movie without resolving references (not self-contained).
`endtime`	30 frame SMPTE timecode (hours:minutes:seconds:-thirtieths of a second)	Indicates the point in the movie where playback should stop.
`height`	A value in pixels; usually the height of the movie	Reserves a space in the page for the QuickTime movie.
`hidden`	Does not take a value; include the parameter only	Tells the QuickTime Plugin not to show the movie. Audio is played, though.

QuickTime Plugin Parameter	*Possible Values*	*Description*
`href`	A URL	A link to go to when the movie is clicked. You can supply either an absolute or a relative URL. QuickTime movies replace the current movie in-place; Web pages open in the browser.
`kioskmode`	true and false (the default)	Eliminates the QuickTime Plugin's controller menu when set to true.
`loop`	true, false (the default), or palindrome	Causes the movie to loop continuously when set to true. The palindrome value causes the QuickTime Player to play alternately forward and backward.
`movieid`	A number	A number identifying the movie so another wired sprite movie can control it.
`moviename`	A number	A name identifying the movie so another wired sprite movie can control it.
`playeveryframe`	true and false (the default)	When set to true, forces the movie to play every frame, even if it must do so at a slower rate than real time. Disables audio and QuickTime Music tracks.
`pluginspage`	`www.apple.com/quicktime`	Where users who don't have QuickTime should be sent to get it.
`qtnext{n}`	A URL	Specifies a movie as being {n} in a sequence of movies. The movie specified in the `src` attribute is movie zero.
`qtnext`	goto{n}	Tells the QuickTime Plugin to open movie {n} in an already specified sequence of movies.

Continued

Table 23-2 *(continued)*

QuickTime Plugin Parameter	***Possible Values***	***Description***
`qtsrc`	A URL	Tells the QuickTime Plugin to open this URL instead of the one specified by the `src` attribute. A way to open files that don't have a .mov file name extension — such as MP3 files — with the QuickTime Plugin, regardless of how the user's system is set up. Use a dummy movie in the `src` attribute.
`qtsrcchokespeed`	movierate, or a number in bytes per second	Downloads the movie specified in the `qtsrc` attribute in chunks; movierate indicates to use the movie's data rate.
`scale`	tofit, aspect, or a number (default is 1)	Resizes the QuickTime Player movie. By setting scale as tofit, you can scale the movie to the dimensions of the embedded box as specified by the height and width values. Setting scale to aspect resizes the movie to either the height or the width while maintaining the proper aspect ratio of the movie. Set to a number, the size of the movie is multiplied by that number.
`starttime`	30 frame SMPTE timecode (hours:minutes:seconds:-thirtieths of a second)	Indicates the point in the movie where playback should start.
`target`	_self, _parent, _top, _blank, a frame or window name or QuickTimePlayer	Enables the link specified in the `href` attribute to be targeted to a specific frame or window. The value QuickTimePlayer causes the movie specified in the `href` attribute to be opened in the QuickTime Player.

QuickTime Plugin Parameter	*Possible Values*	*Description*
`targetcache`	true (the default) or false	Same as the `cache` attribute but for the movie called by a poster movie using the `href` attribute.
`volume`	0 to 256 (the default)	Controls the volume of the audio track(s). Zero is softest; 256 is loudest.
`width`	A value in pixels; usually the width of the movie	Reserves a space in the page for the QuickTime movie.

Tip

Dreamweaver's Plug-in Property Inspector also enables you to enter several other attributes generally used with other objects, such as images. These include `Align` (alignment), `V Space` (vertical space), `H Space` (horizontal space), and `Border` (border). You can also enter a name in the Plugin text box if you plan on referring to your QuickTime movie in a JavaScript or other program.

QuickTime versions

Before inserting a QuickTime movie into a Web page, it's helpful to know what version of QuickTime your movie requires. Because QuickTime movies can contain a variety of track types, each containing a different type of media, some movies may play back with QuickTime 3, while others require QuickTime 4.

You can identify the different tracks in a QuickTime movie by opening it in QuickTime Player and choosing Movie ➪ Get Info. In the dialog box that appears, the options list on the left details the various tracks, as shown in Figure 23-9. If your movie has Flash or MP3 audio tracks, it requires QuickTime 4 for playback. It's a good idea to note this somewhere in your Web page and offer users a link to `www.apple.com/quicktime` so that they can upgrade if necessary.

Playing QuickTime VR

QuickTime VR (QTVR) enables the user to "look around" in a virtual space created from a panoramic image or to rotate an object around its center point in three dimensions ("object movies"). The QuickTime VR author can also designate certain areas in the movie as hotspots that, when selected by the user, activate a link to another page or another movie. Though purists argue that QTVR is not really virtual reality, the technology is a low-bandwidth quick-and-dirty virtual reality that makes sense on today's Web. QTVR is commonly used to show homes, cars, and other products to potential buyers.

Figure 23-9: In addition to the Video track, this QuickTime movie also has a (MIDI) Music track, a Flash track that provides the opening titles and closing credits, and an MP3 audio Sound track.

QuickTime VR movies open in their own special QuickTime Player window, shown in Figure 23-10. Instead of the more-familiar brushed aluminum and round buttons, the QTVR controller has zoom and pan buttons.

Figure 23-10: QuickTime VR's panoramic views enable the user to look around in a panoramic picture by moving the cursor right, left, up, and down.

QuickTime VR <embed> tag attributes are entered in the same manner as other QuickTime Plugin attributes: click the Parameters button in the Plug-in Property Inspector to open the Parameters dialog box (see Figure 23-11) and enter attributes and values. As with a regular QuickTime Player movie, the only required parameters for a QTVR movie are the source file, movie width, and movie height.

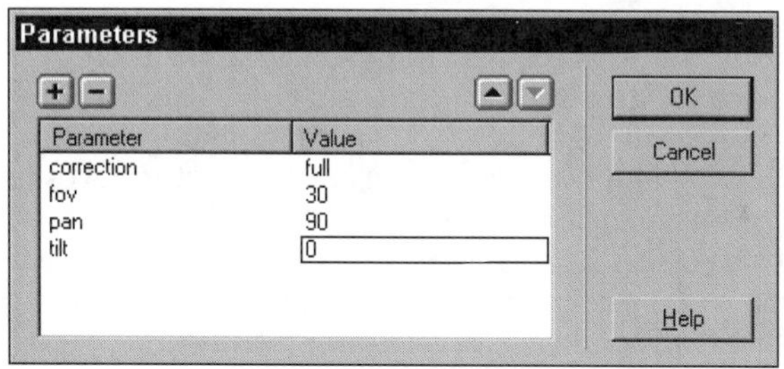

Figure 23-11: Use the Plug-in Parameters dialog box to enter attributes for any plug-in. This example is for a QuickTime VR movie.

Table 23-3 details QuickTime Plugin <embed> tag attributes that work with QuickTime VR only.

Table 23-3
Additional Parameters for QuickTime VR Movies

QuickTime VR Parameter	*Possible Values*	*Description*
`correction`	none, partial, or full (the default)	Applies the correction filter.
`fov`	0 (the default) to 360	Specifies the initial field-of-view angle, in degrees.
`hotspot{n}`	A URL	Defines the URL for any designated hotspot. Replace *n* with the identification number given the hotspot during QTVR authoring.
`node`	A number less than or equal to the number of nodes in the movie	Specifies which node of a multinode movie is opened first.
`pan`	0 (the default) to 360	Sets the initial pan angle, in degrees.
`target{n}`	_self, _parent, _top, _blank, a frame, or window name	Targets the URL of the similarly numbered hotspot at a specific frame or window.
`tilt`	–42.5 to 42.5 (0 is the default)	Sets the initial tilt angle, in degrees.

Some parameters meaningful to regular QuickTime Player movies are not appropriate for QuickTime VR movies. These include autoplay, controller, hidden, href, loop, playeveryframe, target, and volume.

Using a Poster Movie

One of the nicest features of the QuickTime plug-in is the capability to have one movie replace itself with another. This enables you to place very lightweight (low file size), single-image "poster movies" into your Web pages instead of the full clips, so that the rest of the elements in your page load quickly. When the user clicks a poster movie, it replaces itself with your full movie, which begins downloading or streaming immediately. A poster movie can be a preview of the full movie that replaces it or a generic QuickTime image. It's possible to use poster movies to place a number of movies in a single page, enabling the user to pick and choose which ones to view without downloading the rest, as in the following figure.

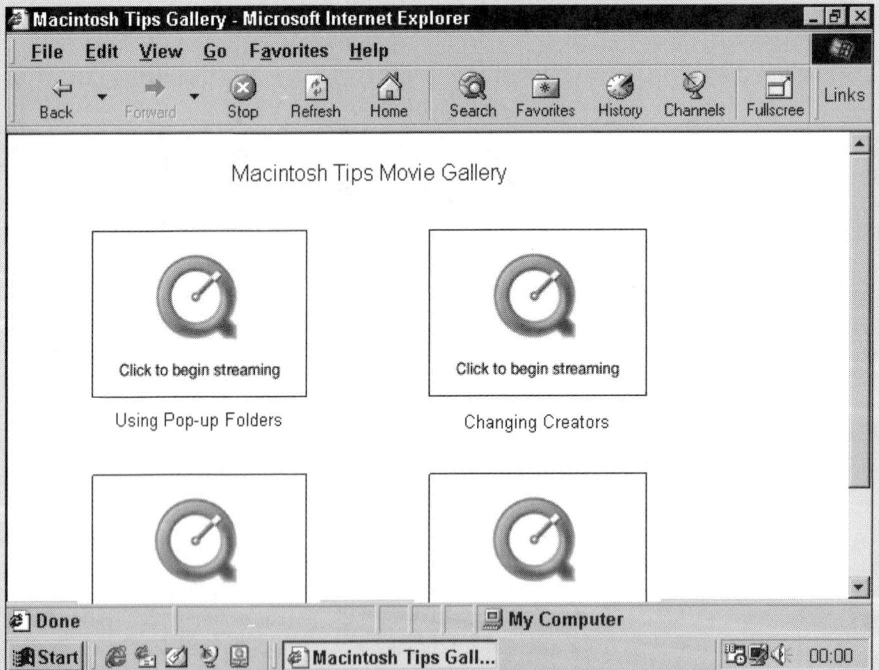

Creating a poster movie requires QuickTime Pro. Simply open your movie in QuickTime Player Pro, move to the frame you'd like to use as a preview and choose File ⇨ Export and select Movie to Picture from the Export options list and Photo-JPEG from the Use options list. This exports the current frame as a QuickTime Image using JPEG compression. Choose

File ➪ New Player to create a new untitled movie and then File ➪ Import to import your picture into this new movie. Save your work as a self-contained movie. A good idea for a file name might be the name of your full movie with "poster" prefixed.

Embed your poster movie in your Web page as discussed previously in this chapter and use the Plug-in Property Inspector's Parameters button to add the `href` attribute with the value set to the URL of your full movie, so that the `<embed>` tag looks like this:

```
<embed src="my_poster_movie.mov" width="360" height="180" ¬
href="my_full_movie.mov"></embed>
```

You can also make multiple frame poster movies if you like. As long as you keep the file size low, your pages will seem to load more quickly, and you'll provide your users more control over the way they experience them.

Streaming with RealMedia

If you've ever downloaded a few minutes of digital video over a slow modem connection, you know the reason why streaming video was invented. In an age when immediacy rules, waiting until the complete video file is transferred and then loaded into the video player can seem to last an eternity. *Streaming*, on the other hand, enables the multimedia content to begin playing as soon as the first complete packet of information is received, and then to continue playing as more digital information arrives. Video is just one form of media to get the streaming treatment: You can also stream audio, animation, text, and other formats.

Regardless of which streaming video protocol you use, the procedure for incorporating the file on your Web page is basically the same, although the details (such as file name extensions) differ. In order to demonstrate the general technique and still offer some specific information you can use, the next section details how to include streaming RealMedia clips with Dreamweaver. Check with the developer of the streaming video format you plan to use to get the precise installation details. Typically, lots of information is available for free on the developers' Web sites.

A RealMedia example

When incorporating RealMedia into your Web pages, you have a variety of playback options. You can set the video so that a free-floating RealPlayer is invoked, or you can specify that the video appears inline on your Web page. You can also customize the controls that appear on your Web page so that only the ones you want — at the size you want — are included.

Tip

Dreamweaver includes a full set of Real media objects—collectively called *RealSystem G2 objects*—which were developed in partnership with RealNetworks. You can find instructions for using these Dreamweaver extensions later in this chapter.

Creating RealMedia metafiles

RealMedia uses its own specialized server software called RealServer to transmit encoded video files. Rather than call this server and the digital video file directly, RealMedia uses a system of *metafiles* to link to the RealMedia server and file. A metafile is an ordinary text file containing the appropriate URL pointing to the RealServer and video file.

The metafiles are distinguished from the media files by their file name extensions:

- ✦ RealMedia files: .rm, .ra, .rp, .rt, .swf
- ✦ Metafile that launches the independent RealPlayer: .ram
- ✦ Metafile that launches the RealPlayer plug-in: .rpm

To create the metafile, open your favorite text editor and insert one or more lines pointing to your server and the video files. Instead of using the `http://` locator seen with most URLs, RealMedia files address the RealServer with an `rtsp://` (Real-Time Streaming Protocol) indicator. The contents of the file should take the following form:

```
rtsp://hostname/path/file
```

where *hostname* is the domain name of the server where the RealMedia files are stored, *path* is the path to the file, and *file* is the name of the RealMedia file. For example, to display a training video, the metafile contents might look like the following:

```
rtsp://www.trainers.com/videos/training01.rm
```

You can include multiple video clips by putting each one on its own line, separated by a single return. RealMedia plays each clip in succession, and the user can skip from one clip to another.

Inserting RealMedia in your Web page

Once you've created both the encoded RealMedia file and the metafiles, you're ready to insert them into your Web page. You have two basic techniques for including RealMedia: as a link and using the `<embed>` tag.

Using a link

Generally, if you want to invoke the free-floating RealPlayer, you use a link; the `href` attribute is set to an address for a metafile, like this:

```
<a href="videos/howto01.ram">Demonstration</a>
```

When the link is selected, it calls the metafile that, in turn, calls the video file on the RealServer. As the file begins to download to the user's system, the RealPlayer program is invoked and starts to display the video as soon as possible through the independent video window, as shown in Figure 23-12. The link can be inserted in Dreamweaver through either the Text or Image Property Inspector.

Figure 23-12: You can set up your RealMedia clip so that it plays in its own RealPlayer window. This is RealPlayer's "Compact" view (compare Figure 23-1).

Using <embed>

If, on the other hand, you'd like to make the video appear inline with the Web page's text or graphics, you use Dreamweaver's Plug-in object to insert an `<embed>` tag. Position the pointer where you want the RealMedia to be displayed, and either choose Insert ➪ Plug-in or select Insert Plug-in from the Objects palette. After the Insert Plug-in dialog box appears, enter the path and file name for the video's metafile in the Plug-in Source text box.

When the Plug-in object representing the RealMedia clip is selected, you can enter values for the `<embed>` tag in the Property Inspector. The only attributes required for a RealMedia clip, as with the QuickTime Player object, are the file source and the width and height of the movie. And, as you can with QuickTime Player, you can choose from a healthy number of attributes to control your RealMedia movie. Enter attributes by selecting the Parameters button on the Plug-in Inspector and entering attributes and their values in the Parameters dialog box (shown earlier in Figure 23-11).

RealMedia attributes are listed in Table 23-4.

Table 23-4
Parameters for RealMedia Movies

RealMedia G2 Parameter	*Possible Values*	*Description*
`autostart`	true (the default) or false	Tells RealPlayer to start playing as soon as content is available.
`console`	{name}, _master, _unique	Determines the console name for each control in a Web page that has multiple controls. Force controls on a page to refer to the same file by giving them all the same name. A value of `_master` links to all controls on a page, whereas `_unique` connects to no other instances.
`controls`	all, controlpanel, imagewindow, infovolumepanel, infopanel, playbutton, positionslider, positionfield, statuspanel, statusbar, stopbutton, statusfield, volumeslider	Enables the placement of individual control panel elements in the Web page. You can use multiple controls in one attribute or multiple `<embed>` tags to build a custom RealMedia interface.
`nolabels`	true or false (the default)	Suppresses the Title, Author, and Copyright labels in the Status panel. If you set nolabels to true, the actual data is still visible.

Using the RealSystem G2 Objects for Dreamweaver

Macromedia has partnered with RealNetworks to provide a full set of objects to ease the implementation of RealMedia in Dreamweaver. The RealSystem G2 Objects for Dreamweaver include drop-in objects for RealAudio, RealVideo, RealPix, RealText, RealFlash, and SMIL presentations. You can also find an array of control panel options for building your own interfaces.

Find the RealSystem G2 Objects for Dreamweaver at Macromedia's Dreamweaver Exchange at `exchange.macromedia.com`.

HTTP Streaming

To gain the maximum throughput of your RealVideo files, it's best to use the RealServer software. However, you occasionally encounter Web site clients who must economize and can't afford the specialized server. Not widely known is the fact that you can use a regular World Wide Web server to stream RealVideo and other RealMedia files over HTTP.

Two prerequisites exist for HTTP streaming: Your system administrator must first correctly configure the MIME types, and you must provide multiple files to match the right user-selectable modem speeds. The proper MIME types are as follows:

✦ audio/x-pn-RealAudio (for .ra, .rm, or .ram files)

✦ audio/x-pn-RealAudio-plugin (for .rpm files)

✦ video/x-pn-RealVideo (for .ra, .rm, or .ram files)

✦ video/x-pn-RealVideo-plugin (for .rpm files)

RealServer automatically selects the right file for the user's modem connection. If you are using HTTP streaming capabilities, you should offer multiple files to accommodate the various modem connection rates, such as 28.8K and 56K.

Other than a reduction in download speed, the other disadvantage to using HTTP streaming over RealServer streaming is the reduced number of simultaneous users who can be served. RealServer can handle hundreds of connections at the same time; HTTP streaming is far more limited.

Installing RealSystem G2 objects

The RealSystem G2 objects need to be installed before they can be used. Naturally, you need the RealPlayer G2 version 6 or 7 on your system as well. To install the objects, follow these steps:

Making a backup copy of your Dreamweaver 3/Configuration folder before using an installer to add extensions helps to guard against accidentally losing custom menu settings or other unforeseen problems.

1. Decompress your RealSystem G2 objects installer (if it isn't already) using one of the following methods:

   • On Windows, open the g2_obj.zip file using WinZip or a similar unzipping utility.

   • On Macintosh systems, use Stuffit Expander or a similar program to open the realg2.sit.hqx file.

2. Run the setup program (setup.exe for Windows and RealSystem G2 Objects Installer for Macintosh) and follow the onscreen instructions.

The RealSystem G2 objects were originally developed for Dreamweaver 2. The Windows Installer complains that it can't find Dreamweaver and offers you a path of C:\Program Files\Dreamweaver 2. Use the Browse button to choose your Dreamweaver 3 folder. The Macintosh Installer says it will install into your Dreamweaver 2 folder but will find Dreamweaver wherever it is. If you have multiple copies and/or versions of Dreamweaver, the installer asks you to pick one.

3. Restart Dreamweaver.

A RealSystem G2 pane has been added to the Objects palette. Objects exist for six media types, including RealVideo, and seven control panel options. You may need to expand or scroll the Objects palette to see buttons for all the objects.

Control options for RealSystem G2 objects

You can also use the RealSystem G2 objects to build your own interface that incorporates parts of the standard control panel. A separate control panel element works with any file or other element with the same console name. For example, if you have two RealVideo files on your Web page, you could have separate Play buttons (each pointing to a different console value, say video1 and video2), while having one volume slider controlling all sound with the console name `_master`. Table 23-5 displays the various control options available to all RealSystem G2 objects.

Table 23-5
RealSystem G2 Control Options

Icon	*G2 Object*	*Description*
	Insert Full Controls	Shows the Control panel, Information and Volume panel, and the Status bar.
	Insert Control Panel	Shows the Play/Pause button, the Stop button, Fast Forward and Rewind controls, and the position slider.
	Insert Play Button	Shows the Play and Pause buttons.
	Insert Stop Button	Shows only the Stop button.
	Insert Volume Slider	Shows the vertical volume control slider.

Icon	*G2 Object*	*Description*
	Insert Status Panel	Shows the Status panel, which displays messages, current place in the presentation timeline, and total clip length.
	Insert InfoVolumePanel Control	Shows the title, author, and copyright information panel, as well as the volume slider.

Inserting a RealVideo object

With the RealVideo object, all you need to know is the name of your source file and its dimensions — all the other factors are handled for you. The RealVideo object inserts a combination of tags to call both an ActiveX control and a plug-in so that the file can be played with both Internet Explorer and Netscape Navigator. You can also add new parameters after the object has been inserted through the Property Inspector's Parameters button.

To insert a RealVideo object, follow these steps:

1. Choose Insert ➪ RealSystem G2 Object ➪ RealVideo or select the Insert RealVideo button from the RealSystem G2 panel of the Objects palette.

   The Insert RealVideo dialog box (shown in Figure 23-13) opens.

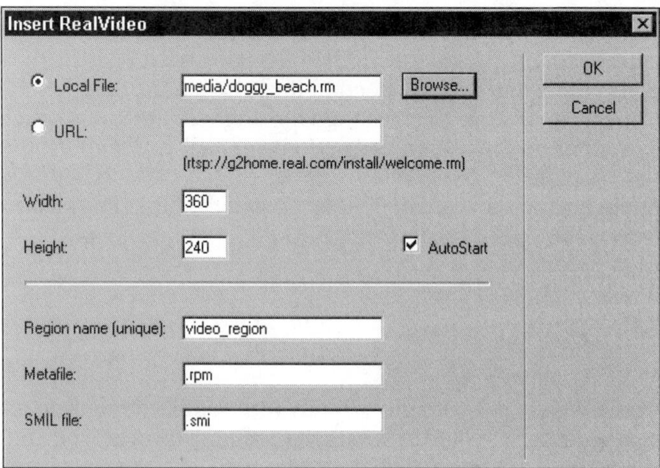

Figure 23-13: The RealVideo object makes inserting streaming video a simple process.

2. Enter the source file by choosing one of the following radio buttons:

   - **Local File:** Enter the path name of a file found on the local system in the Local File text box or choose the Browse (Choose) button to locate the file.
   - **URL:** Enter the absolute address of a file located on the Internet in the URL text box. The example address, `rtsp://g2home.real.com/install/welcome.rm`, is displayed beneath the URL text box.

3. Enter the dimensions of the RealVideo movie in the Width and Height text boxes.

   The default measurements of 192 pixels wide by 112 pixels high are suggestions only and do not necessarily reflect the accurate size of your file.

4. If you don't want your file to begin playing automatically, deselect the Autostart option.
5. The remaining text boxes, Region name, Metafile, and SMIL file, are automatically filled out. Alter any name by entering the modification in the text box.
6. Click OK when you're done.

The RealVideo object creates both a metafile and a SMIL presentation file. When selected by the user to play (or when playing automatically), the original file first calls the metafile, which in turn calls the SMIL file. For this reason, if you ever need to change the source of the original file, you have to open and edit the referenced SMIL file—or delete the RealVideo object and reinsert it with the new file name.

By default, the RealVideo object is inserted with the controls set to the ImageWindow option, which shows only the RealVideo movie with no control panel. To incorporate a control panel into the video file, you need to first choose the Edit Parameters button from the Property Inspector. Next, change the controls attribute from imagewindow to one of the other options, such as All, ControlPanel, or PlayButton.

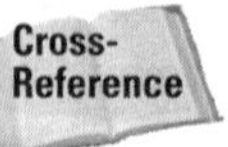

The RealAudio object is covered in Chapter 24 and the other RealMedia objects in Chapter 31.

Summary

Digital video on the Web is in its infancy. Bandwidth is still too tight to enable full-screen, full-motion movies, no matter what the format. However, you can include downloadable as well as streaming video content through Dreamweaver's Plug-in object and Plug-in Inspector.

✦ Even with compression, digital video has steep storage and download requirements.

- ✦ You can include a digital video movie to be downloaded in your Web page by linking to it as if it were a Web page.
- ✦ Use Dreamweaver's Plug-in object when you want your video to be presented inline on your Web page. The Plug-in Property Inspector then enables you to alter the video's parameters for any video architecture.
- ✦ QuickTime is a cross-platform multimedia architecture that offers much more than just video. QuickTime movies can include QuickTime VR, MIDI music, 3D objects, Flash movies and more.
- ✦ To enable your visitors to view your digital video clips as soon as possible, use a streaming video technology such as RealMedia, QuickTime, or Windows Media. Streaming video files can be displayed in a separate player or embedded in the Web page.

In the next chapter, you learn how Dreamweaver helps you incorporate sound and music into your Web pages.

✦ ✦ ✦

CHAPTER 24

Using Audio on Your Web Page

✦ ✦ ✦ ✦

In This Chapter

Digital audio fundamentals

Music files overview

MP3 mini-primer

Linking and embedding sound

Streaming audio

Sonifying with the Beatnik ActionSet Pro

✦ ✦ ✦ ✦

Web sites tend to be divided into two categories: those totally without sound, and those that use a lot of it — there's not much middle ground. Many music and entertainment sites rely heavily on both streaming audio and downloadable audio files such as MP3.

In this chapter, you learn how to use audio in the Web pages you design with Dreamweaver. We look at traditional digital audio formats such as AIFF and WAV, and how you can turn these into files suitable for publishing on the Web, in formats such as MP3 and RealAudio. We also look at music formats such as Standard MIDI files and QuickTime Music.

Lest we forget that we're Dreamweaving here, we look at some Dreamweaver extensions you can use to get audio-enabled sites up and running in no time. But before we leap into those deep waters, let's get an overview of digital audio and its place on the Web.

Because the primary technologies for distributing streaming audio are also the primary technologies for streaming video, you may find it helpful to familiarize yourself with the Big Three streaming media technologies — RealMedia, QuickTime, and Windows Media — introduced in Chapter 23.

Digital Audio Fundamentals

Digital audio files are digitized representations of sound waves. While not as heavy as digital video, digital audio files — even those that have been compressed — are still a strain for today's Web. As usual, minimizing file sizes wherever possible makes for a better experience for users of your Web site.

File formats

Many different formats for digital audio files are in use today across the various computer platforms. The most common formats are described in Table 24-1 and can be identified by their unique file name extensions and/or by their icons on Macintosh systems.

Table 24-1
Web Digital Audio File Formats

Audio Format	*Typical File Name Extension*	*Description*
AU	.au, .snd	Very common on the early Unix-dominated Web. Uncompressed and no longer suitable for Web use.
AIFF	.aif, .aiff	The Audio Interchange File Format was developed by Apple. Uncompressed versions can be played in most browsers, but using AIFF on the Web should be avoided when possible.
Flash	.swf	Not just an animation format, Flash streams PCM- or MP3-compressed audio at various bit rates.
MP3	.mp3, .mp2	The MPEG Audio Layer 3 format features high-quality digital audio files with excellent compression. MP3 has become the standard for downloadable music. It plays in QuickTime Player 4+, RealPlayer G2 6+, Windows Media Player 5.2+, and a whole range of standalone players that work as browser helper apps.
QuickTime	.mov	A QuickTime movie with a soundtrack only.
RealAudio	.ra or .ram	The audio component of RealNetworks' RealMedia. Lots of players. Good quality at low bit rates, but not as good as MP3.
Rich Music Format	.rmf	Beatnik's hybrid audio/music format. Samples are either PCM or MP3 compressed.

Audio Format	Typical File Name Extension	Description
Shockwave Audio	.swa	The audio component of Shockwave, they're low bit rate MP3 files with a different file header. They stream over HTTP, and any MP3 player can play them locally.
WAV	.wav	Codeveloped by Microsoft and IBM, the default audio format for Windows. Uncompressed versions play in browsers, but their use on the Web should be avoided whenever possible.
Windows Media	.asf, asx	Microsoft's streaming media solution.

Which audio format should you choose? That depends on a combination of factors, including your target audience, available bandwidth, and the purpose of the audio's content.

Although most browsers can play standard digital audio files such as AIFF and WAV, the sheer uncompressed bulk of these files makes them unsuitable for the Internet, now that so many highly compressed formats exist. In the early days of the Web, with slower computers and less advanced compression technologies, these uncompressed audio files were the only game in town. But today, fast computers are capable of easily decoding MP3 and RealAudio, and free players for those formats are common.

A live Internet broadcast dictates a streaming solution such as RealAudio, QuickTime, or Windows Media. If you're offering complete songs for download, you may not have to look any further than MP3. It's not uncommon to offer a sound file in multiple formats. Although many users have more than one player, offering your audio in a few formats gives you a better chance of reaching everybody.

Converting between formats

Converting one audio file format to another typically involves opening the source file in an audio editor that can read that format and exporting it in another form at. If you lack a professional audio editor such as SoundForge or Peak, a simple alternative is to use QuickTime Pro; it reads and writes a lot of formats. You can also easily cut and paste sections of files, to remove or add a few seconds of silence, for example.

Making audio files lighter

As well as categorizing by file format, we can also think of audio on the Web as being in one of two categories: uncompressed and compressed.

Uncompressed files

AIFF and WAV audio files come in compressed and uncompressed formats, but only the uncompressed versions play in Web browsers. If you can't compress an audio file in some way, the only way to lower its file size is to lower its quality in one of three ways:

- **Convert a stereo file into a mono file:** a stereo file has two audio channels, while a mono file has only one. Converting a stereo file to mono halves its file size.
- **Lower the bit depth:** for example, from 16-bit to 8-bit. A lower bit depth reduces the accuracy of the stored audio waveforms.
- **Lower the sample rate:** from 44kHz to 22kHz, for example. This lowers the range of audio frequencies in the recording, chopping off the "high end" or treble frequencies.

You can make the preceding conversions by opening the audio file in an application such as QuickTime Player Pro and exporting the file with new properties, as shown in Figure 24-1.

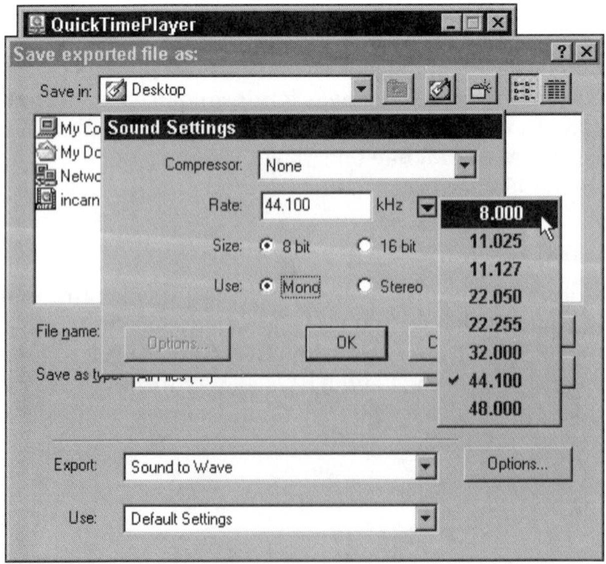

Figure 24-1: Exporting an AIFF as a WAV in QuickTime Player Pro. Converting stereo to mono, 16-bit to 8-bit, and lowering the sample rate from 44.1kHz to 8kHz lowers the file size but drastically lowers the quality.

Compressed files

Network-ready audio file types that were specifically created for the Internet, such as MP3 and RealAudio, are compressed through encoding. Rather than arbitrarily lowering the quality of the file to make it lighter, you pick a target bit rate, as in Figure 24-2, and the encoding software produces the best quality file it can at that bit rate. If you've ever exported a JPEG graphic from an image editor and specified a target file size, the principle is the same.

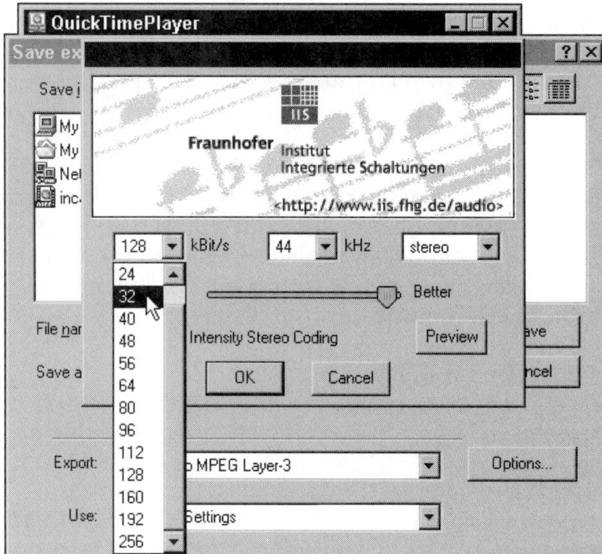

Figure 24-2: Choosing a 32kbs bit rate when exporting an AIFF as an MP3 from QuickTime Player Pro with the Terran Interactive MP3 plug-in

When working with a compressed audio format, you ideally start with the best "master copy" that you have in an uncompressed format, such as AIFF, and then encode that audio file as MP3 or RealAudio. If you want your audio to move quickly, even over dial-up connections, choose a low bit rate such as 24kbs.

Always keep a master copy of your audio file when you're encoding. Encoding a file is often a "lossy" compression; in other words, information is thrown away in order to create smaller files. Although you can convert an MP3 to an AIFF, it will not be the same quality as the original AIFF that the MP3 was made from. The process is similar to converting a TIFF to a JPEG, rather than zipping and unzipping files.

Music Files

In the 19th century, before the technology to electronically record audio existed, a musical performance could be "recorded" by making a series of stipples on a cylinder. The performance could then be played "live" for the listener through a music box. Later, player pianos used rolls of paper with appropriate holes punched in them to cause the piano keys to mimic the performances of far away or long dead musicians. In the early 1980s, electronic musical instrument manufacturers created MIDI (Musical Instrument Digital Interface) to enable the keys of one electronic keyboard to trigger the sounds in another. It wasn't long before somebody realized that the MIDI information that all electronic keyboards were putting out could be recorded and could thus turn any electronic instrument into a modern-day music box or player piano.

The key to using music files on the Web is their very small file size. A music file is the ultimate in compressed sound: the musical instruments aren't even included! For example, a three-minute, full-fidelity, 128bps stereo MP3 file would weigh in at just under 3MB. A QuickTime movie that only contains a music track could give you ten minutes of music for 60k and have similar fidelity, although you're limited to the sounds contained in the QuickTime synthesizer, of course.

Today, music files appear on the Web in one of three ways:

✦ **QuickTime Music:** MIDI information is stored as a music track within a QuickTime movie, and it is played back through the QuickTime software synthesizer (or through a hardware synthesizer such as a sound card if the user has configured QuickTime to use one). The QuickTime synthesizer sounds have often been criticized for being a little bland. Music tracks can coexist with all other kinds of QuickTime media in one movie, so they make excellent soundtracks for digital video tracks. QuickTime movies have a file name extension of .mov.

✦ **Rich Music Format:** Beatnik's hybrid audio/music format. MIDI information is played through the Beatnik player's software synthesizer, which contains generally excellent and often original sounds. Additionally, further instrument sounds can be included in an RMF by adding digital audio samples with the Beatnik Editor for Macintosh. RMF files are unique among music file formats in that the user cannot get the raw MIDI data out of them. Some content authors see this is as an advantage. RMF files have an .rmf file name extension.

✦ **Standard MIDI files:** This is the "raw data" of MIDI music files. The biggest downside is that the Web author has absolutely no idea what kind of synthesizer the user will use to play back a MIDI file. On older Windows machines, this synthesizer may not even include actual instrument sounds, but instead use FM synthesis to come up with very poor approximations. Standard MIDI files have a file name extension of .mid, .midi, or .smf.

Rendering MIDI files

Occasionally, you may want to render a music file as a digital audio file, in order to play it in a situation where a synthesizer is unavailable. Doing this the hard way involves playing the file through a synthesizer and recording the output to a digital audio file. You have an easier way, however, if you have QuickTime Player Pro. Open your QuickTime Music or import your Standard MIDI file into QuickTime Player Pro and then choose File ➪ Export and specify Music to AIFF. QuickTime Player Pro creates a digital audio file of its "performance" of the music using the QuickTime software synthesizer. You can also convert a QuickTime Music track back into a Standard MIDI file. Choose Music to Standard MIDI when you export.

RMF files are designed to disallow this conversion. Always keep the original Standard MIDI file when you create an RMF.

MP3 Mini-Primer

The MP3 audio format has quite simply taken the Web — and the world — by storm. While other downloadable music formats come with caveats such as ownership by one company or built-in limitations on how users can use the files they purchase, MP3 just did the work and got the job done. MP3 software players are common. A range of manufacturers offers MP3 hardware, such as home, car, and personal stereos.

MP3.com remains the one-stop place for information about MP3. Visit `www.mp3.com`.

Generally, the MP3 "scene" has shown interest in new and/or unusual artists, offered a selection of dynamic, full-featured players (see Figure 24-3), and maintained an attitude of music appreciation. Conversely, non-MP3 downloadable music has generally featured bland players, corporate music, proprietary technologies, and an unhealthy fascination with watermarking and controlling content. It's not hard to see why the market chose MP3.

Player support

Table 24-2 lists common MP3 player software — including old friends like RealPlayer that now handle MP3 — and the URLs where they can be found. Many of these applications offer to set themselves up as browser helper applications. You might feature some of these links at the bottom of pages with MP3 content, so users who are new to MP3 can get a leg up.

Figure 24-3: Many standalone MP3 players feature dynamic looks that can even be changed by applying a new "skin."

Table 24-2
Common MP3 Players

Player Software	*URL*
Audion (Mac only)	www.panic.com/ppack/audion
QuickTime Player 4+	www.apple.com/quicktime
RealJukebox	www.real.com/jukeboxplus
RealPlayer G2 6.0+	www.real.com/player
SoundJam MP (Mac only)	www.soundjam.com
Winamp (Windows only)	www.winamp.com
Windows Media Player 5.2+	www.microsoft.com/windows/windowsmedia/en/download

Providing users with a link to MP3.com is another way to offer them a great selection of players.

Encoding MP3

The most common MP3 files are downloadable music files. These files aim for "CD quality" and so are recorded with a bit rate of 128kbs. This works out to a little less than one megabyte per minute for a stereo, 44.1KHz file, which is too heavy to move quickly on today's Web. You can encode an MP3 using a variety of bit rates, though. Lower bit rates mean lower quality, but even at 16kbs, speech sounds pretty good, and the 60k per minute bulk of a mono file will be music to your ears.

Beware of MP3 encoders that sacrifice quality for speed. Many encoders simply throw out the upper audio frequency range so that they can encode the rest in record time. While this might be fine if you're encoding your CD collection into a massive jukebox on your computer, it is less than ideal for content creators who want the best quality encoded files.

Linking to Audio Files

The simplest way to add sound to a Web page is to create a link to an audio file. You enter the path to your audio file in the Link text box in the Text or Image Property Inspector, or select the folder icon to browse for the file. When the user clicks that link, the sound file downloads, and whatever program has been designated to handle that type of file opens in a separate window. The exception to this is the QuickTime Plugin. Instead of opening linked audio files in the QuickTime Player, it opens them within the browser window, as if they were a new Web page. To get back to your Web page, the user clicks the browser's Back button.

Netscape Navigator 4.*x*'s LiveAudio player is the only major audio player that does not yet support MP3, but Netscape has also shipped with RealPlayer G2 for quite some time now, which does play MP3, as shown in Figure 24-4.

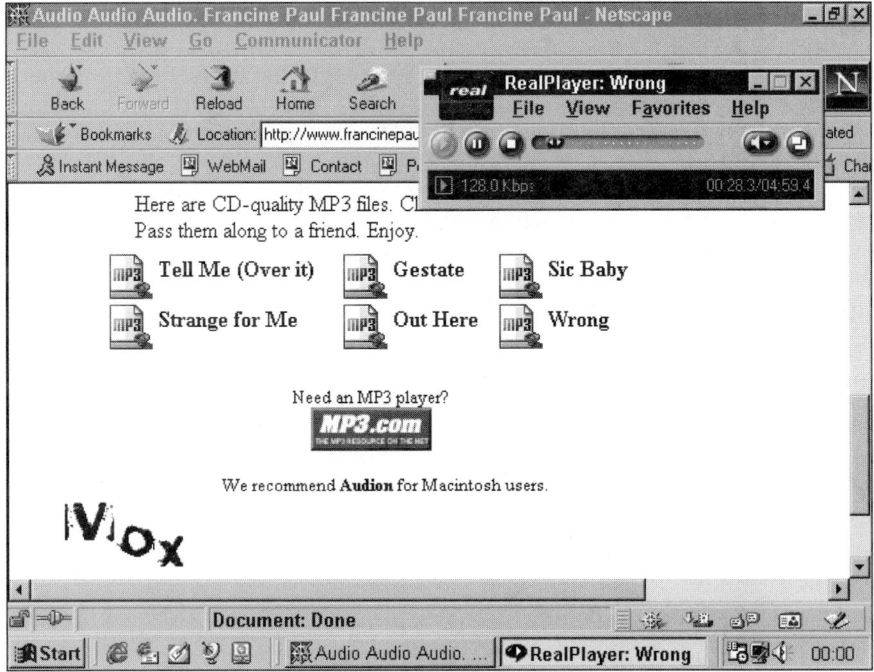

Figure 24-4: A link to an MP3 file in this Web page downloaded and then opened the file in RealPlayer, which was specified as a helper application for MP3 files.

To create a link to an audio file in Dreamweaver, follow these steps:

1. Select the text or image that you want to serve as the link to the audio file.
2. In the Property Inspector, enter the name of the audio file in the Link text box, or select the folder icon to browse for the file.
3. Because audio files can be large, it's good practice to note the file size next to the link name or enter it in the Alt text box for your image.

When you use the link technique for incorporating sound, you have no control over the position or appearance of the player. However, you can control these factors and more by embedding your audio.

Embedding Sounds and Music

Embedding a sound file truly integrates the audio into your Web page. Embedding the sound files also gives you a much higher degree of control over the presentation of the audio player itself, including the following:

- ✦ The clip's play volume
- ✦ Which part, if any, of the player's controls is visible
- ✦ The starting and ending points of the music clip

As with any other embedded object, you can present the visual display inline with other text elements — aligned to the top, middle, or bottom of the text, or blocked left or right to enable text to flow around it. Dreamweaver controls all of these parameters through two different objects: the Plug-in object and the ActiveX object. Each type of object calls a specific type of player. For example, the default Plug-in object calls the LiveAudio plug-in in a Netscape browser and the Windows Media Player control in Internet Explorer. Calling the Windows Media Player as an ActiveX object explicitly enables you to modify a great number of parameters for Internet Explorer — which are completely ignored by Navigator. You learn all of your embedding options, including techniques for cross-browser audio, in the next few sections.

As with the basic video file, Dreamweaver uses the generic Plug-in object to embed audio in your Web page. The object requires only three parameters: the source of the audio file and the width and height of the object. To embed an audio file in your Web page, follow these steps in Dreamweaver:

1. Position the cursor where you want the control panel for the audio file to appear.
2. Insert the Plug-in object by choosing Insert ⇨ Plug-in or by selecting the Plug-in object from the Objects palette.

3. In the Property Inspector, enter the path and file name for your audio file in the Plug-in Source text box. Select Browse (Choose) to choose your file from the Select File dialog box.
4. Use either of the following techniques to size the plug-in placeholder:
   - Enter the appropriate values in the W (Width) and the H (Height) text boxes of the Property Inspector.
   - Or click the resizing handles on the plug-in placeholder and drag it out to a new size.

   For a default audio plug-in, use a width of 144 pixels and a height of 60 pixels. These dimensions are slightly larger than necessary for Internet Explorer's audio controls, as shown in Figure 24-5, but they fit Navigator's controls perfectly, and the control panel does not appear to be "clipped" when viewed through any browser.

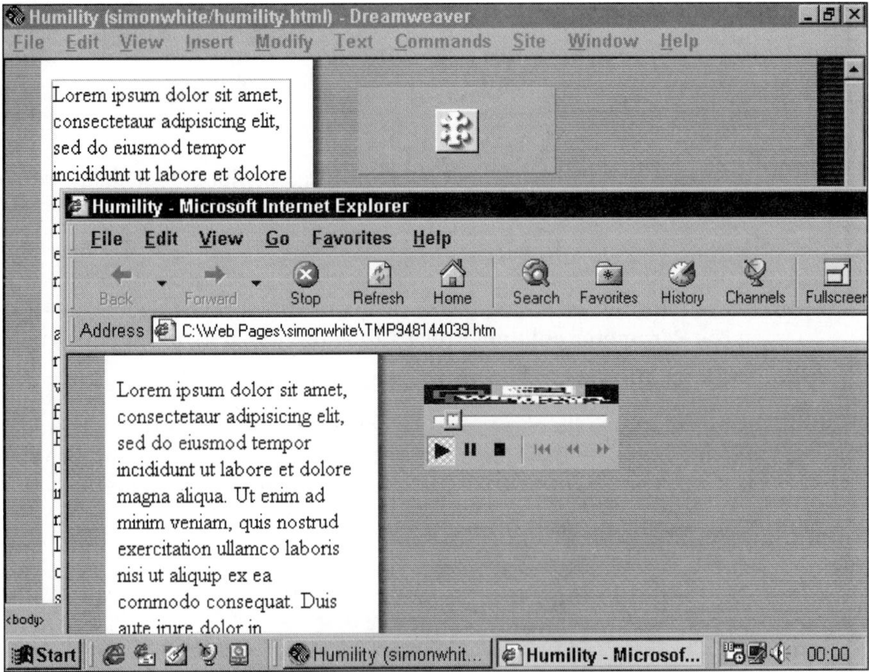

Figure 24-5: Windows Media Player needs less space than Netscape's LiveAudio for its controls, so it fills the rest with a crushed version of its logo.

When the Plug-in object is inserted, Dreamweaver displays the generic plug-in placeholder.

Playing background music

Background music, played while the user is viewing online material, is one of the Web's hidden treasures. When used tastefully, background music can enhance the overall impact of the page.

Making a regular embedded sound into a background sound is as simple as adding a few parameters to the embed tag: hidden tells the browser not to display any controls, autostart tells it to start playback automatically, and loop tells it to play the audio continuously. Although you can add these attributes to the `embed` tag manually in the HTML Source window, it's easier to add them using the Parameters button of the embed tag Property Inspector.

Follow these steps to embed background music in a Web page:

1. Position the cursor near the top of your Web page. Choose Insert ➪ Plug-in or select the Plug-in object from the Objects palette.
2. Enter the path to your audio file in the Plug-in Source text box or select Browse to locate the file.
3. In the Property Inspector, enter **2** in both the H (Height) and W (Width) text boxes.

Entering a width and height attribute is necessary for compatibility with older browsers.

4. Click Parameters.
5. In the Parameters dialog box, select the add (+) button and enter **hidden** in the Parameter column. Press Tab and enter **true** in the Value column.
6. Enter autostart as the next parameter and give it the value **true**.
7. To make the audio clip repeat, enter **loop** as the next parameter, and in the Value column, enter the number of times you want the sound to repeat. To make the audio repeat indefinitely, enter **true** as the value.
8. Click OK to finish.

Targeting Specific Plug-ins

You can exercise a much finer degree of control of the audio in your pages by calling specific plug-ins. The trade-off, unfortunately, is that by designating a plug-in, you reduce the size of your potential audience. Some plug-ins are specific to a browser or browser version. Moreover, plug-ins that aren't distributed with the major browsers face an uphill battle in terms of market penetration. If you use a plug-in, you can always expect some folks to be resistant to downloading the necessary software. Before you incorporate any plug-in, you must weigh these issues against your overall design plan.

A great number of audio plug-ins are available and offer a broad variety of functionality and features. A good place to see a list of those available is the Plug-in Plaza (`www.browserwatch.com/plug-in.html`). In addition to offering complete descriptions, this site also has links directly to the download areas.

Windows Media Player audio

The Windows Media Player is Internet Explorer's multimedia player. As such, you can use it to play the standard audio formats, including MP3, WAV, AIFF, AU, or MIDI files. In fact, when you add an audio file as a link, or embed it without any other specifications, Internet Explorer automatically calls Windows Media Player to play the file. Calling Windows Media Player directly as an ActiveX control, however, gives you far more flexibility over the player's appearance and functionality.

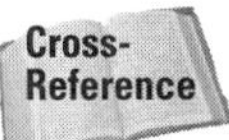

If you're unfamiliar with ActiveX Controls, you might want to look over the section "Incorporating an ActiveX Control" in Chapter 17 before proceeding.

Calling the Windows Media Player ActiveX control

To incorporate the Windows Media Player ActiveX control, follow these steps:

1. Position the cursor where you would like the Windows Media Player control panel to appear. Choose Insert ➪ ActiveX or select Insert ActiveX from the Objects palette.

   The Property Inspector displays the ActiveX options.

2. In the ClassID text box, enter the ID for the Windows Media Player control: **CLSID:22d6f312-b0f6-11d0-94ab-0080c74c7e95**.

If you've entered this long Windows Media Player class ID previously, you can click the arrow button and choose the ID from the drop-down list.

3. Change the width and height values in the W and H text boxes to match the desired control display.

   The Windows Media Player display resizes to match your dimensions as closely as possible.

4. Click Parameters in the Property Inspector.
5. Select the add (+) button and enter the first parameter: `FileName`. Press Tab to move to the Value column.
6. Enter the path and file name for your audio file. Press Tab.
7. Continue entering the desired parameters and values for your audio file.
8. Click OK when you're finished.

The Windows Media Player ActiveX Control has many parameters to choose from — 34, to be exact. Explaining all of these parameters is beyond the scope of this book, but Table 24-3 lists the key parameters that parallel the LiveAudio attributes.

Table 24-3
Windows Media Player Parameters

WMP Parameter	*Possible Values*	*Description*
`AutoStart`	true (default) or false	Determines if the sound begins playing when the download is complete.
`FileName`	Any valid URL	Specifies the sound file to be played.
`PlayCount`	Any integer	Sets the number of times the file should repeat. If the value is 0, the sound loops continuously. The default is 1.
`SelectionStart`	Number of seconds	Determines the beginning point for the audio clip, relative to the start of the file.
`SelectionEnd`	Number of seconds	Determines the ending point for the audio clip, relative to the start of the file.
`ShowControls`	true or false (default)	Hides the control panel if set to true.
`ShowDisplay`	true or false (default)	Hides the display panel if set to true.
`Volume`	Any integer, from 10,000 to 0 (the default).	Sets the loudness of the audio.

Windows Media Player's default volume setting is 0, but this is the highest setting, not the lowest setting. Specifying a higher number for the volume parameter lowers the volume of the sound.

Using Embed with ActiveX

All ActiveX controls are included in HTML's `<object>...</object>` tag pair. Dreamweaver codes this for you when you insert any ActiveX control. Netscape doesn't recognize the `<object>` tag, and Internet Explorer doesn't recognize the `<embed>` tag when it's within an `<object>` tag, so it's possible to target both browsers with one `<object>` and `<embed>` pair.

After you've entered the `FileName` parameter and value for the Windows Media Player ActiveX Control, select the Embed checkbox in the Property Inspector. The same name that you specified as the `FileName` now appears in the Embed text box.

Dreamweaver takes advantage of the fact that Netscape doesn't recognize the <object> tag by inserting the <embed> tag inside the <object>...</object> tag pair. The resulting HTML looks like the following:

```
<object width="200" height="18" classid="CLSID:05589FA1-C356-11CE-BF01-¬
00AA0055595A" border="2">
 <param name="FileName" value="images/BrazMIDI file">
 <param name="ShowDisplay" value="False">
 <embed width="200" height="18" border="2" filename="images/BrazMIDI¬
 file" showdisplay="False" src="images/BrazMIDI file"></embed>
 </object>
```

Note that Dreamweaver picks up the attributes and parameters from the ActiveX control to use in the <embed> tag. You often have to adjust these, especially when specifying a narrow ActiveX control and a taller Netscape object.

Using Netscape's LiveAudio plug-in

LiveAudio is Netscape's default audio player and is used when you do basic embedding of an audio file, as well as when you attach a sound file to a URL. Both of these methods of incorporating audio, however, barely scratch the surface of what LiveAudio is capable of doing. LiveAudio uses up to 13 different parameters to shape its appearance and functionality in the Web page, and also accepts a full range of JavaScript commands.

To take advantage of LiveAudio's full capabilities, you must enter the audio file's parameters and values through Dreamweaver's Property Inspector. Follow these steps to specify the parameters for your Plug-in object:

1. Insert the Plug-in object — either by choosing Insert ➪ Plug-in or by dragging the Plug-in object from the Objects palette to a place on your Web page.
2. From the extended Property Inspector, select Parameters.

   The Parameter dialog box is displayed with its two columns: Parameter and Value.
3. Click in the Parameter column and type in the first parameter. Press Tab to move to the Value column and enter the desired value. Press Tab again to move to the next parameter.
   - Press Shift+Tab if you need to move backwards through the list.
   - To delete a parameter, highlight it and select the minus (–) button at the top of the parameters list.
   - To add a new parameter, select the plus (+) button to move to the first blank line and press Tab to move to the next parameter.
   - To move a parameter from one position in the list to another, highlight it and select the up or down arrow buttons at the top of the parameters list.

For most plug-ins, including LiveAudio, the order of the parameters is irrelevant.

4. Repeat Step 3 until all parameters are entered.
5. Click OK when you're done.

The parameters for LiveAudio affect either the look of the player or the qualities of the sound. The main parameter for altering the player's appearance is `controls`. Depending on the value used, you can display the default control panel, a smaller version, or individual controls.

You can embed individual controls anywhere on your Web page. To link the various controls, you use the `mastersound` keyword in each `<embed>` statement and set the name parameter to one unique value for all files. Finally, set the source in one `<embed>` tag to the actual sound file, and the other sources in the other files to a dummy file called a *stub* file.

Table 24-4 contains all the parameters available for LiveAudio, except those set by Dreamweaver's Property Inspector (source, height, width, and alignment).

Table 24-4
LiveAudio Parameters

Parameter	***Acceptable Values***	***Description***
`autostart`	true or false (default).	If autostart is set to true, the audio file begins playing as soon as the download is completed.
`controls`	console (default), smallconsole, playbutton, pausebutton, stopbutton, or volumelever	Sets the sound control to appear.
`endtime`	minutes:seconds; for example, 00:00	Determines the point in the sound clip at which the audio stops playing.
`hidden`	true	Expressly hides all the audio controls; sound plays in the background.
`loop`	true, false, or an integer	Setting loop to true forces the sound file to repeat continuously until the Stop button is selected or the user goes to another page. To set the number of times the sound repeats, set loop equal to an integer. The default is false.

Parameter	*Acceptable Values*	*Description*
`mastersound`	None	Enables several `<embed>` tags to be grouped and controlled as one. Used in conjunction with the name attribute.
`name`	A unique name	Links various `<embed>` tags in a file to control them as one. Used in conjunction with the `<mastersound>` attribute.
`starttime`	minutes:seconds; for example, 00:00	Determines the point in the sound clip at which the audio begins playing.
`volume`	1 to 100	Sets the loudness of the audio clip on a scale from 1 to 100 percent.

Installing Streaming Audio

Although audio files are not as time consuming as video, downloading them can take a long time. Audio-on-demand — or *streaming audio* — is an alternative to such lengthy downloads.

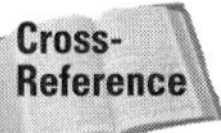

Streaming audio files have a lot in common with streaming video files, as covered in Chapter 23.

For streaming audio, you have the same Big Three choices as with streaming video — RealMedia, QuickTime, and Windows Media — plus Shockwave streaming audio and Flash movies.

Shockwave and Flash are covered in Chapter 25.

Using the RealAudio object

Embedding a streaming audio file has been greatly simplified with the introduction of the RealAudio object. As you can with RealVideo, you can have the RealAudio player appear either free-floating or embedded in the Web page. Embedding a RealAudio file is explained in the next section. To insert a RealAudio streaming audio file with a free-floating player, follow these steps:

1. Select the link or image that you want to use to begin the RealAudio file.
2. In the Property Inspector, enter the path to the RealAudio metafile in the Link text box or select Browse to locate the file.

Make sure that the metafile has the .ram extension.

To learn how to install the RealSystem G2 objects (and attach individual controls), see Chapter 23.

After you've installed the RealSystem G2 objects, you can insert the RealAudio object in one of two ways. You can choose Insert ➪ RealSystem G2 Object ➪ RealAudio, or you can select the Insert RealAudio object from the RealSystem G2 panel of the Objects palette. Once you've inserted the object, the Insert RealAudio dialog box appears, as shown in Figure 24-6. All you need to do is to enter the path to the streaming audio file either in the Local File text box or in the URL text box; be sure to select the appropriate radio buttons for your choice. After you click OK, the object verifies the creation of two additional support files, the metafile and the SMIL file, and your file is ready to stream.

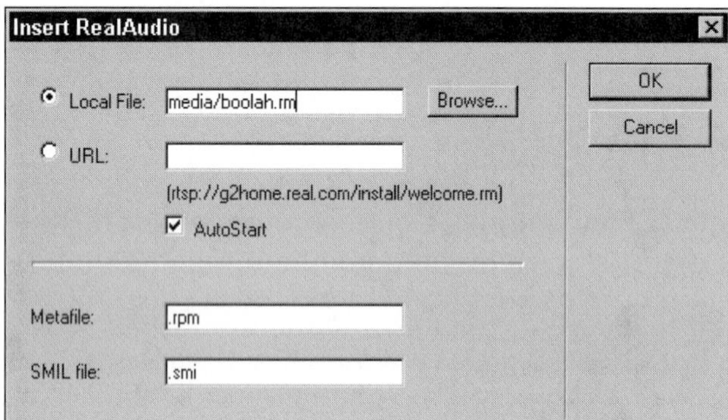

Figure 24-6: The Insert RealAudio object, part of the RealSystem G2 object set, makes embedding a streaming file into your Web page a snap.

Accessing RealAudio parameters

Only the source of the player and the dimensions are required, but it probably comes as no surprise to you that a great number of attributes are available for a RealAudio file. You can add any of the attributes found in Table 24-5 through the Parameters button of the selected RealAudio file's Property Inspector.

Sonifying with the Beatnik ActionSet Pro

While other technologies enable you to use the Web to download or listen to audio, Beatnik is focused solely on making interactive audio part of the Web itself. The Beatnik player links directly with JavaScript to enable a Web author to "sonify" almost any element within a Web page. Add sounds to rollover buttons, form elements, or add tasteful background music to heighten the immersive experience. Because the Beatnik player contains many built-in sounds — called "Groovoids" — the user doesn't need to download anything to hear audio immediately.

Table 24-5
RealAudio Parameters

RealPlayer Attribute	*Possible Values*	*Description*
autostart	true (the default) or false	Enables the RealAudio clip to start playing as soon as content is available.
console	_master or _unique	Determines the console name for each control in a Web page that uses multiple controls. To force controls on a page to refer to the same file, use the same console=name attribute. The console name _master links to all controls on a page; _unique connects to no other instances.
controls	all, controlpanel, infovolumepanel, infopanel, statuspanel, statusbar, playbutton, stopbutton, volumeslider, positionslider, positionfield, or statusfield	Enables the placement of individual control panel elements in the Web page. You can use multiple controls in one attribute, or multiple <embed> tags to build a custom RealAudio interface.
nolabels	true or false (the default)	Suppresses the Title, Author, and Copyright labels in the Status panel. If you set nolabels to true, the actual data is still visible.

The best part of Beatnik for a Dreamweaver user is the free Beatnik ActionSet Pro, a comprehensive collection of Dreamweaver behaviors — 48 in all — that makes sonifying a Web site a point-and-click affair.

A demo version of Beatnik ActionSet Pro 1.1 is available on your Dreamweaver 3 CD-ROM, but Beatnik now offers the Beatnik ActionSet Pro 1.2 for free at www.beatnik.com. The Beatnik ActionSet Lite is no longer available.

The only downside to Beatnik is that it is subject to the problems inherent in using browser plug-ins. Your audience has to have the Beatnik plug-in (or ActiveX Control) installed before it can experience the RMF and Groovoid sounds. The Beatnik player is included with all Intel Pentium III machines, though, and installs automatically on Internet Explorer 4 or above for Windows and on Netscape Navigator 4 or above.

Beatnik is nothing if not well documented. Comprehensive help files, instructional examples, and user forums are available on the Beatnik Web site. If you want to go further with Beatnik than this chapter takes you, check out www.beatnik.com.

Making RMFs

Beatnik's proprietary audio format is Rich Music Format (RMF) files. RMF files can contain digital audio or MIDI data, or a mixture of the two. MIDI data is played back through the Beatnik player's built-in synthesizer, providing consistent fidelity for every user. Digital audio can be MP3 encoded to minimize file size.

You don't have to make your own RMF files to sonify a page — the Beatnik player's built-in sounds are excellent in their own right — but if you want to, Beatnik offers the free Beatnik Converter for Windows and Beatnik Editor for Macintosh. Either one can turn any standard audio format or MIDI file into an RMF. The Macintosh version can also integrate with other music and audio software through Open Music System (OMS), the standard MIDI communication system on the Macintosh. Both tools also come in reasonably priced Pro versions that add MP3 compression features.

Installing the Beatnik ActionSet Pro

Before you can use the Beatnik ActionSet Pro in Dreamweaver, you have to install it. Follow these steps:

1. Close Dreamweaver if it is running.
2. Double-click the installer file to begin the installation process.

Note

The Beatnik ActionSet Pro installers contain a license that says "Beatnik ActionSet Lite" instead of "Beatnik ActionSet Pro", which seems to be a simple mistake and should not affect the installation.

3. Follow the onscreen instructions. On Windows, you are prompted to browse to and select your Dreamweaver installation folder. On Macintosh, the installer finds Dreamweaver for you but asks you to confirm which copy of Dreamweaver you want the installer to target if you have multiple copies or versions.

   When the installation is complete, the documentation for the Beatnik ActionSet Pro automatically opens in your system browser. On Windows, an entry is added to the Add/Remove Programs panel to make uninstallation easier. On Macintosh, the Beatnik Installer leaves a standard installer log called "Beatnik ActionSet Installer Log" in the root folder of your startup drive. It details the names and locations of the files it has installed.

4. When you're ready to begin investigating the Beatnik ActionSet Pro, start Dreamweaver.

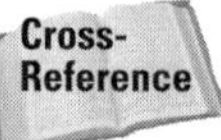

If you've never worked with behaviors before, you might want to review Chapter 19 before proceeding.

Using the Beatnik ActionSet Pro

As befits a revolutionary technology, the Beatnik ActionSet Pro must be used with special care. While it's still possible to use the <embed> tag to insert Beatnik RMF files as detailed later in this chapter, the Beatnik ActionSet Pro works in a significantly different fashion. Following are the key points:

- **Players:** Beatnik, unlike many other Web audio technologies, is capable of playing eight different audio files simultaneously, which is what has enabled it to become so popular for remixing songs in a Web page. When the Beatnik ActionSet is initialized, the eight different voices are established, although one is reserved to play musical notes. Many of the Beatnik behaviors enable you to assign a specific player or use the next available player. Unless you wish to exercise ongoing control over a specific voice, it's generally best to choose the available player option.
- **Interface:** Under the new Beatnik ActionSet philosophy, you won't find a series of control panels from which to choose — in fact, you won't find one. Rather than hard-code a VCR-like panel into the system, all Beatnik audio events occur via user interaction, using either a custom interface or no interface whatsoever. While this may seem daunting at first, it actually gives the Web designer tremendous freedom and works effectively to better integrate the sound design into the page.
- **Settings:** Adding music to the Web page often requires much fine-tuning and trial-and-error. The Beatnik ActionSet includes a series of settings that recognize this real-world requirement. At the least, you'll find Default Settings for using preset configurations, Previously Used Settings from your last configuration, and New Settings, which reflect the latest modifications. You can switch back and forth between these settings to find exactly the right sound.

Initializing a page

Each of the behaviors in the Beatnik ActionSet Pro uses a JavaScript library found in the file beatnik-actionset.js as well as a dummy music file stub.rmf. In order to use any of the behaviors, a page must first be initialized and these files located. To simplify this task, Beatnik includes a special behavior, the Beatnik ActionSet Setup.

To initialize a page for Beatnik behaviors, follow these steps:

1. Select the <body> tag from the Tag Selector in the status bar.
2. Open the Behavior Inspector by choosing Window ➪ Behaviors or selecting the Show Behaviors button from either Launcher.
3. Click the add behavior button (the + sign) and choose Beatnik ActionSet Setup from the drop-down list.

   The Beatnik ActionSet Setup dialog box opens, as shown in Figure 24-7.

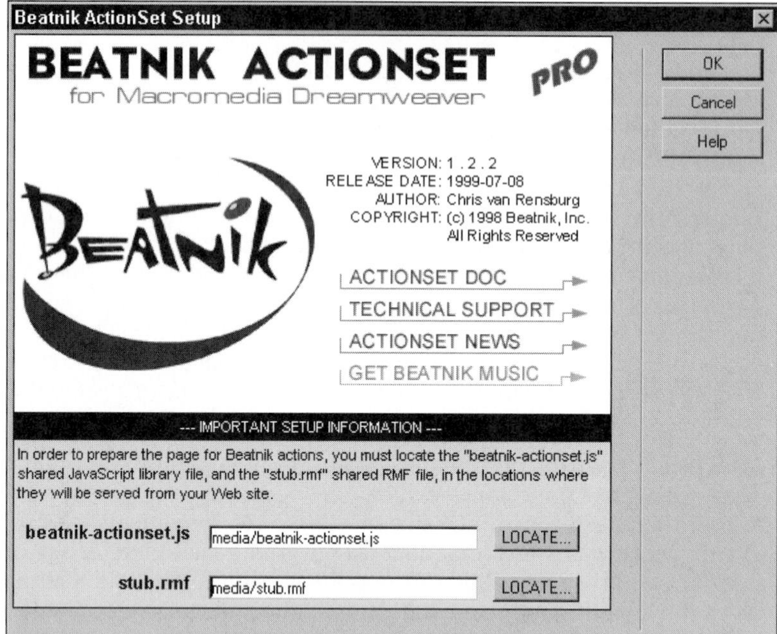

Figure 24-7: You must initialize your Web page with the Beatnik ActionSet Setup before you can use any of the Beatnik behaviors.

4. Enter the path to the beatnik-actionset.js file in the appropriate text box or select the Locate button to browse for the file.

   Initially, the beatnik-actionset.js file is located in the Configuration\Behaviors\Help\Beatnik-ActionSet\javascript folder. It's good practice to copy the file to the local root folder of your working site and assign that file in the Setup behavior. Keeping it in the local root folder makes it easier to upload when publishing the page.

5. Next, enter the path to the stub.rmf file in the text box or select the Locate button to browse for the file.

   You'll find a copy of the stub.rmf file in the Configuration\Behaviors\Help\BeatnikActionSet\music folder. Again, it's a good idea to copy this file to your working site directory and choose that file in the Beatnik Setup.

6. Click OK when you're done.

Should you ever relocate a page that has been Beatnik-initialized, Beatnik (the company) recommends that you use Dreamweaver's advanced Find and Replace features to update the pages with the new location for these two files. Currently, it's not possible to delete and reapply the Setup behavior.

Adding Groovoids

As mentioned earlier, Groovoids are short musical riffs and sound effects intended to add an interactive sound dimension to your Web page. The Beatnik player includes 72 such samples in five categories: User Interface, Hits, Fanfare, Background, and Miscellaneous. Groovoids are used in two different ways:

- ✦ As a repeating background theme, generally begun when the page is loading
- ✦ As an interactive audio cue based on a user's actions and attached to a specific button or link

The Beatnik ActionSet has a section devoted to Groovoids with three behaviors:

- ✦ **Play Groovoid:** Starts a specified Groovoid when triggered.
- ✦ **Pause Groovoid:** Pauses or restarts a Groovoid. The pause can incorporate a fade of user-definable length.
- ✦ **Stop Groovoid:** Stops the specified Groovoid from playing; the Stop action can also fade out.

To insert a Play Groovoid behavior, follow these steps:

1. Set up the Web page as outlined in the section "Initializing a Page," earlier in this chapter, if you've not done so already.
2. Select the tag you'd like to attach the Play Groovoid behavior to.
3. From the Behavior Inspector, choose Beatnik ➪ Groovoid ➪ Play Groovoid.

   The Play Groovoid dialog box opens, as shown in Figure 24-8.

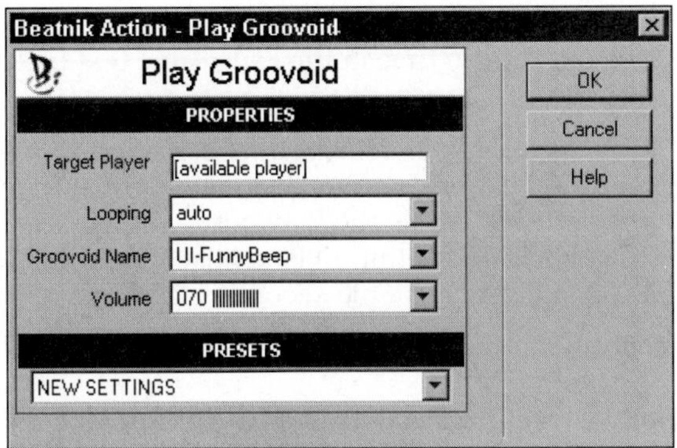

Figure 24-8: Use the Play Groovoid behavior to insert ongoing background music or short user-interface sounds.

4. If desired, enter a unique player name in the Target Player text box. Generally, Groovoids use the [available player] setting.

5. Select the looping option. Choose Yes to cause the Groovoid to repeat, No for it to play once, and Auto for automatic looping. Under the Auto setting, background music loops, and user interface selections do not.

6. Choose the Groovoid Name from the drop-down list. The Groovoids are grouped by category.

7. Select the Volume from the drop-down list, where 100 is the loudest and 0 is mute.

8. To return to the original settings, choose Default Settings from the Presets option box. If you are editing a behavior, you can choose Previous Settings to return to your prior options or New Settings to display the latest changes.

9. Click OK when you're done.

Because of the ongoing nature of the Groovoid background music, it is sometimes helpful to pause the audio. The Pause Groovoid behavior enables you to stop and restart the music from where it stopped. Applying a second Pause Groovoid behavior causes the music to restart, as can triggering the behavior again. Moreover, you can fade the music out and back in again. Naturally, a Groovoid must be playing before it can be paused.

To insert a Pause Groovoid behavior, follow these steps:

1. Select the tag to which you'd like to attach the Pause Groovoid behavior.

2. From the Behavior Inspector, choose Beatnik ➪ Groovoid ➪ Pause Groovoid.

   The Pause Groovoid dialog box opens.

3. Enter the Target Player in the text box, if specified earlier. Otherwise, leave Target Player with its default setting [matching Groovoid].

4. Select the name of the Groovoid you wish to pause.

5. If desired, enter the fade out/fade in time in the Fade Time text box, in milliseconds.

   You can use the VCR-like controls to choose a Fade Time. The Go To Beginning, Fast Reverse, and Reverse buttons decrement your value (0, –1,000, and –100, respectively), while the Play button increases it 100 milliseconds; the Fast Forward button, 1,000 milliseconds; and the Go to End button, 100,000 milliseconds (100 seconds or 1.6 minutes).

6. Click OK when you're done.

The Stop Groovoid behavior is structured exactly like Pause Groovoid and is implemented in the same fashion.

Playing Beatnik music

While Groovoids are great for providing aural feedback or "canned" background music, you can't use them to play user-designated music files. Beatnik supports Rich Music Format (.rmf) and MIDI files (.mid, .midi, and .smf). Unlike Groovoids, these file types have to be completely downloaded before they can begin playing on the user's system. To prevent unwanted delays in playback, Beatnik includes a Preload behavior.

In all, the Beatnik ActionSet provides four commands for working with music files:

✦ **Play Music File:** Starts the selected file to play. The file can also be designated as looping or nonlooping.

✦ **Pause Music File:** Pauses and restarts the selected file with or without fades.

✦ **Stop Music File:** Stops the music from playing with or without a fade.

✦ **Preload Music File:** Loads the selected file into memory before it begins to play.

All of the behaviors function in a similar fashion. Like the Groovoids, a Target Player is chosen initially; however, in the case of music files, it is often better to designate a Target Player, rather than leave the default selection of [available player]. By designating a Target Player, you reserve one of the eight voices for the particular file and are assured of uninterrupted play. You can also adjust the parameters of the music file while it is playing by referring to the Target Player in another behavior.

To use the Play Music File behavior, follow these steps:

1. Set up the Web page as outlined in the section "Initializing a Page," earlier in this chapter, if you've not done so already.
2. Select the tag to which you'd like to attach the Play Music File behavior.
3. From the Behavior Inspector, choose Beatnik ➪ Music File ➪ Play Music File.

   The Play Music File dialog box opens, as shown in Figure 24-9.

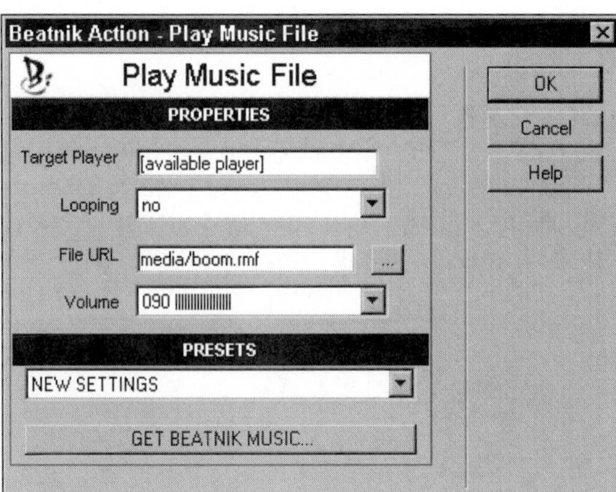

Figure 24-9: Start any RMF or MIDI file through the Play Music File behavior.

4. If desired, enter a unique player name in the Target Player text box. Otherwise, leave the default [available player] setting.
5. To cause a file to play repeatedly, change the Looping option to Yes.
6. Enter the path to the music file in the File URL text box or use the Browse (Choose) button to the right of the text box to locate the file.
7. Select the loudness setting for the file from the Volume option box, where 100 is the loudest and 0 is mute.

The mute or zero setting should be chosen only if you intend to fade up the music at a later time.

8. You can inspect previous configurations by choosing one of the Preset options: Default Settings, Previous Settings, or New Settings.
9. Click OK when you're finished.

The Pause Music File and Stop Music File are used in exactly the same manner as Pause Groovoid and Stop Groovoid. If you've given the music file a unique Target Player name, use that in the Pause and Stop Music File behaviors. If, on the other hand, you left the Target Player at the [available player] setting, choose [matching file] for Target Player and enter the file's path in the File URL text box.

Hitting all the notes

If you're a musician first and a Web designer second, you'll appreciate the total control Beatnik gives you over music. Beatnik has a fully functional built-in software synthesizer that is capable of playing notes over the 16 MIDI channels using any one of over 500 instruments. Moreover, you can alter the velocity, duration or sustain, volume, and pan settings of any note.

You can easily play chords by assigning multiple Play Musical Note behaviors to a single tag and event. Just change the note settings while maintaining the same instrument in all behaviors. Of course, you could also have multiple instruments playing the same note as well.

Only two behaviors are in this category: Play Musical Note and Stop Musical Note. All settings are established in the Play Musical Note dialog box, shown in Figure 24-10. Generally, it's best to leave the Target Player setting at its default [reserved player] setting, although you can also specify a player already declared for a Groovoid or music file. You cannot enter a new, previously unused value. Likewise, leaving the Channel parameter set to [auto] enables the Beatnik Music Management System to handle note assignment. Change this setting to a specific MIDI channel only if you want to halt its playing with the Stop Musical Note behavior at some point.

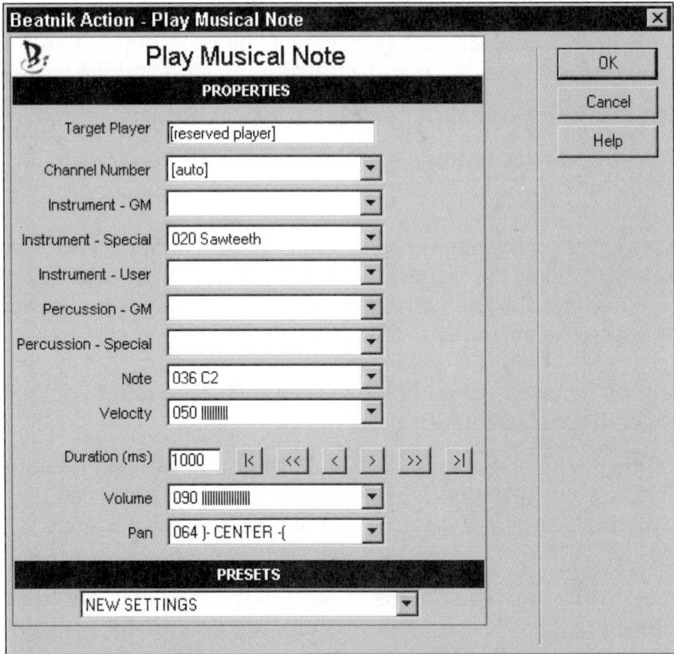

Figure 24-10: Choose from more than 500 musical MIDI instruments to play any of 128 notes over a ten-octave range with the Play Musical Note behavior.

To assign a Play Musical Note behavior, follow these steps:

1. Set up the Web page as outlined in the section "Initializing a Page," earlier in this chapter, if you've not done so already.
2. Select the tag to which you'd like to attach the Play Musical Note behavior.
3. From the Behavior Inspector, choose Beatnik ➪ Musical Note ➪ Play Musical Note.

   The Play Musical Note dialog box opens.
4. Enter a unique name in Target Player text box, if desired. Otherwise, leave the default [reserved player] setting.
5. If a specific MIDI channel is desired, choose a new number from the Channel Number drop-down list. Otherwise, leave the default [auto] setting.
6. Choose a musical instrument from one of the following five categories:
   - **Instrument - GM:** The general MIDI soundbank, modeled after industry-standard instruments.
   - **Instrument - Special:** Variations on the general MIDI soundbank.

- **Instrument - User:** User-defined instrumentation for RMF music files, set up by Beatnik authoring software. (These files are dependent on the selected music file and not present when the stub.rmf file is used.)
- **Percussion - GM:** General MIDI percussive instruments.
- **Percussion - Special:** Variations on the general MIDI percussive instruments.

Although the behavior's user interface enables you to choose multiple instruments from different categories, only the first one is valid. Therefore, make sure that only the final choice is displayed in the chosen category list box; all other list boxes should display the blank value, found at the top of the list options.

7. Choose a note pitch from C-1 (C in octave –1) to G9 (G in the ninth octave) by selecting an option from the Note drop-down list.

   The notes are shown with the corresponding MIDI number (0–127), followed by the musical note name. Middle C, for example, is displayed as 060 C4—which represents the C note in the fourth octave. Sharps are designated with a hash mark (#).

8. Select the velocity (how hard the note is struck) of the musical note from the Velocity drop-down list.

   The Beatnik velocity scale goes from the hardest note struck (100) to the softest (0) and corresponds to the MIDI rates of 127-0. The default is 100.

9. Select the duration for the musical note from the Duration (ms) VCR-style controls.

   The duration is given in milliseconds. The default is 1,000 or 1 second.

10. Choose the loudness setting for the musical note from the Volume option box.
11. Choose the pan setting from the Pan option box.

    The default pan setting is the audio center, between the left and right speakers. Beatnik enables you to choose from 21 pan positions in all, from all the way to the left to all the way to the right.

12. You can inspect previous configurations by choosing one of the Preset options: Default Settings, Previous Settings, or New Settings.
13. Click OK when you're finished.

Incorporating advanced Beatnik features

Beatnik really gets its power from making your Web page audio interactive—and much of that interactivity comes from using the behaviors found under the Beatnik - Advanced category. In all, 22 different behaviors are divided into the four main advanced sections: Channels, Global, Player, and Tracks. Virtually any of the attributes previously explored in the music file or musical note behaviors can be modified on the fly with the advanced behaviors, including the volume, pan setting, and instrument. Moreover, you can adjust the tempo, transpose the music, and instantly mute all but one of the instruments for a solo.

All the behaviors function in a similar fashion to those already described. Rather than detailing the use of each of the 22 behaviors, the remainder of this section describes their effects. The advanced Beatnik behaviors are categorized according to what they control:

✦ **Channel behaviors:** Control individual MIDI channels.

✦ **Global behaviors:** Affect all Beatnik sounds.

✦ **Player behaviors:** Pinpoint specific, named voices or players.

✦ **Track behaviors:** Target any one of the possible 64 tracks in a Beatnik MIDI or RMF composition.

Tip

Any behavior that starts with the word *Adjust*, such as Adjust Channel Pan, is used relatively, while any one that starts with *Set*, such as Set Channel Pan, is used absolutely.

Table 24-6 describes the Beatnik Channel behaviors. These behaviors are applied by selecting a tag and, from the Behavior Inspector, choosing Beatnik - Advanced ➪ Channels and then the desired behavior. In all cases, choose either the matching Target Player or the number of the MIDI channel already playing that you wish to alter.

Table 24-6
Beatnik Advanced Channel Behaviors

Behavior	*Description*
Adjust Channel Pan	Moves the left-to-right speaker pan relative to the current setting.
Adjust Channel Volume	Changes the loudness of the selected player or channel relative to the current setting.
Set Channel Instrument	Selects a different instrument for the selected player or channel.
Set Channel Monophonic	Changes the MIDI setting from polyphonic (multivoiced) to monophonic (single-voiced) or vice versa. A Toggle option enables the setting to alternate each time it is selected.
Set Channel Mute	Turns the mute setting on or off for the selected channel or player. A Toggle option enables the setting to alternate each time it is selected.
Set Channel Pan	Selects a new left-to-right speaker pan setting for the selected player or channel.

Continued

Table 24-6 *(continued)*

Behavior	***Description***
Set Channel Solo	Changes the solo status from the unsolo setting to solo or vice versa. A Toggle option enables the setting to alternate each time it is selected.
Set Channel Volume	Selects a new loudness setting for the specified channel or player.

The Global Beatnik behaviors apply to all eight player voices, affecting every sound emanating from the Beatnik sound engine. Only two behaviors are in this category:

✦ **Set Global Mute:** This behavior effectively mutes or unmutes all Beatnik sound. The behavior can be set to one option or the other, or used as a toggle to alternate between the two states.

✦ **Set Reverb Type:** Reverb can be thought of as the amount of echo in a sound. Beatnik has one reverb setting for all of its sounds, which can be altered globally through this behavior. The six different reverb options are each expressed as the size of a room, ranging from zero to the most reverb:

- No Reverb (Default)
- Closet
- Garage
- Acoustic Lab
- Cavern
- Dungeon

The Global Reverb setting should be judiciously applied. If an instrument relies heavily on reverb for its effect, changing the Global setting significantly alters what is heard.

When you want to alter one of Beatnik's eight players on a page, use one of Beatnik's Advanced Player behaviors. These behaviors can be used in concert with the Channel behaviors to affect the sound experience. Before any of the Player behaviors can be used, a Groovoid, music file, or musical note must be inserted with a named player. Table 24-7 describes the Advanced Player behaviors.

Table 24-7
Beatnik Advanced Player Behaviors

Behavior	*Description*
Adjust Position	Resets the playback position relative to its current position. This behavior can be used to build a VCR-like control with fast-forward and reverse features. A positive value (measured in milliseconds) moves the position forward, and a negative value moves it backward.
Adjust Tempo	Alters the playback speed of a selected player relative to the current speed. Values are measured in beats per minute; a positive number speeds up the music, while a negative number slows it down.
Adjust Transposition	Alters the pitch of a selected player relative to the current setting. Possible values range from up three octaves to down three octaves.
Adjust Volume	Modifies the current loudness setting relative to the current setting for a selected player.
Release Player	Frees one of the eight Beatnik player slots previously reserved.
Set Position	Resets the playback position to an absolute position. This behavior can be used to build a VCR-like control with a Rewind feature. A positive value (measured in milliseconds) moves the position forward, and a negative value moves it backward.
Set Tempo	Resets the playback speed of a selected player to a new speed. Values are measured in beats per minute; a positive number speeds up the music, while a negative number slows it down.
Set Transposition	Resets the pitch of a selected player to a new setting. Possible values range from up three octaves to down three octaves.
Set Volume	Resets the current loudness setting relative to a new setting for a selected player.
Show Copyright Info	Displays the detailed copyright information available in every RMF file in a separate system window.

The final advanced Beatnik category affects music tracks. Both RMF and Beatnik MIDI files enable composers to create their music with up to 64 different tracks. The tracks are identified by their number, 1 to 64. The two Track behaviors are as follows:

✦ **Set Track Mute:** Mutes or unmutes the sound on a specified track. The behavior can be set to one option or the other, or used as a toggle to alternate between the two states.

✦ **Set Track Solo:** Sets a specified track to solo or unsolo status. A toggle option enables the choice to alternate.

Exploring the Pro behaviors

Four more categories of behaviors are included in the Beatnik ActionSet Pro, found under the PRO menu of the behaviors menu:

✦ **Compatibility:** This enables the Web page designer to specify a specific minimum version requirement for the Beatnik player. Without this behavior, any system with the Beatnik player installed — regardless of version — attempts to run the page.

✦ **Dynamic:** Often the difference between a great sound effect and an annoying one is the number of times the same sound is heard. The Dynamic category enables Groovoids, music files, and musical notes to be chosen for a specified group and played randomly, thus varying the musical experience of a Web page.

✦ **Sonification Wizards:** The form is perhaps the most interactive of all Web page elements. Rather than undergo the tedious procedure of adding feedback sounds to each and every form checkbox, radio button, or text box, Beatnik provides a Sonify Forms With Groovoids Wizard (shown in Figure 24-11) for an all-in-one solution. Additionally, form elements can be used to trigger any JavaScript function by using Beatnik's Sonify Forms with Handlers. This behavior extends beyond an audio capability and enables, for example, a layer to be made visible when a text box receives focus, and disappear when it loses focus.

✦ **Synchronization:** With the Synchronization category of behaviors, Beatnik can use events in the music — such as a chorus change or the beginning of lyrics — to trigger specific JavaScript functions. These music events are incorporated into the RMF file by the composer and can be referenced generically (such as all the choruses in a song) or specifically (such as one particular lyric).

The Pro Beatnik behaviors are extremely powerful and enable an integration of music and visuals limited only by the imagination — and, because they're Dreamweaver behaviors, you can do it all without coding the JavaScript.

Embedding a Beatnik object in your page

Once the Beatnik object is installed in Dreamweaver, incorporating RMF and other files to use the plug-in is a very straightforward process. As with other plug-ins, simply position the cursor where you want the Beatnik object to appear and select it from the Objects palette. (You can also choose Insert ⇨ Beatnik from the menus.) When the Insert Beatnik dialog box opens, enter a file source in the RMF File Source text box. This can be the name of any RMF file or other audio format file. As usual, you can also select Browse to choose your file from a Select File dialog box. Click OK when you're finished.

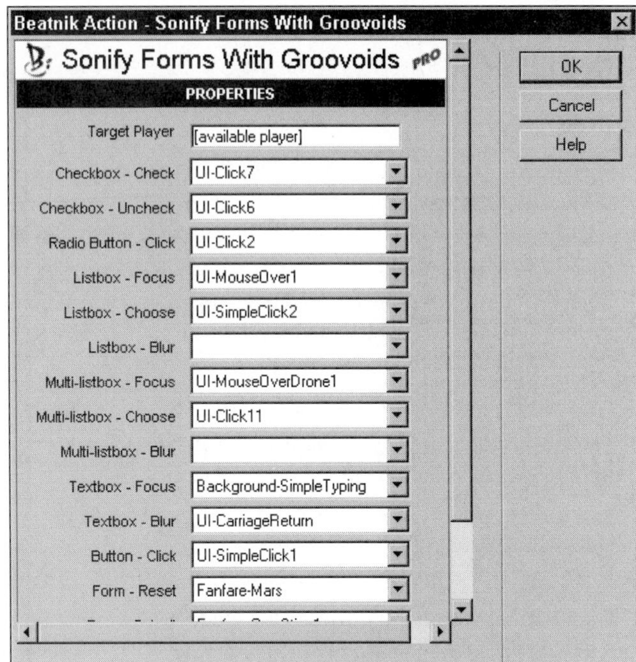

Figure 24-11: The Sonify Forms with Groovoids behavior enables you to attach aural feedback cues to any or all form elements in a page.

After you've picked your file, the Property Inspector displays your file name in the src text box, along with other information about the Beatnik object, including the following attributes:

✦ **Width and Height:** The preset dimensions conform to the size of the default Beatnik controls. As you can with LiveAudio objects, you can vary the size and number of Beatnik controls through the parameters.

✦ **Plg URL:** When a user doesn't have the appropriate plug-in, this attribute provides a link to get one. The Beatnik plug-in URL address is `www.beatnik.com/to/?player`.

At a minimum, always keep the width and height attributes set to a value of at least 2, even when using the `hidden` parameter. Enter the width and height pixel sizes in the W and H text boxes, respectively, on the Property Inspector. Otherwise, your plug-ins are not backwardly compatible with earlier versions of Netscape Navigator.

Beatnik parameters

When you click Parameters in the Beatnik object's Property Inspector, you get access to the parameters described in Table 24-8.

Table 24-8
Beatnik Object Parameters

Beatnik Parameter	*Description*
`autostart`	This attribute is set to true, which enables the audio to begin playing as soon as the file has completely downloaded. Use false if you want to control the playing of the audio independently.
`Display`	Determines which graphic is used to represent the Beatnik object. Options are song, which shows copyright information, or system (the default), which enables the user to toggle between the song information, output meters, or oscilloscope.
`Hidden`	Hides the controls; no value is specified.
`Type`	Sets the MIME type. If the audio file is in RMF format, this attribute is set to audio/rmf.
`mode`	Sets which of three graphics is to be displayed initially as the Beatnik plug-in — scope, meters, or copyright. When `display=song`, only the copyright value is available.
`loop`	If set to true, this attribute causes the file to repeat continuously. If set to false (the default), the file plays once only. The value for loop can also be an integer to determine the number of times the file repeats.
`volume`	Preset to the loudest value (100); this attribute can be any number from 1 to 100.

Summary

Adding sound to a Web page brings it into the realm of multimedia. Dreamweaver gives you numerous methods to handle the various different audio formats, both static and streaming. With custom Dreamweaver objects and actions, enhancing your Web site with audio is a snap.

✦ The common downloadable audio file formats are MP3, AIFF, WAV, AU, and RMF.

✦ The common downloadable music file formats are MIDI, QuickTime Music, and RMF.

✦ You can either link to a sound or embed it in your Web page. With standard audio, the linking technique calls an independent, free-floating player; the embedding technique incorporates the player into the design of the page. Hiding the player creates background music or sound.

- Third-party plug-ins offer far greater control over the appearance and functionality of the sound than relying on a browser's default plug-in; to use a third-party plug-in, however, your user must download it.
- The Beatnik plug-in provides incredible JavaScript interaction, excellent fidelity, and low file sizes.
- Streaming audio gives almost instant access to large audio files; RealAudio is the leader in player deployment, and the inclusion of the RealSystem G2 objects simplifies embedding streaming players.

In the next chapter you learn how to incorporate Shockwave and Flash movies into your Dreamweaver Web pages.

✦ ✦ ✦

CHAPTER 25

Inserting Shockwave and Flash Movies

✦ ✦ ✦ ✦

In This Chapter

Getting to know Shockwave and Flash

Using Shockwave and Flash in Dreamweaver

Managing Flash links

Dreamweaver Technique: Custom controls for Shockwave movies

Dreamweaver Technique: Playing Shockwave movies in frames

Dreamweaver Technique: Triggering behaviors from Flash movies

✦ ✦ ✦ ✦

To many Web designers, Shockwave has represented the state of the art in Web interactivity since Macromedia first created the format in 1995. With Shockwave, multimedia files created in Macromedia's flagship authoring package, Director, could be compiled to run in a browser window. This gave Web designers the capability to build just about anything — from interactive Web interfaces with buttons that look indented when pushed, to arcade-style games, multimedia Web front-ends, and complete Web sites built entirely in Director — bringing a CD-ROM "look and feel" to the Web. Today, Shockwave continues to be an important force on the Web, as the launch of Macromedia's Shockwave.com amply demonstrates.

But Shockwave is not Macromedia's only solution for building interactive, low-bandwidth presentations for the Web. Splash screens, banners, button bars, and other common elements are often built with Flash. Flash combines vector graphics and streaming audio into great-looking, super–low bandwidth files that can be viewed in a browser using the 100k Flash player plug-in. Flash's vector graphics have also turned out to be just the thing for Web-based cartoons. And with version 4, Flash has gained its own scripting language, ActionScript, and added MP3 compression to its streaming audio. With a huge base of installed players, Flash is an excellent way to liven up a Web page.

As you might expect, Macromedia makes it easy to incorporate Shockwave and Flash files into your Dreamweaver projects. Both of these formats have special objects that provide control over virtually all of their parameters through the Property Inspector — and each format is cross-browser compatible by default. To take full advantage of Shockwave's multimedia capabilities, you need to understand the differences between Director and Flash, as well as the various parameters available to each format. In addition to covering this material, this chapter also shows you how to use independent controls — both inline and with frames — for your Shockwave and Flash movies.

Shockwave and Flash: What's the Difference?

Director and Flash share many features: interactivity, streaming audio, support for both bitmaps and vector graphics, and "shocked fonts." Both can save their movies in formats suitable for viewing on the Web. So how do you choose which program to use? Each has its own special functions, and each excels at producing particular types of effects. Director is more full featured, with a complete programming language called Lingo that enables incredible interactivity. And Director movies can include Flash animations. Director also has a much steeper learning curve than does Flash. Flash is terrific for short, low-bandwidth animations with or without a synchronized audio track; however, the interactive capabilities in Flash are limited compared to Director.

Director is really a multimedia production program used for combining various elements: backgrounds, foreground elements called *sprites*, and various media such as digital audio and video (see Figure 25-1). With Director's Lingo programming language, you can build extraordinarily elaborate demos and games, with Internet-specific commands. When you need to include a high degree of interactivity, build your movie with Shockwave.

One of the primary differences between Director and Flash is the supported graphic formats. Director is better for bitmap graphics, in which each pixel is mapped to a specific color; both GIF and JPEG formats use bitmap graphics. Flash, on the other hand, uses primarily vector graphics, which are drawing elements described mathematically. Because vector graphics use a description of a drawing — a blue circle with a radius of 2.5 centimeters, for instance — rather than a bitmap, the resulting files are much smaller. A fairly complex animation produced with Flash might be only 10- or 20K, whereas a comparable digital video clip could easily be ten times that size.

Aside from file size, the other feature that distinguishes vector graphics from bitmap graphics is the smoothness of the line. When viewed with sufficient magnification, bitmap graphics always display telltale "stair-steps" or "jaggies," especially around curves. Vector graphics, on the other hand, are almost smooth. In fact, Flash takes special advantage of this characteristic and enables users to zoom into any movie — an important effect that saves a lot of bandwidth when used correctly.

Figure 25-1: Director works mainly with bitmaps and video, and enables "multimedia programming" using Lingo.

However, these differences were significantly blurred with the release of Director 7, which incorporates its own native vector graphics and introduces the capability to include Flash movies within Director movies. Flash 4 blurred the line the other way by incorporating streaming MP3-encoded audio and QuickTime integration, both things that were traditionally the province of Director.

Flash animations can be used as special effects, cartoons, and navigation bars within (or without) frames. Although Flash isn't the best choice for games and other complex interactive elements, you can use Flash to animate your navigation system—complete with sound effects for button-pushing feedback (see Figure 25-2).

If Flash 4 is a power tool, Director is a bulldozer. Director 7 has been significantly expanded to handle a wide variety of file types, such as QuickTime and MP3, with advanced streaming capabilities. Supporting multimedia interactivity is Director's own programming language, Lingo, which has also been enhanced for version 7. Furthermore, Director 7 includes multiplayer support for network game play and chat rooms, XML parsing, embedded compressed fonts, up to 1,000 sprite channels, and a potential frame rate of 999 frames per second. Luckily, Dreamweaver enables you to pack all that power into a Web page with its Shockwave object.

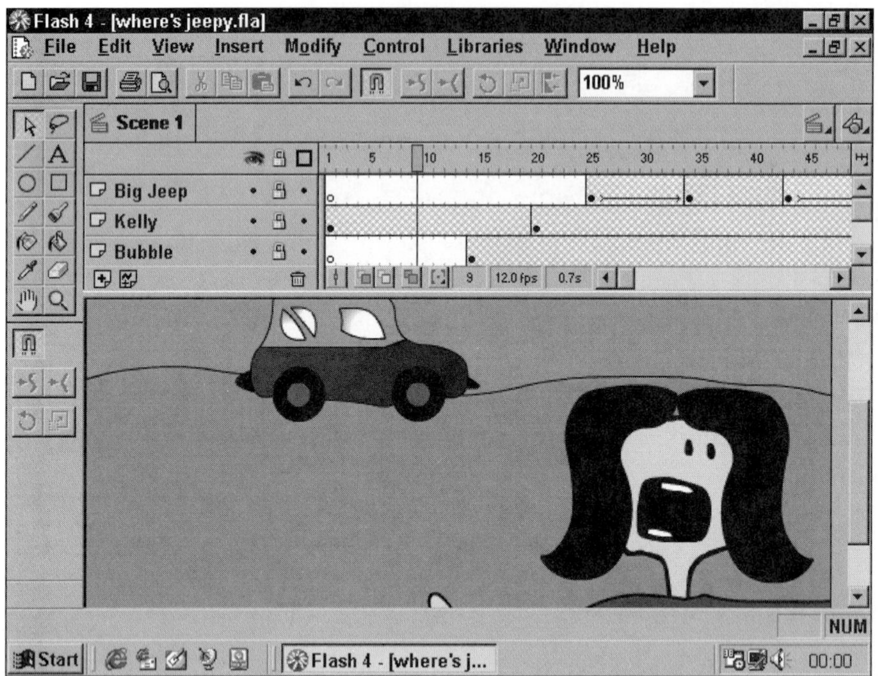

Figure 25-2: Flash movies tend to look more cartoon-like, thanks to Flash's lightweight vector graphics.

Including Shockwave Movies in Dreamweaver Projects

Dreamweaver makes it easy to bring Shockwave and Flash files into your Web pages. The Objects palette provides an object for each type of movie, both located in the Common panel.

Because Shockwave and Flash objects insert both an ActiveX control and a plug-in, Dreamweaver enables you to play the movie in the Document window. First it displays a plug-in placeholder icon (see Figure 25-3).

Before you can successfully include a Flash or Shockwave file, you need to know one small bit of information — the dimensions of your movie. Dreamweaver automatically reads the dimensions of your Flash file when you use the Insert Flash Movie object.

Unfortunately, if you're incorporating a Shockwave movie, you still need to enter the dimensions by hand in the Shockwave Property Inspector.

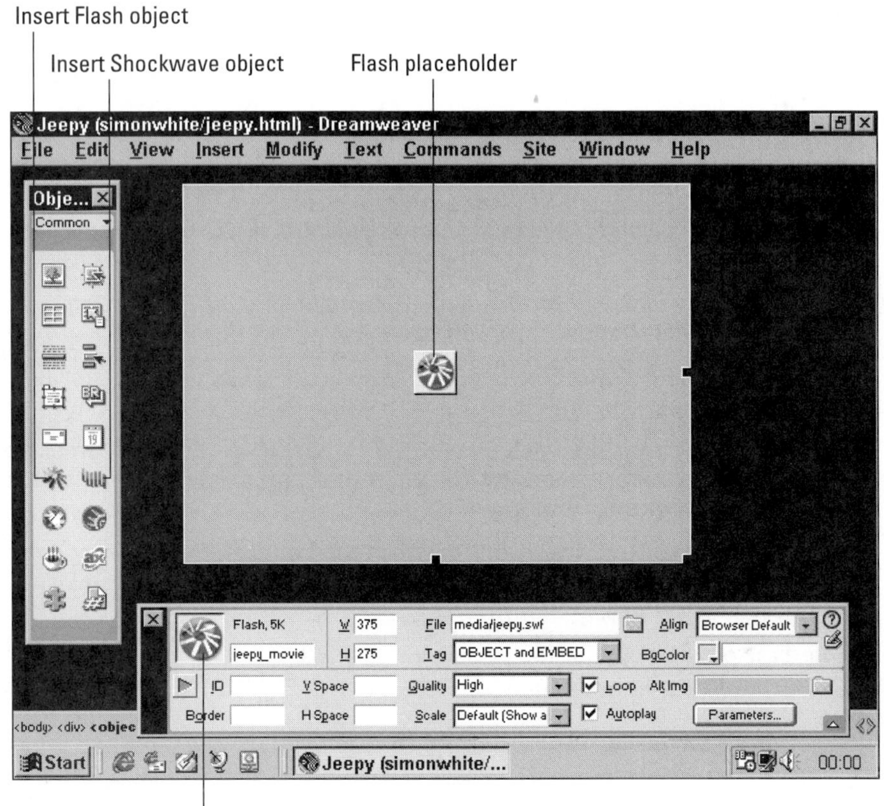

Figure 25-3: Dreamweaver includes many interface elements for working with Shockwave and Flash.

To check the width and height of your movie in Director, load your file and then choose Modify ➪ Movie ➪ Properties to open the Movie Properties dialog box.

Note It is essential to know the movie's height and width before you can include it successfully in Dreamweaver-built Web pages. During the development phase of a Dreamweaver project, I often include the movie dimensions in a file name, as an instant reminder to take care of this detail. For example, if I'm working with two different Shockwave movies, I can give them names such as navbar125x241.dcr and navbar400x50.dcr. (The .dcr extension is automatically appended by Director when you save a movie as a Shockwave file.) Because I consistently put width before height in the file name, this trick saves me the time it would take to reopen Director, load the movie, and choose Modify ➪ Movie to check the measurements in the Movie Properties dialog box.

To include either a Shockwave or Flash file in your Web page, follow these steps:

1. Position the cursor in the Document window at the point where you'd like the movie to appear.
2. Insert the movie using any of these methods:
   - Choose Insert ➪ Shockwave or Insert ➪ Flash from the menus.
   - In the Common panel of the Objects palette, select either the Insert Shockwave or Insert Flash button.
   - Drag the movie object from the Objects palette to any location in the Document window.
3. In the Select File dialog box, enter the path and the file name in the File Name text box or select the Browse (Choose) button to locate the file. Click OK.

   Dreamweaver inserts a small plug-in placeholder in the current cursor position, and the Property Inspector displays the appropriate information for Shockwave or Flash.
4. Preview the Flash or Shockwave movie in the Document window by selecting the Play button found in the extended Property Inspector. You can also choose View ➪ Plugins ➪ Play.
5. End the preview of your file by selecting the Stop button in the extended Property Inspector or selecting View ➪ Plugins ➪ Stop.

If you have more than one Flash or Shockwave movie on your page, you can control them all by choosing View ➪ Plugins ➪ Play All and View ➪ Plugins ➪ Stop All. If your files appear in different pages in a frameset, you have to repeat the Play All command for each page.

As noted earlier, you must specify the dimensions of your file in the Property Inspector before you can preview the movie in a browser; again, Dreamweaver supplies this information automatically for Flash files, but you have to enter it yourself for Shockwave movies. Shockwave and Flash have some different features in the Dreamweaver Property Inspector. These differences are covered separately in the following sections.

You can find a custom Command called Insert Shockwave HTML that automates the process of inserting a Shockwave movie and its Director-generated HTML. Look in the Configuration\Commands folder on CD-ROM 1 that accompanies this book.

Specifying Shockwave Properties

Once you've inserted your Shockwave file, you're ready to begin entering the specific parameters in the Property Inspector. The Property Inspector takes care of all but one Shockwave attribute, the palette parameter. Some of the information, including the ActiveX Class ID, is automatically set in the Property Inspector when you insert the movie.

Generating HTML Within Director

Starting with Director 7, you can now generate a file with all the appropriate HTML code at the same time that you save your Shockwave movie, with just the selection of a checkbox. When you choose File ➪ Save as Shockwave Movie in Director, the dialog box now contains a Generate HTML option. Selecting this option causes Director 7 to save an HTML file with the same name as your Shockwave movie but with an appropriate file extension (.html for Macintosh and .htm for Windows). You can easily copy and paste this HTML code directly into Dreamweaver.

When you open the Director-generated HTML file, you see the name of your file and the Shockwave placeholder, correctly sized and ready to preview. To move this object into another Web page in progress, just select the Shockwave object and choose Edit ➪ Copy. Then switch to your other page and choose Edit ➪ Paste. Naturally, you can also use the keyboard shortcuts or, if both pages are accessible, just drag and drop the object from one page to another.

To set or modify the parameters for a Shockwave file, follow these steps:

1. Select the Shockwave placeholder icon.
2. In the Shockwave Property Inspector, enter the width and the height values in the W and H text boxes, respectively, as shown in Figure 25-4. Alternately, you can click and drag any of the three resizing handles on the placeholder icon.

Pressing the Shift key while dragging the corner resizing handle maintains the current aspect ratio.

3. To designate how the Shockwave HTML code is written, select one of these three options from the Tag drop-down list:
   - **Object and Embed:** This is the default option and ensures that code is written for both Internet Explorer and Netscape Navigator/Communicator. Use this option unless your page is on an intranet where only one browser is used.
   - **Object only:** Select this option to enable your movie to be viewed by Internet Explorer–compatible browsers.
   - **Embed only:** Select this option to enable your movie to be viewed by Navigator/Communicator-compatible browsers.
4. Set and modify other object attributes as needed; see Table 25-1 for a list.

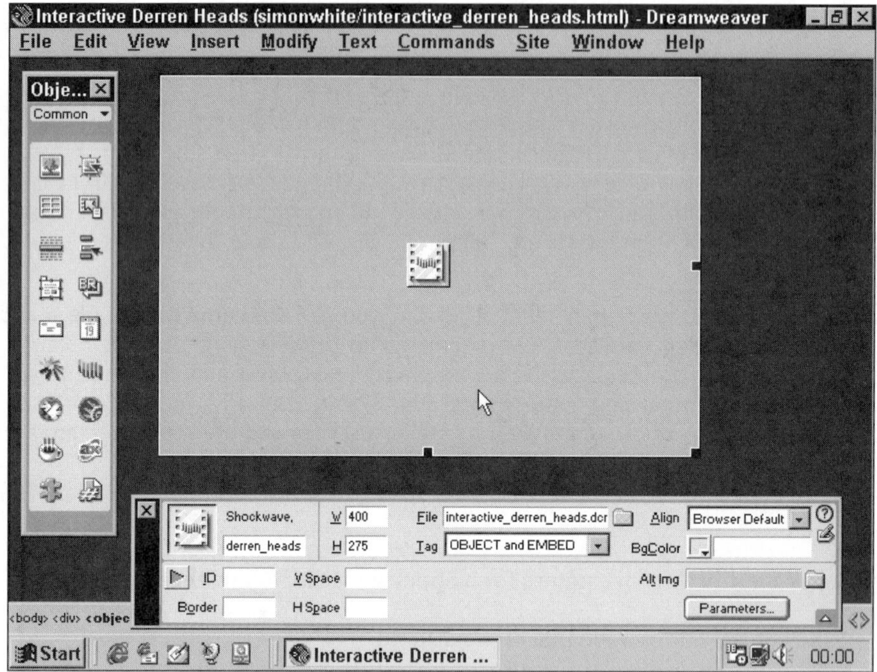

Figure 25-4: Modify parameters for a Shockwave property through the Shockwave Property Inspector.

Table 25-1
Property Inspector Options for Shockwave Objects

Shockwave Property	*Description*
Align	Choose an option to alter the alignment of the movie. In addition to the browser default, your options include Baseline, Top, Middle, Bottom, Texttop, Absolute Middle, Absolute Bottom, Left, and Right.
Alt Image	The Alt Image file is displayed in browsers that do not support the `<embed>` tag and is available if you select Embed Only. This image does not display in Dreamweaver. Enter the path to the alternate image, or select the Folder icon to open a Select Image Source dialog box.
BgColor	The background color is visible only if the width and height of the plug-in are larger than the movie. To alter the background color of your plug-in, choose the color swatch and select a new color from the pop-up menu; or enter a valid color name in the BgColor text box.

Shockwave Property	*Description*
Border	To place a border around your movie, enter a number in the Border text box. The number determines the width of the border in pixels. The default is zero or no border.
H Space	You can increase the space to the left and right of the movie by entering a value in the H (Horizontal) Space text box. The default is zero.
ID	The ID field is used to define the optional ActiveX ID parameter, most often used to pass data between ActiveX controls.
(Name)	If desired, you can enter a unique name in this unlabeled field on the far left of the Property Inspector. The name is used by JavaScript and other languages to identify the movie.
V Space	To increase the amount of space between other elements on the page and the top and bottom of the movie plug-in, enter a pixel value in the V (Vertical) Space text box. Again, the default is zero.

Additional parameters for Shockwave

As you can with other plug-ins, you can pass other attributes to the Shockwave movie via the Parameters dialog box — available by clicking the Parameters button on the Property Inspector. Press the add (+) button to begin inserting additional parameters. Enter the attributes in the left column and their respective values in the right. To remove an attribute, highlight it and select the delete (–) button.

Automatic settings for Shockwave files

When you insert a Shockwave or Flash file, Dreamweaver writes a number of parameters that are constant and necessary. In the `<object>` portion of the code, Dreamweaver includes the ActiveX Class ID number as well as the `codebase` number; the former calls the specific ActiveX control, and the latter enables users who don't have the control installed to receive it automatically. Likewise, in the `<embed>` section, Dreamweaver fills in the `pluginspage` attribute, designating the location where Navigator users can find the necessary plug-in. Be sure you don't accidentally remove any of this information — however, if you should, all you have to do is delete and reinsert the object.

The palette parameter

Only one other general attribute is usually assigned to a Shockwave file, the `palette` parameter. This parameter takes a value of either foreground or background.

✦ If palette is set to background, the movie's color scheme does not override that of the system; this is the default.

✦ When palette is set to foreground, the colors of the selected movie are applied to the user's system, which includes the desktop and scroll bars.

Note that palette is not supported by Internet Explorer.

Web designers should take care when specifying the palette=foreground parameter. This effect is likely to prove startling to the user; moreover, if your color scheme is sufficiently different, the change may render the user's system unusable. If you do use the palette parameter, be sure to include a Director command to restore the original system color scheme in the final frame of the movie.

Designating Flash Attributes

Flash movies require the same basic parameters as their Shockwave counterparts — and Flash movies have a few additional optional ones as well. As it does for Shockwave files, Dreamweaver sets almost all the attributes for Flash movies through the Property Inspector. The major difference is that several more parameters are available.

To set or modify the attributes for a Flash file, follow these steps:

1. After your Flash movie has been inserted in the Document window, make sure it's selected. Dreamweaver automatically inserts the correct dimensions for your Flash movie.
2. Set any attributes in the Property Inspector as needed for your Flash movie. (Refer to the previous descriptions of these attributes in the "Specifying Shockwave Properties" section.) In addition, you can also set the parameters described in Table 25-2.

Table 25-2
Property Inspector Options for Flash Objects

Flash Parameter	*Possible Values*	*Description*
Autoplay	Checked (default)	Enables the Flash movie to begin playing as soon as possible.
Loop	Checked (default)	If Loop is checked, the movie plays continuously; otherwise, it plays once.

Flash Parameter	*Possible Values*	*Description*
Quality		Controls anti-aliasing during playback.
	High	Anti-aliasing is turned on. This can slow the playback frame rate considerably on slower computers.
	Low	No anti-aliasing is used; this setting is best for animations that must be played quickly.
	AutoHigh (default)	The animation begins in High (with anti-aliasing) and switches to Low if the host computer is too slow.
	AutoLow	Starts the animation in Low (no anti-aliasing) and then switches to High if the host machine is fast enough.
Scale		Scale determines how the movie fits into the dimensions as specified in the width and height text boxes
	ShowAll (default)	Displays the entire movie in the given dimensions while maintaining the file's original aspect ratio. Some of the background may be visible with this setting.
	ExactFit	Scales the movie precisely into the dimensions without regard for the aspect ratio. It is possible that the image could be distorted with this setting.
	NoBorder	Fits the movie into the given dimensions so that no borders are showing and maintains the original aspect ratio. Some of the movie may be cut off with this setting.

Setting the scale in Flash movies

Be careful with your setting for the Scale parameter, in order to avoid unexpected results. If you have to size a Flash movie out of its aspect ratio, the Flash player needs to know what to do with any extra room it has to fill. Figure 25-5 demonstrates the different results that the Scale attribute can provide. Only the figure in the lower right is at its proper dimensions. The gray box is the actual size of the authoring canvas.

Tip

Dreamweaver makes it easy to rescale a Flash movie. First, from the Property Inspector, enter the precise width and height of your file in the W and H text boxes. Then, while holding down the Shift key, click and drag the corner resizing handle of the Flash placeholder icon to the new size for the movie. By Shift+dragging, you retain the aspect ratio set in the Property Inspector. This enables you to quickly enlarge or reduce your movie without distortion.

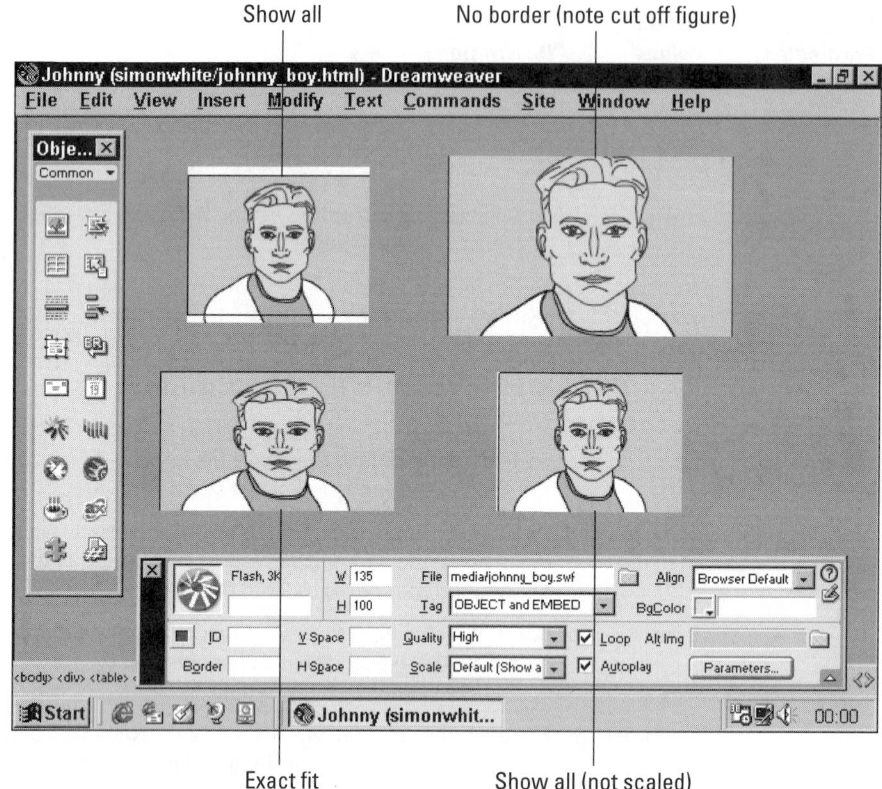

Figure 25-5: Your setting for the Scale attribute determines how your movie is resized within the plug-in width and height measurements.

Additional parameters for Flash

Flash has two additional attributes that can be entered through the Parameters dialog box (click the Parameters button on the Property Inspector): salign and swliveconnect. The `salign` attribute determines how the movie aligns itself to the surrounding frame when the Scale attribute is set to ShowAll. In addition, salign determines which portion of the image gets cut off when the Scale attribute is set to NoBorder. The alignment can be set to L (left), R (right), T (top), or B (bottom). You can also use these values in combination. For example, if you set salign=RB, the movie aligns with the right-bottom edge or the lower-right corner of the frame.

The `swliveconnect` attribute comes into play when you're using FSCommands or JavaScripting in your Flash 4 movies. FSCommands are interactive commands, such as Go to URL, issued from inside the Flash movie. The latest versions of the Netscape browser initialize Java when first called — and if your Flash movie uses FSCommands or JavaScript, it uses Java to communicate with the Netscape plug-in interface,

LiveConnect. Because not all Flash movies need the LiveConnect connection, you can prevent Java from being initialized by entering the `swliveconnect` attribute in the Parameters dialog box and setting its value to false. When the swliveconnect=false parameter is found by the browser, the Java is not initialized as part of the loading process — and your movie loads more quickly.

Configuring MIME Types

As with any plug-in, your Web server has to have the correct MIME types set before Shockwave files can be properly served to your users. If your Web page plays Shockwave and Flash movies locally, but not remotely, chances are good the correct MIME types need to be added. The system administrator generally handles configuring MIME types.

The system administrator needs to know the following information in order to correctly configure the MIME types:

Shockwave	application/x-director (.dcr, .dir, .dxr)
Flash	application/x-shockwave-flash (.swf)

Both Shockwave and Flash are popular plug-ins, and it's likely that the Web server is already configured to recognize the appropriate file types.

Movies made by an earlier version of Flash, called FutureSplash, can also be played by the Flash plug-in — but only if the correct MIME type is added: `application/futuresplash` with the file extension .spl.

Managing Links in Flash Movies with Dreamweaver

Many Web sites rely heavily on Flash movies, substituting movies for entire pages that would otherwise be created with HTML. Others take advantage of Flash's interactivity in their main navigation buttons. Adding links to buttons in Flash is easy, but embedding multiple URLs into multiple SWF files can make modifying a site's structure a nightmare, forcing you to re-create every SWF file in your site. Luckily, Dreamweaver 3 comes to the rescue, with link management features that are SWF-savvy.

Dreamweaver 3 extends its link management to include the links contained in Flash SWF movies. Edit links within a SWF file manually in the Site Map, or move SWF files in the Site Files view and let Dreamweaver clean up behind you.

Within the Site window, you can drag SWF files to new folders just as you would an HTML file. Unless your Update Links preference is set to Never, Dreamweaver will either modify the links in the SWF file accordingly or prompt you for permission to do so.

To modify the links in a SWF file manually, follow these steps:

1. Choose Window ➪ Site Map to view the Site Map.
2. Choose View ➪ Show Dependent Files (Site ➪ Site Map View ➪ Show Dependent Files) to include dependent files such as Flash movies in the Site Map.
3. Locate the SWF file that you want to modify. If it contains any links, a plus sign is shown next to its icon. Click the plus sign to expand a branch of links from the SWF file, as shown in Figure 25-6.

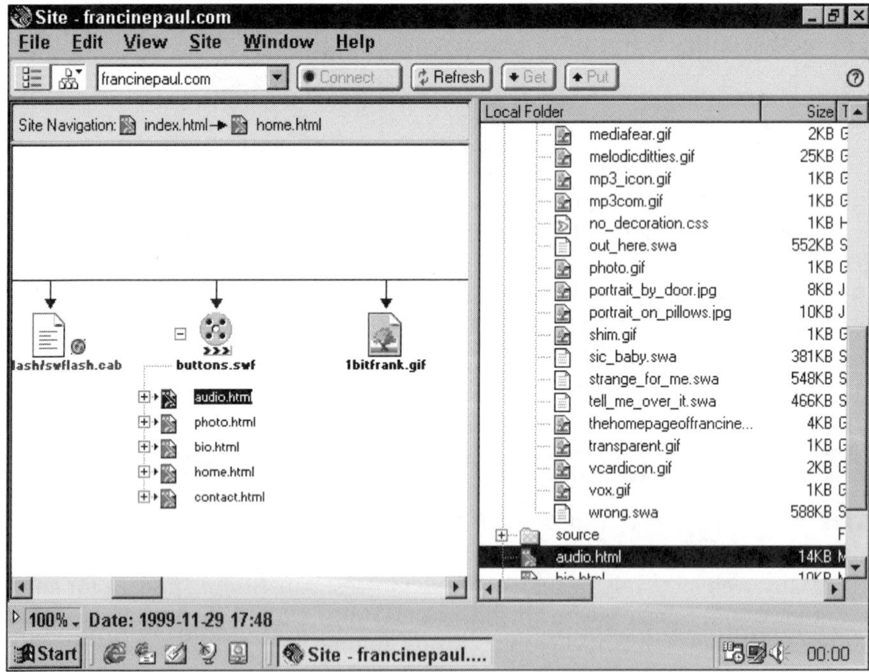

Figure 25-6: Dreamweaver's Site Map displays links contained in Flash SWF movies.

4. To change a link, select it and choose Site ➪ Change Link (Site ➪ Site Map View ➪ Change Link) or use the key shortcut Ctrl+L (Command+L). Alternatively, you can right-click (Control+click) the link and choose Change Link from the contextual menu. Dreamweaver displays a Select HTML File dialog box.
5. Select a new file by navigating to an HTML file or entering an URL. Click OK when you're done.

If your preferences call for Dreamweaver to prompt you before updating links, Dreamweaver will ask you to confirm that you want this link changed.

The link in your SWF file is changed.

Just as with HTML files, you can also remove links from a SWF file by selecting the link and choosing Site ➪ Remove Link (Site ➪ Site Map View ➪ Remove Link) or use the key shortcut Ctrl+Shift+L (Command+Shift+L).

Dreamweaver changes links within SWF files, but the links in the original Flash document that you edit in Flash itself will remain unchanged. Make sure to update your Flash document before exporting a revised SWF file.

Providing User Interaction with Shockwave Movies

What happens once you've installed your Director or Flash Shockwave files? Many movies are set to play automatically or upon some action from the user, such as a mouse click of a particular hotspot within the page. The Show Me movies used in Using Dreamweaver are good examples of the kind of interactivity you can program within a Director Shockwave movie. But what if you want the user to be able to start or stop a movie in one part of the page, using controls in another part? How can controls in one frame affect a movie in a different frame?

Dreamweaver includes a Control Shockwave or Flash behavior that makes inline controls — controls on the same Web page as the movie — very easy to set up. However, establishing frame-to-frame control is slightly more complex in Dreamweaver and requires a minor modification to the program-generated code.

Both of the following step-by-step techniques rely on Dreamweaver behaviors. If you're unfamiliar with using behaviors, you should review Chapter 19 before proceeding.

Dreamweaver Technique: Creating inline Shockwave controls

Certainly it's perfectly acceptable to make your Director or Flash movies with built-in controls for interactivity, but sometimes you want to separate the controls from the movie. Dreamweaver includes a JavaScript behavior called Control Shockwave or Flash. With this behavior, you can set up external controls to start, stop, and rewind Shockwave and Flash movies.

To create inline Shockwave or Flash controls:

1. Insert your Shockwave or Flash file by choosing either the Insert Shockwave or Insert Flash button from the Objects palette.
2. From the Select File dialog box, enter the path to your file in the File Name text box or select the Browse (Choose) button to locate your file.
3. For Shockwave, enter the width and height of your movie in the W and H text boxes, respectively, in the Property Inspector. The dimensions for Flash movies are entered automatically.
4. Enter a unique name for your movie in the text box provided.
5. If you are inserting a Flash movie, deselect the Autoplay and Loop options.
6. To insert the first control, position the cursor where you'd like the control to appear on the page.
7. Select Insert Image from the Objects palette or select some text.
8. In the Link box of the Property Inspector, enter a dummy link or just a hash symbol, #, to create an empty target.
9. Open the Behavior Inspector by selecting the Behavior button from the Launcher or by pressing F8.
10. If necessary, change the selected browser to 4.0 Browsers; you can do this by opening the drop-down list at the top of the Browser Inspector.
11. Select the + (Add) Action button and choose Control Shockwave or Flash from the drop-down list.
12. In the Control Shockwave or Flash dialog box (see Figure 25-7), select the movie you want to affect from the Movie drop-down list.

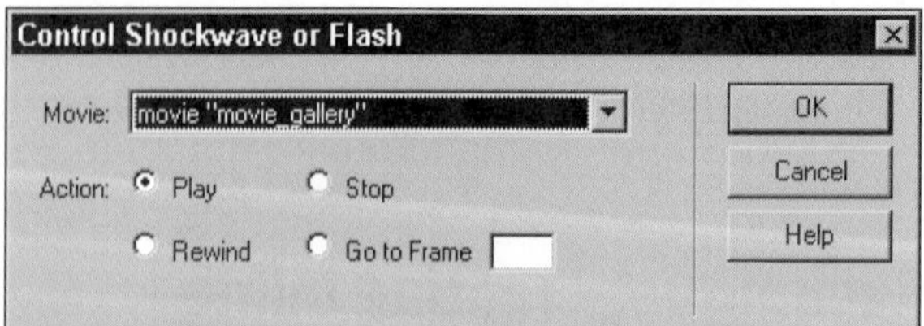

Figure 25-7: In the Control Shockwave or Flash dialog box, you assign a control action to an image button or link.

13. Now select the desired action for your control. Choose from the four options: Play, Stop, Rewind, and Go to Frame. If you choose the Go to Frame option, enter a frame number in the text box.

14. Click OK to close the Control Shockwave or Flash dialog box.

15. Repeat Steps 6 through 14 for each movie control you'd like to add. Figure 25-8 shows a sample Web page with Play and Stop controls.

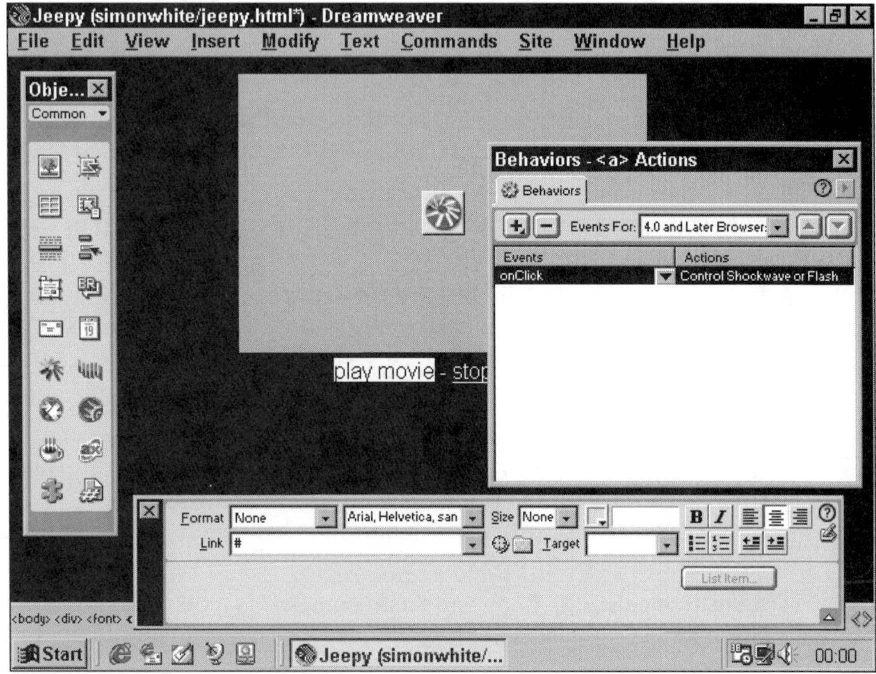

Figure 25-8: This Web page contains Play and Stop controls using the Control Shockwave or Flash behavior.

Dreamweaver Technique: Playing Shockwave movies in frames

Framesets and frames are great for Web sites in which you want your navigation and other controls kept in one frame and the freedom to vary the content in another frame. It's entirely possible to set up your movie's playback buttons in one frame and the Shockwave movie in another. The method and the tools used are similar to those used in the preceding technique for adding same-page controls to a Shockwave movie. For this technique using frames, some HTML hand-coding is necessary, but it is relatively minor — only one additional line per control!

As you saw in the previous section, Dreamweaver's Control Shockwave or Flash behavior lists all the Shockwave and Flash movies in the page and enables you to choose the one you want to affect (as previously shown in Figure 25-7). Unfortunately, the behavior looks on only one page and not through an entire frameset.

However, with a little sleight-of-hand and a bit of JavaScript, you can get the effect you want.

Before you begin applying this technique, you should construct (and save) your frameset and individual frames. Be sure to name each frame uniquely, because you have to provide the names in order to address the correct frames.

To place Shockwave controls in frames:

1. In one frame, insert the images or links that are going to act as the Shockwave controls. (For this demonstration, the control frame is named `frControl`.)
2. In another frame, insert the Shockwave file (either Shockwave or Flash) by choosing the appropriate object from the Objects palette. (For this demonstration, the movie frame is named `frMovie`.)
3. Be sure to modify the Shockwave Property Inspector with the necessary parameters: name, width, height, and source; and, if you're inserting a Flash file, deselect the Autoplay and Loop checkboxes.
4. Copy the Shockwave placeholder by selecting it and choosing Edit ➪ Copy.
5. Position the cursor in the `frControl` frame and paste the placeholder in a temporary position by choosing Edit ➪ Paste. At this point, the placement for the placeholder is not critical, as long as it is in the same frame as the images or links you are going to use as controls. The placeholder will be deleted shortly.

   Instead of using the Copy and Paste commands, you can hold down Ctrl (Command) and click and drag the placeholder to its new temporary position.
6. Now select the first image or link you want to use as a control. As described in the preceding technique, attach the Control Shockwave or Flash behavior to the selected object. As you learned in the preceding exercise, this entails the following actions:
   - With the image or link selected, open the Behavior Inspector.
   - Add the Control Shockwave or Flash action.
   - In the Control Shockwave or Flash dialog box, specify the movie and select the required action (Play, Rewind, Stop, or Go to Frame).
7. The major work is finished now. All you still need to do is add a little HTML. Open the HTML Inspector or use your favorite external editor to edit the file.
8. Locate the image or link controls in the code. Each JavaScript routine is called from within an `<a>` tag and reads something like the following, where `fMovie` is the name of the Flash movie:

```
<a href="#" onClick="MM_controlShockwave¬
('document.fMovie', 'document.fMovie','Play')">
```

9. Wherever you see the JavaScript reference to document, change it to

```
parent.frameName.document
```

where *frameName* is the unique name you gave to the frame in which your movie appears. In our example, `frameName` is `frMovie`, so after the replacement is made, the tag reads as follows:

```
<a href="#" onClick="MM_controlShockwave('parent.¬
frMovie.document.fMovie','document.fMovie','Play')">
```

By making this substitution, you've pointed the JavaScript function first to the "parent" of the current document—and the parent of a frame is the entire frameset. Now that we're looking at the entire frameset, the next word (which is the unique frame name) points the JavaScript function directly to the desired frame within the frameset.

Tip

If you have a number of controls, you might want to use Dreamweaver's Find and Replace features to ensure that you've updated all the code.

10. After you've made the alterations to all of your controls, close the HTML Inspector or external editor.

11. Finally, delete the temporary Shockwave movie that was inserted into the frame containing the controls.

Test the frameset by pressing F12 (primary browser) or Shift+F12 (secondary browser). If you haven't changed the Property Inspector's default Tag attribute (the default is Object and Embed), the Shockwave movie should work in both Netscape Navigator and Internet Explorer.

Dreamweaver Technique: Triggering Behaviors from Flash Movies

Flash 4 includes a number of its own behaviors for creating interactivity, but Flash behaviors don't do JavaScript as Dreamweaver behaviors do. A Flash-heavy project might benefit from Dreamweaver's Open Browser Window or Pop-up Message behaviors as much as the next site. The technique in this section shows you how to trigger Dreamweaver behaviors from buttons in a Flash movie.

What Flash buttons do is specified in the Flash authoring environment, not in Dreamweaver. Dreamweaver can attach behaviors to HTML elements such as anchor tags and body tags but not to plug-ins. The solution lies in creating dummy "buttons" in Dreamweaver and copying the JavaScript code from those links into the actions attached to Flash buttons, within Flash itself.

To trigger Dreamweaver behaviors from Flash buttons, follow these steps:

The following steps require Flash or the Flash trial version available on your Dreamweaver CD-ROM or CD-ROM 1 that accompanies this book.

1. Create a new Dreamweaver document or open an existing one.
2. Create a dummy link that represents a button in your Flash movie. If you want a Flash button to open a new browser window, attach the Open Browser Window behavior to your dummy link, as in Figure 25-9.

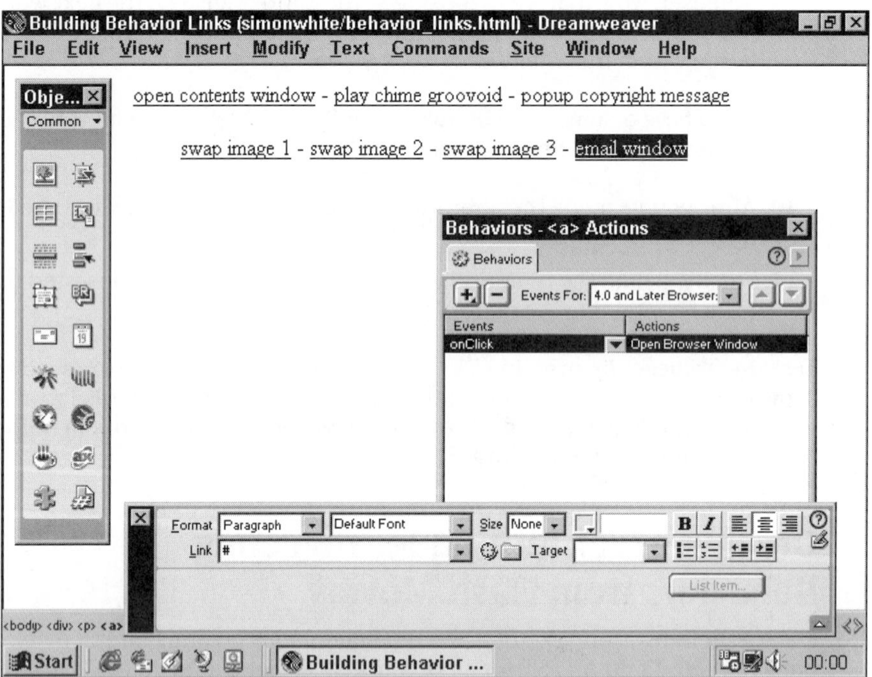

Figure 25-9: Attach a behavior you want to trigger from Flash to a dummy link in Dreamweaver.

3. Place your cursor within the dummy link and choose the <a> tag from the Tag Chooser in Dreamweaver's status bar to completely select the link.
4. Choose Window ➪ HTML Source or use the key shortcut F10 to open the HTML Inspector. Note that the dummy link is selected in the HTML Inspector as well and looks something like this:

```
<a href="#" onClick="MM_openBrWindow('/email.html',¬
'emailWindow','width=250,height=200')">email window</a>
```

5. Select everything between the quotes in the `onClick` attribute — including the parentheses — as shown in Figure 25-10, and copy it to the clipboard. This is the actual JavaScript that we want the Flash button to execute.

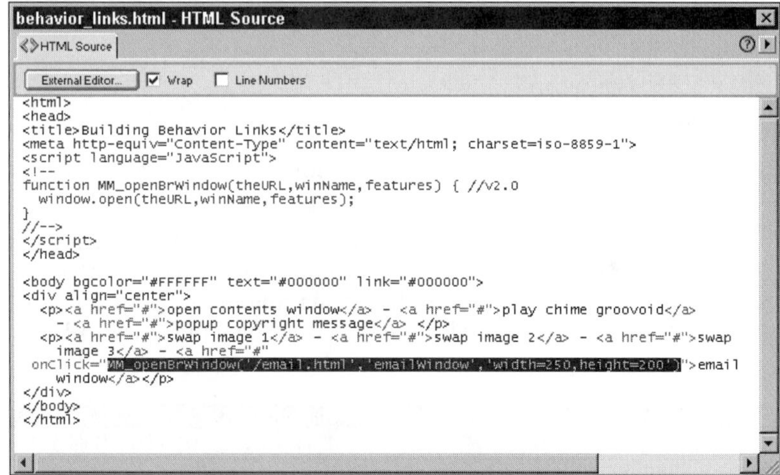

Figure 25-10: Select the JavaScript that the Flash button should execute from within the `onClick` attribute of your anchor tag.

6. In Flash, double-click the button you want to add the Dreamweaver behavior to. The Instance Properties dialog box opens. Select the Actions tab, as shown in Figure 25-11.

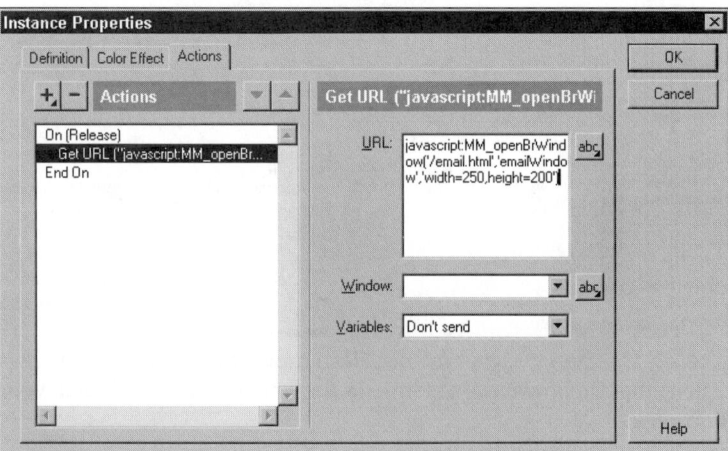

Figure 25-11: Add your JavaScript code to a Flash button Get URL behavior in the Instance Properties dialog box in Flash.

7. Click the + (add) button and choose Get URL to add a Flash Get URL behavior to your Flash button. In the URL box, type:

```
javascript:
```

and then paste the contents of the clipboard — your JavaScript code — so that you have something like this (refer back to Figure 25-11):

```
javascript:MM_openBrWindow('/email.html',¬
'emailWindow','width=250,height=200')
```

Click OK when you're done.

8. Repeat Steps 2 through 7 for each additional button or behavior you'd like to use.

9. Export your Flash movie as a SWF file and place it into the same page in Dreamweaver where you built your dummy links. Note that the `<head>` tag of this page contains JavaScript functions that match your dummy links and the JavaScript inside your Flash movie, as shown in Figure 25-12.

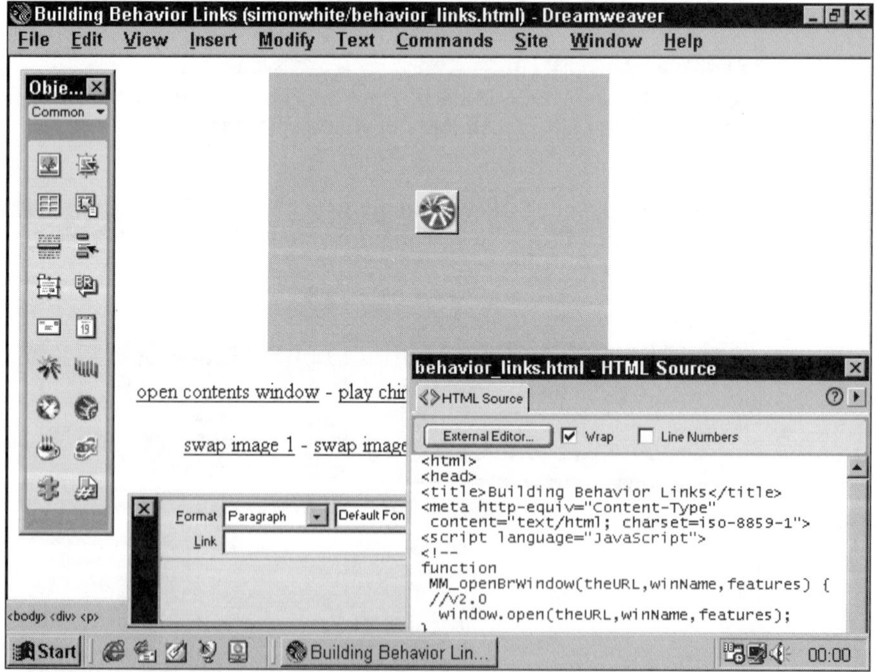

Figure 25-12: The JavaScript in your Flash movie relies on the same JavaScript functions that Dreamweaver inserted in the `<head>` tag as you built your dummy links.

10. Delete your dummy links — but not the JavaScript functions in the `<head>` tag — and publish your page.

When users click the buttons in your Flash movie, `javascript: URL` sends the commands to the browser, executing the JavaScript functions in your Web page. Flash buttons open new browser windows, pop-up messages, and so on. This works in Netscape and in Internet Explorer.

Tip

Shockwave authors can also use JavaScript URLs from Lingo to trigger Dreamweaver behaviors in a manner similar to the preceding. The JavaScript-savvy can also reference their own JavaScript functions using this method.

Summary

Together, the interactive power of Shockwave and the speedy glitz of Flash can enliven Web content like nothing else. Dreamweaver is extremely well suited for integrating and displaying Shockwave and Flash movies.

✦ Saving your Director movies as Shockwave enables them to be played on the Web with the help of a plug-in or ActiveX control.

✦ Flash movies are a way to enhance your Web pages with vector animations, interactivity, and streaming audio. Flash movies require the Flash player plug-in or ActiveX Control.

✦ Dreamweaver has built-in objects for both Director and Flash movies. All the important parameters are accessible directly through the Property Inspector.

✦ You need only three parameters to incorporate a Shockwave movie: the file's location, height, and width. Dreamweaver automatically imports a Flash movie's dimensions. You can get the exact measurements of a Shockwave movie from within Director.

✦ Dreamweaver comes with a JavaScript behavior for controlling Shockwave and Flash movies. This Control Shockwave or Flash behavior can be used as-is for adding external controls to the same Web page or — with a minor modification — for adding the controls to another frame in the same frameset.

✦ Dreamweaver behaviors can be triggered from a Shockwave or Flash movie.

In the next chapter, you begin to learn about Dynamic HTML.

✦ ✦ ✦

Dynamic HTML and Dreamweaver

PART

VI

✦ ✦ ✦ ✦

In This Part

✦ ✦ ✦ ✦

What Is Dynamic HTML?

✦ ✦ ✦ ✦

In This Chapter

Dynamic HTML fundamentals

Using the DHTML features of Navigator

Applying DHTML techniques in Internet Explorer

✦ ✦ ✦ ✦

Dynamic HTML sounds like an ad slogan for the latest technology, doesn't it? In this case, the word *dynamic* refers to the capability to change, evolve, grow, shift, and otherwise metamorphose into a different state. With Dynamic HTML (or DHTML), almost everything on the heretofore static Web page can change. Moreover, these dynamic transitions are not generated from the server side of the Internet; they are inherent in the programming language itself.

Depending on the implementation, Dynamic HTML enables an amazing range of effects:

✦ Objects fly in from all corners of the screen and assemble into a coherent, integrated portion of the page.

✦ Text and logos suddenly materialize and instantly disappear from the screen.

✦ Web pages aren't two-dimensional — now objects can be in front of or behind other objects.

✦ Outlines expand to reveal details and collapse to provide an overview; content changes with the interactive click of a button.

✦ The design on the Web appears as it was designed off the Web; designers can make their Web layouts appear just the way they want, without complicated tables or single-pixel spacers.

✦ Tables are automatically generated according to the data returned from a query, and then updated globally with input from the user.

These capabilities barely scratch the surface of the Dynamic HTML possibilities. With Dreamweaver's advanced interface, challenging and code-intensive projects become intuitively achievable. Dreamweaver was among the first Web authoring tools to take full advantage of Dynamic HTML capabilities.

With its history of open standards and competing commercial visions, however, the Web doesn't yet have a smooth road with Dynamic HTML. In theory, both Netscape and Microsoft have fully embraced DHTML, but the reality is that both companies have adopted divergent models of the standard. Dreamweaver rises above the fray and makes cross-browser Dynamic HTML really work — with little or no assistance from the Web designer.

This chapter has a dual purpose. First and foremost, it introduces you to the concepts of DHTML and provides an overview of the current state of implementation in the two primary browsers. Second, it examines the browser-specific Dynamic HTML features and shows you how to employ them in Dreamweaver.

For a taste of the possibilities with Dynamic HTML, visit Macromedia's Dynamic HTML Zone at `www.dhtmlzone.com` and select the Tutorials option. Once you're in the tutorial screen, click the Launch Superfly button. This demo not only shows the excitement Dynamic HTML can generate, but also acts as an excellent tutorial. (While you're in the Dynamic HTML Zone, be sure to also check out the Spotlight sites for further demonstrations.)

Fundamentals of Dynamic HTML

What makes Dynamic HTML so, well . . . dynamic? No single factor can take all the credit. Rather, DHTML is really a combination of technologies that are coming to be regarded as the next generation of Web development. In this section, you examine the roles of the components that make up DHTML:

✦ **Cascading Style Sheets:** These give the Web designer control over the many characteristics of the Web page, whether designated by a standard or custom HTML tag.

✦ **Absolute positioning:** This feature enables pixel-precise placement of any Web object.

✦ **Dynamic content:** The Web page can have content added or deleted on the fly.

✦ **Downloadable fonts:** Web designers can embed specific fonts to control a Web page's typography.

✦ **Data binding:** Server-side data is linked to a table or form on a Web page, which can dynamically update without redrawing the entire page.

Not all of this functionality is cross-browser, but all these features are possible in one configuration or another. As a whole, Dynamic HTML brings a more responsive, media-rich Web environment to the Web designer's palette — one that more closely resembles multimedia CD-ROM productions, while still maintaining the unique hyperconnectivity of the Internet. Best of all, Dynamic HTML is far more internalized than earlier HTML implementations, relying less on Helper applications and plug-ins to achieve its state-of-the-art effects.

Cascading Style Sheets

As sanctioned by the HTML governing body, the World Wide Web Consortium (W3C), the Cascading Style Sheet (CSS) specification is at the core of DHTML. CSS was the first step toward making traditional HTML more flexible and malleable. In a nutshell, CSS enables a Web designer to specify the attributes of an HTML tag — whether in a single page or through an entire site — with one command.

Take the `<h1>` tag, for instance. Does management want all headlines across the company's Web site during July to be 24-point Helvetica and blue-green? CSS can handle this request in one line:

```
h1 {  font: 24pt Helvetica; color: green}
```

If you're a print-oriented layout artist who has been trying to adjust to HTML, you'll appreciate not only the flexibility and control of Cascading Style Sheets, but also their implementation. CSS uses the well-established language of print designers. Fonts, for example, can be sized in points or picas, instead of with relative sizes 1–6.

The Cascading Style Sheet technology not only affects the standard attributes of HTML tags, but also extends the number and variety of properties that can be modified. For instance, CSS now enables Web designers to specify the line height of any given tag, whether to make a paragraph of text double-spaced or to tighten the leading (line-spacing) for subheads. CSS offers entire categories of new elements, such as boxes, that can be added to the designer's palette and the Web page. Moreover, CSS power is not limited to existing standard tags — you can create custom styles and assign them special characteristics. For instance, a large organization may define a "legal" style to be used in disclaimers and other fine print.

The important aspect of CSS from the standpoint of DHTML is that CSS begins to control the elements on the page in a systematic fashion. In the fullest implementation of CSS, scripting languages such as JavaScript can address any declared style and modify its properties interactively.

Dreamweaver uses an intuitive interface for working with CSS. To learn more about this topic, see Chapter 27.

Absolute positioning

From a print designer's viewpoint, perhaps the single most aggravating aspect of working on the Web has been the inability to easily place type or graphics anywhere on the page. Designers have had to go to elaborate lengths, using complex nested tables and one-pixel images as spacers, in attempts to achieve a faithful online representation of their designs.

An extension of Cascading Style Sheets now provides a more elegant solution: absolute positioning. Known as CSS-P, the standard for positioning has been adopted fully by Microsoft and to a lesser extent by Netscape. CSS-P forms the basis for layers.

Layers are invisible containers that can hold any type and amount of Web elements — and most important, they can be positioned anywhere on a Web page to exact pixel coordinates.

The power of layers goes farther than absolute positioning, however. Layers and their contents can be made invisible or visible with a change of one property. Because CSS employs a concept known as *inheritance*, in which related styles take on the characteristics of the parent style, many layers can be manipulated at once. As the term implies, layers bring an illusion of depth to the Web page. By design, each layer exists in its own three-dimensional plane. You can stack one layer on top of another, or you can change their stacking order interactively.

Just as regular CSS elements can be updated dynamically, the position of layers can too — which makes the look of animation possible. Just as one second in a movie is actually 24 static images shown rapidly, layers can be quickly repositioned, appearing to move from point A to point B. This animation quality is one of the most striking features of Dynamic HTML. For the first time, movement on the Web is not generated from a source external to the Web page itself, whether it is server-push, an animated GIF, or a plug-in. This capability accelerates the display of pages online and enables Web pages to be viewed offline in a more easy and complete manner.

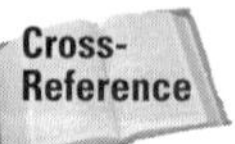

To learn more about absolute positioning and layers, refer to Chapter 28.

Dynamic content

So far, Dynamic HTML can change the look of a Web page's elements with CSS and control the placement of a Web page's objects with layers — but what about the content? Only Microsoft has currently taken the challenge of creating dynamic content. Because Internet Explorer has complete control over the Document Object Model (DOM), any element or tag can be updated on the fly. This capability includes the content or value of tags.

Dynamic content is extremely useful when working with outline-based documents. With dynamic content links, you can show only the heading of a document, which when selected by the user, expands to present the substance — no matter how many paragraphs exist. Select the same heading again, and the expanded outline collapses. Expanding and collapsing outlines can be implemented in all primary DHTML-capable browsers. Only Microsoft, however, uses true dynamic content; Netscape's 4.x browsers use a technique involving layers.

When you build an expanding outline in a Web page, you initially include all the content. Then, you designate the heading and the content and apply the appropriate styles, as illustrated in Figure 26-1.

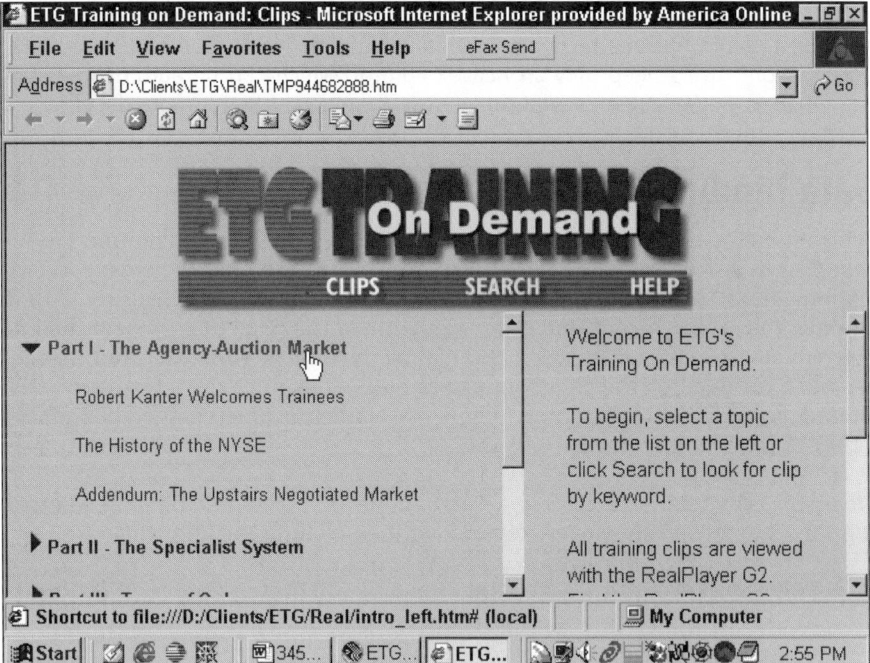

Figure 26-1: Dynamic content enables you to create expanding and collapsing outlines.

Downloadable fonts

Increased font control tops the wish list for most Web designers — and this capability does not mean font size or color. For too long, Web pages have been limited to the most generic of typefaces (primarily Arial, Times, and Helvetica) because HTML could access only the fonts on the user's system. Dynamic HTML promises to change this deficiency with downloadable fonts. As the term implies, downloadable fonts enable the Web designer to embed a specific font within a DHTML page, and the font is temporarily transferred to the Web site visitor's system.

Unfortunately, at the present time, the key word in the preceding paragraph is *promises*. Both Microsoft and Netscape have implemented their own mutually incompatible versions of downloadable fonts. The demand for this capability is so strong, however, that it is only a matter of time before downloadable fonts become a cross-browser reality and a working standard. In the meantime, you can apply Open Font in Internet Explorer and Dynamic Font technology in Communicator simultaneously.

You can embed fonts capable of being read by both browsers with the help of Bitstream's TrueDoc technology. Although it's native to Communicator, Internet Explorer users need only an ActiveX control, which can be automatically downloaded. See Bitstream's Web site at `www.truedoc.com` for more details.

Data binding

Tying an online database to a Web page has never been a trivial matter. Any Web page had to be generated on the server side in order to post the most current information — until the emergence of Dynamic HTML's data binding feature. With data binding, the tables, forms, and other elements of the page that present the information can also receive information and can be dynamically restructured. Once data has been received on the client side, data binding enables the information to be filtered, sorted, and represented — only the elements affected need be redrawn, rather than the entire page.

Presently, only Internet Explorer 4.0 and above supports data binding. Microsoft's support is extensive, however; key innovations include the following:

- ✦ **Full object model access to data binding attributes:** Enables Web designers to use JavaScript to add, delete, and modify bindings at runtime.
- ✦ **Table paging:** Provides the capability to limit the number of records displayed in a repeated table and move the starting record forward and backward in the data set.
- ✦ **Table and form generation:** Offers automatic building of table rows from data records and data-bound form fields.

For more on data binding, see the section "Delivering Data Binding" later in this chapter.

Accessing DHTML in Netscape Communicator

The Navigator component of Communicator contains three features that comprise Netscape's Dynamic HTML effort: style sheets, positionable content, and downloadable fonts. The Netscape version of DHTML only partially conforms to the standard outlined by the W3C. For instance, Netscape supports two different types of style sheets: the W3C-standard Cascading Style Sheets, and the company's own JavaScript Style Sheets (JSS).

The following sections discuss Netscape's methods of implementing Dynamic HTML and show you how to implement those methods in Dreamweaver.

As of this writing, Communicator 4.*x* is the latest browser released from Netscape. Although Communicator 6 promises to enhance the level of support for W3C standards, it is not available at this time for testing and cannot, therefore, be covered in this chapter.

Creating style sheets

Let's take a closer look at Netscape's support of the standard Cascading Style Sheet as well as its own proprietary JSS method. In brief, CSS uses the `<style>` tag to apply new attributes to an existing HTML tag or a custom tag known as a *class*. The CSS style tag format looks like the following:

```
<STYLE TYPE="text/css">
<!--
P {font-size:18pt; margin-left:20pt;}
H1 {color:blue;}
-->
</STYLE>
```

JavaScript Style Sheets also use the `<style>` tag but take advantage of the DOM to format the JSS specifications. The DOM is a hierarchical system that identifies each page element by its type of object (or by its assigned name). Once you have properly identified an element, you can then change its properties. The preceding CSS style sheet example looks like the following in JSS:

```
<STYLE TYPE = "text/javascript">
tags.P.fontSize = "18pt";
tags.P.marginLeft = "20pt";
tags.H1.color = "blue";
</STYLE>
```

Do not use the HTML comment tags with JavaScript Style Sheets.

Dreamweaver outputs CSS-formatted code and previews the changes as well. Although you cannot preview JSS-formatted code within Dreamweaver, JSS renders properly when previewed in a compatible browser.

To be frank, JSS has not received serious support in the Web developer community, and because the standard CSS format works in both browsers, JSS has little chance of becoming popular. If, however, you develop pages that use JSS, you can continue to code them in Dreamweaver—just not as conveniently.

Making positionable content

With positionable content, Netscape again supports two possibilities. Although Navigator 4.0 essentially supports the CSS-P style layers created using the `<div>` and `<span>` tags with the style attributes, it also puts forth its own proprietary `<layer>` and `<ilayer>` tags. Aside from these syntax differences, some differences also exist between what Navigator 4.0 supports in the properties for CSS-P style positioning and the proprietary `<layer>` tags. That said, all of the tags form the basis for layers, which can be placed anywhere on the page.

Note

Netscape has given up on the `<layer>` and `<ilayer>` tag; neither are supported in Navigator 6.

Relative positioning represents perhaps the biggest difference between the two implementations. Usually when you place a layer in your Web page, the left and top attributes define the layer's absolute position on the screen. When the position attribute is set to relative, however, the left and top values relate to whatever contains the layer, whether it is a table or another layer. Relative positioning using the CSS convention of `position:relative` simply doesn't work in the current release of Navigator 4.05. Instead, you should use the `<layer>` and `<ilayer>` tags. The `<layer>` tag is used for absolute positioning, and `<ilayer>` is used for relative positioning—or what Netscape calls *inflow-positioning*. Dreamweaver supports all four of the layer tag variations.

Several other properties for positionable content are supported differently in Netscape than in the CSS standard. In most cases, when Netscape doesn't support the CSS standard, it offers its own variation for the `<layer>` and `<ilayer>` tags and for the CSS style use. Table 26-1 describes these equivalents.

You can include both the CSS standard and the Netscape variation of an attribute in a `<style>` tag for cross-browser compatibility without dire consequences. In Dreamweaver, however, you need to add the Netscape syntax by hand, preferably after the CSS standard syntax.

Table 26-1
Differences between CSS and Netscape Layer Properties

CSS Term	*Layer Property*	*Netscape Equivalent*
`include-source:url ("filename.htm")`	`SRC="filename.htm"`	`source-include:url ("filename.htm")`
`background-color: colorname`	`BGCOLOR="colorname"`	`layer-background color:colorname`
`background-image:url ("filename")`	`BACKGROUND="filename"`	`layer-background image:filename`

Using downloadable fonts

Fonts in HTML have only recently started to get a little respect. A `<font>` tag wasn't supported until HTML 3.2 — and the support is strictly limited. Attributes for the `<font>` tag enable you to specify a number of font face options from which the user's system can choose, such as the following:

```
<font face="Arial, Helvetica, sans-serif">
```

Until Dynamic HTML, however, a designer could not use a typeface that users did not have on their system and still expect to have the layout viewed correctly. Netscape's method for implementing downloadable fonts requires that the fonts be contained in a font definition file on the same Web server as the Web page. When the page is served to the user, the font definition file is downloaded with the HTML file, in the same way as a GIF or JPEG file. The font definition file is loaded asynchronously so that the HTML page doesn't have to wait while the fonts are loading.

To protect the copyrights of font designers, the downloaded font remains on the user's system only while the page is in the browser's cache; the fonts cannot be copied for personal use.

Font definition files are generated with a special authoring tool, such as Typograph from HexMac (`www.hexmac.com`), Bitstream's WebFont Maker (`www.truedoc.com`), or the Font Composer Plug-in for Communicator or CorelDraw 8 and above. The process involves opening your Web page in the authoring tool, selecting text, and applying the font to it. You then burn (process) the file, which saves the document, creates a font definition file containing the fonts used by the file, and also links the font definition file to the document. Font definition files can be used by only one domain at a time, and the domain is specified at the time you burn the file.

Once the font definition file is created, you link the font through a style tag, such as the following:

```
<STYLE TYPE="text/css"><!--
@fontdef url(http://home.netscape.com/fonts/sample.pfr);
--></STYLE>
```

You can also use a `<link>` tag, as follows:

```
<LINK REL="fontdef" SRC="fontdef1.pfr">
```

The final step in getting the user's system to recognize Netscape downloadable fonts adds a new MIME type to the Web server, `application/font-tdpfr`, with a file name extension of .pfr (Portable Font Resource).

Once you've linked the font to your page, you can include it in a font tag, just like a regular system font. For example, if you've included a font called "BurnOut," you could include a font family definition by choosing Text ➪ Font ➪ Edit Font List. Then, when applying the font to a particular bit of text, the HTML could read as follows:

```
"<font face="BurnOut, Arial, Helvetica, sans-serif">
```

To support the new capabilities of downloadable fonts, Netscape includes two new attributes: point-size and weight. The point-size attribute enables you to set exact sizes for your font (unlike the regular `size` attribute for the `<font>` tag, which works relatively). The weight attribute enables you to alter the boldness of the font. The weight value is from 100 to 900, inclusive (in steps of 100), where 100 indicates the least bold value and 900 indicates the boldest value. Specifying the `<b>` tag causes Netscape to render the boldest font possible.

The amount of work involved to achieve downloadable fonts is a factor in Web designers' reluctance to use the technique. As you can see in Figure 26-2, however, the results can be spectacular.

Tip

You can certainly use Netscape's downloadable fonts in Dreamweaver, but keep in mind that you have to add all the special code by hand. Also, Dreamweaver does not preview the font changes.

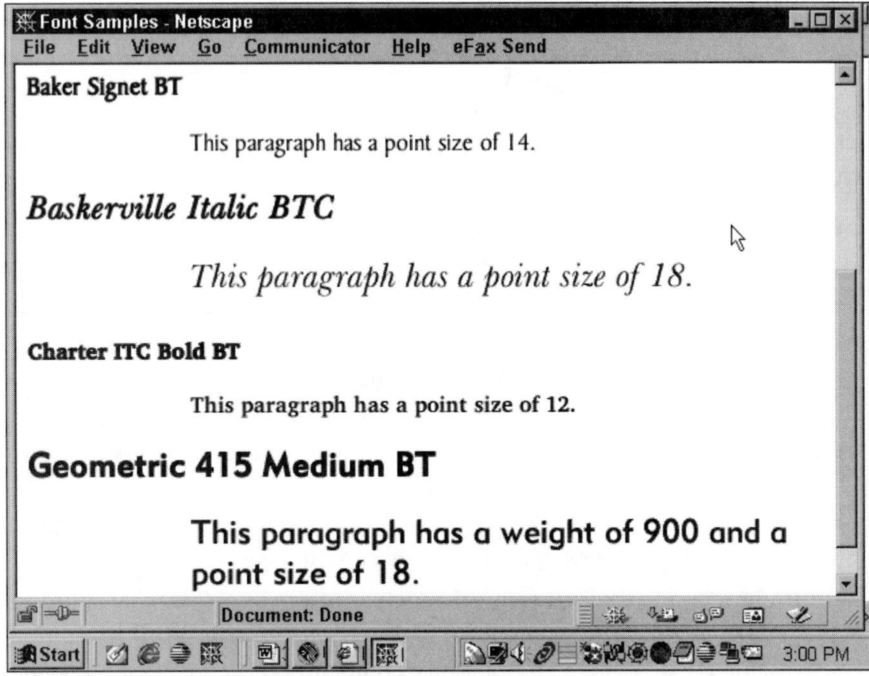

Figure 26-2: You can access a wide range of fonts and font sizes with Netscape's downloadable font technology.

Viewing Netscape Embedded Fonts in Internet Explorer

As noted earlier, Internet Explorer browsers can use Netscape embedded fonts with the aid of a small ActiveX control. The ActiveX control is added simply by inserting the following lines after the `<link>` code:

```
<script language="JavaScript" ¬
src="http://www.truedoc.com/activex/tdserver.js"></script>
```

When the Internet Explorer browser loads the page, the user's system is inspected to determine if the proper ActiveX control is already installed. If not, the user is asked if the ActiveX control should be downloaded.

The easiest way to include TrueDoc fonts in a page is to use Simon White's PFR command, included on this book's CD-ROM 1. The command searches for a PFR file and then inserts the necessary code for the link and the ActiveX control.

Working with DHTML and Internet Explorer

Starting with Internet Explorer 4.0, Microsoft adopted Dynamic HTML with a vengeance. At least partially supporting all the W3C official recommendations as well as numerous proposals, Internet Explorer advances DHTML to the extreme. Included in Microsoft's rendition are the following features:

✦ **Dynamic Styles:** Includes a robust implementation of the CSS Level 1 specification for controlling style sheets.

✦ **Dynamic Content:** Enables the Web page to be redrawn after it has been downloaded.

✦ **Positioning and animation:** Provide a full implementation of the CSS-P specification for layers and movement.

✦ **Filters and transitions:** Permit designers to use special effects applied to images, text, or entire Web pages.

✦ **Open fonts:** Enable the Web page to specify a font that is automatically downloaded, used for that page, and then discarded.

✦ **Data binding:** Links Web elements such as tables to an external source, either a server database or a comma-delimited file, for automatic updating.

✦ **Dynamic HTML Object Model:** Gives complete access to all of the page elements and their properties through an extensive list of events.

Dreamweaver directly supports all the Internet Explorer Dynamic HTML features that are cross-browser compatible, including style sheets, layers, and a large portion of the Object Model. Other elements, such as filters and transitions, can be applied through Dreamweaver's Style Sheet Inspector but cannot be previewed in the Document window.

This book does not cover all the details of Internet Explorer's DHTML implementation, but the remainder of this section covers those features not duplicated in any other browser.

Creating dynamic content

Dynamic content has been made possible by Internet Explorer's complete support of the Dynamic HTML Object Model, a superset of Netscape's own Document Object Model. Essentially, the DHTML Object Model gives you full access to all the elements in a document — and here's the innovation — even after the document has been downloaded to the user.

The most obvious use for dynamic content is with outline-oriented Web pages. Dynamic content enables outlines to expand and collapse at the click of a mouse. The key property to activate dynamic content is the `display` property, because you can name or identify any block of text or element and then alter its `display` property on the fly.

The following code hides the <ul> list elements until the user clicks the heading above them, and then hides the list again when the same heading is double-clicked:

```
<a href=# onClick="javascript:document.all.MyList.style.display = ''" ¬
onDblClick="javascript:document.all.MyList.style.display='none'" border=0>
<h1>Notes on Installation</h1>
</a>
<ul ID=MyList STYLE="display:none" >
  <li>Item #1...</li>
  <li>Item #2...</li>
  <li>Item #3...</li>
</ul>
<p>More information to follow...</p>
```

You see all the elements when viewed in Dreamweaver's Document window, and you must preview it in Internet Explorer to see the dynamic content in action. Currently, you have to code this sort of structure in Dreamweaver by hand or through a custom object.

Using filters and transitions

Looking for a little sparkle in your Web page? Internet Explorer's filters and transitions are quite spectacular. A filter is a special effect, such as a drop shadow, that you can apply to an element (usually text or an image) through CSS. Transitions are used when one image is exchanged with another, or one Web page with another.

The number of available filters and the range of their parameters is mind boggling. The list in Table 26-2 gives an overview of the filters but doesn't hint at the amount of variety available from changing their attributes.

Filters can be coded in the <style> tag or as a `style` attribute and are generally applied to a class object. The syntax follows:

```
filter:filtername(parameter_1, parameter_2, ...)
```

Table 26-2
CSS/Internet Explorer 4+ Filters

Filter	*Description*
Alpha	Sets a uniform transparency level.
Blend	Sets a transition blending between two objects.
Blur	Creates the impression of moving at high speed.
Chroma	Makes a specific color transparent.
DropShadow	Creates a solid silhouette of the object.
FlipH	Creates a horizontal mirror image.
FlipV	Creates a vertical mirror image.
Glow	Adds radiance around the outside edges of the object.
Gray	Drops color information from the image.
Invert	Reverses the hue, saturation, and brightness values.
Light	Projects a light source onto an object.
Mask	Creates a transparent mask from an object.
Shadow	Creates an offset solid silhouette.
Reveal	Sets a transition's revealing of a hidden object.
Wave	Creates a sine wave distortion along the horizontal axis.
Xray	Shows just the edges of the object.

As you can see from Figure 26-3, the effects are quite amazing — especially when you consider that they all can be performed interactively.

Delivering data binding

Much of the business of the Web depends on database-driven Web sites; virtual storefronts, online catalogs, and special information servers all require a strong connection between client-side requests and server-side answers. Microsoft's Dynamic HTML data binding links individual elements in your document, such as tables and forms, to data from another source, such as a database on a server or a comma-delimited text file. When the Web page with the data-bound tag is loaded, the data is automatically retrieved from the source, formatted, and displayed within the tag.

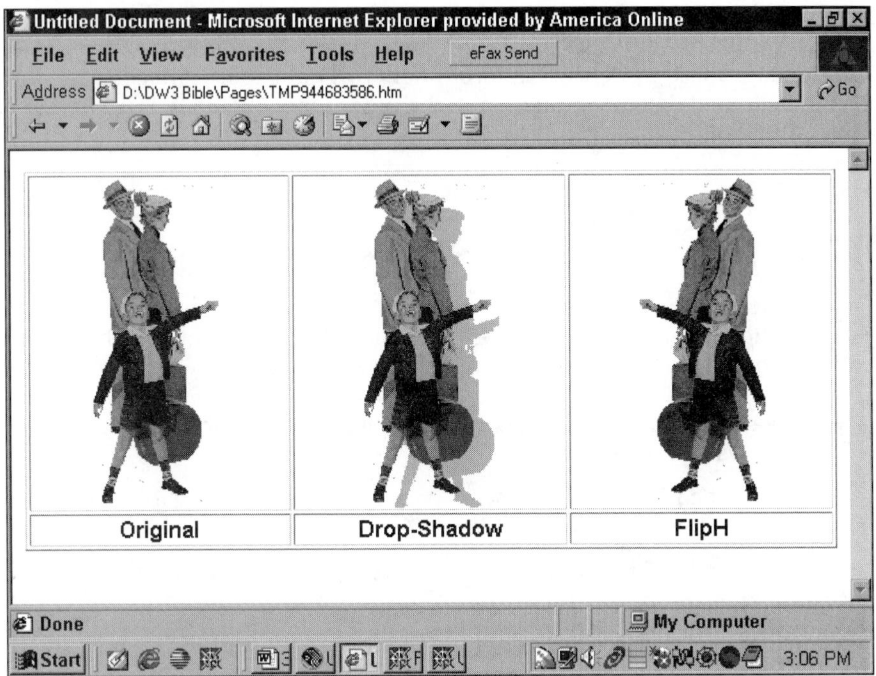

Figure 26-3: Internet Explorer's filters and transitions offer a full spectrum of graphic effects.

You can use Internet Explorer's data binding feature to generate tables in your Web page automatically and dynamically by binding a `<table>` tag to a data source. When the Web page is viewed, a new row is created in the table for each record retrieved from the source, and the cells of each row are filled with text and data from the fields of the record. Because this generation is dynamic, the user can view the document even while new rows in the table are being created. Moreover, once all the table data is present, you can sort or filter it without requiring the server to send additional data. The table is simply regenerated, using the previously retrieved data to fill the new rows and cells of the table.

You can also bind one or more tags in the Web page to specific fields of a record. When the page is browsed, the tags are filled with text and data from the fields in the current record. This technique can be used to generate form letters on the Web from a remote database. You can also bind the form tags to record fields, which gives the user the opportunity to view the information and, if necessary, change it. Then the record can be submitted to the server and reentered into the database.

Data binding requires that a data source object be included in the Web page. A *data source object* is an ActiveX control (or a Java applet) capable of communicating with the data source. Internet Explorer offers two data source objects: one for comma-delimited data in text files, and the other for SQL data in SQL servers and other ODBC sources.

Summary

Dynamic HTML is a quantum leap forward in Web development. Style sheets, layers, dynamic content, downloadable fonts, and other features make the latest generation of browsers faster, more client-side oriented, and more designer friendly.

- Dynamic HTML features work only with Internet Explorer 4.0 and Navigator 4.0 browsers and above.
- Much of the DHTML feature set is based on the Cascading Style Sheet specification recommended by the World Wide Web Consortium.
- The Dynamic HTML components of Netscape Navigator 4.x are a blend of W3C standards and proprietary tags.
- Microsoft's Internet Explorer offers the widest support of Dynamic HTML innovations through its Dynamic HTML Object Model, combined with comprehensive support of the CSS Level 1 standard.

In the next chapter, you study more specifics about how to use Cascading Style Sheets.

✦ ✦ ✦

CHAPTER 27

Building Style Sheet Web Pages

✦ ✦ ✦ ✦

In This Chapter

Cascading Style Sheets basics

Defining and inserting styles

Dreamweaver Technique: Clearing underlines in links

Style sheet options: Eight categories of attributes

Using external style sheets

✦ ✦ ✦ ✦

All publications, whether on paper or the Web, need a balance of style and content to be effective. Style without content is all flash with no real information. Content with no style is flat and uninteresting, thus losing the substance. Traditionally, HTML has tied style to content wherever possible, preferring logical tags such as `<strong>` to indicate emphasis to physical tags such as `<b>` for bold. But although this emphasis on the logical worked for many single documents, its imprecision made it unrealistic, if not impossible, to achieve style consistency across a broad range of Web pages.

The Cascading Style Sheets specification has changed this situation — and much more. As support for Cascading Style Sheets (CSS) grows, more Web designers can alter font faces, type size and spacing, and many other page elements with a single command — and have the effect ripple not only throughout the page, but also throughout a Web site. Moreover, an enhancement of CSS called CSS-P (for positioning) is the foundation for what has become commonly known as *layers*.

Dreamweaver was one of the first Web authoring tools to make the application of Cascading Style Sheets user friendly. Through Dreamweaver's intuitive interface, the Web designer can access over 70 different CSS settings, affecting everything from type specs to multimedia-like transitions. Dreamweaver enables you to work the way you want: Create your style sheet all at once and then link it when you're ready, or make up your styles one-by-one as you build your Web page.

In this chapter, you find out how CSS works and why you need it. A Dreamweaver Technique for removing underlines from links walks you through a typical style sheet session. With that experience under your belt, you're ready for the sections with detailed information on the current CSS commands and how to apply them to your Web page and site. Also, the section on defining styles helps you understand what's what in the Style Definition dialog box. Finally, you learn how you can create external style sheets to create — and maintain — the look and feel of an entire Web site with a single document.

Understanding Cascading Style Sheets

The Cascading Style Sheets system significantly increases the design capabilities for a Web site. If you are a designer used to working with desktop publishing tools, you will recognize many familiar features in CSS, including the following:

- ✦ Commands for specifying and applying font characteristics
- ✦ Traditional layout measurement systems and terminology
- ✦ Pinpoint precision for page layout

Cascading Style Sheets are able to apply many features with a simple syntax that is easy to understand. If you're familiar with the concept of using styles in a word processing program, you'll have no trouble grasping style sheets.

Here's how the process works: CSS instructions are given in rules; a style sheet is a collection of these rules. A rule is a statement made up of an HTML or custom tag, called a *selector*, and its defined properties, referred to as a *declaration*. For example, a CSS rule that makes the contents of all `<h1>` tags (the selector) red in color (the declaration) looks like the following:

```
h1 {color:red}
```

In the following sections, you see the various characteristics of CSS — grouping, inheritance, and cascading — working together to give style sheets their flexibility and power.

Grouping properties

A Web designer often needs to change several style properties at once. CSS enables declarations to be grouped by separating them with semicolons. For example:

```
h1 {color:red; font-family:Arial,Helvetica,sans-serif; font-size:18pt}
```

The Dreamweaver interface provides a wide range of options for styles. Should you ever need to look at the code, you'll find that Dreamweaver groups your selections exactly as shown in the preceding example. Although Dreamweaver keeps each selector in its own rule, when you are hand-coding your style sheets, you can group selectors as well as declarations. Separate grouped selectors with commas, rather than semicolons. For example:

```
h1, h2, p, em {color:green; text-align:left}
```

Inheritance of properties

CSS rules can also be applied to more than one tag through inheritance. Most, but not all, CSS declarations can be inherited by the HTML tags enclosed within the CSS selector. Suppose you set all `<p>` tags to the color red. Any tags included within a `<p>...</p>` tag pair then inherit that property and are also colored red.

Inheritance is also at work within HTML tags that involve a parent-child relationship, as with a list. Whether numbered (ordered, `<ol>`) or bulleted (unordered, `<ul>`), a list comprises any number of list items, designated by `<li>` tags. Each list item is considered a child of the parent tag, `<ol>` or `<ul>`. Take a look at the following example:

```
ol {color:red}
ul {color:blue}
```

With the preceding example, all ordered list items appear in red, whereas all unordered list items appear in blue. One major benefit to this parent-child relationship is that you can change the font for an entire page with one CSS rule. The following statement accomplishes this change:

```
body {font-family: Arial}
```

The change is possible in the previous example because the `<body>` tag is considered the parent of every HTML element on a page.

Tip

There's one exception to the preceding rule: tables. Netscape browsers (through version 4.5) treats tables differently than the rest of the HTML `<body>` when it comes to style sheets. To change the font of a table, you'd have to specify something like the following:

```
td {font-family: Arial}
```

Because every cell in a table uses the `<td>` tag, this style sheet declaration affects the entire table. Dreamweaver 3 is uneven in its application of this treatment. Setting the entire `<body>` to a particular font family is displayed correctly in the Document window, with even tables being affected. However, changing the color of a font in the `<body>` style sheet declaration does not alter the font color of text in a table in the Document window.

Cascading characteristics

The term *cascading* describes the capability of a local style to override a general style. Think of a stream flowing down a mountain; each ledge encountered by the stream has the potential to change its direction. The last ledge determines the final direction of the stream. In the same manner, one CSS rule applying generally to a block of text can be overridden by another rule applied to a more specific part of the same text.

For example, let's say you've defined, using style sheets, all normal paragraphs — `<p>` tags — as a particular font in a standard color, but you mark one section of the text using a little-used tag such as `<samp>`. If you make a CSS rule altering both the font and color of the `<samp>` tag, the section takes on the characteristics of that rule.

The cascading aspect of style sheets also works on a larger scale. One of the key features of CSS is the capability to define external style sheets that can be linked to individual Web pages, acting on their overall look and feel. Indeed, you can use the cascading behavior to fine-tune the overall Web site style based on a particular page or range of pages. Your company may, for instance, define an external style sheet for the entire company intranet, and each division could then build upon that overall model for its individual Web pages. For example, let's say that the company style sheet dictates that all `<h2>` headings are in Arial and black. One department could output their Web pages with `<h2>` tags in Arial, but colored red rather than black, while another department could make them blue.

Defining new classes for extended design control

Redefining existing HTML tags is a step in the right direction toward consistent design, but the real power of CSS comes into play when you define custom tags. In CSS-speak, a custom tag is called a *class*, and the selector name always begins with a period. Here's a simple example: To style all copyright notices at the bottom of all pages of a Web site to display in 8-point Helvetica all caps, you could define a tag like this:

```
.cnote {font-family:Helvetica; font-size:8pt; font-transform:uppercase}
```

If you define this style in an external style sheet and apply it to all 999 pages of your Web site, you have to alter only one line of code (instead of all 999 pages) when the edict comes down from management to make all the copyright notices a touch larger. Once a new class has been defined, you can apply it to any range of text, from one word to an entire page.

How styles are applied

CSS applies style formatting to your page in one of three ways:

- ✦ Via an internal style sheet
- ✦ Via an external, linked style sheet
- ✦ Via embedded style rules

Internal style sheets

An internal style sheet is a list of all the CSS styles for a page.

Dreamweaver inserts all the style sheets at the top of a Web page within a `<style>...</style>` tag pair. Placing style sheets within the header tags has become a convention that many designers use, although you can also apply a style sheet anywhere on a page.

The `<style>` tag for a Cascading Style Sheet identifies the type attribute as `text/css`. A sample internal style sheet looks like the following:

```
<style type="text/css">
<!--
p {  font-family: "Arial, Helvetica, sans-serif"; color: #000000}
.cnote {  font: 8pt "Arial, Helvetica, sans-serif"; text-transform: uppercase}
h1 {  font: bold 18pt Arial, Helvetica, sans-serif; color: #FF0000}
-->
</style>
```

The HTML comment tags `<!--` and `-->` prevent older browsers that can't read style sheets from displaying the CSS rules.

External style sheets

An external style sheet is a file containing the CSS rules; it links one or more Web pages. One benefit of linking to an external style sheet is that you can customize and change the appearance of a Web site quickly and easily from one file.

Two different methods exist for working with an external style sheet: the `link` method and the `import` method. Dreamweaver enables you to choose your preferred method.

For the `link` method, a line of code is added outside of the `<style>` tags, as follows:

```
<link rel="stylesheet" href="mainstyle.css">
```

The import method writes code within the style tags, as follows:

```
<style type="text/css">
@import "newstyles.css";
</style>
```

Between the link and the import methods, the link method is better supported among browsers.

Embedded rules

The final method of applying a style inserts it within HTML tags using the style attribute. This method is the most "local" of all the techniques; that is, it is closest to the tag it is affecting and therefore has the ultimate control — because of the cascading nature of style sheets as previously discussed.

When you create a layer within Dreamweaver, you notice that the positioning attribute is a Cascading Style Sheet embedded within a <div> tag like the following:

```
<div id="Layer1" style="position:absolute; visibility:inherit; left:314px; ¬
top:62px; width:194px; height:128px; z-index:1">
</div>
```

For all its apparent complexity, the Cascading Style Sheets system becomes straightforward in Dreamweaver. You often won't have to write a single line of code. But even if you don't have to write code, you should understand the CSS fundamentals of grouping, inheritance, and cascading.

Creating and Applying a Style Sheet in Dreamweaver

Dreamweaver uses three primary tools to implement Cascading Style Sheets: the CSS Styles palette, the Edit Style Sheet dialog box, and the Style Definition dialog box. Specifically, the CSS Styles palette is used to apply styles created in the Edit Style Sheet dialog box and specified with the Style Definition dialog box. With these three interfaces, you can accomplish the following:

- ✦ Apply styles to selected text or to a particular tag surrounding that text
- ✦ View and edit many of the attributes included in the official release of CSS Level 1
- ✦ Modify any styles you have created
- ✦ Link or import all your styles from an external style sheet

The fourth-generation browsers (and above) support many of the attributes from the first draft of the Cascading Style Sheets standard. Neither Netscape Navigator 4.0 nor Microsoft Internet Explorer 4.0 fully supports CSS Level 1, however. Of the earlier browsers, only Internet Explorer 3.0 supports a limited set of the CSS Level 1 features: font attributes, indents, and color. However, this support is rendered differently in Internet Explorer 3.0 and 4.0. Netscape Navigator 3.0 does not support any of the features of CSS Level 1. On the brighter side, trials of Netscape Navigator 6.0 (unreleased at the time of this writing) show an almost complete compliance of CSS 1 and quite a lot of CSS 2. Internet Explorer version 5 is not as complete, but better than the 4.x versions.

Dreamweaver Technique: Eliminating underlines from links

Because Dreamweaver's interface for CSS has so many controls, initially creating and applying a style can be a little confusing. Before delving into the details of the various palettes, dialog boxes, and floating windows, let's quickly step through a typical style sheet session. Then you can have an overall understanding of how all the pieces fit together.

Don't panic if you encounter unfamiliar elements of Dreamweaver's interface in this introductory technique. You see them at work again and again as you work through the chapter.

Disabling the underline for the anchor tag, `<a>`, which is normally associated with hyperlinked text, is one modification commonly included in style sheets. To accomplish this task, follow these steps:

1. Open the CSS Styles palette by choosing Windows ⇨ CSS Styles or selecting the Show CSS Styles button from either Launcher.
2. In the CSS Styles palette, select the New Style button. This sequence opens the New Styles dialog box.
3. In the New Styles dialog box, select Redefine HTML Tag and choose the anchor tag, `a`, from the drop-down list. Click OK, and the Style Definition window opens.

Tip

You can also select the Use CSS Selector option and choose a:link from the drop-down list. You can even employ the `a:hover` style, which enables text to change color or style on rollover. You must, however, define the four CSS Selector styles in a particular order for them to work correctly. Start by defining the `a:link` class and then proceed to define `a:visited`, `a:active`, and `a:hover`, in that order. Note that theses altered styles do not preview in Dreamweaver.

4. In the Style Definition window, make sure that the correct pane is displayed by selecting Type from the list of categories.

5. In the Decoration section of the Type pane, select the none option. You can also make any other modifications to the anchor tag style, such as color or font size. Click OK when you're done.

Many designers, myself included, like to make the link apparent by styling it bold and in a different color.

The Style Definition window closes, and any style changes instantly take effect on your page. If you have any previously defined links, the underline disappears from them.

Now, any links that you insert on your page still function as links — the user's pointer still changes into a pointing hand, and the links are active — but no underline appears.

This technique works for any text used as a link. To eliminate the border around an image designated as a link, the image's border must be set to zero in the Property Inspector. Dreamweaver handles this automatically when a graphic is made into a link.

Using the CSS Styles palette to apply styles

The CSS Styles palette, shown in Figure 27-1, is a flexible and easy-to-use interface with straightforward command buttons listing all available style items. Like all of Dreamweaver's primary palettes, you can open the CSS Styles palette in several ways:

✦ Choose Windows ➪ CSS Styles.

✦ Select the New Style button from either Launcher.

✦ Press F7.

The CSS Styles palette has several simple but important elements. The Apply To drop-down list shows the current tags available to the present cursor location. The tags in this list correspond to those found in the Tag Selector at any given time. One other item in the Apply To list is Selection, which attaches any defined style to any selected portion of your HTML page. The Apply To list enables you to focus quickly on the portion of the Web page to which you're applying a new style.

The main part of the CSS Styles palette is the list of defined custom styles or classes. Every custom tag you create is listed alphabetically in this window. Once you've chosen the portion of your HTML document that you're stylizing, you can choose one of the custom styles listed here by simply selecting it.

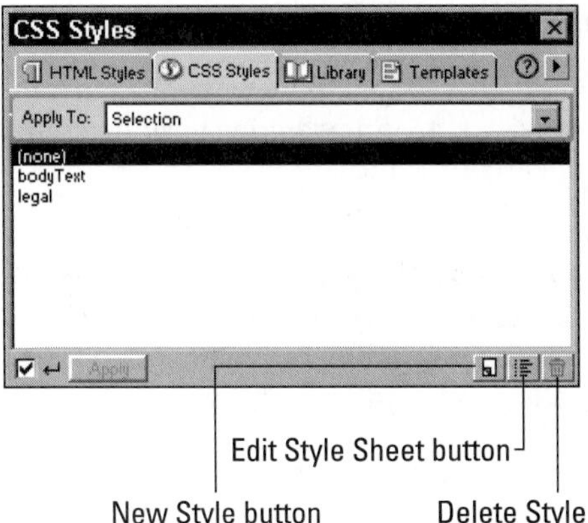

Figure 27-1: The Dreamweaver CSS Styles palette helps you apply consistent styles to a Web page.

At the bottom of the CSS Styles palette are three buttons. Clicking the first — the New Style button — begins the process of defining a new CSS style. The second button, Edit Style Sheet, opens the multifaceted Edit Style Sheet dialog box, in which you can create a new style, link a style sheet, edit or remove an existing style, or duplicate a style that you can then alter. Before you can begin applying styles to a Web page or site, the styles must be defined, and using the Edit Style Sheet dialog box is the pain-free method of accomplishing this task. You can, of course, open the HTML Inspector and add the style by hand, but you can avoid this process with the Edit Style Sheet dialog box. You get a close look at this tool in the upcoming section "Editing and Managing Style Sheets." The final button is for deleting styles once they are defined.

To apply an existing style, follow these steps:

1. Choose Windows ⇨ CSS Styles or select the Show CSS Styles button from either Launcher to open the CSS Styles palette.
2. To apply the style to a section of the page enclosed by an HTML tag, select the tag from the Apply To drop-down list or from the Tag Selector.

   To apply the style to a section that is not enclosed by a single HTML tag, use your mouse to select that section in the Document window. The section is highlighted, and a Selection option then appears in the Apply To list.
3. To apply the style you want to the chosen section of the page, simply select it in the CSS Styles palette.

As you might expect, Dreamweaver offers a second way of applying a style to your pages. The following quick method, using the menus, does not employ the CSS Styles palette:

1. Highlight the text to which you're applying the style, either through the Tag Selector or by using the mouse.
2. Select Text ⇨ CSS Style ⇨ Your Style.

Editing and managing style sheets

The Edit Style Sheet dialog box, shown in Figure 27-2, displays all your current styles — including HTML tags and custom styles — and provides various controls to link a style sheet and edit, create, duplicate, or remove a style.

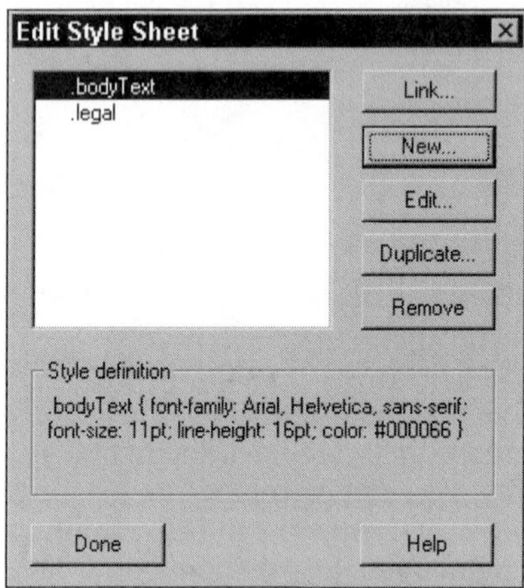

Figure 27-2: The Edit Style Sheet dialog box lists and defines any given style, in addition to presenting several command buttons for creating and managing styles.

To start editing one of your styles immediately, double-click the style in the list window of the Edit Style Sheet dialog box. This sequence takes you to the Style Definition dialog box, in which you redefine your selected style.

Use the five command buttons along the right side of the Edit Style Sheet dialog box to create new external sheets or manage your existing style sheets:

✦ **Link:** Enables you to create an external style sheet or link to an existing external style sheet.

✦ **New:** Begins the creation of a new style by first opening the New Style dialog box, described in the following section.

✦ **Edit:** Modifies any existing style.

✦ **Duplicate:** Makes a copy of the selected style as a basis for creating a new style.

✦ **Remove:** Deletes an existing style.

Defining new styles

Selecting the New button in the Edit Style Sheet dialog box brings up a new dialog box called New Style (see Figure 27-3). In this dialog box, you specify the type of style you're defining, along with its name. The following sections explain the three style types:

- Make Custom Style (class)
- Redefine HTML Tag
- Use CSS Selector

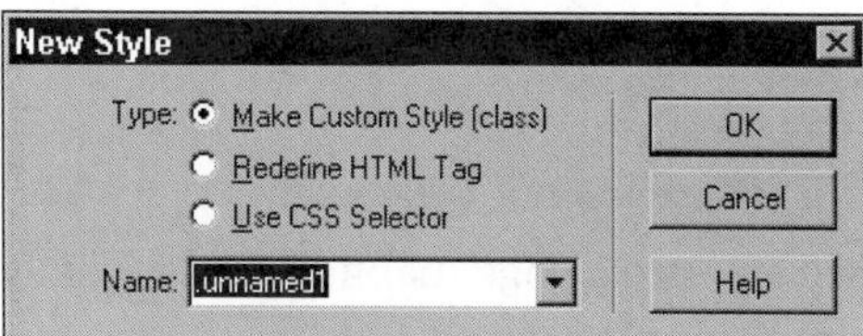

Figure 27-3: The first step in defining a new style is to select a style type and enter a name for the style.

Make Custom Style (class)

Making a custom style is the most flexible way to define a style on a page. The first step in creating a custom style is to give it a name; this name is used in the `class` attribute. The name for your class must start with a period and must be alphanumeric without punctuation or special characters. If you do not begin the name of your custom style with a period, Dreamweaver inserts one for you.

Following are typical names you can use:

```
.master
.pagetitle
.bodytext
```

Although you can use names such as body, title, or any other HTML tag, this approach is not a good idea. Dreamweaver warns you of the conflict if you try this method.

Redefine HTML Tags

The second radio button in the New Style dialog box is Redefine HTML Tag. This type of style is an excellent tool for making quick, global changes to existing Web pages. Essentially, the Redefine HTML Tag style enables you to modify the features of your existing HTML tags. When you select this option, the drop-down list displays over 40 HTML tags in alphabetical order. Select a tag from the drop-down list and click OK.

Use CSS Selector

When you use the third style type, Use CSS Selector, you define what are known as *pseudo-classes* and *pseudo-elements*. A pseudo-class represents dynamic states of a tag that may change under user action or over time. Several standard pseudo-classes associated with the `<a>` tag are used to style hypertext links.

When you choose Use CSS Selector, the drop-down list box contains four customization options, which can all be categorized as pseudo-classes:

- `a:active` customizes the style of a link when it is selected by the user.
- `a:hover` customizes the style of a link while the user's mouse is over it.

The `a:hover` pseudo-class is a CSS Level 2 specification and is currently supported only by Internet Explorer 4.0 and above.

- `a:link` customizes the style of a link that has not been visited recently.
- `a:visited` customizes the style of a link to a page that has been recently visited.

Dreamweaver does not preview pseudo-class styles, although they can be previewed through a supported browser.

A pseudo-element, on the other hand, enables control over contextually defined page elements: Pseudo-elements permit you to style paragraphs within a table differently than paragraphs outside of a table. Similarly, text that is nested within two blockquotes (giving the appearance of being indented two levels) can be given a different color, font, and so on than text in a single blockquote.

Because of their specific nature, Dreamweaver does not display any pseudo-elements in the Use CSS Selector list. You can, however, enter your own. For example, to style text within nested blockquotes, enter the following in the Use CSS Selector field of the New Style dialog box:

```
blockquote blockquote
```

Basically, you are creating a custom style for a set of HTML tags used in your document. This type of CSS selector acts like an HTML tag which has a CSS style applied to it; that is, all page elements fitting the criteria are automatically styled.

Styles and Their Attributes

After you've selected a type and name for a new style or chosen to edit an existing style, the Style Definition dialog box opens. A Category list from which you select a style category (just as you select a category of preferences in Dreamweaver's Preferences dialog box) is located on the left side of this dialog box.

Dreamweaver offers you eight categories of CSS Level 1 styles to help you define your style sheet:

- Type
- Background
- Block
- Box
- Border
- List
- Positioning
- Extensions

You can apply styles from one or all categories. The following sections describe each style category and its available settings.

Dreamweaver doesn't preview all the possible CSS attributes. Those attributes that can't be seen in the Document window are marked with an asterisk in the Style Definition dialog panels.

Type options

The Type category (see Figure 27-4) specifies the appearance and layout of the typeface for the page in the browser window. The Type category is one of the most widely used and supported categories — it can be rendered in Internet Explorer 3.0 and above and Navigator 4.0 and above. Table 27-1 explains the settings available in this category.

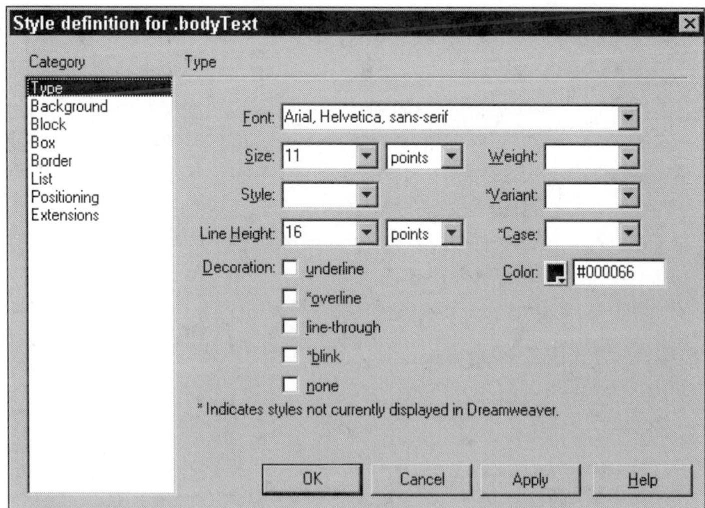

Figure 27-4: Type settings for your style

Table 27-1
CSS Type Attributes

Type Setting	*Description*
Font	Specifies the font or a collection of fonts, known as a *font family*. You can edit the font list by selecting Edit Font List from the drop-down list. (This sequence opens the Edit Font List dialog box, as described in Chapter 9.)
Size	Selects a size for the selected font. If you enter a value, you can then select the measurement system in the adjacent text box (the default is points). The relative sizes, such as small, medium, and large, are set relative to the parent element.
Style	Specifies a normal, oblique, or italic attribute for the font. An oblique font may have been generated in the browser by electronically slanting a normal font.
Line Height	Sets the line height of the line (known as *leading* in traditional layout). Typically, line height is a point or two more than the font size, although you can set the line height to be the same as or smaller than the font size, for an overlapping effect.
Decoration	Changes the decoration for text. Options include underline, overline, line-through, blink, and none. The blink decoration is displayed only in Netscape browsers.
Weight	Sets the boldness of the text. You can use the relative settings (light, bold, bolder, and boldest) or apply a numeric value. Normal is around 400; bold is 700.
Variant	Switches between normal and small caps. Small caps is a font style that displays text as uppercase, but the capital letters are a slightly larger size. The Variant option is not currently fully supported by either primary browser.
Case	Forces a browser to render the text as uppercase, lowercase, or capitalized.
Color	Sets a color for the selected font. Enter a color name or select the color swatch to choose a browser-safe color from the pop-up menu.

Background options

Since Netscape Navigator 2.0, Web designers have been able to use background images and color. Thanks to CSS Background attributes, designers can now use background images and color with increased control. Whereas traditional HTML background images are restricted to a single image for the entire browser window, CSS backgrounds can be specified for a single paragraph or any other CSS selector. (To set a background for the entire page, apply the style to the <body> tag.) Moreover, instead of an image automatically tiling to fill the browser window, CSS backgrounds can be made to tile horizontally, vertically, or not at all (see Figure 27-5). You can even position the image relative to the selected element.

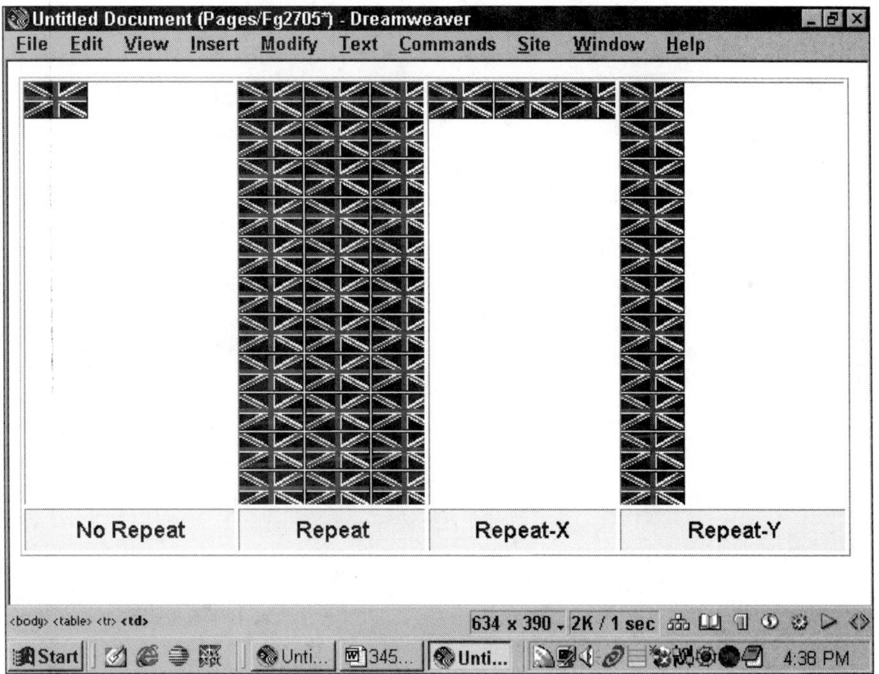

Figure 27-5: You can achieve a number of different tiling effects by using the Repeat attribute of the CSS Background category.

Neither of the primary browsers fully supports the CSS Background attributes shown in Figure 27-6 and listed in Table 27-2. The Repeat attribute enjoys full support, but Positioning and Attachment are rendered only in Internet Explorer 4.0 and above.

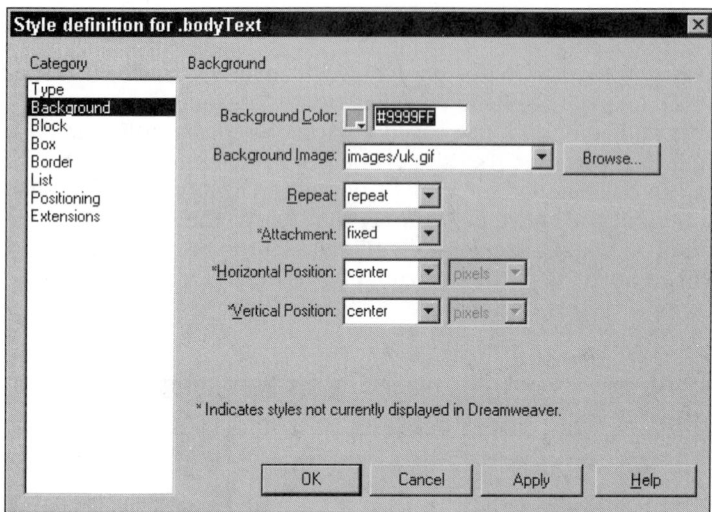

Figure 27-6: The CSS Background options enable a much wider range of control over background images and color.

Table 27-2
CSS Background Attributes

Background Setting	*Description*
Background Color	Sets the background color for a particular style. Note that this setting enables you to set background colors for individual paragraphs or other elements.
Background Image	Specifies a background image.
Repeat	Determines the tiling options for a graphic: **no repeat** displays the image in the upper-left corner of the applied style **repeat** tiles the background image horizontally and vertically across the applied style **repeat-x** tiles the background image horizontally across the applied style **repeat-y** tiles the background image vertically down the applied style

Background Setting	*Description*
Attachment	Determines whether the background image remains fixed in its original position or scrolls with the page. This setting is useful for positioned elements. If you use the overflow attribute, you often want the background image to scroll in order to maintain layout control.
Horizontal Position	Controls the positioning of the background image in relation to the style sheet elements (text or graphics) along the horizontal axis.
Vertical Position	Controls the positioning of the background image in relation to the style sheet elements (text or graphics) along the vertical axis.

Block options

One of the most common formatting effects in traditional publishing long absent from Web publishing is justified text — text that appears as a solid block. Justified text is possible with the Text Align attribute, one of the six options available in the CSS Block category, as shown in Figure 27-7. Indented paragraphs are also a possibility. Table 27-3 lists the CSS Block options.

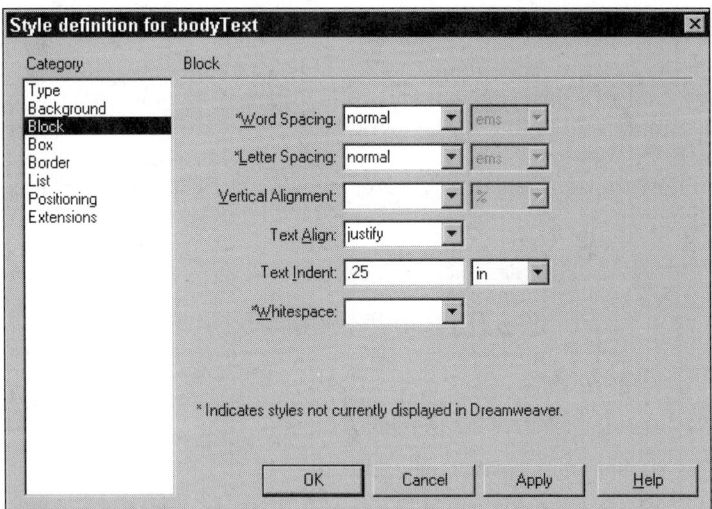

Figure 27-7: The Block options give the Web designer enhanced text control.

Table 27-3
CSS Block Attributes

Block Setting	*Description*
Word Spacing	Defines the spacing between words. You can increase or decrease the spacing with positive and negative values, set in ems.
Letter Spacing	Defines the spacing between the letters of a word. You can increase or decrease the spacing with positive and negative values, set in ems.
Vertical Alignment	Sets the vertical alignment of the style. Choose from baseline, sub, super, top, text-top, middle, bottom, or text-bottom, or add your own value.
Text Align	Sets text alignment (left, right, center, and justified).
Text Indent	Indents the first line of text on a style by the amount specified.
Whitespace	Controls display of spaces and tabs. The normal option causes all whitespace to collapse. The pre option behaves similarly to the `<pre>` tag; all white space is preserved. The nowrap option enables text to wrap if a ` ` tag is detected.

Box options

The Box attribute defines the placement and settings for elements (primarily images) on a page. Many of the controls (shown in Figure 27-8) emulate spacing behavior similar to that found in `<table>` attributes. If you are already comfortable using HTML tables with cell padding, border colors, and width/height controls, you can quickly learn how to use these Box features, which are described in Table 27-4.

Table 27-4
CSS Box Attributes

Box Setting	*Description*
Width	Sets the width of the element.
Height	Defines the height of the element.
Float	Places the element at the left or right page margin. Any text that encounters the element wraps around it.
Clear	Sets the side on which layers cannot be displayed next to the element. If a layer is encountered, the element with the Clear attribute places itself beneath the layer.

Box Setting	***Description***
Margin	Defines the amount of space between the borders of the element and other elements in the page.
Padding	Sets the amount of space between the element and the border or margin, if no border is specified. You can control the padding for the left, right, top, and bottom independently.

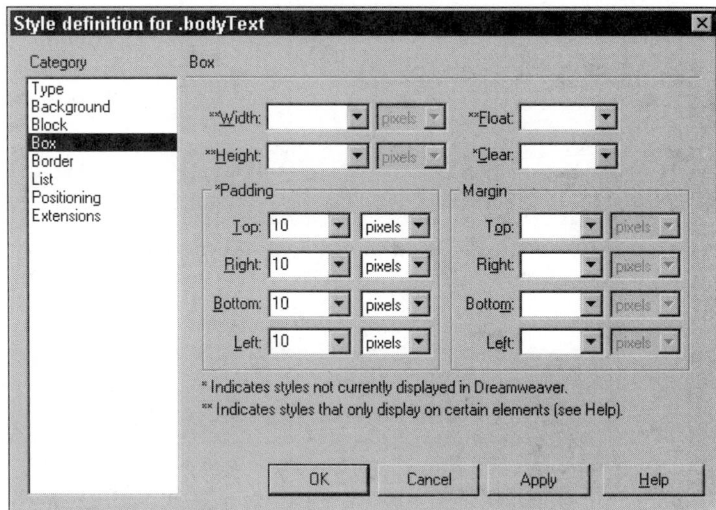

Figure 27-8: The CSS Box attributes define the placement of HTML elements on the Web page.

Dreamweaver imposes some specific restrictions on which Box attributes can and cannot be previewed in the Document window. For example, the Float and Clear attributes can be previewed only when applied to an image. The Margin attributes can be previewed when applied to block-level elements, such as any of the `<h1>` through `<h6>` tags or the `<p>` tag. Padding is not displayed within Dreamweaver.

Border options

With Cascading Style Sheets, you can specify many parameters for borders surrounding text, images, and other elements such as Java applets. In addition to specifying separate colors for any of the four box sides, you can also choose the width of each side's border, as shown in the CSS Border panel (see Figure 27-9). You can use eight different types of border lines, including solid, dashed, inset, and ridge. Table 27-5 lists the Border options.

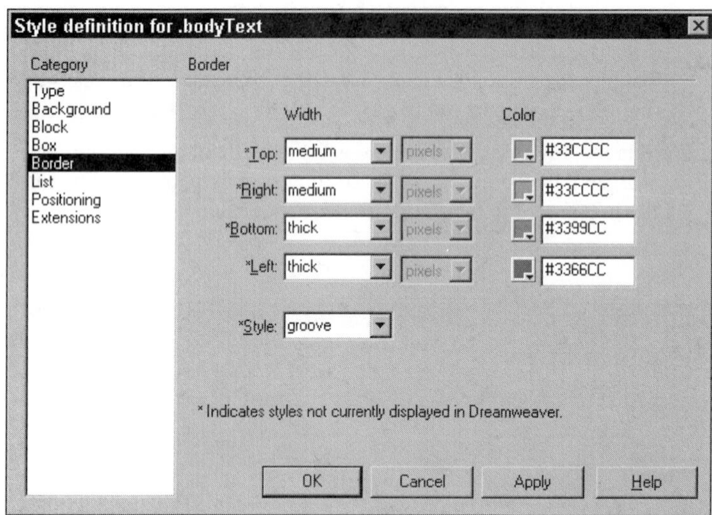

Figure 27-9: Borders are useful when you need to highlight a section of text or a graphic.

Table 27-5
CSS Border Attributes

Border Setting	*Description*
Top	Sets the color and settings for a border along the top of an element.
Right	Sets the color and settings for a border along the right side of an element.
Bottom	Sets the color and settings for a border along the bottom of an element.
Left	Sets the color and settings for a border along the left side of an element.
Style	Sets the style of the border. You can use any of the following as a border: Dotted, Dashed, Solid, Double, Groove, Ridge, Inset, and Outset.

CSS Border attributes are especially useful for highlighting paragraphs of text with a surrounding box. Use the Box panel's Padding attributes to inset the text from the border.

List options

CSS gives you greater control over bulleted points. With Cascading Style Sheets, you can now display a specific bulleted point based on a graphic image, or you can choose from the standard built-in bullets, including disc, circle, and square.

The CSS List pane also enables you to specify the type of ordered list, including decimal, roman numerals, or A-B-C order.

Figure 27-10 shows, and Table 27-6 describes, the settings for lists.

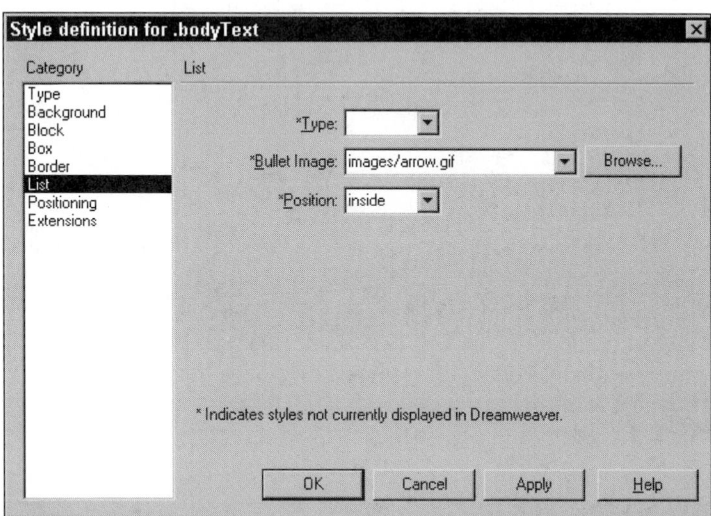

Figure 27-10: Specify a graphic to use as a bullet through the CSS List pane.

Table 27-6
List Category for Styles

List Setting	*Description*
Type	Selects a built-in bullet type. The options include disc, circle, square, decimal, lowercase roman, uppercase roman, lowercase alpha, and uppercase alpha.
Bullet Image	Sets an image to be used as a custom bullet. Enter the path to the image in the text box.
Position	Determines if the list item wraps to an indent (the default) or to the margin.

Positioning options

For many designers, positioning has increased creativity in page layout design. With positioning, you have exact control over where an element is placed on a page. Figure 27-11 shows the various attributes that provide this pinpoint control of your page elements. The options are described in Table 27-7.

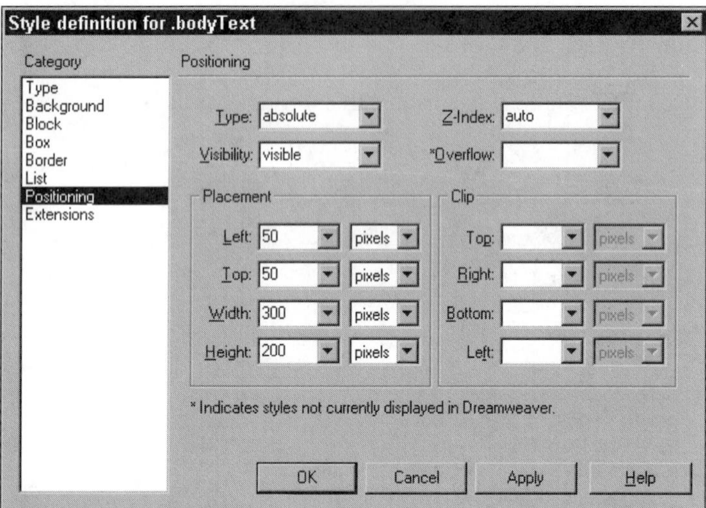

Figure 27-11: Control over the placement of elements on a page frees the Web designer from the restrictions imposed with HTML tables and other old-style formats.

Table 27-7
CSS Positioning Attributes

Positioning Setting	***Description***
Type	Determines whether an element can be positioned absolutely or relatively on a page. The third option, static, does not enable positioning.
Visibility	Determines whether the element is visible or hidden, or inherits the property from its parent.
Z-Index	Sets the apparent depth of a positioned element. Higher values are closer to the top.
Overflow	Specifies how the element is displayed when it's larger than the dimensions of the element. Options include the following: Clip, where the element is partially hidden; none, where the element is displayed and the dimensions are disregarded; and Scroll, which inserts scroll bars to display the overflowing portion of the element.
Placement	Sets the styled element's placement with the left and top attributes, and the dimensions with the width and height attributes.
Clip	Sets the visible portion of the element through the top, right, bottom, and left attributes.

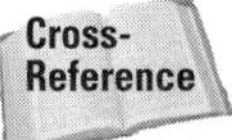

Dreamweaver layers are built upon the foundation of CSS positioning. For a complete explanation of layers and their attributes, see Chapter 28.

Extensions options

The specifications for Cascading Style Sheets are rapidly evolving, and Dreamweaver has grouped some cutting-edge features in the Extensions category. As of this writing, Extensions attributes (see Table 27-8) are supported only by Internet Explorer 4.0 and above, although support is planned for Netscape Navigator 5.0. The Extensions settings shown in Figure 27-12 affect three different areas: page breaks for printing, the user's cursor, and special effects called *filters*.

Table 27-8
CSS Extensions Attributes

Extensions Setting	*Description*
Pagebreak	Inserts a point on a page where a printer sees a page break. Not supported by any current browser.
Cursor	Defines the type of cursor that appears when the user moves the cursor over an element. Currently supported only by Internet Explorer 4.0.
Filter	Filters enable you to customize the look and transition of an element without having to use graphic or animation files. Currently supported only by Internet Explorer 4.0 and above.

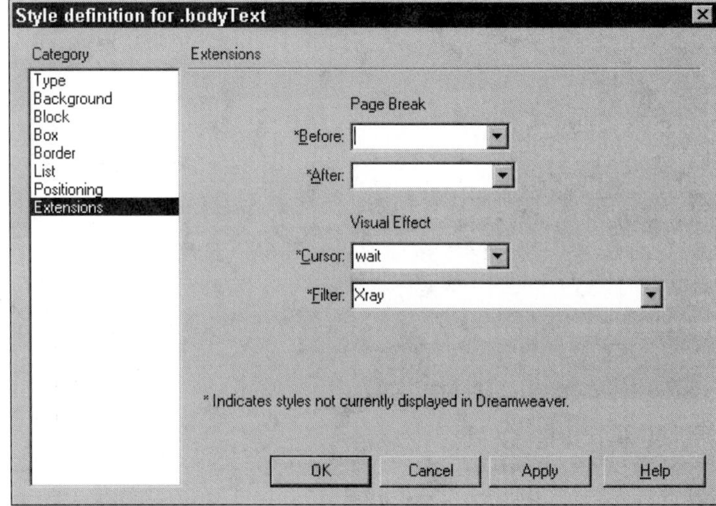

Figure 27-12: The CSS Extensions panel is currently supported only by Internet Explorer 4 and above.

One of the problems with the Web's never-ending evolution of page design is evident when you begin to print the page. The Pagebreak attribute alleviates this problem by enabling the designer to designate a style that forces a page break when printing; the break can occur either before or after the element is attached to the style. Although no browser currently supports this feature, it's a good candidate for support by future browsers.

The Filter attribute offers 16 different special effects that can be applied to an element. Many of these effects, such as wave and xray, are quite stunning. Several effects involve transitions, as well. Table 27-9 details all these effects.

Table 27-9
CSS Filters

Filter	*Syntax*	*Description*
Alpha	alpha(Opacity=*opacity*, FinishOpacity=*finishopacity*, Style=*style*, StartX=*startX*, StartY=*startY*, FinishX=*finishX*, FinishY=*finishY*) *Opacity* is a value from 0 to 100, where 0 is transparent and 100 is fully opaque. *Style* can be 0 (uniform), 1 (linear), 2 (radial), or 3 (rectangular).	Sets the opacity of a specified gradient region. This can have the effect of creating a burst of light in an image.
BlendTrans*	blendtrans(duration=*duration*) *Duration* is a time value for the length of the transition, in the format of *seconds.milliseconds*.	Causes an image to fade in or out over a specified time.
Blur	blur(Add=*add*, Direction=*direction*, Strength=*strength*) *Add* is any integer other than 0. *Direction* is any value from 0 to 315 in increments of 45. *Strength* is any positive integer representing the number of pixels affected.	Emulates motion blur for images.

Filter	*Syntax*	*Description*
Chroma	chroma(Color= *color*) *Color* must be given in hexadecimal form, for example, #rrggbb.	Makes a specific color in an image transparent.
DropShadow	dropshadow(Color=*color*, OffX=*offX*, OffY=*offY*, Positive=*positive*) *Color* is a hexadecimal triplet. *OffX* and *OffY* are pixel offsets for the shadow. *Positive* is a Boolean switch; use 1 to create shadow for nontransparent pixels and 0 to create shadow for transparent pixels.	Creates a drop shadow of the applied element, either image or text, in the specified color.
FlipH	FlipH	Flips an image or text horizontally.
FlipV	FlipV	Flips an image or text vertically.
Glow	Glow(Color=*color*, Strength=*strength*) *Color* is a hexadecimal triplet. *Strength* is a value from 0 to 100.	Adds radiance to an image in the specified color.
Gray	Gray	Converts an image in grayscale.
Invert	Invert	Reverses the hue, saturation, and luminance of an image.
Light*	Light	Creates the illusion that an object is illuminated by one or more light sources.
Mask	Mask(Color=*color*) *Color* is a hexadecimal triplet.	Sets all the transparent pixels to the specified color and converts the nontransparent pixels to the background color.

Continued

Table 27-9 (continued)

Filter	*Syntax*	*Description*
RevealTrans*	RevealTrans(duration=*duration*, transition=*style*) *Duration* is a time value that the transition takes, in the format of *seconds.milliseconds*. *Style* is one of 23 different transitions.	Reveals an image using a specified type of transition over a set period of time.
Shadow	Shadow(Color=*color*, Direction=*direction*) *Color* is a hexadecimal triplet. *Direction* is any value from 0 to 315 in increments of 45.	Creates a gradient shadow in the specified color and direction for images or text.
Wave	Wave(Add=*add*, Freq=*freq*, LightStrength=*lightstrength*, Phase=*phase*, Strength=*strength*) *Add* is a Boolean value, where 1 adds the original object to the filtered object and 0 does not. *Freq* is an integer specifying the number of waves. *LightStrength* is a percentage value. *Phase* specifies the angular offset of the wave, in percentage (for example, 0% or 100% = 360 degrees, 25% = 90 degrees). *Strength* is an integer value specifying the intensity of the wave effect.	Adds sine wave distortion to the selected image or text.
Xray	Xray	Converts an image to inverse grayscale for an X-rayed appearance.

* These three transitions require extensive documentation beyond the scope of this book.

Linking to an External Style Sheet

The external style sheet is an essential tool in the Web designer's CSS toolbox. Certainly, with Cascading Style Sheets, you can change all of a particular tag's attributes in a single page fairly quickly. But changing all the pages on a large Web site can still take an enormous amount of time. With an external style sheet linked to most, if not all, of a Web site's pages, the workload is cut down substantially.

To link to a separate style sheet, follow these steps:

1. Open the CSS Styles palette.
2. Select the New Style button.
3. In the Edit Style dialog box, select the Link command button.
4. The Link External Style Sheet dialog box pops up, where you can access all your style sheets, by browsing and linking (see Figure 27-13).

Figure 27-13: You can link an external style sheet to one Web page or your entire site through the Link External Style Sheet dialog box.

5. Either type in the File/URL path or select the Browse (Choose) button to locate a style sheet; the Cascading Style Sheet file has the .css file name extension on your hard drive. If you have not already created a style sheet, you can do so by locating the place you want the style sheet and then creating a name for it. Useful names for style sheets can be master.css, contents.css, or body.css.
6. Choose either the Link or the Import radio button.

   To add a CSS style to a page, you have to either link or import the file. Both of these features work for linking a style sheet; however, the link method is supported in more browsers.

Tip

Once you've defined your external style sheet, a couple of shortcuts exist for the Edit Style Sheet dialog box. First, you can press the Ctrl (Option) key and click the Edit Style Sheet button in the CSS Styles palette. Rather than displaying the Edit Style Sheet dialog box with a link to your external style sheet (which you'd have to double-click or highlight and select Edit to modify), you'll see the dialog box for the external style sheet immediately.

The second method is useful if you have the Site window open. Just double-click any .css file, and the Edit Style Sheet dialog box for that file opens instantly.

When you go back to the Edit Style Sheet dialog box, you see a link file referenced in the listing above all the styles. You can double-click the linked file to open a new Edit Style Sheet dialog box for your linked style sheet file. The defined styles within the linked style sheet then appear in the CSS Styles palette.

If you've already defined styles in the current document and you want to convert them to an external style sheet, Dreamweaver has you covered. Just choose File ➪ Export ➪ Export CSS Styles and enter a file name in the Export Styles as CSS File dialog box. Follow the directions in this section for linking this newly created file to your other Web pages as a style sheet.

You can also export internal styles to an external style sheet by pressing Ctrl (Command) while clicking the Done button in the Edit Style Sheet dialog box.

Summary

In this chapter, you discovered how you can easily and effectively add and modify Cascading Style Sheets. You can now accomplish all of the following:

- ✦ Update and change styles easily with the CSS Styles palette.
- ✦ Easily apply generated styles to an element on a page.
- ✦ Apply a consistent look and feel with linked style sheets.
- ✦ Position fonts and elements, such as images, with pinpoint accuracy.
- ✦ Exercise control over the layout, size, and display of fonts on a page.
- ✦ Define external style sheets to control the look and feel of an entire site.

In the next chapter, you learn how to position elements on a page in Dreamweaver using layers.

✦ ✦ ✦

CHAPTER 28

Working with Layers

In This Chapter

For many years, page designers have taken for granted the capability to place text and graphics anywhere on a printed page — even enabling graphics, type, and other elements to "bleed" off a page. This flexibility in design has eluded Web designers until recently. Lack of absolute control over layout has been a high price to pay for the universality of HTML, which makes any Web page viewable by any system, regardless of the computer or the screen resolution.

Lately, however, the integration of positioned layers within the Cascading Style Sheets specification has brought true absolute positioning to the Web. Page designers with a yen for more control can move to the precision offered with Cascading Style Sheets-Positioning (CSS-P).

Dreamweaver's implementation of layers turns the promise of CSS-P into an intuitive, designer-friendly, layout-compatible reality. As the name implies, layers offer more than pixel-perfect positioning. You can stack one layer on another, hide some layers while showing others, move a layer across the screen — and even move several layers around the screen simultaneously. Layers add an entirely new dimension to the Web designer's palette. Dreamweaver enables you to create page layouts using layers and then convert those layers to tables that are viewable by earlier browsers.

This chapter explores every aspect of how layers work in HTML — except for animation, which is saved for Chapter 29. With the fundamentals under your belt, you learn how to create, modify, populate, and activate layers on your Web page.

Layers 101

When the World Wide Web first made its debut in 1989, few people were concerned about the aesthetic layout of a page. In fact, because the Web was a descendant of SGML — a multiplatform text document and information markup specification — layout was trivialized. Content and the capability to use hypertext to jump from one page to another were emphasized. After the first graphical Web browser software (Mosaic) was released, it quickly became clear that a page's graphics and layout could enhance a Web site's accessibility and marketability. Content was still king, but design was moving up quickly.

The first attempt at Web page layout was the server-side image map. This item was a typically large graphic (usually too hefty to be downloaded comfortably) with hotspots. Clicking a hotspot sent a message to the server, which returned a link to the browser. The download time for these files was horrendous, and the performance varied from acceptable to awful, based on the server's load.

The widespread adoption of tables, released with HTML 2.0 and enhanced with HTML 3.2, radically changed layout control. Designers gained the ability to align objects and text — but a lot of graphical eye candy was still left to graphic files strategically located within the tables. The harder designers worked at precisely laying out their Web pages, the more they had to resort to workarounds such as nested tables and one-pixel-wide GIFs used as spacers. To relieve the woes of Web designers everywhere, the W3C included a feature within the new Cascading Styles Sheet specifications that allows for absolute positioning of an element upon a page. Absolute positioning enables an element, such as an image or block of text, to be placed anywhere on the Web page. Both Microsoft Internet Explorer 4.0 and Netscape Navigator 4.0 (and above) support layers under the Cascading Style Sheets-Positioning specification.

The addition of the third dimension, depth, truly turned the positioning specs into layers. Now objects can be positioned side-by-side, and they have a *z-index* property as well. The z-index gets its name from the practice in geometry of describing three-dimensional space with x, y, and z coordinates; z-index is also called the *stacking order* because objects can be stacked upon one another.

A single layer in HTML looks like the following:

```
<div id="Layer1" style="position:absolute; visibility:inherit; width:200px; ¬
height:115px; z-index:1"></div>
```

Positioned layers are most commonly placed within the <div> tag. Another popular location is the <span> tag. These tags were chosen because they are seldom used in the HTML 3.2 specification (Dreamweaver supports both tags). Both Microsoft and Netscape encourage users to employ either of these tags, because the two primary browsers are designed to credit full CSS-P features to either the <div> or <span> tag. You should generally use these tags when anything but specific Navigator 4.x compatibility is desired.

Netscape has developed two additional proprietary tags for using layers in its 4.x browser: <layer> and <ilayer>. The primary difference between the two tags has to do with positioning: the <layer> tag is used for absolute positioning, and the <ilayer> tag for relative positioning. Unfortunately, layers created by the <div> tag and the <layer> tag have different feature sets. These tags are no longer supported in Navigator 6.0; instead Netscape's latest browser fully supports the CSS standard tags, <div> and <span>.

Creating Layers with Dreamweaver

Dreamweaver enables you to create layers creatively and precisely. You can drag out a layer, placing and sizing it by eye, or choose to do it by the numbers — it's up to you. Moreover, you can combine the methods, quickly eyeballing and roughing out a layer layout and then aligning the edges precisely. For Web design that approaches conventional page layout, Dreamweaver even includes rulers and a grid to which you can snap your layers.

Positioning Measurement

The positioning of layers is determined by aligning elements on an x-axis and a y-axis. In CSS, the x-axis (defined as "Left" in CSS syntax) begins at the left side of the page, and the y-axis (defined as "Top" in CSS syntax) is measured from the top of the page down. As with many of the other CSS features, you have your choice of measurement systems for Left and Top positioning. All measurements are given in Dreamweaver as a number followed by the abbreviation of the measurement system (without any intervening spaces). The measurement system options follow:

Unit	***Abbreviation***	***Measurement***
Pixels	px	Relative to the screen
Points	pt	1 pt = 1/72 in
Inches	in	1 in = 2.54 cm
Centimeters	cm	1 cm = 0.3937 in
Millimeters	mm	1 mm = 0.03937 in
Picas	pc	1 pc = 12 pt
EMS	em	The height of the element's font
Percentage	%	Relative to the browser window

If you don't define a unit of measurement for layer positioning, Dreamweaver defaults to pixels. If you decide to edit out the unit of measurement, the Web browser defaults to pixels.

Creating layers in Dreamweaver can be handled in one of three ways:

✦ You can drag out a layer, after selecting the Draw Layer button from the Objects palette.

✦ You can put a layer in a predetermined size by choosing Insert ➪ Layer.

✦ You can create a layer with mathematical precision through the CSS Styles palette.

The first two methods are quite intuitive and explained in the following section. The CSS Styles palette method is examined later in this chapter.

Inserting a layer object

When you want to draw out your layer quickly, use the object approach. If you come from a traditional page-designer background and are accustomed to using a program such as QuarkXPress or PageMaker, you're already familiar with drawing out frames or text boxes with the click-and-drag technique. Dreamweaver uses the same method for placing and sizing new layer objects.

To draw out a layer as an object, follow these steps:

1. From the Common pane of the Objects palette, select the Draw Layer button. Your pointer becomes a crosshair cursor. (If you decide not to draw out a layer, you can press Shift+Esc at this point or just click once without dragging to abort the process.)

2. Click anywhere in your document to position the layer and drag out a rectangle. Release the mouse button when you have an approximate size and shape with which you're satisfied (see Figure 28-1).

After you've dragged out your layer, notice several changes to the screen. First, the layer now has a small box on the outside of the upper-left corner. This box, shown in Figure 28-2, is the selection handle, which you can use to move an existing layer around the Web page. When you click the selection handle, eight sizing handles appear around the perimeter of the layer.

Another subtle but important addition to the screen is the Layer icon. Like the other Invisibles icons, the Layer icon can be cut, copied, pasted, and repositioned. When you move the Layer icon, however, its corresponding layer does not move—you are actually only moving the code for the layer to a different place in the HTML source. Generally, the layer code's position in the HTML is immaterial—however, you may want to locate your layer source in a specific area to be backwardly compatible with 3.0 browsers. Dragging and positioning Layer icons one after another is a quick way to achieve this task.

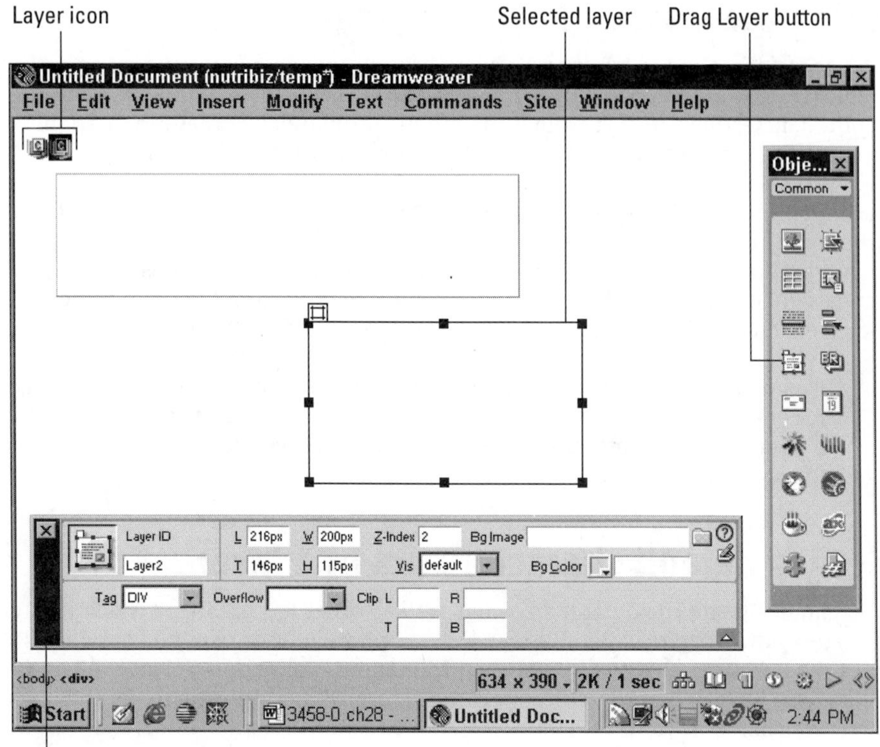

Figure 28-1: After selecting the Drag Layer object in the Objects palette (Common), the pointer becomes crosshairs when you are working on the page. Click and drag to create the layer.

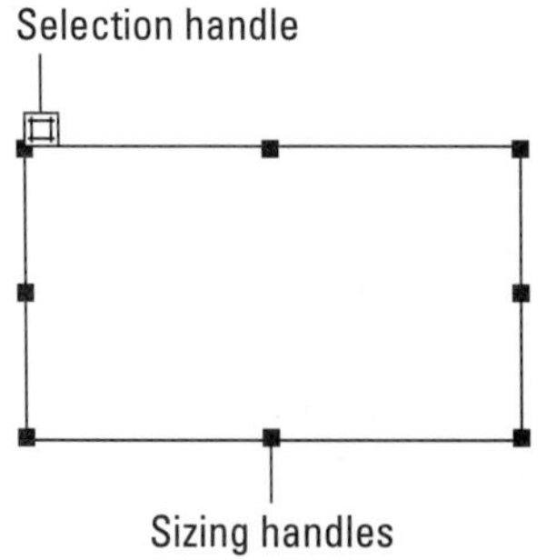

Figure 28-2: Once a layer is created, you can move it by dragging the selection handle and size it with the sizing handles.

Using the Insert ➪ Layer command

The second method to create a layer is through the menus. Instead of selecting an object from the Objects palette, choose Insert ➪ Layer. Unlike the click-and-drag method, inserting a layer through the menu automatically creates a layer in the upper-left corner; the default size is 200 pixels wide and 115 pixels high.

Although the layer is by default positioned in the upper-left corner of the Document window, it does not have any coordinates listed in the Property Inspector. The position coordinates are added when you drag the layer into a new position. If you repeatedly add new layers through the menus, without moving them to new positions, each layer stacks directly on top of one another, with no offset.

It's important for every layer to have a specific position (left and top) assigned to it. Otherwise, the browser displays all layers directly on top of one another. To give a layer measurements, after you've inserted it through the menu, be sure to drag the layer, even slightly.

Setting default characteristics of a layer

You can designate the default size — as well as other features — of the layer that is inserted with Insert ➪ Layer. Choose Edit ➪ Preferences or use the keyboard shortcut Ctrl+U (Command+U) to open the Preferences dialog box. Select the Layers category. The Layers Preferences panel (see Figure 28-3) helps you to set the layer attributes listed in Table 28-1.

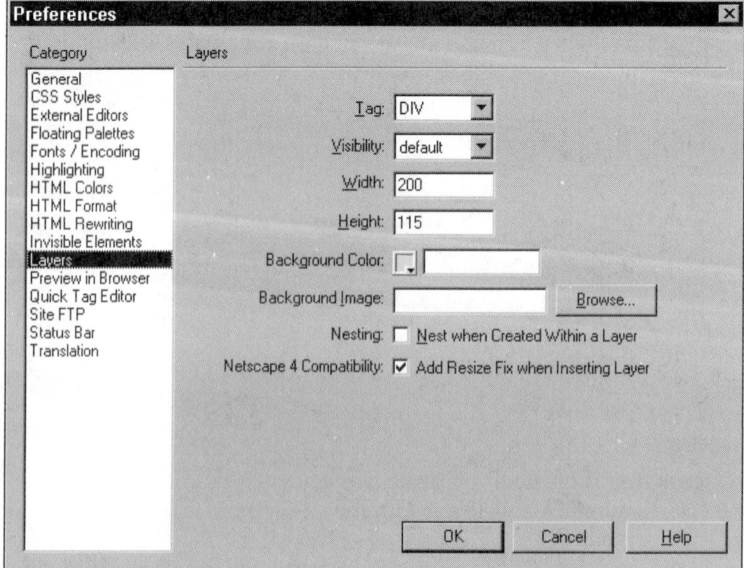

Figure 28-3: If you're building layers to a certain specification, use the Layers Preferences panel to designate your options.

Table 28-1
Layer Preferences

Layer Preference	*Description*
Tag	Sets the HTML code to use when creating layers. The options are `<div>` (the default), `<span>`, `<layer>`, and `<ilayer>`.
Visibility	Determines the initial state of visibility for a layer. The options are default, inherit, visible, and hidden.
Width	Sets the width of the layer in the measurement system of your choice. The default is 200 pixels.
Height	Sets the height of the layer in the measurement system of your choice. The default is 115 pixels.
Background Color	Sets a color for the layer background. Select the color from the pop-up menu of Web-safe colors.
Background Image	Sets an image for the layer background. In the text box, enter the path to the graphics file or click the Browse (Choose) button to locate the file.
Nesting Option	If you want to nest layers when one layer is placed in the other automatically, check the Nest when Created Within a Layer checkbox.
Netscape 4 Compatibility	To add code for a workaround to a known problem in Navigator 4.x browsers, which causes layers to lose their positioning coordinates when the user resizes the browser window, select this option.

Embedding a layer with style sheets

In addition to laying out your layer by eye, or inserting a default layer with Insert ➪ Layer, you can also specify your layers precisely through style sheets. Although this method is not as intuitive as either of the preceding methods, creating layers through style sheets has notable advantages:

✦ You can enter precise dimensions and other positioning attributes.

✦ The placement and shape of a layer can be combined with other style factors such as font family, font size, color, and line spacing.

✦ Layer styles can be saved in an external style sheet, which enables similar elements on every Web page in a site to be controlled from one source.

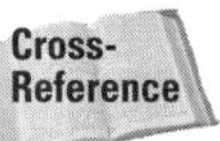

If you haven't yet read Chapter 27, you may want to look it over before continuing here.

To create a layer with style sheets, follow these steps:

1. Choose Window ➪ CSS Styles or select the Show CSS Styles button from the Launcher. This selection opens the CSS Styles palette.
2. From the CSS Styles palette, select the New Style button. This selection opens the Edit Style Sheet dialog box.
3. From the Edit Style Sheet dialog box, select the New button.
4. From the New Style dialog box, keep the Type option set to Make Custom Style (class). Enter a name for your new style and click OK.
5. Next up is the Style Definition dialog box. Select the Positioning category.
6. From the Positioning panel (see Figure 28-4), enter the desired attributes: Type, Visibility, Z-Index, Overflow, Placement (Left, Top, Width, and Height), and Clip settings (Top, Right, Bottom, Left).

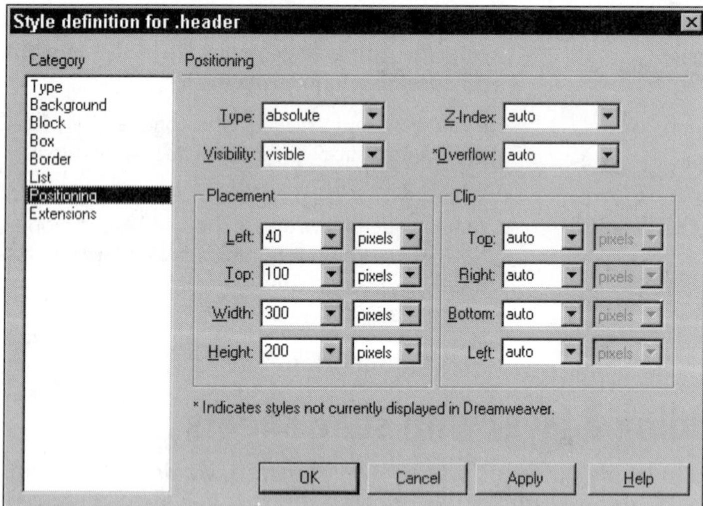

Figure 28-4: Use the Positioning panel of the Style Definition dialog box to set layer attributes in an internal or external style sheet.

The Type attribute offers three options: Absolute, Relative, and Static. While you are familiar with the first two options, the third option, Static, is probably new to you. Use Static when you don't want to add a layer or specify a position, but you still want to specify a rectangular background.

7. If appropriate, select other categories and enter any additional style sheet attributes desired. Click OK when you're done.

Keep in mind that layers are part of the overall Cascading Style Sheet specification and can benefit from all of the features of style sheets. You may decide that a specific area of text—a header, for instance—must always be rendered in a bold, red, 18-point Arial font with a green background, and that it should always be placed 35 pixels from the left margin and 25 pixels from the top of the page. You can place the style sheet within a .css file, link your Web pages to this file, and receive a result similar to what's shown (in black and white) in Figure 28-5. Within one component—the Cascading Style Sheet file—you can contain all of your positioning features for a page's headers, titles, and other text, graphics, or objects. This capability gives you the benefit of controlling the position and look of every title linked to one style sheet.

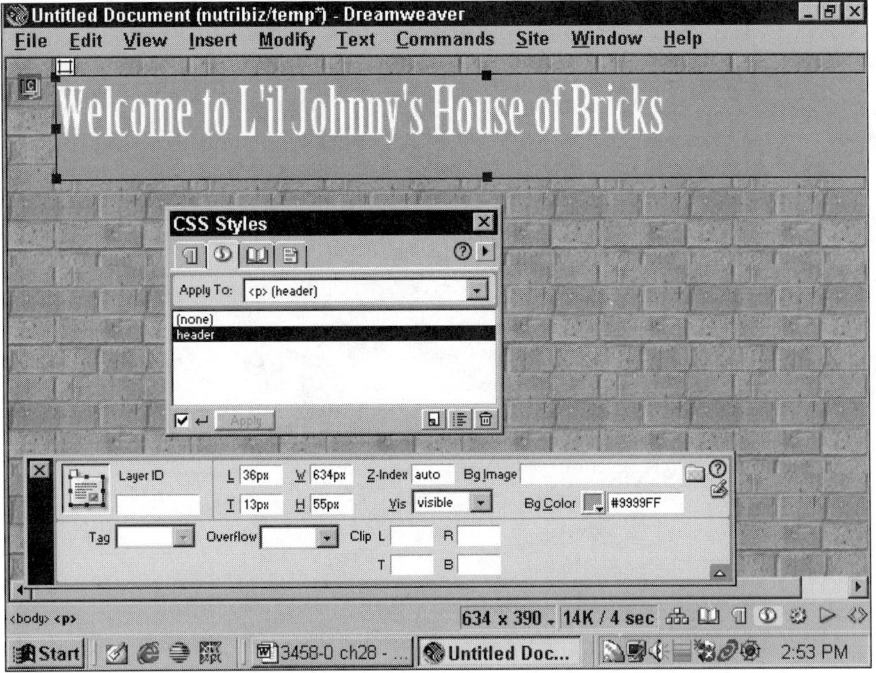

Figure 28-5: You can apply the layer style to any element on any Web page linked to the style sheet.

Choosing relative instead of absolute positioning

In most cases, absolute positioning uses the top-left corner of the Web page or the position where the `<body>` tag begins as the point of origin from which the Web browser determines the position of the text, image, or object. You can also specify measurements relative to objects. Dreamweaver offers two methods to accomplish relative positioning.

Using the relative attribute

In the first method, you select Relative as the Type attribute in the Style Sheet Positioning category. Relative positioning does not force a fixed position; instead, the positioning is guided by the HTML tags around it. For example, you may place a list of some items within a table and set the positioning relative to the table. You can see the effect of this sequence in Figure 28-6. In this illustration's Positioning panel, the Type attribute is set to Relative and the Placement/Left value is set to 0.5 inch for a style applied to the listed items.

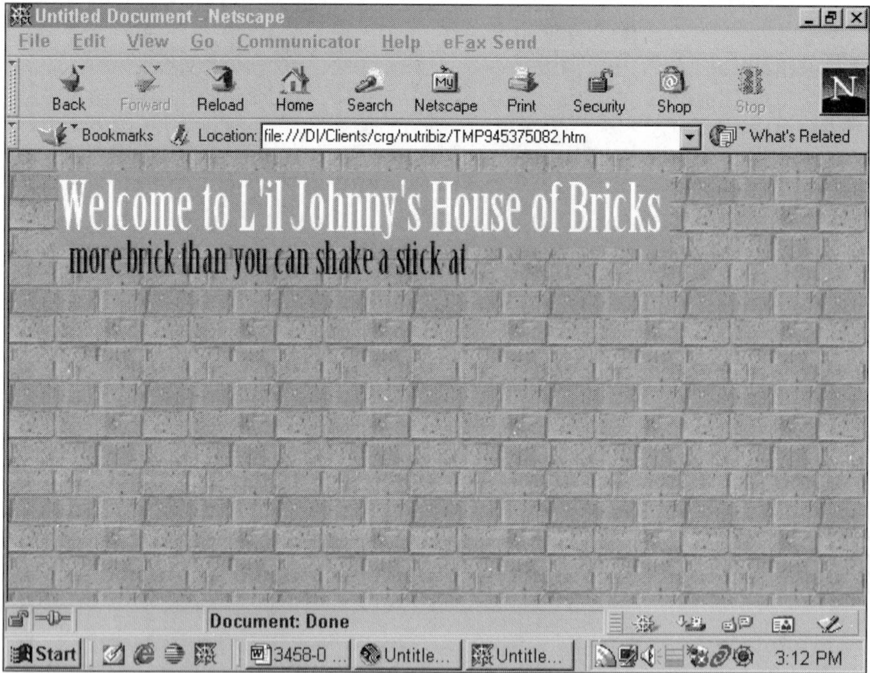

Figure 28-6: Relative positioning through styles can give your document a clean look, although the effect is not previewed in Dreamweaver.

Dreamweaver 3 doesn't preview relative positioning unless you're working with a nested layer, so you should check your placement by previewing the page in a browser, as shown in Figure 28-6.

Relative attributes can be useful, particularly if you want to place the positioned objects within free-flowing HTML. Free-flowing HTML repositions itself if the browser window is larger or smaller than the designer is aware. When you're using this technique, remember to place your relative layers within absolutely positioned layers. Otherwise, when the end user resizes the browser, the relative layers position themselves relative to the browser and not to the absolutely positioned layers. This situation can produce messy results — use relative positioning with caution when mixed with absolute layers.

Using nested layers

The second technique for positioning layers relatively uses nested layers. Once you nest one layer inside another, the inner layer uses the upper-left corner of the outer layer as its orientation point. For more details about nesting layers, refer to the section "Nesting with the Layers Palette," later in this chapter.

Modifying a Layer

Dreamweaver helps you deftly alter layers once you have created them. Because of the complexity of managing layers, Dreamweaver offers an additional tool to the usual Property Inspector: the Layers palette. This tool enables you to select any of the layers on the current page quickly, change layer relationships, modify their visibility, and adjust their stacking order. You can also alter the visibility and stacking order of a selected layer in the Property Inspector, along with many other attributes. Before any modifications can be accomplished, however, you have to select the layer.

Selecting a layer

You can choose from several methods to select a layer for alteration (see Figure 28-7).

Your method of choosing a layer most likely depends on the complexity of your page layout:

- ✦ When you have only a few layers that are not overlapping, just click the selection handle of the layer with which you want to work.
- ✦ When you have layers placed in specific places in the HTML code (for example, a layer embedded in a table using relative positioning), choose the Layer icon.
- ✦ When you have many overlapping layers that are being addressed by one or more JavaScript functions, use the Layers palette to choose the desired layer by name.
- ✦ When you're working with invisible layers, click the `<div>` (or `<span>`) tag in the Tag Selector to reveal the outline of the layer.

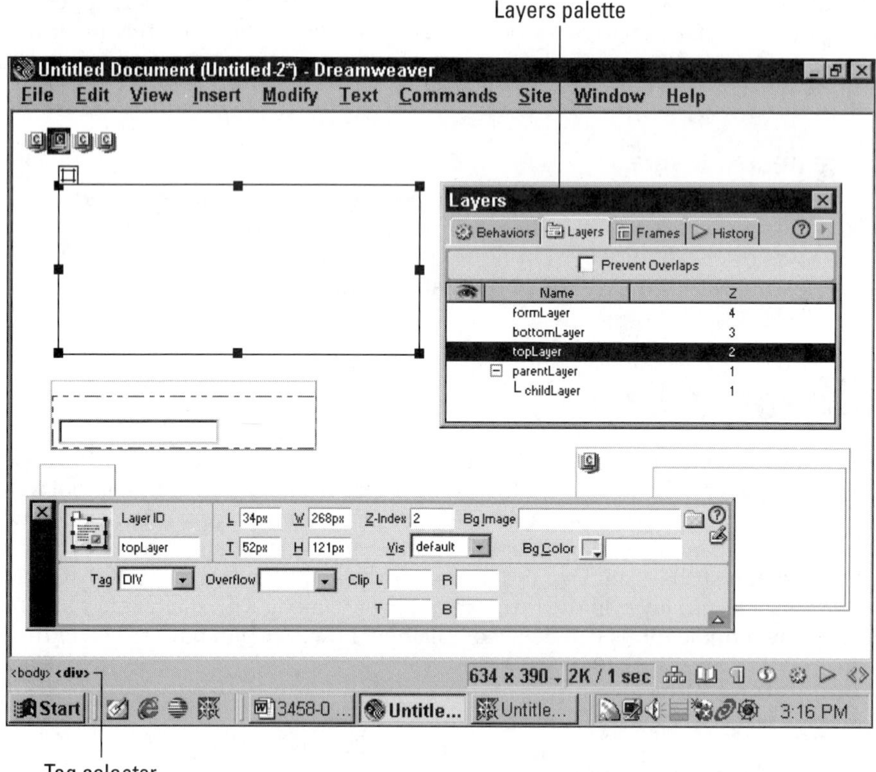

Figure 28-7: You have four different methods for selecting a layer to modify.

Resizing a layer

To resize a layer, position the pointer over one of the eight sizing handles surrounding the selected layer. When over the handles, the pointer changes shape to a two- or four-headed arrow. Now click and drag the layer to a new size and shape.

You can also use the arrow keys to resize your layer with more precision. The following keyboard shortcuts change the width and height dimensions while the layer remains anchored by the upper-left corner:

✦ When the layer is selected, press Ctrl+arrow (Command+arrow) to expand or contract the layer by one pixel.

✦ Press Shift+Ctrl+arrow (Shift+Command+arrow) to increase or decrease the selected layer by the current grid increment. The default grid increment is 5 pixels.

You can quickly preview the position of a layer on a Web page without leaving Dreamweaver. Deselecting the View ➪ Layer Borders option leaves the layer outline displayed only when the layer is selected, but otherwise it is not shown.

Moving a layer

The easiest way to reposition a layer is to drag the selection handle. If you don't see the handle on a layer, click anywhere in the layer. You can drag the layer anywhere on the screen — or off the bottom or right side of the screen. To move the layer off the left side or top of the screen, enter a negative value in the left and top (L and T) text boxes of the Layer Property Inspector.

To hide the layer completely, match the negative value with the width or height of the layer. For example, if your layer is 220 pixels wide and you want to position it offscreen to the left (so that the layer can slide on at the click of a mouse), set the Left position at –220 pixels.

As with resizing layers, you can also use the arrow keys to move the layer more precisely:

✦ Press any arrow key to move the selected layer one pixel in any direction.

✦ Use Shift+arrow to move the selected layer by the current grid increment.

Using the Layer Property Inspector

You can modify almost all the CSS-P attributes for your layer right from the Layer Property Inspector (Figure 28-8). Certain attributes, such as width, height, and background image and color are self-explanatory or recognizable from other objects. Other layers-only attributes such as visibility and inheritance require further explanation. Table 28-2 describes all the Layer properties, and the following sections discuss the features unique to layers.

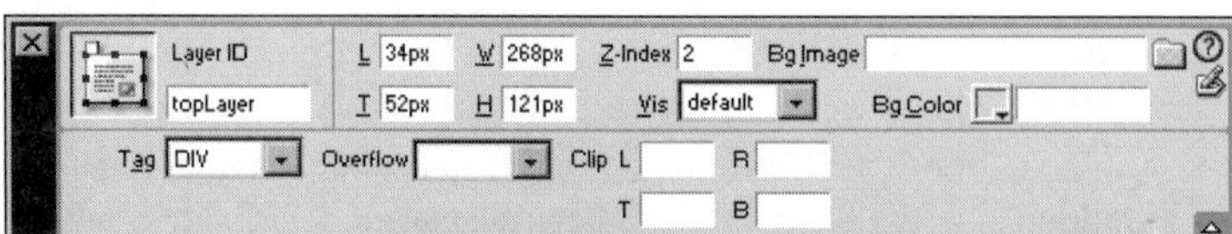

Figure 28-8: The Layer Property Inspector makes it easy to move, resize, hide, and manipulate all of the visual elements of a layer.

Table 28-2
Layer Property Inspector Options

Layer Attribute	*Possible Values*	*Description*
BgColor	Any hexadecimal or valid color name	Background color for the layer.
BgImage	Any valid graphic file	Background image for the layer.
Clip (Top, Bottom, Left, Right)	Any positive integer	Measurements for the displayable region of the layer. If the values are not specified, the entire layer is visible.
H (Height)	Any integer measurement in pixels, centimeters, millimeters, inches, points, percentage, ems, or picas	Vertical measurement of the layer.
L (Left)	Any integer measurement in pixels, centimeters, millimeters, inches, points, percentage, ems, or picas	Distance measured from the origin point on the left.
Name	Any unique name without spaces or special characters	Labels the layer so that it can be addressed by style sheets or JavaScript functions.
Overflow	visible, scroll, hidden, or auto	Determines how text or images larger than the layer should be handled.
T (Top)	Any integer measurement in pixels, centimeters, millimeters, inches, points, percentage, ems, or picas	The distance measured from the origin point on the top.
Tag	span, div, layer, or ilayer	Type of HTML tag to use for the layer.
Vis (Visibility)	default, inherit, visible, or hidden	Determines whether a layer is displayed. If visibility is set to inherit, then the layer takes on the characteristic of the parent layer.
W (Width)	Any integer measurement in pixels, centimeters, millimeters, inches, points, percentage, ems, or picas	The horizontal measurement of the layer.
Z-Index	Any integer	Stacking order of the layer in relation to other layers on the Web page. Higher numbers are closer to the top.

Name

Names are important when working with layers. To refer to them properly for both CSS and JavaScript purposes, each layer must have a unique name: unique among the layers and unique among every other object on the Web page. Dreamweaver automatically names each layer as it is created in sequence: Layer1, Layer2, and so forth. You can enter a name that is easier for you to remember by replacing the provided name in the text box on the far left of the Property Inspector.

Netscape Note: Netscape Navigator 4.x is strict with its use of the ID attribute. You must ensure that you call the layer with an alphanumeric name that does not use spacing or special characters such as the underscore or percentage sign. Moreover, make sure your layer name begins with a letter and not a number—in other words, `layer9` works but `9layer` can cause problems.

Tag attribute

The Tag drop-down list contains the HTML tags that can be associated with the layer. By default, the positioned layer has `<div>` as the tag, but you can also choose `<span>`, `<layer>`, or `<ilayer>`. As previously noted, the `<div>` and `<span>` tags are endorsed by the World Wide Web Consortium group as part of their CSS standards. The `<layer>` and `<ilayer>` tags are Netscape Navigator 4.x proprietary tags, although Netscape also supports the CSS tags.

Indeed, if you are working on a Navigator 4.x-based intranet, you may want to change the default layer tag. Choose Edit ➪ Preferences and then, from the Layers category, select either `<layer>` or `<ilayer>` from the Tag drop-down list.

Visibility

Visibility (`Vis` in the Property Inspector) defines whether or not you can see a layer on a Web page. Four values are available:

✦ **Default:** Enables the browser to set the visibility attribute. Most browsers use the `inherit` value as their default.

✦ **Inherit:** Sets the visibility to the same value as that of the parent layer, which enables a series of layers to be hidden or made visible by changing only one layer.

✦ **Visible:** Causes the layer and all of its contents to be displayed.

✦ **Hidden:** Makes the current layer and all of its contents invisible.

Remember the following when you're specifying visibility:

✦ Whether or not you can see a layer, you must remember that the layer still occupies space on the page and demands some of the page loading time. Hiding a layer does not affect the layout of the page, and invisible graphics take just as long to download as visible graphics.

✦ When you are defining the visibility of a positioned object or layer, you should not use `default` as the visibility value. A designer does not necessarily know whether the site's end user has set the default visibility to `visible` or `hidden`. Designing an effective Web page can be difficult without this knowledge. The common browser default is for visibility to be inherited, if not specifically shown or hidden.

Overflow

Normally, a layer expands to fit the text or graphics inserted into it. You can, however, restrict the size of a layer by changing the height and width values in the Property Inspector. What happens when you define a layer to be too small for an image, or when an amount of text depends on the setting of the layer's overflow attribute? CSS layers (the `<div>` and `<span>` tags) support four different overflow settings:

✦ **Visible (Default):** All of the overflowing text or image is displayed, and the height and width settings established for the layer are ignored.

✦ **Hidden:** The portion of the text or graphic that overflows the dimensions is not visible.

✦ **Scroll:** Horizontal and vertical scroll bars are added to the layer regardless of the content size or amount, and regardless of the layer measurements.

✦ **Auto:** When the content of the layer exceeds the width and/or height values, horizontal and vertical scroll bars appear.

Currently, support for the overflow attribute is spotty at best. Dreamweaver doesn't display the result in the Document window; it must be previewed in a browser to be seen. Navigator offers limited support: Only the attribute's hidden value works correctly and, even then, just for text. Only Internet Explorer 4.0 or above renders the overflow attribute correctly, as shown in Figure 28-9.

Netscape Note: The Overflow property is not recognized by the Netscape Navigator 4.x proprietary layer tags, `<layer>` and `<ilayer>`.

Clipping

If you're familiar with the process of cropping an image, you'll quickly grasp the concept of clipping layers. Just as desktop publishing software hides but doesn't delete the portion of the picture outside of the crop marks, layers can mask the area outside the clipping region defined by the Left, Top, Right, and Bottom values in the Clip section of the Layer Property Inspector.

All clipping values are measured from the upper-left corner of the layer. You can use any CSS standard measurement system: pixels (the default), inches, centimeters, millimeters, ems, or picas.

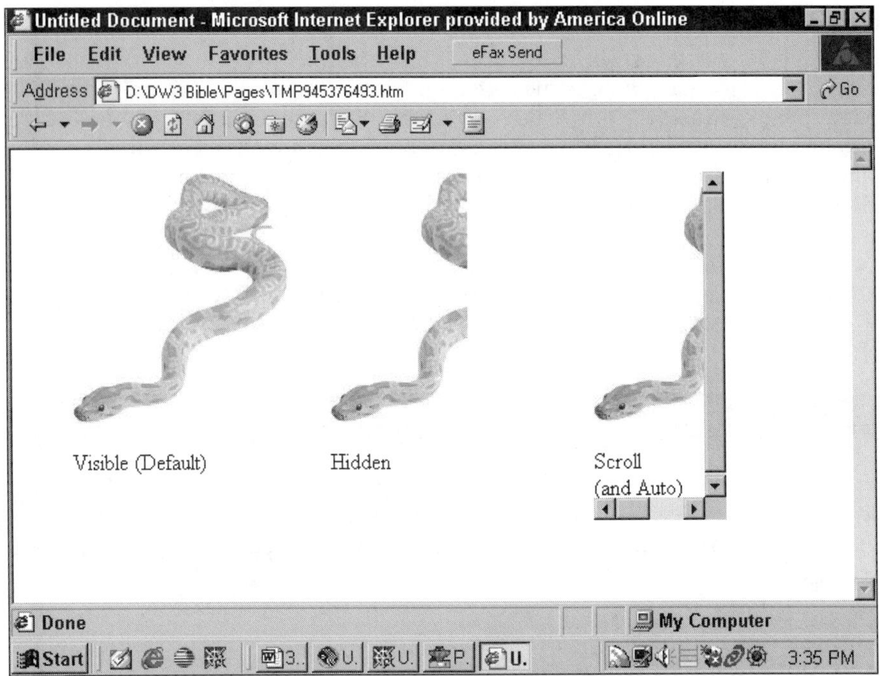

Figure 28-9: When your contents are larger than the dimensions of your layer, you can regulate the results with the overflow attribute.

The current implementation of CSS only supports rectangular clipping. When you look at the code for a clipped layer, you see the values you inserted in the Layer Property Inspector in parentheses following the clip attribute, with the `rect` (for rectangular) keyword, as follows:

```
<div id="Layer1" style="position:absolute; left:54px; top:24px; ¬
width:400px; height:115px; z-index:1; visibility:inherit; ¬
clip:rect(10 100 100 10)">
```

Generally, you specify values for all four criteria: Left, Top, Right, and Bottom. You can also leave the Left and Top values empty or use the keyword `auto`—which causes the Left and Top values to be set at the origin point: 0,0.

Clipping is a powerful function that can be employed in interesting ways. This property is the basis for the image map rollover technique discussed in Chapter 14.

Z-Index

One of a layer's most powerful features is its capability to appear above or below other layers. You can change this order, known as the *z-index*, dynamically. Whenever a new layer is added, Dreamweaver automatically increments the z-index—layers with higher z-index values are positioned above layers with lower z-index values. The z-index can be adjusted manually in either the Layer Property Inspector or the Layers palette. The z-index must be an integer, either negative or positive.

Tip

Although some Web designers use high values for the z-index, such as 3,000, the z-index is completely relative. The only reason to increase a z-index to an extremely high number is to ensure that that particular layer remains on top.

A Visual Clipping Technique

In Dreamweaver, you cannot draw the clipping region visually—the values have to be explicitly input in the Clip section of the Layer Property Inspector. That said, a trick using a second temporary layer can make it easier to position your clipping. Follow these steps to get accurate clipping values:

1. Insert your original layer and image.
2. Nest a second, temporary layer inside the first, original layer (select the Draw Layer button in the Objects palette and draw out the second layer inside the first).

   If you have your Layer Preferences set so that a layer does not automatically nest when created inside another layer, press the Ctrl (Command) key while you draw your layer, to override the preference.
3. Position the second layer over the area you want to clip. Use the layer's sizing handles to alter the size and shape, if necessary.
4. Note the position and dimensions of the second layer (the Left, Top, Width, and Height values).
5. Delete the second layer.
6. In the Property Inspector for the original layer, enter the Clip values as follows:
   - **L:** Enter the Left value for the second layer.
   - **T:** Enter the Top value for the second layer.
   - **R:** Add the second layer's Left value to its Width value.
   - **B:** Add the second layer's Top value to its Height value.

Dreamweaver displays the clipped layer after you enter the final value. The following figure shows the original layer and the temporary layer on the left, and the final clipped version of the original layer on the right.

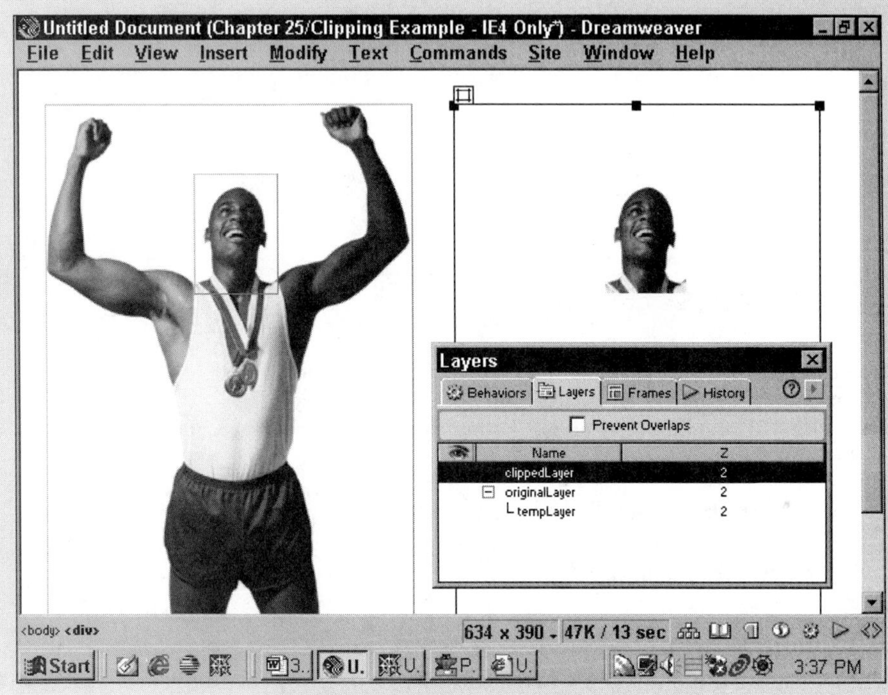

The z-index is valid for the CSS layer tags as well as the Netscape proprietary layer tags. Netscape also has two additional attributes that can affect the apparent depth of either the <layer>- or <ilayer>-based content: above and below. With above and below, you can specify which existing layer is to appear directly on top of or beneath the current layer. You can only set one of the depth attributes, the z-index, or above or below.

Certain types of objects—including Java applets, plug-ins, and ActiveX controls—ignore the z-index setting when included in a layer and appear as the uppermost layer. However, certain ActiveX Controls—most notably Flash—can be made to respect the z-index.

When you designate the layer's tag attribute to be either <layer> or <ilayer>, the Property Inspector displays an additional field: the A/B attribute for setting the above or below value, as shown in Figure 28-10. Choose either attribute from the A/B drop-down list and then select the layer from the adjacent list. The layer you choose must be set up in the code before the current layer. You can achieve this condition in the Document window by moving the icon for the current layer to a position after the other layers. Although you must use either <layer> or <ilayer> to specify the above or below attribute, the layer specified can be either a CSS or Netscape type.

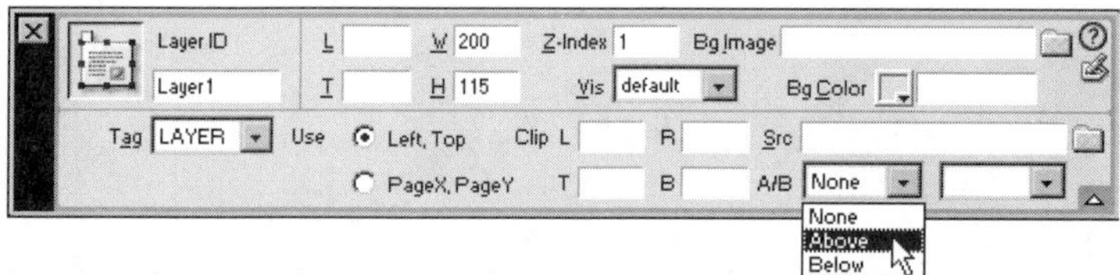

Figure 28-10: Choosing the Netscape-specific tags LAYER or ILAYER from the Property Inspector causes several new options to appear, including the A/B switch for the above/below depth position.

Working with the above and below attributes can be confusing. Notice that they determine which layer is to appear on top of or underneath the current layer, and not which layer the present layer is above or below.

Background image or color

Inserting a background image or color with the Layer Property Inspector works in a similar manner to changing the background image or color for a table (as explained in Chapter 13). To insert an image, enter the path to the file in the Bg Image text box or select the Folder icon to locate the image file on your system or network. If the layer is larger than the image, the image is tiled, just as it would in the background of a Web page or table.

To give a layer a background color, enter the color name (either in its hexadecimal or nominal form) in the Bg Color text box. You can also select the color swatch to pick your color from the color picker.

Additional Netscape properties

In addition to the above and below values for the z-index attribute, two other Netscape variations are worth noting — both of which appear as options in the Property Inspector when either <layer> or <ilayer> is selected as the layer tag.

When either <layer> or <ilayer> is selected, the Page X, Page Y option becomes available as a radio button in the Property Inspector in addition to Left, Top. With Netscape layers, Left, Top places the layer relative to the top-left corner of its parent (whether that's the page or another layer if the layer is nested). Page X, Page Y positions the layer based on the top-left corner of the page, regardless of whether the layer is nested.

The other additional Netscape layer attribute is the source property. You can specify another HTML document to appear within a `<layer>` or `<ilayer>`—much like placing other Web pages in frames. To specify a source for a Netscape layer, enter the path to the file in the Src text box or select the Folder icon to locate the file.

The Layers palette

Dreamweaver offers another tool to help manage the layers in your Web page: the Layers palette. Although this tool doesn't display as many properties about each element as the Property Inspector, the Layers palette gives you a good overview of all the layers on your page. It also provides a quick method of selecting a layer—even when it's offscreen—as well as enabling you to change the z-index and the nesting order.

The Layers palette, shown in Figure 28-11, can be opened either through the Window menu (Window ➪ Layer) or by pressing the keyboard shortcut F11.

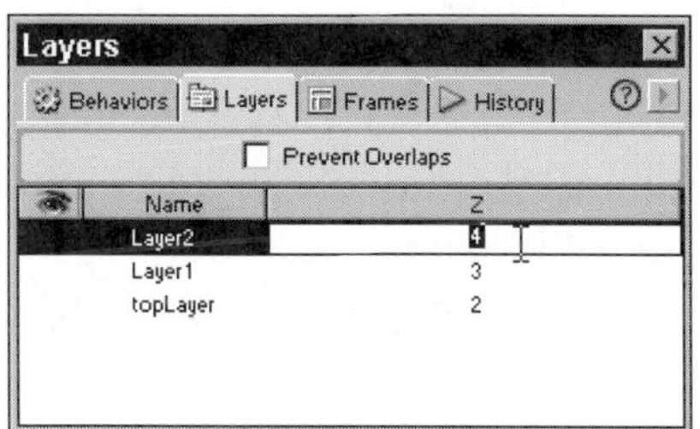

Figure 28-11: Use the Layers palette to select quickly or alter the visibility or relationships of all the layers on your page.

Modifying properties with the Layers palette

The Layers palette lists the visibility, name, and z-index settings for each layer. All of these properties can be modified directly through the Layers palette.

The visibility of a particular layer is noted by the eye symbol in column one of the Inspector. Selecting the eye symbol cycles you through three different visibility states:

- ✦ **Eye closed:** Indicates that the layer is hidden.
- ✦ **Eye open:** Indicates that the layer is visible.
- ✦ **No eye:** Indicates that the visibility attribute is set to the default (which, for both Navigator 4.0 and Internet Explorer 4.0, means inherit).

To change all of your layers to a single state simultaneously, select the eye symbol in the column header. Unlike the individual eyes in front of each layer name, the overall eye toggles between open and shut.

You can also change a layer's name (in the second column of the Layers palette). Just double-click the current layer name in the Inspector; the name is highlighted. Type in the new name and press Enter (Return) to complete the change.

The z-index (stacking order) in the third column can be altered in the same manner. Double-click the z-index value; then type in the new value and press Enter (Return). You can enter any positive or negative integer. If you're working with the Netscape proprietary layer tags, you can also alter the above or below values previously set for the z-index through the Property Inspector. Use A for above and B for below.

To change a layer's z-index interactively, you can drag one layer above or below another in the Layers palette.

Nesting with the Layers palette

Another task managed by the Layers palette is nesting or unnesting layers. This process is also referred to as *creating parent-child layers*. To nest one layer inside another through the Layers palette, follow these steps:

1. Choose Window ➪ Layers or press F11 to open the Layers palette.
2. Press the Ctrl (Command) key, then click the name of the layer to be nested (the child), and drag it on top of the other layer (the parent).
3. When you see a rectangle around the parent layer's name, release the mouse.

   The child layer is indented underneath the parent layer, and the parent layer has a minus sign (a down-pointing triangle on the Mac) attached to the front of its name.
4. To hide the child layer from view, select the minus sign (down-pointing triangle) in front of the parent layer's name. Once the child layer is hidden, the minus sign turns into a plus sign (a right-pointing triangle on the Mac).
5. To reveal the child layer, select the plus sign (right-pointing triangle on the Mac).
6. To undo a nested layer, select the child layer and drag it to a new position in the Layers palette.

When it comes to nested layers, Netscape Navigator 4.0 does not "play well with others." In fact, the expected results are so rarely achieved that it's best to avoid nested layers in cross-browser sites for the time being.

You can use the nesting features of the Layers palette to hide many layers quickly. If the visibility of all child layers is set to default — with no eye displayed — then by hiding the parent layer, you cause all the child layers to inherit that visibility setting and also disappear from view.

Tip

You can also delete a layer from the Layers palette. Just highlight the layer to be removed and press Delete. Dreamweaver does not enable you to delete nested layers as a group, however—you have to remove each one individually.

Aligning layers with the ruler and grid

With the capability to position layers anywhere on a page comes additional responsibility and potential problems. In anything that involves animation, correct alignment of moving parts is crucial. As you begin to set up your layers, their exact placement and alignment becomes critical. Dreamweaver includes two tools to simplify layered Web page design: the ruler and the grid.

Rulers and grids are familiar concepts in traditional desktop publishing. Dreamweaver's ruler shows the x-axis and y-axis in pixels, inches, or centimeters along the outer edge of the Document window. The grid crisscrosses the page with lines to support a visual guideline when you're placing objects. You can e ven enable a snap-to-grid feature to ensure easy, absolute alignment.

Using the ruler

With traditional Web design, "eyeballing it" was the only option available for Web page layout. The absolute positioning capability of layers filled this deficiency. Now online designers have a more precise and familiar system of alignment: the ruler. Dreamweaver's ruler can be displayed in several different measurement units and with your choice of origin point.

To enable the ruler in Dreamweaver, choose View ➪ Rulers ➪ Show or use the keyboard shortcut Ctrl+Alt+Shift+R (Command+Option+Shift+R). Horizontal and vertical rulers appear along the top and the left sides of the Document window, as shown in Figure 28-12. As you move the pointer, a light-gray line indicates the position on both rulers.

By default, the ruler uses pixels as its measurement system. You can change the default by selecting View ➪ Rulers and choosing either inches or centimeters.

Dreamweaver also enables you to move the ruler origin to a new position. Normally, the upper-left corner of the page acts as the origin point for the ruler. On some occasions, it's helpful to start the measurement at a different location — at the bottom-right edge of an advertisement, for example. To move the origin point, select the intersection of the horizontal and the vertical rulers and drag the crosshairs to a new location. When you release the mouse button, both rulers are adjusted to show negative values above and to the right of the new origin point. To return the origin point to its default setting, choose View ➪ Rulers ➪ Reset Origin, or you can simply double-click the intersection of the rulers.

Tip

You can access a ruler shortcut menu by right-clicking (Command+clicking) the ruler itself. The shortcut menu enables you to change the system of measurement, reset the origin point, or hide the rulers.

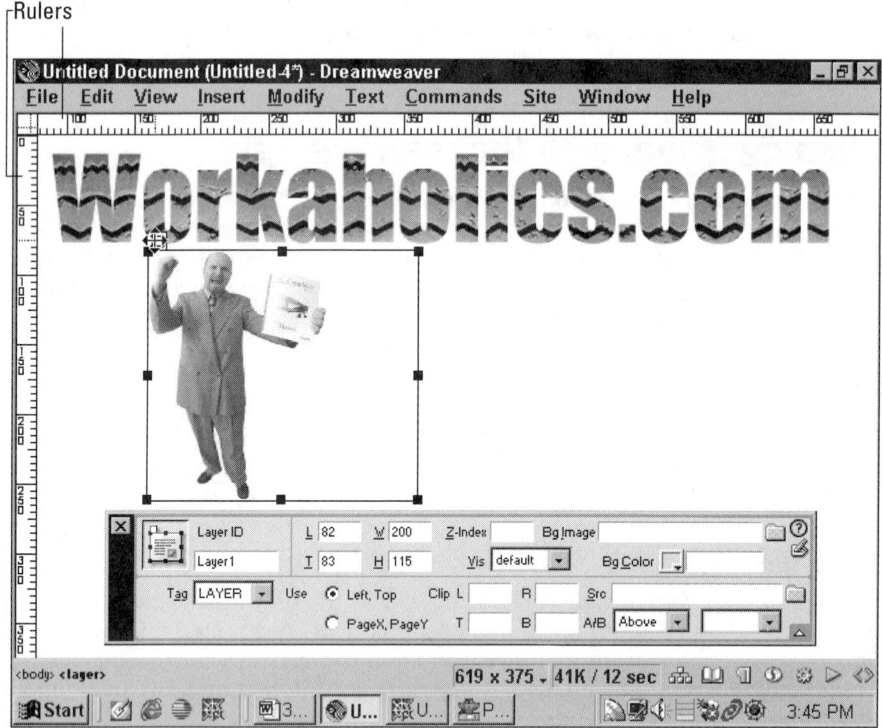

Figure 28-12: Use the horizontal and vertical rulers to assist your layer placement and overall Web page layout.

Lining up with the grid

Rulers are generally good for positioning single objects, but a grid is extremely helpful when aligning one object to another. With Dreamweaver's grid facility, you can align elements visually or snap them to the grid. You can set many of the grid's other features, including grid spacing, color, and type.

To turn on the grid, choose View ➪ Grid ➪ Show or press Ctrl+Alt+Shift+G (Command+Option+Shift+G). By default, the grid is displayed with light-blue lines set at 50-pixel increments.

The snap-to-grid feature is enabled by choosing View ➪ Grid ➪ Snap To or with the keyboard shortcut Ctrl+Alt+G (Command+Option+G). When activated, Snap to Grid causes the upper-left corner of a layer to be placed at the nearest grid intersection when the layer is moved.

Like most of Dreamweaver's tools, the grid can be customized. To alter the grid settings, choose View ➪ Grid ➪ Settings. In the Grid Settings dialog box, shown in

Figure 28-13, you can change any of the following settings (just click OK when you're done):

Grid Setting	*Description*
Visible Grid	Show or hide the grid with this checkbox toggle.
Spacing	Adjust the distance between grid points by entering a numeric value in the text box.
Spacing Unit of Measure	Select Pixels, Inches, or Centimeters from the Spacing drop-down list.
Color	Change the default color (light-blue) by selecting the color swatch to bring up a pop-up menu of color options or typing a new value in the text box.
Display	Choose either solid lines or dots for the gridlines.
Snapping	Checkbox toggle to enable or disable the Snap to Grid feature.
Snap Every	Adjust the distance between snap-to points (the points to which Dreamweaver snaps selected objects). Enter a number in the text box and select the distance measurement unit from the drop-down list.

Figure 28-13: Dreamweaver's grid feature is extremely handy for aligning a series of objects.

Adding elements to a layer

Once you have created and initially positioned your layers, you can begin to fill them with content. Inserting objects in a layer is just like inserting objects in a Web page. The same insertion methods are available to you:

✦ Position the cursor inside a layer, choose Insert in the menu bar, and select an object to insert.

✦ With the cursor inside a layer, select any object from the Objects palette. Note: you cannot select the Draw Layer object.

✦ Drag an object from the Objects palette and drop it inside the layer.

A known problem exists with Netscape Navigator 4.x browsers and nested layers—and layers in general—using the <div> tag. Whenever the browser window is resized, the layers lose their left and top position and are displayed along the left edge of the browser window or parent layer. Dreamweaver 3 includes the capability to insert code that serves as a workaround for this problem. With this code in place, if the browser is resized, the page reloads, repositioning the layers. If you want the code to be automatically inserted the first time you add a layer to your page, select the Add Resize Fix When Inserting Layers option found on the Layers category of Preferences. You can also insert it on a case-by-case basis by choosing Commands ⇨ Add/Remove Netscape Resize Fix. As the name implies, this command also deletes the Netscape Resize Fix code.

Forms and layers

When you're mixing forms and layers, follow only one rule: Always put the form completely inside the layer. If you place the layer within the form, all form elements after the layer tags are ignored. With the form completely enclosed in the layer, the form can safely be positioned anywhere on the page and all form elements still remain completely active.

Although this rule means you can't split one form onto separate layers, you can set up multiple forms on multiple layers — and still have them all communicate to one final CGI or other program. This technique uses JavaScript to send the user-input values in the separate forms to hidden fields in the form with the Submit button. Let's say, for example, that you have three separate forms gathering information in three separate layers on a Web page. Call them formA, formB, and formC on layer1, layer2, and layer3, respectively. When the Submit button in formC on layer3 is selected, a JavaScript function is first called by means of an onClick event in the button's <input> tag. The function, in part, looks like the following:

```
function gatherData() {
  document.formC.hidden1.value = document.formA.text1.value
  document.formC.hidden2.value = document.formB.text2.value
}
```

Notice how every value from the various forms gets sent to a hidden field in formC, the form with the Submit button. Now, when the form is submitted, all the hidden information gathered from the various forms is submitted along with formC's own information.

Netscape Note: The code for this separate-forms approach, as written in the preceding listing, works in Internet Explorer. Navigator, however, uses a different syntax to address forms in layers. To work properly in Navigator, the code must look like the following:

```
document.layers["layer3"].document.formC.hidden1.value=¬
document.layers["layer1"].document.formA.text1.value
```

To make the code cross-browser compatible, you can use an initialization function that allows for the differences, or you can build it into the `onClick` function. (For more information on building cross browser–compatible code, see Chapter 35.)

Creating Your Page Design with Layers

While the advantage to designing with layers is the greater flexibility it affords, one of the greatest disadvantages of using layers is that they are viewable in only the most recent generation of browsers. Dreamweaver enables you to get the best of both worlds by making it possible for you to use layers to design complex page layouts, and then to transform those layers into tables that can be viewed in earlier browsers. Designing this way has some limitations — you can't, for example, actually layer items on top of each other. Nevertheless, Dreamweaver's capability to convert layers to tables (and tables to layers) enables you to create complex layouts with ease.

Using the Tracing Image

Page-layout artists are often confronted with Web-page designs that have been mocked up in a graphics program. Dreamweaver's Tracing Image function enables you to use such images to guide the precise placement of graphics, text, tables, and forms in your Web page, enabling you to match the original design as closely as possible.

In order to use a Tracing Image, the graphic must be saved in either JPG, GIF, or PNG format. Once the Tracing Image has been placed in your page, it is viewable only in Dreamweaver — it will never appear in a browser. A placed Tracing Image hides any background color or background graphic in your Web page. Preview your page in a browser, or hide the tracing layer, to view your page without the Tracing Image.

Adding the Tracing Image to your page

To add a Tracing Image to your Dreamweaver page, select View ➪ Tracing Image ➪ Load. This brings up a Select Image Source dialog box that enables you to select the graphic you would like to use as a Tracing Image. Clicking Select brings up the Page Properties dialog box, shown in Figure 28-14, where you may specify the opacity of the Tracing Image, from Transparent (0%) to Opaque (100%). You can change the Tracing Image or its transparency at any point by selecting Modify ➪ Page Properties to bring up the Page Properties dialog box. You can toggle between hiding and showing the Tracing Image by selecting View ➪ Tracing Image ➪ Show. The Tracing Image can also be inserted directly in the Page Properties dialog box by entering its path in the Tracing Image text box or selecting the Browse (Choose) button to locate the image.

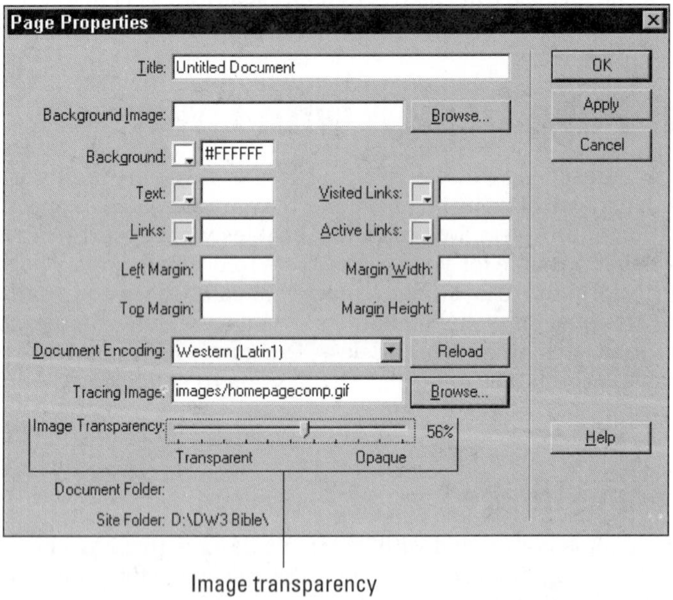

Image transparency

Figure 28-14: Setting the transparency of the Tracing Image to a setting such as 51 percent can help you differentiate between it and the content layers you are positioning.

Moving the Tracing Image

The Tracing Image cannot be selected and moved the same way as other objects on your page. Instead, you must move the Tracing Image using menu commands. You have several options for adjusting the Tracing Image's position to better fit your design. First, you can align the Tracing Image with any object on your page by first selecting the object and then choosing View ➪ Tracing Image ➪ Align with Selection. This lines up the upper-left corner of the Tracing Image with the upper-left corner of the bounding box of the object you've selected.

To precisely or visually move the Tracing Image to a specific location, select View ➪ Tracing Image ➪ Adjust Position. Then enter the *x* and *y* coordinates into the boxes in the Adjust Tracing Image Position dialog box, shown in Figure 28-15. For more hands-on positioning, use the arrow keys to nudge the tracing layer up, down, left, or right 1 pixel at a time. Holding down the Shift key while pressing the arrow keys moves the Tracing Image in 5-pixel increments. Finally, you can return the Tracing Image to its default location of 9 pixels down from the top and 11 pixels in from the left by selecting View ➪ Tracing Image ➪ Reset Position.

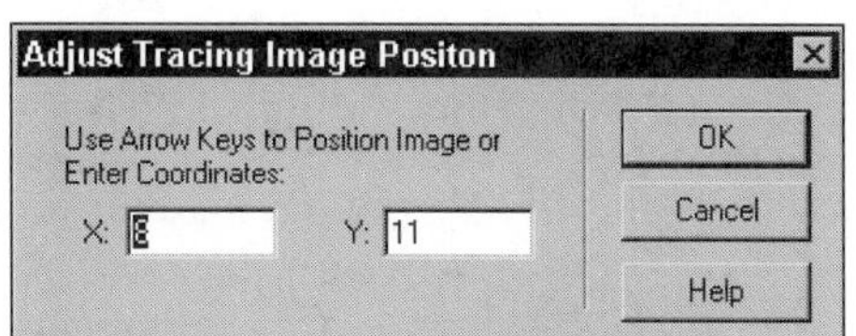

Figure 28-15: Use the Adjust Tracing Image Position dialog box to precisely place your graphic template.

Preventing overlaps

In order to place layers on your page that can later be converted to a table, the layers must not overlap. Before you begin drawing out your layers, open the Layers palette — either by selecting Windows ➪ Layers or pressing F11 — and put a checkmark in the Prevent Overlap box at the top of the Inspector window. You can also select View ➪ Prevent Layer Overlaps to toggle overlap protection on and off.

Designing precision layouts

As noted earlier, layers brought pixel-perfect positioning to the Internet. Now, Web designers can enjoy some of the layout capabilities assumed by print designers. Unfortunately, you need a 4.0 browser to view any page created with layers, and a portion of the Web audience is still using 3.0 or older browsers. Dreamweaver includes layers-to-tables and back again as part of its round-trip repertoire.

Web designers can freely design their page and then lock it into position for posting. Moreover, if the design needs adjustment — and all designs need adjustment — the posted page can be temporarily converted back to layers for easy repositioning. The Convert Tables to Layers and Convert Layers to Tables menu commands work together terrifically and greatly enhance the designer's workflow.

The two commands are described in detail in the following sections, but let's examine a typical Dreamweaver layout session to see how they function together:

1. The Web designer is handed a comp or layout design created by another member of the company or a third-party designer.
2. After creating the graphic and type elements, the Web designer is ready to compose the page in Dreamweaver.

3. Ideally, the comp is converted to an electronic graphic format and brought into Dreamweaver as a Tracing Image.
4. If at all possible, it's best for conversion purposes not to overlap any layers, so the Web designer enables the Prevent Overlap option.
5. Each element is placed in a separate layer and placed in position, following the Tracing Image, if any.
6. With one command (Convert Layers to Tables), the layout is restructured from appearing in layers to being in tables for backward browser compatibility.
7. After the client has viewed the page — and made the inevitable changes — the page is converted from tables to layers. Again, in Dreamweaver 3, this process is triggered by one command (Convert Tables to Layers) and takes seconds to complete.
8. The trip from tables to layers and back again is made as many times as necessary to get the layout pixel-perfect.

Convert Tables to Layers and Convert Layers to Tables is a one-two combination that cuts layout time tremendously and frees the designer to create visually instead of programmatically.

Converting content to layers

Dreamweaver enables you to take any page and enclose all the contents in layers for easy design layout with drag-and-drop ease. Convert Tables to Layers is very flexible and enables the designer to convert pages previously constructed either partially or totally with tables or ones that already have layers in place. You can even quickly convert an all-text page into a layer.

One valuable use for this command is to better prepare a page to use another Dreamweaver feature: Convert to 3.0 Browser Compatible. While you no longer have to have every page element in a layer to use this feature, if you use the Convert Tables to Layers command first, you get better results.

With the page open in Dreamweaver, select Modify ➪ Layout Mode ➪ Convert Tables to Layers to view the command's dialog box, shown in Figure 28-16.

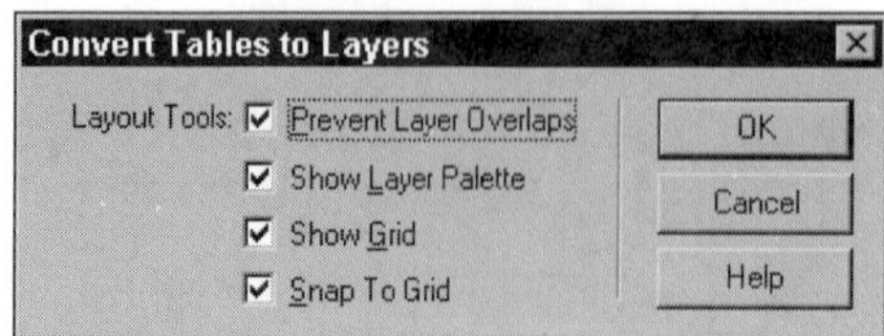

Figure 28-16: Choose the appropriate Layout Tools to help you reposition your content using layers.

By default, each of the following Layout Tools options are enabled:

✦ **Prevent Layer Overlaps:** You want this option turned on if you plan to convert the layers back to a table.

✦ **Show Layer Palette:** This automatically opens the Layers palette for you with each layer given a default name by Dreamweaver.

✦ **Show Grid:** This option reveals the grid overlay that can help with precision layout.

✦ **Snap to Grid:** With this turned on, layers snap to the nearest gridlines as they are moved onscreen.

You can uncheck any of these options before you convert the page.

Tip

Turn off Show Grid and Snap to Grid if you are laying out objects on top of a Tracing Image, as they may interfere with the absolute positions that you are trying to achieve.

Converting layers to tables

To convert a Web page that has been designed with layers into a table for viewing in older browsers, simply select Modify ➪ Layout Mode ➪ Convert Layers to Tables. This opens the Convert Layers to Table dialog box, shown in Figure 28-17, with the following options:

✦ **Most Accurate:** This creates as complex a table as is necessary to guarantee that the elements on your Web page appear in the exact locations that you've specified. This is the default setting.

✦ **Smallest:** Collapse empty cells less than *n* pixels wide: Selecting this option simplifies your table layouts by joining cells that are less than the number of pixels wide that you specify. This may result in a table that takes less time to load; however, it also means that the elements on your page may not appear in the precise locations where you've placed them.

✦ **Use Transparent GIFs:** When you select this option, Dreamweaver fills all empty cells with a transparent spacer graphic to ensure that the table will look the same across a variety of browsers. When Dreamweaver creates the table layout, it places a file called transparent.gif in the same folder as your Web page. You must make sure to include this file when you upload your page to your server in order for it to display correctly.

✦ **Center on Page:** Selecting this option puts `<div align=center>` tags around your table so that it displays in the middle of a browser window. Deselecting this option leaves out those tags so that the table starts from its default position in the upper-left corner of a browser.

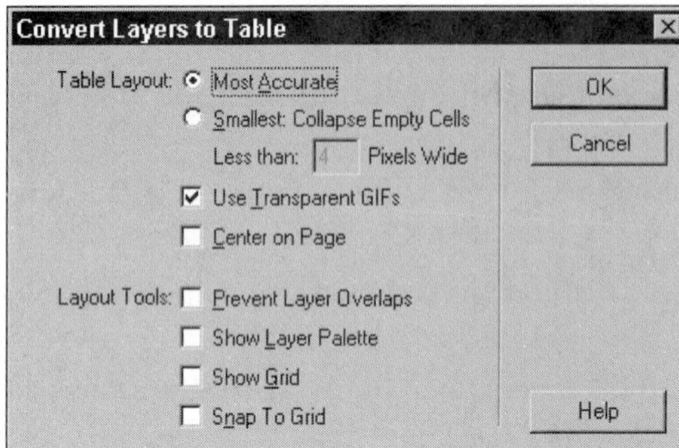

Figure 28-17: Check off the right Layout Tools options to help reposition your content as a table.

Once you have converted your layout into a table, as shown in Figure 28-18, you should preview it in your browser. If you aren't happy with the way your layout looks, or if you wish to do further modifications, you can convert the table back into layers by selecting Modify ➪ Layout Mode ➪ Convert Tables to Layers as described previously, selecting the layers to drag and drop the contents into new positions. Finally, transform your layout back into a table and preview it again.

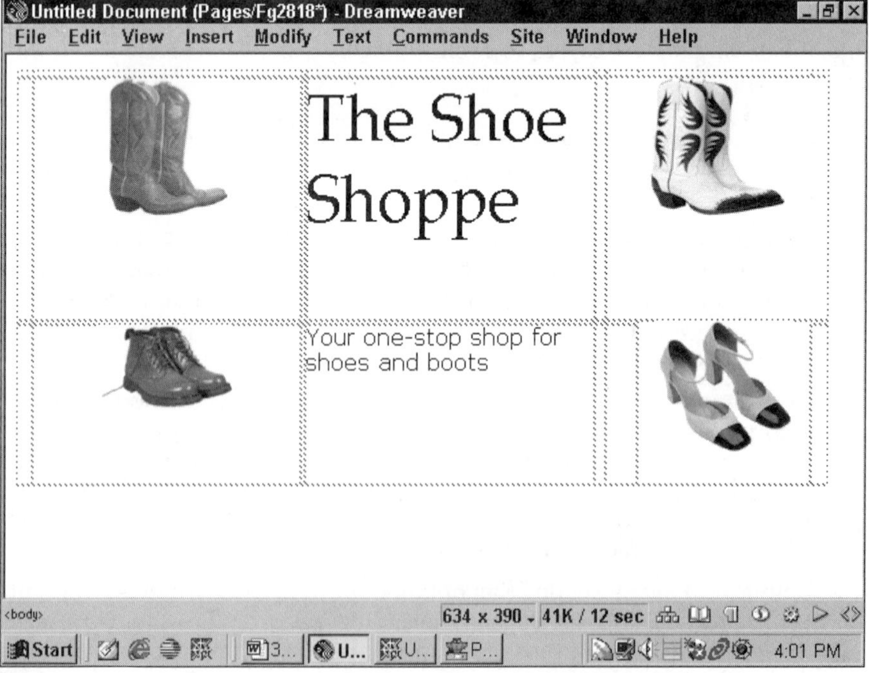

Figure 28-18: The results of transforming layers into a table, using the default settings

It's worth pointing out that the two Modify ➪ Layout Mode commands can be easily reversed by choosing Edit ➪ Undo, whereas the corresponding File ➪ Convert commands cannot.

Activating Layers with Behaviors

While absolute positioning is a major reason to use layers, you may have other motives for using this capability. All the properties of a layer — the coordinates, size and shape, depth, visibility, and clipping — can be altered dynamically and interactively as well. Normally, dynamically resetting a layer's properties entails some fairly daunting JavaScript programming. Now, with one of Dreamweaver's hallmarks — those illustrious behaviors — activating layers is possible for non-programmers as well.

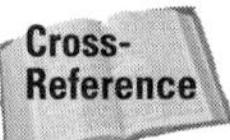

In case you missed it, Chapter 19, describes Dreamweaver's rich behaviors feature.

Behaviors consist of two parts, the event and the action. In Dreamweaver, two standard actions are designed specifically for working with layers:

- **Drag Layer:** Enables the user to move the layer and get a response to that movement.
- **Show-Hide Layers:** Controls the visibility of layers, either interactively or through some preprogrammed action on the page.

You can find detailed information about these actions in their respective sections in Chapter 19. The following sections outline how to use these behaviors to activate your layers.

Drag Layer

For the Web designer, positioning a layer is easy: click the selection handle and drag the layer to a new location. For the readers of your pages, moving a layer is next to impossible — unless you incorporate the Drag Layer action into the page's design.

With the Drag Layer action, you can set up interactive pages in which the user can rearrange elements of the design to achieve an effect or make a selection. Drag Layer includes an option that enables you to execute a JavaScript command if the user drops the layer on a specific target. In the example shown in Figure 28-19, each pair of shoes is in its own layer. When the user drops a pair in the bag, a one-line JavaScript command opens the desired catalog page and order form.

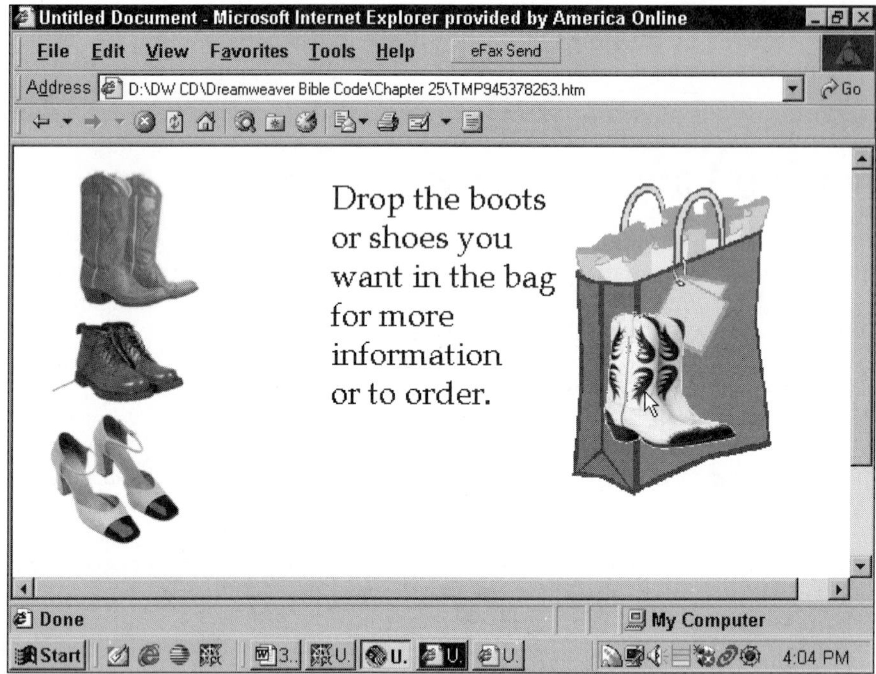

Figure 28-19: On this interactive page, visitors can drop merchandise into the shopping bag; this feature is made possible with the Drag Layer action.

After you've created all your layers, you're ready to attach the behavior. Because Drag Layer initializes the script to make the interaction possible, you should always associate this behavior with the `<body>` tag and the `onLoad` event.

Follow these steps to use the Drag Layer action, and to designate the settings for the drag operation:

1. Choose the `<body>` tag from the Tag Selector in the status bar.
2. Choose Window ➪ Behaviors or select the Show Behaviors button from either Launcher. The Behavior Inspector opens.
3. In the Behavior Inspector, make sure that 4.0 and Later Browsers is displayed in the browser list.
4. Click the + (add) action button and choose Drag Layer from the Add Action pop-up menu.
5. In the Drag Layer dialog box, select the layer you want to make available for dragging.
6. To limit the movement of the dragged layer, select Constrained from the Movement drop-down list. Then enter the coordinates to specify the direction to which you want to limit the movement in the Up, Down, Left, and/or Right text boxes.

7. To establish a location for a target, enter coordinates in the Drop Target: Left and Top text boxes. You can fill these text boxes with the selected layer's present location by clicking the Get Current Position button.
8. You can also set a snap-to area around the target's coordinates. When released in the target's location, the dragged layer snaps to this area. Enter a pixel value in the Snap if Within text box.
9. Click the More Options button.
10. Designate the drag handle:
    - To enable the whole layer to act as a drag handle, select Entire Layer from the drop-down menu.
    - If you want to limit the area to be used as a drag handle, select Area within Layer from the drop-down menu. Enter the Left and Top coordinates as well as the Width and Height dimensions in the appropriate text boxes.
11. If you want to keep the layer in its current depth and not bring it to the front, deselect the checkbox for While Dragging: Bring Layer to the Front. To change the stacking order of the layer when it is released after dragging, select either Leave on Top or Restore z-index from the drop-down list.
12. To execute a JavaScript command when the layer is dropped on the target, enter the code in the Call JavaScript text box. If you want the script to execute every time the layer is dropped, enter the code in the When Dropped: Call JavaScript text box. If the code should execute only when the layer is dropped on the target, make sure there's a check in the Only if Snapped checkbox.
13. To change the event that triggers the action (the default is `onLoad`), select an event from the drop-down menu in the Events column.

Targeted JavaScript Commands

The following simple yet useful JavaScript commands can be entered in the Snap JavaScript text box of the Drag Layer dialog box:

✦ To display a brief message to the user after the layer is dropped, use the `alert()` function:

```
alert("You hit the target")
```

✦ To send the user to another Web page when the layer is dropped in the right location, use the JavaScript location object:

```
location = "http://www.yourdomain.com/yourpage.html"
```

The location object can also be used with relative URLs.

Set Text of Layer

We've seen how layers can dynamically move, change their visibility, and their depth—but did you know that you could also change a layer's *content* dynamically? With Dreamweaver 3, you can do it easily. A new behavior, Set Text of Layer, enables you to swap the entire contents of one layer for whatever you'd like. You're not limited to exchanging just text either. Anything you can put into HTML, you can swap—which, is pretty much everything!

This behavior is extremely useful for putting up context-sensitive help and other information. Rather than construct a series of layers which you show and hide, a single layer is used, and just the contents change. To use Set Text of Layer, follow these steps:

1. Insert and name your layers as desired.
2. Select the graphic, button, or text link you'd like to act as the trigger for your changing the content of the layer.
3. Choose Window ➪ Behaviors or select the Show Behaviors button from either Launcher to open the Behavior Inspector.
4. Choose Set Text ➪ Set Text of Layer from the + (add) action pop-up menu.

   The dialog box (Figure 28-20) shows a list of the available layers in the current Web page as well as providing a space for the new content.

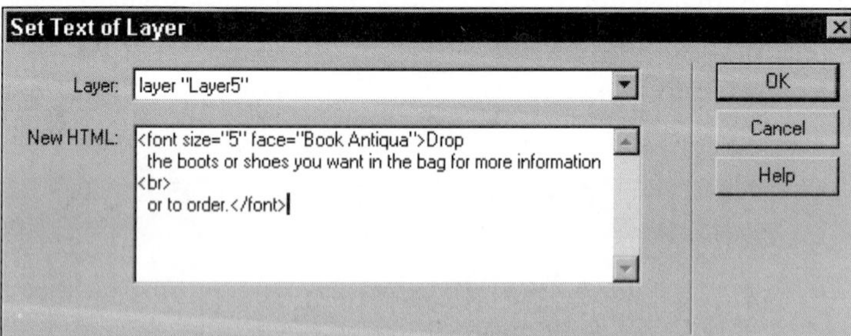

Figure 28-20: Swap out all the contents of a layer using the Set Text of Layer behavior.

5. Select the layer you want to alter from the Layer option list.
6. Enter the text or code in the New HTML text area.

   You can enter either plain text, which is rendered in the default paragraph style, or any amount of HTML code, including `<img>`, `<table>`, or other tags.

If you're entering a large amount of HTML, don't bother doing so by hand—Dreamweaver can do it for you. On a blank page, create your HTML content and then select and copy it. Then, in the Set Text of Layer dialog box, paste the code using Ctrl+V (Command+V).

7. Click OK when you're done.

If you want several layers to change when a single event is triggered, just add more Set Text of Layer behaviors to the same object.

You may need to change the behavior event from its default; to do so select the down arrow in between the Event and Action columns on the Behavior Inspector and choose a new event from the list.

Show-Hide Layers

The capability to implement interactive control of a layer's visibility offers tremendous potential to the Web designer. The Show-Hide Layers action makes this implementation straightforward and simple to set up. With the Show-Hide Layers action, you can simultaneously show one or more layers while hiding as many other layers as necessary. Create your layers and give them a unique name before invoking the Show-Hide Layers action.

To use Show-Hide Layers, follow these steps:

1. Select an image, link, or other HTML tag to which to attach the behavior.
2. Choose Window ⇨ Behaviors or select the Show Behaviors button from either Launcher to open the Behavior Inspector.
3. Choose Show-Hide Layers from the + (add) action pop-up menu. The parameters form (Figure 28-21) shows a list of the available layers in the open Web page.

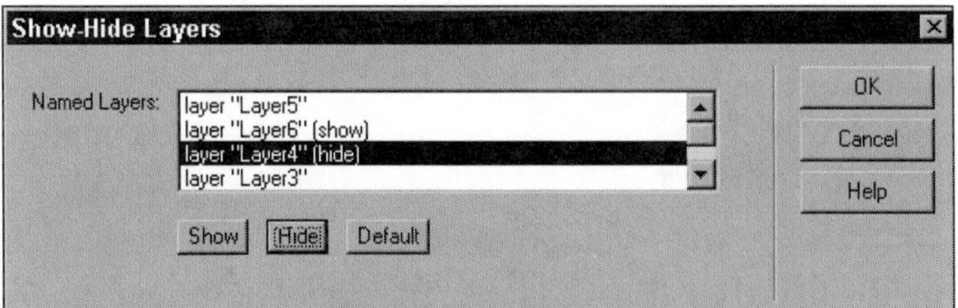

Figure 28-21: With the Show-Hide Layers behavior attached, you can easily program the visibility of all the layers in your Web page.

4. To cause a hidden layer to be revealed when this event is fired, select the layer from the list and choose the Show button.
5. To hide a visible layer when this event is fired, select its name from the list and select the Hide button.
6. To restore a layer's default visibility value when this event is fired, select the layer and choose the Default button.
7. Click OK when you are done.
8. If the default event is not suitable, use the drop-down menu in the Events column to select a different one.

Dreamweaver Technique: Creating a Loading Layer

As Web creations become more complex, most designers want their layers to zip on and off screen or appear and disappear as quickly as possible for the viewer of the page. A layer can act only when it has finished loading its content — the text and images. Rather than have the user see each layer loading in, some designers use a loading layer to mask the process until everything is downloaded and ready to go.

A loading layer is fairly easy to create. Dreamweaver supplies all the JavaScript necessary in one behavior, Show-Hide Layers. Keep in mind that because this technique uses layers, it's good only for 4.0 browsers and above. Use the following steps to create a loading layer:

1. Create all of your layers with the contents in place and the visibility property set as normal.
2. Create the loading layer. (Choose Insert ➪ Layer or select the Draw Layer button from the Objects palette.)
3. Enter and position whatever contents you want displayed in the loading layer while all the other layers are loading.
4. Open the Layers palette (F11).
5. Turn off the visibility for all layers except the loading layer. In essence, you're hiding every other layer.
6. Select the `<body>` tag from the Tag Selector.
7. Choose Window ➪ Behaviors or select Show Behaviors from either Launcher to open the Behavior Inspector.
8. Select the + (add) action button and choose Show-Hide Layers from the pop-up menu.
9. In the Show-Hide Layers dialog box, select the loading layer and then click the Hide button.

10. Select all the other layers and set them to Show. Click OK when you are done.

11. Leave onLoad (the default) as the event to trigger this action.

Now, when you test your Web page, you should see only your loading layer until everything else is loaded, then the loading layer disappears, and all the other layers are made visible.

A loading layer may be the last bastion of the <blink> tag. Created by Netscape fairly early in the history of the Web, the <blink>...</blink> tag pair was grossly overused and is today generally shunned. However, if you apply it (by hand in the HTML Inspector or through the Quick Tag Editor) just to the ellipse following the term "Loading . . ." like this:

```
<h2>Loading<blink>...</blink></h2>
```

you get a small bit of movement on the page, similar to a blinking cursor. The <blink> tag is supported only by Netscape Navigator. You could also use an animated GIF to create the pulsing image for a cross-browser effect.

Summary

Layers are effective placement tools for developing the layout of a page. Anyone used to designing with desktop publishing tools can quickly learn to work layers effectively.

✦ Layers are visible only on fourth-generation and above browsers.

✦ Layers can be used to place HTML content anywhere on a Web page.

✦ You can stack layers on top of one another. This depth control is referred to as the *stacking order* or the *z-index*.

✦ Dreamweaver can convert layers to tables for viewing in earlier browsers, and back again for straightforward repositioning.

✦ Layers can be constructed so that the end user can display or hide them interactively, or alter their position, size, and depth dynamically.

✦ Dreamweaver gives you rulers and grids to help with layer placement and alignment.

✦ Layers can easily be activated by using Dreamweaver's built-in JavaScript behaviors.

In the next chapter, you learn how to develop timelines, which enable layers and their contents to move around the Web page.

✦ ✦ ✦

CHAPTER 29

Working with Timelines

✦ ✦ ✦ ✦

In This Chapter

Adding animation with Dreamweaver timelines

Using the Timeline Inspector

Incorporating timelines

Automatically starting and looping a timeline

Altering timelines with keyframes

Putting behaviors into timelines

Dreamweaver Technique: Creating a multiscreen slideshow

✦ ✦ ✦ ✦

Motion implies time. A static object, such as an ordinary HTML Web page, can exist either in a single moment or over a period of time. Conversely, moving objects (such as Dynamic HTML layers flying across the screen) need a few seconds to complete their path. All of Dreamweaver's Dynamic HTML animation effects use the Timeline feature to manage this conjunction of movement and time.

Timelines can do much more than move a layer across a Web page, however. A timeline can coordinate an entire presentation: starting the background music, scrolling the opening rolling credits, and cueing the voice-over narration on top of a slideshow. These actions are all possible with Dreamweaver because, in addition to controlling a layer's position, timelines can also trigger any of Dreamweaver's JavaScript behaviors on a specific frame.

This chapter explores the full and varied world of timelines. After an introductory section brings you up to speed on the underlying concepts of timelines, you learn how to insert and modify timelines to achieve cutting-edge effects. A Dreamweaver Technique shows you, step by step, how to create a multiscreen slideshow complete with fly-in and fly-out graphics. From complex multilayer animations to slideshow presentations, you can do it all with Dreamweaver timelines.

Note Because timelines are so intricately intertwined with layers and behaviors, you need to have a good grasp of these concepts. Before examining the topic of timelines, make sure to read Chapter 19 and Chapter 28.

Into the Fourth Dimension with Timelines

Web designers in the early days had little control over the fourth dimension and their Web pages. Only animated GIFs, Java, or animation programs such as Macromedia's Flash could create the illusion of motion events. Unfortunately, all of these technologies have some limitations.

The general problem with animated GIF images is related to file size. An animated GIF starts out as an image for every frame. Therefore, if you incorporate a three-second, 15-frames-per-second animation, you are asking the user to download the compressed equivalent of 45 separate images. Even though an animated GIF is an index color file with a limited 256 colors and uses the format's built-in compression, the GIF file is still a relatively large graphic file. Moreover, for all their apparent animated qualities, GIFs enable no true interaction other than as a link to another URL. Animations created with Dynamic HTML and Dreamweaver's timelines, on the other hand, do not significantly increase the overall size of the Web page and are completely interactive.

DHTML is not the only low-bandwidth approach to animations with interactive content for the Web. You can create animations, complete with user-driven interactions, with Java — as long as you're a Java programmer. Certainly Java development tools are making the language easier to use, but you still must deal with the rather long load time of any Java applet and the increasing variety of Java versions. As another option, Macromedia Director movies can be compressed or "shocked" to provide animation and interactivity in your pages. Like Java, the Director approach requires a bit of a learning curve. Shockwave movies can also have long load times and require the user to have a plug-in application.

Macromedia's Flash is another alternative to GIF images, though Flash has its own set of caveats to keep in mind. On the plus side, Flash files are small and can be streamed through their own player. This arrangement is tempting, and if you just want animation on a page, Flash is probably a superior choice to any of the approaches previously described. On the minus side, Flash is limited to its own proprietary features and functions, and every user must have the Flash plug-in or ActiveX control installed. Moreover, you cannot layer Flash animation on top of other layers on a page. Once you or another designer have created a Flash animation, the animation must be edited with the same animation package.

Timeline capabilities

Dreamweaver timelines are part of the HTML code. For the movement of one layer straight across a Web page, Dreamweaver generates about 70 lines of code devoted to initializing and playing the timeline. But just what is a timeline? A timeline is composed of a series of frames. A frame is a snapshot of what the Web page, more specifically, the objects on the timeline, look like at a particular moment. You probably know that a movie is made up of a series of still pictures; when viewed quickly, the pictures create the illusion of movement. Each individual picture is a frame; movies show 24 frames per second, and video uses about 30 frames per second.

Web animation, on the other hand, generally displays about 15 frames per second (fps). Not surprisingly, Dreamweaver's timeline is similar to the one used in Macromedia's timeline-based, multimedia authoring tool and animation package, Director 7.0.

If you have to draw each frame of a 30-second animation, even at 15 fps, you won't have time for other work. Dreamweaver uses the concept of *keyframes* to make a simple layer movement workable. Each keyframe contains a change in the timeline object's properties, such as position. For example, let's say you want your layer to start at the upper left (represented by the coordinates 0,0) and travel to the lower right (at 750,550). To accomplish this task, you need only specify the layer's position for the two keyframes — the start and the finish — and Dreamweaver generates all the frames in between.

Timelines have three primary roles:

✦ A timeline can alter a layer's position, dimensions, visibility, and depth.

✦ Timelines can change the source for any image on a Web page and cause another graphic of the same height and width to appear in the same location.

✦ Any of Dreamweaver's JavaScript behaviors can be triggered on any frame of a timeline.

A few ground rules

Keep the following basic guidelines in mind when you're using timelines in the Web pages you create with Dreamweaver:

✦ Timelines require a 4.0 or later browser.

✦ For a timeline to be able to animate an object, such as text, the object must be within a layer. If you try to create a timeline with an element that is not in a layer, Dreamweaver warns you and prevents you from adding the object to the timeline.

✦ Events don't have to start on the beginning of a timeline. If you want to have an action begin five seconds after a page has loaded, you can set the behavior on frame 60 of the timeline, with a frame rate of 15 frames per second.

✦ The selected frame rate is a "best-case scenario" because the actual frame rate depends on the user's system. A slower system or one that is simultaneously running numerous other programs can easily degrade the frame rate.

✦ You can include multiple animations on one timeline. The only restriction? You can't have two animations affecting the same layer at the same time. Dreamweaver prevents you from making this error.

✦ You can have multiple timelines that animate different layers simultaneously or the same layer at different times. Although you can set two or more timelines to animate the same layer at the same time, the results are difficult to predict and generally unintended.

Creating Animations with Timelines

Dreamweaver provides an excellent tool for managing timelines — the Timelines Inspector. Open this tool by choosing Window ⇨ Timelines, selecting the Show Timelines button from either Launcher, or using the keyboard shortcut F9.

The Timelines Inspector uses VCR-style controls combined with a playback head, which is a visual representation showing which frame is the current one. As shown in Figure 29-1, the Timelines Inspector gives you full control over any of the timeline functions.

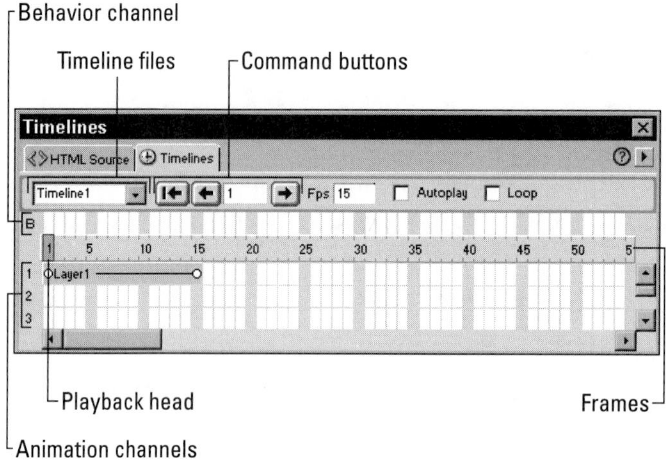

Figure 29-1: Dreamweaver's Timelines Inspector enables you to quickly and easily master animation control.

The Timelines Inspector has four major areas:

- ✦ **Timeline Controls:** Includes the Timeline pop-up menu for selecting the current timeline; the Rewind, Back, and Play buttons; the Fps (frame rate) text box; and the Autoplay and Loop checkboxes.
- ✦ **Behavior Channel:** Shows the placement of any behaviors attached to specific frames of the timeline.
- ✦ **Frames:** Displays the frame numbers for all timelines and the playback head showing the current frame number.
- ✦ **Animation Channels:** Represents the animations for any included layers and images.

Adding Layers to the Timelines Inspector

As with many of Dreamweaver's functions, you can add a layer or an image to the Timelines Inspector in more than one way. You can either insert a layer into a timeline through the menus (Modify ➪ Add Object to Timeline), or you can drag and drop an object into a timeline. The default timeline is set at a frame rate of 15 fps. When you add an object to a timeline, Dreamweaver inserts an animation bar of 15 frames in length, labeled with the object's name. The animation bar shows the duration (the number of frames) for the timeline's effect on the object. An animation bar is initially created with two initial keyframes: the start and the end.

To add a layer or image to the Timelines Inspector through the menus, follow these steps:

1. Choose Window ➪ Timelines or click the Show Timelines button from either Launcher to open the Timelines Inspector.
2. In the Document window, select the layer or image you want to add to the timeline.
3. Choose Modify ➪ Add Object to Timeline. An animation bar appears in the first frame of the timeline, as shown in Figure 29-2.
4. To add another object, repeat Steps 2 and 3. Each additional animation bar is inserted beneath the preceding bar.

Tip

The first time you add an image or layer to the Timelines Inspector, Dreamweaver displays an alert message that details the limitations of timelines. If you don't want to see this alert, turn it off by checking the Don't Show Me This Message Again checkbox.

As previously noted, you can add as many objects to a timeline as you desire. If necessary, increase the size of the Timelines Inspector by dragging any border of its window.

You have a little more flexibility when you add an object by dragging it into the timeline. Instead of the animation bar always beginning at frame 1, you can drop the object in to begin on any frame. This approach is useful, especially if you are putting more than one object into the same animation channel.

To place an object in a timeline with the drag-and-drop method, follow these steps:

1. Open the Timelines Inspector by choosing Window ➪ Timelines or clicking the Show Timelines button from either Launcher.
2. In the Document window, select the object you want to add to the timeline and drag it to the Timelines Inspector. As soon as the object is over the Timelines Inspector, a 15-frame animation bar appears.

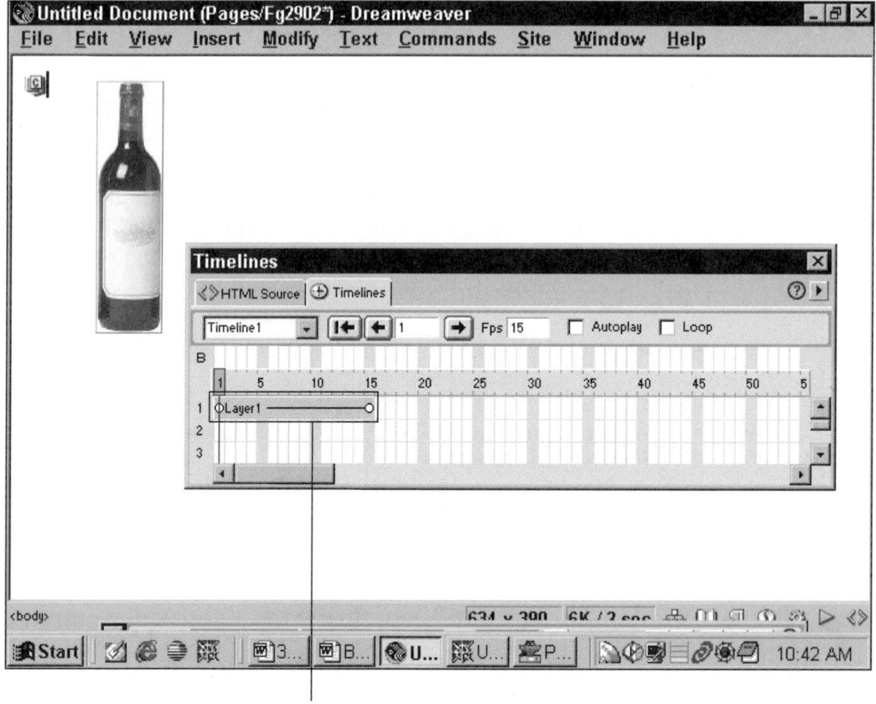

Figure 29-2: The default animation bar is set at 15 frames but can easily be modified.

3. Holding the mouse button down, position the animation bar so that the animation begins in the desired frame. Release the mouse button to drop the object into the timeline.

Your placement does not have to be exact; you can modify it later.

Placing a layer or image on a timeline is just the beginning. To begin using your timeline in depth, you have to make changes to the object for the keyframes and customize the timeline.

Modifying a Timeline

When you add an object — either an image or a layer — to a timeline, notice that the animation bar has an open circle at its beginning and end. An open circle marks a keyframe. As previously explained, the designer specifies a change in the state of the timeline object in a keyframe. For example, when you first insert a layer, the two generated keyframes have identical properties — the layer's position, size, visibility, and depth are unchanged. For any animation to occur, you have to change one of the layer's properties for one of the keyframes.

For example, let's move a layer quickly across the screen. Follow these steps:

1. Create a layer. If you like, add an image or a background color so that the layer is more noticeable.
2. Open the Timelines Inspector (go to Window ➪ Timelines, click the Show Timelines button from the Launcher, or press F9).
3. Drag the layer into the Timelines Inspector and release the mouse button.
4. Select the ending keyframe of the layer's animation bar.

   The playback head moves to the new frame.
5. In the Document window, grab the layer's selection handle and drag the layer to a new location. A thin line connects the starting position of the layer to the ending position, as shown in Figure 29-3. This line is the animation path.

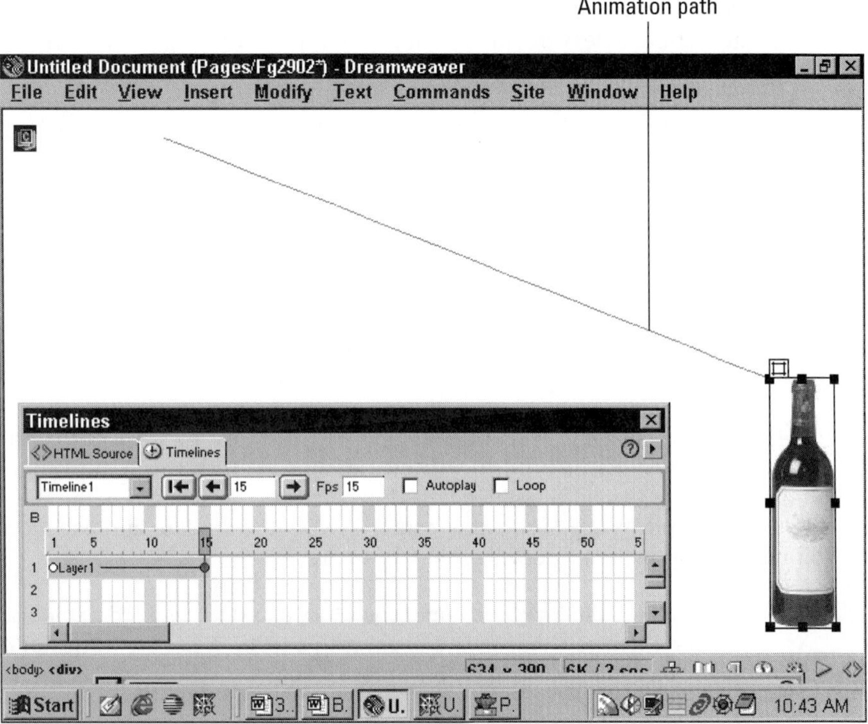

Figure 29-3: When you move a layer on a timeline, Dreamweaver displays an animation path.

6. To play your animation, first click the Rewind button in the Timelines Inspector and then click and hold down the Play button.

If you want to change the beginning position of your layer's movement, select the starting keyframe and then move the layer in the Document window. To alter the final position of your layer's movement, select the ending keyframe and then move the layer.

For more precise control of your layer's position in a timeline, select a keyframe and then, in the layer's Property Inspector, change the Left and/or Top values. You can also select the layer and use the arrow keys to move it.

Altering the animation bars

A Web designer can easily stretch or alter the range of frames occupied by a layer or image in an animation bar. You can make an animation longer or smoother, or have it start at an entirely different time. You can also move the layer to a different animation channel so it runs before or after another animation.

Use the mouse to drag an animation bar around the timeline. Click any part of the bar except on the keyframe indicators and move it as needed. To change the length of an animation, select the first or final keyframe and drag it forward or backward to a new frame.

You can remove an animation bar in two ways: select it and press Delete, or choose Modify ⇨ Timeline ⇨ Remove Object.

Using the Timeline controls

As you probably noticed if you worked through the example in the preceding section, you don't have to use a browser to preview a timeline. The Timeline controls shown in Figure 29-4 enable you to fine-tune your animations before you view them through a browser.

At the top-left corner is the Timeline pop-up menu, which is used to indicate the current timeline. By default, every new timeline is given the name Timeline*n*, where *n* indicates how many timelines have been created. You can rename the timeline by selecting it and typing in the new name. As you accumulate and use more timelines, you should give them recognizable names.

If you change the timeline name, you must enter a one-word name using alphanumeric characters that always begin with a letter. Netscape Navigator 4.x cannot read spaces or special characters in JavaScript.

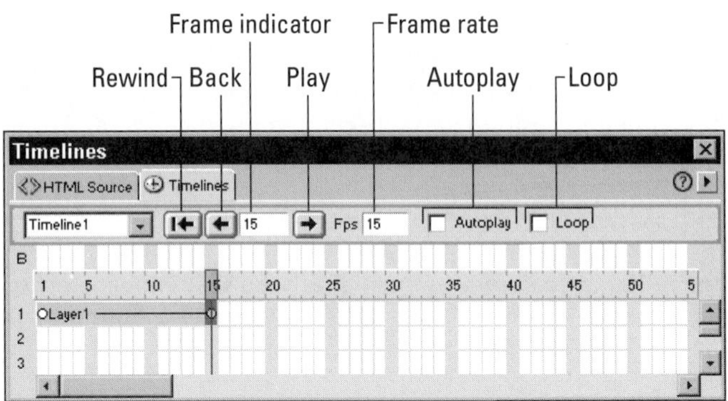

Figure 29-4: The Timeline controls enable you to move back and forth in your timeline, easily and precisely.

The next three buttons in the control bar enable you to move through the frames of a timeline. From left to right:

✦ **Rewind:** Moves the playback head to the first frame of the current timeline.

✦ **Back:** Moves the playback head to the previous frame. You can hold down the Back button to play the timeline in reverse.

✦ **Play:** Moves the timeline forward one frame at a time; hold down the Play button to play the timeline normally. When the last frame is reached, the playback head moves to the first frame of the current timeline and continues playing it.

The field between the Back and Play buttons is the frame indicator text box. To jump to any specific frame, enter the frame number in this box.

The next item in the control bar is the Fps (frames per second) text box. To change the frame rate, enter a new value in the Fps text box and press Tab or Enter (Return). The frame rate you set is an ideal number that a user's browser attempts to reach. The default rate of 15 frames per second is a good balance for both Macintosh and Windows systems.

Because browsers play every frame regardless of the frame rate setting, increasing the frame rate does not necessarily make your animations smoother. A better method for creating smooth animations is to drag the end keyframe farther out and therefore increase the number of frames used by your animation.

The next two checkboxes, Autoplay and Loop, affect how the animation is played.

Autoplay

If you mark the Autoplay checkbox, the current timeline begins playing as soon as the Web page is fully downloaded. Dreamweaver alerts you to this arrangement by telling you that the Play Timeline action is attached to an `onLoad` event. Autoplay is achieved by inserting code into the `<body>` tag that looks similar to the following:

```
<body bgcolor="#FFFFFF" onload="MM_timelinePlay('timeline1')">
```

If you don't use the Autoplay feature, you must attach the Play Timeline action to another event and tag, such as an `onMouseClick` event and a button graphic. Otherwise, the timeline does not play.

Looping

Mark the Loop checkbox if you want an animation to repeat once it has reached the final frame. When Loop is enabled, the default causes the layer to replay itself an infinite numbers of times; however, you can change this setting.

When you first enable the Loop checkbox, Dreamweaver alerts you that it is placing a Go to Frame action after the last frame of your current timeline. To set the number of repetitions for a timeline, follow these steps:

1. In the Timelines Inspector, check the Loop checkbox.
2. Dreamweaver displays an alert informing you that the Go to Timeline Frame action is being added one frame past your current final frame. To disable these alerts, select the Don't Show Me This Message Again option.
3. In the Behavior channel (above the Frame numbers and playback head), double-click the behavior you just added.

When you first add a behavior to a timeline, Dreamweaver presents a dialog box reminding you how to perform this action. Select the Don't Show Me This Message Again option when you've mastered the technique.

The Behavior Inspector opens, with an `onFrame` event in the Events pane and a Go To Timeline Frame action showing in the Actions pane.

4. Double-click the `onFrame` event. The Go to Timeline Frame dialog box opens (see Figure 29-5).

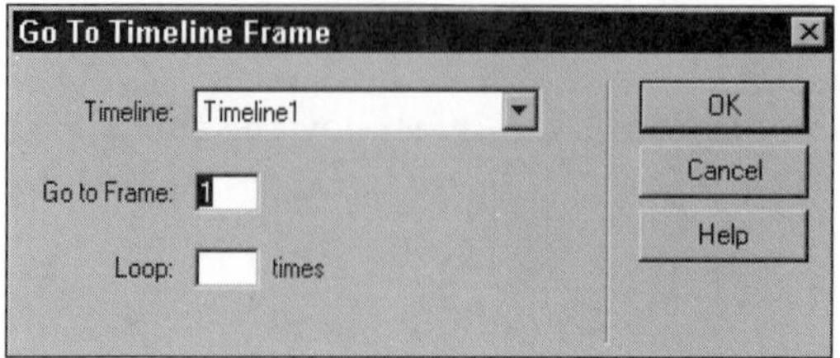

Figure 29-5: Selecting the Loop option on the Timelines Inspector adds a Go to Timeline Frame action, which you can customize.

5. Enter a positive number in the Loop text box to set the number of times you want your timeline to repeat. To keep the animation repeating continuously, leave the Loop text box blank.
6. Click OK when you are finished.

Your animations don't have to loop back to the beginning each time. By entering a different frame number in the Go to Frame text box of the Go to Timeline Frame dialog box, you can repeat just a segment of the animation.

Adding keyframes

Animating a timeline can go far beyond moving your layer from point A to point B. Layers (and the content within them) can dip, swirl, zigzag, and generally move in any fashion — all made possible by keyframes in which you have entered some change for the object. Dreamweaver calculates all the differences between each keyframe, whether the change is in a layer's position or size. Each timeline starts with two keyframes, the beginning and the end; you have to add other keyframes before you can insert the desired changes.

You can add a keyframe to your established timeline in a couple of different ways. The first method uses the Add Keyframe command, and the second method uses the mouse to click a keyframe into place.

Adding keyframes with the Add Keyframe command

To add a keyframe with the Add Keyframe command, follow these steps:

1. In the Timelines Inspector, select the animation bar for the object with which you are working.
2. Select the frame in which you want to add a keyframe.
3. Add your keyframe by either of the following methods:
   a. Choose Modify ➪ Timeline ➪ Add Keyframe.
   b. Right-click (Control+click) the frame in the animation bar and, from the shortcut menu, choose Add Keyframe.

A new keyframe is added on the selected frame, signified by the open circle in the animation bar.

While your new keyframe is selected, you can alter the layer's position, size, visibility, or depth. For example, if your animation involves moving a layer across the screen, you can drag the layer to a new position while the new keyframe is selected. The animation path is redrawn to incorporate this new position, as illustrated in Figure 29-6.

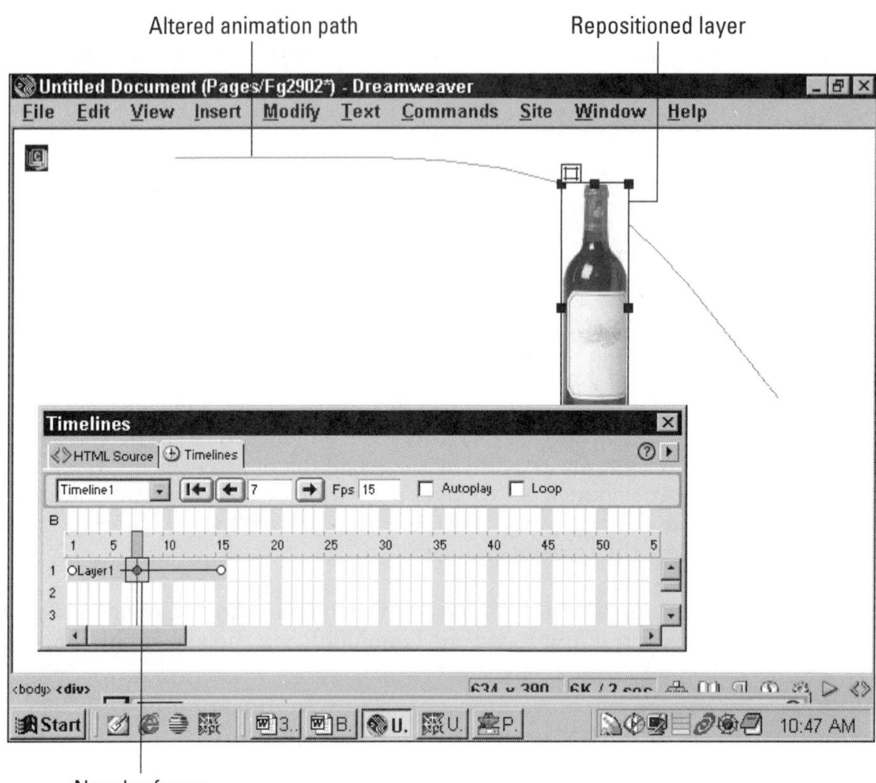

Figure 29-6: Repositioning a layer while a keyframe is selected can redirect your animation path.

Adding a keyframe with the mouse

The second method for adding a keyframe is quicker. To add a keyframe using the mouse, simply hold down the Ctrl (Command) key. Then click anywhere in the animation bar to add a keyframe. Your cursor turns into a small open circle when it is over the Timeline window to show that it is ready to add a new keyframe.

What if you want to move the keyframe? Simply click and drag the keyframe to a new frame, sliding it along the animation bar in the Timelines Inspector.

Tip

If, after plotting out an elaborate animation with a layer, you discover that you need to shift the entire animation—say, 6 pixels to the right—you don't have to redo all your work. Just select the animation bar in the Timelines Inspector and then, in the Document window, move the layer in question. Dreamweaver shifts the entire animation to your new location.

Removing timeline elements

The easiest way to remove an object, keyframe, or behavior from the Timelines Inspector is to select the element and press Delete. You cannot use this technique to delete individual frames or entire timelines, however. For these situations, you must use the menus:

✦ To remove the whole timeline, choose Modify ➪ Timeline ➪ Remove Timeline.

✦ To remove an individual frame, choose Modify ➪ Timeline ➪ Remove Frame.

The Timelines Inspector's shortcut menu also contains all the removal commands. Right-click (Control+click) the Timelines Inspector anywhere below the control bar and, in the shortcut menu (see Figure 29-7), choose the removal command you need: Remove Keyframe, Remove Behavior, Remove Object, Remove Frame, or Remove Timeline.

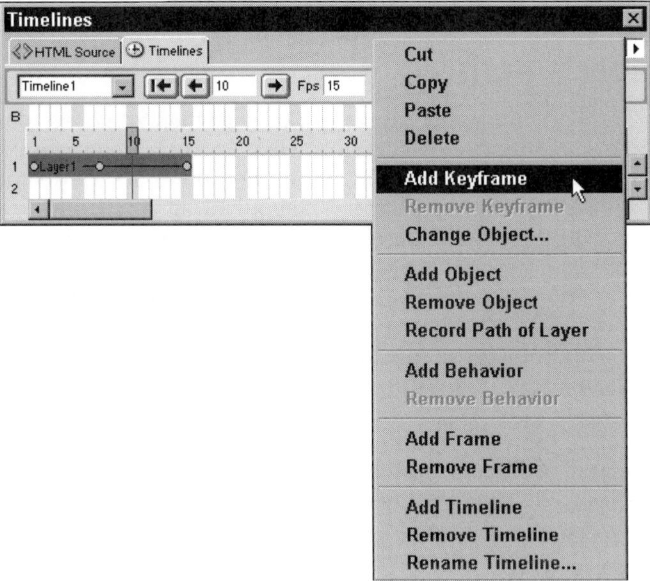

Figure 29-7: The Timelines Inspector's shortcut menu is extremely handy for doing quick edits.

You can also Cut, Copy and Paste Timelines between documents. The Delete command in the shortcut menu is the same as Remove Timeline.

Changing animation speed

You can alter your Dynamic HTML animation speed with two different methods that can be used separately or together.

- ✦ Drag the final keyframe in the animation bar out to cover additional frames, or back to cover fewer frames. Any keyframes within the animation bar are kept proportional to their original settings. This method works well when altering the speed of an individual animation bar.
- ✦ Change the frames per second value in the Fps text box of the Timelines Inspector. Increasing the number of frames per second accelerates the animation, and vice versa. Adjusting the Fps value affects every layer contained within the timeline; you cannot use this method for individual layers.

Browsers play every frame of a Dynamic HTML animation, regardless of the system resources. Some systems, therefore, play the same animation faster or slower than others. Don't depend on every system to have the same timing.

Recording a layer's path

Plotting keyframes and repositioning your layers works well when you need to follow a pixel-precise path, but it can be extremely tedious when you're trying to move a layer more freely on the screen. Luckily, another, easier method exists for defining a movement path for a layer. In Dreamweaver, you can simply drag your layer around the screen to create a path and refine the path or its timing afterward.

The Record Path of Layer command automatically creates the necessary series of keyframes, calculated from your dragging of the layer. To fine-tune your work, you can select any keyframes and reposition the layer or even delete it entirely. This feature is a definite time-saver for quickly inserting your DHTML animation.

Keep in mind that a timeline represents not only positions but also positions over time, and thus, movement. The Record Path of Layer command is very smart when it comes to time; the slower you drag the layer, the more keyframes are plotted. You can vary the positioning of the keyframes by changing the tempo of your dragging. Moreover, the duration of the recorded timeline reflects the length of time spent dragging the layer.

To record a layer's path, do the following:

1. In the Document window, select the layer you are going to move.

Make sure that you've selected the layer itself and not its contents. If you've correctly selected the layer, it has eight selection boxes around it.

2. Drag the layer to the location in the document where you want it to be at the start of the movement.

3. From the menu bar, select Modify ⇨ Record Path of Layer. You can also right-click (Control+click) the selected layer and choose Record Path from the shortcut menu.

   If it's not already open, the Timelines Inspector appears.

4. Click the layer and drag it around onscreen to define the movement. As you drag the layer, Dreamweaver draws a gray dotted line that shows you the path it is creating (see Figure 29-8).

Figure 29-8: To record a layer's path, Select Modify ⇨ Record Path of Layer and then drag your layer in the Document window.

   Each gray dot represents a keyframe. The slower you draw, the closer the keyframes are placed; moving quickly across the Document window causes Dreamweaver to space out the keyframes.

5. Release the mouse. This ends the recording.

   Dreamweaver displays an alert reminding you of the capabilities of the Timelines Inspector. Select the Don't Show Me This Message Again option to prevent this dialog box from reappearing.

After you've finished recording a layer's movement, you see a new animation bar in the Timelines Inspector, representing the motion you just recorded. The duration of the new timeline matches the duration of your dragging of the layer. A number of keyframes that define your layer's movement already are inserted in this animation bar. You can use any of the procedures described earlier in this chapter to modify the timeline or its keyframes. If you select the same layer at the end of the generated timeline and perform the Record Path operation again, another animation bar is added at the end of the current timeline.

Any new paths recorded with the same layer are added after the last animation bar. You can't select a keyframe in the middle of a path and then record a path from that point; the starting keyframe of the newly recorded path corresponds to the position of the layer in the last keyframe.

Triggering Behaviors in Timelines

Adding a behavior to a timeline is similar to adding behaviors to any object on a Web page. Because timelines are written in JavaScript, they behave exactly the same as any object enhanced with JavaScript.

You use the Behavior channel section of the Timelines Inspector to work with behaviors in timelines.

You can attach a behavior to a timeline in four ways:

- ✦ Highlight the frame in which you wish to have the behavior and then right-click (Control+click). Select Add Behavior from the shortcut menu.
- ✦ Highlight the frame in which you want to activate the behavior and choose Modify ➪ Add Behavior to Timeline.
- ✦ Open the Behavior Inspector and click the frame you wish to modify in the Behavior channel.
- ✦ Double-click the frame for which you want to add a behavior in the Behavior channel.

After a behavior is attached to a frame and you open the Behavior Inspector, you see that the event inserted in the Events pane is related to a frame number — for example, `onFrame20`. Each frame can trigger multiple actions.

For more specifics about Dreamweaver behaviors, see Chapter 19 and Chapter 20.

Behaviors are essential to timelines. Without these elements, you cannot play or stop your timeline-based animations. Even when you select the Autoplay or Loop options in the Timelines Inspector, you are enabling a behavior. The three behaviors always deployed for timelines are Play Timeline, Stop Timeline, and Go to Timeline Frame.

If you are not using the Autoplay feature for your timeline, you must explicitly attach a Play Timeline behavior to an interactive or another event on your Web page. For example, a timeline is typically set to start playing once a specific picture has loaded, if the user enters a value in a form's text box or — more frequently — when the user selects a Play button. You could use the Stop Timeline behavior to pause an animation temporarily.

To use the Play Timeline or Stop Timeline behavior, follow these steps:

1. In the Document window, select a tag, link, or image that you want to trigger the event.
2. Choose Window ⇨ Behaviors or select the Show Behavior button from the Launcher to open the Behavior Inspector.
3. In the Behavior Inspector, click the + (add) Action button, and from the pop-up menu choose either of the following methods:
   a. Timeline ⇨ Play Timeline to start a timeline.
   b. Timeline ⇨ Stop Timeline to end a timeline.
4. In the Play Timeline or Stop Timeline dialog box (see Figure 29-9), choose the timeline that you want to play (or stop) from the appropriate Timeline drop-down list.

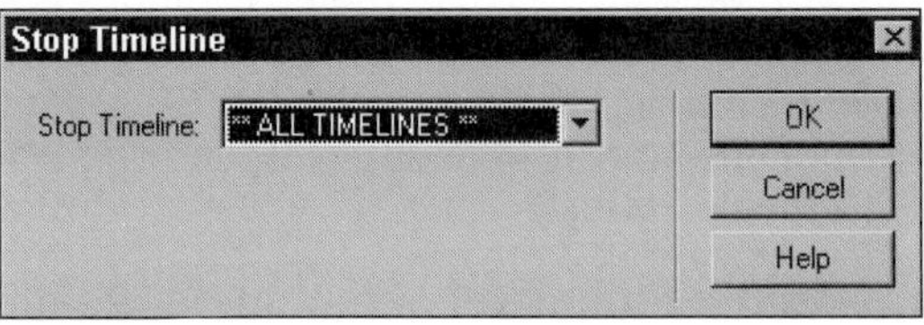

Figure 29-9: You can use the Stop Timeline behavior to stop all timelines or a specific timeline.

5. Click OK when you are finished.
6. Select an event to trigger the behavior from the drop-down menu in the Events column.

When you select the option to loop your timeline, Dreamweaver automatically inserts a Go to Frame behavior — with the first frame set as the target. You can display any frame on your timeline by inserting the Go to Frame behavior manually. To use the Go to Frame behavior, follow these steps:

1. In the Document window, select a tag, link, or image that you want to have trigger the event.
2. Choose Window ➪ Behaviors or select the Show Behavior button from the Launcher to open the Behavior Inspector.
3. In the Behavior Inspector, select the + (add) Action button and choose Timeline ➪ Go to Timeline Frame from the drop-down list.
4. Choose the timeline you want to affect from the Timeline drop-down menu.
5. Enter the frame number in the Go to Frame text box.
6. If you'd like the timeline to loop a set number of times, enter a value in the Loop text box. Click OK when you are finished.

   Remember, if you don't enter a value, the timeline loops endlessly.

Depending on the type of effect desired, you may want to use two of the Timeline behaviors together. To ensure that your timeline always starts from the same point, first attach a Go to Timeline Frame behavior to the event and then attach the Play Timeline behavior to the same event.

Dreamweaver Technique: Creating a Multiscreen Slideshow

Moving layers around the screen is pretty cool, but you've probably already figured out that you can do a lot more with timelines. One of the possibilities is a graphics slideshow displaying a rotating series of pictures. To demonstrate the range of potential available to timelines, the following sample project shows you how to construct a slideshow with more than one screen, complete with moving layers and triggered behaviors.

This technique has four steps:

1. **Prepare the graphic elements.** The process is easier if you have most (if not all) of your images for the slideshow — as well as the control interface — ready to go.
2. **Create the slideshow timeline.** In this project, one timeline is devoted to rotating images on four different "screens."
3. **Create the moving layers timeline.** The slideshow begins and ends with a bit of flair, as the screens fly in and fly out.

4. **Add the behaviors.** The slideshow includes controls for playing, pausing, restarting, and ending the slideshow, which then takes the user to another Web page.

This technique is intended to act as a basis for your own creations, not as an end in itself. You can add many variations and refinements; for example, you can preload images, make rollover buttons, and add music to the background. Following is a fundamental structure focused on the use of timelines, which you can expand with additional objects as needed.

The end result of this Dreamweaver Technique can be viewed only by 4.0 browsers or later.

Step 1: Preparing the graphic elements

Using a timeline for a slideshow presentation has only one restriction, but the qualification is significant — all the graphics in one "screen" must have the same dimensions. The timeline doesn't actually change the image tag; it only changes the file source for the tag. Thus, the height and width of the last image inserted overrides all the values for the foregoing graphics.

Luckily, all major image-processing software can resize and extend the canvas of a picture with little effort. When creating a slideshow, you may find it useful to do all of the resizing work at one time. Load in your images with the greatest width and height — they may or may not be the same picture — and use these measurements as your common denominators for all graphics.

Go ahead and create your interface buttons earlier rather than later. Experience shows that the more design elements you prepare ahead of time, the less adjusting you have to do later. Also, activating a timeline with a behavior is a straightforward process, and a finished interface enables you to incorporate the buttons quickly.

Finally, you should create and place the layers you want to use. The sample Web page in this technique is built of four screens, all of the same dimensions. The four different layers are uniquely named, but they all have the same size.

If you are making multiple versions of the same layer, consider changing the default layer size to fit your design. Choose Edit ➪ Preferences and open the default Layers preferences. Once you've customized the height and width values, all the layers incorporated in the Web page with the Insert ➪ Layer command automatically size correctly. You only have to position these layers.

To recap, use the following steps to prepare your graphics:

1. Create all the images to be used as slides. All the slides must be the same height and width.

2. Prepare and place your interface buttons.

3. Create the number of layers that you need for the different screens in the slideshow.
4. Position your layers so that each can hold a different slide. The preceding example has four layers, centered on the screen in two rows.
5. Insert your opening slides into each of the layers.

Your opening slide doesn't have to be a graphic image. You could also use a solid-colored GIF or a slide with text.

Try to work backward from a final design whenever layer positioning is involved. At this stage, all of the elements are in their final placement, ready for the slideshow to begin (see Figure 29-10). Next, you can activate the slideshow.

Figure 29-10: Before activating any layers or setting up the slideshow, design the layout.

Step 2: Creating the slideshow timeline

For all the attention that timelines and layers receive, you may be surprised that one of the best features of Dreamweaver timelines has nothing to do with layers. You can use timelines to change images anywhere on your Web page — whether or not they are in layers. As explained in Step 1, the timeline doesn't actually replace one `<img>` tag with another, but rather alters an image by swapping the src attribute value.

The src attribute changes just as changes in a layer's position, shape, or depth must happen at a keyframe.

In planning your slideshow, you need to decide how often a new slide appears, because you need to set keyframes at each of these points. If you are changing your slides every few seconds, you can change the frame rate to 1 fps. This setting helps you easily keep track of how many seconds occur between each slide change (and because no animation is involved with this timeline, a rapid frame rate is irrelevant). Note, however, that on the timeline described previously in this chapter that involved moving layers, the frame rate should be maintained at around 15 fps. Each timeline can have its own frame rate.

The only other choices involve the Autoplay and Loop options. As with frame rate, you can set each timeline to its own options without interfering with another timeline. This example has the slideshow loop but does not start automatically. Use the Play button to enable the user to start the show. But first, let's add the images to the slides.

To put images into a slideshow on a timeline, follow these steps:

1. Choose Window ➪ Timelines or select the Show Timelines button from the Launcher to open the Timelines Inspector.
2. If desired, rename Timeline1 by selecting the name and typing your own unique name.
3. Select one image from those onscreen in the positioned layers and drag the graphic to the Timelines Inspector.

Be sure to grab the image, not the layer.

4. Release the animation bar at the beginning of the timeline.
5. Repeat Steps 3 and 4 for each image until all images are represented on the timeline.
6. Change the frame rate by entering a new value in the Fps text box. This example changes the frame rate to 1.
7. Select the Loop or Autoplay options, if desired.
8. On one of the animation bars representing images, select the frame for a keyframe.
9. Choose Modify ➪ Timeline ➪ Add Keyframe, or right-click (Control+click) the frame on the timeline and choose Add Keyframe from the shortcut menu.
10. In the Image Property Inspector, select the Src folder to locate the graphic file for the next slide image.
11. Repeat Steps 9 and 10 until every animation bar has keyframes for every slide change and each keyframe has a new or different image assigned.

This example changes slides every five seconds, as you can see in Figure 29-11 by looking at the keyframe placement. Although the slideshow has all four images changing simultaneously, you can also stagger the timing of the image changes. Simply drag one or more of the animation bars a few frames forward or backward after the keyframes have been set.

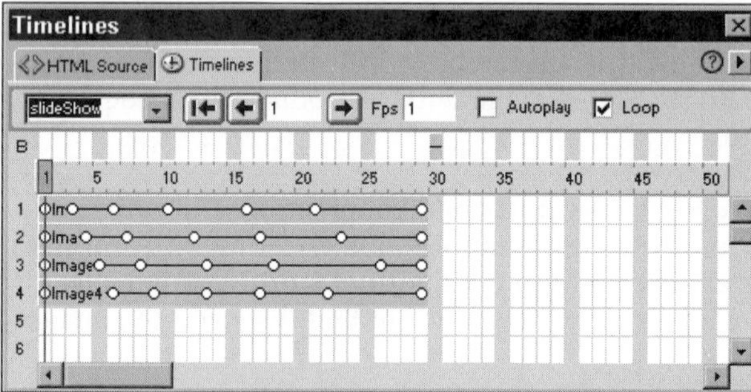

Figure 29-11: Each keyframe on each animation bar signals a change of the slide image.

To preview your slide changes, you don't have to go outside of Dreamweaver. Just click and hold down the Play button on the Timelines Inspector.

Step 3: Creating the moving layers timeline

At this stage, the slideshow is functional but a little dull. To add a bit of showmanship, you can "fly in" the layers from different areas of the Web page to their final destination. This task is easy — to complete the effect, the layers "fly out" when the user is ready to leave.

You can achieve these fly-in/fly-out effects in several ways. You can put the opening fly-in on one timeline and the ending fly-out on another. A more concise method combines the fly-in and fly-out for each layer on one timeline — separating them with a Stop Timeline behavior. After the fly-in portion happens when the page has loaded (because the example selects the Autoplay option for this timeline), the fly-out section does not begin to play until signaled to continue with the Play Timeline behavior.

To create the moving layers' opening and closing for the slideshow, follow these steps:

1. Choose Modify ➪ Timeline ➪ Add Timeline, or right-click (Ctrl+click) the Timelines Inspector and choose Add Timeline from the shortcut menu.

2. Rename your new timeline if desired.
3. Select the Autoplay checkbox so that this timeline begins playing automatically when the Web page is loaded.
4. Select any one of the layers surrounding your images and drag it onto the Timelines Inspector.

This time, make sure you move the layers — not the images.

5. To set the amount of time for the fly-in section to span, drag the final keyframe of the animation bar to a new frame. The example sets the end at 30 frames, which at 15 fps lasts two seconds.
6. From the Document window, select the same layer again and drag it to the Timelines Inspector. Place it directly after the first animation bar. This animation bar becomes the fly-out portion.
7. Drag the final keyframe to extend the time, if desired.
8. At this point, all four keyframes — two for each animation bar — have exactly the same information. Now change the positions for two keyframes to enable the layer to move. Select the first keyframe in the opening animation bar.
9. Reposition the layer so that it is offscreen. Although you can complete this task manually to the right or bottom of the screen by dragging the layer to a new location, you can also use the Layer Property Inspector to input new values directly for the Left and Top attributes.

Use negative numbers to move a layer offscreen to the left or top of the browser window.

10. From the Timelines Inspector, select the last keyframe of the closing animation bar.
11. Reposition the layer offscreen. If you want the layer to return in the same manner as it arrived, enter the same values for the Left and Top attributes as in the first keyframe of the opening animation bar.
12. Repeat Steps 4 through 11 for every layer.

Now, when you preview this timeline, the layers fly in and immediately fly out again. Figure 29-12 shows the layers in the example in mid-animation. In the final phase of the technique, you add behaviors to put the action under user control.

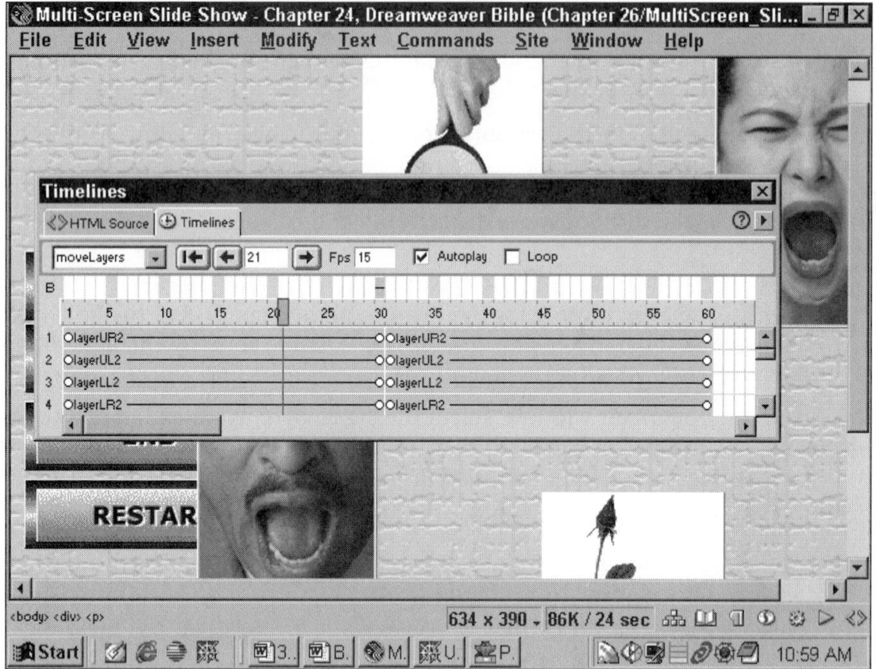

Figure 29-12: You can use two animation bars side by side to achieve a back-and-forth effect.

Step 4: Adding the behaviors

Although it may be fun to watch an unexpected effect take place, giving the user control over aspects of a presentation is much more involving — for the designer as well as the user. The example is ready to incorporate the user-interaction aspect by attaching Dreamweaver behaviors to the user interface and to the Behavior channel of the Timelines Inspector.

Two timeline behaviors have already been attached to the example. When the Loop option is selected in Step 2 for the slideshow timeline, Dreamweaver automatically includes a Go to Timeline Frame behavior after the final frame that sends the timeline back to the first frame. In the moving layers timeline, enabling the Autostart option causes Dreamweaver to attach a Play Timeline behavior to the `onLoad` event of the Web page's `<body>` tag. To complete the project, five behaviors need to be added.

First, you need a behavior to stop the moving layers from proceeding after the fly-in portion of the animation:

1. From the Timelines Inspector, double-click the final frame of the first animation bar in the Behavior channel.
2. In the Behavior Inspector, select Timeline ⇨ Stop Timeline from the + (add) Actions pull-down menu.
3. From the Stop Timeline dialog box, select the timeline that contains the moving layers.
4. Click OK. An `onFrame` event is set for the Stop Timeline action by default.

Second, you need a behavior to enable the user to begin playing the slideshow:

1. In the Document window, select the Play button.
2. In the Behavior Inspector, select the Timeline ⇨ Play Timeline action from the + (add) Action drop-down list.
3. In the Play Timeline dialog box, choose the timeline representing the slideshow.
4. Click OK. An `onMouseDown` event is set to trigger the action by default.

The next behavior enables the user to stop the slideshow temporarily:

1. In the Document window, select the Pause button.
2. In the Behavior Inspector, select Timeline ⇨ Stop Timeline from the + (add) Actions drop-down list.
3. Choose the layer representing the slideshow in the Stop Timeline dialog box.
4. Click OK. An `onMouseDown` event is set to trigger the action by default.

To enable the user to begin the slideshow from the beginning, follow these steps:

1. In the Document window, select the Restart button.
2. In the Behavior Inspector, add the Timeline ⇨ Go to Timeline Frame action.
3. In the Go to Timeline Frame dialog box, choose the layer representing the slideshow.
4. Enter a 1 in the Frame text box.
5. Click OK. An `onMouseDown` event is set to trigger the action by default.
6. Add the next action. In the Behavior Inspector, select Timeline ⇨ Play Timeline from the + (add) Action drop-down list.

7. In the Play Timeline dialog box, choose the layer representing the slideshow.
8. Click OK. An `onMouseDown` event is attached to the action by default.

To end the presentation and move the user on to the next Web page, follow these steps:

1. In the Document window, select the End button.
2. In the Behavior Inspector, select the Timeline ➪ Play Timeline action from the + (add) Action drop-down list.
3. Choose the timeline representing the moving layers in the Play Timeline dialog box and click OK. The timeline begins playing where it last stopped—just before the layers are about to fly out. An `onMouseDown` event is set to trigger the action by default.
4. Add the next behavior. Select the Go to URL action from the + (add) drop-down list.
5. In the Go to URL dialog box, enter the path to the new page in the URL text box or select the Browse (Choose) button to locate the file. Click OK when you are finished.

The project is complete and ready to test. Feel free to experiment, trying out different timings to achieve different effects.

You can test the final working version by using your browser to view the Multiscreen Slideshow Demo in the *Dreamweaver 3 Bible, Gold Edition* Code section of CD-ROM 1 that accompanies this book.

Summary

Timelines are effective tools for developing pages in which events need to be triggered at specific points in time.

- ✦ Timelines can affect particular attributes of layers and images, or they can start any Dreamweaver behavior.
- ✦ Use the Timelines Inspector to set an animation to play automatically, to have it loop indefinitely, and to change the frames-per-second display rate of the timeline.
- ✦ You must use one of the timeline behaviors to activate your timeline if you don't use the Autoplay feature.

In the next chapter, you learn how you can use Dreamweaver to explore the brave new world of XML, the Extensible Markup Language.

✦ ✦ ✦

Creating Next-Generation Code with Dreamweaver

P A R T

VII

✦ ✦ ✦ ✦

In This Part

✦ ✦ ✦ ✦

CHAPTER 30

Extending with XML

✦ ✦ ✦ ✦

In This Chapter

Exploring the basics of XML

Exporting XML from templates

Importing XML into Dreamweaver

✦ ✦ ✦ ✦

XML, short for Extensible Markup Language, is quickly becoming a powerful force on the Web and an important technology for Web designers to master. XML enables the parts of any document — from Web page to invoice — to be defined in terms of how those parts are used. When a document is defined by its structure rather than its appearance, as it is with HTML, the same document can be read by a wide variety of systems and put to use far more efficiently.

Dreamweaver adds *Roundtrip XML* as a complement to its Roundtrip HTML core philosophy. Roundtrip HTML ensures that the defined tags of HTML remain just as you've written them. With XML, no one defined set of tags exists — XML tags can be written for an industry, a company, or just a Web site. Roundtrip XML permits Web designers to export and import XML pages based on their own structure.

You can find XML all throughout Dreamweaver, just under the hood. The Design Notes feature is based on XML, as is the completely customizable menu system and even the HTML Styles feature. The Third-party Tags file is pure XML and can describe any kind of tag. In fact, XML can be used to describe most anything, even HTML. This chapter explores the basics of XML, as well as the implementation of Roundtrip XML in Dreamweaver.

Understanding XML

XML is to structure what Cascading Style Sheets (CSS) are to format. While CSS control the look of a particular document on the Web, XML makes the document's intent paramount. Because there are almost as many ways to describe the parts of documents as there are types of documents, a set language, such as HTML, could never provide enough specification to be truly useful. This is why, with XML, you create your own custom tags to describe the page—XML is truly an extensible language.

XML became a W3C Recommendation in February 1998, after a relatively brief two-year study. The speed with which the recommendation was approved speaks to the need for the technology. XML has been described as a more accessible version of SGML (Standard Generalized Markup Language), the widely used text processing standard. In fact, the XML Working Group that drafted the W3C Recommendation started out as the SGML Working Group.

What can XML do that HTML can't? Let's say you have a shipping order that you want to distribute. With HTML, each of the parts of the document—such as the billing address, the shipping address, and the order details, to name a few—are enclosed in tags that describe their appearance, like this:

```
<h2 align="center"><bold>Invoice</bold></h2>
<p align="left">Ship to:</p>
<p>J. Lowery<br>
101 101st Avenue, Ste. 101<br>
New York, NY 10000</p>
```

With XML, each section of the page is given its own set of tags, according to its meaning, like this:

```
<documentType>Invoice</documentType>
<ship-toHeader>Ship to:</ship-toHeader>
<customer>J. Lowery<br></customer>
<ship-toAddress>101 101st Avenue, Ste. 101<br>
New York, NY 10000</ship-toAddress>
```

Like HTML, XML is a combination of content and markup tags. Markup tags can be in pairs, such as `<customer>...</customer>`, or they can be singular. A single tag is called an *empty tag* because no content is included. Single tags in XML must include an ending slash—as in `<noTax/>`, for example—and are used to mark where something occurs. Here, `<noTax/>` indicates that no sales tax is to be applied to this invoice.

XML tags, again like HTML, can also include attributes and values. As with HTML, XML attributes further describe the tag, much like an adjective describes a noun. For example, another way to write the `<ship-toHeader>` tag would be

```
<header type="Ship To">
```

With a more generalized tag such as this one, you could easily change values, as in <header type="Bill To">, rather than include another new tag.

In all, XML recognizes six kinds of markup:

✦ **Elements:** Elements are more commonly known as *tags* and, as in HTML, are delimited by a set of angle brackets <>. As noted previously, elements can also have attributes set to particular values.

While surrounding values with quotes—such as in color="white"—is optional in HTML, it's mandatory in XML.

✦ **Entity References:** Certain characters in XML, such as the delimiting angle brackets, are reserved in order to permit markup to be recognized. These characters are represented by entities in XML. As in HTML, character entities begin with an ampersand and end with a semicolon. For example <Content> is XML code to represent <Content>.

✦ **Comments:** XML comments are identical to HTML comments; they both begin with <!-- and end with -->.

✦ **Processing instructions:** XML processing instructions are similar to server-side includes in that the XML processor (like the server) passes them on to the application (like the browser).

✦ **Marked sections:** XML can pass blocks of code or other data without parsing the markup and content. These blocks of character data are marked with <![CDATA[at the beginning and]]> at the end. For example:

```
<![CDATA[If age < 19 and age > 6, then the kids are in ¬
school]]>
```

Communication between XML and HTML is greatly eased because large blocks of data can be passed in this fashion.

✦ **Document type declarations:** Because every XML document is capable of containing its own set of custom tags, a method for defining these tags must exist. While a discussion of the formats of such document type declarations is beyond the scope of this book, it's helpful to know that such declarations can be made for elements, attributes, character entities, and notations. Notations refer to external binary data, such as GIFs, that are passed through the XML parser to the application.

XML documents may begin with an XML declaration that specifies the version of XML being used. The XML declaration for a document compliant with the 1.0 specification looks like the following:

```
<?xml version="1.0"?>
```

A much more detailed document type declaration (DTD), in which each tag and attribute is described in SGML, is also possible. XML documents including these types of DTDs are labeled *valid XML documents*. Other documents that respect the rules of XML regarding nesting of tags and other matters, but don't include DTDs for the elements, are known as *well-formed XML*. Dreamweaver exports well-formed XML documents but can import either well-formed or valid XML.

Exporting XML

How do you make an XML page? In Dreamweaver, you can convert an existing document into XML format with one command. Currently, Dreamweaver creates its XML pages based on a template's editable regions. With this approach, the true content of a page — what distinguishes it from all other pages of the same type — can be separated and applied independently of the original Web page. In other words, once the XML information is culled from a Web page, it can be imported into any other application to be displayed, read, spoken, translated, or acted upon.

Dreamweaver templates are composed of locked and editable regions; the locked regions are repeated for each page created from the template, while the content in the editable regions is added per page. The connection between XML and templates is similar to the relationship between a database form and its data. In a database, each field has a unique name, such as LastName, FirstName, and so on. When you create a database form to present the data, the placeholders for the data use the same field names. Then, when data from one record flows into the form, the information from the field goes into the areas with the corresponding field names. Likewise, each editable region has a unique name — in essence, a field name. The content within the editable region is the field's data. When exported as an XML file, the name of the editable region is converted to an XML tag that surrounds its data.

For example, Figure 30-1 shows a Dreamweaver template for a purchase order. On the left are the headings (To, Company, Address, and so on) for the information in a locked area, while the specific shipping data on the right resides in a series of editable regions, each with its own name.

When exported as XML by Dreamweaver, the resulting XML file looks like the following:

```
<?xml version="1.0"?>
<doctitle><![CDATA[<title>Purchase Order</title>]]></doctitle>
<Customer><![CDATA[Jose Bleau]]></Customer>
<Company><![CDATA[Kreamhorn, Inc. ]]></Company>
<Address><![CDATA[155 Somerton Ave.<br>
                  West Therea, TX]]></Address>
<PO_Date><![CDATA[January 2, 1999]]></PO_Date>
<Ship_Via><![CDATA[FedEx]]></Ship_Via>
```

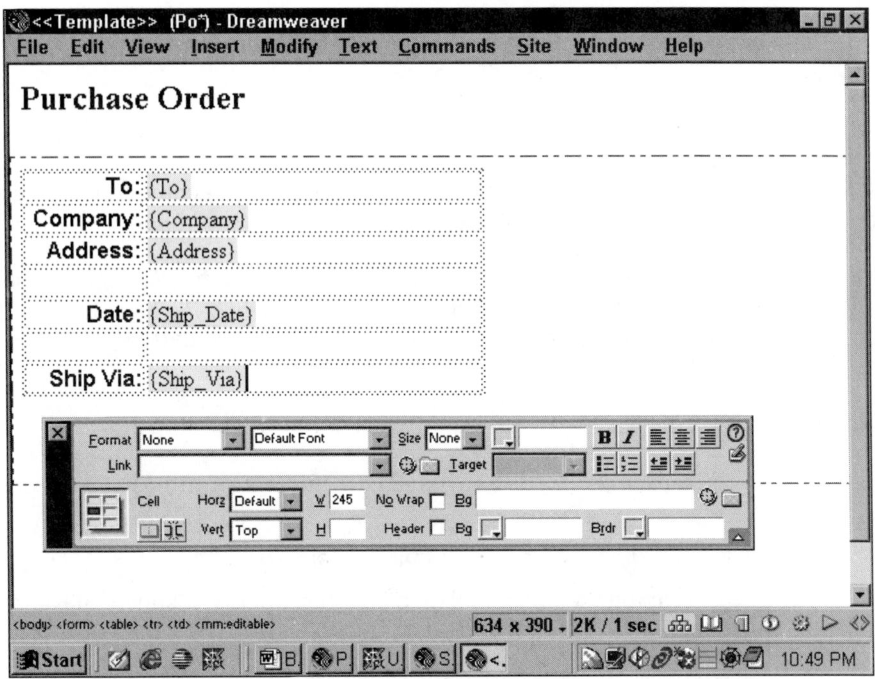

Figure 30-1: Dreamweaver 3 creates XML pages based on templates and editable regions.

To get a better idea of how to use XML, you need to understand Dreamweaver templates. Learn about Dreamweaver templates in Chapter 33.

Note several important items about the XML file. First, notice the use of self-evident labels for each of the tags, such as `<Customer>` and `<Ship_Via>`; such names make it easy to understand an XML file. Even the one tag not based on a user-defined name, `<doctitle>` is straightforward. Second, all the data included in the XML tags is marked as a `CDATA` area; this ensures that the information is conveyed intact, just as it was entered. Finally, if you look at the `<Address>` tag data, you see that even HTML tags (here, a `<br>` tag) are included in the `CDATA` blocks. This practice enables basic formatting to be carried over from one page to the next. You can avoid this by selecting just the inner content — without any of the formatting tags — to be marked as an editable region.

Dreamweaver can create one of two different types of XML tags during its export operation. The first is referred to as *Dreamweaver Standard XML* and uses an `<item>` tag with a name attribute set to the editable region's name. For example, if the editable region was named Ship_Via, the Dreamweaver Standard tag would be

```
<item name="Ship_Via">Content</item>
```

The Dreamweaver Standard XML file has one other distinguishing characteristic. The XML file is saved with a reference to the defining Dreamweaver template, like this:

```
<templateItems template="/Templates/PO.dwt">
```

When importing a Dreamweaver Standard XML file, if the specified template cannot be found, a dialog box appears asking that you select another template.

The other option is to use what Dreamweaver refers to as *Editable Region Name tags*. This method uses the editable region names themselves as tags. In the case of the editable region name Ship_Via, the tag pair under this method would be `<Ship_Via>...</Ship_Via>`.

To create an XML file from within Dreamweaver, follow these steps:

1. Open a Dreamweaver document based on a template that has at least one editable region.
2. Choose File ➪ Export ➪ Export Editable Regions As XML.

   The Export Editable Regions As XML dialog box opens, as shown in Figure 30-2.

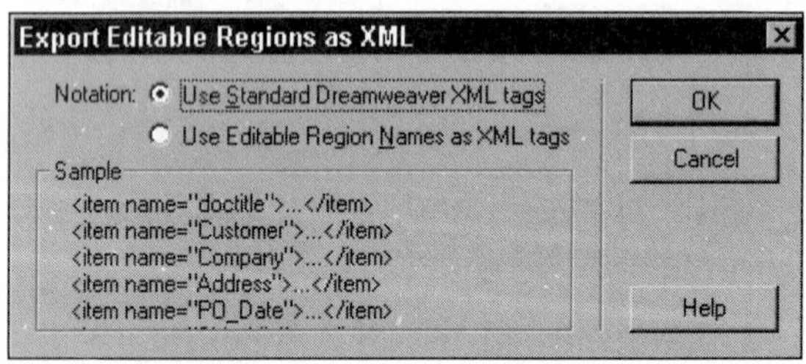

Figure 30-2: Convert any template-based page to an XML document with the Export Editable Regions As XML command.

3. Choose the format for the XML tags by selecting one of the Notation options:
   - **Use Standard Dreamweaver XML Tags:** Select this option to produce `<item>` tags with `name` attributes set to the names of the editable regions.
   - **Use Editable Region Names as XML Tags:** Select this option to produce XML tags that use the editable region names directly.

   Selecting either option displays sample tags in the preview area of the dialog box.

4. Select OK when you're done.

   An Export Editable Regions As XML Save File dialog box appears.

5. Enter the path and name of the XML file you wish to save in the File Name text box or select the Browse (Choose) button to locate another folder. Click Save when you're done.

Importing XML

As part of Roundtrip XML, Dreamweaver 3 includes an Import XML command. Like the Export XML command, Import XML works with Dreamweaver templates. The content information in the XML document fills out the editable regions in the template, much as data fills out a form in a database.

With this import capability, content can be independently created and stored in an XML file and then, to publish the page to the Web, simply imported into the Dreamweaver template.

To import an XML file into a Dreamweaver template, follow these steps:

1. If desired, open a file based on a Dreamweaver template.

You don't have to have a page created from a template open in order to access the XML information — Dreamweaver automatically opens one for you.

2. Choose File ➪ Import XML into Template.

   The Import XML dialog box opens.

Any existing information in the Dreamweaver document in the editable regions is replaced by the information in the corresponding tags of the XML document.

3. Select an XML file from the Import XML dialog box.

4. Choose Open when you're done.

The XML file is imported into Dreamweaver, and the editable region placeholder names are replaced with the data in the XML document.

Summary

XML is a vital future technology that is knocking on the door of virtually every Web designer in business. As the development tools become more common, the Roundtrip XML capability within Dreamweaver makes interfacing with this new method of communication straightforward and effortless. Keep the following points in mind about XML:

- XML (Extensible Markup Language) enables content to be separated from the style of a Web page, creating information that can be more easily used in various situations with different kinds of media.
- Tags in XML reflect the nature of the content, rather than its appearance.
- Dreamweaver includes a Roundtrip XML facility that makes it possible to export and import XML files through Dreamweaver templates.

In the next chapter, you learn how Dreamweaver can extend the multimedia reach of your Web pages through custom objects developed with partners such as RealNetworks, IBM, and Live Picture.

✦ ✦ ✦

CHAPTER 31

Adding Multimedia Extensions

✦ ✦ ✦ ✦

In This Chapter

Building streaming multimedia presentations with SMIL

Creating interactive advertising banners with HotMedia

Using next-generation imaging software from Live Picture

✦ ✦ ✦ ✦

Dreamweaver has become the Web authoring tool of choice among many professionals — especially those designers responsible for building cutting-edge sites. Not only does Dreamweaver integrate well with other hot Web technologies from Macromedia — such as Shockwave and Flash — but also Dreamweaver's extensibility makes it possible to create custom objects for other emerging media. Dreamweaver maintains partnerships with RealNetworks, IBM, and Live Picture that extend Dreamweaver's capabilities into several exciting new areas.

Integrating new technologies into a Web site is far from a no-brainer. Before a Web designer can commit to using any non-standard component — that is, anything not accessible by the basic browser — the market for the Web site must be evaluated. Some Web site audiences follow every trend and always have the latest in browser versions and plug-ins — a crowd such as this is ready for anything new. Other markets are more conservative, and only the most generic Web sites need apply. The general Web audiences are somewhere in between, with pockets of intranets where a particular plug-in is a given.

In this chapter, you explore some of the newest of the new media and learn how Dreamweaver eases the learning curve of adopting a new technology. The first part of the chapter covers streaming multimedia presentations from RealNetworks using the W3C recommendation SMIL to integrate RealVideo, RealAudio, and other Real media types. Next, you see how IBM is integrating multimedia into Web advertising with the HotMedia technology. This chapter also covers a method from

Live Picture for enabling Web browsers to zoom into photographs to reveal astounding detail. No doubt about it: If you're looking for the multimedia edge, you can find it in Dreamweaver.

Understanding SMIL

SMIL, which stands for Synchronized Multimedia Integration Language, truly puts the "multi" back in "multimedia." This new standardized language, developed by the W3C, is used when several streaming media types — video, audio, animation, text, or straight graphics — are displayed in one presentation. SMIL (pronounced "smile") uses a simple markup similar to HTML to coordinate the final display.

RealNetworks is best known for their pioneering efforts in the field of streaming media, primarily audio and video. The latest version of their player, the Real G2 (for Generation 2) Player, can handle far more than single RealVideo or RealAudio files, however. Through SMIL, the RealPlayer G2 plays multiple media streams — whether two or more videos or a video and an audio track. Moreover, additional media types can be integrated into a SMIL presentation:

✦ **RealFlash:** Animated movies in the form of Flash files, synchronized with a RealAudio file and played from a RealServer.

✦ **RealText:** Streaming text files used to create low-bandwidth credits, ticker tapes, or other text-based displays.

✦ **RealPix:** Slideshows of high-quality JPEG photographs, with programmable transitions.

✦ **MP3:** High-quality streaming audio files, widely available on the Web.

The RealSystem G2 objects for Dreamweaver include an object for each of these media types as well as for inserting a completed SMIL presentation. QuickTime 4.1 also supports SMIL.

Streaming audio and video are now mainstays of the Web. To learn more about streaming video, see Chapter 23, and for details on streaming audio, see Chapter 24.

Creating SMIL presentations

Although detailing how you script an entire presentation is beyond the scope of this book, it's interesting to see how the SMIL code works. As with HTML, SMIL is composed of a series of tags with varying attributes — a SMIL document, too, is a text-based file. The basic tag pair is <smil>...</smil>, which forms the shell for any SMIL file. For example, a complete SMIL presentation that displays three streaming audios, one after the other, looks like this:

```
<smil>
  <body>
    <audio src="rtsp://realserver.company.com/one.ra"/>
    <audio src="rtsp://realserver.company.com/two.ra"/>
    <audio src="rtsp://realserver.company.com/three.ra"/>
  </body>
</smil>
```

Note

The rtsp:// prefix seen in the previous example replaces the pnm:// prefix used by RealServer systems before the G2 player was introduced. RTSP is short for Real-Time Streaming Protocol and is a standard adopted by QuickTime as well as G2.

SMIL files can have both <head> and <body> sections, but the <head> section isn't required, unlike in an HTML document. If present, the <head> section is generally used to display information in the RealPlayer, such as creator or copyright information. All tags and attributes are entered in lowercase, although the attribute values, enclosed in double quotes, can be mixed case. Not all SMIL tags come in pairs. As with XML, single SMIL tags, such as <audio> or <video>, end with a forward slash before the closing angle bracket, like this:

```
<video src="video/highlights.rm"/>
```

The src attribute for any media type can be either absolute or relative, as with HTML. Other similarities to HTML include using the same type of comment in SMIL (<!-- -->) as well as identical character entities for special characters such as the quote ("), apostrophe ('), ampersand (&), and left (<) and right (>) angle brackets.

If playing different media in sequence were all that SMIL did, it wouldn't be so exciting. What makes SMIL really shine is its capability to play different media streams at the same time and to synchronize them. To play different media streams simultaneously, use the parallel tag pair, <par>...</par>, as follows:

```
<par>
  <video src="videos/newsong.rm"/>
  <textstream src="lyrics/newsong.rt"/>
</par>
```

In this example, the RealVideo file and the RealText file play together or in parallel. You can also play media in sequence and in parallel in the same presentation. To specify a sequence, use the <seq>...</seq> tag pair. In this example, after the first clip plays, the second and third play at the same time — and when they end, the fourth clip plays:

```
<seq>
    clip 1
    <par>
      clip 2
      clip 3
    </par>
    clip 4
</seq>
```

Synchronizing a parallel presentation can be handled in several ways. You can force all clips in a <par> group to end when one finishes or when they all do. You can also cause them all to stop after a certain time interval. If you wanted to end playback of a streaming audio file when the streaming text file ends, your code might look like this:

```
<par endsync="id(vid)">
  <video id="vid" src="videos/newsong.rm"/>
  <textstream src="lyrics/newsong.rt"/>
</par>
```

The actual presentation could resemble the SMIL screen shown in Figure 31-1.

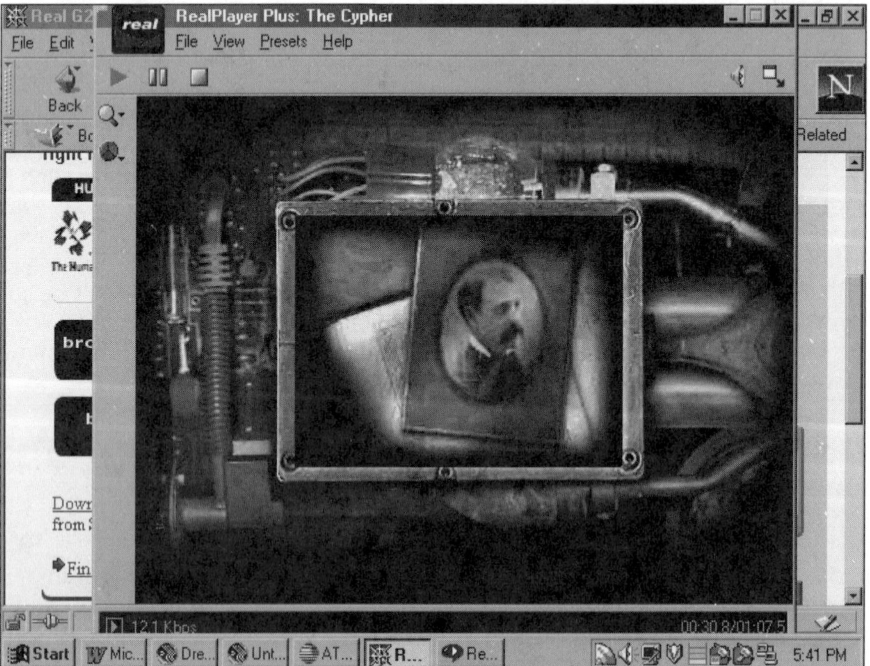

Figure 31-1: SMIL presentations, like any other RealPlayer-supported file, can be shown in a separate player or embedded in the page, as in this example.

The endsync attribute is set to the ID for the streaming video file, vid. Note that the id attribute is used in the `<video>` tag, much like JavaScript uses the name attribute.

Suffice it to say that SMIL is a full-featured language. To learn more about the intricacies of SMIL, visit the Developer Center on RealNetwork's Web site (`www.real.com`) or the Just SMIL Web site (`www.justsmil.com`).

Using the Real G2 objects

In addition to the RealAudio, RealVideo, and control panel control objects (covered in Chapters 23 and 24), the RealSystem G2 objects for Dreamweaver 3 make it easy to insert RealFlash, RealPix, RealText, and SMIL files. Inserting the objects is straightforward—you only need to know the name of the file you're inserting and its dimensions. Currently, SMIL documents themselves must be created by hand, but once that's done, you can easily integrate them into your Dreamweaver pages.

Want to try out the RealSystem G2 objects, but didn't get Dreamweaver yet? No problem—you can find the newest version of the Real objects on the Dreamweaver Web site in the Extensions section (`www.macromedia.com/software/dreamweaver/download/extensions`).

The RealText, RealFlash, and RealPix objects function in exactly the same manner. To insert one of these types of RealSystem objects, follow these steps:

1. Choose Insert ➪ RealSystem G2 Object and select either RealText, RealFlash, or RealPix—or select the desired object from the RealSystem G2 panel of the Objects palette.

Make sure you save your file before beginning to insert any of the RealSystem G2 objects. Otherwise, a system alert reminds you, and you cannot proceed until you do so.

   The appropriate RealSystem dialog box opens. Figure 31-2 shows the Insert RealText dialog box.

2. Enter the source file by choosing one of the following radio buttons:
   - **Local File:** Enter the path name of a file found on the local system in the Local File text box or click the Browse (Choose) button to locate the file.
   - **URL:** Enter the absolute address of a file located on the Internet in the URL text box. The example address, `rtsp://g2home.real.com/install/welcome.rm`, is displayed beneath the URL text box.
3. Enter the dimensions of the RealSystem file in the Width and Height text boxes.

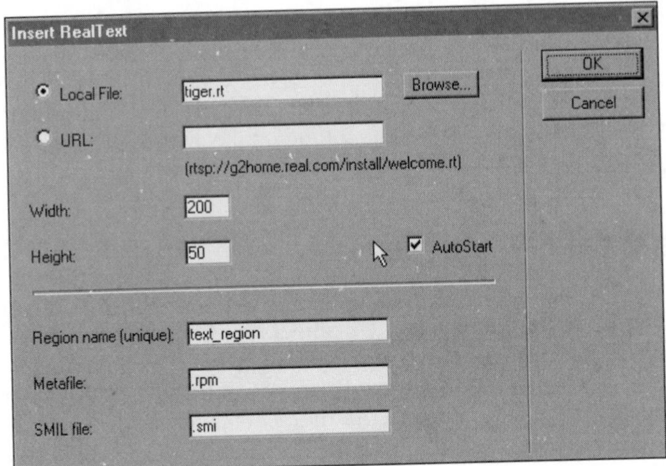

Figure 31-2: The RealSystem objects use simple interfaces such as this Insert RealText dialog box to insert a variety of streaming media types.

Both the RealFlash and RealPix objects suggest dimensions of 320 pixels wide by 240 pixels high; the RealText object uses 200 pixels by 30 pixels as its base. Keep in mind that these measurements are suggestions only and should be altered to reflect the actual size of the player you want to use.

4. If you don't want your file to begin playing automatically, deselect the AutoStart option.
5. The remaining text boxes, Region name, Metafile, and SMIL file, are automatically filled out. Alter any name by entering the modification in the text box.
6. Click OK when you're done.

As with RealAudio and RealVideo objects, these RealSystem objects create both a metafile and a SMIL presentation file. When selected by the user to play (or when playing automatically), the original file first calls the metafile, which in turn calls the SMIL file. By default, the RealVideo object is inserted with the controls set to the ImageWindow option, which shows only the RealVideo movie with no control panel. To incorporate a control panel into the video file, you need to first choose the Edit Parameters button from the Property Inspector. Next, change the `controls` attribute from imagewindow to one of the other options, such as All, ControlPanel, or PlayButton.

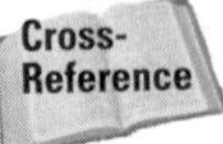

The control panel options — and their corresponding objects — are explained in detail in Chapter 23.

The SMIL object is just a tad different. Because you don't need one SMIL file to play another, only the additional metafile is created for the SMIL object. Otherwise, the procedure is the same: Insert the SMIL object and, in the dialog box, enter the name of the SMIL file or its URL and the dimensions of the player.

If you find that your Real media types are not playing correctly – or at all – check all the paths. The paths to the RealSystem G2 metafiles and SMIL files may need to be adjusted by hand in the code. This is especially true if the HTML page, or any metafile, is moved.

IBM HotMedia

The standard Web ad banner is, at most, an animated GIF linked to the promoter's home page. IBM has developed a Windows-only Java-based technology that significantly sharpens the cutting edge in interactive advertising. With IBM's HotMedia technology, a single ad banner can integrate all of the following:

- ✦ Animated GIFs
- ✦ Panning and scrolling images
- ✦ Multitrack animations
- ✦ 3D object movies
- ✦ Zoomable, multiresolution images
- ✦ Audio and video clips
- ✦ 360-degree panoramas

Unlike many other multimedia solutions, HotMedia requires no additional plug-ins or special server, but rather works with a series of compact Java players published from a standard HTTP server. Taking advantage of Java's inherent modularity, HotMedia delivers only the Java applet code and the source files necessary for the requested display. Moreover, the media itself — such as digitized video — is delivered progressively, in a fashion similar to streaming. Each separate media component can be triggered by mouse-click or set to occur automatically.

HotMedia features

The initial image in a HotMedia file is called a *thumbnail*. A thumbnail is a static image in either JPEG or GIF format. To attract interest to the graphic, HotMedia thumbnails are capable of several effects. The image can scroll from left to right, either smoothly or in frames. The scrolling effect can be set to play once, loop, or ping-pong (go to the end and play in reverse).

Perhaps the biggest innovation, however, is HotMedia's linking capability. Links can call other HotMedia files or jump to a standard Web page. Two different types of links are possible: *spatial* and *temporal*. A spatial link can be placed on objects in any image, panorama, animation, and video media, whereas a temporal link is associated with a specific time in a presentation, such as when an audio announcement says, "Click now!" The Web designer can decide whether or not to display the links as red rectangles.

HotMedia files are composed using IBM's HotMedia Assembly utility. The Assembly program, shown in Figure 31-3, combines output from other programs, such as image editors (for example, Adobe Photoshop or Macromedia's Fireworks) into one file that is saved with a .mvr extension. As of this writing, the current version of the Assembly utility (2.5) supports only the thumbnail and animation media—panorama, audio, and video are still to come.

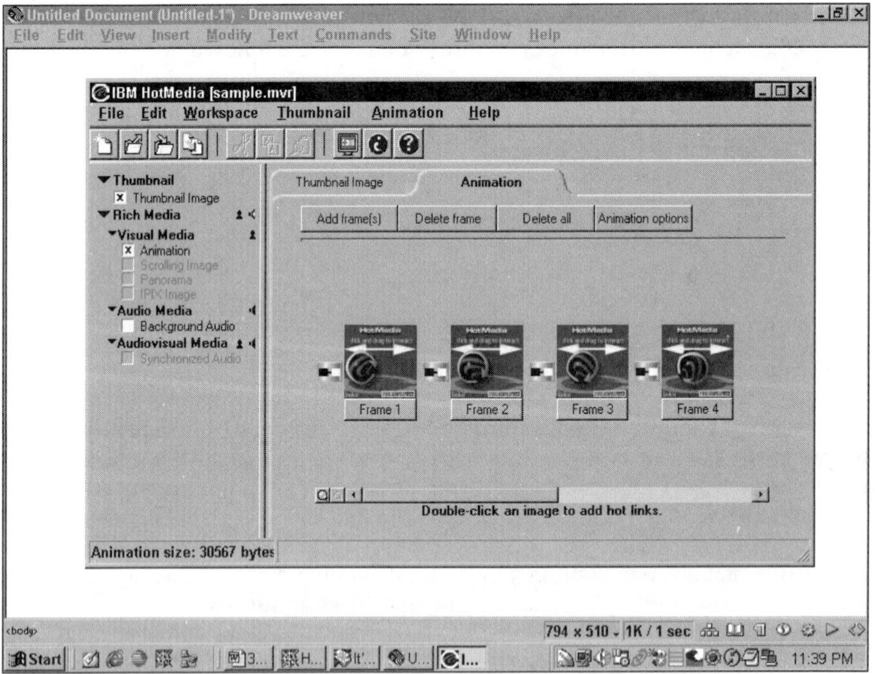

Figure 31-3: The IBM HotMedia Assembly utility combines numerous media types to create compelling interactive advertising.

Currently, the HotMedia Dreamweaver objects are available only for Windows systems; however, the completed files play back on any Java-enabled browser. The HotMedia Assembly program is also cross-platform.

Using the HotMedia object

IBM developed an object to insert the applet code for HotMedia files into your Dreamweaver pages. The HotMedia object is inserted into the Common panel of the Objects palette during the HotMedia installation. The HotMedia Assembly program, with sample files and documentation, is also installed.

Make sure you enable object dialog boxes before attempting to insert a HotMedia object. Otherwise, you get an error message indicating that a file was not chosen — with no option to choose one.

To insert a HotMedia published file, follow these steps:

1. Position your cursor where you'd like the HotMedia file to appear on your page and select the HotMedia object from the Common panel of the Objects palette.

   The Insert HotMediaPlayer dialog box, shown in Figure 31-4, appears.

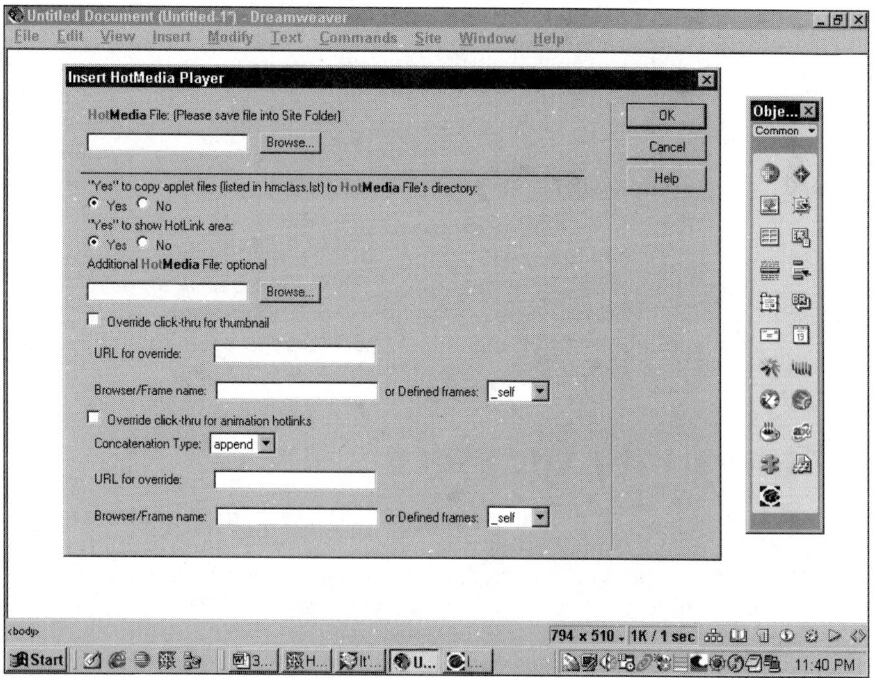

Figure 31-4: With the HotMedia object, you can specify alternative URLs — and even page-specific frames — or additional HotMedia files to link to.

2. Enter the path to the HotMedia file (with file extension .mvr) in the HotMedia File text box or select the Browse (Choose) button to locate the file.
3. To automatically copy the HotMedia .class files to the same directory as the selected file, leave the Copy Applet Files option set to Yes.
4. To display a red rectangle when the user's mouse passes over the defined link area, keep the Show HotLink Area option set to Yes.
5. Enter any additional HotMedia files you wish to link to in the Additional HotMedia File text box.
6. Generally, links are inserted into HotMedia files at authoring time. However, you can specify a different URL in two different locations — in the initial thumbnail image or during an animation:
    a. To insert a different link in the opening thumbnail image, select the Override click-thru for thumbnail image option and then enter the new link in the URL for override text box. If you'd like the URL to appear in a specific browser window or frame, enter its name in the Browser/Frame Name text box or choose one of the frame targets from the Defined Frames drop-down list.
    b. To insert a different link in an animated sequence, select the Override click-thru for animation hotlinks option and then enter the new link in the URL for override text box. If you'd like the URL to appear in a specific browser window or frame, enter its name in the Browser/Frame Name text box or choose one of the frame targets from the Defined Frames drop-down list.
7. Click OK when you're done.

If the browser cannot run the applet, the class files have probably not been found. When the HotMedia applet is selected in Dreamweaver, select the Code Folder icon and choose the HM.class file. This forces the Base value to update properly.

Zooming into Graphics

The standard for photographic images on the Web, the JPEG format, is great for depicting detailed images — but only as a single, flat view. If you try to magnify any JPEG photograph, you quickly find yourself faced with an incomprehensible series of blurred, blocky pixels, and panning anywhere on the image is just not possible. These limitations are not a factor when using technology from Live Picture. This company has developed software that enables users to zoom into photographs with amazing clarity and detail.

Whereas JPEG images with resolutions higher than 800×600 were formerly impractical for the Web because of the extremely large file size, now, using Live Picture's Zoom format, detailed images of 2,000×3,000 are just the beginning. Most important, the special photographic format can easily be inserted into your Web pages using their custom objects with Dreamweaver. The Live Picture technology uses server-side component, Image Server software, to power their enhanced imagery.

Integrating Zoom pictures with Live Picture

With Live Picture Zoom object, each image must be inserted into its own page and displayed independently or, more likely, in a frame as part of a frameset. When inserting the image, all you have to do is select the FlashPix-formatted file — the object does the rest. There are no additional parameters to specify. The control panel is automatically presented underneath the image, and the dimensions of the image are automatically calculated. The Zoom object also takes advantage of Dreamweaver's extensibility and works with a translator to display the JPEG version of the FlashPix image in Dreamweaver.

Note The current version of the Live Picture Zoom object supports zoomable photographs but does not yet support zoomable panoramas and 3D image objects.

Before you can insert a Zoom object file, you must install the Live Picture software. Double-click the `zoomobject` executable to begin the installation process. After following the step-by-step instructions, restart Dreamweaver. To preview the Live Picture file in Dreamweaver, you must first enable the translator. To do this, choose Edit ⇨ Preferences and select the Translator category. From the Translator panel, highlight the FlashPix image translator in the Translator list and then choose the In All Files option under Automatically Translate Server-Side Includes.

Inserting a Live Picture object is a straightforward process. Simply select the page or frame to insert your image in and position your cursor where you'd like the image to appear. Next, select the FlashPix button from the Common panel of the Objects palette. The standard Select Image dialog box appears. Select your .fpx file from the FPX Images folder or one of its subfolders and click OK when you're done. The JPEG preview image is displayed, with the Zoom control panel, in the Dreamweaver page.

Note To interact with the FlashPix file, you must view it through a browser reading the image from a Live Picture Server.

The Live Picture object doesn't insert a modified `<img>` tag like the OpenPix object does. Rather, it inserts a `<meta>` tag that calls the Live Picture Server to deliver the proper image. This is why each Live Picture file must be on its own page.

Once you've inserted the FlashPix file, you can modify its parameters by selecting it and using the custom Live Picture Property Inspector.

The Live Picture Property Inspector gives you access to the following options:

✦ **Filename:** The name of the FlashPix file. You can switch to a different file by selecting the folder icon and choosing a new image.

✦ **Server:** The domain name or IP address of the Live Picture Server to be used.

✦ **Port:** The server port used by the Live Picture Server. By default the port is set to 8087.

✦ **Width:** The width of the image to be displayed. The height is automatically calculated to maintain the proper aspect ratio. Changing the width rescales the final image and the preview image.

✦ **Relative-path:** The path to the selected image, including any folders or directories, on the Live Picture Server.

A known problem exists with early versions of the Live Picture object. When inserting the `<meta>` tag that calls the image, the URL encoding replaces the initial spaces with the Unix code for a space, %20. Check for new versions of the Live Picture object that corrects this problem at `www.livepicture.com/products/misc/dwzoom.html`.

Summary

As the Web strives for a richer media experience, more and more multimedia forms are developed. Dreamweaver's extensibility makes it perfectly adaptable to incorporate new technologies such as SMIL, HotMedia, OpenPix, and Zoom images. When you're looking to expand your Web page beyond the standard media formats, keep the following factors in mind:

✦ The Synchronized Multimedia Integration Language (SMIL) developed by RealNetworks permits multiple media types to be combined into a single streaming presentation.

✦ IBM's HotMedia object enables you to insert interactive advertising with pan-capable images, animation, audio, and programmable hotlinks.

✦ With Live Picture's FlashPix technology, very high-resolution images — with zooming and panning enabled — can be included in your Web pages, but you must have the company's server software installed.

In the next chapter, you learn how Dreamweaver can be used to connect with a variety of database technologies to deliver Web pages with dynamic content.

CHAPTER 32

Building Active Web Sites

✦ ✦ ✦ ✦

In This Chapter

Grasping database fundamentals

Working with active content pages

How e-commerce works

Using cookies to track customers

Merging server-side code with Dreamweaver

✦ ✦ ✦ ✦

The Internet was initially a vehicle for simple documents—basic communication, reports on laboratory findings, and scholarly papers—and the Web consisted of basically static pages, each one separate and independent. As the Web exploded and the need for more up-to-date information grew, the practice of building or continually modifying a Web page soon became impractical. Not only were special skills required, such as an understanding of HTML coding, but also data was often taken from an existing system and reentered onto a Web page, thus duplicating effort unnecessarily. A link between the Web and existing database structures was forged to create dynamic Web pages capable of displaying the most current content in a structured, easy-to-navigate format.

Database connectivity is a strong and growing aspect of the Web. Without a strong connection between the Web and databases, e-commerce could not thrive, news bureaus would be buried under a glut of information, and intranets would be continually out of date. Numerous companies are involved in the field: Microsoft pioneered Active Server Pages for their servers, while companies such as Allaire, Oracle, and Tango produce alternative technologies for others.

Until recently, Internet database connectivity was an art form practiced only by the most adept programmers. If you didn't understand the inner workings of ODBC, SQL, and other database acronyms, you could forget it. However, if you want to keep your client base happy and growing, that won't be an option for long—many businesses are demanding database connectivity for their Web sites. Now, with Dreamweaver, bringing a page to life through active database content is only a click or two away. Dreamweaver has partnered with several of the top companies to smooth this tortuous path. Although specific examinations of all the solutions possible is beyond the scope of this book, this chapter explains the ins and outs of database connectivity and e-commerce—even as more are on the way, thanks to Dreamweaver's inherent extensibility.

Understanding Active Content

For many Web designers, databases are a completely foreign territory—and how you build a bridge from a Web page to a database is a total mystery. Before you implement a database-oriented Web site, it's helpful to understand the fundamentals of databases and gain an overview of the connectivity processes involved. For some Web production companies, the designer is responsible for all aspects of site creation; here, a firm understanding of the new possibilities and technologies of an active content page is essential.

Database basics

Databases store information systematically. Here, the key word is *systematically*. Many other technologies, both low- and high-end, store information—a shelf of books, a shoebox full of receipts, even a collection of Web pages—but few store the information in such a way that retrieval is structured and uniform. Naturally, the precise nature of the structure varies from one type of database to another, but fundamentally, they are all the same.

A database is made up of a series of *records*. Each record can be thought of as a snapshot of a particular set of details. These details are known as *fields*, and each field contains the pertinent information or data. A single database record can be made up of any number of fields of varying types—some fields hold only numbers or only dates, whereas others are open-ended and can hold any type of information. A series of database records, all with the same fields, is commonly referred to as a *table*—a simple table is also known as a *flat-file database*. Like a word processing or an HTML table, a database table has rows and columns. Each column represents a field, while each row represents a record. For example, the following table that I call `BookTitles` describes a series of books:

Title	***Author***	***Pages***	***Published***
JavaScript Bible	Danny Goodman	1,015	1998
HTML Manual of Style	Larry Aronson and Joseph Lowery	385	1997
Netrepreneur	Joseph Lowery	424	1998

The first row in the table contains the field names: Title, Author, Pages, and Published. Each subsequent row contains a complete record. As presented here, this table is in no particular order; however, one of the reasons databases are so powerful is their sorting ability. If I were to sort the `BookTitles` table by page count, listing the books with the fewest pages first, it would look like this:

Title	Author	Pages	Published
HTML Manual of Style	Larry Aronson and Joseph Lowery	385	1997
Netrepreneur	Joseph Lowery	424	1998
JavaScript Bible	Danny Goodman	1,015	1998

Most modern databases can sort a table on any field, using any criteria. Many databases require that a table have an *index field* where each entry is unique, to simplify data manipulation. In the prior table example, the Title field could serve as an index because each title is unique; however, this is often not the case, and a separate field is created.

Index fields, also referred to as *key fields,* become an absolute necessity when two or more tables — or flat-file databases — are combined to create a *relational database.* As the name implies, a relational database presents information that is related. For example, let's say we created another table called `BookSales` to accompany our previous book database example, like this:

Region	Sales	Book
East	10,000	*JavaScript Bible*
South	20,500	*JavaScript Bible*
West	42,000	*JavaScript Bible*
North	25,000	*JavaScript Bible*
East	15,000	*Netrepreneur*
South	12,000	*Netrepreneur*
West	8,000	*Netrepreneur*
North	21,000	*Netrepreneur*
East	8,330	*HTML Manual of Style*
South	6,500	*HTML Manual of Style*
West	8,000	*HTML Manual of Style*
North	7,400	*HTML Manual of Style*

To get a list of authors, sorted according to sales figures, you have to combine or join the two databases. A field common to both tables is used to create the juncture, or *join*—here, the common field is the index field Title. While flat-file databases can be used in many situations, most industrial-strength applications use relational databases to access information.

In addition to changing the sort order of a table, database information can also be selectively retrieved by using a *filter*. A filter is often represented by a *where* statement, as in "Show me the books where regional sales were over 10,000 but under 20,000." Applying this filter to the `BookSales` table would result in the following table:

Region	Sales	Book
East	10,000	*JavaScript Bible*
East	15,000	*Netrepreneur*
South	12,000	*Netrepreneur*

The common language understood by many Web-available databases is SQL, which stands for *Structured Query Language*. A SQL statement tells the database precisely what information you're looking for and what form you want it in. Although SQL statements can become quite complex, a relatively simple SQL statement has just four parts:

- ✦ **Select:** Picks the fields to display.
- ✦ **From:** Chooses the databases from which to gather the information.
- ✦ **Where:** Describes the filter criteria and/or the joins.
- ✦ **Order:** Gives the sorting criteria.

A sample SQL statement translation of our "Show me the books where regional sales were over 10,000 but under 20,000" example would look like this:

```
SELECT Title
FROM BookSales
WHERE (Sales > 10000) & (Sales < 20000)
ORDER by Sales
```

Joins between two or more tables are depicted in SQL with an equal sign and are considered part of the filter in the `WHERE` statement. To show the sales by author's name, I'd have to revise my SQL statement to read as follows:

```
SELECT Title, Author
FROM BookTitles, BookSales
WHERE BookTitles = BookSales & ((Sales > 10000) & (Sales < 20000))
ORDER by Author
```

The quick way to display all the fields in a table is to use a SQL statement with a wildcard, like this:

```
SELECT * FROM Booktitles
```

The asterisk indicates that you want to choose every field.

How active content pages work

The journey for a static Web page from user to server is straightforward, even for the most complex, graphics- and JavaScript-laden page. The user clicks a link that sends a signal to the server to send that page. An active content page — with full database connectivity — travels a much different route, however.

An active content page is a blend of traditional HTML and a database server language, such as Active Server Pages (ASP) or Cold Fusion Markup Language (CFML). When a user accesses an active content page, the requested page is passed through the database server where the code is processed and a new HTML page is generated. This page is then returned to the regular Web server and sent on to the user. Figure 32-1 illustrates this process.

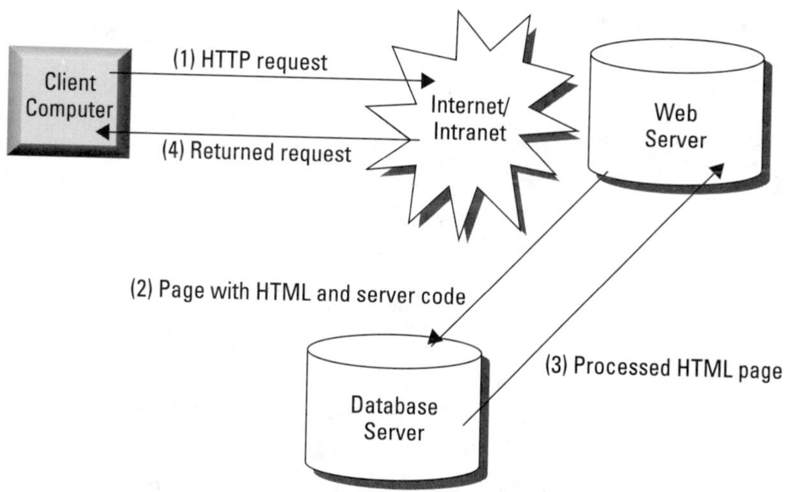

Figure 32-1: An active content page is processed by a database server prior to being sent to the user.

Active content servers can connect to more than databases, however. Other possibilities include the following:

✦ **Directory servers:** Directory servers control the permissions for large corporations and determine who is granted access to what group of files. With a directory server, two people — with different clearances — could see two different pages when clicking the same link.

✦ **Mail servers:** E-mail communication can be fully automated through a mail server: Responses to forms are categorized and forwarded to the proper parties, mass mailings can go out at the click of a button, and messages can be automatically incorporated into Web pages.

✦ **File servers:** By and large, HTML by itself has no file manipulation capabilities. However, with a file server, files can be uploaded, copied, renamed, moved, deleted, and more.

The primary HTML vehicle for interfacing with a database server is the form.

Most Web databases are Open Database Connectivity (ODBC) compliant. ODBC is a standard that enables virtually any type of database to be accessed—if the database has an ODBC driver. Similar to printer drivers that enable your computer to communicate with a wide variety of printers, an ODBC driver translates data to and from the database program. When setting up your database on the Web server, you may need to declare the ODBC driver for the file, as well as establish the Data Source Name (DSN). The DSN is used to simplify query building by giving each database a unique name to be referenced. Most servers require that the ODBC driver and DSN name be handled by the system administrator, or someone with that level of access.

Dreamweaver Database Partners

Developing connectivity for a Web authoring tool requires a close alliance with the database company. Macromedia has established partnerships with several of the leaders in Internet database technology and has released a series of solutions with each of them. As of this writing, the partnership with Allaire has brought the Cold Fusion extensions to fruition, as has a partnership with Pervasive and their Tango extensions. Blueworld built an entirely new product, Lasso Studio for Dreamweaver, around their set of extensions.

Macromedia has instituted similar arrangements with Oracle, Broadvision, and Apple. Oracle has many adherents, and their new technology, Oracle8i, combined with Dreamweaver, promises to be a winning combination. Broadvision is a developer of high-end database solutions used for tracking personal access on the Web; their primary Web development tool is Dreamweaver. Database integration for Broadvision means a much smoother workflow for complex Web sites.

Macromedia and Apple have released a suite of 17 Dreamweaver objects in support of WebObjects. Apple touts WebObjects as the leading application server platform for development of Internet and intranet applications, with more than 3,000 customers globally. WebObjects supports the "Mac OS X, Unix, or Windows NT 4 or 2000 platforms.

Dreamweaver's extensibility makes it the ideal Web authoring tool for customization and use by the various connectivity solutions. Be sure to keep an eye on the official Dreamweaver Web site (`www.dreamweaver.com`) for further announcements and software releases.

E-commerce Solutions

Although the first age of the Internet was widely devoted to information — gathering, storing, archiving, and sharing it — the next era increasingly seems devoted to transactions and business. E-commerce is on the rise; online retail purchases are doubling and tripling each year as consumers feel more secure about shopping over the Web, and business-to-business sales are skyrocketing. You'll find numerous explanations for this explosive growth, but the bottom line is this: Buying and selling online is here to stay.

More and more, Web designers are asked to build storefronts on the Web. Enabling a Web site for e-commerce is not a trivial task, as it requires a blend of Internet security, database connectivity, and marketing savvy. Macromedia has partnered with several leaders in electronic commerce, including iCat, NetStores, and Miva, to develop a series of commands and objects, available on the Dreamweaver Web site, that simplify creating and hosting an online store. Specific discussions of these integration capabilities are beyond the scope of this book; however, the balance of this chapter includes an overview of e-commerce from a Web designer's point of view. Also, along the way, you learn how Dreamweaver can help you with another e-commerce necessity: tracking customers with JavaScript cookies.

Understanding E-commerce

Although there are almost as many variations to how shopping works as there are stores on the Web, many transactions take a similar path. Here's how a typical transaction makes its way around the Internet:

1. The user sees something desirable in the online store and clicks the "Buy" button to put the item in their shopping cart.

   The "Buy" triggers a cookie containing the item number and quantity to be written to the user's system.

2. After shopping for a bit more, the user decides to proceed to the checkout area of the site.

   The link on the Checkout Counter button is to a page on a secure server that employs Secure Sockets Layer (SSL) protocol. An icon on the user's browser — usually a locked padlock or a solid key — indicates the change. All commu-nication between a user and secure server is coded or encrypted.

3. The user is given an opportunity to confirm the current contents of the shopping cart — and, if desired, change the quantity of any item.

   The cookie information (with the information about the selected products) that has been stored during the online shopping trip is read back into the browser.

4. If the customer has shopped at the online store before, a user ID and password are all that are required to retrieve all the pertinent account information: billing and shipping address, credit card numbers, e-mail address, and so forth.

   If the buyer is a first-time customer, forms with the applicable information are filled out, and the data—along with a new user ID and password—is transferred to the store's system over the secure network.

5. The system at the online shop retrieves the order information and decodes it. The transactional information (credit card number, amount of purchase, and so on) is reencrypted and sent over secure phone lines to the credit card clearinghouse with an authentication certificate from the store.

   The order information is entered into the database. Some systems deduct the order from inventory at this point, whereas others wait for the transaction to be confirmed by the bank.

6. The credit card clearinghouse authenticates the merchant and forwards the transaction data to the bank.

7. The bank accepts or declines the charge and sends the result back to the clearinghouse, which then forwards it to the merchant.

8. The merchant sends two electronic confirmations to the customer: one to the browser as a thank-you and one via e-mail with full details of the order and shipping information. Any links from here, back to the main store, end the secure server connection.

As you can see, online selling requires a great deal of behind-the-scenes communication and coordination. However, it all boils down to two primary factors: security and connectivity.

Encryption

The facet of the Web that makes it so compelling—global access—is one of the factors that keeps consumers wary. The common fear is, "If anyone in the world can get online, can't they also get my credit card information?" Grabbing any data as it passes by on the Internet is certainly not a trivial task and is possible for only the most dedicated hackers. Even with the information in hand, however, cyberthieves still haven't made off with the loot—because whatever data they have is meaningless unless it is decoded.

Encryption is handled automatically, with all data passed through a *secure server*. A secure server is one that uses some form of coding, or *encryption*, technology. The most common form of Internet encryption comes from servers with a Secure Sockets Layer (SSL). To secure any information passed over the Web, the page with the form must access a secure server. Links for secure servers begin with `https://`, instead of the usual `http://`—the additional *s* stands, of course, for security.

Depending on the user's browser settings, messages can appear when going from a secure server to a nonsecure server. As these alerts can be disconcerting to the novice user, it's a good idea to continue using the secure server for all Web pages accessed during the sales checkout procedure – even those pages that are purely informational and don't require the secure server to pass data.

Authentication

Encryption solves only half of the problem with online security—the other half requires *authentication*. It does no good to receive an encrypted message from someone if you're not sure they are who they are supposed to be. Because online communication is largely anonymous—there's no visual or aural confirmation of identity—another method of identification is necessary.

The current basic method of authentication involves *digital certificates*. A digital certificate is a type of identity card for companies, Web sites, and online indi-viduals. Digital certificates are issued by established certificate authorities, such as VeriSign (`www.verisign.com`), and are generally automatically transferred by browsers. Companies (or individuals) applying for a digital certificate must prove their identity. With companies, the process is similar to applying for a merchant bank account; you must supply the business' articles of incorporation, tax ID number, and so forth. With individuals, you need enter only an e-mail address. Higher classes of digital certificates include insured protection, which requires a more rigorous identification procedure. Digital certificates are typically offered when a user enters a secure server.

Passing Cookies

As noted earlier, cookies are used to track user information – such as what's in a shopping cart – from one Web page. A *cookie* is a small piece of information that can be passed along with the HTTP header that accompanies every Web page: The Web page is displayed by the browser, and the cookie information is stored on the user's hard drive in a special file. Don't get the idea that cookies are just text files that can be used in any situation. Cookies have a very special format and definite limits.

Each domain is limited to 20 cookies, and a 4-megabyte or 300-total cookie limit imposed by the browser. A cookie generally conveys four pieces of information:

✦ **Domain of origin:** All cookies are domain specific (sent from one particular Internet domain). Only the domain sending the cookie can retrieve it.

✦ **Expiration date:** Many cookies are intended to be active for a single online session; when you leave the Web site, the cookie is no longer of any value. These cookies are maintained in memory only and never written to a file. Other cookies use specified expiration dates to keep the number of cookies down, so new ones can be added.

Continued

Continued

✦ **Path of URL:** You can specify where a cookie is active on your site. Generally, it's best to keep the cookies available in the current directory.

✦ **Name and value pairs:** The name and value pairs are the real content of a cookie. Each variable or name is set equal to a particular value, generally user supplied either directly through a text box or by an action, such as selecting an Add to Shopping Cart button. The name and value pairs are later retrieved by a JavaScript or CGI program when the cookie is read.

Although Dreamweaver 3 doesn't come with any standard cookie behaviors, third-party developers have created a number of them. Generally, cookie behaviors come in a set—one behavior to set the cookie, another to read it, and yet another to remove it entirely. One of the better cookie behavior sets was built by Nadav Silvio of the Webmonkey Web site. With the Webmonkey Set and Read Cookie behaviors, you can even choose a form field on the Web page, such as a text box, to get the cookie from or set it to.

One of the drawbacks to cookies is that they're not universally accepted. Because of the possible security risk involved with any outside system writing and reading information to a local hard drive, browsers enable the user to choose whether they will accept cookies or be warned every time one is passed to their system. Using another third-party extension, the Check Cookie behavior by Jaro von Flocken, you can redirect to another page visitors whose browsers do not have cookies enabled.

Working with shopping carts

Whenever a customer selects an item online with the intent to buy it, the item goes into an online *shopping cart*. Although commonly thought of as a single object, a shopping cart is composed of several key components of a program or programs. Basically, the shopping cart enables the potential customer to tag selected items for purchase and continue shopping. When the customer decides to finalize the purchase, the items are listed on the checkout screen, and a total cost is calculated.

Generally, shopping cart functionality includes the capability to include any number of items and modify the quantity of the items—including changing the number to zero, thus removing it from the shopping cart. Most stores are set up so that items can be added to the shopping cart at any time in one session and checkout is always available.

Because of the complexity of handling complete online shopping transactions and store management—and the inherent expense—several e-commerce solutions have separated the shopping cart component from the all-in-one store solution. Under a shopping cart–only arrangement, your Web pages include Add to Shopping Cart and Proceed to Checkout links that access the e-commerce solution's secure server instead of your own. This is an excellent route for a small business that wants to sell online, but whose business volume doesn't rate an in-house server.

As well as the numerous high-end e-commerce products from such companies as Open Market (www.openmarket.com), Netscape (www.netscape.com), and ICVerify (www.icverify.com), you can also find several full-featured CGI online shopping solutions from such resources as Extropia (www.extropia.com) and the CGI Resource Index (www.cgi-resources.com) for free or at relatively low cost.

Ensuring Dreamweaver Compatibility

Since its first release, one of Dreamweaver's primary selling points has been its claim that it does not alter your code. Unfortunately for many Web designers working with middleware server-side systems that use custom tags for programming, Dreamweaver's claim only extended to HTML code — any other nonstandard tags were often marked as Invalid HTML or, worse, altered significantly.

Recognizing that Web pages aren't just for HTML anymore, Dreamweaver 3 incorporates several new methods to ensure that server-side markup is as protected as HTML. By adjusting Preferences, Dreamweaver can be instructed to adopt a "hands-off" policy for any Web page with a particular file extension, such as .cfm or .asp. Moreover, you can now turn off Dreamweaver's automatic encoding of URLs and/or attributes.

To understand the overall rewriting problem better, let's look at an example. One of the major benefits of active content pages is being able to use a variable as an image's source on catalog-like pages. To do so, you need something like this ASP code:

```
<img src="images/<% = Replace(varGrade," ","%20") %>.jpg">
```

If you tried to include ASP code like this in Dreamweaver 2 or earlier, the crucial %20 value would be stripped out because Dreamweaver interprets %20 as hexadecimal for a space character. Although workarounds exist for situations such as this — you could always assign the offending character or its overall string to a variable and use that within the HTML tag — workarounds take time to implement. An overall solution is far better.

Dreamweaver 3 solves this problem by enabling the user to specify file types that should remain unchanged like HTML. By default, Dreamweaver includes the following file types as being protected when the Never Rewrite HTML option is selected:

File Type	*Server-Side System*
.asp	Active Server Pages
.cfm, .cfml	Cold Fusion Application Server
.ihtml	Inline HTML
.jsp	JavaServer Pages
.php	PHP: Hypertext Preprocessor

You can add as many file extensions as you'd like, although I recommend including only those file types you actually use.

Another potential problem with HTML rewriting stems from URL encoding. In order to ensure universal acceptance of URLs, regardless of the type of server, Dreamweaver automatically encodes nonstandard characters, such as spaces or tildes, entered through the Property Inspector in hexadecimal. Thus, a space is represented as `%20` and a tilde as `%7E`. While this practice is good for standard Web servers, it can raise havoc with application servers. Dreamweaver also extends a similar type of encoding to attributes containing special characters such as angle brackets (< and >), ampersands, and quote marks. Both of these types of encoding can be disabled via an option in Dreamweaver preferences.

It's best to disable the encoding options only if you encounter HTML rewriting issues involving URLs or attributes.

If you find that your active content page code is being rewritten when opened in Dreamweaver, follow these steps:

1. Choose Edit ➪ Preferences.

   The Preferences dialog box is displayed.

2. Select the HTML Rewriting panel, shown in Figure 32-2.

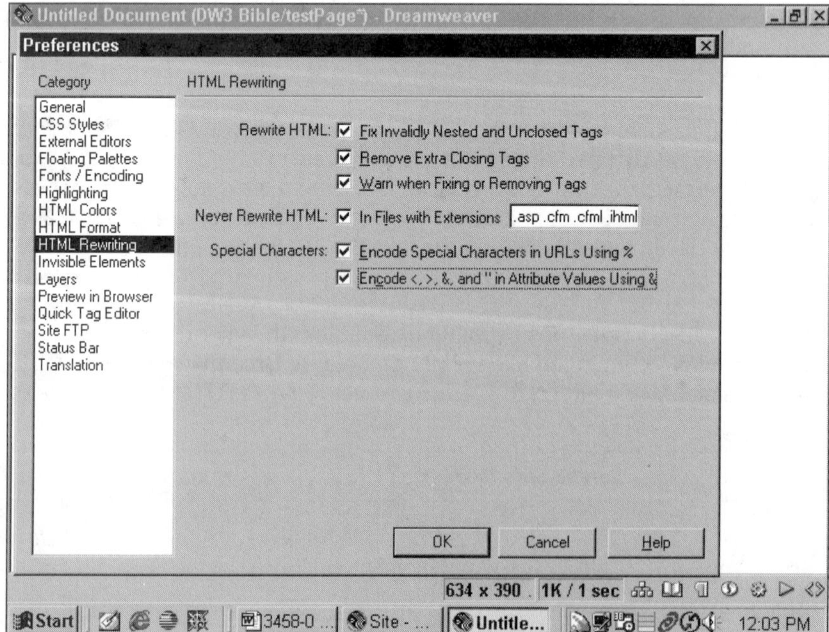

Figure 32-2: Lock out any file type from HTML Rewriting through Dreamweaver Preferences.

3. Enable the Never Rewrite HTML option.
4. Adjust the In Files with Extensions field to include your file type's extension.

   Add new file types separated by a space with a leading period, as in .lasso. Be sure to include all possible variations of the file types, such as .phtm and .phtml.
5. To prevent Dreamweaver from encoding special characters in URLs with hexadecimal values, disable the Encode Special Characters in URLs using % option.
6. To prevent Dreamweaver from encoding special characters in attributes with hexadecimal values, disable the Encode <, >, &, and " in Attribute Values Using & option.

All these Preference changes take place immediately; there's no need to relaunch Dreamweaver.

Summary

It's a pretty safe bet that active content is an issue in every Web designer's future. Not only can database-connected pages serve up simple data in an organized fashion, but images, links, streaming video, and other media are also targetable content. Dreamweaver's extensibility makes it the ideal choice for a Web designer who needs to connect to the ever-expanding world of databases. When you're considering building an active content page, keep the following in mind:

- A database is a structured file for maintaining data. Databases are made up of tables, fields, and records. A database that can use two or more tables together is called a *relational database*.
- Web pages that link standard HTML and elements drawn from a database are referred to as *active content pages*. With an active content page, you change the data, and the Web page is presented with the new information automatically.
- All specialized servers — whether for database-generated pages or e-commerce — use non-HTML code. Dreamweaver 3 offers several Preference options for preserving both HTML and non-HTML code.

In the next chapter, you learn how to create reusable templates within Dreamweaver

✦ ✦ ✦

P A R T

VIII

Enhancing Web Site Management and Workflow in Dreamweaver

✦ ✦ ✦ ✦

In This Part

✦ ✦ ✦ ✦

Using Dreamweaver Templates

✦ ✦ ✦ ✦

In This Chapter

Working with templates

Building your own templates

Working with editable and locked regions

Modifying the default Web page

✦ ✦ ✦ ✦

Let's face it: Web design is a combination of glory and grunt work. Creating the initial design for a Web site can be fun and exciting, but when you have to implement your wonderful new design on 200 or more pages, the excitement fades as you try to figure out the quickest way to finish the work. Enter templates. Properly using templates can be a tremendous time-saver. Moreover, a template ensures that your Web site has a consistent look and feel, which in turn generally means it's easier for users to navigate.

In Dreamweaver, new documents can be produced from a standard design saved as a template, as in a word processing program. Furthermore, you can alter a template and update all the files that were created from it earlier; this capability extends the power of the repeating element Libraries to overall page design. Templates also form the bridge to one of the hottest technologies shaping the Web — XML (Extensible Markup Language).

Dreamweaver makes it easy to access all kinds of templates — everything from your own creations to the default blank page. This chapter demonstrates the mechanism behind Dreamweaver templates and shows you strategies for getting the most out of them.

Understanding Templates

Templates exist in many forms. Furniture makers use molds as templates to create the same basic design over and over again, with new wood stains or upholstery used to differentiate the end results. A stencil, in which the inside of a letter, word, or design is cut out, is a type of template as well. With computers, templates form the basic document into which specific details are added to create new, distinct documents.

Dreamweaver templates, in terms of functionality, are a combination of traditional templates and updateable Library elements. With templates, a new page is created from a mold, or template. Once created, the new document remains attached to the original template unless specifically separated or detached. Because the new document maintains a connection, if the original template is altered, all the documents created from it can be automatically updated, as with Dreamweaver's repeating elements Libraries. In fact, templates can even include Library elements.

Templates are composed of two types of regions: locked and editable. Every element on the Web page template falls into one category or the other. When a template is first created, all the areas are locked. Part of the process of defining a template is to designate, and name, the editable regions. Then, when a document is created from that template, the editable regions are the only ones that can be modified.

Naturally, templates can be altered to mark additional editable areas or to relock editable areas. Moreover, you can detach a document created from a template at any point and edit anything in the document—you cannot, however, reattach the document to the template without losing newly inserted content. On the other hand, a document based on one template can be changed to a completely different look but with the same content, if another template with identical editable regions is applied.

Dreamweaver ships with a tutorial that illustrates the power of templates. The tutorial, found in the Dreamweaver\Tutorial folder, is based on an example Web site for a food company called Scaal Coffee. When you preview the site in a browser, you notice that in the catalog section, all the sample pages for the different products are basically the same—only the product title, description, and images vary. The layout, background, and navigation controls are identical on every page. Each of these pages was created from the template page shown in Figure 33-1. Notice the highlighting surrounding certain areas—in a template, the editable regions are highlighted, and the locked areas are not. When you create a new document based on the template, the reverse is true: The locked regions are highlighted (in a different color), and the editable regions are not.

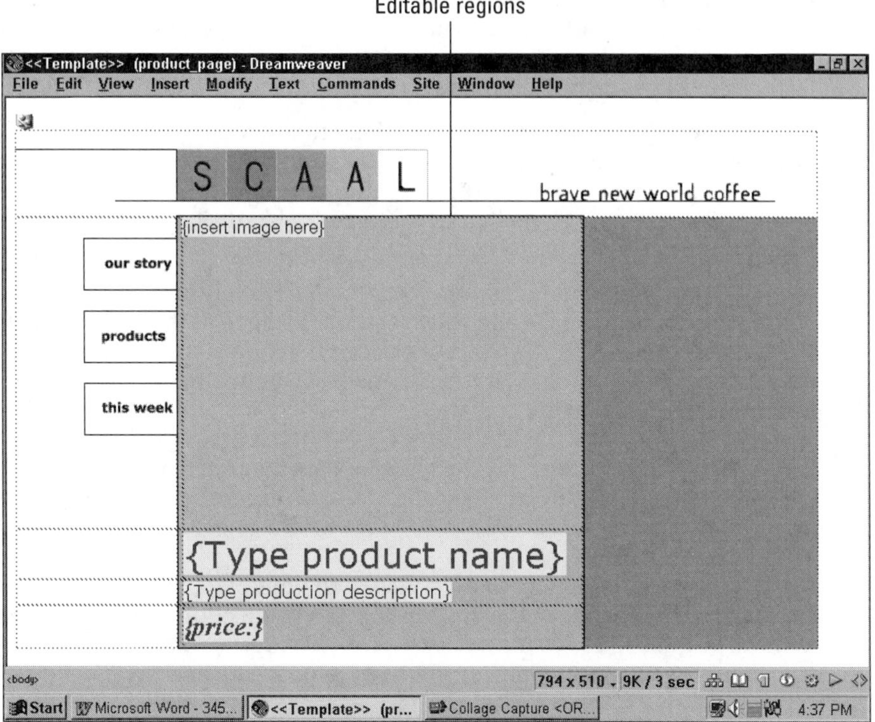

Figure 33-1: In this sample template from the Dreamweaver Tutorial, editable regions are highlighted.

Creating Your Own Templates

You can use any design you like for your own template. Perhaps the best course to take is to finalize a single page that has all the elements you want to include in your template. Then, convert that document to a template and proceed to mark all the changeable areas — whether text or image — as editable regions.

Before you save your file as a template, consider the following points when designing your basic page:

✦ **Use placeholders where you can.** Whether it's dummy text or a temporary graphic, placeholders give shape to your page. They also make it easier to remember which elements to include. If you are using an image placeholder, set a temporary height and width through the Property Inspector or by dragging the image placeholder's sizing handles.

✦ **Finalize and incorporate as much as possible in the template.** If you find yourself repeatedly adding the same information or objects to a page, add them to your template. The more structured elements you can include, the faster your pages can be produced.

✦ **Use sample objects on the template.** Many times you have to enter the same basic object, such as a plug-in for a digital movie, on every page — and only the file names change. Enter your repeating object with all the preset parameters possible on your template page as an editable region, and you only have to select a new file for each page.

✦ **Include your <meta> information.** Search engines rely on <meta> tags to get the overview of a page and then scan the balance of the page to get the details. You can enter a Keyword or Description object from the Head panel of the Objects palette so that all the Web pages in your site have the same basic information for cataloging.

Note

You cannot enter separate <meta> tag information into template-derived pages without inserting it directly into the code. Dreamweaver defines one editable area for the title – your hand-entered <meta> tags should go in this region.

✦ **Apply all needed behaviors and styles to the template.** When a document is saved as a template, all the code in the <head> section is locked. As most behaviors and CSS styles insert code here, this means that documents created from templates cannot apply new behaviors or create new styles.

You can create a template from a Web document with one command: File ➪ Save As Template. Dreamweaver stores all templates in a Templates folder created for each defined site, with a special file extension, .dwt. After you've created your page and saved it as a template, notice that Dreamweaver inserts <<Template>> in the title bar to remind you of the page's status. Now you're ready to begin defining the template's editable regions.

Note

You can also create a template from an entirely blank page if you like. To do so, choose Window ➪ Templates to open the Templates palette. From the Templates palette, click the New button. You can find more information on how to use the Templates palette later in this chapter.

Using Editable Regions

As noted earlier, when you convert an existing page into a template via the Save As Template command, the entire document is initially locked. If you attempt to create a document from a template at this stage, Dreamweaver alerts you that the template doesn't have any editable regions, and you cannot change anything on the page. Editable regions are essential to any template.

Marking existing content as editable

Two techniques exist for marking editable regions. First, you can designate any existing content as an editable region. Second, you can insert a new editable region anywhere you can place your cursor. In both cases, you must give the region a unique name. Dreamweaver uses the unique name to identify the editable region when entering new content, applying the template, and exporting or importing XML.

As noted, each editable region must have a unique name, but the names need only be different from any other editable region on the same page. The name could be used for objects or JavaScript functions, or for editable regions on a different template.

To mark an existing area as an editable region, follow these steps:

1. Select the text or object you wish to convert to an editable region.

The general rule of thumb with editable regions is that you need to select a complete tag pair, such as `<table>...</table>`. This has several implications. For instance, while you can mark an entire table or a single cell as editable, you can't select multiple cells, a row, or a column to be so marked. You have to select each cell one at a time (`<td>...</td>`). Also, you can select the content of a layer to be editable and keep the layer itself locked (so that its position and other properties cannot be altered), but if you select the layer to be editable, you can't lock the content.

2. Choose Modify ⇨ Templates ⇨ Mark Selection As Editable. You can also use the keyboard shortcut Ctrl+Alt+W (Command+Option+W), or right-click (Control+click) the selection and choose Editable Regions ⇨ Mark Selection As Editable from the shortcut menu.

   Dreamweaver displays the New Editable Region dialog box.

If you want the flexibility of adding returns to your editable region, make sure it includes at least one; otherwise, Dreamweaver does not allow any returns, although line breaks are accepted.

3. Enter a unique name for the selected area. Click OK when you're done or Cancel to abort the operation.

While you can use spaces in editable region names, some characters are not permitted. The illegal characters are the question mark (?), double quote ("), single quote ('), and left and right angle brackets (< and >).

Dreamweaver highlights the selection with the color picked in Preferences on the Highlighting panel, if the Show option has been selected. The name for your newly designated region is listed alphabetically in the Modify ⇨ Templates submenu.

If still selected, the region name has a checkmark next to it. You can jump to any other editable region by selecting its name from the dynamic list.

Make sure you apply any formatting to your text—either through HTML codes, such as `<font>`, or CSS styles—before you select it to be an editable region. Generally, you want to keep the defined look of the content while altering just the text, so make just the text an editable region and exclude the formatting tags. It's helpful to have the HTML Inspector open for this detailed work.

Inserting a new editable region

Sometimes it's helpful to create a new editable region where no content currently exists. In these situations, the editable region name doubles as a label identifying the type of content expected, such as `{CatalogPrice}`. Dreamweaver always puts new region names in curly braces as shown here and highlights the entry in the template.

To insert a new editable region, follow these steps:

1. Place your cursor anywhere on the template page.
2. Choose Modify ➪ Templates ➪ New Editable Region. You can also use the keyboard shortcut Ctrl+Alt+V (Command+Option+V), or right-click (Control+click) the selection and choose Editable Regions ➪ New from the shortcut menu.

   Dreamweaver displays the New Editable Region dialog box.
3. Enter a unique name for the new region. Click OK when you're done or Cancel to abort the operation.

Dreamweaver inserts the new region name in the document, surrounded by curly braces, and adds the name to the dynamic region list (which you can display by choosing Modify ➪ Templates).

One editable region, the Web page's title, is automatically created when you save a document as a template. The title is stored in a special editable region called `doctitle`. To change the title (which initially takes the same title as the template), choose Modify ➪ Page Properties and enter the new text in the Title text box. You can also use the keyboard shortcut Ctrl+J (Command+J). Finally, you can select View ➪ Head Elements and choose the Title icon to enter the new text in the Property Inspector.

Locking an editable region

Inevitably, you'll mark a region as editable that you'd prefer to keep locked, or you may discover that every page constructed to date has required inputting the same content, so it should be entered on the template and locked. In either event, converting an editable region to a locked one is a simple operation.

Creating Links in Templates

One of the most common problems designers encounter with Dreamweaver templates centers around links. People often add a link to their template and discover it does not work when the new page is derived from the template. The main cause of this error stems from linking to a nonexisting page or element by hand — that is, typing in the link rather than using the Select File dialog box to choose it. Designers tend to set the link according to their final site structure without taking into account how templates are stored in Dreamweaver.

For example, when creating a template, let's say you have links to three pages, products.htm, services.htm, and about.htm, all in the root of your site. Both products.htm and services.htm have been created, so you select the folder icon in the Property Inspector and select those files in turn. Dreamweaver inserts those links like this: `../products.htm` and `../services.htm`. The `../` indicates the directory above the current directory — which makes sense only when you remember that all templates are stored in a subfolder of the site root called Templates.

Let's assume that the third file, about.htm, has not been created yet, and so that link is entered by hand. The common mistake is to enter it as it should be when it's used: about.htm. However, because the page is saved in the Template folder, Dreamweaver converts that link to /Templates/about.htm for any page derived from the template — and the link will fail. This type of error also applies to dependent files, such as graphics or other media.

The best solution is to always use the folder icon to link to an existing file when building your templates. If the file does not exist, and you don't want to create a placeholder page for it, link to another existing file in the same folder and modify the link manually.

To lock an editable region, follow these steps:

1. Place your cursor in the editable region you want to lock.
2. Choose Modify ⇨ Templates ⇨ Unmark Editable Region.

   The Unmark Editable Region dialog box, shown in Figure 33-2, appears with the selected region highlighted.

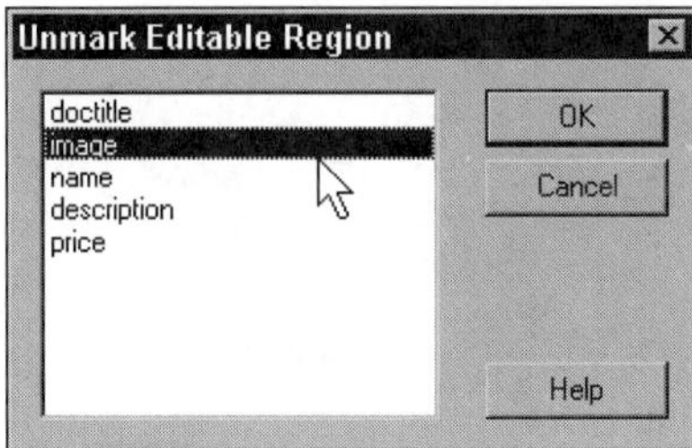

Figure 33-2: Convert an editable region to a locked one with the Unmark Editable Region command.

You don't have to preselect the editable region to unmark it. If you don't, the Unmark Editable Region dialog box opens but doesn't highlight any selection; and you have to choose it by name.

3. Click OK in the Unmark Editable Region dialog box to confirm your choice.

   The editable region highlight is removed, and the area is now a locked region of the template.

Note two concerns when unmarking editable regions. If you are unmarking a newly inserted editable region that is labeled with the region name in curly braces, the label is not removed and must be deleted by hand on the template. Otherwise, it appears as part of the document created from a template and won't be accessible. Also, be careful locking editable regions where pages have already been generated from the templates. On the next update, your page content will be replaced by the new locked region.

Adding Content to Template Documents

Constructing a template is only half the job—using it to create new pages is the other half. Because your basic layout is complete and you're only dropping in new images and entering new text, pages based on templates take a fraction of the time needed to create regular Web pages. Dreamweaver makes it easy to enter new content as well—you can even move from one editable region to the next, much like filling out a form (which, of course, is exactly what you're doing).

To create a new document based on a template, follow these steps:

1. Choose File ➪ New from Template.

   The Select Template dialog box, shown in Figure 33-3, appears.

Figure 33-3: Create a new document based on any template in the Select Template dialog box.

2. If you wish to create a template from a local site other than the current one, select it from the Site drop-down list.
3. Select the desired template from those in the Templates list box.
4. Click OK when you're done.

When your new page opens, notice that the highlighting is now reversed: The locked content is highlighted, and the editable regions are not. You can see this clearly in Figure 33-4, where the template is on the left and the document created from the template is on the right. The highlighting makes it easy to differentiate the two types of regions.

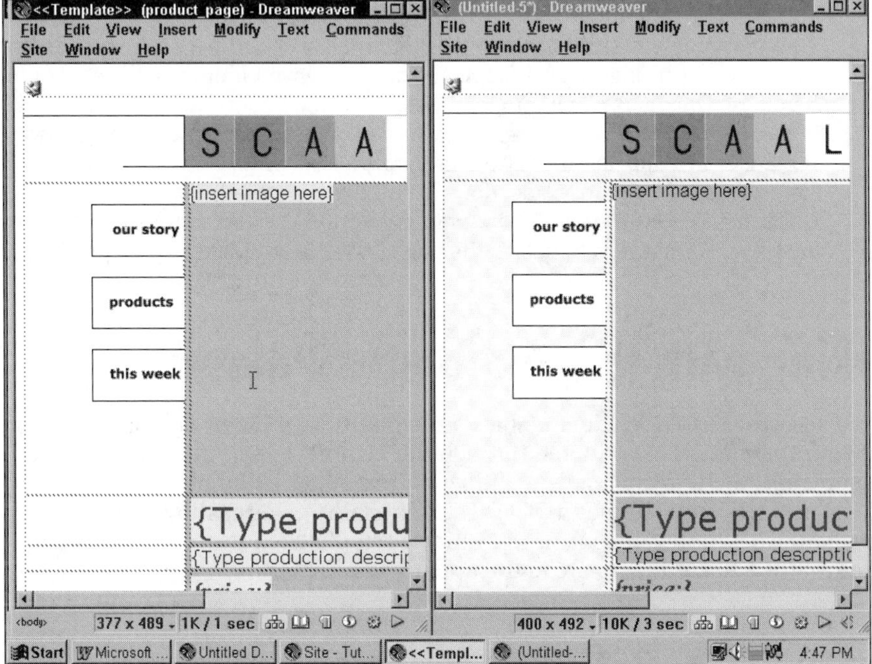

Figure 33-4: The left pane shows the template with the editable regions highlighted; the right pane has the document created from the same template, with the locked regions highlighted.

Generally, it is easiest to select the editable region name or placeholder first and then enter the new content. Selecting the editable regions can be handled in several ways:

✦ Highlight each editable region name or placeholder with the mouse.

✦ Position your cursor inside any editable region and then select the `<mm:editible>` tag in the Tag Selector.

✦ Choose Modify ➪ Templates and then select the name of your editable region from the dynamic list.

If all your editable regions are separate cells in a table, you can tab forward and Shift+Tab backward through the cells. With each press of the Tab key, all the content in the cell is selected, whether it is an editable region name or a placeholder.

Naturally, you should save your document to retain all the new content that's been added.

A known problem exists in using lists in template-based pages. If you attempt to select a series of lines in an editable region and convert them to a bulleted or numbered list, Dreamweaver improperly inserts the code above the lines. This problem is also encountered when indenting a section. One workaround is to use the Quick Tag Editor in Wrap Tag mode to surround the text with `<ul>` tags for a bulleted (unordered) list, or `<ol>` tags for a numbered (ordered) list, and then use the Quick Tag Editor on each line to wrap it with a `<li>` (list item) tag. A less work-intensive alternative is to detach the page from the template, if at all possible.

Working with the Templates Palette

As a site grows, so does the number of templates it employs. Overall management of your templates is conducted through the Templates palette. You can open the Templates palette by choosing Windows ➪ Templates or by pressing the keyboard shortcut Ctrl+F11 (Command+F11). The Templates palette, shown in Figure 33-5, displays a list of the current site's available templates in the lower pane and a preview of the selected template in the upper pane.

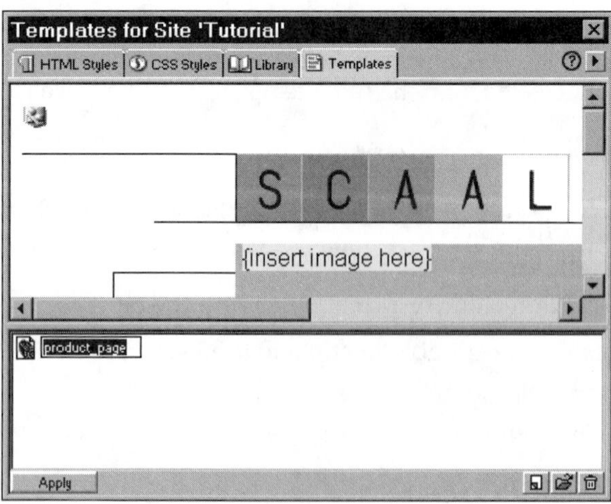

Figure 33-5: Use the Templates palette to preview, delete, open, create, or apply your current site's templates.

Adding Behaviors to Template-Derived Documents

The current implementation of Dreamweaver templates does not enable behaviors to be added to any document created from—and still linked to—a template. If you try, Dreamweaver plays a single note, as it does anytime you try to select a locked region. With behaviors, the <head> section—where the code needs to go—is locked in a template.

You have three ways to handle the problem, however. First, if you're just using the template to get the basic layout of the page and don't need to maintain its link for updating, you can detach the Web page from the template by choosing Modify ➪ Templates ➪ Detach from Template. Second, if all your pages require the same behavior, as in a navigation bar, for example, you can simply add the behavior to the template itself.

The final method is the most involved, but also the most flexible. By adding some code to the original template, new behaviors can be attached, either to the template or to any template-based document. Here are the steps required for the modification:

1. Open the template for editing.
2. Display the HTML Inspector and scroll to the closing </head> tag.

   If you select the <body> tag from the Tag Selector, the closing </head> tag is just above the selected region.
3. Enter this code above the </head> tag:

```
<mm:editable>
<script>
</script>
</mm:editable>

<mm:editable>
<!-- Dummy comment, to be deleted by Dreamweaver -->
</mm:editable>
```

4. Choose File ➪ Save and update any documents linked to the template.

When a document is derived from this modified template, Dreamweaver removes the dummy comment but maintains the <script>...</script> pair, enabling behaviors to be added.

The Templates palette has four buttons along the bottom:

- ✦ **Apply:** Changes the locked region of one document created from a template to a different template.
- ✦ **New Template:** Creates a new blank template.
- ✦ **Open Template:** Loads the selected template for editing.
- ✦ **Delete Template:** Removes the selected template.

Creating a blank template

Not all templates are created from existing documents. Some Web designers prefer to create their templates from scratch. To create a blank template, follow these steps:

1. Open the Templates palette by choosing Window ➪ Templates.
2. From the Templates palette, select New.

   A new, untitled template is created.
3. Enter a title for your new template and press Enter (Return).
4. While the new template is selected, press the Open button.

   The blank template opens in a new Dreamweaver window.
5. Insert your page elements.
6. Mark any elements or areas as editable regions using one of the methods previously described.
7. Save your template.

Deleting and opening templates

As with any set of files, there comes a time to clean house and remove files that are no longer in use. To remove a template, first open the Templates palette. Next, select the file you want to remove and choose the Delete button.

Be forewarned: Dreamweaver does not attempt to stop you or even warn you if files exist that were created from the template you're about to delete. Deleting the template, in effect, "orphans" those documents, and they can no longer be updated via a template.

You can edit a template — to change the locked or editable regions — in any one of several ways. To use the first method, choose File ➪ Open and, in the Select File dialog box, change the Files of Type to Template Files (*.dwt) on Window systems and choose Template Files from the Show drop-down list on Macintosh systems. Then, locate the Templates folder in your defined site to select the template to open.

The second method of opening a template for modification uses the Templates palette. Open the Templates palette by choosing Window ➪ Templates. Then, select a template to edit and choose the Open button. You can also double-click your template to open it for editing.

Finally, if you're working in the Site window, open a template by selecting the Templates folder for your site and open any of the files found there.

After you've made your modifications to the template, you don't have to use the Save As Template command to store the file—you can use the regular File ➪ Save command or the keyboard shortcut Ctrl+S (Command+S). Likewise, if you want to save your template under another name, use the Save As command.

Applying templates

Dreamweaver makes it easy to try a variety of different looks for your document while maintaining the same content. Once you've created a document from a template, you can apply any other template to it. The only requirement is that the two templates have editable regions with the same names. When might this feature come in handy? In one scenario, you might develop a number of possible Web site designs for a client and create templates for each different approach, which are then applied to the identical content. Or, in an ongoing site, you could completely change the look of a catalog seasonally but retain all the content. Figure 33-6 shows two radically different schemes for a Web site with the same content.

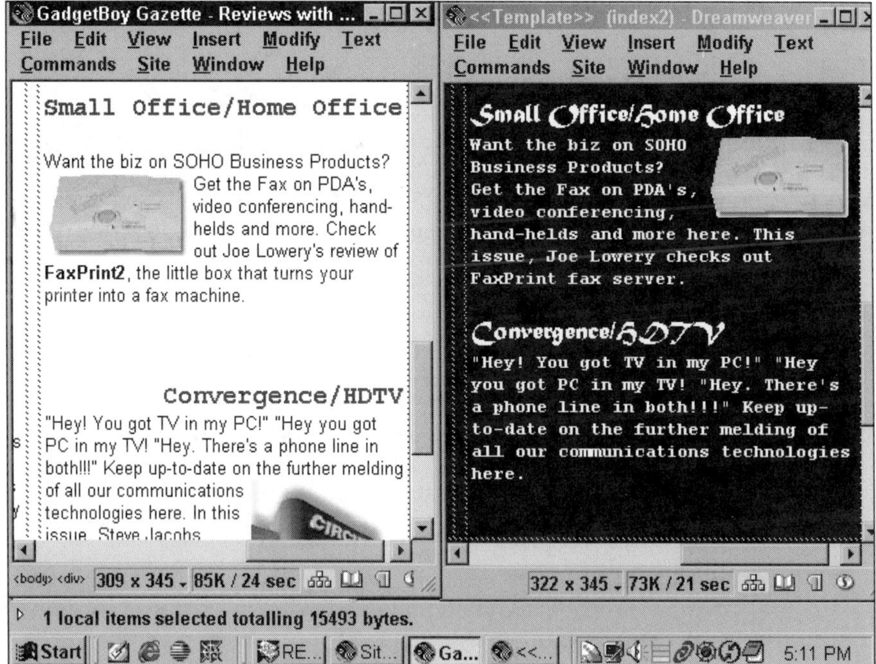

Figure 33-6: You can apply a template to a document created from another template to achieve different designs with identical content.

To apply a template to a document, follow these steps:

1. Open the Templates palette by choosing Window ➪ Templates.
2. Make sure the Web page you want to apply the style to is the active document.
3. From the Templates palette, select the template you want to apply and click the Apply button.

You can also drag onto the current page the template you'd like to apply or choose Modify ➪ Templates ➪ Apply Template to Page from the menus.

4. If a matching editable region contains no content, Dreamweaver displays the Choose Editable Region for Orphaned Content dialog box. To receive the content, select one of the listed editable regions from the template being applied and click OK.

The new template is applied to the document, and all the new locked areas replace all the old locked areas.

Updating Templates

Anytime you save a change to an existing template — whether or not any documents have been created from it — Dreamweaver asks if you'd like to update all the documents in the local site attached to the template. As with Library elements, you can also update the current page or the entire site at any time. Updating documents based on a template can save you an enormous amount of time — especially when numerous changes are involved.

To update a single page, open the page and choose Modify ➪ Templates ➪ Update Current Page. The update is instantly applied.

To update a series of pages or an entire site, follow these steps:

1. Choose Modify ➪ Templates ➪ Update Pages.

   The Update Pages dialog box, shown in Figure 33-7, appears.
2. To update all the documents using all the templates for an entire site, choose Entire Site from the Look In option and then select the name of the site from the accompanying drop-down list.
3. To update pages using a particular template, choose Pages Using from the Look In option and then select the name of the template.

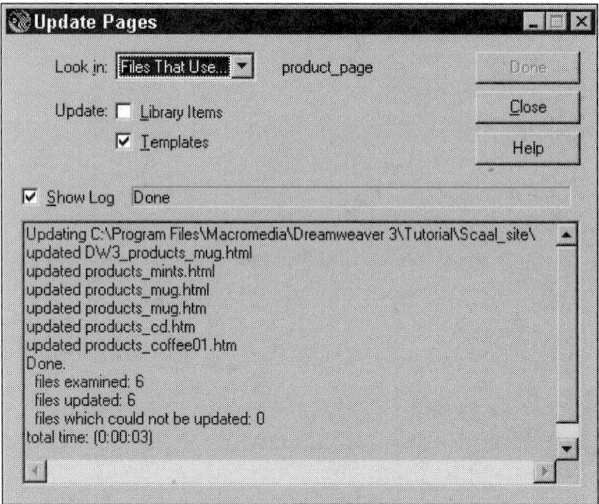

Figure 33-7: Any changes to a template can be automatically applied to its associated files with the Update Pages command.

4. To view a report of the progress of the update, make sure that the Show Log option is enabled.
5. Click Start to begin the update process.

The log window displays a list of the files examined and updated, the total number of files that could not be updated, and the elapsed time.

Changing the Default Document

Each time you open a new document in Dreamweaver — or even just start Dreamweaver — a blank page is created. This blank page is based on an HTML file called Default.html that is stored in the Configuration\Templates folder. The default page works in a similar fashion to the templates in that you can create new documents from it, but no editable or locked regions exist — everything in the page can always be altered.

The basic blank-page document is an HTML structure with only a few properties specified: a document type, character set, and white background for the body:

```
<html>
<head>
<title>Untitled Document</title>
```

```
<meta http-equiv="Content-Type" content="text/html; charset=iso-8859-1">
</head>

<body bgcolor="#FFFFFF">

</body>
</html>
```

Naturally, you can change any of these elements — and add many, many more — once you've opened a page. But what if you want to have a `<meta>` tag with creator information in every page that comes out of your Web design company? You can do it in Dreamweaver manually, but it's a bother, and chances are, sooner or later, you'll forget. Luckily, with Dreamweaver, you have a more efficient solution.

In keeping with its overall design philosophy of extensibility, Dreamweaver enables you to modify the Default.htm file as you would any other file. Just choose File ⇨ Open and select the Configuration\Templates\Default.htm file. As you make your changes, save the file as you would normally. Now, to test your modifications, choose File ⇨ New — your modifications should appear in your new document.

Summary

Much of a Web designer's responsibility is related to document production, and Dreamweaver offers a comprehensive template solution to reduce the workload. When planning your strategy for building an entire Web site, remember the following advantages provided by templates:

- ✦ Templates can be created from any Web page.
- ✦ Dreamweaver templates combine locked and editable regions. Editable regions must be defined individually.
- ✦ Once a template is declared, new documents can be created from it.
- ✦ If a template is altered, pages built from that template can be automatically updated.
- ✦ You can modify the default template that Dreamweaver uses so that every time you select File ⇨ New, a new version of your customized template is created.

In the next chapter, you learn how to streamline production and site maintenance with repeating page elements from the Dreamweaver Library.

✦ ✦ ✦

CHAPTER 34

Using the Repeating Elements Library

✦ ✦ ✦ ✦

In This Chapter

Dreamweaver Library basics

Making and inserting Library items

Managing your Dreamweaver Library

Updating your Web sites with Libraries

Using server-side includes

✦ ✦ ✦ ✦

One of the challenges of designing a Web site is ensuring that buttons, copyright notices, and other cross-site features always remain consistent. Fortunately, Dreamweaver offers a useful feature called *Library items* that helps you insert repeating elements, such as a navigation bar or a company logo, into every Web page you create. With one command, you can update and maintain Library items efficiently and productively.

In this chapter, you examine the nature and the importance of repeating elements and learn how to effectively use the Dreamweaver Library feature for all your sites.

Dreamweaver Libraries

Library items within Dreamweaver are another means for you, as a designer, to maintain consistency throughout your site. Suppose you have a navigation bar on every page that contains links to all the other pages on your site. It's highly likely that you'll eventually (and probably more than once) need to make changes to the navigation bar. In a traditional Web development environment, you must modify every single page. This creates lots of opportunities for making mistakes, missing pages, and adding code to the wrong place. Moreover, the whole process is tedious — ask anyone who has had to modify the copyright notice at the bottom of every Web page for a site with over 200 pages.

Another traditional method of updating repeating elements is using *server-side includes*. A server-side include causes the server to place a component, such as a copyright notice, in a specified area of a Web page when it's sent to the user. This arrangement, however, increases the strain on your already overworked Web server and many hosting computers do not permit server-side includes for this reason. Not to mention you have to know how to install server-side scripts. To add to the designer's frustrations, you can't lay out a Web page in a WYSIWYG format and simultaneously see the server-side scripts (unless you're using a Dreamweaver translator). So you either take the time to calculate that a server-side script will take up a specific space on the Web page, or you cross your fingers and guess.

A better way in Dreamweaver is to use an important innovation called the *Library*. The Library is designed to make repetitive updating quick, easy, and as error free as possible. The Library's key features include the following:

- ✦ Any item — whether text or graphic — that goes into the body of your Web page can be designated as a Library item.
- ✦ Once created, Library items can be placed instantly in any Web page in your site, without your having to retype, reinsert, or reformat text and graphics.
- ✦ Library items can be altered at any time. After the editing is complete, Dreamweaver gives you the option to update the Web site immediately or postpone the update until later.
- ✦ If you are making a number of alterations to your Library items, you can wait until you're finished with all the updates and then make the changes across the board in one operation.
- ✦ You can update one page at a time, or you can update the entire site all at once.
- ✦ A Library item can be converted back to a regular non-Library element of a Web page at any time.
- ✦ Library items can be copied from one site to another.
- ✦ Library items can combine Dreamweaver behaviors — and their underlying JavaScript code — with onscreen elements, so you don't have to rebuild the same navigation bar every time, reapplying the behaviors over and over again.

Using the Library Palette

Dreamweaver's Library control center is, of course, the Library palette. There you find the tools for creating, modifying, updating, and managing your Library items. Shown in Figure 34-1, the Library palette is as flexible and easy to use as all of Dreamweaver's primary palettes, with straightforward command buttons, an alphabetical listing of all available Library items, and a handy Preview pane.

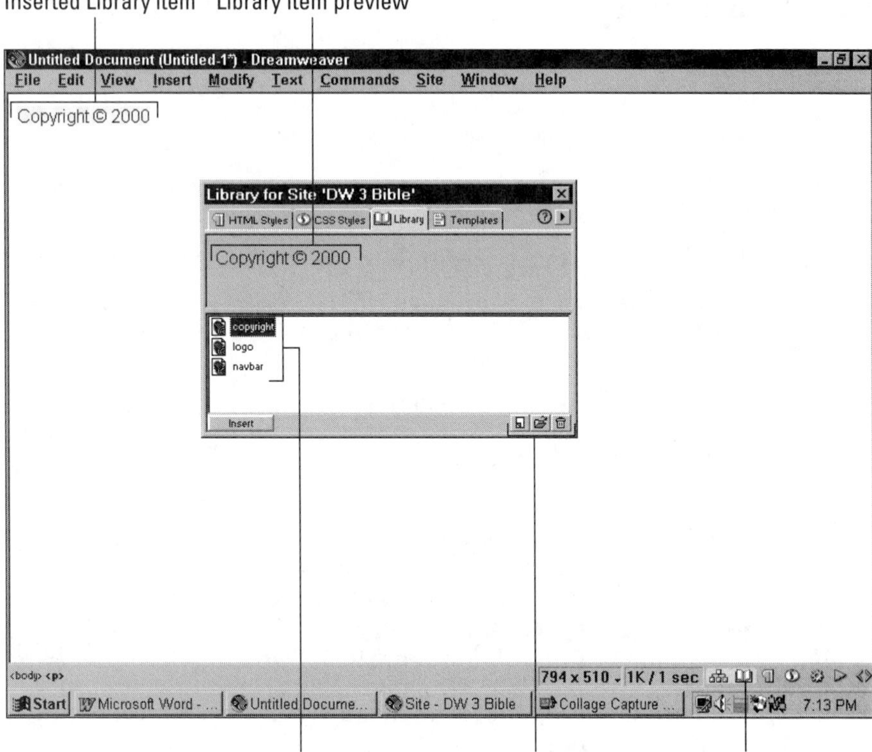

Figure 34-1: With the Dreamweaver Library palette, you can easily add and modify consistent objects on an entire Web site.

As usual, you can open the Library palette in several ways:

✦ Choose Window ➪ Library.

✦ Select the Library button from the Launcher.

✦ Press F6.

To use Library items, you must first create a site root folder for Dreamweaver, as explained in Chapter 6. A separate Library folder is created to hold the individual Library items and is used by Dreamweaver during the updating process.

Ideally, you could save the most time by creating all your Library items before you begin constructing your Web pages, but most Web designers don't work that way. Feel free to include, modify, and update your Library items as much as you need to as your Web site evolves — that's part of the power and flexibility you gain through Dreamweaver's Library.

Adding a Library item

Before you can insert or update a Library item, that item must be designated as such within the Web page. To add an item to your site's Library, follow these steps:

1. Select any part of the Web page that you want to make into a Library item.
2. Open the Library palette with any of the available methods: the Window ➪ Library command, the Library button in the Launcher, or the F6 key.
3. From the Library palette (see Figure 34-1), select the New Library Item button.

   The selected page element is displayed in the upper pane of the Library palette. In the lower pane—the Library item list—a new entry is highlighted with the default name "Untitled."
4. Enter a unique name for your new Library item and press Enter (Return).

   The Library item list is resorted alphabetically, if necessary, and the new item is included.

When a portion of your Web page has been designated as a Library item, a yellow highlight is displayed over the entire item within the Document window. The highlight helps you to quickly recognize what is a Library item and what is not. If you find the yellow highlight distracting, you can disable it. Go to Edit ➪ Preferences and, from the Highlighting panel of the Preferences dialog box, deselect Show check box for Library Items. Alternately, deselecting View ➪ Invisibles hides Library Item highlighting, along with any other invisible items on your page.

At this writing, Dreamweaver can include Library items only in the `<body>` section of an HTML document. You cannot, for instance, create a series of `<meta>` tags for your pages that must go in the `<head>` section.

Drag-and-Drop Creation of Library Items

A second option for creating Library items is the drag-and-drop method. Simply select an object or several objects on a page and drag them to the Library item list of the Library palette; release the mouse button to drop them in.

You can drag any object into the Library palette: text, tables, images, Java applets, plug-ins, and/or ActiveX controls. Essentially anything in the Document window that can be HTML code can be dragged to the Library. And, as you might suspect, the reverse is true: Library items can be placed in your Web page by dragging them from the Library palette list and dropping them anywhere in the Document window.

Moving Library items to a new site

Although Library items are specific to each site, they can be used in more than one site. When you make your first Library item, Dreamweaver creates a folder called Library in the local root folder for the current site. To use a particular Library item in another site, simply open the Library folder from your system's desktop and copy the item to the new site's Library folder.

Be sure to also move any dependent files or other assets such as images and media files associated with the Library items.

Inserting a Library item in your Web page

When you create a Web site, you always need to incorporate certain features, including a standard set of link buttons along the top, a consistent banner on various pages, and a copyright notice along the bottom. Adding these items to a page with the Library palette can be as easy as dragging and dropping them.

You must first create a Web site and then designate Library items (as explained in the preceding section). Once these items exist, you can add the items to any page created within your site.

To add Library items to a document, use the following steps:

1. Position the cursor where you want the Library item to appear.
2. From the Library palette, select the item you wish to use.
3. Select the Insert button. The Library item, highlighted in yellow, appears on the Web page.

Tip

As noted earlier, you can also use the drag-and-drop method to place Library items in the Document window.

When you add a Library item to a page, you notice a number of immediate changes. As mentioned, the added Library item is highlighted in light yellow. If you click anywhere on the item, the entire Library item is selected.

It's important to understand that Dreamweaver treats the entire Library item entry as an external object being linked to the current page. You cannot modify Library items directly on a page. For information on editing Library entries, see the section "Editing a Library Item," later in this chapter.

While the Library item is highlighted, notice also that the Property Inspector changes. Instead of displaying the properties for the HTML object that is selected, the item is identified as a Library item, as shown in Figure 34-2.

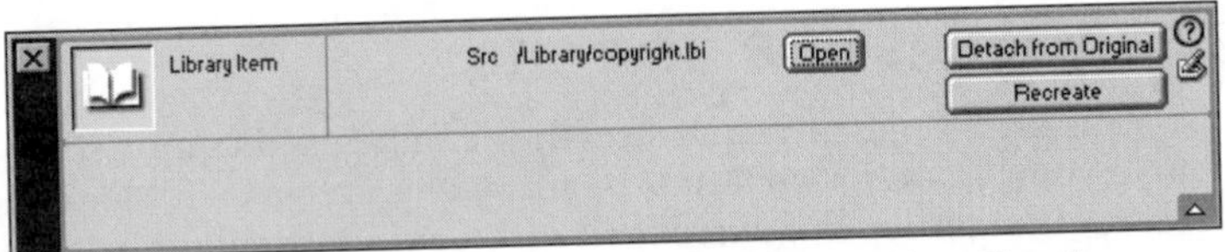

Figure 34-2: The Library Item Property Inspector identifies the source file for any selected Library entry.

You can also see evidence of Library items in the HTML for the current page. Open the HTML Inspector, and you see that several lines of code have been added. The following code example indicates one Library item:

```
<!-- #BeginLibraryItem "/Library/title.lbi" -->
<font color="#FF6633" face="Verdana, Arial, Helvetica, sans-serif" ¬
size="-4">
<b>Copyright &copy; 2000</b></font>
<!-- #EndLibraryItem -->
```

In this case, the Library item happens to be a phrase: "Copyright © 2000." (The character entity `©` is used to represent the c-in-a-circle copyright mark in HTML.) In addition to the code that specifies the font face, color, and size, notice the text before and after the HTML code. These are commands within the comments that tell Dreamweaver it is looking at a Library item. One line marks the beginning of the Library item:

```
<!-- #BeginLibraryItem "/Library/title.lbi" -->
```

and another marks the end:

```
<!-- #EndLibraryItem -->
```

Two items are of interest here. First, notice how the Library demarcation surrounds not just the text ("Copyright © 2000") but all of its formatting attributes. Library items can do far more than just cut and paste raw text. The second thing to note is that the Library markers are placed discreetly within HTML comments. Web browsers ignore the Library markers and render the code in between them.

The value in the opening Library code, `"/Library/title.lbi"`, is the source file for the Library entry. This file is located in the Library folder, inside of the current site root folder. Library source (.lbi) files can be opened with a text editor or in Dreamweaver; they consist of plain HTML code without the `<html>` and `<body>` tags.

The .lbi file for our title example would contain the following:

```
<font color="#FF6633" face="Verdana, Arial, Helvetica, sans-serif" ¬
size="-4">
<b>Copyright &copy; 2000</b></font>
```

The power of repeating elements is that they are simply HTML. There is no need to learn proprietary languages to customize Library items. Anything, except for information found in the header of a Web page, can be included in a Library file.

The importance of the `<!-- #BeginLibraryItem>` and `<!-- #EndLibraryItem>` tags becomes evident when you start to update Library items for a site. You examine how Dreamweaver can be used to automatically update your entire Web site in the section "Updating Your Web Sites with Libraries," later in this chapter.

Deleting an item from the Library

Removing an entry from your site's Library is a two-step process. First, you must delete the item from the Library palette. Then, if you want to keep the item on your page, you must make it editable again. Without completing the second step, Dreamweaver maintains the Library highlight and, more important, prevents you from modifying the element.

To delete an item from the Library, follow these steps:

1. Open the Web page containing the Library item you want to delete.
2. Open the Library palette by choosing Window ➪ Library or by selecting the Library button from the Launcher.
3. Select the Library item in the Library palette's list and click the Delete Library Item button.
4. Dreamweaver asks if you are sure you want to delete the item. Select Yes, and the entry is removed from the Library item list. (Or select No to cancel.)
5. In the Document window, select the element you are removing from the Library.
6. In the Property Inspector, click the Detach from Original button.
7. As shown in Figure 34-3, Dreamweaver warns you that if you proceed, the item cannot be automatically updated (as a Library element). Select OK to proceed. The yellow Library highlighting vanishes, and the element can now be modified individually.

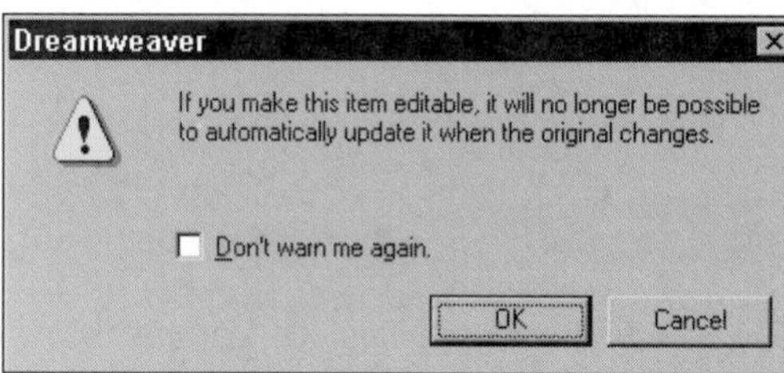

Figure 34-3: When making an item editable from the Library, Dreamweaver alerts you that, if you proceed, you won't be able to update the item automatically using the Library function.

Should you unintentionally delete a Library item in the Library palette, you can restore it if you still have the entry included in a Web page. Select the element within the page and, in the Property Inspector, choose the Recreate button. Dreamweaver restores the item to the Library item list, with the original Library name.

Renaming a Library item

It's easy to rename a Library item, but you should exercise caution when doing so. Renaming a Library item only renames that item in the Library folder—it does not rename the item in any Web page where the item has already been inserted. Should you attempt to modify and update the renamed item, occurrences of the same item under the old name in existing pages are not updated.

To give an existing Library entry a new name, open the Library palette and click the name of the item once. The name is highlighted, and a small box appears around it. Enter the new name and press Enter (Return).

The best strategy to follow when renaming a Library item is to rename it before you insert the entry into any Web pages. If, however, you want to rename the item after it has been included in one or more Web pages, you can take either of two approaches to the renaming task:

- ✦ If the renamed item is included in only a few Web pages, open every Web page containing the Library item that you've renamed. Delete the original entry from the Web page and insert the renamed item.
- ✦ If the renamed item has been included on a number of pages in your Web site, use Dreamweaver's extended Find and Replace feature to change the item's name within the HTML code.

Let's look at an example of the second option. Suppose you've included a Library entry, originally called LibraryItem01, on six or seven Web pages within a site. Later you decide to change the name to something more descriptive, such as CopyrightLine. After you've renamed the item in the Library, you need to correct the previously inserted entries so all future uses of the entry are correct. Because you have numerous entries to fix, you decide to use Dreamweaver's Replace command to change the name within the HTML. You would search for

```
<!-- #BeginLibraryItem "/Library/LibraryItem01.lbi" -->
```

and replace it with

```
<!-- #BeginLibraryItem "/Library/CopyrightLine.lbi" -->
```

Dreamweaver has extremely powerful Find and Replace features that enable you to quickly change all the entries in all the pages of a Web site. You can find the details in Chapter 9.

Editing a Library Item

Rarely do you create a Library item that is perfect from the beginning and never needs to be changed. Whether it is due to site redesign or the addition of new sections to a site, you'll find yourself going back to Library items and modifying them, sometimes over and over again. You can use the full power of Dreamweaver's design capabilities to alter your Library items, within the restraints of Library items in general. In other words, you can modify an image, reformat a body of text, add new material to a boilerplate paragraph, and have the resulting changes reflected across your Web site. However, you cannot add anything to a Library item that is not contained in the HTML `<body>` tags.

To modify Library items, Dreamweaver uses a special editing window that is identifiable by its neutral background. You access this editing window through the Library palette. Follow these steps to modify an existing Library item:

1. In the Library palette, select the item you wish to modify from the list of available entries.
2. Click the Open Library Item button. The Library editing window opens with the selected entry, as shown in Figure 34-4.

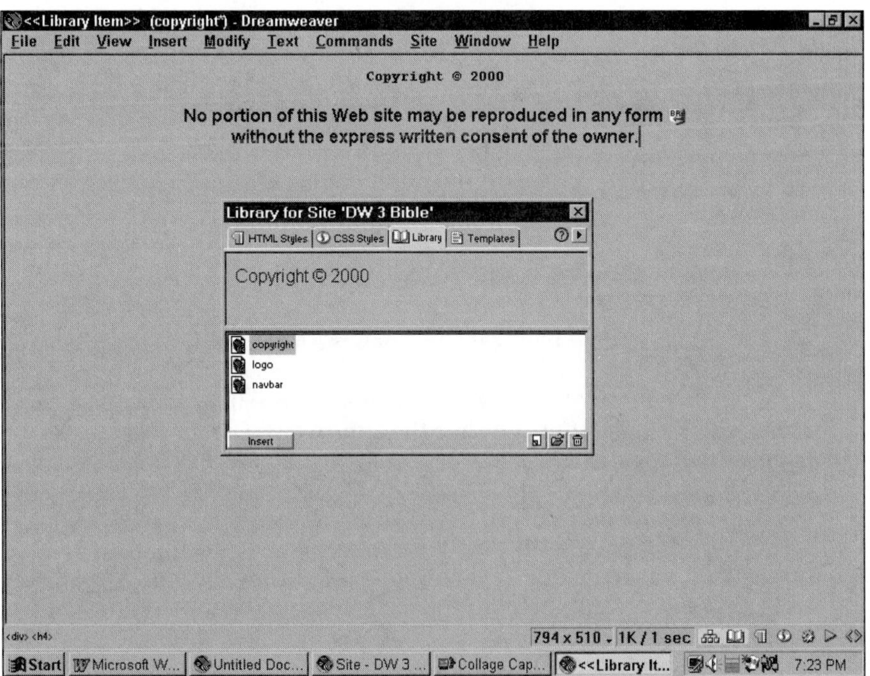

Figure 34-4: Use the Library editing window to modify existing Library items.

3. Make any necessary modifications to the Library entry.
4. When you are finished with your changes, choose File ➪ Save or press Ctrl+S (Command+S).
5. Dreamweaver notes that your Library item has been modified and asks if you would like to update all of the Web pages in your site that contain the item. Select Yes to update all of the Library items, including the one just modified, or select No to postpone the update. (See the next section, "Updating Your Web Sites with Libraries.")
6. Close the editing window by selecting the Close button or choosing File ➪ Close.

Once you've completed the editing operation and closed the editing window, you can open any Web page containing the modified Library item to view the changes.

You cannot use some features when editing Library items. These include timelines, behaviors, and styles. Each of these modifications requires a JavaScript function to be placed in the `<head>` tags of a page—a task that the Dreamweaver Library function cannot currently handle. One workaround is to use a Dreamweaver template to add entire pages with JavaScript functions included, as described in Chapter 33. You could, of course, also add behaviors to an page element before converting it to a Library item.

Updating Your Web Sites with Libraries

The effectiveness of the Dreamweaver Library feature becomes more significant when it comes time to update an entire multipage site. Dreamweaver offers two opportunities for you to update your site:

✦ Immediately after modifying a Library item, as explained in the preceding steps for editing a Library item

✦ At a time of your choosing, through the Modify ➪ Library command

An immediate update to every page on your site can be accomplished when you edit a Library item. After you save the alterations, Dreamweaver asks if you'd like to apply the update to Web pages in your site. If you click Yes, Dreamweaver not only applies the current modification to all pages in the site, but it also applies any other alterations that you have made previously in this Library.

The second way to modify a Library item is by using the Modify ➪ Library command, and when you use this method, you can choose to update the current page or the entire site.

To update just the current page, choose Modify ➪ Library ➪ Update Current Page. Dreamweaver makes a quick check to see what Library items you are managing on the current page and then compares them to the site's Library items. If any differences exist, Dreamweaver modifies the page accordingly.

To update an entire Web site, follow these steps:

1. Choose Modify ➪ Library ➪ Update Pages. The Update Pages dialog box opens (see Figure 34-5).

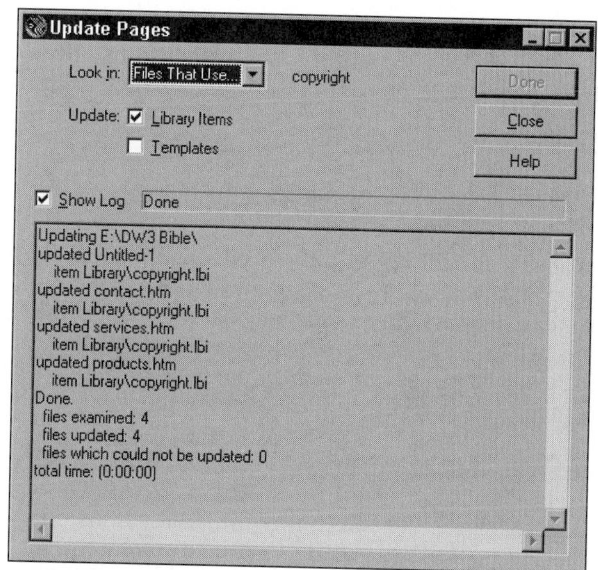

Figure 34-5: The Update Pages dialog box enables you to apply any changes to your Library items across an entire site and informs you of the progress.

2. If you want Dreamweaver to update all of the Library items in all of the Web pages in your site, select Entire Site from the Look In drop-down list and choose the name of your site in the drop-down list on the right. You can also have Dreamweaver update only the pages in your site that contain a specific Library item. Select the Files That Use option from the Look In drop-down list and then select the Library item that you would like to have updated across your site from the drop-down list on the right.
3. If you want to see the results from the update process, leave the Show Log checkbox selected. (Turning off the Log reduces the size of the Site Update dialog box.)

4. Choose the Start button. Dreamweaver processes the entire site for Library updates. Any Library items contained are modified to reflect the changes.

Although Dreamweaver does modify Library items on currently open pages during an Update Site operation, you have to save the pages to accept the changes.

The Update Pages log displays any errors encountered in the update operation. A log containing the notation

```
item Library\Untitled2.lbi -- not updated, library item not found
```

indicates that one Web page contains a reference to a Library item that has been removed. Though this is not a critical error, you might want to use Dreamweaver's Find and Replace feature to search your Web site for the code and remove it.

Applying Server-Side Includes

In some ways, the server-side include (SSI) is the predecessor of the Dreamweaver Library item. The difference is that with Library items, Dreamweaver updates the Web pages at design time, whereas with server-side includes, the server handles the updating at runtime (when the files are actually served to the user). Server-side includes can also include server variables, such as the current date and time (both locally and Greenwich mean time) or the date the current file was last saved.

Because server-side includes are integrated in the standard HTML code, a special file extension is used to identify pages using them. Any page with server-side includes is most often saved with either the .shtml or .shtm extension. When a server encounters such a file, the file is read and processed by the server.

Not all servers support server-side includes. Some Web hosting companies disable the function because of potential security risks and performance issues. Each .shtml page requires additional processing time, and if a site uses many SSI pages, the server can slow down significantly. Be sure to check with your Web host as to its policy before including SSIs in your Web pages.

Server-side includes are often used to insert header or footer items into the `<body>` of an HTML page. Typically, the server-side include itself is just a file with HTML. To insert a file, the SSI code looks like the following:

```
<!-- #include file="footer.html" -->
```

Note how the HTML comment structure is used to wrap around the SSI directive. This ensures that browsers ignore the code, but servers do not. The file attribute defines the path name of the file to be included, relative to the current page. To include a file relative to the current site root, use the virtual attribute, as follows:

```
<!-- #include virtual="/main/images/spaceman.jpg" -->
```

As evident in this example, you can use SSIs to include more than just HTML files — you can also include graphics.

With Dreamweaver's translator mechanism, server-side includes can be visible in the Document window during the design process. All you need to do is make sure that the Translation preferences are set correctly, as described in the section "Modifying Translators," later in this chapter.

One of the major benefits of SSIs is inserting information from the server itself, such as the current file size or time. One tag, `<!-- #echo -->`, is used to define a custom variable that is returned when the SSI is called, as well as numerous *environmental variables*. An environmental variable is information available to the server, such as the date a file was last modified or its URL.

Table 34-1 details the possible server tags and their attributes.

Table 34-1
Server-Side Include Variables

Tag	*Attribute*	*Description*
`<!-- #config -->`	`errmsg`, `sizefmt`, or `timefmt`	Used to customize error messages, file size, or time and date displays
`<!-- #echo -->`	`var` or environmental variables such as `last_modified`, `document_name`, `document_url`, `date_local`, or `date_gmt`	Returns the specified variable
`<!-- #exec -->`	`cmd` or `cgi`	Executes a system command or CGI program
`<!-- #flastmod -->`	`file` or `virtual`	Displays the last modified date of a file other than the current one
`<!-- #fsize -->`	`file` or `virtual`	Displays the size of a file other than the current one
`<!-- #include -->`	`file` or `virtual`	Inserts the contents of the specified file to the current one

Modifying translators

When Dreamweaver displays the contents of the file being called by a server-side include, it has the capability to function like a server — processing the instruction and inserting the file in your page. You can control whether this feature is turned on or in which files such translation occurs. You can even opt to see the translation on a page-by-page basis. The translator controls are handled through the Preferences dialog box.

To change the translator options, follow these steps:

1. Choose Edit ➪ Preferences and then select the Translation category.

   The Translation panel appears, as seen in Figure 34-6.

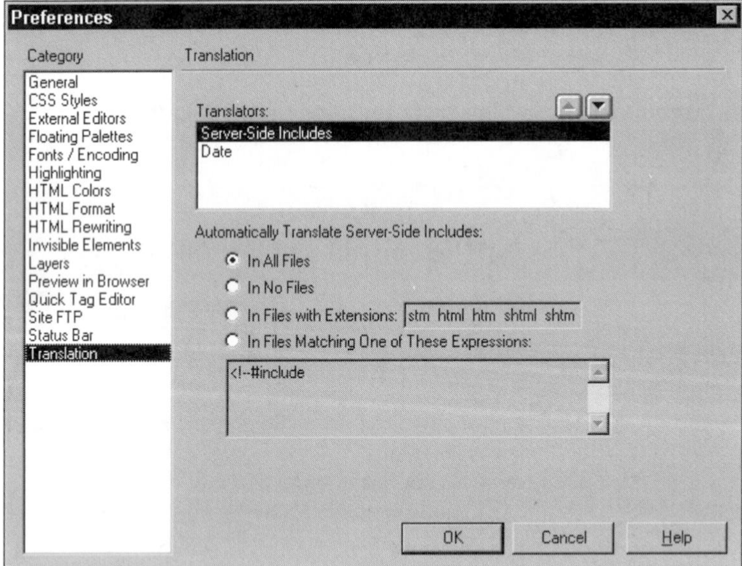

Figure 34-6: In the Translation panel of the Preferences dialog box, you can control Dreamweaver's processing of server-side includes.

2. Select Server-Side Includes from the list of Translators.

   By default, Dreamweaver is set to automatically translate SSI content in all files.

3. To alter the conditions under which translation takes place, select one of the following options under the Automatically Translate Server-Side Includes heading:

   - **In All Files:** Translation occurs whenever a modification is made to the page.

- **In No Files:** Translation must be specified manually.
- **In Files with Extensions:** Only the files with the listed extension are automatically translated.
- **In Files Matching One of These Expressions:** Only the files that include one or more of the listed tags are translated.

4. Click OK when you're done.

If you decide to handle all the SSI translations one page at a time by selecting the Automatically Translate In No Files option, choose Modify ➪ Translate — Server-Side Includes to view a translated page.

Adding server-side includes

Dreamweaver has made inserting a server-side include in your Web page very straightforward. You can use a Dreamweaver object to easily select and bring in the files to be included. Any other type of SSI, such as declaring a variable, must be entered in by hand, but you can use the Comment object to do so without opening the HTML Inspector.

To use server-side includes to incorporate a file, follow these steps:

1. In the Document window, place your cursor in the location where you would like to add the server-side include.
2. Select Insert ➪ Server-Side Include or choose Insert Server-Side Include from the Invisibles panel of the Objects palette.

   The standard Select File dialog box appears.
3. In the Select File dialog box, type in the URL of the HTML page you would like to include in the File Name text box or use the Browse (Choose) button to locate the file. Click OK when you're done.

   Dreamweaver displays the contents of the HTML file at the desired location in your page, if the proper Translation option is enabled. Should the Property Inspector be available, the SSI Property Inspector is displayed (see Figure 34-7).
4. In the Property Inspector, if the server-side include calls a file-relative document path, select the Type File option. Or, if the SSI calls a site root–relative file, choose the Type Virtual option.

Tip

Because server-side includes can be placed only within the body of a Dreamweaver file, the contents of the HTML page that you wish to include should not have any tags that are not readable within the body section of a document, such as `<head>`, `<title>`, or `<meta>` — or the `<body>` tag itself. You can, however, design your HTML page in Dreamweaver, and then use the HTML editing panel to remove any such tags before inserting the page into your document with a server-side include.

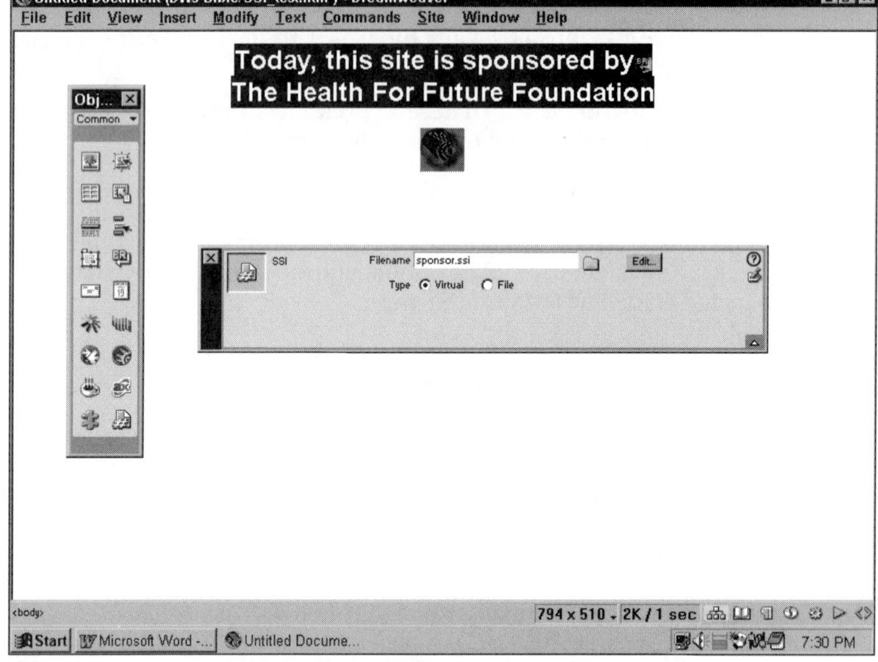

Figure 34-7: The selected text is actually a server-side include automatically translated by Dreamweaver 3, as evident from the SSI Property Inspector.

Editing server-side includes

As is the case with Library items, it is not possible to directly edit files that have been inserted into a Web page using server-side includes. In fact, should you try, the entire text block highlights as one. The text for a server-side included file is not editable through Dreamweaver's HTML Inspector, although the SSI code is.

To edit the contents of the server-side included file, follow these steps:

1. Select the server-side include in the Document window.
2. Select the Edit button from the SSI Property Inspector.

   The file opens in a new Dreamweaver window for editing.
3. When you've finished altering the file, select File ➪ Save or use the keyboard shortcut Ctrl+S (Command+S).
4. Close the file editing window by choosing File ➪ Close.

Dreamweaver automatically reflects the changes in your currently open document.

As is not the case with a Library item, Dreamweaver does not ask if any other linked files should be updated because all blending of regular HTML and SSIs happens at runtime or when the file is open in Dreamweaver and the SSI translator is engaged.

Extending Dreamweaver with XSSI

Both Dreamweaver Library items and server-side includes are useful for easily updating a range of pages when changing one item. But what if you have to change that one item several times a day—or based on which domain the user is coming from? To handle these tasks automatically, a system must support some form of conditional tags, such as `if-then` statements. Such a system is now available through Apache servers and XSSI, extended server-side includes. Most importantly, a full set of XSSI objects, translators, and Property Inspectors for Dreamweaver have been built by the wonderful programmers at Webmonkey (`www.webmonkey.com`). You can find the XSSI extensions on CD-ROM 1 that comes with this book.

In addition to handling standard server-side includes, the XSSI extensions offer a series of conditional statements: `if`, `elif` (`else-if`), `else`, and `endif`. The beauty of the Webmonkey objects is that you can construct or edit these conditional statements through their graphical user interface. The basic syntax of the conditional statements is as follows:

```
<!--#if expr="text_expression" -->
If the above is true, perform this action
<!--#elif expr="text_expression" -->
Else if the above is true, do this
<!--#else -->
Otherwise, do this
<!--#endif -->
```

The XSSI extensions also have the capability of setting an environmental variable so that you can view your page under various conditions. For example, let's say you've written a script that includes a particular file that greets the visitor in a proper way, depending on which browser is being used. Your conditional script would look to the HTTP_USER_AGENT variable to see which message to serve. With the XSSI Set Env Variables command, you could test your script during the design phase without having to visit the server at different times of the day. The following figure displays the Set XSSI Environment Variables dialog box.

Continued

Continued

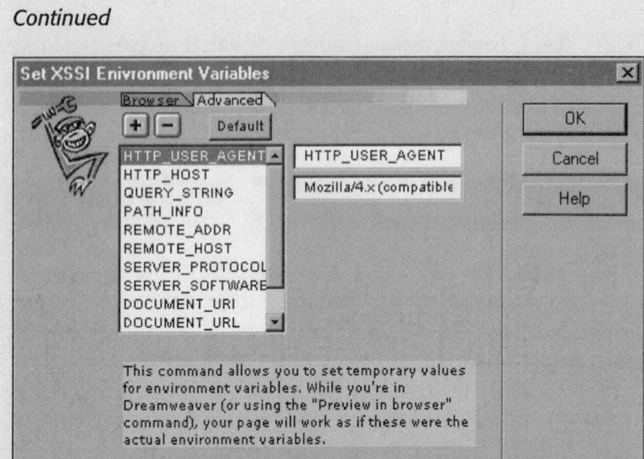

One note of caution: Due to a potential conflict between the two translators, installing the XSSI extensions disables the standard SSI translator. Make sure your system is XSSI compatible (it uses Apache server software) before incorporating the XSSI extensions.

Summary

In this chapter, you learned how you can easily and effectively create Library items that can be repeated throughout an entire site to help maintain consistency.

✦ Library items can consist of any text, object, or HTML code contained in the <body> of a Web page.

✦ The quickest method to create a Library item is to drag the code from the Dreamweaver Document window into the Library palette's list area.

✦ Editing Library items is also easy with the Library palette. Just click the Edit button, and you can swiftly make all of your changes.

✦ The Modify ➪ Library ➪ Update Pages command enables easy maintenance of your Web site.

✦ Server-side includes enable files to be inserted into the final HTML at runtime by the server. Dreamweaver's translation feature enables you to preview these effects.

In the next chapter, you learn how to build Web sites with a team in Dreamweaver.

✦ ✦ ✦

CHAPTER 35

Maximizing Browser Targeting

✦ ✦ ✦ ✦

In This Chapter

Maintaining different versions of Web pages

Handling cross-browser compatibility

Planning for backward compatibility

Dreamweaver Technique: Browser checking

Creating your own browser profile

✦ ✦ ✦ ✦

Each new release of a browser is a double-edged sword. On the one hand, an exciting new array of features is made possible. On the other, Web designers have to cope with yet another browser-compatibility issue. In today's market, you find all of the following in use:

- A rapidly increasing number of 5.0 browsers that, although fairly standards compliant, are still different from each other in implementation
- A host of fourth-generation browsers, widely varying in their capabilities
- A decreasing number of 3.0 browsers, limited in some basic functionality
- A small group of 2.0 browsers in the machines of determined users who have never (and may never) upgraded
- A diverse assortment of browsers outside the mainstream, including Opera, WebTV, and Navigator for Linux
- Various versions of America Online browsers, which range from being completely proprietary to being a blend of current and special technologies; as a specific example, AOL 4.0 is not the same as Internet Explorer 4.0, although it is based on it.

Browser-compatibility is one of a Web designer's primary concerns (not to mention the source of major headaches); and many strategies are evolving to deal with this matter. Dreamweaver is in the forefront of cross-browser Web page design, both in terms of the type of code it routinely outputs and in its specialty functions. This chapter examines the browser-targeting techniques available in Dreamweaver. From multibrowser code to conversion innovations to browser validation capabilities, Dreamweaver helps you get your Web pages out to the widest audience, and with the most features.

Converting Pages in Dreamweaver

DHTML's gifts of layers and Cascading Style Sheets are extremely tempting to use because of their enhanced typographic control and absolute-positioning capabilities. Many Web designers, however, have resisted using these features because only fourth-generation browsers can view them. Though Dreamweaver can't change the capabilities of 3.0 browsers, it can make it easy for you to create alternative content for them.

Dreamweaver makes it possible to convert Web pages designed with layers and CSS into pages that can be rendered by 3.0 browsers. Moreover, if you're looking to upgrade your site from nested tables to layers, you don't have to do it by hand. Dreamweaver also includes a command to convert tables to layers, preserving their location but enabling greater design flexibility and dynamic control. A Webmaster's life just got a tad easier.

To see how to use Dreamweaver's Layers-to-Tables roundtrip features, see Chapter 28.

Making 3.0-compatible pages

It's a slight misstatement that Dreamweaver converts 4.0 feature-laden pages into pages that can be read by 3.0 browsers. Actually, Dreamweaver creates a new 3.0-compatible page based on the 4.0 page—and does it in almost no time at all. Once you've converted your page, you can use Dreamweaver's Check Browser behavior to route users to the appropriate pages, based on their browser version.

Preparing your page for conversion

When Dreamweaver makes a new 3.0-compatible page, layers are converted to nested tables, and Cascading Style Sheet references are converted to inline character styles. You have the option to convert either or both features. To accomplish this conversion of your 4.0 Web page, the document must meet the following conditions:

✦ **All content must be in layers:** Because Dreamweaver converts layers to tables, it must start with everything absolutely positioned.

✦ **Layers must not overlap:** During the conversion process, Dreamweaver warns you when it finds overlapping layers and even tells you which ones they are.

A feature in Dreamweaver prevents you from encountering the problem of overlapping layers in the design stage. Enable the option by choosing View ➪ Prevent Layer Overlaps or clicking the Prevent Overlaps checkbox on the Layers palette. While this can't separate layers that are currently overlapping—you have to do that by hand—it does stop you from accidentally laying one layer on top of another and makes 3.0 conversion a breeze.

✦ **Nesting layers are not allowed:** When one layer is inside another, the inner layer is placed relative to the outer layer. Dreamweaver cannot convert relatively positioned layers.

✦ **The `<ilayer>` tag cannot be used:** Because the `<ilayer>` tag is based on relative positioning, Dreamweaver cannot convert it. Use `<layer>`, `<div>`, or `<span>` instead.

Some Web pages you might like to convert—or devolve—from 4.0 to 3.0 applicability have content both in and out of layers. And, as noted, Dreamweaver needs to have all the Web page elements in a layer before proceeding with conversion. Previously, it was necessary to cut elements outside of a layer and paste them in to prepare the page for conversion. Dreamweaver does it for you—just choose Modify ➪ Layout Mode ➪ Convert Tables to Layers, or choose the keyboard shortcut Ctrl+F6 (Command+F6). In the dialog box that appears, be sure to choose the Select Layer Overlap option to avoid that problem. Click OK, and Dreamweaver places everything in a layer, automatically—without gene-rating a new page. For more on using this new capability, see Chapter 28.

Running the conversion

Once your page is prepped, generating a 3.0-compatible Web page from a 4.0 version is straightforward. You have only a couple of options—whether to convert layers, CSS styles, or both—and once you make your choice and click OK, the rest of the process is almost instantaneous.

To create a 3.0-compatible version of a Web page with 4.0 features, follow these steps:

1. Choose File ➪ Convert ➪ 3.0 Browser.

   The Convert to 3.0 Browser Compatible dialog box opens, as shown in Figure 35-1.

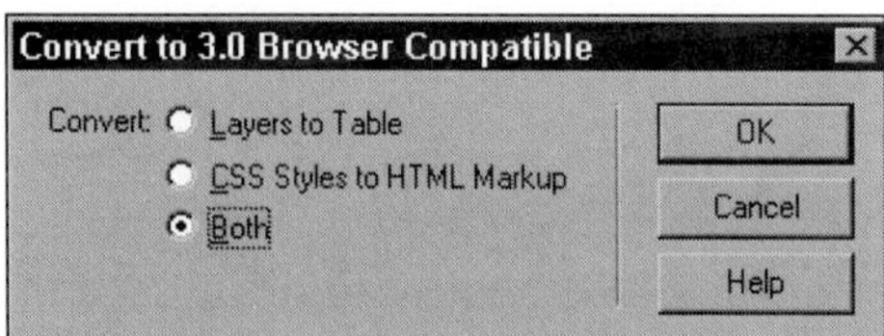

Figure 35-1: Begin to build your cross browser–compatible site with Dreamweaver's Convert Layers to Table command.

2. From the Convert to 3.0 Browser Compatible dialog box, select your options:
   - If you are converting layers to tables only, choose the Layers to Table radio button.
   - If you are converting Cascading Style Sheet styles to HTML tags only, choose the CSS Styles to HTML Markup radio button.
   - If you are making all conversions, select the Both radio button.
3. Click OK, and Dreamweaver starts the conversion. A dialog box informs you if a problem is encountered, such as a nested layer or overlapping layers. If the Web page has overlapping layers, another dialog box (shown in Figure 35-2) tells you which layers are overlapping. Dreamweaver cannot proceed until all conflicts are resolved. If no problems occur, Dreamweaver creates the page in a new window.

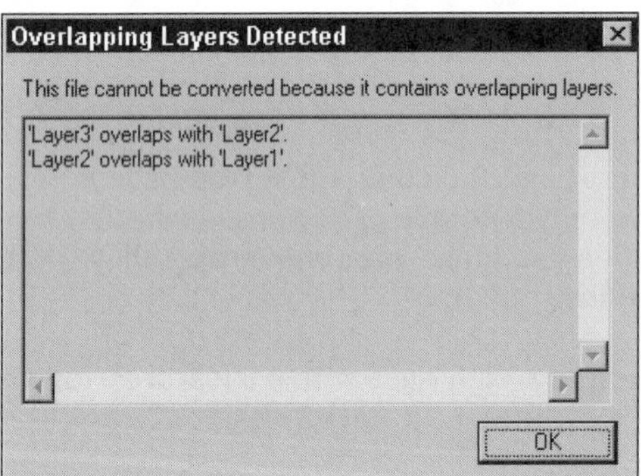

Figure 35-2: On a page with multiple layers, Dreamweaver spots the "illegal" overlapping ones when you try to convert the page to tables.

The CSS-to-HTML conversion disregards any CSS feature, such as line spacing, that is not implemented in regular HTML. In addition, the exact point size that can be specified in CSS is roughly translated to the relative size equivalents in HTML. Any font over 36 points is set to the largest HTML size, which is 7.

Evolving 3.0 pages to 4.0 standards

Web sites are constantly upgraded and modified. You'll eventually need to enhance a more traditional site with new features, such as layers. Some of the older 3.0-oriented sites used elaborately nested tables on their pages to create a semblance of absolute positioning; normally, upgrading these Web pages takes hours and hours of tedious cutting and pasting. Dreamweaver can bring these older pages up to speed with the Convert Tables to Layers command, found under the Modify ➪ Layout Mode submenu item.

The Convert Tables to Layers command can also be used to convert a page created by another Web authoring program (Net Objects Fusion, for example) that uses nested tables for positioning. Once tables have been transformed into layers, the layout of the entire page is much easier to modify. It's even possible to make the switch from 3.0 to 4.0 capabilities, modify your page, and then, with the Convert Layers to Tables command, re-create your 3.0-compliant page.

The name of the Convert Tables to Layers command is another one that's a little misleading. Once you issue this command, every HTML element in the new page—not just the tables—is placed in a layer. Moreover, every cell with content in every table is converted into its own layer. In other words, if you are working with a 3 × 3 table in which one cell is left empty, Dreamweaver creates eight different layers for just the table.

If you want to convert a 3.0-compatible page to a page with layers, but the page has no tables, Dreamweaver places all the content in one layer, as if the `<body>` tag was one big single-cell table.

To convert a 3.0-browser-compatible Web page with tables to a 4.0-browser-compatible Web page with layers, choose Modify ➪ Layout Mode ➪ Convert Tables to Layers. If you need to return to a table-based layout, choose Modify ➪ Layout Mode ➪ Convert Layers to Tables.

Ensuring Browser Compatibility

As more browsers and browser versions become available, a Web designer has two basic options to stay on the road to compatibility: *internal* and *external*.

- ✦ The **internal** method uses scripts on the same Web page; the scripts deliver the proper code depending on the browser detected. Many of Dreamweaver's own behavior functions manage the browser issue internally.
- ✦ The **external** approach examines each visitor's browser right off the bat and reroutes the user to the most appropriate Web page.

Both the internal and the external methods have their pluses and minuses, and both are better suited to particular situations. For example, it is impractical to use the external method of creating multiple versions of the same Web pages when you are working with a large site. Suddenly, you've gone from managing 300 pages of information to 900 or 1,200. Of course, you don't have to duplicate every page—but because of the open nature of the Web, where any page can be bookmarked and entered directly, you have to plan carefully and provide routing routines at the key locations. Conversely, sometimes you have no choice but to use multiple versions, especially if a page employs many browser-specific features.

Don't get the idea that the internal and external strategies are mutually exclusive. Several sites today are routing 3.0 browsers to one page and using internal coding methods to differentiate between the various 4.0 browser versions on another page. This section examines techniques for implementing browser-compatibility from both the internal and external perspective.

Internal coding for cross-browser compatibility

Imagine the shouts of joy when the Web development community learned that the 4.0 versions of Navigator and Internet Explorer both supported Cascading Style Sheet layers! Now imagine the grumbling when it became apparent that each browser uses a different JavaScript syntax for calling them. You get the picture: It all boils down to differences in each browser's Document Object Model.

Although it has not been released at the time of this writing, Navigator 6.0 incorporates the W3C standard for layers, which is also largely supported by Internet Explorer 4.0 and above. Although this will eventually simplify compatibility issues for Web designers, Navigator 4.x browsers will remain in use for some time and the code for handling layers in those browsers must be accounted for.

Calling layers

When referring to a layer, Navigator uses this syntax:

```
document.layers["layerName"]
```

whereas Internet Explorer uses this syntax:

```
document.all["layerName"]
```

The trick to internal code-switching is to assign the variations — the "layers" from Navigator and the "all" from Internet Explorer — to the same variable, depending on which browser is being used. Here's a sample function that does just that:

```
function init(){
if (navigator.appName == "Netscape") {
var layerRef="document.layers";
}else {
var layerRef="document.all";
}
}
```

In this function, if the visitor is using a Netscape browser, the variable `layerRef` is assigned the value `document.layers`; otherwise, `layerRef` is set to `document.all`.

Calling properties

If you're looking to assign or read a layer property, one variable is only half the battle. Another difference exists in the way properties are called. With Navigator, it's done like this:

```
document.layers["layerName"].top
```

and with Internet Explorer, it's as follows:

```
document.all["layerName"].style.top
```

Internet Explorer inserts another hierarchical division, called `style`, whereas Navigator doesn't use anything at all. The solution is another variable, `styleRef`, which for Internet Explorer is set like this:

```
var styleRef="style"
```

And the Navigator `styleRef` is actually set to a *null string*, or nothing. You can combine the two variables into one initialization function, which is best called from an `onLoad` event in the `<body>` tag:

```
function init(){
if (navigator.appName == "Netscape") {
var layerRef="document.layers";
var styleRef = "";
}else {
var layerRef="document.all";
var styleRef="style";
}
}
```

Once these differences are accommodated, the variables are ready to be used in a script. To do this, you can use JavaScript's built-in `eval()` function to combine the variables and the object references. Here's an example that sets a new variable, `varLeft`, to whatever is the `left` value of a particular layer:

```
varLeft = eval(layerRef + '["myLayer"]' + styleRef + '.left');
```

Luckily, the variations between the Navigator and Internet Explorer DOM are consistent enough that a JavaScript function can assign the proper values with a minimum of effort.

Calling objects within layers

There's one other area where the two DOMs diverge. When you are attempting to address almost any entity inside a layer, Navigator uses an additional hierarchical layer to reference the object. Thus, a named image in a named layer in Navigator is referenced like this:

```
document.layers["layerName"].document.imageName
```

whereas the same object in Internet Explorer is called like this:

```
document.imageName
```

This is why the Show-Hide Layers behavior passes two arguments with the affected layers' name: one in the Navigator format and the other in the Internet Explorer syntax.

Designing Web pages for backward compatibility

The previous section describes a technique for dealing with the differences between 4.0 and above browsers, but how do you handle the much larger gap between third- and fourth-generation browsers? When this gap becomes a canyon, with DHTML-intensive pages on one side and incompatible browsers on the other, the ultimate answer is to use redirection to send a particular browser to an appropriate page. However, browsers can coexist in plenty of cases—with a little planning and a little help from Dreamweaver.

When designing backwardly compatible Web pages, browsers generally offer one major advantage: ignorance. If a browser doesn't recognize a tag or attribute, it just ignores it and renders the rest of the page. Because many of the newer features are built on new tags, or on tags such as `<div>` that previously were little used, your Web pages can gracefully devolve from 4.0 to 3.0 behavior, without causing errors or grossly misrendering the page.

Take layers, for instance. One advantage offered by this DHTML feature is the capability to make something interactively appear and disappear. Although that's not possible in 3.0 browsers (without extensive image-swapping), it is possible to display the same material and even enable some degree of navigation. The key is proper placement of the layer code, and not the layer itself.

Browsers basically read and render the code for a Web page from top to bottom. You can, for example, make several layers appear one after another in a 3.0 browser, even if they appear to be stacked on top of one another in a 4.0 browser. All you have to do is make sure the code—not the position of the layers—appears in the document sequentially. You can see this effect in Figure 35-3, where all three layers have the same `left` coordinates. However, the layer symbols inserted by Dreamweaver to represent the actual code appear one after the other with a little whitespace in between. The navigational links in the upper left have two roles: They are linked to the named anchor next to the layer's code and, through the Behavior Inspector, are set to show and hide the appropriate layers when selected (using the `onClick` event).

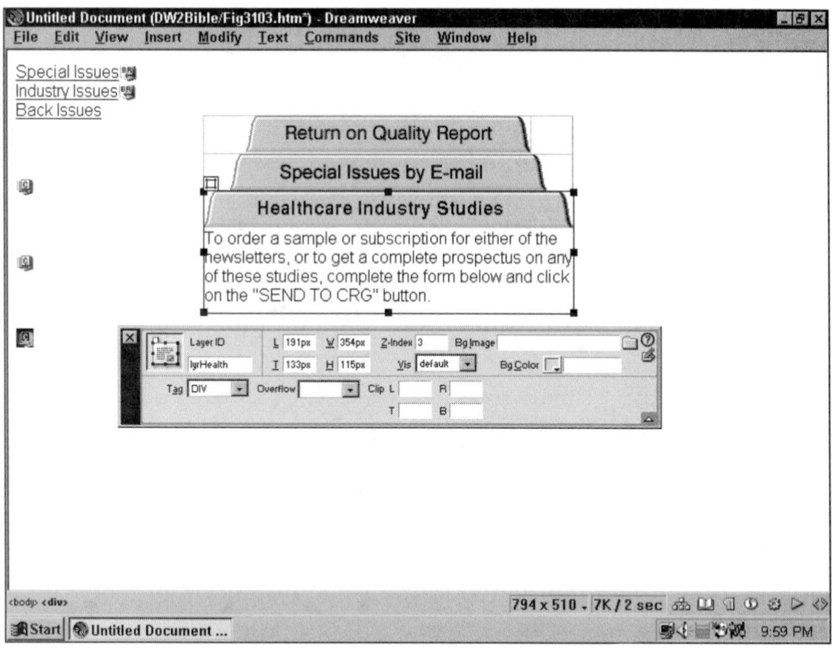

Figure 35-3: Careful placement of the code for layers can be an effective tool for backward compatibility.

Because the code for the three layers is spaced one after the other, browsers that do not understand the `style` attribute in the `<div>` tags — which create the layers — simply render the information contained within all three tags, one after another.

Although it may seem obvious, it bears mentioning that you must preview your pages in a 3.0 browser to see the results of these positioning techniques.

The Dreamweaver Technique in the upcoming section is based on methods used by George Olsen, Design Director of 2-Lane Media (`www.2lm.com`), and on an article by Trevor Lohrbeer in the Dynamic HTML Zone (`www.dhtmlzone.com`).

It's even possible to animate your layers for the benefit of Dynamic HTML-enabled browsers and, at the same time, enable 3.0 browsers to just show the static images. The key is to make sure that your animations begin and end in the same locations.

Dreamweaver Technique: Browser checking

Because of the major differences between third- and fourth-generation and beyond browsers, it is an increasingly popular practice to create a Web page geared to each browser and then use a *gateway* script to direct users to the proper page. A gateway script uses JavaScript to determine a visitor's browser version and route the page accordingly. Dreamweaver includes the Check Browser behavior (see Chapter 19), which makes this process relatively effortless.

For maximum efficiency, the best strategy is to use three pages: one page for 4.0 and above browsers, one page for 3.0 browsers, and a blank page that serves as your home page. Then, the Check Browser action can be assigned to the `onLoad` event of the blank page and can execute immediately. The other alternative is to use only two pages, one for each browser, and then run the Check Browser routine after the page is loaded and send the users of one browser version off to the other page. The disadvantage to this approach is that many of your visitors have to sit through the loading process of one page, only to be whisked off to another to start again.

Other variations besides those encountered in different browser versions may cause you to redirect a visitor to a different Web page. Screen resolution, color depth, MIME types—each comes in myriad possibilities. Using different behaviors, you can detect the differences and direct your users accordingly. You can find a host of these redirection helpers on the Additional Extensions section of CD-ROM 1 that accompanies this book, in the various Behavior folders under each author's name.

The following technique takes you through the conversion of a layers-based page to a 3.0-compatible page, the creation of a new gateway page, and the incorporation of a Check Browser action that automatically directs users to a new page depending on their browser type:

1. In Dreamweaver, construct the fourth-generation browser version of your Web page—the one that uses layers and Cascading Style Sheets—first.

Be sure no layers overlap and that the Web page otherwise meets the criteria noted in the section "Preparing your page for conversion," earlier in this chapter.

2. Choose File ➪ Convert ➪ 3.0 Browser Compatible. Save the new version of the page, created by Dreamweaver, with a name similar to the original (4.0) page but with a different prefix or suffix. For example, you might call the page intended for 4.0 browsers index40.html and the 3.0 version index30.html.
3. Choose File ➪ New to create a new page. This page serves as the gateway for the other two pages.
4. By default, Dreamweaver makes new pages with a white background. To make the gateway page as unobtrusive as possible, it's best to use the same background color as your target pages. To do this, choose Modify ➪ Page Properties. In the Page Properties dialog box, select the color value in the Background Color text box that corresponds to your other pages. You could even position the two pages side-by-side and sample the background color. Click OK to close the Page Properties dialog box.

5. In your blank gateway page, choose Window ➪ Behaviors to open the Behavior Inspector.

6. From the Tag Selector in the status bar of the Document window, select the <body> tag.

7. In the Behavior Inspector, select the + (Add Behavior) button and choose the Check Browser action from the pop-up menu.

8. In the Check Browser parameter form:

   - Enter the URL for your 4.0 browser page in the URL text box or select the Browse (Choose) button to locate the file.
   - Enter the URL for your 3.0 browser page in the Alt URL text box or select the Browse (Choose) button to locate the file.

   Click OK when you are done. If you haven't changed any of the other Check Browser default settings, both 4.0 browsers go to the address in the URL text box, and all other browser versions are directed to the address in the Alt URL text box (see Figure 35-4).

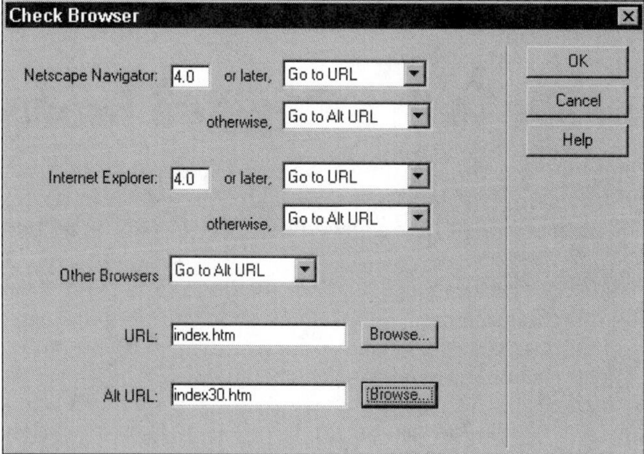

Figure 35-4: The Check Browser behavior can build a gateway script for you with no coding.

9. Save your gateway page. If this page is to serve as the gateway for the home page(s) for your domain, save it as index.html or whatever name your server uses for default documents.

10. The gateway can now be preliminarily tested. However, because any Web page can be an entry point to a site, you also have to use the Check Browser action on each of the version-specific pages. Reopen the 4.0 browser page.

11. If necessary, open the Behavior Inspector by choosing Window ⇨ Behaviors or selecting the Show Behaviors button from the Launcher.
12. Repeat Steps 6 and 7 to get to the Check Browser parameter form.
13. This time, enter the URL for your 3.0 browser page in the Alt URL text box or select the Browse (Choose) button to locate the file.
14. In the sections for both Netscape and Internet Explorer 4.0 (or above), choose the Stay on this Page option from the drop-down list.
15. Select OK when you are finished and save the file.
16. Open the 3.0 browser page. Repeat Steps 12 through 15, but when you get to the Check Browser parameter form, enter the URL for the 4.0 browser page in the Alt URL text box.

Now visitors can come in through the front door of your home page, or through any side door, and be served the correct page. Generally, not all the pages in your site will use the high-end features available to the 4.0 browsers, so you have to create gateways for only those pages that do. If you plan your site with this strategy in mind — and avoid putting a moving layer on every page as a logo, for instance — you can manage your site more effectively.

Testing Your Page with a Targeted Browser

Testing is an absolute must when building a Web site. It's critical that you view your pages on as many browsers and systems as possible. Variations in color, gamma, page offset, and capabilities must be observed before they can be adjusted.

A more basic, preliminary type of testing can also be done right from within Dreamweaver: code testing. Browsers usually ignore tags and attributes they do not understand. However, sometimes these tags can produce unexpected and undesirable results, such as exposing code to the viewer.

Dreamweaver's Browser Targeting feature, File ⇨ Check Target Browsers, enables you to check a Web page — or an entire Web site — against any number of browser profiles. Currently, Dreamweaver comes with profiles for the following browsers:

✦ Internet Explorer 2.0

✦ Internet Explorer 3.0

✦ Internet Explorer 4.0

✦ Internet Explorer 5.0

✦ Navigator 2.0

✦ Navigator 3.0

✦ Navigator 4.0

You can choose to check your page or site against a single browser profile, all of them, or anything in-between. Though not a substitute for real-world testing, Browser Targeting gives you an overview of potential errors and problematic code to look out for.

Testing browser compatibility for a Web page

To check a single Web page against specific browser targets, follow these steps:

Caution: With Browser Targeting, Dreamweaver checks the saved version of a Web page. So if you've made any modifications to your current page, save it *before* beginning the following process.

1. Choose File ➪ Check Target Browsers.

   The Check Target Browsers dialog box opens as shown in Figure 35-5.

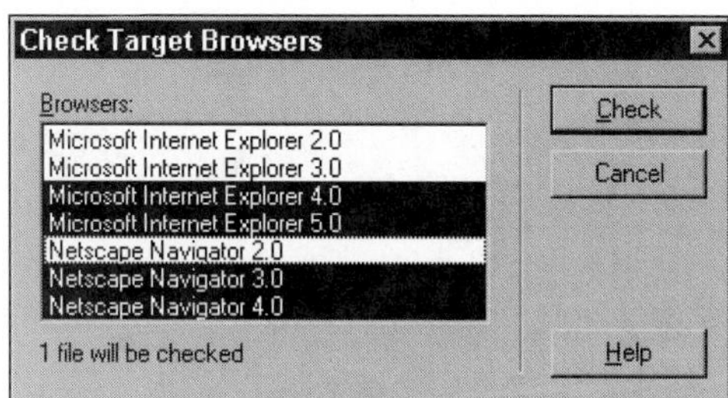

Figure 35-5: Select the browsers on which you'd like to check the code of your current page.

2. Select the browsers against which you want the current page to be checked. The usual selection techniques work in this list: To choose various browsers, press Ctrl (Command) while selecting. To specify a contiguous range of browsers, select the first one, press Shift, and then select the last one.
3. After you've chosen the target browsers, click the Check button. Dreamweaver opens your primary browser, if necessary, and outputs the report to the browser window (see Figure 35-6).
4. Dreamweaver stores the Target Browser Check only temporarily and deletes the file after its use. To keep a record of the report, use your browser's File ➪ Print or File ➪ Save command.

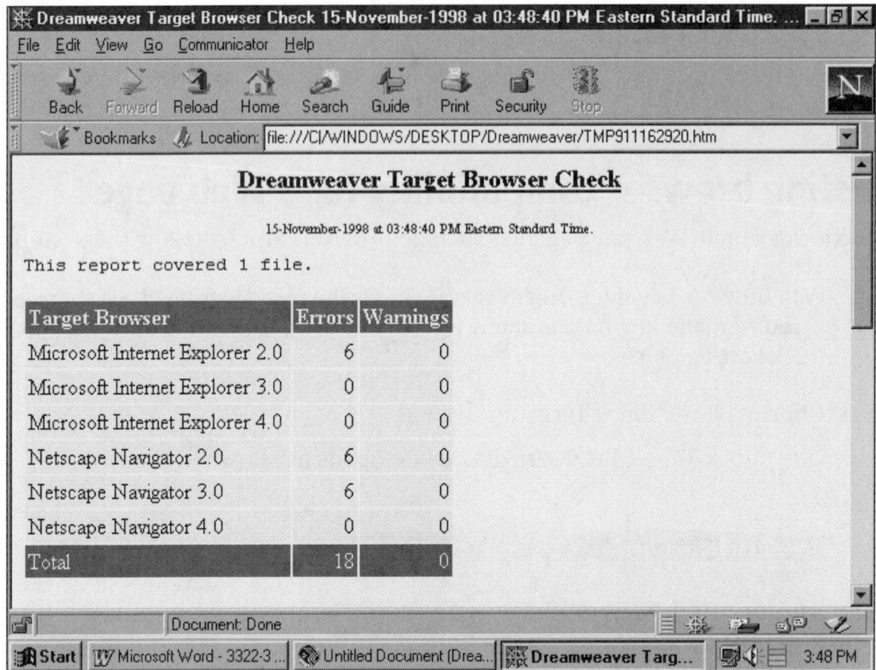

Dreamweaver Target Browser Check

15-November-1998 at 03:48:40 PM Eastern Standard Time.

This report covered 1 file.

Target Browser	Errors	Warnings
Microsoft Internet Explorer 2.0	6	0
Microsoft Internet Explorer 3.0	0	0
Microsoft Internet Explorer 4.0	0	0
Netscape Navigator 2.0	6	0
Netscape Navigator 3.0	6	0
Netscape Navigator 4.0	0	0
Total	18	0

Figure 35-6: The Dreamweaver Target Browser Check displays a summary of all the errors it finds in your selected page. It's a good idea to print the report or save it in a file.

The Dreamweaver Target Browser Check offers both a summary and a detail section. The summary, previously shown in Figure 35-6, lists the browser being tested and any errors or warnings. Totals for each category are listed beneath the columns.

The detail section of the browser check report, shown in Figure 35-7, lists the following:

- ✦ Each offending tag or attribute
- ✦ The browsers that do not support the tag or attribute
- ✦ An example HTML line
- ✦ Additional line numbers where the error occurred

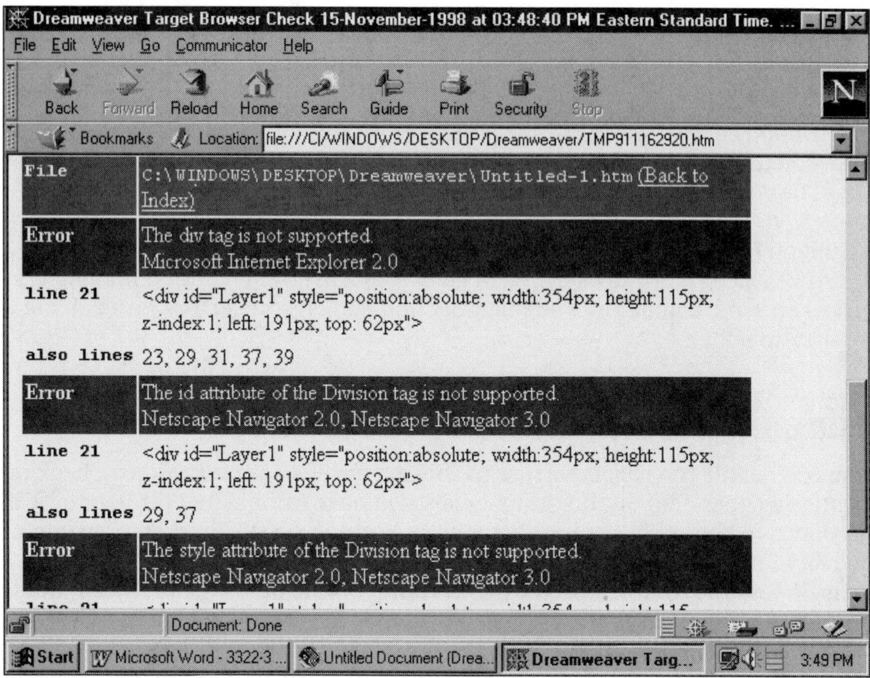

Figure 35-7: You can find detailed information on the lower half of the Dreamweaver Target Browser Check report.

Testing browser compatibility for an entire site

With Dreamweaver, you can check browser compatibility for an entire Web site as easily as you can check a single page. Dreamweaver checks all the HTML files in a given folder, whether or not they are actually used in the site.

To check an entire site against specific browser targets, follow these steps:

1. Choose Window ➪ Site File or select the Show Site FTP button from the Launcher. The Site window opens.
2. In the Site window, select a folder from the Local Folder pane, choose one of the listed sites from the Remote Site pane, or select any number of individual files.
3. Choose File ➪ Check Target Browsers from the Site window menu (while the Site window has focus). The Check Target Browsers dialog box opens, shown earlier in Figure 35-5. Below the list of Browsers is a statement of how many pages are to be checked.

4. Select the browsers against which you want the current site checked.
5. When you're ready, select the Check button. Dreamweaver opens your primary browser, if necessary, and outputs the report to the browser window.
6. Dreamweaver stores the Target Browser Check file only temporarily and deletes the file after its use. To keep a record of the report, use your browser's File ➪ Print or File ➪ Save command.

When you're checking more than one page, the summary section of the Dreamweaver Target Browser Check gives you a list of the files containing errors as well as an error count. The summary section displays the errors for each file grouped together.

Using the results of the browser check

How you handle the flagged errors in Dreamweaver's Target Browser Check report is entirely dependent on the design goals you have established for your site. If your mission is to be totally accessible to every browser on the market, then you need to look at your page/site with the earliest browsers and pay special attention to those areas of possible trouble noted by the report. On the other hand, if your standards are a little more relaxed, then you can probably ignore the 2.0 browser warnings and concentrate on those appearing in the 3.0 and 4.0 categories.

Many items flagged as errors aren't incorrect code—they're just not supported in the targeted browser. For example, checking a page with rollovers against a Internet Explorer 3 profile will always display an error stating "The onMouseOut attribute of the Hyperlink Anchor tag is not supported." Although this means that the rollover won't work in this browser, it also won't create an error message.

Customizing a Browser Profile

In order for Dreamweaver's Browser Targeting feature to be effective, you must have access to profiles for all the browsers you need to check. You can create custom browser profiles to cover any new browser versions or browsers as they become available. The browser profile file is a text file and can be created or altered in any text editor.

This section examines the required structure and format for a browser profile file and the steps for building one based on an existing file.

Understanding the browser profile structure

In order for Dreamweaver to properly process an HTML file using any browser profile, the profile must follow a precise format. Here's a sample taken from the Internet Explorer 3.0 browser profile:

```
<!ELEMENT H1 name="Heading 1" >
<!ATTLIST H1
        Align ( left | center | right )
        Class
        ID
        Style
>
```

As you can see, the HTML tag is listed in a very specific syntax. Here's how the syntax is formed:

```
<!ELEMENT htmlTag Name="tagName" >
<!ATTLIST htmlTag
unsupportedAttribute1 !Error !msg="The unsupportedAttribute1 of the htmlTag ¬
is not supported. Try using thisAttribute for a similar effect."
supportedAttribute1
supportedAttribute2 ( validValue1 | validValue2 | validValue3 )
unsupportedAttribute2 !Error !htmlmsg="<b>Don't ever use this ¬
unsupportedAttribute2 of the  htmlTag !!</b>"
>
```

The variables in the syntax are as follows:

✦ `htmlTag`: The tag as it appears in an HTML document.

✦ `tagName`: Optional; how the tag is known. For example, the `<applet>` tag is called the "Java Applet." If it's noted in the file, the `tagName` is used in the error message; otherwise, `htmlTag` is used.

✦ `unsupportedAttribute`: Indicates invalid attributes so that a custom error message can be offered. Otherwise, all attributes not specifically listed are assumed to be unsupported.

✦ `supportedAttribute`: A valid attribute; all valid attributes must be listed. Only attributes listed without an `!Error` designation are supported.

✦ `validValue`: A value supported by the attribute.

Several other, not-so-obvious rules must be followed for Dreamweaver to correctly read the profile:

✦ The name of the profile must appear in the first line of the file, followed by a single carriage return. This is the profile name that appears in the Check Target Browser(s) dialog box and in the report.

✦ The key phrase `PROFILE_TYPE=BROWSER_PROFILE` must appear in the second line.

✦ On the `!ELEMENT` line, a single space must be used before the closing angle (>) bracket, after the opening parentheses, before the closing parentheses, and before and after each pipe (|) character in the list of values.

✦ An exclamation point, without an intervening space, must be placed before the words `ELEMENT`, `ATTLIST`, `Error`, `msg`, and `htmlmsg`. For example:

```
!ELEMENT, !ATTLIST, !Error, !msg, and !htmlmsg.
```

✦ You can only use plain text in `!msg` messages, but an `!htmlmsg` message can use any valid HTML, including links.

✦ Don't use HTML comment tags, `<!-- -->`, because they interfere with the regular Dreamweaver processing of the file.

Creating a browser profile

As you can see, Dreamweaver browser profiles have a specific structure. Consequently, it's far easier to modify an existing profile than to write one from scratch. The basic procedure takes three steps:

1. Choose an existing profile for a browser similar to the one for which you are creating a new profile. Open the profile in a text editor.

Numerous custom browser profiles appear on this book's accompanying CD-ROM 1. You can copy them directly to your BrowserProfiles folder found in the Configuration folder or use them as models for modification.

2. Add any tags and attributes that are supported in the target browser but not in the existing profile.

3. Remove any tags or attributes not supported by your target browser. Or, you can add an `!Error` message after any attribute to flag it for Dreamweaver's Target Browser Check operation.

For example, take a look at the code fragment illustrated in Listing 35-1; it contains a portion of the browser profile I created for WebTV. Note the custom error messages after the `<applet>` tag and the `rel` attribute of the `<a>` tag.

When saving a new browser profile in Windows, there's a small trick to getting the version number to appear correctly at the end of the browser name, as in "Navigator 3.0." Choose File ➪ Save As from your text editor. Then, in the Filename text box, enter your browser name with the file name extension (.txt), all enclosed in quotes. For example, to save the Web TV 1.0 file, I entered "WebTV_1.0.txt" in the Filename text box.

Listing 35-1: Excerpt from Browser Profile File for WebTV

```
WebTV 1.0
PROFILE_TYPE=BROWSER_PROFILE
-- Copyright 1997 Macromedia, Inc. All rights reserved.

<!ELEMENT A Name="Hyperlink Anchor" >
<!ATTLIST A
        Class           !Error
        HREF
        ID
        Name
        OnClick
        OnMouseOut
        OnMouseOver
        Rel             !Warning !msg "The rel attribute has been modified by ¬
WebTV."
        Style           !Error
        Selected        !Error
        Target          !Error
>

<!ELEMENT Address >
<!ATTLIST Address
        Class           !Error
        ID              !Error
        Style           !Error
>

<!ELEMENT APPLET Name="Java Applet" > !Error !msg "WebTV does not support ¬
Java Applets."
<!ATTLIST APPLET
        Align ( top | middle | bottom | left | right | absmiddle | ¬
absbottom | baseline | texttop )
        Alt
        Archive         !Error
        Code
        Codebase
        Height
        HSpace
        Name
        VSpace
        Width
        Class
        ID
        Style
>
```

Continued

Listing 35-1 *(continued)*

```
<!ELEMENT AREA Name="Client-side image map area" >
<!ATTLIST AREA
        Alt             !Error
        Class           !Error
        Coords
        HREF
        ID
        Name
        NoHREF
        NoTab
        OnMouseOut
        OnMouseOver
        Shape
        Style           !Error
        Target
>

<!ELEMENT AUDIOSCOPE Name="Audioscope" >
<!ATTLIST AUDIOSCOPE
        Align
        Border
        Gain
        Height
        LeftColor
        LeftOffset
        MaxLevel
        RightColor
        RightOffset
        Width
>

<!ELEMENT B Name="Bold" >
<!ATTLIST B
        Class           !Error
        ID              !Error
        Style           !Error
>

<!ELEMENT Base >
<!ATTLIST Base
        HREF
        Target
>

<!ELEMENT BaseFont >
```

```
<!ATTLIST BaseFont
        Size
>
<!ELEMENT BGSOUND Name="Background sound" >
<!ATTLIST BGSOUND
        Loop
        Src
>

<!ELEMENT Big >
<!ATTLIST Big
        Class
        ID
        Style
>

<!ELEMENT Blackface >

<!ELEMENT Blink !Error >

<!ELEMENT Blockquote >

<!ELEMENT Body >
<!ATTLIST Body
        ALink                   !Error
        Background
        BGColor
        BGProperties
        Credits
        LeftMargin
        Link
        Logo
        OnBlur                  !Error
        OnFocus                 !Error
        OnLoad
        OnUnload
        Style                   !Error
        Text
        VLink
>

<!ELEMENT BQ Name="Block Quote" >

<!ELEMENT BR Name="Line break" >
<!ATTLIST BR
        Clear ( left | right | all )
>
```

Summary

Unless you're building a Web site for a strictly controlled intranet, in which case you know everyone is using the BrandX 4.03 browser, it's critical that you address the browser-compatibility issues that your Web site is certain to face. Whether it's cross-browser or backward compatibility you're trying to achieve, Dreamweaver has features and techniques in place to help you get your Web pages viewed by the maximum number of users.

- Dreamweaver takes a Web page built with 4.0 and above features, including layers and CSS, and creates another Web page that is 3.0 compatible.
- Dreamweaver can take a Web page created with layers and create another Web page that uses tables instead. Tools in Dreamweaver, such as Convert Layers to Tables, make it quick and straightforward.
- You can use JavaScript within a Web page to handle cross-browser compatibility problems with 4.0 and above browsers.
- Careful placement of your DHTML objects can help with backward compatibility.
- Dreamweaver enables you to check your Web page, selected pages, or an entire Web site against a browser profile to look for tags and attributes that will not work in a particular browser version.
- Browser profiles can be customized or copied and modified for a new browser or browser version.

✦ ✦ ✦

P A R T

Connectivity with Dreamweaver

✦ ✦ ✦ ✦

In This Part

✦ ✦ ✦ ✦

CHAPTER 36

Activating Database Sites with ASP and Macromedia UltraDev

✦ ✦ ✦ ✦

In This Chapter

Basic ASP techniques

Making connections

Defining recordsets

Managing databases with ASP

Building an Ad Rotator

Introducing Dreamweaver UltraDev

Designing with Live Data

✦ ✦ ✦ ✦

Active Server Pages (ASP) is the most widespread technology for activating Web pages, a pretty amazing reality considering that the servers where ASP is freely available — Windows NT/2000 servers — are in the minority. The popularity of ASP as a connectivity solution is a testament to the technology's power and flexibility. Simple, basic, active-page concepts — such as viewing, adding, and editing records — are well within reach of the novice ASP designer. Yet, ASP is scalable enough to also meet the mission-critical needs of an enterprise IT department.

Dreamweaver offers an open, receptive, but not particularly coddling environment for the ASP Web page designer. Dreamweaver is particularly good at leaving ASP code unchanged, whether it's inserted in another program or in Dreamweaver itself. However, no special extensions accommodate ASP in the standard Dreamweaver package. While this fact may seem to be a hindrance to development, it isn't really, for three reasons. First, because ASP is largely code-driven, many developers are accustomed to hand writing their code and prefer the control that such an approach offers. Second, numerous extensions, written by third-party Dreamweaver extension authors, are available to automate the most common ASP tasks. Finally, there's Dreamweaver UltraDev.

Dreamweaver UltraDev is a new product from Macromedia that combines Dreamweaver's superb layout engine with database connectivity. UltraDev outputs not only ASP code, but code for ColdFusion and Java Server Pages as well. While complete coverage of UltraDev is beyond the scope of this book, the technology is too tantalizing to leave out altogether. After examining how Dreamweaver and ASP can work together, we'll take a brief tour of UltraDev's ASP abilities.

ASP Basics

Many Web designers, myself included, began to pick up the basics of HTML by surfing around the Internet and, when coming upon an interesting Web page, examining the source to see how it was done. Try the same technique with ASP and you'll be sorely disappointed: When you look at any Web page on the Internet with an .asp extension, you'll see just HTML and maybe some JavaScript. That's because the key word in Active Server Pages is the middle one — ASP is a *server*-side technology. After an .asp page has been executed by a server, all the ASP language is removed from the page before it is returned to the client for browsing.

Because ASP code is run (and removed) by the server and not the browser, the HTML `<script>` tag is not necessary the way it is with JavaScript functions. Instead, ASP code is designated using a percent sign delimiter, like this:

```
<%
   'ASP code goes here
%>
```

Everything in between the opening `<%` and the closing `%>` is considered ASP code and will be executed by the server. The only type of statement that is not executed is a comment; comments are indicated with a single quotation mark, as in the example.

ASP code does not have to be a completely separate function; the ability to integrate ASP into HTML is one of the real strengths of the technology. If, for example, you want a different graphic to appear on a Web page at different times of the day, one approach with ASP would be to write a function that first gets the current time and then assigns the URL of a different image to a variable, depending on the time of day. The variable is then inserted into a standard `<img>` tag, like this:

```
<img src="<% = theURL %>" height=100 width=100>
```

Because the ASP code including the variable, `theURL`, is replaced at run-time by the server, a visiting browser would be sent something such as this:

```
<img src="morning.gif" height=100 width=100>
```

or this:

```
<img src="evening.gif" height=100 width=100>
```

You may have noticed that the ASP code included something more than just the variable. The equal sign following the opening ASP delimiter is shorthand for an ASP command, `Response.write`. While this abbreviation is extremely useful, it has a limitation: code following the `<%=` combination all must be on the same line. To span multiple lines, use `Response.write`.

Coding ASP in Dreamweaver

ASP code must be entered in the HTML Source inspector, but Dreamweaver displays an icon for each independent code fragment in the Document window. These ASP icons are only visible under two conditions: first, the Server Markup Tags option on the Invisible Elements panel of Preferences is selected and second, the View ➪ Invisible Elements toggle is enabled.

If the ASP icon is selected, an ASP Property Inspector becomes available. As you can see in Figure 36-1, the ASP Property Inspector only has one button, Edit. Selecting the Edit button opens an Edit Contents dialog box, containing the selected ASP code. The Edit Contents dialog box is good for quick adjustments to your code, but a bit unwieldy for inserting more than a few lines of programming. An alternative method of editing your ASP code in Dreamweaver is to select its icon and then open the HTML Source inspector.

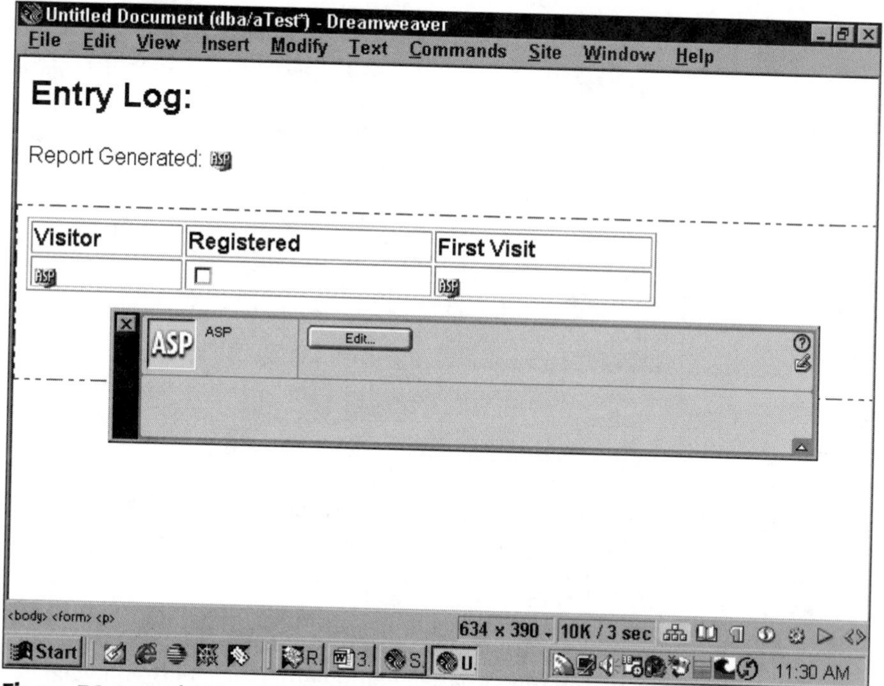

Figure 36-1: In the Document window, Dreamweaver represents ASP code with an icon and permits editing via the Property Inspector and subsequent Edit Contents dialog box.

Although the Edit Contents dialog box reflects the existing formatting for your ASP code, it can be a difficult location in which to format new code. If you use tabs to indent your code, you must press Ctrl+Tab (Windows only) to insert a tab character. Moreover, text in the Edit Contents dialog box does not wrap; to see long lines of code, use the horizontal scrollbar that appears.

ASP code that is entered as part of an HTML tag, like a `src` attribute, is not rendered as an icon, but remains accessible through the Property Inspector. However, many Dreamweaver objects, such as the Image and Flash objects, open a Select File dialog box when the object is inserted. With ASP, the goal is often to incorporate dynamic links to a source rather than a specific file. You can insert a placeholder icon in Dreamweaver by Ctrl+clicking (Option+clicking) the object in the Object palette. To insert the ASP code into an attribute, select the placeholder icon (see Figure 36-2) and enter the code directly into the proper field of the Property Inspector.

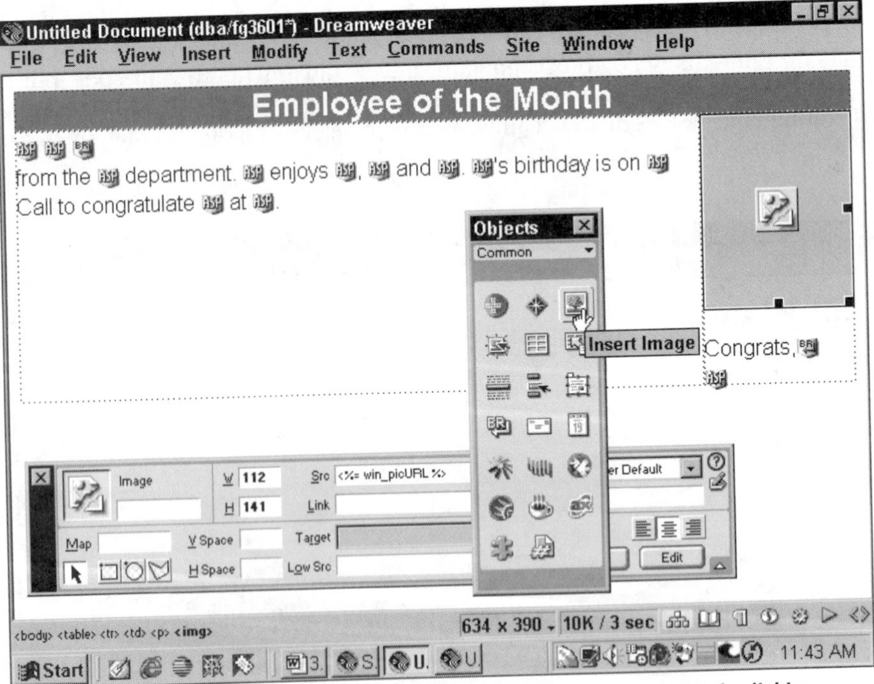

Figure 36-2: Create a placeholder for your ASP-driven images by Ctrl+clicking (Option+clicking) the Image object. After this placeholder was inserted it was resized to match the dimensions of the databased image.

Dreamweaver, by default, is generally good about not altering ASP code; however, you can take additional measures to ensure your page's integrity. Overall you need to be aware of three key preferences when coding ASP pages in Dreamweaver. To see them all (see Figure 37-3), choose Edit ⇨ Preferences and select the HTML Rewriting category.

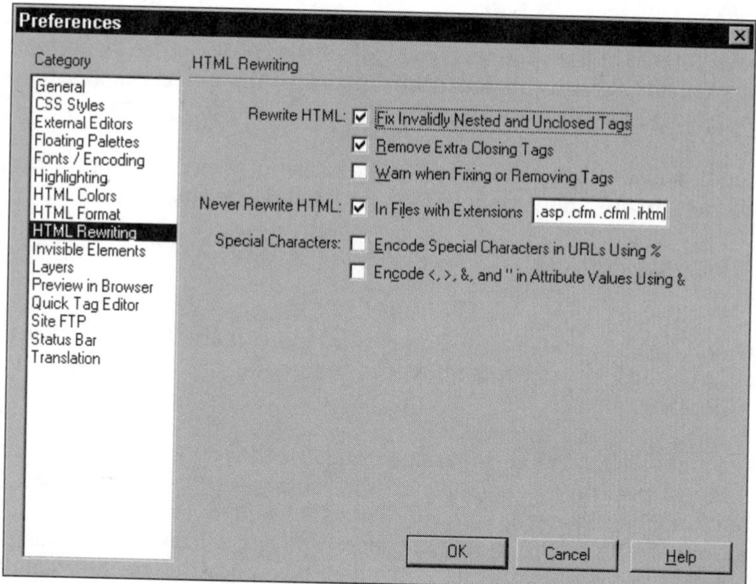

Figure 36-3: Check your Dreamweaver Preferences to assure your ASP code will remain unchanged.

The first notable preference is the Never Rewrite HTML option. When creating or importing ASP pages, make sure that this option is selected and that the .asp file extension is included in the In Files With Extensions list. These options are selected by default, but it's always good to double-check if you run into problems. Note that this preference is especially important when you are opening pages in Dreamweaver that contain ASP code inserted in other programs.

The next two pertinent preferences are found in the Special Characters area. Both are used to control how Dreamweaver handles characters such as spaces, tildes, and ampersands. By default, Dreamweaver encodes these characters so that they can be read by the majority of the servers. However, what's good for one server isn't necessarily good for them all. The first, Encode Special Characters in URLs using %, is concerned with links and the `href` attribute. If your links are supposed to look like this:

```
<a href="EditGeneral.asp?id=<% =rs("id") %>&tab=1">
```

and they end up looking like this (with bold added for emphasis):

```
<a href="EditGeneral.asp?id=<% =rs("id") %>&amp;tab=1">
```

it's time to deselect this option. Dreamweaver does not encode anything it finds within the ASP delimiters, but other characters outside of the `<% %>` markup — such as the ampersand in the example — are fair game.

You won't see the discrepancy between what's entered in the Document window and what's entered in the code until you look at the HTML Source inspector. The Property Inspector displays your link unencoded, so be sure to check the source if problems emerge.

The same encoding issues hold true for values of attributes in other tags. If you were trying to pass an argument via a hidden field value like this:

```
<input type="hidden" value="<% = rs.recipient %>?<% = rs.mail
%>&theSender=theOne" name="hidden">
```

Dreamweaver would again convert the ampersand to its character entity, `&`. To avoid such problems in attributes uncheck the Encode <, >, &, and " in Attribute Values using % option.

One more preference worth customizing if you're creating a lot of ASP pages is the custom extension. On the General panel of Dreamweaver Preferences, select the Add Extension When Saving option and change the field to .asp (note the leading period). Now whenever you save your page with just a base name—using no extension—the .asp is automatically appended. If you need to create a standard HTML file occasionally, just add the .htm or .html to the base name.

Connecting to a data source

While many ASP functions exist, most Web designers want to use the language to access information in a database. Before a database can be accessed in ASP, a connection must be made between the ASP page and the database engine. The connection is established by way of one of the ActiveX Data Objects (ADO), the aptly-named Connection object. Typically the code for connecting to a data source looks like this:

```
<%
Dim myConn
Set myConn = Server.CreateObject("ADODB.Connection")
myConn.Open "bigdb"
%>
```

In this example, the `myConn` variable is first declared, or dimensioned, and then associated with a just-created Connection object. The connection then opens the database known as `bigdb`. Here, `bigdb` represents the simplest type of connection, an ODBC Data Source Name or DSN. ODBC is short for Open Database Connectivity and is a wide-spread method of accessing many popular database formats. A DSN can be thought of as an alias for a database, and is established by the system administrator on the server or on your local machine.

Not all application servers use DSNs. To establish what's referred to as a DSN-less connection, you need to substitute all the details hidden by the DSN in a connection string. For example, to connect to the same database without a DSN, the code might read:

```
<%
Dim myConn, connStr
Set myConn = Server.CreateObject("ADODB.Connection")
connStr = "DRIVER={Microsoft Access Driver (*.mdb)};
DBQ="C:\Inetpub\wwwroot\bigco\data\bigdb.mdb"; UID="admin";
PWD="bigbetter")"
myConn.Open connStr
%>
```

The Driver parameter specifies the type of database, while the DBQ equates to the file URL of the database. To protect usage, this database uses a user ID (UID) and a password (PWD).

Note

While ODBC drivers are installed as part of the Windows operating system, Macintosh users can get them by installing Microsoft Office on the Mac. The ODBC drivers are found in the Value Pack and are an option install.

Defining a recordset

Databases and other data sources can hold a great deal of material, often organized in tables that are composed of separate, but interconnected records. In almost every circumstance, a Web page displays and works with only a portion of that data. This subset of data is referred to as a *recordset*. In ASP, defining a recordset is generally the second step to retrieving information from a data source.

While it's true that one could set up and access a recordset without creating a connection first, the connection is implied. With an implied connection, the default values are used and offer the ASP designer far less flexibility. The majority of ASP pages use both an explicit connection and recordset.

Recordsets are generally defined with a SQL (Structured Query Language) statement. The SQL Select statement filters the database to provide just the desired records, in the proper order and grouping. A simple SQL select statement looks like this:

```
SELECT * FROM employees
```

Translated into English, this example reads "select all the fields from the employees table of the currently open database." Both `SELECT` and `FROM` are keywords. One way the SQL statement can create a recordset is to use the Execute method of the Connection object, like this:

```
<%
  Set rsOne = myConn.Execute("SELECT * FROM employees")
%>
```

As noted earlier, an asterisk in an SQL statement makes all the fields available for display. However, quite often an ASP page requires far fewer fields. To specify the fields, enter their names in a comma-separated list, like this:

```
SELECT id, firstName, lastName, telephone FROM employees
```

The WHERE keyword further filters the recordset. Here's a simple example that selects the Shipping department employees:

```
SELECT id, firstName, lastName FROM employees WHERE department
= "Shipping"
```

Another common addition to SQL select statements is the ORDER BY key phrase. To sort the Shipping departments by the date they were hired, this code could be used:

```
SELECT id, firstName, lastName FROM employees WHERE department
= "Shipping" ORDER BY startDate
```

By default, the ORDER is ascending, but by adding the DESC keyword, the order is changed to descending, according to the field type (alphabetic or numeric).

Obviously, this introduction to SQL barely scratches the surface of what's possible. For a complete reference to SQL—and much more—see the *Active Server Pages Bible* by Eric A. Smith.

As noted in the introduction to this chapter, although no standard Dreamweaver ASP objects exist, a number of such objects have been created by third-party extension authors. Bill Bullman has put together a collection of ASP objects that we examine throughout the chapter. The first relevant object is the Connection object, shown in Figure 36-4.

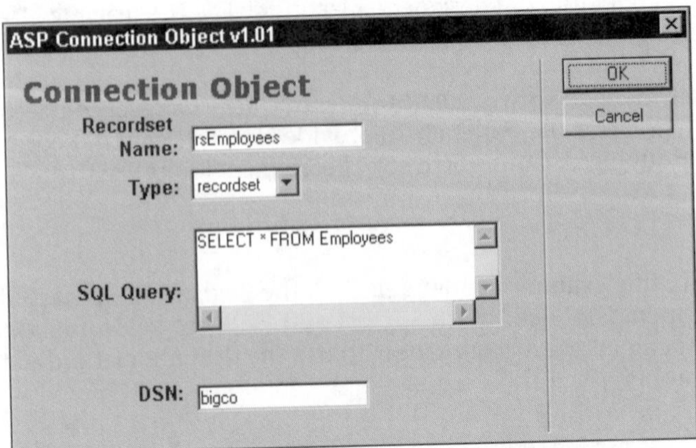

Figure 36-4: This third-party extension, the Connection object, from Bill Bullman simplifies the process of creating an ASP connection.

You can find the Connection object, and the rest of Bill Bullman's ASP objects, on this book's accompanying CD-ROM 2. You can copy the entire ASP folder into your Dreamweaver Configuration\Objects folder and the next time you launch the program, an entire ASP panel will be available.

To use the Connection object, follow these steps:

1. Place your cursor near the top of the page.

   The Connection and Recordset code traditionally are found before other HTML elements.

2. Select the Connection object from the Object palette.
3. In the Connection dialog box, enter name of the desired recordset.

To quickly identify recordsets, ASP coders often begin the variable name with the initials `rs`, as in `rsEmployees`.

4. Select the connection object type, either Recordset or Connection.

   For the code output by this object, it's best to choose Recordset.

5. Type or paste your query in the SQL Query text area.
6. Enter the DSN for the desired data source.
7. Click OK when you're done.

The Connection object inserts ASP code, as marked by the ASP icon. If you open the HTML Source inspector or select the Edit button from the Property Inspector, you'll see code similar to this:

```
<%
 Set rsEmployees= CreateObject("adodb.recordset")
 rsEmployees.Open "Select * From employees", "DSN=bigco"
 %>
```

Although this is not the exact syntax discussed earlier, it serves the same purpose.

Displaying data

Once you've made the database and recordset connection, how do you incorporate data in your Web page? The `Response.write` function handles output in most situations; in fact it's so often used there's a shorthand form of the command: an equal sign. The code

```
<% Response.write rsEmployees("fname") %>
```

is functionally the same as

```
<%= rsEmployees("fname")%>
```

What is being written is a reference to the recordset (here, `rsEmployees`) and a field name (`fname`). This code would output the contents of the `fname` field of the first record of the `rsEmployees` recordset.

To ease the coding, use Bill Bullman's Recordset Output object, found on CD-ROM 2 that accompanies this book. This object, shown in Figure 36-5, only has two parameters: Recordset Name and Field Name. To use it, enter the current established recordset and the desired field name in their respective fields. The object inserts code is the abbreviated format, like this:

```
<%= rsEmployees("fname")%>
```

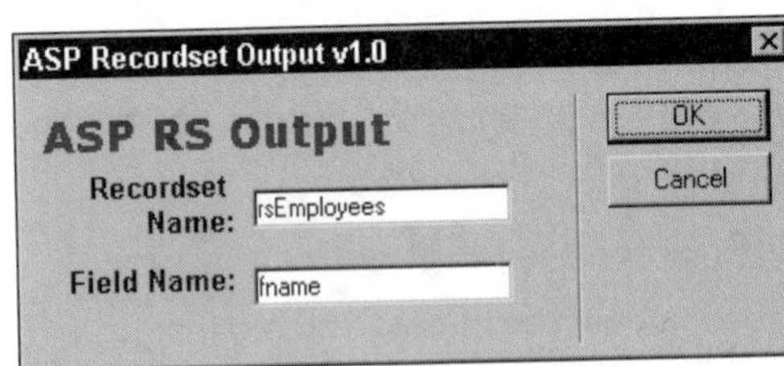

Figure 36-5: The Recordset Output object is used to display information from a data source.

Once inserted, the code can be formatted in Dreamweaver using any of the standard tools. As written, this code only outputs one field; quite often, designers need to display multiple records, one after another. To display multiple records, some type of programmer's looping code is required. The looping code surrounds the HTML and ASP code that is to be displayed.

Another third-party developer, Graison Swaan, has contributed a two-object set to handle the looping code. His ASP Loop Start and ASP Loop Set objects can be used in conjunction with code inserted by hand or with Bill Bullman's objects.

You can find Graison Swaan's Loop Set in Bill Bullman's ASP folder on CD-ROM 2 that comes with this book.

To use these third-party extensions to output all the data from a particular recordset, follow these steps:

1. Use the ASP Connection object to define a recordset as previously described.
2. Choose the ASP Loop Start object from the third-party ASP object palette.
3. In the ASP Loop Start dialog box, enter the name of the recordset being accessed.
4. Choose the Recordset Output object and enter the recordset and the desired field name.

5. Add any required HTML to format the dynamic content.

Tip

To make data appear one line after another, insert a <br> tag at the end of the line.

6. Repeat Steps 4 and 5 to include any other dynamic data.
7. To close the loop, select the ASP Loop End object and, again, enter the recordset's name.

When this page is sent to an ASP capable server, your dynamic content will display until all the records are shown. Often a table is used to hold repeating records. The following code shows how one row of information is repeated until all records — the end of file (eof) — is reached. This code was constructed using the third-party objects and techniques outlined here. I've marked the ASP code in bold for better comprehension:

```
<table width="100%" border="0" cellspacing="0" cellpadding="0">
  <tr>
    <td>First</td>
    <td>Last</td>
  </tr>
  <% do until rsEmployees.eof %>
  <tr>
    <td><%= rsEmployees("FirstName")%></td>
    <td><%= rsEmployees("LastName")%></td>
  </tr>
  <%
     rsEmployees.movenext
     loop
     rsEmployees.close
     set rsEmployees=nothing
  %>
</table>
```

While it's possible to insert this code in the Document window, in practice it's much faster if you keep the HTML Source inspector open to aid in the object placement.

Advanced ASP

Technologies like ASP bring much more to the table than just database connectivity. As a server-side protocol, ASP can authenticate users, integrate client-side details, and schedule dynamic page creation among many other programmable tasks. In this section, we'll look at two important applications of ASP interaction: server variables and rotating advertisements or images.

Uncovering server variables

When a browser requests a page from a server, it's not a one-way street. In addition to sending the requested page to the browser, the server gathers certain information from the client and requesting system, such as the language used, the type and version of browser, the address of the requesting system (both in IP and domain name format), and much more. Collectively this information is known as the server environment variables. Here's one method of using a server variable:

```
Local time is <%= Request.ServerVariables("DATE_LOCAL") %>
```

Naturally, the variable can also be integrated into conditional or other programming. Although they vary from server to server, a listing of the basic variables is found in Table 36-1.

Table 36-1
Basic Server Environment Variables

Variable	*Description*
ALL_HTTP	Returns a list of variables taken from the header of the HTTP request. These variables are separated by a line-feed character. The variables are as follows: HTTP_ACCEPT: Types of content the user's browser will accept. HTTP_ACCEPT_LANGUAGE: The language in use, such as en-us (U.S. English). HTTP_CONNECTION: Kind of connection used, most typically Keep-Alive. HTTP_HOST: Name of machine hosting the ASP page. HTTP_USER_AGENT: Name of the user's browser. HTTP_COOKIE: Value of cookie used to track current session. HTTP_ACCEPT_ENCODING: Compression methods available.
AUTH_TYPE	Kind of authentication used; values include Basic and Integrated Windows NT Authentication.
AUTH_PASSWORD	The user's password, as entered in the authentication dialog box (only available with Basic authentication).

Variable	*Description*
AUTH_USER	The user's username, as entered in the authentication dialog box.
CONTENT_LENGTH	Number of bytes expected by client.
CONTENT_TYPE	The MIME type of the information sent in a POST request.
DOCUMENT_NAME	Current file name.
DOCUMENT_URI	Virtual path to current document.
DATE_GMT	Date and time in Greenwich Mean Time format.
DATE_LOCAL	Date and time in the server's local time zone.
GATEWAY_INTERFACE	Version of CGI specification used by Web server.
LAST_MODIFIED	Date requested page last modified.
PATH_INFO	The path to the requested URL without the domain.
PATH_TRANSLATED	Same as PATH_INFO, but with directories expanded.
QUERY_STRING	The parameters passed in the URL after a question mark, URL encoded.
QUERY_STRING_UNESCAPED	A version of the query string not URL encoded.
REMOTE_ADDR	IP Address of the host requesting the page.
REMOTE_HOST	Name of the host requesting the page.
REMOTE_USER	User name authenticated by server.
REQUEST_METHOD	HTTP request method used, typically either GET or POST.
SCRIPT_NAME	Script program executed; for ASP pages, this value corresponds to the ASP pathname.
SERVER_NAME	Server's host name or IP address.
SERVER_PORT	TCP/IP port number used.
SERVER_PORT_SECURE	Returns 1 when a secure port is used, 0 otherwise.
SERVER_PROTOCOL	Name and version number of Web protocol, such as HTTP/1.1.
SERVER_SOFTWARE	Name and version number of Web server software.
URL	URL requested minus any query string values.

To easily insert a server variable, use Bill Bullman's Server Variables Object, available on CD-ROM 2 that comes with this book. Bill's object, shown in Figure 36-6, offers 44 different variables to choose from, including a full range of those dealing with authentication certificates.

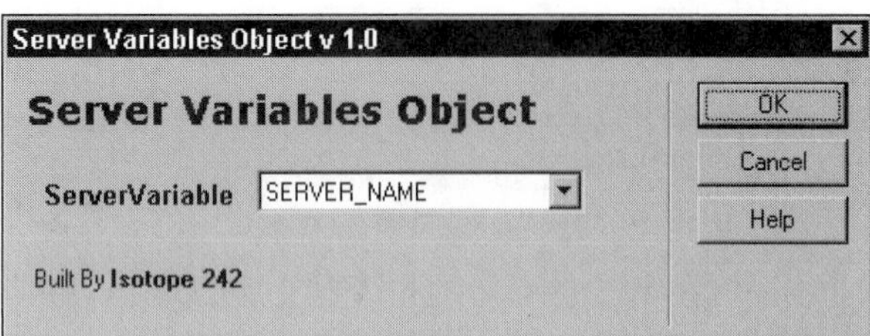

Figure 36-6: Gather data from users via the Server Variables Object.

To use the Server Variables Object, first select it from the ASP panel of the Object palette. Then choose the desired variable from the ServerVariable option list. Only the code for retrieving the chosen server variable is inserted, as in the following example:

```
<% Request.ServerVariables("SERVER_NAME") %>
```

To display it or otherwise incorporate it into your page, other code is required. To display any of the inserted server objects, all you need do is add an equal sign, as the shortcut for `Response.write`. Here's the code for the same variable, set to display on the page:

```
<%= Request.ServerVariables("SERVER_NAME") %>
```

Installing a rotating ad

Banner ads are ubiquitous on the Web. To keep interest up — and to generate more ad revenue — many Web pages rotate ads or show a different ad whenever a new user comes to the site or the page is refreshed. The primary ASP server, Microsoft IIS, offers an ad rotator component that handles the swapping of banner ads. In addition to ASP code inserted into a Web page, this component requires a text file detailing the schedule of rotation (usually called adrot.txt) and, optionally, another file to record the click-thru rate of each ad (usually adRedir.asp).

Bill Bullman's Ad Rotator extension, found on CD-ROM 2 that comes with this book, includes all the necessary files to implement ad rotation. We'll use his implementation to demonstrate this technique.

How does ad rotation work? When the page is loaded, and the ASP is executed, a server-side function, `GetAdvertisement()`, is called. The `GetAdvertisement()` function looks at the rotation schedule file, selects the next ad, and then writes out the HTML required for displaying the banner ad, complete with all the required attributes. If the optional redirection file is available when the user clicks an ad, an ASP program requests the desired page and adds the URL requested to the server logs; the server logs can then be analyzed to determine the click-thru rate of each ad.

It's best to create the rotation schedule first. This text file is divided into two main parts, the global data and the specific ad data. The global data has these four parameters:

✦ **Redirect:** the URL to the optional ASP redirection file

✦ **Width:** the width of the banner ad

✦ **Height:** the height of the banner ad

✦ **Border:** the width of the border surrounding the banner ad, in pixels

Here's an example of a rotation schedule's global section:

```
REDIRECT /asp/adRedir.asp
WIDTH 440
HEIGHT 60
BORDER 0
```

The border is set at one pixel, by default; you have to explicitly set the border value to 0 to disable it.

In the ad specific section of the rotation schedule, each advertisment to be displayed includes values for the source of the image, the link for the ad, the alternative text and the *impressions*, or relative weight of the advertisement. For example:

```
/ads/ad_bigco.gif
http://www.bigco.com
Come to BigCo for all your Big Company Needs
25
```

Although the impression value can be expressed as any number between 0 and 4,294,967,295, it is easiest if you think of the value in terms of percentage. In the example, the advertisement is set to run 25% of the time.

A single asterisk on its own line is used to separate the global section from the ad specific section.

To use the Ad Rotator object, follow these steps:

1. Create a rotation schedule text file and save it in your site as **adrot.txt**.

   The Ad Rotator extension comes with a sample adrot.txt file you can modify or use as an example.

2. If you want to enable click-thru tracking, place a copy of the adRedir.asp file — also included in the Ad Rotator extension — on your site.

3. Place your cursor where you'd like the rotating advertisement to appear and select the Ad Rotator object from the ASP panel of the Object palette.

4. In the Ad Rotator dialog box (see Figure 36-7), enter the path to the `adrot.txt` file in the File field or use the Browse button to locate the file. Click OK when you're done.

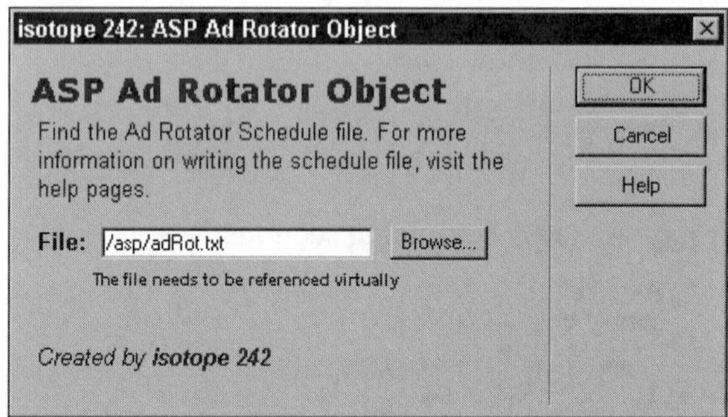

Figure 36-7: The Ad Rotator object inserts code to rotate any number of banner ads on a custom schedule.

Of course, the Ad Rotator object can be applied to more than just ads. You can also use it to show a series of different images on any Web page in the same location; this technique is used by Web designers to keep their home page fresh without having to insert a new image by hand.

Building ASP Pages with Dreamweaver UltraDev

Dreamweaver UltraDev is a new Web application program from Macromedia capable of outputting ASP, ColdFusion, and Java Server Pages (JSP). Why cover another product — even if it does make creating basic ASP pages a snap — inside the *Dreamweaver 3 Bible*? The answer becomes obvious when you take one look at UltraDev: it's Dreamweaver with connectivity features.

Although a full, in-depth discussion of UltraDev is beyond the scope of this book, the fundamentals are not. In the balance of this chapter, we take a look at how UltraDev makes database connections, structures recordsets, inserts database fields, and even enables you to design with live data, from the database, on the page.

Note

As of this writing, UltraDev was still in beta and had not yet been released. Certain descriptions and screen shots here may vary slightly from the final version of the program.

Using UltraDev overview

To gain the most benefit from UltraDev, you need access to a Web server capable of executing Active Server Pages. Many designers use Microsoft's Personal Web Server (PWS) during development and upload their pages to an Internet Information Server or another server running a platform-independent ASP solution like Chili!Soft. UltraDev's ability to work with a Web server during the design-time phase as well as the run-time phase greatly enhances the developer's workflow.

Here's how a typical UltraDev project begins:

1. As in Dreamweaver, a new site is defined; however, in UltraDev one additional step is taken: the application server model — whether it's ASP, ColdFusion, or JSP — is also declared.
2. A data source connection is made, either through a DSN or a connection string.
3. A recordset is defined. UltraDev gives you point-and-click access to all of a database's tables and corresponding fields for straight-forward SQL statement building.
4. The basic page is layed out as in Dreamweaver, with the exception that data elements of the recordset are dragged and dropped on the design.
5. Live Data View is engaged and the formatting of the page is refined.
6. The page is uploaded to the remote server and tested online.

As you can see from this brief overview, the process is much the same as described in the earlier portion of this chapter. UltraDev, however, makes the process relatively intuitive and — with the Live Data View — downright visual. To better understand how UltraDev works, let's look at each of the key steps in-depth.

Defining a data source

UltraDev connects to data sources in a number of ways, including ASP, ColdFusion, and JSP. The first step when working with UltraDev is to begin limiting your toolset; for ASP pages, this process entails selecting the Active Server Pages model and choosing a programming language: VBScript or JavaScript. Although some cross-over exists, the vast majority of ASP developers use VBScript. In UltraDev, the initial server set-up is handled when the site is defined through a new panel in the Site Definition dialog box, App Server Info (see Figure 36-8).

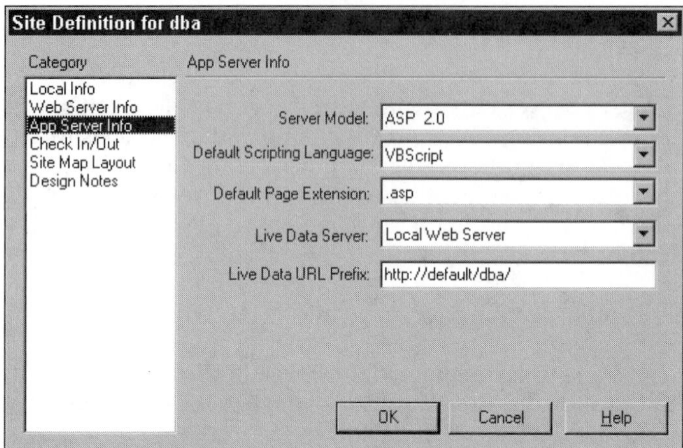

Figure 36-8: Declare your server setup in the App Server Info panel of the Site Definition dialog box.

In addition to selecting a server model and language, the App Server Info panel enables you to choose a default page extension and establish the Live Data settings. As noted earlier, you'll need to establish either a local Web server, like Personal Web Server, or a remote one to take advantage of the Live Data feature.

To define your application server settings, follow these steps:

1. Choose Site ⇨ Define Sites.
2. Select New from the Define Sites dialog box.

   You can apply application server settings to an existing Dreamweaver site by selecting the site name from the list and choosing Edit instead of New.
3. If you're creating a new site, enter the necessary information on the Local Info, Web Server Info and Site Map Layout panels found in the Site Definition dialog box.
4. Select the App Server Info category.
5. On the App Server Info panel, choose ASP 2.0 as the Server Model.
6. Select either VBScript or JavaScript as the Default Scripting Language.
7. Under Default Page Extension, select .asp, .htm or .html.

   If most of your pages are to be executed by the server, select .asp as the default extension; then, when you create a basic HTML page, enter the .htm or .html extension as part of the file name.
8. From the Live Data Server option list, select Local Web Server if you are working with a Web server such as PWS on your system, or select Remote Web Server if you have to connect to a server over a network or via the Internet.

9. If you have chosen the Local Web Server option, enter the Live Data URL Prefix in the appropriate field.

   The Live Data URL Prefix is the standard HTTP path to your site root as defined in PWS or other server. Be sure to end the URL with a trailing slash, /. For example, `http://default/dba` is the Live Data URL for one of my sites where `default` is the name of my computer and `dba` is the name of the virtual directory assigned under Personal Web Server.

   During Live Data Preview, UltraDev saves a temporary file in this folder. The temporary file has a unique name such as `TMP21k01rcc40.asp` and UltraDev uses the Live Data URL Prefix to construct a full address such as:

   ```
   http://default/dba/TMP21k01rcc40.asp
   ```

10. After you've finished entering all of your site definition data, choose OK to close the Site Definition dialog box and Done to close the Define Sites dialog box.

Once the site is defined, the next step is to establish a database connection. UltraDev enables you to connect with or without a Data Source Name (DSN). If a DSN is not available, a connection string, detailing the file path to the data base and other information, is used. A connection string is also known as a DSN-less connection.

Note

To set up a new DSN in Windows, you'll need to open the Control Panel folder and select the ODBC Data Sources (32-bit) program. From there, select the System DSN tab and choose the Add button. You'll need to know the type of driver required to access the particular database.

Once you've defined a connection, it can be accessed from any ASP page within your site. To define a data source connection, follow these steps:

1. Choose Modify ➪ Connections.

   The Connections dialog box, like the Sites dialog box, enables you to add new connections as well as edit and delete existing ones.

2. From the Connections dialog box, select the New button.

   The two-paneled Define Connections dialog box opens, as shown in Figure 36-9.

3. On the Run-Time panel of the Define Connections dialog box, enter a unique name for your connection in the Name field.

4. Select the kind of connection desired from the Type list:

   - Choose ADO (Connection String) if you're not using a DSN; or
   - Select ADO (ODBC Data Source Name) if you are.

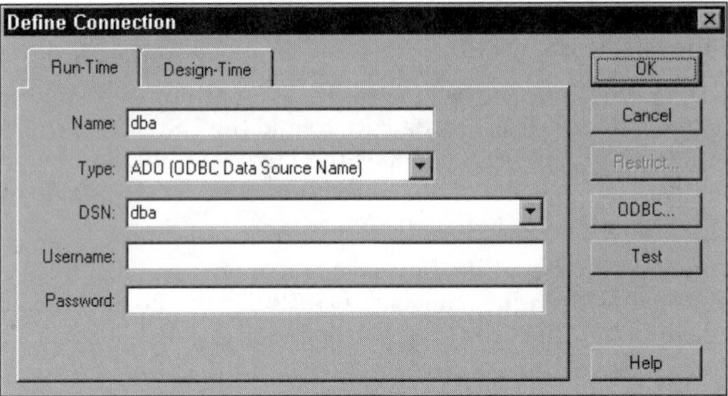

Figure 36-9: With the Define Connections dialog box, you can connect to a database through a DSN during design time and a connection string at run-time.

5. If you choose the ADO (Connection String) type, enter the full text of the string in the Connection String field.

   Each of the connection string segments is separated by a semicolon. For example:

   ```
   DRIVER={Microsoft Access Driver (*.mdb)};
   DBQ="D:\sites\jlowery\db\dbadata.mdb
   ```

   sets up the Access driver and gives the file location for the database to use. User name and password information could also be included in a connection string.

6. If you choose the ADO (ODBC Data Source Name) type of connection, select the data source from the DSN option list.

7. For DSN connections, enter the Username and Password in their respective fields, if necessary.

   The Username and Password are set in the ODBC Data Sources program.

8. You can check your connection by selecting the Test button. UltraDev will inform you if the connection was successful or if a problem occurs.

9. If your run-time connection is different from the design-time connection, select the Run-Time panel; otherwise select OK.

   The information entered in Design-Time is, by default, the same as Run-Time: you are connecting to the same data sources, but the two situations can be set-up independently.

10. From the Run-Time panel, to establish a different run-time connection, deselect the Same As Run-Time option.

11. Repeat Steps 3 through 8 to define the run-time connection.

12. Click OK when you're done.

Establishing a recordset

With one or more connections available for your site, the next step is page specific: defining a recordset. The type of recordset you define depends on the kind of Web application you're developing. Let's say, for example, you have created a mailing list sign-up form. When completed and submitted, this form will insert a new record into the `mailist` table of a larger database, `dbadata`. The record itself consists of basic information fields — like first and last name and an email address — as well as specific interest fields. With a Web application such as this, the recordset will consist of selecting all the fields from the table mailist in the database.

Rather than coding this by hand, UltraDev uses a point-and-click interface that enables you to select each of the relevant elements, in turn, from dynamically generated drop-down lists. When you Select a defined connection, UltraDev presents the various tables associated with that connection's data source. Selecting a table from the drop-down list displays the available fields or *columns*, as they are alternatively known. These columns are then also available for filtering and sorting.

While this type of recordset selection is ideal for many developers, often you need a more hands-on approach . For situations requiring additional coding, UltraDev offers an interface for advanced users that enables direct entry of the SQL statements, combined with point-and-click selection of available fields. Moreover, the code is always accessible through the HTML Source inspector.

Basic recordset definition

UltraDev introduces two new floating palettes to the Dreamweaver interface: Data Bindings and Server Behaviors. The Data Bindings palette is primarily used for inserting dynamic fields into your document, while the Server Behaviors palette shows all the server-side scripts in the current document. Both, however, provide an entry into defining recordsets.

To define a recordset using the standard user interface, follow these steps:

1. From either the Data Bindings or Server Behavior palette, choose Recordset (Query) from the Add button (the plus sign).

   The Recordset dialog box opens, as shown in Figure 36-10.

2. Enter a unique name identifying your recordset in the name field.

   Many developers customarily preface their recordset names with the letters `rs`, as in `rsMailing`.

3. Choose the desired connection from the Connection list.

   If you need to add a new connection or edit an existing one, select the Define button.

4. Select a table from the Table list.

5. If you want to include all of a table's fields in the recordset, leave All option selected in the Columns area.

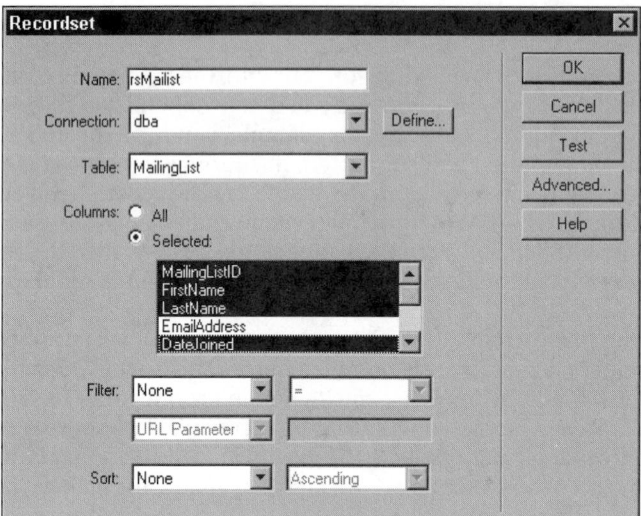

Figure 36-10: UltraDev automatically populates the tables and columns options based on your chosen connection.

6. To limit the selection of fields, choose the Selected option and then Ctrl+click (Command+click) the desired columns.

You can also Shift+click a series of contiguous columns.

At this point, you could select OK to include all the records in the current recordset. However, you can also select a subset of the records by using the Filter options.

7. If you'd like to filter the recordset, follow these steps:

- From the first option list, select the field that will be used in the comparison criteria.
- From the second option list, choose the type of operator to use in the comparison: equal (=), greater than (>), less than (<), greater than or equal to (>=), less than or equal to (<=), or not equal to (<>).
- From the third option list, select the type of value to be compared:

URL Parameter	Used when the method of the requesting form is `GET`.
Form Variable	Used when the method of the requesting form is `POST`.
Cookie	Used when the comparison value comes from a cookie.

Session Variable	Used when the comparison value comes from an ASP sessions variable.
Application Variable	Used when the comparison value comes from an application variable.
Entered Value	Used when the comparison value comes from a static value.

- From the fourth option list, enter the value used in the comparison.

For example, if I wanted to devise a recordset to include only those records from a particular state, I might choose the State field of my database, followed by the equal sign, followed by Entered Value, followed by NY.

8. To order the recordset by a single field, choose that field from the Sort list and then select whether the recordset should be sorted in either Ascending or Descending order.

9. To make sure your recordset returns the expected records, select the Test button.

   Unless there's a problem, UltraDev displays all recordsets 25 records at a time, as shown in Figure 36-11.

10. Click OK when you're done.

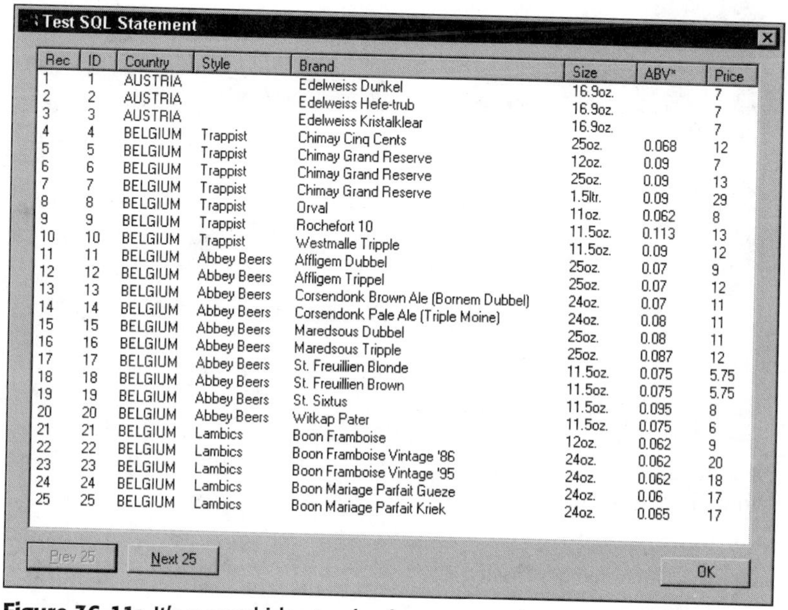

Test SQL Statement

Rec	ID	Country	Style	Brand	Size	ABV*	Price
1	1	AUSTRIA		Edelweiss Dunkel	16.9oz.		7
2	2	AUSTRIA		Edelweiss Hefe-trub	16.9oz.		7
3	3	AUSTRIA		Edelweiss Kristalklear	16.9oz.		7
4	4	BELGIUM	Trappist	Chimay Cinq Cents	25oz.	0.068	12
5	5	BELGIUM	Trappist	Chimay Grand Reserve	12oz.	0.09	7
6	6	BELGIUM	Trappist	Chimay Grand Reserve	25oz.	0.09	13
7	7	BELGIUM	Trappist	Chimay Grand Reserve	1.5ltr.	0.09	29
8	8	BELGIUM	Trappist	Orval	11oz.	0.062	8
9	9	BELGIUM	Trappist	Rochefort 10	11.5oz.	0.113	13
10	10	BELGIUM	Trappist	Westmalle Tripple	11.5oz.	0.09	12
11	11	BELGIUM	Abbey Beers	Affligem Dubbel	25oz.	0.07	9
12	12	BELGIUM	Abbey Beers	Affligem Trippel	25oz.	0.07	12
13	13	BELGIUM	Abbey Beers	Corsendonk Brown Ale (Bornem Dubbel)	24oz.	0.07	11
14	14	BELGIUM	Abbey Beers	Corsendonk Pale Ale (Triple Moine)	24oz.	0.08	11
15	15	BELGIUM	Abbey Beers	Maredsous Dubbel	25oz.	0.08	11
16	16	BELGIUM	Abbey Beers	Maredsous Tripple	25oz.	0.087	12
17	17	BELGIUM	Abbey Beers	St. Freuillien Blonde	11.5oz.	0.075	5.75
18	18	BELGIUM	Abbey Beers	St. Freuillien Brown	11.5oz.	0.075	5.75
19	19	BELGIUM	Abbey Beers	St. Sixtus	11.5oz.	0.095	8
20	20	BELGIUM	Abbey Beers	Witkap Pater	11.5oz.	0.075	6
21	21	BELGIUM	Lambics	Boon Framboise	12oz.	0.062	9
22	22	BELGIUM	Lambics	Boon Framboise Vintage '86	24oz.	0.062	20
23	23	BELGIUM	Lambics	Boon Framboise Vintage '95	24oz.	0.062	18
24	24	BELGIUM	Lambics	Boon Mariage Parfait Gueze	24oz.	0.06	17
25	25	BELGIUM	Lambics	Boon Mariage Parfait Kriek	24oz.	0.065	17

Prev 25 Next 25 OK

Figure 36-11: It's a good idea to check your recordset by choosing the Test button on the Recordset dialog box.

Advanced recordset definition

While the basic Recordset dialog box is sufficient in many cases, you can set up more complex queries using the Advanced Recordset dialog box. In the Advanced dialog box, multiple criteria can be added to the SQL statement, either by pointing and clicking at the dynamically generated table, column, and stored procedure lists, or by entering the code by hand. In addition, any number of variables can be declared and incorporated into your code.

To define a recordset using the Advanced Recordset dialog box, follow these steps:

1. From either the Data Bindings or Server Behavior palette, choose Recordset (Query) from the Add button (the plus sign).
2. Select the Advanced button.

   The Advanced Recordset dialog box opens, as shown in Figure 36-12.

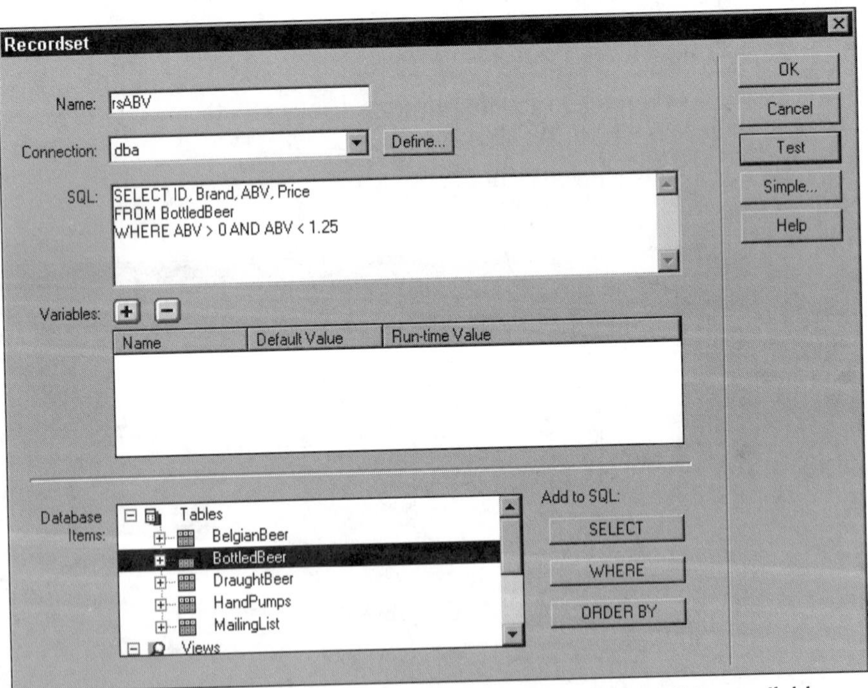

Figure 36-12: Complex recordsets require the enhanced SQL editing available through the Advanced Recordset dialog box.

3. Enter a unique name for the recordset in the Name field.
4. Choose a connection from the Connection option list.

   When a new connection is chosen, UltraDev displays the available tables, columns, views (also called queries), and stored procedures (or macros) in an expandable tree-like structure in the Database Items area.
5. Build in a SQL statement by either:
   - Entering the SQL code by hand in the SQL area; or
   - Selecting a column or other database item and then choosing the Select, Where, or Order By button; or
   - A combination of the two methods.
6. If variables are included in SQL statement, they should be defined in the Variables area. Select the Add button to enter the Name, Default Value, and Run-Time Value.
   - **Name:** the variable's name as used in the SQL statement
   - **Default Value:** the variable's value unless a run-time value is returned
   - **Run-Time Value:** a dynamic value sent by the browser, typically from a server object

Caution

Be sure to use single quotes around your variable name in the SQL statement, as in `SELECT * FROM Mailist WHERE Location = 'varLocation'`. However, quotes should not be used in the Name or Default Value columns.

7. At any point, you can check the validity of your SQL statement by selecting the Test button.

The Advanced Recordset dialog box is very useful for constructing SQL statements with multiple criteria. For example, if you wanted to limit a mailing list recordset to records within a certain set of area codes, your SQL statement might look something like this:

```
SELECT * FROM Mailist WHERE Zip > 10000 AND Zip < 10999
```

In addition, non-arithmetic operators — such as LIKE and NOT LIKE — can be incorporated.

Incorporating data

So far every step we've taken with UltraDev has been preparation; now it's time for that preparation to begin to pay off. From a Dreamweaver user's perspective, one of the best features of UltraDev is how tightly it integrates with Dreamweaver. Table structures are built in the same fashion, text is styled the same way and links are still created in the Property Inspector. Even with the new palettes and much enhanced functionality (noted earlier), the first task of building an UltraDev page is to construct the standard static page first, just as you would in Dreamweaver. After the page is largely complete, the active elements are added.

Adding fields

One of the most common tasks facing the active-page designer is to display data from a database integrated into the page. UltraDev accomplishes this task with drag-and-drop ease. With a connection established and a recordset defined, dynamic text—representing any field and record from the database—can be placed anywhere on the page.

The Data Bindings palette provides the easiest way to include dynamic text. The defined recordsets (multiple recordsets can be defined) are displayed in an expandable/collapsible tree-like structure which make it easy to drill-down to the desired field. Once that field is visible, you can drag-and-drop it anywhere on the page. If the field needs to represent data in a particular format—such as United States currency or European style dates—you can apply or *bind* the formatting to that column. Naturally, you can also format the text using either standard HTML or defined CSS classes.

UltraDev uses a lightning bolt symbol to designate dynamic data. To insert dynamic data into your Web page, follow these steps:

1. Open the Data Bindings palette using one of these methods:
   - Choose Window ➪ Data Bindings
   - Select the Data Bindings button on the Launcher
   - Use the keyboard shortcut, Shift+F10.

   The Data Bindings palette displays all available recordsets in a collapsed form.

2. Expand the desired recordset by clicking the plus sign once.

Be careful not to double-click the name of the recordset as this will cause the Recordset dialog box to open.

3. Select the desired dynamic field and drag it into place on the Web page.

Alternatively, you could first place your cursor where you'd like the data to appear, and then select the dynamic field and choose the Insert button on the Data Bindings palette.

4. The dynamic data appears on your page in the form of *recordsetName.fieldName* (for example, rsMailist.Firstname) for fields, and *recordsetName_recordsetParameter* for the available variables: first record index, last record index, and total records.

Keep in mind that dynamic data can be placed anywhere on a page: inline with graphics, in a layer, or in a table. Tables are frequently used to contain structured data, and prove especially useful in UltraDev for displaying information.

Repeating regions

While fields from a single record are required in many situations, often a Web application is used to present multiple records. UltraDev enables you to repeat data in any selected area on screen. The selected area can be a single field with a separating comma, space, or <br> tag—or it can be an entire row of a table, with each cell containing a different field. When executed, the page repeats the selected region as many times as designated or until all the records are shown.

The Repeated Region command is what is known in UltraDev as a *server behavior*. UltraDev comes with a variety of such commands, all located on the Server Behavior palette as shown in Figure 36-13. Unlike Dreamweaver's standard behaviors—which are, by comparison, client-side—a Server Behavior is not attached to any one tag. Consequently, the Server Behavior palette displays all the server behaviors on the current page.

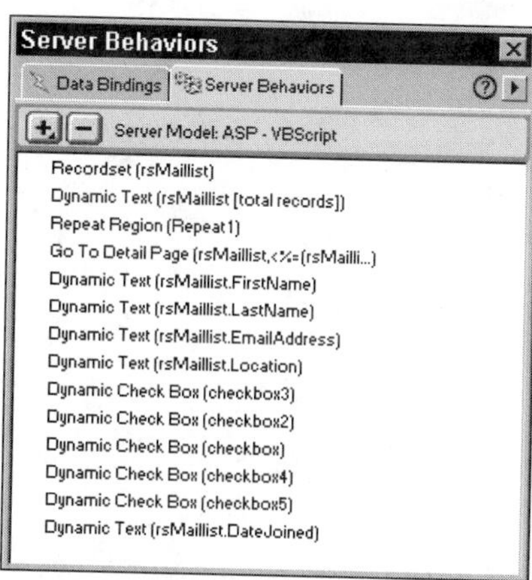

Figure 36-13: The Server Behavior palette displays all the server-side scripts on the current page.

To insert a Repeated Region, follow these steps:

1. Enter your dynamic data on the page.
2. Select the area that you want repeated.

Tip: It's often easier to use the Tag Selector in the Status Bar when choosing the proper elements. This is especially true when selecting the <tr> (table row) tag.

3. Display the Server Behavior palette using one of these methods:
   - Choose Window ➪ Server Behaviors
   - Select the Server Behaviors button on the Launcher
   - Use the keyboard shortcut, Shift+F11.
4. Select the Add (+) button from the Server Behaviors palette.
5. Choose Repeat Region from the list.

   The Repeat Region dialog box appears, as shown in Figure 36-14.

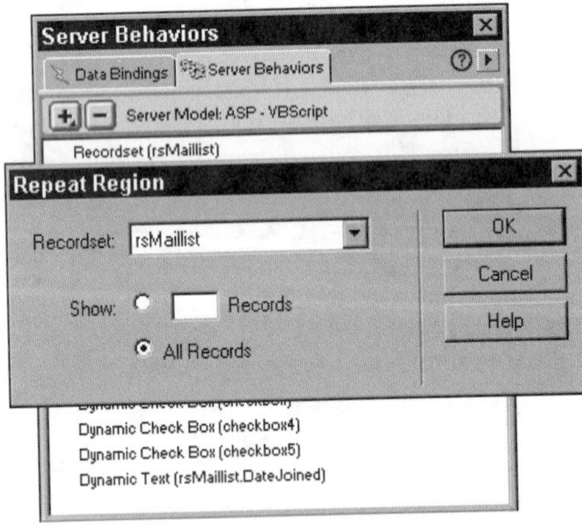

Figure 36-14: With the Repeat Region feature, all or a set number of records can be displayed.

6. Select the desired recordset from the Recordset list.
7. Select the number of records to show at one time by entering a value in the Show Records field or by selecting All Records.
8. Click OK when you're done.

UltraDev highlights the selected region with the color chosen in Preferences and places a Repeat tab above it, as shown in Figure 36-15. The Repeat Region highlight is not visible if View ➪ Invisible Elements is not selected.

Tip

You can alter the number of records at any time by selecting the Repeat tab and changing the value in the Repeat Region Property Inspector.

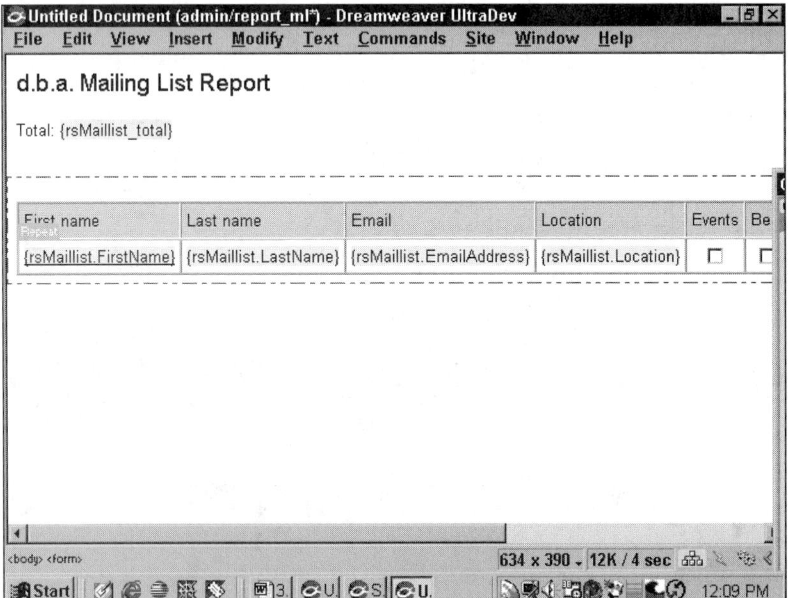

Figure 36-15: A repeated region is marked with the Live Data Untranslated color and a Repeat tab.

Designing with Live Data

Layout is one of the most frustrating challenges facing a Web application designer. Most active-page designers — even those with local Web servers — build their pages with a constant cycle of layout, save, and test. To see how a page will look with real data in it, the page needs to be executed on the server, and most design environments require that the document be stored before it can be "bounced" off the server — most of them, that is, except UltraDev with Live Data.

Live Data is one of UltraDev's most notable features. With Live Data enabled, your page is displayed with actual data from the data source. More importantly, this page is still live and can be edited as usual. This means you can apply formatting — font family, size, color, or whatever — directly to the dynamic text and your format is applied to all the onscreen data. You can also adjust table or column widths as needed and instantly see the results. Moreover, you can also easily set application, session, or other variables to specific values for testing; you can even send the Live Data a series of arguments, typically appended to a URL. All in all, Live Data is a terrific boon to workflow. Let's see how it works.

Viewing Live Data

Enabling the Live Data mode is a snap: select View ➪ Live Data or choose the keyboard shortcut, Ctrl+Shift+R (Command+Shift+R) as shown in Figure 36-16. With Live Data enabled, a new toolbar appears at the top of the screen and the page is sent to the Live Data Server specified in the Site Definition. A small animation of gears turning runs in the right-hand corner of the Live Data toolbar to indicate the progress. After the requested data has been retrieved, it is displayed in locked, translated areas. The data areas are highlighted in the color selected as the Live Data Translated option in the Highlighting panel of Preferences. The highlighting can be toggled on or off by selecting View ➪ Invisible Elements.

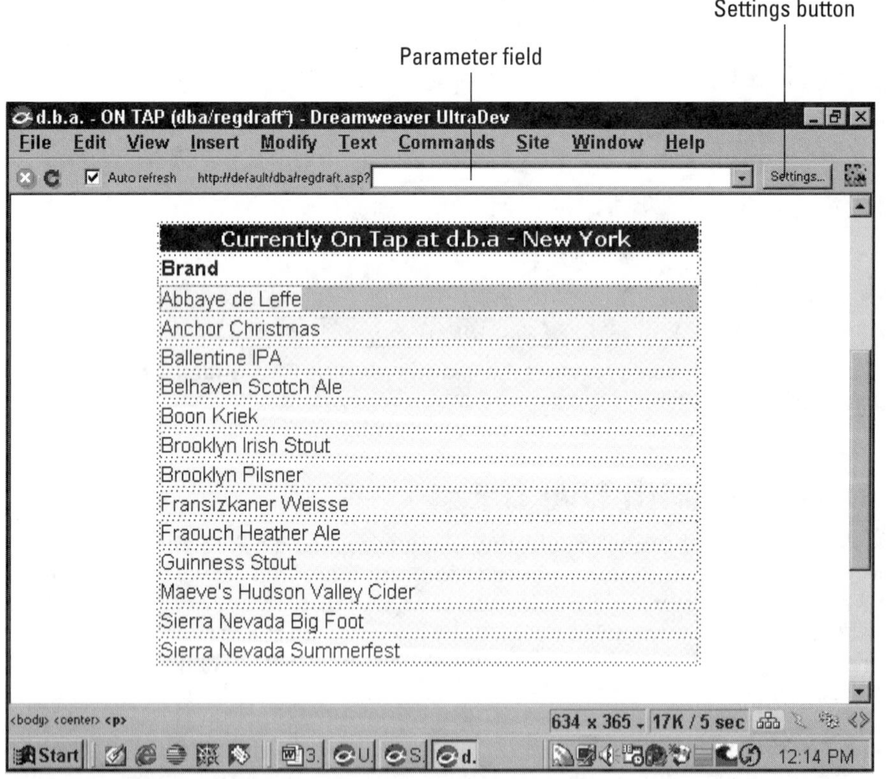

Figure 36-16: UltraDev's Live Data mode lets you preview—and edit—your page with actual data retrieved from the data source.

As indicated earlier, any Live Data area can be selected and formatted. If the dynamic data is in a repeated region, changes should be applied to the initial tags in the region: in other words, the very first row or other area that the Repeat Region behavior was originally applied to. To see the change take effect, select the Refresh button or choose the Auto-Refresh option to have modifications incorporated automatically.

In addition to layout and format alterations, you can also add, change, or remove the dynamic data on a page. With Auto-Refresh enabled, the Live Data server is re-sent the page, and the new or changed data is displayed.

Tip

Processing a Live Data page can take a bit of time. If you realize another change is necessary and you'd rather not execute the page twice, you can abort the Live Data process by selecting the Stop button on the Live Data toolbar.

Live Data settings

Not all data comes straight from a database. The beauty of many Web applications is their flexibility: pages can display different information based on a wide range of variables from the user directly, the user's environment, the server's environment, or any combination of these values. For example, different data could be displayed depending on the contents of a shopping cart cookie or a search request entered in a form. UltraDev gives you the power to preview the results of any of the variables on your page by use of the Live Data Settings.

Of course, before you can preview the results of setting a variable one way or the other, you have to include the variable. Use the Data Bindings palette to add a Request, Session, or Application variable. Once the variable has been added to the page, it becomes available in the data elements tree of the Data Bindings palette and it can be placed anywhere on the page like other dynamic elements.

You can alter the Live Data Settings in two ways:

- ✦ As a series of URL arguments in the Live Data URL field. These arguments follow the *variable01=value&variable02=value* syntax used in forms using the GET method. UltraDev, however, handles all the URL encoding for you; you don't, for example, need to convert a space between words to a `%20`.
- ✦ Choose Settings from the Live Data toolbar and enter the variables and respective values in the Live Data Settings dialog box (Figure 36-17). To enter a variable, select the Add button and input the variable in the Name column, followed by its value in the Value column. The sequence of variables can even be altered by selecting one and choosing the Up or Down arrows.

If the GET method is selected in the Settings dialog box, variables are synchronized in the URL field and the Settings dialog box. If you modify one, the changes are reflected in the other. Should you choose POST, however, the URL field is not displayed, as URL arguments are not used in a POST type form.

Beyond individual variables, Web applications often require some initialization for proper processing. In the executing Web server, such initialization generally takes the form of session variables. UltraDev handles these requirements through the Initialization Script section of the Live Data Settings dialog box.

Note

Any external files required by the page for execution — such as server-side includes — must be uploaded to their proper location on the server for Live Data to work properly.

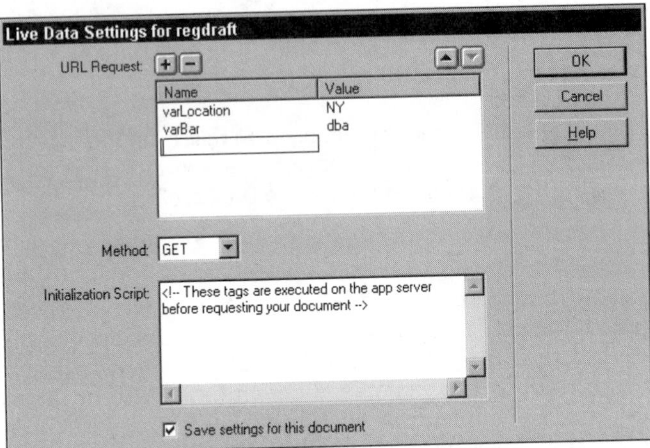

Figure 36-17: Set up variables to preview the results they bring in the Live Data Settings dialog box.

Summary

Active Server Pages are widely used for developing all manner of Web applications. With Dreamweaver's "hands-off" approach to ASP code, you can code your applications in your favorite text editor and still take advantage of Dreamweaver's advanced layout capabilities. Certain frequent operations, such as establishing a connection and recordset, can be facilitated by third-party ASP objects in Dreamweaver. However, for the most robust ASP pages, the clear choice is UltraDev. When looking to develop ASP pages in Dreamweaver, keep these points in mind:

- ✦ ASP uses tags delimited by an opening <% and %> to mark code executed by the server. The end result, returned to the user's browser, is a standard Web page with all the ASP variables replaced by regular HTML.
- ✦ Dreamweaver recognizes anything within the delimiters as ASP tags and substitutes the code with an icon in the Document window. Selecting the ASP icon permits the code to be edited through a Property Inspector.
- ✦ Extension developers, such as Bill Bullman, have developed a variety of ASP objects for entering basic ASP code, including an extremely useful Ad Rotator object.
- ✦ UltraDev, a Web application development program from Macromedia, is based on Dreamweaver and outputs ASP as well as ColdFusion and Java Server Pages.
- ✦ With UltraDev's Live Data feature, you can design your pages using the actual data returned from your Web server. ASP Session and Application variables can be specified through the Live Data Settings command.

In the next chapter, we look at Allaire's ColdFusion and their objects for Dreamweaver.

✦ ✦ ✦

CHAPTER 37

Using Allaire's ColdFusion

✦ ✦ ✦ ✦

In This Chapter

Using and understanding Allaire's ColdFusion

Installing and applying ColdFusion objects

Programming with ColdFusion objects

Accessing other servers with ColdFusion

✦ ✦ ✦ ✦

If you're a Windows Dreamweaver user, you're probably familiar with Allaire, makers of the bundled external editor, HomeSite. Allaire is perhaps better known in the general computing world for ColdFusion, the development system that integrates browser, server, and database technologies. The ColdFusion Application Server, now in version 4.5, works with all major Web servers to deploy active content pages on the Internet.

Using Allaire's ColdFusion

One of Allaire's strongest features is its use of the ColdFusion Markup Language (CFML). Like HTML, CFML consists of a series of tags that are interpreted, at run time, to build a viewable page. The primary difference is that HTML is inter-preted by the browser, or client-side; and CFML is interpreted server-side. The ColdFusion Application server reads a Web page with both HTML and CFML, and processes the CFML tags to convert them to HTML. The real power is when the CFML, processing as database content, is accessed and blended with the existing page before being returned for viewing.

Allaire has partnered with Macromedia to integrate CFML into an advanced Web authoring tool and has recently released a new set of ColdFusion extensions for Dreamweaver. In addition to the 22 objects for inserting CFML tags into the page, the ColdFusion extensions include an equal number of Third-Party Tags and Inspectors. Now, ColdFusion tags can be drag-and-dropped in the Document window and then quickly identified and, if necessary, modified through a Property Inspector. Although this implementation of ColdFusion tags is not exhaustive, most of the commonly performed connectivity tasks are within the Dreamweaver designer's control.

At the time of this writing, the ColdFusion implementation of UltraDev was not available. This technology promises to be extremely powerful, however, and will likely be covered in forthcoming Dreamweaver books.

Understanding ColdFusion

So what does a typical ColdFusion page look like? Let's take a look at a sample application that exports all the information from a small database onto a Web page. To do this, the page first must request or query the database for the data. Then, the data is output onto the page. The code for such a page is a mix of regular HTML and Cold Fusion CFML tags, like the following:

```
<cfquery name="empNames" datasource="employees">
  select * from CurrentEmployees
  order by LastName
</cfquery>
<h2>Current Employee Listing</h2>
<cfoutput query="empNames">
<b>#LastName#</b>, #FirstName#<br>
</cfoutput>
```

In this example, a query is first created from a database with the Data Source Name, "employees." The query itself is named "empNames"; you must name any queries so that they may be referenced later. The CurrentEmployees table is targeted and the query asks that all fields be retrieved and placed in an alphabetical last-name-first order. Next, a heading, "Current Employee Listing," is placed on the page with a regular HTML heading style, `<h2>`. Any HTML tags and content you want—images, layers, or anything else—can be placed here.

The final section, in the `<cfoutput>...<cfoutput>` tag pair determines what form the displayed data takes. Each field called from the CurrentEmployees table of the employees database is marked on either side with hash marks, #. Notice that HTML code as well as regular text can be interspersed with the CFML code to achieve the desired effect. Here, information from the Lastname field is put in bold and followed by a comma. Then the employee's first names are displayed. The line-break tag, `<br>`, is added to ensure that every entry appears on its own line. Figure 37-1 shows how this page looks both in Dreamweaver and in its sample output.

You'll find an evaluation copy of ColdFusion Studio 4.5a on CD-ROM 2 accompanying this book. ColdFusion Studio includes both a design environment, similar to HomeSite, and a full version of the ColdFusion Web Application Server. The ColdFusion Server is restricted to a single computer use and cannot be deployed on the Web, but is ideal for development purposes.

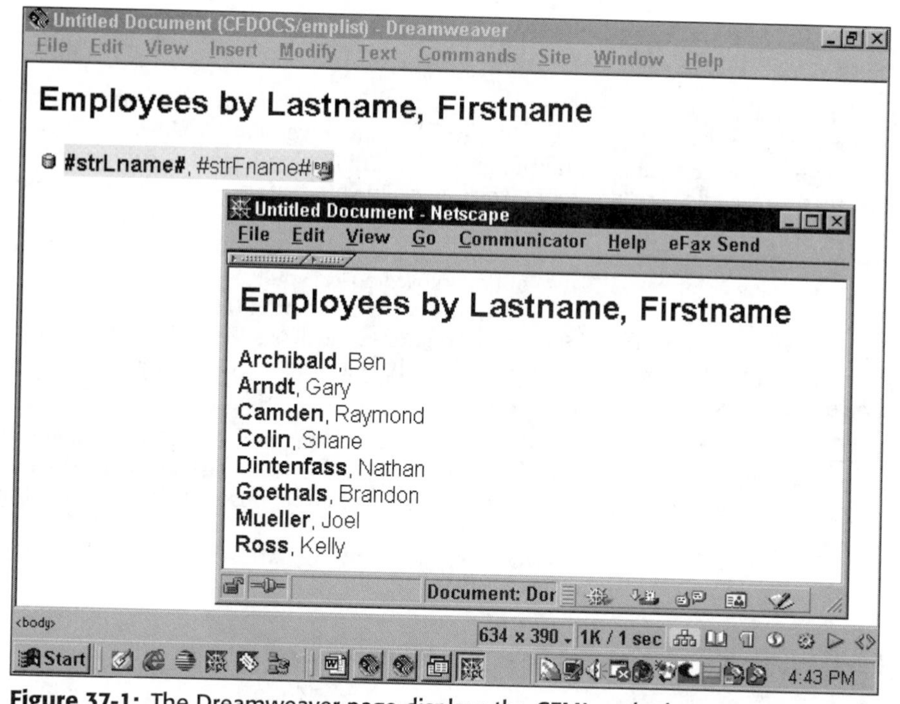

Figure 37-1: The Dreamweaver page displays the CFML code that translates into the browser output, once processed.

Using the ColdFusion Studio

The trial version of the ColdFusion Studio included on this book's CD-ROM 2 offers a unique opportunity for Web developers to get up to speed with database technology on their own systems. If you're new to the server side of Web design, it's important to understand that the ColdFusion Studio works along with Web servers, but does not replace them. To use ColdFusion, you'll need to have a Web server already installed; typical choices are the Personal Web Server from Microsoft, or O'Reilly's WebSite Professional Web Server.

Once you've installed the Web server software, double-click the icon for ColdFusion Server Set-up to start the installation process. Follow the prompts; once it's finished, the program is set to automatically start when your system boots. You'll find a great deal of documentation available in the ColdFusion program group, in HTML format for easy browsing.

Continued

Continued

To preview your new Web documents locally, you'll need to establish a new site where the local root folder points to the public folder of the Web server. With WebSite Professional (and many other servers), this is the htdocs folder. ColdFusion installs a subfolder in the Web server's public folder called cfdocs. You can build your test pages in the cfdocs folder. Before you can preview them locally, however, you'll need to change the Preferences to enable this feature. Choose Edit_ ⇨ Preferences and, from the Preview in Browser tab, select the Preview Using Local Server option. Now you can preview your ColdFusion files using any of the browsers you've set up with the press of a button (F12 or Shift+F12) or the click of a mouse (File ⇨ Preview in Browser). The browser will use the URL `http://localhost/` or a set Internet Protocol (IP) number like 127.0.0.1 as the base address to find the Dreamweaver pages.

You must use caution with this feature, however. If you've enabled the Preview Using Local Server option, you won't be able to preview any sites previously established that aren't included in the Web server folder. To preview these as before, deselect the Preview Using Local Server option.

Installing the ColdFusion objects

The new ColdFusion extensions are packaged in the Macromedia Extension Manager format. As with other Extension Manager files, you can either double-click the ColdFusion.mxp file or select Commands ⇨ Manage Extensions to begin the installation. After you accept the licensing arrangement, the various objects, inspectors and third-party tags will be installed in the proper directories. Relaunch Dreamweaver, and a new panel of objects will be available in the Object palette under the ColdFusion heading.

Applying the ColdFusion objects

Allaire's set of ColdFusion objects greatly simplify the chore of adding CFML code to your HTML page. CFML tags look very similar to the familiar HTML elements. For example, to add a form to your ColdFusion page by hand, you would add the following code:

```
<cfform name="employeeUpdate" action="empUpdate.cfm"></cfform>
```

CFML tags also use attributes and values such as `name="employeeUpdate"`; all CFML tags begin with the ColdFusion initials, `cf`. Like HTML, form elements such as text fields and Submit buttons are placed between the opening and closing tags.

To identify any Web page that should be processed by the ColdFusion Application Server, the file extension `.cfm` or `.cfml` is added. Dreamweaver handles this automatically when you save your document and select ColdFusion Templates from the Files of Type list in the Save File dialog box. If you're working exclusively with ColdFusion files, change the Add Extension When Saving option, found on the General panel of Preferences, to either `.cfm` or `.cfml`.

When a CFML tag is inserted into a Web page in Dreamweaver — whether manually or via one of the ColdFusion objects — Dreamweaver designates it as a third-party tag. As such, it is highlighted in the document, as shown in Figure 37-2, if the Preferences option is enabled. To turn on CFML (and other third-party tag) highlighting, choose Edit ➪ Preferences and select the Highlighting category. Make sure the Show option of Third-Party Tags is selected. If you don't like the default highlight color, choose another one by clicking the color swatch next to the Third-Party Tags label.

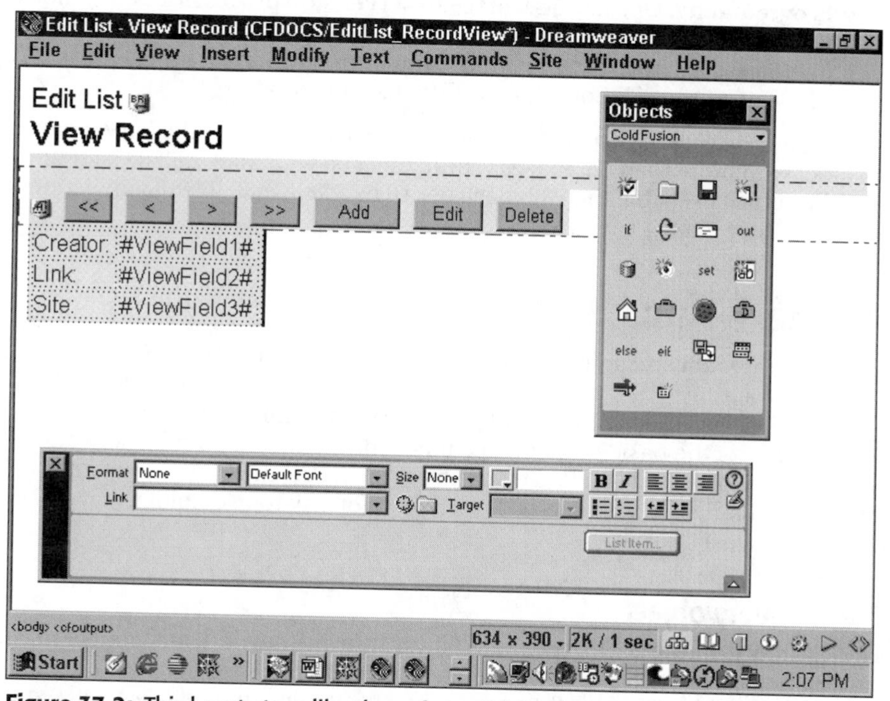

Figure 37-2: Third-party tags like those from ColdFusion can be highlighted in the Document Window.

For some CFML objects, Dreamweaver inserts a generic ColdFusion icon, similar to the Invisible Elements used for the `<br>` tag or layers, as a placeholder to represent the code. Other ColdFusion tags have their own specific icon. You can enable or disable the appearance of either type of ColdFusion icon through the Server Markup

Tags option on the Invisible Elements panel of Preferences. Like all other placeholders, ColdFusion icons can be cut, copy-and-pasted, or moved via the drag-and-drop method. Selecting the icon invokes the tag's Property Inspector, exposing the current attributes and values.

The ColdFusion Dreamweaver objects fall into four categories:

- **Database Setup.** Two objects, CF Query and CF Output, are used for reading information from a database and displaying it.
- **Forms.** Similar to their HTML counterparts, four ColdFusion objects — CF Form, CF Text, CF Checkbox, and CF Radio — receive data from the user. Once that data has been input, the CF Insert and CF Update objects add the information to a data source, or edit it, respectively. The CF Location object specifies the next Web page to load, once the form operation has been completed.
- **Programming.** One key advantage to server-side processing is the ability to use conditional commands, such as the CF Set, CF If, and CF Loop objects found here. Further programming abilities are available through the CF Case, CF Default Case, CF Cookie, and CF Include objects.
- **Other Servers.** As noted earlier, the ColdFusion Application Server can interact with more than databases. These objects — CF Mail, CF File, and CF Directory — enable the Web designer to handle e-mail, file manipulation, and directory management.

Database setup

Two of the arguably most important tags in the ColdFusion Markup Language are `<cfquery>` and `<cfoutput>`. The first, `<cfquery>`, is responsible for establishing a connection with the database and passing SQL statements to it. The second, `<cfoutput>`, is the basic output mechanism for the results of the query and, as such, shapes much of what is seen on the screen. Dreamweaver inserts these two important commands with the assistance of two easy-to-use ColdFusion objects: CF Query and CF Output.

The CF Query object

The CF Query object is the main conduit for transmitting SQL statements to a data source. Generally the SQL statements take the form of a query; however, `<cfquery>`, the tag inserted by this object, is not limited to passing queries — any SQL statement is valid.

The CF Query object, shown in Figure 37-3, has many options, but only the top three are required:

- **Query Name.** A unique name given to the query itself so that it may be called by other tags. The query name must start with a letter and use only letters, numbers, and the underscore character; query names with spaces or hyphens are not acceptable.

✦ **Data Source.** This is the name registered with the DSN program for the database to be accessed.

✦ **Query.** SQL statements define the operation to be performed on the data. Four main types of SQL statements are supported: `Select`, `Insert`, `Update`, and `Delete`.

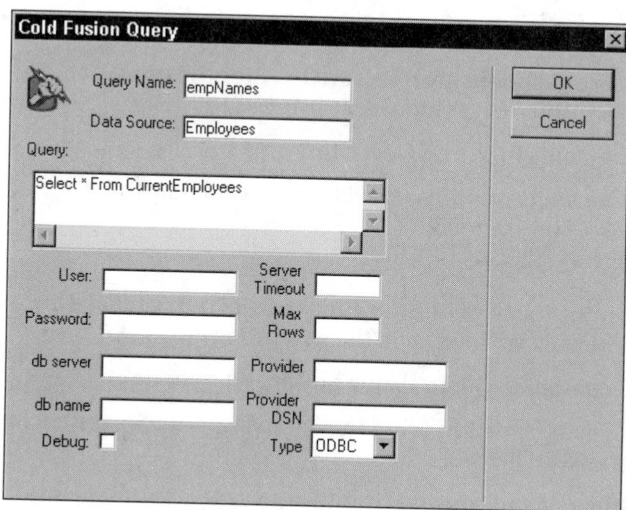

Figure 37-3: The ColdFusion Query object is used to send SQL statements to the selected database.

When the `<cfquery>` tag is generated, the SQL statement is not seen as an attribute of the tag, but of its content, like this:

```
<cfquery name="empNames" datasource="globalcorpdb"
dbtype="ODBC" >Select * from tblEmp Order By strLname</cfquery>
```

The remainder of the ColdFusion Query dialog box is for more advanced, optional settings, such as username and password, a timeout value, and the database type. Each option is discussed individually in the steps following.

Note

The CF Query object must be placed before any other object, such as the CF Output object, that references it on the HTML page. Traditionally, when coding a `<cfquery>` tag by hand, it is placed above the `<html>` tag. However, this is not possible in Dreamweaver and is not necessary if you ensure that other objects are located further down the page.

To use the CF Query object, follow these steps:

1. Place your cursor near the top of the HTML page.
2. Select the CF Query object from the ColdFusion panel of the Objects Palette.

   The ColdFusion Query dialog box is displayed.
3. Enter a unique name for the query in the CF Query Name field. Make sure that the name begins with a letter and does not contain spaces or hyphens.
4. Enter the name of the database in the Data Source field.

   Data source names are case-sensitive. Be sure to enter the exact name as found in the ODBC or other driver manager.
5. Enter your SQL statements in the CF Query text area.

   To define a table from which records should be pulled, enter the name of the table after the phrase. For example,

   ```
   SELECT * FROM Employees ORDER BY Lastname
   ```

   where `Employees` is the name of one table in the selected database and `Lastname` is the field used to determine the sort order.

   The following fields in the CF Query dialog box are all optional.
6. If needed, enter the user name to access the database in the User field and the password in the Password field.
7. Enter a maximum time, in milliseconds, for the query to execute before returning an error message in the Server Timeout field.

Note Currently, only SQL Server version 6.*x* and above support the Timeout feature.

8. To limit the number of rows displayable on the resulting page, enter a value in the Max Rows field.

   The db server, db name, Provider, and Provider DSN fields all relate to the Type of database selected.
9. If you are using a native database driver (for OLE-DB, Oracle 7.3, Oracle 8.0 or Sybase 11), select the proper option from the Type list. Otherwise keep the setting on the default value, ODBC.

Tip While you could get away with keeping the ODBC type even if you are using a native driver, your queries will run much faster if you switch to the correct type.

10. If you changed the Type option to a native driver, enter the data source used by that driver in the db server field.
11. The db name field is used when the Type option is set to OLE-DB or Sybase11 to define the data source.
12. If an OLE-DB is in use, enter the COM provider's name in the Provider field and its data source in the Provider DSN field.

13. To provide debugging information when the query is run, select the Debug option.

    If the query runs with no errors, Debug reports the number of records returned and the length of time the query took to run, and recaps the SQL statements — all at the bottom of the HTML page, after the database output.

Once the CF Query object has been inserted on the page, it can be easily modified. To change the settings or SQL statements associated with a CF Query object, select its icon in the Document Window. The Property Inspector, shown in Figure 37-4 displays all the options chosen in the dialog box — including the SQL statement — and more. One additional attribute is available through the Property Inspector, Blg, which represents the blockfactor parameter. The blockfactor attribute is used with ODBC and native Oracle drivers to set the number of rows to retrieve with each trip to the server.

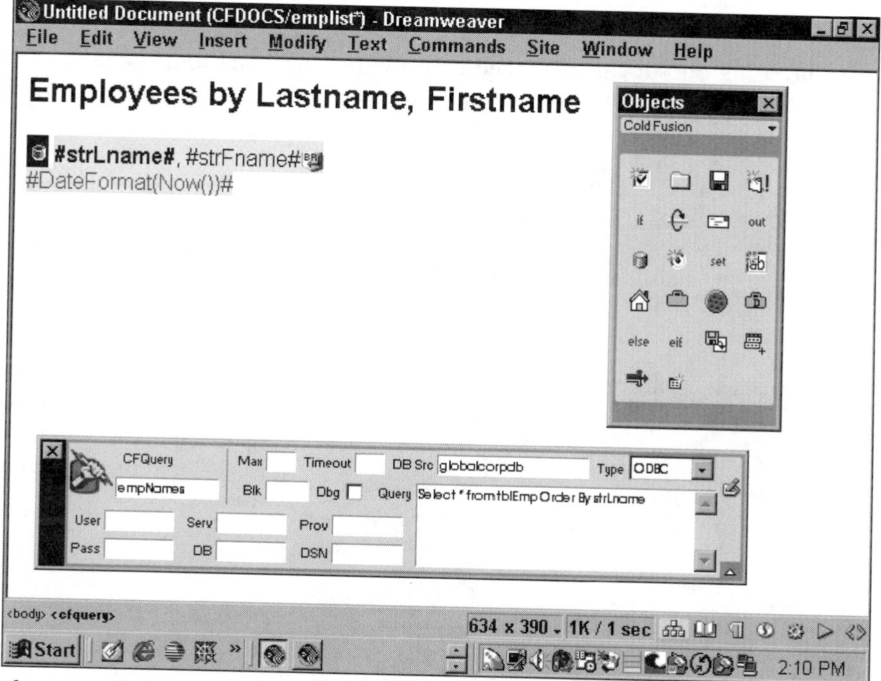

Figure 37-4: Change your ColdFusion query options through its Property Inspector.

To revise the SQL statements of a CF Query object, enter your changes directly in the multiline CF Query field.

The CF Output object

Once the data is retrieved through the CF Query object, the CF Output object displays it, in whatever format specified. While the CF Output object and its corresponding CFML tag, `<cfoutput>`, frequently handle database queries, results from built-in functions—such as those dealing with date and time—are also displayable. The `<cfoutput>` tag is very versatile and can be used as often as required on any given page. You could, for example, use it to create a form letter, filling in the variables (like Name and Address) with information from a database.

While it's possible to nest `<cfoutput>` tags in ColdFusion 4.5, you have to be careful when you do. The outermost tag contains the CF Query information and any Group declarations as well. All inner `<cfoutput>` tags can contain additional Group settings, except for the innermost one.

To use the CF Output object, follow these steps:

1. Position your cursor on the page where you'd like the output to appear.

   The result output can be placed inline with other text on the page or in a separate table. CF Output object results can also be used to populate a drop-down option list.

Keep your Invisible Elements turned on so you can be sure to place the CF Output object after the CF Query object.

2. Select the CF Output object from the ColdFusion panel of the Objects Palette (see Figure 37-5).

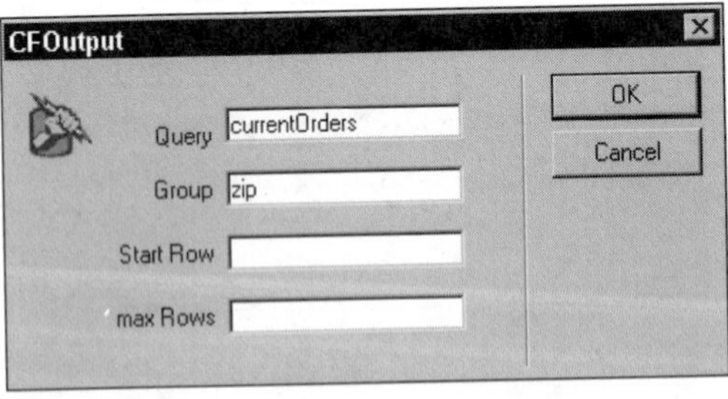

Figure 37-5: The CF Output object controls what is actually integrated into the Web page for viewing – both the content and the format.

3. If you want to display records from a particular query already on the page, enter the name of the query in the CF Query Name field.

4. To begin displaying records other than from the beginning, enter the number of the beginning record in the Start Row field.

5. If you want to limit the number of rows that can be displayed at one time, enter a value in the Maximum Rows field.

6. To eliminate duplicates in a recordset, enter the name of the sort field in the Group field.

   For example, if you wanted to sort some output by state, but only wanted the name of the state to appear once, the State field would be entered in the Group field as well as used in the SQL statement, Order By.

7. Click OK when you're done.

The <cfoutput> tag is entered into the code, but you won't see any indication of it unless View ➪ Invisible Elements is enabled.

8. Position your cursor within the highlighted area, designating the content of the <cfoutput> tag.

After closing the CF Output dialog box, your <cfoutput>...</cfoutput> tag pair is selected, but entering file names and other code immediately erases the tag. You can click into the highlighted area or use two keystrokes – right arrow, left arrow – to place your cursor in the proper place.

9. Enter the desired output format in the CF Output text area.

   Fields are designated with hash marks on either side as in #employees#. HTML code is used to format the CFML field. For example:

```
<cfoutput query="extensions"><a href="#Link#">#Site#</a>:
<font color="red">#Creator#</font><br></cfoutput>
```

   outputs a hyperlink list of Web sites, followed by the name of the site's creator, in red.

You don't have to code anything but the field names by hand. The fields and other embedded functions can easily be formatted using Dreamweaver's text tools, such as font, size, color, and alignment.

Formatting the color of anything within a <cfoutput> tag is a bit troublesome. Normally, Dreamweaver inserts a hexadecimal color value that looks like this: #00FF00. Unfortunately this causes problems for the ColdFusion Server because of the leading number sign, #; the ColdFusion Server sees the number sign and considers it to be the opening mark of a standard ColdFusion tag. Here are two workarounds: first, use a color name, such as "green," wherever possible; second, remove the leading number sign from the code – if you encounter this problem repeatedly, you can automate the procedure with Dreamweaver's Find and Replace feature.

For simple lists, the <pre> tag is often used to format output where the initial field is a constant size, as in this example where the Department ID is always four digits and the phone extension is three:

```
<pre>#dept_ID#    #dept_ext#  #dept_head#</pre><br>
```

ColdFusion Tables

How do you structure output for which the field results are varied in length? Just as you would if you were "hard-wiring" the data on a page—with a table. You have several ways to implement a table in ColdFusion. CFML has its own table tag, `<cftable>`, which uses the `<pre>` tag to line up fields. When used with the `<cfcol>` tag, the heading for each column of data can be specified. For example, this code:

```
<cftable query="tryMe" colheaders>
  <cfcol header="ID" width="5" align="right"
text="<b>#Emp_ID#</b>">
  <cfcol header="First Name" width="30" text="#FirstName#">
  <cfcol header="Last Name" width="30" text="#LastName#">
</cftable>
```

creates a table based on the query `tryMe`. Next, three columns are created, each designated with the label specified by the `header` attribute in the `<cfcol>` tag.

To create an HTML style table with `<cftable>` add the `htmltable` attribute to the CFML tag. With the `htmltable` attribute, column widths are interpreted as percentages, rather than as a number of characters.

Gathering and editing data through forms

Databases aren't necessarily a one-way street. Through forms, you can enable users to insert new information into a database or revise existing information. Both the insert and updating operations are generally handled in two pages: a page that takes in the information on a form, and a page that processes the input and displays a confirmation. In ColdFusion, the form page can use form tags from HTML, CFML, or a combination of both; the processing page, however, must be a CFML page.

The CF Form object

While the regular HTML `<form>` tag can be used without difficulty in ColdFusion, the proprietary `<cfform>` tag—implemented by the ColdFusion Form object—adds a tremendous degree of functionality. In addition to using any of the standard HTML form objects, `<cfform>` also enables its own parallel brand of objects, with the ability to require or validate any response. Moreover, with `<cfform>` you have access to a full complement of Java-based input types, including a tree control for depicting collapsible lists, a grid control for organizing data, and even a slider control for mouse input.

To use the ColdFusion Form object, follow these steps:

1. Position your cursor where you'd like the form to appear on the Web page.

2. Select the CF Form object from the ColdFusion panel of the Objects Palette.

   The ColdFusion Form dialog box appears, as shown in Figure 37-6.

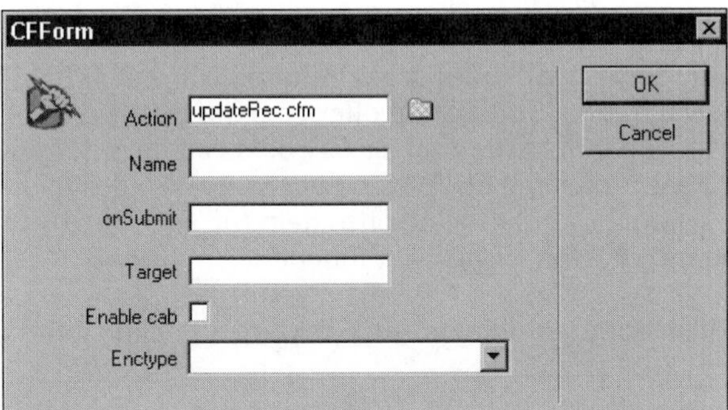

Figure 37-6: With the ColdFusion Form object, a user's input can be automatically validated and the form can include advanced Java input types such as a slider control.

3. Enter a unique name in the Form Name field.
4. Enter the path to a ColdFusion file in the Action field or select the Folder icon to locate the file.
5. If you'd like to preprocess the input before passing it to ColdFusion, enter the JavaScript function to call in the On Submit text field.
6. If the output of your form is a frame or remote window, enter its name in the Target field.
7. To permit Windows Microsoft browser users without the required Java classes to download the necessary cabinet (*.cab) files for the Java applet based controls, select the Enable Cab option.

   Macintosh Internet Explorer users can depend on the Java built into the Mac OS.
8. Specify the format of the information passed by the form in the Enctype field.

   The default enctype is URL encoded, which results in ampersands placed between entries, equal signs linking form element names to their values, spaces as plus signs, and all nonalphanumeric characters in hexadecimal, such as `%3F` (a question mark). The other possible enctypes are text/plain, which presents a series of form field names and their values and multipart/form-data, used for uploading files.
9. Click OK when you're done.

Because the `<cfform>` is not visible onscreen, unlike the standard `<form>` outline, it can be difficult to place input objects inside the tag. I recommend that you keep the HTML Inspector open to ensure that the objects are properly inserted.

The Input objects: CF Text, CF Checkbox, and CF Radio

The key advantage offered by all the ColdFusion input objects — CF Text, CF Checkbox, and CF Radio — is validation. ColdFusion offers ten different types of validation: everything from a date to a credit card number. Any field can be required and numbers can be checked to see if they fall in a particular range. Web designer-defined messages are displayed upon a validation error to help the user. Or, if you prefer, validation can be handled by a custom JavaScript function.

To use any of the ColdFusion input objects — CF Text, CF Checkbox, or CF Radio — follow these steps:

1. Position your cursor where you'd like the form to appear on the Web page.
2. Select the CF Text, CF Checkbox, or CF Radio object from the ColdFusion panel of the Objects Palette.

   The ColdFusion input objects are used like their HTML equivalents. Text enables any user input; Checkbox enables users to select one or several options; and Radio enables a user to select one of a group.

   The specified object's dialog box appears. Figure 37-7 displays the ColdFusion Text dialog box.

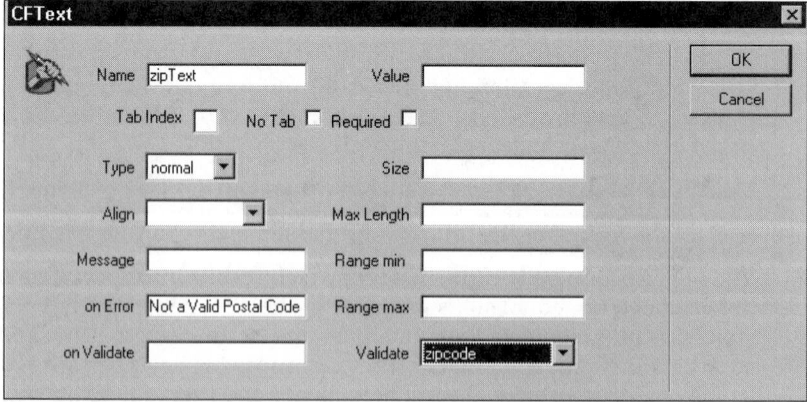

Figure 37-7: ColdFusion input objects, such as the CF Text object, offer a high degree of validation possibilities.

3. Enter a unique name for the input object in the Name field.

4. For a Text object, you can also enter the following information:
   - **Char Width.** The width of the field, in number of characters.
   - **Max Chars.** The maximum number of allowable characters.
   - **Password.** To mask the input, select the Type: Password option.
5. For a CF Checkbox or CF Radio object, you can also select the following options:
   - **Checked Value.** The value that is passed if the check-box or radio button is selected.
   - **Initial State.** Displays the check-box or radio button as selected or unselected.

For a radio button group, make sure that the names of all the buttons in the group are identical.

6. For all ColdFusion input objects, the following validation options are available:
   - **Entry Required.** When selected, the user must enter a value for the field.
   - **Validate.** (Text object only) Select one type of validation.
   - **Date.** Entry must be in U.S. date format: mm/dd/yy.
   - **On Validate.** A custom JavaScript function used to perform validation instead of the selected ColdFusion validation routine.
   - **Message.** Message to be displayed if validation fails.
   - **On Invalid.** A custom JavaScript function that executes if validation fails.
7. The CF Text object has additional validation options:
   - **Range Min.** The minimum allowable value for numeric entries.
   - **Range Max.** The maximum allowable value for numeric entries.

   The following options are selectable from the Validate list:
   - **Date.** Entry must be in a U.S. date format: mm/dd/yy.
   - **Eurodate.** Entry must be in a European date format: dd/mm/yy.
   - **Time.** Entry must be in the form hh:mm:ss.
   - **Float.** Entry must be a floating-point number.
   - **Integer.** Entry must be an integer.
   - **Telephone.** Entry must be in the format ###-###-####, where the first digit is not zero.

- **Zipcode.** Entry must be a five- or nine- digit number in the form #####-####.
- **Credit Card.** Entry must be in a credit card format.
- **Social Security Number.** Entry must be in the form ###-##-####.

To modify any of the input object settings, select their representative icon in the Document window. The appropriate Property Inspector will appear.

In the 2.0.0 version of the ColdFusion objects, no icon for any of the input objects (CF Text, CF Checkbox, or CF Radio) is available; a broken image symbol is displayed instead. Selecting this symbol does display the appropriate Property Inspector though.

One helpful note: Sometimes I've found it difficult to select just the desired input object; often the surrounding `<cfform>` tag is selected as well. If this happens to you, select the input object again and the appropriate Property Inspector will be displayed.

The CF Insert object

To use traditional HTML forms for the input page, you first need to set the `action` attribute of the `<form>` tag equal to the ColdFusion processing page, using the `post` method. Next, the names of `input` tags should match the names of the fields. The `submit` and `reset` buttons do not require any special attention. For example, the following form enables the updating of a Web site link page, taking in the name of the site, its creator, and the link information:

```
<form method="post" action="site_insert.cfm" name="theForm">
  <pre>
   Site: <input type="text" name="Site" size="40"><br>
Creator: <input type="text" name="Creator" size="40"><br>
   Link: <input type="text" name="Link" size="40"><br>
         <input type="submit" name="Submit" value="Insert
Info">  <input type="reset" name="reset" value="Clear
Form"></pre>
</form>
```

To process this `insert` request, you can use one of two methods: via an SQL statement or by use of the `<cfinsert>` tag. On the CFML process page that is called by the action attribute of the form, the code is generally entered at or near the top of the page. The ColdFusion Query object can be used to enter the SQL statements. As before, enter a unique name for the query and the DSN name for the data source. Then the SQL statements are formatted as follows:

```
INSERT INTO TableName (Field1, Field2, Field3)
VALUES ('#Form.FieldName1#','#Form.FieldName2#',
'#Form.FieldName3#')
```

For the balance of the page, you can enter any sort of confirmation message desired, in regular HTML.

The other method for processing is slightly less complicated, especially with the new ColdFusion Insert object. This object inserts the `<cfinsert>` tag, which requires the names of the data source, the table, and the fields. In the previous example, the `<cfinsert>` tag would look like this:

```
<cfinsert datasource="extensions" tablename="Sites"
formfields="Site,Creator,Link">
```

This code is placed at the head of the page listed in the Action attribute for the `<form>` or `<cfform>` tag found on the initial input page. For example, a input page with the code:

```
<form method="post" action="site_insert.cfm" name="theForm">
```

would call the ColdFusion page, site_insert.cfm. The ColdFusion Insert object would be placed at the top of site_insert.cfm. The balance of the page typically confirms the insertion with a message to the user.

The CF Insert object closely resembles the CF Query object and many of the attributes are the same. To use the ColdFusion Insert object, follow these steps:

1. Place your cursor near the top of your page.
2. Select the CF Insert object from the Cold Fusion panel of the Object palette.

   The CF Insert object, shown in Figure 37-8, is displayed.

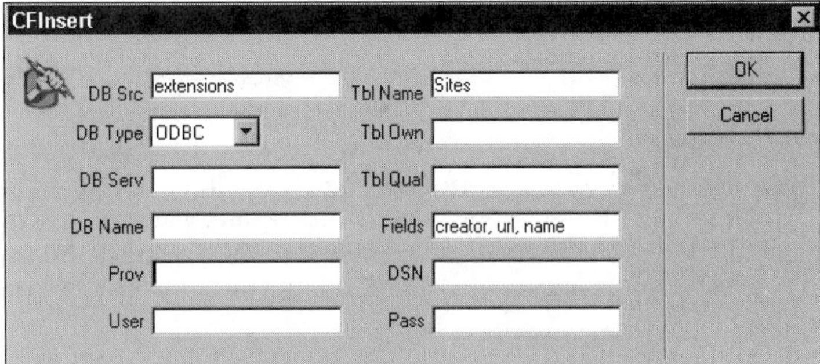

Figure 37-8: The ColdFusion Insert object is placed on the page called by the form action attribute.

3. Enter the data source name for the database to which new records are being added in the DB Src field.

4. Enter the name of the table containing the fields being added in the Tbl Name field.

Caution

For Oracle drivers, the table name must be in uppercase for the Sybase driver, the case must match the name of the table at its creation.

The DB Src and Tbl Name fields are the only two that are mandatory in the CF Insert object.

5. If using a native database driver other than ODBC, select it from the DB Type list.
6. Complete any of the following desired options:
   - **DB Serv.** Used in conjunction with native database drivers, an entry in this field specifies the name of the database server; if used, it overrides the server named in DB Src.
   - **DB Name.** The name of the data source, used only with Sybase 11 and OLE-DB drivers.
   - **Tbl Owner.** Used with data sources that support table ownership, like SQL Server and Oracle databases.
   - **Tbl Qual.** The name of the table qualifier.
   - **Fields.** A comma-separated list of fields to insert; by default (no fields listed) all fields are updated.
   - **Prov.** The COM provider for OLE-DB data sources.
   - **DSN.** The data source name for the COM provider.
   - **User.** The username for accessing the database.
   - **Pass.** The password necessary for accessing the database.
7. Click OK when you're done.

The CF Update object

Editing records, like adding them, is another common database-related task and the ColdFusion Update object is very similar to its Insert one. The primary difference is that, instead of filling out all the fields necessary for a new record, the user is editing a record's existing information. Therefore, the normal course of events for an update operation is:

1. Find the desired record.
2. Display the information in an editable form.
3. Let the user make the changes.
4. Submit the changes to the database.

The Cold Fusion Update object does not come into play until Step 4, when the Submit button is selected. The CF Update object is placed on the page that is called for processing by the Action attribute of the submitted form.

1. Place your cursor near the top of your page.
2. Select the CF Update object from the Cold Fusion panel of the Object palette.

   The CF Update object, shown in Figure 37-9, is displayed.

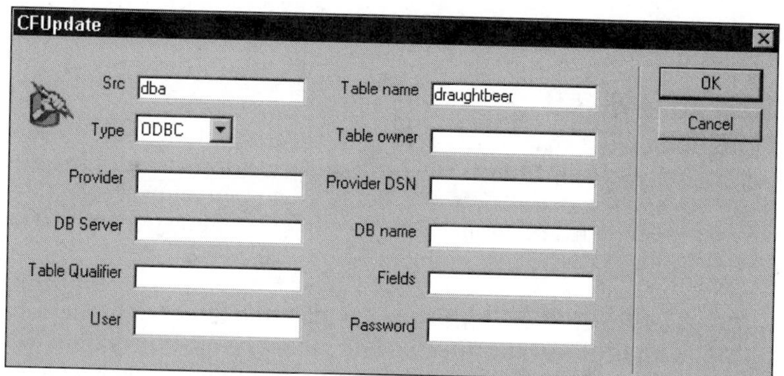

Figure 37-9: Edit existing records through the ColdFusion Update object.

3. Enter the data source name for the database to which new records are being added in the Src field.
4. Enter the name of the table containing the fields being added in the Table Name field.

For Oracle drivers, the table name must be in uppercase. For the Sybase driver, the case must match the name of the table at its creation.

The Src and Table Name fields are the only two that are mandatory in the CF Insert object.

5. If using a native database driver other than ODBC, select it from the Type list.
6. Complete any of the following desired options:
   - **DB Server.** Used in conjunction with native database drivers, an entry in this field specifies the name of the database server; if used, it overrides the server named in Src.
   - **DB Name.** The name of the data source, used only with Sybase 11 and OLE-DB drivers.
   - **Table Owner.** Used with data sources that support table ownership, like SQL Server and Oracle databases.

- **Table Qualifier.** The name of the table qualifier.
- **Fields.** A comma-separated list of fields to insert; by default (no fields listed) all fields are updated.
- **Provider.** The COM provider for OLE-DB data sources.
- **Provider DSN.** The data source name for the COM provider.
- **User.** The username for accessing the database.
- **Password.** The password necessary for accessing the database.

7. Click OK when you're done.

The CF Location object

The CF Location object sends the visitor to a new page, much like clicking on a link. However, the location object puts the browsing experience under the designer's control rather than the user's. The additional advantage of using the CF Location object in an active environment like ColdFusion is the ability to pass arguments that influence the content of the page summoned.

For example, let's say that after the user has updated a record in the database, you want to display the contents of the changed record as a confirmation method. Chances are, a "View Record" page already exists—that's typically one of the steps prior to updating a page—so one method would be to just pass the view record page, the argument necessary to include the altered record. In this situation, the `<cfupdate>` tag would be followed directly by a `<cflocation>`, like this:

```
<CFUPDATE dataSource="company" tableName="employees"
formFields="#Form.FieldList#">
<CFLOCATION url="recView.cfm?RecordID=#Form.EmpID#">
```

Here, the employee identification number—the record's unique ID—of the updated record is retrieved from the form's EmpID field and passed to the recView.cfm page for viewing. Because of this ability to influence a succeeding page, the `<cflocation>` tag has an attribute called `addtoken` that enables user variables to be verified by the ColdFusion management system. For this feature to be used, the `clientmanagement` attribute in the `<cfapplication>` tag must be enabled.

Use of the ColdFusion Location object is very straightforward, as seen in the following steps:

1. Place your cursor where you'd like the CF Location object code to be inserted.
2. Choose the CF Location object from the Cold Fusion panel of the Object Palette.

   The CF Location object dialog box (Figure 37-10) appears.

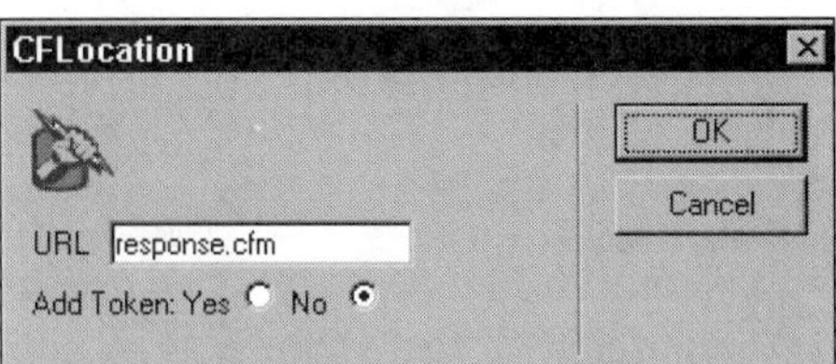

Figure 37-10: The URL of the page you want displayed, entered through the ColdFusion Location object, can call an existing static page or pass an argument to an active page.

3. Enter the absolute or relative of the desired page in the URL field.
4. To verify arguments passed in the URL field, select the Add Tokens option.

There's a known problem with the Add Tokens attribute; selecting either option sets `addtoken="yes"`. To disable the Add Tokens feature, select the Location icon and, in the Quick Tag Editor, change `addtoken="yes"` to `addtoken="no"`.

Programming with ColdFusion objects

Just as client-side scripting is made possible by JavaScript's programming capa-bilities, server-side scripting works with ColdFusion's programming features. The ColdFusion extensions include numerous objects to enable easy code insertion: CF Set, CF If, CF Else, CF ElseIf, CF Loop, CF Switch, CF Case, CF Default Case, CF Cookie, and CF Include.

The CF Set object

The ColdFusion Set object is used to create and define variables through the `<cfset>` tag. Using the Set object is very straightforward. Simply select the Set object from the ColdFusion panel of the Objects Palette and enter the variable and its equivalent value in the dialog box, like this:

```
bookCode = "H23"
```

If a variable has been previously declared, it is set to the new value. The `<cfset>` tag can be used to establish static variables, with strings of text or numeric values, or dynamic variables that depend on a database relationship. To set a variable to the data in a queried field, format the Set object code like this:

```
<cfset currentBook = "bookbase.title">
```

where `bookbase` is the table name and `title` is a field in that table. You can also define a variable to represent a combination of text and dynamic data, like this:

```
<cfset bestBook = "#bookbase.title# is the most frequently read
book this week">
```

You can also use the Set object to represent mathematical expressions, either by themselves or in combination with other text, as in the following examples:

```
<cfset totalTax = (8.25 * 19.95) + 19.95>
<cfset owedAmt = "You owe " & (8.25 * 19.95) + 19.95>
```

Note that an ampersand is used to concantenate a text string and an expression.

The CF If, CF Else, and CF ElseIf objects

Much programming depends on conditionals — if X is true do this; otherwise, do that. ColdFusion uses the <cfif>, <cfelseif>, and <cfelse> tags to create both simple and compound conditional statements. In general, the syntax for a conditional block in CFML is as follows:

```
<cfif expression>
HTML and CFML tags go here
  <cifelse expression >
  HTML and CFML tags go here
<cfelse>
HTML and CFML tags go here
</cfif>
```

Should the expression prove true, the initial statements are processed; otherwise, the <cfelseif> condition is checked and those statements are processed. If both conditions fail, the statements following <cfelse> are executed.

Aside from regular numeric and Boolean operators, ColdFusion also uses a series of decision operators in conditional statements. The decision operators, and their alternative notations, are as follows:

Operator	***Alternative***
IS	EQUAL, EQ
IS NOT	NOT EQUAL, NEQ
CONTAINS	N/A
DOES NOT CONTAIN	N/A
GREATER THAN	GT
LESS THAN	LT
GREATER THAN OR EQUAL TO	GTE, GE
LESSER THAN OR EQUAL TO	LTE, LE

In Dreamweaver, all three conditional statements are accessible through the ColdFusion object. While you can insert conditionals directly in the Document Window, it's a good idea to have the HTML Inspector open, particularly if you are using the CF ElseIf and CF Else forms.

To use the ColdFusion If, ElseIf, and Else objects, follow these steps:

1. Position your cursor where you'd like the conditional block in the code.
2. Select the If object from the ColdFusion panel of the Objects Palette.

   The ColdFusion If dialog box appears, as shown in Figure 37-11.

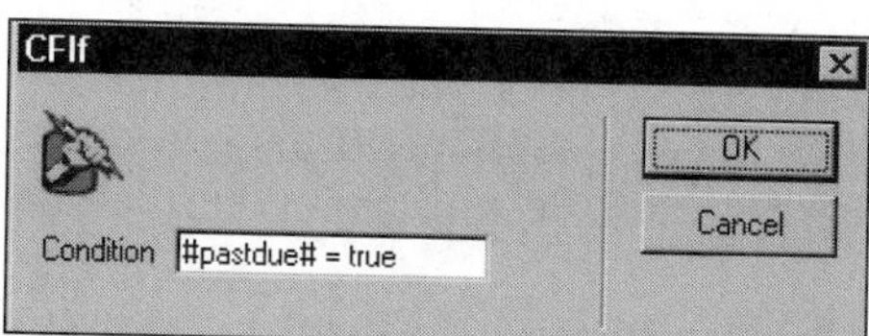

Figure 37-11: Insert the ColdFusion If object before incorporating an ElseIf and/or Else object.

3. Enter the expression to be evaluated in the Condition field and click OK when you're done.
4. In the Document window, enter the statements to be executed should the If expression prove true within the `<cfif>` tag pair.

Tip: As with other ColdFusion objects, it's best to work with the HTML Source Inspector open when inserting the conditional objects.

5. To add an alternative conditional expression, select the CF ElseIf object.
6. Enter the expression to test in the Condition field of the ElseIf dialog box.
7. In the Document window, add the statements to be executed should the CF ElseIf condition prove true.
8. Repeat Steps 5 through 7 for any additional CF ElseIf clauses.
9. To insert an Else condition, choose the CF Else object.
10. Enter the Else condition, if any, in the Condition field of the Else dialog box; click OK when you're done.

Dreamweaver displays all possible outcomes of a conditional statement within the <cfif>...</cfif> tag pair. The CF ElseIf and CF Else objects are represented by onscreen icons; selecting either of them displays the appropriate condition in the Property Inspector. To change the condition of the CF If object, place your cursor within the <cfif> block and choose the <cfif> tag from the Tag Selector, and then modify the condition in the Property Inspector.

The CF Switch, CF Case, and CF Default Case objects

ColdFusion provides an alternative to the CF If/ElseIf/Else conditional series with the CF Switch, CF Case, and CF Default Case objects. While an If/ElseIf/Else conditional statement is fine for simple branching, because a statement must be evaluated for each branch, it can be processor intensive. A CF Switch/Case statement, on the other hand, evaluates the determining statement only once and then, depending on the result, executes the corresponding statements. If none of the stated cases match the result, the default case statements are executed. Here's an example where different headings are written, depending on the customer status:

```
<cfswitch expression="#customerType#" >
  <cfcase value="returning" >
    <h2>Welcome back, #custName#!</h2>
  </cfcase>
  <cfcase value="pastdue" >
    <h2>Your membership dues are in arrears, #custName#!</h2>
  </cfcase>
  <cfcase value="gold" >
    <h2>Special offer now available, #custName#!</h2>
  </cfcase>
  <cfdefaultcase>
    <h2>Please register.</h2>
  </cfdefaultcase>
</cfswitch>
```

The CF Switch, CF Case, and CF Default Case objects work much like the CF If, CF ElseIf, CF Else objects. A CF Switch object is initially inserted and forms an outer defining structure with one attribute, expression. The expression value, often a database field, is then compared with each of the case values. If a match is found, the statements within that <cfcase> tag are executed; otherwise the <cfdefault-case> statements are executed.

Don't be thrown if "CF If" appears as a ToolTip when you move your mouse over the CF Switch object; in the 2.0.0 version of the ColdFusion objects, there's a typo in the object code, but the object still functions as expected.

To use the Switch, Case, and Default Case objects, follow these steps:

1. Position your cursor where you'd like the code to be inserted, making sure that the View ➪ Invisible Elements option is enabled.
2. Select the Switch object from the ColdFusion panel of the Objects palette.

   The Switch dialog box opens.
3. Enter the value to be compared in succeeding case statements in the Expression field and click OK when you're done.

   As noted earlier, the Expression value is often a database field such as `#employeeID#`, but it could also be a mathematical expression or a combination of the two. The `<cfswitch>` tag evaluates the Expression statement before any comparisons are made.
4. Make sure your cursor is in-between the `<cfswitch>` tag pair and select the Case object.
5. In the Case dialog box (see Figure 37-12), enter the value to be compared in the Value field.

Figure 37-12: The Switch/Case construct is a much less server-intensive form of conditional statements.

   Each case can use a series of alternative values. All of these alternatives are entered in the Value field separated by a delimeter, such as a comma or semicolon.
6. If alternative cases are specified and delimited by anything other than a comma, enter the delimiting character in the Delimiter field.

Tip

Make sure that your delimiter is not contained within any of your alternative case values. The pipe, |, makes a good delimiter in many situations.

7. Click OK when you're done to close the Case dialog box.
8. In the Document window, make sure that your cursor is between the just-inserted `<cfcase>...</cfcase>` tag pair and enter the statements you want executed if this case proves true.

9. Place your cursor after the closing `</cfcase>` tag and, if additional cases are desired, repeat Steps 5 through 8.

   After all the cases are defined, you can add a default case code that will execute if none of the other cases are matched.

10. To insert a Default Case object, place your cursor after the closing tag of the last Case object and choose the Default Case object from the ColdFusion panel.

11. Enter the value and delimiters, if any, in the Default Case dialog box and click OK when you're done.

As with If/ElseIf/Else constructions, Dreamweaver displays all possible outcomes in the case statements.

The CF Loop object

Looping, the ability to cycle through a series of operations, is just as important as conditionals in any type of programming. The ColdFusion implementation is especially noteworthy as it supports five different types of loops:

- ✦ **Indexed Loop:** Statements are repeated for a set range of values.
- ✦ **Conditional Loop:** Statements are repeated while a particular condition remains true.
- ✦ **Looping over a CF Query:** Statements are repeated for every record in a range of a recordset.
- ✦ **Looping over a List:** Statements are repeated for every element in a particular list.
- ✦ **Looping over a COM collection:** Statements are repeated for every member of a Component Object Model collection or structure.

The ColdFusion Loop object incorporates all five loop types.

To begin to set up any of the loop types, first choose the Loop object from the ColdFusion panel of the Objects Palette. In the Loop dialog box, select the Loop Type from the drop-down box. For each type, a different set of options is displayed; in every case, the statements to be executed during the loop are entered into the Body text area. Table 37-1 explains the options for each <cfloop> type; optional arguments are marked with an asterisk.

Table 37-1
ColdFusion Loop Types

Loop Type	*Attribute*	*Description*
Indexed Loop	Index Name	Defines the variable that is used as the loop counter.
	From	The initial value of the index.
	To	The ending value of the index.
	Step*	The value that the index is incremented with each loop. The Step value can be a positive or negative whole number where the default is 1.
Conditional Loop	Condition	The expression that is evaluated with each loop. When the expression is no longer true, the loop ends.
CF Query Loop	CF Query Name	The name of the previously defined query that controls the loop.
	Start Row*	The first row of the query to be included in the loop.
	End Row*	The last row of the query to be included in the loop.
List Loop	Index Name	Defines the variable that is used as the loop counter.
	List	The list items to be processed. The items can be directly entered, as in "Baker, Barber, Sailor, Cook," or pulled from a variable.
	List Delimiters	The separators used to divide the list. In the previous example, commas would be listed as the delimiters. Multiple delimiters such as ",.\" can be entered.
COM Collection Name	Collection Name	The name of the COM collection to be accessed during the loop.
	Item Name	The variable assigned from the member of the collection referenced during the loop.

* Optional

The CF Cookie object

Active pages have numerous ways of keeping track of visitors through client and session variables. The use of cookies, however, remains very popular primarily because of its low impact on server performance and ease of use. Briefly, a cookie is Web jargon for a small bit of text stored on the client's system, which can be read by programmed Web pages. Cookies are important because they enable information to persist in between visits to a Web site as well as between pages.

The ColdFusion Cookie object enables you to create and set the cookie values; once the cookie has been set, its values can be easily read. Here, for example, is the code to create a cookie that carries the user's first name (gathered from a form):

```
<cfcookie name="fname" value=theForm.fname>
```

To incorporate the stored name in a ColdFusion page, refer to its name as part of the Cookie object, like this:

```
<h2>Welcome back, <cfoutput>#Cookie.fname#</cfoutput></h2>
```

To use the ColdFusion Cookie object, follow these steps:

1. With your cursor placed where you want the code to be inserted, choose the Cookie object from the ColdFusion panel of the Object palette.

   The Cookie dialog box, seen here in Figure 37-13, appears.

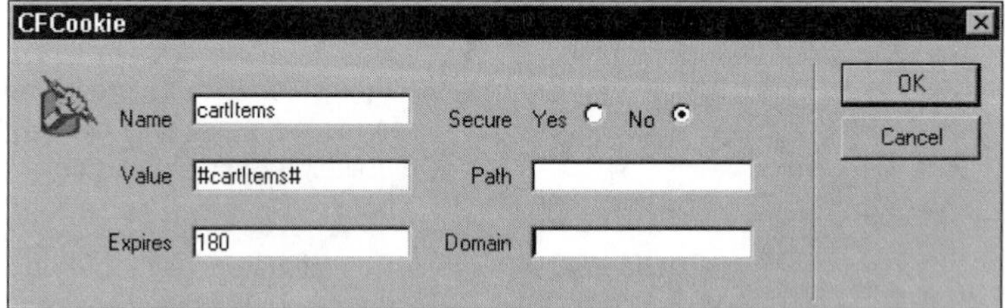

Figure 37-13: One method of tracking visitors uses the ColdFusion Cookie object.

2. Enter a unique name for the cookie in the Name field.
3. Enter the cookie's value in the Value field.

If the value is to be a ColdFusion field or function, be sure to enclose the entry with number signs.

4. Optionally, you can enter an expiration date in the Expires field.

   Possible values for the expiration date are: a standard date format, such as 03/31/01; a date calculation; a number of days such as 15; or the keywords NOW or NEVER. Entering the keyword NOW effectively deletes the cookie.

5. If you want the cookie to be transmitted using Secure Server Layer protocol, select the Secure option.

6. To limit the cookie to a specific area on a Web site, enter the subfolders in the Path field.

   You can enter multiple paths, separated by a semicolon, like this:

   `products/gadgets;products/widgets;products/gidgets`

7. To limit the cookie to a specific domain, enter the abbreviated URL in the Domain field. For example, the domain `www.idest.com` would be entered as `.idest.com`, with the leading period.

If the optional Path value is used, the Domain name is required.

8. Click OK when you're done.

The CF Include object

Frequently, it's easier to include a portion of one Web page when serving up another page. The `<cfinclude>` tag is used in ColdFusion to facilitate the process of inserting entire pages dynamically. You can even use the `<cfinclude>` tag to embed pages recursively.

To insert one page into another using the ColdFusion Include object, follow these steps:

1. Choose the ColdFusion Include object from the Object palette.
2. In the Include dialog box (see Figure 37-14), enter the path to the ColdFusion or HTML page in the Template field or select the folder icon to locate the file using a dialog box.

Figure 37-14: Dynamically build your Web pages by inserting other ColdFusion pages through the Include object.

3. Click OK when you're done.

Accessing other servers

As already noted, the ColdFusion Application Server isn't just for communicating with databases. One of ColdFusion's key advantages is its ability to integrate with a wide variety of server types. For example, because ColdFusion can work with a mail server, it's possible to coordinate mass e-mailings from within the program. Moreover, you can use ColdFusion—and its corresponding Dreamweaver objects—to handle both file and directory functions.

The CF Mail object

E-mail is a fact of modern communication; to some e-mail is the "killer app" for which the Internet was designed. While unsolicited bulk e-mailings (also known as spam) have earned an undesirable reputation, automated e-mails are an effective way for a business to handle today's increased communication load. With ColdFusion, you can output to a mail server to send e-mail just as easily as you can to a Web server to deliver an HTML page.

The ColdFusion Mail object inserts the `<cfmail>` tag, which outputs Simple Mail Transfer Protocol (SMTP) type e-mail. SMTP e-mail is the standard form of text-only e-mail and can be read by all mail programs. The best way to think of `<cfmail>` is as a close relative to `<cfoutput>`—they're identical in functionality except that instead of sending processed output formatted as HTML to a browser as `<cfoutput>` does, `<cfmail>` sends its processed output as e-mail to an SMTP server.

As an example of how `<cfmail>` can automate communication, consider the customer inquiry form. Generally, the interested customer fills it out and clicks the Submit button, where the information may be collected for later retrieval or sent directly to Sales and Marketing. When the Submit button is chosen, if the form has a CFML page set as its `action` attribute, that page is processed by ColdFusion. To automatically send the customer inquiry form to a department (or an individual), the `<cfmail>` tag is added to the CFML page that also serves as a thank-you to the customer. Here's some sample `<cfmail>` code for such an operation:

```
<cfmail from="#form.emailAddress#"
        to="sales@idest.com"
        subject="Sales Inquiry" >
This customer is interested in our product - call today!

Customer: #form.FirstName# #form.LastName#
Product: #form.ProductSelected#

Comments: #form.Comments#
</cfmail>
```

The ColdFusion Mail object has a wide range of attributes that can be employed; however, only a few are required. Parameters such as To, From, and Subject can all be generated on the fly by ColdFusion's database connection, which allows for very flexible mail-management technology.

To insert a ColdFusion Mail object into your Web page, follow these steps:

1. Place your cursor on the page where you want the Mail object code to appear.
2. Choose the Mail object from the ColdFusion panel of the Objects Palette.

   The ColdFusion Mail dialog box appears, as shown in Figure 37-15.

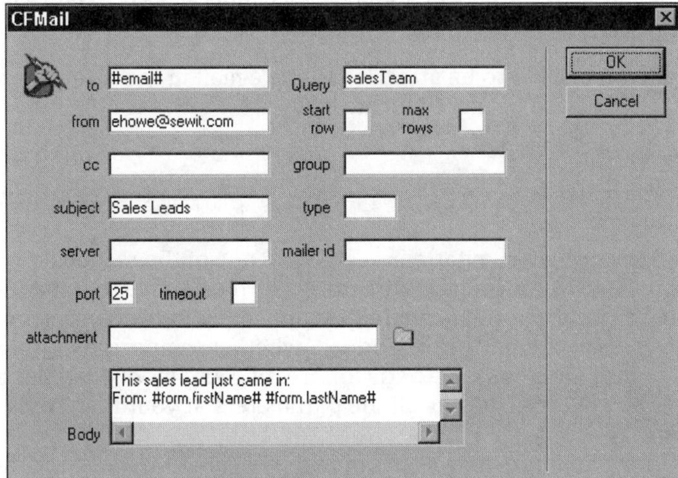

Figure 37-15: Output to e-mail as easily as you output to screen by using the ColdFusion Mail object.

3. Enter the e-mail address of the recipient in the To field (required).
4. Enter the e-mail address of the sender in the From field (required).
5. Enter the e-mail address of any additional recipients in the CC field.
6. Enter the topic of the e-mail in the Subject field (required).
7. Enter the server address of the SMTP system sending the mail. If no server is listed, the server name specified in the ColdFusion Administrator is used.
8. Enter the content of your message in the Body text area.
9. Enter a query name, if any, to be referenced in the CF Query Name field.
10. In the Start Row field, enter the first row in the query to be included in processing.
11. In the Max Row field, enter the total number of rows in the query to be included in processing.
12. In the Group Field, enter the field name of the query to group the results.

13. Enter the mail type, if other than straight text, in the Mail Type field.

Note: As of this writing, the only valid entry here is "HTML."

14. Enter the mail server port in the Server Port field, if different from the standard port number, 25.
15. In the Timeout field, enter the number of seconds to wait before the connection to the SMTP server expires.
16. Enter the path of a file to be attached to the e-mail in the Attachment field or select the Browse button to locate a file.
17. Click OK when you're done.

The CF File object

One of JavaScript's primary limitations — but also one of the reasons it is so widely accepted — is its inability to manage directories or files. While that makes sense for a client-side application, such capabilities are sorely needed in a server-side program. New data is constantly being added, whether temporarily or permanently. ColdFusion provides numerous methods for creating and modifying files as needed, and Dreamweaver's File object puts all the parameters at your fingertips.

Note: If you're having trouble getting results from the File or Directory objects, be sure to check with the ColdFusion administrator for the server. Anyone with administrator clearance can disable file and directory functions.

The File object and its corresponding tag, `<cffile>`, control eight different file operations:

- ✦ **Upload** transfers a file from the user to the server. File types can be limited to specific MIME types and/or file formats.
- ✦ **Move** moves a file from one directory to another.
- ✦ **Rename** renames a file on the server.
- ✦ **Copy** copies a file from one directory to another.
- ✦ **Delete** removes a file from the server.
- ✦ **Read** reads an existing text file, such as an access log.
- ✦ **Write** writes a new text file, including HTML pages.
- ✦ **Append** adds text to an existing text file.

To set up any of the `<cffile>` types, first choose the File object from the ColdFusion panel of the Objects Palette. In the File dialog box, shown in Figure 37-16, select the Action drop-down box. For each `action` type, a different set of options is displayed. Table 37-2 explains the options for each `<cffile>` type; optional arguments are marked with an asterisk.

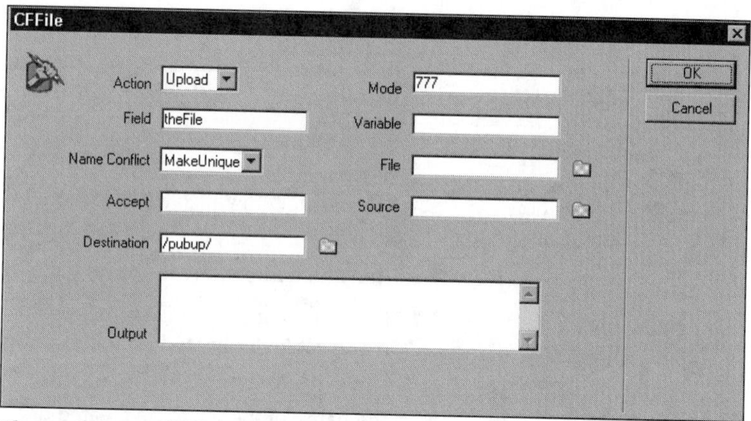

Figure 37-16: All file manipulations are handled through the ColdFusion File object.

Table 37-2 ColdFusion File Object Types

Action	*Parameters*	*Description*
Upload	Form Field	The name of the field in the form that was used to select the file. Do not use hash marks (#) to denote the field.
	Destination	The directory in which the file is to be stored. A full file name must be used.
	On Conflict*	The action taken if a name conflict occurs (the uploaded file has the same name as a file already on the server). The options are as follows: **Error.** File not saved and an error is reported. **Skip.** File not saved, but no error is reported. **Overwrite.** The existing file is replaced. **Make Unique.** A new unique name is created for the uploaded file.
	Acceptable*	Limits uploadable files to MIME types, specified in a comma-delimited list (for example, "image/gif, image/jpg, image/png").
	Mode*	Sets file permissions for uploaded file with `chmod` values such as `666` or `777`. Valid only on Solaris and HP-UX servers.
	Attributes*: Read Only, Hidden, Temp, System, Archive, Normal	Set attributes for uploaded files. All attributes must be explicitly selected.

Continued

Table 37-2 (continued)

Action	Parameters	Description
Move, Rename, or Copy	Source	The path name of the file to be moved.
	Destination	The directory to which the file is moved.
	Attributes	As above.
Delete	File	The path name of the file to be removed.
Read	File	The path name of the file to be read.
	Variable	The variable designated to hold the contents of the file after it is read.
Write or Append	File	The name of the file to be created or added on to.
	Mode	As above.
	Output	The content to be included in the new or modified file.
	Attributes	As above.

* Optional

The CF Directory object

When new files are continually being added to a server, directory management becomes a necessity—otherwise, all the files could potentially end up in one enormous folder. Moreover, it usually takes someone with administrative-level access to even list the contents of a directory. With the ColdFusion `<cfdirectory>` tag, access can be granted on a page-by-page basis.

The ColdFusion Directory object has four different functions:

- ✦ **List** details the contents of the specified folder in a sorted or nonsorted table.
- ✦ **Create** makes the specified folder on the server.
- ✦ **Rename** changes the name of the folder.
- ✦ **Delete** removes the folder and all of its contents from the server.

To set up any of the `<cfdirectory>` options, first choose the Directory object from the ColdFusion panel of the Objects Palette. In the ColdFusion Directory dialog box, shown in Figure 37-17, first enter the name of the directory to be affected. Then, select the Action drop-down box. For each `action` type, a different set of options is displayed. Table 37-3 explains the options for each `<cfdirectory>` type; optional arguments are marked with an asterisk.

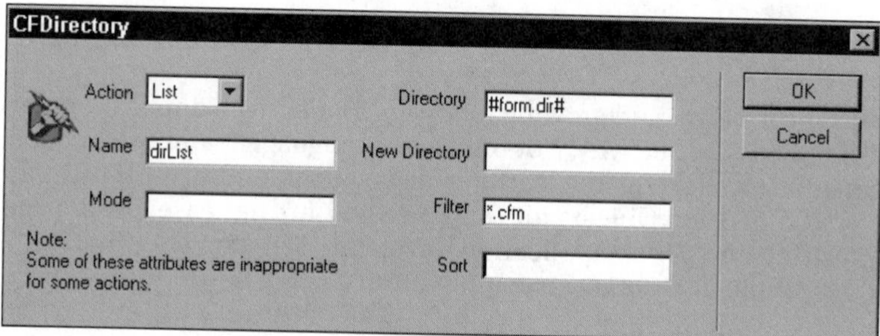

Figure 37-17: The Directory object gives you easy access to any folder on the server.

Table 37-3
ColdFusion Directory Object Types

Action	*Parameter*	*Description*
List Directory	Directory	The name of the directory affected.
	CF Query Name	Name of the output query to be used for listing.
	Filter*	File extension filter used to mask out all other file types, such as `*.cfm`.
	Sort*	Comma-delimited list of query columns to sort results by. The ASC (ascending) or DESC (descending) qualifier can be added for any specified column. For example: `dirname ASC`, `filename2`, `size DESC`.
Create Directory	Directory	The name of the directory affected.
	Mode	Sets the file permission for the new directory. Entry is given in octal values, as in `666` or `777`. Valid for Solaris and HP-UX servers only.
Rename Directory	Directory	The name of the directory affected.
	New Name	The name to be applied to the specified directory.
Delete Directory	Directory	The name of the directory affected.

Summary

ColdFusion has a very loyal and growing following among Web application deve-lopers — and it's very easy to see why. Not only is the language feature-rich, but its markup orientation shortens the learning curve considerably for HTML savvy coders. Allaire's ColdFusion Objects for Dreamweaver further ease a Web page designer's transition into a Web application developer. Here are a few helpful thoughts on this layout and database combination:

✦ Allaire's ColdFusion system works with many different types of servers and uses the ColdFusion Markup Language (CFML) to create a rich server-side language. ColdFusion works with Dreamweaver to enable you to enter CFML tags in your Web pages without programming.

✦ The core of the ColdFusion language revolves around two tags and their corresponding Dreamweaver objects, CF Query and CF Output. The CF Query object provides a direct link to a data source, while the CF Output object structures the presentation of the data on the page.

✦ Although Dreamweaver has a number of form elements, the ColdFusion Objects come with their own version of many of the same objects. Wherever possible, use the ColdFusion form objects to maximize server efficiency.

✦ In addition to maintaining a database connection, ColdFusion can connect to other types of information servers as well, including e-mail and directory servers. The CF Mail, CF Directory, and CF File objects offer management capabilities far beyond database manipulation.

The next chapter shows how the Lasso database system leverages Dreamweaver as an application platform.

✦ ✦ ✦

Integrating FileMaker Pro with Lasso Studio

✦ ✦ ✦ ✦

In This Chapter

Grasping Lasso fundamentals

Rapid Web form development

Accessing the Lasso objects

Using the tag editors

Converting and updating code

✦ ✦ ✦ ✦

Lasso, from Blue World Inc., is a multifaceted Web application system. For a great while, Lasso's main claim to fame was its facility at Web-enabling FileMaker databases. Now, however, Lasso connects to just about every data source under the sun: Access, FileMaker Pro, 4D, Informix, Oracle, MySQL, SQL Server, Sybase, and others. Why should this matter to Dreamweaver users? Because Blue World has built one of the most elaborate extensions to date that combines Dreamweaver's top-of-the-line layout capabilties with Lasso's flexible and powerful tool for creating database-driven Web applications: Lasso Studio for Dreamweaver.

Lasso Studio, in version 1.5 at the time of this writing, sim-plifies many of the mundane Web-development tasks — such as building search and results pages — while keeping more complex applications always accessible. Best of all, pages are designed with your working database layout tightly integrated, and are easily tested on a local Web server before being deployed. Lasso Studio brings a plethora of objects, inspectors, third-party tags, and other extension objects to Dreamweaver, as well as a number of innovations, such as the Database Configuration Wizard and the Site Builder.

Understanding Lasso Studio

Although it comes in many editions and configurations, to handle the various data sources, Lasso is, at its heart, a tag-based system. When a Lasso page is requested by a browser, the LDML (short for Lasso Dynamic Markup Language) that's embedded in the page is processed by a Lasso application, such as a CGI program, plug-in, or Web server. After processing—which may or may not involve integrating information from a data source—the page, stripped of the LDML, is returned to the Web browser for viewing. Lasso is flexible enough to manage most Web application demands: whether it's performing calculations, sending e-mail, reading from or writing to files, you'll find LDML tags appropriate to the task.

A Lasso page can be processed in three ways:

✦ **Form:** When the action of a form specifies a Lasso page, the Lasso application processes the page and returns either a response page in HTML or a page with embedded Lasso tags that are processed on the server.

✦ **URL:** If the user selects a link that specifies a Lasso action, the page will be processed utilizing any arguments appended to the URL.

✦ **Server-side:** When a .lasso page is requested by the browser, the Lasso server intercepts the document, processes it and then returns an HTML page with dynamic content substituted.

One of the first decisions you'll be required to make when you're building a Lasso page in Dreamweaver is whether the document uses Pre-Lasso or Post-Lasso processing, as illustrated in Figure 38-1. If a document uses a form or URL that is submitted to a Lasso action it is considered a Pre-Lasso format; if server-side processing is used, the page is considered Post-Lasso. Pre-Lasso files may not contain any tags that require preli-minary processing by Lasso, such as LDML substitution tags (for example, `[Date]` or LDML process, container tags, or sub-container tags). Post-Lasso pages may contain any LDML tag; however, using the Post-Lasso format for forms (instead of Pre-Lasso) causes the page to be processed twice, lowering performance.

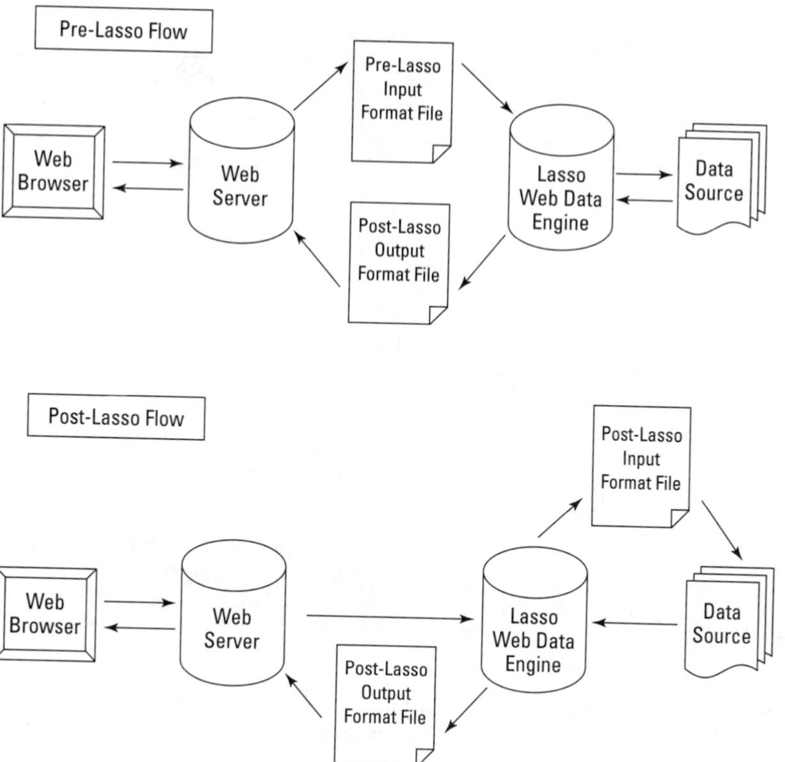

Figure 38-1: The drawing on the top details the data flow during a Pre-Lasso process while the one on the bottom shows a Post-Lasso process.

The tags of the Lasso Dynamic Markup Language can be separated into six different categories:

Type of Tag	*Examples*	*Description*

Action	`-Add`
	`-Delete`
	`-Duplicate`
	`-Search`
	`-Update`
		Informs Lasso of the requested process when a form or URL is submitted. Action tags are designated by a leading hyphen. Unless used in an `[inline]` tag, only one action per form or URL is permitted.

Continued

Type of Tag	Examples	Description
Command	-Database -Response -Email.To -Email.CC	Command tags supplement action tags and provide specific direction. Options to Command tags are designated with a period after the tag name, as in -Email.To.
Substitution	[Date] [Field] [Variable]	When processed, a substitution tag is replaced by data from a data source, server-side calculations or other generated information.
Process	[File_Copy] [Server_Push] [Win_Exec]	Process tags are used to execute a specific server operation. The majority of process tags do not return results.
Container	[If]...[/If] [Loop]...[/Loop] [Rows...[/Rows]	Container tags surround other HTML, LDML or sub-container tags.
Sub-container	[Else] [ValueListItem] [LoopCount]	Sub-container tags work within specific container tags to modify their action or provide a relevant variable.

In Lasso Studio, the Lasso Objects are organized by task rather than by category. In the Object palette, you'll find a mixture of types in the Lasso Programming panel.

Getting Started

Lasso Studio has a number of tools to automate the building of dynamic pages, everything from a Form Builder for the most common types of data source-based pages to a full-fledged Site Builder where multiple pages are generated to your specifi-cations. In addition to building generic pages for easy design modification, the Site Builder can even use Dreamweaver templates to automate the design process.

Both the Form Builder and Site Builder are optional commands; some designers may prefer to create their own pages from scratch. However, one supplied tool, the Configuration Wizard, must be run at least once for every site to gain any benefit at all from Lasso Studio.

Before building pages with Lasso Studio, you'll have to make sure that your system configuration is set up correctly. The Lasso Studio manual has a full chapter on system requirements and installation to assist you.

Configuration Wizard

To display information from a specific data source, you have to know the details of that data source: the names of tables, fields, queries, and so on. Lasso Studio uses a Configuration Wizard to establish a connection to a data source and build a snapshot of the data source's structure or *schema* as well as of your Web server setup. With this data in hand, the developer can embed the data source and field names in Lasso commands that, when submitted to the Web Data Engine, should return the desired results. Moreover, the Web server information enables Lasso Studio to preview and test the work in your development environment.

If you need to reuse the same connection for other pages in your site, the Configuration Wizard provides a method for loading a previously generated snapshot file.

To create a configuration file, follow these steps:

1. Choose Commands ➪ Lasso Configuration Wizard.

   The initial screen of the Configuration Wizard is displayed, as shown in Figure 38-2.

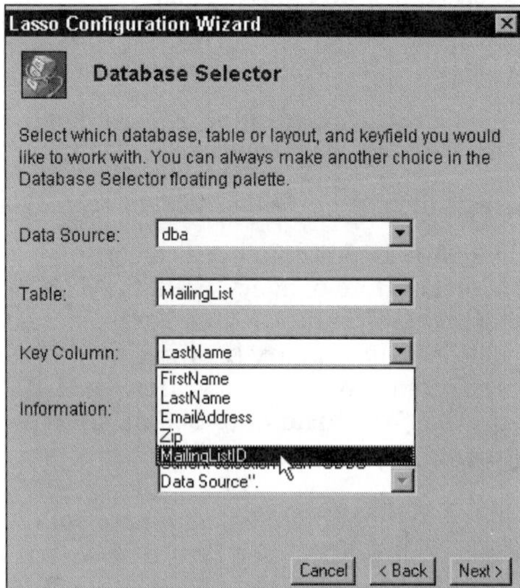

Figure 38-2: You need to step through the Configuration Wizard before building any pages in Lasso Studio.

2. Select the targeted server platform, Macintosh or Windows.

   Lasso Studio needs to know the desired server platform to insert the appropriate version of certain tags. Development does not have to take place on the same platform as deployment.

3. To access a previously created snapshot, choose Load Snapshot File and locate the file.

   Once you've loaded the snapshot file, select Next to proceed to the second screen of the Configuration Wizard, as described in the following section.

4. Enter the URL to the folder that is to contain the snapshots generated. This URL should point to the Lasso\Dreamweaver folder of your Web server root. If you're unsure how to proceed, select the icon to the right of the URL field. Two one-line dialog boxes will appear:

   - In the first dialog box, enter the domain name of your server or the network name of your local system. Many local systems can use an IP address of `127.0.0.0` or the name `localhost`.
   - In the second dialog box, enter the path to the Lasso\Dreamweaver folder. Unless you moved a folder, accept the default path.

Macintosh designers using Web Sharing as their development server can find their machine's IP address by looking at the TCP/IP Control Panel.

5. Select Create Snapshot File to build a new configuration file.

   Before the process actually starts, the Configuration Wizard displays a checklist of prerequisites.

6. When you're sure you've satisfied the prerequisites, select Create Snapshot File.

   Lasso Studio uses Dreamweaver's HTTP API to process a Lasso file on your selected server. The Lasso file makes note of every available data source, their type, and their tables among other information. If an error is encountered, Lasso Studio displays a message in your primary browser. If successful, the snapshot file, an XML file stored as snapshot.txt, is written and Lasso reports the successful operation. Depending on the number of data sources, the process could take a minute or two.

When the snapshot file is completed, you're ready to select a data source to work with. On the Configuration Wizard's second screen (see Figure 38-3), you'll select the desired data source, table, and key field, if required.

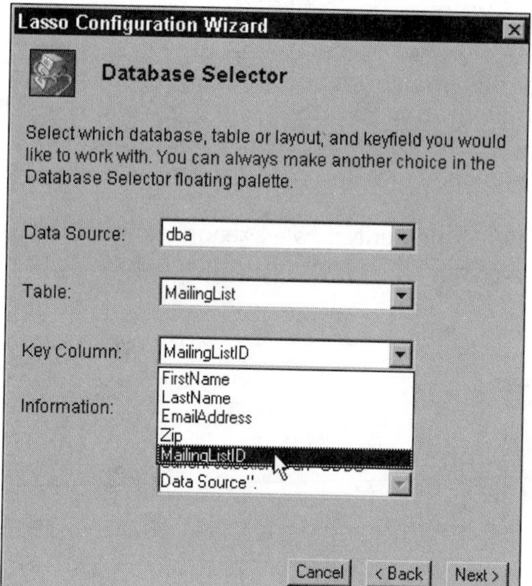

Figure 38-3: Choose the data source, table and, if necessary, the key field in the Configuration Wizard's second screen.

Here are the steps:

1. Choose the data source you want to work with from the Data Source list.

   The other lists are generated dynamically according to your selected data source.

2. Select the table from the Table list.
3. If you're working with an ODBC or 4D database, choose a Key Field from the list.

   After each selection, the Information area at the bottom of the screen displays the number of choices available and the current data source's type.

4. Choose Next to proceed to the final screen of the Configuration Wizard.
5. On the third screen, review your choices. If you want to change anything, select the Back button to return to the previous screens; otherwise, choose Finish.

Database Selector

Once you've established a snapshot file, you've got access to any of the data sources initially displayed in the Configuration Wizard, not just the one you selected. Lasso Studio's Database Selector presents a full list of data sources and their associated tables and key fields.

The Database Selector (Figure 38-4) is implemented as a Dreamweaver palette, also known as a floater so it is always accessible. Moreover, it can be docked with other floaters, custom or standard.

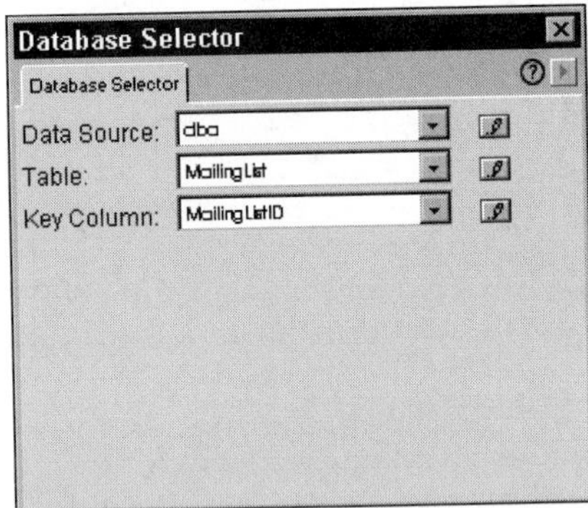

Figure 38-4: Select other data sources or tables from the current snapshot file through the Database Selector.

To use the Database Selector, follow these steps:

1. Choose Commands ➪ Lasso Database Selector to open the floating palette.
2. To choose a new data source, select one from the Data Source list.
3. Select a new table from the Table list.
4. If the chosen data source is in ODBC or 4D format, select a Key Field from the list.
5. You can enter a data source, table or key value not found in the option lists by selecting the pencil button next to their respective fields. Selecting this button opens a Prompt dialog box that enables you to input a value. This value is then temporarily added to the list and selected.

If, after adding a new entry in any of the fields, you change your mind and select another item, the new entry is removed. To select it again, choose the pencil button and re-enter its name.

After changing a data source, table, or key field, the new values become available throughout Lasso Studio.

Although you can't access the Database Manager with one-click from the Launcher, you can open the custom palette with two clicks. Dock the Database Manager with any other standard palette, such as the History palette, by dragging the tab of the Database Manager over the standard palette. Now that it's docked, you can open the group of palettes by selecting the standard History button from the Launcher, and bringing the Database Manager to the front by selecting its tab.

Automating Production

Although the look-and-feel of a Web application may change radically from site to site, the underlying structure often falls into a particular category. Lasso Studio includes two tools that quickly build the basic foundation of a Web application, enabling the designer more time to design the interface. The Form Builder is used for creating portions of separate pages while Site Builder creates all the pages necessary for a particular operation. If you're just starting out in Lasso, the Form Builder and Site Builder are great tools not only for achieving an end-result, but also for understand-ing how all the components work together.

Interacting with the Form Builder

The form is the primary venue for users to interact with an online database. Forms are great for searching databases as well as for adding and updating records. Lasso Studio's Form Builder rapidly creates all the necessary code for all of these operations and more.

The Form Builder primarily inserts forms into existing pages and offers forms for both Pre-Lasso and Post-Lasso processing. In addition to creating forms for searching, adding, updating, and deleting operations, the Form Builder is also capable of inserting the necessary code for displaying fields from a single record or all of the found records. In constructing a Web application, the Form Builder can be used multiple times to make different elements of the application.

Making Pre-Lasso forms

The Form Builder offers three Pre-Lasso operations and seven Post-Lasso ones. The Pre-Lasso operations are:

✦ **Search Database:** Builds a form that enables the user to search a database on any specified field or fields. The form will include search criteria for each field with buttons to find the specified record or all records, as shown in Figure 38-5.

- ✦ **Add Record:** Creates a form that permits the user to add a new record to a database. When built, the form includes selected text fields for inputting the new record information and an Add Record button.
- ✦ **No Database Action:** Creates the shell of a form in which the designer can add form elements. This form includes a Do Nothing button which can be modified.

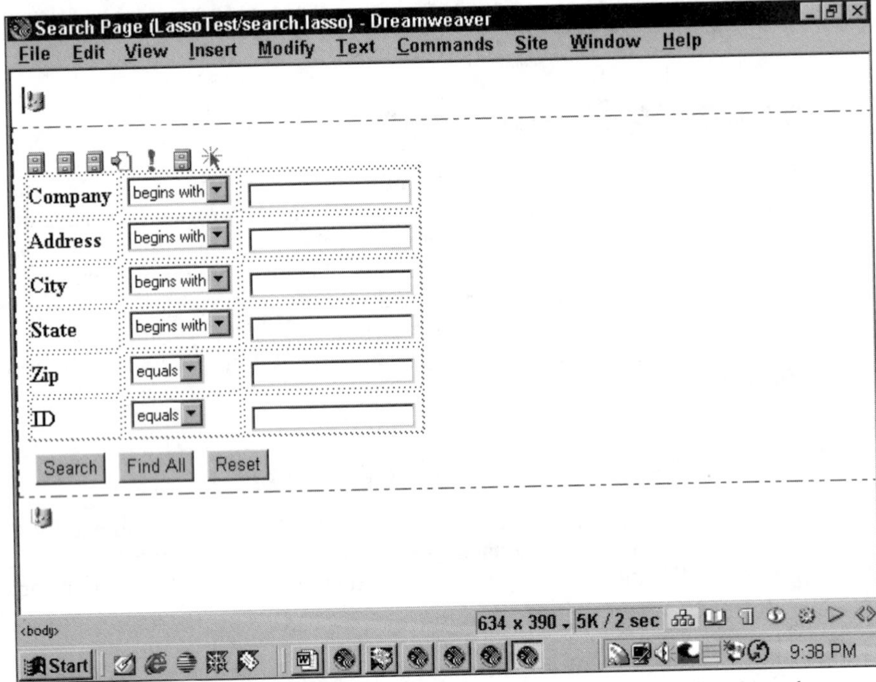

Figure 38-5: This search form, created by the Form Builder, includes drop-down lists for user-friendly search criteria.

All three Pre-Lasso operations require that a response page and an error page be named. Because these pages will require Lasso processing, they should both be Post-Lasso format with a .lasso extension.

While the error and response files don't have to be created before using Form Builder, it's a good idea to create placeholder pages for them. Form Builder does not automatically make either page and you can avoid typographical errors if you use the file selector to locate the files.

To create a Pre-Lasso search or add record form, follow these steps:

1. Place your cursor where you'd like the form to appear and choose Commands ➪ Form Builder.

   The first screen of the Form Builder dialog box appears and displays information about the operation of the command.

2. Select Next to proceed.

3. On the Choose A Form Action screen of the Form Builder (Figure 38-6), choose one of the following from the Pre-Lasso Input area:

   - Search Database
   - Add Record
   - No Database Action

   Choose Next.

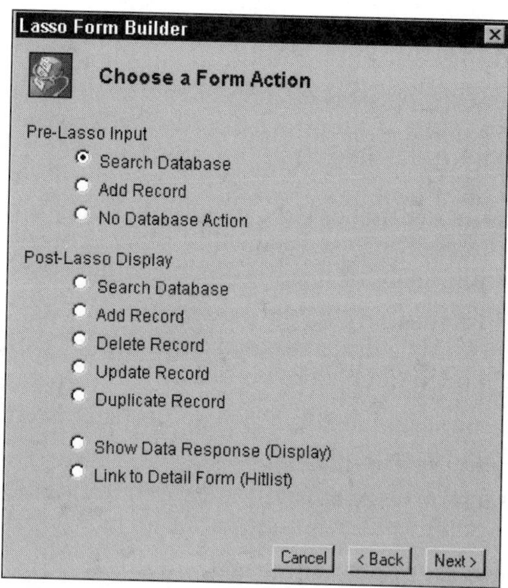

Figure 38-6: The Form Builder is capable of creating a variety of standard form types.

4. On the Choose A Response and Error Pages screen, enter a path and file name for a Response and Error file in their respective fields; use the folder icon to open a Select dialog box to locate the files. Click Next when you're ready to proceed.

   If you chose No Database Action, go to Step 7.

5. On the Choose the Database Fields screen, select the fields from the current database you'd like to appear in the form.

   To select multiple fields, Ctrl+click (Command+click) the field names.

6. If your database supports value lists, such as FileMaker Pro files do, choose how they should be represented from the list: Pop-Up Menus, Checkboxes, or Radio Buttons. Click Next when you're done.

7. On the Review Your Form Selections screen, make sure that all your choices are as desired. To change anything select Back, otherwise choose Finish.

If you have View ⇨ Invisible Elements enabled, you'll notice a number of custom icons above the table enclosing the form elements. These Lasso icons represent tags conveying some of the information selected when using Form Builder, such as type of database action and the paths to the response and error pages. With the Property Inspector open, select an icon to examine it further. The Form Builder also inserts another tag that's not as obvious: a `<meta>` tag that identifies the form as Pre-Lasso. When building a Post-Lasso form, as we'll discuss in the next section, the `<meta>` tag marks the form as Post-Lasso.

Adding Post-Lasso forms

Post-Lasso forms are used whenever a page is directly submitted to the Lasso Web Data Engine or is processed as a result of a previous form action. The five Post-Lasso options that create a form in the Form Builder are:

✦ **Search Databases:** Builds a form that enables the user to search a database on any specified field or fields. The form will include search criteria for each field with buttons to find the specified records or all records.

✦ **Add Record:** Creates a form that permits the user to add a new record to a database. When built, the form includes selected text fields for inputting the new record information and an Add Record button.

✦ **Delete Record:** Creates a form that displays the desired fields of a selected record and includes a Delete Record button.

✦ **Update Record:** Creates a form that displays the desired fields of a selected record and includes an Update Record button, as shown in Figure 38-7.

✦ **Duplicate Record:** Creates a form that displays the desired fields of a selected record and includes a Duplicate Record button.

All of these Post-Lasso options require that response and error pages be identified and fields from the current database be selected. The remaining two options under the Post-Lasso Display section do not create a form and are discussed in the following section. To include a Post-Lasso form on your page, follow these steps:

1. Place your cursor where you'd like the form to appear and choose Commands ⇨ Form Builder.

The first screen of the Form Builder dialog box appears and displays information about the operation of the command.

2. Select Next to proceed.
3. On the Choose A Form Action screen of the Form Builder, choose one of the following from the Post-Lasso Display area:
   - Search Database
   - Add Record
   - Delete Record
   - Update Record
   - Duplicate Record
4. Choose Next.

Not all data source types support remote duplication of records. If the current data source does not, and the Duplicate Records option is selected, an alert is displayed to inform you. You can either choose another option or cancel the Form Builder and select a compatible data source.

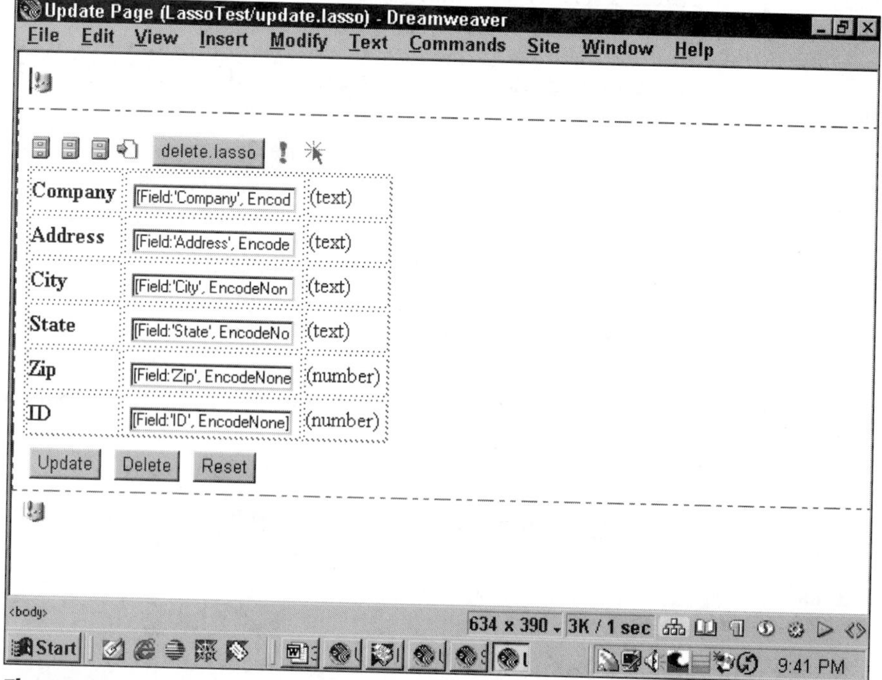

Figure 38-7: The Update Record form enables remote users to edit database records over the Web.

5. On the Choose A Response and Error Pages screen, enter a path and file name for a Response and Error file in their respective fields; use the folder icon to open a Select dialog box to locate the files. Click Next when you're ready to proceed.

   If you chose No Database Action, go to Step 8.

6. On the Choose the Database Fields screen, select the fields from the current database you'd like to appear in the form.

   To select multiple fields, Ctrl+click (Command+click) the field names.

7. If your database supports value lists, such as FileMaker Pro files do, choose how they should be represented from the list: Pop-Up Menus, Checkboxes, or Radio Buttons. Click Next when you're done.

8. On the Review Your Form Selections screen, make sure that all your choices are as desired. To change anything, select Back; otherwise, choose Finish.

Constructing Post-Lasso responses

Most of the forms built by the Form Builder require a response and error page. The error page can be constructed by including Lasso's `[Error_CurrentError]` tag, but what of the response page? The Form Builder includes two display options precisely for the purpose of creating response pages:

- ✦ **Show Data Response (Display):** Shows the selected fields of a single record. This option is generally used in conjunction with the Update, Delete, and Delete form actions.
- ✦ **Link to Detail Form (Hitlist):** Displays selected fields from a number of records, each of which has a link to another response page with a more detailed listing of the chosen record.

To use the Show Data Response option, follow these steps:

1. Place your cursor where you'd like the form to appear and choose Commands ➪ Form Builder.

   The first screen of the Form Builder dialog box appears and displays information about the operation of the command.

2. Select Next to proceed.
3. On the Choose A Form Action screen of the Form Builder, choose the Show Data Response (Display) option from the Post-Lasso Display area.
4. On the Choose the Database Fields screen, select the fields from the current database you'd like to appear in the form. Click Next when you're done.
5. On the Review Your Form Selections screen, make sure that all your choices are as desired. To change anything, select Back, otherwise choose Finish.

Lasso Studio generates a table with the labels and [Field] tags for the requested fields as shown in Figure 38-8.

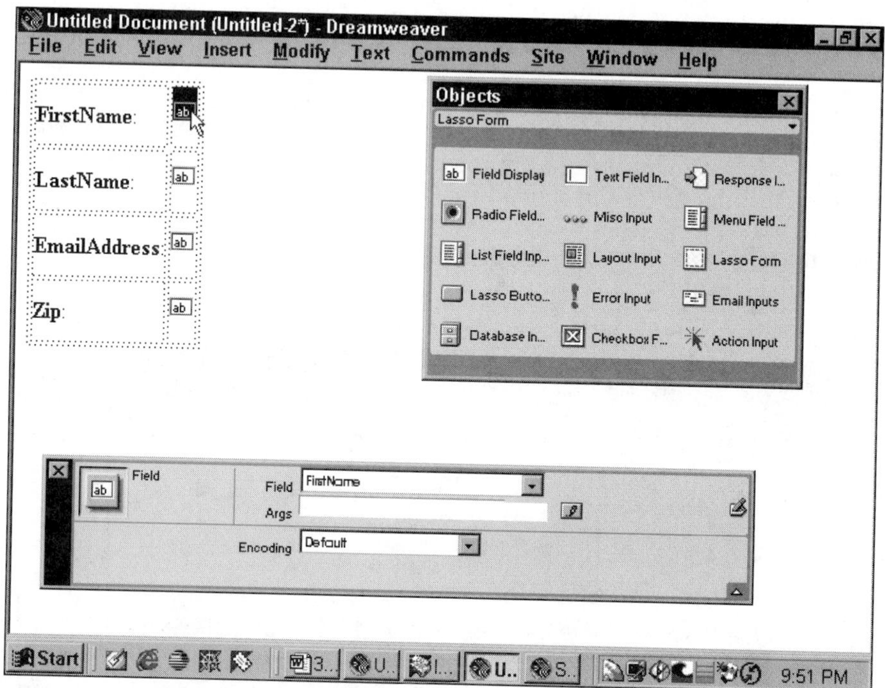

Figure 38-8: The Show Data Response Form creates labels from the field names.

To use the Link to Detail Form option, follow these steps:

1. Place your cursor where you'd like the form to appear and choose Commands ➪ Form Builder.

   The first screen of the Form Builder dialog box appears and displays information about the operation of the command.

2. Select Next to proceed.
3. On the Choose A Form Action screen of the Form Builder, choose the Link to Detail Form (Hitlist) option from the Post-Lasso Display area.
4. On the Choose the Database Fields screen, select the fields from the current database you'd like to appear in the form. Click Next when you're done.
5. On the Select Detail Link Options screen, select the field you'd like to use as a link to a detail record.

6. From the same screen, enter the path and file name for the detail record response page in the Response Page field; use the folder icon to open a Select dialog box to locate the file, if desired. Click Next when you're ready to proceed.

7. On the Review Your Form Selections screen, make sure that all your choices are as desired. To change anything select Back, otherwise choose Finish.

When the Link to Detail Form is complete, Lasso Studio creates a table with the field names for column headings in the first row, as shown in Figure 38-9. The second row appears to contain one instance of each chosen field, but if you examine the code, you'll see that the row is surrounded by a Lasso `[Records]...[/Records]` tag pair which repeats the row until the requested number of records is displayed. The final row contains a More Records button which, when selected by the user, displays the next group of records.

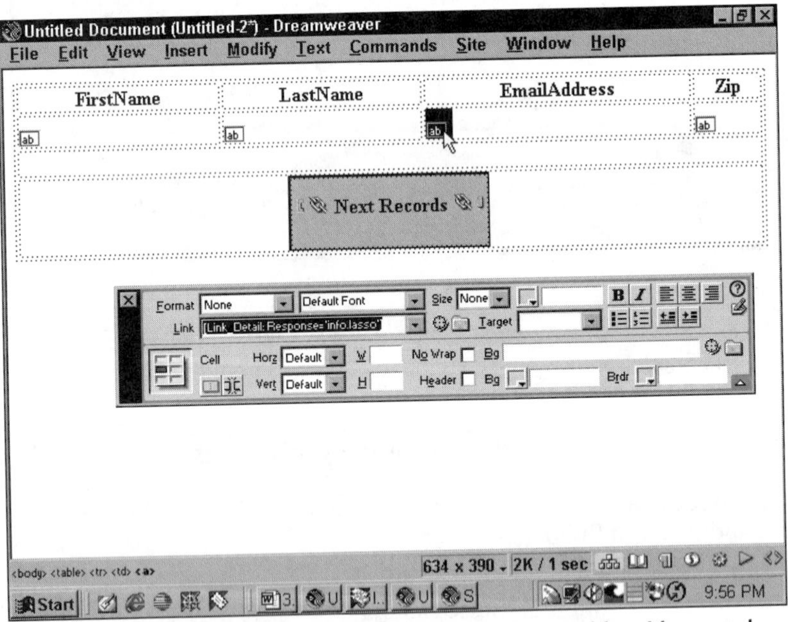

Figure 38-9: The Link to Detail Form option creates a table with a number of rows of records as well as a button for showing the next set of records.

The number of records displayed is set in the form requesting the Link to Detail Form by a Lasso tag, `[-MaxRecords]`. By default, the Form Builder sets this value at 10. You can change it by selecting the `[-MaxRecords]` tag—it's the last Database icon created by the Form Builder's Search Database option—and change the value in the Property Inspector.

Site Builder

Almost every type of Web application — be it search, update, or add records — requires multiple pages, to be really useful. Aside from the initial entry form, generally a resulting detail page and, at the very least, an error page, are called for. Lasso Studio includes a very useful utility that creates all of the needed pages in one operation: Site Builder. Additionally, Site Builder gives you the option of creating a series of bare-bones pages to which design elements are added later, or the option of incorporating the Lasso generated components into a previously designed Dreamweaver template. This is a very powerful feature and has the potential of saving you a great deal of work.

The title, Site Builder, is a bit of a misnomer; it's really an application builder for a portion of your site. Site Builder is capable of creating two different applications — one for searching a data source and another for adding records to a database. Both applications have several branching choices; you can, for example, create a search application that either just displays the results *or* links to an update page with an optional delete button.

As noted, Site Builder works with Dreamweaver templates. The command presents lists of available templates in any given site and all of the editable regions within each template. Site Builder puts the form and other elements it creates within a specified editable region as shown in Figure 38-10. Not only does this facility automate pro-duction while maintaining a consistent look and feel, all of the generated pages are linked to a single template which means that global changes can be affected by altering just one page.

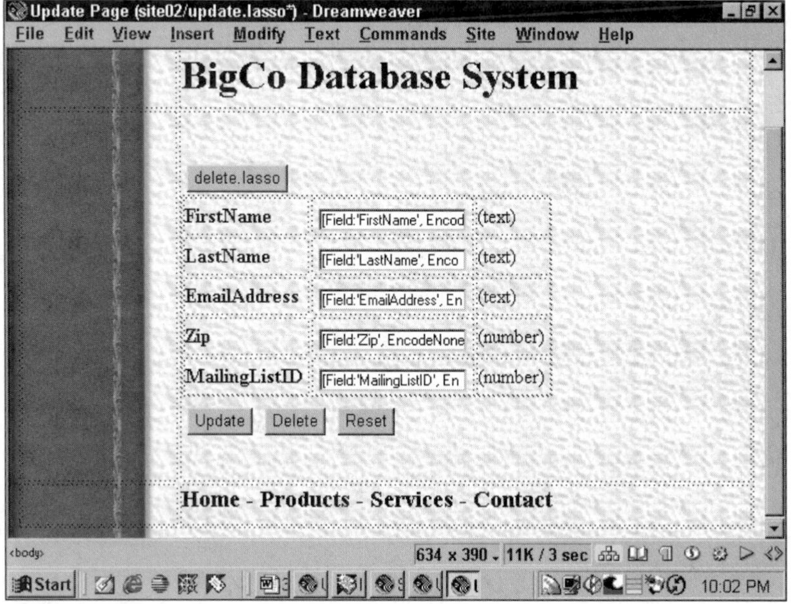

Figure 38-10: Lasso Studio's Site Builder combines the flexibility of Dreamweaver templates with the power of database connectivity.

Creating a search application

Lasso Studio's Site Builder is capable of creating several varieties of a search application:

- One version creates a search form which displays a listing of matched records, each of which is linked to a detail form for showing the entire record.
- Another version makes the search form and listing, but the link goes to a form for updating the selected record.
- The third variation includes search, listing, and update pages as the previously described version did, but also includes a delete button and a page with a response to the delete operation.

The Site Builder displays different screens with different options depending on your previous choices. If, for example, you select to create a display page rather than an update page, you'll never see the option for adding a delete button.

To use the Site Builder for creating a search application, follow these steps:

1. Choose Commands ➪ Lasso Site Builder.

   The Lasso Site Builder dialog box, as shown in Figure 38-11, is displayed.

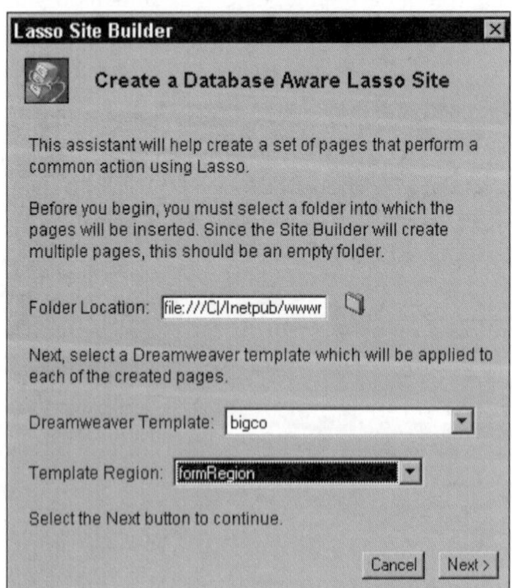

Figure 38-11: The Site Builder stores all created files – up to five in all – in a specified folder.

2. On the Create a Database Aware Lasso Site screen, do the following:
   - Enter the folder path to contain the search application pages in the Folder Location field, or use the folder icon to select a directory. Make sure that the folder is part of the current site.
   - If desired, choose an existing template from the Dreamweaver Template list.
   - If you've chosen a template, select the editable region from the Template Region list to insert the database elements.
   - Click Next when you're done.
3. On the Choose a Site Action screen, make sure the Select Page, Listing Page, with Update or Display option is selected. Click Next.
4. On the Specify a Database Configuration screen, do the following:
   - Choose a data source, table and key column from their respective option lists. The key column need only be selected if you're working with an ODBC or 4D database.
   - In the Site Builder Options area, choose how you'd like the value list to be depicted (if supported) from the Value Lists Display menu.
   - Change the file name of the error page, if desired. The error page must end in a .lasso extension.
   - Click Next when you're ready.
5. On the Create Search Page screen, do the following:
   - Enter a name for the search page in the File Name field.
   - Enter an HTML title for the document in the Search Page Title field.
   - Select the fields you'd like to appear as possible search criteria from the Fields for Search Form list area.
   - If you'd like to insert a button to return all records, choose the Include FindAll Button option.
6. On the Create Results Listing Page (Figure 38-12), do the following:
   - Enter a name for the listings page in the File Name field.
   - Enter an HTML title for the document in the Listing Page Title field.
   - Select the fields you'd like to appear from the Fields for Listing Form list area.
   - If you'd like to insert a button to navigate among the records, choose the Include Next/Previous Buttons option.

- Select the field to be used as a link from the Field for Detail Link list.
- Choose the type of page the results will link to. If the results page should only show the record and not allow it to be edited, choose Display Page; if the results page should allow the user to modify the record, choose Update Page.
- Click Next when you're done.

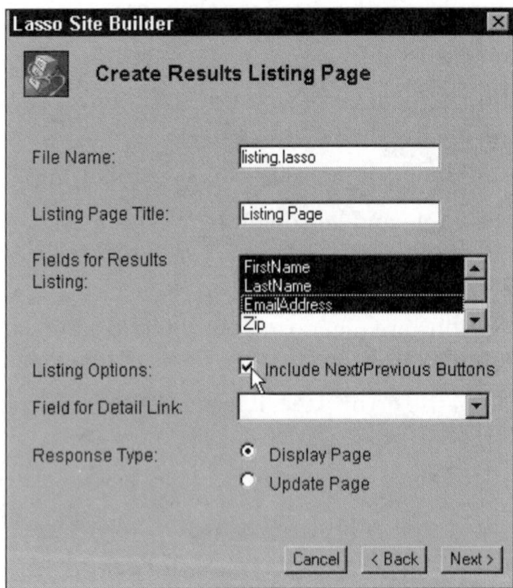

Figure 38-12: Your results listing can automatically include Previous and Next Record navigation controls.

The next screen displayed depends on the type of results chosen. If you chose Display Page, go to Step 7; for Update Page, go to Step 8.

7. On the Create Display Page, do the following:
   - Enter a name for the display page in the File Name field.
   - Enter an HTML title for the document in the Display Page Title field.
   - Select the fields you'd like to appear from the Fields for Display Form list area.
   - Click Next when you're done and proceed to Step 10.
8. On the Create Update Page, do the following:
   - Select the fields you'd like to be able to edit from the Fields for Update Form list area.

- If you'd like the user to have the option to remove the selected record, enable the Include Delete Button option.
- Click Next when you're done. If you've added a delete button, proceed to Step 9, otherwise go to Step 10.

9. On the Create Delete Page screen, do the following:
   - Enter a name for the delete page in the File Name field.
   - Enter an HTML title for the document in the Delete Page Title field.
   - Enter the text you'd like displayed on the delete page in the Delete Message text area.
   - Click Next.
10. On the Review Your Form Selections screen, double-check all of your choices. If you see anything you'd like to change, choose Back; otherwise select Finish.

The Site Builder dialog box stays on the screen while the pages are being generated. After each page is created, it is opened for immediate access.

Incorporating an add record application

Adding a new record to a database is one of the most common Web application tasks. Lasso Studio's Site Builder can automatically produce all the pages necessary for inserting a new record with several variations:

✦ One version builds a new record form and a confirmation page, which displays the just input data.

✦ Another version makes the new record form and an update page to enable any necessary modifications.

✦ A third version creates the new record form and update page and includes a delete button and a page confirming the deletion.

As in the search page Site Builder scheme, all other versions also create an error page.

To make an add record Web application using Site Builder, follow these steps:

1. Choose Commands ➪ Lasso Site Builder.

   The Lasso Site Builder dialog box is displayed.
2. On the Create a Database Aware Lasso Site screen, do the following:
   - Enter the path to folder to contain the search application pages in the Folder Location field or use the folder icon to select a directory. Make sure that the folder is part of the current site.

- If desired, choose an existing template from the Dreamweaver Template list.
- If you've chosen a template, select the editable region from the Template Region list to insert the database elements.
- Click Next when you're done.

3. On the Choose a Site Action screen, choose the Add Page, with Update or Display option. Click Next.
4. On the Specify a Database Configuration screen, do the following:
   - Choose a data source, table, and key column from their respective option lists. The key column need only be selected if you're working with an ODBC or 4D database.
   - In the Site Builder Options area, choose how you'd like the value list to be depicted (if supported) from the Value Lists Display menu.
   - Change the file name of the error page, if desired. The error page must end in a `.lasso` extension.
   - Click Next when you're ready.
5. On the Create Add Page, do the following:
   - Enter a name for the add page in the File Name field.
   - Enter an HTML title for the document in the Add Page Title field.
   - Select the fields you'd like to appear from the Fields for Add Form list area.
   - Choose the type of page the results will link to. If the results page should only show the record and not allow it to be edited, choose Display Page; if the results page should allow the user to modify the record, choose Update Page.
   - Click Next when you're done.

   The next screen displayed depends on the type of results chosen. If you chose Display Page, go to Step 6; for Update Page, go to Step 7.
6. On the Create Display Page, do the following:
   - Enter a name for the display page in the File Name field.
   - Enter an HTML title for the document in the Display Page Title field.
   - Select the fields you'd like to appear from the Fields for Display Form list area.
   - Click Next when you're done and proceed to Step 9.

7. On the Create Update Page, do the following:
   - Select the fields you'd like to be able to edit from the Fields for Update Form list area.
   - If you'd like the user to have the option to remove the selected record, enable the Include Delete Button option.
   - Click Next when you're done. If you've added a delete button, proceed to Step 8, otherwise go to Step 9.
8. On the Create Delete Page screen, do the following:
   - Enter a name for the delete page in the File Name field.
   - Enter an HTML title for the document in the Delete Page Title field.
   - Enter the text you'd like displayed on the delete page in the Delete Message text area.
   - Click Next.
9. On the Review Your Form Selections screen, double-check all of your choices. If you see anything you'd like to change, choose Back; otherwise select Finish.

After the pages have all been generated they are immediately saved and left open for further editing.

Objects

Lasso Dynamic Markup Language (LDML) is an exceptionally rich application language with tags that cover almost every programming possibility. Lasso Studio translates those tags into objects — a lot of objects, representing a lot more tags. In all, Lasso Studio offers 39 objects, spread over four new panels of the Objects palette, which access over 300 Lasso tags. Moreover, all of the objects are represented by onscreen icons which, when selected, give access to the full range of attributes through custom Property Inspectors.

As noted, the objects are grouped, by function, into separate panels on the Object palette. The four panels are:

✦ **Lasso Form:** Objects for building forms including Lasso versions of the various form elements such as text field and radio buttons, as well as objects commonly used in forms like the Email Inputs object.

✦ **Lasso Data Access:** Objects that, in some fashion, connect to the database or Web server and pass or return information.

✦ **Lasso Programming:** Objects for constructing conditional, file, math, and other code.

✦ **Lasso Extensions:** Custom objects that extend Lasso Studio. This panel is discussed later in this chapter.

For the most part, Lasso objects behave like other Dreamweaver objects. You can, for example, insert them by dragging and dropping them onto the page or by selecting them once to add them at your current cursor position.

To see Lasso Studio icons in the Document window, two conditions must be met. First, the Server Markup Tags option on the Invisible Elements category of Preferences must be enabled. Second, the View ➪ Invisible Elements command must be selected.

Form objects

You may do a double-take when you first look at the Lasso Form objects — many of them appear to be identical to their standard Dreamweaver counterparts. That sameness, however, is only icon-deep; the code inserted and the Property Inspectors invoked are very different. The Form object itself is perhaps the best representative of these differences. Where as a Dreamweaver Form object inserts this code:

```
<form method="post" action="">
</form>
```

the Lasso Form object creates code similar to this:

```
<FORM ACTION="action.lasso" NAME="LassoForm.958693820000"
METHOD="POST">
<INPUT TYPE="hidden" NAME="-Database" VALUE="Contacts.db">
<INPUT TYPE="hidden" NAME="-Layout" VALUE="Web">
</FORM>
```

In addition, Lasso inserts a <meta> tag in the <head> section which identifies the form as either Post-Lasso or Pre-Lasso format, like this:

```
<META NAME="LassoForm.958693820000" CONTENT="Pre-Lasso">
```

By default, all Lasso forms are Pre-Lasso although the format can easily be changed through the Property Inspector. To modify the Lasso form object once it's inserted, place your cursor within the form outline and choose <form> from the Tag Selector. The custom Property Inspector, shown in Figure 38-13, makes all the options and attributes available.

Figure 38-13: The Lasso Form Property Inspector lets you change the format from Pre-Lasso to Post-Lasso as well as alter many other attributes.

As you can see, in Lasso, the Form object is much more involved. The underlying philosophy of Lasso Studio is to make this increased complexity transparent to the user for layout, while maintaining its accessibility for editing. This ease-of-use foundation also explains why the Form panel includes objects that, strictly speaking, aren't form elements. Because these objects, such as the Lasso Form Email Inputs object, are frequently used with forms, they are included in this group. All of the objects are described in Table 38-1:

Table 38-1
Lasso Form Objects

Object	***Description***
Lasso Form	Required for providing the necessary surrounding `<form>` tags as well as adding other Lasso specific tags. Inserts several hidden input tags identifying the current data source, table, and (if needed) key value.
Text Field	Functions normally except the Property Inspector allows both database field and form parameter input.
Menu Field	Functions normally except the Property Inspector allows both database field and form parameter input.
List Field	Functions normally except the Property Inspector allows both database field and form parameter input. The difference between the Menu and List Field object is that the List Field is set to display multiple lines initially.
Radio Field	Functions normally except the Property Inspector allows both database field and form parameter input.
Checkbox Field	Functions normally except the Property Inspector allows both database field and form parameter input.
Button	Used for setting the Lasso action. The action options are available from an option list in the Property Inspector.

Continued

Table 38-1 (continued)

Object	***Description***
Action	Sets the action for the form. The default action is `-Nothing`.
Database	Specifies the database used by the action as well as the record affected, the number of records returned and sort order.
Email	Sets up an e-mail to be sent when the form is submitted. Separate Email Editors — one for Pre-Lasso and one for Post-Lasso files — (described later in this section) are initially displayed when this object is inserted.
Error	Sets the page called when an error is encountered on the form being submitted. Allow different pages to be called for different types of errors, such as `-UpdateError` or `-SecurityError`. The default is `-AddError`.
Field	Inserts a field from the current data source as defined in the Lasso Configuration file. Used only with Post-Lasso pages; if you attempt to insert a Field object on a Pre-Lasso page an alert is displayed.
Misc	Six form related tags: `-ClientPassword` and `-ClientUsername` are used for passing values to Lasso to permit the form to be submitted; `-ModuleAdmin` and `-ModuleName` are used to access remote administration pages for a specific module; `-Required` is placed prior to an input field to require that this field be completed; `-Timeout` sets the length of time for Lasso to wait for a response from a database. Measured in seconds, acceptable values are from 10 to 300; the default value is 60. This tag is infrequently used.
Response	Sets the page called as a response to the form being submitted. Different responses may be included for different actions, such as an `-AddResponse` and an `-UpdateResponse`. The default response is `-Response`.

The Lasso Form Email Inputs object is different from the other objects on this panel in one respect, however. It is the only one that opens a separate dialog box; in fact, the Lasso Email object presents two different dialog boxes, one for Pre-Lasso forms and one for Post-Lasso forms. The major difference is that the Post-Lasso forms grant access to processed dynamic data as can be seen in Figure 38-14. With all the fields on the Post-Lasso Email object, selecting the Edit button enables you to enter database field names, form parameters, or other dynamic data.

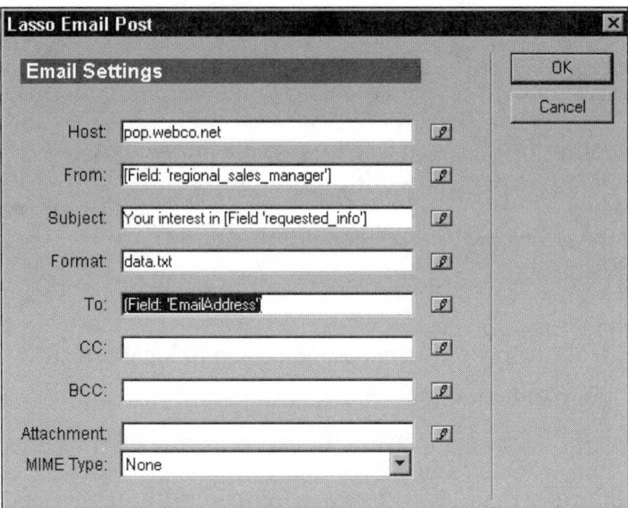

Figure 38-14: With a Post-Lasso Email object, dynamic values for attributes such as the To field.

To use the Lasso Email object on a page, follow these steps:

1. With your cursor placed in a Lasso Form, select the Email object from the Lasso Form panel of the Objects palette.

   If you're in a Pre-Lasso form, the Lasso Email Pre dialog box opens, as shown in Figure 38-15.

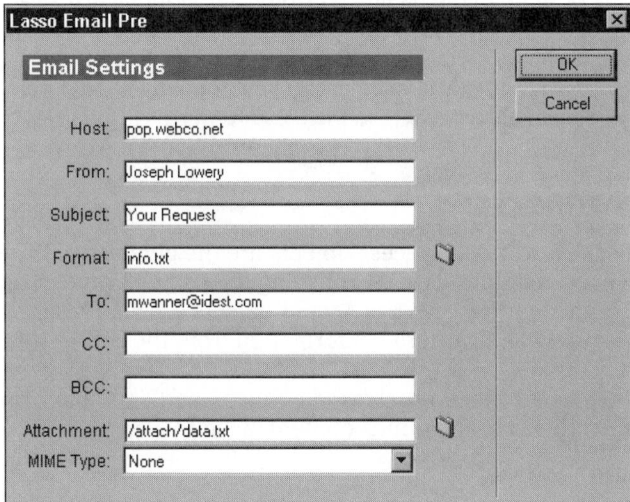

Figure 38-15: The Pre-Lasso Email object only permits static information to be included.

2. Enter the domain name or IP address for the mail server in the Host field. (Required)
3. Enter the name of the sender in the From field. (Required)

Many mail servers require that the From field be a valid e-mail address.

4. Enter the topic of the e-mail in the Subject field. (Required)
5. Enter the path to the file sent as the body of the message in the Format file. (Required)

   On the Lasso Email Pre dialog box, use the folder icon to locate the file.
6. Enter the name of the recipient in the To field. (Required)
7. If you'd like to copy the message to an additional recipient, enter his or her e-mail address in the CC field. If you'd like other recipients to receive a copy of the message, but prefer their identity remain hidden, enter their e-mail address in the BCC field.
8. To send a file along with the e-mail, enter its path in the Attachment field.

   On the Lasso Email Pre dialog box, use the folder icon to locate the file.
9. To send the e-mail in HTML format, change the MIME type from Plain to HTML.
10. Click OK when you're done.

Lasso inserts each of the e-mail parameters as a separate hidden input tag, noted with an e-mail icon in the Document window. You can change the values of any of the parameters by selecting it and then making the modification in the Property Inspector.

If you'd like one or more of the parameters to be a user input, first select the icon of the desired tag in the Document window. Then open the HTML Source inspector and change the <input> tag's `type` attribute from `hidden` to `text`. This will create a text field with an initial value in the field that you should delete. You're free to move the text field anywhere in the Lasso form.

Data Access objects

As their title implies, Lasso's Data Access objects are the glue between a data source and a Web page. In addition to establishing the proper connection and requesting specific information, the Data Access objects are also responsible for formatting code correctly and gathering information from the server.

Several of the Data Access objects, such as `[Records]` and `[Inline]`, are Lasso *container* tags. A container tag surrounds content, as in this code:

```
[Records]
[Encode_URL]
[Field: 'Firstname'] [Field: 'Lastname']<br>
[/Records]
```

In Lasso Studio, container tags are shown with icons for both opening and closing tags, as can be seen in Figure 38-16. Because the enclosed code can be quite complex, particularly if nested container tags are used, Lasso Studio provides a method for finding the opening tag. Choose the closing tag of any container tag and the Property Inspector includes a button, select Matching Open Tag; and select the button to highlight the tag's mate.

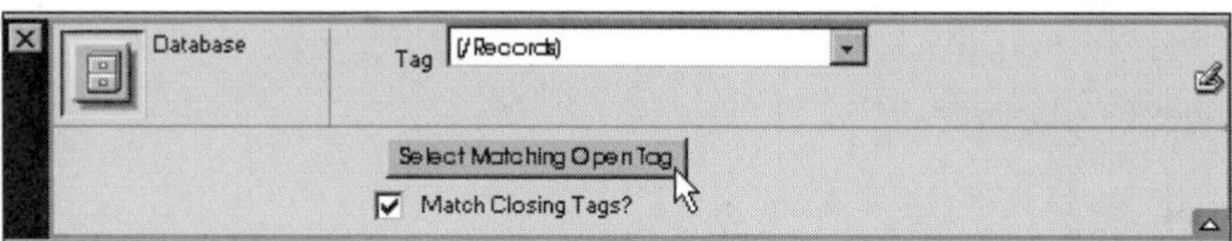

Figure 38-16: Icons for container tags are marked with opening and closing square brackets.

The Data Access objects are detailed in Table 38-2.

Table 38-2
Lasso Data Access Objects

Object	*Description*
Database	Inserts a variety of tags dealing with retrieving data from a data source and presenting it on the page.
Encoding	Encode and decode strings passed to and from a data source.
Field	Displays a field from a database for the current record.
Form Param	Displays a value from the form that called the current page.
Image	Displays an image from a database; either the image data or a link to the image data may be used.
Include	Inserts the contents of a file into the current page.
Inline	Calls a Lasso action outside of a form.
Link	Provides links to returned records or sets of records.
Search	Displays information about the current search.
Server	Displays information about the client and Web browser.

Programming objects

Much of the power of languages such as Lasso is derived from their programming prowess. While complex programming may still be easier to write by hand, Lasso Studio's Programming objects (Figure 38-17) make for quick single tag insertion and alteration of the attributes across the board.

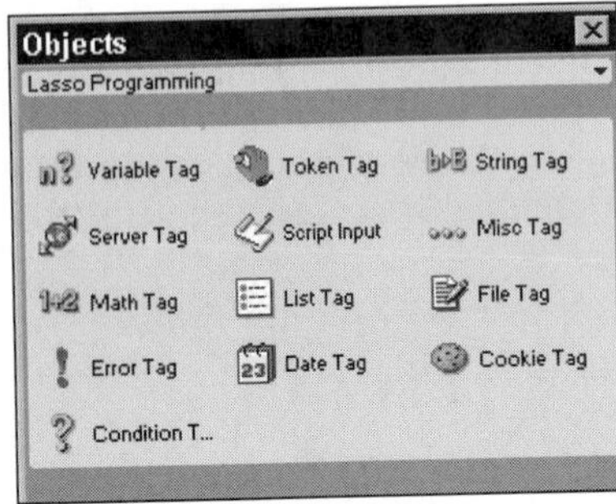

Figure 38-17: Use Lasso Studio's Programming objects to manipulate strings, numbers, or files, among other tasks.

Lasso Studio includes 12 different categories of programming tags in this panel's objects, as detailed in Table 38-3.

Table 38-3
Lasso Programming Objects

Object	*Description*
Condition	Inserts conditional logic tags such as `[If]`, `[Else]`, and `[While]`.
Cookie	Sets and retrieves cookies.
Date	Inserts and formats dates and times.
Error	Displays and sets error codes.
File	Manage files on the Web server; functions include reading, writing, renaming, deleting, and moving, among others.
List	Create and manipulate lists.
Math	Execute mathematical operations such as generating a random number or rounding up a number.

Miscellaneous	The following tags are accessed through this object:
	`[AE_Event]`, `[AE_EventResult]`, `[AE_EventError]`
	`[HTML_Comment]`, `[Lasso_Comment]`
	`[Log]`, `[Roman]`
	`[Valid_CreditCard]`, `[Valid_Email]`, `[Valid_URL]`
	`[Win_Exec]`
	`[4D_RefreshCache]`

Server	Retrieves information about the current Web server and the Lasso implementation.

Object	*Description*
String	Performs string manipulations.
Token	Sets and retrieves a hidden value for passing information from one page to the next.
Variable	Sets and retrieves variables within a page.

Extensions to Lasso Studio

A fourth panel in the Objects palette is installed by Lasso Studio, Lasso Extensions. This panel is intended for custom objects. In general, you add a custom object by installing the HTML and GIF file of the object in the Configuration\Objects\Lasso Extensions folder on your system. Lasso Studio has taken this implementation one step further by providing an example file for creating your own objects that follow Lasso conventions. This technique enables one object to be used to insert multiple tags.

The example file consists of three parts: an HTML file, a GIF found in Objects subfolder, and a configuration file maintained in the Configuration\Lasso\Extensions folder. The three files are used in this manner:

- ✦ **Example.gif:** The image representing the object that appears in the Objects palette.
- ✦ **Example.htm:** The main file executed when the object is inserted. Four variables need to be specified for the object to work properly:
  - `theConfigFile`: The name and path of the configuration file. If no path is given, the file is presumed to be stored in Configuration\Lasso\Extensions.
  - `theCategory`: The name of the objects category which typically corres-=ponds to the Objects palette panel; by default the category is set to "LassoExtensions."
  - `theSubCategory`: The name of the object itself, such as Email. Objects with the same name use the same Property Inspector. (Property Inspectors are not automatically generated and would have to be custom-built.)
  - `theTag`: The default tag to be inserted by the object. If `theTag` variable is left blank, the values are taken from the default attribute of the `<Subcategory>` tag found in the Example.cfg file.
- ✦ **Example.cfg:** An XML file that contains a list of available tags for the object. Each tag is listed separately with attributes for displaying syntax, the type of tag (such as substitution, container, and so on) and any options.

Both the Example.htm and Example.cfg are heavily commented. It's best to create your objects with these files open in a text editor, substituting the values where necessary, but leaving the instructions intact.

Modifying Lasso Studio Code

It's essential for a rich Web application program to be flexible and Lasso Studio meets that requirement with functionality and flair. Once a Lasso object has been inserted, its attributes can be modified to a high degree; not only can static values be entered as attributes, but in many cases dynamic information—either pulled from a data source or entered in a form parameter—may become an attribute's value.

In addition to modifying code on a case-by-case basis, Lasso Studio also includes a couple of utilities for updating your code one page at a time. The Lasso LDML Updater brings code developed prior to Lasso version 3.6.5 up to speed, while the Lasso CDML Converter changes code in FileMaker Pro's 4.*x* syntax to compatible LDML. Both are special use tools, obviously, but, when needed, they'll save you a great deal of work.

Working with Lasso Tag Editors

To make all the various permutations of Lasso tags and attributes available, Lasso Studio uses a series of tag editors. Several of the tag editors are interlinked—you can, for example, add an attribute and value in the primary dialog box, the Lasso Tag Editor, by selecting an Edit button which opens another dialog box; the Name/Value Pair Editor Sub-tags, and even nested sub-tags, are created in the same manner. Another plus is that the tag editors only display which options are available according to the prior choices made.

The primary Tag Editor, as shown in Figure 38-18, is summoned by selecting the Edit button next to the Value field in the Property Inspector. Only those tags that accept attribute values, such as `[Date]`, have an Edit button available. The Tag Editor is basically a series field for ten name/value pairs. The name/value pairs can be edited manually by tabbing from one field to the next. Upon tabbing out of one field, the Code Preview area is updated. If entered manually, names and values are coded exactly as written—the programmer is responsible for making sure that the syntax is correct. For example, all literal values should be enclosed with single quotes and all sub-tags, parentheses.

Although you can type directly into the Code Preview text area, such edits are ignored. Only changes and additions made in the Name/Value pair fields are accepted.

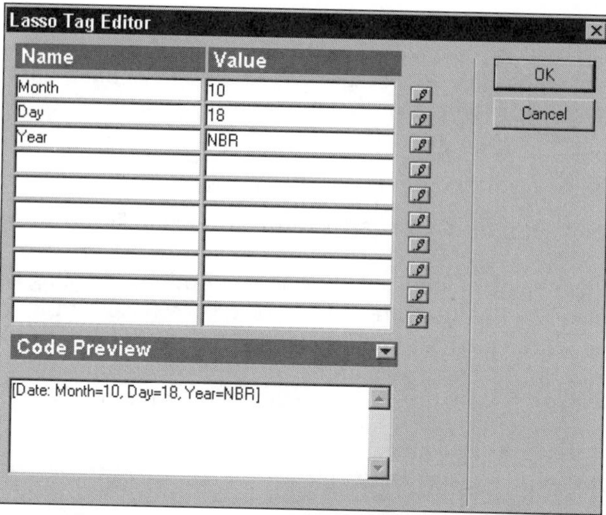

Figure 38-18: Enter Name/Value pairs to build arguments in the Tag Editor.

If you have more than ten arguments to be added to the tag, the additional ones appear in the final Value field of the Tag Editor. Realistically speaking, if you have more than ten arguments, you might need some assistance in keeping all the code straight and that's what the Edit button next to each line is for. Selecting the Edit button on the Tag Editor opens the second of Lasso Studio's tag editors, the Name/Value Pair Editor (Figure 38-19).

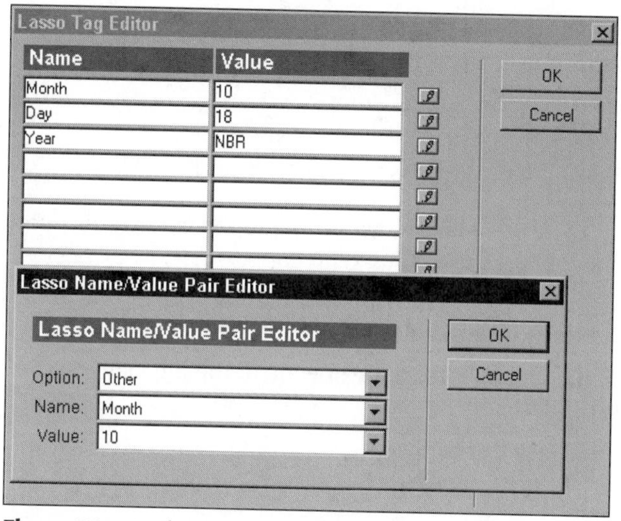

Figure 38-19: The Name/Value Pair Editor presents a limited number of choices depending on the tag that invokes it.

The three lists that make up the Name/Value Pair Editor are used in this way:

- ✦ **Option:** Selects one of eight different categories of Lasso tags, including Database, Action, Search, and Operator. An Other category is used for miscellaneous tags.
- ✦ **Name:** Shows available tags based on the selected Option.
- ✦ **Value:** Lists accepted values for the tag selected in the Name list.

Both the Name and Value lists may include an Other or Edit option. Selecting Other or Edit opens the third Lasso Studio tag-related dialog box, known as the Tag Editor (see Figure 38-20). The Tag Editor, as the name implies, is the most often used of the various dialog boxes. In addition to being available from the Name/Value Pair Editor, many Property Inspectors open it directly when a single value is required.

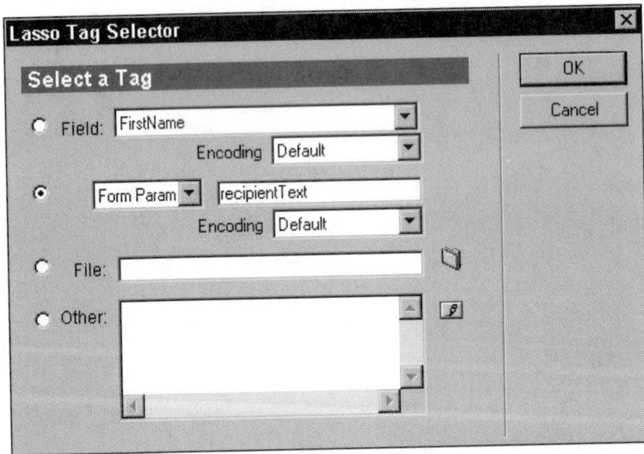

Figure 38-20: The Tag Editor is capable of returning four different types of values.

The Tag Editor is divided into four mutually exclusive areas:

- ✦ **Field:** Provides a list of available fields according to the current data source configuration, with an optional encoding type.
- ✦ **Form Param:** Offers a choice of Form Param, Variable, Cookie, and Token, and enters a value in the adjacent field. Values can also be encoded
- ✦ **File:** Enables a local file path or URL to be specified; the file may also be located by using the folder icon.
- ✦ **Other:** Permits manual entry of values.

Selecting the Edit button next to the final option, Other, opens the fourth tag editor, the Sub-Tag Selector, shown in Figure 38-21. The Sub-Tag Selector is similar to the Name/Value Pair Editor as it enables you to drill-down from category to sub-category to specific tag; each successive list is dynamically generated depending on the previous choice. If the Replace All Existing Content is not selected, the current choice is appended to the existing content of the Other text area. Encoding formats may be added by selecting an option from the Encoding list.

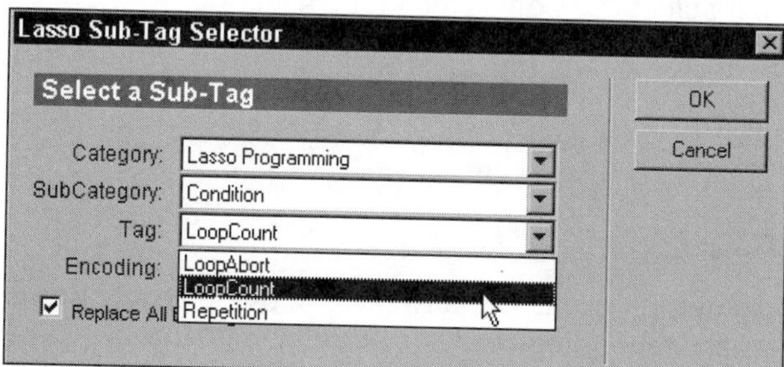

Figure 38-21: Use the Sub-Tag Selector to build nested sub-tags.

Updating pages and converting code

Computer languages are constantly evolving to handle new technologies and add new features and Lasso is no exception. As Lasso is refined, slightly different syntax may be used and an older syntax — while workable on the server — may not be reflected well in Lasso Studio. To ensure that every one is on the same page, Blue World includes a command that harnesses Dreamweaver's automation capabilities to update legacy Lasso documents to the current level. The Lasso LDML Updater works on all Lasso format files from any previous version of the program.

To update the current page of code, select Commands ➪ Lasso LDML Updater. The LDML Update appears as a floating palette with one button, as shown in Figure 38-22. Select Update LDML Code and, after a brief working period, an Update Complete message is displayed.

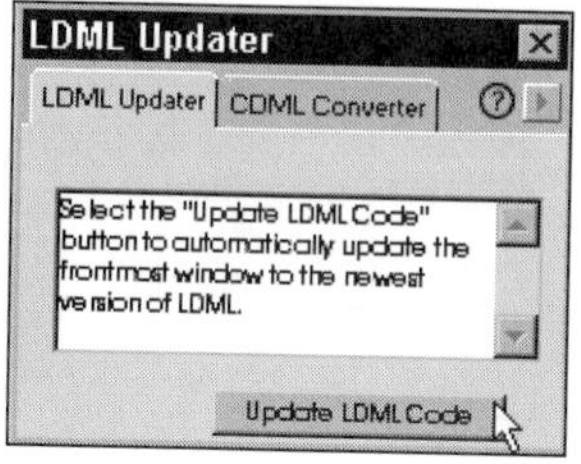

Figure 38-22: Bring your older Lasso pages up to the current version with the Lasso LDML Updater.

While the LDML Updater does a great job, it's prudent to always make an update of your pages before they are modified and to test converted pages heavily.

The other utility provided by Blue World is the Lasso CDML Converter. CDML is generated by FileMaker Pro's Web Companion; the Lasso CDML Converter can convert CDML from FileMaker Pro 4.*x* to the current syntax level. To begin the process, choose Commands ➪ Lasso CDML Converter or, if the Lasso LDML Updater is on the screen, just select the Converter's tab. Select Convert CDML Code to alter the current docu-ment's code from CDML to LDML. Lasso Studio presents a Conversion Complete message when the operation is over.

Summary

Lasso Studio is a very powerful tool for the Dreamweaver active Web site designer. Not only is the underlying Lasso technology very powerful and adaptable, the Lasso Studio integration into Dreamweaver is top-notch. Because the extension has been so completely integrated into the core program, developers can move smoothly from layout to activation. As you start to work with Lasso Studio, keep these points in mind:

✦ The Lasso language, LDML, while tag-based, uses a different syntax than HTML, enclosing tags in square brackets rather than angle brackets.

✦ Lasso Studio offers a number of tools to automate production, including the Form Builder and the Site Builder.

✦ A full range of tags is available through the Lasso Objects. The Lasso Objects are grouped by function into three different panels: Form, Data Access and Programming. A fourth panel, Extensions, serves as a potential repository for future custom objects.

✦ Lasso Studio uses a multitiered series of tag editors for modifying objects and their attributes once inserted. The Edit button on the custom Property Inspectors opens the first of the available tag editors.

In the next chapter, you see how Tango from Pervasive Software integrates with Dreamweaver.

✦ ✦ ✦

CHAPTER 39

Working with Tango

✦ ✦ ✦ ✦

In This Chapter

Understanding Tango application files

Accessing Tango-generated pages

Translating Tango tags in Dreamweaver

Designing with example data

Inserting Tango code through Objects

✦ ✦ ✦ ✦

After you've been immersed in Web development for a while, it's easy to forget that HTML is not necessarily the best environment in which to build an application. The most universal, yes, but certainly not the fastest or the most scalable. Tango has a slightly different solution — why not use a compiled program to generate the HTML as needed? Tango Application Files, recognizable by their `.taf` file extension, are compiled files that are quickly run by the Tango Server. The Tango Server can connect to any ODBC-compliant database, as well as Oracle-specific ones; there's even a special version of Tango for FileMaker databases.

Tango's parent company, Pervasive Software, partnered with Macromedia to deliver a dynamic page solution for Dreamweaver that fits the Tango environment well. Tango Application Files are built in the Tango Editor, which includes various rapid-development tools for automating the process. A number of these tools, such as the Search Builder and New Record Builder, automatically generate HTML forms integrated with the requested database information. These HTML forms can then be easily customized in Dreamweaver for inclusion in your Web site.

Tango uses a series of what it calls *meta tags* that are embedded in the HTML it generates. These meta tags (not to be confused with the HTML `<meta>` tags) always begin with an @ sign, as in `<@if>`. When the Tango Server processes a meta tag, the resulting information is integrated with the HTML and returned to the Web server to be sent back to the browser.

Tango has broken down Web interactivity into its key component parts. In Tango vernacular, any server request — whether to access a database or send out e-mail — is referred to as an *action*. Each action has a limited number of responses and each response corresponds to an HTML page. As an example, let's see how Tango handles a search query:

1. In the Tango Editor, shown in Figure 39-1, you specify the data source you'd like to work with and choose which fields of that data source the user can query.

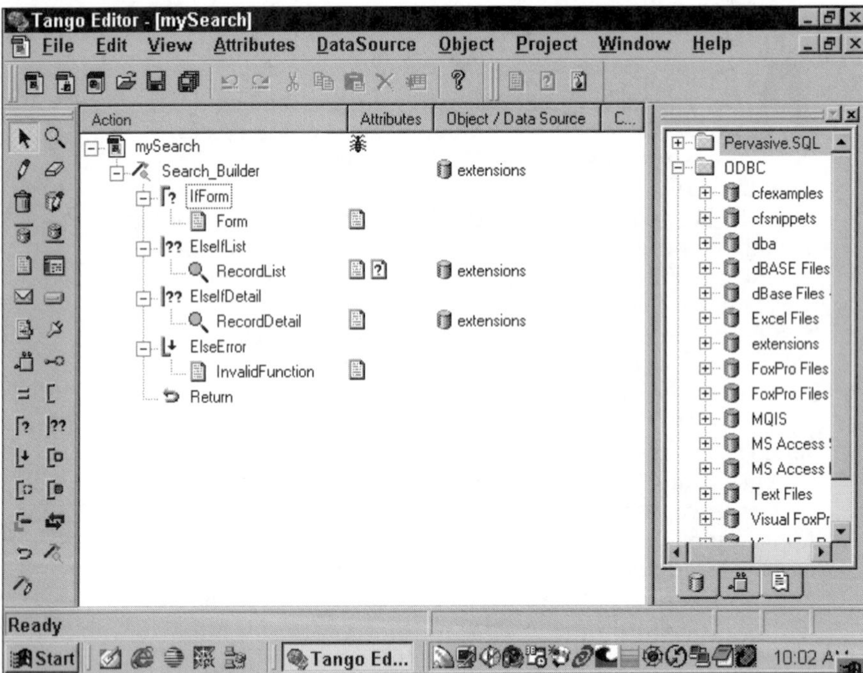

Figure 39-1: Database back ends are developed in the Tango Editor, shown here. The front end, seen by the user, is modified in Dreamweaver.

The form also contains a Submit button and, optionally, a Reset button.

2. You choose which fields from the data source are to be displayed in the record list, as well as any grouping or sorting required.

   Tango builds three different HTML files:

   - The `Results` HTML page, which contains a table of the matches from the specified criteria, and links to additional pages of records, if necessary
   - The `No Results` HTML page, which displays a message indicating that no matching records were found; and a link enabling the user to search again

- The `Error` HTML page, which informs the user of an error encountered when processing the search

3. The Tango Application File can now be saved and run.

Tango builds an HTML page that includes a form to accept the query input. As you might expect, the HTML pages automatically built by Tango are pretty plain — very much "just the facts." Naturally, this is where Dreamweaver comes in. Each of these HTML files can be brought into Dreamweaver, where you can modify their look and feel to integrate them completely into your Web site. Then, the enhanced HTML files are linked back in Tango and saved as part of the Tango Application File. Now, when the `.taf` files are run, you get the power of Tango and the style of Dreamweaver.

Working with Tango and Dreamweaver

Tango has implemented a very robust integration with Dreamweaver. Just how robust? Here's what you get when you install the Tango extension:

✦ Three different translators, including one that permits you to view sample data directly in Dreamweaver

✦ A third-party tag database file that describes 161 Tango meta tags with 25 different icons

✦ Two Property Inspectors — one for conditional tags, such as `<@if>`, and a generic one for all other Tango meta tags

✦ Nine Tango objects, capable of inserting virtually any Tango meta tag or configuration variable

The Tango extension is available on Pervasive's Web site (`www.pervasive.com`). The installation is straightforward. After downloading the Tango file, uncompress the file and double-click the executable to begin the installation. Follow the onscreen prompts and start Dreamweaver.

You have several methods for using the two programs together. One of the best ways I've found is to store the HTML files separately from the Tango Application Files. These files are then accessible for modification by Dreamweaver and inclusion in the Tango Editor. Follow these steps to set up this structure:

1. Use the Tango Editor to make the initial database connection and generate the basic HTML forms.

2. Double-click any HTML form to open its editing window in Tango.

3. From the Tango menus, select the section of the page you wish to copy—typically the <body> section—and then choose Edit ➪ Copy.
4. Switch to Dreamweaver and open a new document, if one is not already available.
5. In Dreamweaver, choose Edit ➪ Paste.

When creating its HTML pages, Tango inserts a doctype declaration before the opening <html> tag. This declaration is used by browsers to determine HTML compatibility at the top of the document. It appears as follows: <!DOCTYPE HTML PUBLIC "-//W3C//DTD HTML 3.2//EN">. If you select the entire Tango HTML document and then paste that code in Dreamweaver's Document window, Dreamweaver inserts this declaration in the wrong location, right after the <body> tag. While this placement is generally ignored by browsers, it can be a potential problem.

You can avoid this situation in two ways. First, copy just the contents of the <body> tag and paste them into Dreamweaver's Document window. Second, after copying all the code in Tango, open Dreamweaver's HTML Source Inspector, and then select all of the existing code and replace it by choosing Paste from the context menu. This ensures that no code is improperly placed.

6. Save this file in Dreamweaver by choosing File ➪ Save.

   Generally, HTML files should be stored in the same folder as or in a subfolder of the Tango Application File.
7. Make any desired modifications in Dreamweaver and resave the file when you're done.
8. Return to the Tango Editor and replace all the HTML in the editor with a link to the file using Tango's <@include> and <@appfilepath> meta tags, as follows:

   ```
   <@include file="<@appfilepath>myResults.htm">
   ```

   Note that the file attribute is capable of mixing meta tags and literal text. The <@appfilepath> meta tag returns the file path for the current application file.
9. Repeat Steps 2–9 for any other HTML file generated by Tango that you want to modify in Dreamweaver.

Now, you—or another member of your team—can continue developing the database application while the front end is being altered in Dreamweaver. Figure 39-2 shows two HTML files for a search page side by side; on the left is the original page as generated by Tango, with all the necessary database elements in place; and on the right is the same page after being modified in Dreamweaver. Because this modified page is now linked to the Tango Application File, it will be called when the application is run.

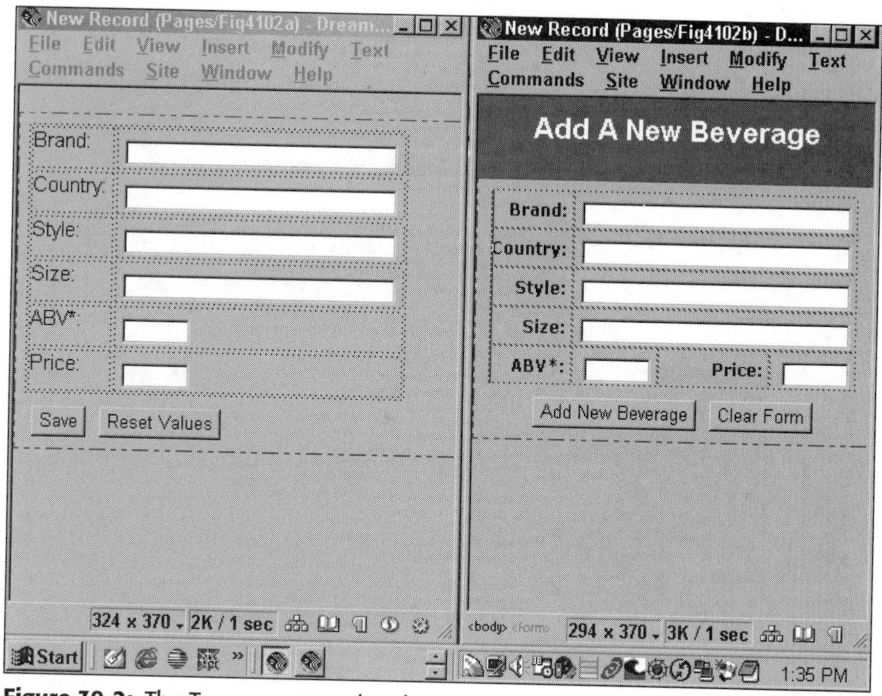

Figure 39-2: The Tango-generated code on the left was transformed into the page on the right in Dreamweaver.

Setting up the Tango Translators

To gain the full effects of the Dreamweaver-Tango integration, you have to make sure the translators are enabled. Translator control is handled through the Translator panel in Dreamweaver's Preferences. Generally, you want the translators to do their job every time any sort of modification occurs on the page. This generalization is certainly true with two out of three of the Tango translators. However, with one of the translators — the Sample Data Translator — it's best to leave off automatic translation; the Sample Data Translator is invoked on an as-needed basis.

By default, the Tango translators are set to work as described in the previous paragraph during installation. To ensure that the Tango translators are set appropriately, follow these steps:

1. Choose Edit ➪ Preferences.
2. In the Preferences dialog box, choose the Translation category, shown in Figure 39-3.
3. From the Translation panel, highlight Tango — Add Attributes Names in the Translators list.

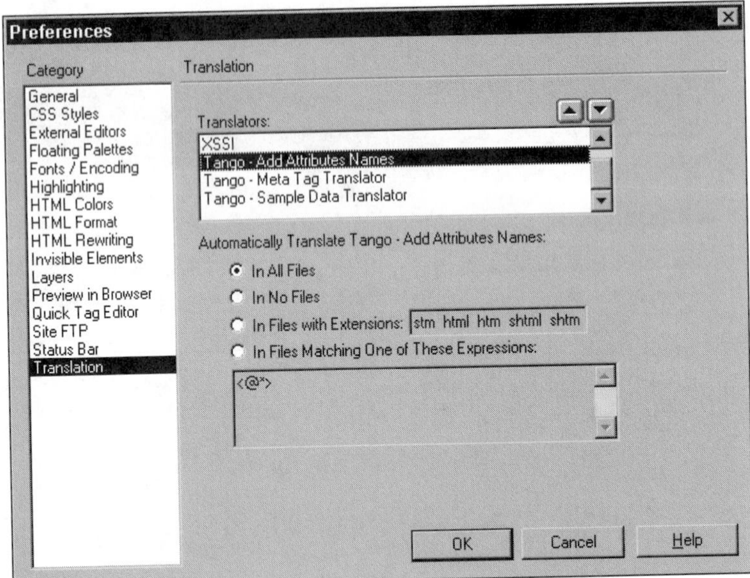

Figure 39-3: Adjust Tango translator settings in the Translation panel of the Preferences dialog box.

4. Select In All Files as the Automatically Translate Tango—Add Attributes Names option.
5. Repeat Steps 3 and 4 for the Tango—Meta Tag Translator.
6. Make sure that the Automatically Translate option for Tango Sample Data Translator is set to In No Files.
7. Click OK when you're done.

Applying the Tango Sample Data Translator

Normally, after you've modified your Tango-generated page in Dreamweaver, you'd view the `.taf` file through the Tango Server in a browser. After processing both the Tango meta tags and the HTML, the Tango Server sends the browser a completed HTML page with the requested data integrated. This is an obvious requirement for finalized pages. However, the Web designer only needs to see an example of the data embedded in the page to complete the job. The Tango Sample Data Translator temporarily pulls in example data and populates the various fields implemented on the page. The command is invoked by choosing Modify ➪ Translate ➪ Tango Sample Data Translator.

Aside from the translator, two other elements are necessary to make the example data appear in Dreamweaver: the Sample Data file and the Sample Data attributes. The Sample Data file is an XML file that lists the data to be presented in

Dreamweaver. Three different data types can be specified: text, numeric, or date. These data types are later used to insert the proper kind of information in the example data showing in Dreamweaver.

The Sample Data file is named tangosampledata.xml and is stored in the Configuration/Tango folder. Regardless of the number of different Tango applications, you can have only one Sample Data file per system. However, the system is flexible enough to provide example data for a range of applications. The XML file follows this format:

```
<tangosampledata>
  <sampledata type="typeData" value="valueData"/>
</tangosampledata>
```

where the possible values for *typeData* are `"text"`, `"numeric"`, and `"date"`; and *valueData* is any string. For example, let's say your Tango application returns a list of contacts and their phone numbers. Such information is always returned in tables, with each column holding a specific field — for this example, we'll presume a four-column table, like that depicted in Figure 39-4 — with column headings Record #, First Name, Last Name, and CustomerID.

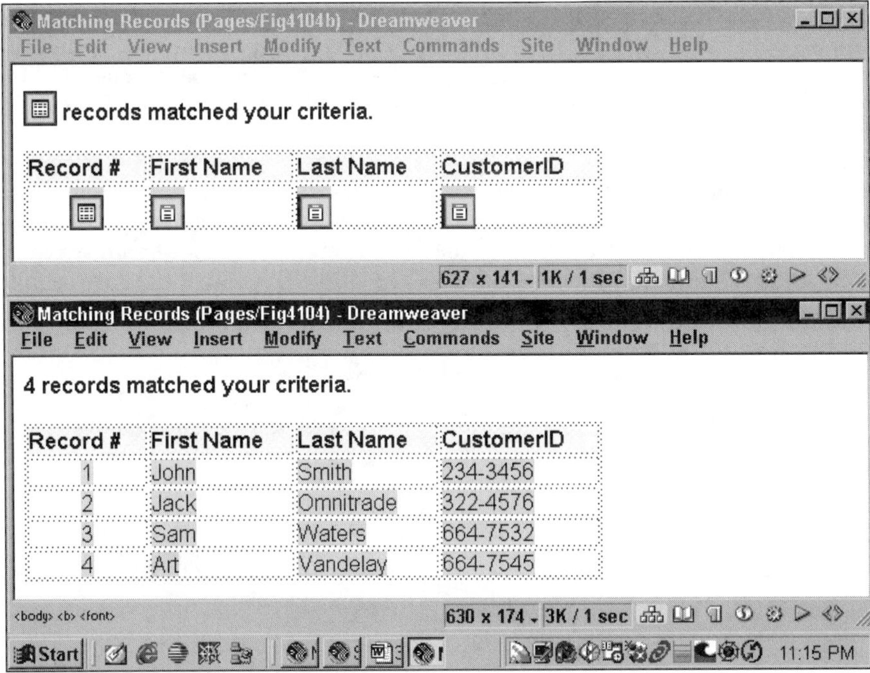

Figure 39-4: Tango's Sample Data feature simulates database output at the design stage. The top screen shows the untranslated page with the Tango icons, and the bottom screen shows the same page after the Sample Data Translator has been called.

The Tango Sample Data Translator reads the XML information sequentially, according to type, so the sampledatafile.xml would read as follows:

```
<tangosampledata>
  <sampledata type="text" value="John"/>
  <sampledata type="text" value="Smith"/>
  <sampledata type="numeric" value="234-3456"/>
  <sampledata type="text" value="Jack"/>
  <sampledata type="text" value="Omnitrade"/>
  <sampledata type="numeric" value="322-4576"/>
  <sampledata type="text" value="Sam"/>
  <sampledata type="text" value="Waters"/>
  <sampledata type="numeric" value="664-7532"/>
  <sampledata type="text" value="Art"/>
  <sampledata type="text" value="Vandelay"/>
  <sampledata type="numeric" value="664-7545"/>
</tangosampledata>
```

If you don't mind repeating the same data over and over again, you could limit the number of <sampledata> tags to the number of fields being filled. The Tango Sample Data Translator loops through the data to fill the fields the required number of times.

In the example, you'll notice that while four fields exist, I've presented example data for only three of them. The first field, Record #, is automatically generated by Tango through the <@currow> meta tag. Values are automatically generated for several other Tango meta tags, including <@absrow>, <@curcol>, <@numrows>, and <@numcols>.

The Sample Data attributes provide the link to the tags rendered in Dreamweaver. When the translator is run, the attributes establish the guidelines for Dreamweaver to integrate the sample data file information, essentially telling Dreamweaver where to put what kind of data and how much. The Sample Data attributes are as follows:

Attribute	*Tag Used In*	*Description*
samptype	<@col> or <@column>	Sets the sample data type to either text, numeric, or date
samplength	<@col> or <@column>	Determines the length of the sample data field
sampnumcols	<@cols>	Sets the number of columns of sample data to display

Attribute	Tag Used In	Description
sampnumrows	<@rows>	Sets the number of rows of sample data to display
samprownum	<@startrow>	Sets a value to represent the starting record number
samptotalrows	<@totalrows>	Sets a value representing the total number of rows to be displayed as part of the sample data

Currently, the Sample Data attributes must be coded by hand in the HTML Source Inspector or your favorite HTML editor. The following code generates the page seen previously in Figure 39-4, with the Sample Data attributes in bold:

```
<html>
<head>
<title>Matching Records</title>
</head>
<body bgcolor="#FFFFFF">
<b><font face="Arial, Helvetica, sans-serif"><@totalrows samptotalrows=4>
records
matched your criteria. </font></b>
<P>
<table border=0>
  <tr valign="top" align="left" bgcolor="#FFFFCC">
    <td><b>Record #</b></td>
    <td><b>First Name</b></td>
    <td><b>Last Name</b></td>
    <td><b>CustomerID</b></td>
  </tr>
  <@rows sampnumrows=4>
  <tr valign="top">
    <td>
      <div align="center"><font face="Arial, Helvetica, sans-serif"><@currow>
</font></div>
    </td>
    <td><font face="Arial, Helvetica, sans-serif"><@col name="Employees.
FirstName" samptype="text" samplength="15"></font></td>
    <td><font face="Arial, Helvetica, sans-serif"><@col name="Employees.
LastName" samptype="text" samplength="15"></font></td>
    <td><font face="Arial, Helvetica, sans-serif"><@col name="Employees.Phone"
samptype="numeric" samplength="11"></font></td>
  </tr>
  </@rows>
</table>
</body>
</html>
```

While the Sample Data Translator is running, you can make changes to any part of the page that does not involve sample data. This facility enables you to design your page around a representative table. To stop the Sample Data Translator, choose Commands ➪ Tango – Untranslate Sample Data.

You can also stop the Sample Data Translator from running by selecting the table containing the sample data and attempting to resize it or make any other change.

Understanding the Tango Meta Tags and Property Inspectors

As of this writing, 161 Tango meta tags are defined in the Third Party Tags XML file. In most cases, any tag created in the Tango Editor will be recognized by Dreamweaver and rendered either with an icon or with its contents displayed. In some cases, as with `<@ifshort>` and `<@scriptshort>`, a tag is used only in Dreamweaver and is automatically translated for the Tango editor when the document is saved in Dreamweaver.

When a particular Tango meta tag is selected, its custom Property Inspector is made available. Four different custom Tango Property Inspectors are available:

✦ **Meta tag** details the attributes and values of most Tango meta tags. Selecting the parameter from the Attribute list displays the corresponding equivalence in the Value text box. Values can be modified in the Property Inspector.

✦ **@if** lists the components of an `<@if>` meta tag: the expression to evaluate and the statements to execute if the expression proves to be true.

✦ **@ifempty** describes the parts of an `<@ifempty>` tag; if a value is an empty string, the supplied string is inserted.

✦ **@ifequal** details the sections of an `<@ifequal>` tag; if `Value1` is equal to `Value2`, the specified string is included.

The conditional Property Inspectors, `@if`, `@ifempty`, and `@ifequal`, enable you to view included `@else` and `@elseif` clauses as well. Choosing a different option from the drop-down list on the Property Inspector displays the appropriate interface.

Inserting Tango Objects

All the Tango code applied in Dreamweaver doesn't have to come from the Tango Editor. The Tango extensions include nine objects that enable you to insert any Tango meta tag, as well as set variables or pull data from database results. After you install the Tango extensions, you can find all objects (described in Table 39-1) on the Tango panel of the Objects Palette. After the objects are inserted in Dreamweaver, you can modify them using the Tango Property Inspectors or through the HTML Source Inspector.

Table 39-1
Tango Objects

Object	*Description*
Insert Action Result Item	Used to reference data returned from an executed action, such as a search.
Insert Current Date or Time	Inserts the current date, time, or timestamp in a given format.
Insert Form Field or URL Argument	Returns the name of a form field or URL argument sent to a Tango Application File.
Insert `@if`	Sets up an `if` conditional statement. A series of statements are executed should a specified expression prove true.
Insert `@if empty`	Inserts an `ifempty` conditional statement. If the expression is true, one statement is inserted; otherwise, another one is included.
Insert `@if equal`	Inserts an `ifequal` conditional statement. If the given value is an empty string, one statement is inserted; otherwise, another one is included.
Insert Request Parameter	Returns one of eight different environmental variables from the server, including Client Name, Client Domain, IP Address, Server Address, Server Port, Referer Page URL, and Method.
Insert Variable	Sets a variable to a specified scope (Local, User, Cookie, Domain, or System). If the variable is an array, the row and column can be specified.
Insert Tango Meta Tag	Enables you to insert any Tango meta tag.

The Action Result Item object

When processing active pages, the fewer trips to the server the better. The Action Result Item gives you access to data returned in the previous Tango action or server request, without processing a new request. Each Action Result Item object returns the value of any one item found in the initial row of returned data; you specify which item by name and the column in which the data is found.

Tip: While the `<@actionresult>` tag, used by the Insert Action Result Item object, retrieves data only from the first row of the current action, you can specify other rows by setting the `resultSet` variable to another number.

To use the Action Result Item object, follow these steps:

1. Place your cursor where you'd like the Action Result Item to appear and choose the Insert Action Result Item object from the Tango panel of the Objects palette.

   The Insert Action Result Item dialog box, shown in Figure 39-5, appears.

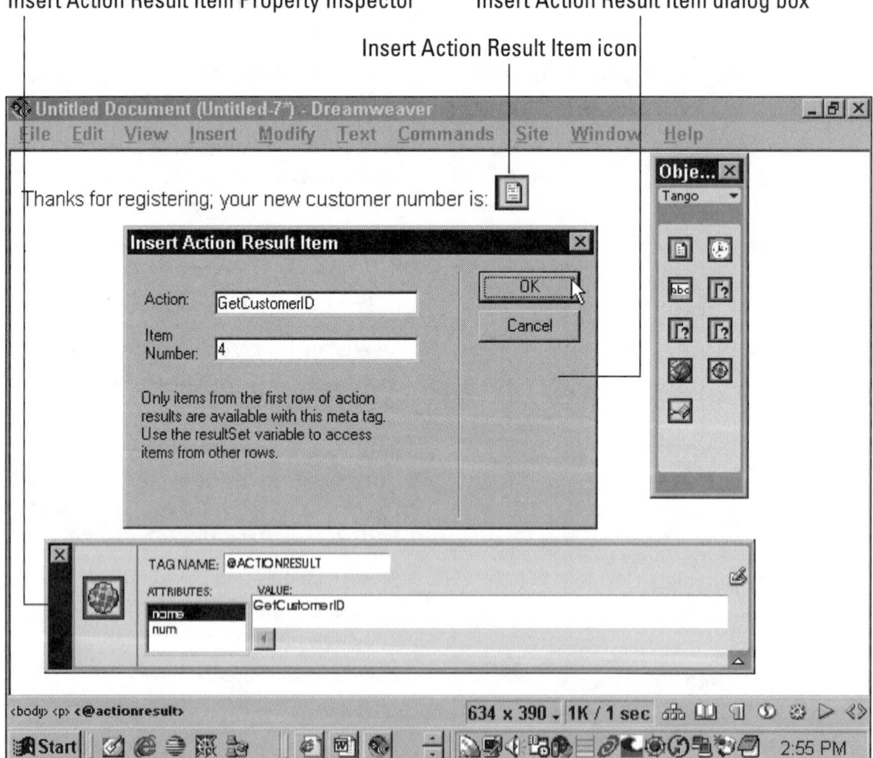

Figure 39-5: Include information from a previously run Tango action with the Insert Action Result Item object.

2. Enter the name of the action that generated the desired result in the Action field.

3. Enter the number of the column in which the desired result appears in the Item Number field.

Remember that unless a `resultSet` variable specifies a different row, only results from the first row are available.

4. Click OK when you're done.

The Current Date or Time object

Tango has a full range of time and date functions. The most commonly used formats are available through the Insert Current Date or Time object. The corresponding dialog box offers three different general functions: Date, Time, and Timestamp (which combines both the current date and time). A wide range of formats is available; if no format is specified, the format is dictated by the Tango server's configuration variables. By default, these variables are set so that March 31, 1984, at 1:05 p.m. would be shown as follows:

✦ **Date:** 03/31/1984

✦ **Time:** 13:05:00

✦ **Timestamp:** 03/31/1984 13:05:00

To use the Insert Current Date or Time object, follow these steps:

1. Place your cursor where you'd like the Current Date or Time object to appear and choose the object from the Tango panel of the Objects palette.

   The Insert Current Date or Time dialog box, shown in Figure 39-6, appears.

2. Select the Current date, Current time, or Current timestamp option.
3. Select the desired format, if any, from the Format option list.
4. Click OK when you're done.

Tip

Tango uses a series of codes preceded by percent signs to specify the different types of formats. For example, the date format for 31 March 1984 is `%d %B %Y`. After you've used the object, when you select the Current Date or Time icon, the format codes appear in the Property Inspector. If you're not familiar with the codes, change the format by deleting the original Current Date or Time object and inserting a new one.

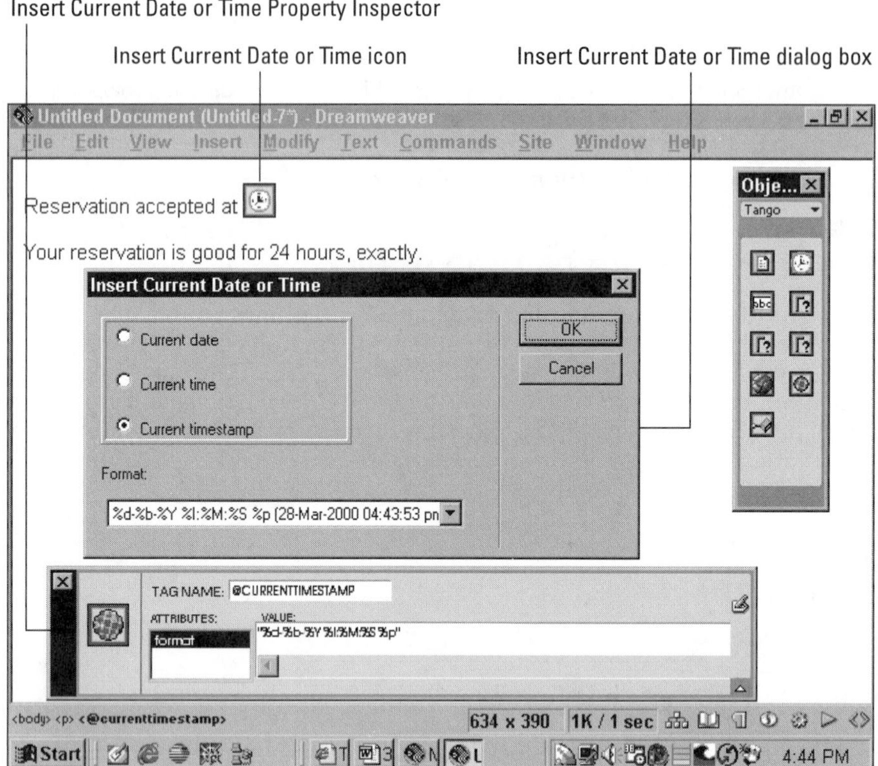

Figure 39-6: Choose from fourteen date formats, four time formats, or eight timestamp formats with the Tango Current Date or Time object.

The Form Field or URL Argument object

Integrating a user's responses is a key concept in building active pages. Whether you're verifying a list selection or reiterating search criteria, Tango offers this facility in Dreamweaver through the Form Field or URL Argument object. On the Web, information from a form is passed either using the Get or Post method. The Post method sends the data in a text packet where each form field is uniquely identified with its corresponding value. The Get method appends a question mark to the linking URL, followed by a series of name=value pairs. The Form Field or URL Argument gives you the option to specify the method used, or to read the value regardless. The information can either be in the form of a single value, such as an entry in a text field, or in an array of values, as when a multiple select list is employed.

To use the Form Field or URL Argument object, follow these steps:

1. Position your cursor where you'd like the Form Field or URL Argument object to appear and choose the object from the Tango panel of the Objects palette.

   The Insert Form Field or URL Argument dialog box, shown in Figure 39-7, is displayed.

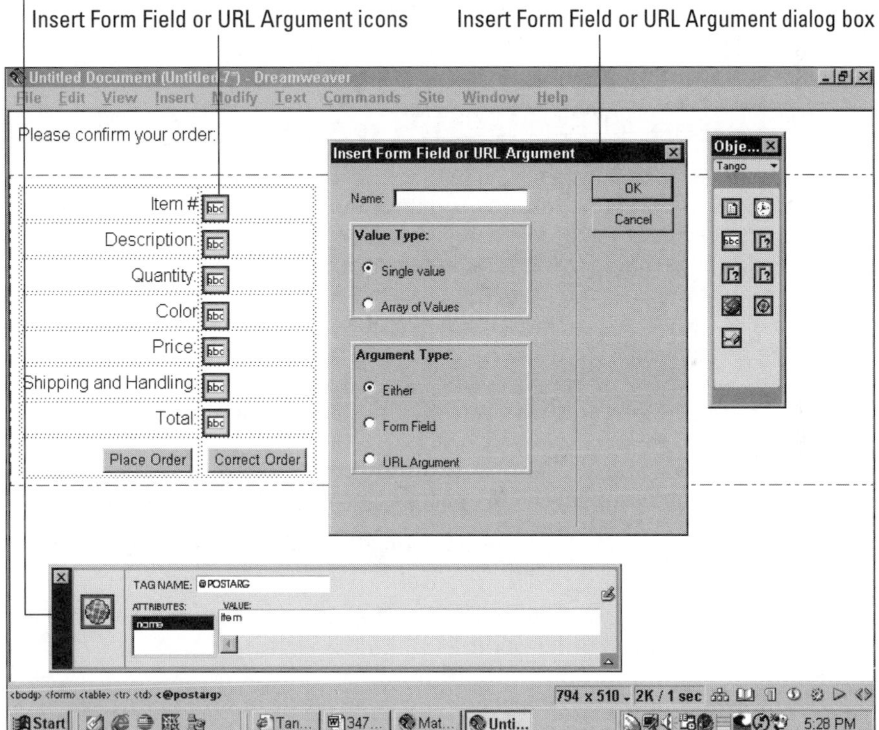

Figure 39-7: Insert values entered by a user on a previous form through the Insert Form Field or URL Argument object.

2. Enter the name of the form field or URL argument in the Name field of the dialog box.

   The name can either be a literal value (such as `firstname`), a value-returning meta tag, or a combination of both.

3. Select whether a single value or an array of values is required from the Value Type options.

4. Choose the Argument Type option:
   - **Either** inserts an `<@arg>` meta tag and can be used with either a form field or a URL type argument.
   - **Form Field** inserts a `<@searcharg>` meta tag.
   - **URL Argument** inserts a `<@postarg>` meta tag.
5. Click OK when you're done.

If you're expecting more than one value, be sure to select the Array option under the Value Type options. By default, Tango returns only the first argument in a series unless an array is specified.

The Insert @IF, @IFEMPTY, and @IFEQUAL objects

You can use conditional statements to insert particular code or to perform a certain action when a stated condition is true. Tango offers three objects for constructing conditional statements in Dreamweaver: `@if`, `@ifempty`, and `@ifequal`. Each of these objects enables you to include alternative responses, known as *Else* conditions. For example, you could test to see if a cookie is found on the user's system and, if so, greet the user with his or her name. If no cookie if detected, the user might be redirected to a sign-up screen to register for the site.

All three objects operate in basically the same fashion:

✦ In the object's dialog box, enter the condition to be tested. This condition could compare a variable and a value or look to see if a value currently exists.

✦ Enter the HTML to be inserted or the Tango meta tags to be executed if the condition proves true.

✦ Optionally, add conditional branches to test other conditions — and if true, display or run other code.

The Tango conditional objects offer a great range of flexibility, particularly when it comes to extending the basic condition. After you've declared the initial expression for either an `@if`, `@ifempty`, or `@ifequal` object, a variety of Else conditions can be added: `@elseif`, `@elseifempty`, `@elseifequal`, and/or `@else`. You can use any or all of these conditional branches.

To use one of Tango's conditional objects, follow these steps:

1. Place your cursor where you'd like the conditional code to appear.
2. Select the desired conditional object from the Tango panel of the Object palette.

The buttons for all three conditional objects on the palette have the same appearance, which can make choosing the correct one difficult at times. Hover your mouse pointer over the button to see the identifying ToolTip. You could also change your Dreamweaver Preferences to display both icons and text in the Object palette; you'll find this option in the General category of Preferences.

3. Depending on which conditional object you're inserting, do the following:
   - For `@if`, enter the expression to evaluate in the `EXPR` field.
   - For `@ifempty`, enter the meta tag or literal value to check in the `VALUE` field, as shown in Figure 39-8.
   - For `@ifequal`, enter the two values to compare in `VALUE1` and `VALUE2`. The values can be meta tags, literal values or a combination of both.

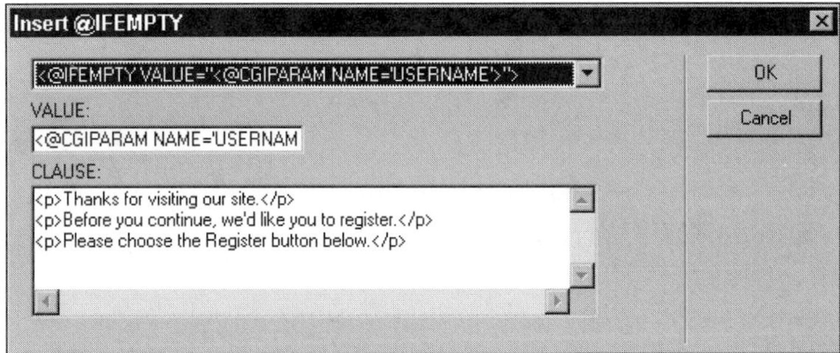

Figure 39-8: The @ifempty object is used here to present a different message to visitors who have not been authenticated by the system (and thus have no value in the Username variable).

4. In the CLAUSE text area, enter the HTML and/or meta tags to be inserted should the condition prove true.
5. To add a conditional Else branch to your object, select the plus (+) button.

   The Add @ELSE dialog box appears, as shown in Figure 39-9.
6. Choose the type of Else condition from the Add option list.
7. Depending on which Else condition you selected, do the following:
   - For `@elseif`, enter the expression to evaluate in the EXPR field.
   - For `@elseifempty`, enter the meta tag or literal value to check in the VALUE field.
   - For `@elseifequal`, enter the two values to compare in VALUE1 and VALUE2. The values can be meta tags, literal values or a combination of both.
   - For `@else`, proceed to the next step.

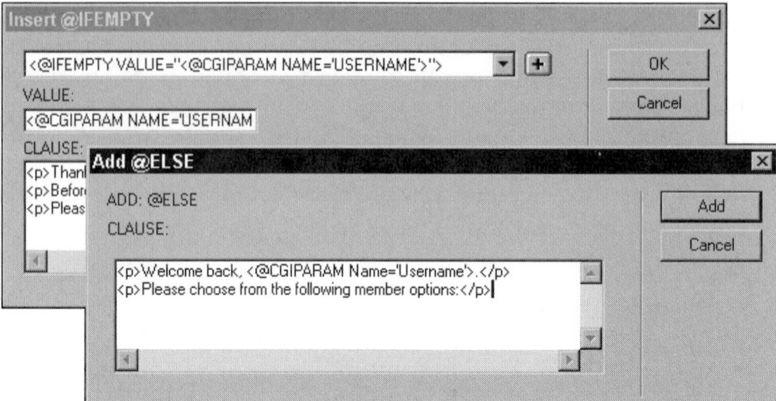

Figure 39-9: With an `@else` conditional branch, authenticated visitors can receive a custom greeting.

8. Enter the HTML code or meta tags to be inserted if the Else condition is met in the CLAUSE text area.
9. Click Add when you're finished with the Else condition.
10. To add additional Else conditions, select the plus button again and repeat Steps 6 through 9.
11. To remove an Else condition, select it from the drop-down list on the @IF, @IFEQUAL, or @IFEMPTY dialog box and choose the minus button.
12. Click OK when you're done.

The conditional statement is represented in Dreamweaver with a highlight behind whichever clause is currently selected. By default, the first clause—where `@if`, `@ifempty`, or `@ifequal` is true—is selected. If the statement has additional Else conditions, the corresponding clause can be displayed in the Document window by selecting the Else clause from the drop-down list in the `@if`, `@ifempty`, or `@ifequal` Property Inspector, as shown in Figure 39-10.

The Insert Request Parameter object

Whenever a user clicks a link, a request is sent to a Web or application server. Along with the URL for the page requested, other information is also sent, including the user's domain, the browser used, and the address for the page containing the link. This information can be incorporated into a Tango page through the Request Parameter object.

The Request Parameter object offers eight different parameters, all of which are inserted as `Name` attributes of Tango's `<@cgiparam>` meta tag. The parameters are detailed in Table 39-2.

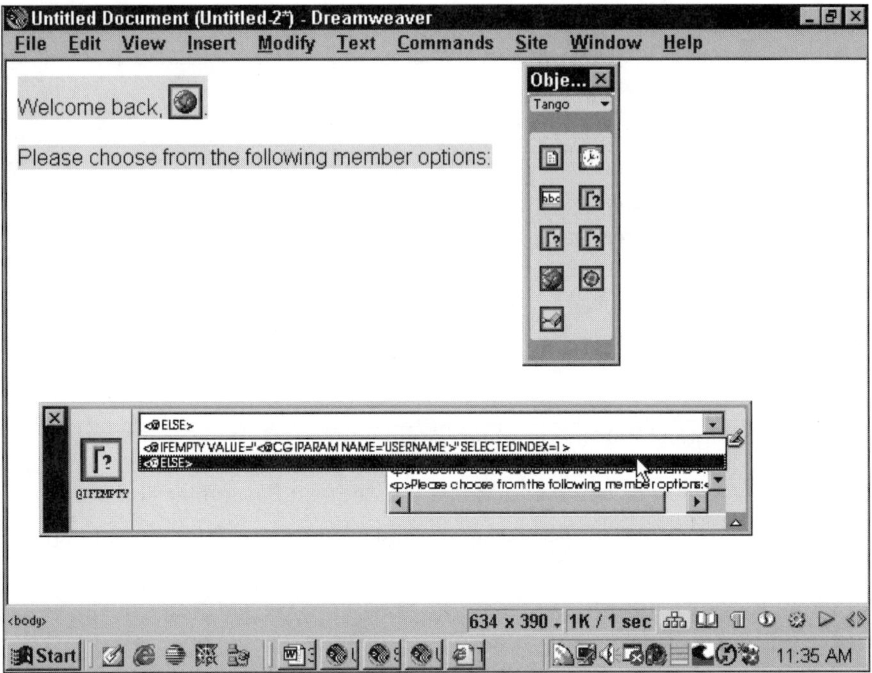

Figure 39-10: Choosing a particular clause in the Tango conditional statement Property Inspector displays the corresponding result.

Table 39-2
Request Parameter Options

Parameter	*Attribute*	*Description*
Client Name	`USERNAME`	The user name, obtained through HTTP authentication, of the user who requested the URL. If the user is not authenticated, this attribute is empty.
Client Domain	`CLIENT_ADDRESS`	The IP address or, if your server is set up for DNS lookups, the user's domain name.
Client IP Address	`CLIENT_IP`	The user's IP address.
Client Browser	`USER_AGENT`	The user's browser.
Server Address	`SERVER_NAME`	The IP address or, if your server is set up for DNS lookups, the domain name of the current server.

Continued

Table 39-2 (continued)

Parameter	*Attribute*	*Description*
Server Port	`SERVER_PORT`	The TCP/IP port on which the Web server is running.
Referer Page URL	`REFERER` (intentionally misspelled for consistent coding)	The URL of the Web page from which the current request was initiated.
Method	`METHOD`	The HTTP request method (either GET or POST) used for the current request.

To include a Request Parameter object, follow these steps:

1. Place your cursor where you'd like the Request Parameter code to appear.
2. Select the Insert Request Parameter object from the Tango panel of the Object palette.

   The Insert Request Parameter dialog box appears, as shown in Figure 39-11.

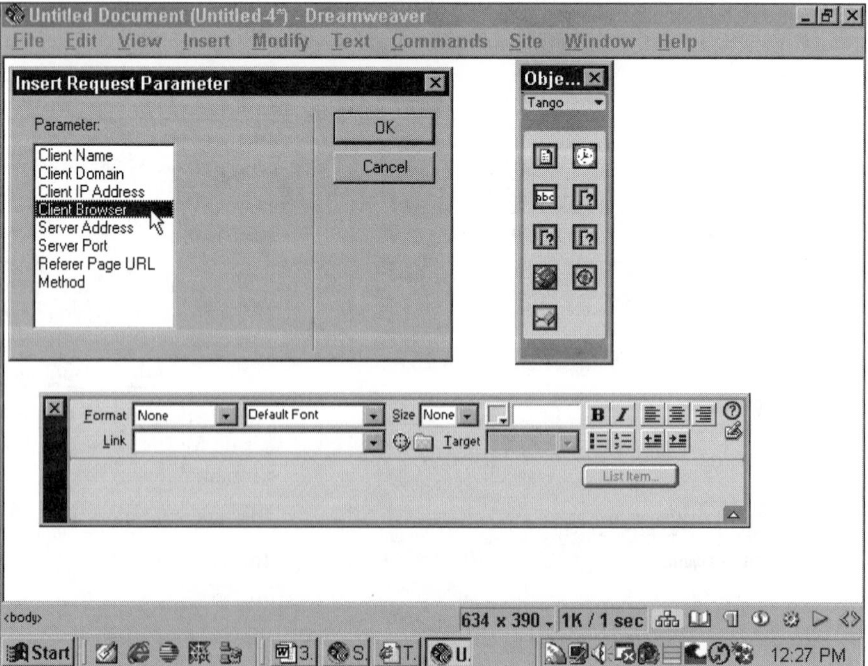

Figure 39-11: Personalize a page by including information about the user through the Tango Request Parameter object.

3. Select the desired attribute from the Parameter list.

Although you can select more than one item from the list, only the first attribute is returned.

4. Click OK when you're done.

The Insert Variable object

Tango variables are retrieved in Dreamweaver through the Insert Variable object. This object enables you to set the scope of the variable as well as work with either single elements or arrays. You can even set a custom scope for a variable, if necessary. The Insert Variable object uses Tango's <@var> meta tag.

To get the value of a variable with the Insert Variable object, follow these steps:

1. Place your cursor where you'd like the Tango variable code to appear.
2. Select the Insert Variable object from the Tango panel of the Object palette.
3. In the Insert Variable dialog box, shown in Figure 39-12, enter the name of the variable in the Name field.

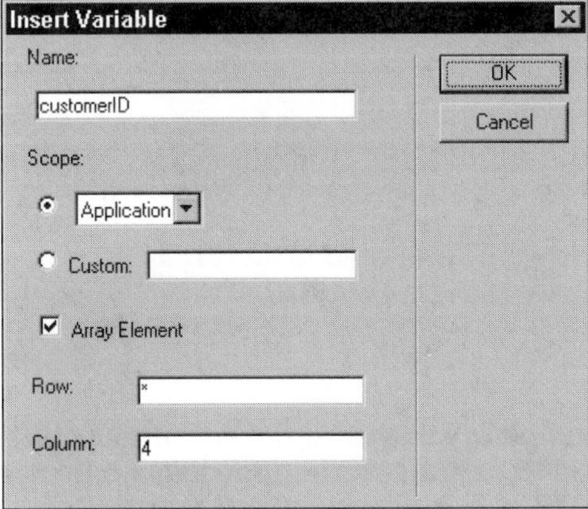

Figure 39-12: Get the values of variables of any scope through the Insert Variable object.

4. Select the scope of the variable from the Scope option list; scope options are Default, Application, Local, Instance, Method, User, Cookie, Domain, and System.

   As an alternative, enter a custom variable scope in the Custom field.

5. If the variable is an array format, check Array Element.

   When Array Element is selected, two additional options become visible, Row and Column. You then use these options to select a portion of the array to retrieve.

6. If the Array Element is selected and you don't wish to retrieve the entire array, enter a number in either (or both) the Column and Row fields. To retrieve all the array elements in a Column or Row, enter an asterisk (*).

7. Click OK when you're done.

The Tango Meta Tag object

For all the tags not available through the previously covered objects, use the Tango Meta Tag object. The Tango Meta Tag object provides a handy way for you to enter code — both Tango-specific and generic HTML — directly without opening the HTML Source Inspector. The meta tags must be entered completely formed because no additional formatting is applied when the code is inserted. In other words, to insert a meta tag such as `@random`, you have to enter

```
<@RANDOM>
```

in the Tango Meta Tag to insert text area, shown in Figure 39-13. Just select the Insert Tango Meta Tag object to open the dialog box and click OK after you've entered your code.

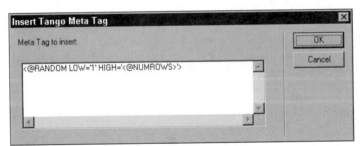

Figure 39-13: Use the Tango Meta Tag object to enter any combination of HTML and Tango code.

Once you insert the meta tag into the Dreamweaver document, selecting it displays one of 22 custom Tango icons. Selecting the icon, in turn, displays the meta tag's attributes in the Tango Property Inspector, where existing attributes can be altered.

While you can only change attributes through the Tango Property Inspector, you could use Dreamweaver's Quick Tag Editor to add new attributes. Once added, the parameters are displayed in the Property Inspector and can be adjusted there, if desired.

Summary

Tango brings a great deal to the Web connectivity table: a full featured application development environment and a robust SQL engine. The Tango Objects for Dreamweaver package is one of the most complete extension packages yet developed and goes a long way toward smoothing the workflow between Web page layout and back-end design. When working with Tango and Dreamweaver, remember these key elements:

✦ Pervasive's Tango uses the Tango Editor to build the database-connected heart of an HTML page, which can then be enhanced and integrated into a Web site with Dreamweaver.

✦ The Tango extensions include a full array of Property Inspectors, objects, third-party tags, and translators to ease design chores.

✦ After developing your basic database pages in the Tango Editor, bring them into Dreamweaver for advanced layout. Then, when you're done, link the Dreamweaver HTML files to the Tango Application File by using Tango's `<@include>` meta tag.

✦ Use the Tango Sample Data Translator to lay out your page with representative database output. You can edit the XML file to add sample data pertinent to your own projects.

✦ Tango uses nine different objects, found on the Tango panel of the Objects palette, for inserting Tango meta tags and their attributes. Once inserted, the meta tags are editable through the custom Property Inspectors.

The next chapter shows you how you can use Dreamweaver to build e-commerce sites hosted by leading vendors.

✦ ✦ ✦

P A R T

Extending Dreamweaver

✦ ✦ ✦ ✦

In This Part

✦ ✦ ✦ ✦

Weaving a Wireless Web

In This Chapter

Wireless markup fundamentals

Building a WML deck

Creating Wireless Content

Working with WBMP graphics

Accepting input over the phone

Testing your cards

Just as the wonders promised by broadband access are being realized, another revolution — at the opposite end of the spectrum — is underway. How could a technology restricted by a tiny screen with limited resolution, low-powered CPUs and a minimal connection speed possibly succeed? By offering mobility and access, that's how. Cellular phones have progressed rapidly since their introduction, both in pervasiveness and features. The feature-set has recently expanded to include communication over the World Wide Web with the development of the Wireless Application Protocol and the Wireless Markup Language.

The Wireless Markup Language (WML) is an application of Extensible Markup Language (XML) which is becoming increasingly familiar to many developers. Much like HTML, WML is used to create pages of content — text, images, and hyperlinks — readable on wireless devices such as mobile phones, pagers, and personal digital assistants (PDAs). A leader in the wireless industry, Nokia, has created an extension to Dreamweaver for building WML content.

While not all Web pages could or should be converted from HTML to WML, much information is well-suited to the wireless Web. As you'll see throughout this chapter, the Nokia WML Extensions to Dreamweaver enable the designer to make the most of this new compact medium. Aside from an intuitive layout engine in the WML Extensions based on Dreamweaver layers, there's even a Preview in Phone command so you can view your creations on a simulated cell phone. As comedian Steve Martin used to say, "Let's get small!"

Understanding WAP and WML

The special characteristics of the wireless medium demand special delivery mechanisms. Just as Hypertext Protocol (HTTP) is used to serve Web pages to browsers, the Wireless Application Protocol (WAP) handles communication to wireless devices. The key language of WAP is Wireless Markup Language or WML.

As noted earlier, WML is an XML application and thus uses XML syntax. A page of WML is identified by the following required lines of code:

```
<?xml version="1.0"?>
<!DOCTYPE wml PUBLIC "-//WAPFORUM//DTD WML 1.1//EN"
"http://www.wapforum.org/DTD/wml_1.1.xml">
```

The WapForum Web address (www.wapforum.org) is a good one for more detailed information about Wireless Application Protocol and WML.

Like other XML languages, WML indicates some tags slightly differently than HTML. While WML elements containing content use both opening and closing tags in the same way as HTML, an empty tag does not. An empty tag, you'll remember, is one that does not surround any text, like the HTML <br> tag. The same tag in WML is represented as <br/> with a slash just before the closing delimiter.

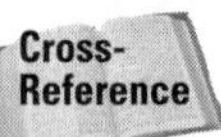

For greater detail about XML syntax, see Chapter 30.

Within WML tags, you should follow a few important rules:

- ✦ All attributes must be in lowercase. For example <card id="firstCard"> is acceptable, but <card ID="firstCard"> is not.
- ✦ All attribute values must be quoted with either single or double quotes.
- ✦ Variables can be specified with a leading dollar sign, such as $amount. To display a dollar sign onscreen, use two dollar signs. For example:

```
<p>The total is $$100.00.</p>
```

A WML page has a different structure than an HTML page. After the initial two lines—one that declares the page to be an XML document and the other specifying the document type as WML, the balance of the page is bracketed by a <wml>...</wml> tag pair. No <html> or <body> tags exist. Instead, the displayed contents of the document are contained within <card>...</card> tag pairs. Here's the basic layout for a WML page:

```
<?xml version="1.0"?>
<!DOCTYPE wml PUBLIC "-//WAPFORUM//DTD WML 1.1//EN"
"http://www.wapforum.org/DTD/wml_1.1.xml">
<wml>
  <card>
```

```
      Displayed content goes here.
    </card>
  </wml>
```

WML pages are referred to as *decks*. Each deck contains one or more displayable screens or *cards*; in WAP, a deck is the smallest unit sent by the server to the requesting user agent, which may be a phone, PDA, or other wireless device. The cards within the decks are distinct—that is, you can't nest one card within another. Each deck may contain one special card called a *template* that defines characteristics for all cards in the deck. For example, a template could define the functionality for a particular function key, so it wouldn't need to be repeated for each card.

To differentiate cards within a deck, each one is named with the id attribute, like this:

```
<card id="first_card">
```

The id attribute is used by one card to reference another within a deck by using a system similar to named anchors. To link to a card in the same deck, a number sign, #, is inserted before the card's name, as in this code example:

```
<card id="first_card">
  Jump to the <a href="#last_card">end</a>
</card>
```

All other links in a card are handled in a similar fashion to standard HTML with either relative or absolute URLs.

Creating a New Deck and Cards

While a fair degree of variation exists in the screen size of wireless devices, one fact is self-evident: they're all small. The maximum display size of the Nokia 7110, a popular model, is 96 pixels wide by 65 pixels high. Rather than try to reduce the Dreamweaver Document window to comparable dimensions, the WML Extensions use precisely sized layers to represent each card in a deck. This type of user interface permits the designer to view several, if not all, of the cards in a deck simultaneously, much like a storyboard.

The Nokia WML Studio is installed via the Extension Manager. After installation, you'll find a new WML menu as well as a WML panel available from the Objects palette.

To create a new deck, choose WML ➪ New WML Deck. This command opens a new WML document and displays the Deck Element and an initial card, as shown in Figure 40-1. The Deck Element contains information about the current deck including the current browser model and the size, in bytes, of the current deck. In addition, the Deck Element enables you to insert and inspect Meta and Access tags, as discussed later in this chapter.

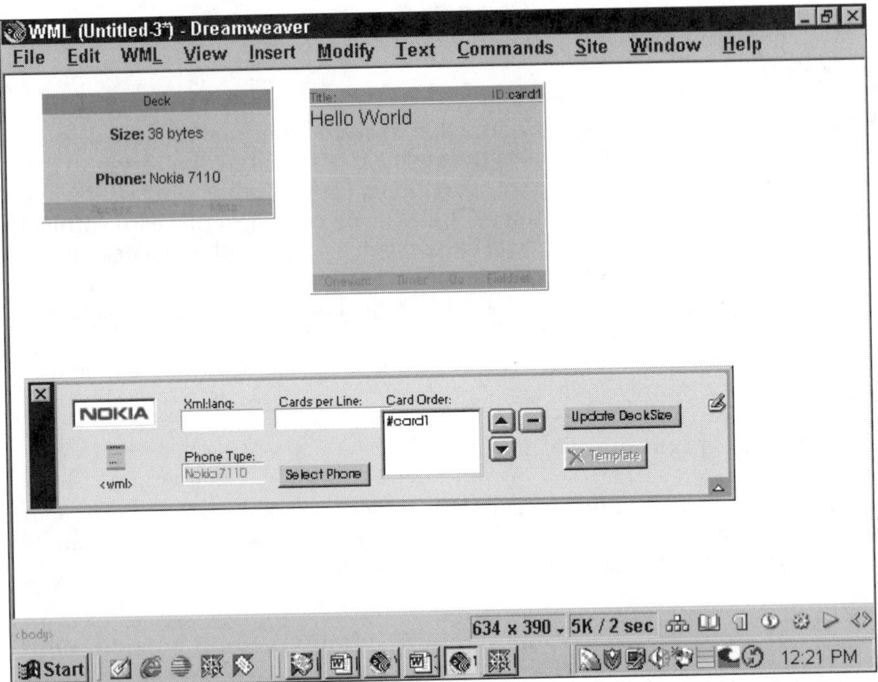

Figure 40-1: The Deck Element shows you at a glance the browser model in use as well as the size of the current deck.

The Size figure refers to the deck's compiled size; unlike HTML, WML files are compiled by the WAP gateway before they are sent to the browser. The deck size is very important because the capacity of the browsers in use — such as phones and other wireless devices — is extremely limited. The Nokia 7110, for example, will not show decks larger than 1,400 bytes. If your deck exceeds the size limitation for the currently selected browser, the Deck Element displays the Size value in red.

The Size values are not calculated automatically, but only when the Update Deck Size button, found on the Deck Property Inspector, is clicked. When this button is clicked, the current deck is processed by a WAP gateway program running in the background. The program returns a precise measurement of the deck size.

In addition to finding the Deck Size, the Deck Property Inspector also has controls for ordering or deleting cards. The Card Order list shows the current arrangement; you can modify the order by selecting a card from the list and choosing the up or down arrows. To delete a card, select its name from the list and click the Remove button.

The Cards Per Line field is used to specify the number of cards Dreamweaver displays in a row. For system resolutions of 640×480 or less, no more than three cards can fit on each row, while for 1,024×768 resolutions, you can show six or more cards, depending on the phone type selected.

Choosing a phone model

The various supported phone models vary in screen size as well as maximum deck size. The screen sizes are reflected in the size of the cards created by Dreamweaver. Here's a breakdown of the supported models and their sizes:

Phone	*Screen Size (in pixels)*
Nokia 6210	120 wide × 70 high
Nokia 6250	130 wide × 80 high
Nokia 7110	140 wide × 90 high
Nokia 7160	140 wide × 90 high
Nokia 7190	140 wide × 90 high

The Nokia 7110 is the default phone model, but you can easily switch to another one. You have two methods to change phone models. You can either first select the Deck Element and then choose the Change Phone Type button or choose WML ➪ Select Phone. With either method, the Select Phone Model dialog box appears, as shown in Figure 40-2. Choose the desired screen size by selecting one of the options from the Phone Model list. For WML screen sizes not listed, choose the Custom option and enter your desired pixel dimensions in the Width and Height fields.

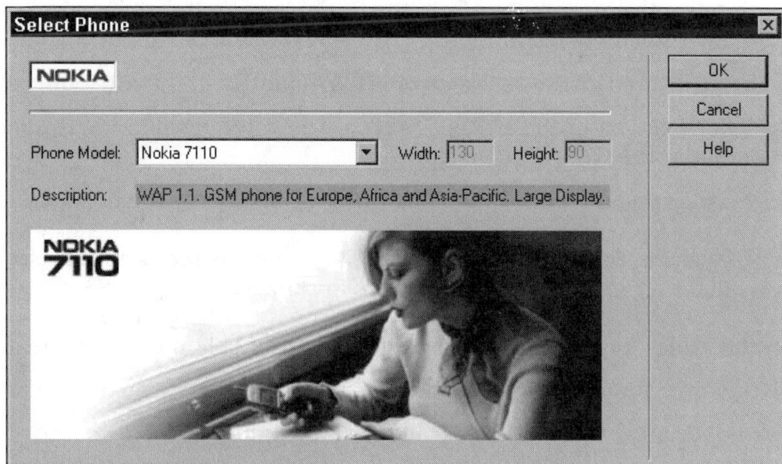

Figure 40-2: Change your card size by selecting a different phone model or choosing the Custom option and entering your own dimensions.

Deck element tags

As noted earlier, the Deck Element offers access to two important tags: Meta and Access. The WML Meta tags are similar to those found in HTML while the Access tags have no parallel. Both tags apply to the overall deck and to all the cards within it. You may have noticed that no `<head>` section exists in a basic WML object. The `<head>` section is automatically created when either a `<meta>` or `<access>` tag is inserted and automatically deleted when neither a `<meta>` or `<access>` tag are in the current document.

WML meta tags

Like HTML `<meta>` tags, WML `<meta>` tags convey information about the overall document. Two types of `<meta>` tags exist: HTTP-Equiv and Name; a `<meta>` tag must have one of these attributes, but not both. The HTTP-Equiv attributes correspond to HTTP headers such as Refresh, Content-Type and Cache-Control. Name attributes are largely used by search engines to index particular pages with values such as Keywords and Description.

With WML, certain meta-information is not intended to be sent to the browser, but rather to be processed by the server. Such `<meta>` tags use the `Forua` attribute set to false to indicate that the tag is server-side only; `Forua`, by the way, is shorthand for "For User Agent," a technical term for the browser.

To insert a WML `<meta>` tag, follow these steps:

1. From the WML panel of the Object palette, choose Insert Meta. Alternatively, you can select the Meta button from the Deck Element, if another `<meta>` tag has already been included in the card, the Insert Meta dialog box opens.
2. Choose the desired attribute, Name or HTTP-Equiv, from the Attribute list.
3. In the Value field, enter the attribute's type. The entered value corresponds to the Content or the HTTP-Equiv value.
4. Select Forua if you intend for the `<meta>` tag to be read by the browser.

Note In most situations, Forua should be selected. If it is not, the server must be set up to strip out the tag before serving the deck to the browser.

5. Enter the values for the HTTP-Equiv or Name attribute in the Content text area.
6. If the Name attribute requires a scheme, enter it in the Scheme text area.

   A *scheme* is similar to a MIME type and describes the type of format used by the document.
7. Click OK when you're done.

Access element

Within WML, access to a particular deck—that is, which other decks can call it—can be restricted to a particular domain or to a particular folder in a certain domain. Some CGI programs use a similar facility to ensure that only pages from the home site are accessing the program; this preserves server resources for those authorized to use them. The WML `<access>` tag performs this function without the use of CGI.

When a browser requests a WML deck, the user agent looks for an `<access>` tag in the requested deck. If one exists, the values in the tag are compared to URL of the requesting browser—in essence, where the link is coming from. Should the requesting URL and the `<access>` values match, the deck is displayed; if not, access is denied. Access can be set to a particular domain, such as `www.idest.com`, or a particular folder on that domain, such as `www.idest.com/dreamweaver`. You can enter the name of a domain or a path or both to restrict viewing.

To establish access control, follow these steps:

1. Choose the Access object from the WML panel of the Objects palette or, if an `<access>` tag is already included, select the Access button from the Deck Element.

   The Access dialog box (see Figure 40-3) is displayed.

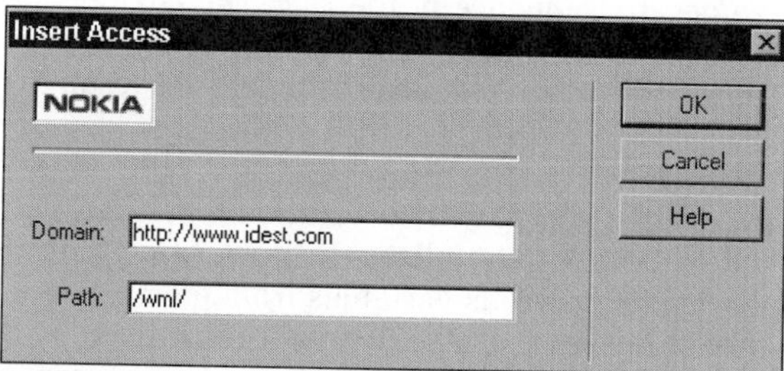

Figure 40-3: Control viewing of your WML decks with the Insert Access object.

2. To limit access to a particular domain, enter it into the Domain field.

   WML looks for a match for the entire domain, not just a portion of the entered value. For example, entering `media.com` does not match `macromedia.com`.

3. To limit access to a particular folder, enter its name in the Path field.

   Tip: Be sure to include any slashes necessary to denote the folder in the Path field, as in `/wml/orders/`.

4. Click OK when you're done.

Adding new cards

You can add new cards at any time in WML Studio. Choose the Card object from the Objects palette to begin the process. The Insert Card dialog box (see Figure 40-4) enables you to insert new events. The events, OnEnterForward, OnEnterBackward, and OnTimer, are discussed later in this chapter.

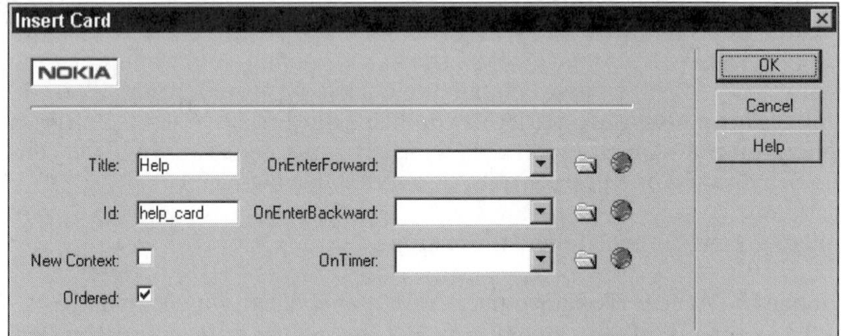

Figure 40-4: Insert as many cards as the wireless model's memory can hold in your deck.

You cannot visually reorder the sequence of the cards. All attempts to drag the card layers to another location are ignored or, in some situations, result in a program crash. Use the Card Order section of the deck Property Inspector to rearrange the card order.

In addition to inserting new events, you have two additional options: Ordered and New Context. The New Context option reinitializes the deck when the card being created is accessed, eliminating all previous variables from memory. The Ordered option adds an attribute that indicates the type of layout to be used by browsers; the `ordered` attribute is referenced if the card contains a series of form elements, such as text fields. If your card contains a series of required fields, enable the Ordered option.

Adding Content to Cards

With WML cards, content is back to the Web basics: text, graphics, and links. Moreover, text is further limited to only one format, `paragraph`, and a handful of markup tags such as `emphasis`, `italic`, and `strong`. Image use is more restricted than with HTML as well — only foreground images are used and a special graphic format, Wireless Bitmap, is required. Links, luckily, work pretty much as expected with the advantage of being easily set to navigate between cards in a deck.

Although the WML cards are presented as Dreamweaver layers, they are not positionable on the screen and cannot be dragged to a new location. Attempting to drag the cards may result in the program unexpectedly quitting.

Each card is presented in the Document window as a presized layer. The size of the layer is determined by the phone model chosen. A card is divided into three regions, as shown in Figure 40-5 — one for title and ID information, one for the displayable content, and one for interactive functions where the code is hidden from the viewer. The title and interactive areas serve as buttons to trigger the various associated Property Inspectors.

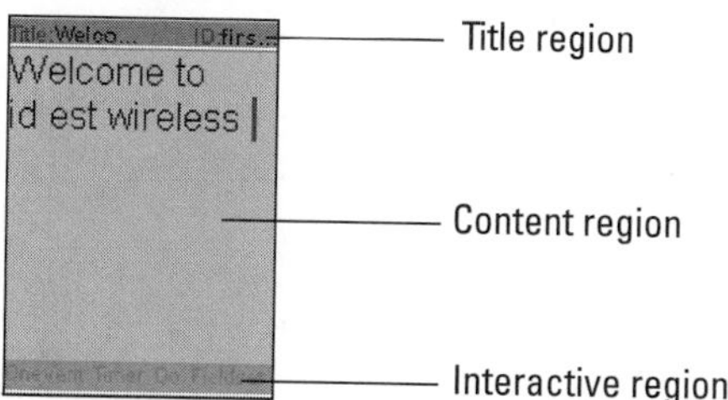

Figure 40-5: Separate regions for title information, the content, and interactive functions make up each card.

Formatting text

Inserting text in a WML card is extremely straightforward: just place the cursor in the card and begin typing. As noted earlier, the `paragraph` format is the only one available for use — none of the heading tags, `<h1>` through `<h6>`, are supported in WML. Moreover, only the default font can be used in WML; `<font>` tags, which control typeface, size and color, are not used. A number of style tags are supported, however:

✦ **Bold:** `<b>`

✦ **Italic:** `<i>`

✦ **Underline:** `<u>`

✦ **Emphasis:** `<emp>`

✦ **Strong:** `<strong>`

✦ **Big:** `<big>`

✦ **Small:** `<small>`

WML Studio includes a special Text Property Inspector (see Figure 40-6) to apply the various styles and alignment. The `big` and `small` tags make the selected text relatively larger and smaller than the standard text. A row of buttons toggles the various styles on –and off, and standard alignment options are also available. All of the WML-supported style tags — including <big> and <small> — are displayed in Dreamweaver.

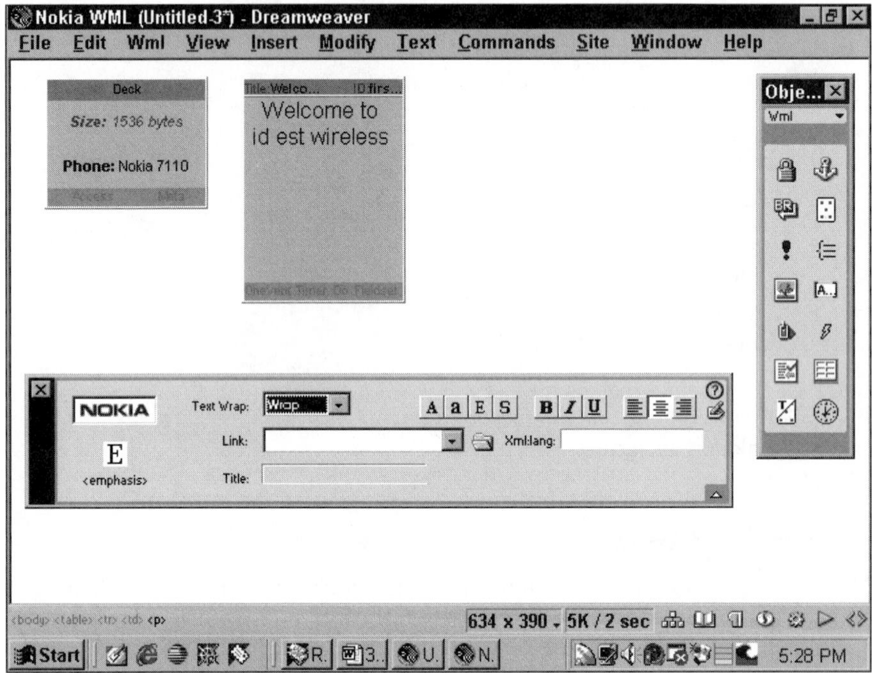

Figure 40-6: WML text is limited to paragraph format with just a few styles such as <emphasis> for variation.

While Nokia WML Studio is WML 1.1 compliant, you have no guarantee that the particular Web phone will render fonts in any of the various styles. For example, neither the Nokia 7110, 6210, or the 5250 models can show different font styles. Just as you should use Dreamweaver's Preview in Browser, it's important to use the WML Studio's Preview on Phone feature to get a truer picture of your final output.

The WML Text Property Inspector also gives you control over line wrapping. In most situations, you'll want to use the default Text Wrap option, Wrap, which permits words to automatically wrap as needed on the browser. With the Non-Wrap mode applied to a paragraph, text does not wrap and the browser must provide scrollbars or some other method of displaying the text. (Reality check: Although the Wrap/Non-Wrap modes are implemented as part of the WML 1.1 specification, currently no Web-enabled phone supports them.)

Tip

If your text contains a fairly long word, you might consider inserting a soft hyphen where you'd prefer the text to wrap, if necessary. A soft hyphen is designated with the character entities `` or `&160;`.

If a second paragraph is entered, all text is automatically placed within `<p>` tags. As in HTML, the `<p>` tag is a block element and lines are separated accordingly. The line-break tag is also supported, but only in the XML syntax, `<br/>`. For this reason, designers must use the Insert Line-Break object from the WML panel instead of using the keyboard shortcut, Shift+Enter (Shift+Return).

Special characters are handled in a special — and seamless — manner in WML Studio. Special entities (such as the trademark or copyright symbol) can be typed in directly or inserted using the Characters objects. Dreamweaver automatically rewrites them to HTML code in the source, as in `©` for (c). However, character entity codes are not valid WML, so when the WML translator is next called, these codes are retranslated to their original representations in the WML source.

Caution

While Dreamweaver does not prevent you from applying `<font>` or other non-WML tags to your text via the menus, when displayed on a WML device, such tags generate an error. The WML Studio includes an error handler, the WML Messages floater, designed to alert you to these problems.

Inserting wireless images

The present severe limitations of bandwidth, color depth, screen resolution, system memory, and CPU speed make it impossible to display standard Web images on a wireless connection. A new format, Wireless Bitmap or WBMP, was created to add a visual element to WML pages. Because WAP devices typically use monochromatic LCD screens — and because of the memory restrictions — the Wireless Bitmap format is restricted to two colors, where one color matches the screen background. Dithering is used to simulate additional colors and shading. Obviously, complex graphics are out of the question here and only the most iconic images — such as the simple corporate logo shown in Figure 40-7 — work well.

capable of displaying GIF, JPEG, and PNG images. In order to display images in the Wireless Bitmap format, the WML Studio uses a graphics converter to create a temporary PNG version of the desired image. A link to the WBMP file is stored in the actual WML document and this link is translated to point to the temporary PNG file during design-time.

Caution

The maximum size for WBMP images is 96 pixels wide by 45 pixels high. Larger images will be displayed in WML Studio, but the Preview On Phone – and a Web-enabled phone – will only display the `alt` attribute text (more information on the `alt` attribute appears in the steps that follow).

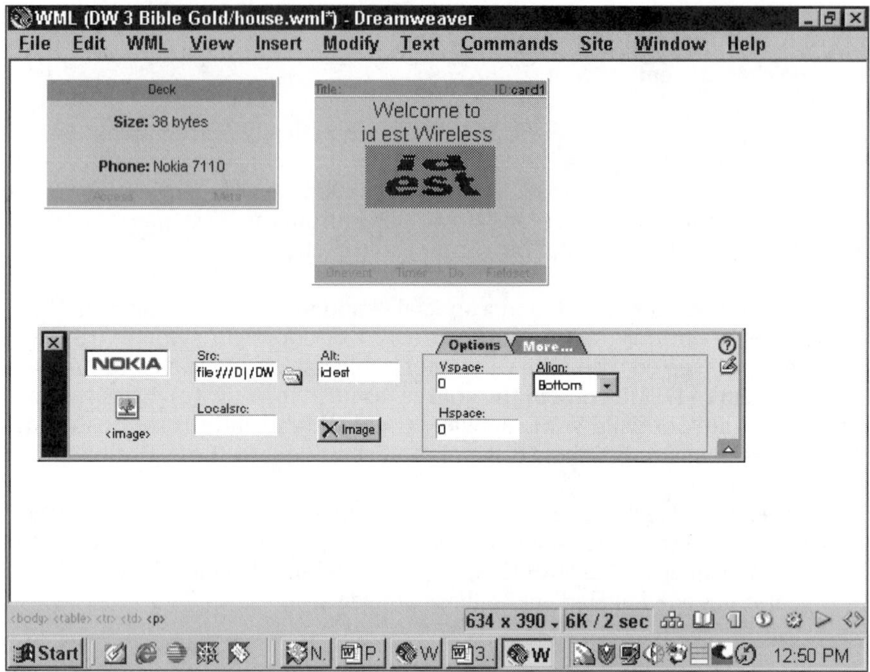

Figure 40-7: Any graphics used in a WML deck must be simple and clear.

As you may remember, Dreamweaver is only Unlike HTML graphics, WML images are not considered to be in-line graphics. In other words, an image cannot be displayed next to text. Another difference found in the WML `<img>` tag is the `localsrc` parameter. Wireless devices have their own series of internal graphics, such as checkmarks, that can be accessed internally rather than downloaded. The `localsrc` attribute, if available, overrides the `src` value.

Although it's part of the WML 1.1 specification, as of this writing no wireless devices have implemented `localsrc` images.

To add a graphic to your WML deck, follow these steps:

1. Place your cursor in the WML deck where you'd like the image to be inserted.
2. From the WML panel of the Objects palette, choose the Image object.

   The Insert Image dialog box (see Figure 40-8) is opened.

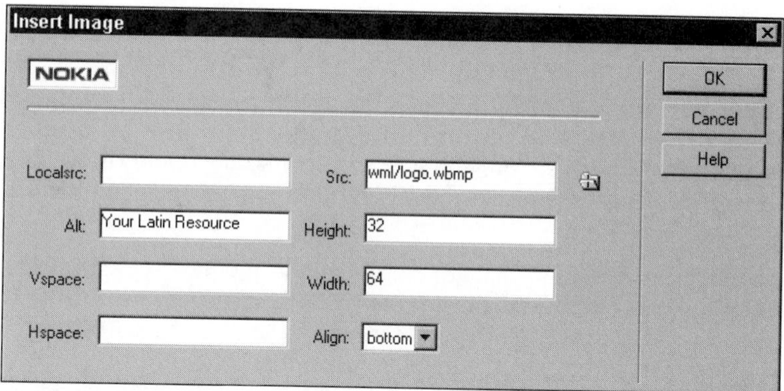

Figure 40-8: For a WML image, only WBMP format files can be specified.

3. If desired, enter the name for the internal image to be displayed in the Localsrc field.
4. Select a Wireless Bitmap format file by choosing the Browse for File button to the right of the Src field.
5. Enter the alternative text in the Alt field.

Tip

While a WML graphic is being downloaded to a wireless device, a rectangular box is displayed with the `alt` (alternative text) value inside. If the user elects to disable images, the rectangle with alt text remains onscreen. To handle this situation, WML Studio uses a default `alt` value if the Alt field is left blank. Therefore, it's highly recommended that you enter your own `alt` attribute for all images.

6. To display the image at its current dimensions, leave the Height and Width fields blank.

   If you'd like to show the image with different dimensions, enter the new height and/or width (in pixels) in the Height and Width fields, respectively. Please note that this does not resample the image and so the quality of the image may lessen.
7. If you'd like to create a margin around the image, enter pixel values in the Vspace field (for margins above and below the image) and/or the Hspace field (for margins to the left and right of the image).
8. Optionally, you can select the vertical alignment of the image from the Align list: `bottom`, `middle`, or `top`.

   The `align` attribute determines where the image is aligned on the corresponding text line. The default value is `bottom`.

WML Graphic Conversion with Fireworks

An additional facet of the Nokia WML Studio is the ability to edit WBMP graphics or convert any graphic to WBMP format in Fireworks. These graphics can then be incorporated into WML cards. WML Studio adds an Xtra and a Export Settings file to the Fireworks configuration; with these files you have all the necessary tools for manipulating Wireless Bitmap graphics.

To convert a graphic to WBMP format in Fireworks, choose WBMP – Best Quality from the Settings option list on the Optimize palette. The WBMP 8 format is invoked, the color resolution is set to Black & White, 2 colors, and the Dithering is enabled at 100 percent. As you can see by the accompanying images, simple logos convert much more effectively than photographic images. You can, however, achieve a wide range of effects by varying the amount of dither applied.

You might observe that two WBMP settings are available: WBMP 8 and WBMP 24. No functional difference exists between the two—they both output 1-bit graphics.

With the Nokia additions, Fireworks also can import an existing WBMP graphic for rescaling, cropping, or other manipulation. The image can then be exported as a Wireless Bitmap or in any other format that Fireworks supports.

Adding links

A key component in any Internet application is the ability to jump from one page to another with hypertext. WML uses a similar system to HTML to implement links—with a twist or two of its own. The primary difference between HTML and WML links to keep in mind is that, in WML, a link is typically activated by the user pressing a key on a wireless device rather than clicking text on a screen with a mouse.

Some difference also exists in how a link is created in WML rather than in HTML. Although the standard link code is acceptable, as in

```
<a href="products.wml">Products</a>
```

WML syntax also enables a link to be created this way:

```
<anchor>Link
  <go href="products.wml"/>
</anchor>
```

Both code styles achieve exactly the same results, but the second WML syntax is more flexible. By formatting the designated link tag in this way, selecting the link activates any actions found within the `<anchor>...</anchor>` tag pair. In other words, a link can do more than just jump to another card. Three major actions—or *tasks* as they are known in WML—are available within an `<anchor>` tag:

✦ **Go.** Loads the card specified in the `href` attribute. The `<go>` tag can, itself, contain the `setvar` and `postfield` tags used for sending arguments along with the requested deck.

✦ **Previous.** A tag, `<prev/>`, is used to go to the previously visited deck. You can nest `setvar` tags to change the state of a variable, if required.

✦ **Refresh.** Used to alter a variable (using `setvar`) and refresh the current card with the new variable in place.

In WML Studio, these tasks are specified after the link is created. To create a link, select the desired text and, from the WML panel of the Objects palette, choose the Insert Anchor object. If the Property Inspector is open, the `<anchor>` default values are shown, as you can see in Figure 40-9.

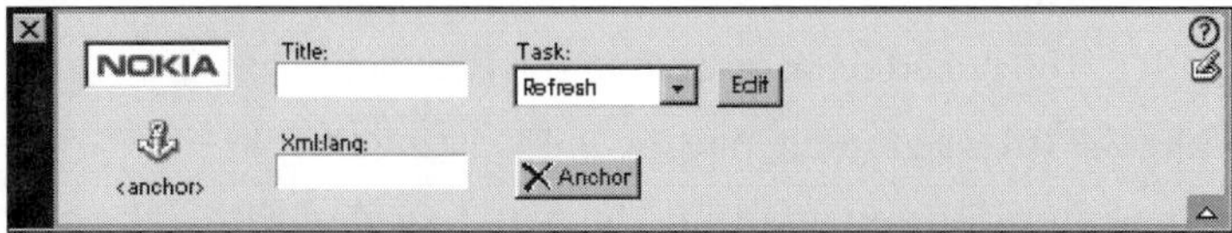

Figure 40-9: The Anchor Property Inspector gives you access to a variety of linkable commands: Go, Previous, and Refresh.

If the link is going to be addressed programmatically, give the current link a unique name by entering it in the Title field. The Xml:lang field is used to specify which language the link uses. For American English, enter `en-us` in the Xml:lang field.

The default task for the `<anchor>` tag in WML Studio is `<refresh>`. To change to a different task, select it from the Task option list. To edit the parameters for the chosen task, select the Edit button. The Edit button opens a different dialog box depending on the task selected.

The Go task

The Go dialog box, shown in Figure 40-10, offers numerous options although only the `href` attribute is mandatory. The dialog box is divided, by use, into two regions: the user interface elements on the right — Href, Method, Accept Charset, and Sendref — are attributes of the `<go>` tag; the remaining elements on the left are concerned with the nested tags, `setvar` and `postfield`.

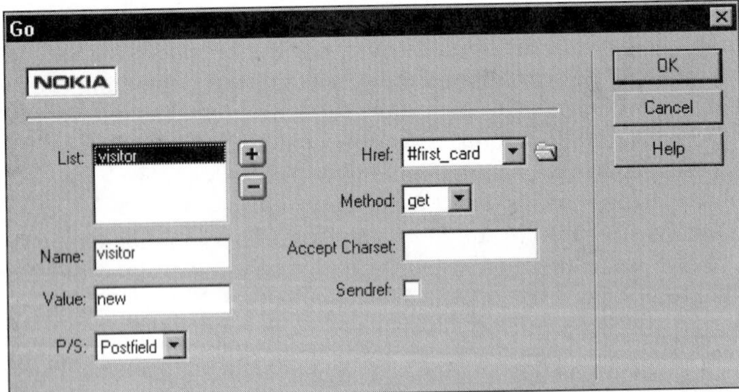

Figure 40-10: Configure your link and various variables by editing the Go task.

To edit the Go task attributes and its nested tags, follow these steps:

1. With your cursor in the link, select Go from the Task option list on the Property Inspector and choose the Edit button.

   The Go dialog box appears.

2. Enter the path to the linked deck or card in the Href field by:
   - Selecting the Browse for File button and locating the file.
   - Choosing Enter URL and inputting the path to a card within the current deck or the file name of a new deck in the Prompt dialog box.

Tip

Remember to enter a number sign before the card's name when navigating to a card in the same deck, like this: #last_card.

3. If necessary, select the desired Method for arguments to be passed from the list: get or post.
4. To specify a list of character encodings, enter the names in a comma-separated list in the Accept Charset field.
5. Choose the Sendref option if you'd like to send the referring address along with the request for the new page. This option is used to authenticate requests.
6. To add a new setvar or postfield nested tag, follow these steps:
   a. Select the Add button (plus sign) next to the List text area. The Name and Value fields are temporarily filled with placeholders.
   b. Replace "New Text" with the variable name.
   c. Replace "New Value" with the value for the variable.
   d. Choose whether the nested tag is to be postfield or setvar by selecting the appropriate name from the P/S list.
   e. Repeat these steps for each additional nested tag.
7. Click OK when you're done.

The Previous and Refresh tasks

Both Previous and Refresh <go> tag options work the same way—they just affect different cards. Choosing Previous from the Task option list on the Go Property Inspector inserts a tag, <prev>, that returns the user to the previously visited card. Choosing Refresh reloads the current card. Both tags accept <setvar> nested tags for altering the value of variables before displaying the requested card.

To reload the current card or revisit the preceding card, follow these steps:

1. With your cursor in the link, select either Previous or Refresh from the Task option list on the Property Inspector.
2. To add or alter variables, choose the Edit button.

   Depending on your task selection, either the Previous (see Figure 40-11) or the Refresh dialog box appears. The two dialog boxes are identical in appearance and use.
3. Select the Add button (plus sign) next to the SetVar List text area. The Name and Value fields are temporarily filled with placeholders.
4. Replace "New Text" with the variable name.

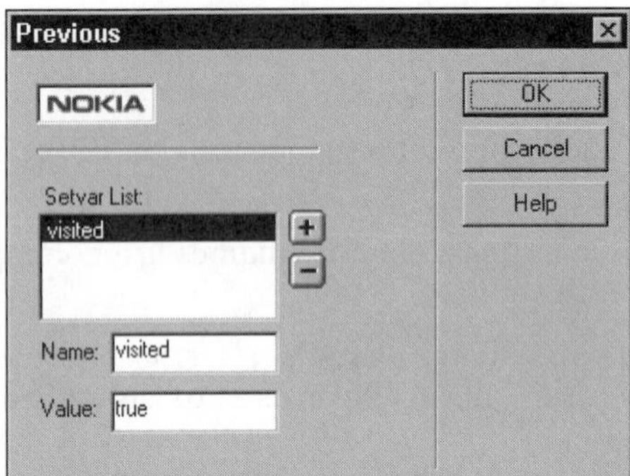

Figure 40-11: Set up a link to the preceding card through the Previous dialog box.

5. Replace "New Value" with the value for the variable.
6. Repeat Steps 2 through 4 for each additional nested tag.
7. Click OK when you're done.

Formatting with tables

Tables are available in WML to display structured data much like in HTML. The WML `<table>` tag, however, is far more limited than the HTML version. With a WML table, column widths cannot be specified in either pixels or percentages and neither background color, image, nor vertical alignment is possible. Furthermore, tables are always drawn with a fixed border, cell spacing, and cell padding. On wireless devices, tables are used for displaying text and images in rows and columns; they cannot be used for layout or sliced images.

To insert a table in your WML card, follow these steps:

1. Position your cursor on the line where you'd like the table to appear in the WML card.

Text cannot be presented next to a WML table and tables cannot be nested.

2. Select the Insert Table object from the WML panel of the Objects palette.

   The Insert Table dialog box, shown in Figure 40-12, is displayed.

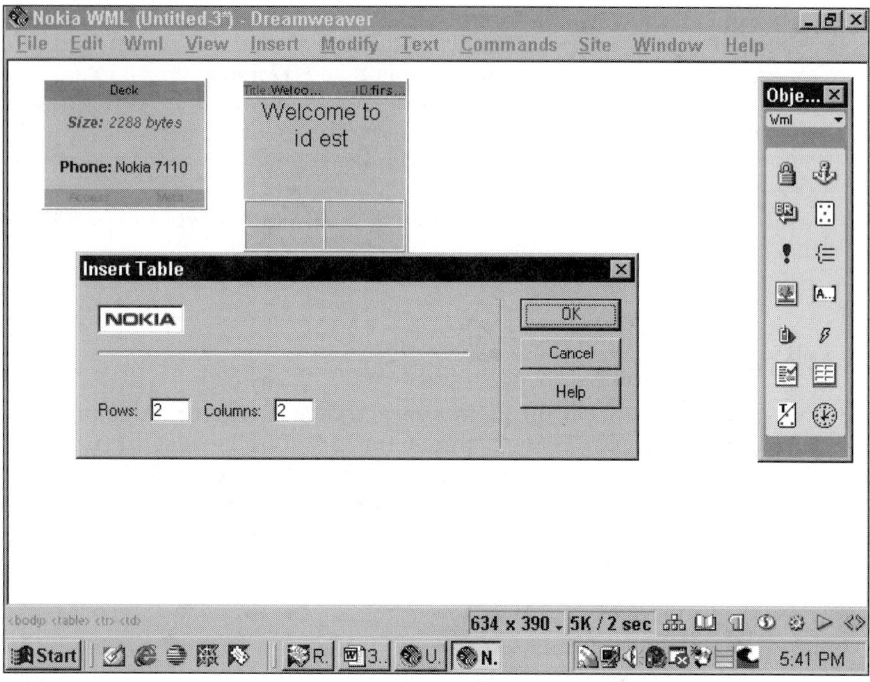

Figure 40-12: Use the Table object for organizing your WML data.

3. Enter the number of rows in the Rows field.
4. Enter the number of columns in the Columns field.
5. Click OK when you're done.

If you need to modify the table, select it either by choosing `<table>` from the Tag Selector or dragging your mouse over the border. The WML Table Property Inspector is then presented with fields for Rows, Columns, Alignment, Title, and `xml:lang` attributes.

Building Interactivity

The wireless device's small screen size intensifies the importance of user input. Unlike with larger HTML pages, specific information should only be presented for a limited number of choices on a single WML card. The restricted display size forces the designer to let the user decide which information is to be displayed.

Here's an example. Suppose your site accepts reservations for a rental car. All the available options — type of car, dates to be rented and returned, and so on — would probably be presented in a single form on an HTML page, with lots of explanatory text and images. A corresponding WML version would display the basic input areas one after another on separate cards, without any of the bells and whistles of a Web page. Information would only be shown when needed, based on previous choices.

In addition to user input, WML supports several other types of events such as timers. These events — and their possible subsequent actions — are coded into specific cards of the deck.

Form objects

Like standard HTML, WML offers a variety of methods for obtaining user input. Unlike HTML, no surrounding `<form>` tag is required — just drop in an input text field and you're ready to receive data. Aside from text fields, WML also supports select lists with either single or multiple selections possible. Moreover, select lists can present groups of options in a hierarchical fashion, which permit visitors to drill down to their choices.

For example, let's say your site hosts a directory of restaurants in New York City. The first grouping of restaurants might be organized by price: Chi-Chi, Mid-Level, and Cheap Eats. Next, the visitor is offered a selection of neighborhoods: Chelsea, SOHO, Upper West Side, and so on. After a browser chooses an area, a variety of menus are offered: Italian, Mexican, Continental, and so on. Finally, a list of restaurants — meeting all the selected criteria — is presented, with a phone number, ready to be dialed.

Text input

On wireless devices, information is gathered from the user through use of the associated keypad. Each device has its own method of accepting text. The text input field in WML can present an initial value, such as `Enter Name`, and display what it receives either as text or as asterisks or bullets when used, as in password mode. WML also offers a fairly robust validation scheme to verify that the user is inputting the correct type of data.

Selecting the WML Studio's Insert Input object does not open a dialog box. Instead default code is inserted in the page with a square bracket pair in the Document window, like this:

```
[...]
```

The designer is then presented with a custom Property Inspector (see Figure 40-13) for modification. Aside from basic information — the input's name, size, maximum characters, and initial value — the Property Inspector is divided into two tabbed areas, Options and More. The Options tab is used to set the input type (text or password) and choose the accepted format. The More panel offers choices for determining the `xml:lang` attribute, the input's title, the tabbing order, and whether it is required or not.

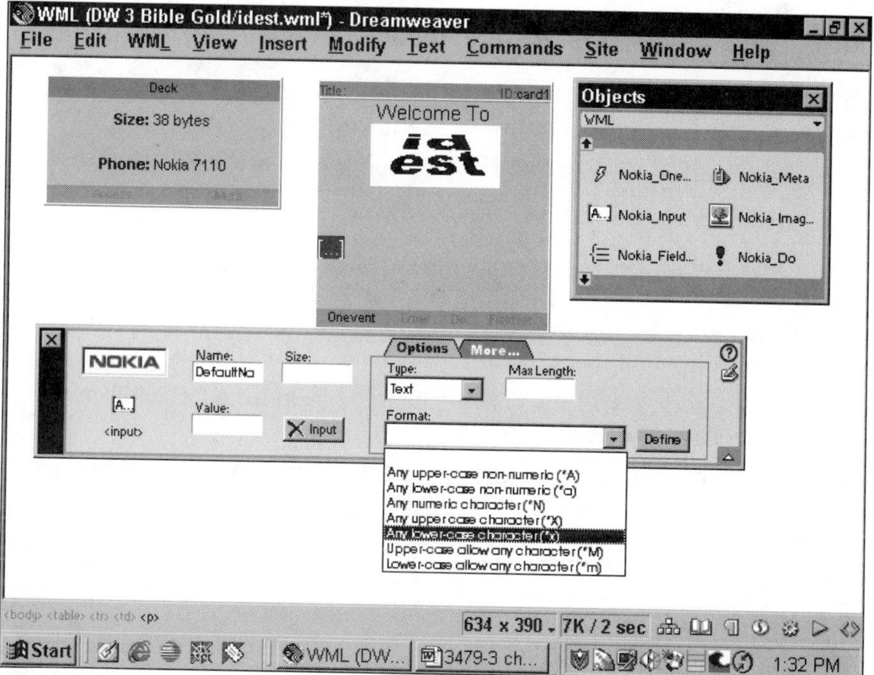

Figure 40-13: The Input Property Inspector is the primary method of configuring WML text input fields.

The Format options, found on the Options tab, control the type of validation applied. The value in parentheses, such as (*A), is the WML code inserted. The default selection is Upper-case allow any character (*M); this format accepts any character which is then uppercased by the browser. Table 40-1 describes the various options.

Table 40-1
WML Text Field Formats

Option	*Example*
Any upper-case non-numeric (*A)	JOSEPH
Any lower-case non-numeric (*a)	joseph
Any numeric character (*N)	55554701234322
Any upper-case character (*X)	MODEL 733P
Any lower-case character (*x)	model 733p
Upper-case allow any character (*M)	669 1ST AVENUE
Lower-case allow any character (*m)	669 1st avenue

To alter the WML input field settings, follow these steps:

1. Set your cursor in a card where you'd like the input field to appear and select the Insert Input object from the WML panel of the Objects palette.
2. In the Property Inspector, change the Name field from DefaultName to something more meaningful, if you like.
3. To alter the dimensions of the input field, enter the number of characters wide in the Size field.

Note: A new Input field size is not represented in Dreamweaver and must be previewed to be seen.

4. To restrict the number of characters to input, enter a value in the Max Length field.
5. To present an initial value to the browser, enter the desired text in the Value field.
6. On the Options tab, select Text or Password from the Type list.
7. Select the type of validation desired from the Format list.
8. From the More tab, you can enter the following options:
   - Specify a language in the Xml:lang field.
   - Add an onscreen title in the Title field.
   - To control the tabbing sequence, enter a number in the Tab field. The entered value is used in concert with other Tab attributes from other input fields.
   - If text input is optional, select the Empty OK checkbox.

Select object

When you want your site visitor to choose among several items, use a Select object. The Select object is similar to HTML's List/Menu object in that a list of items is presented to the user. However, all the items are shown at the same time in WML, instead of through a drop-down list. If the list is longer than the screen, the user can scroll down the page. Both single and multiple selections are supported in WML.

The WML `<select>` tag also supports two programming concepts not found in HTML: option groups and index attributes. An *option group* is a collection of select items set up to permit easy navigation. For example, suppose your site offered a selection of mystery books for ordering. The initial option group might offers several routes for the visitor to search the site:

```
[Author]
[Classic]
[New Release]
[Award Winner]
```

If the user selects the Author option, another option group is presented — this time by genre:

```
[Medical Thriller]
[Police Procedural]
[Political Thriller]
[True Crime]
```

Selecting one of the genres leads to a list of authors, which in turn leads to a list of the author's books.

The other select attribute found in WML but not HTML is index-related. The selected index values — that is, which values in the list will display as selected — can be independently chosen for each select list. With index values (or, in code, the `ivalue`) the first option item corresponds to the number 1; the second one, number 2, and so on. A zero `ivalue` attribute indicates no selection is displayed. A variable, referred to as the index name (`iname`), is also set that allows for dynamic updating. In the following code example, options one and two — Medical Thriller and Police Procedural — would be preselected for the visitor, unless a variable, `i`, was set to another value.

```
<wml>
   <card>
   <p>
   Please select <i>all</i> your favorite mystery genres:
   <select name="genre" iname="i" ivalue="1;2" multiple="true">
   <option value="med">Medical Thriller</option>
   <option value="cop">Police Procedural</option>
   <option value="pol">Political Thriller</option>
   <option value="tc">True Crime</option>
   </select>
```

```
    </p>
    </card>
</wml>
```

You'll notice that multiple selections are handled in a very straightforward manner: the `multiple` attribute is set to true and several `ivalues` are given in a comma-separated list.

The WML Studio Insert Select object is like the Insert Input object; default code for both is inserted when the object is chosen and all modifications are initiated through the Property Inspector. A separate dialog box is available for entering option list and option group items.

To create a select list in WML Studio, follow these steps:

1. Place your cursor in the WML card where you'd like the select list to begin.
2. Choose the Insert Select object from the WML panel of the Objects palette.

   A basic select tag and single option item are inserted in the code while the Document window displays `[ . . . ]` and the Select Property Inspector (see Figure 40-14) is activated.

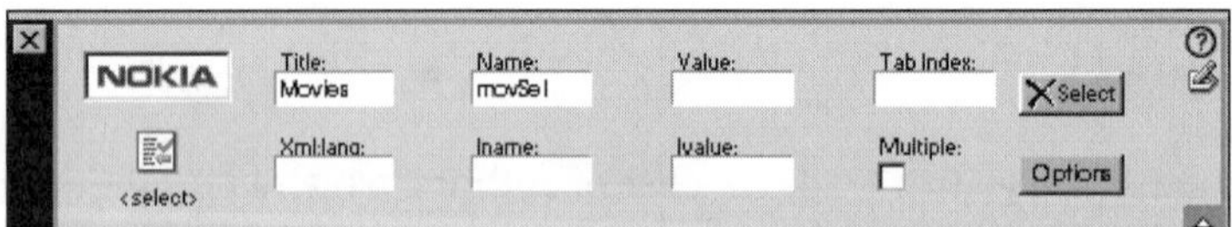

Figure 40-14: Modifying the Select Property Inspector is the first step to inserting option lists in your WML cards.

3. Enter any of the following optional values:
   - **Title.** The title of the select list that may be displayed above it, depending on the browser.
   - **Name.** The name of the select list object, referred to in programming.
   - **Value.** The value of the option item if chosen.
   - **Tab Index.** The relative tabbing position of the select object within the current card.
   - **Xml:lang.** The language of the object.
   - **Iname.** The name of the variable assigned to the index selection.
   - **Ivalue.** The selected indices, given in a series of comma-separated numbers.
   - **Multiple.** An option to enable multiple selections.

4. To enter the option list items and option groups, select the Options button on the Property Inspector.

   The Options & Optiongroups dialog box, shown in Figure 40-15, is displayed.

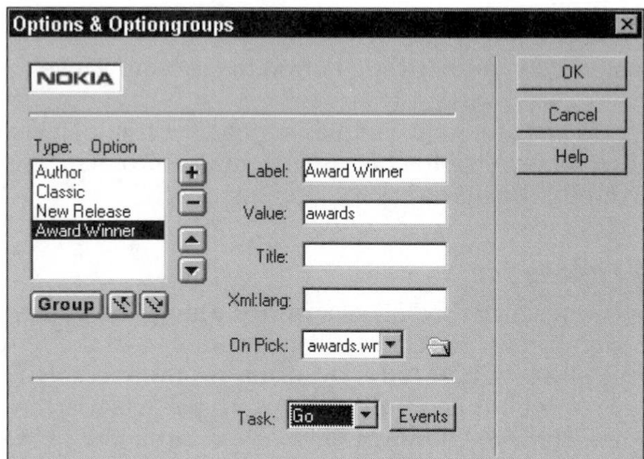

Figure 40-15: Create option groups as well as option items through the Options dialog box.

5. To begin creating an option item, select the NewTitle entry in the list area.

   The preset value and title are shown in their respective fields.

6. Enter the text to be displayed in the Label field.

7. Enter the text to be transmitted as an argument in the Value field.

8. If desired, enter the language for the option item in the Xml:lang field.

9. If the option item is to serve as a jump menu, select a deck with the On Pick field, either by using the Browse for File button to locate the deck or choosing Enter URL and inputting a card in the Prompt dialog box.

10. If the option item is to trigger a task, choose a task from the Task list and use the Edit button to enter the parameters.

    Editing a task's parameters is discussed earlier in this chapter.

11. Select the Add button (plus sign) and repeat Steps 5 through 10 to add additional list items.

12. To begin to create a option group, select one or more option items.

13. With the new items highlighted, choose the Group button.

    The Type changes to OptGroup while the Label and Value fields are deactivated.

14. Enter an onscreen label for the group in the Title field.
15. Repeat Steps 8 through 10 to define the option group item.
16. To enter option items for the current option group, select the Navigate into Selected Option Group button.
17. Repeat Steps 5 through 10 to add each list item.
18. Select the Navigate up to Parent Group button to move up a level.

Obviously, you can create an extremely complex series of option objects using the WML Studio's dialog box. For navigation of this sort, it's best to plan your options carefully to avoid circuitous and unnecessary selections.

Grouping with the Fieldset tag

The `<fieldset>` tag provides a method of encapsulating code and grouping onscreen elements. Although it could be used with any presentation, the `<fieldset>` tag is particularly useful with forms. Because the displays of wireless devices vary so widely in size, the `<fieldset>` tag is used to display a particular arrangement of screen elements together. Think of the use of `<fieldset>` as similar to keeping headings and paragraphs together in word-processing.

Again, the Fieldset object is included for completeness and future compatibility; no Web-enabled phone currently supports the `<fieldset>` tag.

With the WML Studio, marking text with the `<fieldset>` tag is very straightforward. Simply select the text and/or code you wish to group and choose the Insert Fieldset object from the WML panel of the Objects palette. The Insert Fieldset dialog box (see Figure 40-16) consists of a single field, Title. The Title entered is used to identify the portion of the card and should be unique.

Figure 40-16: Group your form elements with the Fieldset object.

After you close the dialog box, the Fieldset indicator along the bottom of the card becomes active. Clicking Fieldset enables the custom Property Inspector that lists all the `<fieldset>` tags in the card, as shown in Figure 40-17. Select an item from the list and the enclosed text and code is displayed in the Property Inspector. You can remove a `<fieldset>` tag by selecting it from the list and choosing the delete button. The Fieldset Property Inspector also permits you to alter the title of the grouping and specify a language in the Xml:lang field.

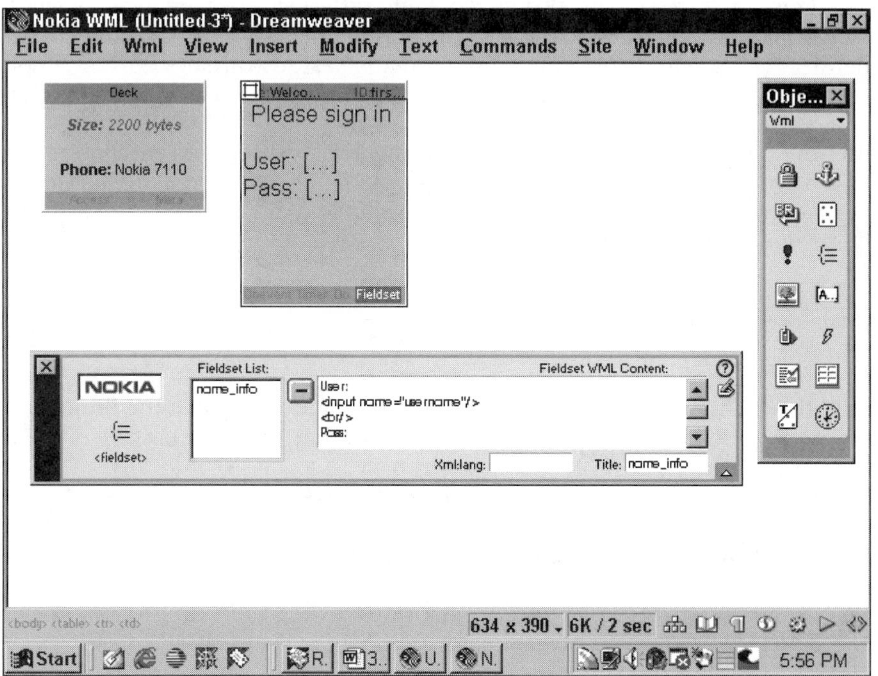

Figure 40-17: Select the card's Fieldset indicator to modify existing `<fieldset>` tags through the custom Property Inspector.

Be careful with your selections when applying a `<fieldset>` tag. Choosing text with the surrounding `<p>...</p>` tag pair is invalid, while selecting just the interior text is not.

Interactive events

Cards can contain actions, such as going to another card, that are triggered by the press of a specified function key on the wireless device, such as the roller on the Nokia 7110. Actions can also be triggered by less overt events, such as entering a card backwards (as if the Previous key was pressed) or a timer elapsing. In the WML Studio, events directly activated by a user are handled by the Do object and those occurring as the result of a user action (or inaction) use the OnEvent object.

The Do object

When the WML Do object is applied, a basic code structure is inserted into the card. Typically, the designer chooses a type first; the type controls the key or other manner in which the event is triggered. Eight different types are available in the WML object: Accept, Delete, Help, Options, Previous, Reset, and Unknown. All of the various types are interpreted differently on various wireless devices, depending on their capabilities.

After the type is determined, the task is assigned. As discussed earlier, the basic tasks are `go` (for accessing another card), `previous`, and `refresh`. The Go object also makes `noop`, short for no operation, available. With the type and task selected, the Do code is inserted in this manner:

```
<do name="doHelp" type="options" label="Help" optional="false">
<go href="#help"/>
</do>
```

Additional `setvar` and `postfield` variables are added through the Property Inspector, which is activated by selecting the Do button at the bottom of the card.

To add a Do event to your WML card, follow these steps:

1. Select the card in which you'd like the code to appear.
2. Choose the Insert Do object from the WML panel of the Objects palette.

   The Insert Do dialog box appears, as shown in Figure 40-18.

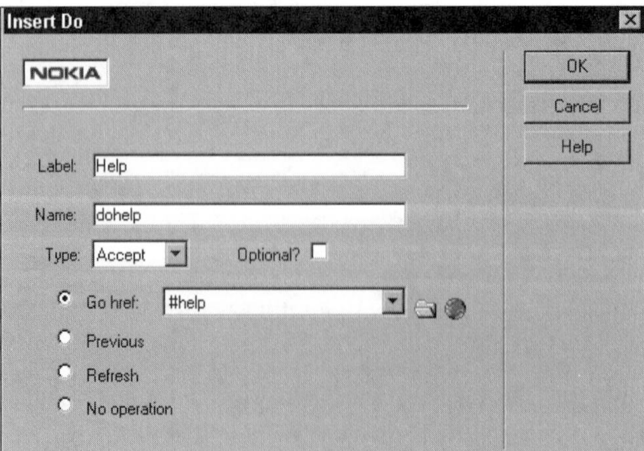

Figure 40-18: Begin to program user keys and other triggers through the Do object.

3. Enter appropriate and descriptive text in the Label field.

   The Label is shown in Option lists and other places in the wireless devices.

4. Enter a unique identification for the Do object in the Name field.
5. Select the triggering mechanism from the Type list.
6. To enable the browser to ignore the Do object, select the Optional checkbox.

   By default, the Optional attribute is false.

7. Choose the associated task: Go, Previous, Refresh, or No Operation.
8. If you selected the Go task, enter a URL by choosing the Browse for File button to locate a file locally or the world button to input either an absolute URL or another card within the current deck.
9. Click OK when you're done.

Once you create a Do object, the Do button becomes active on the bottom part of the card. Select the Do button to enable the Property Inspector; you'll need to have the Property Inspector open to access the custom properties shown in Figure 40-19. To modify an existing Do object, select its name from the list area. To add `setvar` or `postfield` statements, select the Edit button next to the Task list. You can even insert new Do statements by selecting the Add button (plus sign) and altering the appropriate properties.

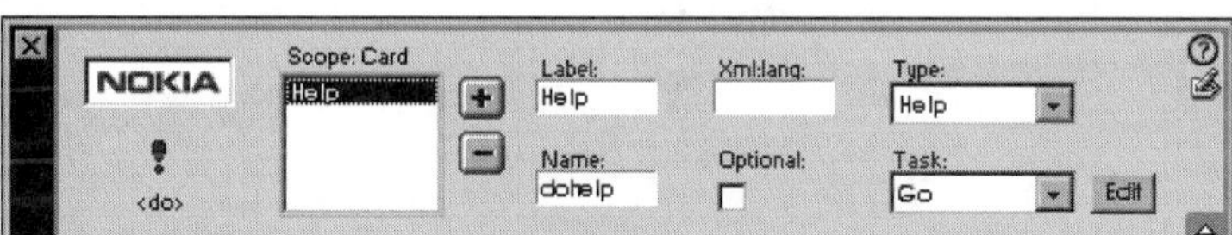

Figure 40-19: Use the Do Property Inspector to add required `setvar` and `postfield` statements.

If Do elements from the Template are inherited in the card inspected, these Do elements are shown in the Property Inspector, but they can only be inspected, not changed. They must be changed from the Do Property Inspector in the Template itself. This also works the same way for OnEvent elements inherited from the Template. The Scope designation changes from Card to Template depending on which items are active.

The OnEvent object

Just as behaviors can be triggered in HTML when a page loads and not just by user action, WML enables certain events to trigger tasks. The four available events are:

✦ **OnTimer.** Provides automatic execution of statements after a designer-set time period has elapsed. When OnTimer is chosen, the Timer object must also be used to set a time.

✦ **OnEnterBackward.** Executes when the current card is revisited by the user.

✦ **OnEnterForward.** Executes when the current card is entered from a standard link.

✦ **OnPick.** Goes to a URL when a particular selection in an option list is chosen by the user.

To use the OnEvent object, follow these steps:

1. Select the OnEvent object from the WML panel of the Objects palette.

   The OnEvent dialog box is displayed, as shown in Figure 40-20.

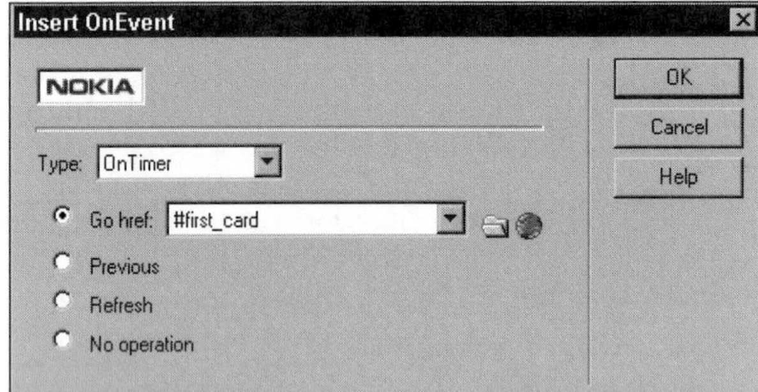

Figure 40-20: With the OnEvent object, tasks can be triggered by the sequence of a user's actions or the expiration of a timer.

2. Select the kind of event you want from the Type list.

The OnTimer event requires that a Timer object also be included as discussed later in this section.

3. Choose the task to perform: Go, Previous, Refresh, or No Operation.
4. If you select the Go task, enter a URL by choosing the Browse for File button to locate a file locally or the world button to input either an absolute URL or another card within the current deck.
5. Click OK when you're done.

As with the Do object, once an OnEvent object is inserted its corresponding button becomes available from the bottom of the card. Selecting the OnEvent button enables the Property Inspector, shown in Figure 40-21. The Property Inspector displays all four possible events; choosing one of them displays the current parameters — and selects the Enabled checkbox — if the event has been included. If an event has not been included, you can add it by choosing the Enabled option, picking a Task from the list, and clicking the Edit button to add any needed statements or values.

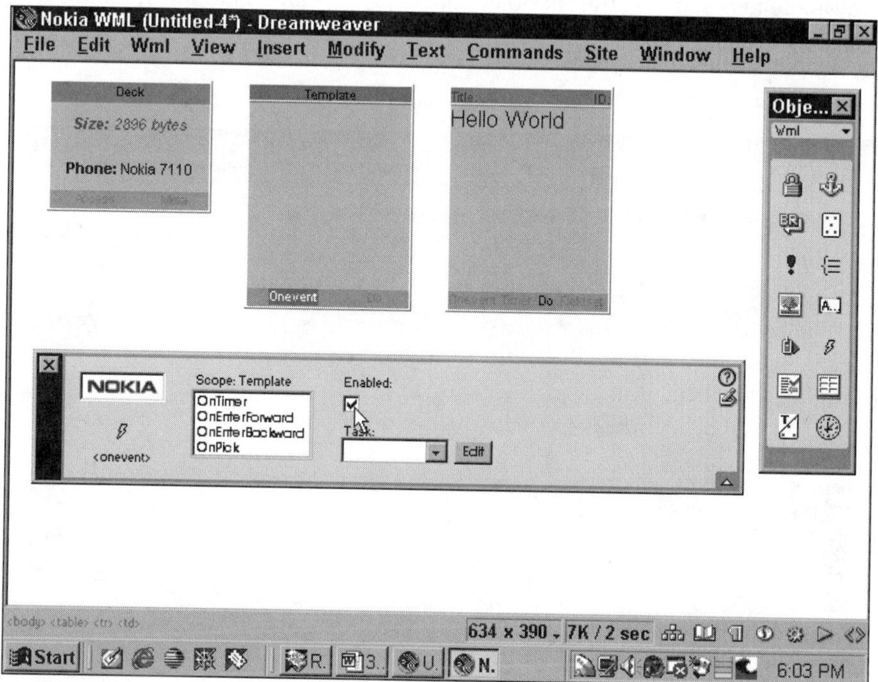

Figure 40-21: You can add new OnEvent items right from the Property Inspector by selecting the Enabled checkbox.

If you select the OnTimer event, you'll need to also use the Timer object to set the value. Choose the Timer object from the Objects palette and, in the dialog box, enter a name for the timer and a value, in seconds. The timer starts counting when the card is initially accessed.

Template creator

Often most cards in a deck will share characteristics. For example, it's not uncommon for all but the first card in a deck to include a Previous button. This is normally accomplished through the use of a Do object set to a Previous task. However, rather than enter the same code on every card, WML permits you to create a *template* and enter the code once there. While any code inserted in a template is available to all cards in a deck, the code can be overridden on a card-by-card basis.

In WML Studio, a new template is created by selecting the Template object. A special card (see Figure 40-22) appears in the Document window — with a red border rather than the standard card green — to represent the template. On creation, URLs can be specified for OnTimer, OnEnterBackward, and OnEnterForward events. To add Do elements, insert the Do object into the template. Like the standard cards, selecting the Do or OnEvent buttons from the bottom of the template card invokes the proper Property Inspector.

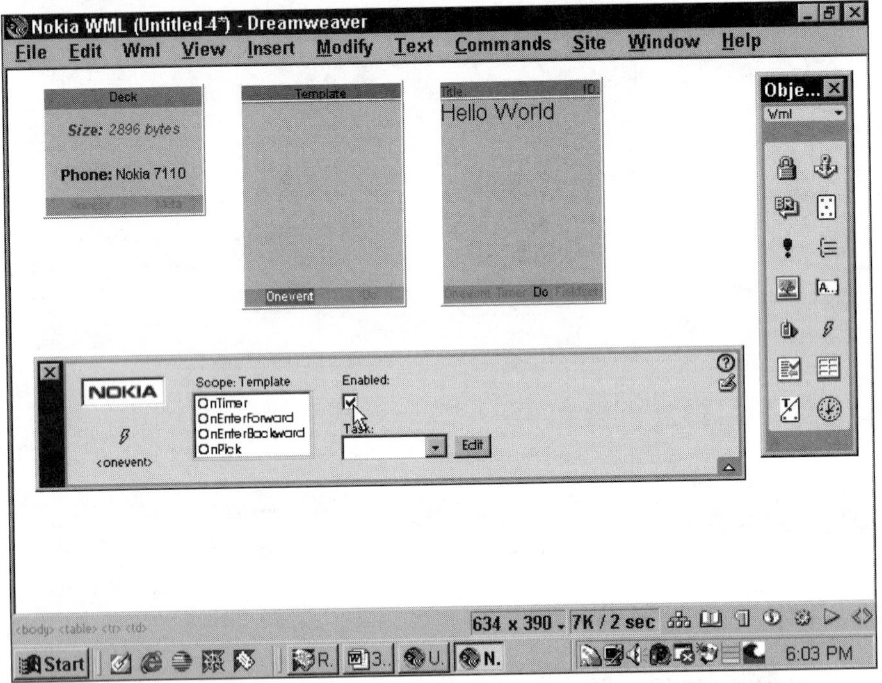

Figure 40-22: A separate card represents the template for the entire deck.

You can override the template events on a particular card by inserting an event of the same name in the card. For example, let's say that the template created a Previous button by way of the Do object named `doPrev` for all cards. To avoid this effect on the opening card of a deck, you would insert a Do object also named `doPrev` in that card. For a task, specify No Operation from the Do object dialog box.

Testing Your Wireless Connection

The HTML developer's tenet of testing your pages online is just as true for the WML developer. While the WML Studio does a good job of representing your cards within Dreamweaver, you have to see them in the environment for which they were intended to get the full effect. Because it's not always possible to fine-tune your designs on a WAP server, WML Studio provides a simulated Web phone for previewing much like Dreamweaver's Preview in Browser feature.

The Preview on Phone command, found under the WML menu, loads the current deck in a simulated Nokia 7011, as shown in Figure 40-23. All of the phone's command buttons are functional to enable you to navigate your deck as the user would. To activate the phone, choose WML ➪ Preview on Phone. The phone simulation runs within your primary browser.

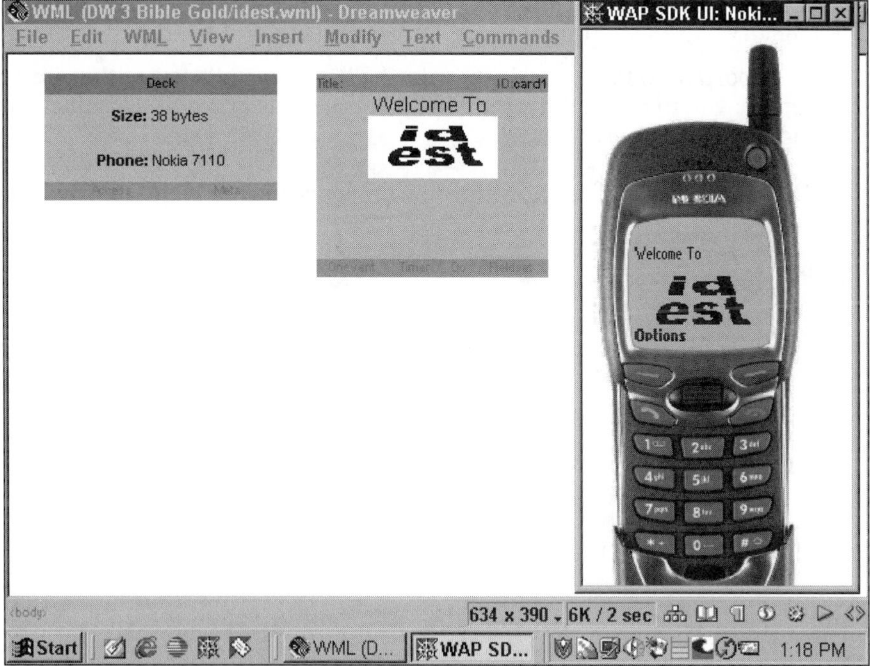

Figure 40-23: Test navigate your deck through the WML Studio's Preview on Phone command.

Summary

The release of the Nokia WML Studio is an important milestone for Web development in general and Dreamweaver in particular. Not only does it signify that the reach of the Web will continue to expand in surprising and innovative ways, it also signals the acceptance of Dreamweaver as a development platform as well as a design program. The WML Studio is sure to open new vistas for Web developers to explore. Before you begin your exploration, consider these points:

- ✦ Wireless Markup Language is an XML-based language with tags similar to HTML, but with a different syntax. Most of the standard Dreamweaver objects will not function properly in the WML environment; the custom WML Studio objects must be used instead.
- ✦ Web-enabled phones have a very limited palette to work with. When designing, the Web developer must be concerned not only with the relative smallness of the screen, the monochromatic screen and, most of all, the limited memory capacity of these particular user agents.
- ✦ It's important to test your decks with the Preview on Phone option. Testing permits you to check the interactivity of the cards as well as see the layout and content properly.

In the next chapter, you'll see how the new Dreamweaver Objects for Aria enable real-time site analysis.

✦ ✦ ✦

CHAPTER 41

Enhancing Site Analysis with Aria Objects

✦ ✦ ✦ ✦

In This Chapter

Aria site analysis fundamentals

Cataloguing content

Tracking visitors

Customizing categories

Following personal choices

✦ ✦ ✦ ✦

ROI: Three initials that any businessperson knows all too well. Return on Investment is key to the success of most every venture — and the Web is no exception. The more extensive a site, and thus the investment, the more important it is to measure the ROI with site analysis techniques. All Web sites generate logs that collect certain basic statistics from all visitors: their referring URL, browser, and even operating system. But the standard logs can't tell you what's really important to the enterprise: what typifies the site's visitors and how their behavior can be objectified to make marketing decisions. This search is greatly hampered in the larger sites that may employ many servers making log comparison a nightmare. Moreover, in these rapidly changing business cycles, site analysis needs to be generated in real time, not once a week.

Macromedia recognized these growing needs and merged with one of the leading players in site analysis, Andromedia. Andromedia's premier site analysis product is Aria, a real-time, enterprise-level statistics solution. Aria side steps the issues associated with server logs by combining a server-side monitor with Web page embedded directives. To facilitate the production of these directives, Macromedia has released the Aria Objects for Dreamweaver. Because Aria has both server and client-side components, proper use of the software requires cooperation between the network administrators and the Web design teams. This chapter explains how the various Aria objects are used on both the page and site level from within Dreamweaver.

Understanding Aria

Aria is capable of producing an amazing number of site analysis reports:

- **Traffic reports:** Basic Web site numbers, including page views, total hits, total visits, and repeat visits.
- **Navigation reports:** Used to track visitor travels to, through, and from your sites. With Previous-Click and Next-Click reports, internal navigation can be mapped.
- **Visitor reports:** In addition to providing traditional Web site information, such as referring domain and browser types, Aria tracks custom Visitor Categories as well as new and repeat visitors.
- **Content reports:** Focuses on the impact your content carries by identifying the content most frequently accessed and most frequently stopped loading, plus new content hits and access failures.

On the server side, the three major Aria components are the Monitor, the Recorder, and the Reporter. The Aria Enterprise Monitor is composed of both a Server Monitor and a Network Monitor; both serve to collect information used in site analysis. The Aria Recorder receives information from the monitors, cross-compiling the data and storing it for retrieval by the Aria Reporter. The Aria Reporter produces reports on demand and on schedule: designated reports can be e-mailed on an hourly basis, if desired. All reports are visible via a standard Web browser, as shown in Figure 41-1.

Much of Aria's technology depends on mapping URIs (Uniform Resource Identifiers) with regular expressions. This technique helps reduce the often overwhelming volume of page hits to a few meaningful categories. The Aria administration team is responsible for mapping the URIs and communicating the resulting Content Categories with the Web design team. To get the most benefit from Aria, it's vital that you insert the precise directives into the site's pages—Dreamweaver's objects streamline the process and reduce user error.

Working with Aria Objects

After installing the Aria Objects for Dreamweaver, you'll find a new panel in the Objects palette and entries in the Insert menu. Digging a little deeper, you'll also find additions to the contextual menu for the Site window. The five basic Aria objects are:

- Title
- Content Category
- Visitor Category
- Key-Value Data
- Persona Data

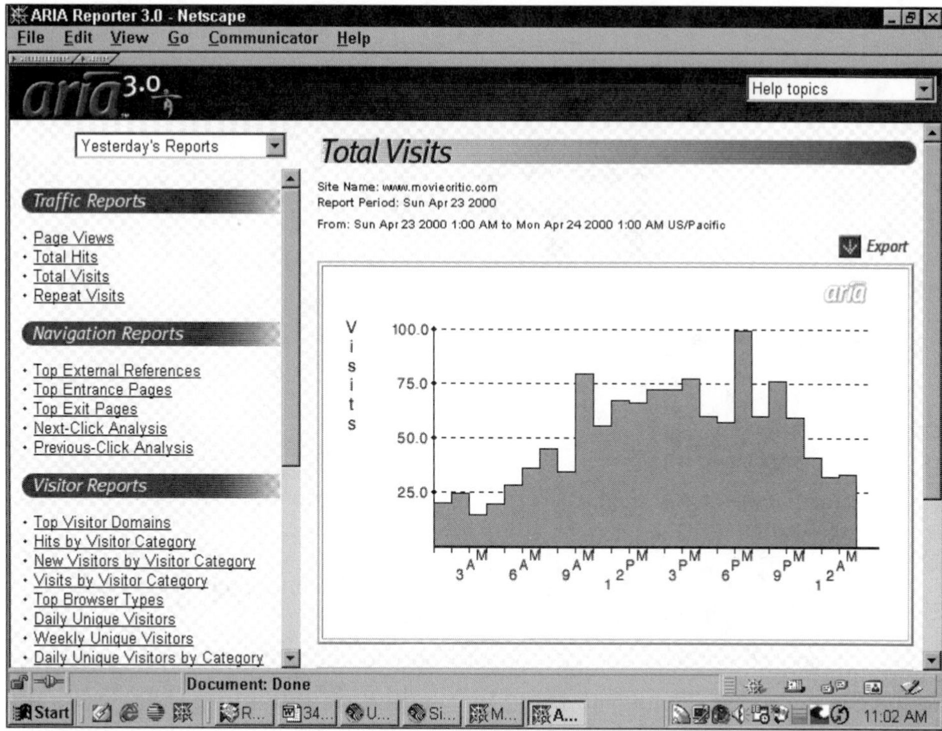

Figure 41-1: With Aria's tracking capability, you can view the peak and low times for total visits over a day.

All of these objects (shown in Figure 41-2) insert the Aria directives as comments in the `<head>` region of a page. This placement enables pages to be quickly scanned by the Aria Monitors and data catalogued by the Recorder. For example, here's the code inserted by an Aria Visitor Category object:

```
<!-- aria add-visitor-category promo_mailing -->
```

Both the Content Category and Visitor Category objects use separate interfaces to define the categories used. These categories are maintained in a text file stored within an Aria folder created for each site when a category is first defined.

You can add up to 200 Content and Visitor Categories on a page, but a high number of categories could degrade server performance.

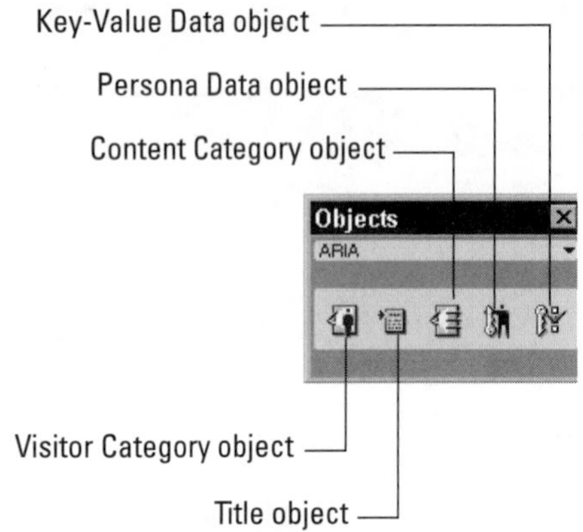

Figure 41-2: Aria installs a new panel in the Objects palette consisting of five objects.

Naming categories and data is very important in Aria, thus you need to keep a few key rules in mind:

✦ Avoid spaces in category and key names. Use underscores, periods, and colons instead. Spaces can be used in values.

✦ Special symbols, such as <, >, or = should not be used in an Aria directive.

✦ Coordinate naming conventions between the Aria administrative and Web design efforts. The names embedded in the Web pages must match the categories analyzed by the server exactly to function properly.

✦ Macromedia suggests that a hierarchical naming convention be adopted to make the most out of Aria's categorization capabilities. For example,

```
services:training:dreamweaver
services:training:fireworks
services:training:ultradev
```

Aria Title

Although the Aria Title object simply writes to the HTML `<title>` tag, its importance cannot be overestimated. Aria uses the document title in both a traditional and innovative manner. Some other site analysis programs incorporate the title (as opposed to the file name) as does Aria; this greatly simplifies reading the reports.

Aria also uses the HTML title to generate entries in its Content and Visitor Categories. Aria compares these categories to the HTML title; if a word in the title matches, the visited page is added to the category. Let's say, for example, that the title of a document is:

```
eHealth Insider: Dot.Com Info for Executives and Investors
```

If Visitor Categories for this site were `investor`, `doctor`, `physician`, and `executive`, Aria would count any visits to this page under the `investor` and `executive` categories.

You can use the standard Dreamweaver method for inserting a title: Choose Modify ➪ Page Properties and enter your text in the Title field of the dialog box. Alternatively, the Aria Title object gives you direct access to the title without opening the larger dialog box. To use the Aria Title object, select it from the Aria panel and, in the dialog box (see Figure 41-3), enter the desired title in the Page Title field.

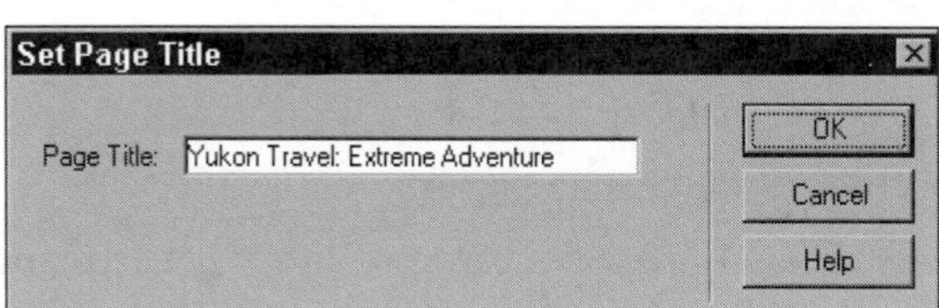

Figure 41-3: Bypass the Modify Properties dialog box and enter the document title through the Aria Title object.

Aria Content Category

As the name implies, you use Aria Content Categories to typify the content of separate Web pages in a site. Content can be broken down to describe page types (such as introduction, description, form, contact, and so on) by the type of multimedia used on the page (QuickTime, Flash, Windows_Streaming, and so on) or in any other pertinent manner. Content Categories can be applied to pages individually or to all pages within a designated folder.

Before an Aria Content Category can be inserted, it must be defined. You have two ways to define Content Categories: one, through the Dreamweaver interface, is best for adding a small number of categories, and the other requires a text editor and is a good way to add many categories at once.

To define new Content Categories within Dreamweaver, follow these steps:

1. Choose Modify ➪ Aria ➪ Define Aria Content Categories.

   The Define Aria Content Categories dialog box opens, as shown in Figure 41-4.

2. Enter the first category in the blank field below the Content Categories list area.

Do not press Enter (Return) after inputting your first field if you'd like to add more fields—to do so will save the category and exit from the dialog box.

3. To add another category, select the Add button to move the category to the list area and reposition the cursor in the blank field.

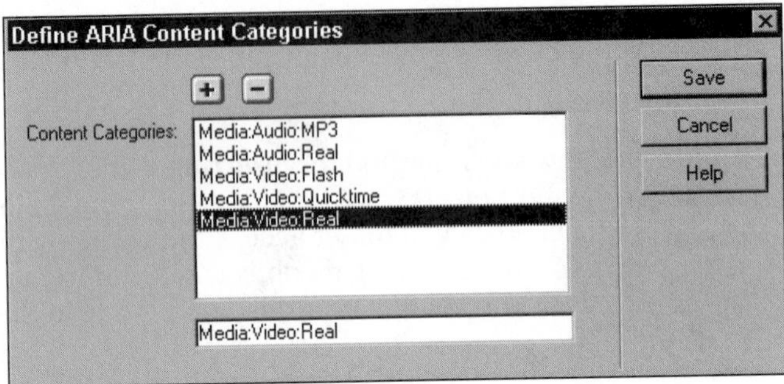

Figure 41-4: Set up Aria Content Categories on a per-page basis from within Dreamweaver.

4. Repeat Steps 2 and 3 to continue adding categories.
5. To remove a category from the list, select the category in the list area and click the Remove button.
6. When you're done, click Save.

As noted earlier, Dreamweaver writes the information to a text file, categories.txt, in the Aria folder. The text file takes this format:

```
[Content categories]
Media:Video:Quicktime
Media:Video:Flash
Media:Video:Real
Media:Audio:Real
Media:Audio:MP3
```

Each of these category lines could have been entered individually through the Define Aria Content Categories dialog box. However, in a situation where many categories are being added at the same time, a better practice would be to open the categories.txt file in a text area and input the categories by hand. You don't have to worry about order: the list is automatically alphabetized by Dreamweaver when presented in the Content Category object.

Once the categories are defined, use of the Aria Content Category object is very straightforward:

1. Select the Content Category object from the Aria panel.
2. From the Content Category dialog box, select the desired category from the drop-down list, as shown in Figure 41-5.

Figure 41-5: The Aria Content Category object presents an alphabetized list of the defined categories.

3. To add or remove categories, select Define.

   Selecting Define displays the Define Content Categories dialog box.

4. When you're done, choose OK.

Often the same Content Category is applicable to all the pages in a particular grouping. If these pages are contained within a single folder, or within successive subfolders, you don't have to enter the Aria categories one page at a time. Dreamweaver can automate the process for you through a command accessible in the Site window context menu.

To insert a Content Category to a series of files, follow these steps:

1. Open the Site window by choosing Window ➪ Sites Files or selecting the Site icon from the Launcher.
2. Select a folder with HTML files you want to insert the Content Category in.

   The same Content Category will be inserted in all the Web page files, including HTML, ASP, ColdFusion, and Java Server Pages.

3. Right-click (Control+click) the folder and choose Aria ➪ Insert Content Category from the context menu.
4. From the Insert Content Category dialog box, select the desired category from the drop-down list.
5. To insert the same Aria directive in all Web page files found in the directory's subfolders, select the Include Subfolders option.
6. Select the Insert button to begin the procedure.

   After all the pages have been processed, Dreamweaver reports the number of pages in which the code has been inserted.

If you mistakenly enter the wrong category, or want to change one category into another, use the custom Aria Property Inspector to make the modification. To access the inserted code, first choose View ➪ Head Content. Next, select one of the Comment symbols. If the chosen comment is an Aria directive, the proper Property Inspector appears, as shown in Figure 41-6.

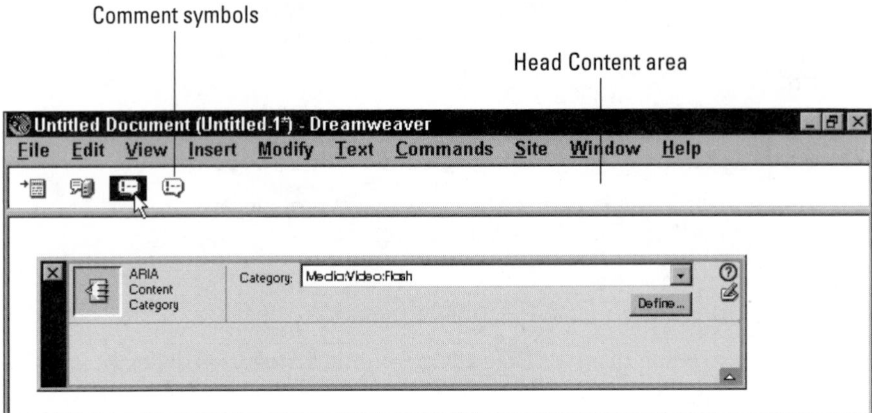

Figure 41-6: From the Aria Content Category Property Inspector, you can switch categories or define new ones.

Aria Visitor Category

Whereas Aria's Content Category directive is concerned with the substance of the Web page, the Visitor Category data is used to classify the people who browse those pages. Aria identifies visitors through the use of a cookie. When a page is requested from an Aria-enabled site, if no Aria cookie is detected on that system, the user is categorized as a first-time visitor and a cookie is sent. The cookie enables Aria to track the visitor throughout the session and on repeat visits.

Aria looks at three other bits of information to segment visitors into distinct categories:

- ✦ **Domain:** The name of the Web site the visitor is coming from, such as Yahoo, C|Net, or AOL.
- ✦ **Referrer:** The page on the other Web site where the link connecting to the Aria-enabled site was selected.
- ✦ **Browser:** The name and version of the browser as well as information on the operating system.

The category definitions that declare how this information is sorted into particular categories are established by the Aria administrator. As with the Content Categories, the page designer is only responsible for inserting the visitor category names in the pages. The process for using the Aria Visitor Category objects is identical to that of using Content Category objects, but the information is repeated here for the sake of completeness.

To define new visitor categories within Dreamweaver, follow these steps:

1. Choose Modify ➪ Aria ➪ Define Aria Visitor Categories.

The Define Aria Content Categories dialog box opens, as shown in Figure 41-7.

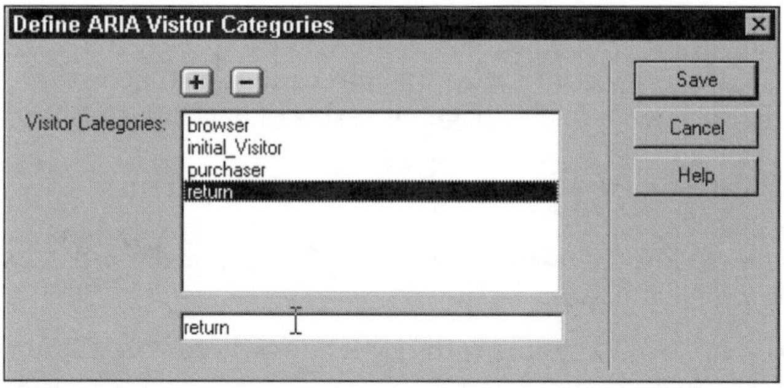

Figure 41-7: Track Web page visitors with the Aria Visitor Categories.

2. Enter the first category in the blank field below the Visitor Categories list area.
3. To add another category select the Add button (plus sign) to move the category to the list area and reposition the cursor in the blank field.
4. Repeat Steps 2 and 3 to continue adding categories.
5. To remove a category from the list, select the category in the list area and choose the Remove button (minus sign).
6. When you're done, click Save.

The defined Visitor Categories are written into the same text file as the Content categories, categories.txt, which is stored in the Aria folder. After the Content Categories section, the Visitor Categories section takes the same format:

```
[Visitor categories]
Referrer:Banner Ad:Lycos
Referrer:Banner Ad:Excite
Referrer:Search Engine:Yahoo
Referrer:Search Engine:AltaVista
```

As with the Content Categories, you have the option of declaring these categories through the Dreamweaver user interface and the Aria Visitor Categories dialog box or by editing the text file.

To insert defined Visitor Categories, follow these steps:

1. Select the Visitor Category object from the Aria panel.
2. From the Visitor Category dialog box, select the desired category from the drop-down list.
3. To add or remove categories, select Define.

Selecting Define displays the Define Visitor Categories dialog box.

4. When you're done, choose OK.

Inserting Visitor Categories can be accomplished on a folder-by-folder basis as well as page-by-page. The Insert Visitor Category command is also accessible in the Site window context menu when a folder, page, or series of pages is selected.

To insert a Visitor Category to a series of files, follow these steps:

1. Open the Site window by choosing Window ➪ Sites Files or selecting the Site icon from the Launcher.
2. Select a folder or variety of files with HTML files where you want to insert the Visitor Category.

   The same Visitor Category will be inserted in all the Web page files, including HTML, ASP, ColdFusion, and Java Server Pages.
3. Right-click (Control+click) the folder and choose Aria ➪ Insert Visitor Category from the context menu.
4. From the Insert Visitor Category dialog box, select the desired category from the drop-down list.
5. To insert the same Aria directive in all Web page files found in the directory's subfolders, select the Include Subfolders option.
6. Select the Insert button to begin the procedure.

   After all the pages have been processed, Dreamweaver reports the number of pages in which the code has been inserted.

Should you ever need to alter or remove the category directives, use Dreamweaver's Find and Replace feature in its HTML Source mode. You can even select specific folders or files in the Site window and modify the directives on all those pages in one operation.

Aria Key-Value Data

Aria key-value data pairs work with both Content and Visitor Categories on specific pages. The *key* element is an information type (defined by the Aria administrator) while the value is a specific subset of that category. For example, say you had an information type, `jobhunter`; jobhunter would be used as the key. The key-value data could be used to extend that category by creating a variety of values associated with it, such as:

```
Jobhunter-California:SanFrancisco
Jobhunter-California:LosAngeles
Jobhunter-California:SanDiego
```

The designer would insert a single key-value data pair on a relevant page; a page with a job offering in San Francisco would use the `Jobhunter-California:SanFrancisco` key-value data pair. This placement enables Aria to put all visitors to this particular page under one grouping (`Jobhunter-California:SanFrancisco`), while visitors to all of the sample key-value data pairs in another (`Jobhunter-California`).

When Aria encounters a key-value data pair on a page, it compares the value to the regular expressions for all related categories. If a match is found, the visit to the page is included in the category.

Because of the interrelated nature of categories and key-value data pairs, it's very important that the defined key-values match those defined in the `cats.sgml` file, which is managed by the Aria administrator.

To insert an Aria key-value data pair in your page, follow these steps:

1. From the Aria panel of the Objects palette, choose the Aria Key-Value Data object.

   The Insert Aria Key-Value Data dialog box appears, as shown in Figure 41-8.

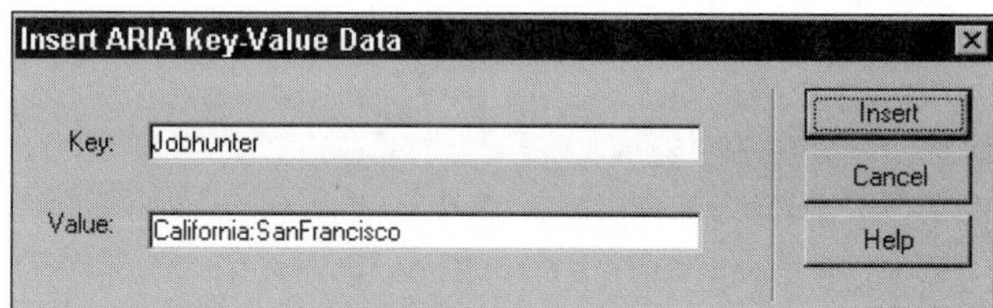

Figure 41-8: Use the Key-Value Data object repeatedly to insert multiple values for each key.

Remember not to use spaces when declaring a key. Use colons, hyphens, or underscores to separate words instead.

3. Enter the key information type in the Key field.
4. Enter the desired value in the Value field.
5. Click Insert when you're done.

As with the other Aria directives, the key-value data can be examined and modified by selecting the appropriate Comment symbol in the Head Content section.

Aria Persona Data

Aria Persona Data is used to build a profile of a Web site's visitors as they navigate throughout the site. Persona Data enables Aria to track items such as the last purchase as well as the last series of visited pages. This technology enables a high degree of customization. For example, suppose that the same visitor looked at a variety of product pages, one of which displayed a ski jacket and the other a pair of ice skates. From this information, it could be extrapolated that the visitor was interested in winter sports. From the marketer's point of view, this is very specific, useful information.

The Persona Data structure follows the key-value data model. To insert an Aria Persona Data pair in your page, follow these steps:

1. From the Aria panel of the Objects palette, choose the Aria Persona Data object.

   The Insert Aria Persona Data dialog box appears.

3. Enter the key information type in the Key field.
4. Enter the desired value in the Value field.
5. Click Insert when you're done.

The Persona Data structure enables Aria to track very specific visitors over time, as shown in Figure 41-9.

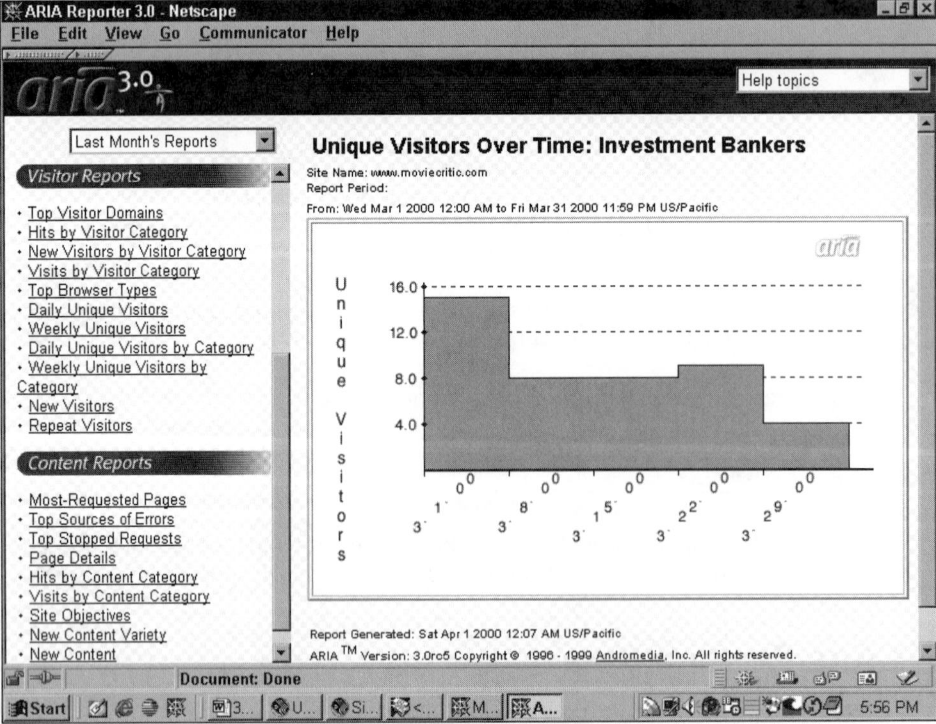

Figure 41-9: Aria Persona Data enables sites such as MovieCritic.com to follow very specific categories of visitors over an extended period.

Summary

For a Web site to be truly effective, some form of dialog must take place between the site creators and the site visitors. All manner of direct feedback is feasible, but often indirect feedback with more of an overview is more telling. Aria mines a variety of user statistics and presents the results for instant analysis; to function properly, Aria depends on metadata and other information embedded in the Web page. The Aria Objects for Dreamweaver provide these necessary tools:

- Aria uses several key components to display on-demand statistics. The Recorder is the server-side component that observes server traffic and extracts information from the embedded Aria objects.
- To analyze what Web site visitors are interested in, Aria employs user-defined Content Categories. These Content Categories are defined within Dreamweaver and then pertinent categories are inserted via the Content Category object.
- Visitor Categories are used to track visitor traffic to and through the Web site. Similarly to the Content Categories, the Visitor Categories are first defined in Dreamweaver and then the proper categories are inserted with the Visitor Category object.
- More specific details about a Web visitor's onsite choices are followed through the Aria key-value and Persona objects. Aria uses regular expressions to detect patterns of interest for Web site visitors.

In the next chapter, you'll see how to easily add extensions to Dreamweaver with the Extension Manager.

✦ ✦ ✦

CHAPTER 42

Customizing with the Extension Manager

✦ ✦ ✦ ✦

In This Chapter

Extension Manager overview

Adding and removing new extensions

Visiting the Exchange

Bundling custom extensions

Submitting extensions to the Exchange

✦ ✦ ✦ ✦

Macromedia had a problem. One of Dreamweaver's most powerful features was misunderstood, hard to use and, largely, unknown to the vast majority of the program's users. The feature in question, Dreamweaver's extensibility, is far more than a single command or dialog box: *Extensibility* is the core facility to shape Dreamweaver to work the way you want — no, need — to work. This facility has inspired a number of third-party individuals and, increasingly, companies to create a wide array of Dreamweaver extensions. Everything from simple objects to site-wide commands to database integration applications are now available for Dreamweaver.

Although all of these extensions are available for Dreamweaver, they are increasingly difficult to install and manage. Macromedia's solution, not only for Dreamweaver but for other programs in their product line as well, is the Extension Manager. The Extension Manager enables you to easily install even the most complex extensions with ease and, if need be, to uninstall them just as easily.

For the Extension Manager to work properly, an entirely new system of assembling extensions was developed. To assist in the distribution of extensions, Macromedia also developed the online center, the Macromedia Exchange. In this chapter you'll see how to install and manage extensions in both Dreamweaver and Dreamweaver UltraDev. When you're ready to don the mantle of Dreamweaver extensionologist, you'll find additional coverage here showing you how to package and distribute your extension to the world, both on the Exchange and off.

Understanding the Extension Manager

Dreamweaver's configuration is basically folder-based. By this, I mean that extensions are initially recognized to be a certain type (Object, Command, Floater, Inspector, and so on) by being stored in the correspondingly named folder. As Dreamweaver matures and extensions grow in complexity, it's not uncommon for an extension to store files in more than one location. A recent version of my BulletBuilder command, for example, requires 36 files spread over six different directories — some of which must be created upon installation. Without the Extension Manager, the instructions for installing such a command would be a nightmare and a potential support bottleneck. The Extension Manager, however, handles the install process swiftly and without errors. Moreover, it keeps track of all the files so that they can be removed or updated when necessary.

The Extension Manager is a separate program that can be run from within Dreamweaver or independently. The core functionality of the Extension Manager is straightforward:

- ✦ New extensions can be installed.
- ✦ Existing extensions, previously set up by the Extension Manager, can be removed.
- ✦ Users can get more extensions from the Macromedia Exchange.
- ✦ Developers can package files as a new extension.
- ✦ Once packaged, new extensions can be submitted to the Macromedia Exchange.

You can start the Extension Manager in a number of ways, but the simplest is to choose Commands ➪ Manage Extensions. As noted earlier, the Exchange Manager is a separate program from Dreamweaver and runs in its own window, as shown in Figure 42-1.

The latest version of the Extension Manager is available from the Macromedia Exchange site at `http://exchange.macromedia.com`. If you're interested in creating your own extensions for distribution, be sure to select the Development Tools option during installation. Mac users should choose Custom Install from the option list and then select the box for Development Tools.

Adding Extensions

One of the keys to the Extension Manager is the Macromedia Extension Package file type. To be installed, an extension must be of this file type that uses the .mxp file extension. An MXP file contains all the required files, plus instructions on where the files should be stored, what the extension does, who the author is, and more.

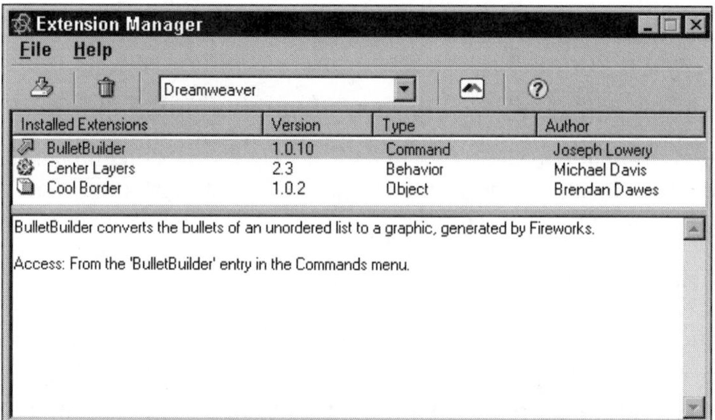

Figure 42-1: The Extension Manager keeps track of all extensions it has installed, providing version and other information about each one.

Although the primary source for Macromedia Extension Package files is the Macromedia Exchange, you can also retrieve these files from other sources such as developers' sites or this book's CD-ROMs. If you've located the MXP file from the Internet, your browser may offer you alternative methods to start the installation:

✦ Download the file to your system and complete the installation once that process is complete.

✦ Install the file directly from the Internet. (Note: This option is not available for extensions housed on the Macromedia Exchange.)

It's a matter of personal preference, but I prefer to store all the extensions locally. The vast majority of them tend to be fairly small and if I need to install them again or on a separate machine, I don't have to go through the download process again. Macromedia recommends that you maintain your extensions in the Configuration\Downloaded Extensions folder, but there's no real benefit to doing so if you'd prefer to store them elsewhere.

To complete the installation, follow these steps:

1. If you chose to open the extension from the Internet, the Extension Manager is automatically launched. If you downloaded the extension, double-click the .mxp file to launch the Extension Manager. In either case, the Macromedia Exchange legal disclaimer is presented.

2. Select the Accept button to continue with the installation or Decline to cancel it.

   After you accept the disclaimer, the Extension Manager informs you whether the installation is successful or alerts you to any errors it encounters, such as existing files with the same name.

If the installation succeeds, the extension is added to your list. The list displays the name of the installed extensions, their version number, the type, and the author.

If you have a great number of extensions, you can sort the list in the Extension Manager by selecting the column heading. To change the display order from ascending to descending (to show, for example, the highest version numbers first) click the heading again under Windows; on Macintosh systems, select the sort-order button on top of the scroll bar.

You can also install an extension from within Dreamweaver by following these steps:

1. Choose Commands ➪ Manage Extensions to open the Extension Manager.
2. Select File ➪ Install Extension or use the keyboard shortcut, Ctrl+I (Command+I). Alternatively, Windows users can also select the Install New Extensionbutton.

   The Select Extension to Install dialog box opens.
3. In the Select Extension dialog box, locate the desired .mxp file on your system and choose Install.

   The legal disclaimer is presented.
4. Select the Accept button to continue with the installation or Decline to cancel it.
5. Once the installation is complete, choose File ➪ Exit (File ➪ Quit) to close the Extension Manager or click the Close button.

Some extensions require Dreamweaver to be relaunched in order to take effect. Unless you're running Dreamweaver 3.01 or higher, you must restart for every extension; failure to restart may result in a corrupted menu file.

Installing in Dreamweaver or UltraDev

The latest version of the Extension Manager offers the ability to install your extension in either Dreamweaver or UltraDev. Although there's no compelling reason to maintain both programs on your system, it's anticipated that initially developers may opt for this route until they're comfortable with UltraDev. With this duality in mind, you choose whether to install an extension in Dreamweaver or UltraDev by selecting one or the other from the drop-down list at the top of the Extension Manager. By default, the intended target is Dreamweaver and if you've double-clicked the .mxp file outside of Dreamweaver\UltraDev or opened the extension from the Internet, the extension is automatically added to Dreamweaver only. To direct an installation into UltraDev, you must choose Commands ➪ Manage Extensions from within Dreamweaver or UltraDev.

With the Extension Manager, extensions can reconfigure your menu for better access. If you ever encounter a problem with the menu system, however, you can always restore your previous menus. When modifying the menus, the Extension Manager always creates a backup of the XML file that controls their structure, menus.xml. The backup is named menus.xbk; to restore your previous configuration, rename menus.xbk to menus.xml.

Removing an Extension

Occasionally an extension outlives its usefulness — perhaps the functionality is incorporated into the core program or maybe another extension does its job better. Whatever the reason, extensions are as easy to remove as they are to install with the Extension Manager. Just select the unwanted extension in the Extension Manager list and choose File ➪ Remove Extension or use the keyboard shortcut, Ctrl+R (Command+– (minus symbol)). Windows users can also select the Remove Extension button, shown in Figure 42-2.

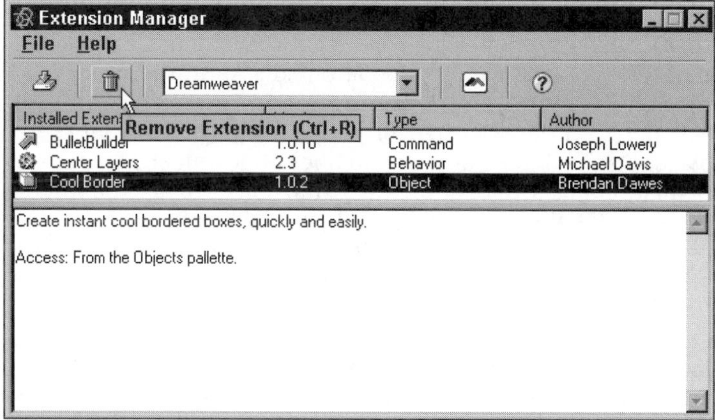

Figure 42-2: To delete an installed extension from your system, select it and choose the Remove Extension button.

Maximizing the Macromedia Exchange

The Macromedia Exchange is the primary venue for Dreamweaver extensions. You can find this addition to the main Macromedia Web site at `http://exchange.macromedia.com` — but you don't have to type in the address to get there. The Web site is accessible both from Dreamweaver and from the Extension Manager. In Dreamweaver, you can get to the Macromedia Exchange if you:

✦ Choose Insert ➪ Get More Objects

✦ Select Commands ➪ Get More Commands

✦ From the Behavior palette, select the Add button and then choose Get More Behaviors from the list

The Extension Manager also gives you a couple of direct connections to the Exchange: Just select File ➪ Go to Macromedia Exchange. Windows users may also select the Macromedia symbol on the toolbar. Either of these methods fires up your primary browser and, if you're connected to the Internet, connects you to the Dreamweaver Exchange home page.

Although it was not open at the time of this writing, Macromedia is expected to launch a UltraDev branch in the Exchange.

What's at the Exchange

The Macromedia Exchange is far more than a list of files to download. Macromedia has taken great pains to bring a degree of stability to the extensions posted, both before and after users add them to their systems. All extensions posted on the Exchange (see Figure 42-3) have been checked by Macromedia quality-assurance personnel to ensure that the files are virus-free and usable, and that they do no harm to your system, the Dreamweaver interface, or Dreamweaver itself. Extensions passing a more stringent series of tests receive a Macromedia Approved classification.

The Exchange also offers a variety of ways for you to decide if you want the extension in the first place. The Exchange lists the number of downloads an extension has received for a quantifiable seal-of-approval. Extensions can also be rated by other users (with a scale of 1 to 5 where 5 is the best). Finally, a discussion group is available for every extension on the site. The discussion group is the perfect place to post a question or comment to the author of the extension or other users.

The Extension Manager and Dreamweaver Exchange work hand in hand. All extensions found on the Exchange use the Extension Manager for installation. Consequently, you won't find any pre-Dreamweaver 3 extensions there, unless they've been converted by the author.

Searching for extensions

The Dreamweaver Exchange is growing by leaps and bounds; the offerings are too many to just browse them all and easily find what you're looking for. To assist you in your search, the Exchange provides both a basic and an advanced search engine. The basic search field is good when you know the name or partial name of an extension. The advanced engine, shown in Figure 42-4, enables you to search by category (discussed later in this section), Dreamweaver type (such as Command, Object, and so on), author's name, the approval code, the rating, the date added, the download popularity and, of course, the name — or any combination of these criteria.

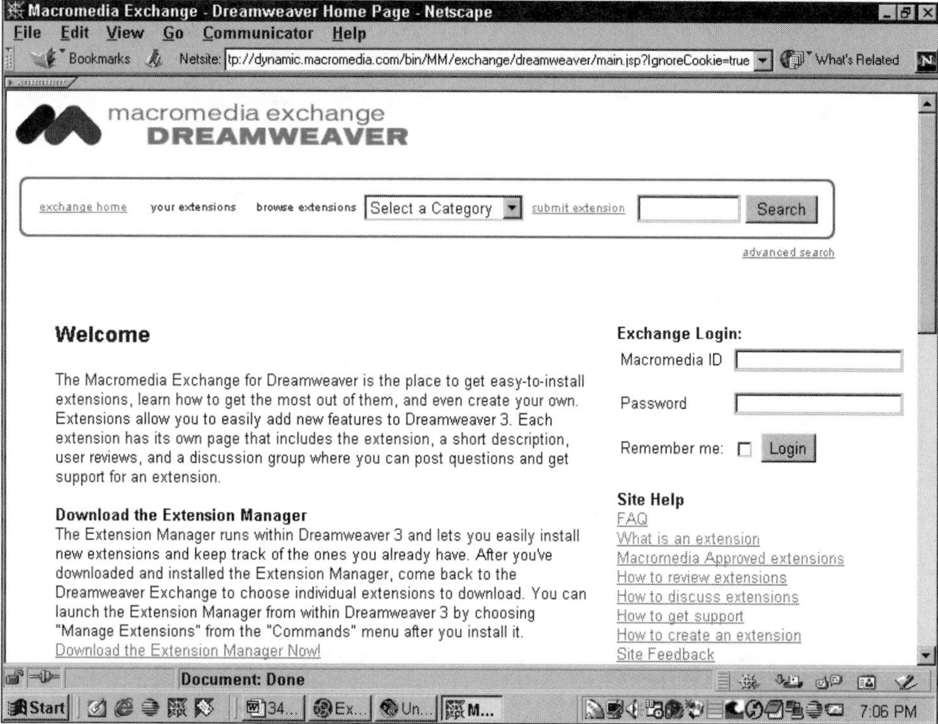

Figure 42-3: The Dreamweaver Exchange is home base for Extension Manager–installed extensions.

The Dreamweaver Exchange search categories offer a more general method of locating extensions — especially useful when you're not quite sure what you're looking for. As of this writing, you can select from 13 different categories:

- **All:** All the extensions currently available.
- **App Server:** Extensions aimed at interfacing with Web application servers such as Allaire's ColdFusion and Blueworld's Lasso Web Data Engine.
- **Browser Compatibility:** Extensions for detecting and redirecting browsers.
- **DHTML:** Extensions for adding Dynamic HTML objects and behaviors.
- **eCommerce:** Extensions designed to help with creating catalogs, tying into existing shopping engine services, or performing transactional processing.
- **Fireworks:** Extensions that use both Dreamweaver and Fireworks. Requires Fireworks 3 or above.
- **Navigation:** Extensions designed to help Web site navigation, including menu builders and frame handlers.

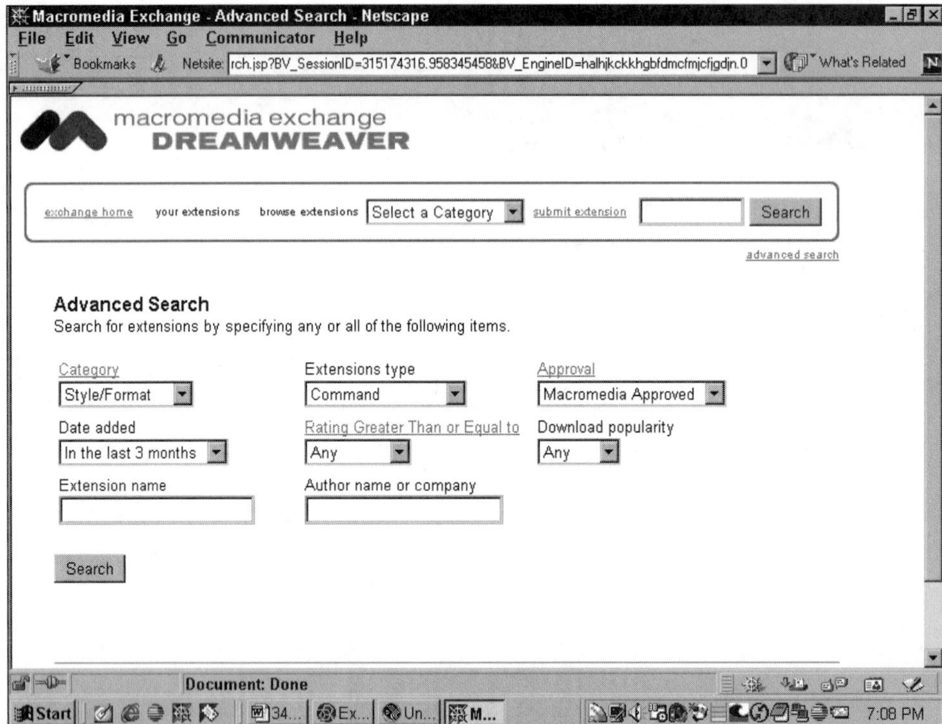

Figure 42-4: Use the Exchange's advanced search engine to narrow down your choices by any combination of search criteria.

- ✦ **Productivity:** Extensions for automating Dreamweaver procedures in Web page production.
- ✦ **Rich media:** Extensions aimed at controlling video, audio, and other media types, both from third parties and from Macromedia.
- ✦ **Scripting:** Extensions for helping with JavaScript editing and example scripts.
- ✦ **Security:** Extensions for presenting and protecting your Web page as intended.
- ✦ **Style/Format:** Extensions to assist in formatting existing text on a Web page.
- ✦ **Tables:** Extensions to manipulate tables.
- ✦ **Text:** Extensions for including special characters and manipulating existing text.

To navigate to a particular category, pick one from the drop-down list on every page of the Exchange and a current list of all those that apply will appear, as shown in Figure 42-5. Once the listing is presented, you can sort by any criteria by selecting the category heading. Selecting the same heading a second time toggles the sort order from ascending to descending.

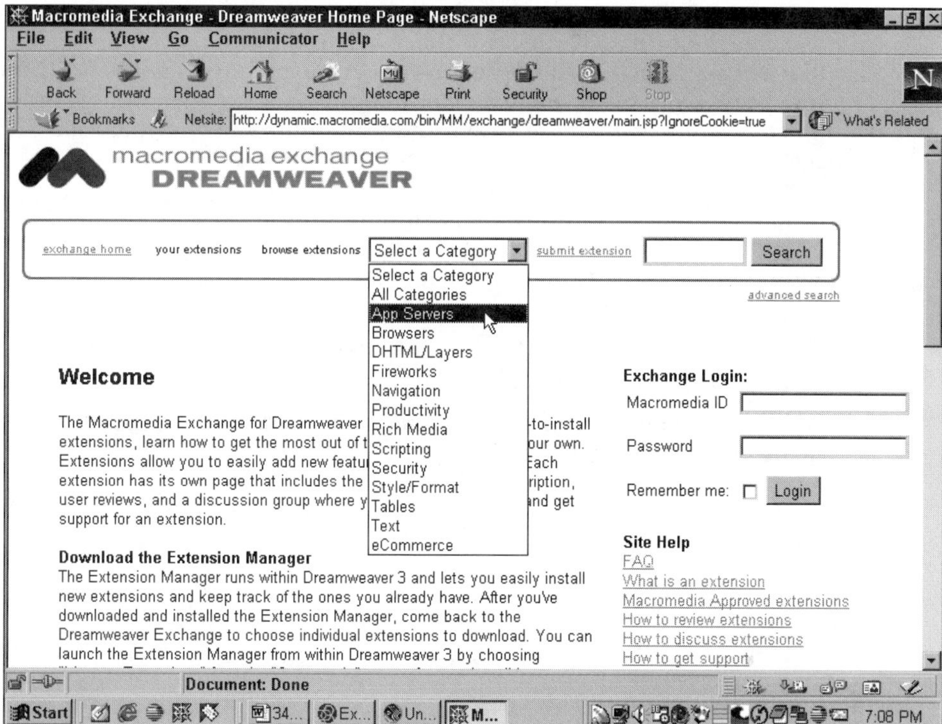

Figure 42-5: The Exchange category listings permit you to browse extensions thematically.

Packaging Extensions

So you've been bitten by the bug and you're ready to become an extensionologist, eh? After you've created your Dreamweaver add-on masterpiece that you're sure will take the world by storm, you've got to make sure the world can install it properly — and that means packaging your extension with the Extension Manager. When you're done, you'll have a nice .mxp file to submit to Dreamweaver Exchange or to distribute on your own. However, to put together the packaged extension, you first need to create a file that describes your product and all the files it uses. This file is called a Macromedia Extension Information file; Windows users might see the .mxi extension identifying this file type.

Note

Any text file will do on the Mac, but a savvy user can give a text file a Creator code of "MMXP" (Extension Manager) and the file will get an icon that matches the Extension Manager application. The .mxi ending is fine too, of course.

A Macromedia Extension Information file is an XML file that the Extension Manager uses to create the extension package. The .mxi file follows a particular format and, as of this writing, must be hand coded. However, the process is not difficult and Macromedia provides blank template files to make the job easier. Nonetheless, it's important to understand the format and your options before you begin to code the page.

A Macromedia Extension Information file has three main parts:

- ✦ A description of the extension (including its name, category, version number, and brief description) and the author's name.
- ✦ A report of every file used by the extension that includes the location in which it is currently stored as well as its installation destination.
- ✦ Details of all configuration changes including the addition or deletion of any menu items and/or keyboard shortcuts.

So what does an .mxi file look like? Here's the .mxi file I used to package an extension of mine called Repeat History:

```
<macromedia-extension
   name="Repeat History"
   version="1.0.0"
   type="Command"
   requires-restart="false">

   <!-- List the required/compatible products -->

   <products>
      <product name="Dreamweaver" version="3" primary="true" />
   </products>

   <!-- Describe the author -->

   <author name="Joseph Lowery" />

   <!-- Describe the extension -->

   <description>
   <![CDATA[
   Use Repeat History to repeat any selected steps in the
History palette, any number of times.
   ]]>
   </description>
```

```
   <!-- Describe where the extension shows in the UI of the
product -->

   <ui-access>
   <![CDATA[
Access: From the 'Repeat History' entry in the Commands menu.
   ]]>
   </ui-access>

   <!-- Describe the files that comprise the extension -->

   <files>
      <file name="RepeatHistory.htm"
destination="$dreamweaver/configuration/commands" />
   </files>

   <!-- Describe the changes to the configuration -->

   <configuration-changes>
      <menu-insert insertAfter="DWMenu_Commands_SortTable">
         <menuitem name="Repeat History"
file="Commands/RepeatHistory.htm" id="jl_RepeatHistory" />
      </menu-insert>
   </configuration-changes>

</macromedia-extension>
```

Because it is an XML file, certain rules of syntax must be followed when the .mxi file is modified. In particular, be careful to always enclose attribute values with a pair of double-quotes (rather than single quotes), like this:

```
name="Repeat History"
```

If you're unfamiliar with XML, you'll also want to be sure to end empty tags properly. You'll recall that an empty tag is one without a corresponding closing tag that is unneeded because an empty tag does not enclose any content. For example:

```
<author name="Joseph Lowery" />
```

Note the closing elements of the tag, `/>`, are positioned next to each other without a space in between.

For more details about XML in Dreamweaver, see Chapter 30.

Describing the extension

The very first thing you might notice about this file is that one XML tag pair, `<macromedia-extension>...</macromedia-extension>`, surrounds all the other tags. Several attributes, within the opening tag, are required for describing your extension. These descriptions are used both by the Extension Manager and by the Macromedia Exchange, if you submit your extension for posting. The attributes and their accepted values for the `<macromedia-extension>` tag are as follows:

Attribute	*Description*
`name`	The name of your extension as it will appear in the Extension Manager.
`version`	The version number of the current extension. Macromedia recommends that you use a standardized numbering scheme where major revision numbers, minor revision numbers, and build numbers are all separated by periods. For example, the version number 2.0.4 would indicated that this is the fourth build of the second major revision.

`type`	The type attribute refers to the Dreamweaver category the extension falls under. The accepted values are as follows:
	`Behavior (or action)`
	`BrowserProfile`
	`Command`
	`Dictionary`
	`Encoding`
	`Floater`
	`JsExtension`
	`Object`
	`Plugin`
	`PropertyInspector`
	`Query`
	`Suite`
	`Template`
	`ThirdPartyTags`
	`Translator`
	For example, `type="Command"`; type values are not case-sensitive.
	A suite is a set of extensions that fall into more than one category. The Nokia WML Studio, for example, includes commands, floaters, inspectors, `thirdPartyTags`, translators, objects, and numerous other custom extensions.

Attribute	*Description*
`author`	The name of the author, to be displayed in the Extension Manager.
`requires-restart`	Accepts a value of either `true` or `false`, If true, the user is informed that Dreamweaver must be relaunched for the extension to work properly. This attribute is ignored on Dreamweaver versions under 3.0.1.

You can enter a more elaborate explanation of your extension in the `<description>` tag. The `<description>` tag uses an XML character data format or `CDATA` like this:

```
<description>
<![CDATA[
Use Repeat History to repeat any selected steps in the History
palette, any number of times.
]]>
</description>
```

The opening `<![CDATA[` and closing `]]>` declarations must be included as shown. Character data differs from standard text in that a couple of formatting elements — namely `<br/>` and ` ` — can also be used. Note that the line-break tag follows the XML convention for empty tags, instead of the standard HTML syntax. There's no set limit on the length of your description that appears in the lower portion of the Extension Manager when your installed extension is selected, as shown in Figure 42-6.

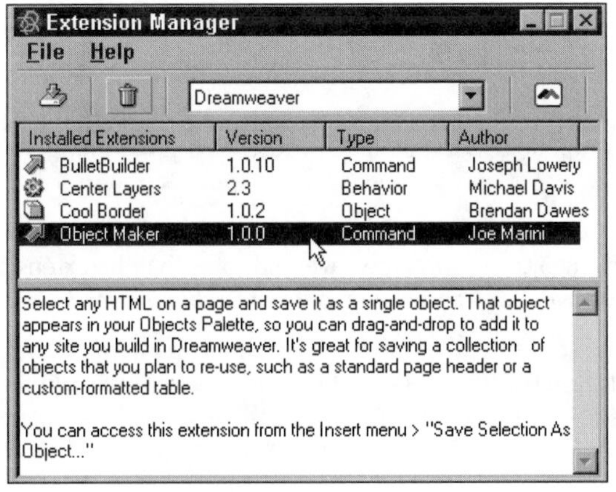

Figure 42-6: The `<description>` portion of the .mxi file is used to describe the extension in some detail.

Another bit of information is displayed in the Extension Manager when an extension is selected: how the user accesses the extension. The `<ui-access>` tag, which also allows character data, informs the user under which menu or on which palette the extension can be found. For example, here's the entry from my BulletBuilder command:

```
<ui-access>
<![CDATA[
Access: From the 'BulletBuilder' entry in the Commands menu.
]]>
</ui-access>
```

Because the `<ui-access>` information appears directly under the `<description>` content, it's a good idea to preface the instruction with a key word or phrase, such as "Access:" or "To get started."

Tip

If you've created an object, be sure to include the name of the Object palette pane that the extension will appear on. The standard installation of Dreamweaver has six different panes initially and you can add any number of custom ones.

The final descriptive tag of the .mxi file lists the compatible Macromedia products and details that are required for the extension to work properly. The `<products>` tag takes this form:

```
<products>
   <product name="Dreamweaver" version="3" primary="true"/>
   <product name="Fireworks" version="3" required="true"/>
</products>
```

Each compatible product is listed in a separate `<product>` tag. The `<product>` tag attributes are as follows:

Attribute	*Description*
`name`	The name of the compatible Macromedia product. As of this writing, the accepted values are `Dreamweaver`, `Fireworks`, and `UltraDev`.
`version`	The lowest version number of the product that can be used by the extension. For example, specifying 3.0.1 for Dreamweaver indicates that the extension works with Dreamweaver 3.0.1 and higher, but not Dreamweaver 3.
`primary`	If multiple programs are listed, the one in which the user interface appears is considered `primary`. For this program, the `primary` attribute would be set to `true`. In the previous code example from the BulletBuilder .mxi file, Dreamweaver is designated as the `primary` program.
`required`	Including a `required="true"` attribute indicates that the named program is necessary for the extension to run properly. If the user does not have a required program, an alert is displayed and the installation is cancelled.

For <products> designated with primary="true", you don't have to also include a required="true" attribute — that's understood.

Detailing the files

Arguably, the <files> section is the real workhorse of an .mxi document. Within the <files>...</files> tag pair, a separate tag declares the source and destination of each file used in an extension. In the most basic command, this might only mean one line, as in this example:

```
<files>
   <file name="RepeatHistory.htm"
destination="$dreamweaver/configuration/commands/"/>
</files>
```

On the other hand, my version of the Nokia WML Studio lists 183 individual files. Why so many? In addition to all the fundamental HTML and JavaScript pages, every graphic in the dialog boxes (such as up and down button images) is also necessary for the extension.

The <file> tag has two key attributes: source and destination. The source attribute is the full path file name, relative to where the .mxi file is saved. In other words, for the command MacroMaker, you might create a new folder called MacroMaker. Within that folder, copies of all the required extension files would be stored, like this:

```
MacroMaker (folder)
- MacroMaker.htm
- MacroMaker.js
   images (folder)
   - logo.gif
   - up.gif
   - down.gif
   scripts (folder)
   - copyMacro.js
   - addMacro.js
   - repeatMacro.js
```

The source attribute includes both the file name and the needed path to find the file. Using the previous example file setup, the source for the logo file would be:

```
source="images/logo.gif"
```

You can also use colons and back slashes, as well as forward slashes, to designate path or folder separators.

Tip

As the example shows, it's best to gather all your required files in a single folder, with subfolders if desired, and store the .mxi file there. Although the Extension Manager copies files into the packaged extension, it's best not to point to the files installed in your own Dreamweaver Configuration folder in the .mxi <file> tags.

The other key attribute, `destination`, names the folder where the given file should be installed. A number of special variables point directly to a program's root folder: `$dreamweaver`, `$fireworks`, and `$ultradev`. To install the MacroMaker command in the Commands folder of Dreamweaver, regardless of where the user installed Dreamweaver, use this syntax:

```
destination="$dreamweaver:Configuration:Commands"
```

Again, path separators can be colons or either type of slash, / or \. Extension files can also be inserted in your platform's system folder by using the `$system` variable; for Windows *9x* users, this variable points to the System folder, while for Windows NT or 2000 users, it points to the System32 folder. The operating system folder in Mac OS through version 9 is /System Folder; on Mac OS X, it's just /System.

Caution

Certain operating systems are case-sensitive when it comes to folder names. Be sure you check both the spelling and case of the intended destination folders.

Three other attributes are applicable to the <file> tag: `platform`, `shared`, and `systemfile`, as follows:

Attribute	*Description*
`platform`	The Extension Manager permits different files to be installed on different systems through the `platform` attribute; accepted values are `win` or `mac`. If no `platform` is specified, the file will be installed on both systems.
`shared`	If a file is used by more than one extension, the `shared` attribute is set to `true`. This attribute prevents a shared file from being deleted if one of the extensions that uses it is removed.
`systemfile`	Designating a file's `systemfile` attribute as `true` indicates that the file is used by the operating system or files other than Macromedia extensions. A file marked `systemfile="true"` is never removed.

Specifying the configuration

Prior to Dreamweaver 3, menu customization was an iffy proposition at best. While you could add items to any menu by editing the InsertMenu.htm and CommandsMenu.htm files, your time-consuming efforts could be obliterated at any turn should you install an extension that rewrote these files to better suit its needs. With the addition of the menus.xml file, menus are far more customizable and flexible — extensions can insert menu items, and even whole menus, without eliminating the existing setup.

Although the InsertMenu.htm and CommandsMenu.htm files are no longer used to control the menus, HTML files added to the Objects subfolders and the Commands folder are still appended to the Insert and Commands menus respectively. To prevent the name of an HTML file from showing up in these menus, insert the code <!-- MENU-LOCATION=NONE --> at the top of the document.

The final portion of a Macromedia Extension Information file is concerned with making your extension accessible to the user. To this end, both menus and keyboard shortcuts are defined within the <configuration-changes>... </configuration-changes> tag pair. All menus, including context (or shortcut) menus, are fair game. You can even add menu items that are extensions in and of themselves.

Before you begin adding — or removing — menu items and shortcuts, you need to understand the menus.xml structure. In brief, the menus.xml file consists of a series of definitions for each menu bar (both window and context menus) that, in turn, contain definitions for each menu and submenu. Within the menu and submenu sections, a separate code line defines every menu item; separators are also declared here. All of the menu bars, menus, and menu items have unique identifiers entered as the id attribute. The id parameter is key to customizing the configuration; once you know the id value of a menu item, you can insert your own menu item before, after, or even instead of the existing item.

To learn more about menu commands and the menus.xml file, see "Managing Menus and Keyboard Shortcuts" in Chapter 21.

Adding a new menu and menu items

Whenever a new menu or menu item is added — by far the most common situation an extension-maker faces — the aptly named <menu-insert> tag is used in the .mxi file. Here's an example of a menu being added:

```
<menu-insert insertAfter="DWMenu_Edit">
  <menu name="WML" id="DWMenu_WML">
  </menu>
</menu-insert>
```

The sole attribute in the <menu-insert> tag places the menu, in this case after Dreamweaver's standard Edit menu. Four placement attributes are possible:

✦ **insertAfter:** Places the menu (or menu item) immediately after the menu (or menu item) identified.

✦ **insertBefore:** Places the menu (or menu item) immediately before the menu (or menu item) identified.

✦ **appendTo:** Adds the menu item to the bottom of the named menu.

✦ **prependTo:** Adds the menu item to the top of the named menu.

One additional attribute, `skipSeparator`, may be used in conjunction with the `insertAfter` parameter. If `skipSeparator=true` is included in the `<menu-insert>` tag and a separator (a line separating menu items) exists, the menu items are placed after the separator rather than directly beneath the existing menu item.

Although the `<menu>` tag encloses no content, a closing tag, `</menu>` is still used in an .mxi file. This structure is designed to parallel the one used in the menus.xml file.

To create a submenu, you need to use the `appendTo` attribute, as in this example:

```
<menu-insert appendTo="jl_Deva">
    <menu name="Create Help Pages" id="jl_Deva_Create" />
</menu-insert>

<menu-insert appendTo="jl_Deva_Create">
    <menu name="TOC" id="jl_Deva_TOC" />
</menu-insert>

<menu-insert appendTo="jl_Deva_Create">
    <menu name="Index" id="jl_Deva_Index" />
</menu-insert>

<menu-insert appendTo="jl_Deva_TOC">
    <menuitem name="Generate TOC" id="jl_Deva_TOC_generate" />
    <menuitem name="Edit TOC" id="jl_Deva_TOC_edit" />
</menu-insert>

<menu-insert appendTo="jl_Deva_Index">
    <menuitem name="Generate Index" id="jl_Deva_Index_generate" />
    <menuitem name="Edit Index" id="jl_Deva_Index_edit" />
</menu-insert>
```

This code would result in a menu structure like this:

```
_Deva_
Create Help Pages
   - TOC
     - Generate TOC
     - Edit TOC
   - Index
     - Generate Index
     - Edit Index
```

Menu items are defined within a <menu-insert> tag. To add four items to the just-created WML menu in the prior example, this code is used:

```
   <menu-insert appendTo="DWMenu_Wml">
   <menuitem name="New Wml Deck" enabled="true"
file="Commands/Nokia_NewDeck.htm" id="DWMenu_Wml_New_Wml_Deck"
/>
      <separator />
      <menuitem name="Select Phone" enabled="true"
file="Commands/Nokia_SelectPhone.htm"
id="DWMenu_Wml_New_Select_Phone" />
      <menuitem name="Preview on Phone" enabled="true"
file="Commands/Nokia_PreviewOnPhone.htm"
id="DWMenu_Wml_New_Preview_on_Phone" />
      <separator />
      <menuitem name="Wml Messages" enabled="true"
command="dw.toggleFloater('Nokia_MsgBox')"
checked="dw.getFloaterVisibility('Nokia_MsgBox')"
id="DWMenu_Wml_Wml_Messages" />
   </menu-insert>
```

The <menuitem> tag is extremely flexible, even, as noted earlier, to the point of enabling JavaScript commands to be attached directly into the item. Numerous parameters can be applied, as discussed in depth in Chapter 21 and listed in Table 42-1.

Table 42-1
Tag Parameters

Attribute	Possible Value	Description
name	Any menu name	The name of the menu item as it appears on the menu. An underscore character causes the following letter to be underlined for Windows' shortcuts—for example, _Frames becomes Frames. The underline is ignored on Macintosh systems. To use an underscore as part of the name, it must be escaped with a percent sign, like this: Frame%_Breaker.
id	Any unique name	The identifying term for the menu item.
key	Any special key or keyboard key plus modifier(s)	The keyboard shortcut used to execute the command.

Continued

Attribute	Possible Value	Description
platform	win or mac	The operating system valid for the current menu item. If the platform parameter is omitted, the menu item is applicable for both systems.
enabled	JavaScript function	If present, governs whether a menu item is active (the function returns true) or dimmed (the function returns false). Including enabled=true assures that the function is always available.
command *(required if the file is not used)*	JavaScript function	Executed when the menu item is selected. This inline JavaScript function capability is used for simple functions.
file *(required if the command is not used)*	Path to a file with JavaScript included	The file is executed when the menu item is selected; the path is relative to the Configuration folder.
checked	JavaScript function	Displays a checkmark next to the menu item if the function returns true.
dynamic	N/A	Specifies that the menu item is set dynamically by the function(s) found in the file.

Should you ever need to remove a previously inserted menu or menu item, use the <menu-remove> tag. The only needed attribute is the id of the element to be removed. For example,

```
<menu-remove id="jl_Deva_Beta">
```

deletes a menu item that is no longer necessary. If the id is not found, no changes are made.

Obviously, you want to use the <menu-remove> tag with great caution. Typically, this tag is only used when your extension is an update to a previous version and the changes affect only your own work.

Including separators and comments

To make a menu easier to read, a separator is inserted between two menu items. The `<separator />` tag is an empty one, with two possible parameters, `id` and `platform`. Again, the `id` attribute is a unique name while `platform` specifies whether the separator should be used only for Windows (`win`) or Macintosh (`mac`); if the `platform` attribute is not included, the separator is added on both systems. The code for separating two line items looks like this:

```
<menuitem name="BulletBuilder"
file="Commands/BulletBuilder.htm" id="jl_BulletBuilder" />
<separator id="jl_builder_separator" />
<menuitem name="StyleBuilder" file="Commands/StyleBuilder.htm"
id="jl_StyleBuilder" />
```

Not only can you make your menus more readable, but you can also make your code easier to understand as well. Two types of comments are available in an .mxi file. The first is a standard HTML comment that is useful for the developer when constructing the file, like this one:

```
<!-- Objects start here -->
```

The other type of comment goes within a `<menu-insert>` tag and is designed to be written into the menus.xml file during installation. This facility enables developers to document their code with comments so that the configuration changes can more easily be identified. Instead of HTML syntax, an XML format is used:

```
<menu-insert insertBefore="DW_Help">
   <comment>The following menu changes were made by the Deva
extension to Dreamweaver</comment>
   [menu items go here]
</menu-insert>
```

Adding and removing shortcuts

Most of the time, shortcuts are added as part of a `<menuitem>` tag through the `key` attribute. However, for shortcuts that do not have a corresponding command file, such as those only used within the Document window, you can still add a keyboard shortcut using the `<shortcut-insert>` and `<shortcut>` tags. These tags work similarly to the `<menu-insert>` and `<menu>` combination.

For example, the following code permits the user to delete the following word by using the Ctrl+Delete (Cmd+Delete) keyboard combination:

```
<shortcut-insert listId = "DWMainWindow">
   <shortcut key="Cmd+Del"
command="dw.getDocumentDOM().nextWord(1,true);dw.getDocumentDOM
().deleteSelection()"
id="DWShortcuts_Main_DeleteNext" />
</shortcut-insert>
```

A single attribute exists for `<shortcut-insert>`, `listId`. The `listId` attribute corresponds to the shortcut list in menus.xml to which the shortcut is to be inserted. Currently, four such lists exist in Windows and three in the Macintosh system:

- ✦ **DWMainWindow:** Shortcuts work within the Document window
- ✦ **DWSiteWindow (Windows only):** Shortcuts used in the Site window
- ✦ **DWTimelineContext:** Shortcuts used in the Timeline inspector
- ✦ **DWHTMLContext:** Shortcuts used in the HTML Source inspector

The shortcut tag, on the other hand, has a number of applicable attributes:

Attribute	*Description*
`key`	The key combination used to activate the command or file.
`id`	A unique identification for the shortcut.
`command`	JavaScript code that is executed when the menu item is selected.
`file`	The path to a file that is executed when the menu item is selected; the path is relative to the Configuration folder.
`platform`	The applicable platform; accepted values are `win` and `mac`.

You can find details on syntax for keyboard shortcuts in Chapter 21.

Running the packager

Now that your extension is built and tested and your .mxi file is complete, all that remains is to package the extension. The procedure is completely automated and, I find, very fast, for even complex multifile extensions. To package an extension, follow these steps:

1. Choose Commands ➪ Package an Extension from Dreamweaver.

2. From the Select Extension to Package dialog box that is displayed, locate your .mxi file and choose OK.

   The next step is to select a location and file name for your .mxp file. The file name should not include spaces and should be valid for both Windows and Macintosh systems. In other words, don't use special characters such as spaces, slashes, backslashes, colons, asterisks, question marks, double quotes, less-than symbols, greater-than symbols, and the pipe.

3. Enter a name for the packaged extension and choose Save.

If you plan on submitting your extension to the Macromedia Exchange, be sure to keep the file's name to 20 or fewer characters. When posted to the Exchange, Macromedia attaches a prefix in the form `MXnnnnn_` where the n's represent a five digit number. For example, my extension, ReplicateSelection.mxp became MX13794_ReplicateSelection.mxp. If your file exceeds the 20-character limit it may not install properly on the Macintosh.

4. If a problem is encountered, Dreamweaver puts up an alert. Otherwise, you'll see a message announcing the success of the procedure.

As in many computing endeavors, occasionally something goes wrong. It's always a good idea to test your own installation process before passing it on to others or submitting it to the Macromedia Exchange.

Submitting Extensions to the Exchange

Ready to share your masterpiece with the world? Post it on the Macromedia Exchange for instant accessibility by over 500,000 Dreamweaver users around the globe. The submission process is not difficult — yet another HTML form — and it's a great way to participate in the growing community of extension authors.

There's one prerequisite to posting your extension: you'll have to become a member of macromedia.com. The membership is free and includes a number of benefits, such as Macromedia's customizable newsletter *The Edge* as well as the ability to participate in the Exchange community, and — of course — submit extensions. The Macromedia Exchange home page contains links to the membership section.

One of the choices you'll need to make when you submit your extension is the desired rating. Macromedia offers two levels of rating your extension: Basic and Macromedia Approved. A Basic rating means that Macromedia found your extension to be virus-free, does what you say it does, and does not affect the system negatively. A Macromedia Approved rating is much more involved. When you apply for this higher rating, Macromedia employees put your extension through a series of quality assurance tests. If issues arise — either problems with the functioning of your extension or incompatibility with Macromedia guidelines — you'll receive an e-mail from the quality assurance team with suggested steps for correcting each situation. Once your extension is accepted for posting (either with a Basic or Macromedia Approved rating) you'll be notified via e-mail.

To help you create your extension so it earns Macromedia approval, the company has created a set of user interface guidelines. These guidelines are available on the Dreamweaver Exchange site. If you selected the Developer Options when installing the Extension Manager, you'll also find a copy of the guidelines and Macromedia's test plan on your system. You can access these documents by choosing Help ⇨ Creating and Submitting Extensions.

Tip

Of course, you can also post your packaged extension on your own to another site instead of the Macromedia Exchange. However, a new MIME type will have to be added to the server so that both Internet Explorer and Netscape Navigator will handle it properly. The MIME type to add is:

```
application/x-mmxp
```

with an `.mxp` extension. If this MIME type is not added, some versions of Netscape Navigator attempt to open it as if it were text, resulting in binary "garbage."

Summary

It's become a truism that the Web is constantly evolving and it's equally true that Dreamweaver's extensibility model is capable of keeping up with the changes. The Extension Manager brings ease of use and a greater degree of control to this powerful feature. Whether you're installing extensions found on the Web at the Macromedia Exchange or creating your own extensions for distribution, the Extension Manager is a valuable asset for customizing Dreamweaver. The key facets of the Extension Manager and the Macromedia Exchange are as follows:

✦ The Extension Manager is a separate program that can be summoned from within Dreamweaver or by double-clicking a Macromedia Extension Package file.

✦ The Extension Manager automates the procedure for installing any type of extension. Once an extension has been installed, the Extension Manager is used to see the author name and other information as well as uninstall the extension.

✦ The Macromedia Exchange is the central warehouse for Dreamweaver extensions. In addition to downloading the latest extensions, you can also rate, review, and seek support for the extension.

✦ Submissions to the Exchange are offered at two levels: Basic and Macromedia Approved. Macromedia Approved extensions comply with user interface guidelines and other stringent criteria.

In the next chapter, you'll see how you can extend Dreamweaver with the additional application programming interfaces (APIs).

What's on the CD-ROM?

✦ ✦ ✦ ✦

The two CD-ROMs that accompany the *Dreamweaver 3 Bible, Gold Edition* contain the following:

✦ Fully functioning trial versions of Dreamweaver 3, Dreamweaver UltraDev, CourseBuilder for Dreamweaver 3, Fireworks 3, and Flash 4

✦ Trial version of ColdFusion Studio 4.5a from Allaire, Inc.

✦ Trial version of Lasso Studio for Dreamweaver from Blue World, Inc.

✦ Code examples used in the book

Also included are hundreds of Dreamweaver extensions from the leaders in the Dreamweaver community, designed to make your work more productive:

✦ Behaviors

✦ Objects

✦ Commands

✦ Inspectors

✦ Floaters

✦ Browser profiles

Using the Accompanying CD-ROMs

The CD-ROMs are what are known as *hybrid CD-ROMs*, which means they contain files that run on more than one computer platform — in this case, both Windows and Macintosh computers.

Several files, primarily the Macromedia trial programs and the other external programs, are compressed. Double-click these files to begin the installation procedure. Most other files on the CD-ROMs are uncompressed and you can simply copy them to your system by using your file manager. A few of the Dreamweaver extensions with files that must be placed in different folders are also compressed.

In the Configuration folder, the file structure replicates the structure that Dreamweaver sets up when it is installed. For example, objects found in the Dreamweaver\Configuration\Objects folder are located on both CD-ROM 1 and the installed program. One slight variation: In the Additional Extensions folder, you'll find the various behaviors, objects, and so on, filed under their author's name.

Files and Programs on the CD-ROMs

The *Dreamweaver 3 Bible, Gold Edition* contains a host of programs and auxiliary files to assist your exploration of Dreamweaver, as well as your Web page design work in general. Following is a description of the files and programs on the CD-ROMs that come with this book.

Macromedia demos

If you haven't had a chance to work with Dreamweaver (or Fireworks or Flash), the two CD-ROMs offer fully functioning trial versions of five key Macromedia programs for both Macintosh and Windows systems. You can use each of the demos for 30 days; they cannot be reinstalled for additional use time. The five trial programs are:

- Dreamweaver 3
- Dreamweaver UltraDev
- CourseBuilder for Dreamweaver 3
- Fireworks 3
- Flash 4

To install any demo, just double-click the program icon in the main folder of the CD-ROM where the demo is located and follow the installation instructions on your screen.

The trial versions of Macromedia programs are very sensitive to system date changes. If you alter your computer's date, the programs will time-out and no longer function.

Trial versions of BBEdit and HomeSite, the external text editors supplied with the commercial version of Dreamweaver, are also included on the CD-ROMs.

In addition to the trial programs from Macromedia, two unlimited-use utilities — the Extension Manager and the Aria Objects for Dreamweaver — are also included. The Extension Manager enables you to easily install and manage Dreamweaver and UltraDev extensions; you'll find details on its use in Chapter 42. The Aria Objects are used in conjunction with the Aria server-side components for tracking and analyzing site visitors, as covered in Chapter 41.

Dreamweaver extensions

Dreamweaver is amazingly extendible, and the Dreamweaver community has built some amazing extensions. In the Additional Extensions folders of the two CD-ROMs, you'll find hundreds of behaviors, objects, commands, inspectors, and more. The extensions are grouped according to author, and within each author's folder they are organized by function. Almost all of these extensions were written prior to the availability of the Extension Manager and do not require that program for installation. Extensions that contain files that must be placed in different folders, such as the Commands and Inspectors directories, are compressed in a Zip format.

Note

Within the Additional Extensions folder, all behaviors are stored in the Behaviors folder to make it easy to access them. When installing, make sure to put them in the Configuration\Behaviors\Action folder on your system and not just the Behaviors folder.

You'll find a ReadMe.htm file in each author's folder, with links to the author's Web site and more information about their creations.

Following is a list of extension authors featured on the two CD-ROMs (alphabetized by first word to match how you'll see them on the discs):

- Al Sparber
- Andreas Spreitzhofer
- Andrew Wooldridge
- Anthony Hersey
- Bill Bulman
- Brendan Dawes
- Eddie Traversa
- Graison Swaan

- Hal Pawluk
- Jaro von Flocken
- Lucas Lopatin
- Marijan Milicevic
- Massimo Foti — The Fantastic Corporation
- Olle Karneman
- Project Seven Development
- Robert Sherman — SnR Graphics
- Simon White — MediaFear
- Subnet Ltd.
- Update Page
- Webmonkey

Dreamweaver 3 Bible, Gold Edition extensions

The majority of the following extensions were built specifically for this book. You can find these extensions in the Configuration folders on the CD-ROMs.

Behaviors

Dreamweaver behaviors automate many functions that previously required extensive JavaScript programming. The behaviors included on the CD-ROMs are in addition to the standard set of behaviors included with Dreamweaver and discussed in Chapter 19. The behaviors on CD-ROM 1 are stored in the Configuration\Behaviors\Actions folder. Copy the behaviors to a similarly named folder in your system installation of Dreamweaver, and restart Dreamweaver to access the new behaviors.

Objects

Much of Dreamweaver's power derives from its extensibility. Each of the standard Dreamweaver objects is based on an HTML file. The CD-ROMs contain various Dreamweaver objects designed to help you create your Web pages faster and more efficiently.

Each Dreamweaver object consists of two files, an HTML file and a GIF file with the same name that is used to create the button on the Objects Palette. For example, the Character Entities object comprises the two files char_entities.htm and char_entities.gif.

To install the Dreamweaver objects, go to Dreamweaver\Configuration\Objects and copy any pair of files from the subfolders Common, Forms, Invisibles, Media, and

New to similarly named folders in your system installation of Dreamweaver. (The Media and New folders are not included in the standard release of Dreamweaver and must be created on your system.) Restart Dreamweaver to access the new objects.

Commands

Commands are proving to be the real workhorses of Dreamweaver extensibility. Not only can they do pretty much everything that behaviors and objects do, but they also have their own capabilities as well. Command files come in many shapes and sizes — from a single file to five or more files split across multiple folders. The commands found in the Configuration\Commands folder on CD-ROM 1 go into the equivalent Dreamweaver folder on your system. The commands are as follows:

- **Repeat History:** Repeats any selected actions in the History palette any number of times. This command requires the Extension Manager to install.
- **Replicator:** Duplicates any selected object, any number of times. Be sure to copy both Replicator.htm and Replicator.js into the Commands folder.
- **Install Shockwave HTML:** Reads an HTML file generated by Director to insert a Shockwave object, complete with proper dimensions and other needed parameters.
- **Change Case:** Converts the case of the selected text to uppercase or lowercase.

Browser profiles

Dreamweaver recognizes the proliferation of browsers on the market today and makes it easy for you to check your Web page creations against specific browser types. The browser targeting capability is available through the use of browser profiles, covered in Chapter 35. In addition to the standard profiles that come with Dreamweaver, CD-ROM 1 contains several browser profiles for checking various implementations of HTML, including the following:

- HTML 2.0
- HTML 3.2
- HTML 4.0
- Opera 3.2
- Pocket Internet Explorer 1.0 (for Windows CE 1.0)
- Pocket Internet Explorer 1.1 (for Windows CE 1.0)
- Pocket Internet Explorer 2.0 (for Windows CE 2.0)

Each additional browser profile is contained in the Dreamweaver\Configuration\BrowserProfiles folder of CD-ROM 1. To install the browser profiles, the files must be copied to a similarly named folder in your system installation of Dreamweaver. Restart Dreamweaver to access the new browser profiles.

Dreamweaver 3 Bible, Gold Edition code examples

You can find example code used in *Dreamweaver 3 Bible, Gold Edition* in the Code folders of the CD-ROMs. Also included and of particular note are the Dreamweaver Techniques from various chapters throughout the book. Each technique contains all the requisite example HTML files and graphics files within its own folder. You can easily view the files through Dreamweaver or your browser without transferring the files to your system. If you do wish to transfer the files, copy the entire folder over to your system.

Dreamweaver style sheets

Dreamweaver makes using a Cascading Style Sheets (CSS) a point-and-click operation. One of the great features of CSS is the capability to link your Web site to external style sheets. CD-ROM 1 contains several external style sheets that you can customize for your Web sites. Each external style sheet comes with an example HTML file that you can view in your browser.

To incorporate the external style sheets in your Web sites, copy the file with the .css extension into your local site root folder. Then follow the instructions in the "Linking to an External Style Sheet" section found in Chapter 27.

Dreamweaver examples

One of the best ways to begin working in Web design is to customize another's designs. CD-ROM 1 includes several Web page examples aimed at giving you a running start in creating your own pages. Each example is found in its own subfolder in the Dreamweaver Bible Code\Examples folder. You can use these examples from within Dreamweaver by opening them directly from the CD-ROM by using the File ⇨ Open command, or by transferring the files to your system and opening them from there.

Online learning

What better place to learn an Internet technology than online? eHandsOn is an online learning company that brings students together with the Web's leading experts. It specializes in media-rich content delivered by industry experts. eHandsOn was founded by Lisa Lopuck, a professional Web graphics designer and instructor. Included on CD-ROM 1 are two sample courses — one on Fireworks 3, taught by Lisa, and another on Dreamweaver 3, taught by me. You can find out more about eHandsOn by visiting its Web site at `www.ehandson.com`.

External programs

To extend their multimedia functionality, browsers use a fair number of plug-ins and external programs. CD-ROM 1 contains one of the most commonly used plug-ins: QuickTime 4.0. To install this plug-in, just double-click the icon in the External Programs folder and follow the instructions on your screen.

As mentioned previously, you'll find numerous trial versions for many of the Web application products discussed in the *Dreamweaver 3 Bible, Gold Edition*, including ColdFusion Studio 4.5a, Lasso Studio for Dreamweaver, and Nokia Americas' WML Studio for Dreamweaver. Each of these products is discussed in great detail in its own chapter.

Web resource directory

The World Wide Web is a vital resource for any Web designer, whether a seasoned professional or a beginner. CD-ROM 1 contains an HTML page with a series of links to resources on the Web; the series contains general as well as Dreamweaver-specific references.

✦ ✦ ✦

APPENDIX B

CourseBuilder for Dreamweaver

Web-based training is an explosive field. With the rise of the intranet, a potential learning delivery system is on every desktop: the browser. To meet the growing needs of corporate trainers, remote educators, and Internet instructors, Macromedia developed a special extension of Dreamweaver called "CourseBuilder for Dreamweaver." CourseBuilder for Dreamweaver extends the standard HTML authoring interface with a CourseBuilder Interaction dialog box designed to simplify the task of creating and testing instructional Web pages. In its earlier versions, CourseBuilder was known both as Dreamweaver Attain and Attain Objects for Dreamweaver.

CourseBuilder for Dreamweaver enables the Web educator to take advantage of the enhancements in Dreamweaver 3 and greatly eases the creation and editing chores. The program now employs Property Inspectors and special Interaction menu commands to facilitate the instructional design. Moreover, any modifications to Interaction parameters are reflected in real time in the Document window, which helps to cut development time significantly.

The intent of this appendix is twofold. First, I'd like to offer an overview of the product for the Web designer unfamiliar with the distance learning market; the need for designers with Web-training savvy is growing by leaps and bounds. Second, this appendix is intended to bridge the gap for educators beginning to explore the Internet as a delivery medium, who may be completely at home with the testing concepts but unfamiliar with Web design possibilities. This appendix is definitely not intended as a CourseBuilder for Dreamweaver instruction manual — a task beyond the scope of this book.

Understanding the CourseBuilder Interface

At the heart of CourseBuilder for Dreamweaver is the CourseBuilder Interaction dialog box. The CourseBuilder Interaction dialog box enables the Web designer to easily insert seven different types of testing objects, ranging from simple multiple-choice questions to complex drag-and-drop representations. The CourseBuilder Interaction dialog box also serves as the command center for interactions between testing conditions and makes it possible for the answer to one question to affect how another is posed. You can also enable tracking with a Computer Managed Instruction (CMI) system such as Macromedia's Pathware or another database setup. Most important, the CourseBuilder Interaction dialog box handles all this complex interactivity through its point-and-click interface without the need for hand-coding HTML or JavaScript.

Although the Insert CourseBuilder Interaction is seen as a single object on Dreamweaver's Objects palette, it acts as the gateway for inserting all the different types of Interactions, such as multiple-choice questions, timers, and text entry boxes. Most of the individual Interactions have a variety of options associated with them — and as you would expect given Dreamweaver's extensibility, new templates can be custom built and called from within the overall CourseBuilder Interaction dialog box.

With CourseBuilder for Dreamweaver, the CourseBuilder Interaction dialog box and the test question structures it generates are far more integrated into Dreamweaver. Special menu options have been added that enable inserted questions to be moved or deleted — without losing the associated code. You can even move any Interaction into a layer to gain the benefits of absolute positions and visibility control.

Using the CourseBuilder Interaction dialog box: An overview

The CourseBuilder Interaction dialog box is a sophisticated tool that interactively assists your Web instructional design. To give you some measure of its complexity, the CourseBuilder Interaction dialog box consists of over 80 layers — most of which are populated at runtime — and uses more than 20 separate HTML and JavaScript scripts. However, for all its behind-the-scenes intricacy, using the CourseBuilder Interaction dialog box is straightforward.

After you've installed CourseBuilder for Dreamweaver, a new object, Insert CourseBuilder Interaction, is added to the Common panel of the Objects palette. Selecting this object opens the CourseBuilder Interaction dialog box, shown in Figure B-1. The actual interface of the CourseBuilder Interaction dialog box varies depending on which implementation of the eight different Interactions you choose to insert; however, you always make your selections from a series of tabbed panels.

Be sure to save your document before opening the CourseBuilder Interaction dialog box; if you start to insert the CourseBuilder Interaction without saving, Dreamweaver gives you the option to store your file.

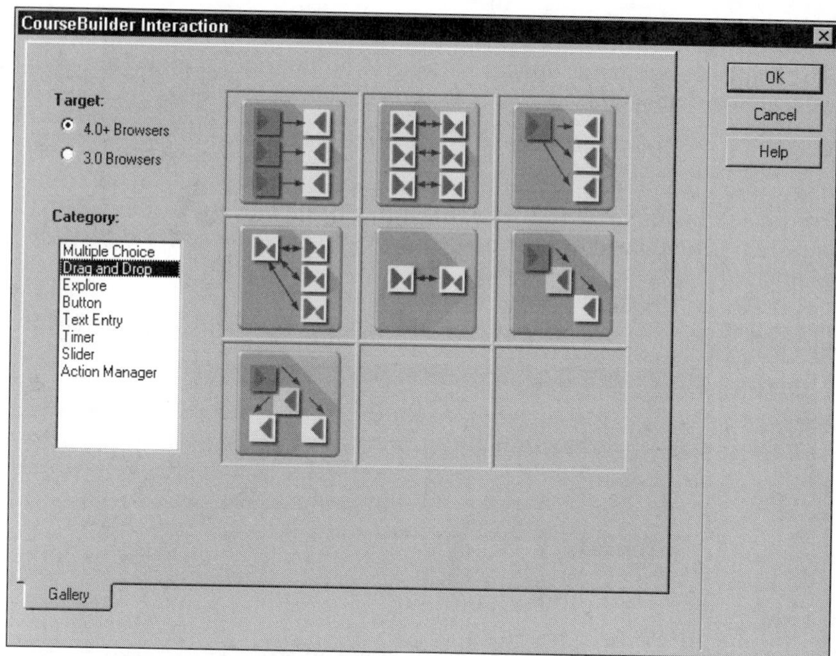

Figure B-1: The CourseBuilder Interaction dialog box is the control panel for almost all of CourseBuilder for Dreamweaver's power.

To give you a better idea of how the CourseBuilder Interaction dialog box works, here are the steps for inserting a relatively simple multiple-choice question that offers visual cues:

1. Position your cursor wherever you'd like the multiple-choice question to appear.
2. From the Objects palette, choose Insert CourseBuilder Interaction.
3. If this is the first time you used CourseBuilder, you are asked if you'd like to copy the support files to the suggested folders.

   Note: It's recommended that you copy the support files within your site. Dreamweaver uploads only those dependent files actually used.

   After the support files are copied, the CourseBuilder Interaction dialog box opens, displaying the Gallery tab.
4. Select the version of browser your Web learning project is targeting by choosing either 4.0+ Browsers or 3.0 Browsers under the Target option.

   Tip: While choosing the 3.0 Browsers option offers the greatest compatibility, none of the 4.0 capabilities, such as layers or CSS, are available to your design.

5. Choose Multiple Choice from the list of Categories on the left.

   The available templates appear in the grid on the right of the CourseBuilder Interaction dialog box.

6. Select the lower-left template with the three graphic symbols.

   The other tabs of the CourseBuilder Interaction dialog box appear, created in response to your selection. Also, the initial design for the multiple-choice question is displayed in the Document window, as shown in Figure B-2.

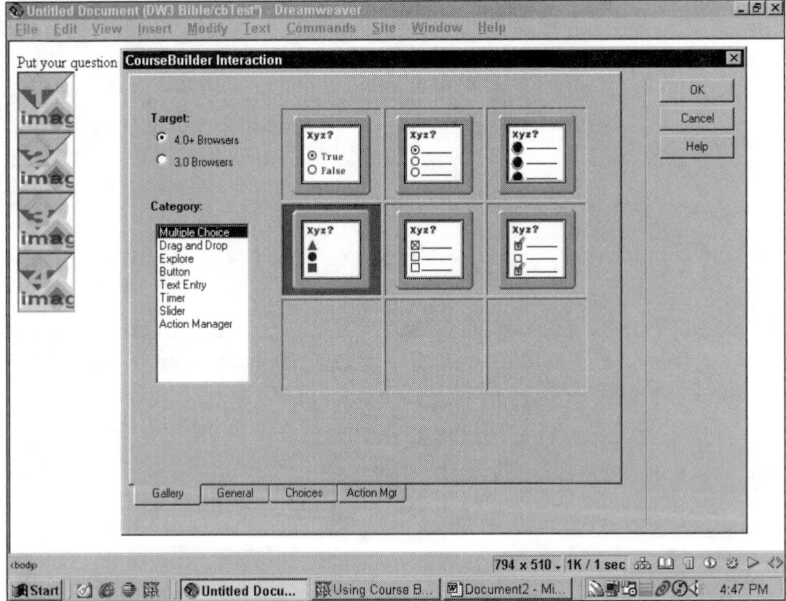

Figure B-2: As you build your Interaction, the elements appear in the Document window.

7. Select the General tab.

8. Enter the particular options that identify this test item, including the following:

   - A unique name, used to identify this particular Interaction.
   - The actual multiple-choice question.
   - The circumstances that determine when the question is judged correct or incorrect. Questions can be judged each time a selection is made or after an entire page of questions is submitted.
   - Whether the results of the question are to be tracked by a test management program.
   - The number of attempts allowed for answering the question.

- A time limit for answering the question.
- Whether a Reset button is to be made available for this question.
- Whether the question should be placed within a layer.

9. If you've opted to send the results of the test question to a management system, select the Tracking tab and enter the necessary identifiers, as well as the relative weight of the question.

10. Select the Choices tab.

11. For each of the placeholders in the Choices list, enter its name, any optional text, the path to the image you want used, and whether or not the choice is correct. If the choice is correct, you can also enter the number of points to add to the user's score.

    Additional choices can be added, or the number of preset choices reduced, by using the Add and Delete buttons at the top of the panel, respectively.

12. Select the Action Mgr (Manager) tab.

    The Action Manager tab lists what actions are taken when the user interacts with the question. Actions can generally be thought of as a series of *If . . . then* statements. *If* a certain condition is met, *then* a defined action is taken. Actions are separated into different *segments*, such as when a particular option is selected. Figure B-3 shows the Action Manager listing for a four-option multiple-choice question.

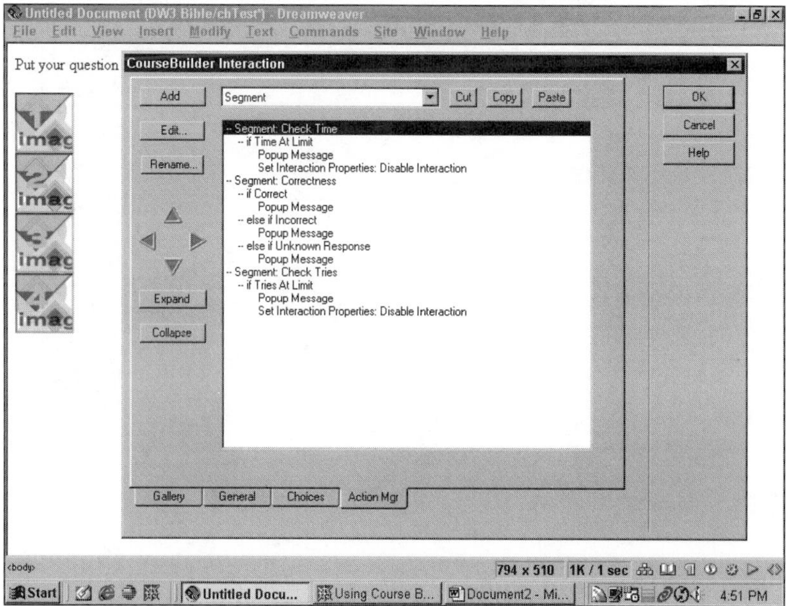

Figure B-3: The Action Manager tab provides an overview of how each question is evaluated at runtime.

13. Segments can be added, deleted, renamed, or repositioned in the Action Manager panel. By accessing the drop-down list at the top of the panel, you can also insert special CourseBuilder behaviors, as well as any standard Dreamweaver behaviors.

14. Click OK when you're done.

Identifying tags and icons

Now that your multiple-choice question has been inserted into your Web page, you can modify its appearance using any of the standard Dreamweaver methods, such as selecting the text of the question and applying a new font face or size. You can also construct an entire page of questions and then use the Style Sheet Inspector to apply a uniform style. CourseBuilder for Dreamweaver makes it easy to identify and select individual Interactions through unique icons and a special tag.

Any inserted Interaction can be chosen by selecting the icon or the tag shown in Figure B-4. The Interaction icon is similar to a layer or form in that, when it is selected, all of the content of the object — the text, images, form elements, and so on — are selected as well. This ensures that any editing includes the whole object. CourseBuilder for Dreamweaver also inserts a special tag, `<interaction>`, which can be chosen from the Tag Selector to achieve the same effect.

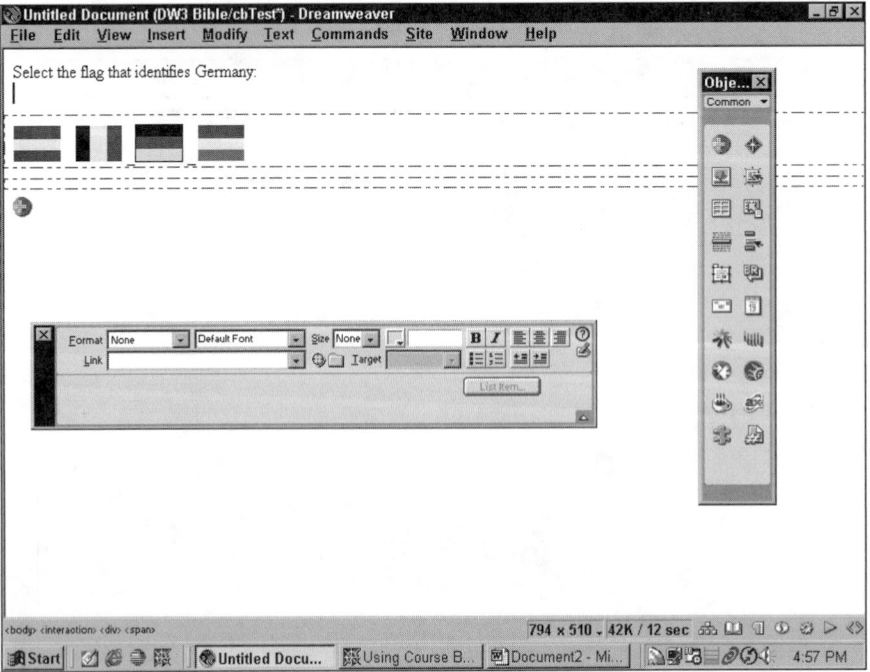

Figure B-4: Select the Interactions by choosing the icon in your Document window or the `<interaction>` tag in the Tag Selector on the status bar.

Working with the Interaction Property Inspectors

When an Interaction is selected, a special CourseBuilder Interaction Property Inspector is displayed. The Interaction Property Inspector, shown in Figure B-5, has three basic functions:

✦ Editing the current Interaction

✦ Selecting other Interactions in the page

✦ Moving the selected Interaction into or out of a positionable layer

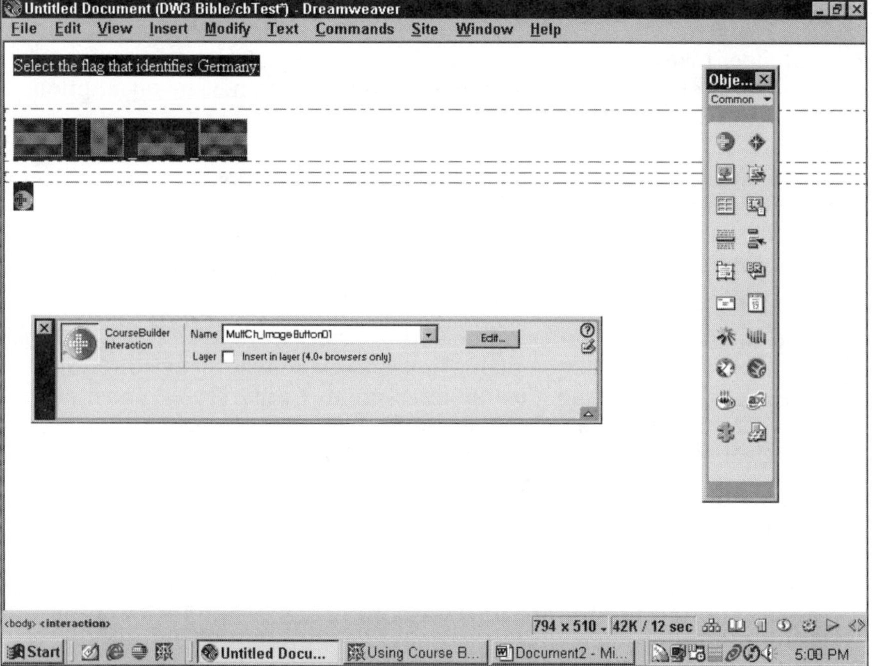

Figure B-5: The Interaction Property Inspector enables you to quickly move from one Interaction to another or to edit the current selection.

To modify an inserted Interaction, select its icon or tag; then, from the Property Inspector, choose the Edit button. A dialog box similar to the CourseBuilder Interaction dialog box opens. The particular options displayed depend on the configuration of the Interaction, but they are generally a subset of the options offered when the object was constructed. The initial Interaction Gallery and its accompanying template variations are not available.

If you have a fair number of Interactions on the current page, you can use the Property Inspector as a navigator of sorts between them. Select the Interaction Property Inspector's drop-down list to reveal a dynamically generated list of the current Interactions. Select any one, and the Document window scrolls to its location, if necessary, and highlights the object.

Finally, the Interaction Property Inspector is useful for moving the individual Interactions into — or out of — layers. In CourseBuilder for Dreamweaver, all Interactions offer you the option of placing the object in a layer at design time. The Property Inspector enables you to change your mind if you so choose by selecting or deselecting the Layer option. Once in a layer, the Interaction can be positioned anywhere on the page, but, of course, layers can be used only in conjunction with 4.0 or later browsers.

Accessing the menus

CourseBuilder takes advantage of Dreamweaver's facility to insert menus wherever appropriate. After installing CourseBuilder, you can find new menu additions in the Modify menu.

Under the Modify menu, you'll find a new CourseBuilder menu option with seven submenu offerings:

- **Edit Interaction:** Opens the CourseBuilder Interaction dialog box with the settings for the currently selected Interaction.
- **Add Interaction to Gallery:** One of the easiest ways to add new options to the CourseBuilder Interaction dialog box is to customize an existing object and then use this command. Custom Interactions can be stored under an existing category (such as Multiple Choice) or under a new category. It's even possible to select and store an entire page as a Gallery item.
- **Copy Support Files:** If you're moving CourseBuilder for Dreamweaver files from one site to another, all you have to do is save the HTML page and then execute this command. All your dependent files, such as graphics and scripts, are copied to the current folder. This command is also used with the next command for updating previous versions of CourseBuilder for Dreamweaver files.
- **Add Template Fix:** Inserts code necessary for attaching Interactions to documents derived from templates.
- **Create Tracking Frameset:** Makes a two-frame frameset for tracking user results to be used by CMI programs other than Pathware.
- **Create Pathware Frameset:** Pathware is Lotus' Computer Managed Instruction program and can be used in conjunction with CourseBuilder for Dreamweaver to track user results. Pathware uses a two-frame frameset structure to display content in one frame and test results in another. The Create Pathware Frameset automatically builds this frameset and loads the current page in the content frame.

✦ **Convert from Previous Versions:** Files created in the earlier versions of CourseBuilder for Dreamweaver cannot be edited in the current version without conversion. After you've loaded the Web page with the Interactions to convert and invoke this command, Dreamweaver stores your old files with a .bak file extension and the converted file under the original name. According to Macromedia, it's best to copy old scripts to a new folder and delete the Scripts folder before beginning the conversion.

Surveying the Interactions

To better understand the capabilities of CourseBuilder for Dreamweaver, you need to know how the various Interactions are used. In all, eight different Interactions exist: Multiple Choice, Drag and Drop, Explore, Button, Text Entry, Timer, Slider, and Action Manager. All but the Action Manager insert an actual object or series of objects in your Web page — the Action Manager controls the interactions between Interactions on the same Web page.

Most of the Interactions have multiple templates to choose from, and all vary in terms of which parameters are available. Some of the objects, such as the Timer and the Slider, are far more useful when working in conjunction with another object. By combining a variety of Interactions, your Web training pages can encompass a wide variety of models and simulations.

Multiple Choice Interaction

The Multiple Choice Interaction encompasses all types of choice questions, not just the traditional pop-quiz type of text questions. This object has four templates:

✦ **Graphic:** Displays images for choices with an optional text line.

✦ **Radio buttons:** Enables one answer to be chosen from a group of possibilities.

✦ **True/False:** Permits an answer to be one of two possibilities.

✦ **Checkboxes:** Enables the user to select any number of answers from a group of possibilities.

All the options enable the designer to specify the text of the question during object setup. You can alter the font face, size, and color — or specify a style — from the Document window.

Drag and Drop Interaction

Computer-based training can be used to simulate the assembly of components or to demonstrate knowledge of the relationship of one object to another. The Drag and Drop Interaction (shown in Figure B-6) enables the user to move one onscreen item and drop it on another. The specified graphics can appear to fit together or lay on top of one another.

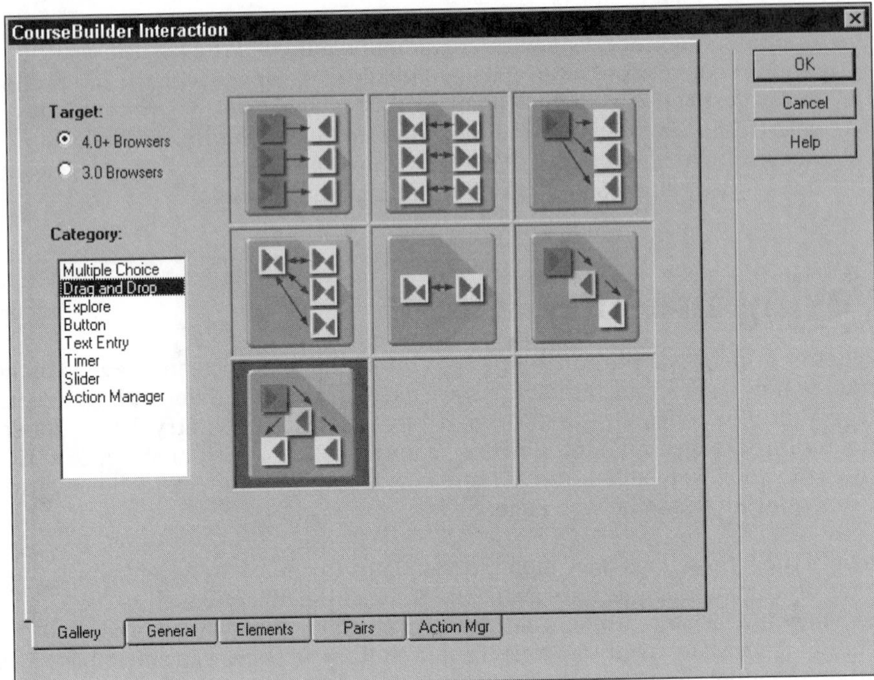

Figure B-6: The Drag and Drop Interaction uses draggable layers that can snap to their targets.

CourseBuilder for Dreamweaver ships with a variety of Drag and Drop Interaction templates:

✦ **One to one matching:** Establishes a series of objects on the left and targets on the right, which must be correctly paired.

✦ **One to one both ways:** Places objects in pairs and enables either object to be dropped on its pair.

✦ **One object to multiple targets:** Used to demonstrate that the object can be associated with any of the onscreen targets.

✦ **One object to many, many to one matching:** Uses four draggable items onscreen; the first object can be dropped on any of the other three items, each of which can in turn be dropped on the first object.

✦ **One object to one, two ways:** Provides two draggable objects, each of which can be a target for the other.

✦ **One object to two targets, in two steps:** Used to demonstrate two-phased operations.

✦ **One object to target, with two steps and one distracter:** Similar to the previously described template, except the second step has one correct and one incorrect target.

The Drag and Drop Interaction is accomplished using layers, and like Dreamweaver's standard Drag Layer behavior, the layer being dragged can be made to snap to specific coordinates when the correct target is approached. Moreover, if the wrong target is chosen, the dragged layer can snap back to its original position.

Explore Interaction

The Explore Interaction uses an image map and a series of hotspots to permit the user to "explore" the onscreen graphic. A click in a particular area — or on a certain part — generates a specific response, which could take the form of a pop-up message or a jump to another URL. Any of the available Dreamweaver behaviors can be attached to a defined hotspot by using the Action Manager tab of the Explore Interaction.

Three templates are available for the Explore Interaction:

✦ **Hotspots at various locations:** Five different hotspots are initially identified, although these can be customized to represent any graphic.

✦ **Transparent hotspots at various locations:** Same as preceding template but with five transparent areas instead of placeholders.

✦ **Hotspots in quadrants:** Use this template when you want to divide an image into four equal areas that cover the entire graphic.

Button Interaction

The Button Interaction is generally used in conjunction with other Interactions on the page to represent selections or choices. One button, when selected, could initiate a series of actions with another button; clicking a button, for example, could start or stop a timer. One bank of buttons could activate another bank of buttons as well.

Although only two templates exist for the Button Interaction — an on/off type switch and a push button — CourseBuilder for Dreamweaver includes eleven different appearances from which to choose, as shown in Figure B-7. The buttons can be set to highlight like a rollover and/or be initially deactivated, if desired.

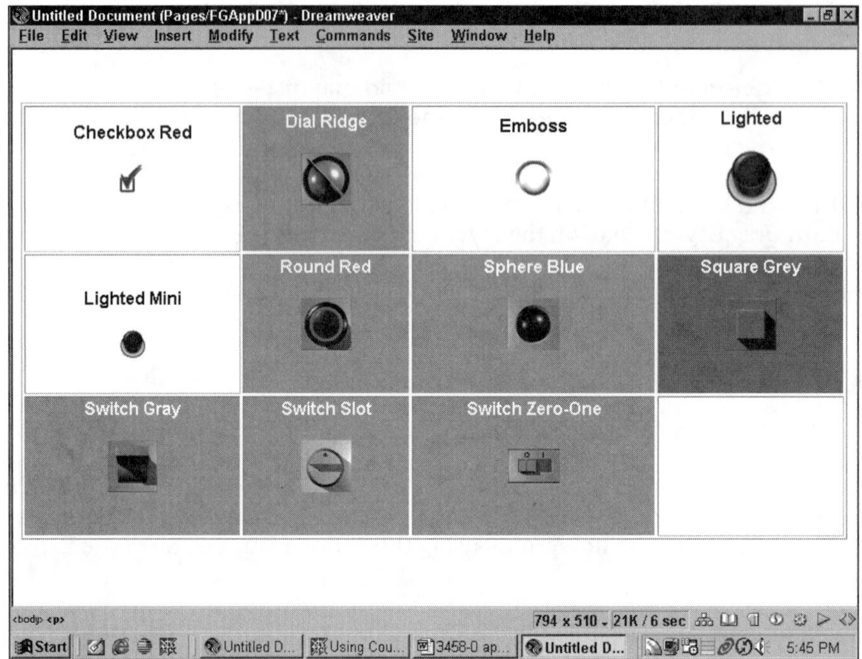

Figure B-7: Choose from any of the eleven different types of buttons included with the Button Interaction.

Text Entry Interaction

While multiple-choice and true/false questions are often used to handle text-based questions, sometimes you want to test a user's retention. The Text Entry Interaction enables you to request information to be keyed in by the user, which can then be judged correct by comparing the input to a specified list of possible answers. You can also use the Text Entry Interaction to request a user ID and password.

The two templates for the Text Entry Interaction are as follows:

- Single line of text
- Multiple lines of text

Timer Interaction

With the Timer Interaction, questions can be judged incorrect if the answer is not chosen within the time limit. An onscreen timer — such as an hourglass, a clap board, or a set of rising bars — can visually mark off seconds or be used as a countdown. Specific triggers can be set at any point in the timeline to activate behaviors such as a pop-up message or a custom function. The two templates for the Timer Interaction enable you to easily choose a count up or count down scenario.

Slider Interaction

The Slider Interaction is similar to the Button Interaction in that it is generally used with other Interactions on the page. However, whereas a button is used to represent a binary set of values, a slider is used to show a linear range of values. CourseBuilder for Dreamweaver includes almost 20 different slider appearances from which to choose; generally, one type of slider is offered in both a horizontal and vertical format. Like the Timer, the Slider Interaction can trigger behaviors at specified points.

You have two Slider Interaction templates to choose from:

✦ **Range of values:** Actions are triggered when the slider is moved anywhere within a set range of values.

✦ **Specific values:** Actions are triggered when the slider is moved to specific values within a specified range.

Action Manager Interaction

The Action Manager Interaction is used to coordinate information from the various Interactions on a given page, whether it is to send all the answers to a database or to switch the interactions from a tutorial to a test. Bear in mind that the Action Manager Interaction is different from the Action Manager panel found in the dialog box, which is used to control a single Interaction.

Generally, the Action Manager object is placed first on the HTML page so that it is set up to interact with all Interactions that follow. Because all customization occurs within the Action Manager object, it has only one template.

✦ ✦ ✦

BBEdit 5.1.1 Primer (For Macintosh Users)

Creating great-looking Web sites is easy thanks to Dreamweaver's visual layout interface. Even so, sometimes it's helpful to switch from Dreamweaver's visual editor mode and edit the underlying HTML (Hypertext Markup Language) source code — particularly when you're troubleshooting HTML documents.

Dreamweaver has a basic built-in HTML editor: the HTML Inspector. When a more advanced code editor is needed, Macintosh users can use the BBEdit application from Bare Bones Software (`www.barebones.com` or `www.bbedit.com`). A trial version of this standalone editor is included on the CD-ROM that accompanies the full version of Dreamweaver.

BBEdit 5.1.1 is the most recent version of this popular, Macintosh programmer's text editor. In recent years, the program has evolved into a feature-packed text-based, pre-Web HTML editor that elegantly exploits the ease-of-use capabilities of the Mac OS. BBEdit is the choice of many Web professionals.

This appendix is written as a basic beginner's guide to BBEdit. The software has a myriad of features and capabilities; some of BBEdit's more advanced features are not covered here.

Note: The trial version of BBEdit included on the CD-ROM is fully functioning with one exception: the program is save-disabled. However, this limitation is not as overwhelming as it may at first appear. You are still able to complete your edits in BBEdit and then save the updated page in Dreamweaver. Optionally, of course, you can upgrade to the full-working version of BBEdit by visiting their Web site or choosing BBEdit Lite, also available there.

Getting Started

You can easily switch between Dreamweaver and BBEdit. A simple click of a button toggles you from one application to the other. Elements selected in one application are automatically highlighted in the other. This capability makes it easy to find your place in the code, and modifications can be made quickly.

Key features

BBEdit is wonderfully full featured and adaptable to your style of working. Just a few of BBEdit's many advantages follow:

- ✦ HTML syntax checking
- ✦ Multiple layers of Undo and Redo
- ✦ Spell-checking
- ✦ Multiple-file Find and Replace
- ✦ Support for files up to 2GB
- ✦ A file comparison feature for locating differences among files
- ✦ HTML syntax coloring
- ✦ "Open from" and "Save to" FTP servers from the File menu
- ✦ Table builder
- ✦ Web-safe color palette
- ✦ One-click preview in any browser

BBEdit installation

BBEdit 5.1.1, like Dreamweaver, runs on Power Macintoshes and compatible computers. Install BBEdit by launching the Install BBEdit 5.1.1 application on the CD-ROM supplied with the full version of Dreamweaver.

BBEdit installs several special folders during the installation process that provide additional functionality. These folders can be removed if you don't need their features. The following items are installed within the BBEdit 5.1.1 folder.

Folder	*Contents*
BBEdit Plug-ins	Modules that offer additional BBEdit features written and contributed by BBEdit users
BBEdit Scripts	AppleScripts ready for execution through the Scripts menu, represented by a script icon, located just to the left of the Help menu
BBEdit Glossary	Text files that can be inserted into an active editing window. Simply add text files to the folder and then use the Glossary command in the Windows menu to insert the contents of a text file.
BBEdit Dictionaries	Dictionaries used by BBEdit's Spell Checker. The User Dictionary stores words you add to this personal dictionary. See the section "Spell-checking," later in this appendix, for more information.
ToolServer Support and ToolServer Tools	Support files for the new ToolServer integration.
MacPerl Support	Support files for MacPerl, a CGI language.
HTML Templates and Example HTML Scripts	Example templates and files to be used.

Working with Dreamweaver and BBEdit

Although Dreamweaver 3 enables you to assign any HTML editor as your external editor, Dreamweaver integrates optimally with BBEdit. Once you set up BBEdit as your default editor, switching between the two editors is just a button click or keyboard shortcut away.

Setting up BBEdit as your default editor

Before Dreamweaver can access BBEdit, you must make BBEdit your default HTML editor. You can make this assignment through the Dreamweaver Preferences by following these steps:

1. In Dreamweaver, choose Edit ⇨ Preferences to open the Preferences dialog box.
2. From the Category list on the left, choose External Editors to display that panel.

3. In the External Editors panel, use the Browse (Choose) button to find BBEdit. Once you pick BBEdit, Dreamweaver offers to enable integration; click in the box that says Enable BBEdit Integration and click OK. The Edit menu option continues to read Launch External Editor.

The External Editor options that control file synchronization between Dreamweaver and BBEdit are explained in Chapter 3.

Switching between Dreamweaver and BBEdit

You have several ways to switch to BBEdit while in Dreamweaver:

- ✦ Click the External Editor button in the top-left corner of the HTML Inspector.
- ✦ Use the Finder.
- ✦ Choose Edit ➪ Launch External Editor.
- ✦ Use the keyboard shortcut, Command+E.

Depending on the file reloading options chosen in the External Editors preferences, Dreamweaver may ask if you want to save the file first before you switch to BBEdit. If you do not save your Dreamweaver file, your modifications do not appear in BBEdit, and vice versa. For this reason, you should set your Reload Modified File option to Always.

After you've made your code modifications in BBEdit and you're ready to return to Dreamweaver, just click the Dreamweaver button near the center of BBEdit's HTML Tools palette (see Figure C-1). The section "HTML Tools Palette," later in this appendix, provides more information about this window.

Disabling BBEdit integration

You may disable BBEdit integration if you prefer working with an older version of BBEdit or if you use a different HTML text editor. Follow these steps:

1. Choose Edit ➪ Preferences.
2. Select External Editors from the category list on the left.
3. Deselect the Enable BBEdit Integration option and click OK.
4. If you like, you can now choose a different HTML editor.

Note

Text selections are not tracked if integration is turned off.

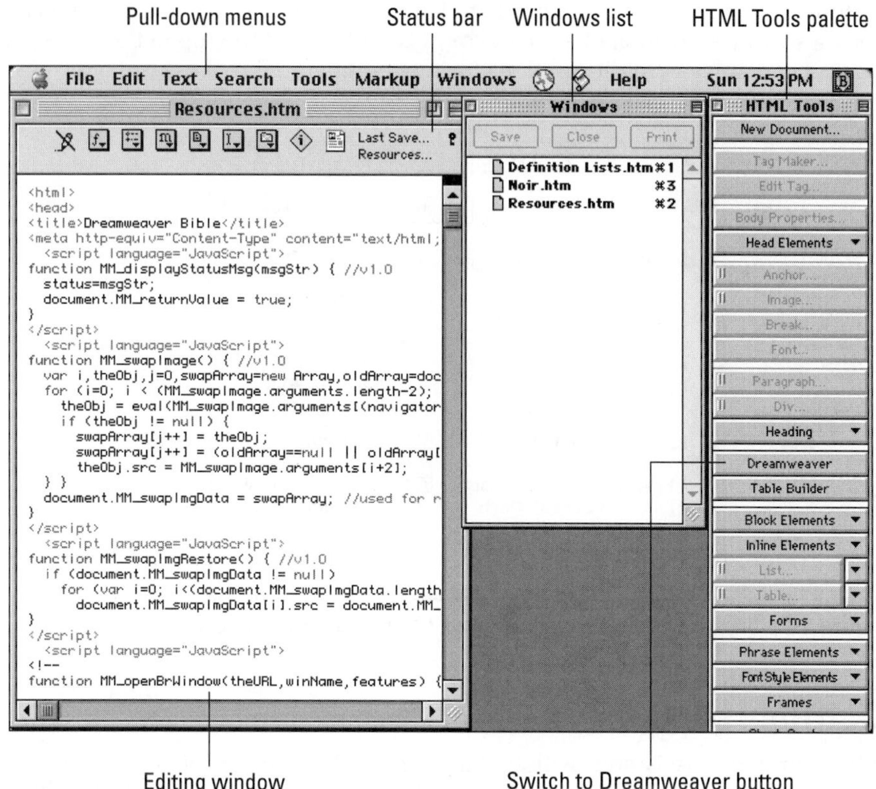

Figure C-1: The BBEdit 5.1.1 workspace

BBEdit menus

Dynamic menus: BBEdit uses an advanced menu system called *dynamic menus*. This system uses the Shift or Option keys to alter menu options while a menu is open.

Keyboard shortcuts: Many of BBEdit's commands have keyboard equivalents. Pull-down menus show keyboard shortcuts. To see the keyboard equivalents for options in a dialog box, hold down the Command key. After a brief delay, the keyboard equivalents appear next to the buttons in the dialog box.

BBEdit preferences

BBEdit offers a wealth of options for customizing the application to meet your needs. Use the Edit pull-down menu to select Preferences. A dialog box appears with several categories of options listed on the left side. When you select a category, a short description of the category is displayed at the top of the dialog box. Figure C-2 displays BBEdit's options for text-editing preferences.

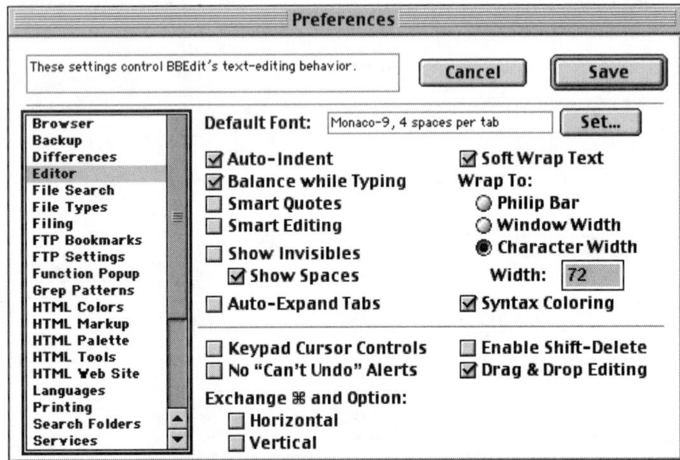

Figure C-2: BBEdit's Preferences dialog box showing Editor options

Getting Help

BBEdit provides assistance with its functions with the Help pull-down menu. You can choose the BBEdit Guide to show a window that offers Help by topic, through an index, or via searching. This choice activates the Apple Guide-style interactive Help in BBEdit. Use the Show Balloons option to display the functions of many buttons and features as you move your mouse over various parts of BBEdit windows. To open the manuals in the BBEdit Documentation folder, the Adobe Acrobat Reader must be installed on your machine.

HTML Document Basics

Once the BBEdit software is installed, you're ready to author HTML documents destined to become great-looking Web pages. This section explains the basics of creating, saving, and opening BBEdit documents.

Creating and saving new documents

Use the File menu to select New; then follow the pointer to the submenu. The most common options are Text Document and HTML Document.

Text Document

This command opens an empty text file with two suboptions:

- **With Selection:** Creates a new document containing text selected in another currently open BBEdit document. This is handy for quickly producing multiple pages that have common elements, such as a sitewide menu or background image.
- **With Clipboard:** Creates a new document containing text copied into the Mac OS clipboard. The text could originate from any application.

HTML Document

Choose HTML Document, and you get a dialog box with options for creating a new HTML-formatted document. This option automatically places the HTML tags you need to begin building a page. This is the best option if you're starting a document from scratch.

Saving your work

When you're ready to save your newly created document, choose File ➪ Save. Give the document a name and choose the location where you wish to save the document.

The Save As command opens a standard Mac OS dialog box. The Option button within this dialog box gives you control over how file attributes are saved. You have two choices:

- **Save As Stationery:** Saves the document as a Mac OS stationery document. Later, when you open this document, BBEdit uses it as a template for a new untitled document. This option is useful for creating multiple Web pages with common elements, such as a sitewide menu or background image.
- **Save Selection Only:** Instructs BBEdit to save only the selected text.

Opening existing BBEdit files

You have three ways to open existing BBEdit documents:

- Drag a file's icon to the BBEdit application icon, or to an alias of the icon. You can place the alias on your desktop for easy access. This option takes advantage of the Mac OS drag-and-drop feature and works for any document with a file type of TEXT.
- Simply double-click a BBEdit file. You can identify BBEdit documents by the associated BBEdit icon.
- With BBEdit launched, use the Open, Open Several, or Open Recent commands from the File menu.

Let's take a look at these File ➪ Open commands.

File ➪ Open

When you select Open from the File pull-down menu, a dialog box gives you the following options:

✦ **Open Read Only:** This command opens the file so it can be viewed but not edited. To make a file editable, simply click the pencil icon in the status bar located at the top of each BBEdit document. (For a description of the status bar, see the section "Editing Documents," later in this appendix.)

✦ **LF Translation:** Translates DOS or UNIX line breaks when you open a file. If this option is not selected, BBEdit leaves the original line breaks untranslated. If your preferred line endings are set to Unix, then the preceding option translates Mac endings to Unix as well.

✦ **File Types:** A pop-up menu enables you to select types of files to open. When the default file type All Available is chosen, BBEdit uses its built-in translation system to open any files it can translate.

File ➪ Open Recent

The Open Recent menu contains a list of files recently opened. To open one of these files, simply choose it from the submenu.

File ➪ Open Several

This command enables you to open multiple files simultaneously. This is particularly useful if you wish to open all the files in a folder — maybe all the HTML documents that make up your Web site. Here are the steps to open several files at once:

1. As you open the File menu, hold down the Option key to enable BBEdit's dynamic menu feature. Select the Open Several command, and a dialog box appears (see Figure C-3).

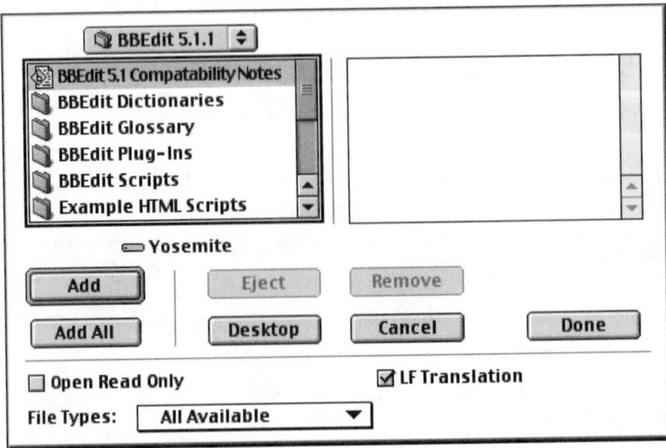

Figure C-3: Opening multiple files

2. Choose a file you wish to open from the list on the left side of the dialog box.
3. Use Add to move the selected file to the list of files to be opened, on the right.
4. Use Add All to add all the files in the folder to the list of files to be opened.
5. Use the Add button to add any other files to the list on the right. Use Remove to eliminate unwanted files.
6. Choose any of the Open options you need (see File ➪ Open, described in the preceding section).
7. Press Done to have BBEdit open the files.

Using file groups

BBEdit enables you to group files in a way that makes managing your Web site easier. You may want to group all the files that make up your Web site or divide them into logical subsections that make sense to you.

A file group is a special BBEdit file that references other files in the file group. Any type of file can be included in a file group.

To start a file group:

1. Select File ➪ New ➪ File Group.
2. The resulting dialog box asks you for a file group name (see Figure C-4).

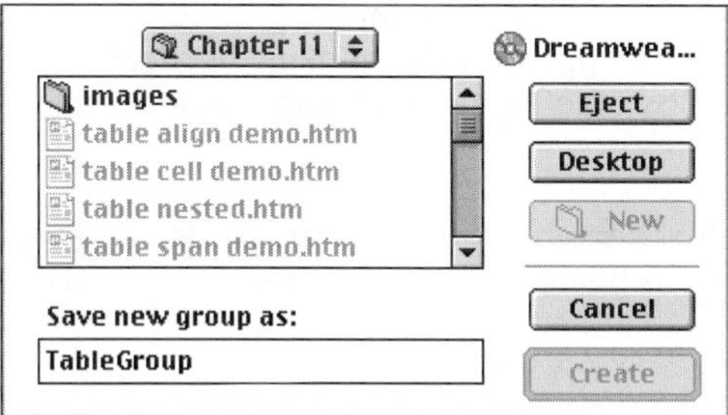

Figure C-4: Creating a new file group

3. Click Create, and BBEdit opens a new empty file group.

To add files to a file group, simply drag any file from the Finder into the file group window (see Figure C-5). Or you can click the Add button to open a dialog box that enables you to choose files.

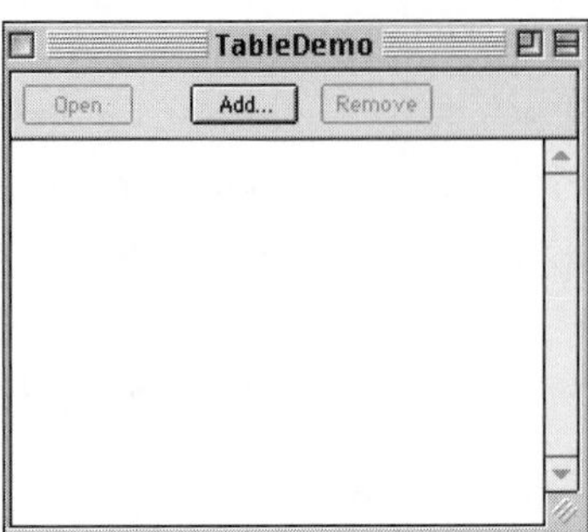

Figure C-5: An empty file group window

To open a file within a file group, double-click the file. Or you can select the file and click the Open button.

If the file is a BBEdit document, then BBEdit opens it. If the file is not a BBEdit document, then the application that created the file is launched.

Editing Documents

This section guides you through BBEdit's menus, windows, and functions.

Basic text manipulation

BBEdit handles text in a way similar to many Macintosh text editors and word processors. Characters typed in BBEdit appear at the blinking vertical insertion point. The insertion point is controlled by placing the mouse in the desired location and clicking.

Click and drag the mouse to select several characters or words. If you select some text and then type, the new entry replaces the selected text. Use the Delete key to remove selected text.

Moving text

To easily move text from one location to another, follow these steps:

1. With the mouse, select the text you want to move.

If you wish to select all the text within a document choose Edit ➪ Select All (keyboard shortcut: Command+A).

2. Choose Edit ➪ Cut (Command+X) to remove the text from the window and store it in the Mac OS clipboard.

3. Find the new place where you wish to move the text and click your mouse at the insertion point.

4. Choose Edit ➪ Paste (Command+V) to place your text.

To copy text into the clipboard without deleting it from its original location, select Copy from the Edit pull-down menu (Command+C).

Dragging and dropping text

A fast and simple method to move text from one place to another takes advantage of the Mac OS drag-and-drop feature. Follow these steps:

1. Select the desired text.

2. Place the mouse pointer within the selected area.

3. Click and hold down the mouse button.

4. Drag the mouse pointer to the new position for the text.

5. Release the mouse button to drop in the text.

You can also use drag-and-drop to copy text to any other open BBEdit window.

Tip

BBEdit enables you to drag and drop a text file from the Finder onto an editing window. Doing so inserts the file's contents where it's dropped.

Undo/Redo

The Edit ➪ Undo command (Command+Z) reverses changes — in chronological order — made to your file. The amount of available memory is the only limit to the number of edits that can be undone.

BBEdit also enables multiple redo's. Choose the Edit ➪ Redo command or use the keyboard shortcut Command+Shift+Z.

Text wrapping

BBEdit wraps text in two ways: *soft wrapping* and *hard wrapping*. You can choose the option that works best for you and have it take effect globally or for just one document.

✦ **Soft wrapping:** Soft wrapping handles text like most word processing software. As the insertion point reaches the limit of the right margin, it automatically moves to the next line. You never need to type a Return at the end of a line unless you are beginning a new paragraph.

✦ **Hard wrapping:** Hard wrapping enables you to type as far as you wish on a single line. You have to enter a Return to end each line in order to begin a new line of text.

To change the text-wrapping option in BBEdit, select Soft Wrap Text from the Window Options pop-up menu in the status bar (see the section "The Status bar" coming up). Or you can choose Window Options via the Edit menu and select (or deselect) the Soft Wrap Text option from the Window Options dialog box.

What's in the BBEdit windows

Basic operation of BBEdit windows follows the standard Mac OS format. BBEdit offers two extra features: the status bar and the split bar.

The status bar

The status bar (see Figure C-6) resides at the top of each editing window. This bar contains buttons and pop-up menus that help you work with the text in the window. Using the status bar you can save your work, show line numbers, display document information, and more.

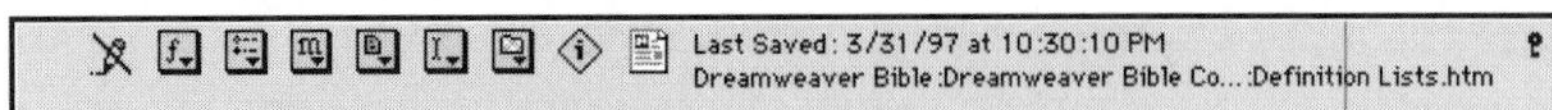

Figure C-6: BBEdit's status bar

Use the Show Balloons option under the Help pull-down menu to show the function of the icons in the status bar. Hide the status bar by clicking the Key icon on the right side of the status bar.

The split bar

Each editing window contains a split bar — it's a small black bar located just above the vertical scroll bar. The split bar divides the window into two panes, which is particularly helpful when you're editing a document in two places. Figure C-7 shows an editing window split into two panes.

To split the window, drag the split bar from the top of the vertical scroll bar into the main window area. You can scroll both windows independently. Return to a full window by dragging the split bar to its original location.

Double-clicking the split bar divides a window into two equal panes or removes the division from a split window.

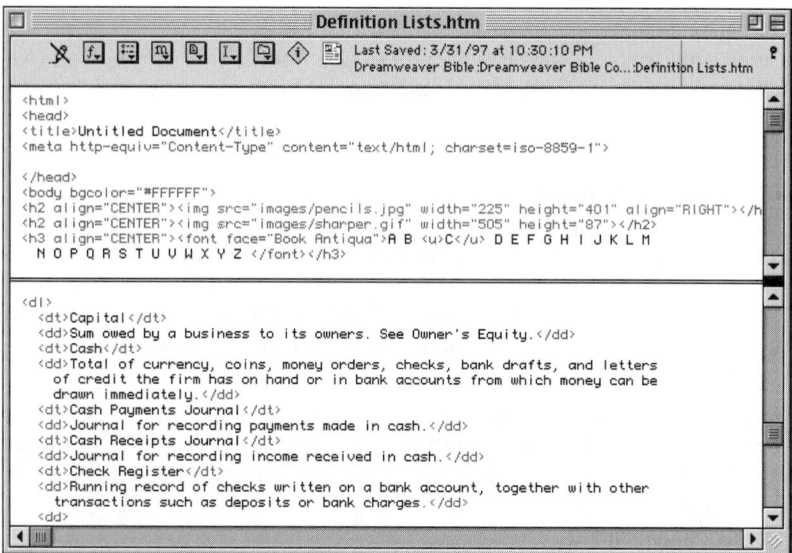

Figure C-7: Use the split bar to divide a window for editing a document in two places.

Markup menu

The Markup pull-down menu and associated HTML Tools palette together offer powerful assistance in designing the layout of your Web pages. In most respects, the Markup menu and the HTML Tools palette function similarly. Following are descriptions of some of the basic Markup menu functions.

Tag Maker command

The Tag Maker command brings up a list of HTML tags or HTML tag attributes that are available for insertion in your file. The command is context sensitive — that is, the list of tags displayed is specific to the location in your document where your cursor is positioned when you choose this command. Select the desired tag or tag attribute from the list and click Insert to add the tag to your file.

Edit Tag command

To use the Edit Tag command, your cursor must be located inside an HTML tag in your document. Selecting the Edit Tag command brings up a context-sensitive dialog box that enables you to edit the attributes of that specific tag.

Head Elements menu

The Head Elements menu contains a variety of commands that enable you to set the properties of an entire HTML page. Examples of head elements are `<meta>` and `<title>` tags.

Body Properties command

The Body Properties command enables you to specify a document's background image, background color, and default text and link colors as follows:

- Select a background graphic by typing the file's name into the Background field or by pressing the File button to bring up a standard Macintosh dialog box.
- Assign a color for the background, default text, and links by checking the box next to the desired attribute and then selecting a color from the pop-up window of 216 Web-safe colors. Hold down the Option key while clicking a color to access the Apple color picker.

Block Elements menu

Insert HTML block elements, such as `<blockquote>`, `<address>`, and `<pre>`, into your page by accessing this menu.

Heading menu

Use this menu to insert the HTML tags appropriate for heading levels 1 through 6, to distinguish the various titles and subheadings within a page.

Lists menu

This menu enables you to organize lists of textual items, with optional indentation and a choice of bullets. BBEdit supports five list types: Unordered, Ordered, Definition, Menu, and Directory.

Tables menu

Tables are a great way to organize your Web page layout. The Tables menu provides the following table-creation tools:

- **Table Builder:** Displays the Table Builder utility. If the cursor is currently positioned within a table, the table is first selected.
- **Table:** Opens a dialog box that enables a variety of table attributes to be specified, including Border, Width, Spacing, Padding, Frame, Rules, Align, Background color, the number of columns, and the number of rows. Inserts a `<table>...</table>` tag pair with the selected attributes, or encloses selected text with the same tag pair.

- **Row:** Opens a dialog box that enables a variety of row attributes to be specified, including Align, Valign, and Background color. Inserts a `<tr>...</tr>` tag pair with the selected attributes, or encloses selected text with the same tag pair.
- **TD:** Opens a dialog box that enables a variety of table cell attributes to be specified, including Rowspan, Colspan, Width, Height, Align, Valign, and Background color; it also determines whether text wrapping is to be turned on or off. Inserts a `<td>...</td>` tag pair with the selected attributes, or encloses selected text with the same tag pair.
- **TH:** Opens a dialog box that enables a variety of table header cell attributes to be specified, including Rowspan, Colspan, Width, Height, Align, Valign, and Background color and determines whether text wrapping is to be turned on or off. Inserts a `<th>...</th>` tag pair with the selected attributes, or encloses selected text with the same tag pair.
- **Caption:** Inserts a `<caption>...</caption>` tag pair, or encloses selected text with the same tag pair.
- **Convert to Table:** Converts the currently selected text to a table format using the parameters set by the displayed dialog box.

Inline Elements menu

An inline element is one that can be inserted next to another element without requiring a paragraph break. Following are some of the most commonly used tags:

- **Anchor:** Inserts an anchor tag with the associated attributes for creating a link or a base anchor.
- **Image:** Places a graphic image at the current insertion point. Size attributes are handled automatically for GIF, JPEG, and PNG files.
- **Font:** Opens a dialog box that enables the specification of a font face, size, and color for the selected text. Click and hold the color chip to bring up a pull-down menu of Web-safe colors, or hold down the Option key while clicking the color to open the Apple color picker.

Font Style Elements menu

Set the size and style of your font through the Font Style Elements menu. You can also open a separate Font Style palette, which contains all of the Font Style Elements commands, by selecting Font Palette from the Font Style Elements drop-down menu on the HTML Tools palette.

The following font style options are available on this menu:

- **Big:** Sets the current text to use the `<big>...</big>` tag pair.
- **Small:** Sets the current text to use the `<small>...</small>` tag pair.

- **Bold:** Sets the current text to use the `<b>...</b>` tag pair.
- **Italic:** Sets the current text to use the `<i>...</i>` tag pair.
- **Strike-Through:** Sets the current text to use the `<strike>...</strike>` tag pair.
- **Teletype Text:** Sets the current text to use the `<tt>...</tt>` tag pair.
- **Underline:** Sets the current text to use the `<ul>...</ul>` tag pair.

Check menu

This set of commands helps you find problems such as bad links and HTML coding errors in your Web documents. Errors are shown in a new window, complete with the line number of the offending HTML code. The Check menu contains the following commands:

- **Document Syntax:** Checks the current document for HTML syntax errors. Faulty HTML may work fine when viewed in one browser but display incorrectly when viewed by another, and this command helps you avoid that problem.

One HTML error can result in the report of multiple subsequent errors. It's best to correct errors from the top of the document and then recheck the document after you correct each error.

- **Document Links:** Verifies that documents linked to a file actually exist, to help you identify bad links in your Web site. The command does not verify that these documents exist on your Web server, but rather that the documents exist in your site root folder (as defined in the HTML Preferences section of BBEdit's Preferences). See the section "Internet Menu," later in this appendix, for information on checking external Web links.
- **Site Syntax:** Similar to the Document Syntax command but checks the syntax of every HTML file in the site root folder.
- **Site Links:** Operates like the Document Links command but checks the validity of link references in every HTML file in the site root folder. No attempt is made to validate external links (such as sites on a remote Web server). See the section "Internet Menu," later in this appendix, for information on checking external Web links.
- **Balance Tags:** Selects the pair of container tags nearest the cursor, highlighting the tags and all the HTML text in between. If you select Balance Tags again, the next pair of tags is selected.

Update menu

This menu replaces all placeholders and includes in the current document (or the current site). See the BBEdit Help system for detailed information on using placeholders and includes.

Utilities menu

The Utilities menu offers a variety of page-oriented tools especially useful for preparing a regular text document for publication on the Web. You can open a separate palette that contains all of the Utilities commands by selecting Utilities Palette from the Utilities pull-down menu in the HTML Tools palette.

The Utilities commands are as follows:

✦ **Format:** Reformats the structure and display of the HTML text. Choose from the following:

- *Hierarchical*—Each set of tags is indented, and tag pairs appear on separate lines.
- *Gentle Hierarchical*—Similar to Hierarchical but anchors within other tags are not indented.
- *Document Skeleton*—Hierarchical style but with everything removed that is not a tag or tag specification (such as all the text). Use this format to create a template.
- *Plain*—Each tag appears on a separate line.
- *Compact*—Deletes any unnecessary whitespace, including tabs, spaces, and carriage returns.

✦ **Optimize:** The Optimize command is similar to the Compact option under the Format command in that it deletes any unnecessary whitespace, but it also removes empty `<font>...</font>` tags, naturalsizeflag attributes, as well as quotes from around tag attributes that don't need them.

✦ **Translate:** Enables a variety of translation options, including conversions between the ISO Latin-1 and Macintosh character set, conversion of 8-bit characters to ASCII equivalents, and conversion of HTML standard characters such as < and > to character entities (and back). Adds or deletes `<p>` tags to or from paragraphs.

✦ **Remove Comments:** Deletes all commented material from the current page.

✦ **Remove Markup:** Deletes all HTML code from the file, yielding a clean text file.

✦ **Comment:** Surrounds selected text with HTML comment tags.

✦ **Uncomment:** Deletes comment tags from selected text.

✦ **Make Tags Upper Case:** Uppercases all HTML tags. Attribute values, such as file names and functions, remain the same case.

✦ **Make Tags Lower Case:** Lowercases all HTML tags. Attribute values, such as file names and functions, remain the same case.

Misc menu

The Misc menu holds a hodgepodge of special-purpose tools, including the following:

- **Dreamweaver:** Returns current document to Dreamweaver.
- **Document Size:** Returns the size of the current document and estimated download times over a variety of modems.
- **Index Document:** Creates an unordered list of all the links and images in every HTML page in the current page. The list appears at the current cursor position.
- **Index Site:** Creates an unordered list of all the links and images in every HTML page in the current site. Aside from the unordered list, four other predefined index styles are available.
- **CyberStudio Cleaner:** Fixes problems associated with Web pages created or edited in GoLive CyberStudio.
- **PageMill Cleaner:** Fixes problems associated with Web pages created or edited in Adobe PageMill, including replacing multiple instances of the `<br>` tag with a single `<p>` tag. Removes the `naturalsize` attribute from image tags and removes empty anchor tags.

Preview menu

This menu loads the active document into the default Web browser defined in the Web Browser section of BBEdit's Preferences.

Preview With menu

This menu enables the selection, from a drop-down menu, of a browser in which to preview the active document. Available browsers can be specified in the Web Browser section of BBEdit's Preferences.

HTML Tools palette

The HTML Tools palette (see Figure C-8) gives you a quick path to the most frequently used functions of BBEdit. You can place this floating palette anywhere on your desktop for easy access.

Several buttons have submenus that appear when you click the button, presenting additional related options. A downward-pointing arrow on the right side of a button indicates a submenu. For example, the Heading button enables the user to select the desired heading level.

Figure C-8: The HTML Tools palette

A double vertical bar on the left side of some buttons (the grip strip) indicates that the button supports drag-and-drop. For example, you can drag the Table button into a document window to place a table at the insertion point. This action brings up the Table dialog box.

Windows menu

It can get confusing when you have many BBEdit windows open simultaneously. The Windows menu helps you manage the clutter.

The Windows List

BBEdit's Windows List helps you gain quick access to the files that make up your Web site. A special floating window (see Figure C-9) lists the names of all the open files.

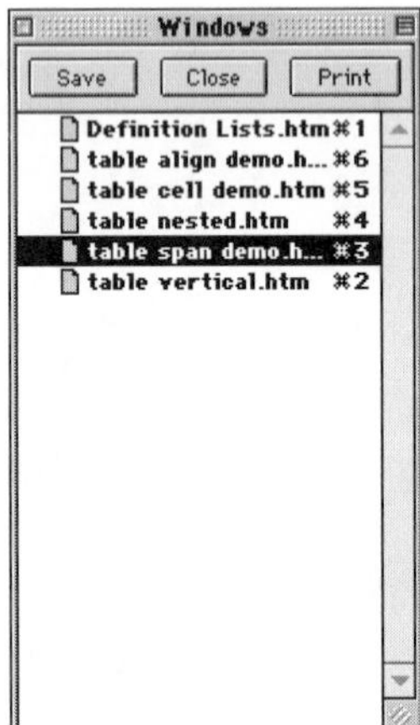

Figure C-9: BBEdit's Windows List

To make a window active, simply double-click its name within the Windows List. In addition, you can open a file by dragging the file's icon into the Windows List. Buttons at the top of the window offer Save, Close, and Print options.

Use your keyboard's Option key to make the action of any button at the top of the window apply to all the files in the Windows List.

HTML Entities

This command displays the HTML Entities dialog box that enables easy entry of HTML character entities.

Web-Safe Colors

This command displays a palette of 216 browser-safe colors. Drag any color swatch from the palette to the document to insert a color value.

Arrange

BBEdit's Arrange command is a tool for organizing multiple windows in the editor. This is particularly helpful if you're using a small monitor to create your Web pages. When you select Window ⇨ Arrange, you get a dialog box from which to choose an arrangement for the windows.

Get Info

This command displays a dialog box that lists the number of characters, words, lines, and pages in any selected text (as well as the document). This same information is available by clicking the Info button on the status bar.

Reveal in Finder

Reveal in Finder is a handy feature with which you can quickly find a particular file without leaving the BBEdit application. This command opens the Mac OS Finder window that contains the active file.

Select the text of a file name (for example, index.html) within a document and hold down the Option key while opening the File pull-down menu. Choose the Reveal Selection command to open the Finder folder that contains that file. You can also click once on the document's icon in the status bar for the same effect.

Send to Back

This command places the front window behind all other windows.

Exchange with Next

This command enables you to switch your screen between the front two windows.

Synchro Scrolling

Synchro Scrolling enables multiple files to scroll in unison — the files in all open windows scroll when you scroll just one. This feature is great for comparing two versions of the same file.

Window Names

All the open windows are listed at the bottom of the Windows pull-down menu. Simply select one to make it active.

Internet menu

If your computer is connected to the Internet — and it undoubtedly is — BBEdit offers additional valuable features. In order to use these features, you must you have the application Internet Control Panel installed and configured. To make the Internet menu available from your menu bar, do the following:

1. Choose Edit ⇨ Preferences to open the Preferences dialog box.
2. From the Category list on the left, choose Services to display that panel.
3. Click in the box that says Internet Control Panel and click OK. You must restart BBEdit for the Internet menu to appear.

The Internet menu is identified by a globe icon in the menu bar. An especially helpful feature of the Internet menu is Resolve URL.

Follow these steps to check the validity of an URL:

1. Make sure you have an active connection to the Internet.
2. Place the insertion point anywhere within the URL.
3. Open the Internet menu and choose the Resolve URL command. BBEdit launches your default Web browser. (If the Web browser can't be found, an alert beep sounds.)

   Note that you can Command+click anywhere in an URL to resolve it.
4. If the URL is invalid, an alert beep sounds.

   If the URL is valid, you can view the site in your browser.

Printing

To print a document, select the Print command from the File menu. A standard Mac OS Print dialog box appears, with a few special BBEdit printing options. Each printer type presents its own options, of course; Figure C-10 shows the printer options associated with an HP LaserJet 4ML.

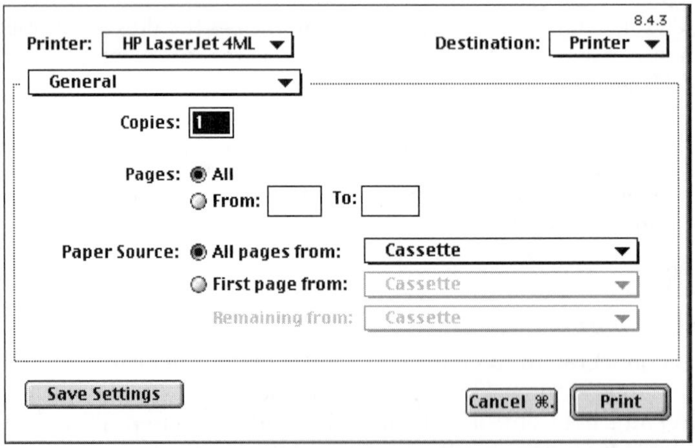

Figure C-10: The Print dialog box for an HP LaserJet 4ML

Click the Options button to see which options are available for your printer (or, on the HP LaserJet 4ML printer shown in the figure, select General and then choose the options you want to view and/or change). Some of the commonly used options are outlined in the following table.

Print Option	***Description***
Print Page Headers	Prints the page number, file name, time, and date from the header of each page.
Print Line Numbers	Displays line numbers along the left margin of the document. This is useful when debugging a file because error reports point to actual line numbers within a file.
Print Two-Up	Use this option to save resources by printing two BBEdit pages on one sheet of paper.
1-Inch Gutter	Leaves a one-inch margin along the left side of the paper. Allows space for notes in the margin, for instance, or to accommodate placement in three-ring binders.
Print Full Pathname	Prints the full path name of the file, from the header.
Time Stamp: Date Last Saved Date of Printing	This option enables you to decide whether the header date is the date the file was last modified or the date the file was printed.
Print Rubber Stamp	You can specify a message to be printed diagonally across the page in gray (or outline). This feature may not work on all printers.

Other Useful BBEdit Features

This section takes a look at some selected BBEdit features that you may find useful.

Spell-checking

The Check Spelling command on the Text menu launches BBEdit's built-in spelling checker. The Spell Checker compares each word in the document with words in the Spell Checker's dictionaries. If a word can't be found in a dictionary, BBEdit attempts to offer a possible correction.

If the questioned word is actually spelled correctly, you can add the word to the User Dictionary or simply skip the word. BBEdit ignores HTML code and checks only the text that will actually appear in your Web page.

If you've used any spell checkers at all, these steps are familiar:

1. Select Text ➪ Check Spelling.
2. To limit spell-checking to only selected text, choose the Selection Only option.
3. Click Start to begin spell-checking.

4. If a Questioned Word is misspelled, choose the correct word from the Guesses list or type a replacement word in the Replace With box.

   If a Questioned Word is not misspelled, choose the Skip command or use the Add command to enter the word into your personal User Dictionary.

Altering the User Dictionary

BBEdit's User Dictionary is a simple editable text file that you can alter yourself. You can add and delete words quickly and easily.

Open the User Dictionary by double-clicking the file located inside the BBEdit Dictionaries folder within the main BBEdit 5.1.1. folder. Each dictionary word must be entered on a separate line. Edit the file just as you would any other BBEdit text file.

Do not alter the coded number that appears at the top of the file. This code enables BBEdit to recognize the file as the User Dictionary.

Comparing files

BBEdit's Search menu contains a Find Differences command for comparing two files. For example, you may want to compare a file you have been working on locally to a file you just retrieved from a server, to find differences between the two. Figure C-11 demonstrates this feature at work.

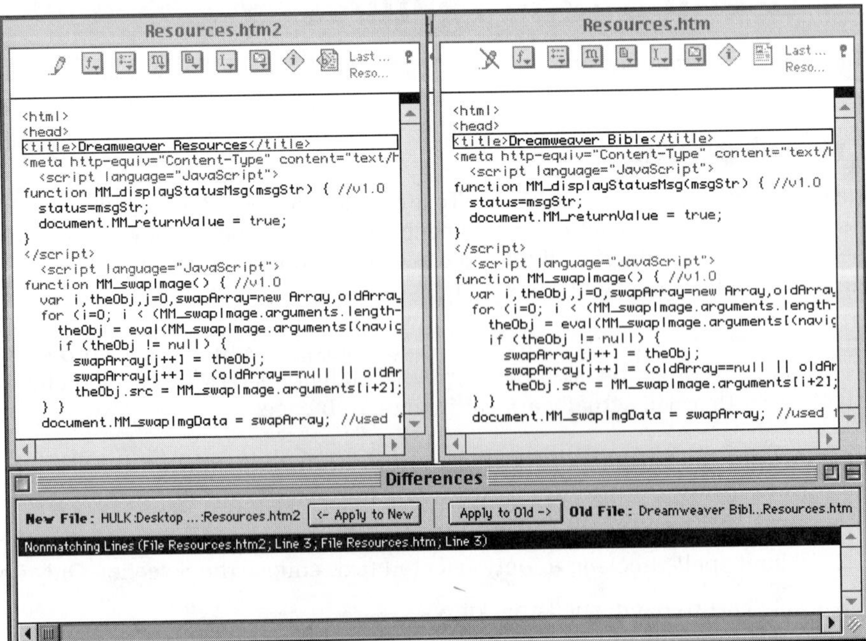

Figure C-11: Comparing differences in BBEdit files

Follow these steps to use the comparison features of the Find Differences command:

1. Choose Search ➪ Find Differences. The Find Differences dialog box appears.
2. Use the New and Old pop-up menus to choose the files you wish to compare. You can also drag file icons from the Finder into the New and Old portions of the dialog box.
3. Select the appropriate options — Case Insensitive or Ignore Leading Space — for your situation.
4. Click Compare to start the file-comparison operation.

If BBEdit finds differences, the two files appear side by side. In addition, a Differences pane detailing the found differences appears at the bottom of the screen (as previously shown in Figure C-11). You can copy a line from one file to another by selecting the line and choosing either Apply to Old or Apply to New. BBEdit italicizes the line in the Differences pane to indicate the change has been applied.

Search menu

BBEdit's Search and Search and Replace features work on a single file or multiple files. Follow these steps to search and/or replace text in the active window:

1. Select Search ➪ Find.
2. Enter the text you wish to locate in the Search For box.
3. To enter a replacement string, do so in the Replace With box. Otherwise, leave this box empty.
4. Choose any options you wish to apply to the search, including the direction of the search (Start at Top, Wrap Around, or Backwards), the selection, and case sensitivity.
5. Click any of the buttons along the right side of the dialog box to begin the search operation: Find, Find All, Replace, Replace All, Don't Find, or Cancel. Don't Find saves the settings of your search without actually performing the search.

One of the options in the Search command's dialog box enables you to search and/or replace text in multiple files. A handy use for this feature is updating each occurrence of a revised file name in several related HTML documents.

Follow these steps to perform multifile searches:

1. Select Search ➪ Find.
2. Enter the text you wish to locate in the Search For box.
3. To enter a replacement string, do so in the Replace With box. Otherwise, leave this box empty.

4. Find the Multi-File Search option and click the triangle to reveal the Multi-File Search options. (This portion of the dialog box may already be visible.)
5. Choose the files you wish to search, using the buttons and pop-up menus in the bottom part of the dialog box.
6. Select any other options you wish to apply to the search, as you would in a single-file search.
7. Click the appropriate button along the right side of the dialog box to begin the operation.

Go To Line command

It's easy to move the insertion point instantly to a specific line in your document. Use the Go To Line command under the Search menu. Enter the line number in the dialog box and click Go To (see Figure C-12).

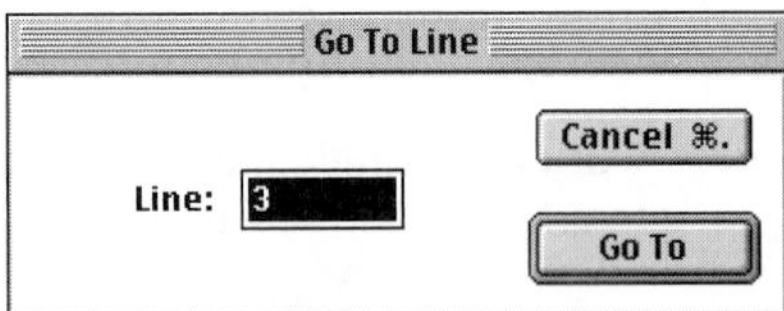

Figure C-12: The Go To Line dialog box

Markers icon

BBEdit's markers enable you to quickly and easily move to a particular section of your file. You can give the marker a unique name that makes sense to you and helps you find it later. This feature helps you stay on track in a large HTML file.

To set markers:

1. First select the section of your document you wish to mark.
2. Click the Markers icon in the status bar and select Set Marker from the pop-up menu.
3. In the Set Marker dialog box, enter a name for the marker and click the Set button.

   Once markers are established, the marker names appear at the bottom of the Mark pull-down menu. Simply select the marker name to take you to that location in your document.
4. When you want to clear markers you don't need anymore, click the Markers icon and select Clear Markers from the pop-up menu. In the Clear Markers dialog box, choose the marker you want to delete and click the Clear button.

Syntax coloring

To make editing easier, BBEdit displays HTML tags in colored text. Be sure to save your HTML documents with the .html or .htm extensions to enable this feature. If you want to change the colors BBEdit uses for syntax coloring, you can do so in the Text Colors portion of the Preferences dialog box.

Working with servers

You will be placing your completed Web files on a public server that enables people to view your masterpiece worldwide. The public server uses the File Transfer Protocol (FTP) to send and receive files. Dreamweaver has built-in FTP capabilities that enable you to connect to a remote server to save (upload) and open (download) files; see Chapter 7 for more information on FTP publishing. In addition, BBEdit offers the following FTP capabilities.

Saving to a server (uploading)

Follow these steps to upload to a server:

1. With a document open in BBEdit, select File ➪ Save to FTP Server.
2. To connect to a server, enter the name of the server. You can choose from previously used servers in the pop-up Server menu.
3. Enter your user name and password.
4. Click the Connect button to begin an FTP session.
5. Choose the destination directory on the server by using the standard Mac OS directory pop-up menu.

BBEdit remembers your password if you desire. Auto-Connect instructs BBEdit to automatically connect to a server using your saved password the next time you begin an FTP session.

Opening from a server (downloading)

If you wish to retrieve files from a server, use the File ➪ Open From FTP Server command. The steps are similar to those for saving to an FTP server in the preceding section.

Once the connection is made, use a standard Mac OS directory pop-up menu to navigate through the directories — just as you would if the files were stored locally on your Mac. Once you have located the file you desire, choose Save to begin the downloading process. After the file is completely downloaded, BBEdit displays the file in a new text-editing window.

✦ ✦ ✦

HomeSite 4.5 Primer (For Windows Users)

Designing and creating Web sites is intuitive and easy with Dreamweaver's visual interface. Yet you may want to leave the visual editor at times and get your hands on the underlying HTML code. In some cases, Dreamweaver's built-in HTML editor is all you need. Whenever you need a more advanced HTML editor to add features or troubleshoot your page, the Windows version of Dreamweaver includes a complete registered version of HomeSite 4.5. This standalone HTML editor package for Windows works with Dreamweaver. HomeSite is one of the most popular HTML editors available today. It enables you to produce HTML files without actually memorizing HTML tag commands.

This appendix provides instructions about how to access HomeSite's basic features. You can also access an Online User Manual and other invaluable help resources by clicking the Help tab in the Resources area of the HomeSite screen. (Remember that you can resize this frame by clicking and dragging the borders to make reading the help resources easier.) Also, you can visit Allaire's HomeSite 4.5 Web site at `www.allaire.com`.

Getting Started

It's easy to switch between Dreamweaver and HomeSite. A simple click of an icon toggles you from one application to the other. Elements selected in one application are automatically highlighted in the other, making it easy to keep your project organized.

Key features

"Full-featured" just scratches the surface when it comes to describing HomeSite. Many of the tools are the perfect complement to Dreamweaver's visual editor; others serve to make straight coding as efficient as possible. Here are just a few of the HomeSite highlights:

- Multiple layers of Undo
- Spell checker
- Site link validation
- Automatic color-coding of HTML, CFML, and other scripts
- Collapsible code
- Extended Find and Replace capabilities for making global edits
- Tag Insight, offering a list of attributes and attribute values as you enter tag code
- Customization of main and tag toolbars
- Wizards for complex tasks, including incorporating Dynamic HTML, RealAudio, and RealVideo
- Toggle capability between multiple documents
- Drag-and-drop from image libraries into the page
- Access to remote sites via built-in FTP
- Estimates of document sizes and download times
- Management for Cascading Style Sheets, CFML server-side tags, Netscape and Internet Explorer HTML extensions, embedded multimedia and plug-ins, and ActiveX and Java controls
- Web-safe color palette
- HTML syntax checking
- One-click preview in any browser
- Design View WYSIWY Need Editing
- Style Editor for applying CSS styles
- SMIL support, with tags for multimedia applications

The HomeSite 4.5 interface

The HomeSite interface is simple and logical, making even the most demanding programming projects easier to accomplish. The workspace (see Figure D-1) has three primary areas: the Editor/Browser and Resource windows, and the command bars.

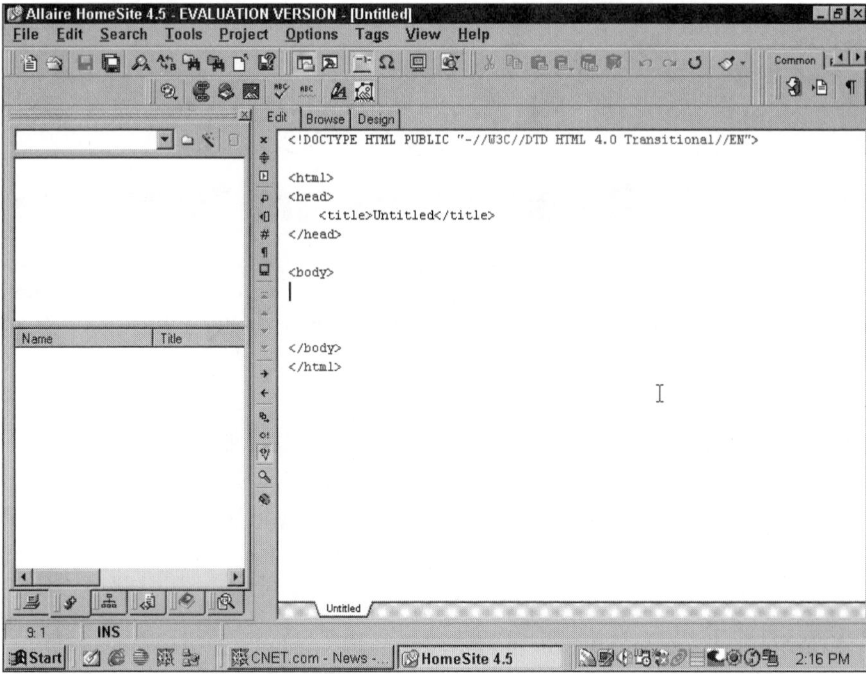

Figure D-1: The HomeSite 4.5 workspace

Editor/Browser window

Toggle between these two screens with F12. The Editor screen is where you enter HTML tags and place page content. The Browser screen is where you render the current document in the browser you choose.

Resource window

Click the tab buttons at the bottom of the Resource window to access areas where you manage files, custom tags, and online help areas. From left to right, the tabs represent the following groups of resources:

- ✦ **Local:** Use the Directory and File panes to access local and network drives.
- ✦ **Projects:** Create and manage HomeSite projects.
- ✦ **Site View:** Provides a graphic view of the links in a document.
- ✦ **Tag Snippets:** Store code for later use; see the section "Inserting Tags in a Document," later in this appendix.
- ✦ **Help:** Access help files, including user manual, FAQ, HTML reference files, and more.
- ✦ **Tag Inspector:** Displays all the tags in your document in a hierarchical tree, along with a list of properties for editing them.

Command bars

A rich supply of menus and toolbars is available throughout the HomeSite workspace, which you read about as you work through this appendix.

Working with Dreamweaver and HomeSite

Although Dreamweaver enables you to assign any HTML editor as your external editor, it integrates best with HomeSite. Once you've set up HomeSite as your default editor, switching between Dreamweaver and HomeSite is just a button click or keyboard shortcut away.

Setting up HomeSite as your default editor

Before Dreamweaver can access HomeSite, you must make HomeSite your default HTML editor. You can make this assignment through the Dreamweaver Preferences by following these steps:

1. In Dreamweaver, choose Edit ⇨ Preferences to open the Preferences dialog box.
2. From the Category list on the left, choose External Editors to display that panel.
3. In the External Editor panel, enter the path to the HomeSite executable. The easiest way to do this is to select the Browse button and locate the file. If you installed HomeSite according to the defaults, this path should read C:\Program Files\Allaire\HomeSite4\homesite4.exe.
4. Click OK when you've finished.

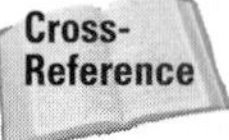

The External Editor options that control file synchronization between Dreamweaver and HomeSite are explained in detail in Chapter 4.

Switching between Dreamweaver and HomeSite

When you're in Dreamweaver, you have three ways to switch to HomeSite:

- ✦ Click the External Editor button in the top-left corner of the HTML Inspector.
- ✦ Choose Edit ⇨ Launch External Editor.
- ✦ Use the keyboard shortcut, Ctrl+E.

You can also select the other program's button on the taskbar or use the Alt+Tab method to switch between applications, but the file integration does not work under these circumstances.

Depending on the synchronization options chosen in the External Editor preferences, Dreamweaver may ask if you want to save the files first before you switch to HomeSite. If you do not save your Dreamweaver file first, your modifications do not appear in HomeSite (and vice versa). For this reason, I recommend setting your synchronization options to Always.

After you've made your code modifications in HomeSite and you're ready to return to Dreamweaver, you have three methods for switching back:

- ✦ Select the Dreamweaver button on HomeSite's Editor toolbar.
- ✦ Choose View ➪ Open in Macromedia Dreamweaver.
- ✦ Use the keyboard shortcut, Ctrl+D.

If HomeSite doesn't switch to Dreamweaver using any of the methods just given, check your HomeSite settings. Choose Options ➪ Settings (or press F8) to open the HomeSite Settings dialog box and select the HomeSite reload options from the Dreamweaver and File Settings tabs.

Disabling HomeSite integration

You can disable HomeSite integration if you prefer working with an older version of HomeSite or if you use a different HTML text editor. Here's how:

1. Choose Options ➪ Settings.
2. Select the Dreamweaver tab.
3. Turn off Enable Dreamweaver Integration and click OK.

Creating Pages: Making HTML Files

You have a couple of ways to work with HTML files. You can either create a new file or open an existing one and edit it. This section shows you how to create, open, apply tags to, and save Web pages in HomeSite. Remember: Even if you create a Web page in another application, you can still edit the page with HomeSite.

If you're starting from scratch to create a new file, HomeSite offers the following ways to create a new document:

- ✦ Select File ➪ New to open the New HTML Document dialog box. Select a blank document, one of the templates, or use any HTML file as a template. Template files are stored separately from the source documents, so you can modify the template files without worrying about changing the originals.

- ✦ Click the New button on the main toolbar to open a new document based on your default template. Change the default template by choosing Options ➪ Settings (F8) and selecting the Locations tab. Then enter the address of the file you would like to use as a template in the Default Template field.
- ✦ Use the Quick Start Wizard. Click the Quick Start button on the Common tab of the Tag Chooser (see Figure D-2) and follow the steps to design a new page or build your own template.
- ✦ Select File ➪ Convert Text File to convert an ASCII text file to an HTML file.

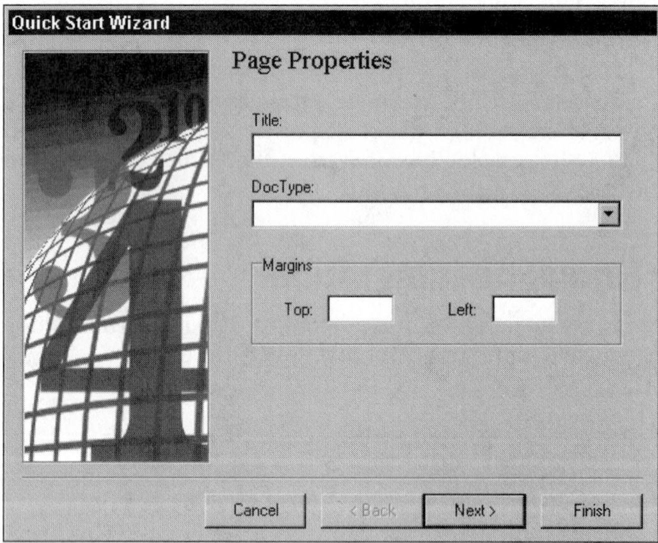

Figure D-2: Use the Quick Start Wizard to build a new page or template.

Opening an existing Web page

Another way to create a new HTML document is to start with an existing Web page. Use any of the following methods to open files:

- ✦ Select File ➪ Open (Ctrl+O).
- ✦ Click the Open button on the main toolbar.
- ✦ In the Open HTML Document dialog box, double-click a file listed in the Local Files view of the Resource tab.
- ✦ To open Web files directly, select File ➪ Open from the Web. Type in a URL or select a URL from your Favorites or Bookmarks list.
- ✦ Select File ➪ Recent Files to see a list of recently used files.

HomeSite treats read-only files differently from other files. These files are marked with a small red dot in the Resource window file list, and a warning message pops up if you try to open one. You cannot edit read-only files, but you can change the attribute on the file by right-clicking it, selecting Properties in the shortcut menu, and then deselecting the read-only attribute.

Inserting tags in a document

Of course, you can type codes directly into the document in the Edit screen, but the following methods are usually more efficient. To have HomeSite add tags for you, choose among these commands:

- ✦ Select Tools ➪ Tag Chooser (Ctrl+E). Select from the Chooser list (see Figure D-3), which contains the complete HTML tag set as well as CFML, HDML, SMIL, VTML, and custom tag sets. Double-click a tag to insert or to display a dialog box in which you can add tag-specific attributes and then click Apply to add the tag to your document.
- ✦ From the Tags menu, choose from a basic set of formatting tags.
- ✦ Select Options ➪ Settings (F8) and select the Tag Help tab to enable the display of options for Tag Insight and Tag Completion. The following sections describe these three tools and their benefits.
- ✦ Select Options ➪ Settings (F8) and open the HTML tab to set alignment and centering tags and to toggle the case of inserted tags.
- ✦ To repeat the previous tag, select Edit ➪ Repeat Last Tag (Ctrl+Q).

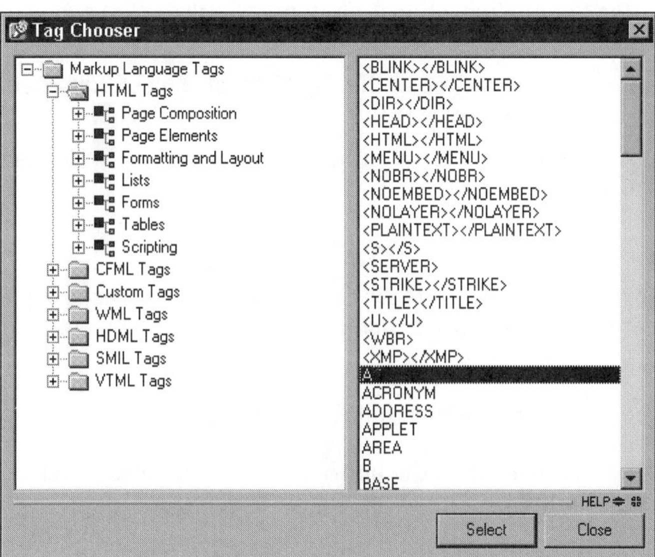

Figure D-3: Access any HTML tag — and many other varieties — through the Tag Chooser.

Using Tag Insight

The Tag Insight tool is a valuable aid to all Web designers, even beginners. It's a quick way to develop a tag as you type it by displaying a drop-down list of attributes and values for each tag. Click the Tag Insight button on the Editor toolbar to enable this feature. Or you can turn off Tag Insight in the Tag Help tab of the Settings dialog box (Options ➪ Settings, or F8). Finally, you can use it only when needed by pressing Shift+F2 when your cursor is in the first tag of a tag pair.

When Tag Insight is turned on, follow these steps to use this helpful feature:

1. Place the cursor in front of the start tag's end bracket (>). Press the spacebar to open the attribute list.
2. To add an attribute to the tag, double-click the attribute in the list. The cursor then moves between the double quotes of the attribute's value.
3. A list of values appears if the attribute has a fixed set of allowed values. To select a value from the list, press the spacebar. Once the value is inserted, the cursor moves in front of the closing bracket.

   If no allowed values appear, the attribute accepts programmer-specified values.
4. Continue selecting attributes until the tag code is complete.

Using Tag Completion

The Tag Completion feature automatically inserts the end tag after you type the start tag. Here are the steps to use this feature:

1. To enable Tag Completion, choose Options ➪ Settings (F8) and, in the Tag Help tab, check the Tag Completion box.
2. In the Tag Completion section of the Tag Help tab, select Edit to change the syntax of a selected tag.
3. You can use the Add and Delete buttons in the Tag Completion section to manage the list.

Tag Snippets

You can save portions of HTML code for easy recall in other files, using the valuable Tag Snippets feature. It's a lot easier than copying and pasting blocks of code from various files.

To save HTML code as a Tag Snippet, follow these steps:

1. Click the Tag Snippets tab at the bottom of the Resources panel to open the Tag Snippets window.
2. Right-click in the empty pane and select Create Folder from the drop-down menu.

3. Name the folder from which you want to save code and press Enter.
4. From the Tag Snippets window, right-click the folder and select Add Snippet from the shortcut menu to open the Custom Tag dialog box.
5. Type the start and end tags or paste them from another file. Click OK to save the tag in the folder created in Step 2.

To add more snippets to a folder, right-click the snippet folder in the Tag Snippets window and select Add Snippet from the shortcut menu. You can delete or rename folders as well, from the right-click shortcut menu.

To insert a Tag Snippet you've saved, follow these steps:

1. In the Editing window, place the cursor where you want to insert the tag.
2. Open the Tag Snippet window using one of the methods described previously.
3. Double-click the folder that holds the snippet you'd like to enter.
4. Double-click the snippet you wish to insert into your document.

Entering text in a document

In HomeSite's Editor window, you can type in page content and tags directly or use the numerous shortcuts to speed up the process. To check your work, toggle to the Browse mode by pressing F12 or click the Browse tab button on the Editor toolbar. Here are some examples of entering text in a document:

✦ To change the defaults for paragraph tags and file name cases, access the HTML tab by selecting Options ➪ Settings (F8).

✦ To create a link, drag and drop a document file into the Editor window.

✦ To insert an image or other media file, drag and drop it into the Editor window to insert it.

✦ To insert an HTML, ASCII text, or Cascading Style Sheet file into a document, select File ➪ Insert File.

✦ To display a menu of special and extended characters, select View ➪ Special Characters (Ctrl+Shift+X). In the Special dialog box (see Figure D-4), click a character to insert it into your document.

✦ To insert text from any application into your document, use the standard Windows Copy, Cut, and Paste commands.

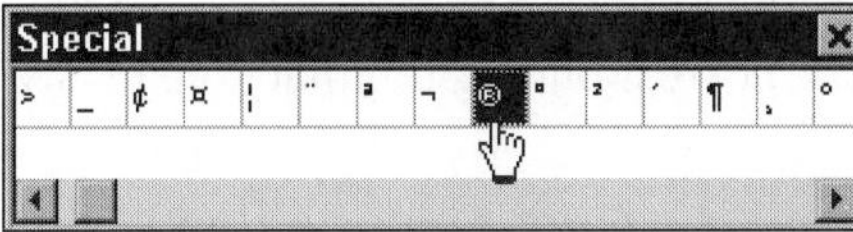

Figure D-4: Insert extended ASCII characters through the Special dialog box.

Saving files

When you view an unsaved document in either the internal or external browser, HomeSite saves a temporary copy of the file in memory. Thus, you should always save documents with new links in them before viewing them in a browser, to ensure that the file paths are identified.

To set the default file format:

1. Select Options ➪ Settings and click the File Settings icon, shown in Figure D-5.

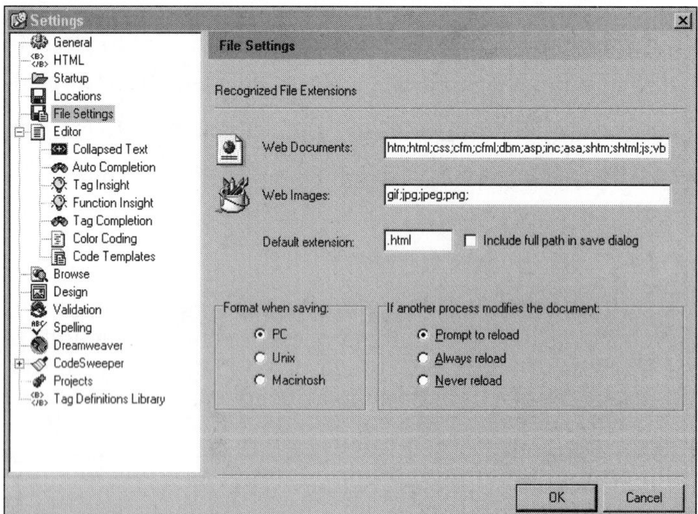

Figure D-5: HomeSite's Settings dialog box features many different options for customizing your work environment.

2. Check a format radio button among the Format When Saving options.
3. Now select one of the four Save commands from the File pull-down menu:
   - **Save (Ctrl+S):** Saves the current document.
   - **Save As (Ctrl+Shift+S):** Select a file name and click the Local tab to save the document locally, or click Remote to save the document to a server.
   - **Save All:** Saves all open documents.
   - **Save As Template:** Saves the HTML file as a template. Template files have the .hst extension and are stored separately. Later changes to the source document do not affect the corresponding template file in any way.

Browsing pages

It's imperative that you view your HTML pages in more than just one browser. HomeSite provides many browser options so you can test your pages against the array of available browsers.

Internal browser

If HomeSite 4.5 detects Microsoft Internet Explorer on your system during installation, you have the option of selecting it as the default HTML browser (see Figure D-6). Netscape Navigator cannot be used as the internal browser in HomeSite.

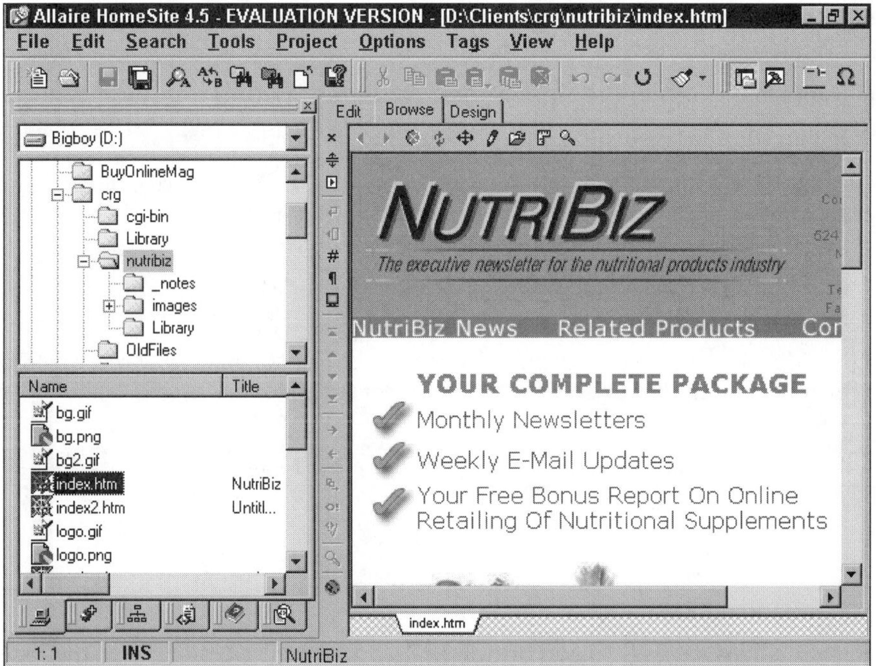

Figure D-6: Use HomeSite's internal browser to preview your Web pages.

If you don't want to have to toggle between the Editor and Browser windows, you can view both at once by clicking the Show Browser Below Editor button in the editing panel (the magnifying glass icon above the Dreamweaver button). You must be in the Editing pane for this button to be available. When you have HomeSite set up this way, you can see the changes you make to your code reflected in the Browser window instantly — without having to toggle the display. Remember that you can resize the Browser view by clicking and dragging the borders.

Mapping Your Web Site

HomeSite's Default Mapping feature sends a document through the specified Web server. If you don't run your own Web server, leave the mapping settings blank. If you do run your own server, here's how to set a default mapping for your Web server:

1. Access the Browse icon by selecting Options ⇨ Settings.
2. Check the Use Microsoft Internet Explorer box.
3. Select the Enable Server Mappings option.
4. Select the Add button to open the Mapping dialog box.
5. In the Mapping dialog box, enter the path of the folder to be mapped in the Map From text box.
6. Enter the URL of the server in the Map To text box. Click OK when you're done.
7. To add additional mappings, select the Add button again and repeat Steps 5 and 6.

You also have the option to map any particular path to a file with a specific URL. This mapping capability enables you to use your remote server to preview server-side includes and other types of files. To define a separate mapping for a project:

1. In the Projects panel of the Resources window, right-click a project and select Properties.
2. In the Project Properties dialog box, access the Server Mapping tab. Enter the local path in the first text box and the URL you want to use for that project in the second text box. Click OK.

Now, if you open this file from the project tree, the project mapping overrides the default mapping.

External browser

HomeSite makes it easy to add browsers — and browser versions — to the External Browser list. To add, delete, or reconfigure an external browser, access the External Browsers panel by selecting Options ⇨ Configure External Browsers. When you add a new browser to your list, you have the following options in the External Browsers dialog box (shown in Figure D-7), which affect your current document when you launch an external browser:

- ✦ Prompt to save changes to current document.
- ✦ Automatically save changes to the current document.

✦ Browse using a temporary copy (no need to save). This is the default setting; it enables you to view your current document without having to save the document itself. Thus, you can get a quick look at your current code without saving over the previous version of the file, in case you don't like what you see.

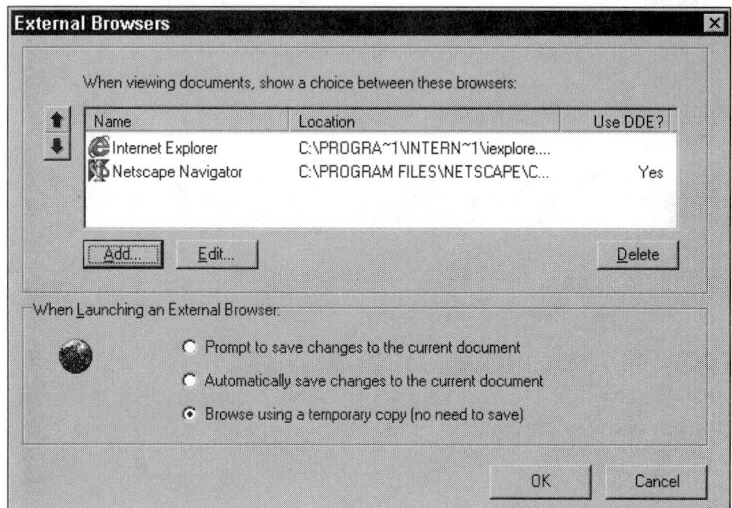

Figure D-7: Add more browsers for testing in the External Browsers dialog box.

Once you add at least one external browser to HomeSite, you can then choose a browser from the list when you click the Launch External Browser button on the main toolbar. Alternately, pressing F11 loads the current document in the first listed browser. To place your preferred browser at the top of the list, open the External Browsers panel, click the browser, and click the blue arrow buttons to move it to the top. Then click OK to save the change.

Setting up an FTP server

To establish an FTP server, follow these steps:

1. Open the Remote tab in the Resources area.
2. Right-click in the top pane of the Remote tab panel and select Add FTP Server to open the Configure FTP Server panel (see Figure D-8).

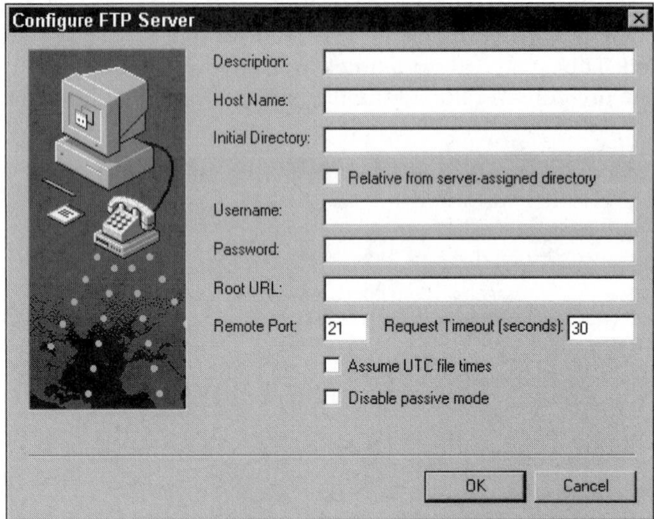

Figure D-8: Set up your FTP server so you can publish directly to the Web from within HomeSite.

3. At a minimum, complete the following fields:
   - **Description:** The name of the server
   - **Host Name:** The FTP address
   - **Username:** Your login name
   - **Password:** Your password, if any
4. Change the default Remote Port entry as needed.
5. Click OK to close the dialog box. Right-click and select Refresh to update the server list.
6. Once you've established an FTP server, right-click the server name and then select Connect. You see the server directory tree if you've connected correctly to the server.

To open a file on a server, you access the remote server's files directly. (To change server settings, right-click a server name and then select Properties to open the Properties panel.) Here are the steps for opening a file:

1. Click the Remote tab in the Resources window and double-click the Remote Servers icon in the top panel to display the server's directory tree.
2. Double-click an FTP icon to open a connection to the server.

3. Double-click a file to open it in the Editor window.

Remote files have a small dot on their file name tab at the bottom of the Editor window. To save changes to a remote file, click the Save button on the main toolbar.

Editing and Enhancing Your Pages

HomeSite makes it easy to customize your working space, modify HTML code, and add bells and whistles to your pages.

Changing how the Editor window looks and works

You can customize the Editor window's appearance as well as its operation to your liking.

- ✦ To remove any of the three toolbars from the screen, toggle them off from the View menu.
- ✦ To switch between open documents, click the tabs at the bottom of the window. If you've made changes to a document since the last time it was saved, the file name is blue.
- ✦ To adjust the size of the text line in the Editor window, click the Toggle Word Wrap button on the Editor toolbar or select Options ➪ Word Wrap.
- ✦ To view your document with an internal browser, press F12 or click the Browser button on the Editor toolbar. To enable the internal browser to Microsoft Internet Explorer, select Options ➪ Settings and open the Browse tab.
- ✦ To view your document with an external browser, press F11 to open the current document in the first browser in your External Browser list. Or click View External Browser List on the main toolbar and select a browser from the list.
- ✦ To have HomeSite insert ending tags automatically after you type in a start tag, toggle the Tag Completion button on the Editor toolbar.

Tag attribute values

Many HTML tags have attribute values that may enable you to define the tag's appearance or its usefulness. You can set attribute values as you create a tag, or later after you've previewed the page in a browser and you need to adjust the display. You can edit a tag with the Tag Inspector using any of the following methods:

- ✦ Right-click any start tag and select Edit Tag.
- ✦ Place the cursor in a start tag and press F4.
- ✦ Select Tags ➪ Inspect Current Tag.

To set or change attribute values with the Tag Editor, follow these steps:

1. Select a start tag, or place the cursor inside it and then right-click and select the Edit Tag option or choose Tags ➪ Edit Current Tag.
2. Enter new values or edit the existing values in the Tag Editor panel; the options for `<body>` are shown in Figure D-9.

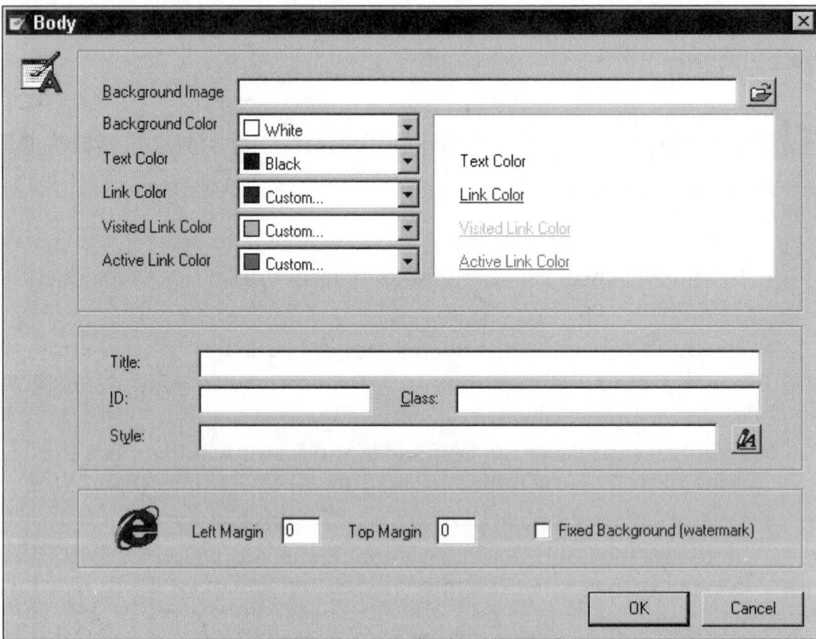

Figure D-9: The Tag Editor shows all of the options for any selected HTML tag.

3. Complex tags may have multiple tabs in their Tag Editor windows. Click the tab names at the top of the Tag Editor panel to access the other attributes.
4. Click the OK button to close the Tag Editor and have the attribute changes appear in the document.

Using bookmarks

You can set up to ten bookmarks in a document — very handy for finding a given spot in a large HTML file. To set and use bookmarks, follow these steps:

1. Select Edit ➪ Set Bookmark (Ctrl+K) to add a bookmark.
2. To go to the next bookmark, select Edit ➪ Go to Next Bookmark (Ctrl+Shift+K).

Using search

HomeSite has two levels of search and replace. Basic searches scan only the currently open document. Extended searches scan more than just the open document. Thus, it's easy to make global changes.

Performing basic searches

To search for a string in the currently open document, select Search ⇨ Find (Ctrl+F). Then, if you want to replace a matching string in the currently open document, select Search ⇨ Replace (Ctrl+R).

If the search panel is closed and you want to resume the previous search, select Search ⇨ Find Again (F3).

Performing extended searches

To search for a string among all open documents (or all HTML files in a particular directory, folder, or project), follow these steps:

1. Select Search ⇨ Extended Replace (Ctrl+Shift+R).
2. Enter your selections in the Extended Replace dialog box, shown in Figure D-10.

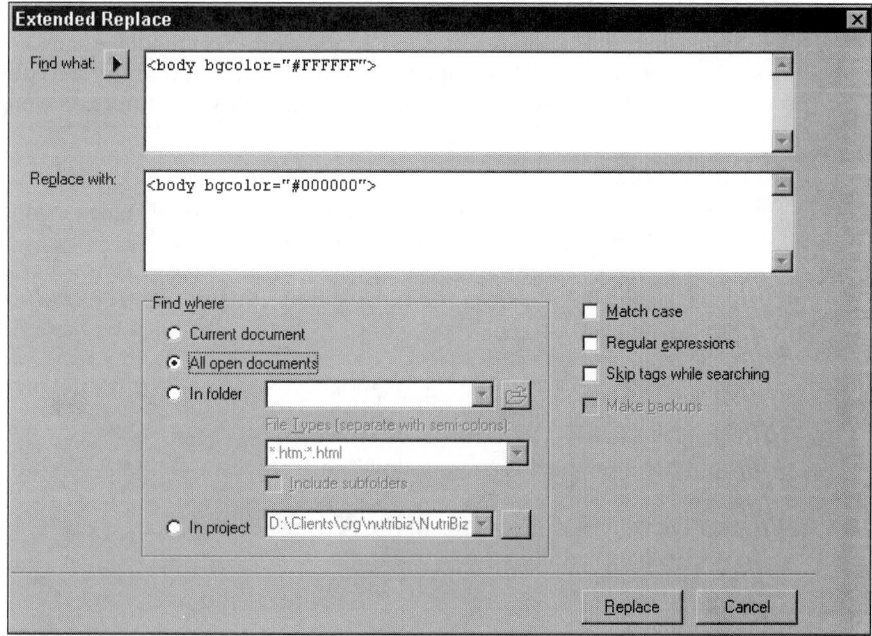

Figure D-10: HomeSite's Extended Find and Replace feature is extremely powerful and flexible.

3. Click the corresponding radio button to search all open documents or to specify a folder or project in which to search.
4. Select the Replace button.
5. You can see all of the matches in the Search Results tab. Double-click any match in the list to go directly to that file. Note that read-only files are not searched and that you are not prompted to confirm each replacement.

Spell check

HomeSite takes the normal spell-checking operation to the next level by providing a multilanguage Spell Check feature. When you install HomeSite, you can select additional language dictionaries to use. To run Spell Check, use any of the following methods:

✦ Select Tools ➪ Spell Check (F7) to scan your current document for spelling errors.

✦ To configure the Spell Checker to skip all text within HTML tags, select Options ➪ Settings and open the Spelling tab. In this tab, you can also select the dictionaries you want the Spell Checker to use.

Using color-coded tags

To facilitate the quick scanning of documents, HomeSite displays tags in distinct colors. This includes all HTML tags, quoted attributes, and script and object tags. You can change the default colors used and create custom colors as well.

Changing colors

To change color coding, access the Color Coding panel (see Figure D-11). Click HTML in the scheme panel and select Edit Scheme.

You can also assign a color from the Basic palette to any tag. Open the drop-down list for the tag you want to color and choose Custom. This opens the color palette. Pick a basic color and click OK.

Creating new colors

To create a custom color for a tag, follow these steps:

1. Open the Color Coding panel in the Settings dialog box. Select HTML from the list and click the Edit Scheme button.
2. Open the color palette by clicking the Foreground button.
3. Drag the arrow on the brightness scale to set a level.

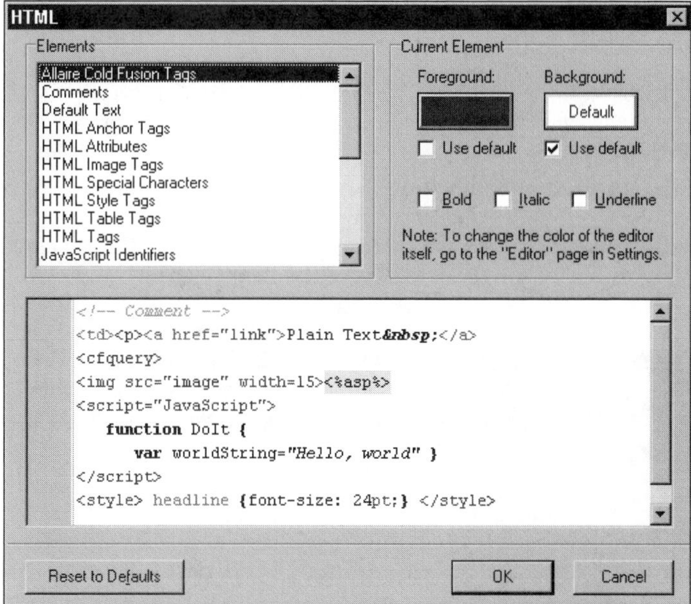

Figure D-11: Color-code your HTML to easily find specific or different kinds of tags.

4. Drag the color pointer to define a color. The color values display as you move the pointer, and the color displays in the Preview box.

5. Click Add to Custom Colors; then click OK to enter the color for the tag.

Adding colors

Wise use of color can make the difference between uninspired and exciting Web pages. HomeSite provides some easy ways to add and change colors in your pages. To insert a color value using Tag Insight:

1. Open Tag Insight by placing the cursor in front of the start tag's closing bracket and pressing the spacebar.

2. Double-click Color from the pop-up list.

3. Double-click a color from the drop-down menu.

HomeSite provides a list of colors to choose from, or you can select a specific color from a variety of color palettes. To insert a color from a palette:

1. To open a color palette, double-click the Custom button from the Colors drop-down list. This opens the Palette pane.

2. Position the cursor over any palette color to display its name or hexadecimal value.
3. Click a color to insert it into your document.

Working with palettes

To open a different palette from which to select colors, follow these steps:

1. Access the Palette drop-down menu, shown in Figure D-12, by clicking the Open Palette button on the left side of the Palette pane.

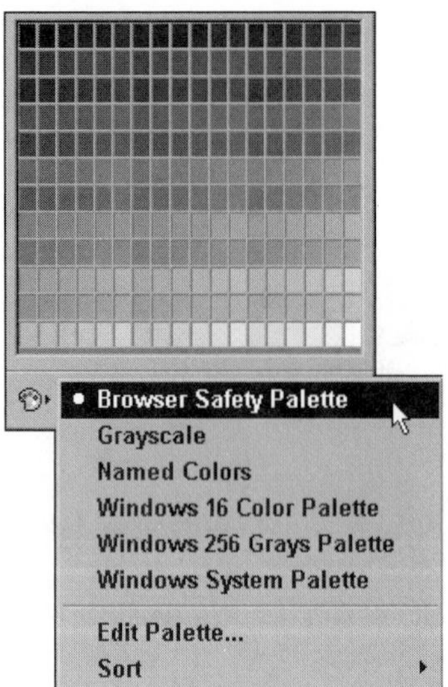

Figure D-12: Switch among any number of color sets through the Palette drop-down menu.

2. Click a palette to open it in the Palette pane.

You can edit and delete existing palettes from the Open Palette dialog box. You can create a new palette, too. Follow these steps:

1. From the Open Palette drop-down menu, select Edit Palette.
2. In the Palette dialog box, click the New Palette button.
3. Select RGB values, or click the Eyedropper button and drag the dropper over the color spectrum to create a color.
4. Once you create a color you want to add to your palette, click the Add button.
5. When you are done creating a new palette, click the Save button and enter a name for the palette. The new file is saved with a default .pal extension in the Palettes subdirectory.

Adding a palette from Paint Shop Pro

Paint Shop Pro is an excellent graphic editor that comes free with HomeSite and is available to Dreamweaver users who register HomeSite online. Follow these steps to bring a Paint Shop Pro palette into HomeSite:

1. In Paint Shop Pro, select Colors ➪ Save Palette to open the Save Palette panel.
2. Enter a name for the palette.
3. Set the Save As type to PAL-JASC Palette.
4. Save the file in the HomeSite\Palettes directory.

Adding images

HomeSite supports the standard Web graphics formats: GIF, JPG, PNG graphics files, and BMP (Internet Explorer only). To see all of your image files, right-click in one of the file list resource tabs, select Filter, and then select Web Images to limit the file display to images only. If you want to view thumbnails of the image files, click the Thumbnail button in the Resources menu bar.

To add an image to the current document, follow these steps:

1. Select an image in the file list and drag it directly into your document. The default image width and height appear in the tag code.
2. Place the cursor anywhere in the image tag, right-click, and select Edit Tag.
3. Change the image settings in the editor as needed. You can click the Clear button to delete the current entries.

Testing Your Pages

Before you launch your Web site, you should test your code. HomeSite has several key features — HTML Validation, Link Checking, and Document Weighting — to put your Web page through its paces.

HTML validation

Before you FTP your files up to the remote server, it's a good idea to verify that your HTML code is sound. HomeSite includes a powerful tool for checking and reporting on HTML syntax errors. Although it won't automatically correct errors, it identifies them and gives you a list of errors and comments. Double-click an error message to highlight the offending code in your document.

To set the HTML Validator options:

1. Select Options ➪ Settings and choose the Validation tab. Click the Validator Settings button to open the dialog box shown in Figure D-13.

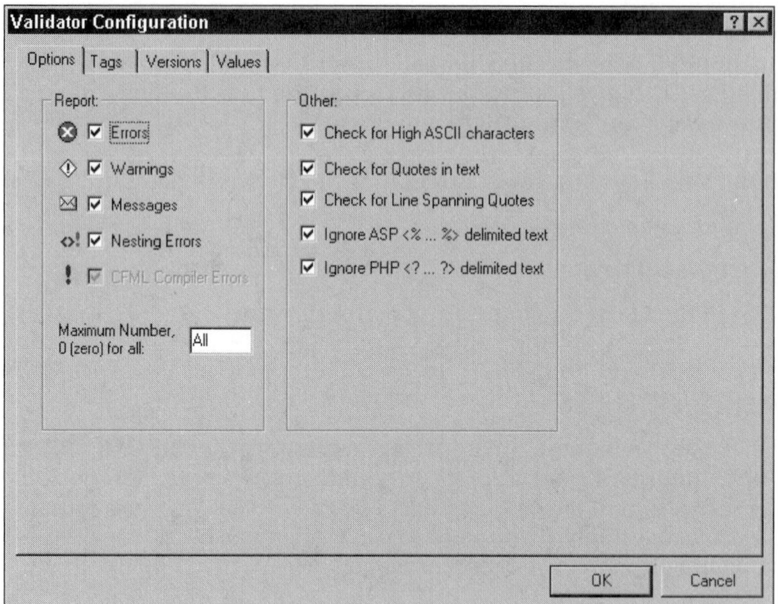

Figure D-13: Set up the HTML Validator to your specific parameters with the Validator options.

2. Complete the settings for Options and then do the same for the Tags, Versions, and Values tabs.
3. Click OK to save your changes.

When you have validation set up as desired, you're ready to use it to test code in your current document. Click the Validate Document button on the main toolbar or select Tools ⇨ Validate Current Document. The results from the validation test appear in a new window below the current document. To find the code that corresponds to any error message, double-click it in the list.

Testing your links

Links change often, so it's important to do regular testing of your documents' links. HomeSite makes the task easier with its built-in Link Checker. Besides testing URLs, it also checks directory paths of images and other Web page elements specified in the current HTML document.

Note that the Link Checker can't verify links to secure pages, FTP links, and mailto: links. You need an active Internet connection to check remote URLs.

Follow these steps to use the Link Checker:

1. To start the Link Checker working on your current document, click the Verify Links button on the main toolbar or select Tools ⇨ Verify Links. A list is generated with each link's URL or path.
2. If you need to change the URL or the local directory, do this by first selecting the Set Root URL button next to the list of links. Next enter the new root URL in the Set Root URL text box that is displayed, or select the folder icon to set the root directory and drive against which local links should be tested.
3. Click the Start Link Verification button, the right-pointing triangle found next to the list of links, to begin the verification. The status of each link is updated as it is processed.
4. A checkmark tells you that the link works. An X indicates that it's a failed link, which means that the document or file couldn't be located. Double-click an item in the Verifier List to find the code that corresponds to the failed link.

Document weight

This handy feature estimates the upload time of your current page. To find out how long it takes to upload a page, select Tools ⇨ Document Weight. The Root URL setting in your FTP configuration is used to determine the relative path to files, and the results are displayed in the Document Weight dialog box (see Figure D-14).

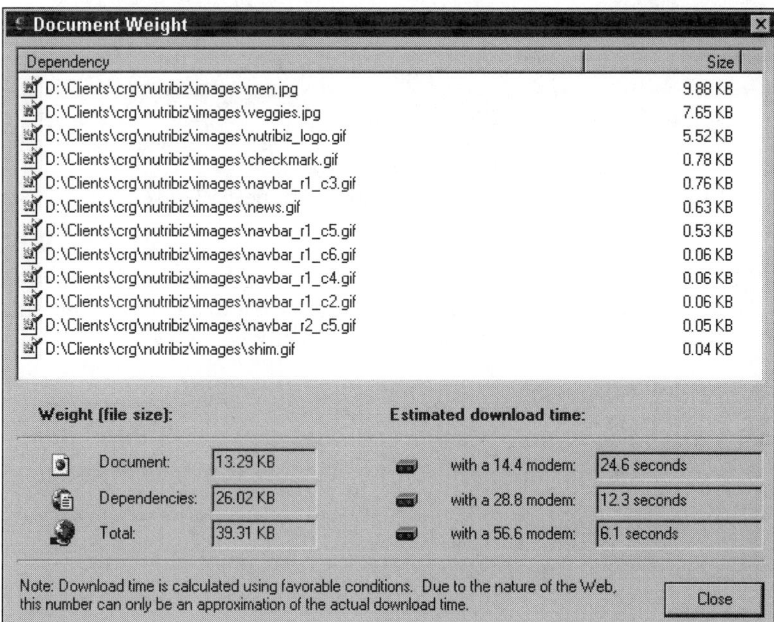

Figure D-14: It's a good idea to check on the probable download time for your Web page.

Creating Projects

If your Web site contains multiple files, you can probably benefit by grouping the files as projects. HomeSite contains powerful project management features that help you organize your site or a collection of sites.

To create a new project, start by clicking the Projects tab at the bottom of the Resources window. From there, you have several alternatives. You can create a new project or import a project from an existing directory folder. To open the New Project dialog box shown in Figure D-15, right-click anywhere in the Project folder area or select Project ➪ New Project.

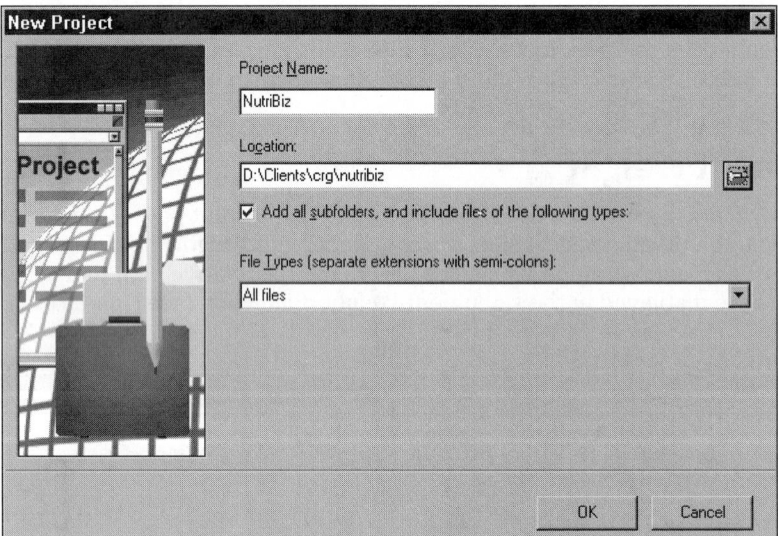

Figure D-15: Use the New Project dialog box to start your new Web site.

The project workspace gives you easy and organized access to related documents and files. The files in the project folders are pointers to your HTML documents. The documents are not physically moved or modified in any way.

Projects toolbar

When the Projects tab is open in the Resources window, you have access to the following tools:

- ✦ **Open Project:** Opens up a project from a local or remote folder.

✦ **New Project:** Brings up the New Project dialog box.

✦ **Upload Project:** Opens the Upload Project dialog box.

Uploading a project to a server

Use the Upload Project icon to select and upload project files to a server. You can select from the list of server connections you have established in the Remote tab.

To upload a project, follow these steps:

1. First, open the Upload Project dialog box by clicking the Upload Project button in the Project tab.
2. In the Upload Project dialog box, select whether you want to upload the entire site or upload only new or modified pages. Click Next.
3. Select the target server from the list in the Upload locations. (If the server you want is not on the list, close the dialog box and set up a protocol for an FTP connection as described earlier.)
4. Click OK to start the upload. The uploaded files are displayed in the file list.

Keyboard Shortcuts

As an alternative to using the pull-down menus, HomeSite 4.5 provides a full complement of keyboard commands, listed in Tables D-1 through D-4.

Table D-1
File Menu Keyboard Shortcuts

File Command	*Keyboard Shortcut*
Open an HTML document	Ctrl+O
Save current document	Ctrl+S
Save As	Ctrl+Shift+S
Print current document	Ctrl+P
Close current document	Ctrl+W
Close All	Ctrl+Shift+W

Table D-2
Tag Selector Keyboard Shortcuts

Tag	*Keyboard Shortcut*
Open the Tag Chooser	Ctrl+E
Open the Editor for the selected tag	Ctrl+F4
Open the Quick Anchor dialog box	Ctrl+Shift+A
Open the Image dialog box	Ctrl+Shift+I
Insert a paragraph tag	Ctrl+Shift+P
Insert a break tag	Ctrl+Shift+B
Insert a nonbreaking space	Ctrl+Shift+spacebar
Insert a bold tag	Ctrl+B
Insert an italic tag	Ctrl+I
Insert a center tag (div align="center") by default	Ctrl+Shift+C
Insert a comment tag	Ctrl+Shift+M
Find matching tag	Ctrl+M
Repeat last tag	Ctrl+Q

Table D-3
Edit and Search Menu Keyboard Shortcuts

Edit Command	*Keyboard Shortcut*
Select all text in the current document	Ctrl+A
Copy selected text to the clipboard	Ctrl+C
Cut the selection to the clipboard	Ctrl+X
Paste selection from the clipboard	Ctrl+V
Insert bookmark at the current line	Ctrl+K
Go to the next bookmark	Ctrl+Shift+K
Open the Find dialog box	Ctrl+F
Run the Find command again	F3
Open the Replace dialog box	Ctrl+R

Edit Command	***Keyboard Shortcut***
Open the Extended Find and Replace dialog box	Ctrl+Shift+R
Open the Go To line number dialog box	Ctrl+G
Undo the previous edit	Ctrl+Z
Validate HTML in the current document	Shift+F6
Spell-check the current document	F7
Open the special/extended character list	Ctrl+Shift+X
Indent the selected text block	Ctrl+Shift+. (period)
Unindent the selected text block	Ctrl+Shift+, (comma)

Table D-4
General Workspace Keyboard Shortcuts

Workspace Command	***Keyboard Shortcut***
Toggle the Quick toolbar	Ctrl+H
Display Help for current tag	F1
Open the Options ⇨ Settings menu	F8
Toggle the Resources tab	F9
Toggle Full Screen view	Ctrl+F12
Toggle Editor/Browser views	F12

✦ ✦ ✦

APPENDIX E

Fireworks 3 Primer

Fireworks was designed to meet a need among Web artists — to simplify workflow. Before Fireworks, designers typically used different programs for object creation, rasterization, optimization, and HTML and JavaScript creation. Fireworks combines the best features of several key tools — while offering numerous innovative additions of its own — into a sophisticated interface that's easy to use and offers many surprising creative advantages. Once you discover the power of Fireworks, it's hard to design Web graphics any other way.

With Fireworks, the designer has tools for working with both vector-based objects and pixel-based images. Typically, you work in Fireworks just as you would in a vector graphics application, such as Macromedia FreeHand, by creating and transforming shapes. When you do want to work at the pixel level — in a style more similar to working in Photoshop — you can access Fireworks' Image Edit Mode simply by using a pixel-only tool such as the Marquee. By enabling you to switch effortlessly between paths and pixels, Fireworks smoothly integrates them both.

The advantage of working mainly at the vector level is that virtually every aspect of a Fireworks graphic can be altered at any stage. In other words, in Fireworks everything is editable, all the time — even Photoshop-compatible image filters can be applied to vector objects and then edited, removed, or reordered later. Not only is this a tremendous time-saver, but it's also a major production enhancement — and the Web requires an extraordinary amount of material and maintenance. Not only are new sites and Web pages constantly going online, but existing pages need continual updating. The underlying philosophy of Fireworks — everything editable, all the time — reflects a deep awareness of the Web designer's real world situation. Changing one aspect of a graphic — without having to rebuild the image from scratch — is one of Fireworks' key strengths.

With version 3 of Dreamweaver and Fireworks, Macromedia increased the integration between the two applications and made it clear that they want Fireworks to be the image editing application of choice for Dreamweaver users. Both applications now feature common interface elements like the Commands menu and History panel, lessening the learning curve as you move from one application to the other.

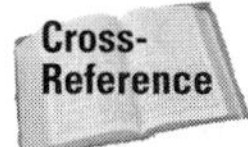

See Chapter 22 for more about the integration features of Dreamweaver 3 and Fireworks 3.

Understanding the Interface

Whether you start your graphics session by creating a new document or loading in an existing one, you'll find yourself working within a complete creative environment that includes menus, a toolbox, one or more document windows, and a large selection of floating panels. Many of the elements of the Fireworks interface will be familiar to you if you've used other graphics applications. In fact, many Fireworks elements were deliberately designed to be familiar to Photoshop and FreeHand users in order to lessen the learning curve.

Feature for feature, Fireworks for Macintosh and Fireworks for Windows are nearly identical. Both include the same menus, toolbox, and floating panels. However, each application also goes out of its way to conform to the user interface standards of the platform it runs on, so some differences exist.

Fireworks for Windows (see Figure E-1) uses the multiple document interface, common to Windows applications, where all interface elements are contained in a larger, parent window. Fireworks for Windows also includes convenience toolbars, providing easy access to features that are also found in the menus or floating panels. The parent window includes a context-sensitive Status bar that provides hints as you work. Toolbars, and even the toolbox, can be docked to the parent window or floated as desired.

Fireworks for Macintosh (see Figure E-2) uses the single document interface of the Macintosh platform, where each interface element is contained in its own window, and other applications are visible beneath.

We'll examine each element of the complete Fireworks interface. Remember to refer back to Figures E-1 or E-2 at any time if you find yourself losing track of a particular item.

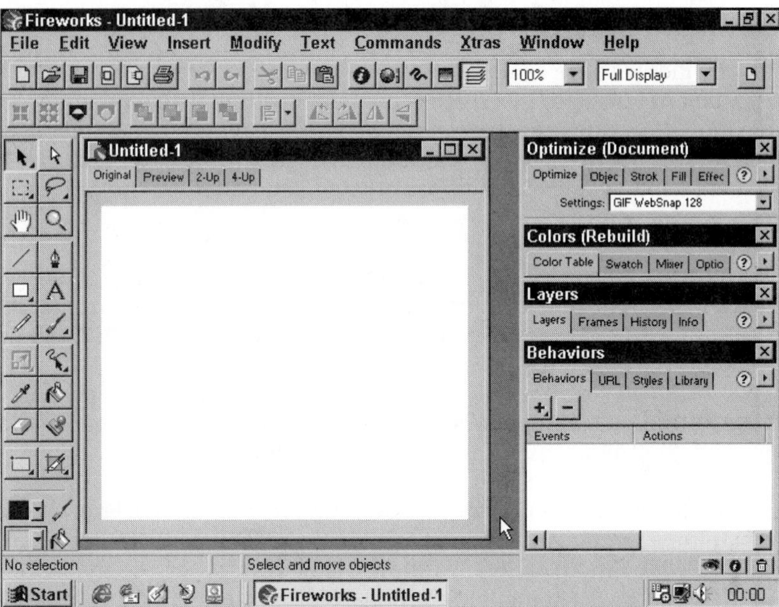

Figure E-1: The Windows version of Fireworks has additional toolbars and uses a multiple document interface.

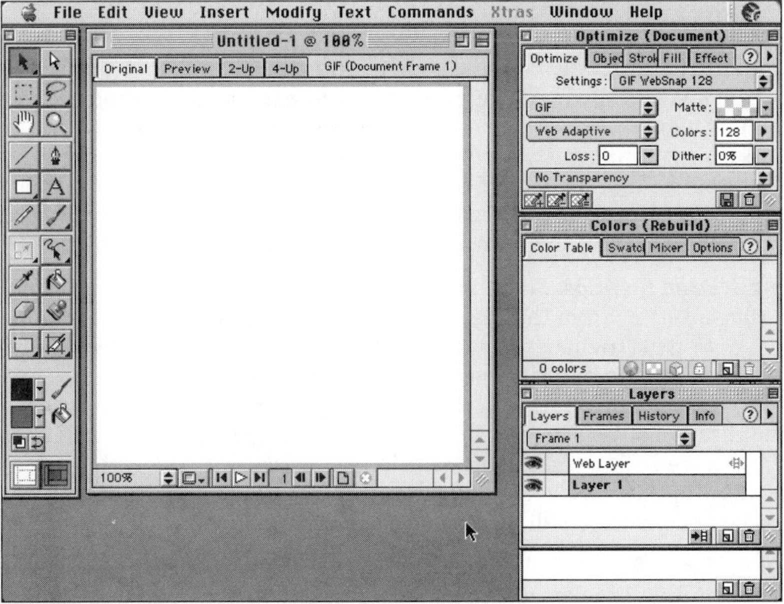

Figure E-2: Fireworks for Macintosh uses the single document interface of the Macintosh platform.

The Document window

The document window is the central focus of your work in Fireworks. Each Fireworks document you open or create is contained within its own document window, and multiple documents can be opened and displayed simultaneously. The menus, toolbox, floating panels, and toolbars (Windows only) affect the active document window only. Objects are created and edited on the canvas within the document window.

You can also hide document windows that you're not currently using. Windows users can click the Minimize button on a document window to minimize its title bar to the bottom of the parent window. Windows users can also click Maximize to dock a document window to the parent window, hiding all other windows. Clicking the document window's Restore button undocks it. Macintosh users can click the Windowshade button on a document window to hide all but the title bar, and click the Windowshade button again to restore the document window.

In addition to multiple document windows for multiple documents, Fireworks can also display multiple document windows for the same document. To open a new view of a selected document, choose Window ➪ New Window or use the key shortcut Ctrl+Alt+N in Windows (Command+Option+N for Macintosh). The new view opens at the same magnification as the previous image, but you can easily zoom in for detail work on one view while displaying the overall effect in another.

Fireworks enables you to control what you see in a document window in a number of ways:

- **Original/Preview Tabs.** Preview your work as it will appear in your final, exported image(s) by choosing the appropriate tab along the top of the document window. When you open or create a document in Fireworks, the document window is set on the Original tab, so that you can create and interact with objects on the canvas. Choose one of the other tabs at any time and Fireworks will create and display a single, two-up or four-up preview of your work according to the settings in the Optimize panel.
- **Magnification Settings.** Zoom in or out, from 6 percent to 6,400 percent, by choosing a setting from the View ➪ Magnification submenu or the Magnification option list. Because Fireworks objects are always rendered as pixels (even when they're based on vectors), the magnification settings are predefined to offer the best image pixel to screen pixel ratio and the most accurate representation of your image. In addition to specifying a zoom setting, you can also have Fireworks fit the image in the current window with the Fit All in Window option. Fireworks zooms in or out to the maximum magnification setting possible while still displaying the entire image.
- **Display Mode.** Choose Full Display or Draft Display from the Display Mode option list. Draft Display shows all vector-based objects with one-pixel-wide outlines and no fill; pixel-based images are shown as rectangles with an "X" in the middle.

✦ **Page Preview.** Click the Page Preview button to see a quick dimensional overview of the current document. The width, height, and resolution are displayed in a small pop-up window. On Windows, click once to activate the control, and once again to deactivate it. On the Mac, click and hold to activate; release to deactivate.

✦ **Animation controls.** With these VCR-like buttons — on the document window in Macintosh and on the Status bar in Windows — you can play a frame-based animation straight through, using the timing established in the Frame panel. You'll also find buttons that enable you to move through the animation a frame at a time or to go to the first or last frame.

✦ **Exit Image Edit Mode button.** Click the "stop" button, on the bottom of the document window on the Macintosh and on the Status bar in Windows, to quickly exit Image Edit Mode and to enter Object Mode. When you're already in Image Edit Mode, the stop button is grayed out in Macintosh and invisible in Windows.

Opening the toolbox

All Fireworks drawing and editing tools can be found in the Toolbox. Most tools work with both pixel-based images and path-based objects, although some change their behavior in order to do so. The eraser, for example, becomes a knife when you're working with paths.

Tools that are similar, such as the Lasso, Polygon Lasso, and Magic Wand, are grouped together into tool groups and accessed through a flyout. A tool group can be recognized by the small triangle in the lower-right corner of the button; clicking and holding the button causes the flyout to appear. Once the tool group is visible, you can select any of the tools in the group by moving the pointer over the tool and releasing the mouse. Figure E-3 shows the toolbox with all of its flyouts *out*.

Tip

Windows users have the option of floating the Toolbox or docking it to the Fireworks window. Double-clicking the title bar of the toolbox docks it to the parent window. Dragging it back out undocks it.

All of the tools have keyboard shortcuts. As befits a program that incorporates both pixel- and vector-editing tools, these single-key shortcuts parallel the shortcuts for some of the pixel-based tools in Photoshop, and vector-based ones in FreeHand. If two or more tools share a keyboard shortcut (as with M for Marquee and Ellipse Marquee), the key acts as a toggle between the tools; the letter R toggles through seven tools: the rectangle, the ellipse, and all of the Web tools. You can find the button for each tool, as well as its keyboard shortcut and a brief description the tool, in Table E-1. More detailed information on each tool is presented throughout this book when the tool is used for various operations. In Table E-1, tools that are new or have moved in Fireworks 3 are displayed in bold text (Crop and Polygon Slice).

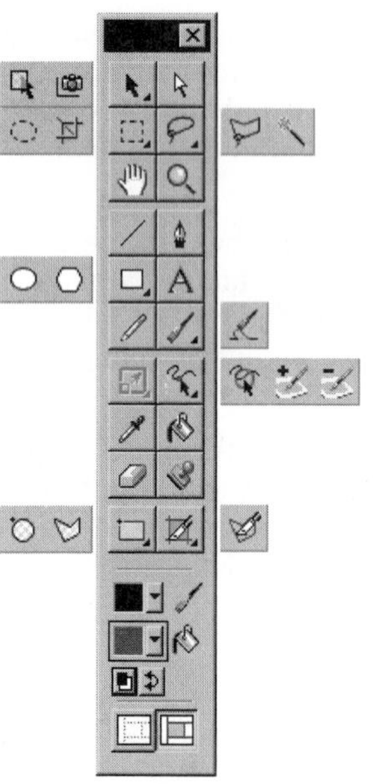

Figure E-3: The Toolbox contains 37 different creation and editing tools for both graphics and Web objects.

Table E-1
Fireworks Tools

Button	*Name*	*Shortcut*	*Description*
	Pointer	V or Zero	Selects and moves objects
	Select Behind	V or Zero	Selects and moves objects that are behind other objects
	Export Area	J	Exports a selected portion of a document
	Subselection	A	Selects an object within a group or points on a path
	Marquee	M	Selects a rectangular portion of a pixel image
	Ellipse Marquee	M	Selects an elliptical portion of a pixel image
	Crop	C	Increases or decreases canvas size
	Lasso	L	Selects a freely drawn area of a pixel image

Button	***Name***	***Shortcut***	***Description***
	Polygon Lasso	L	Selects a polygon-shaped area of a pixel image
	Magic Wand	W	Selects similar color areas of a pixel image
	Hand	H or press and hold spacebar	Pans the view of a document
	Magnify	Z	Increases or decreases the magnification level of a document by one setting
	Line	N	Draws straight lines
	Pen	P	Adds points to paths
	Rectangle	R	Draws rectangles, rectangles with rounded corners, and squares
	Ellipse	R	Draws ellipses and circles
	Polygon	G	Draws polygons and stars
	Text	T	Inserts text objects
	Pencil	Y	Draws single-pixel freeform strokes
	Brush	B	Draws strokes using the Stroke panel settings
	Redraw Path	B	Redraws portions of a selected path
	Scale	Q	Resizes and rotates objects
	Skew	Q	Slants, rotates, and modifies the perspective of objects
	Distort	Q	Reshapes and rotates objects
	Freeform	Period	Pulls or pushes a path with a variable-size cursor
	Reshape Area	Period	Reshapes an object's area with a variable-size cursor

Continued

Table E-1 (continued)

Button	Name	Shortcut	Description
	Path Scrubber (+)	U	Increases the stroke settings that are controlled by cursor speed or pen and tablet pressure
	Path Scrubber (–)	U	Decreases the stroke settings that are controlled by cursor speed or pen and tablet pressure
	Eyedropper	I	Picks up color from anywhere onscreen and applies it to the active color well
	Paint Bucket	K	Fills the selected area with color, gradients, patterns, or textures and enables fills to be adjusted
	Eraser/Knife	E	Deletes pixels from pixel-based images and cuts the paths of vector-based objects
	Rubber Stamp	K	Repeats portion of pixel images
	Hotspot	R	Draws an image-map hotspot area in a rectangular shape
	Ellipse Hotspot	R	Draws an image-map hotspot area in an elliptical shape
	Polygon Hotspot	R	Draws an image-map hotspot area in a polygonal shape
	Slice	R	Draws a slice object in a rectangular shape
	Polygon Slice	R	Draws a slice object in a polygonal shape

Certain tools have keyboard shortcuts that enable you to temporarily replace the active tool. Press and hold Ctrl (Command) in order to switch to the Pointer temporarily, and press and hold Alt (Option) in order to switch to the Eyedropper. You can also press and hold Ctrl+spacebar (Command+spacebar) in order to access the Zoom tool. Holding down the spacebar by itself temporarily retrieves the Hand tool.

Floating panels

Fireworks maintains a great deal of functionality in its floating panels. In all, the program offers 19 different panels for modifying everything from the stroke color to a JavaScript behavior.

Toggling, whether a particular panel is shown or hidden, is as simple as choosing its name from the Window menu or pressing its shortcut key. Although you have an almost dazzling array of panels to choose from, the effect is not overwhelming because panels are docked together into groups. When a panel is docked behind another one, click its tab to bring it to the front.

By default, Fireworks combines the floating panels into four different groups, but you can customize the groupings to fit the way you work. If you're working with dual monitors, you might want to dedicate one display to an impressive array of side-by-side floating panels. On the other hand, if screen real estate is tight, you could dock all of the panels into one supergroup, with tabs visible for each individual panel. The middle ground, though, is probably the best for most people: some docked, some not, and commonly used panels always visible.

Grouping and ungrouping floating panels is a straightforward process. Drag panels into or out of groups by their tabs. Fireworks provides visual feedback as you drag and drop.

In addition to the grouping or hiding individual panels, floating panels can also be manipulated in the following ways:

✦ **Showing and Hiding.** Choose View ➪ Hide Panels or press the Tab key to toggle the visibility of *all* of the floating panels.

✦ **Moving.** Individual panels or groups of panels can be moved by dragging their title bar. Panels snap to the borders of the document window or another floating panel as you drag them, creating an attractive arrangement.

✦ **Sizing.** Panels can be sized above their minimum by dragging their edges on Windows, or by dragging the resize widget located in the lower right corner of a panel on the Macintosh.

✦ **Windowshade.** Individual panels or groups of panels can be "windowshaded" by double-clicking their title bars. This "rolls up" the panel into the title bar, like window blinds, saving screen space. This has long been a standard behavior in Mac OS 8 and 9, but is found in the floating panels on both Macintosh and Windows versions of Fireworks.

✦ **Panel Layout Sets.** Once you've discovered a particular arrangement of the floating panels that works well for you, Fireworks 3 enables you to save that arrangement as a Panel Layout Set. Choose Commands ➪ Panel Layout and enter a name for your new Panel Layout Set in the dialog box that appears. Your arrangement is saved and added to the Commands ➪ Panel Layout Sets submenu. Choose a Panel Layout Set from this submenu to recall it. If you want to save your current panel layout, do so before accessing a saved Panel Layout Set.

Although each floating panel does something different, they all share common interface elements, as shown in Figure E-4. Many of the features, such as sliders and option lists, will be familiar to users of most any computer program.

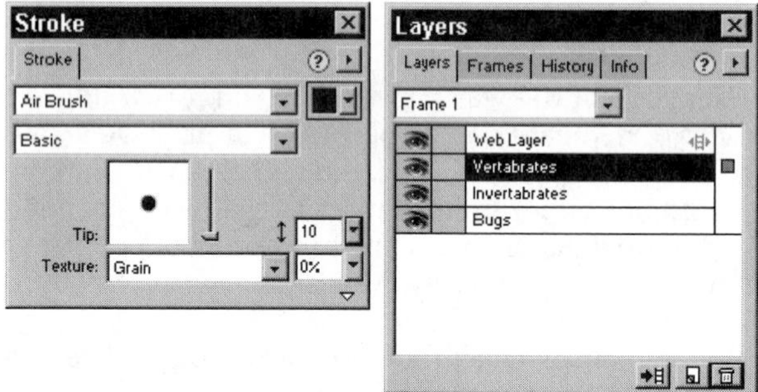

Figure E-4: Fireworks' floating panels use a variety of interface elements.

Some of the more Fireworks-specific interface elements you'll encounter are:

- ✦ **Pop-up menus.** All floating panels except for the Tool Options panel have a number of different options that you can access by selecting the pop-up menu button (a right-pointing arrow) in the upper right of the panel.
- ✦ **Help button.** All floating panels have a context-sensitive Help button that opens Using Fireworks at the appropriate page to help with the current operation.
- ✦ **Color wells.** Any color selection in Fireworks is handled through a color well that displays the current color for a certain aspect of the image. Click the color well to pop up the color picker with the active swatch. All color pickers have an Eyedropper tool for choosing onscreen colors and a Palette button for opening your operating system's color picker(s). Most Fireworks color pickers also have a No Color button for deselecting any color.
- ✦ **Numeric sliders.** Any entry that requires a numeric value — whether it is a percentage, a hexadecimal value, or just a plain number — uses pop-up sliders. Selecting the arrow button next to a variable number, such as a stroke's tip size, pops up a sliding control. Drag the slider and the numbers in the text box increase or decrease in value. Release the mouse button when you've reached the desired value. You can also directly type a numeric value in the adjacent text box.
- ✦ **Expander arrow.** Several floating panels — Stroke, Fill, and Effect — have an additional preview section that you can reveal by selecting the expander arrow.

Table E-2 details each of the floating panels and briefly describes its function.

Table E-2
Floating Panel Functions

Floating Panel	*Description*
Optimize	The Optimize panel enables you to specify export settings for the current document. Choose a file type and file-type specific settings, such as Quality for JPEG images, and palette for GIFs. Depending on which file format you choose, the available options change accordingly.
Object	The Object inspector is primarily responsible for displaying and controlling how a selected object (or objects) interacts with the canvas and other objects in your document. This floating panel displays one of nine different interfaces, depending on what is selected.
Stroke	Any object created using one of the vector drawing tools — Pen, Brush, Rectangle, Ellipse, Line, or Text tool — is initially constructed with a path, the outline of the object. When a path is visible, it is said to be *stroked*. In Fireworks, strokes can be as basic as the one-pixel Pencil outline or as complex as the multicolored Confetti. The Stroke panel controls all the possible path settings and is a key tool in a graphic artist's palette.
Fill	Just as the Stroke panel controls the outline of a drawn shape, the Fill panel controls the inside. Fills can be a solid color, a gradient, a pattern, or a Web dither. All fills can have textures applied with a sliding scale of intensity; moreover, textured fills can even appear transparent. Once you've chosen the type of fill from the Fill panel, you can go on to pick a specific color, pattern, edge, or texture.
Effect	The Effect panel provides access to Fireworks' always-editable Live Effects, detailed later in this chapter under Live Effects and Xtras.
Color Table	The Color Table panel displays the current export palette when working with 8-bit images, such as GIFs. The Color Table panel provides feedback that enables you to minimize the file size of exported GIF images by reducing the number of colors in their palette.
Swatches	Whereas the Color Mixer defines the color universe, the Swatches panel identifies a more precise palette of colors. As the name implies, the Swatches panel contains a series of color samples. With the commands in the pop-up menu, you can switch to standard palettes (such as the Web 216, Windows, or Macintosh system palettes), save and recall custom palettes, or access the current export palette.
Color Mixer	Web designers come from a variety of backgrounds: some are well-rooted in computer graphics, others are more familiar with print publishing, while an increasing number know only Web imagery. The Color Mixer lets you opt for the color model that you're most familiar with and that is best suited to your work.

Continued

Table E-2 *(continued)*	
Floating Panel	***Description***
Tool Options	Many tools from the Fireworks Toolbox have configurable settings accessible through the Tool Options panel. To expose the Tool Options panel for a specific tool, select a tool in the Toolbox and choose Window ➪ Tool Options, or just double-click a tool and Fireworks opens its Tool Options panel automatically.
Layers	Layers in Fireworks enable the creation of extremely complicated graphics, as well as compatibility with files stored in Photoshop format. Fireworks layers permit multiple images and objects—each with their own stacking order—to be treated as a group and, in turn, placed on top of, or beneath, other layers. Moreover, each layer can be hidden from view for easier editing of complex images, and can be locked to prevent accidental editing. Layers can be shared across frames, enabling you to instantly add a static element to every frame of an animation.
Frames	Frames have two primary uses in Fireworks: rollovers and animations. When used to create rollovers, each frame represents a different state of the user's mouse with up to four frames being used. To create an animated GIF, each frame in Fireworks corresponds to one frame of the animation. You can use as many frames for your animation as necessary (although file size often dictates that the fewest frames possible is best).
History	The History panel enables you to step back through your previous actions, or save them as Commands. The History panel is detailed later in this chapter under Undo, Redo, Commands, and the History Panel.
Info	Often it's necessary to check an object's size or position when you're creating an overall graphic. The Info panel not only provides you with that feedback, but it also enables you to modify those values numerically for precise adjustments.
Behaviors	One of the key features of Fireworks that separates it from other graphics programs is its capability to output HTML and JavaScript code along with images. The code activates an image and makes it capable of an action, such as changing color or shape when the user passes the mouse over it. The code is known in Fireworks as a *Behavior*. A Behavior is actually composed of two parts: an action that specifies what's to occur, and an event that triggers the action. Behaviors require a Web object, such as a slice or a hotspot, to function. After you've selected the desired Web object, you assign a Behavior by choosing the Add Action button (the plus sign) from the Behavior inspector. Fireworks comes with four groups of Behaviors from which to choose: Simple Rollover, Swap Image, Set Nav Bar Image, and Set Text of Status Bar. All assigned Behaviors for a given Web object are listed in the Behavior inspector.

Floating Panel	*Description*
URL	The URL panel greatly eases the work required for managing URLs by listing all of the Internet addresses inserted in the current session or loaded from an external file.
Styles	In Fireworks, a *Style* is a collection of attributes that can be applied to any object. The Styles panel is preset with a number of such designs, which appear as graphical buttons and text, with many more available on the Fireworks CD-ROM. To apply a Style, select the object and then select the Style; you can even select multiple objects (such as a row of navigation buttons) and apply the same Style to them all with one click. Styles are a terrific time-saver and a great way to maintain a consistent look and feel. To create your own Styles, just highlight the object with the desired attributes and select the New Style button on the Styles panel.
Library	The Library panel is a central storage place for Symbols. Symbols are master copies of Fireworks objects that can be inserted into documents as Instances. Instances are similar to Windows file shortcuts or Macintosh aliases, right down to the arrow badge. Changes made to Symbols are inherited by Instances, making updating similar objects a snap.
Find and Replace	Because Fireworks objects are always editable, the Find and Replace panel makes updating a series of Web graphics a snap. You can change all of the graphics in a selection, a file, a frame, or a series of files. Moreover, Find and Replace can handle more than just text; you can also alter fonts, colors, and URLs, or even snap all of the colors to their nearest Web-safe neighbor.
Project Log	The Project Log panel tracks changes made to your documents, such as Find and Replace operations.

Using the menus

The cross-platform, almost universal access of the Web is achieved with limitations. Although many different image file formats exist, browsers are currently limited to displaying only three of them: GIF, JPEG, and PNG. What's more, only GIF and JPEG enjoy truly wide acceptance. Bandwidth is severely limited for the mass market: while an increasing number of Web surfers enjoy the speed of a DSL or cable modem, the vast majority still view the Internet through a 56K dial-up modem.

These limitations make optimizing and exporting graphics a necessity and not just a nicety. Your work in Fireworks has to be exported in the correct format and with the smallest file size possible. Macromedia realized the importance of export features when it created Fireworks; much of the program centers around making the best-looking graphic, with the smallest file size, in an accepted format. The features covered in this chapter rank among the best available with advanced controls, such as lossy GIF and color locking. Fireworks takes the limitations of the Web and turns them into an art form.

- ✦ **File.** It's standard practice to place basic computer operations — creating, saving, and printing files — in the File menu. Fireworks follows this practice and also includes commands for importing and exporting, scanning, previewing your work in a browser, and more.
- ✦ **Edit.** As evidenced by its name, the Edit menu holds the standard editing commands, such as Undo, Cut, Copy, and Paste. Numerous commands are also specific to Fireworks graphics, such as Paste Inside and Crop Selected Image.
- ✦ **View.** The View menu commands control a Web artist's views during the creation phase. In addition to numerous magnification commands, the View menu also contains helpful layout aids, such as Rulers, Grids, and Guides. You'll also find several features to help you see just the graphic when you need to have a clear, uncluttered perspective.
- ✦ **Insert.** The Insert menu contains commands for inserting Buttons, Symbols, Hotspots, Layers, Frames, and more.
- ✦ **Modify.** Once you've created your basic objects, you'll undoubtedly spend as much, if not more time, tweaking and modifying them in order to get them just right. The Modify menu contains commands for scaling, modifying and arranging objects and more.
- ✦ **Text.** Text in a traditional graphics program plays a relatively small, but key role. In a Web graphics program such as Fireworks, text becomes more important because graphics are the only way to incorporate heavily styled text into Web pages. The Text menu commands offer many shortcuts that enable you to manipulate text objects without opening the Text Editor.
- ✦ **Commands.** The Commands menu is new in Fireworks 3. Commands are a way for the Fireworks user to extend the basic feature set and are relatively easy to create because they're written in JavaScript. The Commands menu reflects the Commands that are stored in your Fireworks\Settings\Commands folder.
- ✦ **Xtras.** In Macromedia parlance, an Xtra is a plug-in that extends the capabilities of a program. With Fireworks, Xtras are primarily image filters. Fireworks comes with four groups of filters, plus two Eye Candy filters, referred to as Eye Candy LE. Because Fireworks can read most Photoshop filters and plug-ins, you can greatly extend the available Xtras, either by including them in Fireworks' Settings\Plug-ins folder or by assigning another folder in Preferences.

✦ **Window.** The Window menu commands give you access to all of Fireworks' floating panels and toolbars. In addition, several commands help you work with multiple images or multiple views of the same image.

✦ **Help.** Everyone needs help now and then, especially when working with a program as rich and deep as Fireworks. The Help menu provides quick access to *Using Fireworks*, various online resources, and a number of key tutorials that explain the basics of the program.

Working with Documents

A Fireworks session can often require you to work with quite a few unique image files, in a number of formats. The most basic workflow involves your master document — a Fireworks PNG file — and the image or images you export for the Web, usually in GIF or JPEG format. Fireworks can also import and export a number of other common formats.

Creating a new document

Before you actually begin work, it's best to consider what you are aiming to create. The better you can visualize the final result, the fewer modifications you'll have to make along the way. This is not to say that trial and error is out of the question, but a little planning can save a lot of time and trouble later.

A fundamental question that you have to answer before you even choose File ➪ New is what approach you're going to take in creating the multiple image files that typically make up Web pages. You can take either of two basic approaches:

✦ Create multiple small images in multiple Fireworks documents and assemble them into a Web page later in another application, such as Dreamweaver.

✦ Populate one Fireworks canvas with a complete Web page design, including all of the navigation elements, text, and images.

The method you choose is a matter of your personal preference, of course. I'll go on record, though, recommending the one-canvas approach. Fireworks excels at one-stop Web graphics, and an integrated approach takes full advantage of the variety of tools Fireworks places at your disposal.

To create a new document, follow these steps:

1. Choose File ➪ New or use the key shortcut Ctrl+N (Command+N). Windows users can also click the New button on the Main toolbar. The New Document dialog box, shown in Figure E-5, opens.

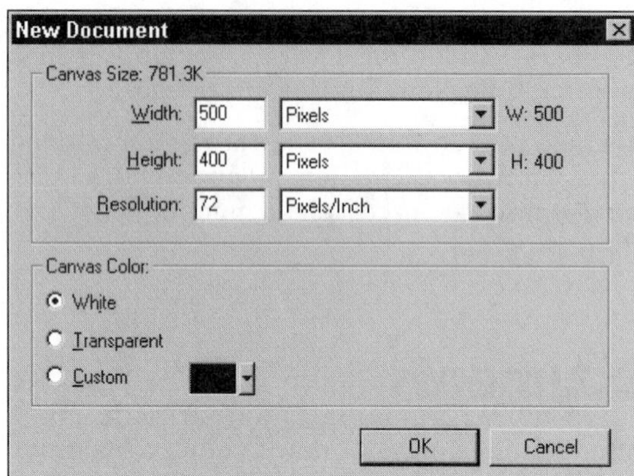

Figure E-5: Set your document's dimensions, print resolution, and canvas color in the New Document dialog box.

2. To change the horizontal measurement of the canvas, enter a new value in the Width text box.

Tip

Press Tab when you're done to move on to the Height text box.

3. To change the vertical measurement of the canvas, enter a new value in the Height text box.

Tip

Don't be afraid to make your canvas a little bigger than you actually require. I find that a little elbow room is nice while drawing, especially when using a pen and tablet . . . you can experiment with strokes in the extra space before marking up your actual work. When you're done, delete the test strokes and choose Modify⇨Trim Canvas to quickly get rid of the extra space and get your document ready for export.

4. To enter a new (print) resolution for the canvas, enter a value in the Resolution text box. The default resolution in Fireworks is 72 pixels per inch on both Macintosh and Windows. Unless you have a specific reason to change it, leave it at 72.

5. To change the measurement systems used for Width, Height, or Resolution, select the arrow button next to the corresponding list box. You can choose Pixels, Inches, or Centimeters for both Width and Height; with Resolution, you can select either Pixels/Inch or Pixels/cm (centimeter).

Note

Whenever you switch Width or Height measurement systems, Fireworks automatically converts the existing values to the new scale. For example, if the new canvas was originally 144 pixels wide at 72 pixels per inch resolution, and the Width measurement system was changed to inches, Fireworks converts the 144 pixels to 2 inches. No matter which system you choose, Fireworks always displays the dimensions in pixels on the right side of the dialog box as W (width) and H (height).

6. Select a Canvas Color: White, Transparent, or Custom Color.

Tip

Canvas color is very important, but also very flexible in Fireworks. When you're creating Web graphics, the canvas color often needs to match the background color of a Web page. You don't have to match the colors when creating your new page, but if you can, you should, and it will save you a step or two in the near future. You can modify the canvas color at any point in Fireworks by choosing Modify ➪ Canvas Color.

7. To choose a Custom Color, select the arrow button next to the color swatch and pick the desired color from the pop-up color palette.
8. For a more extensive color choice (beyond the 216 Web-safe colors in the pop-up display), either select the Palette button on the pop-up display or double-click the swatches to reveal the system color picker(s).
9. Click OK when you're done.

Tip

The New Document dialog box remembers your last settings the next time you create a new file, with one exception. If you've cut or copied a graphic to your system's clipboard and you select File ➪ New, the dialog box contains the dimensions of the image on the clipboard. This makes it easy to paste an existing image into a new file.

Opening and importing

Because Fireworks is terrific at optimizing images for the Web, you're just as likely to find yourself opening an existing file as creating a new one. Opening a regular PNG file is just like opening a Fireworks document. Opening a file of another type creates a new Fireworks document that will need to be saved as a Fireworks PNG-format document under a new name. Export GIF, JPEG, or other files from your Fireworks document as required.

Tip

Use a lossless file format such as PNG or TIFF to move images between applications. The GIF and JPEG formats are unsuitable for use as master copies because information—and quality—is thrown away when you create them in order to achieve a smaller file size.

As most anyone who's ever touched a computer graphic is aware, different computer programs, as well as platforms, store files in their own file format. Fireworks opens a wide range of these formats. With formats from advanced graphic applications, such as Photoshop, Fireworks retains as much of the special components of the image — like layers and editable text — as possible. You can even open ASCII or RTF (Rich Text Format) files to bring text into Fireworks.

Table E-3 details formats supported by Fireworks.

Table E-3
Supported File Formats

Format	*File Name Extension*	*Macintosh Type Code*	*Notes*
Fireworks File Format	.png	PNGf	A PNG file with Fireworks-only information such as vectors added.
Fireworks 2.0	.png	PNGf	Converted to Fireworks 3 when opened, but can optionally be saved again as Fireworks 2 for later editing in Fireworks 2.
Fireworks 1.0	.png	PNGf	The Background is placed on its own layer.
Portable Network Graphic	.png	PNGf	Standard PNG documents that don't have extra Fireworks information.
Photoshop Document	.psd	8BPS	Version 3.0 or later only. Layers, editable text, and Layer Effects are preserved.
FreeHand Document	.fh7 or .fh8	AGD3	The vector-based format of FreeHand 7 or 8.
Illustrator 7 Document	.ai	uMsk	Adobe Illustrator 7's vector-based default format.
CorelDraw 8 Document	.cdr	CDR8	CorelDraw's vector-based format must be saved without CorelDraw's built-in bitmap or object compression in order to open it in Fireworks.
GIF	.gif	GIFf	Graphics Interchange File Format. Static or animated. Each frame of an animated GIF is placed on its own frame in Fireworks.
JPEG	.jpg or .jpeg or .jpe	JPEG	Avoid importing JPEG images due to their lossy compression scheme and low quality.
Targa	.tga	TPIC	Common Unix image format.
TIFF	.tif or .tiff	TIFF	Tag Image File Format. High-quality lossless compression similar to PNG.
ASCII Text	.txt	TEXT	Plain text.
Rich Text Format	.rtf	RTF	Microsoft's styled text format, easily exported from Word.
Microsoft Bitmap	.bmp	BMP	Default image format for Windows 3+.
PICT (Macintosh only)	.pct or .pict or .p	PICT	Default image format for Mac OS 1-9. Combination vector/bitmap format. Fireworks renders any vectors as bitmaps.

To open or import an existing file, follow these steps:

1. To open a document, choose File ➪ Open or use the keyboard shortcut, Ctrl+O (Command+O). Windows users can also select the Open button from the Main toolbar. Alternatively, to import a document, choose File ➪ Import.
2. An Open dialog box appears.
3. Select the desired file in the Open dialog box. Fireworks identifies the file and displays a thumbnail of the image for certain file types in the Preview section of the dialog box.
4. To open a copy of the graphic, choose the Open as "Untitled" option. Click OK when you're done.
5. If you are opening a vector graphics format such as FreeHand, or a Photoshop document, Fireworks presents you with a dialog box, enabling you to choose from a range of format-specific options. In most situations, the defaults work just fine. Click OK to continue.
6. If you are opening a document, Fireworks opens the file while, if necessary, reducing the magnification so that the full image is displayed.
7. If you are importing a document, Fireworks changes the mouse cursor to an import placement cursor that looks like a right-angle. Click once anywhere on the canvas to place the imported object(s), or click and drag out a box with the import cursor to fit the imported information to the size of the box.

It's the rare Web page that has but a single image on it. Most Web pages contain multiple graphics and, occasionally, a designer needs to work on several of them simultaneously. With the Open Multiple command, you can select as many files as you want to load into Fireworks, all at the same time. The files can come from the same folder or from different folders, if necessary. Select a range of files to open or double-click each file to add it to the List Window. You can easily remove files from the List Window, and when you're ready, Fireworks opens and displays all the files in a series of cascading windows.

Opening Photoshop Files

Fireworks makes it relatively easy to open and work with Photoshop images. When you open or import a Photoshop file, Fireworks displays a dialog box to enable you to adjust how the file will be converted. By default, Fireworks maintains Photoshop's layers and editable text, but you can also choose to flatten the file if you don't need to edit it in Fireworks. Photoshop masks created from grouped layers are converted to Mask Groups, and Photoshop's Layer Effects are converted to editable Fireworks Live Effects. Fireworks 3 now retains Photoshop 5's Layer Effects and converts them to editable Live Effects, retaining a very similar look, and most importantly: editability.

Macintosh users can also open multiple Fireworks documents by selecting a group of them in the Finder and double-clicking. Multiple image files that don't have a Fireworks Creator code can be selected as a group in the Finder and dropped on the Fireworks icon.

One significant advantage to the Open Multiple command: you can use it to create animated GIFs. In Fireworks, an animated GIF is a series of frames. When you choose the Open as Animation option in the Open Multiple dialog box, Fireworks inserts each chosen file into a single graphic on an individual frame. You can preview the animation using Fireworks VCR controls or adjust the timing in the Export dialog box.

Optimizing and exporting

As mentioned previously, the cross-platform access of the Web is achieved with limitations. Browsers are currently limited to displaying only three image file formats: GIF, JPEG, and PNG—and PNG hasn't yet gained wide acceptance. More and more Web surfers enjoy the speed of a DSL or cable modem, but most still view the Internet through a 56K dial-up modem. These limitations make optimizing and exporting graphics a necessity and not just a nicety. Your work in Fireworks has to be exported in the correct format and with the smallest file size possible.

Although it's possible to use a graphic stored in Fireworks native format, PNG, in a Web page, this really isn't practical, nor is it the intention of the program for you to do so. Every graphic produced in Fireworks should really be stored in two files: a Fireworks-format PNG master file, and an exported format to be published on the Web. Think of the Fireworks PNG file as an original, and the exported file as a photocopy ready for wide circulation. Working hand-in-hand with selecting an appropriate file type is the other main goal of exporting: *optimization.* Optimization is the process of producing the best-looking, smallest possible file. An optimized image loads faster, without sacrificing perceived quality.

Optimizing and exporting in Fireworks is focused around the preview tabs of the document window, the Optimize panel, and the Color Table panel (Figure E-6). Adjusting settings in these panels is a necessary precursor to choosing File ➪ Export to create your exported image file. Once you've made these settings, they are saved with your Fireworks PNG file for next time. Export settings are as much a part of a document as the kinds of fills or strokes you use.

The hardest part of optimizing is finding a balance between image quality and file size. Fireworks takes a lot of the guesswork out of this task by providing up to four comparison views of different formats at various color resolutions or compressions.

Here's an overview of the typical procedure to use when optimizing a file:

1. Create your image with optimization in the back of your mind at all times; scale and crop images as small as possible, and create large areas of flat color or horizontal stripes of color to make the smallest GIFs.

Figure E-6: Preview and optimize your work right in the workspace using the document window's in-place previews and the Optimize panel.

2. Select a file format in the Optimize panel, based on the type of image you're working on. Choose an indexed color format such as GIF for illustrations and flat-color artwork, or a continuous-tone, True Color format such as JPEG for photographic images.
3. For indexed color images, reduce the number of colors as much as possible, using the setting in the Optimize panel in concert with the Color Table panel. Reducing the number of colors is the primary method of reducing the file size of indexed color images. The fewer colors used, the smaller the file.
4. For the JPEG format, use the Quality slider in the Optimize panel to choose the lowest acceptable quality in order to achieve the smallest file size.
5. Select any additional format-specific options in the Optimize panel, such as Interlaced GIF or JPEG Smoothing.
6. Choose File ➪ Export to export your document and create the optimized file.

The two most common image formats for Web publishing are GIF and JPEG. Each format is suitable for a different kind of image and requires a different approach for optimization.

Optimizing GIF images

Images that have large areas of flat color (typically illustrations, as opposed to photographic images) and that can get by with only a limited number of colors are exported in an indexed color format, such as GIF. Indexed color formats have a maximum of 256 different colors, also known as 8-bit color. Which specific colors a particular image file contains is maintained in a color index inside the file, hence the name *indexed color.*

Color palette

A *palette* is the group of colors actually used in the image. Fireworks offers nine preset palettes in the Optimize panel's Indexed Palette option list, plus the Custom setting that refers to a deviation from one of the preset palettes. After you customize a palette, you can store it as a preset and add it to the Indexed Palette option list.

Each of the nine different palettes (available to all indexed formats, not just GIF) accesses a different group of colors. The WebSnap Adaptive and Web 216 palettes are the choices generally made for Internet graphics, although other palettes are appropriate in some situations. The following are the nine preset palettes:

- **Adaptive:** Looks at all the colors in the image and finds a maximum of 256 of the most suitable colors; it's called an *adaptive* palette because, instead of a fixed set of colors, it is the best 256 colors adapted to the image. If possible, Fireworks assigns Web-safe colors initially and then assigns any remaining non-Web-safe colors. The Adaptive palette can contain a mixture of Web-safe and non-Web-safe colors.
- **WebSnap Adaptive (listed as Web Adaptive on the Mac):** Similar to the Adaptive palette insofar as both are custom palettes in which colors are chosen to match the originals as closely as possible. After selecting the initial matching Web-safe colors, all remaining colors are examined according to their hexadecimal values. Any colors close to a Web-safe color (plus or minus seven values from a Web-safe color) are "snapped to" that color. Although this palette does not ensure that all colors are Web-safe, a greater percentage of colors will be Web-safe.
- **Web 216:** All colors in the image are converted to their nearest equivalent in the Web-safe range.
- **Exact:** Uses colors that match the exact original RGB values. Useful only for images with less than 256 colors; for images with more colors, Fireworks alerts you that you should use the Adaptive palette.
- **Macintosh:** Matches the system palette used by the Macintosh operating system when the display is set to 256 colors.
- **Windows:** Matches the system palette used by the Windows operating system when the display is set to 256 colors.
- **Grayscale:** Converts the image to a grayscale graphic with a maximum of 256 shades of gray.

- **Black & White:** Reduces the image to a two-tone image; the Dither option is automatically set to 100 percent when you choose this palette, but this setting can be modified.
- **Uniform:** A mathematical progression of colors across the spectrum is chosen. This palette has little application on the Web, although I have been able to get the occasional posterization effect out of it by reducing the number of colors severely and reducing the 100 percent Dither setting that is automatically applied.
- **Custom:** Whenever a stored palette is loaded or a modification is made to one of the standard palettes, Fireworks labels the palette Custom. Such changes are made through the pop-up menu found on the Options panel.

Given all of these options, what's the recommended path to take? Probably the best course is to build your graphics in Fireworks by using the Web Safe palette, and then export them by using the WebSnap Adaptive palette. This choice ensures that your image remains the truest to its original colors while looking the best for Web viewers whose color depth is set to 24-bit or higher, and still looking good on lower-end systems that are capable of showing only 256 colors.

Keep in mind that even if you use all Web-safe colors in your graphic, the final result won't necessarily be completely within that palette. Fireworks generates other colors to antialias, to create drop shadows, and to produce glows, and the colors generated may not be Web-safe. This is why either the Adaptive palette or WebSnap Adaptive palette often offers the truest representation of your image across browsers.

Number of colors

One of the quickest ways to cut down a GIF image's file size is to reduce the number of colors. Recall that GIF is referred to as an *8-bit format;* this means that the maximum number of colors is 256, or 8 bit planes of information — higher-math lovers will remember that 256 is equal to 2^8 (2 raised to the 8th power). Each bit plane used permits exponentially more colors and reserves a certain amount of memory (but also increases the file size). This is why the Number of Colors option list contains powers of 2, 4, 8, 16, 32, 64, 128, and 256.

For complete control of individual colors, the controls on the Color Table panel enable you to add, edit, and delete individual colors, as well as store and load palettes. Fireworks enables you to select a color from the swatches and then lock it, snap it to its closest Web-safe neighbor, or convert it to transparent by clicking one of the Color Table panel buttons, or choosing a command from its pop-up menu.

Locking one or more colors in your graphic ensures that the most important colors — whether they're important for branding, a visual design, or both — can be maintained. After a color is locked, it does not change, regardless of the palette chosen. For example, you could preview your image by using the Web 216 palette, lock all the colors, and then switch to an Adaptive palette to broaden the color range, but keep the basic colors Web-safe. Web-safe colors are displayed in the swatches with a diamond symbolin them, and locked colors are identified by a square inthe lower-right corner of the swatch, as shown in Figure E-7.

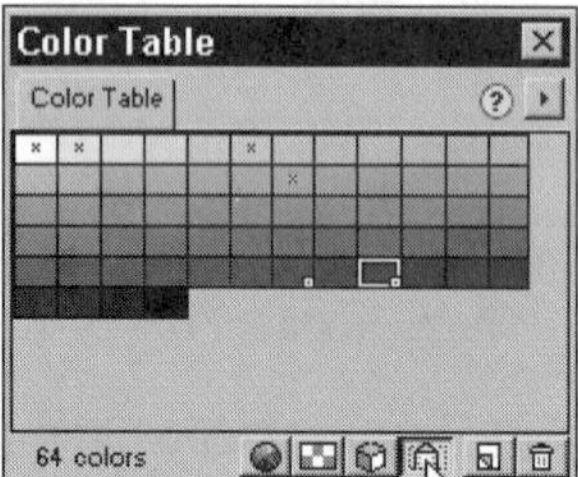

Figure E-7: The Color Table panel is your window into an image's color index.

Dithering

One way — although not necessarily the best way — to break up areas of flat color caused by the lower color capabilities of GIF is to use the Dither option. When the Dither option is enabled, Fireworks simulates new colors by using a pattern of existing colors — exactly how the Web Dither fill is created. However, because dithering is not restricted to a single area, but instead is spread throughout the graphic, the dithering can be significantly more noticeable — dithering makes the image appear "dotty," as shown in Figure E-8, and usually increases your file size. The degree of dithering is set by changing the Dither Amount slider or by entering the amount directly in the text box.

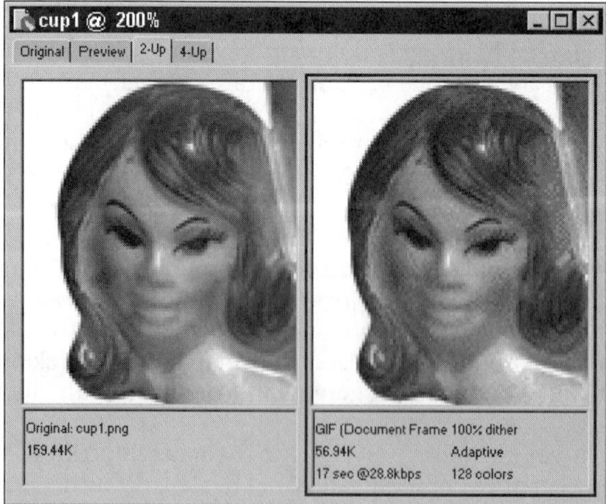

Figure E-8: The image on the right was produced with dithering at 100 percent, causing the solid color to be heavily dotted.

Transparency

One of the main reasons GIF is often selected as a format over JPEG is GIF's ability to specify any one color — and thus certain apparent areas — of the graphic transparent. As mentioned previously, transparency is the key to making nonrectangular-shaped graphics, and the Fireworks transparency controls (see Figure E-9) are the key to making transparency.

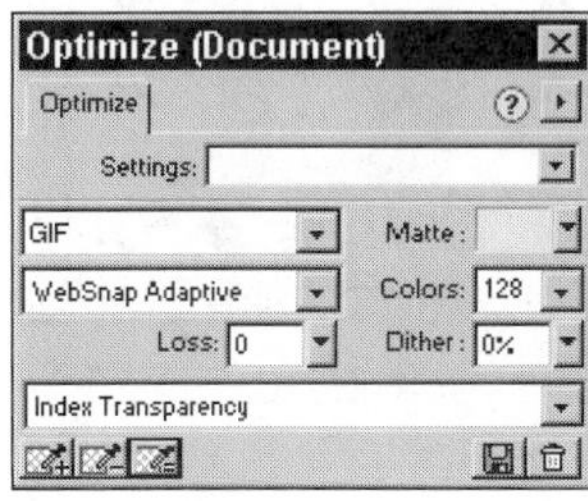

Figure E-9: The Optimize panel enables you to adjust the transparency of the GIF image you're exporting.

The transparency controls in detail are as follows:

- ✦ **Type of Transparency option list:** Choose either No Transparency, Index Transparency, or Alpha Transparency to specify the transparency type. The canvas color is initially made transparent, by default.
- ✦ **Add Color to Index Transparency button:** Enables you to choose additional colors to make transparent, either from the swatch set or sampled directly from the previewed image.
- ✦ **Remove Color from Index Transparency button:** Converts transparent colors to their original color, either from the swatch set or sampled directly from the previewed image.
- ✦ **Set Transparent Index Color button:** Select to choose a single color to be transparent, either from the swatch set or sampled directly from the previewed image.

When a color is made transparent, its swatch and pixels in the Preview image are replaced with a gray-and-white checkerboard pattern, as shown in Figure E-10. You can choose as many colors as you'd like to make transparent.

To make portions of your GIF image transparent, follow these steps:

1. Select a document window preview tab to view a preview of your document.
2. If the Optimize panel is not visible, choose Window ➪ Optimize to view it.
3. If necessary, select GIF from the Optimize panel's Export Format option list.
4. To make the canvas color transparent, select Index Transparency from the Type of Transparency option list.

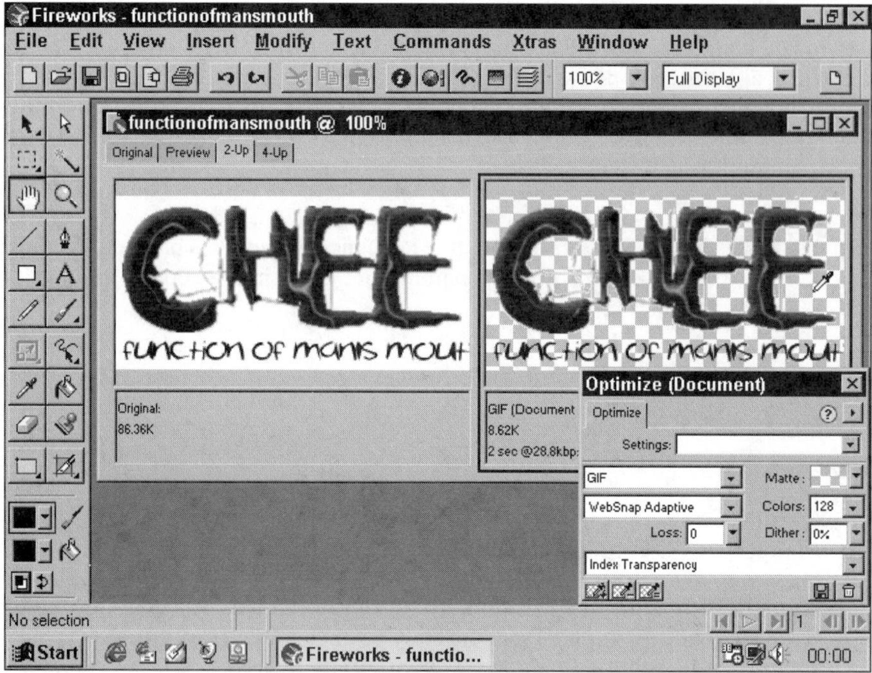

Figure E-10: Part of the power of the GIF format is the ability to make any color transparent.

5. To make a color other than the canvas transparent, click the Set Transparent Index Color button and sample a color either from a swatch or from the preview image.

Tip

If you want to select a small area in your image for transparency, use the Zoom tool to magnify that selection before choosing the color.

6. To make more colors transparent, click the Add Color to Index Transparency button and sample the colors either from the swatch or from the Preview image.
7. To restore a transparent color to its original color, click the Remove Color from Index Transparency button and select the color either from a swatch or from the Preview image.
8. For even greater control, select a color or colors from the Color Table panel and click the Transparent button.

As noted in the Transparency option list description, two different types are available: Index and Alpha Transparency. Index Transparency enables you to make any color totally transparent — think of it as an On/Off switch; the color is either transparent or it isn't. Alpha Transparency, on the other hand, enables degrees of transparency — you can create tints and shades of a color.

Index Transparency is generally used for the GIF format, because, technically, only the PNG format truly supports Alpha Transparency. However, the Fireworks engineers have left Alpha Transparency enabled for GIFs, to achieve a slightly different effect. When Alpha Transparency is chosen, a new color register is created for the canvas and then made transparent. How is this different from converting the canvas color to transparent, as occurs with Index Transparency? If you've ever created an image where part of the graphic is the same color as the background — the white of a person's eyes is also the white of a canvas — you'll quickly understand and appreciate this feature. Basically, Alpha Transparency, as applied in Fireworks' GIF format, leaves your palette alone and just makes the canvas transparent.

Remove Unused Colors

The Remove Unused Colors option — which is enabled by default — is a Fireworks-only feature that causes the program to discard duplicate and unused colors from a palette. This can seriously reduce your file size, particularly when choosing one of the fixed palettes, such as Web 216 or either of the operating system palettes. Find the Remove Unused Colors option on the Optimize panel's pop-up menu.

Interlaced

The Interlaced option on the Optimize panel's pop-up menu enables a GIF property that displays a file as it downloads. The file is shown in progressively finer detail as more information is transferred from the server to the browser. Although a graphic exported with the Interlaced option won't download any faster, it provides a visual cue to Web page visitors that something is happening. Interlacing graphics is a matter of taste; some Web designers don't design a page without them, others are vehemently opposed to their use.

Fireworks' Optimize panel also contains saved optimization settings. Saving your own favorite settings cuts down on optimization time later. Click the Save Optimization as a Setting button (diskette icon) on the Optimize panel to save your current optimization settings and add them to the Saved Settings option list.

Optimizing JPEG images

Photographic images are most often displayed in 24-bit True Color, in a format such as JPEG, rather than the limited palette of an indexed color image, such as a GIF. Photographic images contain subtle gradations that are not easily reproduced in fewer colors and yet are dithered quite serviceably by the browser if the client machine is running in a 256-color video mode.

Additionally, the JPEG format excels at compressing the smooth tones of a photographic image down to unbelievably small file sizes, without an appreciable loss of quality. The fact that the JPEG format is so good at the things the GIF format fails miserably at, is part of the reason for their enduring reign as the king and queen of Web graphics formats.

Whereas GIFs generally become smaller from lowering the number of colors used, JPEGs use a sliding scale that creates smaller file sizes by eliminating pixels. This sliding scale is built on a *lossy* algorithm, so-called because the lower the scale, the more pixels are lost. The JPEG algorithm is a very good one and you can significantly reduce the file size by lowering the JPEG Quality setting.

Other characteristics of the JPEG format include:

- ✦ JPEG images are capable of displaying over 16 million colors. This wide color range, also referred to as *24-bit,* enables the subtle shades of a photograph to be depicted easily.
- ✦ Although JPEG images can display almost any color, none of the colors can be made transparent. Consequently, any image that requires transparency in a Web browser must be stored as a GIF.
- ✦ For JPEG images to be viewed as they are downloaded, they must be stored as Progressive JPEGs, which appear to develop onscreen, like an interlaced GIF. Progressive JPEGs have a slightly better compression engine and can produce smaller file sizes.

Internet Explorer doesn't fully support Progressive JPEGs. They are displayed just as if they were not Progressive, though, so there's no harm in using them.

Quality

The major method for altering a JPEG's file size is by changing the Quality value in the Optimize panel. In Fireworks, the Quality value is gauged as a percentage, and the slider goes from 0 percent to 100 percent. Higher values mean less compression, and lower values mean that more pixels are discarded. Trying to reduce a JPEG's file size by lowering the Quality slider is always worthwhile; you can also enter a value directly in the text box. The JPEG compression algorithm is so good that almost every continuous-tone image can be reduced in file size without significant loss of quality, as shown in Figure E-11. On the other hand, increasing a JPEG's Quality value from its initial setting is never helpful. Whereas JPEG is very good at losing pixels to reduce file size, adding pixels to increase quality never works — you'll only increase the file's size and download time.

With the JPEG image-compression algorithm, the initial elements of an image that are "compressed away" are least noticeable. Subtle variations in brightness and hue are the first to disappear. With additional compression, the image grows darker and less varied in its color range.

A good technique for comparing JPEG images in Fireworks is to use the 4-Up preview option. The upper-left pane shows your original document, so that you always have an image on which to base your comparisons. In another view, reduce the Quality to about 75 percent or so. If that image is acceptable, reduce the Quality setting to 50 percent in another view. By then, you'll probably start to get some unwanted artifacts, so use the fourth window to try a setting midway between the last acceptable and the unacceptable Quality settings, such as 65 percent. Be sure to view your images at 100 percent magnification. That's how your Web audience will see them, so you should too.

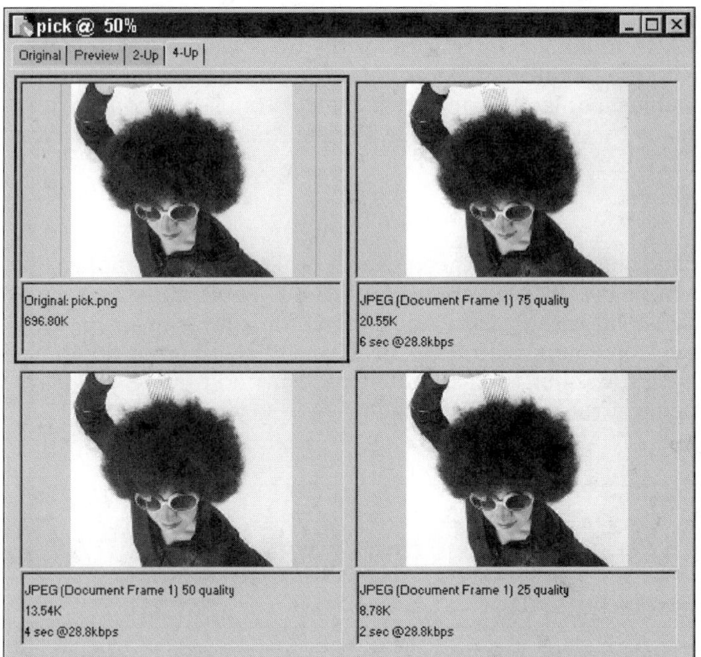

Figure E-11: Each of the three previews uses a different JPEG quality value (the first picture at the top left shows the original image); only when the quality is lowered significantly does the image become unacceptable.

Tip

Don't forget that you can stretch the document window to a larger size to increase the size of the multiple preview panes.

Other options

Additional methods for reducing JPEG file size are:

✦ **Sharpening edges.** JPEG is far better at compressing gradations than it is at compressing images with hard edges and abrupt color changes. To overcome these obstacles, use Fireworks' Sharpen JPEG Edges option, which can be found on the Optimize panel's pop-up menu. As the name implies, Sharpen JPEG Edges restores some of the hard-edge transitions that are lost during JPEG compression. This is especially noticeable on text and simple graphics, such as rectangles, superimposed on photographs.

✦ **Smoothing.** The more that a JPEG file is compressed, the "blockier" it becomes. As the compression increases, the JPEG algorithm throws out more and more similar pixels — after a certain point, the transitions and gradations are lost and areas become flat color blocks. Fireworks' Smoothing feature slightly blurs the overall image so that any stray pixels resulting from the compression are less noticeable.

✦ **Progressive.** To most, Progressive JPEG is seen only as an incremental display option for JPEGs, much like Interlaced for the GIF format. The Progressive JPEG option on the Optimize panel's pop-up menu is more than that though: it actually enables a different compression algorithm — a second generation one — that many times offers lower file sizes at the equivalent quality of the original JPEG compression.

Other formats

In addition to GIF and JPEG, Fireworks can export other common graphics file types, detailed in Table E-4. You can choose from 8-bit, 24-bit, and 32-bit variations of most formats. The 8-bit versions are indexed color images, similar to GIF. The 24-bit versions are true color, similar to JPEG. Images with 32-bit color depth have the same number of colors as 24-bit images, but include an additional 8-bit, grayscale alpha mask that defines transparency.

Table E-4
Fireworks Export Formats

Format	*Description*
PNG	Portable Network Graphic. Offers lossless compression that results in larger file sizes than JPEG – often much larger – but maintains pristine quality. Also has better transparency and color matching features than GIF.
TIFF	Tag Image File Format. Print artists commonly use 24- and 32-bit TIFFs, although they are not suitable for the Web.
BMP	Microsoft Bitmap image. The native graphics format of Microsoft Windows 3.0 and later. Not suitable for the Web, but a good way to share images between Windows applications.
PICT (Macintosh only)	Macintosh Picture. The native graphics format of Mac OS 9 and earlier. Vectors are not supported by Fireworks. Not suitable for the Web, but a good way to share image files between Mac applications.

Using the Export Wizards

Fireworks' export options are very full-featured and can certainly be overwhelming if you're new to Web graphics. If you're not even sure how best to begin optimizing your image, let one of Fireworks' Export Wizards guide you. The Export Wizard command has three primary uses:

✦ To help you select an export format.

✦ To offer suggestions to optimize your image after you select an export format.

✦ To recommend export modes that will reduce a graphic to a specified file size.

To use the Export Wizard to select an export format, follow these steps:

1. Choose File ⇨ Export Wizard.

   The initial screen of the Export Wizard appears, as shown in Figure E-12.

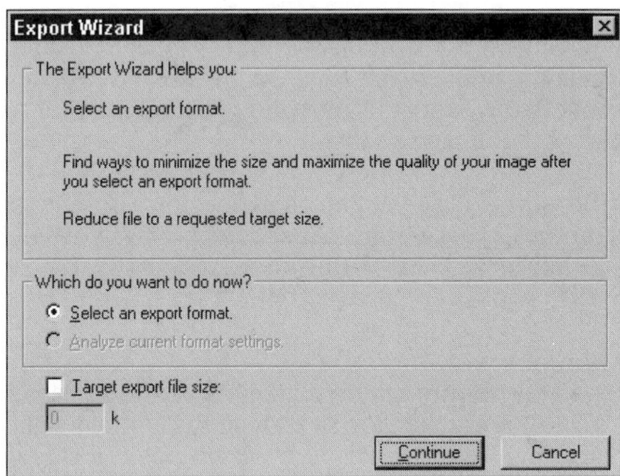

Figure E-12: The Export Wizard provides a good launchpad for export selections.

2. With the "Select an export format" option selected, click Continue.
3. The next screen of the Export Wizard appears and offers four choices for the graphic's ultimate destination:
   - **The Web:** Restricts the export options to the most popular Web formats, GIF and JPEG.
   - **An image-editing application:** Selects the best format for continuing to edit the image in another program, such as Photoshop. Generally, Fireworks selects the TIFF format.
   - **Desktop publishing application:** Selects the best print format, typically TIFF.
   - **Dreamweaver:** The same as The Web option, restricts the export options to the most popular Web formats, GIF and JPEG.

Note

If your graphic uses frames, the Export Wizard asks instead whether your file is to be exported as an Animated GIF, a JavaScript button rollover, or a single image file.

4. Click Continue after you make your choice.

   Fireworks presents its analysis of your image, with suggestions on how to narrow the selection further, if more than one export choice is recommended.

If you select Animated GIF as your destination for your multiframe image, you must select the resulting Preview window to display the details in the Options panel.

5. Click Exit to open the Export Preview dialog box and complete the export operation.

If you choose either The Web or Dreamweaver for your graphic's export destination, Fireworks presents you with two options for comparison: a GIF and a JPEG. The file in the upper Preview window is the smallest file size. Fireworks is fairly conservative in this aspect of the Export Wizard and does not attempt to seriously reduce the file size at the cost of image quality.

If you'd like to limit the file size while selecting an export format, select the "Target export file size" option on the Export Wizard's first screen. After you enable this option, you need to enter a file size value in the adjacent text box. File size is always measured in kilobytes. After you enter a file size, click Continue for Fireworks to calculate the results.

In addition to specifying a file size through the Export Wizard, you can choose the Export to File Size Wizard by clicking the button on the Options panel of the Export Preview dialog box. The Export to File Size Wizard opens a simple dialog box that asks for the specified file size. The major difference between this wizard and the Export File Size option on the Export Wizard is that the Export to File Size Wizard works only with the current format — no alternative choices are offered. Consequently, the Export to File Size Wizard is faster, but it's intended more for the intermediate-to-advanced user who understands the differences between file formats.

Live Effects and Xtras

In the early days of the Web, special graphics effects like drop shadows and beveled buttons required many tedious steps in programs, such as Photoshop. These days, Fireworks enables you to apply wondrous effects in a single step through the Effect panel. More importantly, like everything else in Fireworks, the effects are "live" and adapt to any change in the object. And you can easily alter them by adjusting values in the Effect panel.

The Effect panel options list contains the actual effects, split into two groups. The top group are Fireworks built-in effects. The bottom group are Photoshop-compatible image filters from your Fireworks Xtras folder and from another folder if you specified one in Fireworks Preferences.

Caution

Although Photoshop-compatible filters remain editable when applied with the Effect panel, applying them from the Xtras menu flattens path objects into bitmaps and removes your object's editability.

Fireworks is shipped with a range of useful Live Effects built-in, contained in the following submenus of the Effect panel's Effect Category option list:

- **Adjust Color:** Auto Levels, Brightness/Contrast, Curves, Hue/Saturation, Invert, Levels
- **Bevel and Emboss:** Inner Bevel, Inset Emboss, Outer Bevel, and Raised Emboss
- **Blur:** Including Blur, Blur More, and Gaussian Blur
- **Other:** The unclassifiable Convert to Alpha and Find Edges
- **Shadow and Glow:** Drop Shadow, Glow, Inner Glow, Inner Shadow
- **Sharpen:** Including Sharpen, Sharpen More, and Unsharp Mask

Choosing an effect from the Effect panel option list applies it to the current selection and adds it to the active list in the Effect panel. Once an effect is in the active list, you can check or uncheck the box next to it in order to enable or disable it.

Selecting the *i* button next to an applied effect's name enables you to modify its settings. Photoshop-compatible filters each have their own unique dialog boxes. Many of Fireworks' built-in Live Effects open a small, pop-up edit window with their settings. Clicking anywhere outside the pop-up edit window dismisses it. Raised Emboss is an example of an effect with a pop-up edit window, shown in Figure E-13.

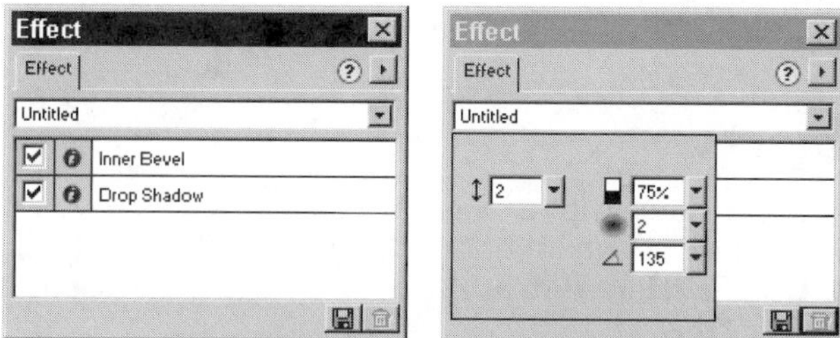

Figure E-13: The settings for some Live Effects are displayed in an unusual pop-up edit window, such as this one for Raised Emboss.

As you develop specific effects, you can save them for later use with the pop-up menu commands listed in Table E-5.

Table E-5
Effect Panel Pop-up Menu Commands

Option	*Description*
Save defaults	Saves the current setup as the default for new effects
Save Effect As	Saves the current effect settings under a new name
Rename Effect	Re-labels the current effect settings
Delete Effect	Removes the current effect from the menu
All on	Turns on all the effects currently active in the Effect panel
All off	Turns off all the effects currently active in the Effect panel
Locate Plug-ins	Shows a dialog box that enables you to select a folder of Photoshop plug-ins

Effect settings are also retained in Fireworks Styles. If you create a combination of stroke, fill, and effects settings that you'd like to save for future use, use the Styles panel to create a new Style based on your object.

Exploring Fireworks Objects

If you have previous experience with a vector drawing application such as Macromedia FreeHand, Adobe Illustrator, or Corel Draw, you'll find that this serves you well when working with Fireworks. One key difference to keep in mind: Fireworks uses vector objects and vector drawing tools as a method to create bitmaps.

Creating path objects

Objects begin as *paths.* Paths are lines with at least two points. Whether you draw a squiggly line with the Pencil tool or a multi-point star with the Polygon tool, the outline of your drawing is what is referred to as the path. By themselves, paths are invisible. Don't believe me? Try this:

1. Start up Fireworks and open a new document by choosing File ➪ New.
2. Select the Rectangle tool from the Toolbox.
3. Draw out a shape by clicking on the canvas and dragging the mouse out to form a rectangle.
4. Release the mouse when you have a visible shape. You'll see the path in the default highlight color, as shown in Figure E-14.

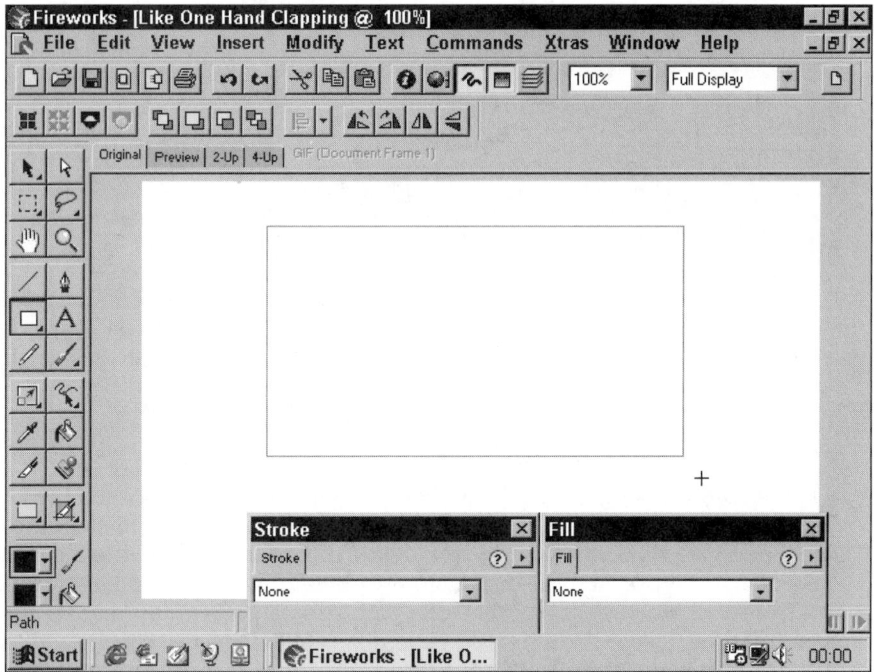

Figure E-14: Drawing out a rectangle — with no stroke or fill selected — leaves you with just the path.

5. Choose the Pointer tool from the Toolbox and click anywhere on the document, outside of the just-drawn rectangle. The highlight — and the rectangle's path — disappears.

6. If you pass your pointer over the existing rectangle, it will highlight temporarily so that you can select it again.

Applying a stroke

To make a path visible, you have to apply a *stroke* to see the outline. You can quickly apply a stroke to a selected object by choosing a color from the Stroke color well, located on the Toolbox or on the Color Mixer. This action applies a Pencil-type stroke five pixels wide with a soft or *antialiased* edge. Strokes can vary in color, width, softness, texture, and type of brush to name a few characteristics; several examples of different strokes are shown in Figure E-15. You'll notice in the figure how, regardless of their different attributes, strokes always follow the path of an object.

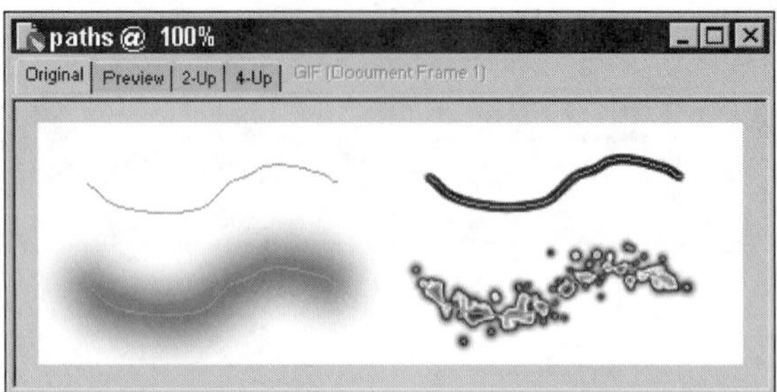

Figure E-15: You can see the same path in each of these different strokes.

Part of Fireworks' power is derived from the wide range of strokes possible. To learn more about strokes, see Chapter 8.

Open and closed paths

Paths come in two types: *open* and *closed*. The difference between the two is simple: a closed path connects its two endpoints (the start and finish of the line), and an open path doesn't. Closed paths define different shapes, whether standard — such as an ellipse, square, or polygon — or custom — such as a freeform drawing. Just as a stroke gives the outline of a path substance, a *fill* makes the interior of a path visible. Like strokes, fills come in different categories, colors, and textures. In addition, a *pattern,* created from a PNG file, can be used as a fill. You can even change the softness of a fill's edge. As Figure E-16 shows, regardless of what the interior fill is, it always follows the established path.

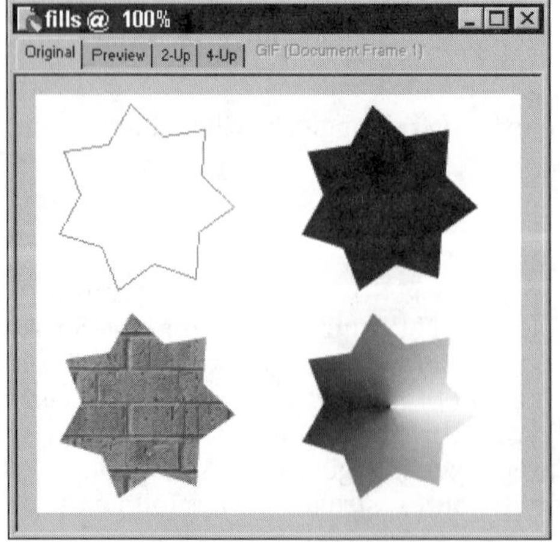

Figure E-16: An object can be filled with a solid color, a gradient, or a Pattern.

Even though fills are most often applied to closed path objects, it's perfectly legal to apply a fill to an open path object – although the results are not as predictable. But then, that's one of the beauties of computer graphics – try it and if you don't like it, undo it.

Center point

One common feature that all objects in Fireworks share is a *center point*. A center point is an invisible point in the middle of any path; if the path is open, the center point is on the line. If the path is closed, it's inside the object. Center points are useful when you need to rotate an object. You can also adjust the center point of an object when its transform handles are visible, in order to rotate it around a different axis, or control how its center aligns to other objects.

Chapter 9 explains how to work with rotation.

Starting from shapes

Most Fireworks documents are amalgams of many, many objects of different types, sizes, colors, and attributes. Drawing shapes sounds easy, but you must master the capabilities of each basic object to get the greatest effect in the shortest amount of time.

Fireworks provides tools for creating a series of basic geometric shapes — rectangles, ellipses, and polygons — as well as those for drawing structured and freeform lines. All of these tools will be familiar to anyone who has worked with a vector drawing program in the last few years. In fact, most of the key shortcuts are industry-standard. This appendix, though, is written for the complete novice. Even if you've never used a computer to draw before, you'll have a full understanding of the basic tools in Fireworks after working your way through this chapter.

If you have access to a graphics tablet, don't be afraid to use it here. Drawing is always easier with a pen and tablet than with a mouse.

The quickest way to create a Web page design, particularly the often-required navigational buttons, is to use one of Fireworks' shape-building tools. Although at first glance there only seems to be three such tools — the Rectangle, Ellipse, and Polygon — these tools each have options that enable them to produce a wide range of objects.

Using keyboard modifiers

You can use two keyboard modifiers with the Rectangle tool, Shift and Alt (Option), in order to apply two very commonly required behaviors.

✦ **To create a square:** You can easily make your rectangle into a square by pressing Shift while you drag out your shape. Unlike some other graphics programs, you don't have to press Shift before you begin drawing; pressing Shift at any time while you're drawing causes Fireworks to increase the shorter sides to match the longer sides of the rectangle to form a square.

✦ **To draw from the center:** To draw your rectangle from the center instead of from the corner, press Alt (Option) when dragging out the shape. While Alt (Option) is held down, Fireworks uses the distance from your originating point to the current pointer position as the radius rather than the diameter of the shape. As with Shift, you can press Alt (Option) at any time when drawing to change to a center origin.

Tip

Of course, you can use Shift and Alt (Option) together to draw a square from the center.

You can use the Info panel to check the pixel placement of your rectangle while you are drawing. One section displays the Width and Height (marked with a W and H) dynamically, while another displays the upper-left point of the rectangle, even if it is being drawn from the center.

Creating rounded corners

The standard rectangle and square, by definition, are composed of four right angles. However, Fireworks can create rectangles with rounded corners — and you can even set the degree of "roundness." The corner setting is visible on the Tool Options panel when the Rectangle tool is selected. The quickest way to access the Rectangle Tool options is to double-click the Rectangle tool; the Tool Options panel will automatically open. You can also display the Tool Options panel by choosing Window ➪ Tool Options or using the keyboard shortcut, Ctrl+Alt+O (Command+Option+O).

Once the Tool Options panel is available, choose how rounded you want the corners of your rectangle to appear by entering a value in the Corner text box or by using the Corner slider. The Corner scale is percentage-based: 0 represents a standard rectangle and 100 creates a fully rounded rectangle — also known as a circle. As Figure E-17 shows, the higher the Corner value, the more rounded the rectangle's corners become.

Exactly how Fireworks applies the corner percentage is most easily explained with an example. Let's say you draw a rectangle 100 pixels wide by 50 pixels tall, and choose a Corner value of 50 percent. Fireworks plots the points of the corner 50 pixels along the top edge (50% of 100 pixels = 50 pixels) and 25 pixels along the side edge (50% of 50 pixels = 25 pixels). The resulting arc makes the corner. If you created an ellipse with a horizontal diameter of 50 pixels and a vertical one of 25, it would fit right into the newly rounded corner.

Tip

Be sure to set the desired corner percentage on the Tool Options panel before you draw your rectangle. You can't convert a right-angle rectangle to a rounded-corner rectangle (or vice-versa) after it's been created.

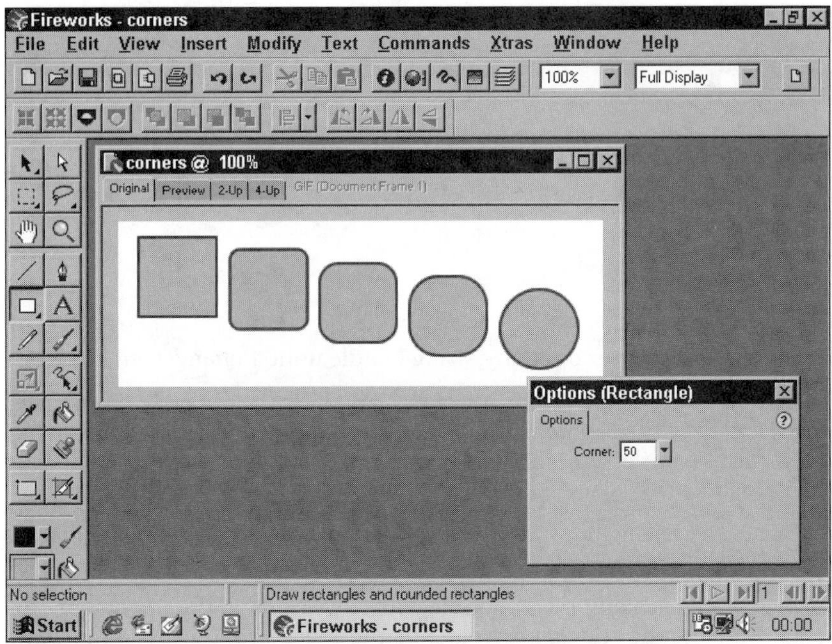

Figure E-17: Use the Corner setting from the Rectangle Tool Options panel to determine the degree of roundness for your rectangle or square's corners before you draw them.

Scaling and transforming objects

In Web design, the size of an object frequently needs adjustment. Sometimes a button is too large for the current navigation bar or the client wants the "On Sale" notice to be much bigger. Other times a graphic just looks better at a particular size. Regardless of the reason, Fireworks gives you a quick way to resize an object—either up or down—through the Scale tool.

The Scale tool is the first of three transformation tools in the Toolbox that become active when an object is selected. Choose the Scale tool (or use the keyboard shortcut, Q) and the standard selection highlight is replaced with a transforming highlight, as shown in Figure E-18. Eight sizing handles exist—one on each corner and one in the middle of each side—and a centerpoint on the transforming highlight. You can drag any of the sizing handles to a new position in order to resize the selected object. Dragging any corner handle scales the object proportionately.

To resize an object using the Scale tool, follow these steps:

1. Select the object you want to resize.
2. Choose the Scale tool from the Toolbox or use the keyboard shortcut, Q. Alternatively, you can use the menu command, Modify ➪ Transform ➪ Scale. Sizing handles and a centerpoint appear on the selected object.

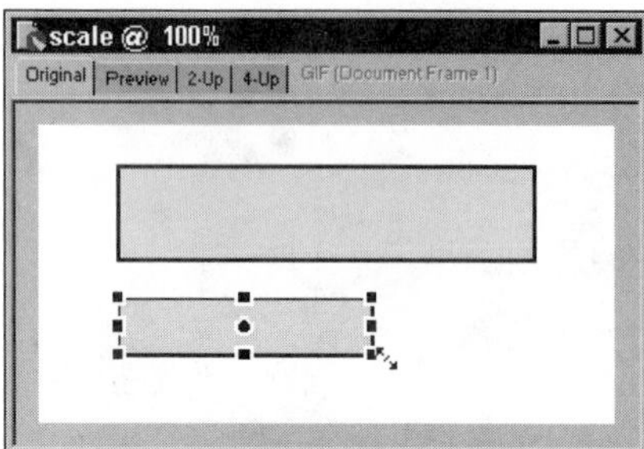

Figure E-18: Choose the Scale tool and sizing handles, and a centerpoint appears on the selected object.

3. Position your pointer over any sizing handle until it changes into a two-headed arrow.
4. Click and drag the sizing handle in the direction you want the object to grow or shrink. To scale an object while maintaining the current proportions, click and drag a corner sizing handle.
5. To cancel a resizing operation and return the object to its original dimensions, press Esc.
6. To accept a rescaled object, double-click anywhere on the document. You can also complete the resizing by selecting the Transform button in the Options panel, if it's visible.

In addition to sizing vector objects, Fireworks provides two other transform tools, on the same toolbox flyout as the scale tool:

- **Skew tool.** Use the Skew tool to move one side of an object while the opposing side remains stationary. Select the Skew tool by clicking and holding the Scale tool until you can choose the Skew tool from the flyout, or by pressing the keyboard shortcut Q twice. Selecting the Skew tool causes transform handles to appear on the selected object, just like selecting the Scale tool. Drag any middle Skew handle in order to slant that side of the object. Drag any corner Skew handle in order to slant that side and the opposing side in the opposite direction.
- **Distort tool.** With both the Scale and Skew tools, entire sides move when one of the transform handles is adjusted. The Distort tool (the third tool on the transform flyout) removes this restriction. When the Distort tool is selected, you can adjust the bounding box surrounding the selected object by dragging the handles in any direction. The object is then redrawn to fit within the confines of the new bounding box shape.

You can also move or rotate an object when any of the transform tools are selected. When the pointer is positioned within the selected object and it becomes a four-headed arrow, click and drag the object to a new position. If the pointer is outside of the selected object's bounding box, the pointer turns into a rotate symbol; clicking and dragging when this occurs rotates the object around its centerpoint. An object can rotate through a full 360 degrees.

Working with bitmaps

Path-based objects are the backbone of Fireworks, and are perfectly suited for the bulk of the work a Web artist does: building navigation bars, drawing shapes and lines, and inserting editable text. These design elements benefit from the precision that vector drawing provides, and are the kinds of things you're likely to draw right from scratch in Fireworks.

Some kinds of images won't benefit from a path-based substructure, though. Photographic images that started out life in a digital camera or scanner are pure bitmap, through and through. Think of product photographs for an online store, or digitized paintings for an online art gallery. Incorporating them into a Web page won't involve drawing. Instead you'll cut and paste pixel selections and manipulate alpha masks and blending modes.

Almost all work with images takes place in Fireworks' Image Edit mode. Fireworks enters Image Edit mode whenever you use a bitmap tool such as the Magic Wand. It will seem like a subtle transition, but it's an important one. You're telling Fireworks to stop moving groups of pixels around in convenient vector containers; to shift gears and focus instead on the pure pixels themselves.

Examining Image Edit mode

As you can see, manipulating path-based objects and pixel-based images are two completely different operations. For that reason, Fireworks has two different modes: an Object Edit mode for vector objects (discussed in Chapter 5) and an Image Edit mode for bitmap images. Some tools work in one mode but not the other, whereas some tools seem to work the same, but actually return different results. It's not that one mode is better than the other, they are just used for different purposes.

You can ask Fireworks to change over to Image Edit mode, but you don't have to. Mode changes are tool-driven: start to use an image-editing tool and you automatically enter Image Edit mode. Pick an object-editing tool, start to work, and you're back in Object Edit mode. Sometimes the transition is accompanied by a helpful message from Fireworks explaining that the change is necessary. For example, if you try to use the Reshape Path tool in Image Edit mode, Fireworks warns you that it's only good for paths.

The mode-shifting warnings all include a "don't show again" checkbox, so you can switch them off when you feel comfortable enough to do so.

All of the objects you use in Fireworks start out in one camp or the other — either they're all pixels or all paths. However, eventually the lines begin to blur (pun intended, maybe) and you find yourself moving back and forth between the two modes effortlessly and with no real conscious thought.

Starting Image Edit mode

In addition to automatically invoking Image Edit mode by choosing a particular tool, you can also enter it explicitly in several ways:

- ✦ Double-click an image object with the Pointer or Subselection tool. This is probably my most commonly used technique for accessing Image Edit mode.
- ✦ Choose Modify ➪ Image Object, or use the keyboard shortcut, Ctrl+E (Command+E).
- ✦ Choose Insert ➪ Empty Image, or use the key shortcut Ctrl+Alt+Y (Command+Option+Y). This creates a new image object, which you can paint with pixel-based tools.

It's easy to tell when you're in Image Edit mode; in fact, Fireworks offers multiple visual cues, as shown in Figure E-19. First, a striped border surrounds the canvas, unless you uncheck the "Expand to Fill Document" preference; in which case the striped border only surrounds the image object itself. Second, you'll notice the phrase "(Image Edit Mode)" in the Title Bar of the graphic you're working on, and also in the title bar of the Object panel. Finally, the status bar Stop button (a white X in a red circle) is active instead of grayed-out.

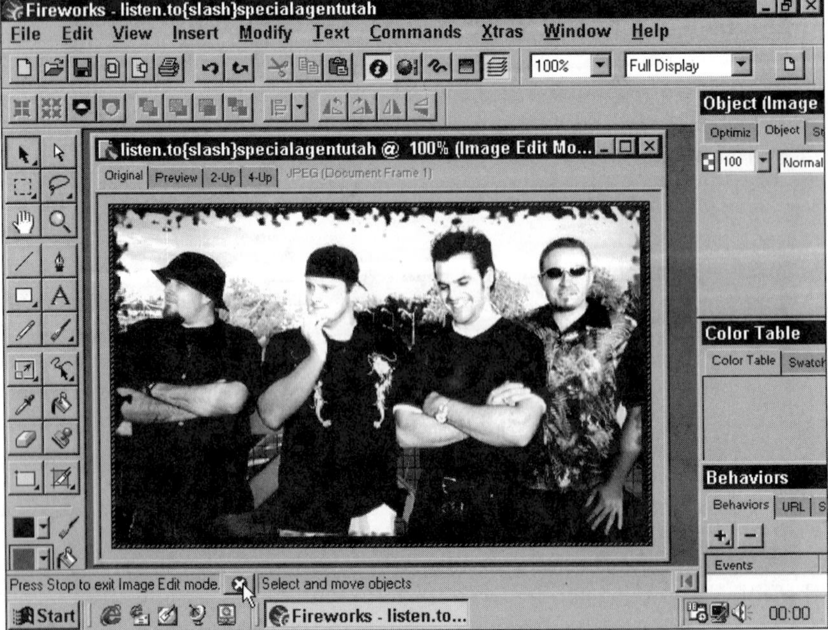

Figure E-19: Fireworks tells you that you're in Image Edit mode in a number of ways. Note the ToolTip describing the function of the Stop button.

Tip

Windows users will also see the helpful hint "Press Stop to exit Image Edit mode" right next to the stop button itself.

Leaving Image Edit mode

When you leave Image Edit mode, any bitmap image, if selected normally, has a bounding box around it. In Fireworks, images can also be manipulated — moved, resized, aligned, distorted — as image objects. In Object Edit mode, image objects act like rectangular path objects filled with a bitmap image. You can even apply an effect, such as a drop shadow, to a selected image object.

The most obvious way to leave Image Edit mode and go to Object Edit mode is to select the Stop button. However, the Fireworks team created a number of other exits, as well. Here's a list of all the methods for leaving Image Edit mode:

✦ Choose Modify ➪ Exit Image Edit or use the key shortcut, Ctrl+Shift+D (Command+Shift+D).

✦ Press the Stop button on the Status bar.

✦ If the Image Edit border surrounds just the image object and not the canvas, then the cursor changes into a Stop button when it's not over the object itself. Click once when you see the Stop button cursor.

✦ If the Image Edit border surrounds the entire document, choose a selection tool (Marquee, Ellipse Marquee, Lasso, Polygon Lasso, or Magic Wand) and double-click any open area.

To specify whether the image border surrounds just the image object or the whole canvas:

1. Choose File ➪ Preferences.
2. Select the Editing tab in the Preferences dialog box.
3. Uncheck Expand to Fill Document under When Editing Images.
4. Choose OK.

The change takes place immediately.

Why would you want to have the Image Edit border surround more than just the image? Quite often, you need to expand the area of an image while you're editing — to blur the edges or make the shape nonrectangular, for example. If the Image Edit border tightly hugs the bitmap graphic, there's no room for expansion. By enabling the Expand to Fill Document option, you have plenty of canvas in which to maneuver. You're still just editing the one image object.

Examining other Image mode functions

The other two options under the Editing tab in Preferences — Open in Image Edit Mode and Turn Off "Hide Edges" — can also prove useful. The Open in Image Edit Mode option (checked by default) tells Fireworks to automatically go into Image Edit mode when you open a document that doesn't contain any path objects — in other words, a single image. If you prefer, you can uncheck this option and always start out in Object Edit mode. You have to quit and restart Fireworks to enable changes in Preferences.

As helpful as the striped — also known as the barber-pole — border is in identifying Image Edit mode, though it can be a bit of a visual nuisance. To temporarily view your image without the striped border, choose View ➪ Hide Edges or the key shortcut Ctrl+H (Command+H). When you change modes, the Hide Edges command is automatically unchecked. If you'd prefer the edges stay hidden, uncheck Turn off "Hide Edges" (it's checked by default). This option takes effect immediately.

Scaling images

Changing the size of a pixel-based image is something we probably take for granted, but it's actually a pretty complex task, requiring Fireworks to literally create a new image — with the newly specified dimensions — by analyzing the old image. Fireworks looks at groups of pixels and basically makes a best guess about how to represent them with either more or fewer pixels. Coming up with intermediate values based on analysis of known values is called interpolation.

Fireworks offers you four interpolation methods:

- **Bicubic:** With bicubic interpolation, Fireworks averages every pixel with all eight pixels surrounding it — above, below, left, right, and all four corners. This scaling option gives the sharpest results under the most conditions and is recommended for most graphics.
- **Bilinear:** Bilinear interpolation is similar to bicubic, but only uses four neighboring pixels (above, below, left, and right), instead of eight.
- **Nearest Neighbor:** The Nearest Neighbor algorithm causes Fireworks to copy neighboring pixels whenever a new pixel must be interpolated. Consequently, the Nearest Neighbor scaling option creates very pixelated, stairstep-like images.
- **Soft:** Soft interpolation was the original scaling option used in Fireworks 1 and it offers a smoothing blur to the scaled-down images. The Soft Interpolation scaling option is a good choice if your images are producing unwanted artifacts using the other scaling images.

I've found that although I tend to use Bicubic Interpolation most of the time, I do turn to Bilinear and Soft Interpolation in some cases, usually when small text is involved. I haven't found much use for the blockiness produced by the Nearest Neighbor scaling option. Experimenting with the different interpolation methods is the best way to become familiar with their results.

Using the Text Editor

In Fireworks, all text creation and most modification takes place in the Text Editor. The Text Editor, shown in Figure E-20, is a separate window with a full range of text controls and its own preview pane. After the text is created, a text object appears in the current Fireworks document, surrounded by a bounding box. The text object has many, but not all of the properties of a path object — you can, for example, use the transform tools such as Skew, but you can't use Reshape Area to warp the text as you can a path. On the other hand, text objects have features unlike any other object — for example, the capability to be aligned to a path such as a circle. If necessary, it's possible to convert a text object to a path object or an image object, but the text can no longer be edited.

Figure E-20: The Text Editor is used to compose and edit text in Fireworks.

The Text tool in the Toolbox is your initial gateway into the Text Editor. The Text tool can be used two ways:

✦ Click once on the canvas with the Text tool to set a starting point for your text. If necessary, the text flows to the edge of the current document and expands downward toward the bottom of the document.

✦ Drag out a rectangular text region with the Text tool. The text created in the Text Editor wraps on the horizontal boundaries of the established region and, if necessary, expands downward.

The general steps for inserting text into a Fireworks document are:

1. Select the Text tool from the Toolbox or use the keyboard shortcut, T
2. Set the text area by:
   - Clicking once on the document where you'd like the text to start
   - Dragging out a text area for the text to fit into

   Either method opens the Text Editor.
3. From the Text Editor, choose text characteristics such as font, size, color, and alignment.
4. Click in the Preview pane and input the text. If Auto-Apply is enabled, Fireworks updates the text object in the document after each keystroke.
5. Click OK when you're done.

Pressing Enter (Return) when your cursor is in the Preview pane adds a line break, as you might expect. Unfortunately, the OK button in the Text Editor is highlighted, and that may tempt you to hit Enter (Return) to dismiss the Text Editor dialog box. Press the other Enter (Enter) on the numeric keypad to dismiss the Text Editor.

Once the text object is onscreen, you move it as you would any other Fireworks object, by clicking and dragging with the Pointer tool. To adjust the shape of the text object, drag any of the six handles that become available when the object is selected.

Dragging a text object's handles doesn't resize the text itself, but instead changes the outside boundaries of the text object, after which, the text reflows through its new boundaries. A text object can only be vertically resized to fit the current text it contains. If you want your text object to take up more vertical room, select it and choose a larger font size from the Text ⇨ Size menu.

When you need to edit an existing text object, you have several ways to open the Text Editor. You can select the text object as you would any other Fireworks object, and then choose Text ⇨ Editor. Alternatively, once the text object is selected, you can press the keyboard shortcut, Ctrl+Shift+E (Command+Shift+E). You can also choose the Text tool from the toolbox and hover it over an existing text object; when the I-beam cursor gains a small right-pointing triangle, click once to open the Text Editor. Finally, the most efficient method (and certainly my most used one) is to double-click the text object with the Pointer or Subselection tool.

Choosing basic font characteristics

Within the Text Editor, you have full control over the look and style of your text. The Text Editor offers two methods of working, just like a word-processing program. To set your options, use either one of the following techniques:

✦ Set the font attributes prior to entering text into the Preview pane.

✦ Select the text you want to modify in the Preview pane — all or a portion — and then alter the attributes.

The core characteristics are all found at the top of the Text Editor. The basic attributes are very straightforward to establish:

✦ **Font:** To choose a typeface, select a name from the Font list. The Font list displays all the available TrueType or Type 1 fonts on your system.

Windows users can also select the Font list itself and, either use the cursor keys to move up or down the list one font at a time, or type the first letter of a font's name to jump to that part of the list.

✦ **Size:** Choose the text size using the Text Size slider or by entering a value directly in the Text Size box. Size is the height of a font in points. Fireworks accepts sizes from 4 to 1,000 points, although the slider only goes from 8 to 128.

You can also adjust text size by using the Scale tool on your text object, just as you would resize any other object. Although the text remains editable, its point size in the Text Editor doesn't change as you resize it. This can become confusing when you attempt to edit a huge text object and find that it says it's 10pt in the Text Editor.

✦ **Color:** Initially, the Text Editor applies the color specified in the Fill color well. However, you can easily choose a new text fill color by selecting the option arrow next to the color well in the Text Editor. The standard pop-up color picker is displayed with the current swatch set. Each character in your text object can have its own color.

✦ **Style:** Choose from Bold, Italic, and Underline styles for your text; each style button is a toggle and any or all can be applied to one text object.

All of the basic attributes are applicable on a letter-by-letter basis. You can — although you're not advised to for aesthetic reasons — change every letter's font, size, color, or style (ransom notes were never easier).

Commands and the History Panel

The History panel, shown in Figure E-21, enables precise control over Fireworks' multiple level Undo command. The Undo Marker points to your preceding step. To roll back to even earlier steps, slide the Undo Marker up one or more notches. The number of steps the History panel keeps track of is the number of Undo steps you have specified in Fireworks preferences.

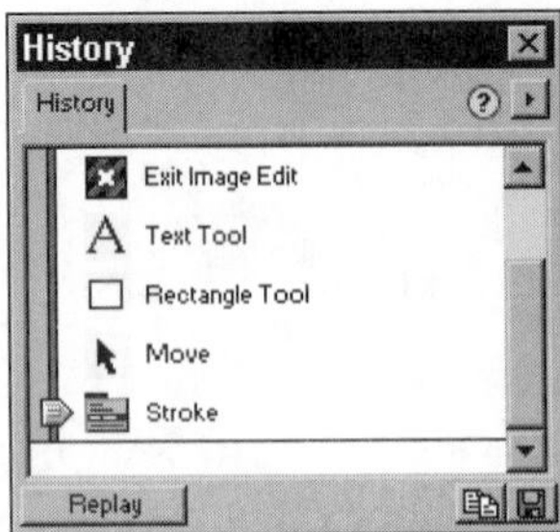

Figure E-21: The History panel contains a record of your actions.

The maximum number of Undo steps you can specify in Fireworks for Windows is 100. On the Mac, the number of Undo steps is limited only by the amount of RAM Fireworks has access to.

The ability to save or replay your steps makes the History panel more than just an enhanced Undo. Saving your previous steps as a Command enables you to automate almost anything you do in Fireworks. If you have a project that requires you to tediously edit a number of images in the same way, do it once and save the steps as a Command that you can run on all of the other images.

To save History panel steps as a Command, follow these steps:

1. Perform an action or a consecutive series of actions that you'd like to save as a Command. Following are examples of steps you could perform before saving them:
   - Create a standard copyright/legal footer for your Web site, with associated text formatting and precise canvas placement.
   - Create a circle object, duplicate it five times, select all six objects, align them horizontally, and distribute them to widths, creating a basic button bar that can be easily built upon or modified.
2. If you want to save just one step as a Command, click that step in the History panel to select it. To save multiple steps, hold down Shift and click the first and the last step in the series that you want to save. Ctrl+click (Command+click) noncontiguous steps to select them.

   The selected steps are colored a dark selection color.
3. Click the Save Steps as Command button in the History panel.

   Fireworks displays the Save Command dialog box, as shown in Figure E-22.
4. Enter a name for your new Command. Click OK after you're done.

Your steps are saved as a Command and added to the Commands menu in alphabetical order. To apply your Command, choose Commands ⇨ and the name of your new Command.

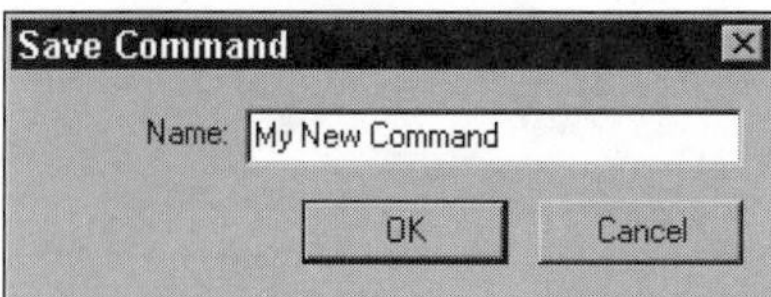

Figure E-22: Enter a name for your new Command in the Save Command dialog box.

Note two caveats when saving steps as Commands:

- Some actions, such as drawing a shape with the Brush tool, are nonrepeatable. Fireworks marks these steps with a red *X*, as shown in Figure E-23.
- Fireworks places a separator in the History panel (also shown in Figure E-23) when you change your selection. Replaying steps across a separator can have unpredictable results because some objects can't be modified in the same way as other objects.

Figure E-23: Items with a red *X* next to them are nonrepeatable. A separator line indicates a change in selection, which can lead to unpredictable results.

When you attempt to save steps that include either of these potential problems, Fireworks notifies you with a dialog box, indicating that there may be a problem and offering you the opportunity to continue or cancel.

Although storing and running your own Commands is perhaps the primary purpose for the Commands menu, the menu arrives from the factory with a group of built-in Commands that enable you to take Fireworks extensibility for a test drive. After a couple of turns around the block, I found myself amazed that these kinds of features can be added to Fireworks using JavaScript, and in some cases without even writing a line of code! The built-in Commands are wonderfully useful additions to the Fireworks toolkit.

✦ ✦ ✦

Index

Continued

B

Continued

Continued

C

Continued

D

E

F

Continued

H

I

J

K

L

M

O

Q

R

S

V

W

X

Y

Z

IDG Books Worldwide, Inc. End-User License Agreement

READ THIS. You should carefully read these terms and conditions before opening the software packet(s) included with this book ("Book"). This is a license agreement ("Agreement") between you and IDG Books Worldwide, Inc. ("IDGB"). By opening the accompanying software packet(s), you acknowledge that you have read and accept the following terms and conditions. If you do not agree and do not want to be bound by such terms and conditions, promptly return the Book and the unopened software packet(s) to the place you obtained them for a full refund.

1. **License Grant.** IDGB grants to you (either an individual or entity) a nonexclusive license to use one copy of the enclosed software program(s) (collectively, the "Software") solely for your own personal or business purposes on a single computer (whether a standard computer or a workstation component of a multiuser network). The Software is in use on a computer when it is loaded into temporary memory (RAM) or installed into permanent memory (hard disk, CD-ROM, or other storage device). IDGB reserves all rights not expressly granted herein.

2. **Ownership.** IDGB is the owner of all right, title, and interest, including copyright, in and to the compilation of the Software recorded on the disk(s) or CD-ROM ("Software Media"). Copyright to the individual programs recorded on the Software Media is owned by the author or other authorized copyright owner of each program. Ownership of the Software and all proprietary rights relating thereto remain with IDGB and its licensers.

3. **Restrictions On Use and Transfer.**

   (a) You may only (i) make one copy of the Software for backup or archival purposes, or (ii) transfer the Software to a single hard disk, provided that you keep the original for backup or archival purposes. You may not (i) rent or lease the Software, (ii) copy or reproduce the Software through a LAN or other network system or through any computer subscriber system or bulletin-board system, or (iii) modify, adapt, or create derivative works based on the Software.

   (b) You may not reverse engineer, decompile, or disassemble the Software. You may transfer the Software and user documentation on a permanent basis, provided that the transferee agrees to accept the terms and conditions of this Agreement and you retain no copies. If the Software is an update or has been updated, any transfer must include the most recent update and all prior versions.

4. **Restrictions on Use of Individual Programs.** You must follow the individual requirements and restrictions detailed for each individual program in Appendix A of this Book. These limitations are also contained in the individual

license agreements recorded on the Software Media. These limitations may include a requirement that after using the program for a specified period of time, the user must pay a registration fee or discontinue use. By opening the Software packet(s), you will be agreeing to abide by the licenses and restrictions for these individual programs that are detailed in Appendix A and on the Software Media. None of the material on this Software Media or listed in this Book may ever be redistributed, in original or modified form, for commercial purposes.

5. Limited Warranty.

(a) IDGB warrants that the Software and Software Media are free from defects in materials and workmanship under normal use for a period of sixty (60) days from the date of purchase of this Book. If IDGB receives notification within the warranty period of defects in materials or workmanship, IDGB will replace the defective Software Media.

(b) **IDGB AND THE AUTHOR OF THE BOOK DISCLAIM ALL OTHER WARRANTIES, EXPRESS OR IMPLIED, INCLUDING WITHOUT LIMITATION IMPLIED WARRANTIES OF MERCHANTABILITY AND FITNESS FOR A PARTICULAR PURPOSE, WITH RESPECT TO THE SOFTWARE, THE PROGRAMS, THE SOURCE CODE CONTAINED THEREIN, AND/OR THE TECHNIQUES DESCRIBED IN THIS BOOK. IDGB DOES NOT WARRANT THAT THE FUNCTIONS CONTAINED IN THE SOFTWARE WILL MEET YOUR REQUIREMENTS OR THAT THE OPERATION OF THE SOFTWARE WILL BE ERROR FREE.**

(c) This limited warranty gives you specific legal rights, and you may have other rights that vary from jurisdiction to jurisdiction.

6. Remedies.

(a) IDGB's entire liability and your exclusive remedy for defects in materials and workmanship shall be limited to replacement of the Software Media, which may be returned to IDGB with a copy of your receipt at the following address: Software Media Fulfillment Department, Attn.: *Dreamweaver 3 Bible, Gold Edition*, IDG Books Worldwide, Inc., 10475 Crosspoint Blvd., Indianapolis, IN 46256, or call 1-800-762-2974. Please allow three to four weeks for delivery. This Limited Warranty is void if failure of the Software Media has resulted from accident, abuse, or misapplication. Any replacement Software Media will be warranted for the remainder of the original warranty period or thirty (30) days, whichever is longer.

(b) In no event shall IDGB or the author be liable for any damages whatsoever (including without limitation damages for loss of business profits, business interruption, loss of business information, or any other pecuniary loss) arising from the use of or inability to use the Book or the Software, even if IDGB has been advised of the possibility of such damages.

(c) Because some jurisdictions do not allow the exclusion or limitation of liability for consequential or incidental damages, the above limitation or exclusion may not apply to you.

7. **U.S. Government Restricted Rights.** Use, duplication, or disclosure of the Software by the U.S. Government is subject to restrictions stated in paragraph (c)(1)(ii) of the Rights in Technical Data and Computer Software clause of DFARS 252.227-7013, and in subparagraphs (a) through (d) of the Commercial Computer—Restricted Rights clause at FAR 52.227-19, and in similar clauses in the NASA FAR supplement, when applicable.

8. **General.** This Agreement constitutes the entire understanding of the parties and revokes and supersedes all prior agreements, oral or written, between them and may not be modified or amended except in a writing signed by both parties hereto that specifically refers to this Agreement. This Agreement shall take precedence over any other documents that may be in conflict herewith. If any one or more provisions contained in this Agreement are held by any court or tribunal to be invalid, illegal, or otherwise unenforceable, each and every other provision shall remain in full force and effect.

CD-ROM Installation Instructions

The *Dreamweaver 3 Bible, Gold Edition* CD-ROMs contain trial versions of Dreamweaver 3, Flash 4, Fireworks 3, and CourseBuilder for Dreamweaver 3, in addition to an online training trial, a host of extensions, objects, and commands, and code from this book.

Accessing the Programs on the CD-ROMs

The trial programs on the CD-ROMs are in a compressed installation format: Double-click these files to begin the installation procedure and follow the offered prompts. In the Additional Extensions folder, most files are uncompressed and can simply be copied from the CD-ROM to your system by using your file manager. However, some extensions use more files, which must be copied to the proper place in the Dreamweaver\Configuration folder. These extensions all include Read Me files to help you with the installation.

Generally, the file structure of the CD-ROMs replicates the structure that Dreamweaver sets up when it is installed. For example, objects found in the Dreamweaver\Configuration\Objects folder are located in both the CD-ROM and the installed program.

For a detailed synopsis of the contents of the CD-ROMs, see Appendix A, "What's on the CD-ROM?"

Installing Dreamweaver

To install Dreamweaver on your Windows system, follow these steps:

1. Insert the *Dreamweaver 3 Bible, Gold Edition* CD-ROM 1 into your CD-ROM drive.
2. Double-click the Dreamweaver.exe file to unpack it and begin the installation process.
3. Follow the onscreen instructions. Accept the default options for program location.

Changing the Windows read-only attribute

You may not be able to access files on the CD-ROMs after you copy the files to your computer. After you copy or move the entire contents of the CD-ROMs to your hard disk or another storage medium (such as a Zip disk), you may get the following error message when you attempt to open a file with its associated application:

```
[Application] is unable to open the [file]. Please make sure
the drive and file are writable.
```

Windows sees all files on a CD-ROM drive as read-only. This normally makes sense because a CD-ROM is a read-only medium — that is, you can't write data back to the CD-ROM. However, when you copy a file from a CD-ROM to your hard disk or to a Zip disk, Windows doesn't automatically change the file attribute from read-only to writable.

Installation software normally takes care of this chore for you, but in this case, because the files are intended to be manually copied to your disk, you have to change the file attribute yourself. Luckily, it's easy — just follow these steps:

1. Click the Start menu button.
2. Select Programs.
3. Choose Windows Explorer.
4. Highlight the file name(s) on the hard disk or Zip disk.
5. Right-click the highlighted file name(s) to display a pop-up menu.
6. Select Properties to display the Properties dialog box.
7. Click the Read-only option so that it is no longer checked.
8. Click the OK button.

You should now be able to use the file(s) with the specific application without getting the annoying error message.